Praise for  netbooks™

In bookstores now!

NetSpy

Become an online sleuth! Now the ordinary computer user can tap into the information and data that credit agencies, lawyers, research companies, government departments, and other investigative and "snooping" firms have used for decades. Leave no relevant Web page unscrolled as you locate lost family members and check out potential employers.

ISBN
0-679-77029-1
US: $12.95
Canada: $17.50
200 pages

NetCollege

NetCollege gives you a crash course on how to get into the college of your choice—the online way! Visit virtual campuses. Stop by cyber-admissions offices. Get some SAT practice. Sort through financial aid info online. And, soon enough, find out the good (or bad) news via email.

ISBN 0-679-77380-0
US: $19.95
Canada: $27.00
400 pages

NetStudy

Where can I get help with my algebra homework? My English paper's due tomorrow and the library's closed. I don't understand frog anatomy. From the beginner studying astronomy to the math whiz taking AP calculus, *NetStudy* can help students get an education online. Includes Internet resources for teachers and parents.

ISBN 0-679-77381-9
US: $22.00
Canada: $30.00
400 pages

NetDoctor

NetDoctor offers a powerful cure for medical ignorance—the Internet! Packed with thousands of sites that let you diagnose your own maladies and lead you to the latest research on ailments ranging from AIDS to cancer to the common cold, this is the only book you'll ever need to stay healthy.

ISBN 0-679-77173-5
US: $22.00
Canada: $30.00
400 pages

Fodor's NetTravel

Fodor's NetTravel—from Fodor's and the creators of *NetGuide* and the NetBooks Series—tells you how to find the best online travel sites. Find your way to brilliant travelogues and wonderful travel secrets—plus subway maps, restaurant and hotel guides, movie listings, and train schedules.

ISBN 0-679-77033-X
US: $22.00
Canada: $30.00
400 pages

NetMarketing

NetMarketing is the first book that spells out strategies for how corporate marketers and mom-and-pop businesses can use the Net to powerful advantage. It includes hundreds of successful Web sites, a primer for getting started, and a directory of more than 1,000 marketing sites.

ISBN 0-679-77381-9
US: $22.00
Canada: $30.00
400 pages

NetGames 2

NetGames 2 is the all-new, updated edition of the original bestseller. It covers more than 4,000 games, including *Doom, Marathon, Harpoon II, Myst*, and more than a hundred MUDs, MUSHes, and MOOs, plus demos, tips, and free upgrades!

ISBN 0-679-77034-8
US: $22.00
Canada: $30.00
UK: £20.49 Net
400 pages

NetJobs

NetJobs tells you how to take advantage of the Iway to land the job you've always wanted. It includes the email addresses of over 1,000 companies, special tips for '96 college grads, and a complete directory of online classifieds, help wanted, and job notice boards.

ISBN
0-679-77032-1
US: $12.95
Canada: $17.95
UK: £11.99 Net
200 pages

Just arrived!

NetSci-Fi

The ultimate guide for science fiction fanatics! *NetSci-Fi* covers topics from *Aliens* to *The X-Files*— and everything in between. Want to work on a *Battlestar Galactica* revival campaign or learn about the value of those old *Star Wars* trading cards? *NetSci-Fi* will unlock a new universe of sci-fi trivia and fandom.

ISBN 0-679-77322-3
US: $22.00 / Canada: $30.00
400 pages

Coming soon!

NetKids

The first Internet guide written by kids— for kids! What are the best playgrounds in cyberspace? Where are the toothiest shark and dinosaur sites? How can I find a new pen pal? *NetKids* is the first comprehensive guide to age-appropriate activities for kids in cyberspace—from pirates to pop culture. Our junior Web masters rank the sites and tell us where the action is online.

ISBN 1-889-670-08-1
US: $19.95
Canada: $27.00
200 pages (11/96)

NetShopping

Cybercommerce is booming and *NetShopping* will show consumers how to shop big-name retailers and mom-and-pop virtual store fronts from their home computers. Special section on the top 100 FREE products and services in cyberspace.

ISBN 1-889-670-09-X
US: $22.00
Canada: $30.00
400 pages (11/96)

NetLove

Looking for love in all the wrong places? Spend your next Saturday night cuddled up with *NetLove* and start finding passion in the right places. Follow online sexpert and NetHeat columnist Alison Grippo as she feels her way across the most erogenous zones in cyberspace.

ISBN 1-889-670-00-6
US: $12.95
Canada: $17.00
200 pages (1/97)

NetBaseball

Every fantasy season means a mad scramble for last-minute information and a string of calculations to prepare for the draft-even in an online league. *NetBaseball* will help you find a playing field, make smart trades, manage your team, and even keep up with the real Major League game.

ISBN 1-889-670-01-4
US: $12.95
Canada: $17.00
200 pages (2/97)

To order, call 1-800-NET-1133, ext. 1300

Instant

Visit Your Personal Net at

Updates.

http://www.ypn.com

Your Guide to the Best of Everything on the Net

A MICHAEL WOLFF BOOK

For free updates visit Your Personal Net at http://www.ypn.com

New York

WOLFF NEW MEDIA

The NetBooks Series is published by Wolff New Media LLC, 520 Madison Avenue, 11th Floor, New York, NY 10022, and distributed by National Book Network, 4720 Boston Way, Lanham, MD 20706, as agent for Wolff New Media LLC.

NetGuide has been wholly created and produced by Michael Wolff & Company, Inc. and Wolff New Media LLC. *NetSci-Fi, NetSpy, NetCollege, NetStudy, NetDoctor, NetMarketing, NetVote, NetJobs, NetGames2, NetTravel, NetTaxes, NetMusic, NetGames, NetChat, NetMoney, NetTech, NetSports,* Your Personal Net, the Your Personal Net Logo, NetBooks, NetHead, NetSpeak, NetBest, and CyberPower are trademarks of Wolff New Media LLC. The Net Logo, What's On In Cyberspace, and YPN are registered trademarks of Wolff New Media LLC. The trademark NetGuide, created by Michael Wolff & Company, Inc., is now owned by CMP Media, Inc., and is used under a license from CMP. The book *NetGuide* is an independent publication not affiliated with CMP or any CMP publication. All design and production has been done by means of desktop-publishing technology. The text is set in the typefaces Champion, Century 725, Eldorado, and Zapf Dingbats.

Published simultaneously in the U.S. and Canada by Wolff New Media LLC

0 9 8 7 6 5 4 3 2 1

ISBN 1-889670-07-3

The authors and publisher have used their best efforts in preparing this book. However, the authors and publisher make no warranties of any kind, express or implied, with regard to the documentation contained in this book, and specifically disclaim, without limitation, any implied warranties of merchantability and fitness for a particular purpose with respect to listings in the book, or the techniques described in the book. In no event shall the authors or publisher be responsible or liable for any loss of profit or any other commercial damages, including but not limited to special, incidental, consequential, or any other damages in connection with or arising out of furnishing, performance, or use of this book.

All of the photographs and illustrations in this book have been obtained from online sources, and have been included to demonstrate the variety of work that is available on the Net. The caption with each photograph or illustration identifies its online source. Text and images available over the Internet and other online services may be subject to copyright and other rights owned by third parties. Online availability of text and images does not imply that they may be reused without the permission of rights holders, although the Copyright Act does permit certain unauthorized reuse as fair use under 17 U.S.C. §107. Care should be taken to ensure that all necessary rights are cleared prior to reusing material distributed over the Internet and other online services. Information about reuse is available from the institutions that make their materials available online.

Trademarks

A number of entered words in which we have reason to believe trademark, service mark, or other proprietary rights may exist have been designated as such by use of initial capitalization. However, no attempt has been made to designate as trademarks or service marks all personal-computer words or terms in which proprietary rights might exist. The inclusion, exclusion, or definition of a word or term is not intended to affect, or to express any judgment on, the validity or legal status of any proprietary right which may be claimed in that word or term.

Manufactured in the United States of America.

New York

WOLFF NEW MEDIA

Michael Wolff
Publisher and Editor in Chief

Kelly Maloni
Executive Editor

Stevan Keane
Editor

Research Editor: Kristin Miller
Senior Editor: Dina Gan
Managing Editor: Donna Spivey

Creative Director: Stephen Gullo
Associate Art Director: Eric Hoffsten
Assistant Art Director: Jay Jaffe

Editor of *NetGuide*: Hylton Jolliffe

Associate Editors: Deborah Cohn, Lev Grossman
Staff Writers: Henry Lam, Wendy Nelson, Stephanie Overby
Copy Editor: Sonya Donaldson
Editorial Assistants: Jennifer Levy, Vicky Tsolomytis
Research Assistants: Max Greenhut, Rachel Kleinman
Production Assistants: Alex Fogarty, Jackie Fugere, Gary Gottshall
Contributing Writers: Christine Cooper, Juan Gan, Keith Hays, Bennett Voyles, Eric Zelko

Vice President, Associate Publisher: Carol Lappin
Vice President, Marketing: Jay Sears
Advertising Director: Michael Domican
Advertising Sales: Eric Oldfield, Bob Treuber
Marketing Coordinator: Amy Winger
Marketing Assistant: Joanna Harper

YPN Development Producer: Jonathan Bellack
Associate Directory Editor: Richard Egan
YPN Managing Editor: Mila Shulkleper
YPN Producers: Molly Confer, Rachel Greene, Alison Grippo, Jonathan Spooner

Systems Administrator: Jonathan Chapman
Database Administrator: Graham Young
Database Technician: Toby Spinks

Administrative Assistant: Ann Peters

Wolff New Media LLC

Michael Wolff
President

James M. Morouse
Executive Vice President

Alison Anthoine
Vice President

Joseph Cohen
Chief Financial Officer

Special thanks:

NetResponse—Tom Feegel, Richard Mintz, Adam Behrens, Luis Babicek, Bob Bachle, Max Cacas, Cheryl Gnehm, Paul Hinkle, Larry Kirk, Chris Quillian, Jonathan Rouse, Brent Sleeper, and Pete Stein

And, as always, Aggy Aed

The editors of *NetGuide* can be reached at Wolff New Media LLC, 520 Madison Avenue, 11th Floor, New York, NY 10022, or by voice call at 212-308-8100, fax at 212-308-8837, or email at editors@ypn.com.

CONTENTS

PART 5: Home & Health

PART 6: The Digital World

PART 7: Education & Culture

PART 8: Identity & Society

Contents

FAQ

"Frequently Asked Questions" about the Net and NetGuide

I. Big as this book is, and it is *big*, it isn't as big as the entire Internet, is it? What will I find here that I won't find online?

YOUR POINT IS WELL MADE, and we are happy to oblige. The key issue is that while there is nothing within these pages that you won't find online, without this book, you will have a lot more trouble finding it. Here are some other points to consider:

• If you are new online and looking for a book that will guide you to the sites you *really* want to see—from a range of topics that expands by the second— then this book has everything you need.

• If you have quite a bit of online experience, yet require a direct, easy-to-follow, and carefully researched map of the very best the Net has to offer, then this book has everything you need.

• If you are an expert netsurfer and fancy a fresh set of bookmarks with considered, critical synopses of their content, then this book has everything you need.

• If you are a netmaniac and feel every second that you spend offline is time squandered, then this book has everything you need—you can't use your computer to check out new Web sites when you are in the bath, in bed, or on a bus.

2. So how easy is it to find my way around this book?

FOR EXPERIENCED NETSURFERS it's easier than checking email. If you already know what you're interested in, just turn to the *NetGuide* index. If you are of a more systematic leaning, then you may wish to browse the book, section by section. Accordingly, *NetGuide* is divided as follows:

- **Entertainment**
  If it's at the movies, on TV, at the video store or on the radio, it's online

- **Sci-Fi & Fringe**
  If it hadn't been invented, the Net would have been a sci-fi dream

- **Fun & Games**
  We all like a laugh every now and then

- **Recreation**
  Exercise other than just bashing the keyboard

- **Home & Health**
  From online doctors to bringing up children

- **The Digital World**
  A beginners guide to the slickest computing and Internet resources

- **Education & Culture**
  An introduction to what is becoming an encyclopedia of all knowledge

- **Identity & Society**
  The Internet is not just for pale males with wrist cramps

- **Virtual Newsstand**
  All the news that's fit to digitize—and more

- **Politics & Government**
  Giving democracy a shot in the arm

- **Dollars & Sense**
  Can you make secure transactions online? Bank on it.

 If you want to take a rapid tour of the book and only look at the sites we have deemed the very best in any category, look for the target symbol next to our Click Picks.

3. I get it. This book will guide me to the parts of the Net I actually *want* to see! So, what exactly is the Net?

THE NET IS THE FUTURE of communications, and the largest part of the Net is the Internet, the global, noncommercial system that has more than 30 million computers communicating through it. The World Wide Web, email, Usenet, FTP, telnet, and IRC are all available via the Internet.

Most other Net traffic passes through the commercial online services, such as America Online and CompuServe. Running on their own networks, commercial services are generally more secure than the Internet and some people are more comfortable using them for online financial transactions. You can also use them for email, and most offer gateways to the Internet.

The Net is most commonly used to exchange email, and unless you have spent the last two years in an ashram on Venus, you will know that the second most commonly used area of the Net is the World Wide Web.

4. Ah, the World Wide Web. How does it work ?

THINK OF A HOUSEHOLD BRAND NAME. Prefix it with a "www." and suffix it with a ".com". Chances are you will have come up with a functioning Web address. The Web is the hypertext-based information structure that now dominates Internet navigation. In its early days, people described it as being like a house in which every room has doors to a number of other rooms. Today, most people recognize that a computer screen invariably has an option in which words, icons, and pictures on a page are connected to elements on other pages not only on the same machine, but anywhere in the world. If you know exactly where you want to go on the Net and don't want to wade through Net directories and indexes, you can type a Web address, known as a URL (uniform resource locator). The URL for Your Personal Net, for example, is www.ypn.com. Prototypes of machines you can use to browse the Web on your televison set exist, but until they arrive on the market you will need a computer and a modem to get online and find your way around.

5. **What computer and modem do you recommend?**

OPEN A NEWSPAPER AND YOU will see endless advertisements for powerful home computers with built-in modems and extraordinary processing power. Wait six months and you will see the same package for much less money. It's infuriating, but eventually you will have to take the plunge, and the standard advice to anyone buying a computer is: Decide what you want it for. Gamers will likely want the fastest processor and a fast CD-ROM. If you want a computer for design, you may want a Mac. Either way, you will want a 28,800 modem—which transfers data at speeds up to 28,800 bits per second (bps)—built into your system or plugged in externally. You should be able to pick one up for about $100, if you shop around. Finally, you'll want a telephone line. If that's still not fast enough, you could install an ISDN line, which conveys data up to five times the speed.

6. **And what kind of account?**

A COUPLE OF YEARS AGO the easiest way to play online was to sign up with one of the big services, usually America Online, CompuServe or Prodigy. These days most people know that a free-standing online service can't give you the diversity of information and entertainment you will find on the World Wide Web. As a result, all online services are now repurposing themselves as Internet gateways with bells and whistles. For the time being, the most popular way to access the Net is through an Internet Service Provider, and the simplest way to find the nearest one to you is, oddly enough, to look them up online. At www.thelist.com you'll find a directory of many of the ISPs in the country. Most will provide you with a basic package of software you wil need, and not you can get the friend who showed you the list's Web site to download it for you.

For your information, here are some of your current access choices:

Email Gateway

This is the most basic access you can get. It lets you send and receive messages to and from anyone, anywhere, anytime on the Net. Keep your eye open for free (i.e., ad-sponsored) services like Juno.

Online Services

Online services are cyber city-states. The large ones have more "residents" (members) than most U.S. cities—enough users, in other words, to support lively discussions and games among their membership, and enough resources to make a visit worthwhile. They generally require special start-up software, (Hint: Look for the inescapable starter-kit giveaways.).

Internet Providers

As explained in question 4, there are many full-service Internet providers. Dial-up SLIP (serial line Internet protocol) and PPP (point-to-point protocol) accounts are currently the most popular types of Internet connections. Even faster connection methods like ISDN, ASDL, and cable modems are hovering on the horizon).

BBSs

BBSs range from mom-and-pop, hobbyist computer bulletin boards to large professional services. What the small ones lack in size they often make up for in affordability and homeyness. Unfortunately, the scenic byroads off the infobahn are becoming obsolete. On the other hand, many of the largest BBSs are almost as rich and diverse as the commercial online services. BBSs are easy to get started with. If you find one with Internet access or an email gateway, you'll get the best of local color and global reach at once. You can locate local BBSs through the Usenet discussion groups alt.bbs.lists and comp.bbs.misc, the BBS forums of the commercial services, and regional and national BBS lists kept in the file libraries of many BBSs. Many, if not most, local BBSs now offer Internet email, as well as live chat and file libraries.

Direct Network Connection

The direct network connection is the fast track of college students, computer scientists, and a growing number of employees of high-tech businesses. It puts the user right on the Net, bypassing phone connections. In other words, it's a heck of a lot faster.

7. Email? Will it replace the telephone?

WITH EMAIL, YOU CAN WRITE to anyone on a commercial service, Internet site, or Internet-linked BBS, as well as to those people on the Net via email gateways, SLIPs, and direct-network connections.

An Internet address is broken down into four parts: the user's name (e.g., wolff), the @ symbol, the computer and/or company name, and what kind of Internet address it is: **net** for network, **com** for a commercial enterprise—as with Your Personal Net (ypn.com) and America Online (aol.com)—**edu** for educational institutions, **gov** for government sites, **mil** for military facilities, and **org** for nonprofit and other private organizations. For instance, the address for one of the designers of this book, who, despite one impossible creative challenge after another, continues to show up in the office dressed like a Victorian banker would be jaffe@ypn.com.

8. What about these newsgroups?

THERE ARE MANY PLACES in cyberspace where netsurfers can post their opinions, questions, and comments, but the most widely read bulletin boards are a group of over 10,000 "newsgroups" collectively known as Usenet. Usenet newsgroups are global, collecting thousands of messages a day from whomever wants to "post" to them. Everything is discussed here. Check out www.dejanews.com for comprehensive lists and searchable archives. To cut back on repetitive questions, newsgroup members often compile extensive lists of answers to frequently asked questions (FAQs). Many FAQs have grown so large and so comprehensive that they are valuable resources in their own right, informal encyclopedias (complete with hypertext links) dedicated to the newsgroup's topic.

9. Mailing lists?

MAILING LISTS ARE LIKE NEWSGROUPS, except that they are distributed by Internet email. The fact that messages show up in your mailbox tends to make the discussion group more intimate, as does the proactive act of subscribing. Mailing lists are often more focused, and they're less vulnerable to irreverent and irrelevant contributions.

To subscribe to a mailing list, send an email to the list's subscription address. You will often need to include very specific information, which you will find in this book. To unsubscribe, send another message to that same address. If the mailing list is of the listserv, listproc, or majordomo variety, you can usually unsubscribe by sending the command **unsubscribe ‹listname›** or **signoff ‹listname›** in the message body. If the mailing list instructs you to "write a request" to subscribe ("Dear list owner, please subscribe me to..."), you will probably need to write a request to unsubscribe.

10. And telnet, FTP, gopher? Can you explain?

Telnet

When you telnet, you're logging on to another computer somewhere else on the Internet. You then have access to the programs running on the remote computer. If the site is running a library catalog, for example, you can search the catalog. If it's running a live chat room, you can communicate with others logged on. Telnet addresses are listed as URLs, in the form **telnet://domain .name:port number**. A port number is not always required, but when listed, it must be used.

FTP

FTP (file transfer protocol) is a way to copy a file from another Internet-connected computer to your own. Hundreds of computers on the Internet allow "anonymous FTP." Since the advent of Web browsers, netsurfers can transfer files without using a separate FTP program. In this book, FTP addresses are listed as URLs, in the form **ftp://domain.name/directory/filename.txt**. And here's a bonus—logins and passwords aren't required with Web browsers.

Gopher

A program that turns Internet addresses into menu options. Gophers perform many Internet functions, including telnetting and downloading but have now been superceded by the Web. Any gopher addresses you might access through the addresses in this book will be accessible via your Web browser.

II. So the addresses will look how exactly?

ALL ENTRIES IN *NETGUIDE* have a name, review, and address. The site name appears first in boldface, followed by a review of the site. After the review, complete address information is provided. The name of the service appears first: **WEB** to designate the World Wide Web, and so on. The text following the service tells you what you need to do to get to the site. When you see an arrow (→), this means that you have another step ahead of you. Bullets separate multiple addresses.

If the item is a Web site, an FTP site, telnet, or gopher, it will be displayed in the form of a URL. FTP and gopher sites will be preceded by **URL**, while telnet sites, which cannot be launched directly through a browser, will be preceded by **TELNET**. If the item is a mailing list, the address will include an email address and instructions on how to subscribe. IRC (Internet Relay Chat) addresses indicate what you must type to get to the channel you want once you've connected to the IRC server. Entries about newsgroups are always followed by the names of the newsgroups.

In an online service address, the name of the service is followed by the keyword (also called "go word"). Additional steps are listed where necessary. In addition, there are a few special terms used in addresses. *Info* indicates a supplementary informational address. *Archives* is used to mark collections of past postings for newsgroups and mailings lists. And *FAQ* designates the location of a "frequently asked questions" file for a newsgroup.

12. Great! What else can I do?

WE AT NETBOOKS ARE CHARTING the whole range of human existence as it is represented online, and we probably have exactly what you're looking for. Try one of these for size: *NetChat, NetGames, NetSports, NetMusic, Fodor's NetTravel, NetVote, NetJobs, NetMarketing, NetTech, NetDoctor, NetStudy, NetCollege, NetSpy,* and *NetSci-Fi.* Lined up for the future we have *NetMoney, NetTravel USA,* and *NetLove.* Just around the corner, look out for *NetKids* and *NetShopping.* Happy hunting!

INFOSEEKING

Infoseek's Top 10 rules for searching the Internet

RULE 1. **Ask whatever you want**

THE FIRST TIME YOU USE a search engine you may want to see just what it's got. You may want to test drive it. You may want to ask it a question you imagine it has no hope of answering. Suppose you are planning a trip to a little-known corner of the planet. You type in: **Get me a hotel in Harrogate, now!** Were you to ask this of some search engines, you would be given an indiscriminate list of sites with the words "Harrogate" or "hotel" in them. Or nothing. Type the question into Infoseek and the first thing you see is the Harrogate Hotels Directory Index. This is followed by a list of hotels, guest houses and local information about England's premier northern Spa town.

Infoseek also seems to understand that a stay in Harrogate may not be the pinnacle experience of a transatlantic tour, so alongside this information it includes topics that begin with "Hotels and Resorts in Europe." Of course you may not need a hotel. Maybe you want to know **What are the lyrics to Penny Lane?** Try it!

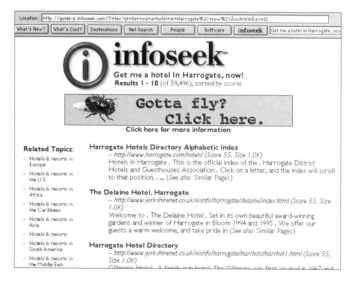

RULE 2. **Say what you mean**

WHILE IT IS POSSIBLE for a search engine to ignore some words, others might simply confuse it. A question that often rears its head in art circles is **Was the Renaissance good for Michelangelo or was it the other way around?** Type that in and you'll find yourself taking a virtual tour of Italy. Happy Fresco. If what you really want is a Michelangelo biography, why not try **Michelangelo biography?**

RULE 3. **Watch your spelling**

ANYONE WHO HAS READ email knows that literacy has never been at a premium on the Internet, but as more and more information is added to the online database, seeking it out will require a commitment to some conventions of accuracy. If you're looking for information on David Schwimmer (of the TV series *Friends*), don't spell his name "Swimmer" or "Schimmer." Why? Because you'll get swimming information with the former, and nothing with the latter.

RULE 4. **Know where to look**

NO POINT LOOKING UP newsgroups on mailing lists, or Web sites on a search engine devoted to newsgroup posts. Make sure that you've directed your search engine to look at the right section of the Internet—it's huge, and you don't want to be looking in the wrong place. For example, you may be looking up a long-lost relative, a business contact, or to see if the bank robbery you just committed has been reported yet. At the Infoseek home page you can specify the area of your search by using the pull-down menu, which offers email addresses, the World Wide Web, Usenet newsgroups, and special options like "Timely News" and "Company Directory."

RULE 5. **A phrase is a phrase is "a phrase"**

YOU DON'T HAVE TO PLACE quote marks around a phrase to limit your search, "but it helps!" For example, if you're searching for information on the film *First Wives Club*, put the title in quotes—otherwise, you'll get a page that contains firsts, wives, and clubs. Goldie, Bette, and Diane will be nowhere to be seen. You want to know who said **Tomorrow and tomorrow and tomorrow?** Make sure you use the quotes, otherwise the rest of Macbeth's maudlin meanderings will be beyond the grasp of your browser.

RULE 6. **Be proper**

AS IN LIFE, SO ON THE WEB. Suppose you are a Prince fan and interested in knowing what became of his 1986 black and white movie, *Under the Cherry Moon*. Attempt a search without capitalizing the movie's full name and you will find a list of nightclubs called "Cherry Moon" that is as long as a Nelson Rogers guitar solo.

RULE 7. **Take direction**

ONCE IN A WHILE YOU'RE going to switch on your machine and you won't have a clue where to begin. Something has happened and you really need to know the answer, quick. You could type **Get me a new job**, but better yet, you could take a tour of the careers directories accessible through the Infoseek home page.

RULE 8. **Take exception**

MOST SEARCH ENGINES allow you to eliminate search terms from a sentence. For example, you want to know everything about baseball but you aren't interested in that fantasy stuff. You want nothing to do with office gambling. You want nothing to do with rotisseries. So, were you searching on Infoseek this would be your search sentence: **+baseball and -rotisserie**

RULE 9. **Think "site & title"**

THERE'S A HUMORIST OF DISTINCTION named Joe Queenan. Someone told you about this hilarious piece he wrote. He thinks it was in a site called Mr. Showbiz, or something. You have nothing else to go on. You type **site: mrshowbiz joe queenan** into your Infoseek search window. Up comes a list of the estimable author's latest rants. Bingo! Say you need a used car but you don't know one online used car dealership. Type **title: used car** and you will be presented with all Web sites that have the phrase "used car" in them. Now you're driving! Try this with other search engines and you're stuck in the slow lane.

RULE 10. **Look carefully**

THE WEB ISN'T JUST words, remember. There are millions of fascinating pictures. If you want to search for one of them, don't waste your time with a normal search sentence—most images won't be caught. Instead, use Infoseek's special search facilities and type the name of the person or thing you want to see pictured. Whatever you want to see, from portraits of James Bond to paintings of the world's cathedrals, you'll find them here. Another feature you might find useful is the opportunity to see where you're going. Literally. Suppose you need to meet someone in Washington, but you're not sure how to get there. They give you the address—1600 Pennsylvania

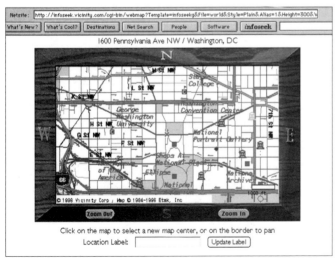

Avenue—and you have no idea where it is, what it's near... nothing. Go to Fast Facts, look under the heading Street Maps and type in the address. You'll never have trouble meeting up with Chelsea again!

PART I
Entertainment

Entertainment

CLICK PICKS
The very best on the Net

Showbiz

No need to hit the road for Hollywood. It's all on the Net

SHOW BIZ SHINES like never before on what could ultimately become the biggest marquee ever—the Internet. As gods and goddesses of glamor go digital, the gossip factory that is Tinseltown is beginning to generate a multitude of news channels, movie review pages, photo galleries, clipping services, fan-worship pages, episode guides, parody pages, and countless more resources that make the Net a haven for celebrity-struck surfers. The newest on the big-screen luminaries, the archives on the classics, and the future of film and television, and theater wait at your popcorn-buttered mousepad for the curtain to rise and the show to begin. Sites, camera, action!

09/04 TV Actor Brandon Call Shot In LA Traffic Dispu

LOS ANGELES (Sept. 4) - Actor Brandon Call, who appeared in the TV sitcom "Step by Step", was shot in both arms during an apparent traffic dispute, police said on Wednesday.

The 19-year-old Call, who played J.T. Lambert on the show starring Patrick Duffy and Suzanne Somers, was listed in good condition Wednesday at UCLA Medical Center.

Police said he had been driving home Tuesday night when he was shot in the Mid-City section of Los Angeles. His car had at least four bullet holes in the driver's side and windshield.

A police spokesman said Call had tried to avoid a car that was pursuing him following an apparent dispute. He drove into a dead-end street and when he turned around, he was shot by the occupants of the other car. The suspects

SHOWBIZ NEWS & INFO

AMERICA ONLINE *keyword* showbiz news

Broadway has its theaters. Hollywood has its movie studios. And this area on **AOL** has links to the big names in entertainment: *Entertainment Weekly*, *People*, the *New York Times*'s Arts & Leisure section, an entertainment newswire with photos, and several movie-review services—everything you could ever want to know about Tinseltown from box office bombs to blockbusters. Babble about your special celebrities in the chat room, post picture requests on the message board, or sally forth into star-studded cyberspace.

Starting points

AOL Live! More than 35,000 AOL members (5,000 in each of seven auditoriums) can attend AOL Live events at any one time, and when the forum hosts the biggest big names in showbiz, the music industry, or politics, its auditoriums fill to capacity. On any given evening, a supermodel might be chatting with AOLers in one auditorium while a senator is fielding questions in another, and a star athlete in another. Yeah, right. At least that's the theory, anyway. Nevertheless, like Carnegie Hall in New York or Hammersmith Odeon in London, AOL Live consistently draws big-name guests: Mick Jagger, Peter Jennings, Ted Kennedy, Armand Assante, Victoria Principal, Ice-T, Cheap Trick, Sally Jesse Raphael, Conan O'Brien, The Doors, Billy Joel, and many more. Visit the huge archives for transcripts of past events and publicity photos of the guest stars.
AMERICA ONLINE *keyword* centerstage

The Biz The Biz offers a typical array of tabloid-style TV, movie, and music news. What makes The Biz a little different is its consideration of new media and advertising as entertainment, as well as an enormous archive of QuickTime music videos. If for nothing else, use it as a link to the hourly Reuter/Variety news updates.
WEB http://pathfinder.com/bizmag

English Server Film and Television A collection of essays produced by the English Server, a cooperative that has published humanities texts on the Internet since 1990. Topics range from discussions of PBS and the nature of corporate ownership of broadcasting to an interactive story involving Theodore Tugboat, the cheerful star of a Canadian TV show.
WEB http://english.hss.cmu.edu /FilmandTV.html

Entertainment Encyclopedia Who says encyclopedias are dry?

This gold mine of entertainment information includes a list of celebrity birthdays (Mary Tyler Moore is a Capricorn, Lyndon Johnson was a Virgo, and Sly Stone is a Pisces); prime-time TV schedules, a Beatles tour history; Oscar, Tony, and Grammy Award winners; and an A-Z listing of pop and rock musicians that includes the release dates for all albums and singles.
COMPUSERVE *go* hhl-249

Extra Keep in mind that as a joint venture of Time and Warner Bros. Extra is very

"You talkin' to *me*?"
http://www.mrshowbiz.com

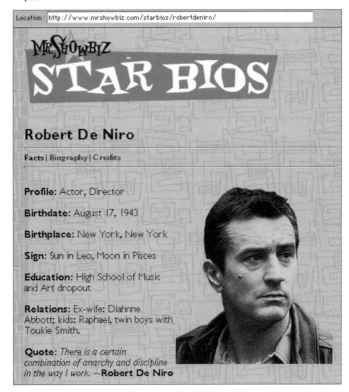

Location: http://www.mrshowbiz.com/starbios/robertdeniro/

MrSHOWBIZ
STAR BIOS

Robert De Niro

Facts | Biography | Credits

Profile: Actor, Director

Birthdate: August 17, 1943

Birthplace: New York, New York

Sign: Sun in Leo, Moon in Pisces

Education: High School of Music and Art dropout

Relations: Ex-wife: Diahnne Abbott; kids: Raphael, twin boys with Toukie Smith.

Quote: *There is a certain combination of anarchy and discipline in the way I work.* --**Robert De Niro**

often repackaged doo-dads from *People, Time, Sports Illustrated*, and promos for Warner Bros. pictures. The result is a tabloid with some fairly dubious original features, as this sampling of headlines will attest: "You Can Live to 100 Yet Stay as Lively as a Teenager," "Last Lepers in Hawaii Tell How They Beat This Frightening Disease," "The Search is On at *Playboy* for Hardbody Bunnies," and "Elvis' Vacation in 1956." Movie reviews and star interviews save this site from being relegated to the ranks of supermarket checkout fare.
WEB http://www.extratv.com

Hollywood Wrap Pop quiz, hot shot: You're out of the broadcast range of KCRW radio, but you can't bear to miss Nikki Finke's weekly interviews with Hollywood heavyweights. What do you do? Just speed over to the Hollywood Wrap page and start downloading from the generous selection of RealAudio feeds. Anyone interested in movie and TV production will want to catch this show. Aside from talking heads, Finke's program also features stories ranging from the revamping of television to the difficulties of screenwriting. Information on upcoming shows and an archive of past

programs are available as well.
WEB http://www.kcrw.org/hw

Showbiz Media Forum Starstruck fans could get lost in this forum's library with its photos of actors and actresses, celebrity FAQs, sound clips from popular movies (listen to Stallone deliver the line "Judge This!" or Lori Petty exclaim "Faaabulous!"), QuickTime previews of upcoming movies, episode guides and trivia lists, and provocative photos of famous women (Elle Macpherson nude, Drew Barrymore nude, Uma Thurman topless, Winona Ryder in the tub, etc.). And the message boards

 # ENTERTAINMENT WEEKLY
WEB http://pathfinder.com/ew

Interested in who scored and who bored this season? Want to read about "the stars of the digital age"? Or maybe you want a lesson on how to be a star from everybody's favorite *ER* nurse, Julianna Margulies? It's all here, along with interviews, message areas, and reviews of movies, TV

shows, as well as an excellent multimedia section that is sustained by withering reviews of CD-ROMs and generous ones of Web sites. In the section labeled Critical Mass Interactive, netsurfers can check out the grades given to movies by reviewers and audiences—and even cast their own votes.

Location: http://www.hyperlink.com/muse/95/7_8/dance/contemp.

A little twist on the Macarena
http://www.hyperlink.com/muse

aren't exactly dull; forum members gossip about celebs, respond to Roger Ebert's latest movie reviews, discuss foreign films, and consider the issues of film production.
COMPUSERVE *go* showbiz

Commentary

Beck/Smith Exclusive Which series have been canceled? What's the score with the new John Grisham film? And which actor's been picked up for drug possession? Marilyn Beck and Stacey Jenel Smith report on the entertainment industry in a syndicated column for hundreds of newspapers and the CompuServe community.
COMPUSERVE *go* beck

Critics' Choice Its goal: to prevent you from spending hard-earned money or valuable time with recreation that's just not going to pay off. Its method: detailed reviews. Its coverage: movies, television, videos, books, music, and games. This online guide not only reviews the movies currently at the box office or the games hitting the stores next week, it also customizes some of the reviews—e.g., there are separate reviews for each movie based on its appropriateness for kids. The forum also carries daily news coverage of the entertainment industry and hosts a message board where AOLers themselves can be the critics.
AMERICA ONLINE *keyword* critics

Entertainment Drive Take a seat and click on over to movie talk, movie reviews, celebrity photos, video trailers from current movie blockbusters, sound clips, *Playboy* photos, and soap summaries. And, wait, is that Tom Hanks, Lori Petty, or Brandon Tartikoff in the conference room? (EDrive regularly hosts live conferences with big stars.) But if video clips and live conferences aren't enough, head to the Entertainment Drive Forum where movie fans are discussing classic Hollywood films, dead celebrities, the theater, and hot stars of the moment. The forum is home to more than showbiz oohing and aahing, it's also filled with Letterman Top Ten lists, Rex Reed reviews, star photos, and movie clips—and there's the *Baywatch* library.
COMPUSERVE *go* edrive

Film Comment This real-world prototype for the alt.movies newsgroup started in 1962 as a magazine devoted to documentaries and "serious" film fodder. Now, two decades after its peak years championing directors like Robert Altman and Martin Scorsese, *Film Comment* has gone digital with all its charms intact: its yearly Ten Best, Grosses Glosses (a review of what rocked and what tanked at the box office) and the fun Guilty Pleasures page, wherein famous directors admit to less-than-honorable favorite films.
MSN *keyword* filmcomment

Hot Hollywood Gossip Hung over from the online Hollywood hype? Steve Gordon administers the perfect antidote—a parody of celebrity gossip. Gossipy Gordon tosses out the latest outrageous tabloid tidbit, and readers submit their most clever standup replies. Unfortunately, the call-and-answer technique fails to provoke its promised wit. But the celebrity bytes are mildly amusing, conjuring images of Jack Nicholson whipping his women with a ping-pong paddle, or shaking an upside-down Tori Spelling to see what falls out.
WEB http://members.aol.com/editor man/gossip.html

The Movie Critic Become a bona fide movie critic here. Rate 12 movies of your choice for admission into the Movie Critic archive where you'll get film recommendations from viewers like yourself. Enter the directory to browse movie reviews, star profiles, catchy quotes, credits, and nearly anything else you'd want to know about a film.
WEB http://www.moviecritic.com

Mr. Showbiz This online magazine features editorials on the showbiz world, movie reviews, illustrated movie satire, and gossip. It also solicits your vote on a weekly issue: Did the media overexpose the Hugh Grant scandal? You make the call. Mr. Showbiz is also home to online fiction and games like "Plastic Surgery Lab" to round off an entertaining page.
WEB http://www.mrshowbiz.com

The Muse An artsy monthly electronic magazine "reflecting on the Creative Arts, Music, Cinema, Books, Dance and Theatre." Typical fare includes a profile of Roman Polanski, a feature on Laurie Anderson, and a review of the Pushpalata Dance Company. Back issues are also archived at the site.
WEB http://www.hyperlink.com/muse

People Online Are you mad about Brad? Interested in the $145,500 paid for the white polyester suit worn by John Travolta in *Saturday Night Fever*? Head to *People* for feature stories and photographs, along with reviews and lots of

MovieWorld

WEB http://www.movieworld.com

Hello, and welcome to MovieWorld. If you'd like to check out today's price for your Viacom Stock, press one. If you want to surf the sites of movie critics, from Mr. Cranky to Joe Bob Briggs, press two. If your modem is running well and you'd like to download our animation clips, press three...

You get the idea—Hollywood Insider news, reviews, artwork, links—the works. But what we'd really like to know is whether Orville Reddenbacher is a silent sponsor of MovieWorld. That would explain the abundance of near-subliminal popcorn screens at most links.

Location: http://pathfinder.com/@@uW5*0QcAUAyHA3yz/people/sp/bikini/index.html

BIKINI BIRTHDAY ONE-HALF CENTURY OF THE TWO PIECE

- BIKINI MOMENTS
- BIKINI LINE
- BIKINI BINGO

People ONLINE

People magazine celebrates the anniversaries that really matter
http://pathfinder.com/people

celebrity news. Check out The Insider for the scoop on private rehearsals, celebrity reunions, and disappearing characters on your favorite TV shows. Scan celebrity bios from Fiennes to Fawn Hall.
WEB http://pathfinder.com/people

Saturday Review Online It was a magazine for the cultured, the refined, the aesthetically inclined. It folded after more than 50 years of tasteful publishing. Now the *Saturday Review* returns as an online venture, bringing essays about art and the information age, announcements of museum exhibit openings, works of fiction, reviews of theater performances, and areas with resources for and discussions by classical music enthusiasts, politics buffs, and avid readers.
AMERICA ONLINE *keyword* saturday review

Screen Shot Nice graphics, ancient content. End of story. Screen Shot promises "exclusive interviews with the hottest stars," but most archive entries of RealAudio interviews are over three years old. Do you still really want to hear Arnold Schwarzenegger talk about *Last Action Hero*? The available film reviews are not quite as moldy, but you'd have better luck finding the movies they're talking about in a video store than in a movie theater.
WEB http://www.screenshots.com

Somethin' Juicy Fresh-squeezed daily gossip on the movie and TV world's megawatt stars, delivered in quick cyberbytes with the sass of the E! cable channel. That comes as no surprise, since one of the reviewers, Flo Anthony, is a former E! writer, a former soap-opera actress, former sports writer at

the *New York Post*, and a former PR rep for Muhammad Ali. Plenty of tabloid tidbits to keep the seekers of the sensational happy.
WEB http://www.dnx.com/gossip

TimeOut Covering Europe and New York, *TimeOut* online posts calendars of arts and entertainment events in Amsterdam, Berlin, London, Madrid, New York City, Paris, and Prague, as well as dozens of articles on such topics as the bar scene in Paris, sightseeing in Prague, and coffee shops in Amsterdam.
WEB http://www.timeout.co.uk

Industry

And the Winner Is... Admit it: Even if you've never heard of a particular award ceremony, you do want to know who won. Here's a virtual banquet of rans and also-rans, from the big Kahunas—The Oscars and the The New York Film Critics Awards—to more quirky festivities like the Berlin and Cannes Festivals.
MSN *keyword* and the winner is

Bill Mead's Entertainment Technology Page Hypertext links to the Web pages of film studios, movie theaters, film magazines, and companies and institutes involved in audio and video product development.
WEB http://www.cinenet.net/users /wmead/ca_tech.html

The Casting Forum If your six-year-old has star quality, your

girlfriend is better looking than Linda Evangelista, or you're an aspiring actor with more talent than opportunities, why not take a chance in the Casting Forum? Upload a resume and photo (only one each) and maybe a casting director or modeling agency will call. Maybe.
AMERICA ONLINE *keyword* casting

Hollywired A useful piece-by-piece breakdown of everything you'll need to produce your own film. Choose a location, then zoom in on the resource you require whether it's lighting, make-up, or the regional weather forecast. A handy tool for would-be directors.
WEB http://www.hollywoodwired.com

The Internet Entertainment Network, Inc. Targeting aspiring actors, directors, and screenwriters, this site features monthly columns, contests, and tips from the pros. Facilities include a directory of entertainment-industry contacts and organizations, entertainment-law information, scriptwriting resources with a registry and library, and a shopping service with books, software, celebrity photos, games, souvenirs, trade publications, and videos. Chat loungers post questions and comments to Hollywood professionals on a number of topics—you can chat with your favorite *The Price Is Right* star and even relax with a game of Trivianet.
WEB http://hollywoodnetwork.com

The Talent Network This polished site aspires to be a directory of performers and production personnel (hair stylists, sound technicians, set designers, location managers, etc.). Email the site for information on how to get listed.
WEB http://www.talentnet.com
EMAIL webmaster@talentnet.com ✍
Write a request

Women in Film & Television This Australian organization works to promote the position of women in film and television, by providing detailed actress information, advice, links to gopher related sites, and contact with other women in the industry.
WEB http://www.deakin.edu.au/arts /VPMA/wift.html

Celebrities

alt.binaries.nude.celebrities Post your yearnings for nude pictures, complaints about porn site disappointments, flames, me-toos, fakes, and even nude pictures of the unfamous, usually scanned from men's magazines.
USENET alt.binaries.nude.celebrities

alt.binaries.pictures.celebrities More or less the same as alt.binaries.nude.celebrities, except the descriptions of the pictures occasionally include the phrase "no nudity." This group seems to be a magnet for spams, scams, and get-rich-quick posts. Only the gullible need apply.
USENET alt.binaries.pictures.celebrities

alt.celebrities Primarily a request site for celebrity information. Newsgroup regulars discuss the celebrity scandal of the week and speculate on sexual orientations of the famous, while collectors search for pics.
USENET alt.celebrities

alt.fan.actors The usual tabloid discussion of celebrity scandals and requests for addresses.
USENET alt.fan.actors

alt.fan.teen.idols *Tiger Beat* meets NAMBLA. A more-or-less equal mix of young, starstruck fans seeking tidbits about their idols, and somewhat older gentlemen interested in the teens.
USENET alt.fan.teen.idols

alt.fan.teen.starlets A forum for discussions of the talent, looks, and attributes of nubile and nearly nubile actresses. Most of the messages are requests for info and pictures of young girls.
USENET alt.fan.teen.starlets

alt.showbiz.gossip A very popular group. Common threads revolve around "Who's gay?" "Who's fat?" and "Who's askin'?" Celebrity deaths often result in an RIP notice to this group, usually followed up with sincere expressions of condolence.
USENET alt.showbiz.gossip

Bitesite: Celebrity Bites Earsful of an extensive list of stars, plus thumbnail sketch biographies. Hear why Kyra Sedg-

wick acts, where Matthew McConaughy was discovered, and which is Sean Connery's favorite James Bond film. A growing, well-structured archive for getting to know celebrities.
WEB http://www.bitesite.com/celeb /bsceleb.html

Celebrity Circle Sent Sandra Bullock hundreds of fan letters? Fought your way through the crowds at an autograph signing for Alicia Silverstone? Maybe there's an easier way. This site, sponsored by Oldsmobile (yes, the car manufacturer), features celebrity biographies and photos, a schedule of upcoming celebrity appearances in cyberspace, and nightly events.
AMERICA ONLINE *keyword* celebrity circle

Cinemania A labor of love by people seriously in love with the movies. Most of what goes on movie-wise on MSN can be found here in a truly impressive database that includes biographies of film stars and creators, obscure films, photo archives, and downloads of every imaginable stripe along with access to select Web/film pages.
MSN *keyword* cinemania

Real Names of Stars Get the skinny on stage pseudonyms. Bo Derek was born Cathleen Collins. Rita Hayworth was originally Margarita Cansino. Elton John changed his name from Reginald Dwight. And John Wayne was known to his parents as Marion Morrison. If showbiz trivia is your thing, check out this long list of

famous stars and their original names.
AMERICA ONLINE *keyword* showbiz→ Libraries→origst.nme

rec.arts.movies.people According to the FAQ, "this newsgroup contains discussions of actors, actresses, directors, writers, composers, film critics, etc. with focus on their skills, styles and other characteristics of the person(s) discussed. It also contains celebrity gossip." In practice, the newsgroup has a more scholarly tone than some of the other related newsgroups—gossip hounds may be disappointed. Many posters appear to be researching books, articles, or possibly— obsessions.
USENET rec.arts.movies.people

Silver Screen Siren Website See the sleek starlets of the past at this large photo gallery. Feather boas and diamond earrings sparkle off the likes of Ginger Rogers, Ingrid Bergman, Audrey Hepburn, and many more classic kittens of stardom.
WEB http://users.deltanet.com/users /dstickne

Theatre and Television Obituaries Obituaries of recently deceased professionals in television and the theater. Many entries contain links to biographies and filmographies. The glamorous graves of the famous, once famous, and obscure form a fascinating history of the entertainment business.
WEB http://catless.ncl.ac.uk/Obituary /theatre.html

Looking for screen sirens? Chew on this
http://users.deltanet.com/users/dstickne

Movies

FROM THE BIG SCREEN TO THE LITTLE SCREEN,
THE NET IS THE ULTIMATE SOUNDSTAGE

THE CENTURY'S FIRST mass medium is finding a home on the century's latest. The Internet is dense with fan pages devoted to actors and directors, review databases, and even movies (clips of classics and short, experimental videos); which isn't to say that the big studios have been slower on the uptake, both in terms of capitalizing on what's hot and marketing at the appropriate point in a movie's life-cycle. Still, what the sites lack in savvy they usually make up for in browser-crunching, state-of-the-art multimedia. Clear your cache log and check 'em out.

CINEMEDIA

WEB http://www.afionline.org/cinemedia

From the mainstream to the obscure, 6,000 category-indexed links point cinema-savvy netsurfers to whatever they're looking for: film home pages, film production company pages, animation and silent-film sites, scripts and screenwriting resources, film production resources, and dozens of cinema archives, institutes, and guilds. An in-house search engine makes finding the right sites easy. If your ever-burgeoning list of bookmarks can hold only one movie site, make it CineMedia.

Multiplexes

All Movie Guide This database doesn't appear to be superior to several like it on the Web, but it is certainly a substantial repository of film information. The most useful feature is the "If You Like This... " section of many of the entries, which lists movies that fans of one particular movie might also like. Fans of *Billy the Kid vs. Dracula*, for example, are advised to give *Godzilla* a whirl.
COMPUSERVE *go* all-movie guide

Cinema Sites If you want to broaden your cinematic knowledge beyond Hollywood, Cannes, and Sundance, cinephile David Augsburger has done a tremendous job of collecting bits and bytes from all corners of the film world. Want to learn about the vanishing cinemas of Paris? Brush up on the history of Thai film? Listen to movie sounds from *Caddyshack*? You can do any of those, or just read the latest issues of *Kulture Void* (an indie Web journal) or iNR's *Digital Matinee* (a newsletter for digifilmmakers). It's all here, including a few oddball subjects for TV buffs, such as the link to The Lurker's Guide to *Babylon 5*.
WEB http://www.webcom.com /~davidaug/Movie_Sites.html

Guide to Film and Video Resources on the Internet An index of Net addresses for hundreds of reviews, film discussions, filmographies, and searchable

Redneck reviews packed with paradigm
http://hotx.com/joebob

movie databases.
WEB http://http2.sils.umich.edu /Public/fvl/film.html

Joe Bob Briggs Drive-In America He's the pride of Grapevine, Texas, a man who knows, to the nearest decimal point, the number of "nekkid breasts" in every B-movie ever made. This cowpoke is Joe Bob Briggs, and he's the fastest gun west of the Mississippi when it comes to reviewing really bad movies with a surplus of really bad jokes. Mosey on over to his Web site to wrassle up his latest take on the type of movie they used to show in drive-in theaters, then shuffle through his vaguely-titled humor column, "America." And yes, he really will tell you how many naked breasts appear in each movie.
WEB http://hotx.com/joebob

Marquee You'll have to see if your tastes coincide with those of Seattle movie critics Doug

Thomas and Bob Cappel. We think they're fairly easy to please. You can also get their reviews emailed to you each week, if you decide their movie taste jibes with yours (or if you're just lonely). Marquee is well-organized, broken down into simple sections, including Continuing Runs, Pick of the Week, and What to Rent When the New Release Shelf is Empty.
WEB http://www.marquee.com

Movie Mom's Guide to Movies and Videos for Families This movie mom writes a guide to the latest to see and what not to see with your budding cineasts.
WEB http://www.pages.prodigy.com /VA/rcpj55a/moviemom.html

Movie Review Query Engine The good news is that you can search here for 19,576 reviews of 4,480 movies. The bad news is that when we tried it, the engine had trouble turning over at all. The quality of the reviews ranges from the sopho-moric to the professional.

WEB http://www.cinema.pgh.pa.us /movie/reviews

Movie Reviews on AOL The movie review section includes links to professional reviews from such sources as *The New York Times* and a bulletin board of messages from movie-goers about all the recent movies.

AMERICA ONLINE *keyword* movie reviews

rec.arts.movies.announce Dedi-cated movie mavens post the impressive efforts of their hard work in the form of compre-hensive listings about all mat-ters regarding the serious and sublime in filmdom. Typical subjects include worldwide box-office gross reports, an A to Z list of Oscar-eligible films, and lists of celebrity birthdays and obituary anniversaries.

USENET rec.arts.movies.announce
FAQ: **WEB** http://www.cis.ohio-state .edu/hypertext/faq/usenet-faqs /bygroup/rec/arts/movies/top.html

rec.arts.movies.current-films When choosing a film, do you base your decision on media reviews or a friend's recom-mendation? What about a

good middle ground—cyber-friends who publish in this newsgroup? Moviegoing fans gossip and speculate on current Hollywood and indie films, including some very thoughtful film critiques filled with literary references and analogies; post responses to the reviews of national film critics; discuss special effects and inflated blockbuster budgets; and pub-licly submit love and hate notes to the stars.

USENET rec.arts.movies.current-films

ReelViews Archives Don't fall victim to video store paralysis ever again. With a choice of

FILM.COM

WEB http://www.film.com/film

Designed for and by film critics, industry professionals, and movie buffs, Film.com's fascinating cinematic collection aims to bring an interactive and critical perspective to the world of film by offering newspaper reviews of current movies, reports of box-office receipts, and even an email column where you can see your own film comments listed on an indexed page of contributors. The Web site also sponsors a message board; discussions flourish on such topics as The All-Time

Winners, where you vote for your most and least favorite films, and Tarantino-ville, a section in honor of the world's most famous ex-video store clerk. Film.com has a film-fes-tival circuit report, video and laserdisc databases, essays on soundtracks, reports on movie-related newmakers and socio-political issues, and an index of links to other film resources on the Web.

Netsite: http://www.obs-us.com/obs/english/films/mx/deadman/pics/dead04.jpg

From Miramax, Johnny Depp plays William Blake in Jim Jarmusch's *Dead Man*: "Recite 'Tiger' or I'll pump you full of lead!"
http://www.miramax.com

more than 900 thorough, well-written reviews, you'll never worry about bringing home another boring flick.
WEB http://www.cybernex.net /~berardin/archives.html

T@p Film & Video A refreshing break from the same-old sites on movie stars and Hollywood blockbusters, T@p has something to offer fans on the fringes of movieland as well, with links to sites on cult, student, and retro films. Download shorts of student flicks, such as *Tapehead*, the touching story of a video camera and some Scotch, masking, and packaging tape; or the bizarre *Das Feet*. For Quentin Tarantino fans, there's an ezine: a demented little home for those crazy kids.
WEB http://www.taponline.com/tap /movie.html

Studios

Fine Line Features From the art-house division of New Line Cinema comes a site for fans of off-the-beaten-track films, with quickie seminars for would-be filmmakers and critics. Check up on this (and last) year's Fine Line releases, listen (via RealAudio) to three panel discussions on how films get made, and pore over cast-and-crew bios and production notes for each picture. Basically, it's an online press kit, with some film classes thrown in for good measure. Film clips can be downloaded in the new Vivo format, which is something like RealAudio, but with pictures.
WEB http://www.flf.com

MGM/UA—The Lion's Den The official Web site of MGM-United Artists is skillfully and

artfully presented, giving you a clickable guide to all the cubbyholes in the Lion's Lair, from what's the latest in MGM's home video line to the newest interactive video releases. Of course, the focus is on the motion picture division, and you'll find thumbnail sketches of many of the past, present and future offerings of the studio that Agent 007 brought back from the dead. Don't miss the link to the "reVamped" *Showgirls*, now playing the midnight circuit. And please don't feed the lion.
WEB http://www.mgmua.com

Miramax Miramax has managed to couch its menu of flicks in a fun-to-navigate virtual cafe. Lime and lavender acid-tinted screens with images of Siamese twins coming out of a manhole cover serve as the screen entrée to Counter Culture, the section for such offbeat flicks as *Dead Man*. There's a Blood and Guts gallery (for their offshoot, Dimension films) for all you gore fans, and Buzz, a helping of promo pieces updated every Friday, which is, after all, movie day. The site also boasts a terrific selection of downloadable trailers (more than many sites), and a gallery of stills from Miramax movies past and present.
WEB http://www.miramax.com

Sony Pictures Classics Sony's definition of "classic" means its roster of current independent and foreign films. Links to film synopses, cast/crew bios and credits, a contest to win a soundtrack, and some multimedia stills and clips are provided.

WEB http://www.spe.sony.com /Pictures/SonyClassics/index.html

Sony Pictures Entertainment: Movies Sony makes it easy to read about their latest movies with a giant scrollable billboard bringing you descriptions of current and upcoming films. You can also download screen savers and read the rules for entering your child in a casting call for an upcoming film, which, if nothing else, saves the site from becoming self serving.

WEB http://www.spe.sony.com /Pictures/SonyMovies/index.html

United International Pictures (UIP) Home Page This international film distributor offers links to the MGM/UA, Universal Pictures, and Paramount movie studio Web sites and their current film releases. You can view the pages in English, French, German, Spanish, or Dutch.

WEB http://www.uip.com

Universal V/IP MCA/Universal Pictures wants you to feel like a VIP when you screen pictures at their Visual/Interactive Previews Web site. Although there's nothing very special here, you can get preview information about scripts, production and costume design, and cast and crew biographies

for a few upcoming Universal releases.

WEB http://www.mca.com/universal _pictures

Walt Disney Pictures Enter the Magic Kingdom's family film site by clicking on the logo of the film of your choice. Surfing around is guaranteed to knock at least ten years off your age while you're there—and serve as a worthy cyberbabysitter for the young 'uns. At the *James and the Giant Peach* page, when you click onto a new screen, it magically goes from black-and-white to color, (shades of *The Wizard of Oz*). You can read story books of the films, print out pictures of Disney characters to color in, or do

 PARAMOUNT

WEB http://www.paramount.com

Enter the famous studio gates and get a virtual look at the latest exploits of the Paramount Pictures family. You'll be able to see posters for their feature films, icons for home video releases, images from the TV divisions lineup, and even previews for this evening's features on *Entertainment Tonight*. Click on any of these icons and get whisked to movie and TV pages so thick they could be a Web site of their own. The playful online extensions of such Paramount presentations as *Mission: Impossible* and *Star Trek: Voyager* are most impressive, with terrific graphics and

downloadable clips, audio, and, in the case of the latter page, some Web-exclusive material, for all you *Trek* completists. Some great ShockWave games are also available; the general rule of thumb seems to be that the better the movie, the worse the game.

Location: http://www.sirius.com/~sstark/mkr/cb/cb-one1.jpg

Craig Baldwin's *O No Coronado!*, from the Flicker Web site
http://www.sirius.com/~sstark

serious, grown up things—like downloading a trailer.
WEB http://www.disney.com/Disney Pictures/index.html

Warner Bros. Warner Bros. Online is like a funhouse of things to do on a rainy day that just happens to tie into the studio's pics. Listen to the original *Superman* radio broadcasts from five decades ago; croon along to Looney Tunes in the Karaoke section; or just check out Warner's latest films by clicking on icons resembling baseball cards. These motion picture tie-ins are often imaginative interactive games to coincide with new releases. One such offering allowed visitors to chase *Twister* as part of an experiment of the Severe Weather Institute Research Lab.
WEB http://www.warnerbros.com

Independent

Alternative Access Expressing the opinion that cable and regular TV have failed to serve the computer-driven videomaker, this page hopes to change that with easily downloadable, QuickTime works from the student body of the University of Texas. A bit scatter-headed, the page is not without merit; there's some good work here.
WEB http://www.piglet.cc.utexas.edu /~bulls/altacc.html

Alternative Cinema Magazine No, "alternative cinema" does not refer to the art (and it is an art) of paying for one movie and sneaking into another at the multiplex. It is, instead, a little-appreciated school of filmmaking (often deservedly so), and this is its flagship magazine. Download front and back cov-

ers of the print version or preview the most recent issue's features. If you want Adobe Acrobat Reader (and you do, if you intend to play here), the link has been kindly provided. But even with a 28.8 hookup it takes half an hour—just so you know.
WEB http://www.members.aol.com /acmagazine/ac.html

Beyond Eerie post-industrial/ gothic graphics lead us through the disturbing world of cinematographer/director Zoe Beloff. Explore "monsters created by the marriage of Freud and Edison" in QuickTime downloads. Serious Teutonic weirdness.
WEB http://www.users.interport.net /~zoe

Documentary Film Site As matter-of-fact as its name, this Holland-based site is a sober affair, with an impressive, world-wide database of documentary films, distributors and a vast film library accompanied by downloadable QuickTime clips. There is also Chat Communication, and email offers for every imaginable job for every imaginable film on every imaginable topic.
WEB http://www.dds.nl/~damocles

Filmmakers Anonymous Who but Leni Riefenstahl, Nazi-regime femme fatale of filmmaking, would make a suitable mascot for cinematic unknowns working their way through the bottom rungs of the independent and video film circuit? For

aspiring directors, you'll get a complete listing of every festival and individual call for entering your 28-minute masterpiece. You wouldn't want to miss the deadline this year for Meatfest, Thaw '96, or the Festival of Films in Languages of Limited Diffusion, now would you?
WEB http://www.gl.umbc.edu/~kburdel

Flicker Past a bright front page neatly organized by artist, film, venue, resource and images, this site quickly turns as dark and gritty-looking as a back-

alley editing suite. You'll find text that ranges from hardcore art theory jargon, to wiseacre commentary, and lots of downloadable JPEGs and QuickTime shorts (these averaging about 5.5Mb). Typical fare is Craig Baldwin's *Tribulation 99*, an amazing combination of filmed TV shows, UFO theory, "appropriated" weird images, and more, all set to an Yma Sumac soundtrack; it's not available for listening, although thumbnail sketches of scenes from the movie are.
WEB http://www.sirius.com/~sstark

Independent Film and Video Makers Internet Resource Guide This reference guide to resources for film and videomakers discusses—in serious, intellectual terms—the impact and meaning of the Net upon independent media artists. Learn what sorts of competitions are available to get your work shown, what technologies are becoming available for your own computer, and how to become politically active in the long, losing battle for arts funding.
WEB http://www.echonyc.com/~mvidal /Indi-Film+Video.html

The Sundance Channel

WEB http://www.sundancechannel.com

Since 1981, Robert Redford's Sundance Festival has supported independent filmmakers; now the Festival offers this site as a tie-in to its subscriber TV channel. Bring up this sharp, *très moderne* page, and you'll see a clever animated "film strip" and click-on-graphic access for ordering the channel. But the real reason to hang here is to see items such as the "filmmaker focus," a list of

past Sundance directors (from Spielberg to Greg Araki), a cool day-to-day log of events at Sundance, and ample info on current festival offerings such as *I Shot Andy Warhol* and *Welcome to the Dollhouse*. Then download select QuickTime preview files. A "personal note" from Redford claims this as "a place where work and play are one and energy arises from it... this is all for and about filmmakers." That may sound a bit like spacey southwest talk, but the page itself really delivers the indie goods.

The Independent Film Channel
Mainly a guide to IFC's 24-hour, off-Hollywood programming, this page has the additional attraction of boasting directing kingpins Scorsese, Altman, Lee, and others on its advisory board. What this means is that you get nice quotes and profiles on these and less-renowned directors. There are also links to film schools and some impressively obscure magazines. If you're tired of surfing, visit the online classifieds for independents in search of gear and crew.
WEB http://www.ifctv.com

Independent Films Here's a home page for all those independent moviemakers in Austin, Texas. The site links to resources for filmmakers in the hottest state, including sites dedicated to film production, festivals, equipment, and scripts.
WEB http://www.eden.com/~delta-9/index.html

Low Res Film and Video Festival
A singular festival page, zeroing in on artists making "films" using home video, computers, and digital tools. Along with a list of upcoming festivals, the downloadable QuickTime movie clips make one want to actually *see* these unique works, even if (or because) they tend to have titles like *Godzilla Christ Superstar*. The featured directors (or shall we say artists) are nobody you've heard of—yet.
WEB http://www.lowres.com/menu.html

New Realities Video Old hippies never die—they just make whacked-out pages like this one. Basically an entry point for lots of "counterculture" pages ("Timothy Leary," "Eye Candy," and articles focusing on things like the "Cannabis Club Video" and books by the likes of Allen Ginsburg). "I like to screw around with what some people call reality" says designer Richard J. Gaikowski. Nostalgically interesting, complete with animated psychedelic email icon and groovy graphics.
WEB http://www.slip.net/~richgaik

> ❝ **Where else are you going to have access to production companies with names like 'Leather Tongue' or 'Big Lizard'?** ❞

Northwestern University Image Vault Quick access to the multimedia works (ranging from claymation to CGI animation) of the students and faculty of Northwestern University. Download an eclectic (and often theory-based) set of QuickTime and MPEG films, along with loads of pictures.
WEB http://www.rtvf.nwu.edu/production/image-vault.html

!Pixin(*) Compendium! "Transpixin" is Northwestern University's word for "the digital Internet movie," which means an array of interesting, bizarre animated and computer-generated QuickTime, MPEG and .AVI student films.
WEB http://www.rtvf.nwu.edu/compendium

Qualia-Net Underground Film Archive "The Qualia-Net Comprehensive, Annotated, Independent Film-O-Link" claims to be the "largest list of independent film-related links on the Web!" The snotty attitude may get to be a bit much, but where else are you going to have access to production companies with names like "Leather Tongue" or "Big Lizard," or get sneak thumbnail previews of psychotronic features like *Satan's Vampire Lovers*? Definitely R-rated, by the way.
WEB http://www.qualia-net.com/film

t@p Student Film and Video A look at intriguing student efforts, some downloadable in QuickTime format, plus useful links to studio resources and amusing mainstream film reviews.
WEB http://www.taponline.com/tap/entertainment/film/stud.html

Virtual Film Festival This page brings together media-makers, the public, and the business community. VFF offers independent film festival coverage, realtime chat rooms, helpful sources for post-production

services and ordering info on select indie films.
WEB http://www.virtualfilm.com

World Cam Although it calls itself "The World's Moving Picture Show," this site is actually a collection of downloadable short films, a sort of hit parade of the indie MidWest. An unexpected kick is the amusing sound file of the page's theme song.
WEB http://www.worldcam.com

Directors

Director's Guild of America
What's your union done for you lately? If you're one of the 10,000 card-carrying members of the Director's Guild of America (a necessary step for entree into the creative film community), you can find out the latest news and review your organization's esteemed history. If you currently dream of sitting in that canvas chair (and who doesn't?), you can research membership qualifications and read the latest issue of the official mag of the DGA, where you'll find some superlative interviews with heavy-hitting film directors.
WEB http://www.leonardo.net/dga

Woody Allen "What if everything is an illusion and nothing exists? In that case I definitely overpaid for my carpet." So sayeth Allen Stewart Konigsberg (a.k.a. Woody Allen). In addition to some of the Woodster's more inspired quotes, get the latest on his new projects

(Allen is notoriously secretive about his upcoming movies). But be forewarned, the entries may be rife with speculation. Fans can learn a new trivia bit or study the crib sheets on all of Allen's films, but don't expect photos of Soon-Yi.
WEB http://www.idt.unit.no/~torp /woody

The Hitchcock Page Good evening... Hitch makes much more than a cameo appearance on this home page. There are direct links to descriptions of his films at The Internet Movie Database, plus links to his bio, awards won, info about the Hitchcock TV shows, a very-low-tech frame-by-frame animation of the renowned shower sequence in *Psycho*, and a listing of Hitchcock's movie cameo appearances.
WEB http://www.primenet.com/~mwc

Hitchcock: The Master of Suspense This Web site offers links to a rear window into the director's life, a career-encompassing 1925-1976 filmography with some reviews by Leonard Maltin, a descriptive listing of Hitchcock's trademark cameos, cast and crew lists, some of Hitch's wittier quotes ("Always make the audience suffer as much as possible") and sources for videos and laserdiscs.
WEB http://nextdch.mty.itesm.mx /~plopezg/Kaplan/Hitchcock.html

The Kubrick Page A packed site with links to Web pages at The Internet Movie Database for Stanley Kubrick's films. There are also many images and sound clips from *2001: A Space Odyssey*, *A Clockwork Orange*, and *The Shining*.
WEB http://www.lehigh.edu/~pjl2 /kubrick.html

Woody and Mia in happier times
http://www.idt.unit.no/~torp/woody

Stanley Kubrick Home Page A man watches silently, his face angled downward, but his eyes looking as far up as they can possibly stretch. If this image of a particularly psychotic-looking hombre seems familiar, you're probably thinking of one of the films of legendary director Stanley Kubrick: *A Clockwork Orange*, *Full Metal Jacket*, *The Shining*, perhaps? This virtual shrine to the British mastermind behind these films and other classics like *2001: A Space Odyssey* and *Dr. Strangelove*, begins with a photo of the man himself, looking like a hyperintelligent character from a Dostoyevsky novel. A link makes it a snap to dip into the FAQ archive at alt.movies.kubrick. Visitors will also be treated to such info-bites as a profile of Kubrick on the set of *2001*. Thankfully, the page is updated at a greater frequency than Kubrick's actual oeuvre.
WEB http://www.Krusch.com/kubrick/kubrick.html

Francois Truffaut A pleasing royal blue, black-and-white design helps make this scrapbook so easy to understand, you won't have any trouble following the fun, even if you don't speak French (the English version isn't yet available). Jean-Luc Godard discusses his colleague and competitor; correspondence between Truffaut and H. P. Roche are available. The filmography includes published articles of Truffaut. Most noticeable is the fabulous

Hitchcock makes yet another cameo
http://nextdch.mty.itesm.mx/~plopezg/Kaplan/Hitchcock.html

chronology which is really a family scrapbook, with pics from films and life, important events from birth to death, and a list of more great links to check out when you've exhausted this lovely tribute to a wonderful filmmaker and a fascinating man.
WEB http://outlet.imag.fr/fberard/grougne/Truffaut.html

Also playing

Hong Kong Cinema A collection of links to the searchable Hong Kong movie database, an FTP site with film info, box-office reports, film-industry articles, the 1994 Golden Statue and Golden Banana Awards, and California's Bay Area listings of theaters and video stores.
WEB http://www.egret0.stanford.edu/hk/index.html

Hong Kong Movies Home Page Features a searchable database of Hong Kong movies, film and actor lists, filmographies, interviews, movie reviews, FAQs, photos, and a tribute to Jackie Chan—Hong Kong's premier action superstar who is making box office waves stateside.
WEB http://www.mdstud.chalmers.se/hkmovie

James Bond Movie Page A Bond movie-lover's paradise. Full of essential information plus original scoops on Her Majesty's top special agent. For each film, Bond fans can get detailed information on leading ladies, theme songs, bad guys' plans, production trivia, downloadable poster art, press clippings, and reviews.
WEB http://www.dur.ac.uk/~dcs3pjb/jb/jbhome.html

The Official Unofficial Marx Brothers Web Site Just reading the lines of the Marx Brothers isn't the same thing; you really need Groucho's unmistakable voice to bring them to life—as they've done at this site—with several dozen zingers in quick, easy-to-use .WAV format. Download a few and hear them whenever your computer warms up. As for the rest of the site's offerings, webmaster "Hackinbush" plays no favorites. Every movie—even *Love Happy*—is represented, and the photo gallery offers several treats. This is a friendly place for fans to meet, so take the quiz and get yourself on the list.
WEB http://users.aol.com/hackinbush /private/marx.html

The Rocky Horror Picture Show Find out everything you need to know to fit in at a showing of *The Rocky Horror Picture Show*. The script is broken down into principal segments, and the site has a prop list with directions, credits, character bios (with photos), and links to other *RHPS* sites are included.
WEB http://www.cs.wvu.edu/~paulr /rhps/rhps.html

Silent movies

alt.movies.silent A group for serious buffs of Hollywood's silent days, when acting, not special effects, carried a movie. Newsgroup readers and disciples of actors such as Charlie Chaplin, Buster Keaton, D. W. Griffith, and Harold Lloyd dis-

cuss the little tramp's wardrobe and his authorship of film scores, Griffith's political incorrectness, regional and local silent film conferences, and the availability of memorabilia.
USENET alt.movies.silent

Chaplin Film Locations Then and Now Who knows why there are no great Charlie Chaplin pages yet? Maybe fans have inherited their hero's distrust of technology. This one, anyway, has a peculiar melancholy interest: The webmaster has collected film stills of old scenes shot on location and contrasted them with contemporary photos. Things have changed, as you might guess.
WEB http://www.members.aol.com /summitl085/gerald.htm

 ## The Tarantinoverse
WEB http://rmd-www.mr.ic.ac.uk/~dan/tarantino/tarantino.html

This Tarantino universe is populated with links to information about *Reservoir Dogs* (including an FAQ, video clips, and philosophical stuff), *Pulp Fiction* (an FAQ which addresses such mysteries

as the contents of the briefcase and the movie's nonlinear plot, movie poster scans, Christopher Walken's "Gold Watch" speech text, and scenes that didn't make the final cut), screenplay resources, a transcript from the boy-auteur's interview on the *Charlie Rose Show*, and assorted film Web sites.

Douglas Fairbanks & Mary Pickford Home Page Back in the 1920s two actors ruled Hollywood—Doug Fairbanks and Mary Pickford. A fair attempt at capturing the feel of his action classic, *Mark of Zorro*, is the key feature of this underdeveloped fan-tribute site. Links have improved, but the site is still marred by sloppy writing and spelling mistakes. The founders of United Artists and builders of Pickfair deserve far better.
WEB http://www.157.242.97.98/Silents/pickfair.html

The Louise Brooks Society This mysterious siren of the Jazz Age appeared in movies for only a few years, then quit. She was celebrated in her day, and has been rediscovered every 20 years or so since then. "Describing Louise presents its difficulties. She is so very Manhattan. Very young. Exquisitely hard-boiled. Her black eyes and sleek black hair are as brilliant as Chinese lacquer. Her skin is white as camellia. Her legs are lyric," wrote one Brooks-struck interviewer in 1926. Find out what all the fuss was, is, and will be about at this detailed site, which is heavy on biography and reprints of interviews from the '20s, and light on the multimedia.
WEB http://www.slip.net/~thomasg/brooks.html

Project Buster Old Stone Face doesn't have a home on the Web yet that does him justice, but the webmaster of Project Buster is trying hard. His Buster Keaton home page includes .MOV clips, stills, sound bytes, a filmography—and as perhaps befits a tribute to a silent movie star, very few words.
WEB http://www.netbistro.com/buster/clips/train.zip

Silent Movies Stars and filmmakers of the Silent Era are honored here with text, still images, and a few video clips. Charlie Chaplin, Buster Keaton, Lillian Gish, Douglas Fairbanks, and Mary Pickford have home pages; there's also the *Taylorology* newsletter about the life and unsolved murder of William Desmond Taylor, and information about the preservation of silent films.
WEB http://www.cs.monash.edu.au/~pringle/silent

Scripts/screenwriting

Drew's Scripts-O-Rama Links to more than 500 screenplays are available at Drew's Scripts-O-Rama, both classic (such as *Star Wars* and *The Godfather*) and less than classic. Scripts are also available for obscure, yet deliciously creative titles, such as *Monkeybutt, Zombie Killer, The Plaintive Song of the Curious Boy*, and several other unproduced originals that may or may not be coming to a theater near you. But don't even think about stealing any lines from the screenwriters. Drew warns: "Their lawyers will have you crushed faster than a stray pork rind on Newt Gingrich's chair."
WEB http://home.cdsnet.net/~nikkoll/nontable.htm

Essays on the Craft of Dramatic Writing Script doctor Bill Johnson explains it all for you. If you are interested in writing a screenplay, or in reworking one that's moldering in a bottom drawer, you'll find many tips on how to make your story work.
WEB http://www.teleport.com/~bjscript/index.htm

Internet Screenwriters Network This may be the best site online for screenwriters; parts are meant for pros and "semipros" (i.e., you must have written at least one screenplay to join), but most sections are open to the public, including more than 25 forums in which you can post your questions to a variety of industry experts.
WEB http://www.screenwriters.com/hn/writing/screennet.html

Screenwriters Online The main features of Screenwriters Online are an online magazine ($38.70 for a year's subscription), which includes interviews with and articles by many working screenwriters, and a free online chat room. The director of the site is Lawrence Konner, half the writing team that brought you *Star Trek VI* and *The Beverly Hillbillies*. Don't bother looking, you won't find Quentin Tarantino here.
WEB http://www.screenwriter.com

Encyclopedias/trivia

The Internet Movie Database No matter what your film query, you'll find the answer here. There are more than 75,000 titles in this database, from *Express Train on a Railway Cutting* (1898) to several currently in production. The database includes 14,000 biographies, one million filmography entries, and credit information for more than 300,000 people involved in movie production.
WEB http://wwwus.imdb.com/tour.html

Movie Trivia A list of thousands of movie and TV trivia entries featuring on-the-set in-jokes, cameo appearances, crazy credits, and casting and crew decisions. Did you know that *Aladdin*'s animator claimed the character was based on Tom Cruise? Or that Carrie Fisher was originally cast as the star of the film *Carrie*, but refused to do nude scenes and swapped roles with Sissy Spacek who was already cast in *Star Wars*?
WEB http://www.cis.ohio-state.edu /text/faq/usenet/movies/trivia-faq /faq.html

Diversions

American Memory ShockWaved to death? In the mood for a different kind of movie site? Take a look at early films in .AVI format from the Library of Congress's American Memory site. Many of these short early films are street scenes from the early part of the century, but some are a bit more dramatic—a clip of the electrocution of President William McKinley's assassin, for instance. One warning: These files are huge—10, 20, even 30 megs. To avoid frustration, create a new window or browser and surf elsewhere while the file downloads.
WEB http://rs6.loc.gov/amhome.html

Bernard Herrmann Web Pages Even if you haven't heard of

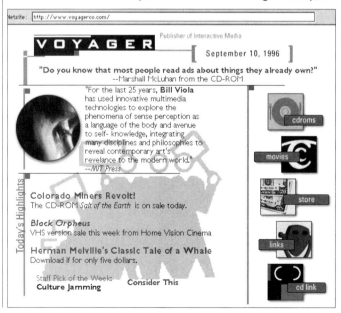

VOYAGER CO.
WEB http://www.voyagerco.com

This well-designed and arty Web site showcases Voyager's media products, including the Criterion Collection of Laser Discs (*Citizen Kane* was the original disc), CD-ROMs (indexed by title and category), and Expanded Books (interactive books published on floppy disks). There are also daily and weekly sales. But for all of its commercial aspects, the site is a great resource for film buffs, with features and filmographies for heavy hitters like Bergman, Kubrick, Kurosawa, and Welles.

Bernard Herrmann, you have heard him. You've probably even whistled him. The music for the Alfred Hitchcock Show? That was Herrmann. So was the theme to *The Twilight Zone*. So were the scores to both *Citizen Kane* and *Taxi Driver*. This nicely laid out page includes sound clips of low quality that still satisfy (check out the overture to *The Day the Earth Stood Still*); a list of Herrmann's credits in film, radio, TV, and concerts; and a biographical note.
WEB http://www.uib.no/People/midi /soundtrackweb/herrmann

Corinth Video A master catalog of videos as well as a browseable catalog of dance, opera, theater, classic and foreign films, and classic television. Includes movie- and video-related links to other Internet resources.
WEB http://www.awa.com:/softlock /video

Ephemeral Films: 1931-1961
What's an ephemeral film? TV commercials and corporate propaganda, used, forgotten, and now used once more by American cultural historians. This site is an overview of Rick Prelinger's Ephemeral Films, a Voyager CD-ROM based on Prelinger's collection of thousands of ephemeral films. Four film clips and a gallery of stills are featured.
WEB http://www.voyagerco.com/CD /ph/p.ephemeral.html

The Movie Sounds Page From one-liners to the background

What's an ephemeral film? Television commercials used, forgotten, and used once more by cultural historians.

music in Looney Tunes 'toons, it's all here. You can also listen in on a Mystery Sound pick of the week and post your best guess. Asked to describe *The Ref*, a 1994 Denis Leary comedy from Disney, one guy wrote in that "this isn't some namby-pamby goody-two-shoes pre-pubescent Disney crap." On top of that, link to other sound pages, from a Cary Grant Shrine to the latest mega-Hollywood hit's home page.
WEB http://www.moviesounds.com

Movietone News Online Before Dan Rather, before Walter Cronkite, even before Edward R. Murrow, there was the *Movietone News*. Download one or two sections of newsreels (in .MOV or .AVI format) from a limited digital archive, write a caption to a goofy newsreel still, or send an historical picture postcard across the Net.
WEB http://www.iguide.com/movies /movitone/contents.htm

The Palace Audio clips, JPEG photos of a range of cinema classics, and movie posters are the highlights of this site. There are also some interesting bits of film criticism and history. Not a comprehensive site, but you'll find some real goodies here.
WEB http://www.scruz.net/~mmills /palace

Sound Files from the Balcony In addition to information about The Balcony film discussion group, The Balcony Web site offers an excellent selection of sound clips, from "Here's looking at you, kid," to *Frankenstein*'s "It's Alive"
WEB http://www.balcony.com /quotes.htm

Video Wasteland If you can't get enough sleaze and cheese in your local video store, consider rental by mail. The aptly named Video Wasteland specializes in horror, exploitation, and B movies. The tapes aren't cheap—a six-day rental will cost you $7.50, with a two-tape minimum.
WEB http://www.slaughter.net /VideoWasteland

www.filmmusic.com This is a comprehensive site for information on film soundtracks, with links to sound clip archives. It's nicely laid out and easy to use. If you want to learn more about one of the most important parts of the movies, this is a good place to start.
WEB http://www.filmmusic.com

Television

IF TV IS THE OPIATE OF THE MASSES, THEN THE
INTERNET IS A DRUG DEALER ON THE PLAYGROUND

WELCOME TO TV PARADISE, the place where tubeheads meet to discuss their favorite shows and stars. Do Archie Bunker, Samantha the witch, and Gilligan ring a bell? What about Letterman, Leno, and Conan? Discuss the latest plot twists, attacks of melodrama, and character flaws revealed on the daytime soaps. Decode the diabolical, subliminal messages embedded in the body language of characters on *Friends*. Debate with other telephiles the conspiracy behind the termination of *Northern Exposure*. Television "culture" has never been subject to such public attention, and forums abound where the most esoteric questions are frequently asked and answered. You may even be privileged enough to be initiated into the profound secrets of the esoteric art of TV Zen.

Location: http://www1.ridgecrest.ca.us/~eclipse/Pictures/f&t.jpg

TV NET
WEB http://tvnet.com/UTVL
picture: WEB http://www1.ridgecrest.ca.us/~eclipse/files.htm
When you enter the TV Net, you've hit the mother lode of online television-program indexes, the home base of the boob tube. At last count, TV Net offered 6,021 links to servers and newsgroups for 925 shows, including 1,294 Web pages. This hub meticulously breaks down all that ever was and is broadcast with ease. Too lazy to browse? Search by show title or genre. Not even those often deplorable miniseries or public-access cable programs can escape the reach of TV Net. If TV Net doesn't know about it, it's not out there.

CLICK PICKS

Starting points

Academy of Television Arts & Sciences For those who consider television to be the greatest combination of art and science the twentieth century has produced, the ATAS has something for you—the latest TV news, with the official update on the Emmy organization. Not a lot of gossipy stuff here. View some great .GIFs from Emmys past, such as snapshots of a young and beautiful Dinah Shore receiving one of her first Emmys, and *Taxi*'s Judd Hirsch taking home one of his own.
WEB http://www.emmys.org/tindex .html

CineMedia Television Sites This site covers the television world in North America, Europe, Australia, and Asia. Resources include a worldwide TV networks index and individual program home pages, 6,000 connections to the hottest TV spots on the Web and to episode guides (these are great if you catch a show late in its run and want to know what happened in earlier seasons), and a database of TV regulations. The recently added channel-changing console below flourescent frames and a weekly selection of a top TV site will keep you glued.
WEB http://www.gu.edu.au/gwis /cinemedia/CineMedia.home.html

Doug Krause's WWW TV Server A four-thrusted foundation of television and entertainment:

Netsite: http://www.emmys.org/gallery/Taxi.gif

Judd Hirsch and Shelly Long with their Emmys from the 1982-1983 season
http://www.emmys.org/tindex.html

network addresses, selected show and ad archives, humor, and links. If you really need to know ABC's address, you could check here, but for entertainment, delve into the archives— *M*A*S*H* is particularly well-represented, with wonderful photos and the entire theme song available to download—as well as the standard episode listings and generic boob-tube attractions. Mr. Krause adds scanned-in comedy strips and Official Site TV links as an afterthought for your viewing pleasure, but definitely check out the Mentos section for quirky research on that Freshmaker with the cult following.
WEB http://www.lido.com/tv

Internet TV Resource Guide Wondering if there's a home page for *Twin Peaks*? How about *Are You Being Served?* or *Max*

Headroom? Whether you're looking for the No. 1 sitcom in the U.S.A. or a little-known Japanese actor, this comprehensive index is an easily navigated means of finding servers and newsgroups around the world for your favorite show, actor, or actress. The alphabetical listings make searching painless, but it's also fun to browse and discover such gems as the Web page of Xuxa, a Brazilian actress/kiddie-show hostess who's more famous in South America than Pamela Anderson.
WEB http://www.teleport.com/~celinec /tv.shtml

Letterboxed Movies on TV History For the cinema buff in the family. This is a list of all letterbox-format movies playing on cable movie channels (HBO, TMC, Showtime, etc.) for the current month. Clicking on

titles connects you to Cardiff's Movie Database for more in-depth information.
WEB http://www.cheezmo.com/lbx .html

P.O.V. Interactive On the cutting edge of new technologies, P.O.V. Interactive is "an evolving experiment in the use of online technologies to provide TV viewers with opportunities to share their reactions." The site, tied to the *P.O.V.* showcase for independent, non-fiction films, is available in graphic or text modes, and opens with helpful suggestions about modem speed, downloading time, and such options as the disabling of the "Auto Load Images" Netscape feature to make things move quickly.
WEB http://www.pbs.org/pov

rec.arts.tv This high-volume group is all over the board, from the mainstream (*ER*, *Mary Tyler Moore*) to the obscure (*Land of the Lost*) to the truly *recherché* (jingles of Coke ads from the '70s). Posts include FAQs, fan club news, episode guides, discussions of TV-related products (especially photos and videos of prize episodes), and trivia queries. A caveat for Canadians—TV in the Great White North is a source of endless derision here.
USENET rec.arts.tv

Sky Internet A guide to sports, weather, and other programming, Sky Internet combines two obsessive passions—the Internet and television—into

one easy-to-use package. The graphics are quick to load but not excessively minimalist, and the information is clearly and sensibly organized.
WEB http://www.sky.co.uk/main.html

Television and Radio Couch-potato heaven, with links to the big three networks, MTV, a variety of cable channels—from Comedy Central to Court TV to C-SPAN, and those are only the C's—and dozens of message boards.
AMERICA ONLINE *keyword* tv

Television Pointers Quite simply, this is a gold mine for anyone with a well-developed sense of humor and off-the-wall tastes. It doesn't even pretend to be comprehensive; it's the site's selectiveness that adds to the appeal. Link to various pages on *The Simpsons*, *Monty Python*, David Letterman's Top Ten List, or even the Mentos Page. Browse through a fine selection of science-fiction sites and listen to a cache of catchy jingles, including the classic tunes of *Schoolhouse Rock*. Even without fancy photos and graphics, this is everything a pointer page should be—it doles out just the good stuff, and plenty of it.
WEB http://www.cs.cmu.edu/afs/cs .cmu.edu/user/clamen/misc/tv /README.html

The TV Plex One has to wonder if The TV Plex is truly putting its best foot forward as a component of a megaplex including music, art, food, travel,

A BRUSH WITH FRESHNESS

Commercial Synopsis: Through the Car (or *The 3 Second Car Jacking*)

There is little peace in the land of Mentos, as yet another teen is faced with a distressing problem. While crossing the street, he is separated from his friends, and nearly from his legs by an over anxious motorist. Finding himself needing to traverse the street, but without a normal means to do so, he again thanks his lucky stars he remembered the freshmaker. His supply is reduced by one, but his freshness is increased exponentially. Opening the rear door, he climbs through the auto, while the driver looks over his shoulder in astonishment. Upon exiting, the youth shrugs at the motorist, Mentos in hand. Although a bit shaken, the passenger acknowledges the carefree youths with an approving glance as he speeds away. "Wait till the wife hears of my brush with freshness!"

—from Doug Krause's WWW TV Server

books, and other leisure activities. The top of the opening page recently had a grainy black-and-white photo of Matt LeBlanc with the primate costar of his movie *Ed*, and a link to a gag-inducing interview filled with such witty repartee: "Q: You're cast as a baseball player in this film; are you a jock? A: I played Little League for awhile. I played one game and I was shipped off to right field after being nicknamed Scatter Arm!" The Plex provides some juicy TV tidbits with studio updates and star interviews while plugging merchandise for T-shirt hungry watchers.

WEB http://www.gigaplex.com/tv/index .htm

September in the City—*NYPD Blue* on ABC
http://www.abctelevision.com

Broadcast networks

ABC Did you lose the *TV Guide*? Not to worry—the ABC schedule is right here. The network doubles its online efforts with new season show profiles, broadcast breakdowns, and a day-by-day calendar describing shows with a .GIF of the cast. The news section features regional RealAudio headlines for daily updates. Skip to the top-rated show sections which are better maintained.

WEB http://www.abctelevision.com

ABC Online Capital Cities/ABC, which is now part of the Disney empire, has a wonderful Web site on the AOL commercial service, with links for early-morning chat, daytime soaps, educational programming the nightly news, the network's venerable sports department, and its prime-time line-up.

AMERICA ONLINE *keyword* abc

CBS Television Home Page The CBS eye focuses a bit more on the Net these days. Catch the programming updates for sports events, season previews, and listings. Find a news channel here, along with an online merchandise catalog, kids stuff, and (of course) a link to *The Late Show with David Letterman*, the buoy that keeps this waterlogged network afloat.

WEB http://www.cbs.com

FOX Broadcasting In addition to the standard programming info, this site contains links to individual shows with their own episode guides. You can also download scripts and quotes. Fox knows its market, and doesn't suppress other links—there are many *Simpsons* and *X-Files* resources, and the *Animaniacs* page connects to other animation-related sites.

WEB http://www.eden.com/users/my -html/fox.html

NBC Supernet Must-see TV and more. A television addict's mainline to all in the world that's NBC: a guide to programming, live chat with network celebs, an invite to join the NBC Viewer's Club and even an NBC screensaver download. One feature here of use to everyone is the Intellicast, a minute to minute weather update accessed via a click-on map of the country.

MSN *keyword* nbc

NBC.COM Soap operas, Saturday-morning cartoons, Tom Brokaw... the complete spectrum of everything the National Broadcasting Channel has to offer online can be found here. Access daily soap updates, the NBC news server, and then gawk at their collection of animated peacocks. Additional links will take you to your local station or such NBC shows as *Seinfeld* or *Late*

Night with Conan O'Brien, but the most interesting linked sites are only nominally affiliated with NBC, most notably the Studio Noir page for jazz and blues.
WEB http://www.nbc.com

PBS National programming, which includes a "daily trivia challenge" (today's mind-bending quiz: "What cold-blooded animal is included in the normal diet of the Bald Eagle?"), home pages for PBS programs, learning services, and a quilt-like clickable map of the U.S. that serves as a directory of local PBS stations.
URL ftp://ftp.pbs.org • gopher://gopher.pbs.org
WEB http://www.pbs.org

Universal Channel Universal series represented here include *Sliders*, *Weird Science*, *Partners*, *Law & Order*, *Dream On*, *Hercules*, and *Xena: Warrior Princess*. Background information, character bios, production notes, and credits are available for each of these series. In addition to downloadable .GIFs, audio, and video clips, if you can bluff the online Guard, you'll learn the secrets of the Backlot's Closed Sets! There is a great sense of whimsy here and they have devised a complicated graphics-rich game called Zapper's Lounge that will keep you busy for a while. The Hercules series has its own 3-D gallery.
WEB http://www.mca.com/tv

WGBH—NOVA Pictures and descriptions of *NOVA* specials and their videos (at present there are three—*This Old Pyramid*, *In Search of Human Origins*, and *The Miracle of Life*, with its incredible photography of the human body).
WEB http://branc.com/nova/nova.html

Cable networks

A&E The Arts and Entertainment channel offers a well-planned, classy-looking site. The pages for *Biography* give ample background on the shows, but not so that you feel like you're doing research. Excerpted articles from monthly print magazine are

 ## AMERICAN MOVIE CLASSICS
WEB http://www.amctv.com

Wander the grounds of a movie studio backlot during the golden age of American films—American Movie Classics has marvelously captured the mystique and glamour of it all at this absolutely stellar Web spot. After checking out the cable channel's schedule, peek into the virtual dressing rooms of James Dean or Marlene Dietrich, or enjoy the in-depth portraits of the artist of the month. AMC treats the presented films not as musty relics, but as vibrant, timeless works of art. In this new framed medium, the magic of the movies continues to shine.

Location: http://www.amctv.com/dressingrooms/bettedavis/index.html

Bette Davis' Dressing Room

short and interesting.
WEB http://www.aetv.com

BETN (Black Entertainment Television Network) The Black Entertainment Television Network offers an impressive range of music and information, but their home page barely represents that array. Visitors can link to cable listings, jazz servers, and pay-per-view offerings through a virtual skyline, or connect to BETN's magazines *Emerge* and *YSB*. The on-site information is limited to program schedules and tables of contents, offering little that can't be found in any TV listings.
WEB http://www.betnetworks.com
MSN *keyword* bet

Bravo Get the requisite cable schedule listings, but give the network a little something of your own. Bravo has a call for paintings, poetry, and anything else that can be shown online. You can even try to sell your art at the site. Now that's an arts network. The show descriptions could be more informative, but what it lacks in depth it makes up in scope. Literature and movie sections make this stop "arts central."
WEB http://www.bravotv.com

C-SPAN Democracy is online, and much of it is here. Hear RealAudio clips of important political speeches, investigate the information available on current election campaigns, and even read the first chapter of books featured on C-SPAN's

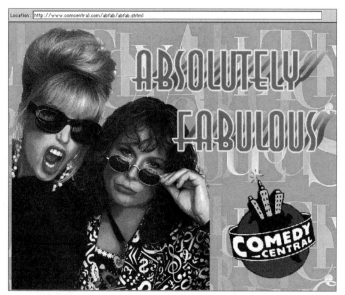

Location: http://www.comcentral.com/abfab/abfab.shtml

Wheels on fire, still rolling down the road at Comedy Central
http://www.comcentral.com

Booknotes. A daily schedule is provided as well as lesson plans for classroom use to keep the world politically informed.
WEB http://www.c-span.org

CNN Forum The CNN Forum not only delivers the top news around the clock—just like the network on television—but also gives dedicated CNN junkies a place to discuss their favorite network. Talk Hiroshima or Bosnia, or forward a question about national affairs to CNN. Maybe Bernard Shaw will show up at your house to give you an answer.
COMPUSERVE *go* cnnforum

CNN Interactive As they have done repeatedly, CNN takes the lead in bringing news to the American people—this

time through their impressive and comprehensive online presence. Whether you want detailed coverage of the elections in India or last night's playoff scores, CNN dispatches a wealth of easy-to-access information in every conceivable news area, with numerous photographs and graphics. For a lark, check out the Orwellian link called Watch Us Work—it updates a live shot of the frantic CNN newsroom every two minutes.
WEB http://www.cnn.com

CNN Internet Newsroom The Web site brings six weeks' worth of daily news—including today's—from the people who brought you Tiananmen Square and the Gulf War. Download a MPEG movie of the latest news item, and read submissions from CNN's contributors.

WEB http://www.nmis.org/NewsInter
active/CNN/Newsroom/contents.html
URL gopher://eis.calstate.edu:7I/II/cnn

alt.tv.comedy-central In-depth discussion of Comedy Central's top shows—*Absolutely Fabulous* is very hot here. Comedy Central contests launched with each new big show are frequent topics of discussion. And if your VCR fell down on the job, don't worry—videos of missed episodes can be sought out from fellow CC fans.
USENET alt.tv.comedy-central

Comedy Central Home Page This site has the same boys'-locker-room, Penn-&-Teller ambiance as the station itself. Besides the Silly Noise Depository—a depositiory for silly noises, of course—there are QuickTime videos (*Monty Python*, *Kids in the Hall*, *MST3K*, etc.), a place to send hate mail to select celebs and politicians, the day's schedule, and an *Absolutely Fabulous* archive.
WEB http://www.comcentral.com

Court TV This clear-headed link to the law, those who practice it, and those who break it, is the online version of the cable

staple. After updating yourself with coverage of the day's hot cases, you can check program schedules, link to online legal advice, or access an archive of O.J. Simpson trial depositions. Most intriguing is Arthur Miller's Courtroom Challenge, where, with all relevant information and precedents at your fingertips, you get to play lawyer and tackle a controversial issue.
WEB http://www.courttv.com

Discovery Channel Online An extensive program guide for the Discovery and Learning channels, with a "Topics of the

 MTV
WEB http://www.mtv.com

For the Post-Industrial, Post-Cold War, Postmodern, Post-Ism & It generation, which has been assigned the media-branded logo "X," MTV has come to represent the epitome of the sell-out, the pinnacle of pop. But MTV does at least offer an Underground Connection that links to as yet unsigned, up-and-coming bands marketed with "BuzzClips." Haymarket Riot, for instance, is not just a band, we're told, but an event. And if you find yourself struggling for an identity, what better place to shop for the subculture that fits you best, or take a dive into the world of pop (read: cor-

porate) culture. Which summer concert tour is right for you? Try Select-o-Tour in the Music Feature area or browse info about channel shows on Tubescan. You'll also find links to your favorite MTV shows and hosts. Complete with trendy colorful doodads and gizmos for clicking around what's cool. And, it should go without saying, plenty of Jenny McCarthy.

Month" feature for major categories like History, Nature, Science, People, Exploration, etc.
WEB http://www.discovery.com

Disney TV Plex As with all Disney animation, this one is lovely to look at, swell to behold, but download an image and consider it sold. The exquisitely illustrated gateway foretells of the colorful fun inside, but don't forget to read the copyright rules and registration at the bottom of each page, so you know you won't get sued for use. All warnings aside, there are beautiful audio/visual clips from *Toy Story*, *The Lion King*, and many others; games to put on your computer; and coloring-book pages to print out and fill in. Check out the cartoon show spinoffs and Disney schedule.
WEB http://www.disney.com/TVplex

ESPNET Sports Zone Sports fans will love this site. Why? Top sports stories of the week, scores for the game you missed, trivia, athlete bios, a program schedule, and live-chat rooms for various sports. There are even audio clips of your favorite sports show's theme music.
WEB http://espnet.sportszone.com

fX The real star of this network is the Manhattan apartment where its live shows are shot, and you can take a point-and-click tour of it here. Click on the bedroom and a colorful image of it appears for your

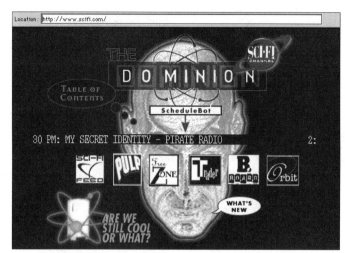

Enter the Sci-Fi Channel's dominion, and jack your brain at the door
http://www.scifi.com

perusal. Downloadable .GIFs, video, and sounds are available for each of fX's live shows. There's also a program guide for these shows as well as the network's baby-boomer nostalgia programs like *Batman* and *Family Affair*, or follow whatever's made fresh daily.
WEB http://www.fxnetworks.com

HBO Home Video HBO can be a great station, but its home video department lacks substance. Unrecognized coming attractions *Sugar Time* and *Three Wishes* don't get you running to your local video store, do they? What else? Well, here are a few better known titles—*Circle of Friends*, *Tyson*, and... *Exit to Eden*. You'll find little more than promotion, but, sometimes you need a break from this month's airing of *Police Academy*.
WEB http://www.hbohomevideo.com

The History Channel It's a sad fact that much of humanity's history has been written by the victors of war. The History Channel is hardly one to break with tradition, and the graphics at their Web site attest to the importance placed on military history. Visitors will find a program schedule (filled with history-of-war shows), cantankerous Marvin Kitman's monthly column (usually about George Washington's military genius), and links geared toward teachers. The This Day in History portion is truly fascinating—even more so because you can select any day of the year.
WEB http://www.historychannel.com

alt.tv.nickelodeon Wasn't Ivan on Nickelodeon's *Roundhouse* in that Pringle's ad? At this newsgroup you will find the answer to that question as well as many a nostalgic discussion of your favorite classic TV

shows. There are also good FAQs for various Nickelodeon shows and plenty of discussion about *Ren and Stimpy*.
USENET alt.tv.nickelodeon

Sci-Fi Channel: The Dominion
The Dominion is a vast domain for quenching your sci-fi thirst. Get a dialogue going in a chat room to trade your sci-fi collectibles, or download video clips of UFOs (pie pans or ETs: you be the judge). You'll find more standard video clips, stills, and audio. In addition to a program guide for the Sci-Fi Channel, there's a link to SF-themed comic strips. Go ahead, fertilize your imagination.
WEB http://www.scifi.com

Showtime Online The Shockwave-enabled Showtime Online does a great job, employing some eye-catching motion and excellent graphics that are just repetitive enough to make downloading quick and still keep it interesting. There are Now Playing and Coming Soon departments full of interesting titles, synopses, and teasers. There's also a fair amount of space devoted to Showtime original programming, such as *Zalman King's Red Shoe Diaries*. Well put-together and worth a look.
WEB http://showtimeonline.com/INDEX.HTM

Turner Classic Movies Want to see what's on Turner Classic

Movies right now? The cable channel's Web site has a function that will show you what's being broadcast at this very moment—just reload for new images. This pleasant presentation also gives you the month's TCM schedule, a classic-movie quiz, QuickTime classic-movie trailers, a real-time chat room, and looks at upcoming TCM features. Fans of the channel will enjoy its online presence.
WEB http://www.turner.com/tcm

Daytime

alt.tv.talkshows.daytime Is daytime TV trash TV? Or is daytime TV a cathartic force that responds to psychological pres-

NATIONAL TALK SHOW GUEST REGISTRY

WEB http://ourworld.compuserve.com/homepages/ntsgr

Where do you think Geraldo finds those women who pick up men at the mosh pits of benefit concerts for lesbian acrobatic groups? Through the National Talk Show Guest Registry, of course! Now you too can submit your story online to the NTSGR. If you think you're a "potential talker," the NTSGR will give you advice and guidance for presenting yourself, while matching your yarn to the

likeliest talk show. A few helpful tips are even offered for potential guests; the writers remind us to "avoid wearing reflective clothes," "never change your story," and "never physically lash out at anyone!" Jenny Jones, here we come!

sures within the American psyche, thrusting embarassing secrets forth, stripping them of their shame, and ultimately cleansing? Boon or menace? You be the judge. Watch out, though—you'll have to wade through Lake country, Oprahland, and the purgatory that houses such "talents" as Jenny Jones, and Rolanda—before you can make up your mind.
USENET alt.tv.talkshows.daytime

Good Morning America Online
What's on *Good Morning America* this morning? Maybe a chef demonstrating how to cook barbecued chicken. Maybe a movie star touting his new film. Before you start the day with the smiling face of Charles Gibson on *GMA*, preview your good morning at this site, which includes recipes, a list of guests, a library, and more.
AMERICA ONLINE *keyword* gma

Oprah Winfrey Just the basics here: the address of the show, and phone numbers for tickets and general information. There's even a 900 number for Rosie's recipes.
WEB http://www.wvectvl3.com/wvec /releases/entry-9.html

Ricki Lake The .GIFs, videos, and audio clips are not the highlights here. No, the highlights would definitely be the roster of Ricki's killer show topics ("Lose Weight or Lose Me"),which are fun browsing whether you're a fan of the show or not.
WEB http://www.spe.sony.com /Pictures/tv/rickilake/ricki.html

Tempestt Tempestt Bledsoe (Vanessa from *The Cosby Show*) now has her own Sony-produced show designed as a companion to Ricki Lake. The one-hour spectacle airs daily and focuses on the trials and tribulations of relationships.

You can download .GIFs and audio of the rising star.
WEB http://www.spe.sony.com /Pictures/tv/tempestt/tempestt.html

Soaps

rec.arts.tv.soaps.abc Delicious catty remarks about fashion no-nos on the ABC lineup: "Maria's hair seems to be turning very *That Girl* Marlo Thomas. Amusing threads on continuity glitches: "Felicia has been to Luke's club before; she had a baby there for God's sake!" Plot twists, desired and abhorred, and predictions for the future.
USENET rec.arts.tv.soaps.abc

Soap Links Your one-stop soap shopping mall on the Web. Resources include a graphically rich index of all the main U.S. soaps and some non-domestic favorites as well—*East Enders* and *Coronation Street*. There are connections to newsgroups and chat conferences. Some of the online soaps available here—*As the Web Turns*—can be pretty entertaining.
WEB http://members.aol.com /soaplinks/index.html

Soap Opera Forum What is a soap, exactly? Well, daytime dramas are soaps, of course—*Another World*, *The Bold & The Beautiful*, *General Hospital*, and *The Young & The Restless*. But according to this forum, prime-time serials like *ER* and *Chicago Hope* also qualify, as do the brain candies

Biker-dude makeovers, best friends stealing boyfriends, and men behaving badly
http://www.spe.sony.com/Pictures/tv/rickilake/ricki.html

peddled by the Spelling empire—namely, *Melrose Place* and *Beverly Hills 90210*. Libraries contain pictures of fans, plot summaries, and information about international soaps.
COMPUSERVE *go* soapforum

Soapline Daily A daily newsletter for soap fans, plus links to some of ABC's most popular daytime dramas—*All My Children, General Hospital, One Life to Live*—that furnish cast photos, a library of past plots, and chat in both real-time and message board formats. And if you feel in need of a little soap-related product, visit the ABC SoapStore, which sells hats, t-shirts, and keychains (but no soap).
AMERICA ONLINE *keyword* abc soaps

Oakdale Online (*As The World Turns*) If you like, you can point-and-click your way through Virtual Oakdale (Oakdale being the setting for *ATWT*, of course) for soap news. When you're done with that, view character bios or play the *As The World Turns* Trivia game. You can even share your favorite memories of 40 years in Oakdale.
WEB http://www.clic.net/~birdy/atwt

Port Charles Online (*General Hospital*) Scoops, spoilers, and daily synopses so that you never have to miss out on an affair, murder, or spell of amnesia in Port Charles again. The site also contains a ton of downloadable sights and

---

ROSIE ROCKS THE HOUSE

Nancford wrote:

〉Finally the folks at WPVI Channel 6 in Philadelphia got their act
〉together—Rosie will now be on at II A.M. (starting Monday,
〉September 9th). Too bad Ricki Lake—you now have the I2:05 A.M.
〉slot.

Which is **EXACTLY** where she should be. Ricki is nothing but trash and I cannot **STAND** her show. Rosie replaced her here, too. I would **MUCH RATHER** see Rosie than Ricki (or Montel, or Geraldo, or Richard Bey, or Sally, etc. They're all **TRASH**).

〉Just a quick question—What happened to all the Rosie posts—Am
〉I suddenly in the wrong news group? There used to be a lot of
〉Rosie posts to this site, but I only saw one in the last week (mine
〉will make 2)???

There's now a rosie newsgroup. It's called alt.fan.rosieodonnell. It was just formed. Come join us!

—**from alt.tv.talkshows.daytime**

---

sounds and all the vital statistics on the cast members, past and present (Did he win an Emmy? Was she in *Batman*?).
WEB http://www.cts.com/browse /jeffmj/GeneralHospital.html

The Guiding Light page If you're dying to know how some plot line turns out, the "spoilers" provided here will put you in the know. There are links to newsgroups, IRCs, FAQs, and character polls (A.M. Spaulding is a favorite). This is also a homebase of the "Keep the Light Burning Campaign" to save this soap from extinction. If you'd like to help, come visit.
WEB http://server.Berkeley.EDU /soaps/gl

The Loving Home Page If you love that *Loving* theme song, you can download it here. The site also features FAQs, daily synopses, information on newsgroups, and links to other soaps.
WEB http://server.Berkeley.EDU /soaps/loving

One Life to Live This site links to Web pages for *One Life to Live* characters, picture archives, an episode guide, and explanations of show history and plot, including a character study of Vicki (all her personalities) and a chart of the *OLTL* family tree.
WEB http://www.tvnet.com/cgi-bin /utl?card+II76

alt.tv.real-world This is the newgroup for MTV's *Real World* series. You can find out that "the camera people do live in the house" with the "characters" of this *cinema verité* soap, as well as other background information. Several threads want to know, "if this is so real life, where are the gay people in *RW4*?"
USENET alt.tv.real-world

Game shows

alt.tv.game-shows A fun, freewheeling group with discussion of shows from *Family Feud* and *Joker's Wild* to *21* and *Jeopardy!* Many of these netheads say they've been on the shows, and share their stories ("I found Alex to be a really neat guy," etc.) while speculation revolves around new guests and shows.
USENET alt.tv.game-shows

〝 Donald wants ads for Nutter Butter. Email him if you've got one on tape. 〞

The Game $how Page! A great spot for game-show lovers, with a list of game-show board games, lyrics to theme songs, a video collection, calls for contestants, FAQs, and rules of shows from *The Hollywood*

Watch the synapses spark on *Jeopardy*
http://www.spe.sony.com/Pictures/tv/jeopardy/jeopardy.html

Squares to *The Newlywed Game*. The site provides links to related newsgroups and Web sites.
WEB http://silver.ucs.indiana.edu /~wlambert/GameShows.html

JEOPARDY! Home Page This site's got video and audio clips, photographs of the charismatic Alex in action, pages of questions, an address for potential contestants, and info on the CD-ROM game.
WEB http://www.spe.sony.com /Pictures/tv/jeopardy/jeopardy.html

Wheel of Fortune Home Page Hey, wheel watchers, see that mesmerizing wheel spinning on your monitor? Yep, here's your spot for *Wheel of Fortune* video and audio clips ("I will solve the puzzle, Pat"), along with photographs and bios of cute hosts Pat Sajak and Vanna

White. Better yet, play the game here with an interactive online version.
WEB http://www.spe.sony.com /Pictures/tv/wheel/wheel.html

Commercials

alt.tv.commercials Donald wants ads for Nutter Butter. Email him if you've got one on tape. Yep, it's a zany group, with rants and praise for commercials of all types, whether for Clearasil or Zima.
USENET alt.tv.commercials

alt.tv.infomercials "What's the difference between the Super Slicer and the V-slicer? Which is better?" Sincere discussions of the products and personalities of infomercials, whether for hair extensions, ab enhancers, or nail products.
USENET alt.tv.infomercials

Infomercial List A basic list of infomercials for everything from Acne-statin to the Great Wok of China. The guide includes brief product descriptions and the name of the infomercial's star. Richard Bey, Vanna White, and other prime-time rejects seem to dominate.
WEB http://www.best.com/~dijon/tv /infomercials/info-list.html

Prime time

alt.tv.nypd-blue Arguments flare now and then over which cop drama show is better, *NYPD Blue* or *Homicide*. Generally, though, this newsgroup is a quiet spot, with calm discussion of such topics as Andy's marriage, the real NYPD, and the occasional nudity (i.e., butt shots) on the show.
USENET alt.tv.nypd-blue

Sitcom Page From the famous (*Seinfeld*) to the infamous (*Saved by the Bell*), the classic (*All in the Family*) to the forgettable (*My Two Dads*), Sitcom Page is a solid server for 21 comedies that have graced (or disgraced) the television screen since the late seventies. While they're graphically static, the links bring you details about where each sitcom aired, thegenesis of the show, and a brief episode guide. Thumb through like the back issues of *TV Guide*.
WEB http://pmwww.cs.vu.nl/service /sitcoms

The Official Baywatch Website The bodacious *Baywatch* squad is featured in gorgeous color, and the site links to such hard-core fan attractions as "Meet David Hasselhoff and

the Cast of *Baywatch*" and episode updates, as well as the essential picture gallery and series archives.
WEB http://baywatch.compuserve.com

Beverly Hills 90210 A sharp, professional break-down of the show by cast, episodes, and creators. Some behind-the-scenes bits, brief bios and facts, as well as sharp photographs of the glamour "kids." Find out what goes through writers' minds, and how the finished product evolves. See an interesting glimpse of episode creation through the eyes of a production assistant, as well as a glossary of production terms and the hierarchical breakdown of the hit show's creators.
WEB http://www.cu-online.com/~adept /90210/homepagl.htm

Cheers Home Page Publicity stills of Sam, Rebecca, Cliff, Woody, Carla, and the rest of the gang, along with the theme song, an episode guide, a trivia quiz, sound bytes, merchandise, and a collection of Normisms.
WEBhttp://s9000.furman.edu/~treu /cheers.html

The Chicago Hope Homepage Lots of information here on the "other" doctor drama, including an episode guide, a drinking game, bios of the cast, a picture gallery, audio clips of the theme song, and best lines from the series.
WEB http://www-cs-students.staford .edu/~clee/chicagohope.html

Kelly's the slut, Donna's the virgin, Valerie's the bitch, and Claire's the... uh... uh...
http://www.cu-online.com/~adept/90210/homepagl.htm

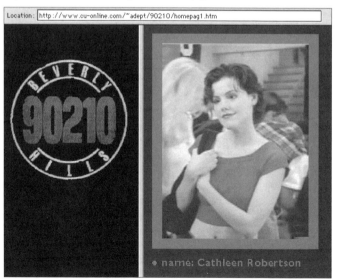

Location: http://www.cu-online.com/~adept/90210/homepag1.htm

• name: Cathleen Robertson

LIFE LESSONS FROM *MELROSE PLACE*

All women are size 6 or smaller.

There is only one bar in Los Angeles (Shooters).

All men are seducible if they are straight.

Gay couples rarely kiss... and if they do it's reported by the major networks.

No one ever dies from being sick/shot/blown-up once their picture appears in the opening credits.

In medicine, you can work your way up the ladder from resident to chief of staff in 2 seasons.

In advertising, you can work your way up the ladder from receptionist to VP in 2 episodes.

There are no Latinos or Asians in Los Angeles.

You can fall off a ten-story building and emerge unscathed as long as you fall on top of another body. (Even if you were shot in the chest at point blank range two weeks earlier.)

—from 4616 Melrose Place

The Official E.R. Homepage NBC lays out a typical prime-time breakdown of the show. Here one finds cast bios, episode schedules, photos, and show credits. An authoritative fan's Web site should be up soon to overtake this one.
WEB http://www.nbc.com /entertainment/shows/er/index.html

Forever Knight Home Page This site includes history and background for the now-defunct show starring Geraint Wyn Davies as Detective Nick Knight, information on the cast and crew, episode guides, information on fan clubs, and links to related sites.
WEB http://www.hu.mtu.edu/~gjwalli /fktoc.html

Frasier Program Guide Descriptions and titles of each episode, along with a list of cast and crew members. The guide provides a list of guest callers, writing and directing credits, and lyrics to the show's theme song.
WEB http://www.cis.ohio-state.edu /hypertext/faq/usenet/tv/program -guides/frasier

Friends on the WWW The cast winks out at you as three pages of theme song lyrics and photos flicker by. Then enter a solid hub to fans of the top twentysomethings show. Complete with cast bios, extensive resources to links for episode guides, articles on the show, and several other features for *Friends* junkies.
WEB http://watt.seas.virginia.edu /~acs5y/friends/friends.html

alt.tv.highlander "Is it me," wrote one *Highlander* fan, "or do a lot of the immortals that Duncan deems to be his close friends go crazy, turn against him, etc., and thus he ends up having to kill 'em all?" Nope, someone responded, it's just that the turncoats and the psychos "make for more interesting story lines." A reasonable theory if you actually believe that the fictional character has a lot of healthy relationships off-camera. You'll find lots of talk about airdates, time inconsistencies, and debates over "the Quickening" (a mystical process that's got something to do with beheading immortals). These fans don't talk about the *Highlander* movies and TV shows like they're high art, but they're not likely to agree with the reviewer who called the latest movie "brainless fodder for undiscriminating audiences." The review, posted to the group, got a blow-by-blow refutation ("*H3* gets bad rap" was the title of the post). Not a group dominated by science-fiction fans. One of the regu-

lars jokingly referred to *Star Trek* as Star What?
USENET alt.tv.highlander

Home Improvement Home Page
The site includes press materials, info on the cast and crew, an episode guide, scripts, and interviews with Tim Allen from publications such as *Time* and *Playboy*.
WEB http://www.diku.dk/students /normann/hi

Homicide, Life on the Web Lots of *Homicide* files and info at this well-designed site, including an FAQ, an episode list, photographs, and a good selection

of sound clips. Too bad they couldn't incorporate that soothing cinema verité camerawork.
WEB http://www.gl.umbc.edu/~jlempkl /page2.html

Law & Order Production notes, pages for the show's stars, and a story by the show's head writer about combining accuracy and dramatic storytelling. An interactive feature puts you on the set of the show, looking for a missing prop.
WEB http://www.mca.com/tv/laworder

alt.tv.lois-n-clark Patty has never understood why Lois, this great journalist, can't figure out

that Clark is Superman: "Come on, Lois. DUH!" These fans mull over every detail in *Lois & Clark*, from the reasons why Lois has so few female friends to the variety of Superman's powers.
USENET alt.tv.lois-n-clark

Mad About You Download a *Mad About You* screensaver for Macs or PCs. View an outtake of the Helen and Paul characters boxing. Take the *Mad About You* baby poll. Get free tickets for the tapings. Something of a *Mad About You* theme park, this highly slick site offers the usual cast pho-

Encyclopedia Brady

WEB http://www.primenet.com/~dbrady
picture: WEB http://www.teleport.com/~btucker/bradys.shtml

With the big-screen Bradys stirring up Bradymania, this is a must-see site for any twentysomething who wants to keep up with nostalgia minutiae. Where did Alice's cousin go to military

Location: http://www.teleport.com:80/~btucker/bbcast1.jpg

school? What was Marcia's campaign slogan? Who sold Greg that beat-up convertible? Someone combed every episode for the most minute details, and this is the result: an interactive reference to the 117 episodes of *The Brady Bunch*. This site's for people who are just dying to know the title of Marcia's math workbook (*Exercises: Exploring Modern Mathematics*). Also includes an episode guide.

tos, too, plus links to other television sites.

WEB http://www.spe.sony.com /Pictures/tv/mad/mad.html

Bundyland, Home of MWC Everything from diagrams of the Bundy homestead to biographies of the cast. Bundyland offers fans of *Married with Children* an episode guide, photos, lots of audio and video clips, and information on getting tickets to the show and buying t-shirts and other goods.

WEBhttp://mwc.telescope.org/index .html

4616 Melrose Place Opening with a graphic of the doorbell nameplate featuring Jake, Matt, Alison, Amanda, Jane, Jo, Sydney, and Billy, the Melrose Place site is notable for cast photos, which are accompanied by character bios like this one: "Hey, I am Alison Parker. Originally from Wisconsin but now a true L.A. girl. Advertising is my game, but that's not all I do..." For true devotees only.

WEB http://melroseplace.com

alt.tv.melrose-place Since the *Melrose Place* fan sites seem to have been all shut down by Aaron Spelling Inc., this is a precious site to learn about what's happening on *MP*. Typical topics include "Best in bed on Melrose," "Kimberly is a bitch," and "Brooke's thighs." These netheads have a fun time rating the characters, making fun of them, and

Laura Leighton, *Melrose Place*'s ditzy but devious diva
http://www.intergate.net/uhtml/sam/Melrose

guessing what's going to happen next. Also has some threads about *Party of Five*.

USENET alt.tv.melrose-place

Melrose Space *Melrose Place* is one of those shows that calls for a periodic gathering of devotees, whether to praise or lambaste the most recent episode. One place for such fans to meet is Melrose Space. If you can't want to find out what's going to happen to Jane, Jake, Amanda, and the rest of those quiet, unassuming residents, you can read the plot summaries of shows that have yet to air. And there's more than just plot outlines. You can participate in the madness by posting your own inanities, such as an *MP* top-ten list.

WEB http://www.intergate.net/uhtml /sam/Melrose

My So-Called Life An excellent selection of video and sound

clips, along with scripts, fan fiction, and quotes ("I want anger. I want honesty. I want nakedness"). The FAQ includes an episode guide, a list of who's who on the show, and "goofy trivial information." How to support "My-So-Called-Petition," and other info about fans' efforts to bring the cancelled show back. After two years, maybe the fans should get a so-called clue.

WEB http://www.tc.umn.edu/nlhome /g564/lask0008/mscl.html

My So-Called Life Homepage This site has scripts, bios of the cast (did you know that Jared Leto used be called Jarhead in college?), an episode guide, a picture archive, a list of songs from the show, and "The So-Called Drinking Game." A well-designed site, with lots of unique info.

WEB http://www.ilstu.edu/~jmhutch /life.html

alt.tv.northern-exp Call it "NX" and you'll be welcomed in this group of devoted *Northern Exposure* fans (still obsessed even after the show's cancellation). Plans for a convention, and lots of talk of the relationship between Maggie and Joel—"he is a technocrat and she an emotionalist," etc.—and the unpredictable career moves of Rob Morrow.
USENET alt.tv.northern-exp

The Moose's Guide to Northern Exposure A large archive of material about the quirky CBS drama, arranged so clearly and simply that even a moose could understand.
WEB http://www.netspace.org/~moose /moose.html

Party of Five Did you know that the actress who plays Bailey's girlfriend once co-starred in a Barbie workout video? This site has facts on the cast and characters, along with a list of music from the show, a selection of quotes, and links to related sites.
WEB http://found.cs.nyu.edu/tkbalt /salingers

The Unofficial Picket Fences Strange things are happening. Again! This page collects resources on the award-winning CBS drama, including an episode guide, images, sounds, and information on the show's mailing list and newsgroup.
WEB http://www.lewis.edu/fences /fences.html

alt.tv.roseanne An odd mix in this group, with lots of anti-*Roseanne* posts. But the *Roseanne* fans prevail, discussing upcoming episodes and the characters' travails.
USENET alt.tv.roseanne

Roseanne Why is Roseanne so important to the economy of the Netherlands? She's not, really, but she does have some fans across the Atlantic, and they've generously provided the TV star with her own fan page. Get episode titles, plot summaries, and more.
WEB http://pmwww.cs.vu.nl/service /sitcoms/Roseanne

alt.tv.seinfeld "I bet if the producers knew what was going

THE DUKES OF HAZZARD HOME PAGE

WEB http://www.ghgcorp.com/rbigoness/hazzard.html
Tighten your silver belt-buckle, shine your boots, and slide across the General Lee! Rosco Peco Train's on your tail and Daisy's waiting back home. Luke and Bo ain't goin' nowhere as these good old vigilantes elude Boss Hog and the gang for rubber-burnin' excitement in cyberspace! A totally

cool aerospace engineer Ray Bigoness really knows what he's doing, and he loves it! Any child of the eighties who relied on this program for a weekly fix of at least three car chases is bound to appreciate the best collection of *Dukes* images and info on the Web, all combined in quick, easy formats, just like the show. Rejoice with Ray that *Dukes* has returned to the air, and when you're done, follow his well-selected links to other TV sites.

on in this newsgroup, they'd probably make an episode on this alone." Just as on the sitcom, humor is derived from microscropic observations, but instead of Manhattan, the subject is the latest episode and, to a much smaller degree, the tabloid details of Seinfeld's real-life romance. Characters' selfish flaws are angrily defended, even venerated and every couple of days a new "Is _____ Jewish" thread starts up. One regular poster compiles a "laugh analysis" of which character gets the most laughs per show (George) and which the "most thoughtful tee-hees" (Jerry).
USENET alt.tv.seinfeld

Seinfeld Home Page "It's the funniest show and it's about... well, it's about nothing and everything." So says the description of *Seinfeld* at this official site, which offers video and audio clips, photos of the cast, and details on upcoming shows.
WEB http://www.spe.sony.com /Pictures/tv/seinfeld/seinfeld.html

Twin Peaks Billed as the "Ultimate *Twin Peaks* Reference Page," this site is maintained by Jon Yager, who admits in his introduction that "over the years [he] has become obsessed with the show, and with the other works of David Lynch," and that he's planning on using his Web site to "spread the 'gospel' of *Twin Peaks.*" Features include cast bios, an episode guide, Log Lady

Time for some stupid human tricks
http://WWW.CBS.COM/lateshow/lateshow.html

intros, info on the film, an FAQ, and links. A site bound to become more authoritative with a promising future looming in the green mist around the page.
WEB http://www.xmission.com /~jonyag/TP/Twin-Peaks.html

Late night

alt.fan.conan-obrien As such things go, this site is hipper and *less* juvenile than its (older, dumber) brother late-night sites. Lots of discussion about the writers and Conan's Harvard days.
USENET alt.fan.conan.obrien
FAQ: **WEB** http://www.cis.ohiostate .edu/hypertext/faq/usenet/conan-obrien-faq/faq.html

alt.fan.howard-stern "Penis" and "incest" are the major buzzwords. There's also lots of talk about objects inserted in the anus. And many of these

posters would love nothing better than to be spanked by Horrible Howard. Not a repository of sparkling intellectual insights, the newsgroup is like the show—crass, crude, and sometimes hilarious.
USENET alt.fan.howard-stern

alt.fan.jay-leno "Is Jay dying out?" queries one concerned fan. Aside from discussions relating to the fate of late-night television, you'll discover that Letterman isn't the only one with a frat-boy following. Speaking of Letterman, there's a surprisingly large amount of Letterman discussion and debate on this list.
USENET alt.fan.jay-leno

alt.fan.letterman Insomniacs and would-be television insiders go over the most recent installments of Dave's show with a fine-tooth comb and dissect the performances of celebrity guests. Unlike most of the alt.fan newsgroups, the show and show business are the center of discussion here. Occasional groupie posts (from, say, admirers of Dave's accumulation of speeding tickets) are generally ignored by the amateur analysts who fine-tune their network savvy here. Running tallies track which guests have the rare power to make Dave uncomfortable (Madonna, Sandra Bullock, Richard Simmons, Cher) and which earn his bullying wrath (Howard Stern, Shirley Maclaine). Much overlap and jousting with the alt.tv .talkshows.late newsgroup. **USENET** alt.fan.letterman

alt.tv.talkshows.late Anybody have the transcripts for last night's *Politically Incorrect*? Analysis of the late-night horse-race between David, Conan, and Jay is hot and heavy here. One-stop shopping for Late-Talk trivia and information. Find out what happened on the other guy's show. **USENET** alt.tv.talkshows.late

Hereeeeeeeeee's Conan The feeling here is that the underdog just might pull it off and shoot to #1. Come for Conan sounds and many images of his very popular forehead. Summaries of episodes are available by date. **WEB** http://styx.ios.com/~damone /gconan.html

King of All Media Fans' Home Page Where is Robin Quivers' hawking her book this week? You can find out here. There is also a connection to a Howard Stern newsletter and to chat groups. Do you want an audio clip of the infamous exchange between Howard and Linda Rondstadt? It's here, along with many other downloadable .GIFs and sounds. **WEB** http://krishna.cs.umd.edu/stern

The Late Late Show with Tom Snyder Find out what scintillating personality is on the show tonight. Send Tom your questions, and maybe he'll even answer them on the air. **WEB** http://www.cbs.com/snyder

VANDERBILT TELEVISION NEWS ARCHIVE
WEB http://tvnews.vanderbilt.edu
picture: WEB http://www.veronica.nl/events/wlc/TheConcert/Artists/cronkite.html
Current-events researchers, take heart. In 1968, when folks realized that it might be nice to record news broadcasts for future reference, this seriously impressive archive was created, making

abstracts and transcripts of network news programming permanently available to all. Now this organization is online, and they're offering inexpensive video cassettes of the programs. This exceptional resource may not be fancy, but it offers complete coverage of ABC, NBC, CBS, CNN, and, in its special-edition section, even some news magazines like *Nightline*.

Late Show News The current edition of this terrific newsletter is available online, or you can subscribe to have it emailed to you via their live link. Read opinionated articles from the front lines of the late-night talk-show battles, or just check to see who's on this week; except for a few random listings like *Nightline*, this almost exclusively covers Leno, Letterman, Kinnear, and O'Brien.
WEB http://www.worldwidenews.net /lateshow/home.html

The Late Show with David Letterman An archive of Dave's Top Ten lists, a list of tonight's guests, and a link to a *Late Show* merchandise order form where you can buy hats, keychains, and real-hair replicas of Dave's toupée (but not World Wide Pants).
WEB http://WWW.CBS.COM/lateshow /lateshow.html

The Tonight Show with Jay Leno At this site you can download videos of last night's highlights, view amusing typos from the newspapers, venture behind the scenes, and view the week's line-up of guests.
WEB http://www.nbctonightshow.com

Upcoming Guests on The Tonight Show with Jay Leno Besides the roster of guests for the week, there is a listing for European air-times. You can also download an audio clip of the theme song here.
WEB http://pmwww.cs.vu.nl/links/TV /JayLeno/tonight_show_us.html

Location: http://www.clever.net/wiley/anghst.htm

And my name is Tom Arnold; they work for me
http://www.clever.net/wiley/charliea.htm

Syndicated

'80s Television Homepage "ABC, NBC, and CBS are my second set of parents," confesses the couch potato engineer of the '80s Television Homepage. If you're a TV orphan as well, yearning for the glory days of *Dallas* and *Punky Brewster*, lost without those *Cheers* mugs and *Dukes of Hazzard* bumper stickers, here you'll feel right at home. It's loaded with yearly Nielsen ratings, plus rotating descriptions of hot (and not-so-hot) shows, with audio and video clips. The best feature? A sampling of canned audience sounds—from tinny laugh tracks to the contrived "Awww!"
WEB http://www.megahits.com /quickcam/80stv.html

All in the Family A sound file of the theme song, an episode guide, and pictures of Archie, Edith, Meathead, and a stunning, svelte Gloria.
WEB http://pmwww.cs.vu.nl/service /sitcoms/AllInTheFamily

The Bewitched and Elizabeth Montgomery Page A close up of *Bewitched* star Elizabeth Montgomery, including an interview and articles. Recent chat forum transcripts, rotating picture and sound galleries, and simple design make this a worthwile visit for fans of Samantha and her magical family.
WEB http://www.erols.com/bewitchd

The Bewitched Home Page Make a stop at this product of

Samantha-simpatico and share stories, sound bites, trivia, and a truly expert sense of design. The background is rich and the cartoons cute, but the sounds aren't yet up to speed.
WEB http://www.sappho.com /bewitchd

The Unofficial Brady Bunch Home Page An extensive selection of *Brady Bunch* memorabilia, including scripts, photos, sound clips, blueprints, and a series of photographs of the Brady house—the real thing— as it has aged over the past 25 years.
WEB http://www.teleport.com /~btucker/bradys.htm

Charlie's Angels Home Page Just who was Charlie anyway? Many an adolescent boy couldn't have cared less; all they needed to know was what night of the week Farrah Fawcett, Jaclyn Smith and the other Angels would grace the screen. Bone up on the show's history, including the premise, the cars they drove—all Fords, including an orange Pinto—and the author's favorite episodes.
WEB http://www.clever.net/wiley /charliea.htm

Just One More Thing... The Columbo Home Page Despite the site's well-kept design, the most lovable slob since Oscar Madison calls it home—page, that is. You can ask other *Columbo*-obsessives "just one more thing" or subscribe to the *Columbo* newsletter. The *Columbo*-loving Web master

has even started an original mystery story starring the absent-minded detective. You'll find the goofy genius in all his glory, from the original NBC series through the current ABC movies and critically acclaimed novels.
WEB http://members.aol.com /kevinglove/columbo.html

The Gilligan's Island Homepage If not for the courage of this web page, *Gilligan* fans would be lost, er, maybe. The page, like the Minnow, is small and could easily be swept away by a more avid fan, so the skipper ought to add more to it. But the essentials are there: audio clips, a couple of cast photos, and an episode guide that includes cast bios and the lyrics to the theme song. This ship also navigates your *Gilligan* daily programming, cites print resources, links, trivia,

and requests fan feedback. Stay tuned for more.
WEB http://www.epix.net/~jabcpudr /gilligan.html

Hawaii Five-O Home Page "Book 'em, Danno!" The *Five-O* wave is surfable on the Net. "Five-O Oddities, Goofs and Trivia" collects a number of strange occurrences from the show, while the FAQ covers the basics, such as Jack Lord's height and real name, and the evil Wo Fat's criminal undertakings. Also included: an episode guide and an audio clip of the theme song, fan links, snips from the media on the show, and updates on *Five-O* exposure.
WEB http://web20.mindlink.net /a4369/fiveo.htm

I Love Lucy Trivia Challenge Get your one-a-day trivia dose of the small screen's wackiest red-

Just sit right back and you'll hear a tale...
http://www.epix.net/~jabcpudr/gilligan.html

Location: http://www.best.com/~dijon/tv/gilligan/images/cast-photo.jpg

head right here! Amass points based on your recollection of Magillicuddy as Lucy's maiden name, or that miracle product "Vitameatavegamin." Or just wander through the list of past questions for a boost to your memory-lane morale.

WEB http://www.mtwinc.com /~brettsch/Trivia/Lucy_Ball

The Fans from U.N.C.L.E. Information on *The Man From U.N.C.L.E.*, the TV series that ran for four seasons in the sixties, with episode guides, cast information, and a look at the Women of U.N.C.L.E., a small group of fans who gather at local conventions to buy, sell, and cry uncle.

WEB http://www.greatbasin.net /~kuryakin/uncle

alt.tv.mash What's your favorite Frank line? How about this one: "I'm all for individuality as long as we're all doing it." Lots of *M*A*S*H* talk and trivia. And remember: Frank Burns eats worms.

USENET alt.tv.mash

M*A*S*H Archives So what if the show lasted longer than the Korean War it chronicled through the eyes of Hawkeye, Radar, and Major Houlihan. This site offers cast photos, a sound clip from the theme song, an episode guide, a list of characters, and a FAQ with *M*A*S*H* quotations and lyrics to the now-grating "Suicide is Painless."

WEB http://www.best.com/~dijon/tv /mash/index.html

The Monkees Home Page Hey, hey it's the... fake Fab Four! Or at least a reasonable facsimile thereof, featuring a playable theme song, silly pics to ogle, and updates about the quasi-Beatles, all accessible via full-color photo buttons. These guys are so wonderfully funny, it's hard to imagine why they haven't gone on tour with Spinal Tap.

WEB http://www.primenet.com/~flex /monkees.html

The Rockford Files Homepage Here lies everything *Rockford* —info on James Garner's series, a detailed episode guide, a picture gallery, and a list of phone messages from the opening credits.

WEB http://falcon.cc.ukans.edu /~asumner/rockford

Sketch comedy

alt.tv.kids-in-hall Kids No More? Find out all rumors, gossip and news, as well as happy reminiscing about gay subtexts and Canadian humor.

USENET alt.tv.kids-in-hall

alt.tv.snl Discussion of *Saturday Night Live*, with most of the talk focused on the current cast—though arguments flare, now and then, over whether Chevy Chase did a better "Weekend Update" than Dennis Miller.

USENET alt.tv.snl

Saturday Net Wondering what year Dan Ackroyd left *Saturday Night Live*? Check out the Cast Member Timeline at this *SNL* site. Other highlights

Lasting proof that television isn't (all) trash
http://www.best.com/~dijon/tv/mash/index.html

Location: http://bau2.ulbk.ac.at/sg/python/Images/fork.jpg

And now for something completely different... Python madcaps mug for the camera
http://www.iia.org/~rosenrl/python

include a detailed episode guide, a list of celebrity hosts and musical guests, and a schedule of TV reruns.
WEB http://ccwf.cc.utexas.edu/~serpas/snl.html

Saturday Night Archives Detailed info on cast members from Dan Akyroyd to Danitra Vance, along with FAQs on recurring characters, band info, "Wayne's World," commercial parodies, and song lyrics.
WEB http://www.best.com/~dijon/tv/snl/index.html

British

rec.arts.tv.uk.comedy Talk of British comedy shows, from *Absolutely Fabulous* to *The Young Ones*, with lots of bashing of fare from across the Atlantic (one active thread was titled "American Comedies—Crap").
USENET rec.arts.tv.uk.comedy

alt.tv.ab-fab Nitpick, obsess, and carp about *Absolutely Fabulous*—the political persuasions of various characters, the unlit joint Edina was holding in one episode, the characters' last names. Fervent fans.
USENET alt.tv.ab-fab

Are You Being Served? Well, are you? Not unless you check out this site's sound clips ("Come and sit next to me, Mr. Humphries, and give me a baby"), episode guide, and an interview with John Inman, who played Mr. Humphries.
WEB http://www.webcom.com/~jrice/aybs.html

James Dawe's Avengers Home Page Your assignment: Investigate *Avengers* history from Cathy Gale to Tara King using articles, trivia games, and images in the online files of one James Dawe. Find Steed and Mrs. Peel in every conceivable

pose and scrape (like most *Avenger* fans, Diana Rigg's turn as Steed's leather-clad partner is Dawe's favorite). Read behind-the-scenes trivia and steal looks at photos detailing Emma Peel's erotically athletic manner of adventure.
WEB http://nyquist.ee.ualberta.ca/~dawe/avengers.html

BBC Television Whether you're trying to sell comedy scripts and want some helpful hints or you need to know the BBC's weekly on-air schedule, this site offers Anglophilic Americans and homesick Brits a wealth of TV information. The pages are text-heavy, but there are some visually appealing hot-links graphics. Using the site is as easy as clicking the remote control for the telly.
WEB http://www.bbcnc.org.uk/tv/index.html

rec.arts.tv.uk.coronation-st Why does Ken hate Baldwin? Did Andy ever fall for a co-worker? Much *Coronation Street* talk, with the focus on plot twists and favorite episodes of the longest-running soap opera in the world.
USENET rec.arts.tv.uk.coronation-st

East Enders Information on the people and places of this very British soap, along with spoilers, plot synopses, and a special feature that selects the character of the week. Anglo-serial addicts can get connections to other U.K. soaps here.
WEB http://www.cybernetics.net/users/emmett/tv/ee.html

BONUS BUTTOCKS

Eric Idle: And now for something completely different. A man with three buttocks!

Host (John Cleese): I have with me Mr. Arthur Frampton who... (pause) Mr. Frampton, I understand that you—um—as it were... (pause) Well let me put it another way. Erm, I believe that whereas most people have—er—two... Two.
Frampton (Michael Palin): Oh, sure.
Host: Ah well, er, Mr. Frampton. Erm, is that chair comfortable?
Frampton: Fine, yeah, fine.
Host: Mr. Frampton, er, vis a vis your... (pause) rump.
Frampton: I beg your pardon?
Host: Your rump.
Frampton: What?
Host: Er, your derriere. (Whispers) Posterior. Sit-upon.
Frampton: What's that?
Host (whispers): Your buttocks.
Frampton: Oh, me bum!
Host (hurriedly): Sshhh! Well now, I understand that you, Mr. Frampton, have a... (pause) 50% bonus in the region of what you say.
Frampton: I got three cheeks.
Host: Yes, yes, excellent, excellent. Well we were wondering, Mr. Frampton, if you could see your way clear to giving us a quick... (pause) a quick visual... (long pause). Mr. Frampton, would you take your trousers down.
Frampton: What? (to cameramen) 'Ere, get that away! I'm not taking me trousers down on television. What do you think I am?
Host: Please take them down.
Frampton: No!
Host: No, er look, er Mr. Frampton. It's quite easy for somebody just to come along here claiming... that they have a bit to spare in the botty department. The point is, our viewers need proof.
Frampton: I been on Persian Radio, and the Forces' Network!

—from Monty Python Home Page

duced will turn mild giggles into outright guffaws before long. Plain and simple cast and episode lists are the basics, and that's about as far as it goes— but with the brilliant text of John Cleese's scripts available, it might just be enough.
WEB http://www.cm.cf.ac.uk/htbin /RobH/Fawlty_Towers

Monty Python Home Page The site includes songs from the series, pointers to *Monty Python* sound clips, biographical info on members of the troupe, and transcripts of sketches from "Australian Table Wines" to "Spot the Brain Cell."
WEB http://www.iia.org/~rosenrl /python

Archives & episodes

Footage.net If you ever wondered where documentary filmmakers manage to get just the right shot of an obscure event, you can find the answer here. Footage.net helps film production professionals get stock footage for virtually anything. Just put in a topic and get a list of stock footage dealers who can sell you the film and videotape clips you need.
WEB http://www.footage.net:2900

Internet TV Ratings Looking for thumbs up, stars, or kudos for films? Get quick movie scores here. There is an FAQ describing in detail the informal nature of this ratings system. Ratings cover only the broadcast networks (not PBS) and

rec.arts.tv.uk.eastenders Lots of chat about upcoming episodes, who's shagging who, and the characters' psychological profiles. Hilarious and volatile.
USENET rec.arts.tv.uk.eastenders

Fawlty Towers Information You won't be graphically stimulated in this gray area, but the recounting of "memorable moments" of what is perhaps the greatest sitcom ever pro-

syndicated shows now in production (e.g., no *Star Trek: TNG*). You can subscribe here to participate in the weekly ratings' survey and supply information on your daily viewing habits.
WEB http://tvnet.com/misc/ratings.html

Shokus Video Ah, the good old days—the Golden Age of television. Hard to believe those classics led to *Mighty Morphin Power Rangers*. If you're into the black-and-white, innocent era of TV, take a trip down this memory lane; it'll cost you nothing. But if you want to order some vintage footage of Art Linkletter in *People Are Funny*—before he started hocking insurance, that is—or

Roy Rogers in *The Roy Rogers Show*, before he started pitching burgers, it'll cost you. VHS or Beta tapes (remember those?) generally run about $20 each, plus shipping and handling. You can place your orders on impulse and online.
WEB http://www.rahul.net/shokus

Wiretap TV Episode Guides Episode guides for dozens of television shows from *Alf* to *Young Indiana Jones*. Each guide arranges episodes by season and gives a plot summary of each episode along with acting, writing, and production credits. Some guides also have series-related information—upcoming books or the lyrics to a show's theme song. The guides concentrate

on the cheesy (*The A-Team*), the popular (*Cheers*), the cultish (*Twin Peaks*), and the obscure (remember *Parker Lewis?*).
URL gopher://wiretap.spies.com/11/Library/Media/Tv

Listings

Cable Movie Guide Movie listings guide for 27 mainstream cable and broadcast networks plus Fox (no PBS, UPN, or WB). Listings include notations about program violence and sexual content, format (is it letterboxed?), etc. Clicking on a movie title will take you to the Internet Movie Database for more detailed information on the movie. There are also features on stars, links to sport-

TV Guide Online

 WEB http://www.iguide.com/tv

It's possible to become so engrossed with *TV Guide* Online you can forget to check the listings. Discovering how Tom Selleck was all choked up about playing Courtney Cox's love interest on *Friends*, or devouring the gossip about whether Darlene from *Roseanne* was contemplating her

own spin-off can be thoroughly overwhelming. Indeed, the listings are there too, segmented by region. Overall, it's a good, well-written product, just like its paper-bound cousin— except that it's free, and you don't have to try to hide it under your lettuce at the checkout line.

ing event pages, and a search engine for major sports events.
WEB http://emporium.turnpike.net/W/wto/tvguide.html

TV Schedules of the World Put your 600-channel satellite dish to work. With TV schedules for every nation from Estonia to the United States, it's a dish jockey's dream come true. Catch that upcoming soccer match from Brazil without having to miss the latest episode of your favorite British sitcom. Nicely organized and professionally assembled, this operation is presented by the Buttle Broadcasting Group of independent producers; should you tire of clicking through the intricate satellite listings, link to Buttle's home page to see what some cutting-edge TV folks are doing.
WEB http://www.buttle.com/tv/schedule.htm

❝ Want to hear Ross from *Friends* say 'Here's my monkey' over and over? ❞

TVI With free customizable television listings, TVI has the potential to be an invaluable service for both the occasional viewer and the relentless couch potato. After a quick registration, you can assemble your own personal TV guide by program category, specified channels, and/or desired viewing times. Or you can browse through the complete television listings for your area up to six days in advance.
WEB http://www.TVI.com

TVNow You have to download the shareware version of the browser (Windows and DOS; the Mac version is supposed to be ready soon) to read the listings here. Listings are for movies only and include information for over 70 channels. You get the data monthly or bimonthly, here or by email. There is an 800 number to get the registered browser, which reads listings for movies, series, sports, specials, etc., and allows you to choose which of the channels to get information for.
WEB http://tvnet.com/TVNow/tvnow.html

Theme songs

alt.binaries.sounds.tv Want to hear Ross from *Friends* say "Here's my monkey" over and over? Never tire of Edina saying "Sweetie! Darling!"? This is the place. It has a small selection of audio clips.
USENET alt.binaries.sounds.tv

TV Bytes—WWW TV Themes Home Page Nothing perks up a drab operating system more than a few well-placed sound files. Replace those boring generic beeps and chords with the themes from your favorite old TV shows and watch your coworkers perk up. After registering, listen to a few new clips every day from sci-fi classics, cartoons, and every other type of show imaginable. The possibilities are wondrous.
WEB http://themes.parkhere.com/themes

Stations & cable

alt.cable-tv.re-regulate The pros and cons of cable monopolies; descramblers and digital TV; Hollywood's attempts to take over the cable industry; and explanations of arcane cable legislation. Discussion here is for the truly hard-core cable fan or professional.
USENET alt.cable-tv.re-regulate

U.S. TV Stations Home Pages Connections to Web pages of many local TV stations. You can get video and audio clips of the latest local news in Huntsville, Ala., or a bio of the weatherperson in Gainesville, Fla.. Most have programming guides as well. Far-flung but not comprehensive yet.
WEB http://tvnet.com/misc/Resources/stations.html

World TV An index of links to TV station home pages around the world, from Afghanistan to Zimbabwe. Many listed countries have no actual links as yet. Information ranges from the elaborate listing of all local TV and radio stations, to a brief mention or cursory description of one or two.
WEB http://tvnet.com/WORLDtv/worldtv.html

Music

IN THE '80S; VIDEOS REINVENTED THE MUSIC INDUSTRY. WELCOME TO THE ONLINE REVOLUTION

MUSIC AND THE WEB didn't always go hand in hand. When HTML first became a tool of the masses, it was individuals who chose to create small cyberaltars to their favorite performer or genre, from hip-hop to opera, from old-fashioned to rock and roll. A mere three or four years later, and the corporate world has embraced the new medium with cacophanous passion. Every new band and record now gets a simultaneous push on the radio, TV, the music press, and the Net. Artists without Web pages are almost deemed "uncool." It all comes down to the very essence of the Net—it's a virtual space for the worldwide sharing of information. And music, as we all know, is a universal language.

Location: http://www.iuma.com/IUMA-2.0/home.html

 IUMA
WEB http://www.iuma.com

One of the most impressive sites in cyberspace, the Internet Underground Music Archive houses Web pages for a number of labels from the tiny (Blue Goat) to the enormous (Warner Bros.), designs home pages for individual bands, and hosts a number of ezines. It's divided into four sections—Bands, Record Labels, Publications, and What's Brewin'. Band or individual artist pages include audio clips, pictures, profiles, and a section for comments and reviews. Record Labels offers more than 20 labels that use the Web to announce new releases, publicize artist tour dates, link to their artists' Web pages, and even sell from their catalogs. And the half-dozen or so publications available offer critical reviews, interviews, music news, and a lot of attitude.

Starting points

All Music Guide Forum Sponsored by the creators of the All Music Guide, a resource that covers thousands of musicians, this forum is one more area for fans to discuss their favorite musicians and styles. Unlike the usual gossip and zealous ravings of music fans, this discussion is more information-oriented. Everything from easy listening to heavy metal is on topic, and specific songs like Ray Davies' poignant "Days" come under intense investigation. Have any ideas for a classical piece of music suitable for flute and guitar to play while people file into church for a wedding? Feel free to share your opinions.
COMPUSERVE *go* amgpop

Fan Club Forum Music fans flock to this forum to discuss, investigate, and gossip about their music idols. They come to report Elvis sightings, describe getting Elton John's autograph, review an Annie Lennox concert, and discuss the Artist Formerly Known as Prince, among other things. Sections are set up for fans of Queen, Aerosmith, Rick Springfield, Barry Manilow, Elton John, Madonna, Live, Pearl Jam, Chicago, and many other artists and groups. If your favorite group doesn't have its own section, just hang around for a while and holler a lot—section topics are not set in stone. Download tour dates, a biography of Jimi Hendrix, a

Sex Pistols, Soundgarden, Smashing Pumpkins—Now that's variety
http://www.imusic.com

Madonna screen saver, Barry Manilow sound clips, a Queen FAQ, and other musical artifacts from the libraries.
COMPUSERVE *go* fanclub

iMusic Once you get past the flashy ads, you'll find audio files from new albums by the likes of Elvis Costello and Soundgarden, chat rooms, live broadcasts from Moe (one of Seattle's top alternative clubs), music news, record reviews, a concert calendar, and links to more than 100 other top music sites.
WEB http://www.imusic.com

Library of Musical Links This elegant site breaks music resources down into Web sites, FTP sites, mailing lists, gophers, and newsgroups. Not only is it easy-to-use, it's got information on everyone from Tori Amos to Oingo Boingo. It's certainly not the largest music index on the Net, but its

collection of Web sites and newsgroups rivals those of the larger, corporate sites.
WEB http://www-scf.usc.edu/~jrush/music/index.html

Music & Bands How do you dance the "Macarena?" Buried in the middle of the Entertainment Drive Forum, the Music & Bands topic is home to a small group of fans who convene to weigh in on the musical issues of the day. Has Courtney Love ever been photographed topless? Where are the Afghan Whigs playing? What do people think of Alanis Morrisette? "She expresses what we've all felt at one time or another," writes one fan.
COMPUSERVE *go* eforum→Libraries or Messages→Browse→Music & Bands

Music/Arts Forum Ethnic music? Barbershop? Opera? For the most general music chat and resources online, visit the Music/Arts Forum, where posts

range from queries for information on songs featured in commercials to requests for Duran Duran memorabilia. The board is divided into dozens of discussion and library sections, including The Blues, Opera, Dance, Religious Music, Classical Music, and Pop/Rock. Pick up Nirvana pictures, Beethoven sound clips, and artist FAQs in the libraries.
COMPUSERVE *go* musicarts

MusicSpace AOL's lineup of music companies makes this one of the hottest music hangouts in cyberspace. Read the entertainment section of *The New York Times*, download

goodies from Warner Brothers and Virgin Records, and shop at Tower Records. Music fans can gossip and exchange news in forums run by MTV and ABC, ones dedicated solely to rock, and even some exclusively created for Grateful Dead fans. Check out new alternative bands at the BMG section, and use MusicSpace to get news and record reviews, download pictures and sound clips, and even locate a nearby concert. If music fans are looking for more, AOL has also built in a directory to the range of musical sites accesible via the Web.
AMERICA ONLINE *keyword* music

Perpetual Music "If music be the food of love, then play on..." So you want to find music on the Internet? You know it's there, everywhere. This Web page is a great place to start your adventure; it leads off with comments and critiques of music sites and finishes with a mid-sized index of sites, most of which are band pages.
WEB http://www.cs.umd.edu/~lgas /music

RockWeb Interactive The staff of RockWeb Interactive is anxious to help up-and-coming bands create their own Web pages—for a price. After you

WILMA TOUR DIRECTORY

WEB http://wilma.com/tour.html

Space-age cartoon design only enhances this huge index of concert and venue information links to city guides, tour schedules, and even concert reviews. Visitors can search hundreds of cities for information about arenas, clubs, theaters, colleges, and coffeehouses. In many cases, venues have

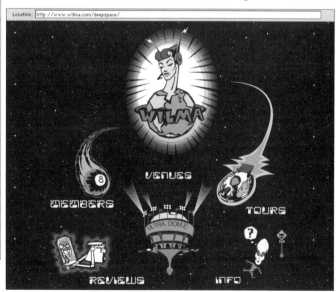

their own home pages (The Knitting Factory in New York City, for instance) and the Wilma Tour Directory links directly to these pages. Wilma also offers a directory of artists who are currently on tour, and features links to tour schedules and concert reviews.

Netsite: http://www.sonicnet.com/ontour/ad_main.html

Who's coming to your corner of the galaxy?
http://www.sonicnet.com

ante up, your group's cyberpropaganda will be part of a rich site that includes celebrity interviews, music news, chat rooms, artwork, videos, and the latest and coolest applications of new technologies like Shockwave, Java, and RealAudio.
WEB http://www.rockweb.com/rwi

SonicNet SonicNet, the NYC-based source for music online, is quite simply one of the most active and creative resources for alternative music on the Internet. Everyone from Dick Dale to KMFDM to Ozzy Osborne makes an appearance in some form on SonicNet, and the variety is never too much. The site has chats, contests, and cybercasts, and includes an archive of almost everything it's ever been involved in. Transcripts of SonicNet-sponsored artist chats reveal the lighter side of some groups; Dean Wareham of Luna recently responded to a fan's compliment in the following

way: "Thank you. What are you wearing, PopStar?"
WEB http://www.sonicnet.com

The Vibe Former MTV veejay Adam Curry left the music giant and formed Metaverse—a Web site that serves as the online headquarters for several high-profile events, some musical (the Grammy awards) and some not (the NFL Draft), and also has a number of more specific rock resources which range from music reviews to celebrity interviews to columns. The coolest part of Vibe is its Sleaze section, which features daily celebrity gossip, from overdoses to business breakups.
WEB http://metaverse.com/vibe

Web Wide World of Music There are never enough ways to organize the thousands of music sites on the Internet. At least that's the philosophy of this fabulous Web site, which breaks sites down into ezines,

charts, discussion forums, directories, band pages, and lyric servers. Each section comes with its own series of options. However you decide to browse, don't miss the site's Ultimate Band List—one of the best places in cyberspace for band information. The Web Wide World of Music also lets visitors vote on sites they like and sponsors live chat sessions with musicians. Check the calendar for events. While the site is designed for ease of navigation, you may get lost here on purpose; it's just that good.
WEB http://american.recordings.com/wwwofmusic

On stage

Musi-Cal A worldwide listing of live musical performances that you can search by performer, city, venue, or event. Want to know where Neil Young is playing in upcoming months? Enter his name, designate "performer," and search. Looking for something to do this Saturday night? Search by city name (not just the big cities), and listings for performances at local nightclubs, bars, colleges, and arenas are retrieved. Listings include dates, performers, and contact numbers. While the site is certainly not comprehensive, it's pretty amazing.
WEB http://www.calendar.com/concerts

Pollstar For years, Pollstar has been the music industry's No. 1 source for touring information. It has now opened up shop on

the Net, and that's a great thing for fans of live music and industry types alike. Not only does the site include the magazine's special features, it has an extensive, searchable database of concert listings.
WEB http://www.pollstar.com

Lyrics

alt.music.lyrics You can talk about lyrics almost anywhere in the online music world, but this is one newsgroup where lyrics are always on the menu. Alt.music.lyrics is composed of two kinds of posts—lyrics requests and lyrics answers for an artist range so wide it features both Suzi Quatro and Portishead.
USENET alt.music.lyrics

HeadBang's Home Page "You want it all but you can't have it/ It's in your face but you can't grab it," sang Mike Patton of Faith No More. HeadBang's collected an archive of hard rock and alternative lyrics organized by band name. Blur, Nirvana, and Sepultura are here, along with many more. There's also an image gallery featuring selected artists from Biohazard to Weezer.
WEB http://www.stack.urc.tue.nl/~niels

The Ultimate Band List Lyrics Organized by band name, this Web page indexes hundreds of sites with band and artist lyrics—from Harry Chapin to The Cure to Alanis Morrisette.
WEB http://american.recordings.com /WWWoM/ubl/lyric_list.shtml

Labels

Arista You may not have known that the Grateful Dead, Annie Lennox, and Whitney Houston are all on the same record label; now you do. The Arista site has information on the label's entire stable of artists, which also includes groups like Ace of Base and TLC. The content varies by performer, but most have images and audio bites; many have links to other fan or official sites on the Web. Their Virtual Conference room, when completed, will be a great place to talk with other fans.
WEB http://www.aristarec.com

Atlantic Records In the days before Hootie, Atlantic Records was just another of the

ADDICTED TO NOISE

 WEB http://www.addict.com/ATN

An excellent online music magazine that covers the cutting edge as well as venerable artists who haven't lost their currency. With news updates, profiles, interviews, and reviews, *ATN* is also one of the best-written rock mags around, with regular contributions from music journalism gurus Dave Marsh and Greil Marcus. The *ATN* folks have also recently launched a chat area in Sonic Lodge, where you can prattle on to your heart's delight. If they ever get T-I connections to the great gig in the sky, this is the ezine Lester Bangs will write for.

Netsite: http://www.subpop.com/

S·U·B P·O·P online

"One World, One Network"

A step below the rest
http://www.subpop.com

nation's major labels, with an artist roster that included All-4-One, Victoria Williams, and Billy Pilgrim, and a back catalog stocked full of classic rock and R&B (Led Zeppelin, Ray Charles). Thanks to Tori, Weiland, and the guys in Bad Religion, Atlantic is riding tall in the saddle again, and the label's beautiful Web site shows off its newfound prosperity. New bands like Yum Yum, Seven Mary Three, and Poe are featured here. Chew the fat with other fans in Atlantic's online chat room, or download sound and movie clips. The Atlantic Web site also serves as a promotional site for Spew+, a high-tech, high-energy enhanced CD-ROM promo tool. If you're using the latest version of Netscape, buckle your seatbelts—Atlantic has built in some special features for netsurfers on the cutting edge of browser technology.
WEB http://www.atlantic-records.com

Elektra Records As major labels go, Elektra is one of the best, with a roster that includes AC/DC, Bjork, They Might Be Giants, Ween, and dozens more mainstream and alternative artists. The site includes pages for individual artists as well as information about the label's marketing, publicity, and A&R departments. Unsigned bands can take heart from this encouraging message from Ben, a member of the A&R staff: "I work in the Elektra A&R (Artists & Repertoire, not Angst & Rejection) department. We're the department that discovers new artists, oversees the recording of their albums, helps select singles, and generally helps to guide the creative aspects of their careers. It's my job to find artists across the country that have developed a strong buzz at a local and regional level. Once I hear of a happening band, I bring the music to the rest of the folks in A&R to let

them listen and decide whether it's something we want to pursue further. Please don't send us any unsolicited tapes! We just don't have the time to listen to everything. If you have a band that's really good, we'll catch up to you. Thanks."
WEB http://pathfinder.com/elektra

Geffen/DGC Records Though Geffen arrived on the Web later than most other majors, the label has made up for lost time with a Web site that emphasizes recent releases (including those by Beck and the Cowboy Junkies), a full artist roster (including Maria McKee and Hole), and even links to other music sites. Also, tune into the Geffen site for its new related labels: Almo Sounds (featuring Garbage) and Outpost Recordings.
WEB http://geffen.com

Grand Royal Home of the Beastie Boys, as well as affiliated artists such as Luscious Jackson, the Grand Royal Web site is also a lesson in how to establish a beautiful and functional Web presence. Tour dates, news, and new artists like Butter are presented with class, as is the Milarepa Organization, a group to which Beastie M.C.A. belongs. Check your head before you enter—you'll be swept away.
WEB http://grandroyal.com

MCA Records This is the home to *AMP*, MCA's Web 'zine, which reviews music and movies and publishes tour

schedules for bands distributed and publicized by the Music Company of America. Although it's got loads of information and interviews, its attempts at humor and cutting edge design fall on the lame side.
WEB http://www.mca.com/mca_records

Sony Music The giant entertainment company's music division furnishes information for hundreds of artists in rock, pop, folk, jazz, and classical genres. From Alice in Chains to Michael Jackson to the Presidents of the United States of America, this is one of the best places to start browsing for pop music information. This highly recommended site is not just a great source of information,

including sound and audio clips for almost all their artists, it's one of the better designed corporate sites on the Web.
WEB http://www.music.sony.com /Music/MusicIndex.html

Sub Pop The influential Seattle independent wasn't always so huge, but they always had the good taste to deal with bands like Sebadoh, Velocity Girl, the Spinanes, and the Friends of Dean Martinez. Get the latest dope on the hottest indie bands here, along with a lavish electronic 'zine. Don't miss out on the hottest new bands— groups like the Afghan Whigs and Six Finger Satellite got their start at Sub Pop HQ.
WEB http://www.subpop.com

Warner Bros. Records One of the largest record companies in the world, Warner has been expert at spinning out successful imprints like Slash, Reprise, Luaka Bop, Maverick, and Paisley Park. Unfortunately, its site is limited and, surprisingly, poorly designed. While the AOL site isn't updated as often as it should be, it is an impressive source of multimedia press kits and sound clips.
AMERICA ONLINE→*keyword* warner
WEB http://www.wbr.com

Magazines

BigO "Asia's coolest rock magazine" has enough content and style to rival *Rolling Stone*. Features on bands like Folk

NME
WEB http://www.nme.com

Britain's best music rag brings its informed combination of music news, features, and reviews to the Web in a colorful, friendly fashion. Artists such as Björk, Depeche Mode, Bis, Blur, and Pulp are the chorus here, and *NME* helps alternative-minded Americans stay ahead in the "you hear it

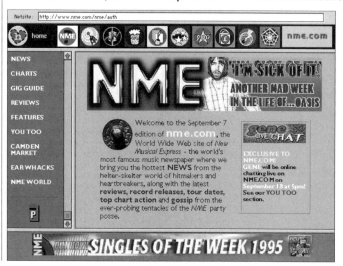

first" game. The United Kingdom's charts are available, along with gossip, the Gig Guide, and an online shopping area cleverly called Camden Market. Remember, the prices are in pounds, not dollars.

Location: http://pathfinder.com/@@iwbNcQQAOhin*3es/Vibe/

VibeOnline—In your face in cyberspace
http://www.pathfinder.com/Vibe

Implosion and Pavement fit right in with their expansive fan base in the west, as do live concert reviews of bands like Filter. Music isn't the only thing on tap at BigO; movies and culture are also featured. A recent issue included an interview with Akira creator Katsuhiro Otomo.
WEB http://www.asia-online.com/bigo

Rolling Stone Online Although not yet up and running at presstime, *Rolling Stone* magazine's Web site should be one of the best online resources for rock and roll animals. Forums for discussion on hip-hop, country, R&B, rock-and-roll, alternative, and metal will find fans posting reviews of the concerts they went to last night, discussion of the annual Lollapalooza festival and speculation about upcoming tours and albums. Expect the typical *RS* features: high-profile interviews, gonzo journalism, and hard-hitting commentary on national affairs.
WEB http://www.rollingstone.com

Spin Bob Guccione, Jr.'s music magazine was once a young upstart taking on *Rolling Stone*. More than ten years later, it's older and wiser, with a by now familiar mix of excellent coverage, self-indulgent reporting, and low-rent sensibility. AOL's *Spin* Online includes daily rock news updates along with a generous helping of content from the print magazine. In the Chat Pit, rant about groups like Paw, Magnapop, and Oasis. The photo gallery has some beautiful images of the late, great Kurt Cobain.
AMERICA ONLINE *keyword* spin

Stereo Review The audiophile's dream, Stereo Review listens to CDs not only for their creative content, but for their technical expertise. Learn all about new recording procedures, and whether the naked ear can detect any difference, then get the latest on home stereo systems. Check out the product reviews and the news on the hottest new gear. Music isn't music if you can't hear it properly.
AMERICA ONLINE *keyword* stereo

VibeOnline Though it's mostly about soul and hip-hop, *Vibe* —the urban-music magazine of the Time-Warner empire—covers movies, celebrities, sports, and more. *Vibe*'s photos are beautiful, its attitude strong, and its articles are well-written with a refreshing point of view.
WEB http://www.pathfinder.com/Vibe

Networks

alt.tv.mtv MTV, a network that has defined a generation (or so it's said over and over, ad nauseam), is a network of music videos, right? Not quite. The network also produces cartoons, dramas, sport, and even game shows. It also covers the news and elections, does annual award shows, and focuses on fashion. But what

about the music? Newsgroup members also seem more concerned with the politically-conservative-big-mouth-airhead-of-a-VJ Kennedy than videos. But what about the music? Well, the folks on this newsgroup spend a lot of time arguing about the balance, defending their favorite shows, and spewing venom at the corporate big-wigs at MTV's parent company, Viacom. But what about the music? Well, that's a pretty big topic of discussion here, too. Come by and ask.
USENET alt.tv.mtv

MTV Online MTV's site on the Web is a comprehensive guide to the network's programming, profiling both regular shows and special features, and also featuring daily music news

updates, message boards for music fan discussions, concert and album reviews, and multimedia downloads. Shows like *Beavis and Butt-Head* and the *Real World* have great pages, and Kurt Loder's news corner is always a realm of insightful data. MTV's proactive "Choose or Lose" campaign is also featured, with links to voter registration sites for interested cybercitizens.
AMERICA ONLINE→*keyword* mtv
WEB http://www.mtv.com

Rockline *Rockline*, the nationwide call-in radio show that allows fans to talk to their favorite rock stars, has been broadcasting for almost 15 years, bringing rock news and opinions to the nation—as the press materials note, the show

even broadcast on Jan. 17, 1994, despite the fact that the studios were almost completely destroyed by the San Francisco earthquake. The busy AOL forum includes lists of upcoming *Rockline* guests, both on the radio and online, a catalog of memorabilia from the Rock Shop, and information about other shows (like Live from the Crazy Horse, an hour of the finest new country music). There are some less serious features as well—RockThrobs, a file of rock-related supermodels and image-obsessed rock stars, and Bite This, a collection of sound clips and .GIFs that includes a *Rockline* listener photo gallery.
AMERICA ONLINE *keyword* rockline

VH-1 MTV's sister (although some might claim "mother") station, VH1 was created with an older, more mellow audience in mind. Stereotypically, it's viewed as a haven for easy listening artists like Michael Bolton and Barbara Streisand. But actually, watching VH1 can be a vacation from being bombarded by MTV and all of its non-music programs. The Web site is also a change from MTV's—information here is presented clearly and quickly, with easy-to-understand graphics and links. Message boards are active and intelligent, including sections such as Live Performance and 8-Track Flashback. Program guides are also helpful. A definite treat for most any music fan.
WEB http://www.vh1.com

From the small screen to the smaller screen
http://www.mtvcom

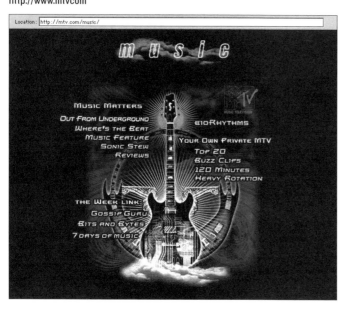

Location: http://www.cipsinc.com/jack

The Guillotine staff have lost their heads
http://www.cipsinc.com/jack

Hip hop

Davey D's Hip-Hop Corner Bronx Prince Davey D has assembled one of the most extensive hip-hop sites on the Web. While the focus is primarily on Bay Area hip-hop (including history, artist bios, and local newsletter), D also features interviews (such as his talk with Ice-T), hip-hop news updates of tour dates and arrests, and album and movie reviews ("The book *Waiting to Exhale* may have been all dat," says D, "but the movie is wack!"). The nicest touch is the Hip-Hop Freestyle Message Board, where you can post your rhymes. Just be prepared for some fierce feedback.
WEB http://www.daveyd.com

Guillotine Check out the subtleties of the Cypha where the rhymes move in circles, injected with the colorful metaphors and lyrical flavors of myriad MCs. Peep in on the poetics of the Vibe Chameleons and other talented rappers at this hip-hop rag loaded with photos set against a background of lightning bolts. With audio files and a stunning sketchbook featuring the work of cutting edge street artists, this is as real as it gets.
WEB http://www.cipsinc.com/jack

The Hip Hop Hotlist Recently updated, this busy site includes a Top 10 chart created by Net voters, and a huge list of hip-hop links, including pages for dozens of artists such as Wu-Tang Clan, Nas, Kris Kross, and The Fugees. The News sections features up-to-date notices about rap and R&B artists.
WEB http://mmm.mbhs.edu/~cmccoy

Hip-Hop Lyrics Home Page If you've ever had a hard time understanding exactly what artists like Doug E. Fresh, EPMD, or Das EFX say in their songs, this is a site you don't want to miss. The site's creator has assembled a fresh library of lyrics to rap songs—from the classics to the newest. It's frequently updated, and contributions and corrections are always welcome.
WEB http://www.public.iastate.edu/~krs_one/lyrics

Internet Ghetto Blaster Clayton Wynter's brilliantly titled Internet Ghetto Blaster features well-written notes on recent albums and mix tapes, but functions best as a communications station for the hip-hop community. Speak Ya Clout polls browsers on important social questions, while the Shout-Outs! section gives you a chance to do just that. Past shouters have hailed from Sweden, Australia, and, of course, Brooklyn.
WEB http://www.seas.upenn.edu/~cswynter/jams.2.html

rec.music.hip-hop / alt.rap Rap longevity is measured in months rather than years, so don't come to this newsgroup with archival concerns—if you're still moving to the rhythm of Boogie Down Productions, step off, and step back on for Mobb Deep, Coolio, and Biggie Smalls. International rap and other hip-hop styles (trip-hop, acid jazz, etc.) are discussed as well. The murder of Tupac Shakur caused frenzy on these groups.
USENET rec.music.hip-hop • alt.rap

Spoonfuls of Hype Hip to the Hop and the Hype never stops! Headz ain't ready for this heady 'zine. A unique spin on American and Canadian hip-hop, broken down into well-organized subdivisions. Check out Listen Up and Backspinz for interactive single and album reviews, The Writtens for interactive lyrics complete with sound samples, and Word? for essay and commentary on the culture of rhythm and rhyme.

WEB http://www.neocom.ca/~jaypee /index.html

Metal & punk

alt.punk What does SNFU stand for? Society's Not For Us, according to a seemingly knoweldgeable voice on alt.punk. No longer just a clan

of youths with green mohawks in London's Piccadilly Circus, punks are around the world, and this is where they talk. For any and all questions and issues regarding punk rock or just being a punk, this is the place to hang. Discussion hits upon the Sex Pistols, veganism, and regional punk scenes. Grab your Doc Martens, dog collar, and Manic Panic! Let's rock!

USENET alt.punk

alt.rock-n-roll.metal Everything from glam talk to Metallica sell-out threads are a permanent feature at this newsgroup. New bands, record sales, and tours are discussed in a generally open atmosphere. Reviews

of Lollapalooza shows and bands like Judas Priest make apperances. People looking for information abound, like the Type O Negative fan who wrote: "I need some help. In the song 'Christian Woman' off *Bloody Kisses*, what the f**k does he say before the 'Body of Christ' part? (in the real deep voice). It sounds something like 'Corpus Christi," or something. Somebody has to know it."

USENET alt.rock-n-roll.metal

Flexbook When was the first Social Distortion record? How many albums did X make? Flexbook is a huge discography that covers the North American punk scene, from its

 Jᴀᴍᴍɪɴ Rᴇɢɢᴀᴇ Aʀᴄʜɪᴠᴇ
ᴡᴇʙ http://orpheus.ucsd.edu/jammin
picture: ᴡᴇʙ http://www.oanet.com/homepage/sleeper/scratch.htm
This home page features an extensive collection of links to reggae archives, including a newsgroup FAQ, Rasta/Patois dictionary, catalogs, tour schedules, lyrics, discographies, articles, periodicals,

Location: http://www.oanet.com/homepage/sleeper/scratch3.gif

©Dave Hendley Trojan

pictures, shops, clubs, books, dub mailing list info, album cover art, artists, interviews, video clips, and a list of reggae stage names. As if that's not enough, the page also features links to sound samples of recent releases, other reggae home pages, Bob Marley pages, radio shows' pages, FTP sites, record company sites, newsgroups, and other reggae-related pages. Rhygin'!

late-seventies beginnings to its early-nineties explosion, with bands like Nirvana and Green Day.
URL ftp://ftp.uwp.edu/pub/music/lists /flex

Hard Rock/Metal Message Center
Korn? Sepultura? Galactic Cowboys? With names like these, the music must be something else. In this active forum, America Online users discuss the aforementioned artists, along with Christian Hard Rock, 1980s Heavy Metal, and body art/rock outfit the Genitorturers. Favorite musicians range from Mark Slaughter to Ted Nugent, so all tastes are obviously welcome.
AMERICA ONLINE *keyword* rock→Rock Messaging→Hard Rock/Metal

Reggae

Dub Page With a definition of dub, a list of artists and labels, reviews of the latest releases, links to other pages, and a brief history of the genre, this page offers a good starting point for dub enthusiasts. If you have suggestions or comments, submit them electronically, and they'll be displayed on the dub page forum alongside the remarks of other dubbernaughts.
WEB http://www.mw3.com/electro /dub-pg.htm

rec.music.reggae Don't worry, be happy. Everyt'ing under the sun, from Sunsplash updates to history lessons to lyric sheets. The newsgroup is the

Location: http://www.nwu.edu/WNUR/jazz/artists/braxton.anthony/

The Jazz Web **People in Jazz** **WWWNUR** Northwestern University

Anthony Braxton (born 1945)

alto saxophone, all other saxophones and clarinets, flute, piano, electronics, percussion

- Anthony Braxton and the Tri-Centric Foundation home page
- Biography from AACM Web Site
- Interview with Anthony Braxton at the New Albion Records site
- The Jazz Photography of James Radke includes one photo of Anthony Braxton

Listen to the legends and learn
http://www.nwu.edu/jazz/artists

best place for regular postings of the reggae FAQ and updates from the Jammin' Reggae Archive.
USENET rec.music.reggae

Reggae Chordbook More than just guitar tabs. Learn to play your favorite reggae hits, from "Sitting in Limbo" to "Kaya" to "Satta Amassagana." There are also images and links to many other reggae sites on the Web. Pay attention to the Javascript at the bottom of the window to learn a little more about the Rastafari philosophy, while you're at it.
WEB http://www.yamamura.material .tohoku.ac.jp/~endo/index.html

Ska FAQ Few Jamaican dance music styles are as infectious as ska. Where did ska come from? What is ska-core? What is skanking? Are there any feature-length ska films? Jo can find all de answers here, mon. An informative site—this FAQ also includes a list of dozens of

ska artists, from A-Kings to Zwit.
WEB http://www.cis.ohio-state.edu /hypertext/faq/usenet/music/ska-faq /top.html

Jazz

InterJazz: The Global Internet Jazz Plaza With a directory of jazz clubs and venues, record labels, booking agencies, and show promoters, as well as individual artist biographies and a link to JazzIRC—a program that allows jazz fans to talk to their favorite artists over IRC—this is one of the most innovative and comprehensive sites on the Web.
WEB http://www.webcom.com/~ijazz

Jazz With links to Usenet newsgroups from alt.music.ragtime to alt.blues, and a users library of downloadable .GIFs of contemporary riff masters such as Pat Metheny and George Benson and loads of style-focused "BBSs," this is

the place for the opinionated jazz fan. Once a week, improvise live in a scheduled chat room after dark.
MSN *keyword* jazz

Jazz Clubs around the World
Mostly U.S. listings, but also a sprinkling of European clubs and even a few from Israel. The clubs are listed by cities and the info is limited to phone numbers and addresses. There are no reviews and the list doesn't specify whether the clubs are exclusively jazz venues.
WEB http://www.acns.nwu.edu/jazz /lists/clubs.html

JAZZ Online Full of slick graphics, this page links to general info, a blues room, industry label pages, and news. Festival and conference listings are growing, as are the links to jazz labels like Verve and JVC Jazz. The sleek design and interviews with artists like Christian McBride make getting hip to cool jazz that much easier.
WEB http://www.jazzonln.com

Jazz/Big Bands By far the busier of CompuServe's two jazz message boards, this group covers everything from Jelly Roll Morton to Miles Davis to the entire Marsalis family. Jazz festivals from Newport to Istanbul are cherished; and music from such strange arenas as the sound-track to *Harriet the Spy* is brought up and shared. Fan reviews also come through, whether they're slams or praises. One fan recently wrote of *After Hours*: "A solid collection of songs and the John Pizzarelli delivery make for yet another winning album. Highly recommended, a perfect late-evening album!"
COMPUSERVE *go* musicarts→Libraries or Messages→Jazz/Big Bands

JazzNet While it's not really limited to jazz—there's plenty of blues information here, too—this site contains a wealth of resources for jazz fans. Want updates on the Monterey Jazz Festival or the San Francisco Blues Festival? Interested in

THE BLUE HIGHWAY
WEB http://www.vivanet.com/~blues

Graham Parker once sang, "Get on the blue highway / Follow the blue highway / to where the real America lies." Parker probably wasn't talking about the Web, but he might have been referring to this site, which traces the history of blues. The site includes bios and pictures of major blues artists,

as well as a map of the Mississippi Delta, the fertile stretch of blues history that runs between the Mississppi River and the Natchez Trace. Not only is this an informative site, it's one of the most beautiful and carefully organized out there. Highly recommended.

learning about the the hottest new jazz ensembles worldwide? You can do all those things from this page, and check on labels, artists, newsletters, and academic resources as well.
WEB http://www.dnai.com/~lmcohen

rec.music.bluenote What color is jazz? Blue, of course. Internet jazz chat is blue, too, mostly because there's so much to talk, and so little time. What are the best CDs of solo drumming? What rock bands have most successfully integrated jazz signatures into their work? What's the best septet ever? When they're not comparing lists, fans are talking about jazz movies (the Oscar-nominated documentary, *A Great Day in Harlem* gets high marks), wishing Louis Armstrong a happy posthumous Fourth of July (and a very happy birthday), and wondering what jazz songs are being used as the soundtracks for network TV shows.
USENET rec.music.bluenote

People of Jazz Index Northwestern University's WNUR has created dozens of profiles for jazz artists, from the major (Louis Armstrong, Miles Davis, Chet Baker) to the minor (Shaun Baxter, Tatsu Aoki), and they're all here, along with well organized discographies, biographies, and supplementary links to other jazz sites.
WEB http://www.acns.nwu.edu/jazz /artists

BluesNet boasts the last known photograph of Blues great Albert King, left
http://dragon.acadiau.ca/~rob/blues/blues.html

Blues

The Blues CompuServe's blues music board isn't terrifically busy, but if you're interested in the chord box, Skip James, or Memphis Minnie, pop over here for blues chat. Talk of blues around the country, as well as greats like B.B. King and Buddy Guy.
COMPUSERVE *go* musicarts→Libraries or Messages→The Blues

Blues World *Blues World* ezine is dedicated to the blues. The pieces featured are genuinely interesting, right down to a recent feature on the race record advertisements of the 1920s. Photographers' exhibitions and record reviews are standard parts of the online collection; you'll also find helpful links, although one, for some reason, profiles the sad story of a drug-addicted, HIV-positive, teenage prostitute.
WEB http://www.bluesworld.com

BluesNet "Opinionated and proud of it," is how Excite described this useful Web resource for fans of the blues. The people behind those opinions are the real stars of the site, since they've selected one expert for almost every popular blues artist. If you got a question about any of the blues greats, just click on the respective expert's name and send it off. Besides this helpful list, there are also images and a suggested reading list on the blues included.
WEB http://dragon.acadiau.ca/~rob /blues/blues.html

rec.music.bluenote.blues Discuss Tampa Red's hokum blues, the blues-rock flights of the Allman Brothers, the fate of Canadian blues, Fenton Robinson, and the mysterious death of Robert Johnson on this active and well-informed newsgroup.
USENET rec.music.bluenote.blues

Country

Country Chat The big winners on AOL's country music board are the women of modern country—Trisha Yearwood, Reba McIntyre, and Suzy Boggus. Why are they the big winners? Because they have hundreds of messages from adoring fans who pore over the smallest details of their catalog. Who are the losers? In fandom, there are no losers, but there are artists who have less active message boards. Compare notes on the big, the small, the old, the new, and the rest.
AMERICA ONLINE *keyword* mmc→ Country/Folk→Country/Western

❝ Hang out in the malt shop talking about the sock hop and staring at all the bobby soxers. ❞

Country Connection The largest site on the Web for country music is also one of the easiest to use, with a huge artist reference guide, TV and radio listings, and links to country 'zines and record labels. Its site sports a search function that should help you locate the information you need.
WEB http://digiserve.com/country

Country Music Online A Patsy Cline convention may not be big news to everyone, but the event is highly respected here. This site has few graphics but a straightforward layout with loads of information. A large list of country links including magazines, newsgroups, songs, radio stations, concerts, fan clubs, and artist sites (most of which are accompanied by online images).
WEB http://www.tpoint.net/Users /wallen//country/country.html

rec.music.country What's old-time country? Hank Williams, certainly, and Jimmie Rodgers, and Bob Wills, and Roy Acuff. What's not? Anything that has happened in the last ten years, since new superstars like Garth Brooks, Keith Whitley, Clint Black, Lorrie Morgan, Mary-Chapin Carpenter, and Dwight Yoakam have changed the way America thinks about this genre. The newsgroup offers country fans a place to fuss, fight, and then make up. Engaging conversation is the standard.
USENET rec.music.country

Oldies

alt.rock-n-roll.oldies Stay up all night with this musical version of *American Graffiti*. This newsgroup gives oldies fans a place to share info about their favorite classic songs. Artists like the Everly Brothers and Jan and Dean are discussed, as well as lyrics and one-hit wonders.
USENET alt.rock-n-roll.oldies

American Oldies Diner Hang out in the malt shop talking about the sock hop and staring at all the bobby soxers. Drop a nickel in the jukebox and listen for the rave-up sounds of Gene Vincent. Then talk all you want about Elvis, rockabilly, surf, the Beatles, vintage labels, and oldies from the 1950s, 1960s, and 1970s. Whether your tastes run toward the Hollies or Paul Revere and the Raiders, this is the place for you.
COMPUSERVE *go* oldies

Classical

All Music Guide Classical Section This enormous classical music recordings database can help you get your hands on that hard-to-find recording of Chopin's "Aeolian Harp Etude" or give you details on the latest from Kronos Quartet. Search the database by any of the following criteria: performance, performers, composer, instrument, period, and rating. Every release is described by listing its composer, title, genre, period, form, instrument, key, date, number, performance quality, performers, and the record company that released it.
COMPUSERVE *go* amgclassical

Classical is Cool The Web is cool, and so is classical music, or so the keepers of this vault maintain. With a user-friendly style and loads of information, Classical is Cool puts netheads in touch with their orchestral

roots, linking to sites on dozens of composers and musical periods. There's multimedia, information on radio shows, and a place to vent your feelings on the site, classical music on air, and the genre in general.
WEB http://www.classicaliscool.com

Classical Music America Online's home for classical music is its own harmonious masterpiece. With lists of classical Web sites, online classical events, and even a classical music chat room, the area is a must-visit for any aficionado. Message boards provide an additional arena for sharing requests, favorites, and news. (Find out here why Beck's favorite composer is Schubert.)
AMERICA ONLINE *keyword* music→ genres→classical

Classical Net Like a symphony, this is a large site with many important parts, each of which stands on its own, but makes an awe-inspiring noise when considered as a group. A Basic Repertoire List, which is organized by musical period, provides a guide to assembling a well-rounded library of classical recordings. The Buying Guide lists classical-music recording companies and several publications that feature classical reviews. For even more suggestions on what to buy and listen to, the Recommended Classical CDs section lists nearly 2,000 that have been deemed exceptional (That should jumpstart your Christmas list). Background information about composers is in the Composer Data section, and links to classic-related

Web sites and newsgroups round out this extensive site.
WEB http://www.classical.net

The Great Composers All the masters, from Albeniz to Mozart to Wagner, are profiled at this comprehensive site. In fact, this is one of the few places on the Net to get a quick sketch of the lives of major composers such as Schubert, Stravinsky, Handel, and Hayden. Locate your favorite by searching the index alphabetically by name or by period. This site is brought to the Net courtesy of the folks at BMG Classics as part of their beautiful, extensive Web site.
WEB http://www.classicalmus.com /bmgclassics/comp-index/index.html

rec.music.classical Are you a tubist looking for work? Need to sell a cello? Looking for a conductor? Besides basic fiscal queries that will be of interest to any starving musician or composer, this newsgroup serves as the central clearinghouse for classical music chat—from polls inquiring about your favorite sublime musical fragments to debates on using a pedal when playing Scarlatti (purists would say you shouldn't even play it on a piano). Whether you are looking for a favorite "Figaro" recording, used record stores in Boston, or a Stravinsky biography, you will find ample attention here. If you don't want to sort through the general list messages, check out the rest of the groups in the hierarchy,

Cage rubs elbows with Chopin at The Great Composers site
http://www.classicalmus.com/bmgclassics/comp-index/index.html

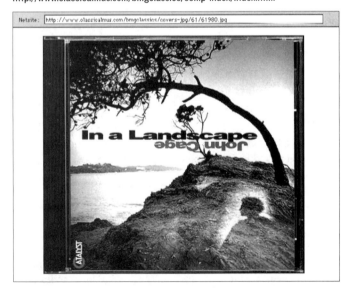

which focus specifically on classical guitar, performance techniques and announcements, and recordings.
USENET rec.music.classical

rec.music.classical.recordings
There must be hundreds of recordings of Beethoven's Ninth available in some shape or form, even 8-track, so if you would like them all, you would do well to consult the record collectors who assemble here. And if you are not lusting for more Ludwig, there's plenty of other composers treated by the group regulars, who offer recommendations, reviews, and feedback on classical recordings past and present.
USENET rec.music.classical.recordings

New Age

Music for a New Age "Alas, it's unfortunate that some marketing types coined the term 'New Age' to describe a form of music that, by its very nature, defies definition. After all, when you combine the modern-day sounds of electronic synthesizers with the droning of the ancient aboriginal didgeridoo, what are you going to call it? Hence the term 'New Age.' The long-term affect of this appellation has been derision and confusion; many people believe that New Age music is meant only to be listened to during meditation, mud baths, or mystic activities. And while any of these activities may be appropriate for this type of music, it is my belief

Location: http://www.windham.com/

Don't forget the Chardonnay
http://www.windham.com

that music should be enjoyed for its value to the listener, whatever that may be." The author of these words, Fred Puhan, also created this encompassing collection of New Age links. Organized into several sections—record companies, artists, radio stations, and miscellaneous resources—the links here will take you into the new age and beyond.
WEB http://www.his.com/~fjp/music .html

rec.music.newage Why bother sending away for the Hearts of Space playlist when you can download it here? These days, "New Age" refers to any type of music with spacey bleeping sounds and a generic synth sound in the background. Ambient music. Meditative music. Sculptural music. Records are reviewed and sold via this newsgroup, from Mike Oldfield's pre-New Age *Exor-*

cist soundtrack to Mychael Danna's recent music for Exotica. Whether you're looking for the Kitaro Web site or upcoming gigs in your area, you'll find New Age information and camaraderie aplenty here.
USENET rec.music.newage

Windham Hill Records Known as the granddaddy of New Age record companies, this label offers the recordings of William Ackerman, Gaia, Ray Lynch, and Torcuato Mariano, among others. Each of Windham's artists is profiled here with a short bio, a discography, tour information, and sound clips. Of course, all of the recordings listed can be ordered online.
WEB http://www.windham.com

Opera

Cyberspace Opera An opera is being composed online, and you can contribute by sending

in rhymed couplets based on concepts or quotes from the storyline. The couplets will then be set to music and incorporated into a real opera to be performed in Austin, Texas. The opera's working title is "Honoria in Ciberspazio," and its main characters include Rez, a passionate young writer and philosopher of virtual communities, and Sandy Stone, a cyberspace goddess who "flips her long black hair before saying something wonderfully brilliant." It's opera for the computer age.
WEB http://www.en.utexas.edu/~slatin /opera

Field Notes of a Rookie Opera Lover If you think opera music is something you only listen to when you are at the dentist's office, these "field notes" might make you take a more serious look at the genre. A mysterious opera fan identified only as Weaver has collected loving observations of the many performances he attended over a seven-year period.
WEB http://www.alaska.net/~hweaver /opera-index.html

Opera Want to discuss the Japanese production of "La Boheme" or argue if there are world-class American opera singers performing today? Would you like to cast your vote for Cheesiest Baritone on the worldwide opera stage? The message board at this site is the place to post your opinion on these and all other opera topics. The boards aren't just

for fans, either; it's common for singers to meet here to discuss their profession and current productions. In the library, you can read discussions among directors, stage hands, singers, and opera lovers about numerous subjects, including the popular topic of stage direction in different houses worldwide.
COMPUSERVE *go* musicarts→Libraries or Bulletin Board→Libraries→Opera

Opera Schedule Search this worldwide opera schedule by artist, location, or time to find out when and where the next performance of your favorite opera is taking place.
WEB http://www.fsz.bme.hu/opera /main.html

rec.music.opera Put a bunch of opera buffs in the same room and there is bound to be trouble. "Has anyone read a review of Renata Scotto's recent Der Rosenkavalier performance?" "'Execrable' was one comment I read, but I can't remember where." If you're having trouble choosing between a Bartoli or Larmore "Barber of Seville" recording, don't expect any straight answers. You'll most likely be buried in piles of recommendations, along with a combination of some on-the-nose and some long-winded reviews. And when the fans leave, the performers remain behind, exchanging performance tips, tipping each other off to potential gigs, and recommending instructors.
USENET rec.music.opera

Dance

Fly! zine If you fancy being eckied out of your box—that is, if you like tripping on Ecstasy— you'll love Mystic Mick's Love Signs, a sexually overtoned horoscope for the clubbing scene. A forecast for Libras in September: "If you accept an invitation at the start of the month, don't be too surprised if an unusual sexual encounter is the end result." In addition to their dance, jungle, house, garage, techno and ambient album reviews, the staff of *Fly!* also include features and interviews with artists such as Afrika Bambaataa and the Dust Brothers. Don't miss their invaluable radio, club, gig, and specialty record store guides.
WEB http://www.fly.co.uk

Inter DanceWeb ;-) mEg@ZINE! This "is for everybody who is interested in every kind of danceable music, eurodance, techno, rave, house, hip hop, trip hop, swing beat, trance, ambient (the after party music)...etc." Or so they claim. It's hard to believe that the IDW team of "weirdos" would be able to satisfy fans of so many genres with their small site. They have two charts— Club Trip 20 and The Heavenly Eleven—where artists like Orbital and Meat Beat Manifesto get top billing. IDW's page of links features dozens of clubs, labels, and artists, but needs some TLC before it's truly an extensive resource.
WEB http://www.idw.be

PART 2
Sci-Fi & Fringe

Sci-Fi & Fringe

CLICK PICKS
The very best on the Net

Sci-Fi

RESISTANCE IS USELESS, SCIENCE FICTION IS THE FUTURE—IF THAT'S NOT ALREADY OBVIOUS

THE INTERNET ITSELF is straight out of science fiction—a kind of diaphanous Big Brain transmitting our ideas, thoughts, and passions through an oxygen-less ether. So it should be no surprise to sci-fi fans that social Terrans have taken to the Web as dystopians predicted they would. The Net is a home to the friendliest and most diverse crowd of sci-fi fans to be found anywhere—whether you're looking for a full-fledged science fiction celebration, a chatty news magazine, or the most obscure detail from a TV show that only lasted five episodes in 1967, it's out there somewhere in the parallel universe known as cyberspace, the final frontier—for now.

Location: http://www.filmzone.com/~vkoser/vader/starwars/pics/people/HAN-AND-.jpg

FANDOM DOMAIN
WEB http://www.sff.net/sff/sflinks
picture: WEB http://www.filmzone.com/~vkoser/vader
The site that makes all others obsolete. Whatever your fantasy, however fictive your science, the Fandom Domain contains links for you and your ilk. Read up on the genre you love best, through links to more than 35 fanzines online. Love Pern? Goth? *Trek*? Furries? The good *Doctor Who*? Links to fan pages for these subgenres and many of their cousins are all here, plus, games, art, anime, reviews, and lots more. Do not miss this site—it's almost like seeing *Star Wars* for the first time. OK, it's not quite that good, but almost.

Starting points

Beyond the Farthest Star A highly detailed list of links with minimal graphics and a ton of information, organized into sensible categories that make finding info quick and easy. Topics include Organizations, TV Shows and Listings, Animation, Games, Stores, FAQs, and Zines.
WEB http://www.cs.swarthmore.edu /~binde/sf/index.html

Giant Science Fiction Gophers Ceaseless in their pursuit of links, these sci-fi gophers have created connections to archives of sci-fi 'zines, the full-text of sci-fi novels, FAQs for every sci-fi discussion group on the Net, newsletters from publishing houses, convention schedules, fan club information, author biographies, image and sound clip collections, and lists galore.
URL gopher://marvel.loc.gov:70/II /employee/clubs/scific • gopher: //wiretap.spies.com/II/Library/Media /Sci-Fi

The Linköping Science Fiction and Fantasy Archive For any fan looking to vent, or to find out what to read, see, or think next in the realm of sci-fi, this archive is the place to visit. Linköping collects texts, especially reviews, related to authors, books, and movies. Full versions of online sci-fi newsletters and magazines such as *Ansible* are gathered here, too, along with publicly available fiction, art, and

SF and fantasy, live from Linköping!
http://sf.www.lysator.liu.se/sf_archive

guides to the craft and the genre.
WEB http://sf.www.lysator.liu.se/sf _archive

Nathan's Fandom Page It isn't nearly as comprehensive as Fandom Domain, but it is attractive and easy to use, with topics like Fantasy (four links) and Fandom (seven links). The links are quality, and Nathan's use of frames is intelligent. Sci-fi fans particularly interested in filk, megafandom (Goth), or The Artemis Society will want to visit Nathan's other Web sites devoted to these topics.
WEB http://members.tripod.com /~Aelffin/sfandom.html

Rutgers Archive Having trouble remembering that *Star Trek* episode in which people were turned into green styrofoam dice and crushed by a childish god? How about the first scene of *The Flash*? You'll find the

answers here, in Rutgers' huge collection of science-fiction TV show episode guides, with entries on shows ranging from the immensely popular to the barely remembered. Annotated links to hundreds of sci-fi Internet sites are organized into archives, authors, awards, bibliographies, bookstores, fandom, fiction, movies, publishers, reviews and criticism, role-playing games, television, Usenet newsgroups, and fanzines. The Rutgers archive also contains other documents of interest to science-fiction fans, including a UFO guide, a list of Nebula award winners, and a large archive of *SF Lovers* digest.
URL ftp://sflovers.rutgers.edu/pub /sf-lovers/Web/sf-resource.guide .html

Science Fiction Earth Links at One World Network Are you fannish but frenzied? Then you'll

appreciate this index to the sci-fi Web. Each link is listed next to the most complete annotations available (outside of this book, of course!), so there's no time wasted. Categories cover the whole SF spectrum, including more rarely seen topics like sci-fi artists or bookstores. The site also provides plenty of news on its frequent updates and evolution.
WEB http://www.oneworld.net/SF

Science Fiction Forum A heavy concentration of literature, which means there's traffic for readers of any popular author from Stephen Donaldson to William Gibson to Robert Heinlein. It also means that many of the postings are fans' notes—gushing appraisals of classic works ("Bradbury's

Martian Chronicles is the most completely imagined science fiction novel ever"), arguments over originality (should we credit the invention of robots to Karl Capek or Isaac Asimov?), and even clarifications of picayune points in massive epics (how exactly does mind-reading work in Frank Herbert's *Dune*?). Looking to read even more sci-fi adventures? The Interactive Fiction Library (a subset of the Science Fiction Libraries) has stories, poems, and songs written by other AOL members. Plenty of people love related media, of course, and there are some fascinating discussions on film and TV. Don't expect much esoterica here: Spielberg and Lucas rule the libraries. *Star Wars* fans have packed a sepa-

rate library with images, timelines, FAQs, and newsletters.
AMERICA ONLINE *keyword* scifi→ Science Fiction

The Science Fiction Gallery
Thoughtful, interactive, and conducted like a write-in symposium on classic and recent SF, the Science Fiction Gallery is more interested in words and ideas than flash and technogeekery. Its Science Fiction in Literature section offers the more print-minded denizens of SF land the cyberequivalent of a wing chair, slippers, and a place to call home.
WEB http://www4.onestep.com/scifi

Science Fiction Weekly An online venture that may appeal to beginning fans more than those who have found a niche. This

THE SCI-FI SITE

WEB http://www.abacus.ghj.com/sci_fi/default.htm
picture: WEB http://www.3gcs.com/tron
Offering a choice of enhanced graphics or text only, and delivering plenty of great features in either format, The Sci-Fi Site is like visiting an SF convention and wandering from exhibit to exhibit. Over here, some fans to talk to, over there, an episode guide, and way over there are a few more

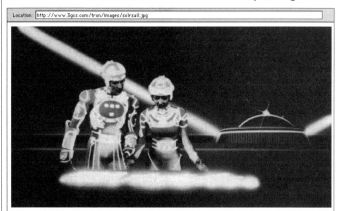

people trading the latest science-fiction (mostly non-*Trek*) rumors. The webmasters' interest in feedback and interactivity gives the site a personalized yet random feel of those conversations you stumble onto in convention center elevators.

Everything but the spiders from Mars
http://smash.cs.com

slick and pretty production reviews the recent sci-fi nascences and newsmakers. The best section by far is News of the Week, with its well-written and suitably brief updates to sci-fi events, including awards and hot shows. The reviews, on the other hand, are more plot summary than critique, and some show little knowledge of sci-fi. However, for sheer elegance, this magazine deserves a place in the forefront of similar media, and many online fannish types point to it as an authority.
WEB http://www.scifi.com/sfw

SF-Lovers No, the name of this digest does not refer (specifically anyway) to the incestuous world of cyberpunk authors, Captain Kirk's seduction of green, half-dressed princesses,

nor the late-night action at a science fiction convention. All science fiction and fantasy themes are game, and much of the digest material comes from the rec.sf.* newsgroup hierarchy. Saul Jaffe, the moderator, speaks of the digest as a magazine, and brings a strong sense of decorum to his editorial choices. The flame-free result is really the only human way of keeping up with the hyperactive newsgroups for literature, TV, and movies. The digest is still huge, though—monthly compilations available from the immense FTP archive average about 1.25 meg.
EMAIL sf-lovers-request@rutgers.edu
✍ *Write a request*

SF-News: Mr. Data's Data An electronic news column covering the sci-fi media—from *Dr.*

Who to *Star Trek*—on a monthly basis. Culls gossip, rumor, and hard news about shows from all the sci-fi newsgroups and mailing lists, offline fan clubs and newsletters, and the press. Where are the plot twists of your favorite show heading? What shows are being threatened with cancellation and which are being revived?
EMAIL majordomo@stargame.org ✍
Type in message body: subscribe sfnews

SMASH! The Cyber-Zine! Collectors, comic-book readers, and TV junkies (especially the X-Philes) will delight in the freshness of this comprehensive, no-frills newsmag. The home page greets visitors with the question "What's New?" in any one of six categories, including anime, cards, and science fiction. The features are especially geared to collectors and comics fans, but one much-needed section, The Dead Zone, lists all series (comics, cards, and shows) that have been recently canceled or are doomed. How sad that the world of science fiction (like Rodney Dangerfield) gets no respect. Computer and other-electronic games are included.
WEB http://smash.cs.com

Chat

....

alt.fandom.cons Those with any doubts about the unlimited depths to which fandom can go will find them erased after a perusal of just a few of the posts in this celebration of cons, the ultimate fan gatherings. Those who know nothing about cons will find little here, other than a certain knowledge that cons attract an inside crowd. Those who have attended one, two, or umpteen cons, and don't already know about this busy newsgroup will find the ultimate handbook and insider's guide.
USENET alt.fandom.cons

Cybertown You'll be glad to learn that Cybertown is popu-lated mostly by people from Earth, probably because it's not far from this galaxy. It's a fully realized virtual community of folks looking to pretend that the Internet has literally taken over the Earth sometime in the late twenty-first century. Get a VR apartment, join in the entertainment, and generally lose yourself in a fun, role-playing Web tour, which is really what this is.
WEB http://www.cybertown.com

rec.arts.sf.fandom This newsgroup seems to exist to prove two points: (a) Fandom is a complex operation with its own history and culture, and (b) sci-fi fans like to talk about plenty besides sci-fi. The threads that don't discuss nam-

 PLANET X
WEB http://www.planetx.com/PlanetX
Transhumanism and political humor are just two of the topics that the "science fiction-obsessed" residents of Planet X love to discuss. These are netizens who—gasp—know each other well and get together in real life for yearly reunions. New members join all the time. Head to Immigration and Naturalization Services to join the mailing list and find out the dirt. "Don't be offended" and "R.A. Heinlein and Larry Niven are Gods" is a preview of the advice you'll get. Good luck: It's a hairy planet.

Location: http://www.planetx.com/album/gang2.small.jpg

LIFE ON MARS? PONDER THIS

Let's say there is life in a solar system for every pick-six matchup out of your machine. If you run that machine as many times as there are solar systems in the universe, I think you'll discover plenty of life, if you could actually detect it.

Pick bigger odds, say a trillion to one. There are so many solar systems in the universe you still end up with life all over the place.

Now, pick odds so that you have the number of solar systems in the universe to one (us). Now you'd have to justify yourself for picking those odds, and you'd probably turn to religion for help.

—from rec.arts.sf.science

ing your cat or embarrassing typos are about fandom itself, and often involve passing on lore about con etiquette and the pre-Net days. Discussions are extremely long-winded; nearly every thread has more than a dozen posts in it, and many have more than 100. It's a polite, thorough, and (almost) always interesting bunch, even when they're not discussing science fiction in the least.
USENET rec.arts.sf.fandom

rec.arts.sf.marketplace What's the story with the X-rated C-3PO card? "I believe that's due to a printing error," wrote one collector, "C-3PO looks like he has a... um, male member." Another disagreed: "Printing error, nothing. Somebody *airbrushed* a little manhood onto that droid." Whatever the case, the card goes for $50. Any takers? Looking for *Star Wars* figures in mint condition? How

about a complete set of *Star Trek* cards? If you're in the market for such wares, you've come to the right place, as long as you've got a credit card, cash, or something to trade. This is the place to visit if you want to buy, trade, or just chat about sci-fi stuff—everything from Harlan Ellison books to videos of Gene Roddenberry.
USENET rec.arts.sf.marketplace

rec.arts.sf.misc Anybody remember the TV series *Quark*? Who is the typical SF reader? Where can I get a story that I vaguely recall from 20 years ago? This newsgroup is like a deluxe pizza—it's never the same twice, but it always tastes delicious. Do not venture here if you're looking for something specific. It's not the busiest newsgroup in the world, so if you only like *The X-Files* or are deep into Robert Jordan and nobody else, there are no guarantees that anyone

is already discussing something of interest to you. But in the uncrowded environment of this ever-changing group of general sci-fi fans are plenty of do-it-yourself experts eager to solve any sci-fi mystery. So do visit if you have an unanswerable question to post, or seek a source of unending trivia, news, and miscellaneous knowledge from those who really know their stuff. If you get tired of the trivial, rec.arts.sf.misc is also home to posters like this guy, who thinks too much for his own good: "I was just wondering what the effect on the Earth would be if the Moon suddenly winked out of existence?"
USENET rec.arts.sf.misc

❝ What's the story with the X-rated C-3PO card? The card goes for $50. Any takers? ❞

rec.arts.sf.science Private space exploration, cold fusion, personality cloning, and other candidates for the year 2000 edition of the Sharper Image catalog. Speculative science at its best—nowhere else outside of the physics lab do people argue as intelligently about "ways around the Heisenberg

Uncertainty Principle" and other basic assumptions of modern science. The most skillful posters make the scientific seem absurd and the fictitious sound plausible.
USENET rec.arts.sf.science

Science Fiction Fandom AOL's Science Fiction Fandom board covers a broad spectrum of sci-fi topics, from general categories (the best and worst sci-fi movies of all time) to more specific concerns (How are women depicted in sci-fi? Where can you see footage of a naked David Duchovny?). If it doesn't always go where no man has gone before, it does provide a friendly environment for discussion and gentle disagreement.
AMERICA ONLINE *keyword* scifi→ Science Fiction→Science Fiction Fandom Board

Spaced Sci-Fi Discussion List This list is home to a busy and intense bunch of subscribers who love to criticize everything that is sci-fi pop culture. Their focus is primarily on TV and movies, both the latest (*Independence Day*) and the greatest (the original *Star Trek*). The discussion is generally playfully rude, but those who tread into the obnoxious zone will be flamed unmercifully. Newbies are warmly welcomed, although most commonly the posts are by the same few list junkies.
EMAIL majordomo@branson.org ✎ *Type in message body:* **subscribe spaced**

Sci-Fi Movies

ALIENS, DUNE, STAR WARS... AN ALPHABET OF ALIEN LIFE

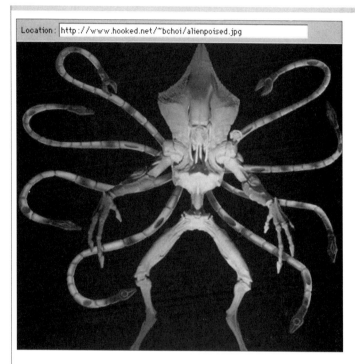

Location: http://www.hooked.net/~bchoi/alienpoised.jpg

 ## WWW SCI-FI FILM PAGE
WEB http://weber.u.washington.edu/~ataraxus /sfmenu.html
picture: WEB http://www.hooked.net/~bchoi/alienpoised.jpg
"There is nothing wrong with your computer terminal... Do not attempt to adjust the picture... We are controlling transmission... Psychotronic Cinema." Through automatically loading pages, the designers blitzkrieg these words on your screen to make you feel even more powerless over your already stubborn desktop computer. What do you get for this momentary lapse of control? You get more than 150 alphabetically and chronologically arranged reviews of well-known and obscure sci-fi films.

Starting points

rec.arts.sf.movies In this forum, participants scheme to pitch ideas to Steven Spielberg, rewrite scripts for their own satisfaction, and debate the merits of any given sci-fi flavor of the month. Although discussions are dominated by issues concerning contemporary releases, you will find topics devoted to classics like "Godzilla v. Destroyer: Why!?!." Note the oft-ignored newsgroup FAQ request that *Trek* newsgroup post to the appropriate newsgroup, rather than here. To some participants' ire, William Shatner's acting, ego, and hair occasionally turn up as subjects.
USENET rec.arts.sf.movies

Aliens

Al's Alien Homepage Who would've ever thought to be considerate where *Aliens* are concerned? Unlike most others, this thoughtful Web site gave *Alien* and *Alien3* equal time with Cameron's standout, *Aliens*. You can get collages of screen shots from all three movies, plus intermittent quotes. The casting page, while not a unique idea in itself, give all the usual info and kindly includes the mugs of all the characters to jog our failing memories. There are also QuickTime movies of missing footage found on the laserdisc versions.
WEB http://ng.netgate.net/~alvaro /alien/alien.htm

Aliens: The Web Site The meatiest part of this Web site is the catalog of the aliens encountered so far, as well a description of their reproductive cycles. Other parts of Aliens: The Web Site feel more like Aliens: The Vacant Room, largely because the trilogy (and not Dark Horse Comics' expanded universe, for example) serves as its only information source. The section devoted to "Company" technology, for instance, is restricted to androids, cryotubes, and atmospheric plants. Nonetheless, where there is no substance, there is at least style—the well written text suitably draws you into the *Alien* universe and the design looks clean and professional. Perhaps when the potentially exciting page of 3-D VRML-rendered models fleshes out, the site may as well.
WEB http://www.viscon.com/aliens /welcome.html

Blade Runner

Blade Runner Although the site isn't much to look at—opening with a weak facsimile of the movie's logo—the material is of primo quality. Check out the Memorable Quotes section, which offers dialog or voice-overs as text, but links to images and sound files. "The light that burns twice as bright burns half as long... and you have burned so very, very brightly, Roy." Indeed.
WEB http://www.uq.oz.au/~csmchapm /bladerunner

Blade Runner Trivia A fanatic's dream! Religious and philosophical parallels, as well as the symbolism of the eye are discussed here. Most exciting, however, is the "Did You Notice?" section, which includes everything from Pris' incept date (Valentine's Day) to the sheet music on Deckard's piano (Vivaldi's "Concerto in D major for Guitar, Strings and Continuo").
WEB http://dingo.cc.uq.oz.au /~csmchapm/bladerunner/trivia.html

Dr. Strangelove

Dr. Strangelove "I can no longer sit back and allow Communist infiltration and indoctrination, Communist subversion, and the international Communist conspiricy to sap and impurify all of our precious bodily fluids..." General Jack D. Ripper loses his mind, succumbing to his theories of Communist conspiracy, and the world's fate lies in his hands. For years, fans have celebrated this film, another one of Stanley Kubrick's influential science-fiction masterpieces. This black-and-white page, created by a fan, features audio clips and image files from the 1964 movie also known as *How I Learned to Stop Worrying and Love the Bomb*.
WEB http://www.lehigh.edu/~pjl2/films /strangelove.html

Voyager's Dr. Strangelove Released just two years after the Cuban Missile Crisis, Kubrick's film was almost a refreshing way to look at the impending destruction of the planet as instigated by human irrationality. Movie clips, images, and a great essay about the film are provided for fans and those unfamiliar with the classic, no matter how distant the situation may currently seem.

WEB http://www.voyagerco.com/CC /ph/p.strangelove.html

Dune

alt.fan.dune "I was just thinking about this the other day, how Luke's [Skywalker] home planet, and Arrakis are very much the same. Both have fringe cultures, large, dangerous animals, no surface water,

and are deserts. I'm not sure what I'm trying to say, maybe George Lucas based his planet on *Dune*?" wrote a fan in a recent post to this active and interesting newsgroup. Discussion erupts about topics such as Arabic and Islamic themes in the movie, the director's cut, favorite characters, and even homophobia in relation to the film.

USENET alt.fan.dune

FAQ: **URL** ftp://nctuccca.edu.tw /USENET/FAQ/alt/fan/dune

Dune Page Get ready for the ultimate *Dune* site. Behindthe-scenes details, cast information, and even the entire script. Find cut scenes, mistakes, laser disc and sound-

track information, as well as links to other *Dune* sites on the Web.

WEB http://phymat.bham.ac.uk /BennetMN/dune/dune.html

Star Wars

David's Star Wars Hub If there's a bright center to the online *Star Wars* galaxy, this is it. Follow the terrific graphics to a gold mine of Internet resources, linking you to image servers, sound files, fiction, comic books, computer game; the list goes on, but we won't. Suffice it to say that it's a Bantha-sized heap o' stuff. Unique to David's Hub is his Forceful presentation of some awesome starship blueprints and his

ALIEN SAGA

WEB http://found.cs.nyu.edu/michael/alien

While most pages will give you the requisite biographical information on the main characters of the *Alien* trilogy, or show the creepy reproduction cycle of the buggers, this page incorporates key features rarely found at one site alone. For one thing, scenes cut from the theatrical releases are

summarized to help fill in some plot gaps. In addition, the Dark Horse Comics' *Alien* universe is detailed, revealing an expanded, more absorbing addition to the *Alien* mythos than even David Fincher's *Alien^3* could offer.

Location: http://www.abacus.ghj.com/sci_fi/apes/apes.htm

Ape icons in '70s chic
http://www.abacus.ghj.com/scifi/apes/apes.htm

server for collectible *Star Wars* cards. And if you've been hunting all over for a TIE Interceptor Pilot action figure, the free listings on the Jawa Trading Post might help you find what you're looking for.
WEB http://161.32.228.104/david.htm

Hose Beasts' Star Wars Page
Billing itself as a catalog-in-process, this *Star Wars* index already seems as large as the Death Star (the second, unfinished one). Hose Beast has worked harder than a Jawa in a junkyard to amass an array of literature—from early screenplay drafts to humor articles like, "Everything I Know I Learned from *Star Wars*." There are also links to the role-playing game, theoretical technical information, and plenty of online fiction. The volume of *Star Wars* versus *Star Trek* stories is truly astronomical, and

it's no surprise that the Empire usually creams the Federation.
WEB http://www.break.com.au /~hbeast/3-1-txts.html

rec.arts.sf.starwars Much talk about *Star Wars* toys and the next trilogy. Would you buy a Darth Vader carrying case for $200? No? Well, someone will. One thread was titled, "Why hasn't Luke gotten laid yet?" "I think it's about time," Anton wrote. "Heck, I bet even the Wookie sneaks out for a little nookie. Luke gets the award for being the most sexually represed hero ever." But, soap-opera-like worries aside, this is a sci-fi savvy group of regulars with lots of Star Wares. When the conversation veers from Obi-Wan and Luke, it often turns to *Star Trek*, with Corey contending a battle between the *Enterprise* and the *Star Destroyer* would be "very

close," while Joshua trashes transporters as "the most contrived and moronic devices, ever." Hey, try and say that in rec.arts.startrek.fandom, bud!
USENET rec.arts.sf.starwars
FAQ: **WEB** http://bantha.pc.cc.cmu .edu:1138/INFO/faqrass.html

Star Wars Standing head and shoulders above all other sci-fi action movies, George Lucas's 1977 film and its two sequels forever changed the habits and expectations of movie audiences worldwide. In the AOL *Star Wars* discussion, fans fret over rumors of new *Wars* films ("The only thing definite about this movie is that nothing is definite"), point out inside jokes in other Lucas efforts (in *Indiana Jones and the Temple of Doom*, there's a nightclub named for Obi-Wan Kenobi), and bemoan the diminished employment prospects of *Star Wars* star Mark Hamil ("Time has not been kind to Hamil... and neither was *Corvette Summer*"). Except for the occasional dig, this message board is one big love-in that embraces Luke Skywalker, Darth Vader, Princess Leia, Han Solo, et al.
AMERICA ONLINE *keyword* scifi→ Science Fiction →Star Wars Fan Forum→Message Boards

Star Wars Multimedia Archive
Before jetting here at sub-light speed, make sure your computer can handle RealAudio and QuickTime—otherwise this archive will only remind you of all the swell *Star Wars*

stuff you're missing. Covering the multimedia gamut from movie trailers to film stills to the NPR radio dramas, this is a *Star Wars* smorgasbord for your eyes and ears. But even if you can't listen in or watch things in motion, the General Information text links will feed your curiosity—particularly the hefty Bloopers Guide that tracks every minute gaffe in the *Star Wars* saga.
WEB http://bantha.pc.cc.cmu.edu :1138/SW_HOME.html _pictures/12/index.html

Planet of the Apes

The Forbidden Zone This site is a useful resource for *Planet of the Apes* fans. There are articles

and excerpts and trivia, as well as an episode guide to the *Return to the Planet of the Apes* animated television series. Images, sound bites, and movie clips can be found within the great music hall.
WEB http://members.aol.com /rogerapple/forbiddenzone.html

The Sci-Fi Site: Planet of the Apes Main Page Burke, Urko, Galen, and Virdon: only a few of the many characters of the film and television series. This dedicated home page features everything from an episode guide to a collection of articles related to *Planet of the Apes* and its cast. Be sure to catch the sometimes confusing but highly enlightening document,

the Chronological History of *Planet of the Apes*.
WEB http://www.abacus.ghj.com/sci_fi /apes/apes.htm

2001

2001: A Space Odyssey—30 Years On The somewhat anonymous author (we know only that he's male and Australian) has created a thorough site of information and discussion about *2001*. Using an interface that's heavy with graphics but light on load-in time, the site points you to everything from transcripts of HAL's conversations to "fan" mail for the site itself. Section such as Connection, Vision, Discourse, and Interchange guide fans to interest-

OFFICIAL BLADE RUNNER ONLINE MAGAZINE

WEB http://www.devo.com/bladerunner

From its electric sheep counter on, the *Official Blade Runner Online Magazine* is as thorough and exciting as any Web page could be. A visit makes the complex world of Los Angeles in the year 2019 much more comprehensible. Not only is it clearly designed in terms of both appearance and

navigation, it's an extensive site with lots of information. You'll find such great material as Philip K. Dick's last interview, in which he explains what he saw as the meaning of his story. "In his job of hunting and killing these replicants, Deckard becomes progressively dehumanized," Dick said. "At the same time, the replicants are being perceived as becoming more human."

DUM, DUM, DUM... DA-DUM!

Arthur C. Clarke's novel, *2001: A Space Odyssey*, is the most obvious book to turn to for anyone looking for the answers to the movie—but the novel is not the final authority on the film. Clarke's novel is based upon an earlier version of the movie screenplay; he and Kubrick co-wrote the story while the movie was in production, and Kubrick made many changes to the film after the novel was finished and before the movie was released. Therefore, there are passages within the novel that do not take place in the movie at all, and likewise there are elements of the film that are not found in the book. For instance, in the novel the spaceship *Discovery* travels to the planet Saturn and its moon Japetus, while in the movie the destination is Jupiter. Hal (the computer) opens the airlock doors and lets all of the air out of the spaceship *Discovery* while Dave Bowman is still aboard in the novel; in the movie he lures Dave into outer space and refuses to let him back into the ship. The idea of letting the air out of *Discovery* had been included in the screenplay to the movie (which is why we see Dave wearing a spacesuit and helmet during his attack on Hal's memory banks), but it was later cut.

Clarke himself was confused by many elements of the movie. He tried to offer concrete, rational explanations of some of the questions raised by the film in his book, and in doing so he took many creative liberties. However, the answers offered in the novel are often contradictory and even inaccurate. They do offer clues and, in some cases, explanations to the symbolisms and behind-the-scenes action that takes place in the movie, but because of the differences between the novel and the film, the novel cannot be considered the last word on *2001*. To discover the subtleties and concepts of the movie, the best course of action is to watch the film carefully and make your own conclusions.

—from And Beyond the Infinite

The 2001 Internet Resource Archive The obligatory collection of photos, sounds, links, and movie clips for the *Space Odyssey* fan is only one of the things you'll find at this constantly updated site. Interesting stuff, but the coolest thing, by far, is an early version of the film's entire script, with some additional scenes and voiceovers. Find it under Other Resources.
WEB http://www.design.idg.no/2001/index.html

Others

Back to the Future ... the Web Page The only site you'll really ever need for *BTTF* information. There are throrough biographies on all of the cast members, information on joining the worldwide fan club, and even a time travel chronology of all three films. *This Week in Hill Valley*, the fan club's newsletter, includes cast members' upcoming online events. This site is well-designed, well-written, and well worth any fan's surfing time. Its background image is the famous California "OUTA-TIME" license plate, and Deloreans zip around and disappear. There are also links to other *BTTF* sites, but you probably won't need to visit them. Brilliant work.
WEB http://www.hsv.tis.net/~bttf/main.htm

Hypermedia Brazil What does the singing telegram girl sing? What do all the signs say?

ing discussion pieces; themes and issues such as suspicion and lasting images are deftly handled. Die-hard fans will enjoy the site creator's 20,000-plus word opus on the films, their history, and their impact. "Every frame is full of imagery, every element is exquisitely positioned and lit, every visual proportion is exact. There is no denying that Kubrick got a few things wrong, but I imagine even Michelangelo got a few brush strokes out of place," he writes. This home page is frequently updated and is the ultimate *2001* resource on the Net.
WEB http://www.peg.apc.org/~pjv

This FAQ should help answer the most elusive questions, as well as the more obvious ones, such as "I didn't understand the film at all. What's it all about?" That's a tough one, but the answer is thorough and includes informative quotes from director Terry Gilliam.
WEB http://www.minet.uni-jena.de /~erik/brazil

Voyager: Close Encounters of the Third Kind In 1977, Teri Garr and Richard Dreyfuss acted as our ambassadors to the alien visitors. The impact this film has had on us is most definitely immeasurable. The Criterion Collection's advertisement for the movie features a few clips, along with an essay about the history and making of Steven Spielberg's sci-fi blockbuster. It's definitely an amazing story.
WEB http://www.voyagerco.com/CC /ph/p.closeencounters.html

The Day the Earth Stood Still Homepage This is one of the only Web sites for this influential 1950s sci-fi flick starring Michael Rennie as the alien, Klaatu, whose request for a government audience is denied. Not surprisingly, he gets pretty upset, although he doesn't allow that to affect his impeccable manners. Strangely, the site has nothing more than an overview of why the site was created, and an incomplete cast list. Perhaps fans of the movie will put their knowledge of page design together and create a site that's out of this world. "Klaatu Barada Nikto."
WEB http://admin.inetport.com /~rgylford/klaatu.html

Escape Fans everywhere still enjoy their memories of that classic futuristic thriller, *Escape from St. Louis*, right? Wrong. In fact, the entire 1981 movie *Escape from New York* was filmed in the great state of Missouri. Weird. More factoids, pictures, and ecstatic plot summary here. Follow links to The Snake Plissken Page.
WEB http://vlsi2.elsy.cf.ac.uk/bright /escape.html

THE BANZAI INSTITUTE
WEB http://bbs.annex.com/relayer/bbanzai.htm

Blue Blaze Irregulars: Whenever you need inspiration to carry on with your mission, take a tour around the Institute and surrounding areas. Yoyodyne offers extensive information, including images and sound files, on the Lectroid/Adder War and the two sanctions behind it. The Conference room offers info on other BB sites on the Net, as well as one part of the press packet sent out by 20th Century Fox announcing the Banzai Institute's cooperation with the studio in dramatizing one of Buckaroo's adventures. This document gives the background info on Buckaroo

and Professer Hikita. In the Lab, you'll find Dr. Caryl Sneider's paper on the movie's particle physics theories, the formula for the antidote to the Lectroid Electronic Brainwashing, quizzes, puzzles, and the offical answer to the Watermelon Question. Remember: Wherever you go... there you are.

The Unofficial Flash Gordon Movie Page News Flash: This site will answer your most pressing questions about everybody's favorite 1980 movie. Who played the Arborian initiate? What are the words to the song "Flash," by Queen? How can you get your mitts on a picture of Max von Sydow in full imperial regalia? Where are other fan pages on the Web? It's all here on the unofficial site. By the way, there is no official *Flash Gordon* site.
WEB http://www.geocities.com /Hollywood/4262/index.html

Forbidden Planet The home page for the film that science forgot is packed with pictures of Robby the Robot and pals, a guide to the Krells, movie credits, an analytic essay, JPEGs of the beautiful, original posters, and, of course, sounds. This site should be the first step in a *Forbidden Planet* Web tour.
WEB http://www.tizeta.it/home/duo /fbhome.htm

The Ghost in the Shell A truly amazing interactive multimedia kit, despite annoying and repetitive music and overly enthusiastic prose. No, really, it's fun! There is a game, movie credits, character information and more, all in a fascinating interface. But return to this Web site for the rest of the goodies, including video, pictures, sounds, notes, and the complete movie trailer.
WEB http://www.hollywood.com /movies/ghost/bsghost.html

Location: http://www.hollywood.com/movies/ghost/photo/motoko2.html

©1995 Shirow Masamune/ Kodansha Bandai Visual/ Manga Entertainment.

I am not an Anime!
http://www.hollywood.com/movies/ghost/bsghost.html

Official Hackers Site Do all computer geeks have such expertly uncoiffed hair? Pull a "hairy hack" with the *Hackers* game, and suck up more non-lingo in the other areas of this dark and gloomy site. Visit the part of the site which may or may not have been hacked and destroyed by "real" hackers, possibly employees in MGM/UA's marketing department. Then check out information about the movie, its characters, and all its fast-paced cyberpunkness.
WEB http://www.mgmua.com/hackers

Independence Day (Official Site) Those who were first in line to get tickets for 1996's most hotly anticipated blockbuster will find plenty to see and do at this official site. Not only does it provide the typical sound-and-video promotion (including two surprisingly challenging text-based adventure games), it also provides enough background on alien lore and the real Area 51 to satisfy anybody's desire for a close encounter. Unlike most movies' official sites, this one may actually warrant a second visit.
WEB http://www.id4.com

Voyager: Invasion of the Body Snatchers When a typical '50s drive-in date movie turns into a cult feature to outlast any other, even "serious" sci-fi fans pay attention. Such is the case with *Body Snatchers*, offered here in a new laserdisc edition. Helpful and fascinating background information, credits, and—bonus!—film clips. Now anybody's computer can say, "They're like huge seed pods!"
WEB http://www.voyagerco.com/CC /ph/p.invasion.html

Official Johnny Mnemonic Site If you blinked once, you may have missed the rapid-fire opening and closing of *Johnny Mnemonic*, starring Keanu Reeves. But it was a banner event in the lives of William

Gibson's cyberpunky fans, who anxiously awaited Gibson's script. This official site is now largely abandoned, but still contains audio, video, and stills, as well as a "virtual reality experience in William Gibson's Cyberspace."
WEB http://www.spe.sony.com /Pictures/SonyMovies/06jonmnu .html

Unofficial Jurassic Park Home Page A fan's love for *Jurassic Park* can be as hard to contain as a hungry T-Rex, and this site is a testament to that kind of fierce ardor. It is constantly updated, and full of dinosaur roars and actor screams in sound and video. Don't forget to follow that the link at the bottom of the home page to the

first draft of the screenplay by Michael Crichton.
WEB http://uslink.net/~warrior

La Jetée Perhaps best known as the source for Terry Gilliam's *12 Monkeys*, *La Jetée* is a post-apocalyptic vision of what passes for life after world destruction. This site has a background synopsis, but that's not all: Click under the picture to find more than 30 stills from the film. Follow them by clicking on the airplanes; they're supposed to be arrows, although that's not especially obvious!
WEB http://www.favela.org/frenzy /lajette/lajette2.html

Voyager Review "Released the year before *Close Encounters* of

the Third Kind and *Star Wars*, Nicolas Roeg's *The Man Who Fell to Earth* is a science-fiction film without science, a terrestrial space opera minus matte shots, models, or pyrotechnics that leaves us not wondering at the stars but grieving for ourselves." This in-depth look at the 1976 sci-fi film also discusses the original novel, inspired casting choices (David Bowie as the alien, Newton), and the fact that after all, this movie is just "a love story."
WEB http://www.voyagerco.com/CC /sfh/manwhofell.html

The Metropolis Home Page Reviews, commentaries, and excerpts from books on Fritz Lang and his work are included here, along with

STAR WARS HOME PAGE AT U. PENN

WEB http://force.stwing.upenn.edu/01/~jruspini/starwars.html

So, you want an explanation of hyperspace travel, a list of Kenner action figures, a catalog of missing scenes from the trilogy, or the rules of the *Star Wars* drinking game? This huge (and we mean Jabba-sized) home page includes *Star Wars* news, scripts of the trilogy, images and sound files,

information on the trilogy and *Star Wars* collectibles, guides to *Star Wars* role-playing games, nit-picking and bloopers lists, trivia, Lucas Arts pages, and a guest book. Also featured is a huge section of news and FAQs about the series.

great, high-quality images from the film. It's an insightful resource, reflecting the genuine interest the site's creator has in the film and sharing it with the rest of the world. He's even put a very touching obituary on the site in honor of Brigitte Helm, the actress who played Maria and the evil robot, who passed away half-way through 1996. Links to other worldwide *Metropolis* sites are included, up near the top of the page.
WEB http://members.aol.com /PolisHome/metropolis.html

Plan 9 from Outer Space Vampira, the pale, buxom beauty who was Elvira's inspiration, not only performed in Ed Wood's "classic"; she also starred in *The Magic Sword*, *Sex Kittens Go To College*, *The Beat Generation*, and *Night Of The Ghouls*. Here's a brief, but informative review of *Plan 9* with background information on the cast of the movie voted "The Worst Film of All Time" in a 1980 poll.
WEB http://www.iguide.com/movies /mopic/pictures/IO/IO755.htm

The Criterion Collection: RoboCop "This future is a technological nightmare that all workers fear: Star Peter Weller, as the murdered officer who gets recycled into the half-machine, half-man of the film's title, plays a supporting role to his character's robotic armature. And the Detroit of the future, its mirror-and-steel skyscrapers reflecting crumbling, crime-ridden slums, is less metropolis than war

zone," writes Carrie Rickey of the influential Reagan-era film. Look into the heart of the film with this in-depth essay.
WEB http://www.voyagerco.com/CC /sfh/robocop.htm

" The U.S. government decided to combine human DNA with that of another life form. "

Species In 1993, the U.S. government decided to accept the invitation from another world to combine human DNA with that of another life form. A new life—a token of the union of two species across the void of space—and woman was created. So begins the movie, *Species*. At this official MGM site, you can take on the role of the new species in their Web Adventure—your instincts and survival skills are put to the test as alien and human psychology go to war inside your mind. If that's a little too intense for you, simply visit the Species Inventory of exclusive information on the making of the movie.
WEB http://www.mgmua.com/species /index.html

Stargate Indiana Jones meets *Close Encounters* in this story

of a mysterious artifact unearthed at the pyramids at Giza, which turns out to be a stargate—a portal to another world. This site is a multimedia melange of info about the movie, clips from the film and the soundtrack, the behind-the-scenes cast and production scoop, details on the CD-ROM, *Secrets of Stargate*, and the video game.
WEB http://www.mgmua.com /STARGATE

Terminator Home Page You'll say "hasta la vista" to other *Terminator* pages once you've visited this all-inclusive site. Its *T2* FAQ presented in hypertext form includes explanations of different movie versions, detailed listings of available soundtracks, and speculation on whether or not there will be a third movie. Also, a scripts page, featuring *Terminator*, *T2*, unofficial *T3* scripts (they're betting he'll be baaack), and loads of images and sounds.
WEB http://www.contrib.andrew.cmu .edu/~atreides/Terminator/welcome .html

The TRON Home Page Twenty-somethings can relive eighties arcade chic in all its computer-blipping splendor. For those who believe that *TRON* was the defining movie of that era (and there are plenty of them here), this page is paradise. *TRON* images and sounds, chat rooms and links to fellow *TRON* fans around the world, and even a list of arcades

around the country that still have the *TRON* game.
WEB http://www.aquila.com/guy .gordon/tron/tron.htm

12 Monkeys Talk about the power of promotion. This first-class site is truly interactive; it has the feel of a CD-ROM. Register as a volunteer and find out that "Prison Block 675/B accepts no liability for personal injury to volunteers, whether physical or psycholog-ical in origin." Then, tour through such areas as a decont-amination unit and the streets of Philadelphia. Get close to the bulletin board in the engine room and read news clippings about the disappearance of Dr. Kathryn Railly (Madeleine Stowe). There are interviews and movie clips available, and you can even read excerpts from Jack Lucas's book, *Van-ishing Act: The Making of 12 Monkeys*. That is, if you can find it. (Hint: Look for the broken window.)
WEB http://www.mca.com/universal

War of the Worlds, The (original movie) Sounds "... and now, fought with the terrible weapons of super-science, menacing all mankind and every creature on earth, comes..." Susan Powell! Nah, just Martians with death rays. Get all the cool sound effects and the best quotes from the original movie (nothing from Orson Welles' radio broadcast, unfortunately).
WEB http://www.geocities.com/ Hollywood/1158/warworld.html

Sci-Fi TV

WE'VE COME A LONG WAY FROM THE DAYS OF *CAPTAIN VIDEO*

Location: http://www.scifi.com/freezone/images/gargoyles2.jpg

 ## THE SCI-FI CHANNEL

WEB http://www.scifi.com/sforiginals
AMERICA ONLINE *keyword* scifi channel

It may look a little dense, but there's logic behind the design. With the frenetic quality of *Blade Runner* billboards, the vari-ous graphic menus transport you to the frontlines of science fiction, from late-breaking news to trippy nostalgic flashbacks that include A/V clips and downloadable images. On Sci-Fi's Pulp page, you'll find online excerpts from sci-fi magazines. If you decide to try the BBoard Dominion Chat, arm yourself. All in all, the Sci-fi Channel Web site is about as orderly a sci-fi site as you'll find.

Starting points

rec.arts.sf.tv With so many different allegiances, you'd think it would be hard to make your way through the flame wars in a place like this, but it's not. Sci-fi fans can find common ground now and then, and they do, more often than not, in this freewheeling newsgroup. *Battlestar Galactica, Lost in Space, Space: 1999*— it's all fair game here (along with all likes of *Trek*, of course). But if you criticize *The X-Files*, watch out. One guy called it "a waste of time," saying the show belongs alongside *Weekly World News*. The response? Much anger against his "wild ravings." It's a good spot to talk about the shows you still love, or want to discuss, even if they were only on the air for a season or two.
USENET rec.arts.sf.tv

Science Fiction Episode Guides Essentially an online card catalogue featuring highlights and greatest hits from the Science Fiction Repository at Rutgers, SFEG lists more than 30 noted SF shows within the Episode Guide folder. The listings are accessible by episode and broken down into brief plot summaries and info-bits (mostly cast and crew facts) that are either highly significant or useful mostly as answers to trivia questions, depending on your perspective. There is also a TV show FAQ folder, and a folder for movies. Because the movies page contain many broken links to movie home pages, the TV episode guide remains the best resource at this site.
URL ftp://sflovers.rutgers.edu/pub /sf-lovers

The Ultimate TV List: Science Fiction List This can be your lifeline to TV shows that other Web sites overlook. Sure, this sci-fi list features *Planet of the Apes* and *The Outer Limits*, but you'll also find *Automan*, *The Powers of Matthew Star*, and their ilk, plus a complete list of invaluable links to episode guides, newsgroups, FAQs, mailing lists, and Internet Movie Guide's vast cast/credits info.
WEB http://www.tvnet.com/UTVL/sci _list.html

Battlestar Galactica

Battlestar Galactica Homepage Click here to find that rare thing—a slick site that uses high-concept graphics, yet respects the fact that information can travel the Web only at limited speed. The info is cleanly organized into archives, images, dialog and sound effects, fan-created stuff, and software. There's also the obligatory info about the campaign to revive the show.
WEB http://mcmfh.acns.carleton.edu /BG

Buck Rogers in the 25th Century

Buck Rogers in the 25th Century Did you know that the same actor, Buster Crabbe, played both Buck Rogers and Flash Gordon in their respective 1930s film serials? Crabbe's bio and other fascinating facts are all part of this history of Buck Rogers—from his inception in a 1928 serialized Armageddon novel, through his reincarnation (in the guise of actor Gil Gerard) in the 1979 movie and subsequent short-lived TV series, and to the character's current popularity as a role-playing game model. The site will link you to a few of the games starring the twenty-fifth century's most famous hero.
WEB http://www.attistel.co.uk:8000 /jnp/br25c.html

Dr. Who

Doctor Who Home Page Any site claiming to cover the longest running sci-fi series in history (26 seasons, to be exact) would have to be huge. And this one is—looming as large as the revered series does in the minds of *Who* watchers. One of the more interesting pages in this all-encompassing *Who* hub is devoted to lost and found episodes. How do episodes get lost? Well, sometimes it's the fault of film archivists, and sometimes they slip through a rip in the fabric of time. But with so many devoted *Dr. Who* fans working to rescue them, they won't stay away long. This area has a dual function, serving as both a warehouse of information on episode retrieval and rescue, and as a headquarters for the ongoing recovery effort.

Another list pays homage to the people related to the series who have died. Any necrology for a series with such a lengthy run is bound to be substantial, and this document lists the *Dr. Who* alums who have passed on to that big junkyard in the sky. There are some more lighthearted lists housed in this *Who* archive. Rounding out the site are the Doctor Who FAQ, a program guide, other roles of series actors, and a current list of stations carrying the show.
WEB http://nitro9.earth.uni.edu/doctor/homepage.html

rec.arts.drwho More *Who* than you'll know how to handle, from the subsequent careers of the show's stars, to the latest in *Who* publications and paraphernalia. You'll hear endless debate about rumors of a new series. Will it be yet another regeneration? Or will it be a remake of the original series? Lots of guesses, but no real answers. Some fans, apparently, have limits to their devotion. One *Who*-man decided to sell his *Dr. Who* scarf, which was made by a friend's mother; he was looking for the best offer ("looks like the real thing—incredibly cool for the Tom Baker look-alike"). It helps if you know the lingo for this group. These people like acronyms, especially NA (new adventures, referring to *Dr. Who* novelizations) and MA ("missing adventures," another series of books).
USENET rec.arts.drwho

Earth 2

New Pacifica Reruns! We have reruns! *Earth 2* fans are cheered by the news that the Sci-Fi Channel will be rerunning episodes—soon! Also cheering is this page, containing an episode guide, actor bios, pictures, sounds, fan fiction, and fan club info. Links to other *Earth 2* sites and a how-to guide to help get the show back on the air are also offered. *E2* is out of production, but not out of fans' hearts.
WEB http://www.serve.com/e2cheer/earth2.html

DR. WHO—A BRIEF HISTORY OF TIME (TRAVEL)

WEB http://www.physics.mun.ca/~sps/drwho.html

A good mix of old and new *Who*. This site includes a complete guide to the original show, from season one ("Into the Unknown") to season twenty-six ("Journey's End"). The Eighth Doctor page is dedicated to exploring the attributes of the latest regeneration of the good doctor: "Like the Fifth

Location: http://www.physics.mun.ca/~sps/whoq.html

Doctor, he exhibits an endearing vulnerability, but this is contrasted by a sense of urgency and decisiveness. He also demonstrates a flippant sense of humor reminiscent of, though not identical to, the Second and Fourth Doctors." And for all the latest in the effort to resuscitate the all-but-dead Doctor, click to the Dr. Who News Page. Questions about what is and isn't in the works on the screen and the page are answered here.

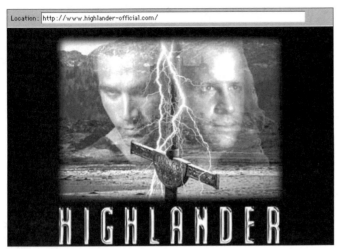

Location: http://www.highlander-official.com/

Scotland, Swords, and Slabs of Euro Hunk
http://www.highlander-official.com

The Sci-Fi Site: Earth 2 Devon Adair would never have left Earth 1 if she knew that this stuff was available on the Net! Anything an *E2* fan might desire is here, from very recent news to photos and detailed descriptions of villains from Terrans to Gaal (Funny, he looks an awful lot like Tim Curry). This site is a must-see.
WEB http://www.abacus.ghj.com/sci_fi /earth2/e2_main.htm

Highlander

Duncan Flag Wavers International (DFW) The phrase "cult of personality" springs to mind after visiting this site. The central force behind this collective of (mostly) women is a devotion to Duncan MacLeod—his righteousness, his loyalty, his eclectic taste in clothing, and the way he swings that sword during the opening credits, his bare, lithe muscles gleaming

with sweat... oh, sorry, got a little carried away there. Duncan's appeal is generously attributed to the actor who plays him on TV, and, thus, Adrian Paul—despite his unfortunate eyebrows—occupies more than one page at this site. Celebrating those who bring them joy, the DFWers proclaim their motto: "Once you lose sight of fantasy, it's only a matter of time before reality will finish you off."
WEB http://www.mt.net/~satori/DFW /DFW.html

Glenfinnian Rysher Television has put together this official site with actor bios, synopses and credits for *Highlander* episodes, links to *Highlander* Fan Clubs, airing schedules, and lots and lots of pictures of Duncan MacLeod (played by Adrian Paul). Since it is an "official site," one should probably take the producers' claims

that "Adrian has been described as a cross between Errol Flynn and Douglas Fairbanks but most of his fans liken him to a young Sean Connery" with a grain of salt. Particularly interesting is the tempered surprise with which the producers discuss how a single screenplay, unassumingly filmed, has grown into an legend replete with TV shows, cartoons, action figures, memorabilia, and a rabid band of fanatics who clamor for more.
WEB http://www.rysher.com/highlander /index.html

Highlander—The Official Site This elaborate, media-rich hubsite covers the entire *Highlander* universe with enormous features on the films, the television series, even the cartoon— all Shockwaved and Quick-Time VR'd to the gills. One of the most impressive features is "The Travels of Duncan MacLeod," which offers a Shockwave map of Duncan's adventures through time. Click on your favorite period and place—1815 at the battle of Waterloo, 1750 in Eurasia, 1637 in Verona (doesn't he look dashing in that cape?)— and you'll find, not an episode synopsis, but an enlightening history lesson covering the culture and politics of the period and region. The section on the animated series includes excellent images, character profiles, and, of course, info on how to buy the action figures. If you're more interested in the film versions, you'll find tons of multi-

media, behind-the-scenes production notes, and Lambert-trivia, including the reasons he was cast as Conor MacLeod in the first place. Probably that convincing accent.
WEB http://www.highlander-official.com

Land of the Lost

Land of the Lost Those cheesy dinosaurs, those ultra-cheap floods, and those unconvincing time-vortex effects. Yes, it's none other than Sid and Marty Krofft's *Land of the Lost*. The page is about as basic as the show, but that helps to capture the feel; a high-tech Java-powered site just wouldn't be right for one of the lowest budget sci-fi shows ever made. This presentation will bring back memories if you were one of those who woke up early on Saturdays to see the misadventures of Rick, Will, and Holly. Learn to speak Pakuni, read an extensive episode guide, and even get pictures of Sleestaks and the Marshalls.
WEB http://www.execpc.com/~nolsen/lotl/lotl.html

Lost in Space

Alpha Control: Lost in Space Every space chariot should stop here, for a cute and colorful look at one of 1965's contributions to pop culture (There may have been a couple of Beatles songs, too). See pictures of the major players, read a detailed episode guide including inside dirt on each

Location: http://www.scifi.com/lostnspace/

The Jetson's alter ego's
http://www.scifi.com/lostnspace

episode's scrapped plot twists or "firsts," and download photos, movies, and sounds. Click on Virtual Dr. Smith for a silly Shockwave goodie in which Dr. Smith spontaneously generates insults for Robot. Return to the intro to find out when the Sci-Fi Channel will be airing reruns.
WEB http://www.scifi.com/lostnspace

Lost in Space Page The poor Robinson family, lost in space in 1997. That's right, 1997, which must have seemed like a distant future when the show was first aired, during the same years as the original *Star Trek*. A superfan has put up this extensive site, including the most current information about the rumored movie, magazine articles, and more for *Lost in Space* fans who are more than casual about it. Plenty of sounds, movie clips, and pic-

tures, of course, plus a hugely long, alphabetized list of robotic insults: Lead-lined Lothario! Silver-plated Sellout! Danger, Will Robinson!
WEB http://www.snowcrest.net/fox/Space.html

Max Headroom

The Max Headroom Squares The Sci-Fi Channel is rerunning the ill-fated pioneering cyberspace drama *Max Headroom*. To celebrate, the Sci-Fi Channel's staff created a fun online game that actually works. The game is based on *The Hollywood Squares*, and even has audio-clip commentary from Max. The questions are easy and the prize is a link to an episode guide that you can find elsewhere anyway—but the game itself is an impressive piece of Web writing.
WEB http://www.scifi.com/headroom

LONG, LONG AGO IN THE LAND OF THE LOST: THE ORIGINAL JURASSIC TRAILER PARK

Land of the Lost began as an exceptional show. The first season is arguably the finest from any children's science fiction series. The special effects were very good (even real dirt on cave floors); the 200-word Pakuni language also gave realism to the show. Most notable, however, were the sense of real danger (the Marshalls acknowledged their hostile natural environment, as well as the risks of experimenting with the unknown around them) and the intelligent plots that often dealt with complex moral issues. The combination of an adequate budget, very good writing and excellent directing established *Land of the Lost* as first-class science fiction show for both children and adults.

The second season saw somewhat of a decline in quality; perhaps due to demands from parents and the network, the shows were no longer truly scary. (During the 1st season, at the age of 8, I distinctly remember finding the Sleestak to be humorous clods, but come night time I was deathly afraid.) Some episodes still provided intelligent adventures and moral challenges, but others had tacky humor apparently to cater to more dim-witted kids. Some of the special effects got cheaper (cave floors were unrealistically flat and clean), and too many episodes dealt with the Pakuni.

The third season was mostly a pathetic embarrassment. Spencer Milligan (Dad) quit the show, and Ron Harper (Uncle Jack) took his place; the Marshalls also moved their residence into the Temple (At least some of the changes were involuntary; it is rumored that the original set had burned up in a fire). The show now catered to an audience of simpletons; almost all of the plots were shallow and/or outrageously far-fetched. This last season was filled with a plethora of monsters and guest stars, most of which were intolerable if not inexcusable. Holly grew several inches, Will sang awful songs, and Cha-Ka's character declined to little more than making moronic comments. Both Cha-Ka and the Sleestak Leader miraculously spoke in English. Enik declined into someone who was always making harsh warnings or threats; he kept running around saying "not logical" in a cheap take-off of Mr. Spock. Both he and Uncle Jack willingly deceived whomever they pleased, eroding the show's original stance on ethical behavior. Bad, inconsistent writing and horrible directing in the third season had *Land of the Lost* digging its own grave.

—from **Land of the Lost**

MST3K

alt.tv.mst3k/alt.fan.mst3k/rec.arts .tv.mst3k/rec.arts.tv.mst3k.misc
Cynical and hilarious, much like the show itself. Fans of *Mystery Science Theater 3000* revel in their ruthlessness. After all, the show relies on viewer disdain for movies like *Invasion USA*, *The Creeping Terror*, and *Teenagers from Outerspace*. One fan, upset by recent screenings of such pictures as *Racket Girls* and *Red Zone Cuba*—they weren't bad enough?—posted a plea for "dumb Japanese monsters" and "stupid alien movies": "We want to leave the sleazy '50s-'60s underworld films (YAWN!) mercifully buried and happily decaying into a puddle of ooze!" Newbies, beware. Post a sincere question to this group and you're asking for a flame. Plenty of talk of sci-flicks such as *Logan's Run*, *Nightfall*, and *Fire Maidens of Outer Space*. Celebrity mentions should be particularly severe, with posts judged by their level of ridicule. After Kathy Ireland was called "the dumbest celebrity," one regular wrote: "If you ever get a chance, listen to Nancy Sinatra. She makes Tony Danza and Sylvester Stallone look like Mensa members."
USENET alt.tv.mst3k • alt.fan.mst3k • rec.arts.tv.mst3k • rec.arts.tv.mst3k .misc

Big Ole Mystery Science Theater 3000 "Some eye creatures are born with scaly, protective cov-

ering. Others are born with hundreds of eyes protruding from fleshy knobs. Still others, like this whisper-thin fellow, are born with tight, acrylic, wool-blend turtle-neck sweaters from Chess King." As Tom Servo would say, "Hodgeka, that's comedy!" Nearly every sketch, every song, every wacky, loony, loopy, cock-eyed moment of hilarity is painstakingly reproduced here for your reading pleasure. Oh, and there's an episode guide, too.
WEB http://www.slinknet.com /~wmorgan/mst3k.html

Index—Deus Ex Machina SCARIER than Santa Claus

Conquers the Martians! BIGGER than the Amazing Colossal Man! Better SORTED than the M& Ms backstage at a Stones concert. Prepare to be SHOCKED out of your seats! It's Deus Ex Machina, Web site of TERROR! Watch in HORROR as a mild mannered college student is impelled by an unknown force to collect dozens and dozens of Web sites, ALL DAY, ALL NIGHT! Is it ALIEN MIND CONTROL? A government experiment gone HORRIBLY WRONG? And what is his UNEARTHLY goal? FIND OUT, if you dare...
WEB http://sunsite.unc.edu/lunar /mst3k/mst3k.html

Mystery Science Theater 3000 A great hangout for MiSTies and MiSTics, with folders called Joel vs. Mike, Satellite of Love, Favorite Running Gags, and lots of other goodies. The quotes in the Favorite Quotes folder include "Bite me, it's fun," and "We come bearing honey-baked yams." Check out the Itchy Mango folder for an add-on story: "Create absurd situations, zany characters, and disgusting plot conveniences. In jokes—a plus. You (all of you) are responsible to keep the wacky adventures of Ms. Itchy Mango alive and kicking. Post away!" This is a raucous and fun-loving bunch. Never a dull moment, with

 # TOM SERVO FAN CLUB
WEB http://sebago.internet.com/tsfc

Patrick is a big *MST3K* fan. It's his *raison d'etre*. His entire life seems to be devoted to watching the show. And you are the beneficiary of his obsessive compulsion! You have to take a test to get into the exclusive club, and those who fail are tarred and feathered in the public square. What members

Location: http://sebago.internet.com/tsfc/Gallery/gallery4.html

actually do in this club is shrouded in mystery—the info page talks of revolution and *CHIPs*, and little else. For non-members, there is still lots to do at this site—image and video galleries, episode lists with quotes ("Nobody drinks from my girl!"), an **FAQ**, and a viewing schedule, The **TSFC** Homepage is a testimony, not just to one of the most beloved television shows of all time, but to a man obsessed, a man devoted, a man with far too much time on his hands.

A STILL TONGUE MAKES A HAPPY LIFE

I will not be pushed, filed, stamped, indexed, briefed, debriefed, or numbered! My life is my own.
—No.6; "Arrival"

New No.2: Good day, Number Six.
No.6: Number what?
New No.2: Six. For official purposes. Everyone has a number. Yours is number 6.
No.6: I am not a number, I am a person.
—"Arrival"

We're all pawns, m'dear.
—The Ex-admiral; "Arrival"

No.2: What you should do is find yourself a nice young lady for the carnival. You're too independent. Now, they're pretty and unattached...
No.6: What about her? (points to The Observer)
No.2: Quite unsuitable.
No.6: I'm independent, don't forget.
—"Dance of the Dead"

The Observer: [The Village] has been going a long time'
No.6: Since the war? Before the war? WHICH war??
The Observer: A long time!
—"Dance of the Dead"

Never trust a female; even the four-legged variety.
—No.6; "Dance of the Dead"

—from The Prisoner U.S. Home Page

caustic comments appreciated. One MiSTy's thoughts on "Kitten with a Whip": "My, this movie was putrid... What cheese!" The best of the worst for students of cinema absurdité; *Cahiers du Cinéma* this ain't.
AMERICA ONLINE *keyword* scifi→Star Trek/Comics/TV/Star Wars Boards →Mystery Science Theater 3000

Outer Limits

The Outer Limits: The Original Series Neat-looking Java that mimics the famous sine-wave opening sequence of the groundbreaking sci-fi show from the '50s greets you upon arrival. Download the "control voice" to complete the effect: "There is nothing wrong with

your television set..." A collection of historical facts, an episode guide, and images make this a must-see for anyone even remotely intrigued by not only this show, but any science-fiction TV.
WEB http://www.webzonel.co.uk/www /brendan/outer.htm

The Prisoner

Sci-Fi Channel: The Prisoner Click anywhere on this map of Your Village—the Town Hall, the Hospital, the Citizen's Advice Bureau—to start a virtual trip through the world of *The Prisoner*. While other sites are full of interesting information, series trivia, and fanatics arguing about whether the butler was No. 1, or a symbol of the oppressed working class, this page is a series of links that lead in circles, rather frustrating games, and flurries of images and sounds. It has perfectly captured the atmosphere of the show. Be warned! Trying to get to any part of The Village you don't have access to sets off an orange alert, if you're lucky. If you're not, let's just say we won't be seeing you again.
WEB http://www.scifi.com/prisoner /index.html

Quantum Leap

The Accelerator Chamber How do you leap through time? With high-technology, a healthy respect for twentieth-century American social history, and a little luck. And how do you leap through cyberspace? With a well-designed Web site devoted to *Quantum Leap*, especially one that includes general information such as fan club listings and an episode guide. The user-friendly Accelerator Chamber even has a map of the site with descriptions of each feature. A fanatics' look at the life of Dr. Samuel Beckett is one of the most interesting parts of the site—you learn that the character "could read at age 2, do advanced calculus in his head at 5, went to MIT at age 15..." Links are provided, of course, and so is an in-depth look at the Quantum Leap Project: "This top secret project is

located in a cavern in New Mexico in 1995 (at the time of the pilot episode; it's now sometime in 1999). By fall 1996, it's cost $43 billion of our tax dollars, with $2.4 billion a year operating funds."
WEB http://www-usacs.rutgers.edu /funstuff/quantum-leap

Quantum Leap Archive Take one drink when someone makes a remark about Sam's "Swiss cheesed" memory (the words "Swiss cheese" must be used). Take two when Sam pretends to talk on the phone so he can talk to Al. Huh? Rules to the clever *Quantum Leap* drinking game are posted here. If you're not too drunk and want some

more *QL* goodies, also guides, archives of mailing list posts, tape lists, interview transcripts, and FAQs for the show are also featured.
URL ftp://ftp.doc.ic.ac.uk/pub/media /tv/collections/tardis/us/sci-fi /QuantumLeap

Red Dwarf

David's Smegi Page-A-Rooni As well-designed as the Cat's wardrobe, as big as the curry stain down Lister's shirt, as informative as Holly (actually more so, thankfully), and with almost as many features as Kryton—even without the groinal socket. OK, so the site ripped off all the sounds,

 # The Prisoner U.S. Home Page

WEB http://www.cis.yale.edu/~rdm/pris.html
picture: WEB http://pantheon.yale.edu/~rdm/i_resign.gif
Ignoring the maxim, "A still tongue makes a happy life," this site is the most analytical, verbose page on the series. The Beginners Page offers an in-depth introduction not only to the plot, but to the philosophy behind the show, as well as "Kent Notes" which attempt to detangle the more confounding aspects of the series.

At the core of the page, is discussion of and theorizing on every nuance of the show— What does the Butler's umbrella symbolize? Did we ever find out where The Village is located? What's the deal with the glowing rover in "Free For All"? The page also houses an intensive analysis of Episode Order, and the best *Prisoner* index on the Net.

Location: ftp://ftp.queeg.crater.com/pub/red-dwarf/pictures/DemAng.gif

Red Dwarf: British style is the envy of the world
http://www.queeg.crater.com

images, and video from the Queeg site, but, as the Cat would say, style is the important thing. It does provide its own FAQ and a timeline taking us from the birth of Chu Ch'ang-lo Kuang Tsung to the End of Time Itself, which the Inquisitor has visited and doesn't much like. This is one of the better places to go for scripts—there is one for every episode and they're available in HTML instead of .ZIP files. But the coolest thing here is the Inconsistencies page, with thousands of nit-picks. They even nit-pick the smeg-up video!
WEB http://www.ozramp.net.au/~rocky /rdwarf.html

Krosis' Red Dwarf Pagearoonie
Step onto the Express Lift (patent applied for) for a tour of *Red Dwarf*. First level: Quote of the Week—"KRYTEN: The poor devil scrawled it in his death throes, using a

combination of his own blood and even his own intestines. RIMMER: Who would do that? LISTER: Someone who badly needed a pen." Second Level: *Red Dwarf* FAQ— Under Construction, please remain in the lift. Third Level: Guides to the *RD* Books and Videos—be sure to check out *Better than Life*, where we find our heroes (and the git) living in their dream worlds (and you know how scary their dreams are!). Fourth Level: Episode Scripts—go back to the first episode, it's still bloody funny (even in the late eighties, Grant and Naylor managed to keep their sense of humor). Fifth Level: Mailing list info. Sixth Level: Personnel files on the boys. It reads like a *Playboy* centerfold, but thankfully they keep their clothes on. Seventh Level: Links. The cute borg at the end is Krosis (see what kind of costumes you get when you spend a million dollars an

episode instead of 30 pounds and a tub of Nutella?).
WEB http://www.louisville.edu/~atjewe 0l/reddwarf.html

Queeg's Red Dwarf Archive This is where the other site authors dip their sticky little hands to get multimedia files and everything else that they're too lazy to create themselves. There are hundreds of files in this archive. If it has anything to do with vindaloos and swimming certificates, its here—reviews, bios, birthday lists, space corp directive lists, fan fiction, even the *Red Dwarf* fishlist which documents every fishy moment, word or action in the entire series. But, you say, it's about as stylish as Dwane Dibbly, about as entertaining as Hammond Organ music, about as funny as Henny Youngman. But that's the point, innit? It's Queeg, right, so it's efficient and humorless, see?
WEB http://www.queeg.crater.com

seaQuest DSV

alt.tv.seaquest David wants the writers of *seaQuest, DSV* to have enough creativity not to steal characters and episodes from *Star Trek: The Next Generation*. "If you're going to steal stories," he wrote, "at least don't make them WORSE than the original!" Another viewer—not a fan, exactly— dubbed this show "Fish Trek, 90H20" for its combination of hardbodied hunks and salvaged *Trek* plots. You'll find ample comparisons of captains

Kirk and Picard to *SQ*'s Captain Bridger. "Let's face facts," one person wrote, "Bridger doesn't and can't compare to either of those captains." Aside from the *Trek* references, this group is heavy on science, with plenty of arguments about proper air pressure and vertebrates with gills.
USENET alt.tv.seaquest

Sliders

Sliders Webmeister Tim Lucas has done a great job of cataloging all of the alternate earths and personas from *Sliders*, the Fox sci-fi show about a group of people who "slide" from one parallel earth to another. The show is always under the threat of cancellation (perhaps on a parallel world the show is highly rated), but it has a group of devoted fans, who can check out this address to see a photo gallery, actor and character bios, and an interview with series star and NYU grad Jerry O'Connell.
WEB http://washington.xtn.net/~lucast /sliders/sliders.html

Universal Channel: Sliders
Shameless commercialism reigns in this self-promoting coverage of Universal's sci-fi show. All the standard series info is there, but you can also play the *Sliders* WWW game—which is fun—even if you don't know anything about the show. Feel compelled to express yourself on the burning issues of *Sliders*' quality, the stories and characters? Or do

you just have the hots for one of the main actors? You can send email to the cast, writers, or producers.
WEB http://www.univstudios.com/tv /sliders

Space: Above and Beyond

Mission Status: Space: Above and Beyond Whether you've only seen half an episode or follow the series religiously, Mission Status is the ideal Web resource to Fox's *Space: Above and Beyond*. With this encyclopedia of info, you can decipher the show's many acronyms, translate the characters' military lingo ("Zoomie" means pilot),

and learn more about their technology. The timeline and episode guide helps put the plot in perspective, while the episode reviews remind you that this is only a TV program. Most intriguing is the Wild Card MOO area, which allows you to not only interact with other visitors but also with the rooms themselves on board the Saratoga space carrier.
WEB http://www.microserve.net/space :aab

Studio Tours: Space: Above and Beyond A day in the life of the crew of the 58th United States Space Aviator Cavalry stationed on the USS *Saratoga*. Tour the flight deck, the air

---

V FOR VILIFIED

My opinion: *V* is okay, but only as fairly mindless, Saturday-afternoon-type skiffy. It got a lot of praise, mainly due to all the hype it got when it originally aired, than it deserves. *V* is one cliché after another. It's Nazis from outer space! It's Europe in WII fighting back! They are big lizards disquised as people. They are here to eat us! Etc. etc. etc. And the characters are just as cliched. The science of the science fiction is REALLY weak; they not only want to EAT us, they want to steal our water! (Oh, please!)

The first 2-parter is better than the second 3-parter. The second mini-series started to show the major weaknesses of the whole *V* premise, which were glossed over by some decent effects (the ships coming in, hanging over the cities (later to appear in *ID4*)) and the shorter length. It didn't have the depth of story to last as a series and it came as not the slightest surprise to me when it end after a season (or less, I seem to I remember).

V is okay if you turn off the critical thinking of your brain when you watch it. But that is about it.

—from rec.arts.sf.tv

X marks the award-winning spot
http://www.foxhome.com/trustno1

lock, the Armored Personnel Carrier cockpit, the bunk room, and Tun Tavern—the only place to unwind after a full day of fighting Chigs and A.I.'s. Never mind that the show's been canceled. Suspend disbelief for a bit—this is science fiction, after all.
WEB http://www.fox.com/st2spce.htm

Twilight Zone

Twilight Zone Episode Guides
Remember the first *Twilight Zone*, from 1959? That would have been "Where is Everybody?" with Earl Holliman, which told the story of a man stranded in a deserted city. Or maybe you'd rather spend your time reviewing such classics as "Stopover in a Quiet Town," or hit-and-miss efforts such as "Caesar and Me." This document lists all the episodes from the original run of the show, along with credits for writers,

directors, and actors, a brief synopsis, and a capsule review.
URL ftp://sflovers.rutgers.edu/pub /sflovers/TV/EpisodeGuides/twilight -zone.guide

V

"V" Home Page An index of links, and so much more. Even if you know a lot about the series, check out the "history" of *V* feature, which offers long synopses of lost scripts, articles about the show's creator and it's later creative problems, and background on all the various versions, formats, and spin-offs that the series produced.
WEB http://www.prairienet.org/~drthiel /v.htm

The X-Files

Official Web Site The mysterious agency which has created this official site is rumored to have something to do with Fox Tele-

vision. Is it a trap? Will an unsuspecting special agent be kidnapped by aliens from the marketing department? Will they spend, spend, spend in the online merchandise store? No. An anonymous source has told us that the site is safe if you trust no one (and cut up your credit cards). Listen to Sunset Boulevard's talking *X-Files* billboard (the whole file is 20 minutes long), find out about Chris Carter or the characters, and read an extensive episode guide. Finally, take a test and (possibly) win a T-shirt.
WEB http://www.thex-files.com

> ## " Suspend disbelief for a bit—this is science fiction, after all. "

Official X-Files Site We suspect this site of brainwave manipulation, and frankly, we're shocked. Hang on, there's a mix-up here. What we meant to say was that this site uses Shockwave, but you don't have to be Shocked to enjoy it. The Fox official *X-Files* site is subtle marketing disguised as a fan page, but gosh, it's more fun than a hot tub of humanoids. Also, because it's legal promotion, we know that the copyright hitmen won't be stalking

it as they do the sites created by dispensable fans. So put on your trench coat, grab some sunflower seeds, and go "undercover" to meet creator Chris Carter (a former editor of *Surfing* magazine), the writers, directors, or special effects crew. This section also provides the slick info about Scully, Mulder, and the gang, along with interviews and reviews. Classified Tapes offers delightful clips from the recently-released videos of what they term "six of the finest episodes": "Pilot," "Deep Throat," "Conduit," "Ice," "Fallen Angel," and "Eve." X-Quest (an interactive simulation) and X-Sightings (fan merchandise and Operation X, a most excellent trivia contest) round out this conspiracy to make you watch no other show.
WEB http://www.foxhome.com/trustnol

The X-Files Episode Guide The episode guide is out there... look, here it is—the ultimate amateur episode guide, referenced by everyone and written by superfan Cliff Chen. It's in unattractive ASCII format, but for the detailed dirt (including an FAQ and lots of miscellaneous resources and information), it can't be missed. When you get bored reading the summaries in English, you can finish the rest in Finnish. If you ever find an *X-Files* trivia contest that requires answers in Finno-Ugric, you know where to go.
WEB http://bird.taponline.com/~cliff

Sci-Fi Literature

From Asimov to Wells, the last written word on Sci-Fi

Location: http://www.bmk.hu/dune/images/movie/09.jpg

Museum Arrakeen
WEB http://www.bmk.hu/dune

Finally! Somebody's jazzed up a simple index into a Web page; and it's actually entertaining. It's in the guise of a role-playing, choose-your-own-adventure game, but don't be fooled. It's really just a tour through all aspects of the world of *Dune*. There are several rooms in the museum, beginning with the Music Chamber, where Gurney Halleck offers sound clips. The Holo-Photo Wing houses movie pics, and the Information Desk hosts an FAQ. Other rooms include the Document Archives, Gaming Chamber, the Grand Portrait Wing, and the News Room. This virtual museum is a must-see for anyone even marginally interested in Frank Herbert or *Dune*... or anyone about to post another annoying, dry index.

Douglas Adams

alt.fan.douglas-adams If consciousness is a dense, blurry fog, then the humor of Douglas Adams is an out-of-control lorry that emerges from that fog, rebounds off street signs and the occasional pedestrian, before crashing through the window of a fish-and-chips shop. Of course, if you've read Adams's *Hitch Hiker's Guide* trilogy (which comes in five volumes), you know this already. Vogon poetry. Pan-Galactic Gargle Blasters. The end of EOEAWKI (Existence On Earth As We Know It) and the answer to the question of life, the universe, and everything. Alt.fan.douglas-adams, where the guide series and other snarky bits of Adams' universe are discussed, showers readers with incredibly unenlightening points of philosophy, anecdotes of how the number 42 has influenced/changed/ended their lives, and loads of Favorite Lines. Like its cousin, alt.fan.pratchett, it has an extensive international following, with posters chiming in from all corners of the Sceptered Isle and its colonies, in addition to the good old U.S. of A. While old reports suggested that Adams was a no-show at the group, new surveillance has revealed that the head honcho himself does occasionally drop by for a laugh or two. That is, when he's not in the bath.
USENET alt.fan.douglas-adams

Enter the galaxy of the imagination that is the work of Isaac Asimov
http://www.clark.net/pub/edseiler/WWW/asimov_home_page.html

Deep Thought The answer to the Great Question... Of Life, the Universe, and Everything... is 42, according to Deep Thought in *The Hitch Hiker's Guide*. Elvis Presley died at the age of 42. A Playtex Wonderbra consists of exactly 42 parts. The city of Jerusalem covers 42 square miles. Coincidence? Hundreds of DNA fans think not, though Adams has tried to dispel any myths about the number by posting to Usenet, "The answer to this is very simple. It was a joke. It had to be a number, an ordinary, smallish number, and I chose that one. Binary representations, base thirteen, Tibetan monks are all complete nonsense. I sat at my desk, stared into the garden and thought '42 will do'. I typed it out. End of story." Nonetheless, the leg-

end of 42 lives on, and this page takes a lighthearted look at the hundreds of "significant" sightings of the number throughout history, from the first recorded appearance in 2 Kings 2:23-34 to the fact that there are 42 Oreo cookies in a one-pound bag. You can also contribute your own close encounters with the uncanny numeral.
WEB http://www.empirenet.com /personal/dljones/index.html

Isaac Asimov

alt.books.isaac-asimov There's a lot of debate over the lineage of Asimov storylines now that they're being farmed out to other science-fiction writers (à la the post-Fleming 007). The most soulful participants are making repeat pilgrimages through the *Foundation* series and wondering out loud about character motivations with the kind of active curiosity that would make a high school English teacher think she had been transported to a parallel universe. Perhaps because so many of the group members have shared experiences treading through Asimov's work, the conversation tends to be extremely polite and reasoned, even when debating the data storage potential of black holes. **USENET** alt.books.isaac-asimov

Isaac Asimov Home Page A collection of Asimov resources almost as comprehensive as the works themselves. An FAQ, a list of his works, the best places

to go to get your hands on the books, Asmiov's publishers on the Web, links to reviews, a list of worlds mentioned in the *Foundation* series, and a guide to Asimov's short fiction and essays. This site even provides a graph of the number of books Asimov published each year throughout his career. Apparently, it took 19 years for Ike to publish his first 100 books, 10 years to publish the next 100, and only 5 more years to bring the total up to 300. **WEB** http://www.clark.net/pub/edseiler /WWW/asimov_home_page.html

J.G. Ballard

J.G. Ballard From a photo of Ballard to the latest on the

movie version of *Crash*, fan Craig has collected it here. His Ballard page is the only place to read *JGB News*, an infrequent fan newsletter. You'll also find bibliographies with synopses, info on the *JGB* mailing list, links to interviews, and much more. **WEB** http://www.simons-rock.edu /~craigs/ballard.html

J.G. Ballard: What I Believe Message to the creators of this site: OK, so now we know that you can use frames. But did you know that each frame is supposed to say something different? This site is a hypertext version of Ballard's powerful statement of self, a credo that acknowledges the absurdity,

 VOGON'S HITCH-HIKER'S GUIDE TO THE GALAXY
WEB http://www.vogon.com/megadodo
picture: WEB http://www.msms.doe.k12.ms.us/~mlargent/hhx.html
"When you've been thrown out of an airlock into the cold vacuum of space... stuck on prehistoric Earth for ten years, stopped in for the end of the universe and breakfast at Milliways... had your

planet blown up to make way for a hyperspace bypass or, in general, you've lost your towel, **DON'T PANIC!** Reach for your handy, new, expanded and revised, *Hitch-Hiker's Guide to the Galaxy!*" This Web version of Adams' electronic encyclopedia allows you to look up entries on everything from the Annual Ursa Minor Alpha Recreational Illusions Institute Awards Ceremony to Zaphod Beeblebrox.

WHAT? NO ANCHOVIES?

Ray Bradbury's Recipe For Liquid Pizza

Ingredients:
I can Campbell's Tomato Soup, I lb. soda crackers, salt, I quart milk, I pint half-and-half.

Instructions:
Pour can of soup into a large pot. Add milk instead of water as instructed on the can. Begin to heat soup. As soup warms to a boil, add I/4 lb. of crumbled soda crackers. Add a little half-and-half as you stir (don't overdo the stirring). When the soup is ready to serve, there should be a thick crust on the top and you should be able to stand a spoon up in it. Make a furrow down the middle with your spoon. Do the sides cave in immediately? If so, add more crackers.

Ray's Liquid Pizza is now ready to eat! As you eat, feel free to add more half-and-half to taste.

—from Ray Bradbury

beauty, tragedy, and treasure of human life. The site's authors have linked many of the operative words in the statement to Ballard-related quotes and sites. They claim that this is to celebrate Ballard's principle of connectedness within disparate objects. It is a thought-provoking and affecting presentation.
WEB http://www.cnw.com/~miki/index .html

Frank Herbert

alt.fan.dune "After reading the scene in *Dune Messiah* when the stone burner blinds Paul and a bunch of his Fedaykin," one fan wrote, "I'm wondering, What is a stone burner?" Fans scurry to their much-valued copies of *The Dune Encyclope-* *dia* whenever there's a question like that one. Every once in a while they're stumped. Stone burner? Perhaps it was just a "plot device," a way to induce temporary blindness without any contextual or cultural justification. Contributors have expansive knowledge of all aspects of *Dune*-dom; books, the movie, or MUSH simulations of the *Dune* universe.
USENET alt.fan.dune
WEB http://www.princeton.edu/~cgil more/dune/faq/afdFAQ.html

Dune "Since the release of the *Dune Chronicles,* a six-book series, the world of science fiction has never been the same," claims this page. There are bundles of *Dune* sites on the Net, and legions of fans

MUSHing and FAQing all over the place. Alex Dunkel has collected links to some of the best, but he has already created some of the most impressive *Dune*-related Web resources himself. Fans can find sounds from *Dune,* a complete guide to each of the Chronicles, a great .JPEG of the Arrakis Map, Terminology of the Imperium, and sound files from each of the songs on the *Dune* soundtrack.
WEB http://www.ECNet.Net/users /murjd5/Dune

George Orwell

Newspeak and Doublethink Homepage The year 1984 has come and gone, but was Orwell's vision of the future so far-fetched as we were all led to believe? The author of this page thinks that newspeak and doublethink have never been so prevalent as they are today. He cites political correctness, employee drug testing, affirmative action, and other common "whipping boys" as evidence that Big Brother is getting bigger. He is also convinced that the government is spying on him through the microphone in his telephone. Even Orwell would run from this nutty page.
WEB http://aloha.net/~frizbee/index .html

Terry Pratchett

L-Space Web What's L-Space, you say? From the *Discworld Companion,* "Knowledge =

Power = Energy = Matter = Mass; a good bookshop is just a genteel Black Hole that knows how to read. Mass distorts space into polyfractal L-space, in which Everywhere is also Everywhere Else." L-Space is kind of like the Web, with its links from here to there and elsewhere. Or so the Pterry fans and founders of this site think. Practically speaking, L-Space Web is the permanent home of the frequently linked-to random quote generator, a Terry Pratchett Who's Who covering everyone from Angua to Esmerelda Weatherwax, the Clarecraft catalog of figures and figurines, and fandom facts on fan clubs, fanzines, and forthcoming events, as well as the all-important Annotated Pratchett File, the Pratchett Quote File, and the FAQs. Even more whimsical are the Recipe Exchange and the "Let's Cast a Discworld Movie" thread from alt.fan .pratchett.
WEB http://www.lspace.org

The Terry Pratchett Archive Site
Terry Pratchett's work is full of references, allusions, parodies, and insider jokes. The Pratchett faithful have collected 1,300 such annotations in a huge document called the Annotated Pratchett File (or APF) here. Regulars on alt.fan.pratchett respectfully request that newbies check here before posting "to make sure you are not wasting bandwidth on something we already know." This anonymous FTP site also con-

Location: ftp://ftp-us.lspace.org/pub/people/pratchett/images/bookcovers/interesting-times.jpg

May you live in *Interesting Times*
ftp://ftp-us.lspace.org/pub/people/pratchett

tains an FAQ, bibliography, and many other items of Pratchettian interest, such as a quotes file with almost 500 entries, the rules to the Cripple Mr. Onion card game, several versions of "The Hedgehog Song," and scanned images of most of the original covers of the novels.
URL ftp://ftp-us.lspace.org/pub/people /pratchett

H.G. Wells

The Time Machine In 1898, Herbert George Wells posited a fourth dimension, time. Our consciousness moves across it like any other dimension, why not our bodies? he asked, before sending his anonymous Time Traveller on his way. The rest is history—or is it?
WEB http://www.literature.org/Works /H-G-Wells/time-machine

The War of the Worlds Home Page The year 1997 marks the centennial of the serial publication of *The War of the Worlds*, and little Woking, England (where the book is set) is having a party. There are walks, newspaper stories, and schedules (diaries, to the British). Do you feel like making a pilgrimage?
WEB http://www.dircon.co.uk/mjbstein /warhome.htm

Others

Ray Bradbury This site is a must on a Bradbury site-seeing trip. If you'll step this way, please, you'll see a biography and bibliography, many photos of the author of *Fahrenheit 451* and *The Illustrated Man*, and even a nauseating recipe for liquid pizza. Why not stop into the library and pause briefly to read several stories and

excerpts from the master, including "Pendulum" and "A Sound of Thunder."
WEB http://www.on-ramp.com/johnston /bradbury.htm

Anthony Burgess Reading *A Clockwork Orange* Many authors are the best readers of their own work. They know where the nuances lie, and how the rhythm should flow. When they speak their characters' lines, they speak them as they should be spoken, with proper emphasis. Here, Burgess speaks Nasdat, the language he invented, as it would be spoken.
WEB http://town.hall.org/Archives /radio/IMS/HarperAudio/070494 _harp_ITH.launch.html

❝ L. Ron Hubbard, if his agent is to be believed, was nothing short of the Messiah. ❞

Orson Scott Card Discussion Mailing List A very busy discussion group devoted to Card, but not in awe of him. Most of OSC's most fervent Web fans, including Barbara and Khyron, are frequent posters here. A recent lurk on the list revealed thought-provoking examinations of the unpleasant strains in Card's work, ranging from anti-Semitism to pederasty.

One poster even spawned a thread discussing whether all Mormons are racist. In fact, plenty of posters want to know about OSC's Mormonism, and how it affects his literary take on the world. The give-and-take is enormously polite—in fact, truly exceptional for the faceless Internet world. Any suggestions, however offensive to diehard fans, are discussed, rather than flamed to death. That makes for a refreshing change as well as intriguing dialogue.
EMAIL majordomo@hundred.acre .wood.net ✍ *Type in message body:* subscribe orsoncard
WEB http://haw.usfca.edu/~khyron /card/cardlist.html

Ellison Webderland The Web site with the seal of approval of H.E. himself, Webderland explores Harlan Ellison the persona and phenomenon rather than Ellison the serious author. This official site features frequent updates about publishing events and Harlan's health (since quadruple-bypass surgery), a one-of-a-kind photo gallery, biographies (real and surreal) and reviews. There's even an online store stocked with Ellison books and recordings, and a page of his quotes titled "Everything I Needed to Know I Learned from Harlan."
WEB http://www.menagerie.net /ellison/INDEX.HTM

The L. Ron Hubbard Literary Site Seek not, ye sci-fi fans, for an objective viewpoint of the guru

here. Master storyteller and Scientology pedagogue Lafayette Ronald Hubbard, if his literary agent is to be believed, was nothing short of the Messiah. So why do we get the feeling that hidden behind the can-ya-believe-it bio is the biggest nerd in school? You decide. Anyway, there is a lot of good stuff here. Many of L. Ron's books are available at a 20-percent Internet discount—the intros and first chapters are entirely online, and there's beautiful artwork from the books throughout.
WEB http://www.Authorservicesinc .com

Island Web Does the idea of a psychedelic utopia appeal to you? Help these "hyper dimensional cyber elves" build one at Island Web, an interactive community based on ideas in Huxley's last novel, *Island*. While such LSD-loving froth seems hopelessly sixties, it's always interesting to see what an author will do to justify anything.
WEB http://www.island.org

Kurt Vonnegut Would you let this guy mind the baby? He looks creepier than Woody Allen in a sorority house, as befits a former in-law of Geraldo Rivera. But this home page is packed with Vonnegut-related links. Of particular interest is the link to an online Vonnegut story called "Sun Moon Star."
WEB http://www.cas.usf.edu/english /boon/vonnegut/kv.html

Star Trek

You think you know everything about *Trek*? Well, there's a whole new universe online

You, too, can boldly go where many have gone been before. Mr. Data! *Yes, Captain?* How can we get onto the Federation-approved Internet? *Well, we might be able to harness the warp phasers and turn them back around in order to reset the holodeck to play itself in a fight to the death, which might assist us in harnessing the inverse energy of the missing black hole to augment the energy we need to harness from the failing dilithium crystal!* How long would that take? *About three years.* We only have 20 minutes. What else can be done? *Well, we could simply follow the helpful suggestions listed below this paragraph.* Good work, Data. *Thank you, Captain.* Geordi! You heard Mr. Data. Make it so.

Location: http://www.cdsnet.net/vidiot/

Welcome to the Vidiot Web Pages
Your source for Star Trek & UPN Info

Vidiot Home Page
WEB http://www.cdsnet.net/vidiot

Wouldn't you like to own a house next to Rick Berman or have a friend who worked on the set of *Voyager*? Ahh, for the inside scoop on storylines. Here's the next best thing. Mike Brown's *Trek* pages have a somewhat official air about them, and since they often reveal news about upcoming episodes and Paramount decisions, they may be the closest you get to an inside source. Each *Trek* series has its own page, with casting news, air dates, images, and episode summaries. If you have a graphical Web browser, be sure to check out the image pages—especially those for the premiere episode of *Voyager* and the movie *Generations*. The images take a while to load, but they're well worth the wait.

Starting points

alt.sex.fetish.startrek Are you curious about which of the *ST* women have done photo spreads "out of uniform"? (Denise Crosby, Marina Sirtis, but never Gates McFadden.) Do you wonder which of the male officers on deck has the biggest Ten-Forward? (Apparently, at least as far as *TNG* is concerned, the Captain's Log is most impressive, with No. One a close No. Two.) Ever wished that phasers had a setting marked "stimulate"? Well, then, post haste to alt.sex.fetish .startrek. One of the few sex.fetish groups dominated by female posters, it is a remarkably close-knit community, bound by an intense and absolutely serious lust for the men and women of *Trek*'s past, present, and future.
USENET alt.sex.fetish.startrek

FAQs by Category The staff at Oxford University has done what they do best; namely, list things. In this case, they've undertaken the task of compiling a list of all available *Star Trek* FAQs. But read the page carefully and you'll discover that no person actually performed this chore: the stuff is churned out automatically. Oxford has a staff of robots that spends all day (weekends too— what a bunch of slave drivers), finding categories to make lists. Their robots have won awards for being hyper-efficient little list makers. It's rather spooky, the idea of robots compiling

Early model *Enterprise*, circa 1976
http://images.jsc.nasa.gov/html/ALT.htm

Star Trek information that you can access from your home computer.
WEB http://www.lib.ox.ac.uk/internet /news/faq/by_category.star-trek.html

NetTrekker's Complete Stardate Index A comprehensive chronology noting the stardates of hundreds of *Trek* adventures, including all events portrayed on television and in movies, books, and comics. Adventures are cross-listed if the story used flashbacks, time travel, or visions of the future. Each listing is also tagged with the type of story (e.g., Pocket Books *Deep Space Nine* novel; Animated Series episode). Compiled by Dayton Ward, an active member of AOL's *Star Trek* club, the list also includes a detailed set of footnotes that often preempt arguments over an event's occurrence.

WEB http://users.aol.com/nettrekker /its-net.htm

Nitpickers Central Phil Farrand watches way too much *Star Trek*. He has written five books "of minute and usually unjustified criticism" that nip away at every little plot oversight, equipment oddity, and production problem in the *Trek* universe. At his Web page he has assembled a legion of fellow nit-pickers—more than 4,500—fans who love to tear apart their favorite shows. Warp here to apply for membership and peruse the weekly persnickety newsletter for the latest nits. The best online feature is the Glossary, pointing out hilarious stuff like the "He's Dead, Jim" and AOTW (Alien of the Week) Syndromes.
WEB http://members.gnn.com /nitcentral/thisweek/thisweek.htm

The Particles of Star Trek "Wait a minute, wait a minute... if the food replicators are connected to the warp core and then the ship performs a baryon sweep, there might be enough reserve energy for a single plasma discharge that will vacate all of the onboard lavatories." Find out if this is at all possible in the world of *Star Trek* at this page, which references all particles on every show, including the original series (remember quadrotriticale with the Tribbles?), *TNG* (on which we were introduced to psilocynine, which pulled Deanna out of hallucinations), the movies (trilithium, natch), and *Voyager* (tricobalt). And you can use the Particle Generation Form to submit the names of new discoveries.
WEB http://www.hyperion.com/~koreth/particles

Star Trek Trivia Chats "RED ALERT!! Classic Stumper Questions Coming!!" The 48 room members quiet down briefly to watch for the upcoming question: "Who did the voice for Alice in Wonderland in 'Once Upon a Planet?'" (Oh no! It's the *Trek* Animated Series!) Hope you've got the answer because "HAILING FREQUENCIES CLOSED!!" Time's up—did you guess Majel Barrett? Or perhaps Abe Vigoda, as some chose to answer? The correct answer is "Nichelle Nichols." BirdOfPrey and DocObee, two AOL *Trek* Club forum staffers host a real-time trivia game every Saturday night at 11 p.m. ET. Another real-time trivia game, based on *The Next Generation* and hosted by NetTrekker and Data1701D, is held every Friday night at 11 p.m. ET on The Bridge, the *Star Trek* Club forum's live chat room. Both of these games are extremely popular, and The Bridge is always filled to capacity with trivia-meisters, so get there early to get a place on board.
AMERICA ONLINE *keyword* trek→The Bridge

 STAR TREK NEWSGROUPS (REC.ARTS.STARTREK*)
USENET rec.arts.startrek*
picture: WEB http://shuttle.nasa.gov/sts-71/images/sts-63-imax/low_0005.jpg
The heart of Net Trekdom is the rec.arts.startrek.* news hierarchy, which consists of two primary groups: rec.arts.startrek.current (discussion of first-run and forthcoming *Trek* shows, books, movies, and paraphernalia) and rec.arts.startrek.misc (discussion of *Trek* in general). For more

advanced Trekkers, the hierarchy also includes rec.arts.startrek.fandom (fan conventions and politics), rec.arts.startrek.tech (brain-bending physics and fancy), rec.arts.startrek.info (FAQs and announcements) and rec.arts.startrek.reviews (critical analyses). Quirkier, non-rec.arts.startrek* fixes are in the alt hierarchy—alt.sex.fetish.startrek and alt.wesley.crusher.die.die.die among them. Engage!

The Star Trek Zone Ranking *Trek* sites on the ol' starship scale, the Star Trek Zone is no USS *Defiant*, but it's not a shuttle craft either. Think of it as the USS *Grissom*—visually appealing without packing all that much firepower. Full of graphics, there are scads of pretty pictures, yet nothing that any *Trek* fan hasn't been exposed to many times before. The listing of actors' birthdays is rather unique, but the trivia questions are fairly unchallenging and most of the links are unremarkable. One notable exception: a connection to the "music" of the *Star Trek* actors, including Brent Spiner's unforgivable *Ol' Yellow Eyes is Back*. As Spock would say, "Argh—pain! Pain!"
WEB http://wane-arc.scri.fsu.edu /~janecek/trekkie.html

The Terran Web Node of Andrew C. Eppstein If you can tolerate his interminable boasting about attending Yale, the Terran Web Node of interstellar blowhard Andrew C. Eppstein is an above-average nexus of *Star Trek* bric-a-brac. Andy does have a springy sense of humor with which he peppers his page, as well as the good taste to present only the finest (but least widespread) graphics. His offering of links is rewarding, particularly since he offers a synopsis of each one so you won't be clicking away blindly. No visit would be complete without a stop to the hilarious "Captain Kirk Sing-A-Long" and the ludicrous "Particles of

Care Bear assimilation
http://www4.ncsu.edu/eos/users/d/dsaraned/WWW/borg.html

Star Trek." Finally, as proof that he has friends, he offers links to his cronies' non-*Trek* pages.
WEB http://pantheon.cis.yale.edu /~acepps/acepps.html

Aliens

alt.shared-reality.startrek.klingon
The Klingon role-playing newsgroup is similar to long-established newsgroups such as alt.dragons-inn and alt.callahans: Users post role-playing style messages for others and collectively create stories in which all play a part. Please be aware that a.s-r.s.k is not for people to come in, post a one-liner, and then wait for someone to respond. Messages are expected to be fairly lengthy, with a description of your character's participation in the story as well as the surroundings and

character development such as inner thoughts, life history, plans, and dreams. New characters can join—for example, if after reading a series of messages, you could create the role of a Klingon crewman in for a drink at the bar, walk into the bar and "note the fist fight between the two drunken officers, pay it no heed, and step over the comatose form of Captain Krang on the floor next to the Terran jukebox..." and go on from there.
USENET alt.shared-reality.startrek .klingon

alt.startrek.bajoran Clear away the deep drifts of spam and you'll find some Bajoran-related discussions here, but the forum, at the moment, tends to slip into various marginally related topics. Your best bet for

finding a thread of interest is to start one—the area is visited often, and you never know who might show up.
USENET alt.startrek.bajoran

alt.startrek.klingon The newsgroup for those who find mainstream *Star Trek* fandom too milquetoast and sissified—you might call them the Weathermen of the Trekkers. This is a group of irritable idealists who seem to have an insane amount of free time on their hands—enough to have learned Klingon, the velar- and glottal-laden tongue spoken by the warlike aliens. Want to know the Klingon for "meter maid?" Someone did, because the readers of this newsgroup had a whole

thread about it. Alt.startrek.klingon also takes time out to discuss Klingon customs and technology: One discussion centered on the question of how a hostile race could survive to the point where they developed spaceflight. The highlight of this group is the translations of Klingon dialog in the movies and TV shows. If the readers here are telling the truth, the Klingons we see onscreen have a very (ahem) spicy vocabulary.
USENET alt.startrek.klingon

alt.startrek.romulan After a thorough application of Spam-B-Gone, this area will yield some pretty decent Romulan news and information, including the

name and address of an international club sponsoring everything from War College classes and fanzines to a bimonthly newsletter for beings whose blood runs green.
USENET alt.startrek.romulan

The Cardassian Page Every aspect of *Star Trek* has its own group of fans. Cardassians are the none-too-handsome tyrants of *Star Trek: Deep Space Nine*. The fans of the ugly despots have set up an Internet home, albeit a tiny one, and joining their club gets you a T-shirt. Free online features include Cardassian wallpaper, image and sound files, plus a lot of gossip on the actors who seem to be genuinely nice people

Trek Reviews Archive

WEB http://www.mcs.net/~forbes/trek-reviews

picture: WEB http://sunsite.doc.ic.ac.uk/media/visual/collections/icdoc

If you haven't visited the rec.arts.startrek.reviews newsgroup lately, or if you want to know what they think of anything even remotely *Star Trek*-related, transport yourself to this spot and indulge in volume after volume of reviews. The busy fingers of this group have touched upon every episode

Location: http://sunsite.doc.ic.ac.uk/media/visual/collections/

past and present, plus all the movies and most of the books. The index is easier to read than an Academy star map, so finding some opinions on the latest *Deep Space Nine* episode is no problem. Those who post here are also very spoiler-conscious, and will give you plenty of fair warning before ruining any episode for you with their review.

under all that gruesome makeup. How they remain pleasant after enduring those torturous makeup sessions, we'll never know.
WEB http://members.gnn.com /cardassia/prime.html

Klingon World Home Page At long last, the Klingons have a site that rivals what those gee-whiz, high-tech goody-goody Federation folks offer. Klingon World Home Page has an interface like the computers on the Klingon ships, an online encyclopedia, and all the other goodies you'd expect in a top-notch resource for a sci-fi show. You've got info on fan clubs and soon-to-be-released CD-ROMs, plus the answer to that all-important question: Just where do they get those impressive leather uniforms?
WEB http://www.itw.com/~zer0

Kronos (the Klingons) The Klingon discussion "We are Klingons!" became so large, they gave the Klingons a per-manent folder on AOL's *Star Trek* Club. If you've longed to try Boiling Worm Wine and Slimy Tongue Balls, but just can't find the recipes, stop by. A great resource for Klingon warriors-in-training, you can talk about anything here as long as it's Klingon. Are Klingons alien Samurai? Well, did you know, for instance, that the Klingon martial art, Mok'bara, is based on Tai Chi? Or that the bat'telh, the Klingon "Sword of Honor," is based on an ancient Chinese

battle sword? You can also get information on Klingon ships, the Klingon Assault Groups, the Klingon Language Institute, and the myriad other Klingon organizations.
AMERICA ONLINE *keyword* trek→ Message Boards→Kronos (the Klingons)

The Q Continuum Presented in a straightforward manner, but stuffed with delicious and numerous Q-ish links, The Q Continuum explores various aspects of Q-ness, from inquiries into the nature of their being to news about *Trek* stars' (particularly John De Lancie's) personal appearances and conventions.
WEB http://www.europa.com /~mercutio/Q.html

Vulcan-L Do you fancy yourself a sort of Surak, a man who will lead his society out of vio-lent turmoil into a New Eden of logical precision? Do you have a second eyelid? Or are you just hungry for a little *Pon farr*? If you've answered yes to any of these questions, you may want to subscribe to the Vulcan mailing list, which dis-cusses issues of Vulcan cul-ture, philosophy, physiology, and technology. Regular con-tributors include several stu-dents of extraplanetary studies at the Science Academy in the Eridani system (on the planet "which you call Vulcan") who claim to patch into the Inter-net through subspace frequen-cies. As is the case in most *Star Trek* forums, members

just can't resist speaking in character. Those whose ear-points have been worn dull through misuse or neglect need not apply.
EMAIL majordomo@netcom.com ✎
Type in message body: subscribe vulcan-l ⟨your email address⟩

The Wonderful World of Borg You will come to this page. Resistance is futile. Wallpaper your screen with images of Locutus or the whole wacky collective. Check out the cheesy puns—Why wasn't Jean-Luc naturally a Borg? Because he wasn't Bjorn Borg—who knew they were such fun-lovin cut-ups? Study Cubism (the archi-tecture for Borg ships) at the Borg Institute of Technology. Sing along with the dowload-able Borg Theme Song, or hear the Borg recite such memorable zingers as "Surrender or we will destroy your ship" or "Death is irrelevant." You might as well bulk up on your Borg lore now, because they will assimilate you.
WEB http://www4.ncsu.edu/eos/users /d/dsaraned/WWW/borg.html

Federation

Starfleet Intelligence Cardassian agent Lt. Durham has infiltrat-ed Starfleet data banks through a security feed at Deep Space Nine. As a result, information on everything from Vulcan philosophy to Ferengi slang to Klingon chocolate has been forwarded to Cardassian lead-ers. That same information was also inadvertently posted

on Earth's World Wide Web. Which is fortunate for us, as this is a great selection of *Star Trek* links that pays particular attention to the various races in the *Trek* universe. Jump from here to language generators, characters' home pages and even a wide variety of newsgroups and newsletters. And be sure to take a look at the Borg Institute of Technology, where "Graduation is Futile."
WEB http://www.wctc.net/~durham

United Federation of Planets Like most enormous bureaucracies, the United Federation of Planets does things the hard way and does it poorly. Swearing to "Promote all that is good and remove all that is evil" (funny, we don't remember that slogan from any episode), the UFP offers a ponderous search engine coupled with shreds of text-only information on the Starship *Enterprise*. In fact, most of the links here take you to non-*Trek* shareware and FTP programming campaigns. You come away with the feeling that this Federation is actually a cartel of alien computer geeks posing as intergalactic politicians.
WEB http://www.ufp.org

Fan fiction

alt.startrek.creative There's a lot of general *Trek* discussion here, but this is also the best place to discuss the hundreds of *Trek* books in circulation, and discover the freshest fan fiction. Anything goes here—including slash fiction, interspecies sex, and just plain strange couplings (Janeway and Riker? Unlikely.) If your tastes don't run to erotica, you have two choices: go elsewhere, or post your own story. In fact the non-erotic fan fic tend to be some of the best around—after all, what is *Trek* without dialogue like this: Kes sits back, and sighs. Tuvok is about to say something, but she's too quick for him... "Mister Tuvok! You said that with a positive twinkle in your eye! It looks to me like you've discovered the comic potential of hyperbole." "That would be

THE COLLECTIVE
WEB http://webpages.marshall.edu/~swann1/borg.htmlx
picture: WEB http://www.wu-wien.ac.at/usr/h92/h9200084/gfe.html
Trekkers who "wish to improve themselves" or find their "defensive capabilities useless" may want to lose all sense of individuality, join the collective, and even email the Borg. There are the requisite episode summaries, but The Collective's webmaster goes one step further, presenting a few

"lost" episodes. For fun, find out just how screwed Bill Gates would be if he took on the Borg, and discover secret connections with *The Simpsons*. There's also a top ten list, which informs you of ways in which you can surmise whether or not your roommate is a Borg ("Your entertainment center disappears, and two days later he's wearing it").

ALL ABOUT THE BIG E

WEAPONS AND FIRING DATA

Beam Weapon type: FH-15
Number: 1
Firing Arcs: 300
degreee collimator arc
Missle Weapon Type: FP-10
Number: 4
Firing Arcs: 3

OPERATION CAPABILITIES

Crusing Range: 25,570
light years
Expected lifetime: 35 years
Average time until resup-
ply: 12 years
Estimated time between
refittings 5 years

POWER GENERATION

Primary: Third Generation
Multi-Field Warp Drive
Secondary: Chioks Fusion
Reactors A-D
Tertiary: Mark-9 Solar
Battery Collectors

POWER OUTPUT

Maximum Speed: Warp
9.95 l
Interval from Subspace to
warp l: 1.2 microseconds

—from United Federation of Planets

impossible. You know as well as I, Kes, that my eyes do not twinkle."
USENET alt.startrek.creative

LCARS: Alexi Kosut's Star Trek Page While this Web page links to some of the more serious *Trek* sites on the Net, its focus is on *Trek* fun. Drop by to read the Silly Top Ten lists, *Trek* filks, or Alexi Kosut's own fan fiction—*Star Trek: Affliction of Paradise* and *Star Trek: Return to Hellgate*.
WEB http://www.nueva.pvt.kl2.ca.us /~akosut/startrek

Trek Fan Fiction In the story "Star Trek: Destinies," the author writes "Time is about to meet its end..." In "Nightmares from a Distant Time," the story is one "of loyalty tested, of friendship held, of faith's tenaciousness. It's the story of the heart of a Bajoran..." And, in "Kirk's Other Enterprise," the story suggests an alternative to the movie *Generations* in which Kirk doesn't buy the farm. Written by AOLers, these are just a few of the *Trek* stories, parodies, and filks archived in the *Star Trek* Club.
AMERICA ONLINE *keyword* trek→ Record Banks→Fiction

Fan clubs & conventions

Star Trek Conventions This is the only place you need to aim your mouse for online information on *Star Trek* conventions. A far-ranging listing of national and international cons, the only drawback is that they're listed by date, so it takes a measure of browsing to find one in your area. Postings are free, so gatherings both large and small are available. The site also sponsors a convention of sorts every night with live chat from 9 p.m. to 9 a.m. EST. Since this site is a subsidiary of World Wide Collectors Digest, you can also link to info about all kinds of collectibles, from pogs to telephone cards.
WEB http://www.wwcd.com/shows /strekconv.html

Games

alt.starfleet.rpg Ensign Fred(dy) Krueger of the USS *Excalibur* detects an energy build-up on Mockra IX. "I have never seen such immense energy concentrated in one place," he reports to his superiors. "Perhaps this is a new type of power generator the Borg are after." Meanwhile, Lieutenant Cameron Raeghar of the U.S.S. *Caesar Augustus* tests the distortion field and works on modifications to the third warp nacelle. It's a tough job, but somebody's got to do it. In this active role-playing club loosely based on *Star Trek: The Next Generation*, members create characters and weave an action-oriented interactive fiction. To get started, look for the Starfleet Command document SF.RPG FAQ, frequently posted to the group and available at the newsgroup's Web site. Before you join, be sure to read the FAQ, the Starfleet Manual, and the etiquette document. You'll start off as a lowly ensign, but you can move up the ranks quickly; your progress is gauged by the skill and frequency of your posts. Become a regular, and you'll be at the front lines staving off the Borg in no time.

USENET alt.starfleet.rpg

Archives: **WEB** http://rzstudl.rz .uni-karlsruhe.de/~ukea

Starfleet Online (SFOL) So you want to explore the universe? Interested in making friends from distant planets? Wesley and Nog are your role models? Consider joining Starfleet. You'll have to attend the Academy, where you'll learn how to role-play *Trek* adventures: an attack by the Borg, a plot contrived by the Romulans, a Klingon trial of honor, a warp drive failure, etc. Even if in an alternate universe (or different Net site) you had risen to the position of captain

or admiral, you still have to begin as a cadet here. Drop by the Starfleet Resource Center and the Starfleet Misc Articles archive in Starfleet Online for some background on what SFOL is and what you need to know to get through the Academy. Here in the bowels of the libraries, you'll be able to read the cadet manuals on ships, ranks, races, locations, and technology.

AMERICA ONLINE *keyword* academy

Star Trek Tridimensional Chess Another set of rules for the multi-level chess game made popular by Kirk and Spock which continues to be played by members on *DS9*. No set of rules for the game were

revealed on the show, but *Trek* fans have come up with their own.

AMERICA ONLINE *keyword* trek→ Record Banks→Text/Other Files→ Tri-Dimensional Chess Rules

Books & collectibles

Playmates Toys Few people understand the unadulterated joy of finding an unopened Playmates figure that you've despaired of getting because you live in the only town in America that doesn't have its *Trek*-collectibles-act together. Sigh. But here, the success stories just roll in. From Utah: "I just got back from my local toy store with Data in dress uniform and ENSIGN RO!" From

Star Trek Club

AMERICA ONLINE *keyword* trek

One of America Online's most active areas, the Star Trek Club is host to several live *Trek* trivia games each week (quick, what's the name of Jean-Luc Picard's sister-in-law? And name the three actors that have played Picard), a monthly club newsletter, new stories submitted every day by

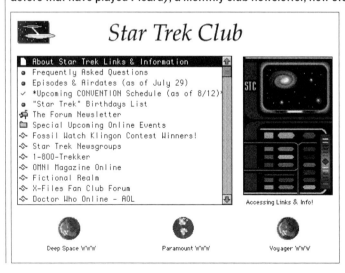

Deep Space WWW   Paramount WWW   Voyager WWW

aspiring *Trek* writers, and suitably passionate discussions about *Trek* aliens, spaceships, *Deep Space Nine*, and the Prime Directive. The club menu features a schedule for the current series, a list of upcoming conventions, a schedule of Club activities, a message board, file libraries, and The Bridge (live chat). If you have any questions, transport to the Promenade and visit the Questions/Help w/Datatl7OID topic.

Knoxville, Tenn.: "You can find everything at Wal-Mart." And, in Virginia, there's both success and failure: "Just found the Klingon Generations Bird of Prey! It is absolutely BEAUTI-FUL. The lights and stand and everything makes it, what I believe, to be the best ship produced yet! Definitely better than the battle-damaged *Enterprise*." But... "Hugh Borg is not that abundant."
AMERICA ONLINE *keyword* trek→ Message Boards→The Promenade→ PLAYMATES Buy/Sell/Trade

TNG Books/Mags Everybody here has a favorite *Trek* book to recommend—though be warned —they're not part of the *Trek* canon. But, given that *TNG* episodes are now only in syndication and movies only happen every couple of years, *TNG* books will be the only steady source for new adventures with Picard and crew. When a high school English teacher asked for help picking her first *Trek* novel (she loved the episodes "Offspring" and "Inner Light"), a fellow teacher responded: "Being an ex-high school/university English instructor, I, too, prefer books with strong character development over those with a lot of special effects and 'battle scenes.' My favorite four are 'Imzadi' (a MUST read!), 'Q-in-Law' (funniest *Trek* book yet), and 'Q-Squared'—all by Peter David—and 'Guises of the Mind' (great discussions on religious tolerance and Data's search for God) by Rebecca Neason."

AMERICA ONLINE *keyword* message boards→The Next Generation→ TNG Books/Mags

Treknology

rec.arts.sf.science The regulars of this newsgroup don't limit their conversations to the pseudo-science of sci-fi; discussions also include hyperspace, intelligence enhancement, and the possibility of receiving phone calls from the future. One thread concerned the writing of a "future history." Some of the predictions for the next couple of centuries: genetic tailoring of bacteria, education by virtual reality, the arrival of alien missionaries. This is a friendly and intelligent group of sci-fi-addicted science types, including some youngsters; Damian, an eighth-grader into astronomy, posted a question about chaos theory.
USENET rec.arts.sf.science

rec.arts.startrek.tech The heart of *Star Trek* may well be its human (and alien) relationships, but its soul, surely, is its new machines. Where would *Trek* be without the flash of phasers, the zoom of silver ships, the mix of whimsy and hard science in the Cochrane Drive? Well, it wouldn't be in eternal syndication and box-office nirvana, anyway. Rec.arts.startrek.tech is perhaps the most curious of the rec.arts.startrek* groups, requiring its participants to find semi-rational explanations for

implausible, and often inconsistent, Treknology. How does a deflector shield work? A warp drive? A phaser? A transporter? (This last one, at least, is easy—it has something to do with Heisenberg Compensators and Annular Confinement Beams.) This is the most male-dominated of the rec.arts .startrek* groups, since it caters expressly to boys-and-their-toys conversation. Still, always an interesting read—not least when RAST'ers gather together to pound *Trek* for tripping itself up with YATIs (Yet Another Technical Inconsistency). Back to the drawing boards...
USENET rec.arts.startrek.tech

Battle of the captains

Kirk v. Picard Over the last couple of years, countless threads have debated the relative merits of the two captains. This is a collection of some of those lists, including the top 100 reasons why Kirk is better than Picard and a point-by-point response by Picard fans. Just listen: "Kirk has sex more than once a season." Rejoinder: "Sex with Picard is worth waiting for a whole season." "Kirk never once stood up and had to straighten his shirt." Rejoinder: "Picard never once stood up and had to suck in his gut." "Kirk never asks his bartender for advice." Rejoinder: "Picard never asks his Chief Medical Officer to be bartender." And, that's only three.
WEB http://ftp.cis.ksu.edu/pub/alt.star trek.creative/misc/Kirk.v.Picard.zip

Reasons Why Captain Janeway is Better Than Captain Picard The top 73 list, because you demanded it. And it goes beyond the expected hair jokes by entry number three—hey, now that's an accomplishment by itself.
WEB http://hou.lbl.gov/~gmonsen/janeway.html

The original series

Largent's No New Trek Guide Webmaster Largent waxes nostaligic about a time when *Trek* depended more on imagination than special FX. To that end, he dedicates this guide to the original series'

crew and villains, with episode guides that contain a little bit of trivia and a lot of memories and opinions about each show. The site may not have much new information, if any, but Largent's enthusiasm and point of view will invigorate many TOS fans.
WEB http://www.msms.doe.k12.ms.us/~mlargent/Trek.html

Star Trek: The Original Series Central Do you want a picture of Captain Sulu aboard the *Excelsior* signed by George Takei? Or pictures of many of the members of the TOS crew, autographed by the actors? Of course you do. Surf to yet

another of Jeff "Koganuts" Koga's picture galleries for nice (but static) publicity photo shots from the later *Trek* movies. Aside from being a great source for pics, Koga's pages (there are similar offerings for the other shows) are also fantastic starting points for linking to sites about *Trek* and other SF entities.
WEB http://underground.net/~koganuts/Galleries/sttos.html

The Next Generation

alt.sexy.bald.captains Dominated by a group calling itself the Patrick Stewart Estrogen Brigade ("that's PSEB, with a

THE CAPT. JAMES T. KIRK SING-A-LONG PAGE

WEB http://www.ama.caltech.edu/users/mrm/kirk.html

No matter what his other accomplishments may be, fans will never forget, or let William Shatner live down, his 1968 album *The Transformed Man*. It's in such demand that collectors will gladly

Location: http://www.ama.caltech.edu/users/mrm/kirk.html

"Quit playing on the Web you geeks! Get a life!"

part with an arm or an antenna for the original pressing. Exactly why is one of the great mysteries of the universe. If you want to hear bits of the songs at a bargain price, download them for use with the Netscape audio player. Then you'll see why Shatner never hit the top of the charts.

NO TREK LIKE THE FIRST TREK

"Space: the final frontier..." There's magic in those words. As a child, those words guaranteed incredible adventures on unimagined worlds. With the U.S. space program still in high gear, I could let myself believe that someday, maybe in my lifetime, we would live that dream. Of course, that didn't happen; but I didn't let go of the dreams.

Star Trek was an incredible vehicle for the imagination. Cops and Robbers, Cowboys and Indians, all those childhood games paled next to playing *Star Trek*. In *Star Trek*, there were no limits, no boundaries. My backyard became another planet (so did the front-yard, for that matter), and with the mind's eye, it was far more exciting, far greater, far more wonderous than the bleak stretch of grass and dirt it was in reality.

To those unlucky children who grew up too late, *Star Trek* may seem unrealistic, but that just shows that they've got underdeveloped imaginations. When you can make an old sprayer nozzle from a kitchen sink a phaser and believe in it, you don't need special effects.

So that's it. If you came here thinking that I was going to have a huge debate about which Trek is better, then you've been led astray. There is no new Trek here, because this is a page dedicated to what inspired my imagination as a child. If you're one of those lucky ones like me, then go through these pages and remember the magic, the wonder, and the dreams.

—from Largent's No New Trek Guide

silent P, as in psychotic," notes one member). Devotees post their desire to "grope him like a piece of meat." Three members visited New York to see Stewart in "A Christmas Carol," and after the show, they got to touch him! ("Yes, my shaking little hand reached out and gently stroked the captain's l-l-l-leather jacket. It was lovely.") Of course, Picard's not the only bald captain to lust after... there's always *The Love Boat*'s Captain Stubing.

This is certainly one of the strangest spots on the Net; an amusing frontier for lurkers.
USENET alt.sexy.bald.captains

Star Trek: The X Generation The USS *AMC Pacer* treks through space with Captain Jean-Luc Slackard in command, to boldly go... in style. Much of the crew spends most of their time thinking up cool band names, playing air guitar, and getting tattoos. Most inspired casting is Lt. Waif, a painfully

thin Klinger (the codependent version of Klingons) with stringy hair who enjoys walking about the starship in designer jeans and no top. It's a cool mix of social and *Trek* commentary, with no real fiction yet, but the webmaster welcomes more ideas to expand this slacker universe.
WEB http://www.netaxs.com/~tgi /stxgen/xgen.html

Starbase 211 The well-executed main information kiosk lets you interface with a Starfleet computer and access the Federation database. Starfleet vessel specs, with each ship's complement of crew members and maximum speed and ordnance capabilities, are the type of stats you'll be able to access. Visit the Klingon, Romulan, or Ferengi home worlds. Take the Starfleet Academy entrance exam (this is pretty serious stuff—if you get more than 15 out of 30 right you might want to seek professional help), and see if you've got what it takes to fly around the Milky Way in a brightly colored, crotch-grabbing jumpsuit.
WEB http://www.efn.org/~d_mills /top.html

Warped Trek: The Next Generation A site that was initially developed at Paramount, Warped Trek soon went independent for various reasons, and it puts most other fantasy-team matchup pages to shame. Hear compelling sound clips as different TOS and *TNG* characters square off against

one another. Will Spock out-logic Riker? Does Crusher's feminine perspective give her an edge over Bones? With such forceful questions nicely illustrated with color pics, you may not need to follow the links to other *Trek* sites.
WEB http://www.gj.net/~pcconfig/warpl.html

Deep Space Nine

The Deep Space Nine Archive *DS9* fans can come up with their own Rules of Netquisition—patterned after the Ferengi's Rules of Acquisition—for a contest sponsored at this spot. Many of the submitted rules are silly and sound as if Quark himself thought them

up. This information-packed page also boasts episode synopses and production data from the first four seasons of Paramount's *TNG* follow-up. Find out what episode of *DS9* is currently airing in Finland, Japan, New Zealand, and a host of other countries.
WEB http://www.bradley.edu/campusorg/psiphi/DS9

Deep Web Nine Although this site comes with a title that someone, sooner or later would have to have used, the good news is that this is a site that delivers everything you need to know about the shows, and probably more. What about the season-ending cliffhanger on *Star Trek:*

Voyager? What's this about *Star Trek* TOS helmsman Sulu, a.k.a. George Takei, guest-starring on *DS9?* The webmaster quotes the Ferengi Rules of Acquisition ("Keep your ears open") and certainly lives up to it by providing a tremendous, almost intimidating amount of data. Not only can you read about aspects of all the *Trek* series and movies, you can also catch up on the current doings of cast members (guess who's starring in the latest *Trek* CD-ROM interactive game?).
WEB http://www.tut.fi/~pekka

Oops Homepage Welcome to Operations control, the center for *DS9* humor. While some

STAR TREK: THE NEXT GENERATION

WEB http://home.sprynet.com/sprynet/laforge
The well-designed but slightly overwhelming graphics were obviously created with frame-capable browsers in mind. But if you have the equipment, you can access Starfleet personnel profiles and

Location: http://home.sprynet.com/sprynet/laforge/computer.htm

Patrick Stewart on his favorite episode:

The Offspring because it represents all of the things that we have always tried to do on Star Trek: The Next Generation. Also, it has another brilliant performance from Brent Spiner matched by an equally fine performance by Hallie Todd, and because it marked the first opportunity given by the studio for one of us to direct an episode, which Jonathan Frakes did outstandingly.

keep up to stardate on your favorite crew members' stats. *ST: TNG* fonts and screensavers, as well as Jerry Goldsmith's wonderful theme music are available in the file library, but they're Windows-compatible only. Is your warp theory a little rusty? Brush up in the document library. Before you leave, check out the Letterman-esque top ten lists.

bits are inevitably silly (e.g., the long lost Shakespeare play "Deep Space IX"), most of what's here is fairly intelligent and funny. The Plot-o-matic plays on the series' predictability. Bright spots (Why is Sisko better than Picard? He punched Q instead of hiding in his ready room.) will leave you asking for more. Check out the list of famous last words for the series, including this zinger: "I let Nog and Jake take the Defiant out for a spin."
WEB http://metro.turnpike.net /anomaly/oops.htm

Voyager

Adventure: Voyager This beautiful page features an animated starship *Voyager*, Yahoo! *Trek* links, and the webmaster's *Trek* fiction (he's come up with an alternate ending to *Star Trek Generations* that may finally satisfy fans). But this guy isn't just a Trekkie; he's also got sports info here and links to the official sites of the University of Manitoba and *Late Show with David Letterman* (good for keeping up with Brent Spiner interviews.)
WEB http://home.cc.umanitoba.ca /~umsharif

alt.tv.star-trek.voyager The more than 1,000 messages here tell you a hell of a lot about *Trek* fans—chiefly their barely masked misogynist attitude toward Captain Janeway. Besides the expected plot nitpicking, it seems every other message deals with how she

> **ff Why is Sisko better than Picard? He punched Q instead of hiding in his ready room. JJ**

screwed up, how her character is badly written, or how she sounds like Katharine Hepburn on helium. You'll also find the usual rumors (Will the show be canceled? Will Wil Wheaton be added to the cast? Did Robert Picardo actually storm the shores of Normandy on D-Day?) and, of course, discussions about the latest cliffhanger (Should Chakotay have gone after the kid? Why didn't

the Kazon kill them all?).
USENET alt.tv.star-trek.voyager

Riker's Voyager Homepage
Devoted exclusively to Captain Janeway and her crew, this comprehensive page features an updated episode list with corresponding stardates, a healthy selection of *Voyager* images—including some pics that you probably haven't seen a hundred times over—and a generous helping of *Star Trek* links. The original content offered on this page is prefaced with a link to a picture of the webmaster sitting, in full Starfleet regalia, in the captain's chair at the Star Trek Adventure—a theme-park experience that allows you to be a crew member on the *Enterprise*. Is that haircut regulation, Captain?
WEB http://www.itek.net/~riker

Is it me, or does he look *exactly* the same out of makeup?
http://www.calweb.com/~erj/spock_sings.html

Location: http://www.calweb.com/~ejr/spock_sings.html

Fringe

YOU'RE NOT ALONE IN THINKING WE'RE NOT ALONE. FIND AN EMPATHETHIC EAR ONLINE

ALIENS ON THE BRAIN? Literally? That's a problem, but fortunately, you are not alone. Or rather, we are not alone. But you knew that already, if you can remember what happened before the abduction. Maybe you are currently having an out-of-body-experience, in which case you are merely watching yourself read this. But you might want to revisit the corporeal and explore your very own haunted house. Poltergeists, spirits, and hopping ghosts alike are welcome. Skepticism (which is caused by government conspiracy, as you well know) can be an asset when you're learning how to build crop circles or trying to find out who really shot JFK. Anyway, you'll enjoy your venture into the paranormal side of the Internet—that is, if They aren't preventing, through the control chip in your earlobe, any chance you have for future happiness.

Location: http://www.aufora.org/pics/archive/alien00.jpg

AUFORA WEB

WEB http://ume.med.ucalgary.ca/aufora

Did you see flashing lights? A big saucer in the sky? Have a close encounter of the first, second, or third kind? Report it to the Alberta **UFO** Research Association. **AUFORA** Web contains news from that other world of ufology, a guide covering everything from crop circles and cattle mutilations to Area 51 and the Roswell incident, an explanation of **AUFORA**'s investigation procedures, and a picture archive. **AUFORA** Web not only provides links to all the **UFO** sites, newsgroups, and commercial service forums, it also rates them for you. You'll appreciate it once you realize the hundreds of unidentified flying resources that are out there.

Starting points

alt.paranet.* Believers, skeptics, experts, and amused bystanders jump among the family of paranet newsgroups—alt .paranet.abduct, alt.paranet .paranormal, alt.paranet .science, alt.paranet.skeptic, and alt.paranet.ufo—in ongoing discussions about the possibility of aliens and a world beyond. Discussion on these groups tends to be more scientific and serious than its newsgroup counterparts.
USENET alt.paranet.*****

alt.paranormal A well-trafficked newsgroup, despite the fact that most who believe in the paranormal either (a) focus on specific interests, like psychic activity, witchcraft, or alien abduction—which have their own newsgroups—or (b) are members of the somewhat more "serious" alt.paranet groups. Alt.paranormal mostly has dilettantes talking about personal experiences and dabblers asking querulous or curious questions. The gender ratio is fairly even, and the environment relatively flame-free.
USENET alt.paranormal

The Anomalist A twice-yearly periodical reporting on anomalies not only in science, but in history and nature as well. Created by writers, scientists, and investigators, rather than believers or skeptics, expect a balanced publication with justified questions and criticism. Not the place to report Batboy

sitings or musings on when the Venusians are going to return Elvis.
WEB http://cloud9.net/~patrick /anomalistp

Committee for Scientific Investigation of Claims of the Paranormal Home to the *Skeptical Inquirer*, a publication devoted to debunking everything from alien abductions to floral health remedies, this site also lists events sponsored by CSICOP and reprints articles about the organization. One question: If the committee's mission is one of investigating scientific and pseudoscientific events, why didn't its members select the name Scientific Committee for Investigation of Claims of the Paranormal, which would have permitted the acronym SCI-COP?
WEB http://iquest.com/~fitz/csicop

Encounters Forum Associated with the Fox network's *Encounters: The Hidden Truth*, this forum sets out to prove that the world is not an empiricist prison, and that things happen every single day that simply cannot be explained by reasonable scientific minds. The subscribers seem dead serious about their lunch dates with aliens; as one man says, "When my wife started coming up with memories and dream recollections that made me suspect she was a possible abductee, I couldn't ignore it any more. Funny how a thing like that turns your thinking around." *Encounters* also cov-

ers ghosts, spiritualism, possession, and announcements of spoon-bending parties. The staff of the *Encounters* television show frequents this forum looking for stories (strange kangaroo behavior in Australia, sidewalk eating blobs from the sky in San Francisco).
COMPUSERVE *go* encounters

Fortean Times: The Journal of Strange Phenomena One of the more creative paranormal magazine sites, *Fortean Times* has press clippings of reports on UFOs, creationism, and other concepts that are a little hard to swallow. The site contains an image archive of "20 Years of Fortean Photo-Highlights," short stories, and tables of contents for the current and back issues. Oh, and did we mention the page also houses excerpts from the *FT Book of Weird Sex*? Well, you're probably not interested in that kind of thing.
WEB http://alpha.mic.dundee.ac.uk/ft

Paranormal Belief Survey Do you believe in the Loch Ness monster? Do you think the government regularly engages in widespread conspiracies? And most importantly, do you believe that Elvis is still alive? Participate in this survey and make your beliefs and/or paranoia known. The latest results reveal that more than 90 percent of people believe in the existence of extraterrestrials, but only 5 percent think the King lives on.
WEB http://galileo.metatech.com /surveys/paranorm/paranorm.htm

ParaScope An online forum dedicated to exploring the mysteries of the unexplained and unexplainable, from conspiracies and UFOs to paranormal phenomena. Contributors search for concrete answers to some of life's most puzzling mysteries, fostering an atmosphere where cyberbelievers can explore ideas and concepts ignored or ridiculed by the mainstream media. The Matrix area covers conspiracies and scandals. Enigma covers paranormal phenomena. Nebula focuses on aliens and UFOs. And Dossier offers "evidence" in the form of government reports, corporate memos, and more.
AMERICA ONLINE *keyword* **parascope**

PAW Resources for the paranormally-inclined, organized by preternatural pages covering tarot, astrology, palmistry, ouija, occult resources, and parapsychology.
WEB http://www-scf.usc.edu/~siddique/PAW.HTML

The Shadowlands Vampyres, and ghosts, and witches. Oh my! Plus a wealth of information on spirits, the supernatural, the occult, horror, psychic subjects, Big Foot, Loch Ness, UFOs, the Bermuda triangle, folklore, ancient mysteries, and other unknowns. This site is overseen by the Shadow Lord, of course.
WEB http://www.serve.com/shadows/index2.htm

Unexplained Phenomena Strange things happen, and sometimes they happen within earshot of people who subscribe to CompuServe. For instance, 1,700 head of cattle might disappear from a heartland farm or a 17-year-old girl in Palisades Park might suddenly begin to speak fluent Egyptian. What can account for these mysterious events? Well, according to CompuServe's Unexplained Phenomena message board, the answer is simple: aliens! This is not just a place for speculation on the extraterrestrial and/or paranormal (for that, see CompuServe's Encounters forum). There's also plenty of entertaining chat about the Kennedy assassina-

THE GHOSTWATCHER

WEB http://www.flyvision.org/sitelite/Houston/GhostWatcher/index.html

Do you ever hear strange sounds coming from your closet or worry about what may lurk underneath your bed? June does. Help her get a good night's sleep. Through the magic of the CU-SeeMe cam, you can keep an eye on the platform under her bed, inside her trunks, and on strategic points in her basement while she gets some shuteye. Some volunteer ghostwatchers advise June to be

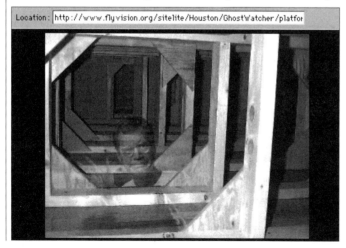

assertive: "If your ghosts are acting up **GET RID OF THEM.** Get a priest, get a medium, get *Sightings* to come in and broadcast live from your house. But get them out. If they're just causing a lot of noise, and you can live with that, then by all means, let them stay. Just remember who's the boss of the house."

tion and unorthodox techniques for scuba breathing. **COMPUSERVE** issues→Libraries *or* Messages→Unexplained Phenomena

The WWW Virtual Library: Paranormal Phenomena Archive X is devoted to maintaining a record of the supernatural sightings and experiences of cybersurfers. Submit or scroll through ghost stories and folklore, angel encounters, channelings, near-death experiences, and UFO sightings. Leave your email address and you'll be notified each time new experiences are posted. **WEB** http://www.crown.net/X

Hauntings

A Spectre Search Some folks turn to Zagat's, or Fodor's, or even AAA to decide how to spend their dining and entertainment dollar. Others use the Spectre Search, a travel directory of haunted dining and lodging in the U.S. For an unexpected (and undead) guest at dinner, try the Crier in the Country Restaurant in Glen Mills, Penn. Or try the Captain Lord Mansion in Maine, and keep an eye out for the captain's widow who floats across the floor in the Lincoln Room and on the stairs. Don't worry about the rates—the extra spirits in your room stay free. **WEB** http://web2.airmail.net/spectre1 /source/page0.html

alt.folklore.ghost-stories Keeping the oral tradition alive in the

COME ON, LET'S NOT GET PARANOID HERE

"It's pretty amusing, when you think about it. The number of individuals claiming abduction is so great I'm surprised there's room in the sky for vehicles of Earth origin. Don't these ET's have lives?"—Bill

"Goin out for an abduction, Ma. Be back for dinner."—Eric

"Don't forget your genital probes, dear."—Bryan

"If the number of persons allegedly abducted is even 10-percent of those reported, it's the greatest case of mass-kidnapping ever conceived. I would expect the Guvmint to be saying: uh, excuse me. What are you guys doing with our citizens?"—Jethro

"Currently, I'm favoring the theory (reported in *X-Files* scripts and elsewhere) that the Guvmint itself is behind the abduction phenomena."—Bubba

"It's doing something with its citizens and planting false memories."—Bill

—from alt. paranet.abduct

age of cyberspace, talk here tends to focus on the spreading of supernatural tales. You'll also find plenty of discussion of ghost-themed movies and ghost mythos surrounding the making of them. **USENET** alt.folklore.ghost-stories *FAQ:* **WEB** http://www.lib.ox.ac.uk /internet/news/faq/archive/folklore .ghost-stories.html

The Ghost Pages Become a ghost links research assistant. If you've seen a ghost, be prepared to provide not only the who, when, and where of the sighting, but also answers to such questions as, "What color was the ghost?" "Did it glow?" and "Did it try to communicate

with you?" All you'll get in return, however, is the satisfaction of helping one researcher with his work in the spirit world. **WEB** http://www.lookup.com /Homepages/71229/home.html

Ghosts What's the difference between a ghost and a ghoul? A poltergeist and a psychopomp? This haunting site contains a guide to the undead, with such entries as radiant boys (also know as *kindermordernin*, boys murdered by their mothers), spunkie (a goblin or trickster ghost), and golem (an artificial human made by magical means). An index of hauntings, a ghost

bibliography, and links to other sites of the supernatural are also available.
WEB http://star06.atklab.yorku.ca /~peterpan/ghost.html

The Phantom's Closet Ghost hunter Richard Senate invites you into his closet and provides you with a list of everything you'll need when in hot pursuit of the undead and the best places to search for the specters. What you do with the ghost when you catch it is up to you. They make a great baby shower gift; who needs another Gund Bear?
WEB http://www.phantoms.com /~phantom/ghost.htm

What Is a Hopping Ghost? The Chinese honor their dead, and for good reason. They believe an unsatisfied soul can become a ghost and make life unbearable when, in some cases, they literally become hopping mad. This page answers questions on one of their more animated apparitions making star appearances on the Hong Kong movie scene.
WEB http://www.resort.com/~banshee /Misc/hopping_ghost.html

Where the Ghouls Are Skeletons in the closet? A one-page listing of the most noteworthy haunted houses according to international "authority" on the topic, Dennis William Hauck, from Chatham Manor in Fredericksburg, Va. to the White House across the river.
WEB http://www.obs-us.com/obs /english/books/pg/pg527.htm

UFOs & aliens

Alien Exploratorium A cyberclearinghouse of alien "intelligence," including stories of mass abductions, abductions at the White House, a rundown of types of aliens from the Greys to lizard people, as well as government conspiracy and coverup theories. Note: Information on alien autopsies and cattle mutilations, however implausible, is not for the faint of heart.
WEB http://area51.upsu.plym.ac.uk /~moosie/ufo/aexplo.htm

Aliens, Aliens, Aliens If you have question about whether there's other "intelligent" life out there, put them to rest with one visit here. After perusing some

of the posts of visitors to this page: "Aliens rule. I want to be abducted, and lose my virginity to some terrestrial chick," your new question will be, "Is there intelligent life down here?"
WEB http://www.xensei.com/users /john9904

alt.alien.visitors The group that epitomizes the kook ecosystem, alt.alien.visitors is almost equal parts *True Believers*, scientists, Net bystanders, and kookwatchers—existing, if not in harmony, then in synchronicity. Discussion of crop circles, the "Greys" (insectoid ETs whose activities have been documented, sort of), Erich Von Daniken, and biblical proof of aliens sits side by side

Norman Bates' oceanfront property
http://web2.airmail.net/spectrel/source/page0.html

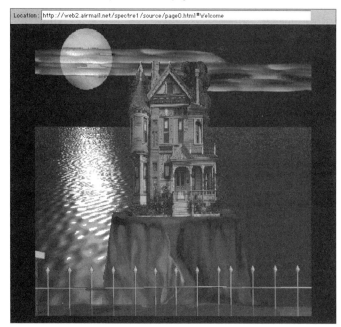

Location : http://web2.airmail.net/spectre1/source/page0.html#Welcome

with utterly hilarious posts mocking the UFO party line. One ongoing, somewhat paranoid thread concerns whether alt.alien.visitors is now "moderated," i.e., screened for improper—or overly revelatory?—posts. The conclusion anyone might draw from actually reading alt.alien.visitors is: No. If you're a True Believer or Scientific, watch for the posts of Earl Dumbrowski, a level-headed, empirical researcher and enthusiast of UFOs. If you're more inclined to see the whole thing as a gas, watch for the posts of the Hastings UFO Society, which claim to be channeled onto the group by a psychic named Madame Thelma. The posts, documenting the activities and beliefs of a UFO club somewhere out in Hooterville, are so strange and well-written, you might just believe—for a second—that the society exists, before you fall down laughing.
USENET alt.alien.visitors

The EBE Page The Extraterrestrial Biological Entity Page is actually a list of links to more than 200 sites categorized by The Roswell Incident, Area 51 at Groom Lake, unidentified flying objects, abductions, crop circles, Internet resources, off-the-Net resources, multimedia, and personal experiences.
WEB http://sloop.ee.fit.edu/users /lpinto/index.html

Faking UFOs The cybercharlatan's guide to making people think they've seen a UFO.

Some of these actually might work if you have a lot of time on your hands. Roel van der Meulen provides how-tos for creating close encounters using hang gliders and balloons as well as instructions for leaving crop circles. Wacky antics and emotional breakdowns are sure to follow!
WEB http://www.strw.leidenuniv.nl /~vdmeulen/Articles/UFOfake.html

Internet UFO Group IUFOG is not a formal UFO investigative organization. Instead, it is an attempt to organize WWW and traditional authors of UFO and EBE pages into one cohesive cybermovement. It appears the effort was not in vain. Some must-reads: "The Ten Most Compelling UFO Cases in History," "Cosmic Conspiracy: Six Decades of Government UFO Cover-ups" (from *OMNI*), and "Stupid Government Tricks." The IUFOG site also includes a database of research, events, and sightings; a media page of clippings and press releases; and a library of books, periodicals, and 'zines.
WEB http://members.aol.com/iufog /index.html

Skywatch International A pilot in California reports two large, bizarre red lights hovering "at 245 degrees, 45 degrees up" which fade sequentially. The same night, an anonymous female caller reports that multiple observers see two bright red lights hovering in night sky. Across town, a man also

reports two bright red lights hovering together "35 degrees to the left of Venus" which move in formation to the left and disappear. Is it a bird? Is it a plane? No, it's one of hundreds of sightings maintained by the National UFO Reporting Center. At Skywatch International, you'll find the center's monthly reports with accompanying maps as well as a gateway to a galaxy of UFO and EBE information, including photos of UFOs, government documents, and another "authentic alien autopsy." Jonathan Frakes is on the case.
WEB http://www.wic.net/colonel /ufopage.htm

UFO Folklore Whether it's up-to-date UFO news and press releases, Freedom of Information Act documents, or speculation about the vaults at Wright-Patterson Air Force Base, cattle "moo-tilations", and the MJ-12 documents, each piece of evidence at this site is treated with appropriate skepticism until it is proven fact. Among the more interesting tidbits of trivia in this comprehensive collection of extra-terrestrial information is a U.S. law on the books in 1969 that specifically prohibited astronauts from making contact with aliens.
WEB http://www.qtm.net/~geibdan /framemst.html

The UFO Guide Area 51. Crop Circles. Greys. CE1s, CE2s, CE3s. If it all makes about as much sense to you as a message from outerspace, Nick

Humphries' UFO Guide may be just what you need to brush up on the basics. This extraterrestrial encyclopedia covers the A to Z of UFOs from George Adamski to Zeta Riticuli.
WEB http://www.rahul.net/rogerd /ufo.guide.html

UFO-L Biblical references to UFOs, the disappearance of the Mars observer, lost Soviet probes—what on earth can it all mean? This bunch approaches the idea of extraterrestrial life thoughtfully and seriously. A relatively flameless list for the curious and the almost-convinced to figure it all out together.

EMAIL listserv@brufpb.bitnet ✍ *Type in message body:* subscribe ufo-l ⟨your full name⟩

The Ultimate UFO Page Ufology 101. Touting itself as a rational approach to ufology, TUFOP includes articles exploring whether the alien autopsy film is a scam, the complete Roswell primer, and a survey you can complete electronically to help them out in their UFO/alien abduction research.
WEB http://www.serve.com/tufop

Unexplained Phenomena: Crop Circles A cyber-resource guide to the crop circle phenomenon, in which geometrically intricate

circles appear mysteriously in farmlands. Eighty percent of sightings occur in England, but circles are also reported in Australia, Italy, the U.S., Norway, and Canada. This site points you to the answers which have been formulated to explain the circles and the more puzzling questions that still remain, like: Who are the circle makers? What explains the sound and light which sometimes accompany the appearance of the ancient symbols? And why in the world would aliens want to spend all of their time in a wheat field in Devonshire?
WEB http://www.vuw.ac.nz/~broche /crop.htm

50 Greatest Conspiracies of All Time

WEB http://www.webcom.com/~conspire

This site is so incredible, you'll probably spend all your time on it, drive up phone bills, and not finish any of your other work. And it seems quite likely that your spouse would then have an excellent excuse to divorce you and get the kids. AT&T and Sprint would then drain every last dollar from your savings. And the guy who sits next to you at work would be in a perfect position to take your job. Not

that you should be paranoid. This site was created to advertise a book titled *50 Greatest Conspiracies of All Time*, and includes descriptions of the prize winners (from Kennedy to Jonestown to the Freemasons), offers weekly conspiracy reports, houses an archive of dozens of conspiracy-related interviews and articles, sponsors a contest of "find Oswald," and even links you to the CIA home page.

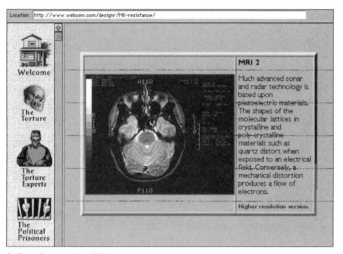

Location: http://www.webcom.com/designr/MK-resistance/

Welcome

The Torture

The Torture Experts

The Political Prisoners

MRI 2

Much advanced sonar and radar technology is based upon piezoelectric materials. The shapes of the molecular lattices in crystalline and poly-crystalline materials such as quartz distort when exposed to an electrical field. Conversely, a mechanical distortion produces a flow of electrons.

Higher resolution version.

A slice of supernatural life
http://www.webcom.com/designr/MK-resistance

To Brian, these are clear signs of psychiatric torture perpetrated by the federal government. Brian exposes "proponents" of these mind games and their torture techniques, explores the unanswered questions of Jonestown, and shares the stories of fellow victims. A side note to would-be flamers —whatever the actual cause, he certainly has enough problems without your comments, don't you think?
WEB http://www.webcom.com/designr/MK-resistance

Conspiracies

alt.conspiracy From the murder of JFK (The Mafia? The Pope?) to the ineffable workings of the Secret Persuaders, alt.conspiracy is perhaps the most "serious" of the "kook" newsgroups. It has the highest ratio of True Believers to kook-watch and flamer types. Which isn't to say there aren't flames here: Everyone's got an agenda or an idiosyncratic belief, and most of them contradict. Wanna watch irresistible forces hit immovable objects? This is a good place to do it. The "NY News Collective—All the News that Doesn't Fit" posts reprints of articles condemning government activities. Meanwhile, on an individual basis, Brian Redman keeps flames high with his "Conspiracy of the Day" posts, lengthy digressions on topics ranging from the International AIDS Con-

spiracy to, yes, the assassinations of JFK and Martin Luther King, Jr. Lengthy threads include discussions of the redesign of U.S. currency, the national debt, and ongoing talk about standby subjects like skinheads, the anti-Holocaust movement, and Waco.
USENET alt.conspiracy

alt.conspiracy.area51 Distrustful discussion of the government land north of Las Vegas, rich in UFO lore. Visitors here believe that everything imaginable— captured aliens to underground bases—has existed on the shore of Groom Lake, and that the U.S. government, as always, is covering it up.
USENET alt.conspiracy.area51

Brian's Government Psychiatric Torture Website Check out MRI scans of Brian's brain, taking great care to notice the "inexplicable foreign objects" there.

❝ Ed's remote controllers talk to him through radios, TVs, cars, trains... ❞

Mind Control Forum Homepage
Ed claims he's a captive of the mind-control "cabal's" microwave anti-personnel projects. His remote controllers talk to him through radios, TVs, cars, trains, and airplanes and hail from areas like Minot AFB, the Florida Keys and somewhere on the grounds of Nellis AFB in Nevada (Area 51 territory). Ed's forum provides archives of his and others' experiences with psychiatric torture, news in the field, and other resources.
WEB http://members.gnn.com/fivestring/index.htm

PART 3
Fun & Games

Fun & Games

CLICK PICKS
The very best on the Net

Comics & Cartoons

WHETHER YOU WATCH *THE SIMPSONS* OR COLLECT VINTAGE *VALIANT*, YOU'LL BE DRAWN ONLINE

IN A WORLD that does not concern us here, asthma-hound chihuahuas don't live with pneumatic cats, Pocahontas was a kidnapped child, uncanny mutants have the life expectancy of mayflies, peanuts are the soggy droppings you find in bowls on bars, and the Tick carries Lyme disease. In the real world, Dilbert never gets a raise, Homer never beats his wife, Aeon Flux never falls out of her leather bindings, and the Tick is just too fine. In cyberspace the two worlds combine in a crazed concatenation of creative combobulation (Thank you, Mel Blanc!). The online world wants to refract comic reality through its own, and every nuance of every character of every show gets a working over here, every plot detail a rating. Do you think *The Simpsons* is genuinely the most subversive show on American television? Meet your friends here.

LOONEY TUNES HOME PAGE

WEB http://www.usyd.edu.au/~swishart/looney.html

Visiting this Aussie toon site is like entering a virtual theater—the background image evokes the feeling of heavy, blue curtains, and the *Looney Tunes* characters, including Bugs, Daffy, and Elmer, appear for all to see. Besides a spectacular archive of pictures of Michigan T. Frog, Pepe Le Pew, and other Warner Bros. characters, webmaster Stuart Wishart provides many great links, including a colorful Marvin the Martian page, the Road Runner Homepage, and even one dedicated to the venerable Acme Co. Fans also get obscure trivia from the FAQ, such as the name of the monster in Bugs' adventure "Hair-Raising Hare?" and details about the time Wile E. Coyote actually caught the Road Runner. Rounding out the lunacy are downloadable .WAV files, including Porky Pig's famous last words, "Be'db, That's all, folks!"

The drawing board

alt.binaries.pictures.cartoons
Whether you're looking for pics of Bambi and Thumper, the Tasmanian Devil, or Rogue and Storm from *The X-Women*, this image-filled newsgroup is likely to carry them. Lots of polite requests, such as *"Far Side* stuff, please" and "Please post *Beauty and the Beast* pictures."
USENET alt.binaries.pictures.cartoons

Animation Resources on the Net
Interested in attending the Ottawa International Animation Festival? You can learn a bit more about it by following the link from this surprisingly graphics-free site. Organized by *The Magazine of Animation on Film and Video*, this extensive list of animation links connects visitors to sites ranging from the Winnie the Pooh FAQ to the Association for Japanese Animation. The list covers everything from cartoons in American film and TV to Japanese anime and manga.
WEB http://www.cam.org/~pawn /ANIMRES.html

Cartoon Network A snazzy spot for 'toon lovers. Want to read about Snagglepuss or Scooby-Doo? Check out Hanna Barbera's Cartoon Network Hall of Fame. Interested in the use of Silicon Graphics workstations and "performance animation" in the creation of 'toons? Then click on that Moxy icon. The 'Toon Boutique sells T-shirts, caps, and other 'toon-

A million alternative universes in one convenient place
http://www.comicsworld.com/cw

ware, while 'Toon Studio serves as a spot for live chat with cartoon creators. As Snagglepuss might say, "Heavens to Murgatroyd! Exit stage right!"
AMERICA ONLINE *keyword* cartoon network

The Cartoons Forum Interested in the art of cartooning? The business side of the craft? Or just viewing comics? The cartoons available here include *Modern Wonder, McHumor, CompuToon,* and Mike Keefe's editorial cartoons. If you want to share your work, upload it to the folder labeled Your Cartoons.
AMERICA ONLINE *keyword* cartoons

The Comic Strip *Dilbert, Marmaduke,* and the *Peanuts* gang are on display at this comical site run by United Media. More than a dozen other online comics are featured as

well, including *The Buckets, The Born Loser,* and *Robotman.* Each page features a sample strip, plus information about its creator and links to related pages. The Dilbert Zone, for example, includes character descriptions, a photo tour demonstrating a day in the life of Scott Adams (from morning coffee to avoiding tripping over the pet cats on the way to the studio to making ideas come to life at the drawing board), and a link titled "Early photos of me (may frighten young children)." Fun, but the plethora of picture files can make this site agonizingly slow loading.
WEB http://www.unitedmedia.com /comics

Comics 'n' Stuff It takes a guy with attitude to build such a vast library of comics, and Christian's just perfect. "Censorship sucks!" he proudly pro-

claims. His site includes an area for real-time comics chat and links to hundreds of comics that are uploaded onto the Net. Look into such strips as *Angus Og* and *Dave's Brain*. Also check out *CultuRe Trap*, Christian's own comic creation.
WEB http://www.phlab.missouri.edu /~c6l7l45/comix.html

Comics Publishers Forum "I agree completely that something absolutely fantastic can be completely ignored until someone somewhere calls it great," writes Phil in a thread on self-publishing. In this forum, there are sections for several comic book publishers, from Marvel Comics to Rip-Off Press. The library includes an assortment

of images and excerpts from soon-to-be-released comic books.
COMPUSERVE *go* comicpub

Comics/Animation Forum An active spot for discussing, reporting, and sharing favorite examples of animation, cartoons, and comics. Discussion threads focus on anime and manga, Disney, writing and drawing, collecting, and conventions. In the library sections, you'll find icons for *Batman* and the *Animaniacs*, software for tracking comics, and a treasure trove of sound and image files, including original work from forum members.
COMPUSERVE *go* comics

ComicsWorld Fans will love this easy-to-use comics treasure chest. Not only does it list every comic publisher's upcoming releases—with trade paperbacks and books for mature readers clearly labeled —it also lists upcoming comics-related film and TV projects. Read interviews and reviews, see if you want to invest in that new title, and try the fun trivia contest. The highly interactive Comics-World also invites browsers to write stories for them.
WEB http://www.comicsworld.com/cw

The Kids' WB Shows Plotting to take over the world? Pay a visit to the *Pinky and the Brain* section at this fun offshoot of the

ANIME WEB ARCHIVE

WEB http://soyokaze.biosci.ohio-state.edu/~jei/anipike

picture: WEB http://www.tc.umn.edu/nlhome/m432/edwa0089/anime/akira/images/bike2.jpg

Hundreds of links jammed onto one site make for a useful resource, and it appears that the archives haven't missed a single anime-related link. The standard commercial pages get top billing, but so do anime club pages, fan pages, conventions, and image galleries. There's fan fiction, newsgroups, mailing lists, and even a miscellaneous pages section with links to music, fanzines, and hentai (erotic) pages. Without question this is any anime fan's best resource for finding his or her favorite type of 'toon on the Net.

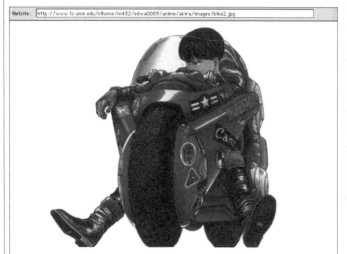

Netsite: http://www.tc.umn.edu/nlhome/m432/edwa0089/anime/akira/images/bike2.jpg

Warner Bros. animation page and perhaps gain some insight into why those two wacky rodents' outrageous plans for world domination never seem to come to fruition. Read all about the characters (and the actors whose voices are behind them) and download terrific audio and video clips from this and other WB shows, including *Animaniacs*, *Freakazoid!*, *The Sylvester and Tweety Mysteries*, and *Earthworm Jim*.
WEB http://www.wbanimation.com /cmp/ani_kdsh.htm

The Philadelphia Inquirer Now you're reading with power! The future of the custom-built newspaper is on display at the wackiest of places—the Philly *Inquirer*'s custom comics section. There are old favorites, such as *Family Circus*, *Andy Capp*, and *Peanuts*, as well as newer creations, including *Bent Halos*, and, for the Net-savvy, *PC and Pixel*. But, it's not the variety that matters here (although the great selection makes the site that much better), it's your options. Not only can you choose the daily comics you wish to view, you can also define the order. Or, if you'd like to visit the same strips every day, use the power comics button to select your faves. Then, bookmark the resulting page for return visits.
WEB http://www2.phillynews.com /comics

rec.arts.animation Does Disney have a monopoly on animation features? Is it a stretch to call

Disney "the Microsoft of the entertainment industry?" Most of the people who speak up on this newsgroup feel that way, and they're definitely not afraid to say so. The newsgroup is a great resource for keeping on top of animation-related issues, whether you want to find out about animation festivals, trade art, learn about the process of directing a cartoon, or just try to find some sort of redeeming qualities in the latest Disney release.
USENET rec.arts.animation
FAQ: **WEB** http://www.cis.ohio-state .edu/hypertext/faq/usenetfaqs /bygroup/rec/arts/animation/top .html

rec.arts.comics.info News related to comic books, including announcements about new releases, Web sites, conventions, and interactive chat appearances. Look for the New Weekly Releases post to stay up to date with the latest from Caliber, DC, Marvel, Warp, and other publishers. The group also carries reviews of comic books, including "Thrasher's Sporadic Reviews" and "Pick of the Brown Bag." Several documents have been produced by and for the group, including a glossary of comics terms, guides to comics-related resources on the Net, netiquette rules, and an FAQ with answers to questions such as "Where are the 'real' locations of Metropolis, Gotham City, Hub City, etc., in the DC Universe?"
USENET rec.arts.comics.info

FAQ: **WEB** http://www.cis.ohio-state .edu/hypertext/faq/usenet-faqs/by group/rec/arts/comics/info/top.html

rec.arts.comics.misc This is a gathering place for mavens and manifesto-writers whose seething obsessions are sequential art, graphic novels, and similar euphemistic synonyms for comic books. It's one of the largest groups on Usenet and growing every day. The newsgroup gets upwards of 300 posts a day. Unlike most Usenet communities, rec.arts.comics.misc is vertically integrated, which means that in addition to a roiling mass of fanboys (and a few fangirls), there are owners of comic-book shops, indie 'zine publishers, fan-convention organizers and a few professional artists and writers who read RACM regularly. One notable celebrity poster is Peter A. David, perhaps the most successful comic-book writer of modern times, plotter of *Spiderman 2099* and *The Incredible Hulk*, among other series. Retailers and first-in-line fans post advance reviews of what to buy and what to avoid. Be prepared to read this group nightly if you wish to keep up.
USENET rec.arts.comics.misc

rec.arts.comics.other-media "Why does Hollywood insist that every action star must have a woman to fall in love with or rescue?" Regulars to the newsgroup agonize over this and other issues involved in the adaptation of comic books for

Netsite: http://www.wbanimation.com/cmp/ani_kdsh.htm

Welcome to The Kids' WB! Shows!
Click on your favorite character to visit their web page.

Undisputed king of kids' cartoons
http://www.wbanimation.com/cmp/ani_kdsh.htm

films and TV shows.
USENET rec.arts.comics.other-media

rec.arts.comics.strips Fun, free-wheeling discussion of comic strips from *Dick Tracy* to *Doonesbury*. Discussions focus on Charlie Brown's hometown, the top 10 strips, and the ups and downs of various artists. No strip dominates the group; most of the fans, it seems, are happy to discuss their faves and learn about the likes and dislikes of others.
USENET rec.arts.comics.strips
FAQ: **WEB** http://www.cis.ohio-state .edu/hypertext/faq/usenet-faqs/by group/rec/arts/comics/strips/top.html

Toontalk *Ren & Stimpy*, *The Brothers Grunt*, and *Timon and Pumbaa* are the headliners here. While some of the animated characters are created for adults, the talk is often puerile: "Beavis is stupid and Butt-Head has some common

sense. They used to be cool but they've gotten old." Whether you're transfixed by the *Lion King*, amused by *Animaniacs*, or conducting an academic investigation into the motif of cross-dressing in classic Warner Bros. cartoons—Bugs in the dress and Elmer at the altar—this message area is, in the words of breakfast cereal huckster Tony the Tiger, "grrrrreat!"
AMERICA ONLINE *keyword* cartoons→ Toon Talk

Disney

alt.disney Random and unfocused without enough of a mission to make things truly interesting. Some people show up to sell Disney videos. Others post Disney-related questions. Serious fans want to compare *Aladdin* and *Beauty and the Beast*.
USENET alt.disney

FAQ: **WEB** http://www.cis.ohio-state .edu/hypertext/faq/usenet-faqs/by group/alt/disney/top.html

alt.disney.collecting David's thinking about selling an animation cel of Flora the orange fairy from *Sleeping Beauty*. Interested? No? How about a Mufasa and Simba keepsake ornament from Hallmark? Videos, cards, lithographs, and all of the other Disney products are on sale here.
USENET alt.disney.collecting

Crystal's Disney Home Page It's a small world, after all, and this Web site brings the entire Disney experience that much closer to home. Crystal has assembled pages for almost every Disney character and film, including *Who Framed Roger Rabbit?*, *Aladdin*, and *Sleeping Beauty*. There are pages for individual rides and hot spots at the Disney parks such as the eerie Haunted Mansion and the breathtaking Pirates of the Caribbean. Pages for new and old movies—everything from *Pete's Dragon* to *Oliver and Company*—are promised; all we can hope for is a more solid foundation of information.
WEB http://www.launchsite.com /riddler/crystal/disney.htm

#disney They have nicknames like Rhett, DWDucky, and Dopey; they're regulars on the IRC channel #disney, and they're profiled at this Web site. The FAQ answers questions about #disney, including

the average age of participants—generally, late teens
and early twenties—and the
most frequent hours of operation. There are scores of
images and QuickTime movies
of the regulars; watch these
Disney fans meet at the airport
and show each other their tattoos. In addition, the site offers
a great set of Disney links,
including video clips, FAQs,
images, and more.
IRC #disney
Info: **WEB** http://www.umich.edu
/~mingchen/disney.html

Disney.com Okay, Joe Schmo,
webmaster and avid fan of
Mickey, Minnie, and Donald
Duck (and with a certain perverted predilection for Pocahontas), you've just lost your
multi-million dollar battle over
copyright infringement with
Disney before the Supreme
Court. What are you gonna
do? Uh, go to Disneyworld?
Disney will win. And when
they do, when every last unofficial site has been squelched
by their corporate lawyers, it's
a good thing this site will be
around for all those wayward
Disney fans wandering the
cyberstreets. If you've ever
pondered Pooh, wanted to
explore Epcot, or had a query
about Quasimodo, this is the
official place to do it. Travel
and purchase information,
news on upcoming releases,
and even live chats with Disney-related artists (Robin
Williams, voice of the genie
from *Aladdin*, was a guest)
abound on this colorful, infor-

mative Web site.
WEB http://www.disney.com

Disney FAQ Is Walt Disney preserved in cryogenic suspen-
sion? No, the FAQ says—
that's an "urban legend." Is
Goofy a dog, a horse, or what?
A dog. The FAQ answers
questions about buying animation cels, finding Disney .GIFs
and lyrics, acquiring videos,
and purchasing Disney stock.
It includes an extensive and
detailed list of books about
Disney parks, movies, and
characters—and about Walt
himself. For those planning to
hang out in Disney cyberspots,
check out the list of Disney
acronyms (BatB for *Beauty and
the Beast*, MK for Magic Kingdom, etc.).
WEB http://www.cis.ohio-state.edu
/hypertext/faq/usenet/disney-faq
/disney/faq.html

Doug and Lisa's Disney Home Page
Divided into sections on Disney parks, animated feature
films, art, pictures, and miscellaneous items, this site offers a
voluminous amount of info on
all things Disney. Traveling to
Disneyland? Then check out
the list of attractions and a map
of the park. If you're into Disney films, take a look at the
images from *Dumbo*, *The Lion
King*, and other flicks. The site
also includes a list of Disney
characters, images of Disney
dollars (it's not illegal to scan
fake currency), and links to
other Disney sites.
WEB http://www.best.com/~dijon
/disney

Frank's Disney Home Page Frank's
site features a comprehensive
list of links for Disney's animated features, beginning with
1937's *Snow White and the
Seven Dwarves* and running
through 1996's *The Hunchback
of Notre Dame*; for each film,
the list includes reviews,
images, lyrics, credits, and
more. The site provides scripts
for *Sleeping Beauty*, *The Little
Mermaid*, *Beauty and the Beast*,
Aladdin, and *The Lion King*,
along with a selection of fairy
tales, such as *Cinderella*.
WEB http://www.uni-frankfurt.de/~fp
/Disney

Anime

alt.binaries.pictures.anime
Robby's searching for pics of
mech warriors, while Patrick
wants to see the art from *Fatal
Fury*. And James has just
posted a dozen images from
Sailor Moon. A variety of
images pass through this newsgroup, along with talk about
where to find other anime pictures online.
USENET alt.binaries.pictures.anime

alt.binaries.pictures.erotica.anime
A popular group with images
labeled "Suffering Girls,"
"Lovely Lady Leopard Shows
'Her Spots,'" and the like. It's
primarily a place to download
from or trade anime-style erotica. Requests accepted.
USENET alt.binaries.pictures.erotica
.anime

Anime and Manga Resources List
Basically a big, sprawling list

of links to hundreds of sites with info on Japanese animation and comics, including art galleries, fan fiction, and anime clubs, along with general information, and an answer to the question, "What are Manga and Anime?"

WEB http://www.csclub.uwaterloo.ca/u/mlvanbie/anime-list

Anime Picture Archive Looking for *Vampire Princess Miyu*, *Angel Cop*, and *The Desire Series*? Here's a collection of anime pictures of all types, from *Akira* to *Sailor Moon*. Click the Anime Archive Slideshow, select from a large list of anime series and programs, and a new image will pop up on your screen in increments of 10 to 120 seconds.

WEB http://se.animearchive.org/index.html

rec.arts.anime* Big sparkly eyes, perky girls in sailor suits, giant robots, psychics, and many-tentacled beasts—it takes a certain sensibility to be a fan of Japanese animation. This group is extremely high-volume, with daily check-ins necessary to avoid unmanageable posting buildup. It is divided into just about a half-dozen linked subgroups: rec.arts.anime.info, rec.arts.anime.marketplace, rec.arts.anime.creative, rec.arts.anime.fandom, rec.arts.anime.misc, rec.arts.anime.models, and rec.anime.music.

USENET rec.arts.anime*

FAQ: **URL** ftp://rtfm.mit.edu/pub/usenet-by-hierarchy/rec/arts/anime

Animation

IT TAUGHT US ONE THING: SENSELESS VIOLENCE IS *FUNNY*

Location: http://www.acm.uiuc.edu/rml/Gifs/Simpsons/simpsons-at-home.gif

THE SIMPSONS ARCHIVE

WEB http://www.snpp.com/index.html

picture: WEB http://www.acm.uiuc.edu/rml/Gifs/Simpsons

¡Ay caramba! The world's finest mass satire is as much an online institution as it is an onscreen one. *Simpsons* sites abound, but this is one of the finest. Including FAQs, an episode guide, and links to other *Simpsons* pages, it also has the invaluable list of "chalkboard gags," which includes, "I will not drive the principal's car," "I will not Xerox my butt," and "I will not instigate revolution." D'oh!

Animaniacs

alt.tv.animaniacs With a rabid following—especially after *Animaniacs'* near-cancellation by Fox—alt.tv.animaniacs is one of the freshest, most creative newsgroups around. Many posters compare the adventures of Wakko, Yakko, and Dot to the classic chaos of the Warner Bros. cartoon heyday; others just love the constant cultural referencing and clever punnery. Light volume, but building, all types of people visit the group including general fans, collectors, and even a few people looking to write for Warner Bros.
USENET alt.tv.animaniacs

Animaniacs Mega Lyrics File They're tiny, they're toony, they're just a little looney, and boy, do they like to sing! One thing they are known for is the power of caricature. This file has nearly every song from the show, be it parody or original material. You'll find lyrics from episodes like "Les Miserani-mals," "Taming of the Screwy," and "Hooked on a Ceiling." For the uninitiated, a sample from "West Side Pigeons": "Carloota! / I just met a bird named Carloota. / And please don't think me rude / But I think I'd like to brood with Carloota!" And this is for kids?
WEB http://members.cruzio.com /~keeper/AMLF.html

Beavis & Butt-Head

Beavis and Butt-Head Home Page "Enough whining, just tell me what can I find here, Dill-weed!" Well, lots of stuff. The *Beavis and Butt-Head* episode guide, information about the show's creator, Mike Judge, and "the brand spanking (heh hmm, I said spanking) new *Beavis and Butt-Head* FAQ" are available at this site. Links are also provided for *Beavis and Butt-Head* sounds, pictures, and related Web pages. Most fascinating, perhaps, is Chris' (the site's honest creator) story of trying to get the torrid *Singled Out* off the air, and the evil (although completely falsified) email he received as part of his "Jenny McCarthy-should-shut-the-hell-up campaign." That would be cool.
WEB http://calvin.hsc.colorado.edu

Duckman

Duckman Do you really give a flying duck? If you do, and you can put up with his atti-tude, visit the Duckman's offi-cial site. Since he was "webbed before it was cool," you can expect loads of goodies cour-tesy of the feathered freak. Take a tour of his house, read his daily schedule, and take a peek at the Hollywood sign via a spy cam. And if you're hun-gry, Duckman can really help—there are dozens of links to nationwide fast food joints. Pizza, pizza!
WEB http://www.duckman.com

I guess Lucky Pariah is kind of an abstract concept to illustrate
http://www.duckman.com

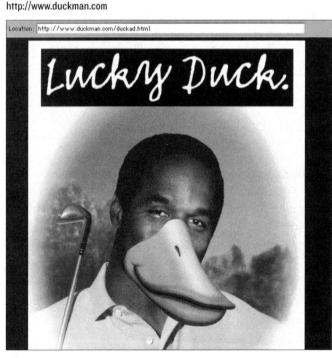

Location: http://www.duckman.com/duckad.html

Lucky Duck.

The Duckman Information File If you're a serious fan of the duck detective, this page carries episode synopses with information on guests whose voices you may have recognized, including Crispin Glover, Tim Curry, and Sally Struthers, while the pictures offer *Duckman* images from publications such as *Wired* and *TV Guide*. For a few laughs, read the transcript of a CompuServe Q&A session with the always irreverent Duckman: "The Internet? I thought it was that new kind of support-hose you slip dollar bills into at the Chicho Mundy's Tick-Tock Lap Dance Palace and Canola Mart." **WEB** http://bluejay.creighton.edu /~jduche/duckfaq.html

Ren & Stimpy

Ren & Stimpy Information What is it about *Ren & Stimpy* that makes it such an underground hit? "The show's attraction is its shameless and gross physical humor, often consisting of nose-picking and farts (though there's more to it than that). It is suitable (and funny) for the whole family, though some have called it an acquired taste." Basic coverage of the show, with an encyclopedia, an episode guide, and an FAQ which provides information on the show's producers, *Ren & Stimpy* paraphernalia, and the pronunciation of Ren's last name. The episode guide makes for amusing reading (even if you've never seen the show) with its descriptions of Ren and Stimpy's antics. The encyclopedia lists episodes, quotes, and bumpers. **WEB** http://www.lysator.liu.se/~marcus /ren_stimpy

Ren & Stimpy Page You eeeeeediot! Why haven't you visited this page before? It's a great site for *Ren & Stimpy* data, with links to libraries and files all over the Web dedicated to the ever-chipper chihuahua and his fat feline friend. You'll also find FAQs, sound files, song lyrics, and QuickTime movies. Happy happy! Joy joy! **WEB** http://www.cris.com/~lkarper /rands.html

 # THE AUTHORITATIVE BEAVIS & BUTT-HEAD PAGE
WEB http://www.columbia.edu/~gan3/bnb.html

Any Ivy League student worth his or her salt knows that a little copyright infringement is enough to get the attorneys of huge media conglomerates on the hunt. But until Viacom's corporate lawyers trudge up Broadway from their offices at 45th Street to the Columbia campus at 116th, this site will

Location: http://www.columbia.edu/~gan3/bnb/grapes.jpg

be a great resource for sound, images, and great video clips including "I am the great Cornholio. Come out with your pants down!" When this intrepid webmaster does finally get the ax, just head to MTV's site for all stuff *Beavis and Butt-Head*. You know the address.

The Simpsons

alt.tv.simpsons A great spot for fans of *The Simpsons*, with the best posts devoted to uncovering the things you're liable to miss while watching, like the church sign advertising "Bingo night" and a "Big trip to Reno" after Rev. Lovejoy's sermon on the evils of gambling. Other posts focus on "butts in *The Simpsons*," "the best Homer lines," and "best sign sayings," such as "Springfield Nuclear Power. As seen on *60 Minutes*."
USENET alt.tv.simpsons
FAQ: **WEB** http://www.cis.ohio-state .edu/hypertext/faq/usenet-faqs /bygroup/alt/tv/simpsons/top.html
FAQ: **URL** ftp://rtfm.mit.edu/pub /usenet-by-hierarchyalt/tv/simpsons

The Tick

The Incredibly Complete Tick Links Page There are links to *Tick* comics, the cartoon, and shrines to *The Tick*. The webmaster also reveals her choices for the top three *Tick* sites. But the most fun section is monickered Strange and Wonderful Things, which features *Tick*-related games. Play a *Tick* dart game and choose your targets —from Bill Gates to Garfield.
WEB http://www.intranet.org/~maggi /tick.html

The Original Tick Homepage He's big. He's blue. He's nigh invulnerable. He's the Tick! Get a taste of *Tick* justice here. With spoilers for each episode, a picture archive of good guys

"Don't you know cartoons will ruin your mind?"
http://www.cris.com/~lkarper/rands.html

and bad guys, the Tick FAQ, and an online newsletter, you'll feel like you haven't missed a single episode. Fans of *The Tick* comic book—the even funnier predecessor to the cartoon—will also find links to sites devoted to their favorite do-gooder.
WEB http://www.cu-online.com /~phyber/tick/tickpage.html

The Tick Page The beefy, blue comic book hero has survived the journey from comics to cartoon show remarkably intact. This fan-created page is one of the most extensive *Tick* sites; it opens with a friendly, "Yoo-hoo! Are there any villains out there?" Read character bios, episode descriptions, and Tickisms ("City, it is I, the Tick, your destined defender... show me where it hurts!"). The site's most original touch are the browsers who sign on as

Do-Gooders or Evil-Doers, then describe their super powers.
WEB http://www.cipsinc.com/TICK

Other shows

Rocky and Bullwinkle-Frostbitely Asked Questions Fans nostalgic for Bullwinkle and Rocky will love this straightforward page of answers to questions about the dimwitted moose and his high-flying sidekick. For example: What is the population of Frostbite Falls, the home of our heroes? What's Bullwinkle's middle initial? There are no pics of the pair, who were created by Jay Ward for the '60s shows *Rocky and His Friends* and *The Bullwinkle Show*— intelligent, deconstructionist cartoons way ahead of their time—but you get links to plot summaries and info about the cast and characters, including

June Foray, Paul Frees, Dudley Do-Right, and of course, Boris and Natasha.
WEB http://mindlink.bc.ca/Charles_Ulrich/faq.html

Space Ghost Coast to Coast As we all know, the Cartoon Network reincarnated the straight-laced Space Ghost (of the 1966 Hanna-Barbera cartoon) as an idiotic talk show host whose goal is to end the talk-show wars. The smarmy TV series lends itself perfectly to a similarly smarmy (though graphically sophisticated) site. There's not a whole lot of information about the show here, but you can go on some interactive journeys, either underground or sifting through a cartoon-like hallway. It's suprising that Cartoon Network hasn't really taken the time to give this *Space Ghost* site more bite.
WEB http://www.filmzone.com/SpaceGhost/index.html

Speed Racer Fans of the series should rev to this address for a tribute to this early star of Japanese animation. Get episode synopses and Go Team info, download snappy pictures, and locate hard-to-find merchandise. Instructions for a paper model of the Mach Five are groovy, but the brightest spot is the audio clip of Speed's theme song—one of the all-time catchiest. The University of Delaware student who created this fun site gives you the lyrics so you can sing along.
WEB http://www.eecis.udel.edu/~markowsk/anime/speed

Strips

From Snoopy to Sandman, if it's in print, it's online

The Dog House
WEB http://www.unitedmedia.com/comics/peanuts

Snoopy, the little round-headed kid who feeds him, and the rest of Charles M. Schulz's endearing *Peanuts* gang are all at this fun address. Enter The Dog House to find a two-week archive of recent comic strips, a *Peanuts* timeline dating back to the strip's premiere in 1950, and a fascinating bio of Schulz. You can get background info on all the beloved characters (including Linus, Lucy, Sally, Schroeder, Woodstock, Peppermint Patty, Marcie, and even Pig Pen), each accompanied by some wonderful insights from their creator, "Sparky" Schulz.

Alternative

Alternative Comics: A WWW Guide
An extensive, well run site for "alternative/underground/non-mainstream" comics. Its creator, Michael Fragassi, offers pithy reviews of the comics, helping visitors decide what links (Alleged Literature? Young Geezers?) to follow. Aside from the links, the site offers a great selection of its own pages about comics, including reviews, interviews, essays, and FAQs.
WEB http://copper.ucs.indiana.edu /~mfragass/altcom.html

rec.arts.comics.alternative Are you a fan of comics like *Go-Go Boy*, *Sin City*, *Jar of Fools*, and *Cerebus*? This newsgroup hosts nonstop discussions about alternative, independent, and non-traditional comic books, including analyses of the best indies being published. Many inkers looking for feedback on their work also participate.
USENET rec.arts.comics.alternative

Tank Girl First there was Brenda Starr. Then Wonder Woman. Now there's Hewlett & Martin's comic chick for the '90s, Tank Girl, and she's taking no prisoners. So, who is that lovable rogue Tank Girl? Enter her punkster world here—with links to newsgroups, an FAQ, and information on the various media *Tank Girl* has appeared in—to find out.
WEB http://www-dept.cs.ucl.ac.uk /staff/b.rosenberg/tg/index.html

• http://ocaxpl.cc.oberlin.edu /~jdockhor/tg

Calvin and Hobbes

Calvin and Hobbes Comics Gallery
Tour this cybergallery dedicated to everyone's demonic inner child, Calvin, and everyone's favorite virtual tiger, Hobbes. Spend a rainy afternoon enjoying the antics of Spaceman Spiff, defying death on a speeding sled, and torturing Susie from next door. Beware the Deranged Mutant Killer Monster Snowgoons.
WEB http://infolabwww.kub.nl:2080 /calvin_hobbes

The Calvin & Hobbes Jumpstation
Henrik Erikkson asks: "Can anyone have enough *Calvin and Hobbes* links?" Apparently not, as there are more than 80

URLs listed for fan sites on Bill Watterson's inventive strip, which came to an end in 1995 after a highly successful run. Newsgroups, FTPs, and gophers are also listed. Curious fans (and what Calvin fans aren't?) may want to peek at pages in Norway, Italy, and Finland for a glimpse at the universal appeal of Watterson's humor. Be warned: The officials behind Watterson's cartoon strip have been sending out cease-and-desist orders to a number of Calvin sites, so you may find more and more inoperative links as time rolls on.
WEB http://www.csd.uu.se/~d94her /calvin/jumpstation.html

The Last Day of Calvin and Hobbes
When Bill Watterson ended his marvelously drawn and written *Calvin and Hobbes* car-

---

Out of circulation? Not online!
http://infolabwww.kub.nl:2080/calvin_hobbes

Location: http://infolabwww.kub.nl:2080/calvin_hobbes/index.html

toon strip, many of his fans were shocked and upset. You can sense some of that at this sincere tribute, which features the first and last *C&H* strip, affectionate tributes from fans, and great *C&H* debates (Is Hobbes real? What is the nature of Calvin's relationship with Susie?). Webmaster Jeff Manson also promises to pass along any messages for Watterson via the cartoonist's publisher.
WEB http://www.goldenfrog.com/ch

Classic

alt.comics.classic Not a highly trafficked spot, but one that's useful for collectors of older comic books, including *Spiderman*, *Hulk*, and *Captain America*. Much of the discussion centers around buying, trading, and determining the value of vintage comics.
USENET alt.comics.classic

Dilbert

Dilbert OD on *Dilbert*. The site includes info on Dilbert and his creator, copies of the current strips, an archive of classics, and a gift shop. Dilboard, the site's discussion area, includes topics such as "Dogbert could kick Snoopy's ass" and an active thread on "The Worst Comic Ever" includes such posts as "Dave Must Die" and "Put Mutts to Sleep!"
AMERICA ONLINE *keyword* dilbert

The Dilbert Zone It's no secret that Dilbert and his creator

Scott Adams have quite a fan following, especially among netheads. There's no greater proof to this than the dozens of sock puppet pages featured on Adams' official *Dilbert* Web site. There's an open post for pictures of Web surfers with sock puppets at their computers; Adams publishes all sock puppets that he receives, and boy, are there a lot of 'em! If you're not really interested in the sock puppet pics, get your *Dilbert* fix—there's an FAQ, information on Scott Adams, and a two-week *Dilbert* archive so you can catch up on all the trials and tribulations of Dilbert, Dogbert, and their just-another-cog-in-the-wheel compatriots.
WEB http://www.unitedmedia.com /comics/dilbert

DC Comics

DC Comics Unfortunately, this isn't much more than a generic Warner Bros. commercial, headlining comics involving best-sellers *Batman* and *Superman*. You don't get much more than thin press-release info and short previews, and you certainly won't find fan-caliber perspective or gusto. Still, it's nice to see online re-broadcasts of the original *Superman* radio serial.
WEB http://www.dccomics.com

DC Comics Online With areas for the various divisions of DC, such as *MAD* magazine, Milestone Media, and Paradox Press, this forum has libraries

IT'S NOT LIKE THE SIMPSONS DIED

There are no guarantees that all friendships will last forever. This year has been the year of ending friendships for me. I guess it is fitting that my friendship with *Calvin & Hobbes* would end on this day. There will always be new friends to fill the space I now have empty. I'm looking forward to this new year as I begin to fill my blank page.

I think Bill Waterston has done the right thing. There wasn't much more he could have said or done without repeating himself. We all need to end something so we can start something else. Imagine if Bill had never stopped doing what he was doing before he started *C&H*! I'll be ending school in June and I can't wait to end this period of my life. What I'll find ahead will only be imagined if I don't start exploring today.

—from The Last Day of Calvin & Hobbes

full of goodies, including images from vintage comic books and stats on characters such as Aquaman, Catwoman, and Superboy. The message areas can be fairly juvenile, with lots of the "This is weird" and "*MAD* rules!" variety of posts.
AMERICA ONLINE *keyword* dc comics

THE BIG MISTAKE

A while back I was reading the older stories again from The Greatest Superman Stories book, and I was surprised how much I enjoyed them. Superman was different than the Silver Age one I grew up with, but it didn't matter to me exactly how or when they incrementally changed him. He was the same Superman, that was the same Luthor. But today, I can't buy a comic with those characters. They were all wiped out in the crisis. That rule that Superman never really dies doesn't apply. He died, and his whole universe—his whole history—was wiped out.

Time for a revamp that sets thing right. Why don't they merge the last ten years with a huge blob of protoplasmic time, drain from the blob those stories and events that can fit in the pre-1987 framework, stuff what's left in a bottled city called The Big Mistake, and send it to a parallel universe called Elseworlds-2.

Oh, and let Ma and Pa Kent out of the blob before they stuff it.

—from rec.arts.comics.dc.universe

DC Heroes Appollo had his fiery steeds, Santa his bounding reindeer, and Aquaman his trusty dolphins. If all you remember of Aquaman is his fleet of flippers, this Web site should help you flesh him out along with other DC heroes, from Abra Kadabra to Zatannna. Equipped with vital stats and loosely codified power rating, this site is good for those interested in RPGs or for those who always wondered how Catwoman would fare against Wonder Woman. By the way, Aquaman's Achilles' heel is— you guessed it—no water.
WEB http://copper.ucs.indiana.edu /~rmaple/table.html

Fizban's Guide to DC Comics This charming tour gives vital stats on key figures of the DC Universe, such as Azrael, Batman, the Flash, Green Lantern, Superman, and Wonder Woman. If you're tired of those superheros and the fact that they always prevail, head to the small section on their villainous counterparts. Although the Events and News pages are strong, the rest of the site could use some beefing up. Still, it's worth a look for a quick dalliance in the DC universe.
WEB http://expert.cc.purdue.edu /~fizban/dc/dc.html • http://www .santarosa.edu/~sthoemke/x/x.html

rec.arts.comics.dc.universe You can join discussion on the limits of super strength, Wonder Woman's muscle definition, the amount of skin revealed by the characters' costumes, plot lines, and favorite characters. But there are also arguments about the superheroes' political views—or lack of them—and the ways comic books handle deaths. "I don't like Legionnaires dying just because," wrote one fan. "I like 'em to go out heroically. I like 'em to die for a reason."
USENET rec.arts.comics.dc.universe

ElfQuest

alt.comics.elfquest Flame *ElfQuest*, as one person did ("All Elves Must Hang!"), and you risk being called a troll and a snotling. Discussion on the newsgroup ranges from the possibilities for an *ElfQuest* movie to the most appropriate music to listen to while reading *ElfQuest*. Some say folk music, but one fan said "folk was the *last* music to come to mind." He went on to add that he favors the Sex Pistols, Black Flag, and the Circle Jerks.
USENET alt.comics.elfquest

Elfquest.com Sometimes an official site really is the best resource for information and not just a cheap promotional tool. Although Warp Graphics does include purchasing options and information to fans of the mythical comic, most of the pages of the Elfquest.com site are replete with goodies. Fans will find graphics, previews, character biographies, and updates for the upcoming film.
WEB http://elfquest.com

rec.arts.comics.elfquest Lots of *ElfQuest* diehards are online at this newsgroup offering newbies advice on which *ElfQuest* books to read first and where to find them. Perhaps the most sensitive topic is the question of who would do the voices in an *ElfQuest* movie.
USENET rec.arts.comics.elfquest

Marvel

MAWORLD! While a little content-shallow, this Web site is good for all sorts of Marvel Universe links. The best are the *Spider-Man* and *X-Men* links, but you'll also find *Daredevil*, *Avengers*, *Power Pack*, *Silver Surfer*, and *Hulk* links.
WEB http://www.teleplex.bsu.edu /pages/bneely/index.htm/maworldl.htm

The Mutant Pages Perusing this home page is like surfing in a tsunami. Information flies in front of you, to the left of you, to the right, and sometimes over your head. Despite the orderly menu selection, this home page is frenetic and only sporadically informative. Brief yourself with the X-tinction Agenda Issue Guide, the X-Cutioner's Song Issue Guide, the guide for the New Mutants, or other storylines that you may have missed. If you'd like to find the time-traveling Cable, his past (or rather future) appearances are followed in The Cable Guide. Also worth skimming is The Angst Guide, which, like a John Hughes' film, posits that teenage angst is what makes

Location: http://www.cad.uni-sb.de/elzer/fsfiles/fs0jpg.html

Pete's All-Time-Favorite Far Side cartoon

I'll tell you what this means, Norm—no size restrictions and screw the limit.

© Chronicle Features/FarWorks, Inc.

More subtle social commentary from Gary Larson
ttp://www.cad.uni-sb.de/elzer/farside.html

the world go 'round. Each character's past is analyzed, and then rated numerically to determine their angst quotient. The brilliant Beast grew monstrously and sprouted blue fur. Is he in angst? What do you think? If you've braved the site and want more, see the voluminous resource links.
WEB http://www.santarosa.edu /~sthoemke/x/index.html

rec.arts.comics.marvel.universe When someone openly asked the group which Marvel hero they'd like to be, one honest guy replied, "Mr. Fantastic. Why? Can you say 'Rad Sex'?" Well, if you like frank conversation, this newsgroup is definitely the place for you. Discuss movies, conspiracy theories, and new releases. Or, find postings about merchandise for sale, collector conventions, or people just saying hello.
USENET rec.arts.comics.marvel .universe

Peanuts

alt.comics.peanuts Discussion of Charlie Brown, Woodstock, Snoopy, and the other *Peanuts* characters. Threads focus on the best and worst of the TV specials, what's known about the adult characters in the strip, and creator Charles Schulz.
USENET alt.comics.peanuts

Other comics

The Far Side by Gary Larson Conniving cows, driving dogs, and beehived women named Sylvia populated Gary Larson's hilariously weird daily cartoon until 1994, when he retired the strip. But for webmaster Hans Peter Elzer, the cows and their ilk live on. Elzer has compiled 70 of his favorite *Far Side* cartoons, in glorious full color. You may not find your favorite *Far Side*—remember, this is Pete's page, not yours—but any Larson fan will appreciate this fine collection.

WEB http://www.cad.uni-sb.de/elzer
/farside.html

Kev's World A cop leans out of a
nethead's computer monitor,
shouting, "Internet police, sir.
Are you sure you really want to
post that unflattering comment
about your mother-in-law?"
The full-color *Kev's World* is
the creation of Kevin Nichols,
a skilled illustrator and cartoonist. High-quality work.
WEB http://www.S2F.com/kevsworld
/index.html

NetBoy "Unix type flesh must
taste good," says one of the
offenders in "When Computer
Peripherals Attack"—one
episode of NetBoy Theater.
Netboy is a comic guide to Net
culture, cartoon-style. Primi-
tively drawn, sure, but the
prose is amusing, with an
interesting, refreshing take on
what's happening on the electronic frontier.
WEB http://netboy.com

Rock-It Comix A site for comic
books inspired by rock 'n' roll
stars. The comics feature stories based on acts from Black
Sabbath and Ozzy Osbourne
(yep, they're big on metal) to
Carlos Santana. In the Santana
comic book, the artist traces
"his roots from his dishwasher
days, to his moment of musical
epiphany, through his chemi-
cally distraught years, to his
inspirational now." Keep your
eyes peeled for Yes, Marilyn
Manson, and a four-issue tribute to The Doors. Rock-It
offers sample pages from the

Be a part of it!
http://www.tooluser.com

comics online.
WEB http://www.musick.com/Rockit

Strange Matter A popular online
cartoon, *Strange Matter* is
posted to the Internet from
New Zealand. Many of them
focus on science, with their creator, Nick Kim describing his
cartoon as a "thinking man's"
version of *Far Side*, *Bizzaro*, or
Quiqman. The *Strange Matter*
FAQ at this site offers an amusing bio of Kim, a chemist from
New Zealand, and the genesis
of the cartoon ("It all began in
the mist-covered mountains of
the Yukatoblerone").
WEB http://galadriel.ecaetc.ohio-state
.edu/tc/sm

Marketplace

rec.arts.comics.marketplace
Imagine a huge bazaar with

comic books everywhere. And
not only comic books, but
everything remotely related to
them—trading cards, action
figures, animation cels, and the
like. The items for sale in this
thriving cybermall range from a
$700 Batman statue to issues
of *Spiderman* selling for less
than $1 each.
USENET rec.arts.comics.marketplace

**Tool User Comics' World Wide Web
Comics Project** Tool User
Comics sells comic books and
strips over the Web. The site
provides an alphabetical listing
of Tool User's offerings, complete with short descriptions,
biographical data on artists,
and links to sample pages. The
works of cartoonists such as
Ted Rall, Stan Mack, and Tom
Tomorrow are online as well.
WEB http://www.tooluser.com

Video Games

THERE'S MORE TO VIDEO GAMES THAN SOLITUDE. ON THE NET, YOUR ENEMIES ARE ALIVE

WHETHER YOU'RE INTO role-playing adventure games or the retina-searing graphics of run-and-gun shooters, the video game industry is sure to have something to suit your taste. And once the manufacturers have your needs pegged, they'll keep on coding away until you're stuffed: Unlike Hollywood movies, video games thrive on sequels. Just look at ORIGIN's *Ultima* series, which is on its ninth installment (one more than the *Friday the 13th* slash-a-thons), or the popular arcade phenomenon *Street Fighter*, which is closing in on its seventh —it's come out swinging more times than Rocky Balboa, and, unlike the Italian Stallion it's still going strong. See these pages for the latest technologies, the hottest format, and the scorching code of the moment.

Location: http://happypuppy.com/games/index.html

HAPPY PUPPY GAMES
WEB http://happypuppy.com

The puppies here have every reason to be happy—they're wallpaper for the most comprehensive video game site on the Net. The frequently updated Happy Puppy has an impressive breadth of coverage, including demos and shareware for Mac (*Descent 2*, *Barrack*) and PC (*Quake*, *Firefight*), features that cover the industry (a virtual tour of E3), and gaming columns. This Web site has so much information delivered with style and character (think: "Puppy Press"), things can get a little congested: Page after page of frames and menus make navigation somewhat of a headache. Even so, the content more than makes up for it. Let the dog feed you for once.

Starting points

Game Zero For those hip to the gaming world, *Game Zero* is a familiar name. This huge online magazine covers a spectrum of gaming delights from fantasy to sports, from 3-D to *Mortal Kombat*. *Game Zero* has inside information on the biggies like Nintendo, Crystal Dynamics, and ORIGIN, so you can get a glimpse of the new Nintendo Ultra 64 and PlayStation programs before they hit the stores.In its regular Head to Head feature, the magazine pits similar games from different systems against one another, like *Battle Arena Toshinden Remix* on the Sega Saturn vs. *Battle Arena Toshinden* on the PlayStation. Note: Updates are less than lightning-quick. If it were faster, this ezine would definitely be A-list.
WEB http://www.gamezero.com

The Games and Recreation Web Site If you're yearning to get out of the mainstream of graphic glitz and stereo surround sound, this Web site might give you the breather you're looking for. Links to MUSHs, MUDs and RPGs, card games, board games, miniature-based games, and table games. A miscellaneous link to the Scottish Tiddlywinks Association is accompanied by the dire warning, "Do not underestimate the complexity of tactics in this game."
WEB http://www.cis.ufl.edu/~thoth /library/recreation.html

New Type Gaming Magazine A magazine that tries hard to exude attitude and edge, covering dedicated consoles, PC games, Mac games, and arcade games. They pick up on some items that aren't found anywhere else, like an arcade preview of Midway Williams' *War Gods* and the fabulous looking first-person shooter *Tenka* for the PlayStation. However, the overall content doesn't rise above mediocrity. The reviews menu is organized by the title's first letter, not by the title itself, which makes quick scans difficult, at best. There's probably some good information somewhere at this site, but be prepared to negotiate the terrain.
WEB http://Web.Actwin.Com/newtype

Revolutions One of the better ezines, both in content and organization. *Revolutions* has collected more than 50 tiny preview images of *Mario 64*! Short articles that digest the gaming world's current events, such as one on Nintendo's pricing policies, and a behind-the-scenes look at *PilotWings 64*. Also available are interviews with a Nintendo rep for the Ultra 64, an EA designer, and other industry people looking to plug their products.
WEB http://www.therevolution.com /menu/menu.htm

Online Gaming Review *OGR* is paradoxical: It's both ahead of the game and behind the times. It's great for reliable daily news updates on the gaming indus-

try, but its games review section lags a little, with a couple of current releases noticeably missing, although games released half a year ago are still occupying server space. It's best to go to *OGR* for its newswatch, or to check out its extensive links to software development companies for the latest in news, software, and patches.
WEB http://ogr.nrgroup.com

Ultimate Gaming Resource The freshest information here is for the release dates of games on consoles and for the PC. The Rumors page also has intriguing tidbits about the next generation of Sony PlayStation and possible industry mergers, but we wouldn't go buying stock or anything without some more authoritative confirmation. Try their selection of demos, alphabetized from A-Z, but be wary of dead links.
WEB http://www.nai.net/~duane /previews/previews.htm

Video Game Yellowpages Everything gets a Yahoo!, including video games. The pages of this vast, burgeoning industry are sorted, packaged, and redistributed by Video Game Yellow Pages, which, like Yahoo!, is searchable by category. The News option turns up more than 20 Web sites with reliable news updates. If you want to peruse sites on your favorite dedicated console, there are fan and company home pages.
WEB http://www.gamepen.com /yellowpages

Arcade

Classic Arcade Games Sounding like your folks? Waxing nostalgic for a time when things were simpler? Namely coin-op video games. Sure, 64-bit games are all the rage and the action and graphics dwarf those of their forebears, but really, can anything compare to the heady days of video gaming? Can playing *Virtua Cop 3* or *Bandicoot* really match the exhiliration of mastering *Donkey Kong*, *Centipede*, or *Dig Dug*? This true fan has culled many of the resources available on the Net as well as posted some of the early advertisements and links to sounds from such games as *Donkey Kong Junior* and *Moon Patrol*. You'll never forget your first *Tempest*.
WEB http://www.coinop.org/sharkie/vids.html

Coin-Ops Don't you love the smell of carnage in the morning? Find discussions on all the monster-hit action arcade games here. Just wash your hands before dinner: If you get blood stains on the linen, your family will throw a fit.
COMPUSERVE *go* vidgam→Libraries *or* Messages→Coin-Ops

rec.games.video.arcade Groundzero for discussion of coinoperated and home-system video games, ranging from the practical (cheat sheets) to the technical (maintenance, retrofitting, and pirating) to the metaphysical (are you addicted?). The most useful

Location: http://www.coinop.org/sharkie/coinop/images/XEVIOUS.JPG

The coffee machine in the middle was actually an exciting submarine game
http://www.coinop.org/sharkie/vids.html

information is quickly incorporated into the FAQs that are posted on the newsgroup and archived. Discussion of hot new games is practically simultaneous with their release.
USENET rec.games.video.arcade

Video Game FAQ Archive Listed by system, there are FAQs at this site for arcade games, the Sony Playstation, 3DO, the Atari Jaguar, the Sega Saturn, the Sega Genesis, Super Nintendo, Nintendo 8-bit, portables, and the Philips CD-I, the *Titanic* of CD Consoles (this one sank, too).
WEB http://www.flex.net/users/cjayc/vgfa/index.html

BattleTech

BattleTech VR FAQ *BattleTech VR* is an arcade war simulation in which the participants pilot a battlemech—a walking tank

of sorts—within a "pod" that projects the virtual environmen, with which they interact. This Web site explains the concept, the execution, and the mechanics of *BattleTech VR*, which FASA developed from its role-playing story line. But before exploring the *BT* resources here, click on the Mood Music button and get into the spirit of thing. For newbies, the page's *BT* FAQ will answer fundamental questions like "What is a Red Planet?" and "Won't I get slaughtered? I've only played twice!" The FAQ also contains some hints and tips for the intermediate player. All *BT* aficionados will enjoy the picture and QuickTime galleries at the Web site, but approach these loads only if you have a long afternoon on your hands.
WEB http://http.bsd.uchicago.edu/~c-henkle/html/btech.html

FAQs for last year's Christmas present
http://www.flex.net/users/cjayc/vgfa/index.html

Btech 3056 As the ComStar in the year 3056 gears up for its next battle with the Clans, it's a time of transition and intrigue in the *BattleTech* universe. Gigantic ten-meter robots, called the BattleMechs, duel for supremacy; MechWarriors who pilot the BattleMechs are the heroes of this age. *Btech 3056* is huge, crowded, and complicated, but if you're a *BattleTech* junkie with a penchant for combat, it's also a lot of fun. There's a sophisticated combat system that can support fights between dozens of robots at the same time (not that there won't be some lag), allowing players to battle opponents in simulations, skirmishes, and full-blown invasions. (Your ability to kill, and kill quickly, is more important than your talent for role-play.) Come here to chat about *BattleTech*, kibitz with members of your faction, and

fight. Your first goal on the MUSE will be to join one of the factions which are always eager to recruit anyone who knows one end of a laser from another. Enter the hotel lobby and read all the newbie topics you can—you'll be lost otherwise. Look at the faction Leader Info to find out which leaders are connected, then try to buy a ticket from Raglin's Robo Vendor to visit the Faction of your choice (not always easy, but you're in a room with other newbies, so talk it through). When you've bought your ticket, hop on the elevator and go talk to your preferred Faction about recruiting possibilities. Don't worry. If they don't want you, the ticket's round trip. Newbies have the run of the hotel, so do explore. Players are allowed to program on *Btech 3056*, and it's recommended that you learn how.

Make sure you know something about *BattleTech* before you try this MUSE, otherwise the thirty-first century could be a little lonely.
TELNET telnet://btech.netaxs.com:3056
Info: **WEB** http://btech.netaxs.com

Slayer's Battletech Page Fans of the Battletech RPG should not miss this one: It's probably the largest compilation of *Battletech* links available. Its resources include lists for mechs, vehicles, aerospace vehicles, and weapons. Also available are clan data, various gam rules, record sheets and other RPG materials. To keep you in touch with the online *Battletech* community, the Web site offers downloadable Zipped newsgroup files and links to other fan home pages with general info, clan pages, merc pages, multimedia links, *Mechwarrior 2* links, and a few FTP sites.
WEB http://www.geocities.com/Times Square/3058/index.html

Chat

alt.games / rec.games While alt.games gives reviews of games and discusses various technical issues, "HELP!!!" is the cry most often heard from these desperate posters. What the hell does the Synonium Device for *Xcom—Terror from the Deep* look like? Where is the conservatory in *Phantasmagoria*? Why do I keep dying when I get to the *Burn: Cycle*'s Buddha? There are often more questions than answers on the board, but at least you'll know you're not alone in your confusion. Rec.games is basically alt.games's scraggly cousin; only a handful of people post, perhaps because they're clueless about alt.games.

USENET alt.games • rec.games

Game Company Support Leave messages for and read posts from editors of game industry and gamer-oriented magazines and newsletters in the Publications choice. Download game rules, updates of game manuals, character sheets, newsletters, and journals in The GCS File Library; retrieve company catalogs from the GCS Catalogs and Boards; write to representatives of several game companies (e.g., Atlas Games, FASA Corporation, Mayfair Games, Ragnarok Enterprises, White Wolf Game Studio, and World Building magazine) in the Gaming Support Messaging area. And visit the Gaming Playtest Center, where these companies run playtests of their still-unreleased products.

AMERICA ONLINE *keyword* gcs

Game Publishers These forums are divided into four areas, A through D, each covering a specific group of game publishers. Within each area are Messages and Libraries sections, which contain support, discussion, files, patches, and upgrades and the generally skinny on the game companies in question.

COMPUSERVE *go* gambpub

rec.games.misc If the game you want doesn't have a newsgroup, and you don't mind the baggage carried over from other gaming newsgroups and a lot of loud whining for hints and cheats, stop by here.

USENET rec.games.misc

Video Games A general forum for discussing video games and VR. Hints and game codes, especially for *NBA Jam* and *Mortal Kombat II*, are in the Hints, Pics & Sounds Library. Press releases for games and gaming systems can be found in the News and Previews section of the main window.

AMERICA ONLINE *keyword* video games

Cheats

The 3D Gaming Scene-Cheats The webmaster's intro says it all: "Here you can find cheat codes for *Blake Stone*, *Catacomb Abyss*, *Corridor 7*, *Dark Forces*, *Descent*, *Descent 2*, *Doom*, *Doom II*, *Duke Nukem 3D*, *Fury3*, *Greed*, *Heretic*, *Hexen*, *HiOctane*, *Magic Carpet*, *Magic Carpet 2*, *Mechwarrior 2*, *Powerslave*, *Quarantine*, *Radix*, *Rise of the Triad*, *Roadwarrior*, *Slipstream 5000*, *Spear of Destiny*, *Strife*, *Tekwar*, *Terminal Velocity*, *Terminator: Future Shock*, *Witchaven*, and *Wolfenstein 3D*." There's also a link to the main page, with summaries and screen shots for the same games, and a download page gives you the shareware and add-ons.

WEB http://www.pol.umu.se/html/ac/cheats.htm

alt.binaries.doom The genius of *Doom* is the open architecture for plugging in new features. Data files that augment *Doom* —like replacing sounds with Clint Eastwood saying "Make my day"—are posted here. You can find all sorts of stuff in alt.binaries.doom, from levels inspired by movies like *Aliens* and *Blade Runner* to games with a slightly spicier bent. X-rated levels exist, even if blowing away "bimbos" is passé.

USENET alt.binaries.doom

The Cheater's Guild-Recreation: Computer Games: Cheats and Hints As cheat resources go, this list is relatively small. Nonetheless, it covers the games that deserve it, and also includes a few "dirty tricks." Currently available are some really nasty but effective *MechWarrior 2* strategies that only truly demented minds (or truly idle ones) could produce.

WEB http://www.inetport.com/~kenb

Dragon King—Video Game Tips Main Page When Mr. Dragon King isn't presiding over the brood, he likes to kick back and compile cheats and hints for numerous consoles and portable game equipment. If you have a 32X, 3DO, Arcade, Game Gear, GameBoy, Genesis, Jaguar, Lynx, Master System, Neo-Geo, Nintendo, PlayStation, Saturn, Super NES, SuperGrafx, TurboDuo, or Virtual Boy, this Web site may be worth your time.

WEB http://www.winternet.com/~markhjOI/videogametips

Game Cheats from the Game Page

Far from complete, but still extensive, this page features codes for some games that others miss, like *System Shock*, and that old classic *Defender of the Crown*. Don't use this list unless you know the game you're looking for: The only point of reference is the name of the game, and nothing more.
WEB http://www.xs4all.nl/~gzbrn /Cheats/Game-Cheats.html

Help for Gamers

Not extremely large, but it has cheats for some of the favorites, like *Wing Commander IV*, *Warcraft II*, *Quake*, *SimCity*, *Dark Sun*, *Descent*, and *Lemmings*.
WEB http://members.tripod.com /~game29/strategy.html#cheat

Mike's Hint Shop List—Game Hints

You'd never think to juxtapose the classic *Bard's Tale* with the hi-tech *Bioforge*, but Mike has done it here, with an alphabetized listing of PC game cheats. Almost all the *Ultimas*, those back-breaking, time-devouring RPGs by ORIGIN, have codes on this page, as do LucasArt's *Tie Fighter* and *Dark Forces*, but not (gasp!) *X-Wing*.
WEB http://www.ozemail.com.au /~mharvey/pages/hints.htm#ulist

rec.games.computer.doom.editing

This newsgroup is the cathedral of the religion of *Doom*-hacking. And make no mistake—it's serious business. Take this example of the philosophy of *Doom* programming: "No product is ever revolutionary in its field, if you understand how science evolves. Each person builds on the next. Some more than others." Admittedly, these discussions frequently involve the construction of WAD files to turn imps into Energizer Bunnies and demons into Pac Men. If you're looking for the WAD files themselves, head for alt.binaries.doom.
USENET rec.games.computer.doom .editing

Skalathill's Video Game FAQ Archive

Since most cheat code pages focus on PC games, this frames-optional site is a welcome addition for console gamers. The FAQs and cheats are divided into Fighting, Action, RPG, Sports, and System (hardware) categories. The codes here are wide-ranging, not only in terms of the number of titles, but also the number of codes included for each title. Worth a peek, a dalliance, and even an extended visit.
WEB http://198.76.12.50/~diamante /vgfaqs.ht

Command & Conquer

The Command and Conquer Dial Up Home Page

Sometimes your best friends can be your greatest enemies. This is certainly the case with multi-player games like *Command & Conquer*, which allow networked play. But in case your friends don't have computers, or if you simply have no friends to begin with, a database of *C&C* players like the *Command & Conquer* Dial Up Homepage, which will summon up a list of players in your area code, would be ideal. With 300 listings in the U.S., Asia, South America, Africa, Australia, and Europe, the database grew so large that the busy webmaster was forced to charge a nominal fee for anyone who wanted to place their names on the list; or at least that's the story he's going with. Note, however, that viewing the database is absolutely free.
WEB http://www-public.rz.uni -duesseldorf.de/~ritterd/main.htm

Command & Conquer Games Page

All Those C & C Notes... This webmaster was so moved by *C&C* that he wrote a 13-part strategy guide to beating the original missions (expansion packs aren't included). If repeated bouts with the artificial intelligence have left you a bit jaded, there's a page with instructions and initialization strings for popular modems, as well as fairly thorough Kali setup instructions.
WEB http://www.netcom.com/~moises /ccnotes.html

Command and Conquer Games Page

Most notable are the international modem players list and the well-used message board for the *C&C* Internet community. Also available are game edit tools and a large archive of new levels, like the intriguing "Chemical Brothers" and "2 MCVs and Tyrannosaurus Rex".
WEB http://www.pernet.net/~rlongl /c&cframe.htm

Command & Conquer: Tiberian Dawn Home Page The official page of *C&C* also happens to be one of the best designed. It's clean, with an archive of great graphics—worthwhile if you want to make your own *C&C* home page. Also worth looking at are the stunning original movie clips from the game's intro; they'll push your PC to the limits, and your eardrums as well. Tiberian Dawn also offers some significant content that the others do not—an extensive summary on the story line and profiles of the two warring sides, the Brotherhood of NOD and GDI. **WEB** http://www.westwood.com/ccl /ccinfo.html

Consoles

Dave's Sega Saturn Home Page As the Saturn satiates many a gamer's longing for unbeatable 32-bit fighting games, Dave's Web page satisfies every Saturn lover's need to stay on top of things. First and foremost, Dave gives a wealth of information concerning new releases for the next four months. Previews, like the great preliminary shots of the arcade version of *Virtua Fighter 3*, will give you a great idea of what to expect down the line. Also, the huge list of current Saturn games, which inches ever closer to completion, provides reviews, pix, and basic info on most games on the market for this console. The page of Tips & Tricks, a dense but welcome eyesore to die-hard gamers (where do you start?!), is also very extensive. **WEB** http://www.sega-saturn.com

Mike Ferrell's Ultimate Gamer's Page Deals primarily with the leading console systems. Rumors about Sony's PSX 2 are bandied about here, as are cheat codes and release dates for the Saturn. Don't bother with any of the "latest news" options, as they're usually over a month old. The best features at the Ultimate Gamer's Page are the screen captures from a mountain of games for the Saturn, the PlayStation, and video capture previews of Nintendo

 ## THE ULTIMATE COMMAND AND CONQUER
WEB http://www.k2.org

With more than 60 links to other fan, archive, and resource pages, a more apt name would be the Ultimate Link collection—but that's just the first page. Clicking the Ultimate File Collection hypertext takes you to a veritable gold mine of *C&C*-related files. Most of them are downloadable fan-

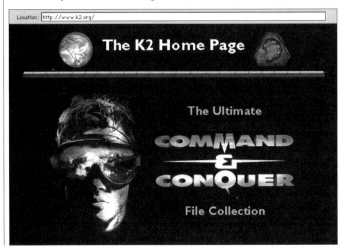

created missions divided into single-player, multi-user, and campaign categories, but you'll also find cheats, game FAQs, *C&C* and Win95 map-making tools, and editing tips. There's a lot here to help rejuvenate your *C&C* gaming scene, especially if you've finished the original missions and are yearning for more.

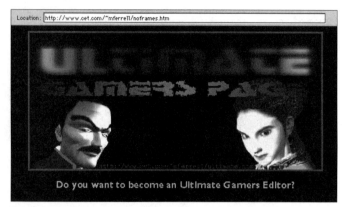

Location: http://www.cet.com/~mferrell/noframes.htm

Do you want to become an Ultimate Gamers Editor?

Father-daughter reunions can be a painful affair at Mike Ferrell's place
http://www.cet.com/~mferrell/ ultimate.htm

Ultra 64 games, which are circulating rapidly around the Internet. The *Star Wars: Shadows of the Empire, Mario 64, PilotWings, Doom 64, Turok: Dinosaur Hunter,* and *Mission: Impossible* 64-bit teasers should be checked out—both pictures and movies are available for each game.
WEB http://www.cet.com/~mferrell /ultimate.htm

Nintendo Net Boogerman and Earthworm Jim are two points in any Web site's favor. This well-designed page, which is devoted to Nintendo (not just Ultra 64!), is covered with yummy graphics of those guys from *Clay Fighter 3*, as well as senior Nintendo celeb *Donkey Kong*. Naturally, previews for the highly anticipated Ultra 64 games like *Robotech: Crystal Dreams, Star Fox 64, Body Harvest,* and *Super Mario Kart R* are available, plus information on the games' development. The Cheat Codes page will help you beat the SNES:

Need 50 extra lives in *Donkey Kong Country?* How about a Bonus Game in *Super Mario World 2*, or invulnerability, free play, and Silent Turbo modes for *Primal Rage?* If you want to visit the companies that develop games for Nintendo, links take you to Viacom New Media Interplay, EA Sports, LucasArts, Namco, Capcom, and, of course, Nintendo.
WEB http://member.aol.com/WJrandon /welcome.htm

Playstation Codes Multiple visits to this voluminous warehouse of PSX cheat codes should be a moral imperative for all PSX owners. It's an unbeatable resource that will bring down the walls between you and the finish line, so to speak. There are so many codes here that you'll get scroll headaches, but that's a minor price to pay for this rewarding experience. Perhaps you'd like to get the full arsenal of weapons and invincibility in *Assault Rigs*, or play *King's Field* not merely with

the usual infinite hit points/ magic points/gold advantages but also Mega Offense, Mega Defense, and rapid weapons usage. Plug in a few of these and you'll have your PSX console begging for mercy.
WEB http://ourworld.compuserve.com /homepages/rwhite/games.htm

The Unofficial Nintendo 64 Headquarters Consummate professionals run this Web site, which provides some of the meatiest editorials about the Ultra 64 on the Web. The news department is on the ball, with articles on Nintendo's deliberate Ultra 64 retail shortage—it prolonged demand—and announcements on shipping dates, new software projects, and Japanese releases. The departments are updated weekly, and stamped with a last-revision date to let you know you're not getting a history lesson. Weekly editorial features cover Nintendo's marketing strategies and offer meditations on the cartridge-CD debate, all written in the knowing style of industry veterans. While the site is peppered with good insights into industry mechanics, the excessive moral support for Nintendo found in most console-specific gaming Web sites is also present here. A bit more critical objectivity and a bit less preachiness would give this page an even advantage over the competition, but the dense features are definitely worth a look.
WEB http://www.nauticom.net/www /capscott

Doom

The All-Time Best Doom Levels
Reviews and downloading instructions for the best *Doom* add-ons, including the famous Aliens adaptation—you can even get in the big yellow mobile exoskeleton suit to take on the Queen Mother.
WEB http://doomgate.cs.buffalo.edu /~williams

DoomGate You'll know as soon as you see the immense *Doom* logo that this is the definitive site for the popular run-and-gun game. A visually intense Web site with links to an incredible range of *Doom*-related resources online—from dozens of personal home pages to FAQs to a list of *Doom* mailing lists. DoomGate has been steadily absorbing smaller *Doom* sites all year—don't be surprised if your favorite *Doom* resource has disappeared from its original home, leaving behind nothing but a "Gone to Doomgate" sign behind.
WEB http://doomgate.cs.buffalo.edu

Official Doom FAQ A great user-friendly guide, the Official *Doom* FAQ begins with "What is *Doom*?" and ends with a poem called "The Night Before *Doom*." Includes hardware troubleshooting and net-working how-tos as well.
URL ftp://ftp.cdrom.com/pub/doom /docs/faqs/dmfaq66.zip
WEB http://doomgate.cs.buffalo.edu /docs/FAQ/doomfaq

Duke Nukem 3D

A Tribute to Duke Duke Nukem is now a confirmed celebrity. His 3-D lifestyle has been caught in 2-D stills on this Web page as he slips in an out of various high profile situations: He's seen kickin' it to a groovy tune as an animated Disco Duke; it's revealed that Duke is the lost Beatle; and Duke's debating the presidential incumbent, sound clip

 # MULTIPLAYER GAMES AND SIMULATIONS
WEB http://www.teleport.com/~caustic
picture: WEB http://www-home.calumet.yorku.ca/dcardoso/www/quake2.htm
If you were stranded in cyberspace and could access but one address, this might not be a bad choice: It's a comprehensive resource for simultaneous multiplayer gaming. Enter this labyrinth and you'll find lists of gaming groups worldwide, lists of individual players, and even more lists of

Location: http://www.stomped.com/monsters/grunt.jpg

the games they play. The page divides the teeming world of modem-to-modem gaming into Internet gaming, online gaming, BBS servers, and free and commercial services. Note that the site is somewhat outdated, and some information is now obsolete: You won't find Mplayer, TEN, or battle.net info here, though there's a goldmine of Kali instructions and an obituary for the departed MILK.

I THINK I CLAN, I THINK I CLAN

Clan Steel Viper presents something of a paradox. They follow more fiercely the Clan way and the code of the warrior than any other Clan, and at the same time believe in a unique vision that may ultimately temper the aggression of the Clans. This seeming paradox rises from the Vipers' deeply held conviction that they alone understand that Nicholas Kerensky's true vision called for the Clans to conquer the former worlds of the Terran Hegemony and then to restore the Star League, not by coercing the people of the Inner Sphere to accept Clan leadership, but by cooperating with the existing Great Houses to reestablish one proper government. Because they alone understand this vision, the Viper also believe that their destiny is to lead the restoration of the Star League as ilClan.

—from Xtreme Battletech

included! Also, there's a photo gallery of pix from fans who've spotted Duke in other strange places. See? These games really can be creative.
WEB http://duke.intersphere.com

The Adrenaline Vault—Duke Nukem 3D Site Hey, if aliens shot up your ride, would you call the cops like a little post-apocalyptic weasel or would you mow the perps down with your chain gun? If that dilemma is an easy one, so is overcoming any reservations you may have over using *Duke* cheats to boost the blood-letting. The AV site for *Duke Nukem 3D* has codes that allow you to use the entire arsenal of weapons, give you access to all doors, and make the good Duke invincible in "God mode," among other things. Don't forget to get the maps, the map editors, a *Duke* screensaver, and some hints,

tips, and game secrets.
WEB http://www.avault.com/duke.html

Fighting games

Brawl An FTP site that offers FAQs and other basic information on fighting games: the *MK*s, the *Virtua Fighter*s, the *Street Fighter*s, *Tekken*, *X-Men: Children of the Atom* (also guides and pictures), *Killer Instinct I & II*, and *FX Fighter*.
URL ftp://brawl.mindlink.net/pub

Fighting Games—Realm of Warriors This list o' links spotlights *Ultimate Mortal Kombat 3* and *Killer Instinct*. Beyond that, there's a big list of miscellaneous links to other fan pages and FAQs for popular games: *Tekken*, *Virtua Fighter*, *Street Fighter*, *FX Fighter*, *Samurai Showdown*, *WWF Wrestling*, *Primal Rage*, etc.
WEB http://po-2.clinton.k12.ia.us/ccs /Student/O'Lone/Fighting.HTML

USA*F Index Moves, combos, and codes for *MK3* and *Street Fighter Alpha*, There are links here to numerous FAQs for *Mortal Kombat 3, Street Fighter, Dark Stalkers, Killer Instinct, King of Fighters, Tekken, WWF,* and *X-Men*.
WEB http://www.cris.com/~Bktwist /indexI.shtml

Flight sims

Air Warrior FAQ The popular online multiplayer flight sim, which allows almost 100 players simultaneously to engage in cross era (WWI, WWII, Korea) combat missions, is explained in depth in this FAQ. Whether you've got a question about *AW* technique ("Everyone is able to out-turn me, and I die every time I go up. What am I doing wrong?") or tech ("I downloaded SVGA *Air Warrior* but when I try to run it I get "Unable to find TERMDATA.BIN." Where do I find this file?"), you'll find the answers here.
WEB http://ddi.digital.net/~rocket/faq /faq.html

Air Warrior on CRC Net From this site—a great resource for the *AW*er—you can telnet directly to CRC, where you can download the game and other *AW* files, get images and sound clips, and participate in a flight sim forum. It also offers a quick path for scenario registering, current and upcoming scenario info and schedules, and links to historical, aviation, and gaming sites of interest to the *Air War-*

rior community and the flight sim community at large.
WEB http://www.shebop.com

comp.sys.ibm.pc.games.flight-sim
Flying fans discuss the ins and outs, ups and downs, and loop-the-loops of flight simulation: *X-Wing*, *Aces Over Europe*, *Falcon 3.0*, the Microsoft *Flight Simulator*, and of course, the new *Air Warrior II*, about which the newsgroup is all abuzz.
USENET comp.sys.ibm.pc.games .flight-sim

Falcon 3.0 and Modem Lobby Help
Download this file for detailed step-by-step instructions for hooking up your *Falcon 3.0* to the Modem-to-Modem Lobby, where you can compete against other *Falcon* pilots in real time.
COMPUSERVE *go* mtmforum→Libraries *or* Messages→*Search by file name:* F3.MTM

Historic Air Combat Duels are proposed and postponed over this forum, and there's constant jabber about the Fighter Duel Ladder and the PAW (Pacific Air War) Ladder. Naturally, really bad fighter pilot metaphors ("at your six") are used shamelessly, but that's part of the fun. What would the Red Baron make of it all? This niche community is heavily into its own jargon, but it's open and friendly nonetheless.
COMPUSERVE *go* mtmgames→Libraries

MiG-29 Challenge Ladder Rules
So, comrade, you've got 36,600 lbs. of deadly thrust blowing

out of twin Isotov RD-33 engines—but so does the other guy. See who wins accolades from the Central Committee and a virtual pic in *Pravda* when you compete against other MiG aces on the Challenge Ladder. Download this file for complete details. Competitive flytime takes place in the Modem-to-Modem Lobby.
COMPUSERVE *go* mtmforum→Libraries →*Search by file name:* **MIG29.RUL**

Modern Air Combat The nitty-gritty of the sims—from *Falcon 3.0* to *F-14 Fleet Defender*—is discussed on the Flight Sim Forum's Message board. For utilities and flight films, check out the Forum's Library. Need even more utilities? Visit CompuServe's Modem-to-Modem Forum Library. The Modem-to-Modem Message board discussion centers around the challenge ladders—this is a competitive place!
COMPUSERVE *go* mtmforum→Libraries *or* Messages→Modern Air Combat

The Usenet Guide to Falcon 3
Spectrum Holobyte created one of the most sophisticated and realistic flight simulators in the multi-user *Falcon 3.0*. This site archives the collected wisdom of three years worth of *Falcon* fan exchanges, covering tech issues like system requirements and setup procedures as well as tactical matters such as dogfights and bombing runs. The advice oscillates between congeniality and practicality.
WEB http://cactus.org/~knutson /UGF3/UGF3.book.html

The XPilot Page The whole shooting match, the FAQ, access to *XPilot* Servers (sites where you play the game), information on the game's inventors, and access to sites which will let you play *XPilot* with sound effects!
WEB http://www.cs.uit.no/XPilot/

XPilot Newbie Manual Shade and Zoff guide newbies through the game of *XPilot* with a hypertext manual that covers both beginning and advanced play. There's also a full-service glossary of *XPilot*.
WEB http://bau2.uibk.ac.at/erwin/NM /www

Magic: the Gathering

MtG on IRC There's a certain blind faith involved in playing a card game against someone you can't see. For all you know, they could be making it up as they go along. But on the understanding that no-one who can be bothered to play the game online would actually cheat, it's an uncertainty that doesn't hinder hundreds of *MtG* players from coming here every night. Ask if anyone wants to play, and you'll get a /msg back suggesting a private room where you can meet to compete. There's a slightly arcane code used to transmit moves, but once you pick this up you'll find that IRC is actually a fun way to play—it's fast-paced, the competition is good, and there's always someone ready when you are.
IRC #magic

rec.games.trading-cards.magic .misc Those lucky devils at Wizards of the Coast! *Magic: the Gathering* may be the most successful (and addictive) trading-card game of all time. Drop by this newsgroup for discussion of new cards and sets, rants and raves, and misplaced traffic that should go in the rules, strategy, or marketplace subgroups.

USENET rec.games.trading-cards .magic.misc

rec.games.trading-cards .marketplace.magic.trades Before there was money, there were barter societies. Then, there was money. Now there are barter cybercommunities. "Three of my uncommon revised cards for one of the cards in an unlimited edition." "My Lord of Atlantis for your Mirror Universe." "I have a Beta Cyclopean Tomb in near mint condition to trade for a Jihad in similar condition." These aren't your daddy's baseball cards.

USENET rec.games.trading-cards .marketplace.magic.trades

Marathon

Bungie Software The company behind the best use to which you and your buddies can put your networked Macs, has a functional and commercially acceptable Web site. Delving into the mysterious and diverse dimensions of the *Marathon* game's plotline is left to the fansites. Here, the closest you can get to an insight into your

onscreen alter-ego—besides the opportunity to download demos and purchase full versions of all Bungie productes from *Pathways into Darkness* to *Abuse*—is a hint book that spells out the whole plot. Nevertheless, this is an essential stopping point for any Mac owner with a modem.

WEB http://www.bungie.com

Marathon Central *Marathon* arrived as such an improvement on *Doom*, the iconoclastic PC game from id software, that its launch presaged a huge burst of interest in a machine that until then had not been thought of as much of a games platform. Subsequent generations of the game have ensured *Marathon* remains Mac users' favourite form of bloodletting. Visit AMUG (Arizona Macintosh Users Group) and discover how passionate Marathoners can be and why you scarcely need look anywhere else for the secrets of the Pfhor.

WEB http://www.bungie.com

MechWarrior2

Activision Home Page This multiplayer video game derived from the *BattleTech* universe has a very different online culture from its RPG brethren—one might say as different as live chat from email. The battling brothers of *MechWarrior* are adrenaline addicts of the real-time variety; no dice, no rule books, no charts or tables to slow down the pace. They all

have the URL of the official company bookmarked and memorized, if only for the *MW2* index. Activision offers the latest *MechWarrior 2* updates online, news on expansion packs, and demos to make your PC purr months before the actual releases. Also, there's information on the networking program that brings players together, Netmech. It's a little advertisement-heavy, but the toys will keep you glued to the site.

WEB http://www.activision.com /netmech/index.html

alt.games.mechwarrior2 In all likelihood, the "Thrust master Problem" posting is not a male plumbing problem, though there are numerous other posts (most are random insults) that simply fly way off topic in this newsgroup. While the conversations have a tendency to be vulgar and random, advice for the troubled player still manages to creep into the postings. Lot's of setup questions like "Can't connect Netmech via modem. Help!" and "3DPro won't work with GBL (Ghost Bear's Legacy)" are asked and answered.

USENET alt.games.mechwarrior2

MechWarrior 2 Add-Ons & Patches Don't use this Web site if you value your honor. It aspires to collect all available patches for *MW2*, and then some. The Enzo cheat, which supposedly allows you to access three new mechs, has caused much grief since the hulking Battlemaster

mech didn't turn out to be playable. There's a patch here that fixes that problem, so armchair mechwarriors can terrorize the universe to their hearts' content.
WEB http://arbornet.org/%7Elokety /mw2_addon.html

MW2 Player Directory Players from more than 20 countries have joined this registry in order to find modem opponents in their areas. Welcome Mexico, Switzerland, Philippines, and the U.K., the new additions to the list.
WEB http://arbornet.org/%7Elokety /mw2_pd.html

Modem play

AppleTalk Games Over the Internet FAQ Shatter the myths and outsmart the troubleshooters in the AppleTalk world. This page offers great support for those who want to play games like *Minotaur* and *Air Combat* using an AppleTalk connection. Get how-tos and free software for IPRemote, IPTnnl, and Async Atalk. Lots of discussion about what games run best and where.
WEB http://www.xmission.com /~morrison/AoI/home.html

battle.net Blizzard Entertainment plans to make available a free multi-player network service called battle.bet for Blizzard games. Players with TCP/IP connections will be able to connect to the service just by clicking on a button from a game's main screen.

Location: http://www.3drealms.com/graphics/duke3d/dukesmurf4.gif

A Duke a day keeps the Smurfs away
http://www.3drealms.com/duke3d.html

The upcoming releases from Diablo and Starcraft, which will work with both the PC and Mac, will be the first of a long line (Blizzard hopes) specially designed to support battle.net. At press time battle.net, which will run 24 hours, seven days a week, has not been given a starting date.
WEB http://www.battle.net

DWANGO! The irreverent name is actually an acronym for Dial-up Wide Area Network Game Operation, a service that links vast numbers of users together for intense multiplayer action in games like *Doom I & II*, *MechWarrior 2*, *Heretic*, *Hexen*, and *Descent II*. The content is not exclusive, since several other companies offer similar services at competitive rates, but the performance is more than adequate.
WEB http://www.dwango.com

Game Publishers Lobby The lobby has busy message boards filled with lengthy discussions of what to do with the Windows 95 software when dealing with pre-existing games. The new game *Steel Panther* seems to get the most attention these days, along with the seasonal sports games. If it's happening in life, it's in here: Your hockey team against mine. 9 p.m. CompuServe. Be there.
COMPUSERVE *go* mtm games

Internet Modem Players Listing A server listing gamers interested in playing modem-to-modem games. Players are listed by area code, email address, and the modem games in which they're interested. The email server allows players to add their name, search for other players, and get help.
WEB http://www.xmission.com /~morrison/IMPL/home.html

Modem-to-Modem Challenge Board A directory of CompuServe gamers looking for opponents. Search by game title, phone number, or name. Players may choose either to connect via the MTM Gaming Lobby or to call each other directly.
COMPUSERVE *go* mtmchallenge

Modem-to-Modem Gaming Lobby If all your favorite PC game lacks is a living opponent—*Tom Landry Strategy Football* and *Empire Deluxe* are much more fun when the enemy is flesh and blood—and if the game (commercial or shareware) has modem-to-modem capabilities, CompuServe is the place to dig up opponents. Who cares where your adversary lives, as long as he or she likes—and owns—the same game? Once you and your opponent are connected, just exit your communications program (probably Information Manager) and run the game. Set up the game as if you were connected directly, rather than via modem, since the connection is already established. Reduced rates are in effect, and support is available in the evening.
COMPUSERVE *go* mtmlobby

Multi-Player Games Forum Looking for help with *Island of Kesmai* or *MegaWars*? Fellow gamers, designers, and CompuServe staffers are here to share their gaming secrets. There are messages and files related to *MegaWars I*,

MegaWars III, Island of Kesmai, British Legends, You Guessed It, Sniper, and the *Entertainment Center*.
COMPUSERVE *go* mpgames

Multiplayer Internet Gaming Programs and instructions for playing modem games over the Net via gaming networks like Kali, Internet Head-to-Head Daemon, iFrag, IPTunnel, Milk, JServe, and BBS Game Servers.
WEB http://www.teleport.com/~caustic /internet.shtml

TEN—Total Entertainment Network Another gaming service that's grabbing a lot of press is TEN. The Total Entertainment Network was in beta-testing at press time, with registered users logging on with free testing accounts. Whether you join before or after beta, you'll be able to test your mettle with an ever-growing number of games: *Duke Nukem 3D, Terminal Velocity, Deadlock, Warcraft, Civnet, Magic: The Gathering*, and *Dark Sun Online*. *Dark Sun Online* is notable as one of the few RPGs Online in a sea of action/adventure and strategy games. TEN hopes to maintain 400 players at once in this *AD&D* universe of deserts, magic, city-states, and dragons.
WEB http://www.ten.net

Welcome to Kali! Kali boasts that it's the largest Internet gaming system in the world—there are more than 35,000 registered users worldwide. Although it's

notoriously slow under certain conditions, the one-time flat fee (about twenty sponduliks) is too attractive for many players to pass up, in light of the fact that most other services will charge per minute, hour, or month. Kali supports games that are IPX compatible—the network protocol that it emulates to connect players—so popular games like *Descent, Command & Conquer, Duke Nukem 3D, Quake, MechWarrior 2, Heretic, Mortal Kombat 3*, and *Nascar Racing* are all basically Kali-ready. This updates page will give you the latest news as well as the current BETA version of Kali95. You'll get a basic rundown on how Kali works, info on the system minimums you need to make Kali run, and instructions on how to use it.
WEB http://www.axxis.com/kali/index .html

MUDs & MUSHes

Hall of MUDs With a jolly, nostalgia-inducing skeleton knight welcoming new players, this sitelets players to jump straight into any one of several score of it's webmaster's favorite adventure MUDs. There's a separate section just for new MUDs, including the intriguing Nanny MUD, and a link to a similar but much larger and less exclusive resource, the MUD Connector. Even non-players will enjoy the "Cool Mud Hero" feature.
WEB http://scuba.uwsuper.edu /~sfenness/mud.html

History of MUDs A long, long time ago, the Spanish discovered America. A long time ago, man first visited the moon. And not so long ago, MUD worlds were created. Read a brief history at this site and learn how Roy Trubshaw and Richard Bartle helped create these entertaining havens.
WEB http://www.shef.ac.uk/uni /academic/I-M/is/studwork/groupe/tl .html

The MUD Resource Collection Maintained by Amberyl— long-time MUDder, moderator of the newsgroup rec.games .mud.announce, and author of the MUSH manual—this site brings together virtually all of the resources a beginning (and even experienced) MUDder is likely to need. MUD lists? Got

'em. Links to the MUD newsgroups? You bet. The most current version of the MUD FAQ and Amberyl's MUSH manual? Of course. The MUD Resource Collection also links to MUD encyclopedias, large MUD sites, articles about MUDding, and much more. How much more? Well, Amberyl is a role-player, and she's added the World of Darkness FAQ and a list of Tolkien games to her site. She's also helped to administrate MUDs in the past, and offers resources for the coder, programmer, and beginning builder.
WEB http://www.cis.upenn.edu/~lwl /mudinfo.html

rec.games.mud.announce Carries announcements about new

MUDs, lamentations for deceased MUDs, updates on site changes, and regular postings of the multi-part MUD FAQ. If your favorite MUD is down for a long period of time, check here for an announcement about why, when, or if it's expected back up. The MUD FAQ is perhaps the best source of information on the Net for the new MUDder. It includes an introduction to the basic vocabulary of the MUD world, hints on how to start (what to do and what not to do), and an extensive list of client programs that players can use to make MUDding easier. Descriptions of the clients include info about the programs and addresses where you can download them.
USENET rec.games.mud.announce

 DR. SHAREWARE
WEB http://www.rbi.com/~salegui/jim
picture: WEB http://www.bungie.com
Marathon Infinity continues the action of the popular *Marathon 3-D* shooter for the Macintosh, and you can download its demo from this Web site. The webmaster has a lot to offer, like *Ultima 3, Odyssey I.4, Citadel of the Dead, Battle Planets, Doom, Escape Velocity, Mortal Pongbat,* and

Maelstrom. The Good Doctor even gives brief descriptions of each game, in case you're having trouble deciding which version of *Cheese Toast* to grab. There are definitely some games here worth your time. If you don't crave them, your Mac will. It's hungry.

Quake

Mr. Wolf's Quake Den News and links, plus cheats, sites to download the game and software add-ons, help documentation, configuration tricks, Deatmatch servers, and more news and links. In a flood of *Quake* sites (mixed disaster metaphor duly noted), Mr. Wolf's Quake Den is better organized and more regularly updated than most.
WEB http://www.vvm.com/~hfowler /hug.htm

Quake Mania! The page could stand some reorganization, but if you're looking for links to new *Quake* levels, maps, textures, fixes, tools, and hacks created by gamers. For each program or guide listed, there's a name, a brief description, the size of the file, and a link. Quake Mania! also points to other fan pages.
WEB http://www-home.calumet.yorku .ca/dcardoso/www/quake2.htm

The Quake Mini-FAQ The not-so-mini FAQ answers questions about hardware and system requirements for playing the game, links to sites where you can download the software and other documentation, and collects links to *Quake* FTP and Web sites.
WEB http://www.geocities.com/Athens /1802/Quake-Mini-FAQ.html

Quake Modem Player Directory A directory of modem players organized by area code. Sign up and add your name to the list or search for an opponent. Each listing includes a player's handle, email address, state, and a brief description of skill level and playing preferences. If you've found a player but aren't sure how to get a game started, click the Modem Help link for instructions.
WEB http://members.aol.com /whitejazz7/qmodem/index.htm

Quake News Regular reports from the front lines of *Quake*. The site links to news from id, the best and worst of *Quake* happenings on the Net, new releases of programs and editing tools, and interviews with *Quake* developers. Visit often.
WEB http://web.inter.NL.net/users /L.J.Noordsij

Telefrag Interested in playing on a *Quake* team? Getting together with other players on the Net to dominate cyberspace? The Quake Wars page is hell-bent on creating rivalries among *Quake* teams across the Internet. But first, it's helping to organize players into teams. Stop by and try out. Sharing news of scientific advancements, discussing censorship, and finding a date are all worthwhile online endeavors, but the Net may well be at its best when it's used to organize a gaming community—even if the community is based on violent competition and carnage. Let the *Quake* Wars begin. If CNN isn't covering them, this site will be.
WEB http://www.hom.net/~stagger /telefrag.html

Warcraft

EvilByte's Warcraft 2 Library This is the Internet equivalent to buying fireworks in Times Square on July 4th. Though nothing needs to be purchased here, you can get some discreet program that removes the CD check from the *WC2* program. Also, there are a few game editors to help you experiment with the game and some cheats to make game play more interesting. Don't forget to download the pack of almost 50 PUDs for hours more of play.
WEB http://www.cuug.ab.ca:8001 /~bereznii/war2.html

Madman's Multi-Player PUD's Madman has done *WC2* fans a great service by posting a number of downloadble PUDs along with thumbnails of maps.
WEB http://www.itsnet.com/~madman /puds.htm

WWGhomepages Another league to which you can apply your honed *WC2* wrist-mouse skills. From this page, you can join up, see their rules and requirements, check up on tournaments, and download official WWG PUDs (add-on levels for *WC2*). If you wish to join, you'll need the permission from the leader of the clan that you wish to join; their email addresses are listed on the membership page, along with other membership instructions.
WEB http://www.premier1.net/~emlaug /war

Humor

BOSS GETTING YOU DOWN? LAUGH AT HER EXPENSE.
SNICKER WHILE YOU SURF ON COMPANY TIME

UMOR HUCKSTERS, stand-up comedians, offbeat satirists, penny panto-
mimes and other laughmongers bring you World Wide Weirdness on
such a grand scale, it makes Comedy Central look like amateur night.
This Web of laughter is bound to bring you to your knees, with everything
from droll song parodies and political satire, to *bon mots* and filthy jokes
that will make your coworkers convulse in disgust and delight. Or just chuckle ruefully at the asinine and ridiculous things our political and celebrity luminaries have uttered, especially that punching bag of a former Vice-President, Dan Quayle: "I love California; I practically grew up in Phoenix."

Location: http://www.thecorporation.com/oneoffs/96/kittyporn/index.html

The problem is growing.

Each day it is estimated that as many as twenty pictures of young cats go up on the Internet without their knowledge or consent. With a computer and phone line, anyone, even children, can easily find and view these pictures. In fact, in a frightening new trend children themselves are increasingly responsible for taking and distributing these startling pictures. What is to be done? Where does free speech end and compassion begin?

 ## THE CORPORATION
WEB http://www.thecorporation.com
The Corporation knows exactly where you're funny bone is located and goes after it with truly novel content. This professional parody paints broad strokes of yellow into cyberjournalism, and with a style all its own. Check out the latest headlines in The Corporation Times, or catch the Humor Product Archive's hilarious pitch for Kitty Porn, the Carpal Tunnel Workshop, or the CyberAtlas. Ground zero for brilliant, offbeat satire.

Starting points

Adrian's Humor Collection The categories in this eclectic collection of hilarious email and anecdotes include Computers and Programming, Gender and Sex, *Star Trek*, Science, Religion, and University Life. The section titled "25 Ways to Cope with Stress" offers suggestions ranging from "Braid the hairs in each nostril" to "Make a language up and ask people for directions in it." Other files include the "Professor Translation Guide," "Problems with Soap and Hotels," and "Alternate MS Bob personalities." Find your way to even more laughs with Adrian's extensive list of links.
WEB http://gpu.srv.ualberta.ca /~apowell/humor.html

alt.folklore.urban Did you know Grand Central Station is radioactive? Have you heard about the latest fad in Japan— hydrogenated beer, which is green and yields Hinden- burgesque, inflammable burps? If you enjoy walking the fine line between entertainment and deceit—a practice known on alt.folklore.urban as "trolling" —you will enjoy this news- group. Unfortunately, several months ago, James "Kibo" Parry outlawed trolling on the newsgroup; since then, the only legends posted here are those whose veracity has been confirmed. For example: The more milk you drink, the more mucus your body produces. Rumor (what else) has it that

Douglas Adams is a devotee. No smileys allowed.
USENET alt.folklore.urban
*FAQ:***URL** ftp://rtfm.mit.edu/pub/use net-by-hierarchyalt/folklore/urban

alt.humor.best-of-usenet Come here to the virtual dumping ground for many of the light and loopy things uttered on Usenet. A kid in rec.food.veg talks about his vision of the Garden of Eden: skateboard ramp, monster-truck pit, and "a meat locker the size of a 7-11 store." A college student gets flamed, amusingly, for asking for a 10-page paper on Buddhism. Learn to "lighten up: buy a puppy, smoke some dope, torture small rodents, etc." Humorous posts from newsgroups from rec.backcountry to gnu.emacs .vm.info.
USENET alt.humor.best-of-usenet

The Biggest List of Humor Links on the Web Interested in a little funny business? It's long, it's not selective, and it's definitely not pretty. It's just an endless list of humor links.
WEB http://mars.superlink.net/~zorro /humor.htm

Centre for the Easily Amused Creators Dave and Cathy have compiled a campy entertainment link fest here. This straightforward, award-winning page hooks you up to some of the most amusing hubsites around. Your virtual remote control to Internet lounging and laughing.
WEB http://www.amused.com

NEW MEDIA WOLF

The pigs leapt to their window and saw bulldozers, cranes, steamrollers and flatbed trucks, shaking the earth and filling the sky with acrid black smoke. At the head of this devilish parade, studying maps and blueprints with great interest, were four dangerous-looking wolves in expensively tailored suits.

—from Politically Correct Bedtime Stories

Comedy Connection This is best for its scheduled chat sessions, which are organized according to their adult-content level. For some real groaners, check out the Joke BBS (an inadvertent pun?) and downloadable .WAV files.
MSN *keyword* comedy

The Funny Pages Looking for "50 Great Things to Do in an Elevator?" Try selling Girl Scout cookies, or giving religious tracts to fellow passengers. Or maybe you're more interested in "105 Ways to Drive Your Roommate Crazy," "19 Ways to Be Offensive at a Funeral," or "Why God Never Received Tenure at Any University." Paco divvies his laughs into factual humor, fictional humor, and computer jokes, with the requisite links to more online humor and comics.
WEB http://uvacs.cs.virginia.edu /~bah6f/funnies

The IMPROVisation Online A spot for anyone in search of a laugh, including aspiring writers and performers. The Comedy Chatter message board offers folders on dirty jokes, the best comedians, and news from comedy clubs. Jokesters can post their best material in The Schticks Library. The site also includes a list of IMPROVisation clubs from Hollywood to Washington, D.C.
AMERICA ONLINE *keyword* improv

LaughWeb Interested in the "Top Ten Signs You Are an Internet Geek?" If you refer to your children as "client applications" and introduce your husband as "my domain server," you probably qualify.

See the Laugh of the Day or Month, check out the demo version of "Bill Gates in Heaven," and get lost in the jokes and stories split into categories such as business humor, puns and groaners, and insults. The site even offers a ratings system to warn prudish visitors, with an "L" for strong language, an "R" for risque, an "S" for sexist, and an "*" for gross and disgusting. All this, plus a jokes archive and links for guaranteed fun.
WEB http://www.misty.com/laughweb

The Matrix: Humor Are you an Internet nerd? Take the test—with questions about your email address and the time it took you to construct your

.SIG file—to find out. An enormous number of humor-oriented lists can be found at this site, with everything from "10 Things Not to Say When Pulled Over By a Cop" ("Back off Barney, I've got a piece") to "101 Ways to Say No" ("I've dedicated my life to linguini"). Other files include "The Muppet Massacre," "Mental Disease of the Month Club," and countless other humorous stories and parodies.
WEB http://www.marshall.edu /~hartwell/humor.html

The Mother of All Humor Archives Country-western song titles ("Drop Kick Me, Jesus, Through the Goalposts of Life," "Get Your Tongue Outta

ORACLE SERVICE HUMOR ARCHIVES
 WEB http://www.synapse.net/~oracle/Contents/HumorArch.html

The super-deluxe, streamlined, side-splitting source for humor on the Web. Expertly crafted and thoroughly hilarious. "Grab your funny bone and dive in" for rapid-fire laughs including 100 Jokes to Play While Ordering Pizza, Unabomber Haikus, an Elvis Versus Jesus send-up, all among funny

lists, dirty jokes, and political humor. Check out "How to Know if You're a Redneck" in Oracle's Favorites, or the uncategorizable "Warm Fuzzies" from a collection of snippets from newsgroups, email, and chain letters. The enormous archive will have you in stitches. Includes an excellent links department rated with Oracle stars.

My Mouth 'Cause I'm Kissing You Goodbye," "I Wanna Whip Your Cow," etc.). Other files in this voluminous collection include "Geek Code," "Dictionary of Dating," an "Explanation of Stupidity," and many links across the seemingly infinite universe of online humor.
WEB http://www.cs.cornell.edu/Info /People/ckline/humor.html

Online Humor Collection Why did the chicken cross the road? Karl Marx: "It was an historical inevitability." Timothy Leary: "Because that's the only kind of trip the Establishment would let it take." And so forth. A large collection, alphabetically arranged, with files from "Alligator Bites Penis" to "Wife vs. Email." Mostly amusing snags from postings to newsgroups.
WEB http://www.csua.berkeley.edu /~benco/humor.html

rec.humor Last night at the party, your new girlfriend wasn't vomiting. Sure, she drank too much and she was leaning over the toilet clutching her stomach, but she wasn't vomiting. What was she doing? "Driving the porcelain bus," "The Technicolor yawn," "Involuntary personal protein spill": all purported euphemisms for throwing up, and all available on this newsgroup, in a lengthy thread titled "How many ways can you say 'puke'?" Rec.humor is the Internet's clearinghouse for the funny, strange, and juvenile. Read and post jokes and stories

It's just one joker after another at the *Daily Muse*
http://www.cais.net/aschnedr/muse.htm

here, or request them ("Michael Jackson jokes needed," "Need lawyer jokes," etc.).
USENET rec.humor

Your Mom An off-the-wall humor ezine specializing in lowbrow laughs. It's got a goofy smell to it, comprised of comedic articles such as "7 Reasons why Oranges are Better Than Navel Lint," "Evan's Walrus Training Facility," and "An Interview With A Potato." The authors feel "it takes a hell o' work to put this thing together. Is it worth it? Well, my mind says no, but the little gerbil that talks to me in my sleep says yes." Surf on in for armpit noises and fart jokes you'll never outgrow.
WEB http://bird.taponline.com/yourmom

Parody & satire

Bill TV Groove with the funky green boob tube on centerstage of Bill TV. The site is a four-

channeled mechanism of funny clips from varying topics of the paranormal, paradoxical, or just plain entertaining. A neat layout with some clever animation any couch potato can appreciate, plus amusing links.
WEB http://ourworld.compuserve.com /homepages/billtv

The Daily Muse The *Daily Muse*, a.k.a. Technophobics Anonymous, has its finger on the pulse of the American political scene. With a newsy outlook, this simply designed ezine snaps up current events and spits them out with an entertaining spin.
WEB http://www.cais.net/aschnedr /muse.htm

Deep Thought of the Day "If you're a horse, and someone gets on you, and falls off, and then gets right back on you, I think you should buck him off right away," quips *Saturday Night Live*'s Jack Handy

A DAY WITH UNCLE JACK

One thing kids like is to be tricked. For instance, I was going to take my little nephew to Disneyland, but instead I drove him to an old burned-out warehouse. "Oh, no," I said, "Disneyland burned down." He cried and cried, but I think that deep down he thought it was a pretty good joke. I started to drive over to the real Disneyland, but it was getting pretty late.

—from **Deep Thought of the Day**

ogy, student humor, and several other specifically designed laugh channels.
WEB http://miso.wwa.com/~boba/bob/parody.html

The Keepers of Lists The masters of humor, a mysterious lineup of Gregorian-cloaked critters, are "keepers of the Lists." They 're busy compiling quite a collection of "X number of reasons why..." lists on which readers may vote.
WEB http://www.dtd.com/keepers

Monday Morning Briefs No, this site's not about what underwear you start the week with, but it might be funnier if it were. Its collection of "Bravos" may be earned from mild chuckles garnered by Biographical Biopsies, the Trite List and the Briefs which sketch pathetic souls in the news with puns and parody. Easily digestible, light humor—like a caffeine-packed coffee on a Monday morning.
WEB http://members.aol.com/MMBRIEFS/index.htm

News Grief "Take the concept of a daily news brief, add plenty of satire, sarcasm and cynicism and you have the ingredients for giving grief back to the news with our own unique Skewpoint." This is the ticker-tape of scathing satire, worth a daily glance at the newsgrief article of the moment by renowned muse Bob Hirschfield.
WEB http://www.newsgrief.com/index.htm

beside a beautiful landscape .GIF. A fun stop on your daily surf.
WEB http://www.eecs.nwu.edu/cgi-bin/deepthought

Gallery of Advertising Parody Good at inventing bad ads? Interested in skewering the commercials you see on TV? Visit this page, which includes parodies of famous campaigns-for products such as Absolut Vodka, Benson & Hedges, IBM, the Gap, and many more.
WEB http://www.dnai.com/~sharrow/parody.html

It's Time to Parody A parody panorama of links. Categories carved up by smiley faces include political satire, Microsoft-busting links, kibol-

True A delightful showcase for Daryl Cagle cartoon enthusiasts. View the cartoons, and know the motives behind them with this informative look at cartooning, divided into categories such as Rush Limbaugh, Sex, and Fat. Cagle delivers as a first-class social lampooner equipped with a creative pencil and a quick wit.
WEB http://www.pacificnet.net/art/DarylCagleDailyCartoon.html

Jokes

Fun Email Fun Email's creator, David Krider, sends amusing messages to unsuspecting people with interesting Web pages; once he gets a response, he includes links to those pages and the relevant correspondence. To the creator of the Nice Page—a site that includes a logo reading, "Mean People Suck"—Krider wrote, "Where have all the nice people gone?" He got a response with theories about "the rise of materialism," "the money-is-God attitude," and appreciation for his concern about "the declining numbers of nice people." Strange and compelling, this online version of Don Novello's Lazlo Letters displays one of the few genuinely creative uses of the electronic medium.
WEB http://www.cco.caltech.edu/~ekrider/FunEMail/funemail.html

Joke Wallpaper Dedicated to finding those amusing needles in the Web's haystack. The folks at Joke Wallpaper create a collage of funny email mes-

sages, stories, and links with the simplistic style of an old friend fiddling around the Net.
WEB http://www.iquest.net/~skremer

Mirsky's Worst of the Web For sites so awful, Mirsky sure spends a lot of time looking at them. For those fascinated with the ridiculous use of the Internet, browse Mirsky's choices and chuckle away at his rips on them.
WEB http://mirsky.com/wow

Loonie Bin A handy pocketbook of jokes to add a little spice to any collection of bookmarks. Bugs Bunny looks amused above a list running the gamut of top ten lists, Your Momma jokes, and one liners.
WEB http://www.NorCom.mb.ca/deedee/loonbin.htm

Practical Jokes Learn the art of exploding salt shakers, Chinese fire drills, and hear the shenanigans of college students and laugh-seekers snipped from various newsgroups.
WEB http://www.umd.umich.edu/~nhughes/htmldocs/pracjokes.html

Newsgripes

alt.aol-sucks When America Online added Usenet access to its services, thousands of newbies flooded in. Usenet posts from aol.com outnumbered posts from any other domain in a matter of weeks. And AOLers (known on this newsgroup as "AOLusers"), like all newbies, committed gaffes. The AOL company is bashed here for its corporate paranoia, schoolmarmish chiding ("We would like to remind you that our Terms of Service prohibit vulgar or sexually oriented language..."), and time-wasting and fee-escalating interface. AOLers themselves are mocked as point-and-click consumers, too out of it to know what they're missing, or too Pollyanna-ish to protest. If you're logging on from AOL itself, this newsgroup has the euphemistic name "Flames and Complaints about America Online."
USENET alt.aol-sucks

alt.devilbunnies A fantasy realm where users interactively construct a new reality online. "Fudds"—self-appointed defenders of humanity—hunt down bloodthirsty rabbits worldwide. "We are the only thing that stands between a disbelieving human race and horribly, inescapable, fluffy doom," reads the FAQ. A huge, arcane lore has grown up around the battles, the participants and their tribes, and their technology (a "cuteness geometer?"). Patience and a high tolerance for nonsense are required for participation in this highly social environment. Once you're initiated, however, you're free to steer the action in pretty much any direction your fantasy might roam.
USENET alt.devilbunnies
FAQ: **URL** ftp://rtfm.mit.edu/pub/usenet-by-group/alt.answers/devilbunnies-faq

alt.elvis.king From Graceland West, in reply to a request for an Elvis fanclub mailing address: "Death To All Drooling Zombie Memorabilia Freakazoid Elvis Fans! Take that 'fan' shit elsewhere, please. This is the place where Elvis's quasi-evil, pirate, anti-Graceland, money-grubbing, Scientology, Inc. minions are hanging, examining important questions like: 'If The King blows out the seat of his jumpsuit in deep space with a King-sized fart, does it make any sound, and what does it smell like here on Earth?' Let's celebrate E as The King, and not just a cash cow for latter-day wannabe Col. Parkers. This opinion not endorsed by Elvis Presley Enterprises, Graceland, Lisa Marie, Lucky "Michael"

Jackson, or L. Ron Hubbard. Elvis (The King) however endorses it wholeheartedly." Much cross-posting to the likeminded alt.elvis.sighting. **USENET** alt.elvis.king

alt.flame Post-adolescents spew hate in cyberspace. The group also cultivates a Harvard-Yale type rivalry with alt.bigfoot— periodically the two newsgroups invade each other. Pyrrhus never had it so bad. Drop by if you feel the need to call someone stupid. Be careful not to respond to any posts whose follow-up has been set to misc.test. **USENET** alt.flame

alt.tv.dinosaurs.barney.die.die.die Whose language on the Net is most laced with vitriol and hostility? No it's not some militia's hateful utterances deep in the heart of Montana. The answer: Barney-bashers, driven to homicidal rhetoric by the grinning purple dinosaur who sings simple-minded children's songs on PBS. According to the Jihad, a group sworn to the destruction of said reptile, his message of love is an insidious media virus. A place to both vent and draw up battle plans. **USENET** alt.tv.dinosaurs.barney.die .die.die

Off beat

Adventures of Cyber-chicken Questing for cult status, this cartoon ezine beckons: "Follow the daily madcap adventures of a cybergenetic chicken hellbent on mayhem and destruction!" He's the buffest piece of poultry you've ever seen, comin' at ya with a colorful cartoon strip, feather-brained advice forum, and merchandise to boot. Revel in the henhouse madness: "Cluck here!" **WEB** http://www.whoa.ca

The Bathrooms of Madison County "As we drove away from Winterset, Janice pointed out how we'd visited more bathrooms than bridges in Madison County. "Hey," she said, "that would make a cool book..." and thus began this amusing spoof on the Robert James Waller bestseller. Click your way through this seven-page tale of diner stools and bathrooms in the county with covered bridges. **WEB** http://www.nutscape.com/~fluxus

 ## Hecklers Online
WEB http://www.hecklers.com/index.shtml

A universe of comedy unto itself, spanning from a *Bob Dole in Space* cybernovel to raunchy pickup lines. The Hecklers comedic stew is spiced with the range and style to satiate any grin-glutton with

Location: http://www.hecklers.com/rennais/digital/mona/mona.htm

off-the-wall jokes, stories, and satire, plus picture galleries and prodigious punch lines; they break it all down into Happenings, Heckler's HQ, Headlines, Renaissance, and Interactivities. Surf sparingly, or you may never leave.

Gallery of the Absurd "These little bits of popular culture will make you laugh, they'll make you cry, and maybe, just maybe, you'll learn a little bit about yourself," warns the Gallery, before bombarding you with a full course meal of vomit-inducing advertisements, shop fronts, and signs. Click to view the "Grocery Jackpot," "Clabber Girl Baking Powder," "S&M Shopping Arcade," or the "Super Massager" and wretch 'till your heart's content. **WEB** http://omni.cc.purdue.edu /~royald/absurd.htm

Grouchy Cafe This page deftly captures the coffeeshop counterculture. Grouchy proprietors poke fun at the freaks in the corner who mumble to themselves, the left wingers completing their manifestos, and the crust that forms on the rim of your mug. Wake up and smell the coffee like you never have before. **WEB** http://www.echonyc.com /~cafephrk/cafe.html

Hacker Barbe Dream Basement Apartment Surprise: These pages poke fun at the Barbie phenomenon through pictures of those lovable plastic babes in compromising poses. Investigate the "twisted delights" of Barbe and her true blond pal Madge, the Internet hunter, as they explore the info highway, chanting "the only good Internet is a dead Internet." Scenes from Barbe's dark past at the No-Tell Motel are unsuitable for children.

Who called me chicken?
http://www.whoa.ca

WEB http://www.catalog.com/mrm /barbe/barbe.html

The Lost Elvis Diaries "Just imagine. A day-to-day account of the private thoughts of the most famous man in the world. Yes, that would bring a pretty penny..." And so Jasper Journalist embarks on the quest for the holy grail of souvenirs by the hip swinger himself. A complicated mystery unfolds weekly by short chapters devoted to unlocking the secrets of the true Elvis: "They discovered major discrepancies in the texts such as repeated references to Elvis' father as "Al" and other references to Elvis' biggest hits as "Blue Suede Skis," "Heartburn Hotel," and "(You Are Nothing If Not A) Hound Dog." The online saga wades through the media scams and weaves in the laughs for hooked readers. **WEB** http://home.mem.net/~welk /elvisdiaries.html

Migraine Boy Migraine Boy is just trying to do his thing. He always has a headache. You'll laugh until you have one, too. He comes with Java and RealAudio add-ons, and special *Migraine Boy* merchandise as well. Knock yourself out. **WEB** http://www.visualradio.com /migraineboy

Needful Things The needful things are... you guessed it, barf bags! Enjoy the colorful display of Scandinavian travel-sickness, with a tidy bag that has tic-tac-toe on the back, or check out other major airlines' puke pouches. Vomit can be funny, but scary to think someone finds it that funny. **WEB** http://www.pvv.unit.no/~bct /spypose

News of the Weird Archive Life surely is stranger than fiction, and it doesn't get any stranger than *News of the Weird*. Read all about the chiropractor who

"tried to market a hypnosis service for breast enlargement," the boyfriend who attempted to wed his girlfriend's corpse, or cows killed when high winds carried them into treetops. This is a collection of Chuck Shepherd's classic news articles. Each week he selects items in the mainstream press that strike him as unimaginable, perverse, or just plain odd.
WEB http://www.nine.org/notw /archive.html

Soundbites A spot featuring hundreds of professionally produced "audio cartoons" that satirize people, events, and issues in the news. The credo of Soundbites: "There are no sacred cows, only steak sauce."

The subjects of Soundbites' satire include everyone from Jeffrey Dahmer to Jocelyn Elders. Typical titles include "Real Welfare Queens Play Golf," "Clinton Pounds His Podium," "Recycling as a Lifestyle," and "Boxers or Briefs?" The message boards include folders for jokes on everyone from Rush Limbaugh to Bill Clinton, with the attempts at humor veering off topic now and then—and heading into political bickering and name-calling, with such pithy comments as "I think you're stupid."
AMERICA ONLINE *keyword* **soundbites**

SPAM Haiku Archive "I inserted SPAM / In the VCR. It played/

dull pink movie." Join the fascination with the world's most entertaining "meat" product, SPAM! Worthy of slaughterhouses full of limericks, sonnets, and best of all, haikus (Spamku), the Hormel blue-canned phenomenon lives on.
WEB http://www2.best.com/~tyrtle /aunt.html

Wall O' Shame Shamefulness of all sorts displayed at this site, whether it's "normal shamefulness," as in the guide dog supposedly responsible for the deaths of four owners (see Lucky Dog), or "visual shamefulness" (check out the Waterproof Home, wherein a housewife sprays the couch with a hose. Items culled from the

POLITICALLY CORRECT BEDTIME STORIES
WEB http://w3.macdigital.com/macdigital/pcbs

Come one, come all to the unbiased, unprejudiced Politically Correct world spawned in James Garner Finn's Politically Correct Bedtime Stories. Promising "Cybersensitivity for our life and times," Simon & Schuster scripters and artists have put their heads together and generated a brilliant page parodying the funniest of fairy tales. Open your eyes to Goldilocks' "Grant Proposal to The Department of the Interior." What was Little Red Riding Hood doing with M.C. Snoop Wolfy Wolf in the woods, and why should Snow White "stay away from free apples and invitations to the Viper Room"? Part book promotion, part social satire, pure comedy!

press and from spots on the Net.

WEB http://www.milk.com/wall-o -shame

Yep, It's Barney's Page What would the officials at Barney Inc. think about this site, which houses a Barney shotgun target and Barney's case history from "the asylum" in which the cuddly purple dinosaur fantasizes about choking Big Bird? Sound clips titled "Barney Meets the Gestapo" and "When Barney Met Sally" may offend some younger viewers. Barney will answer questions posted here, although he insists his sex life is a private matter.

WEB http://asylum.cid.com/barney

Sci-fi humor

alt.tv.mst3k / alt.fan.mst3k / rec.arts.tv.mst3k A cynical and hilarious set of newsgroups, much like the show itself. Fans of *Mystery Science Theater 3000* revel in their ruthlessness. After all, the show relies on viewer disdain for movies like *Teenagers from Outerspace*. One fan, upset by recent fare like *Racket Girls* and *Red Zone Cuba*—they weren't bad enough?—posted a plea for "dumb Japanese monsters" and "stupid alien movies": "We want to leave the sleazy '50s-'60s underworld films (YAWN!) mercifully buried and happily decaying into a puddle of ooze!" Newbies, beware. Post a sincere question to this group and you're asking

Location: http://asylum.cid.com/barney/godbarn.gif

Need a light, Barney?
http://asylum.cid.com/barney

for a flame. Plenty of talk of sci-fi flicks, including *Logan's Run*, *Nightfall*, and *Fire Maidens of Outer Space*. Celebrity mentions should be particularly severe, with posts judged by their level of ridicule. After Kathy Ireland was called "the dumbest celebrity," one regular wrote: "If you ever get a chance, listen to Nancy Sinatra. She makes Tony Danza and Sylvester Stallone look like Mensa members."

USENET alt.tv.mst3k • alt.fan.mst3k • rec.arts.tv.mst3k

Good Ol' Geeky Star Trek Stuff Still in its infancy, the site includes *Trek* skits (e.g., "Microsoft—The Next Generation") and a few sound clips for the easily amused Trekkie.

WEB http://kelp.honors.indiana.edu /%7echrome/trek/index.html

LCARS: Alexi Kosut's Star Trek Page While this Web page links to some of the more serious *Trek* sites on the Net, its focus is on *Trek* fun. Drop by to read the Silly Top Ten lists, *Trek* filks, or Alexi Kosut's own fan fiction—"Star Trek: Affliction of Paradise" and "Star Trek: Return to Hellgate."

WEB http://www.nueva.pvt.k12.ca.us /~akosut/startrek

Mystery Science Theater 3000 A great hangout for MSTies and MSTics, with folders called We Love Joel Club, Cultural Chaos, How dumb are ya, Uncle Dad?, and lots of other goodies. The quotes in the Favorite Quotes folder include "Bite me, it's fun," and "We come bearing honey-baked yams." This is a raucous and fun-loving bunch. Never a dull

DID WE SAY WEIRD?

Oslo, Norway, police inspector Leif Ole Topnes admitted in July that "our body-search techniques aren't good enough." He was commenting on a male prisoner's having been locked up for two weeks in the women's jail despite having been "body-searched" at the Sola Airport and then "strip-searched" at the jail. The man was wearing female makeup and had hormone-treatment breasts, but Topnes admitted that otherwise he was obviously a man and should have been detected as such. [*New Haven Register*-AP, 7-19-96]

Jeffrey J. Pyrcioch, 19, and an alleged accomplice were arrested in West Lafayette, Ind., in May on theft and fraud charges. Pyrcioch allegedly cashed checks that he had written with disappearing ink, apparently believing the checks would be blank by the time they were presented to the bank for collection. However, traces of ink remained, and police said Pyrcioch would have a better chance of getting away with it if he had not used checks pre-printed with his name and account number on them. [*Washington Post*, 6-2-96]

In April in Providence, R. I., Anthony "The Saint" St. Laurent, Sr. pleaded guilty to an organized-crime charge and took a 10-month prison sentence. He said he pled guilty only because an intestinal illness would have made it impractical for him to sit through a lengthy trial: "How can I go to trial with (the 40-50 daily) enemas I got to take?" [*Providence Journal-Bulletin*, 4-22-96]

—from News of the Weird

moment, with caustic comments appreciated. One MSTy's thoughts on "Kitten with a Whip": "My, this movie was putrid... What cheese!" **AMERICA ONLINE** *keyword* scifi→ messageboards→Mystery Science Theater 3000

Trek Plots Fan Warren Siege takes on TOS and *TNG* with parodic plot summaries. "The Galileo Seven-Eleven," in which "Spock takes the shuttlecraft to make a quick stop at a local planet to get a Slurpee,

but the natives refuse to accept his Vulcan Express card." Then there's "Skin of Evil," in which "the *Enterprise* is attacked by a being of pure acne." **WEB** http://www.cosy.sbg.ac.at/ftp /pub/trek/fun/trek-synopsis-humor .html

Nerds

Geek Site of the Day "Geek Site of the Day—because I'm a loser, and you are, too." This is your compass to those techni-

cally terrifying, monumentally mundane sites for the beloved geek. **WEB** http://www.owlnet.rice.edu /~indigo/gsotd

Greg's Micro$oft Humor Page Bitter about the Gates Empire? Log on for rants, raves, and geeky giggles about poor interface and networking nightmares. Jokes also available in Windows and DOS flavors. **WEB** http://www.cs.bgu.ac.il/~pribushg /jokes.html

Nerdity Test Does a Friday night mean a good long download and hanging ten on the Net? Do you speak Unix-ese? Are you torn between Kirk and Picard? Check the appropriate boxes to ascertain your nerd quotient. **WEB** http://gonzo.tamu.edu/nerd.html

Love

Cyrano Server For the romantically disinclined, the Cyrano Server is your savior! Plug in your favorite parts of speech for a mad lib that will make your honey howl. Can even assign a tone—steamy, desperate, indecisive, poetic, etc. **WEB** http://www.nando.net/toys /cyrano.html

Foolproof Guide to Making Any Woman Your Platonic Friend Joe Logon claims to be the expert on "he said, she said." The guru of interpreting the "I just want to be friends" and other romance-razing remarks offers a safe haven for the misunder-

stood. Laugh at his breakdown of the platonic symptoms, and keep your head up, you really are a special person!
WEB http://www.phantom.com /~joelogon/platonic.html

Abuse

Abuse-A-Tron A simple concept. Click on the "Heap Abuse Upon Me" button, and you get insulted. Click again, another insult. And so on. Here's a sample, worthy of the best of alt.flame: "You roll in smelly stuff to disguise your scent, you drooling, fungus picking, frog exploring, unhinged accident of a maso-chistic-submissive parliamen-tarian." If you don't enjoy this site, it's probably because you're a simpering whelp of a dyspeptic cannibal.
WEB http://www.xe.net/upstart/abuse

Auntie Lois The sign "Advice you did not ask for, from a woman you will not like" greets those seeking humorous counsel here. Auntie Lois has successfully offended regular toothbrush users, barefoot wanderers, and soggy avengers among a cast of thousands who venture her way for her two cents' worth. Read her feature article or hear her voice and get to know this snappy comedienne who dares to lend an ear.
WEB http://www2.best.com/~tyrtle /aunt.html

Automatic Complaint Generator A graphically challenged page,

The power of positive thinking, revisited
http://www.visualradio.com/migraineboy

you'll enter with a beef about someone, and leave with a mouthful. The page specializes in using your "plug ins" to generate paragraphs upon paragraphs about why your tar-get is no good.
WEB http://www-csag.cs.uiuc.edu /individual/pakin/complaint

Word play

Dorktionary Remember Rich Hall's "Sniglets"? They were the sensation of the early eight-ies, words that perfectly defined previously uncaptured experiences. The Dorktionary, which operates on the same principle, isn't quite as clever—some of its entries, like "cheesy" and "old fart," aren't exactly cutting-edge coinage. But "gasino" (a trashy roadside mini-mart) has a nice ring to it. Primarily computer-related.
WEB http://www.latech.edu/~jlk/jwz /dorktionary/index.shtml

Madlib! Yep, generated by com-puter. You type adjectives, _____ (part of speech), adverbs, nouns, and the com-puter generates a _____ (a quan-tity) lines or so of mala-propisms. Here's a _____ (adjective) excerpt from one: "Single cool male... I like to program, take long keyboards by the mouse pad, or just love with a good monitor. If you enjoy surfing, loving or going out for folder, then this could be the CD-ROM you're look-ing for."
WEB http://www.mit.edu:8001/madlib

The Pun Starts Here Surely a site for sore eyes, the pun page lists the extravagant and the expec-ted plays on words that you may have heard, but didn't care to. The smiley-faced sections fare the best; the better part of the list will make you groan.
WEB http://gdbdoc.gdb.org/~nazar /puns/punpl.html

PART 4
Recreation

Recreation

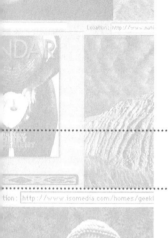

CLICK PICKS
The very best on the Net

Sports

IF THEY WOULD ONLY INVENT A COMPUTER THAT CAME WITH A REMOTE, LIFE WOULD BE PERFECT

IT MAY BE A LONG WAY from the La-Z-Boy reclining chair to your multimedia computer, but it's worth the effort. With Web sites offering virtually instantaneous updates, aficionados can get the scoop on Major League Baseball's 1996 home run bonanza or commentary on the New York Knicks' post-Riley facelift—everything up to and including Dennis Rodman's newest dye job/wedding/supermodel girlfriend. Though life beyond the TV, the hoagie, and the brew is hard to envision for some, sites like The World Wide Web of Sports can make the transition from watching to playing easier with its recreational sports links. With this kind of coverage, the Web can be more valuable to the sports fan than the boob tube.

THE SPORTS NETWORK

WEB http://www.sportsnetwork.com

This wonderful Web site is more journalistic than most other sports pages, and far less self-indulgent. Forgoing the whole style vs. substance debate, these guys make substance their style, creating an Online sports section that covers three or four other sites-worth of material. While it isn't the single most comprehensive sports site, you do get daily news flashes on football, baseball, basketball, tennis, hockey, and other major spectator sports, delivered in one informative and no-nonsense package called Daynotes.

Starting points

America's Sports Headquarters
Don't look here for anything other than links to elsewhere. This mammoth site is a well-stocked database of sports on the Web, from fantasy-team pages to sport employment opportunities to three (count 'em, three) Web pages devoted to Shoeless Joe Jackson. A wide range of choices is available, including such far-flung topics as broomball and kinesiology, as well as the standard fare. The site is divided into categories—Spectator, Outdoor Adventure, and Recreational—and then subdivided by sports category. The spectator sports page will take you to, say, the Major League Baseball menu and then the Atlanta Braves official home page. The Recreational option offers links to a wide spectrum of sports-related links, from A (aerobics) to Y (Yo-Yo). Headquarters is a great place to start a search for athletic information if a general Web search hasn't turned up what you're looking for.
WEB http://www.sport-hq.com

Brian's Ultimate Sports Link
Meticulous sports enthusiast or post-employment hobbyist? You be the judge, when you peruse Brian's NASCAR, NFL, NBA, and NHL links, and some for college as well. The B-Man has even incorporated a menu to make his thousand plus baseball links accessible to non-obsessive human beings. Through this page,

All the sports info you could ever want.
http://www.sportszone.com

you'll gain access to commercial pages like those of Nando and the NBA, but also to Mitchells's Knicks page and Mikey's Bulls page. Come here if you like options and don't mind plowing through links.
WEB http://falcon.jmu.edu/~hamricba/slink.html

Computer Sports Rev.2 The sports of Computer Sports Edge are the non-strenuous ones: computer sports and fantasy leagues. Fans of the former will find a small sampling of news bits and recent-release reviews, while league enthusiasts have a few linked competitions (baseball, football, and basketball) to choose from, as well as a CSE-sponsored contest.
WEB http://www.compsportsedge.com/cse_toc.html

ESPNET The ESPNET features resemble some fraternity Super

Bowl party conversations, where the hosts miraculously gain moments of eerie clarity and jock-minded insights into the world of sports. In a good way, though. These articles (some free, others subscription-based) touch upon topics such as why the increasingly belligerent Olympic "dream teams" don't deserve our applause, and how Michael Jordan vaulted over the salary cap. There's also a meditation on Andre Agassi's '96 season downturn. Meanwhile, newsflashes cover all the breaking stories in professional sports. ESPNET delivers exactly what you'd expect it to—competent, timely news reporting with heaping portions of respectable editorial.
WEB http://www.sportszone.com

The Grandstand Skiers, karate experts, horse riders, and race car drivers (not to mention,

baseball, football, hockey, basketball, and soccer fans), come together for a brief time in this sports center before heading off to their own discussion groups and libraries. For almost every major sport, The Grandstand has message boards, schedules, news, libraries packed with images, logos, and stats. And what about bowlers, hunters, tennis players, and track and field stars? Check the "Whole 9 Yards" area. They get their say, too.
AMERICA ONLINE *keyword* grandstand

Nando.Net Sports Server If there were a playoff for sports Web sites, this one would probably meet ESPNET SportsZone in the World Series. The busy site has a wealth of resources for

the sports fan, from sports news briefs to statistics to team home pages. And when a sporting event the size of the NCAA Final Four or the World Series comes around, expect special coverage.
WEB http://www.nando.net/Sport Server

Sport World Where else can you go to find the North American Orienteering home page, sail with the Goowla Regatta Club of Australia, or catch the latest Hong Kong soccer results? Featuring a point-and-click map of the world to connect you to the sporting events of various continents, Sport World is an easy-to-use and refreshingly cosmopolitan connection to international sports.

Coverage of Olympics sites is also featured, and external submissions are encouraged.
WEB http://susis.ust.hk/~danny/sport /sport.html

The Sports Forum Tyson's next bout is covered in the Ring Things topic, Jordan's latest record is being discussed in the Pro Basketball topic, Andy Pettitte's pitching performance is recounted in the Baseball topic, and Sabatini's record is analyzed in the Golf/Tennis topic. Is the reality of last night's game too limiting? Have some fun with the sports world—put Shaq and Jordan on the same team in a fantasy basketball league. And while the message boards are full of sports fans arguing strategy,

Fox Cyber Scoreboard
WEB http://www.igiude.com/sports

A cool, black background and straightforward design greet you upon arrival at this network site. The latest scores are divided into categories: NFL, NHL, MLB, NBA, and Fox (yes, they are in a

league of their own). Read transcribed interviews with celebs like Mighty Duckster Paul Kariya or Bulls coach Phil Jackson. A Fox Fanatics chat area gives you a chance to get your opinion heard, and there's an interesting plug for *In the Zone*, a show that gives kids a chance to live out their sports fantasies.

speculating about upcoming games, and playing in fantasy leagues, the library, divided by sport, is filled with software, images, stats, schedules, logos, and sound clips.
COMPUSERVE *go* fans

USA Today Sports Like father, like son. The online version of *USA Today Sports* gives you the *USA Today* experience without ever having to touch paper. You'll get pre-game coverage of basketball, baseball, football, and hockey games slated to be played today, with a rundown of the pitchers, the clubs' win/loss streaks, and the previous performance of both. The Scoreboard will give baseball box scores from the previous day and a play-by-play of the highlights. With professional sports relationships as fleeting as those of *Melrose Place*, the transactions link will wire you to the latest marriages between player and team. While you won't suffer from information indigestion, you might yearn for something more substantial.
WEB http://www.usatoday.com/sports /sfront.htm

World Wide Web of Sports This no-frills Web site is a comprehensive bridge to sports online. Just about any sporting activity that you can imagine, and some you can't, can be investigated via links from this page. Far from being elitist, or even discriminating, more than 80 categories, from the obvious to the obscure, are covered, Hol-

land's Korfball, for instance. "The Only [gender] Mixed Sport," has been given some play time on this page for interested, experiment-minded folk. Check it out when you have some free time.
WEB http://www.tns.lcs.mit.edu/cgi-bin /sports

The World-Wide Web Virtual Library: Sport Pages Actually, this library functions more as a links library, since almost all its information comes from outside it. The voluminous selection is a grab-bag, with some interesting links and also some duds. In spite of it all, you may find this site useful indeed. One winning characteristic is the representation of foreign countries: From Taiwan's basketball team the Hung Kuo Elephants to an Italian baseball team the B.Est Group, this Web site emphasizes the global appeal of baseball, basketball, soccer, and other popular sports.
WEB http://www.atm.ch.cam.ac.uk /sports/sports.html

Archery

alt.archery The traditionalists and the non-traditionalists talk bowstrings and feathers on this newsgroup, but beware the political twists the group can sometimes become embroiled in. Politics in the archery community can be vicious, and the direction of archery in the U.S. and the balance of power between different archery organizations are often the subjects of bitter debate. But equipment

and technique are not overlooked either. Are feathers better than vanes? The group's divided evenly. Which is better: right or left helicol? "Doesn't matter" was the overwhelming response. "I've shot five-inch feathers and vanes, four-inch feathers and vanes and three-inch feathers. The helical provides spin, just like the rifling in a gun barrel, which makes them inherently more accurate," explains Stephen of the Maurice Thompson Archery Association.
USENET alt.archery
FAQ: **WEB** http://www.dcs.ed.ac.uk /home/ajcd/archery/faq/index.html

Archery on the Internet A comprehensive list of online archery resources, broken down by country, with a special section for Olympic archery pages. A brief summary of each site is given to help you find exactly what you're looking for. The list itself tells an interesting story—whereas the rest of the world is mostly interested in the challenges of the sport and in mastering the skills involved through competition, America's numerous sites seem mostly concerned with the process of killing big (and not-so-big) game and boasting about it online.
WEB http://www.ilinkgn.net/commercl /author/links.htm

Auto racing

In the Pits/Motor Sports Talk tracks. Talk tires. Talk tur-

bochargers. And do it in AOL's auto racing area, which has a variety of message boards on auto racing topics ranging from equipment to collectibles. If you're not chat-oriented, visit the In the Pits library, which is filled with JPEGs of racing vehicles. And don't forget the simulation racing game.
AMERICA ONLINE *keyword* gs auto

Physics of Racing Series A compendium of things that affect racecar drivers each and every time they get behind the wheel—weight transfer, traction, grip angle, and braking force. Brian Beckman, a physi-

cist and a member of the No Bucks Racing Club in Southern California, guides netters through the fascinating world of auto physics. Learn why "one braking maneuver in our 3,200 pound example car causes 640 pounds to transfer from the rear tires to the front tires," and how to figure your car's movement in terms of kinematics.
WEB http://reality.sgi.com/employees /rck/PhOR

Racer Archive A classy page from the University of Hawaii, complete with full-season Formula One, IndyCar, and

NASCAR synopses by race. Each weekend is divided by first- and second-day practice and qualifying laps, as well as the starting grid and race results. This archive is hands down the best organized motorsports page on the Net.
WEB http://www.eng.hawaii.edu/carina /ra.home.page.html

Tracks Around The World The next time you're in Czechoslovakia, you might want to stop by the Automodrom in Brno. And if you're planning an Australian jaunt, make sure to take a few laps at Amaroo. This rapidly expanding guide to

SI ONLINE

WEB http://pathfinder.com/si

While some Web sites function superbly with a succinct voice, *Sports Illustrated*'s official home page excels in its garrulousness. It is filled with dense, well-written sports features, with the journalistic quality commonly associated with *Sports Illustrated*. An article on Marge Schott, the

Location: http://pathfinder.com/@@kH7ENAQAKxzLdYHO/si/athens/daily/july31/act.html

STonline OLYMPIC DAILY

PHOTO ACT

Athletes' Feet

They give competitors two legs to stand on and a chance to make a push for greatness

owner of the Cincinnati Reds baseball team, for example, profiles the life of the acerbic old woman with enough embarrassing anecdotes of her vitriol to capture anyone's attention, baseball fan or not. While *SI Online* serves you best with its meditation and digestion of professional sports, it also keeps you on top of things with the latest in sporting news.

tracks, courses, and speedways around the world includes address and phone information, track histories, and driving tests.
WEB http://www.bath.ac.uk/~py3dlg /tracks.html

Baseball

Baseball Historian's Guide to Internet Resources A Web page as accurate and specific as its name: Essentially a hypertext card catalog for baseball historical data in the broadest possible sense, it includes general information on baseball as a pop-culture fixture within specific historical periods. Dry, dry, dry. But if it's the significant spot baseball occupies in our national historic consciousness you're after, start flipping pages. Also includes a page for trading and selling memorabilia and historically valuable items.
WEB http://rampages.onramp.net /~wordwork/index.html

Baseball Library A library filled with trivia quizzes, team logos, stats management shareware programs, little league scheduling software, historical stats databases, Major League Baseball schedules, rulebooks, baseball poetry, proposals for fan strikes, and player interviews.
COMPUSERVE *go* fans→Libraries→ Baseball

CNN-Sports-Baseball The moment this page is called up, its crispness and clarity lends it an air of brand-name recogni-

tion and reliability. The table of contents gives today's scores, yesterday's scores, the current standings, stats leaders, and a break down of the teams' win-loss records. Directly below the TOC is a neatly organized grid of team links taking you to team rosters, batting averages, pitching stats, and games schedule for every team in the Majors.
WEB http://cnn.com/SPORTS/BASE BALL/index.html

> **"For those who find reading yesterday's sports news in today's paper a jarring experience, this Web site is worth a look. "**

The Dugout Cincinnati Reds fans are speculating about the depth of their pitching staff on the Professional Baseball message board while would-be baseball managers are building teams for AOL's Fantasy Baseball League. Clemson and Rice fans are arguing about the NCAA pennant race on the College Baseball message board and gamers with baseball simulators are playing in

the forum's ongoing simulation league, raiding the library for files of favorite ballparks and memorable games. And while they're in the library, fans are collecting images of Ty Cobb, Yaz, Roberto Clemente, and the Yankees logo. This elaborate baseball resource and entertainment center also features team schedules, baseball news, and live baseball chat.
AMERICA ONLINE *keyword* gs baseball

Fastball Despite being third in line on the basic menu that runs across the top of this page, the "1000+ Stories" option will undoubtedly catch your eye. Naturally, anyone who is intrigued by the immediacy of news and information will appreciate this site, which is updated so often that each news item has a time stamp on it. A certain depressing kind of power trip comes over you (starting at your finger tips), when you click on news items time-stamped at 6:57 A.M., before most people even wake up. For those who find reading yesterday's sports news in today's paper a jarring experience, this Web site is worth a look. Also interesting are the baseball anecdotes, funny stories, myths, or quips that true fans will love. As for the other news options, they're cluttered, busy, and less inviting.
WEB http://www.fastball.com/mlb /at539999.htm

John Skilton's Baseball Links A handsome and extensive catalog of baseball links—almost

1,000 and growing daily—John Skilton's Baseball Links is a must for all boys and girls of summer. Every imaginable aspect of baseball—buying and selling, fantasy/rotisserie leagues, official and unofficial team hangouts, trivia contests—are represented in this obvious creation of a high priest in the church of baseball. **WEB** http://www.pc-professor.com /baseball

MLB S.W.A.T. *USA Today Sports*, ESPNET: SportZone, *SI Online*, and Fastball are each large, dense, and frequently unwieldy. Aside from their inherent clutter, each Web site is better at select news items. MLB S.W.A.T. reigns them all

into one manageable, nonintimidating service. This All-Star caliber line-up of some of the best news services covers transactions, injuries, standings, pitcher matchups, comprehensive team digests, and of course, statistics. *USA Today* will give you the daily news and notes of the American and National Leagues, ESPNET will bring you Box Scores and standings, and *SI Online* will rundown the current events for every team. Clicking the NL or AL icons will let you access baseball by league and by team. The only unfortunate thing is, as the services tend to overlap in their coverage, so do these links, on occasion. Redundancy notwithstanding, this

thorough Web site is not to be missed. **WEB** http://www.ici.net/customers /rickw/mlb

NCAA Baseball If you want to see the College World Series, then you want to see this page. For Divisions I, II, and III information is given for the dates and sites for the championships, a telephone number for tickets, and a schedule for televised games. Also, check out the results of the CWS for every year since 1947. **WEB** http://www.ncaa.org/champs /baseball

Other College Baseball Homepages From A (Abilene Christian University) to Y (Yale), this

MAJOR LEAGUE BASEBALL @BAT

WEB http://www.majorleaguebaseball.com

As the official site of Major League Baseball, this graphics-heavy page is worth the wait for access. In addition to snazzy photos, you'll find complete box scores for each day's game, links to every team, and profiles of each league's player of the week. Features abound: One covers the latest baseball video games, while another waxes on about that most important of ballpark treats—the food. For a nostalgia kick, check out the fascinating This Day in Baseball History page. True fans can also order team merchandise.

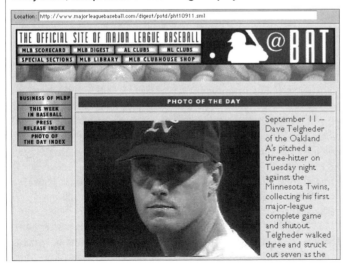

index of universities link to each school's baseball team home pages. The hypertext will also take you to tournament and conference pages that will keep you one step ahead of the games.
WEB http://stimpy.ame.nd.edu/gross /baseball/other.html

Total Baseball Online The online home of the incomprehensibly vast *Official Encyclopedia of Major League Baseball* is a window into history. This tome features bios of baseball legends from Lou Brock to Cy Young, team histories, and "comprehensive stat summaries of every player who's ever put on a professional uniform." If you're looking for baseball milestones, peruse the encyclopedia's record books for batting, base running, fielding, and pitching all-time leaders, plus the numerous featured articles covering everything from players to statistics to history. "Robinson Signing," for instance, explains Branch Rickey's plan to integrate African-American players beyond Jackie Robinson, though he was ultimately halted by political pressure. There are no wasted words, spaces, gimmicks, or colorful excess to cloud the functional beauty of the site. It is handsomely designed and elegantly written, capturing the spirit and the palpable mythos behind the game. This Web site is a winner, and is without a doubt better than any other Web site at what it does—

BELLE BLASTS HOMER

... and he wasn't nice to Bart, either
http://www.fastball.com/mlb/at539999.htm

making the history of baseball come alive.
WEB http://www.totalbaseball.com

Basketball

The Basketball Highway Former college player and coach Alan Lambert has made a resourceful site for basketball coaches at any level. Lambert has created an effective virtual community for coaches, providing job listings, basketball camp information, coaching articles, downloads, links to software providers, and anything else a coach could need. With pleasing graphics and a user-friendly, simple format, TBH is ideal for those who feel more comfortable with the basketball net than the Internet.
WEB http://bbhighway.com

Fantasy Basketball Shaq kicks it out to Stockton, and Stockton

dishes it inside to Kemp, who turns on the afterburners for a monstrous tomahawk dunk... Wait a second. Shaq on the same team as Stockton and Kemp? In your dreams—or in AOL's fantasy league. First you sign up for a team, then you draft players in a live chat area, and then you begin to move your squad into competition against other fantasy teams. Fantasy basketball players can download rulebooks that contain information about trades, roster changes, scoring, statistics, and other facets of the fantasy league.
AMERICA ONLINE *keyword* fantasy basketball

Fantasy Basketball Let your paper tigers roar in CompuServe's Fantasy B-Ball league. How much will it cost to have Larry Johnson on your team? How about Dennis? Can you

release David Benoit and activate Kevin Johnson? That depends on the needs of other players, and the approval of the league. The Fantasy Basketball message board is too committed to official business to be interesting, and the real meat of the forum is in its library, which stocks rosters and stats for fantasy teams (all named after NBA greats). Keep track of stats, engineer blockbuster trades, and worry that injuries to real players will disable your imaginary cagers.
COMPUSERVE *go* fans→Libraries *or* Messages→Fantasy Basketball

GNN Basketball A marvelous hubsite for hoops fans, with sections on the NBA, men's and women's college basketball, and international basketball. Fans of the old GNN sports center will be pleased with this recent version, which streamlines the design and makes stats and news even easier to find.
WEB http://gnn.com/gnn/meta/sports /basketball/index.html

The Journal of Basketball Studies Every Monday, fans across the country get together to discuss which NBA player should be traded and why. Now, webmaster Dean Turcoliver, a former college-level player with a Ph.D., has unleashed his statistical formula for trading players upon an unsuspecting world. Most of the results, he tells us, are surprisingly counter-intuitive. His professional-looking site makes a science of the various statistics and strategies of the game. Analytical articles and an online book, *Hoopla*, make this a complete resource for those who want to take the guesswork out of the sport.
WEB http://cmr.sph.unc.edu/~deano /bball/index.html

NBA Chat Wanna talk basketball but you're not into stats? Sick of chat sites where you pick up an itinerant pest who dogs you for the rest of your cyberlife? You can block messages from specific annoyances, attach that favorite .GIF of Patrick Ewing's eye-popping dunk to

NBA.com
WEB http://www.NBA.com

No surprise here. A slick site from the league that brought top-notch marketing to professional sports. The NBA's up-to-the-minute pro-basketball magazine presents constantly updated articles on teams and players. Sports celebs like Reggie Miller are featured in interviews—discussion

ranged from the Dream Team to his life on and off the court. Info on upcoming games, weekly news, and complete season stats are easy to find, and interviews are available with highlight clips in .AVI and QuickTime formats. For those-who need more than downloads, the Online catalog has official NBA merchandise, including everything from clothes to ceiling fans.

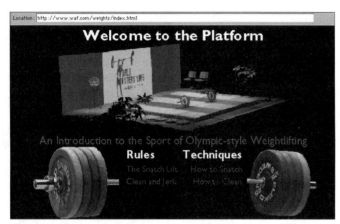

Olympic-style platform lifting is where Ah-nold pumps you up
http://www.waf.com/weights/index.html

your own tagline, and rail on into the night about the best team on Earth—whichever one you happen to think it is.
WEB http://www.irsociety.com/cgi-bin/webchat_doorway.cgi?Room=NBA_Chat

On Hoops Love talking, thinking, and reading basketball? These guys ("Los Chucks") definitely have too much free time on their hands, but that works to the advantage of every true basketball fanatic. Hear inside information. Read and post theories and gossip on such topics as Nellie's departure from the Knicks, the Lakers' serial referee-bumping, and Rachel meeting her basketball hero. Or vote for the chump of all time. Everybody here loves not only the game, but the culture of basketball.
WEB http://onhoops.com

Pro Basketball What's here? NBA, College, Fantasy Leagues, and more. While the

NBA is still patently a league of superstars—Michael, Shaq, Sir Charles, and company—there's ample chat about lesser-known players, and you can even get into a heated debate over the talents of Rex Chapman if you'd like. Or maybe you'd rather spend time in the libraries, looking at NBA logos for real teams (the Rockets) and imaginary ones (the New Jersey Fire Dragons).
COMPUSERVE go fans→Libraries or Messages→Basketball

Billiards

Pool and Billiards FAQ Useful primarily as a guide to billiards terms and basic rules, this FAQ is perfect for the beginning pool player who can't make heads or tails of head spots or end rails, and it will even teach you how to pull off a jump shot. But if you're looking for hints on more difficult trick shots or advice on sharking, you'll have to turn elsewhere.

WEB http://nickel.ucs.indiana.edu/~fulton/Pool/PoolFAQ

Bodybuilding

The Male Bodybuilder Curiously, there are few profiles of the athletes, and the few that are offered tend to be long and superficial—the kind that tell you the color of professional bodybuilder Michael Francois' dream car. Lists of events and muscle-magazine subscription addresses are de rigueur, but it's nice to see links to sites for female bodybuilders, nutrition, and training. Numerous JPEG pics are available for a long list of pumped-up pros.
WEB http://bb.acc.stolaf.edu

misc.fitness.misc You won't find any Jenny Craig loyalists in this newsgroup. This serious group of fitness folks talks incessantly on numerous exercise topics, and practically never deviates into inanity. The Schwarzenegger-Lite dialogue covers a lot of ground, from moderate weightlifting to aerobic exercise to proper nutrition. Though the newsgroup tends to raise more questions than answers, you'll still find helpful people who are willing to offer their own experiences. Currently, the most sought after knowledge concerns the effectiveness of the "Ab-Roller" variety exercise equipment, the messianic fitness contraption that has relegated all Thigh-Masters to near phantom presence.
USENET misc.fitness.misc

Weights-L Nutrition, injuries, workouts—it's all fair game on this active list. You don't have to be an experienced body-builder to join, although many of the contributors clearly know their stuff—and have strong opinions—when it comes to such issues as diet supplements and steroids (you'll find lots of arguments about the latter). "If the Republicans are serious about 'getting government off our backs,'" wrote one lifter, "then they should be at the forefront of restoring our freedom by repealing the laws that make some drugs legal (alcohol, caffeine) and others not (steroids, marijuana, etc.)." You can get advice for beginners, learn about exercises to flatten your stomach, or lurk for a while and hear lots of talk about ephedrine and Creatine. Women are well-represented on the list.

EMAIL weights-request@fa.disney.com
✐ *Type in message body:* subscribe weights-l ⟨your full name⟩

Welcome to the Platform: Olympic Style Weightlifting You've probably never had the nerve to go up to that massive guy in the gym and ask, "Hey, how do you do that clean and jerk?" This address not only tells you what a clean and jerk is, it tells you how to do it—with photo illustrations. No-nonsense facts about history, competition, and rules make this an intelligent, well-conceived, even welcoming site. The nicest feature is the Athlete of the Month—nominate your friends! A photo and a straightforward Q&A with each month's winners help to inspire the aspiring.
WEB http://www.waf.com/weights/index.html

The Women's Bodybuilding Forum It's a good thing that female bodybuilders have broad backs, because they have to bear the brunt of numerous stereotypes about physically powerful women. Are they all stupid? Are they all lesbians? Are they all Germans injected with enough testosterone to keep a pro football team in clover for months? Absolutely not, and this forum does its best to help combat prejudice against muscular femmes. With discussion

The Nando Basketball Server
WEB http://www.nando.net/SportServer/basketball/nba.html

Nando Net is heaven on earth for sports fans with Web browsers. Why? Well, the North Carolina-based *News and Observer* publishers have put together an excellent basketball site, with a college home page, a pro home page, and dozens and dozens of levels of stats, scores, standings, and

Location: http://www.nando.net/newsroom/sports/PressBox/special/colbkb/a10pics.html

HOOPLA: The 1996 Atlantic 10 Tournaments

schedules, not to mention in-depth analysis. There are home pages for every pro team and many college conferences; once you start linking it's possible the ball may never stop rolling.

about sexual orientation, sexual potency, and the rules of attraction interleaved with weights and workout talk, this is a list with a social conscience. Did your husband look at you strangely when your bulging abs started picking up distant radio stations? Did your boyfriend break up with you when you dead-lifted his Volkswagen Rabbit? Toss that wimp aside and subscribe to this list.

EMAIL femuscle-request@lightning .com ✍ *Write a request*

Bowling

alt.sport.bowling How do you get a hook on a ball? What's the proper way to clean a ball during play? Do instructional videos work the way they're supposed to? The lane rangers in this newsgroup consult one another on every aspect of their favorite sport. While most of the posts relate personal experiences, a decent number of Net bowlers want advice, some of them are so detailed they'll bowl you over: "A friend of mine is giving me a Ninja RPM, because he's going to 15 lbs. The ball is drilled axis leveraged and left-handed. I'm right-handed. The ball is 16 lbs, 2" pin-out, with a 3.5 oz top weight. Should I: (a) Plug the thumb and finger, and keep it axis leveraged. (b) Plug all the holes and drill it "over label" (c) Keep it left-handed and try bowling left handed. (Yeah Right!)."

USENET alt.sport.bowling

Bowling While there's a fair amount of talk about pro favorites, youth bowling, bowling oddities, and the most satisfying kinds of strikes, most of the bowling chat on this bulletin board focuses on equipment concerns. Shoes, gloves, and balls are the order of the day. Consider this post from a Senior PBA member: "I'm continually testing new equipment. I just bought an Omega and I hate it! After three days of trying to get it to work on synthetic lanes I have about given it up. The best surface I have found for synthetics is Brunswick's purple and teal Rhinos."

AMERICA ONLINE *keyword* gs other→ Bowling Area

Boxing

Boxing News and Notes A wealth of boxing discussion, including archived threads on topics ranging from Roberto Duran's

umpteenth comeback to the sketchy future of the strawweight division. In addition, this area includes a comprehensive list of champions that is updated every few months and links to the boxing/ wrestling library, which contains AOL's ring report.

AMERICA ONLINE *keyword* gs boxing→ Grandstand Boxing Area

The Cyber Boxing Zone Study the long history of the sweet science at this respectful, intelligent, and humorous site. Fans of pugilism can check out news and reviews, link to AOL's *Boxing Newsletter*, and read excerpts from boxing bios. Click to the list of every heavyweight of the Queensbury era, starting with bare-knuckled John L. Sullivan. Only two of the more contemporary champs—Ali and Tyson—are currently profiled, but this zone is an up-and-comer.

WEB http://cyberboxingzone.com

Hey—them's fighting words
http://www.cyberboxingzone.com

rec.sport.boxing Come back to the five and dime, Mike Tyson, Mike Tyson. The former heavyweight champion and convicted rapist eats up much of the talk on this newsgroup. When the discussion does turn to other fighters, it's usually to review a round, or complain that a fighter was robbed by poor officiating. And then there are the never-ending lists of the top ten heavyweights of all time (Gene Tunney? Larry Holmes? And how about that guy who floats like a butterfly and stings like a bee?). **USENET** rec.sport.boxing

Canoeing & kayaking

Water Sports and Activities With folders on whitewater, canoeing, kayaking, and other paddleboat sports, this is one of the best commercial service sites for river talk. The Whitewater Paddlers folder fills with cheers when the weather is good, and there's even occasional advice about equipment: "Try the Prijon Hurricane—I own a kayak shop and they are hot sellers. Boat is rockered and has rails that makes it great for surfing and popping in and out of eddies. My husband and I have paddled them for a year now and we love them." **AMERICA ONLINE** *keyword* exchange→ Outdoor Activities→Water Sports and Activities Board

Caving

alt.caving While low-profile cavers do not approve of this "renegade," unmoderated newsgroup—many, in fact, campaigned against its creation—it still provides a good place for people curious about caving to make contact with experienced cavers in their locale. The main fear is that "spelunkers" (that's what true cavers, speleologists, call yahoos who cave with only flashlights, ignoring helmets, safety gear, extra batteries, etc.) will post exact cave locations and that rescues and cave closures will result. Still, now that the initial debate has died down, almost every wired caver at least lurks on the newsgroup, even if they won't admit it above ground. **USENET** alt.caving

Climbing

Big Wall Climbing Home Page Finally discover exactly what a Double Portaledge looks like. John Middendorf and A5 Adventures of Flagstaff, Ariz. have put together this homage to the most challenging climbs in the world. This is a serious climber's site, complete with a hypertext guide to equipment. The page also clarifies climbing difficulty ratings—A5 denotes climbs that "take many hours to complete and require the climber to endure long periods of uncertainty and fear, often requiring a ballet-like efficiency of movement in order not to upset the tenuous integrity of marginal placements." And then they'll tell you where to find 'em in detailed, geologically-specific wall descriptions (Diorite ledges and all). Further whet your appetite with the pictures of Big Walls of the World and the many trip reports supplied by those who have braved the ultimate climbing challenges. **WEB** http://speleology.u.washington .edu/cavers

The Climbing Archive Endless information for the avid rock hound. There's even a search function to find exactly what you're looking for. Check out The World of Climbing for mountaineering insights, peruse the schedules of upcoming climbing events, and consult the lists of gyms, guides, and specialty shops. The wild spirit of the climbing community is illustrated in the climbing stories, songs, and poems posted to the archives by rock fans. Do trip reports titled "Lurking Fear" or "A Cheap Way to Die" fill you with a sick sort of pleasure? If so, you may have finally found paradise. **WEB** http://www.dtek.chalmers.se /Climbing/index.html

Climbing FAQ Everything you need to know to stay alive during a climb. Collected from informative answers posted to rec.climbing, these FAQs cover a wide variety of topics, from avalanche information to the ethics of bolting. There is a lot of information here for beginners, including an introduction to the philosophy of rock climbing, and new climbers will want to check out the glos-

sary so they can talk about "onsight flashes" with confidence.
WEB http://www.dtek.chalmers.se /Climbing/Training/FAQ/index.html

GORP—Climbing Resource on the Internet All the information you'll ever need to conquer the summits of the world, from Tasmania to Tennessee. In addition to GORP's own estimable resources, the page includes a plethora of climbing links—everything from general information about climbing to descriptions of local sites to lists of climbing clubs and outfitters to technical information. And check out the Online bookstore for synopses of climbing-related literature.
WEB http://gorp.com/gorp/activity /climb.htm

Curling

International Curling Information Network Group ICING The International Curling Information Network Group (ICING, to the cognoscenti) makes the bold claim on its home page that "millions of people around the world are involved in the sport of curling, thus information about the game and its participants is almost limitless." ICING does its best to support that claim, offering news and information about curling, history, rules, organizations and clubs across the world, a mailing list and newsgroup section, and links to coaches, ice-makers, collectors, and merchants of brooms, brushes, and curl-

ing clothing. Some links are still under construction and there isn't much to look at, but the information is thorough and useful.
WEB http://www.netaccess.on.ca/icing /icehome.htm

What is Curling? Good question. It's an ice sport, that much is certain, and it's played between two teams of four players. Each team must send eight "rocks" —large stones similar to giant hockey pucks—skidding across the ice, and attempt to place them closest to the bulls-eye of the far target. In short, ice shuffleboard! This document explains the basics of the sport, from the composition of the rocks (granite) to the layout of the target area.
WEB http://www.cs.cmu.edu/afs/cs .cmu.edu/user/clamen/misc/Sports /posts-archive/Curling-Desc.html

Cycling

BikeNet—The Bicycle Network This forum is one of the most impressive biking sites in cyberspace, featuring representatives from the biggest biking organizations in the country (the Bicycle Federation of America, the United States Cycling Federation, and the League of American Bicyclists, and others). Its biking message center has garnered more than 25,000 messages in categories such as components, accessories, classifieds, racing, training and fitness, regional trails and tours, and mountain bikes. Live BikeNet chats happen

several times a week here and there's always a schedule for the chats posted in the conference folder. The Software Exchange area of the forum stores biking images, FAQs, guides, tip sheets, chat logs, and a large collection of biking software.
AMERICA ONLINE *keyword* bikenet

Rec.bicycles FAQ Mike Iglesias, rec.bicycles* moderator of sorts, compiled a list of answers to questions that have been repeatedly asked on the seven biking newsgroups, and the result was a huge reference guide to biking and biking resources online. How do the organizers determine the ratings for the climbs in the Tour de France? What exactly is Polarlite? What are the pros and cons of Terrybikes for women? Can you reuse old spokes in new wheels? Why do heavier people roll down hills faster than little scrawny people? These and hundreds of other biking questions are addressed, primarily in the form of answers that have been posted to the newsgroup.
URL ftp://draco.acs.uci.edu /pub/rec.bicycles/faq • gopher:// draco.acs.uci.edu.:1071
WEB http://www.cis.ohio-state.edu /hypertext/faq/usenet/bicycles-faq /top.html

rec.bicycles.misc Stephen is getting a vasectomy and wonders how soon he can cycle afterwards (a week according to the several men who responded). Mark is explaining to Dwaine the issues involved with seat placement when using aero-bars. Ed is advising fellow bikers on cleaning up after riding in messy weather. And, dozens of members are fighting over the issue of carrying guns while riding a bike. For exposure to a broad range of biking issues and advice, this newsgroup leads the pack. It's also the best place to learn about new biking Web sites.

USENET rec.bicycles.misc

WOMBATS on the Web Female mountain bikers of the world have united. This fun arena features women helping each other stomach and surmount the mountain-biking community's omnipresent macho lingo and techno obsessions. Talk about biking, form a group, learn about events in your area, or just vent through the reader's forum; you're bound to feel better after you visit with these noncompetitive, pro-personal-best women.

WEB http://www.wombats.org

Equestrian

alt.sport.horse-racing "Did anyone see Urgent Request's odds fall from 8-1 to 5-2 in one flash with one minute to post time shortly before he went wire to wire in the one million dollar Santa Anita Handicap today? Someone must have made a lot of money!" Yeah, and that someone has a piece of the horse, according to the gossip on alt.sport.horse-racing: "When the horse ran the first

time last season in the U.K. the odds tumbled from 25:1 to 8:1. I think that a certain Mr. Aitken owns the horse and he is a very shrewd gambler. I remember him backing a horse over here from 33:1 down to 5:1 Fav and the horse duly obliged in the Ebor Handicap, which is one of the best Hcaps run in the U.K." The talk in this newsgroup isn't all this witheringly specific—much of it centers on general opinions about betting systems, racing collectibles, and other online sites that meet the needs of racing fans.

USENET alt.sport.horse-racing

Derby Right out of the gate, the discussion here is intense, with serious handicappers and horse trainers discussing the world of derby racing. Discussion moves from a critique of Phar Lap's training regimen to thoughts on the book *The Fit Racehorse II* by Tom Ivers to the determination of track vari-

ants in calculating the early speed of horses to reminiscing about the race when Angel Cordero rode a race without a saddle. Odds for upcoming races and results of races recently run are posted as well on this incredibly active list.

EMAIL derby-request@inslab.uky.edu
✍ *Write a request*

The Hay Net: An Exhaustive List of Horse Sites on the Internet Many sites say they can tell you how to find a stud. The Hay Net breaks it down into categories for you: quarter horses, ponies, etc. Anything related to raising and caring for horses (including the personal Web pages of people who just love them) is categorized on this plainly laid-out list of links. But if all you want is racing results, you've come to the wrong place.

WEB http://www.freerein.com/haynet

PoloNet Calling polo the "world's oldest sport," the webmasters here say their mis-

Ralph Lauren's favorite sport
http://www.cts.com/browse/polonet

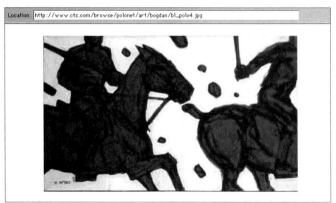

Location: http://www.cts.com/browse/polonet/art/bogdan/b1_polo4.jpg

sion is to provide communication between players, clubs, teams, and associations; to educate the curious; and to promote their sport and the Web. They succeed on all counts. Learn all about polo (and such polo alternatives as polocrosse, bike polo, canoe polo, and cowboy polo). View paintings, photos, and drawings from fans and players, and read postings detailing polo events from around the world. The most original bits are the witty quotes placed around the site, such as Winston Churchill's "A polo handicap is your passport to the world." **WEB** http://www.cts.com/browse /polonet

rec.equestrian All things equine are fair game on this newsgroup, whether it's a post from a world traveler with information about the Queen of England's master saddler or a James Herriot-esque anecdote from a horse owner: "Mud season has started here, and yesterday the man I board with decided to put the horses' hay down on a long sheet of plastic, to keep it out of the mud. At first they were a bit skeptical, but by today, there was a three way tug of war going on in the field. Three horses had each grabbed a corner of the heavy plastic sheet in their teeth, and were dragging it back and forth, pulling and flapping. It was hysterically funny to watch." Rude bicyclists banging into animals on trails? Bandage problems

delaying healing of a bad leg cut? An endurance horse sidelined by equine protozoal myelitis? Everything you always wanted to know about the knights on life's chessboard, and more. **USENET** rec.equestrian

Winner's Circle A thoroughbred among the Net's horse-sport sites, the Winner's Circle includes track news from six U.S. regions (West Coast, Southwest, Midwest, Northeast, Mid-Atlantic, and Southeast), as well as an area for Track Talk, a collection of horse racing photos, a historic Gallery of Champions, and even a detailed glossary of racing terms. This is truly the mane event. **AMERICA ONLINE** *keyword* abctrack

Fencing

Fencing FTP Site An archive of information and illustrations related to fencing, swords, and sword play. Line drawings of everything from an epée (a type of fencing sword) to a plastron (a quilted pad worn by fencers). The text here ranges from the by-laws of the Durendal Fencing Club in Madison, Wisc. to a list of fencing concepts and terms. The document fensafe.txt outlines the "inherent risks in the activity." **URL** ftp://bbs.macc.wisc.edu/pub2 /fencing

rec.sport.fencing Discussion here varies from debate about the merits of the French grip

vs. the pistol grip to talk of interesting club names, like the Vampire Fencing Club, Foiled Again!, and Swash and Buckle. A friendly yet serious group gathers to talk about rules and strategy. Posts about tournaments are always welcome. **USENET** rec.sport.fencing *FAQ:* **WEB** http://www.ii.uib.no/~arild /fencing/faq/Top-view.html

Fishing

alt.fishing The oldest of the fishing newsgroups, alt.fishing was suppose to be superseded by the rec.outdoors.fishing newsgroups. Someone tell its members. The group consistently generates hundreds of messages a week on topics ranging from trolling for trout to bass fishing in Massachusetts to deep sea fishing. "Anyone have experience with big game fishing around Zanzibar?" Betcha, someone does. **USENET** alt.fishing

Fishing Archive A fly fishing FAQ, recipes, and several fishing software programs are archived here. For Mac users, there's FlyBox, a HyperCard program that catalogs Fly dressings—stats and illustrations. FishLog for IBM-compatibles is a database for recording your catches—know when and where you've caught the biggest and the best. Fish Scales, a program available for both platforms, calculates the weight of your fish (enter the length, fish type, and fish fatness). In addition to several

Location: http://www.inetmkt.com/fishpage/pics.html

"Brookie caught by Jenni Kirkham in Henry's Lake 6/94"

You're never too young for bloodsports
http://www.eskimo.com/~baubo/wfp.html

other fishing software programs, the site stores hundreds of images, including diagrams of fly patterns, great catches, fishermen, and fishing waters. **URL** ftp://ftp.geo.mtu.edu/pub/fishing

rec.outdoors.fishing Dave's going bass fishing in Dallas and is looking for a guide. Jeff was there a few months ago and recommends Lucky Lee's Guide Services—"tell him Jeff and Don said hello!, the boys from LA!" Robby's heading to Lake Rodman and wants a fishing report. And Mark's trying to explain to Lee that there isn't a perfect lure for catching large mouth bass, that it's a matter of preference: "My brother has often told me that he would rather catch *one* bass on a buzzbait than five on any other lure—go figure." Covering fishing worldwide, the group is a mix of fishing stories and advice, hard information and reports, and discussions about lures, rods, and

fishing lore.
USENET rec.outdoors.fishing

rec.outdoors.fishing.fly With several hundred messages a week, this newsgroup is home to an active online community of fly fishermen. Beginners to old timers exchange information and tips here. Mike and Marie, for instance, are trying to sell old equipment. Brian is looking for hints on beading hooks. Dozens of organizations are announcing classes and trips. And, everyone seems to be looking for a good guide.
USENET rec.outdoors.fishing.fly

The Virtual FlyBox... No one here but us flies. There are descriptions of several variations of dry fly dressings, wet fly dressings, streamer dressings, and other fly patterns as well as illustrated diagrams of a widespread fiber spinner wing, a no hackle spinner proportion, a dry fly proportion, the spinner wing tying method, and the

Devaux method. Hatching charts for the Delaware River and the Eastern and Western U.S. are also available.
URL ftp://anonftp.geo.mtu.edu:/pub /fishing/from_nicb/flys.htm

Women's Fishing Partnership Yes, this site is intended to lure female flycasters, but don't let that scare you away, men— there are links available to almost every fishing resource a serious fisher could ever need. Sample the Fish Page for starters, where, you can buy tackle, trade fishing gear, read product reviews, join fishing clubs, or plan a flycaster's dream vacation. You can learn about fishing regulations and licensing requirements within your state by clicking on the State Fishing Resources Page. However, there are some goodies for women only. Perhaps you're tired of always fishing with the guys, or you're looking to swap fish stories, trade expertise, or learn new fishing tips from other women. If you're someone who'd rather "go fish" with the girls, the Women's Fishing Partnership wants to help. Just email the Partnership and let them know you'd like to plug into the network. Or try the Links to Women's Resources.
WEB http://www.eskimo.com/~baubo /wfp.html

Footbag

Official Rules From Footbag Golf to Footbag Consecutive, from Footbag Net to Footbag

Freestyle, there are plenty of sports that use the little bag more commonly known as a Hackey-Sack™. This site lists all the rules, and even contains short histories of each sport—footbag golf, in case you were wondering, debuted in Portland, Oregon's Delta Park in August 1982.
WEB http://ifab.Footbag.ORG//contents.html

The Sport of Footbag Footbag is not Hackey-Sack™. Really. Hackey-Sack™ is a trademark registered to the Wham-O company. Wham-O also makes the Frisbee™. But footbag is not Hackey-Sack™, and flying disc is not Frisbee™. This footbag page links to footbag pictures and events, as well as the rules of various footbag sports.
WEB http://gregorio.stanford.edu/footbag/footbag.html

Football
....
ESPNET NFL Here's why ESPN has the best all-around sports coverage in the world. Check out SportsZone for breaking news and in-depth analysis of everything that's happening in the National Football League: from draft-day bargains to statistical rankings and breakouts to exclusive interviews, this site has football knowledge coming out of its ears. One caveat: If you want it all, it'll cost you. SportsZone only gives a taste of what it has to offer for free; most stories and services require a monthly subscription.
WEB http://espnet.sportszone.com/nfl

Fantasy Football League drafts, starting lineups, prime time players—AOL's fantasy football is almost like the real thing. And when you're done absorbing the important stuff, consult the Miscellaneous Provisions section, which reiterates that "all owners are expected to act in a mature and sportsman-like manner." Are you listening, Al Davis?
AMERICA ONLINE *keyword* fantasy football

Fantasy Football What's your football fantasy? How about Montana rolling and passing to Rice again, or Jim Brown taking the handoff from Sid Luckman and then blowing by Kellen Winslow on the way to the end zone? Fantasy football doesn't exactly work that way—most leagues only allow you to pick current players, and to use their stats to build a paper squad. But dreams die hard.
COMPUSERVE *go* sports→Libraries *or* Messages→Fantasy Football

Football Get your fill of pigskin in AOL's football area, which includes a wide variety of message boards, libraries, and news services devoted to the game that brought new meaning to the phrase "illegal motion." Start out talking NFL at the pro football message board, then relive your days rooting for Notre Dame or Nebraska on the college football message board. Check out the scores, news, and especially the file libraries, which

are filled with .GIFs of team logos, rosters, and even some wonderful multimedia clips.
AMERICA ONLINE *keyword* gs football

Football Server Nando is football. Or maybe football is Nando. Whatever the case, the Nando football server is one of the best places on the Web for gridiron fans. Link to college and pro scores, news reports, statistics, and even previews for upcoming games. On the NFL page, you'll find a complete resource to the world of pads and end runs, including highlights from past seasons, news and views from around the NFL, and conference-by-conference breakdowns. Fans who follow conference links can find individual home pages for each team, which contain stats, rosters, schedules, and historical information.
WEB http://www.nando.net/SportServer/football

NFL on Fox Now, this place is well-organized. Instead of giving headings as links and requiring you to jump to another page, Fox uses tables to narrow your choices and ease your way through their site. Pick from a group of categories, click "go," and know exactly where you're headed. What's more, the tables are carried over to the new pages, so you don't have to go backwards or reload to get a new search. It's an effective search engine that leads to an array of scores, news, schedules, commentary, and statistics, all on an attrac-

tive design and intuitive layout.
WEB http://fyionline.com/mci-news
/newsroom/NFL/scoreboard.html

Golf

golf.com One of the most comprehensive golf sites on the Web, with information on 15,000 American courses; discount coupons for those courses; online subscription information for a variety of golfing publications (Northeast Golfer, Par Excellance); playing tips from a PGA player (Jeff Maggert); an electronic golf shop; an electronic travel service; and a listing of more than 300 golf schools. While

this site is a pay service ($4.95/month), it also has a selection of materials available for free, including essays on famous courses such as Turnberry and a program guide to The Golf Channel.
WEB http://gdol.com

Golf Information Service This is one of the best online services for golfers seeking to plan a links trip or to locate a golf course near their homes. Search the gigantic golf course database to find a course that suits your needs, get a list of all golf resorts in your area, order merchandise, or scan lists of golf schools, publications,

organizations, and tournaments. The page also contains a list of tournament results.
AMERICA ONLINE *keyword* golfis

rec.sport.golf This is a huge newsgroup, with thousands of posts on hundreds of topics ranging from balls to clubs to shoes to blues. While posts occasionally discuss pro golfers, most of the traffic is concerned with golfing as a participatory rather than spectator sport, and the group has a number of fascinating threads about the dangers of golf ("Golf as a contact sport"), cost-cutting while putting ("Budget golf"), and the sport's steep learning curve

 TEAM NFL (OFFICIAL)
WEB http://www.nfl.com

It's official—the official **NFL** home page, that is, which means they must have tons of money and the resources to make it look pretty cool. They have posted some great photos and the latest team logos here. But still, they're trying to make money by advertising and selling official merchandise to you, the product-hungry fan. You can find links to every team as well as continually updated **NFL** news, courtesy of an agreement with ESPN's SportsZone. Don't look for any exposés here on

Location: http://www.nfl.com/steelers/index.html

PITTSBURGH

drug use in the league, though. You'll have to settle for how the World League is breaking attendance records and similar one-sided stuff. Team NFL also offers complete schedules for the coming year, forums for idea exchanges and gridiron talk, an **NFL** history, a football search engine, and the occasional interview.

TEAM STATS
ROSTER
DEPTH CHART
COACHING
FRONT OFFICE

Sack lunches

The loss of Greg Lloyd to a season-ending injury hasn't slowed the Pittsburgh Steelers, which clamped down on the Ravens last week and looks for more of the same this week in a Monday night showdown with the Buffalo Bills. Players like Rod Woodson, with two interceptions, and Kevin Henry, pictured, have stepped up the defense without Lloyd, recording six sacks over the first two weeks.

("New course = higher score?"). There's even a thread about the legal ins and outs of cloning popular club designs.
USENET rec.sport.golf

The Virtual Golfer The Virtual Golfer has lots of Java and tables on it, which is fun unless you're Netscape-deprived. It's also got golf chat and a Virtual Golfer Message Board where you can communicate with the similarly fanatical. Your golf-talk options include clubhouse talk, a PGA "pool" where you can pick the winners, a locker room, and a classifieds area for hockers, hackers, and buyers.
WEB http://golfball.com

Gymnastics

Gymn: an electronic forum for gymnastics What are the standings for the men's prelims in the Pan American Games? How about the final standings for the women's American Classic Senior All-Around? Brought to you by the same folks that run the Gymn mailing list (an archive of the list is available here), the site reliably tracks results at recent meets, features a calendar of gymnastic events, and monitors the collegiate rankings. And that's just the beginning. Check out the *Gymn Reporter*, an on-site newsletter, indexed for easy use, that provides professional commentary on meets and training tips. You can also look up the address of the Azerbaijan National Olympic Committee in the list of gymnastics

Location: ftp://ftp.cac.psu.edu/pub/gymn/Images/96euros/khork4.jpg

Gymn Photography (c) Debbie Poe

No holds barred
http://www.rmii.com/~rachele/gymnhome.html

organizations or get details on other gymnastics publications.
URL ftp://ftp.cac.psu.edu/pub/gymn
WEB http://www.rmii.com/~rachele/gymnhome.html

Hockey

The Blue Line For the past few hockey seasons, AOLers have bickered over a few key hockey points: Who's the NHL's best looking player? (Writes Kathy, one of the hundreds of fans who responded, "I love Kovalev's mouth, so very kissable looking. Chelios is handsome in a menacing sort of way. I love Eric Lindros's body.") Who's the best goaltender? Who's the best center? And, who are the best officials? These and similar discussions continue through the seasons, engaging fans of all teams. But team talk is big here as well. The professional hockey bulletin board includes folders for every NHL team and the college board is home to a few

college teams. Hockey fans also get together in the Grandstand's chat rooms for live discussions.
AMERICA ONLINE *keyword* gs hockey→ Hockey (Professional) *or* Hockey (College)

Fantasy Hockey Days after the NHL drafts its players, CompuServe hockey fans can do the same—draft NHL players, that is. Although the forum often runs more than one league, the goal in all of them is the same: assemble a team of players with the best possible stats. Line-ups, trade talk, and player transactions are posted in the message boards, and standings and game files are available in the libraries. Prizes are sometimes awarded at the completion of a season.
COMPUSERVE *go* sports→Libraries→ Fantasy Hockey

NHL Open Net (official) Featuring warp-speed interstellar graphics á la *Trek*, this official

site of the National Hockey League provides links to statistics, standings, individual teams, rosters, and the All-Star Celebrity League—not a bad offering at all. Make sure you have a frame-enabled browser before you drop by, though—otherwise, you could get caught in a perpetual loop between the home page and frame windows. Kind of like doing serious time in the penalty box.
WEB http://www.nhl.com

SportsLine USA NHL Rink
Another entry in the ever-growing list of comprehensive hockey news pages, SportsLine boasts neat graphics and extensive information. What makes

this site most original, however, is only available to paying subscribers. Your standard stats, previews, and scoreboards are free for the viewing, but if you want real content, you've gotta pony up $4.95 a month or $39.95 a year. For that you get fun columns, .WAV audio clips, and a plethora of news stories.
WEB http://www.sportsline.com/u/hockey/index.html

Usenet/WWW Hockey Draft The popular Usenet hockey draft grew from 20 teams in 1987 to 342 teams in 1994. In 1995, it added a Web dimension with easy-to-use forms for player transactions and the number grew to more than 700. To play

in the season-long competition, you must choose a team before the hockey season begins by purchasing players (any player, any team) with the uniformly allotted 1,000 points. The goal is for your players to score more points than you pay for them in the preseason drafts and midseason trades and acquisitions. Standings as well as rules and other information are maintained for every participant at the Web site.
WEB http://geocities.com/Colosseum/3216

WWW Hockey Guide We went to a fight last night, and a hockey game broke out. If you've heard that one before, you've likely seen a slapshot or two in

 THE NANDO HOCKEY SERVER
WEB http://www.nando.net/SportServer/hockey
One of the largest hub sites on the Net for hockey information—and one of the slickest. Created by The News & Observer Publishing Co. (publishers of the *Charlotte Observer*), this Web site publishes full-length hockey articles and statistics as well as maintaining Web pages for individual

hockey teams. Link to the Bruins page, for instance, and get a team roster, schedule, statistics, news stories and game reports, and a column of notes and quotes about the team that shares the Fleet Center with the Celtics.

Location: http://www4.nando.net/newsroom/sports/hkn/1995/nhl/edm/arts/pix.html

Edmonton Oilers Pictures

your day. Maybe you're even missing a few front teeth. If you're a hockey enthusiast, you can link to more than 1,100 hockey sites, including professional and college leagues, rotisserie leagues, and roller and field hockey resources. Navigating from this index is fairly painless, and you can also access an intimidating array of hockey-related newsgroups.
WEB http://www.hockeyguide.com

Hunting

rec.hunting "Take the tenderloin and back strap fillets of Venison and cut them into one-inch cubes and fondue!," recommends one member. That's after you've shot the deer. Hunters discuss all aspects of the hunting experience, from the politics to the equipment and guns to the technique to the recipes. Terry's talking about mountain lion hunting in California, Tawashi wants to know where he can hunt wild turkey in Vermont, and dozens of members are trading tips on training hunting dogs. Discussions can be quite informative like a recent thread on bear attacks which provoked a lengthy analysis of bear attitudes and fighting styles. "As a behavior mechanism, bears often employ a bluff charge. They pop their jaws, growl, and charge—up to about 15 feet where they stop and go through more threats. Sort of a bear version of 'chicken.' Then, if combat isn't offered,

they tend to back off as gracefully as they can."
USENET rec.hunting

The Shooting Page Whether you like to blow clay disks out of the sky or shred stationary targets from 20 yards away, you'll find detailed technical and historical information here to a wide variety of shooting competitions for rifles and handguns. Plus, learn about such esoteric goings-on as muzzle-loading conventions—complete with muskets and eighteenth-century costumes—or "action shooting" matches where professionals take out five targets in less than three seconds. Don't fire until you see the whites of their eyes.
WEB http://www.wsa.com/ool/misc .files/shootmain.html

Ice skating

ABC Figure Skating Need to know the difference between a camel spin and a death spiral? Look up skating terms and lingo in the figure skating glossary, read skaters bios and personal interviews, and skim through USFSA info. A good place for spectators to learn the basics, ABC's site even has a Fun Facts area that lists endless championship trivia.
AMERICA ONLINE *keyword* ABC→Figure Skating

CTV Sports: The Rink Figure skating snuck into Americans hearts and televisions as quickly as the infamous lackey Shawn Eckardt crept up on

Nancy Kerrigan with that fateful pipe. Figure skating competitions—high drama, sequined glamour and all, are one of America's most watched sporting events, including The World Figure Skating Championships. This Web site gives you the standings, marks, scoring, and evaluations of Michelle Kwan, Elena Liashenko, Lu Chen, and others during this figure skating Super Bowl.
WEB http://www.CTViSTAR.COM

Recreational Figure Skating FAQ With this FAQ, learn the ABCs of figure skating terminology, like the differences between counter, three-turn, rocker, and bracket turns, or the difference between crossover strokes and progressives. It will explain the purchase, use, and maintenance of skating equipment, different skating styles, and some techniques to practice on the rink. Whether you hit the ice, or it hits you, you had better note the five basic types of skating injuries you can sustain. "Bruised ego, bruised body, pulled muscles or ligaments, broken bones, concussion," and the appropriate prevention techniques explained here. This FAQ is great for learning the sport from the bottom up.
WEB http://www.crc.doc.ca/~kbryden /recreationalSkating

Martial arts

MARS—Martial Arts Resource Site One of the most impres-

sive martial arts resource pages in cyberspace. The site links to several essays including "Ki Breathing" and "The Real Meaning of the Black Belt," texts like "The Art of War" and "Tao Te Ching," terminology lists and bibliographies for several forms of martial arts, dozens of FAQs, and many other martial arts-related Net sites.
WEB http://www.lehigh.edu/~sjb3 /martial.html

rec.martial-arts Is Tae Kwon Do or Judo more effective on the street? Do Aikido or Jujitsu techniques work better against resistance? Rivalries among the martial arts run rampant here ("I'm sorry but there isn't a Tae Kwon Do stylist who's come to our Judo club to learn grappling who's lasted more than three weeks. They all quit because they got hurt and bruised and humiliated a bit too much for their liking"). Even video game fighting simulations come into the mix ("Did anyone see the game *VirtuaFighter*? The moves are pretty impressive and look authentic.... Why pay fifty dollars a month for lessons when you can learn cool moves, fighting strategy, and stances for a few quarters?" And the response? "Umm, excuse me, but are you high? Watching moves doesn't make you skilled anymore than brushing up on *Batman* reruns will help you build his utility belt... *VirtuaFighter*: Cool to watch. Pretty unrealistic.... Until TRUE VR, complete with impact and maybe even pain, comes about, video games won't be that useful for training."). The newsgroup is a great place for movie IDs when you just can't remember where that fantastic fighting scene came from.
USENET rec.martial-arts

Motorcycles

Harley Owner's Group A prepossessing home page for owners of the timeless marque. Besides being true to the Harley heritage, the HOG is also dedicated to the corporate folks in

SKATEWEB: THE FIGURE SKATING PAGE

WEB http://www.cs.yale.edu/homes/sjl/skate.html

You can feel the love for the sport emanating from this home page. It has a load of **FAQ**s and reference material concerning various federations, associations, and competitions, rules and regulations. Skating tips and attire are also subjects given some consideration. Fans of the professional

Location: http://haskell.cs.yale.edu/sjl/skate-images/misc/ob-cs-07.jpg

skaters will be happy to find that the webmaster has provided numerous links to fan pages as well. This well-maintained page has lively links and an up-to-date schedule of upcoming events. It's enough to make you get up and try a grafstrom spin.

OK, I'M NAKED. LET'S GO!

I don't know how the martial arts community can consider judo a self-defense form since it is considered more of a sport like you see on the Olympics. Furthermore, how are you able to grab a hold of someone and do a throw for instance if they are not wearing a martial art uniform??? Anyhow give a couple of good reasons of why this martial art can be considered a self-defense system!!!!!!!!!!

Judo is descended from JuJitsu, the empty handed art of the Samurai. It involves throws, joint locks, arm and leg bars, chokes and more. Need a uniform to hold on to? The Samurai had armor. Do you wear a suit, or are you a jeans and T-shirt kind of guy? Do you wear a belt? Even if you are naked a good judoka will find something to grab onto.;) However, the most devastating Judo techniques, IMO, do not involve the use of the gi. Naked chokes, arm/leg bars, throws using the arm or leg all leave a person more vulnerable than their counterparts using the gi.

—from rec.martial-arts

Milwaukee, from whom they are seeking permission to make the site official. In the meantime, check out World Wide Glide, with its neat pictorial on the history of Harley engines ("My Grandaddy was a Knucklehead!") and the Official Harley-Davidson Art Collection with its groovy (and pricey) bike art.
WEB http://www.magicnet.net/mni/hog .html

Motorcycle Online The Bimota of Net biker services, except MO is free and won't start pinching you after 200 miles of sweepers on Highway 1. This one-stop resource offers everything ranging from new-model reviews to as-it-happens race coverage and product evaluations. Motobytes, Buyer

Beware, and particularly the Skeptics Society are helpful and informative pages that virtually write the book on how to put together a leading Web site.
WEB http://motorcycle.com/motor cycle.html

rec.motorcycles.racing Scott Russell wins the Daytona 200. Howard marvels at the success of Cadiva against much larger European conglomerates. And William believes that Doug Chandler "suffered a compound fracture of his ego." Whether you want to talk about new equipment, old injuries, or the eternal questions of motorcycle racing— how many notches should you leak out the needle if you depart from stock settings?

what's the value of an F2 frame?—you'll have to type fast and corner well.
USENET rec.motorcycles.racing

Outdoor sports

rec.backcountry With threads like "dehydrated fowl" and "high altitude snakes," how can you go wrong? These folks are enthusiastic about their ramblings, posting trip reports and reminiscing about favorite hikes. Wilderness pros pass on tricks like lighting a stove from a flashlight battery and steel wool or the best way to conquer the Pacific Crest Trail. Advice on all aspects of enjoying the outdoors in relative comfort is freely offered here— so start whipping up that homemade beef jerky!
USENET rec.backcountry

Paintball

alt.sport.paintball Guns, guns, guns. Is that all paintballers ever talk about? Well, pretty much. There's occasional talk of paintball courses, newly designed games, and ethical issues in the world of Gotcha! Most of the discussion on this newsgroup consists of equipment comparisons, classified ads, and recommendations for the best way to blow an opponent to kingdom come.
USENET alt.sport.paintball

WarPig Paintball Server When paintball players get together to talk about the online resources for their sport, the first name raised is usually WarPig. As the first server devoted entirely to paintball, the page has a certain paramilitary air, and dozens of fascinating links— from listings of paintball fields to plans for custom weapons to detailed reviews of production air cannons and other equipment.

WEB http://www.warpig.com

Racquetball

Racquetball FAQ General questions, techniques, and rules for the sport of kings (some say horse racing is the sport of kings, but they're the kind of people who get snowed by a lots of loud noise and big prize money). What racquetball

videotapes are available? Are there any good mail order supply houses for racquetball aficionados in the boondocks? And what happens if you bust your racket over an opponent's head and the strings make that "whang, whang, whang" noise that busted rackets do in cartoons?

WEB http://www.mcs.com/~toma/www /files/rqb.faq.html

Roller sports

alt.skate-board Skateboard culture's a free-for-all. Postings range from "I think skating is sh*tty now, everything has turned dumb... 40s, pot, and chicks, that's it," to "Smokin' herb is out, going to Raves on

rollerblades on ecstasy with a big wallet chain is here to stay," to "I would never do pot or alcohol when skating." Although the arguments can get infinitely more banal, including arguments about the energy value of grilled cheese vs. peanut butter & jelly sandwiches—"You cannot compare a GCS to a PBJ. Where I live you could get shot for doing such a thing"—the skateboard discussion group remains a good source for information on where to find old school paraphernalia and boards, tips on getting yourself sponsored, as well as first-hand reviews of the latest and hippest Adidas skate shoes.

USENET alt.skate-board

GORP—GREAT OUTDOOR RECREATION PAGES

WEB http://www.gorp.com

Thinking of a trip that doesn't include a Hilton and a hairdryer? **GORP** undoubtedly has the best source of outdoor information on the Web. These intertwined pages of Net links provide tons of information for trip-planning and some useful outdoor advice. There are plenty of descriptions of

Location: http://www.gorp.com/gifs/gorp/activity/paddle/mctwist.jpg

everything our great nation has preserved for us: wildlife refuges, national battlefields, parks, forests, and monuments, too. There are also links to hiking, biking, climbing, fishing, skiing, paddle sports, and bird watching sites. GORP is also home to the Adventurous Travel Bookstore, a searchable database of 1,200+ books and maps, with an online ordering facility.

Inline Online The best of the Inline Skating Web 'zines, *Inline Online* sports links to profiles of companies and products, skate park addresses worldwide, archives of an email list on inline skating, a movie and picture archive, individual and team profiles, and classifieds for skating equipment. Inline Skating is in the process of building a mini-empire of online skate 'zines, offering space and links to such 'zines as *Daily Bread, Box, Roller Hockey,* and *XSk8.*
WEB http://galaxy.einet.net/galaxy /Leisure-and Recreation/Sports /daniel-chick/io_org.html

Inline Skating FAQ Looking for first-hand tips on how to perform a front-side curb grind? Can't decide whether to buy the Hyper Hop-Up kit or the Lazzy Legs? If you're confused about which features are a priority, here is where you can learn to decipher SSHA ("Silly Sales Hype Acronyms"). Net skaters can look up local skating clubs in their area, and accessory hounds will find a full listing of retail outlets around the world.
WEB http://www.skatefaq.com

Tumyeto Home Page Billed as "the 'premier' digital forum of skateboarding information source" (aren't there a few too many nouns in that sentence?), this page is a relatively intensive trip through the world of skateboarding, complete with news briefs, events listings, companies, organizations, and

a continually expanding list of world skate parks.
WEB http://skateboard.com/tydu /skatebrd/skate.htm

Rowing

Rowing FAQ If you're thinking about trying out for crew, check out this FAQ to learn all of those weird rowing terms, like coxless pair, skeg, and rigger. It covers types of boats, weight classes, race formats, regatta information and ergometers. The FAQ includes a useful list of books, magazines, and rowing-related addresses. It even attempts to answer the question, "Why do we do this?"
WEB http://www.rpi.edu/dept/union /crew/public_html/faq.html • http:// riceinfo.rice.edu/~hofer/Rowingfaq .html

Things You Don't Want to Hear What are the things you don't ever want your coxswain to say? How about "It looks shallow here..."? Here's a list of about 50 more examples.
WEB http://wsnet.com/~jiml/mrc /cox.html

Rugby

Rugby Server It's rugbymania at this site, which include the basics of rugby, rules of rugby, rugby trivia, country-specific information, schedules of international games, scrumptious rugby songs, and more, more, more.
WEB http://rugby.phys.uidaho.edu /rugby.html

The Rugby Union WWW Home Page This definitive site covers the basic rules of traditional rugby, international game schedules, match results, video clips, and words to some infamous (and unprintable) rugby songs and jokes. In addition, there is a very good copy of the Laws of the Game designed to be searched and links to other Internet resources. The FAQ for the Usenet newsgroup rec.sport.rugby is maintained on this site.
WEB http://rugby.phys.uidaho.edu /rugby

Running

Dr. Pribut's Running Injuries Page Meet Dr. Stephen Pribut, D.P.M., F.A.A.P.S.M.—he must know what he's talking about, with that many initials after his name. So listen up as he shares a wealth of information on everything from such common injuries as iliotibial band syndrome to stretches that will treat or prevent injuries. Pribut also offers handy health tips for running in any kind of weather and buying the right kind of running shoe. After all, the best medicine is preventative.
WEB http://www.clark.net/pub/pribut /spsport.html

Internet Resources for Runners If you're a hard-core runner, the Internet Resources for Runners page is worth a bookmark. We found the most valuable link on the site: the injury resource library. Manned by Dr. Fer-

nando Dimeo, there are common diagnoses, cures, and insights to even the most minor problems runners encounter. And naturally, there are links to studies, industries, standings, and post-mortems on just about every running event.
WEB http://irfr.com

rec.running No pain, no gain. If you run a lot, then you probably won't squirm when people start recounting the details of their various knee injuries or the bunions they can't get rid of, and, most of all, how much it hurts. Besides countless postings on where to run, local running clubs, and first-hand feedback from runners about the latest footwear, debates run

wild over how to handle those ferocious dogs in the park. When the solution to kick, hit, or spray ammonia in the face of a dog is suggested, users might get a warning: "If you ever kicked/hit/punched my dog in the face or ribs or anywhere I would take this as an act of animal cruelty and as an attack on what is basically 'my child'. In other words, I would do my best to make you regret the hell out of such vicious behavior." Runners of the world may not unite, but they sure like to fight and complain.
USENET rec.running

The Running Page Going to L.A., Portland, and Florida but afraid you won't know how to

fit in your workout? This is a great place to get detailed information on running scenes around the world. Dedicated to linking you to information about running organizations on the Web, it is a good starting point for information about upcoming races, local clubs, and becoming a member of USATF (USA Track and Field). You can also post your own running tips or compare personal bests.
WEB http://sunsite.unc.edu/drears /running/running.html

Sailing

The America's Cup Regatta Not only will you get an extensive history of the America's Cup

DANSWORLD
WEB http://www.cps.msu.edu/~dunhamda/dw/dansworld.html

If you're looking to find out who "started a fight with two guys he didn't know were professional kickboxers," check out Rick's Gossip! pages at *Dansworld*, the self-proclaimed first skateboarding Web 'zine. Industry announcements, the history of skateboarding, excerpted newspaper and mag-

azine articles, and links to other skateboard sites are accessible from this fast growing site. QuickTime videos and high-quality JPEG pics capture hot skateboard tricks. An excellent FAQ tells you everything you ever wanted to know about ramp & street skating, board prices, 'zines, New School vs. Old School styles, and "Flip Essentials."

Regatta, but there are separate Web pages dedicated to the Cup defender and each challenger. Start with the history of the three cups. Can Dennis Conner do it again? Then explore each boat through design blueprints and boat biographies. Pick a crew member to root for. How about Yann Gouniot, Mainsail trimmer on the French entry, or Merritt Carey from Tenants Harbor, ME on the America3 all-women's team. Then get down to racing. Follow (or relive) the Cups with online race results, scoreboard, commentary, and pictures. Don't miss the FAQ or the America's Cup merchandise sold here.
WEB http://ac95.org/index.shtml

Mark Rosenstein's Sailing Page
This well-appointed Web site is undoubtedly the best port from which to begin sailing the Net. You can finds other sailors hanging about in the archives of boating mailing lists and newsgroups accessible from this hub. Get pointers on tuning your sails from the Laser WWW Server. There are design resources here too, for those eager to trust themselves in a hull of their own building. Looking for a local moorage or regatta? Home pages for sailing clubs from New Zealand to San Francisco are listed here. If you fancy tracking Intrepid 'round the world races, jump to the BOC challenge page. Don't miss Mark's collection of tall ship information, or his links to maritime literature and

The Soling World Championships 1996
http://helsinki.fi/~avnurmin/soling.html

history sites. Mark's even added a link to The Gutenberg Project's online novels so you can relax with Captain Ahab. Really longing to run away to sea? Try the rec.boats .crewlist, where captains search for able hands.
WEB http://community.bellcore.com /mbr/sailing-page.html

rec.boats Where the sailors and the motorheads meet to talk water. In this very active newsgroup, all boating and sailing topics are up for discussion. Nick asks about noseplugs and Thomas wonders about Kevlar running rigging. And then there are those who come to share boating pranks and jokes or seek help in naming the newest member of their family (a JY, not a kid). Drop by. You never know who you might meet when you're looking for a sextant.
USENET rec.boats

Soling A Web site with probably everything you ever wanted to know about soling. At this home page for the International Soling Class, interested browsers will find the history and even the blueprints of this Olympic-class keelboat for three. Racers might want to look back at the 1994 World Championship through images and articles, or make plans to race themselves after checking here for this year's international and Finnish schedules.
WEB http://helsinki.fi/~avnurmin /soling.html

YachtNet/Intersail This attractive Web site has its own newsletter with interesting articles on match racing, boat building, marine ecology, and regattas. If that weren't enough, there are links to many of the best sailing sites on the Web. There's also an online store that sends you to the purveyors of nautical

wares Web-wide. Check back for shorelife and real estate databases.
WEB http://www.best.com/~ychtnt

Scuba

Aquanaut *Aquanaut* may bill itself as "the Internet's first online magazine" dedicated to scuba, but that's not all it is. First, there's the awe-inspiring collection of scuba links. Head here to find out about training, dive destinations, and clubs worldwide. Specialized information on everything from Nitrox to shipwreck locations is only links away. There's also a map of the latest global sea surface temperatures, classified ads, and a diving gear market-place. This multimedia extravaganza also has loads of camcorder movies and underwater pictures uploaded by enthusiasts.
WEB http://www.aquanaut.com

Scuba Chat At 4, 7, or 10 p.m. daily (EST), you can talk scuba with serious and not-so-serious enthusiasts. Just pick an alias and join in. What makes this chat room hip? The atmosphere, dude. Participants are encouraged to upload a funky scuba-themed graphic—perhaps a drunken sea turtle or a squirmy blue octopus—which appears every time they speak.
WEB http://www.4-lane.com/sportschat/newsc/sc_index.html

Scuba Diving Information Page John Gross has dedicated much of his free time to collecting Internet resources for others who share his passion for scuba. In addition to bigger sites like *Aquanaut*, the Comdive Archives, and Yee's Scuba archive, this hubsite has links to several lesser known, but fascinating, resources. Check out, for instance, a page dedicated to scuba diving in Singapore, or sign up for the Divers Environment Survey. Another highlight of John's page is his admirable collection of dive-related software for Mac, DOS/Windows, and Unix.
WEB http://www.ssc.com/~jong/scuba/scuba.html

BEAUTY MAGAZINE
WEB http://www.beauty.se

No, this ezine is has nothing do with cosmetics. But it does have everything to do with beauty—at least, as it relates to the art of hang-time. Indeed, humans have learned to fly, thanks to the invention of the snowboard. Packed with action shots, this slick site is entirely devoted to boarding. It

focuses on competitions in Sweden, but "Tales from the Hill" brings you the latest news, anecdotes, and gossip form the world of boardom. Get up-to-date world rankings, tour the photo gallery, or jump to other snowboarding pages.

Skiing & snowboarding

GORP Internet Skiing Resources
There are certainly other Web sites with more comprehensive ski coverage, but GORP's numerous links are well organized and annotated. Select World Ski Reports to see where the powder is best, and then head to the local resort pages for prices and pictures of Bozeman, Mont. or Sunday River, Maine. If you're looking for ski buddies try GORP's list of ski clubs. Cross country advocates will find links to several good Nordic pages.
WEB http://www.gorp.com/gorp /activity/skiing.htm

Other Ski Info The rather modest title does this page a huge disservice. No other Net ski site has more links to worldwide ski areas, from Slovenia to Santiago, than this one. What can you expect to find? Most local sites provide their slope details, as well as prices, local tourist information, and often trail maps and enticing pictures. This is a great place to dream, and to comparison shop—jump easily from Sugarloaf to Sunday River. If that's not enough, there's an impressive collection of weather links, ski clubs, ski sites, and retail Web pages on board. Ready to go? The collection of travel links here can help with air fares and adventure vacations through a dozen online travel services.
WEB http://gamera.syr.edu:2345/SKI ING/other.html

Location: ftp://ccadfa.cc.adfa.oz.au/archives/aus-snow/Pictures/olympo09.jpg

A schusser takes his turn on the Web
http://rmd-www.mr.ic.ac.uk/snow/snowpage.html

Ski Map Server Maps, yes, but so very much more. This massive site has everything a Net skier could possibly need, with links to ski sites from around the world. Try the Snow Page's European ski collection or jump to Ski Colorado. There are also gopher and FTP links for the truly slope obsessed. Finally, there are the maps, more than 70 to date, collected by the site's creator and downloaded by other eager Web skiers. If you want to relive your last trip to Sundance, there is a map here for you. Have recurrent James Bond super-skier fantasies? Take a look at the map of Murren in Switzerland, the site of the Bond film *On Her Majesty's Secret Service*. Missing Aspen? There always Beau Jo's pizza menu to bring back the whole Colorado experience.
WEB http://www.cs.umd.edu/~regli/ski .html

The Snow Page This is the best skiing site going—a massive collection of links to resorts, newsgroups, archives, and home pages worldwide. There are also maps, conditions reports, travel services, and online ski shops to assist in every aspect of a cyber ski-bum's life. You can jump to several online cyberzines or find out about the "snow people" on the Net by linking from here to their home pages. Email them with comments through the Snow Page's automatic email link. And if all that's not enough, there's a large picture gallery and 900 skiing-related documents to while away many sultry summer hours.
WEB http://rmd-www.mr.ic.ac.uk/snow /snowpage.html

Skydiving

rec.skydiving FAQ This newsgroup is packed with informa-

tion about the sport, announcements about equipment for sale, and reviews of drop zones. Jumpers with stories to tell are also here in great numbers. And, yes, there are more than a few people asking that perpetual question: "What if my parachute doesn't open?" No one answers from experience. Information on how to learn to skydive, costs, physical requirements, and movie myths are also described in the FAQ.
FAQ: **WEB** http://www.afn.org/skydive/faq/faq.html

Skydive Archive Jump to this site to explore an amazing range of skydiving resources. Once you've mastered the no-jumping-over-airports rule, you

might want to memorize the article (one of many on the site) titled "Live to survive in 1995!" by Pat and Jan Works which describes how to avoid in-air collisions. You can also link from here to a site for weather forecasts, look back over the archives of the rec.skydiving newsgroup, connect to the Web sites of close to a hundred skydivers with personal web pages, keep abreast of equipment recalls, and read the FAQ.
WEB http://www.afn.org/skydive

Skydiving AOL's skydiving center hosts one of the most consistently active skydiving discussion groups in cyberspace. It also has a photo album of

jumps made by its members. Maybe you have questions about USPA or AFF certification and have discovered their folders. The Golden Knights are here with official representatives responding to fan questions. Dozens of active folders based on regional jumping fill the forum. The forum's FAQ is a work-in-progress—not much information except for a brief list of acronyms that have been defined.
AMERICA ONLINE *keyword* fly→General Aviation→Skydiving

Soccer

A Short History of Soccer This chronicle details the development and refinement, includ-

---

 ## Soccer America Online
WEB http://www.sportsite.com/SA

Gooooaalll! *Soccer America* Online is good-looking, well-organized, and has both domestic and international coverage. This electronic version of the soccer-based news weekly has a lot more to offer than your average magazine. The Top Stories column is a near-endless litany of soccer sites

Soccer America **Silver XI**

Giorgio Chinaglia

from across the planet, the Q & A is a full letters page, Ask a Star puts your questions to top players, and SA Graffiti lets you demonstrate civilized restraint in an unmoderated environment. Clean, lean, and firmly on the ball.

ing all rule changes, that have made football the crowning glory of British gaming. Did you know that today's rules are a combination of the Sheffield and Football Association charters? Ever wonder what compels those refs to make the calls they do, what the standardization of the soccer ball means to play, or how to explain the vagaries of off-sides rules to a novice? All this and more are available in this factually fabulous forum.
WEB http://www.innotts.co.uk/~soc cerstats/histl.htm

International Soccer Cybertour
True to its name, International Soccer Cybertour will take you around the World Wide Web, Usenet, and beyond in order to find the soccer resource or article you seek. ISC is good for the professional soccer enthusiast, amateur, coach, or parent. An abundance of background art can make some pages slow at lower speeds, but at 28.8 Kbps, the art adds a great deal to the site, making it much more interesting. The proprietary search engine works well.
WEB http://www.cybergoal.com/soccer

Pure Web No soccer-related site in cyberspace has missed being caught in Pure Web. Start out with up-to-the-hour scores provided by Premier League Soccer Results and clarify the name of the goalkeeper for Italy in the '72 World Cup at the International Soccer Server. There are links to club pages from the Tottenham Hotspurs

to the Zurich Grasshoppers; and competitions from the Coca-Cola Cup to the venerable European Cup. Last but not least, there are links to a U.S. TV soccer programming schedule and an FAQ about the World Cup.
WEB http://www.atm.ch.cam.ac.uk /sports/webs.html

rec.sport.soccer This newsgroup is sometimes as much a political science primer as a site for soccer discussion. In the midst of a Croatia supporter's tussle with a Slovenia fan comes a discussion of just what happened to those Yugoslav players when the country split up. If you take note of the vituperative accusations of hooliganism flying between fans, it's obvious that the union of England and Scotland under James I (VI) in 1603 has yet to take root. Someone will always be here willing to rate players, share stories of the most unusual goals and greatest games, and wonder fearfully about Tony Adams's recovery.
USENET rec.sport.soccer

Rec.sport.soccer—The Web Page
The worldwide online rant tank for fans of "the gentlemen's game played by ruffians," helpfully broken down by category: FIFA rules, computer soccer games, and a fairly comprehensive guide to mailing lists. You'll find a good assortment of trivia, too, of course: Did you know that while purists still call it "foot-

ball," the term soccer, for those in the know, is a play on the second syllable of association, with the English-schoolboy affectation "er" tacked on? Now you do.
WEB http://www.atm.ch.cam.ac.uk /sports

The Soccer Homepage For fans on a quest for the ultimate Internet tour guide for soccer, this is it: current standings for the Olympics, U.S. major leagues, and many other worldwide divisions, soccer servers from Algeria to Peru, youth soccer teams, soccer camps, women's soccer, you name it. Includes strange soccer stories, like the one of the fan in Manchester, England who brings a fresh chicken dubbed Frank to every game, clapping its wings for team support—and cooking it afterward. Sounds like a *Twilight Zone* ad for Zacky Farms.
WEB http://www.distrib.com/soccer /homepage.html#USISL

Sumo

SumoWeb If you want to amaze friends and impress aficionados with your mastery of sumo arcania, stop here. Illustrated with delicate yet powerful images of sumo bouts, and offering links to sumo news sources, international sumo associations, and other sumo resources on and off the Web, this elegantly designed resource also features a helpful glossary of the sport. The carefully detailed and gracefully presented glossary serves as an introductory guide to the sport. Did you know that the ceremony performed to purify the clay ring in which a match takes place is called the Dohyo-matsuri? Sure you did. **WEB** http://www-bcf.usc.edu/~tmccarth /sumo.htm

Surfing

alt.surfing Why does a twinzer work better than a thruster? And what the hell are twinzers and thrusters, anyway? Well, they're types of surfboards, and they're also topics of discussion on the very active newsgroup. Whether members are naming favorite beaches, musing about insuring surfboards for air travel, or recommending surf literature, the culture is completely covered. **USENET** alt.surfing

Surf Lingo Dozens of surf terms, from "aerial" to "trough." Many of the terms are commonly known—reef, rocks—but some of the lingo, like "goofy foot" and "lid kid," requires the experience of a veteran surfer. **WEB** http://www.sd.monash.edu.au /~jasonl/Dropin/lingo.html

Swimming

rec.sport.swimming Looking for the perfect off-season workout? Need advice for a good stretch program to alleviate cramps? Even if you're simply suffering through a swimmer's fashion dilemma, like whether mirrored swimming goggles will go down well at the local Y, this discussion group has no deep end to be scared of. **USENET** rec.sport.swimming

SwimChat The next best thing to actually swimming is, of course, talking about swimming. Swimmers and fans who start feeling a little out of their element on dry land need only dial SwimChat to get right back into the—swim of things. There are three daily discussion groups at 4, 7, and 10 p.m. (EST)—and options are available for private conversations. There's also a subscrip-

 ## LaJolla Surfing Page
web http://facs.scripps.edu/surf/surfing.html

While some sedentary fans can hardly bring themselves to stand for the wave, real men and women, like the creators of this site, can hardly sit still waiting for the next series of good waves to come ashore. With gallons and gallons of weather and oceanographic links, this is a swell site for

surfers who want to let their Powerbooks tell them whether or not the waves are worth it. Log into the Southern California Coastal Marine forecast, check out tropical storm projections, or download Mercator maps of Hawaii. The site includes dozens of surfing links and a picture gallery with stunning shots of ten being hung at a range of angles.

tion option to notify those interested of scheduled chats.
WEB http://www.4-lane.com/sports chat/newsc/sw_index.html

Swimnews Online After the obligatory bragging about its Web awards, *Swimnews* Online opens with a sharp index of its various components, including the magazine, a photo library, meet results, rankings and records, a calendar, and a list of links. The index is easy to use, and the rankings come up quickly and cleanly. There are no excessive graphics to slow things down, just stats and stats and stats. It took only a few clicks and almost no time at all to learn, for example, that on day one of the April 21 swimming races in Sydney, Australia, it was Susan O'Neill who placed first in the women's 100-meter freestyle, with a time of 56:24.
WEB http://www.swimnews.com

Table tennis

rec.sport.table-tennis For no apparent reason someone's compiling a list of famous Barrys in ping-pong, and Tubby has another name to add to the list—Rutledge Barry, former U.S. Junior Champion from the 1970s, made the semifinals of the U.S. Nationals in 1978 or 1979, now semiretired, but still ranked in top 30. Not all the chat on rec.sport.table-tennis is this obsessed with minutiae— there are listings of tournaments, tips on play, and even posts about table-tennis demo-

graphics ("At the place where I work, the population of table tennis players are 80% blue collar and 20% white collar").
USENET rec.sport.table-tennis

Table Tennis FAQ As FAQs go, they don't get much more businesslike than this one, which has information on rankings, players associations, scoring, and the terminology of the game (ball, racket, and the ever-popular speedglue). Did you know that in Spanish this sport is called *el tenis de la mesa*, which translates literally as "the tennis of the table"?
WEB http://peacock.tnjc.edu.tw/ADD /sport/faq.html

Tennis

rec.sport.tennis If you post "Agassi's a boring player," don't plan to walk away from this group flame-free. "Get a life, buddy," one fan replied. Another praised Agassi for playing "rock 'n' roll tennis." O.K., enough about Agassi. Didn't you know that "Sampras is God"? Fan talk aside, there are a lot of serious discussions here, like the one about whether you get more power with looser strings and the thread about the sexiest woman player. Again, fan talk isn't easy to keep on the sidelines here.
USENET rec.sport.tennis

Tennis Country Billing itself as "the total tennis site on the Internet," Tennis Country is packed with information.

Using it makes you feel like you're walking through the doors in the opening-credits of *Get Smart*. The information, once you get to it, is very good, and the graphics, once they load, are equally impressive. You enter this site, which fancies itself a club, by signing up as a member or by visiting as a guest. Once inside, the areas of interest include a playing-hint library, fitness tips, and a guide to resorts and camps where tennis is celebrated and elevated.
WEB http://www.tenniscountry.com

The Tennis FAQ Wondering who's got the highest number of career singles titles? Connors has 109, but Martina Navratilova is way out in front with 167. How about the type of racquet Agassi uses? A Head Radical Trisys 260, strung at 75 pounds. The FAQ is divided into sections on tournaments, rankings, players, equipment, media, and a section of miscellany, like tips for alleviating tennis elbow ("stretch the tendon before you play") and the origin of the scoring system ("said to derive from the usage of the four quarters of a clock, 15-30-45-60, used to score a game in the pre-modern era"). If you need to bone up on tennis trivia, this is your source for study.
WEB http://www.tennisserver.com /Tennis.html#Rules

Tennis Information A general hubsite for tennis scores, rankings, tour results, and player stats, these pages are deep

enough to contain singles title-match results from 1980 on forward. Check out TV listings for local tennis broadcasts, match your knowledge of tennis against the comprehensive FAQ list, and get news from the numerous stories that are linked from this page.
WEB http://www.mindspring.com/~csmith

The Tennis Server An atmospheric painting of a tennis racquet and a palm tree greets the netheads who visit this attractive site, which is anchored by links to the best tennis info on the Web. Aside from the usual info on equipment and rankings, you'll find .GIFs of Steffi Graf, Michael Chang, Stefan Edberg, and others, along with a "Player Tip of the Month" offering detailed advice on such topics as "the role of the server's partner in doubles." ("Failing to go back and cover the mid-range lobs over your head encourages your opponents to lob more often.") And the titular pun just can't be beat.
WEB http://www.tennisserver.com/Tennis.html

Ultimate

The Ultimate Players Association
What happens when you mix football, soccer, and a flying disc (a.k.a. Frisbee™)? You get the team sport called "ultimate" that has plastic discs whistling across college campuses from Hampshire to Stanford. The Ultimate Players Association

TAKING CONTROL AT THE NET

Controlled anger sometimes proves useful on the tennis courts. John McEnroe may be best remembered for his violent and maniacal temper tantrums. He was actually a brilliant strategist who used anger to distract opponents, while maintaining internal control. Perhaps he wasn't angry at all, but only made it appear so to gain an advantage! I am not recommending that anger be used in this manner, but stay extra focused when your opponent gets mad!

Getting mad at yourself after unforced errors might sometimes be useful, because it shows that you value consistency. But remember to stay in control and move mentally to the next point or you may find yourself distracted and unable to perform your best.

Here are some further ways to control anger:
1. Use your anger to focus intensely on what you will do next rather than on the mistake you just made.
2. Negative self-talk is a killer. Learn to recognize when it happens and get angry that you are thinking negatively. Use this anger to transform negative thoughts into positive ones.
3. When anger is overwhelming you, do anything to break the pattern. Tie your shoelaces, count to 10, breathe deeply and slowly, write a letter to your grandmother, and get in the mindset of playing each point one at a time.
4. Use imagery to practice dealing with situations that have caused anger in the past. Imagine yourself handling these situations successfully.

Anger is quite a force, but like most energy it can be harnessed for your benefit or allowed to roam wildly and destroy you. Understand and conquer this madness!

—from The Tennis Server Home Page

oversees varsity and club competitions in the U.S., so you can zip over to see how your college team is doing in the polls. If you just can't get enough of the sport that uses an adjective as a noun, you can link to multiple newsgroups, currently featuring heated discussions on various pressing

matters of the ultimate concern.
WEB http://komodo.hacks.arizona.edu/~upa

The Ultimate Timeline A history of the Frisbee™, from Fred Morrison's historic disc of solid tenite (first carved in 1947 and manufactured in the mid-

fifties by Wham-O) to the proliferation of summer Ultimate leagues across the United States. The page also includes famous Frisbee quotes (including the ultimately pretentious "Ultimate doesn't build character, it reveals it").
URL ftp://pipkin.lut.ac.uk/pub/gumpf /Ultimate/ultimate_timeline

Volleyball

rec.sport.volleyball Does anyone have any experience with torn tendons? Can anyone think of any really wild (but perfectly legal) plays? When not concerned with serve reception tactics, jumping shoes, and tournament announcements, the group's participants sometimes veer into odder areas, such as this agonized, if not exactly lucid, lament by a high-school v-ball coach: "We coaches have to be very careful. Can you believe that you can be successfully sued by a player for not teaching them everything you said you would? If I tell Molly Middlehitter that I'll teach her how to set and I'm unsuccessful, she can sue my tail off for 'breach of verbal contract' or something like that."
USENET rec.sport.volleyball

Volleyball WorldWide With its thoughtfully highlighted new entries and links to everything from the Olympics to sources of volleyball history, rules, books and magazines, clothes and decals, and various local, regional, and national organiza-

Profiling the accomplishments of women athletes
http://www.womensports.com

tions, Volleyball WorldWide hopes to be your one-stop news and information center for this popular and growing sport. Not notable for its graphics, the site stakes its claims to excellence on the completeness and thoroughness of its links—the idea being that if it isn't here, you don't need it.
WEB http://www.volleyball.org

volleyball-FAQ.Z Dealing mostly with rules, regulations, and equipment, this FAQ for the newsgroup rec.sports.volleyball breaks down basic play and discusses treatment for common volleyball-related injuries. In an effort to be helpful and avoid legal reproach, the Web master who penned the FAQ, an aficionado himself, repeatedly warns that the document should not be construed as official in any sense, especially the medical advice toward the end. Nonetheless, its casual tone and its cautiously informative

passages make this page an ideal resource for volleyball enthusiasts.
URL gopher://wuecon.wustl.edu:671 /00/volleyball-faq.Z

Women

Women Sports This well-laid-out site has all kinds of sports that involve women, mostly on the collegiate level, including volleyball, basketball, skating (figure and speed), soccer, softball, gymnastics, golf, and tennis, as well as a mysterious section called Athletics, which consists basically of track and field. Each sport is represented by a selection of news items, opinion pieces, schedules, and statistics, although for some of them the information is a bit scant. There is also, of course, a special section on the Olympics. It almost makes up for the lack of coverage of women's sports an other sites.
WEB http://www.womensports.com

Travel

80 DAYS? ONLINE, YOU CAN CIRCLE THE WORLD MORE THAN A DOZEN TIMES IN 80 MINUTES

VACATIONS CAN BE HELL. The average American worker has less than two weeks of respite in which to de-stress, decompress, and return completely refreshed. For most, this means going somewhere far, far, away. But sometimes traveling can seem more like a travail. Where in the world should you go? What should you see while you're there? How can you make reservations that will help you stick to a budget? The Internet makes answering these questions easy, *if* you know where to look. Find out where to go, discover travelers' tips and traps, and even book a tour or a flight online. If you can't afford the time or money for a vacation and your only mode of transport is your modem, you can simply take a virtual vacation on your lunch break.

Location: http://www.travelchannel.com/images/pgimages/pg161.jpg

 CITY.NET
WEB http://www.city.net

This site combines tourism and cultural information on cities worldwide and should be a mandatory stop for armchair travelers and vacationers. You can explore the world by region, country, or city (they are listed alphabetically). A jaunt to Paris rewards you with street and subway maps; an insider's guide to the city, complete with hotel and restaurant recommendations; language tips; and weather forecasts. For a less urban trek, visit the Grampian Highlands of Scotland through online pictures and narrative, including a visit to a twelfth-century cathedral and a trip down the Malt Whiskey Trail.

Around the world

Around the World in 80 Seconds

Allot more than 80 seconds to explore this collection of links—you'll hardly have time to catch your breath as you connect to information on more than 80 destinations worldwide. The site begins with a link to Hampton Roads, a page featuring hotel and restaurant descriptions, and an events calendar for tourist towns in the Chesapeake Bay area. After contemplating vacation resources in southeastern Virginia, you can head to the Windows-to-Russia Home Page, which serves up a full helping of reports on Russian arts, culture, and businesses, and virtual tours of the Kremlin and the Soviet Archive. This comprehensive collection of travel links ends with a stop at the All Languages of the World page where you'll find dictionaries and glossaries there to help you decipher hundreds of languages. Along your way, there are plenty of fun detours such as Yahoo! Travel Sites and the Virtual Tourist, as well as sites dedicated to Northern Spain and Caribbean Culture.
WEB http://www.infi.net/~cwt/travel .html

CheckIn: The Tourism Database

Check in with tourism boards across the county (from Alaska to Wyoming) and around the world (Algeria to Zimbabwe).
WEB http://www.checkin.com /database.html

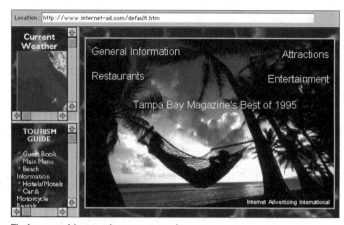

The Internet—It's everywhere you want to be
http://www.internet-ad.com/default.htm

CyberTrip Cybertrip's travel kit includes links to a visa FAQ, currency exchange converters, current weather conditions, time zone information, maps, and guides. Also available are links to destinations, accommodations, online travel agents, airlines, trains, rental cars, and cruise lines.
WEB http://www.cybertrip.com

eGo Travel With information on popular travel destinations in every state (except North Dakota), eGo Travel focuses on quality travel links, not quantity. Click on a state on the interactive map to access destination links, travel tips, and travelogs.
WEB http://www.ego.net

ExpressNet Travel American Express sponsors this full-service travel forum. The Global Guide offers detailed guides to major cities, including shopping and night club suggestions, articles from *Travel &*

Leisure magazine and major newspapers, and lists of AmEx services and offices nationwide. If you have specific questions about a particular destination, post your request on ExpressNet's active message boards where fellow travelers go to exchange advice and tips. You can also participate in regular online conferences which feature topics including tricks to hosteling, the rebirth of Shanghai, and live chat with travel luminaries like Arthur Frommer. ExpressNet also has links to *Frommer's City Guides* and *Fodor's World View*, adding the resources of two more excellent travel guides to those of the Global Guide. Don't miss the savvy Travelers Weekly Hot Tips section for bargains on air fares, cruises, and hotels. If all that's not enough to build the perfect travel site, American Express is available to put plans into action with online booking. Don't leave home—

or stay home—without it.
AMERICA ONLINE *keyword* expressnet
→Travel Info & Reservations

Family Travel Network Though the words "family vacation" can strike terror into the hearts of even the most well-balanced families, this AOL forum actually celebrates family travel. Folks young and old will want to visit this area where they can talk to other parents, kids, and experts about vacation destinations, off-beat travel activities, weekend getaways, super deals, travel tips, and resources.
AMERICA ONLINE *keyword* ftn

Index of Hotels and Travel on the Net This Web site offers a collection of links to the home pages of numerous hotels and resorts worldwide, including Best Western International, Novotel, Westin Hotels and Resorts, and Hyatt. In addition to the hotel links, the site also links to many airlines (Air France, Lufthansa, and Air Canada) and cruise lines (Norwegian Line and Royal Caribbean Line).
WEB http://www.webscope.com/travel/homepage.html

Interactive Travel Guides' Travel Page An attractive and easy-to-follow presentation of Web links awaits you at Interactive Travel Guides. You can hop from here to the beaches of Cancun Online or to the banks of the Vistula on Warsaw's home page. At every stop cybertravelers can collect helpful info on local lodgings and restaurants as well as view enticingly beautiful images of exotic locations. If you're looking for hotel, resort, or cruise recommendations, Interactive Travel Guides offers an "Our Favorites" section which reviews tourist stops it finds exceptional—the Royal Horseguard Thistle Hotel in London received the highest possible rating (four stars) for its balconies overlooking the Thames.
WEB http://www.travelpage.com

Internet Travel Directory Flying from Cairo to Stockholm? Check here for quotes on wholesale air fares or to order tickets online. Ticket discounts are always appreciated, but the real premium at this site is the Special Internet Travel Direc-

WORLD TRAVEL NET
WEB http://www.world-travel-net.co.uk/default.htm
A virtual encyclopedia of travel at your fingertips. World TravelNet not only includes the basic airline, cruise, and rail guides and the typical weather, currency, and accommodation links; it also

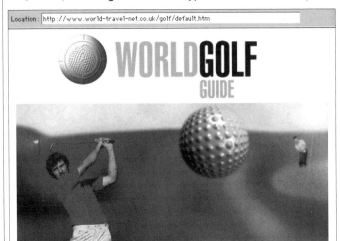

contains such gems as a world health and spa resort guide, a world theme park guide, and a world apartment guide. The amount of links amassed here has to be seen to be believed; so you'd better leave some of your vacation time open for surfing.

tory, which provides the names and numbers of tour operators specializing in theme vacations from antiquing to whitewater rafting. If you want to spend your next vacation tending llamas on the plains of Argentina, then stop here first.
WEB http://oim.com

Internet Travel Mall (ITM) Let's say you want to go to Fredericksburg, Texas. With online navigation tools, you can explore various accommodations in the Lone Star State and learn about the region from the publicity materials provided by each hotel or lodge. The Web page for the Inn on the Creek Bed & Breakfast, for instance, includes room rates and breakfast schedules and describes the history of the area. If it's Utah and not Texas that you're traveling to, you might be interested in the link to information on a paragliding school just outside of Salt Lake City. For now, the pickings are a little slim, but more attractions will certainly be added. The Mall also contains dozens of useful 800 numbers, including listings for airlines, car-rental companies, motorcoach lines, international rail lines, cruise lines, and hotel/motel/resort chains.
WEB http://www.travelmall.com

Rec.travel Library Whether your travel plans are taking you to Albuquerque or Africa, the rec.travel library is a good starting point for research and

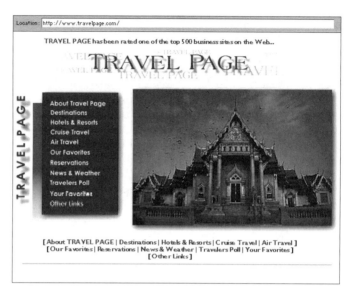

Location: http://www.travelpage.com/

TRAVEL PAGE has been rated one of the top 500 business sites on the Web...

TRAVEL PAGE

About Travel Page
Destinations
Hotels & Resorts
Cruise Travel
Air Travel
Our Favorites
Reservations
News & Weather
Travelers Poll
Your Favorites
Other Links

[About TRAVEL PAGE | Destinations | Hotels & Resorts | Cruise Travel | Air Travel]
[Our Favorites | Reservations | News & Weather | Travelers Poll | Your Favorites]
[Other Links]

"It's a *wat*." "What?" " Yeah" "It's a what?" "Yeah, it's a *wat*." "No really, what is it?"
http://www.travelpage.com

planning. Links to sites, pages, and cyberdocuments around the Web and around the world from the Cottage Country Locator to the Gateway to Antarctica.
WEB http://WWW.Solutions.Net /rec-travel

Tourism Info Internet Annotated in both German and English, this series of pages links travelers to airline home pages, subway and railway information, and accommodations worldwide—from American B&Bs to resorts in southern Spain. There are also travel reports gathered from the wisdom of Usenet newsgroups (including rec.travel.misc) and links to destination-specific information (like a link to a virtual tour of Johannesburg). Unfortunately this Web site's online newspaper, *Touristic News*, is

available only in German, and their "last-minute offers" only apply to certain regions in Germany.
WEB http://www.tkz.fh-rpl.de/tii/tii-e .html

Tourism Offices Worldwide Directory Contact information for tourism offices worldwide. Type in "Austria" on the search form and the names of more than 30 Austrian tourism offices in Austria and elsewhere appear on the screen. Some of the offices even offer links to their home pages. Canada and the U.S. can be searched by country and city name. For international destinations , the database is searchable only by country, so don't get careless and type in just "Paris."
WEB http://www.mbnet.mb.ca/lucas /travel

Travel File Can't remember when Monaco's circus festival will be held? Have a hankering for the corn dogs and cucumber pickles of the Iowa State Fair of days gone by? The EZ destination search promises to deliver information on everything from Illinois state parks to a calendar of sport and cultural events worldwide, by a mere flick of the search button and the stroke of a few keys.
WEB http://tfsrvr.travelfile.com

Travel Forum This forum acts as an informal guide book, allowing netters to post travel questions and have them answered by fellow cyberspace travelers. On the message board, Sue asks for recommendations for a good restaurant in Key West—Ken answers that The Old Conch Inn is very good. Dan is traveling to Las Vegas soon, and he wants to know which casinos' blackjack tables are best—Walter recommends a trip to the Stardust. Trish has even volunteered her own personal ratings of hotel pools in New York City. Pose your questions, and somebody in the great big CompuServe world will be your virtual guide.
COMPUSERVE *go* travsig

Travel Forum This site is a good first stop for prospective travelers. A filing cabinet of articles provides information on everything from travel insurance to Eurail pass bargains. The library is equally well stocked with articles, software (from

Amtrak schedules to Disney-world guides, to an I-95 exit list), and photos. A traveler's bookstore reviews new travel-related titles and offers book-club member discounts. State Department travel advisories ensure that you don't plan any untimely trips to Libya or attempt to enter Mongolia without a visa. For the personal touch, try the travel message boards or the live-time travel cafe, where journeyers meet to talk about everything from fear of flying to singles cruises.
AMERICA ONLINE *keyword* travelforum

Travel.org Can't think of anywhere exciting to explore on your next vacation? Browse the extensive Travel.org directories, search the files on any country that strikes you, and see what sparks your imagination. Birdwatching in Panama? Spelunking in New Jersey? A great point of reference from which to cull ideas, although the travel agent and lodging sections are somewhat thin.
WEB http://www.travel.org

Travel Source Fancy yourself a modern-day Dr. Livingston? Click on Safaris and get contact info for companies that specialize in bringing people nose to nose with African rhinos. Prefer a quieter time? Glance at the Blackbird Cave Resort page (it's on the Turneffe Reef Atoll). Most links are commercial in nature—Club Med and the Marble Mountain Ranch advertise their services here—but the scope is wide, encom-

passing sites designed for those who like to put on plaid and shout "fore!" as well as those who like to wear wet suits and stare down sharks.
WEB http://www.travelsource.com

Travelers Corner Dominating this forum are U.S. and international destination profiles with details on the doings in more than 221 countries and 9,000 cities, provided by Weissman Travel Reports. Traveling to Tuscaloosa on business? Why not take a drive to Moundville Archeological Park—the most important prehistoric Indian settlement and ceremonial center of the South? Must-sees when you're in Copenhagen? A trip to the top of Rundetarn (Round Tower), midnight fireworks at Tivoli Gardens, and the view of Rosenborg Castle from Kongens Have. Other notable nodes of info featured are the Exotic Destinations message center, Late-breaking Travel News, and Seasonal Features.
AMERICA ONLINE *keyword* travelers corner

TravelLinks Hundreds of links and descriptions of Web sites in the categories of agencies, destinations, ezines, lodging, services, shopping, sports travel, and transport. Travel-Links also maintains its own ezine, *TravelTips*.
WEB http://www.trvltips.com

Travelonline An unabashedly self-promoting site—but what does Travelonline offer? So far

HIT THE ROAD, JACK

For anyone out there who is interested, I just got back from a two-month whirlwind tour of the "world" and thought I would share a few things that I learned. First, two months is WAY too short. I could have easily spent another 6 months on the road and still had a list a mile long of the things that I missed. Everyone we met along the way was out for at least 4 months, but usually 6 to 12 months (and of course some out indefinitely). Two, bring pictures of your life to show to people from other counties. They love to see pics of the West and really warm up to seeing things like your big house, significant other, relatives, anything really. The wonderful mountain people we met in Nepal loved the pics that my buddy brought. Three, bring a decent camera and don't be afraid to take people shots (but always ask first). Oh, and be concerned about foreign x-ray machines. I had one roll that meant a lot to me screwed up somewhere along the way. Four, when Lonely Planet jokes about packing... leave half at home and take twice the money... listen. Five, we didn't have a tightly planned itinerary and it worked wonderfully. The fewer constraints, the more fun you will have just seeing what each day brings. Chances are that you will meet others and you all will do all of the cool stuff anyway. Time constraints just lead to stress. Six, don't fly Pakistan Air.

We went to Hong Kong, Thailand, Nepal, India, Egypt, Greece, Italy, and France. I would be more than happy to share my experiences with anybody. Drop me a line here. Everyone has asked me where my favorite place was... and since it is impossible to name one place, I usually say Nepal, Paris, and Egypt (in that order). Nepal was unforgettable...

Wish all a great trip and if you're still out there next year... may see ya there!

—from AOL's Travelers Corner

TravNet International TravNet International bills itself as the worldwide home of cyber-tourism. The centerpiece of the service is a database itinerary planner available through a telnet link. Simply submit the names of your destinations, and TravNet draws up a customized map showing accommodations, restaurants, and attractions neatly plotted along the route. TravNet promises to put 4,000 pages online eventually; currently links lead to such diverse information as dialysis services for travelers and slide shows designed to lure the weary to lush locales.
WEB http://comdinet.com/comdinet.htm

Travel services

Airline Tickets Wholesale Find an online rates-request form here for Travel Discounters, where they guarantee to save you $50 to $150 on published airline domestic fares above $300. This site also features monthly specials, tips for getting the lowest fares, and an FAQ.
WEB http://www.traveldiscounters.com

American Express Cardholders looking for the best deal of the day on AmEx value flights or those who want to check out all the discounts available for members and avoid voice-mail hell, will be pleased to learn that American Express has made their lives a little easier. A comprehensive menu of travel-related specials is

there are beautifully constructed search forms that reward users with zero hotel listings for Santa Fe, N.M., and only ten entries for New York City accommodations. Hitting the bargain page may be the best bet. Travelers will find everything from discount

three-day packages at the Park Hotel in Hong Kong to special rates at the Minneapolis Hilton Towers. Travel Online promises to add entertainment and dining guides soon, so you can make your online reservations with confidence.
WEB http://TravelOnLine.com

offered, from trips to Disney World where kids eat and stay free to European tour packages. You can even get weather forecasts for Berne, Berlin, and Bemidji (and other cities not necessarily beginning with the letter B) in the travel resources section.
WEB http://www.americanexpress.com/travel

Genie Travel Services Submit a fare-request form online for flights worldwide and Genie will call you back with available rates. Or, take matters into your own hands and search the vast Genie database of discounted prices to international destinations.
WEB http://www.xnet.com/~genie/home.cgi

Internet Travel Network Once you've registered with ITN, you'll be asked to fill out your traveling profile. It's well worth the time. Every time you search for flights and airfare, ITN asks you questions such as: How many listings do you want to see? What are your priorities? Window or aisle? What travel agency do you want to buy your ticket from? If you fill out the profile, the service will automatically fill in the answers to these questions whenever you search. ITN uses the Apollo reservation service and, while using the site appears to be fairly simple, we found that more often than not, airfares were high and flights were closed.
WEB http://www.itn.net

National Center For Educational Travel Just fill in this online questionnaire with some basic information (departure date, departure city, destination city, return date, etc.), and NCET emails you with the lowest rate it can find. Group rates are also available through this service.
WEB http://www2.ios.com/~ncet

Official Airline Guides Travel Service Full lists of all airline flights, schedules, and fares. The service is rather pricey, with access running $10 per hour during off-peak hours and soaring to $28 per hour in the heart of the business day. Still, the resources are impressive: For any route, OAG displays all flights and combinations of flights currently available,

AIRLINES OF THE WEB

WEB http://www.itn.net/airlines
picture: WEB http://www2.twa.com/TWA/Airlines.fcgi/flights/ap727.htm

The fruit of a graduate dissertation on the airline industry, this collection of airline information is the most comprehensive on the Web. The airlines listed range in size from the small (Mount Cook

Airways, serving only New Zealand) to the massive (globe-trotting TWA). Links are also provided to cargo carriers, aviation newsgroups, airport pages, frequent flyer information, and car-rental operations. If you're interested in a piece of the airline action, this site even provides a link to airline stock quotes.

along with all possible fares. If your choice is available, you can book it immediately. Hotels and motels can also be reserved through OAG, and the guide offers a number of specialized databases on cruises, skiing, resorts, discount travel, frequent flyer programs, and weather.
COMPUSERVE *go* oag

PC Travel It ain't pretty nor is this the easiest service to use, but PC Travel has the distinction of being the first airline reservation service to operate on the Internet and it boasts a much better collection of travel resources than its competitors. If you're here to book a ticket and not to browse, however, you're going to have to work a bit. Begin by filling out a brief travel profile; the site will try and get you to join its Web-Net Travel club which offers airfare discounts. Click "Check Availability or Make a Reservation" to get to the reservation system. You'll be asked to enter departure and destination city codes. There's a table of the codes if you don't know them. On the same page, you'll have to select departure and return dates and times. Then, the site makes you move through a series of pages confirming departure info, selecting flights, confirming destination info, selecting flights, reserving or rejecting a car reservation, and then, last but not least, requesting fare info. PC Travel, like the Internet Travel Network, uses the

Apollo reservation system. Once again, we weren't very impressed with the fares.
WEB http://www.pctravel.com/pctravel .html

Preview Vacations Use this online travel agent, which is sponsored by MCI, to plan and book vacations with friends and family. Read about the service's various tour packages or catch up on travel industry news. Try the active message board for advice from real travelers on cruises, honeymoons, and the relative charms of Antigua and Anguilla. After you've decided where you want to go, head to the booking information online to seal the deal.
AMERICA ONLINE *keyword* vacations

Travel Agent Indexes There is no shortage of travel agents online. Some specialize in travel to certain destinations. Others cater to certain classes of travelers—the budget, business, etc. Still, others offer the world to anyone ready to use their credit card. Customer service, fares, and selection vary from agency to agency. Only some offer online booking. Shop around.
WEB http://www.travelhub.com

Travelocity Fairly new to the world of Internet travel services, Travelocity has a pretty powerful partner. EAASY SABRE, the reservation system that books a significant percent of world's airline reservations, provides online users

with the same flight and fare information that the professionals get—including the discounts. The site provides an easy-to-use interface to the EAASY SABRE system and conveniently lets users store travel preferences (window or aisle? smoking or nonsmoking?), payment information, and other contact info. As long as you've registered with the service—it's free—and faxed or called in your credit card number, which Travelocity permanently keeps on file, you can buy tickets online. More than just a booking service, Travelocity also flashes announcements about current bargains, remembers information about your past reservations, and regularly hosts live chats on topics ranging from Frequent Flyer Tips to Hawaiian Getaways. Air fares are pretty good too.
WEB http://www.travelocity.com

TravelQuest A one-stop shop for links to airlines, cruise lines, rail companies, major hotels, car rental agencies, road maps, travel condition sites, and tour operators. You'll also find essential information for the traveler from weather to travel warnings, medical alerts to currency exchange info. Among the original services provided by TravelQuest are an airlines reservation form for making flight arrangements online and a destination search by which you can collect data on the city of your choice. Users can enter as many user profiles as they

like to distinguish between their business and personal travel needs, as well as plan trips for others. A good tool for executives, as well as executive assistants.
WEB http://www.travelquest.com

TravelShopper Browse through airline listings, compare prices, or even make a reservation with this online service. Simply choose a departure point, destination, and travel dates, and TravelShopper will generate a list of all available flights. Then fill out a brief personal profile to determine fare eligibility, select the cheapest flight still remaining, and book your tickets. Because the service is affiliated with TWA, Delta, and Northwest, you must fly one of

those carriers to have the tickets mailed to you directly. Otherwise, your tickets will be mailed to a nearby affiliated travel agent or be waiting for you at the airport.
COMPUSERVE *go* worldcim

Wholesale Travel Centre Enter where you're flying from and your destination and the system returns flight options. Choose one. If the flight you choose is too expensive, click "Find Value Fare" to get a list of less expensive flights. Online booking is available. Deals are not always better than the other online reservation services, despite the company's name.
WEB http://206.235.50.10/wtc/index .htm

Planes

Airport Directory A comprehensive collection of links to airports indexed by city, as well as a list of air parks, fixed base operators, heliports, air harbors, and airport-related organizations on the Net.
WEB http://w3.one.net/~flypba /AIRLINES/airports

InsideFlyer Frequent flyers can learn how to earn the most miles and points possible, redeem the best awards available, manage their growing number of miles and points, sort through the maze of partners, and get advice from the frequent flyer guru himself, Randy Petersen, in this AOL version of *InsideFlyer* maga-

THE AIR TRAVELER'S HANDBOOK HOMEPAGE
WEB http://www.cs.cmu.edu/afs/cs/user/mkant/Public/Travel/airfare.html

The Air Traveler's Handbook is the collected knowledge of the folks at rec.travel.air. Eventually, there will be an offline version of the handbook, which will contain four times as much info as the Web site. That's hard to imagine, and you'll see why, once you explore the vast resources available

Location: http://mmink.com/cayman/cayman_islands.html

Destination Cayman Islands

Seven Mile Beach...

here. The handbook offers airline and travel agency contact info, airport layouts, links to online reservation systems, lists of courier agencies and ticket consolidators, hotel info, listings of travel book publishers, and much more, designed for those who have terminally restless feet.

IN MY VIEW

It is extremely difficult to rank scenic flights. The appreciation of beauty is very personal. Based on my personal experience, I would earmark (without any ranking):

* Lima-Tacna over the multicolored desert of Southern Peru

* Seattle-Anchorage in the evening, along the St. Elias and other ranges

* Honolulu-Hilo, if you happen to fly (as I once did) right over the summit of Haleakala Volcano

* A night arrival from the North into JFK, going down the Hudson river, parallel to Manhattan

* Landing at Orly airport in the 1970s (before they had double day-light savings time) at precisely 2200 on Bastille day (July 14), when all the fireworks were going up over Paris

* Any flight over Greenland during the summer

Actually, I would say that it is a rare flight in daylight and with good weather, that is not in some way interesting (granted, **LAX-HNL** may not qualify). Simply, the different nature of the soils, the patterns of farming, the development of cities, can make for very enriching observation.

All of this of course, assuming that you are not chastised by a flight attendant insisting that you should pull down your shade, so that TV-intoxicated passengers can watch commercials, rather than partake in an educational occasion, i.e., the study of geography, or simply an artistic one, i.e., experiencing beauty.

—Emile

—**from rec.travel.air**

out with links to major airport Web sites from Amsterdam to D.C.
WEB http://www.quickaid.com /airports.html

rec.travel.air When we visited, it was abuzz with discussion of air travel safety in the wake of the TWA Flight 800 disaster, but this newsgroup is normally filled with the exchange of air travel tips, insider information on the latest airfare bargains, and airline travel anecdotes of the nightmare variety.
USENET rec.travel.air

Space Available Travel on Military Aircraft A "military hop" is not a variation of the Lindy performed in uniform. It's soldier-speak for the free flights available to qualified military personnel on some U.S. Department of Defense aircraft. Also referred to as "Space-A" travel, the rules and regulations for participation are outlined here.
WEB http://www.ee.umd.edu/medlab /spacea/spacea.html

Web Flyer If you're one of the estimated 35 million people who participate in frequent flyer programs, you may want to visit Web Flyer, sponsored by *InsideFlyer* magazine. It's the only Web publication devoted to keeping track of frequent flyer bonus news and updates. Best of all, frequent fliers of all ilks can register here each week for a chance at the 1,000 free miles given away on American, Continental, Delta,

zine. The mile-hungry will want to check out Want Miles each week for the 500-mile Friday giveaway. For those who live to fly for free.
AMERICA ONLINE *keyword* insideflyer

QuickAid Airport Directory Need directions to O'Hare? Flying through Frankfurt soon? Curious about the ground transportation options at JFK? This site may be able to help you

Up, up and away...
http://www.webflyer.com

Northwest, United, or USAir each Thursday.
WEB http://www.webflyer.com

Trains

Amtrak's Station on the World Wide Web Everything Amtrak, from routes and schedules to a company history to travel tips. Which trains have space for storing automobiles? Can you take your pet iguana on the train? Stop here for the answers. All aboard!
WEB http://www.amtrak.com

Commuter Railroad Schedules in the U.S. and Canada Need to know how long it will take to get to your coworker's suburban wedding? To the shopping mall in Jersey City when you're in Montclair? From the Alaska Railroad to Connecticut's Shore Line, you can download maps (which include connections to Amtrak and Via Rail) and view schedules and fares

for commuter rail lines in more than 20 major cities.
WEB http://www.libertynet.org/~dvarp/other.html

Deutsche Bahn TrainsEuropean Railway Schedules In Europe, riding the rails can often save time and multiply your destination options. Deutsche Bahn AG and CompuServe have joined forces to provide this extensive booking and browsing service for European railways. Learn about all available trains, their services (sleeper car, dinettes), and prices. Consult the station appendix to find out if you can rent a car when you arrive. At this time, you can only book if your travel plans include Germany, but schedule information is transnational.
COMPUSERVE *go* railway

misc.transport.urban-transit There's plenty of transit talk from around the world here.

Should subways be bilingual (as in Brussels, Montreal, and New York)? "What's the new light rail line in Denver like?" "Fast and smooth," replies Michael. "Try it!" A wide range of issues is discussed, including fare increases (which everyone unanimously opposes), crime, and where new rail systems should be routed (lots of NIMBY here). Read the postings from New York and Chicago—they might improve your appreciation of the system in your city.
USENET misc.transport.urban-transit

Rail Europe Homepage Everything you always wanted to know about Eurail rates, schedules, the sleek Eurostar, youth passes, and booking information.
WEB http://www.raileurope.com

Railroad Related Internet Resources Come here for a depot full of links. You can reach pages about city subways, Amtrak schedules, and newsgroups dedicated to the discussion of the finer points of riding the rails. For those planning a European vacation, the link to train schedules in cities across the Atlantic is especially useful.
WEB http://www-cse.ucsd .edu /users /bowdidge/railroad/rail-home.html

Subway Navigator Traveling underground might bewilder you, whether you're in Amsterdam, Athens, or Atlanta. Demystify the experience with subway maps and a database

which plots your route, including transfer points, and gives you an estimated travel time for cities around the world.
WEB http://metro.jussieu.fr:l000l/bin /cities/english

Automobiles

Alamo Rent A Car: Freeways Booking a car may lead the list of things to do on the Alamo Web site, but Alamo doesn't just hand travelers the keys. The site delivers travel tips, information on destinations across the U.S., Alamo locations, directions for getting around popular U.S. cities, coupons for tourist sites, and even links to other travel, map, and weather sites. Knowing that travelers like to talk about their trips, Alamo offers a forum for customers to give advice on road-side food, hotels, restaurants, and sightseeing.
WEB http://www.freeways.com

The Auto Europe Website Auto Europe is an independent car rental company with 4,000 car rental locations worldwide, including Europe, the U.S., Canada, the Caribbean, South America, Africa, and the South Pacific. At its Web site, you can request brochures or make reservations at the location nearest you or at your destination.
WEB http://www.wrld.com/ae/index .html

Avis Rent-A-Car In addition to the typical reservation and rate info you'd expect, the Avis

Galaxy contains more than 6,000 pages of information you might not expect, including a map database.
WEB http://www.avis.com

Car Rental Shoppers Guide The Transportation Reservation Network provides a central online reservation system with more than 3,000 car rental locations throughout the U.S., Canada, and the U.K.
WEB http://www.rent-cars.com

Rent-a-Wreck "Don't let the name fool you." This site features contact information for the company's 400 U.S. and 8 international locations.
WEB http://www.rent-a-wreck.com

Thrifty Home Page Make reservations at any of Thrifty's worldwide franchises in Asia, Canada, the Caribbean, Europe, Latin America, the Middle East, South America, or the good old U.S. of A. You can also check up on current promotions.
WEB http://www.thrifty.com

Cruises

2 Cruisin Some people are obsessed with trains, others with planes, and still others with cruise ships. And while this Web site caters to the cruise ship hobbyist by featuring the dimensions of several cruisers, it also meets the needs of tourists. The site outlines shore excursions, the latest liners to hit the oceans, and weekly specials for different

lines. Book a voyage yourself by filling out 2 Cruisin's online survey. The company will make a tentative booking for you, which you later confirm with your credit card.
WEB http://www.crocker.com/cruisin

Cruise Critic Whether you're looking to go on a Caribbean cruise, a romantic sailing expedition, or a ship set for exploring Alaskan wildlife, Cruise Critic is the best online cruise guide for in-depth and candid reviews of more than 100 cruise ships worldwide. You'll also find the latest cruise bargains, cruise tips, and the advice of your fellow AOL cruisers. The Cruise Selector is an interactive ship finder for locating the best boats for your personal criteria. And the Cruise Boards, a collection of cruising message boards, are always lively. There are the usual categories segregated by cruise line, as well as travel tips, FAQs, and shore excursions. Then there are the online "personals" in Going My Way? where people tell you when and what ship they are traveling on, describe themselves and ask if you'd like to "hook up." Veteran cruisers may find nostalgia in Whatever Happened To...? Virtually any issue, from family cruising to theme cruising to cruising other passengers on the sun deck, can be discussed here.
AMERICA ONLINE *keyword* cruise critic

K.L. Smith's CruiseLetter *The CruiseLetter* is filled with articles of interest to veteran and

virgin cruisers alike. Editor K.L. Smith stuffs every issue with reviews of recent launches, tips on dress codes, stories about gastronomic delights on the high seas, notes on trouble-free air connections to different ports of embarkation, and highlights from various shore excursions.
WEB http://www.chevychase.com /cruise

rec.travel.cruises Some people on this active newsgroup are planning a cruise and looking for feedback about the ships they're considering; others are seeking companions who may be traveling on the same cruise. Although the newsgroup tends to be information oriented (cruise recommendations, ticket sales, and travel-agent advertisements are typical fare), it is also a comfortable forum for sharing cruise experiences: Ron speaks of surviving the maiden voyage of Carnival's *Sensation*, whose passengers included Kathie Lee and Frank Gifford (with Cody); Aggie raves about her cruise aboard the *Tropicale*; while Shaun laments that modern cruise ships look like floating apartment buildings. If the topic is cruises, you can climb aboard this newsgroup to discuss it.
USENET rec.travel.cruise

Lodging

All the Hotels on the Web A mammoth network of more than 10,000 individual pages and links that, if you're able to get

COSTUME CUSTOMS

My wife and I will be travelling on HAL for a seven day cruise this weekend. The pre-cruise material indicates that HAL has a costume party on all cruises longer than four days. We're considering renting nice costumes and bringing them with us. Has anyone been to a costume party on a cruise? If we are in nice costumes, will we look like idiots, are will there be fellow travelers similarly attired?

Thanks for any input.
—Zeb

We've been on four different HAL ships (5 cruises), and have yet to have seen a Costume Party. Maybe it was some minor afternoon event that we forsook for the pool. Better to use the rental fees for a nice bottle (or two) of wine at dinner...
—Ray

In my experience very few people actually dress in costumes even though many lines do have 'costume' nights.
—Annette

With a professional costume you won't look like an idiot, but some passengers may assume you're a staffer! The trick is to get a costume that looks like you cobbled it up yourself or that's nautical—such as a parody of a ship's captain.
—Al

—from rec.travel.cruises

past the busy home page, has its rewards. While hotel information in many countries is limited to international chains—in India, for example, only Holiday Inns and Hyatt are included—properties closer to home (England) are related in their full glory, many with online reservations capabilities. If you're thinking of traveling through Europe, you might want to make this the first stop on your itinerary.
WEB http://www.all-hotels.com

B&Bs on the WWW Not to be confused with AAA. This is a virtual guidebook to a host of bed and breakfasts around the world, from County Meath to wilderness guest ranches in Utah. Some guest houses have more complete information than others, with the best of them giving you a list of churches, pubs, hikes, and local flora and fauna, for starters.
WEB http://www.webcom.com /~neatstuf/bb/home.html

Biztravel; for the business traveler in all of us
http://www.biztravel.com/guide

Comfort Zone For those who plan on visiting for long spells and need an apartment, Global Travel Apartments offers flats for rent in 125 cities, in 26 countries, from the Channel Islands to Saigon. Select from standard or deluxe accommodations, including parking options, or an extra bedroom for the kids; then email your request, which is confirmed within 24 hours. Through this service, you can ask for someone who speaks English or Esperanto (to make you feel a little more at ease) and book your flight.
WEB http://www.globaltrvlapt.com/gta

Hospitalitynet "Dew Drop Inn" to this inviting collection of lodging links. Hospitalitynet will take you to hotel sites all over the Web, including the home pages of major hotel chains (Best Western, Holiday

Inn, Hyatt, Novotel, etc.), Small Luxury Hotels of the World, and GENinc Bed and Breakfast Inns.
WEB http://www.hospitalitynet.nl /index/chain.htm

Inn and Lodging Forum Find out if that picturesque little inn in Maine really lives up to the description in its brochure or if it actually has soggy toast and even soggier mattresses. Both inveterate travelers and B&B proprietors use the message board at this forum to exchange advice on inn-related issues ranging from access for the disabled to the best B&B in Bloomsbury. The inn industry makes its presence known in the library of this forum— companies like Homewood Suites and Embassy Suites post information on their accommodations.
COMPUSERVE *go* lodging

InnRoads Brought to you by the editors of *America's Wonderful Little Hotels & Inns*, InnRoads offers everything from the 15 commandments of vacation travel ("#1: know yourself") to extensive national listings with personal testimonial ("Our favorite rooms come with private hot tubs") to the inngoers' bill of rights (right #1: "the right to fair value"). And if you think you're the only one who's had a disappointing inn stay, check out the InnRoads newsletter's pet peeve section ("breakfast was preceded by a lengthy prayer").
WEB http://www.inns.com

Internet Guide to Bed & Breakfast Inns Can't quite remember more than one word in the name of that quaint little Vermont inn you loved so much? Plug in that word and see what comes up in this database of 3,000 B&Bs. If nothing rings any bells, chances are something else will pique your fancy, with many B&Bs offering complete virtual tours of your prospective home away from home.
WEB http://www.ultranet.com/biz/inns

Lanier's Bed and Breakfast Guide Online A listing of bed-and-breakfasts in the United States, Canada, and the Caribbean, courtesy of Lanier Travel Guides. The site offers information on more than 11,000 inns, including their phone numbers and descriptions of their services, the types of meals they serve, accessibility for the handicapped, accommodation for children and pets, and price range.

COMPUSERVE *go* inns

Leading Hotels of the World This Chicago marketing organization highlights properties in one country at a time. If $700 room rates in Courchevel are your style ("as luxurious as a palace and as warm as a chalet"), write down the phone numbers and call this service for more information or to make reservations. The site also offers a link to the Hotel Reservation Center.

WEB http://www.interactive.line.com /alan/lead

National Hotel Directory An online database available for downloading to your computer, First Look is a hotel directory with information on 1,100 properties in 25 major U.S. cities. While the listings are not as detailed as those at some other Web sites, the Directory has its advantages— if you're looking to hold or arrange a business function, handy meeting-space listings will aid you in your search.

WEB http://www.evmedia.com

The REGISTER Directory of Bed & Breakfasts, Inns, and Small Hotels TravelAssist's registry offers pictures and descriptions for hundreds of B&Bs nationwide. The listing is organized by geographical area—New England, Midwest, Rocky Mountain, etc. There are also listings for a few B&Bs in England,

France, and Mexico.

WEB http://travelassist.com/reg /reg_home.html

Travel Web An online lodging network with databases of hotel chains and independent hotels. Simply plug in your desired destination—Fiji, Cleveland, or Cancún. You'll then get capsule descriptions of properties, complete with price and amenities info. You can limit your search by type of lodging (B&B, resort, guest ranch, etc.). The site also offers links to other travel sites on the Net, including the Internet Guide to Bed & Breakfast Inns and Club Med.

WEB http://www.travelweb.com

Business travel

Association of Business Travelers A club that provides business travelers with hotel, restaurant, and transportation discounts. A lost-luggage tracing service is also provided.

WEB http://www.hk.linkage.net /markets/abt

Biztravel.com Biztravel.com contains valuable information on destinations worldwide, geared toward the business traveler. In its feature on the United Kingdom, for instance, there is information on where to get a furnished office, obtain a cellular phone, rent a car, or perform a large currency transaction. The site also has the very latest business travel news.

WEB http://www.biztravel.com/guide

Corporate Rate Hotel Directory Find the most competitive corporate hotel rates online. Listed by state (in the U.S.) or by country, information is available about hotels and amenities, as well as special rates. Email addresses are provided for reservations and for verifying information.

WEB http://www.ios.com/corphotels

Craighead's Business Travel Library Planning a business junket to Estonia to check out the possibilities of becoming an Internet Service Provider to the Baltics? For a thumbnail sketch of local business etiquette and such basics as which calling cards actually work there, the time difference, and how long it takes to get from Tallinn-Ulemiste airport to the Estonia Sheraton downtown, Craighead's is a decent starting point. But you're bound to have more questions. For in-depth answers, you'll have to shell out $49.95 for the Craighead Business report on the region to which you're traveling.

WEB http://plaza.interport.net /craighead

Getting Through Customs There's much more at this site than advice on how not to look like a drug smuggler when leaving Istanbul. Explanations of business practices and protocol, cultural customs, negotiating strategies, and even "cognitive styles" for hundreds of countries are on file here. Don't risk losing the big deal in Malaysia

by putting your feet on the desk, or offending the Swedes by not introducing yourself to everyone in the room upon entering. This site will guide you through the customs of different countries. The libraries hold additional information on world leaders and local transportation. Get set for the global economy now.
COMPUSERVE *go* gtc-7

Venue Finder If you're a meeting planner seeking the perfect spot, this Web site is worth a visit. You can search a directory of business venues or hotel chains (Radisson, Swissotel, Hilton, for example) by nation or city. Each search will retrieve contact information for hotels and conference locations that meet your criteria. Often, a listing will link to the Web site for a specific hotel or city. You can also get calendars of upcoming events for the location you're considering. After you've made your choice, check back to see if your meeting listed is here. If not, send details to the site's webmaster.
WEB http://www.webcom.com/~venues

Budget travel

American-International Homestays "Fulfill your travel dreams without emptying your pockets." A homestay lets you enjoy the hosts' warmth and hospitality and eat authentic, home-cooked meals. American-International Homestays represents hundreds of homestays worldwide. At the Web

site you can read about the company's history and its homestay opportunities and request additional information through the mail.
WEB http://www.spectravel.com /homes

Council Travel Students and budget travelers now have access to Council Travel's services on the Net. If you want to check airfares, find hostel listings, purchase railpasses, or find summer employment abroad, CT is your source. They have offices worldwide; get the full listing here or contact them online. They also offer travel insurance, language programs, car rentals, and youth tours.
WEB http://www.ciee.org/travel.htm

The Hitching Packing List If you've thought about sticking out your thumb and seeing where it would take you, this is the site for you. A Norwegian hitchhiker offers the benefit of the experience he gained hitching from Oslo to Paris with only $2 in his pocket. Though the guide has a northern European slant, the information is pretty universal. What to pack, what to wear, even where to stand—it's all in here. You wouldn't usually pack a shiny bit of plastic to attract drivers, now would you? So what is the best way to get drivers to stop? Wash! The most essential item? Humor!
WEB http://www.solutions.net /rectravel/general/packing_list hitching.html

Hostelling International Homepage A non-profit organization whose goal is to "help travelers gain a greater understanding of the world and it's people through hostelling." HI lists hostels in the U.S. and around the world, including addresses, contact details, and descriptions of the facilities (there's even a note if the hostel takes credit cards). One lucky hostel is featured as the Hostel of the Month with a pic, a descriptive essay, and links to resources on local attractions and nearby cities. Note: American entries are much more detailed than their international counterparts.
WEB http://www.taponline.com/tap /travel/hostels/pages/hosthp.htm

Hostels Europe Inveterate hostelers rate accommodations that vary from a charming lodging in the medieval French city of Carcasonne to a rowdy party crib in Frankfurt.
WEB http://www.tardis.ed.ac.uk/~og /hostels.html

Interactive Travel Guide Check here for Eurail and cheap flight information and for budget-travel insight on everything from car rentals to hostels to hitchhiking. Newly added destination features, discount news and travel updates, and an exchange board have beefed up the site.
WEB http://www.developnet.com /travel

International Student Travel Confederation Brought to you by the makers of those little green

International Student cards that get you discounts on hotels, train tickets, and museum fees the world over. This page tells you where you can get a card, and a list of savings and benefits it can bring you. The country-by-country guide is an education in itself. Who'd have thought an ISIC card would get you a ten-percent discount at the Taco Bell in Accra, Ghana?
WEB http://www.istc.org

rec.travel.marketplace You know that section in the *New York Times* devoted to good deals and advice on travel accommodations? This is much better. Ask about international air fares, and travel agencies will post their best offers. Inquire about a cheap hotel in Amsterdam, and you'll get recommendations like "Stay at BOB's Youth Hostel if you don't mind a bunch of students who just like to kick back and get stoned!" Discount fares, time shares, and apartment sublets are posted regularly.
USENET rec.travel.marketplace

Student and Budget Travel Guide
This guide for student and low-budget travelers is packed with penny-pinching tips and links to relevant newsgroups (rec.travel.marketplace), informative Web sites (STA Travel), and country home pages (from Angola to Zimbabwe).
WEB http://asa.ugl.lib.umich.edu /chdocs/travel/travel-guide.html

TravelGram Published every Saturday, TravelGram reports the latest travel discounts, including specials offered by all the major airlines, hotels, and car-rental agencies. TravelGram also provides a list of toll-free numbers for airlines from Aer Lingus to Zambia Airways.
WEB http://www.travelhub.com /travelgram

World Wide Courier Association
With airfares at such a tremendous discount, who wouldn't want to be a courier? For a yearly fee, the people at World Wide Courier Association will help you realize that dream— as long as you're over 21 and have a "clean cut" appearance.
WEB http://www.wallstech.com

Shoestring Travel Ezine
WEB http://www.stratpub.com
picture WEB http://www.lechateau.com/cruise/1996/group_large.html
If you're sick of wading through commercial postings in travel newsgroups, this is the site for you. The site's creator does all the hard work, collecting tips from rec.travel newsgroups and presenting the most useful nuggets on how to eat, sleep, and travel cheaply. There are also links to other relevant travel sites and info on registering as an independent travel agent. A site that makes traveling on a shoestring easy.

Adventure travel

Adventurous Traveler Bookstore
Don't spend hours fingering dusty volumes in cobweb-filled bookstores to find the travel title you crave! Just come to this site and take advantage of the travel literature warehouse at Adventurous Traveler. Search their catalog of more than 2,200 titles by keyword (a search on "France" yields the *Western European Phrasebook*, *France by Bike*, and *Whitewater Gems of the High Alps*, among 50 other titles). Or you can click on indexes that organize titles by geographic area or by activity (hiking or scuba diving). For a hotlist of new books for the current season, just hit the New Titles and Additions links for the latest in travel guides and literature. After filling your virtual back pack, you can order your choices online, call the telephone numbers listed here, or download an order form to snail mail your requests.
WEB http://www.AdventurousTraveler.com

The Outdoor Sports and Travel Directory This site is for the seriously hardy. Rugged outdoors people find links to scuba, fishing, and biking info—all sports and fixations are served here. Search for adventure by location, too— how about ice climbing in Norway or an Amazon canoe trip? If nature's your game, there's a wealth of links to environmental and educational associations and eco-tour operators. Plus, you can get outfitted online through links to stores that sell ice picks and insect repellent. Start any cyberadventure here.
WEB http://ecotravel.com

The Polar Regions Home Page
Find details on the coolest new vacation destinations. First, get acquainted with the local residents—bears, seals, penguins (and scientists). Get serious by linking scientific explorations of the regions— block of ice in the north, great white fields in the south. There are even live links to research stations. Once you're fully acclimated, you can get travel information for the beginner's polar regions in Alaska, Norway, and Canada, or head right to the links leading to travel services promising Antarctic expeditions and circumpolar navigation around the North Pole.
WEB http://www.stud.unit.no/~sveinw/arctic

Health & safety

CDC Home Travel Information Page You'll find the Centers for Disease Control's list of cholera warnings, cruise-ship inspection ratings, and up-to-the-minute news on contagious-disease outbreaks. General travel precautions are also included— e.g., boil water in Guatemala. Find out what shots you need for that visit to Djakarta.
WEB http://www.cdc.gov/travel/travel.html

Comprehensive Healthcare For International and Wilderness Travelers There's more to wilderness health than how to deal with snake bites and bear attacks. Stanford's travel medicine service provides good general advice for all travelers, including what to include in a first-aid kit, how to deal with Montezuma's revenge, and what insect repellents actually repel insects, rather than fellow travelers.
WEB http://www-leland.stanford.edu/~naked/stms.html

> **❝ Find out what insect repellents actually repel insects, rather than fellow travelers. ❞**

Global Emergency Medical Services Info on Global Emergency Medical Services, an organization that provides medical services worldwide through a network of English-speaking doctors and clinics.
WEB http://www.globalmed.com

MCW International Travelers Clinic The site carries the Medical College of Wisconsin's guide to a healthy vacation. It recommends that travelers pack a medicine kit with antihistamines and topical steroid

cream, explains the immunization requirements for different countries, and gives advice on dealing with altitude and motion sickness. True hypochondriacs can check the graphic description of the incubation periods and symptoms of infectious diseases.
WEB http://www.intmed.mcw.edu /travel.html

Safety and Scams Collection
Some of the information on this list borders on the paranoiac: "Always assume you're being watched," and "Find out what the favorite scams are locally." The list goes on to explain some of the more common (and more entertaining)

scams: "Yuppie in distress lost wallet; pregnant woman (pillow) needs bus money; kids surrounding you using cardboard or magazines to block your view; purse snatchers on scooters; drop change or spill food on you so you will put your bags down at airport or train station; cutting open backpacks; sleeping gas in trains or buses; drugged cups and drinks; fake porters taking your bags; snare bags under seats with umbrella."
WEB http://www.solutions.net /rec-travel/general/safety.txt

Travel Health Online Whether you're taking off for Bahrain or Bermuda, you'll want to review

the country profiles archived here. Updated daily, Travel Health Online also provides a list of travel medicine providers, summaries of travel illnesses, and explanations of preventative medications and vaccines as well as U.S. State Department publications.
WEB http://www.tripprep.com/index .html

Magazines & newsletters

21st Century Adventures Targeted at adventure travelers, the Web site for this travel magazine carries articles on such subjects as the undiscovered Indonesia and white-water kayaking. But

EPICURIOUS TRAVELER

WEB http://travel.epicurious.com

Travel tips are added daily to the online version of *Conde Nast Traveler* housed here, so check often for information on cheap rooms and European rail strikes. The site also has several ways to

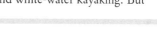
Location: http://travel.epicurious.com/traveler/photo_gallery/show_photo.cgi?path=./Europ

find the ideal vacation destination. The island finder, for example, suggests the perfect getaway for seven different personality types—from Ivana Trump to Margaret Mead. Click on the beach and island atlas for the lowdown on Capri or Rio. Or just plug in your traveling priorities (cost, setting, activities, etc.) and the Web site's "concierge" will suggest destinations.

Location: http://www.travelersguide.com/destinations/issue4/gifs/steak1.jpg

From *Destinations* magazine: Hope that beef's not from Britain...
http://www.travelersguide.com/destinations/destcovr.htm

the site also features an interactive travel quiz (which helps refine your vacation needs), travel advice from industry professionals, and an online traveler's forum to answer those perplexing where-, how-, and when-to-go questions. Let's all meet up in the year 2000.
WEB ttp://travelassist.com/mag/mag_home.html

Country Inns Magazine
Experience the life of gracious homes and country cottages. Illustrated articles from each monthly issue are online here—stories cover topics ranging from fall romance in the Berkshires to the Inn of the Country Inns.
WEB http://www.virtualcities.com/~virtual/cinn/cinn01.htm

Destinations Magazine Not available at the corner newsstand, this online magazine takes readers on a virtual vacation. All tastes are catered to here—the most recent issue focused on seaside Victoriana in Cape May and the search for the perfect steakhouse. A calendar of events covers state fairs and tennis championships, and travel news and bargains are available as well. Check the classified ads for a chance to trade a studio in Manhattan for a villa in France.
WEB http://www.travelersguide.com/destinations/destcovr.htm

Give Yourself a Break A weekly newsletter that compiles news from across the travel industry. If security is tightened at JFK in response to terrorist threats

or if America West reduces fares to Phoenix, Mexico City, and Los Angeles, you can read about it in *Give Yourself a Break*.
WEB http://www.access.digex.net/~drmemory/giveyour.html

Roam When in Roam... check out the latest from this online 'zine's traveling correspondents. In the premiere issue, they start in Toronto, head across the Atlantic and into the heart of Amsterdam's red light district. They then drive across France and over the Pyrenees to run with the bulls in Pamplona, Spain. The interactive travelogue is updated daily and editors welcome email requests, criticism, pictures, suggestions, stories, and dares.
WEB http://www.roam.org

Travel Holiday Magazine More than just previews of the newsstand version, the *Travel Holiday* site presents the full text of current and back issues. Browse or search a wide variety of articles—a search on "mysteries" produced rhapsodies on "Gauguin's Lush Marquesas" and a piece on Morocco's hotels. The online site features travel news, discounts, a worldwide calendar of events, and a directory of travel resources and contacts to help you realize your travel dreams. To get the first crack at upcoming bargains, join the site's mailing list. *Travel Holiday* also makes the full wisdom of its editors available with

accommodation, dining, and getaway suggestions. While exploring this wealth of resources, don't neglect *Travel Holiday*'s message board, especially the entertaining and invaluable topic Worst Vacations Ever.
AMERICA ONLINE *keyword* travel holiday

Travel Industry Magazine
Although *Travel Industry* is billed as a publication for travel professionals, it covers plenty of stories of interest to amateurs. Read travel-related stories off the UPI, AP, and Reuters newswires.
WEB http://www.newspage.com /NEWSPAGE/cgi-bin/walk.cgi /NEWSPAGE/info/dl9/dl

Travel & Leisure The pages of *Travel & Leisure* entertain you with both traditional travel writing and offbeat features (like a guide to European flea markets or a humorous feature on spas by playwright Wendy Wasserstein). Articles from back issues can be searched by locale, and a large library here contains hundreds of maps for downloading. Get on the message board for advice on cruises and frequent-flyer perks, as well as tips for trips— how about a side trip to the walled city of Cesky Krumlov in Bohemia or a stay at the Mayan Inn in Chichicastenango, Guatemala.
AMERICA ONLINE *keyword* travel & leisure

TravelASSIST Magazine For exciting travel adventure stories and tantalizing travel photographs, view the full text of articles and pictures from current and past issues of *TravelASSIST*. Find out how to choose a perfect travel companion, float down the Yangtze River, or luxuriate in the Pink Palace (at the Beverly Hills Hotel).
WEB http://travelassist.com/mag /mag_home.html

Travelmag Not the usual "Best Beaches" travel magazine articles. *Travelmag*, an electronic magazine, delivers reader-contributed articles on subjects like canoeing the Amazon or Moroccan marriage markets.

FODOR'S
WEB http://www.fodors.com

Need to locate a top hotel in Atlanta or a mid-priced trattoria in Rome? Maybe you're just curious about German customs and duties laws—can lederhosen be seized at the border? Fodor's has been guiding smart travelers for 60 years, and if you're smart, you'll let the venerable travel pub-

Location: http://www.fodors.com/features/parks/animamr.html

RAINIER OR SHINE: Clouds often obscure such views

lisher continue to guide you. Contains thousands of listings for restaurants, hotels, and activities in cities worldwide, as well as a wealth of practical travel info that ranges from the general (senior citizens should mention their age to airlines; they may qualify for a discount) to the witheringly specific (the best auto racing in New England occurs at Lime Rock Park in Lakeville, Conn.). Information can also be searched by keyword.

Africa—Ankole cattle at sunset
AOL keyword pictures

Other features cover travel bargains, health advisories, and bizarre news from around the world.
WEB http://www.travelmag.co.uk /travelmag

Web Travel Review If this magazine came in hard copy, postal workers would be miffed—it stands now at 600 Web pages, with more than 2,000 photographs. Here the Net's own travel-writing guru, Philip Greenspun, posts his award-winning travel compendium.
WEB http://webtravel.org/webtravel

Guides

Adventures in Travel CompuServe's resident travel writer Lee Foster pens these articles on the special spirit of places like the Galapagos Islands or Dutch cheese country. There is practical information amidst Foster's feature articles—take a look at the cruise reviews and strategies for eco-tours in

Brazil or theater weekends in London's West End.
COMPUSERVE *go* AIT-I

Around the World in 80 Clicks The world map at this site is covered with red dots. Play connect-the-dots with your mouse, and you'll access 80 different guides to destinations worldwide. Click on that dot over Chile, and it yields the Chilean Ski Guide. Hit that red dot over Japan, and you'll get a guide to dining, shopping, and going out in Japan. Click on the dot over Alaska to learn about Alaskan politics, literature, radio stations, and tourism. More dots, and guides, are added to the map each week.
WEB http://www.coolsite.com/arworld .html

Frommer's City Guides For the urban sophisticate in all of us—city guides that let you act like a native in either Albuquerque or Paris. In addition

to language primers, and lodging, dining, shopping, and sightseeing recommendations, these guides provide detailed historical and cultural background information for each locale; they even suggest books and films to give you the flavor of the city—Luigi Barzini's *The Italians* and Roberto Rossellini's *Open City* are among the many recommendations for Rome. Most major U.S. and international cities are included, but there are some surprising omissions— Berlin, Barcelona, and Mexico City—perhaps they'll be added later. Frommer's also sponsors travel chat sessions and connects to the American Express online booking center. You can order the guides online here, too.
AMERICA ONLINE *keyword* frommer's

Gay Travel Connection Written by Ernie Alderete, these travelogues report on over 20 intimate U.S. and international destinations like the Flex Complex in Phoenix, Az. and the Inca Spa in Peru. Some reviews contain adult subject matter and sexually explicit language.
WEB http://www.travelxn.com/gay /homepage.htm

International Traveler's Guide Spend some armchair leisure time reading the illustrated travel essays at this site—climb snowcapped peaks in the Canadian Rockies, commune with the Conch people of Key West, or cruise the Exuma

chain in the Bahamas. Dining, accommodation, and recreation information is also available for selected cities in Italy, the Caribbean, and Iceland.
WEB http://www.iisys.com/www/travel/world.htm

Internet World Travel Review A collection of essays on a number of locations worldwide, including Canada, Rio, Norway, Switzerland, Hong Kong, and Japan. This guide is a great source for a short history of the country, air travel, hotel recommendations (which include pricing info), tips on local attractions (shop the large bazaar in Dhaka for bargains on leather goods, fabrics, and jewelry), and hints on when to visit certain countries for maximum travel enjoyment. Tip:

Don't visit Bangladesh from May through October unless you like rain. There are also a few links here to other travel sites online.
WEB http://www.stempler.com/punchin/internet.html

Onward Travel Stories This growing collection of travelogues gathers the stories and photographs of a handful of amateur writers and photographers. The collection includes "Big Bend," one man's tale of the biggest national park in Texas, and "No Simple Highway," a photo and text journal of a trip from Maine to Arizona during the fall and winter of 1991-1992. Beatniks will appreciate the homage to *On the Road* in "Remembering Jack."
WEB http://sunsite.unc.edu/onward

Pictures from Around the World Pack your Brownie before you head for Jamaica! Browse this collection of lavishly illustrated articles and images and then head to the library for picture-taking tips and creative inspiration. The libraries are organized by continent (Africa, Asia, Antarctica) and subject (waterfalls, buffalo, cathedrals). Head to the message boards for advice from photographic professionals.
AMERICA ONLINE *keyword* pictures

Road Trip USA A guide in progress to the roads less traveled. This cross country compendium will cover five routes for seeing the U.S. from behind the wheel—U.S. 50, U.S. 93, up the east coast, U.S. 2, and U.S. 83—some of

 ## LONELY PLANET
WEB http://www.lonelyplanet.com

The bible of travelers and trekkers the world over, Loney Planet has tackled yet another frontier—the Web. Would *Conde Nast Traveler* mention the Tupac Amaru revolt when discussing Peru? Perhaps not, but Lonely Planet, the publishers of the ecologically and politically correct travel

guides, surely would. At its online outpost, use the interactive map to gain excellent, illustrated descriptions of the climate, history, economy, and culture of countries worldwide. Postcards from travelers in far-flung spots (greetings from Turkmenistan!) and dispatches from guide writers on the road are included.

which are already complete. Each of the routes will be profiled, with a map (click on any of the sights along the way for a brief description of the attraction), a history, and a description of what you'll see in every state you pass through.
WEB http://www.moon.com/rt.usa /rdtrip/rdtrip.html

Rough Guide HotWired and Rough Guide (the renowned publishers of more than 70 travel guidebooks, phrase books, and music-reference titles) have paired up to offer a database of travel info for the U.S., Canada, and Mexico. The database features recommendations of hotels, restaurants, coffee shops, bars, nightclubs, sporting events, and festivals nationwide with a focus on budget. Click on the map and browse down to any state or city in the U.S. or click on the Rough Search button to

hunt for data by location or subject. The detailed listings are linked to a discussion space where you can read what others have to say about their experiences with roughing it.
WEB http://www.hotwired.com/rough

Round-the-World Travel Guide So you've got at least 80 days and a pair of comfortable shoes— this guide helps make a wild dream into a reality. Conveniently divided into sections such as Major Decisions, Transportation, Money Matters, Communications, and People, this guide offers practical tips on rail travel and bargaining, suggested travel routes, and a good bibliography for further research. It also offers links to offbeat travel sites like freight ships that take passengers, and dispenses advice on working abroad. Don't miss the section on packing your bags: You'll learn

to pack everything you think you need, then cut the load in half.
WEB http://www.solutions.net /rec-travel/rtw/html/faq.html

Travelbase A guide to some very specific resources in the U.S. Click on the Miami Beach, Orlando, and Key West topics here and read Travelbase's comprehensive listings of restaurants, hotels, and events in each city. If you're researching a tennis, scuba, or skiing vacation, Travelbase offers searchable databases of hotels and resorts that specialize in sports themes. Just enter the state and the sports you like, and the database pulls up the addresses, phone numbers, and a short description for all appropriate facilities in that state.
WEB http://www.travelbase.com

Travels with Samantha After the death of his beloved dog George, author Philip Greenspun recuperated from his loss by touring North America with Samantha, his trusty Powerbook, for the summer of 1993. Philip fought traffic on I-93 going through Boston, met a group of Jewish bikers in Minnesota, and almost froze to death in the Canadian Rockies. Travels with Samantha is a touching account of a man working through the loss of a dear friend, and a great source of practical travel info for North America. It also contains beautiful photos of his journey.
WEB http://www-swiss.ai.mit.edu /samantha/table-of-contents.html

That there, you city bumpkins, is what we call a sail
http://travelassist.com/reg /reg_home.html

Location: http://travelassist.com/mag/a59.jpg.html

You're Reading TravelASSIST MAGAZINE

Sex

SOME JUST TALK ABOUT IT. OTHERS DO IT. STILL OTHERS DO IT AND THEN TALK ABOUT IT ONLINE

WHEN SURFING THE SEA of Internet sex resources, the phrase "whatever floats your boat" takes on a new and occasionally alarming significance. There seems to be no limit to the variety of sites, newsgroups, and mailing lists you may happen upon. From masturbation to polyamory, intergenerational sex to infantilism, hair to foot fetishes, furries to bears (there is a bit of a difference), there's something in cyberspace to suit every sexual taste. But lest you think only the freaks come out on the Net, there's plenty of straightforward, old-fashioned (sort of) sex floating around, too, of the heterosexual, gay, lesbian, and bisexual varieties. So, go ahead. Get your feet wet or dive on in head first. Bathing suits are optional.

Location: http://www.tantra.com/books2.html

SOCIETY FOR HUMAN SEXUALITY

WEB http://weber.u.washington.edu/~sfpse

picture: http://www.tantra.com/books2.html

Birds do it, bees do it. But there isn't a critter on earth that does the nasty with as much variety, mythology, or self-importance as humans, who write books, sing songs, paint paintings, and even set up institutions, associations, and societies to study their own pleasure. Many of the documents at this site use frank sexual language, so parents should not use it as an *Am I Normal?* tutorial for latchkey kids. But for adults, there are plenty of diverting and stimulating documents. Curious about blow-job technique? Need pointers on Tantric-orgasm etiquette? With dozens of articles on such topics as body modification, massage, fetishes, and prostitution, this site serves as a clearinghouse for things libidinal.

Starting points

Adult Site of the Day Xpics has amassed a hodgepodge of sites for the seriously horny, from Amateur Hardcore to CyberErotica. Xpics also oversees the A.S.S. Awards (adult sex site, not to be confused with alt.sex.spanking), given each month in 31 categories.
WEB http://www.xpics.com

Annie Sprinkle's Home Page at Gates of Heck The original goddess of female ejaculation, Annie Sprinkle has brought feminism to heretofore unexplored levels. Sexual healing, performance art, and unabashed support of the sex industry—these are the cornerstones of Sprinkle's invaluable work. At her home page, Sprinkle instructs women in the fine art of the energy orgasm, lists 41 uses for sex, and provides a suggestion of self-examination techniques. Visitors are also encouraged to buy Annie's feminist erotic playing cards.
WEB http://www.infi.net/~heck /sprinkleshow.html

Charles Haynes: Radical Sex Filling a perceived void on the Net, Charles Haynes lists links to sex sites deemed "radical" by Pat Califia's definition: "Being a sex radical means being defiant as well as deviant." Haynes' defiance is exemplified in his tirade against the Galaxy Web-indexing service, which, he believes, displays blatant prejudice toward the gay and lesbian online community. Haynes' sexual and political links focus on the bondage, S/M, and transgender communities.
WEB http://www.fifth-mountain.com /radical_sex

CyberPorn Sex Links With an extensive variety of links, arranged by genre (and laid out in phallic splendor), this is a great resource for the curious and the downright addicted.
WEB http://www.cyberporn.inter.net /indexl.html

Introduction to Sexology Read up on the history of sexology and turn your favorite hobby into an intellectual pursuit.
URL ftp://ftp.u.washington.edu/public /sfpse/sex/sexohist

Industry

alt.sex.services Curious about the current status of that massage parlor you used to visit on the outskirts of Minneapolis? Or about the gay strip club near the Tenderloin that gave new meaning to the term pole-dancing? Aficionados of such establishments flock to alt.sex.services, where they chat about the past, present, and future of the sexual service industry.
USENET alt.sex.services

alt.sex.strip-clubs This newsgroup provides nationwide recommendations for strip clubs and other sex establishments. Curious about the quality of the waitresses/prostitutes in

The Brass Rail in Omaha? Worried that the massage parlor you used to frequent in San Francisco may have taken a turn for the worse? Pay a visit to this group; it's a Michelin Guide for the groin.
USENET alt.sex.strip-clubs

Grimace Nudie Club Listings If you're in Times Square, you probably don't need this list—just walk outside and look for the guys on the street corner handing out promotional flyers. If you're in Delaware, Oregon, or Florida, though, you may need to point and click, so to speak, to find your way to the best in adult entertainment. This guide to U.S. and Canadian strip clubs, topless clubs,

and adult-sex clubs incorporates pictures, maps, videos, and even coupons.
WEB http://www.access.digex.net/~ldgrim/nudeclub.html

Prostitutes' Education Network
Learn what it's like to work in a Nevada brothel; chat with the Scarlet Harlot, San Francisco's premier prostitute activist; and learn the ins and outs of safety. This site focuses on decriminalization, education, and rights for prostitutes worldwide.
WEB http://www.creative.net/~penet

The Ultimate Strip Club List With more than 1,000 strip clubs listed—some descriptions are written by the staff of the Ultimate List, some are submitted

by netters—this is the best place to go for advice on where to find a little skin and sin. While the descriptions can swell into mini-narratives of libidinal frustration ("I wasn't sure I was going to do anything other than watch the show until one dancer came over and laid her head on my shoulder..."), the guide tries to keep the froth to a minimum—entries include house specialties, cover charges, a brief history of the club, and bios of specific dancers/performers. Bone up on New York's Scores, Colorado Springs' Deja Vu, and Memphis's Platinum Plus—where the "skinny (almost scrawny) redhead with almost no chest" dances "upside down with her head

between your ankles and her legs locked around your head." The easy-to-use set of icons divides clubs into bikini (clothed on top and bottom, pasties included), topless (nipples must be visible), and full nude (for those with absolutely no imagination).
WEB http://www.paranoia.com/~express/strip.html

The World Sex Guide Though prostitution is technically illegal in Thailand, the nation has one of the most active sex industries in the world, and for 1,000 baht ($40), the Thai prostitutes will stay all night. New York City streetwalkers frequent 11th Avenue between 24th and 30th Street and 9th Avenue between 44th and 50th Street. In

BIANCA'S SMUT SHACK
WEB http://bianca.com/shack

"Bianca greets you with open arms, embracing all who would come to the Shack and contribute their wisdom, talents and love to bianca's growing community." Make yourself at home—scrawl on the walls or step into any of the rooms. Start out in bianca's foyer; make your way to the bedroom

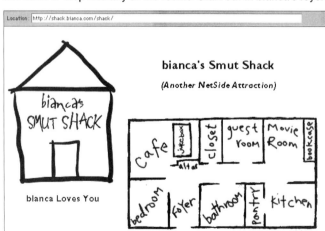

where the sex toys, bianca's diary, and her Dreambooks are kept; and get really raunchy in the bathroom. Whatever you do, make sure to leave your mark before you leave—it's visitors like you who bring this love shack to life.

Location: http://www.infi.net/~heck/sprinklecardshow.html

Excerpts from Annie Sprinkle's Post-Modern Pin-Ups

This is my latest project, and I'm proud to present selections from this updated "stacked" deck on the Internet. These Pleasure Activist Playing Cards feature 56 of my favorite full-color photos of my favorite pleasure activists, with a 64-page booklet of biographies and information about pleasure activism.

These women are straight, queer, all ages shapes and sizes, with plenty of tattoos, piercings, strap-ons and fetishes! The cards emphasize safer sex and are intended for an audience of

No sign of Rita Hayworth
http://www.infi.net/~heck/sprinkleshow.html

Christchurch, New Zealand, bathhouses (brothels) are advertised in the daily newspaper. Find out these facts and more flesh-for-currency tidbits at this site, which collects articles on the sex industry for more than 20 nations.
WEB http://www.paranoia.com/faq/prostitution

Sex talk

alt.sex FAQ "Alt.sex receives significantly more traffic than your typical newsgroup," begins this FAQ file, and upon reading the first few questions and answers, it's easy to see why. For the Internet sex neophyte, especially one with an interest in exploring the erotic splendors of Usenet, there is no better place to begin. While some of the questions deal with general sexual how-tos (e.g.

"How does one give a hand job?"), the majority refer to the various possibilities of the Usenet medium itself (e.g. "Where can I find binary pictures and/or movies?") Of course, for anyone who has logged significant hours into their exploration of Internet sex, this FAQ is simplistic and redundant.
URL ftp://ftp.u.washington.edu/public/sfpse/sex/sexfaq

alt.sex.wanted Demands, demands, demands. That's all you're going to get on alt.sex.wanted, a nationwide newsgroup that offers a forum for sexual requests. As in most of the sex groups, the users are predominantly male, and they seem uniformly interested in having assorted acts performed upon them.
USENET alt.sex.wanted

Sex-L Sure, everyone knows about dental dams and French ticklers, but has anyone ever had a nose bridge? Don't answer yet. First make sure you know what a nose bridge is. The Sex-L mailing list is one of the most explicit sites on the Net, whether subscribers are announcing secret desires ("I have a fantasy of sucking the breasts of a lactating young mother. If you are one, what would you think of a request from a friend, not necessarily a lover, who would ask you to let him taste your milk?") or asking for practical advice ("If it wasn't so 'ergonomically' uncomfortable, I could lick her for hours. But it hurts my neck. What's wrong?"). While many of the postings maintain this compelling texture, a fair number slide into ordinary macho-bewildered stupidity. In the end, sex remains the most fascinating of all human behaviors, and the subscribers to this mailing list chow down at the buffet of eros and libido. Any other questions? Oh, yeah—the nose bridge. Drum roll, please, as a man from the great state of Indiana explains it all to you: "That reminds me of one of the funniest times. We were making love, I was trying to keep sweat from dropping off my face onto hers, when a small, sensual drip ran to the tip of my nose and onto the tip of hers. It was as if we had a 'nose bridge.'"
EMAIL listserv@tamvml.tamu.edu ✉
Type in message body: subscribe sex-l ⟨your full name⟩

Masturbation

alt.sex.masturbation When it comes right down to it, this is the only honest alt.sex group on the Internet; when you're sitting at a keyboard imagining ecstasy, one-handed typing is the most common form of pleasure. This newsgroup hosts a wide range of users, from Danish teens to fortysomething American lawyers. Men and women alike are represented, and the entries range from the erotic to the spiritual (the great Tantric group orgasm). The group's FAQ tackles the basic questions of how, why, and how often.
USENET alt.sex.masturbation
FAQ: **URL** ftp://ftp.u.washington.edu /public/sfpse/sex/masturba

Bianca's Masturbation Index Having fun touching yourselves down there? Well, don't listen to your parents and your clergyman when they tell you that it's wrong. You won't go blind. Go right ahead, and rub until you feel like it's the Fourth of July inside your brain. This site, devoted to the pleasures of self-stimulation, reviews the major autoerotic techniques (clitoral, G-spot, and anal stimulation for women; and penile and prostate simulation for men), debunks myths about masturbation's harms, and even collects stories about masturbation ("I want to confess that I masturbate every day. I like. Everyone should do it every day!"). And one more thing— if you still can't bring yourself to masturbate, ask a friend to lend a hand.
WEB http://shack.bianca.com/shack /goodvibe/masturbate/index.html

Synonyms for Masturbation Those searching for alternatives (to the word, not the deed) need look no further. The synonyms for male masturbation—buffing the bishop, buttering the corn, caning the vandal—far outweigh those for the female version—doing my nails. But we suppose it's only fair since more than 90 percent of men as opposed to 60 percent of women admit to spending a little quality time with themselves from time to time.
WEB http://www.compbio.caltech.edu /~dliney/pics/in_tray/synonyms.html

 ## INTERNET SEX ROAD
WEB http://www.elogica.com.br/imagger/isr

The Brazilians are understandably proud of this remarkable free service, which lists more than 2,000 URLs, "more than any other adult service" (or so they claim, in charming, broken English).

There is something for every taste here, arranged alphabetically and with little regard to genre. Obsessive Meg Ryan sites sit alongside the scantily clad "Men on Net," as tastes converge to form a harmonious, horny whole.

IT'S NOT JUST FOR BREAKFAST ANYMORE

1. Sex as a sedative. It helps you go to sleep.
2. Sex to fight addictions. It helped me quit smoking.
3. Sex as a laxative. Regular sex helps you have regular shits.
4. Sex to get to know somebody. You can tell a lot about a person by fucking them.
5. Sex as meditation.
6. Sex to relieve boredom.
7. Sex to improve concentration.
8. Sex to make money.
9. Sex to create magic. Some witches believe that the most powerful time to cast a spell is during orgasm.
10. Sex for manipulation. It can get you what you want.
11. Sex for a reward. Either to yourself or to someone else.
12. Sex for relaxation.
13. Sex for rejuvenation. It keeps you looking and feeling younger.
14. Sex to increase energy. A great pick-me-up.
15. Sex to cure an asthma attack. I saved a man's life once.
16. Sex to make you laugh. Sex can be hilarious.
17. Sex as a gift. A present for birthdays, anniversaries, Bar Mitzvahs...
18. Sex to get high.
19. Sex to achieve an altered state.
20. Sex to create life.

—from Annie Sprinkle's Home Page at the Gates of Heck

Advice

alt.sex.first-time Some members preach the virtues of virginity or waiting ("As someone who 'lost it' a number of years after age 18, I believe there is more to life than just banging away at the first opportunity"). Others are waging war to keep the group safe for sex talk ("In my august opinion, anyone who is a virgin after the age of 18, male or female, is a weak-kneed lunatic.") If you can work your way through the flames and the "help, I wanna do it with a hottie" posts, this group promises to satisfy the insatiable curiosity netters have about other netters' sex lives. **USENET** alt.sex.first-time

An Approach to Manual Vaginal and G-Spot Stimulation "First, clip your fingernails..." Need we say more? **URL** ftp://ftp.u.washington.edu/public /sfpse/sex/mvgstim

Ask the Expert How did Kim Martyn get to be an expert in sexual matters? Through years of blood, toil, tears, and sweat in Toronto, answering questions on topics such as birth control, sexually transmitted diseases, and human sexuality. Unlike most advice columns, Ask the Expert uses high-end technology to satisfy curious readers; Kim's answers to questions such as "Is it common to fantasize about someone else while having sex?" and "My partner complains that I'm too large for her" (yeah, right) come complete with fancy graphics (a response to a reader who complains that the thrill is gone is decorated with a cartoon of a man and a woman in bed separated by a television). **WEB** http://www.cycor.ca/TCave /netrek.html

Oral Sex For those seeking tangible advice on oral loving, these anonymously-written essays are the real goods. In typical phallocentric fashion, the essay on pleasing a woman is the last and the shortest of the series, but at least the information is out there for anyone willing to read it. The essay itself is surprisingly well-written, and makes a convincing case for the perfecting of this underrated skill: "I know a man who's a lousy f***, simply lousy, but he can eat p***y like nobody I know and he never has trouble getting a date." **WEB** http://www.jmk.su.se/jmk/stud /magen/g-guntin/cock.html

Performing Cunnilingus Yet another detailed guide dedicated to the indoctrination and

basic training of that rare commodity, the unselfish male.
URL ftp://ftp.u.washington.edu/public/sfpse/sex/cunnfaq

Performing Fellatio If for no other reason, the Internet is remarkable for its wealth of well-written fellatio guides. This one may win the award for both wit and attention to detail. Its writer is sympathetic to the perils of the gag reflex, especially as it relates to the technique known simply as "deep throating." The beginner may want to stick with lessons one through five (the basic blow job), before moving on to the more advanced techniques, such as "the traveling figure eight."

URL ftp://ftp.u.washington.edu/public/sfpse/sex/fellatio

Safer Sex With titles like "Hot and Safe: Warming Up to Latex" and "Safe Magic for Gay Men," this archive of articles pushes the positive side of safe(r) sex.
URL ftp://ftp.u.washington.edu/public/sfpse/safersex

Sex FAQ Of all frequently asked questions, those about sex are perhaps the most urgent and fascinating. What's a safe word? How can you practice sexual sorcery? Is it true that Barbra Streisand starred in a porn movie before she became famous? Browse this collection of sex-themed FAQs for infor-

mation about fetishes, bondage, and adult movies.
WEB http://www.cis.ohio-state.edu/hypertext/faq/usenet/alt-sex/top.html

The Sex Skill Men Really Love (and How to Do It Well) Call me naive, but I've always grouped *Redbook* with the likes of Martha Stewart, a world in which Ricki Lake seems risqué. That the ladies' mag endorsed this article on the quest for oral perfection is as astounding as the finished product is informative. For bona fide entertainment, witness the journalist walking that fine line between refinery and out-and-out smut. Case in point: "I took Marjorie, a 38-year-old mother of twins, to

THE MASTURBATION HOME PAGE

WEB http://www.neosoft.com/~mick/auto.html
picture: WEB http://ee.tut.fi/~no104956/sb.html
"This area is dedicated to what we all do, but don't talk about." Fed up with the spamming in the newsgroups, Mick set up this site for the collection of personal masturbation stories, not that

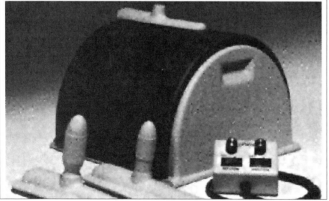

Location: http://ee.tut.fi/~no104956/sba.html

Syblan provides you the opportunity to be one of those consistently orgasmic women.

there's such a thing as impersonal masturbation stories. You'll find true tales from self-pleasuring guys and gals, the best of the alt.sex.masturbation newsgroup, the *Masturbation Newsletter*, and works of reader-submitted fiction bearing such curious titles as "A Good Hair Day" and "Suzanne and the Vacuuming."

dinner and waited patiently until we'd finished a glass of wine before blurting, 'Please tell me the secret to great oral sex!'" Actual advice runs the gamut from the subtle to the blunt. Unfortunately, the more specific tips are few and far between, and a bit too much is left to the imagination.
WEB http://homearts.com/rb/life /llsexsfl.htm

Sexual Positions That Work Best With Fat People From alt.sex.fat, this instructional essay is out to prove that size really doesn't matter. Hefty women can learn to use the missionary position without crushing their partners' little missionaries. They can also give and receive oral pleasure—although not without some logistical difficulty—and engage in creative sexual acts for which size doesn't matter.
URL ftp://ftp.u.washington.edu/public /sfpse/sex/fatposit

Toys & games

Adam and Gillian's Whips Adam and Gillian design good whips for "bad" people, or so the story goes. The whip-wielding couple have earned kudos from sensual shoppers around the world and have been featured on HBO's *Real Sex 6*. Cats, floggers, and tresses are custom-made to suit any pain quotient.
URL ftp://ftp.u.washington.edu/public /sfpse/catalogs/adamgil

Penis Enlargement Pump Be the talk of the locker room with

Dr. Joel Kaplan's Penis Enlargement Vacuum Pump. According to the good doctor, "The process for penis enlargement via the vacuum pump is medically referred to as hyperemiation. Individuals have been using vacuum devices for penis and scrotum enlargement for centuries. However, vacuum pump methods are now finally being recognized as an effective and sage method for penis enlargement." Big words from a big man.
WEB http://www.gayweb.com/406 /kaplan.html

Sex Games Tired of Trivial Pursuit? Frankly bored by Monopoly? Swingers and the wife-swapping derbies may belong to an earlier era, but why limit your retro fashion to bell bottoms and guitar rock? This informative page is based on the sagacious assumption that "some group sex events are best facilitated with some structure," and it is in this spirit that the party games are offered. With spaces on the board like "The Naughty Little Boy" and "The Sweet Candy," this game is not likely to be mistaken for the latest offering from Parker Brothers.
URL ftp://ftp.u.washington.edu/public /sfpse/sex/sexgame

Sybian A page dedicated to the Sybian Machine, the so-called "joystick extraordinaire." It's such a hard sell (ahem), that even if it doesn't induce you to shell out the big bucks for a chance to ride the vaginal stim-

ulator, you'll be cheering for the thousands of lonely housewives who do. You can read Jessica West's essay describing her introduction to the Sybian, a realistic rubber penis mounted on a vinyl seat, capable of rotating and gyrating at break-neck speeds, in no uncertain terms: "Just watching that thing gyrate made me instantly wet and horny." When the Sybian's inventor, David Lambert, asks the author if she'd like to take his machine for a test drive, the real fun begins.
WEB http://ee.tut.fi/~nol04956/sybian .html

Queer sex

alt.binaries.pictures.erotica .amateur.male Prudes beware. This is the place to download "Scans of my dick" and "mycock.jpg." If you prefer checking out somebody's lover over an airbrushed photo scanned from Honcho, check out this clearinghouse of amateur homemade porn photos.
USENET alt.binaries.pictures.erotica .amateur.male

alt.binaries.pictures.erotica.male Looking for pictures of a well-endowed cop? How about some homo high jinks in a dorm room? Maybe just a peek at Bruce Willis's private parts will satisfy your erotic online cravings. Both commercial and homemade male porn pictures are posted.
USENET alt.binaries.pictures.erotica .male

alt.binaries.pictures.lesbians
Whether this site is compromised of porn for lesbians or lesbian porn for straight men is open to debate—the voyeurism-for-straights quotient of photos like "My Wife in Black Teddy" and "Japanese School-teacher Duo" is suspiciously high—but those interested in downloading pictures of two women making the beast with two backs will find their El Dorado here.
USENET alt.binaries.pictures.lesbians

alt.personals.bi Gene, a fiftyish divorcee in the St. Louis area, wants to expand his horizons by tending to the homosexual fantasies that have been with him since his teens. Susan, a

self-professed "hardcore Brooklyn dyke," is looking for a submissive woman to serve her. And Andy in Seattle is sending out a call for any gay filmmakers interested in collaborating in art and life. This newsgroup provides a nation-wide network of personal postings for bisexual men and women. While some of the other personals sites tend toward the smarmy, alt.person-als.bi maintains a fairly high level of dignity and civility, and while most of the postings are from bisexual men and women seeking or responding to search parties, some of the messages are from curious het-erosexuals touring in the land of the polymorphous. If you're

unsure which way to swing, you'll probably want to let your pendulum pass through this newsgroup.
USENET alt.personals.bi

alt.sex.bears "To beard or not to beard" is the most common facial fur question in this dis-cussion group. Other topics include cross-dressing bears, bear code, and glossaries of handkerchief codes. Learn how to say "armpit freak," "hosting an orgy," and "new in town" with only three multicolored hankies in your back pockets. Or, just say "woof!" And while online, look for your daddy dream date, from the Gulf Stream waters to the New York island: "S.E. Tenn Cub ISO

 GOOD VIBRATIONS
WEB http://www.goodvibes.com
Magic wands, dildos, and pleasure nubs of all shapes and sizes—order your equipment from the infamous experts. You'll also find books and videos aplenty. For a little history, check out the Antique Vibrator Museum, with models dating as far back as the nineteenth century when genital

massage was used to treat hysteria in women. A tongue-in-cheek section on Famous Users asserts that Queen Victoria had to use a wooden-crank model while Virginia Woolf had the benefit of elec-tricity. "Is it not possible that the author had other things beside writing in mind when she spoke of women needing 'a room of one's own?'"

Daddy Bear For Fun" (south-eastern Tennessee cub in search of daddy bear for fun) is a typical post.
USENET alt.sex.bears

alt.sex.pictures.male Pictures of "White Muscle Studs," "Black Muscle Studs," "Hispanic Muscle Studs," and "Chris O'Donnell—Shirtless." Sigh.
USENET alt.sex.pictures.male

alt.sex.trans Moderate traffic, but with an unusual poignancy. Most of the postings, in fact, are cries for help—men who can't stop wearing their wives' clothes and can't stop worrying that they are consigning themselves to an afterlife filled with sulfur and brimstone. The group also serves as a forum for discussion of transsexual practices, and even accommodates the occasional personal ad.
USENET alt.sex.trans

Androgyny RAQ After beginning with a didactic digression about the difference between an FAQ (Frequently Asked Questions list) and RAQ (Rarely Asked Questions list), this document goes on to furnish a glossary for androgynes (those are "people whose biological sex is not readily apparent, whether owing to heredity or choice"). Learn about hermaphrodites, gender dysphoria, gender refuseniks, Necked cubes, and pre-operative Minnesotans.
WEB http://www.wavefront.com /~raphael/raq/raq.html

A Badpuppy walking the dog
http://badpuppy.com

Badpuppy Online Services "The total queer experience." If you're new and just checking things out you can gain access to the puppy pen for $5. You'll be able to browse through 3,000 Pictures, the Gay and Lesbian Travel Guide, G-Rated Pictures of the Badpuppy Models, and the Cool Links page. For once, being in the dog house will mean a step up—that's where you'll be if you pay $10 a month for full access. For that you'll get access to more than 400,000 pictures, an email account and a Web page on badpuppy.com, and free reign in the searchable indexes, databases, and personals.
WEB http://badpuppy.com

Euro Boybabes in Cyberspace
Jason Storm has amassed a collection of boy babes for your viewing pleasure. The Boybabes Gallery and Young and Hung are filled with thumbnail pics of male flesh which you can click on for a large(r) version. Hot fiction and videos keep you current on gay erotica in all its forms. And those having problems with their own boybabes can submit them by email for electronic counseling. Those seeking some all-American boybabes can link to the U.S. version here, too.
WEB http://www.boybabes.com

The Gay Male Paradise The cybercousin of Lesbian Lovers. At this XXX On-Ramp page, $10 buys you admission to view 100 hunks in various states—"sensual sex shots, solo shots, gang bangs, fisting, cum shots and whatever else you can imagine!"
WEB http://www.tppal.com/cgi-bin /gay.pl

GayWeb While the links here are not exclusively sexual, the

X-rated section is comprehensive and diverse, including everything from screensavers to video resources.
WEB http://www.gayweb.com/menu.html

Lesbian Lovers "Everything from soft, sensual kissing to hardcore anal fisting." For $10 you can download as many of the 100 pictures housed here as you can in 30 days. Straight males welcome, and expected.
WEB http://www.tppal.com/cgi-bin/les.pl

Lesbians of the Month Of course, nobody's fooling anybody: These extremely explicit, free photos of gorgeous women in graphic mid-coupling are not on anyone's gay agenda. That shouldn't discourage the straight male contingency from spending some serious ogle/download time of this page, though.
WEB http://www.inetnow.net/~happyman/lotm.htm

Men On The Net Looking for California Muscle? Home-grown-nude photos from exhibitionist men? How about semi-nude pics from underwear catalogues? Chris's list of nude male photo galleries on the Net will keep you downloading for hours. While the International Male photos can be accessed by anyone, the semi-explicit nude picture galleries require that you be at least 18 years of age.
WEB http://www.emailaddress.com/men

OLD MEANING OF THE TERM "GOOD VIBE"

What, you must ask, were these esteemed physicians doing with their vibrators? They were treating hysteria the most common health complaint among women of the day. While the existence of hysteria as a disease was debunked in the 1950s, medical experts from the time of Hippocrates up to the 20th century believed that hysteria expressed the womb's revolt against sexual deprivation. A woman's display of mental or emotional distress was a clear indication of her need for sexual release. Genital massage was a standard treatment for hysteria; its objective was to induce "hysterical paroxysm" (better known as orgasm) in the patient. Obviously such treatment demanded both manual dexterity and a fair amount of time, so turn of the century physicians were delighted with the efficiency, convenience and reliability of portable vibrators.

—from Good Vibrations

Nifty Alternative Sexualities Erotic Stories Archive This archive-on-the-run has resided in a variety of different locales before settling into its current home, the library of the Gay Cafè. Lesbian, bisexual, and, especially, gay stories are housed here, sorted by date and category, and culled from various erotica newsgroups. The diverse categories include "Incest," "Camping," "Authoritarian," "Military," and "Adult Youth."
WEB http://library.gaycafe.com/nifty

Resources for Bears Many bear techies are online, which means resources are plentiful for those interested in furry, cuddly men with beards. The site features a breakdown of the bear classification system, where you'll learn how to decipher codes for beard length, body hair, enthusiasm for groping, and ruggedness as well as links to Bear

Club home pages, the Bears in Movies list for filmographies of actor bears from James Brolin to Sebastian Cabot, and BearClipArt, too.
WEB http://www.skepsis.com/.gblo/bears/index.html

BDSM

alt.binaries.pictures.erotica.bondage Get tied up, beaten, dominated, and then get shot—but with a camera. This newsgroup collects images of trussed men and women.
USENET alt.binaries.pictures.erotica.bondage

alt.personals.spanking Jack in Oregon has enjoyed being spanked by his sex partners for as long as he can remember. Since his divorce, though, he can't find a woman who will redden his bottom, and Jack is despairing. "I am looking for a woman of any age in the Portland area for regular spanking experience, the more intense the better. I am willing to drive up to three hours." Although not everyone on alt.personals .spanking is as eager as Jack, all of the participants of this newsgroup find sexual pleasure in the act of spanking, and are trying to find others who share their predilection. Because this is a personals newsgroup, it doesn't offer a tremendous amount of insight into the erotic life of a spanker; most postings, in fact, are open invitations rather than confessions or anecdotes. The traffic is hot and heavy, though, and after a few minutes browsing, any would-be spankers or spankees will be absolutely slap-happy. **USENET** alt.personals.spanking

alt.sex.bondage FAQ From the basics of topping and safe words to the ins and outs of genitorture, this FAQ informs, explains, and debunks the cultural stigmas attached to the leather scene. **WEB** ftp://ftp.u.washington.edu/public /sfpse/bdsm/bdsmfaq

alt.sex.femdom The first newsgroup for dominant females, alt.sex.femdom serves as a meeting place of sorts. Want a submissive in the Seattle area? Interested in climbing aboard in Boston? In addition to wish lists, the newsgroup provides a forum for the pressing emotional and cultural issues facing femdoms in the nineties. **USENET** alt.sex.femdom

alt.sex.spanking If spankers and spankees decided to secede from the United States and create their own nation, alt.sex .spanking would be the first place to look for their Congress. Old and young, men and women, of all races, creeds and colors, the users of this newsgroup—with the acronym A.S.S.—share one passion: They like to take a slap across the bottom, or to dispense one to a willing partner. Sound fun? Come along. For a group with such a narrow focus, it has an unusually high rate of traffic, and there are brand-spanking-new insights each and every day. **USENET** alt.sex.spanking *FAQ:* **URL** ftp://ftp.u.washington.edu /public/sfpse/bdsm/asspfaq

S&M Bibliography A summer reading list for the S&M student, including works of fiction, how-tos, magazines, and criticism. **URL** ftp://ftp.u.washington.edu/public /sfpse/bdsm/smbib

Without Restraint... Online The home page of New York's Eulenspeigel Society (a non-profit organization interested in exploring "the erotic exchanges of power") explores all manners of consensual dominance and submission. With links to the S&M/Leather/Fetish Online Resources Directory, a calendar of S&M events, and an online edition of the organization's quarterly BDSM journal, this is a good place to visit for information on single-tail

whips and leather cabaret. **WEB** http://www.mcsp.com/tes /welcome.html

Fetish

alt.binaries.pictures.erotica.fetish Pictures of, by, and for foot fetishists, hair fetishists, shaving fetishists, and more. **USENET** alt.binaries.pictures.erotica .fetish

alt.sex.breast Subscribers to *Jugs* and other mammocentric magazines will love alt.sex .breast, an erotic newsgroup devoted entirely to the most conspicuous of all fetishes. Like 'em big? Like 'em small? Interested in learning the seven different kinds of nipples? While traffic is mostly male, a few women check in now and then to offer firsthand experience on the topic. **USENET** alt.sex.breast

alt.sex.enemas That's right. Never has the rear emetic been so celebrated for its erotic potential as in alt.sex.enemas, where the mostly middle-aged subscribers get together to trade stories and tips about rectal fluid injection. Unlike some other newsgroups, this one does not contain many old messages, and seems to be emptied out regularly. **USENET** alt.sex.enemas

alt.sex.fetish.diapers Have you ever made your wife wear Pampers all night long, and begged her to urinate into them rather than get up and go to the bathroom? No? Move along, then. Otherwise, slip out of those briefs and boxers and slip into something more disposable. Deftly combining excremental and infantile fetishes, diaper-wearing has a following that seems to be confined mostly to thirtysomethings—those with children, perhaps, reusing the material of their life for erotic purposes. As Simon, a straight Chicagoan who can achieve an erection only while wearing diapers, puts it, "There's nothing I like better than the freedom of a diaper: you can literally let it all hang out."

USENET alt.sex.fetish.diapers

FAQ: **URL** ftp://ftp.u.washington.edu/public/sfpse/fetish/inffaq

alt.sex.fetish.fashion FAQ Why was this newsgroup created? "To spread the knowledge about fetish fashion and dressing for pleasure; what it is, why we wear it, where to get it, and so on. To show that we're not perverts, weirdos, psychopaths, or worse, but only regular people with a special taste in clothing and/or footwear." Here you'll find answers to questions about the materials (leather, PVC, spandex, rubber); the shoes; the designers; and literature, comics, music, movies, and TV shows with fetish fashion elements.

URL ftp://ftp.u.washington.edu/public/sfpse/fetish/fashion

alt.sex.fetish.feet If you think that foot fetishists are relics of a bygone era, it's time to get in step. Whether spotting podiatric treats in centerfolds—check out the big toe on *Penthouse*'s Miss May!—or otherwise celebrating sole food, the participants in this newsgroup, mostly young men, do their best to sustain the cult of the foot.

USENET alt.sex.fetish.feet

alt.sex.fetish.hair A newsgroup that contains two newsgroups within it, alt.sex.fetish.hair caters both to those who experience orgasm while they are getting perms—a substantial percentage of the population,

THE STEAMROOM

WEB http://steam.creative.net

"For the man who wants to know where to meet men for sex," proclaims the opening page. In the Sex Spots Around the World section, users read the ins and outs of "getting it on" in various global locales. The tips themselves are sent in by readers, who, for one reason or another, are experts on the location in question. Of the Paradise Adult Boutique in Phoenix, Arizona, an anonymous writer

Location: http://steam.creative.net/

remarks: "In the mini-theater I watched, first, a fellow on his knees go down on five guys standing next to each other against a wall; then two other guys going down on each other in their seats." Other sections contain such articles as the subtly titled "The Whores of San Francisco." In the age of rampant STDs, The Steamroom is something of an anachronistic fossil. But you can't beat it for pure entertainment value.

apparently—and to those obsessed with body hair, pubic and underarm primarily. The body-hair contingent dominates the group, with plenty of requests for .GIFs of hirsute men and women and stories of ecstasy among the follicles. But it's the haircut segment that manages to provide the most interesting commentary, such as an extended discussion on the political and erotic effects of the Citadel's decision to order a crew cut for their groundbreaking but short-lived female cadet Shannon Faulkner.
USENET alt.sex.fetish.hair

Anime Picture Archive Not just your everyday anime page: This one allows you to preview .GIF and JPEG images from your fave Japanimation films via a slide show option that plays dozens of great stills until you've made your download decision. Also featured are updated hentai and manga news, FAQs regarding censorship, and a viewer feedback page. High quality all around.
WEB http://se.animearchive.org/index .html

Pervertual Reality Because one man's pleasure is another man's pain, and we are all vacillators on the Kinsey scale, Pervertual Reality celebrates the wide world of kinky pleasure. Includes detailed listings of web resources for BDSM, fetish fashion, fetish art and photography, scene-related events, "and other assorted kinky stuff."

Location: http://konpeito.bekkoame.or.jp/~adolf/web/boobs/pics/shinobu/frame/shih03.htm

That day at the beauty salon, things got a bit out of hand in the steam room
http://konpeito.bekkoame.or.jp/~adolf/web/home.html

WEB http://members.aol.com/ratch01 /index.html

TokyoTopless Yes, half of this is in Japanese, but this is such a strange page, we don't think subtitles would make a difference. What we could make out involved things like the "Tokyo Oddity Organization." "The Web Knows No Night," "Boobs Fetish" and enough bondage, big breasts, and just plain odd JPEGs (a close-up of some naked hands, for example) to make this a bafflingly erotic visit.
WEB http://konpeito.bekkoame.or.jp /~adolf/web/home.html

Polyamory

alt.personals.poly A catchall for personal ads: couples looking for bi women to complete threesomes, gay men looking for partners, married businesswomen itching to be scratched

at a conference. The clientele is nationwide and diverse, and consequently difficult to classify, but it seems to comprise roughly the same population as the alt.personals group. This is a smaller and less crowded version of the larger personals newsgroups.
USENET alt.personals.poly

Poly Replacing the triples list, Poly is an extremely high-volume mailing list for those interested in discussing extended, multi-adult, non-monogamous intimate relationships. According to the Poly Home Page, "it covers all the ground from polyfidelity (a closed, committed relationship in which the members do not have sex with outsiders) to polyamory (openly and honestly having more than one lover at a time, but allowing those lovers to have other lovers). The focus is on honest long-term relation-

ships rather than one-night stands, 'cheating' or 'swinging.'" At the home page, you can also access a glossary of polyamory terminology and a collection of posters' mini-biographies.
EMAIL listserv@lupine.org ✍ *Type in message body:* subscribe poly (your full name)
Info: **WEB** http://www.owlnet.rice.edu/~ert/poly

Exhibitionism & voyeurism

alt.sex.exhibitionism Not as single-minded as its name might indicate, alt.sex.exhibitionism is a grab bag of an erotic newsgroup, filled with assorted .GIFs, stories, and opinion pieces. Anything goes, really, from anecdotes of public sex to discussions of sex in movies. Dominated by male users, the group does have a small but steady lesbian membership (or are they?).
USENET alt.sex.exhibitionism

alt.sex.voyeurism If you're the kind of person who watches *Rear Window* for strategy, this sexually explicit newsgroup is the place for you. Alt.sex .voyeurism users—almost exclusively male and techno-obsessed—offer tips on wiretaps, review the pros and cons of bathroom video monitoring, recommend specific hotel rooms, and trade both stories of sexual espionage and erotic .GIFs culled from their excursions. If you're a woman, this newsgroup may be a source of some discomfort: Every time you shower or undress, it seems, some cybergeek has a lens trained on you from across the courtyard.
USENET alt.sex.voyeurism

V-Man's Voyeurism and Exhibitionism Pages Whether you're looking for exhibitionism ("Guy has his very cute younger cousin visiting from Alabama. Girl gets happy and on a whim the guy talks her into doing a little dance for his friends, one gets the camera! Good move. The young lady willingly agrees and puts on a cute spirited little show") or voyeurism

ALT.PERSONALS.BONDAGE

USENET alt.personals.bondage
picture: WEB http://www.lovecuffs.com/Products
Open the closet of this newsgroup, and you'll be confronted with rows and rows of straps and whips and studs. Lots of leather, doms seeking subs, couples interested in trying out tripartite

handcuffs with a willing third party. Despite the fairly diverse clientele—men and women, straight and gay, old and young alike—alt.sex.bondage somehow seems unified, and the massive amount of traffic— more than 100 new messages every day—has the unmistakable feel of a zeitgeist. Score another victory for the ties that bind.

("It's girl's night at a popular club and drinks for the girls are free. Sometimes the inexperienced young girls have a bit too much to drink and stagger out in the parking lot sometimes having to sit on the ground to collect their wits before attempting to drive. Well, all this makes for some great up-skirt opportunities"), you'll find the appropriately inappropriate images here. Also available are stories, links, archives, and video information.
WEB http://pages.prodigy.com/vman /index.htm

Magazines

alt.mag.playboy Despite occasional kamikaze raids by enraged women, this newsgroup is primarily devoted to the history of the magazine, pictorials, and even articles (seriously!). Get in a huff over Hef.
USENET alt.mag.playboy

alt.sex.magazines.pornographic There's a scene in a Woody Allen movie in which Woody is trying to buy a porn mag. Embarrassed, he sandwiches it between a pair of reputable magazines, only to have the cashier hold it aloft and bellow for a price check. That was the seventies. Now, in the nineties, porn mags seem sort of retro, trapped forever in the world of print. But as this newsgroup proves, plenty of publications are still flourishing despite the onrush of high-

tech erotica. And not just *Playboy* and *Penthouse*; in addition to these old standbys and their less reputable cousins (*Hustler, Swank*), there are dozens and dozens of less familiar offerings—*Leg Show, Red Muff*, and *Barely Legal*, just to name a few. Though the discussion of these periodicals is dominated by netboy libido, there's a decent amount of gay and lesbian traffic, and even a discussion over whether horny straight women should hone in on gay men's magazines. So before you go to the newsstand, do your research here.
USENET alt.sex.magazines.pornographic

Body Politic This British magazine toes the fine line between erotica and smut, with gender un-specific articles, art, and political dissemination of sexual mores. The latest issue deals with issues of sex and power, and includes articles on female domination, prostitution and pornography, and parenthood.
WEB http://the.arc.co.uk/body/home .html

CyberPorn (tm) Adult Online Magazine Conventional smut, at a lower cost than the old standards (*Playboy, Penthouse*, and *Hustler*), *CyberPorn* taunts and titillates with waist-up cutouts of the explicit photos available to subscribers. Back issues require a separate purchase, but with such artistic photos as Tonya receiving "critical care" from Nurse Dixie, there's no

question that *CyberPorn* is worth every penny.
WEB http://www.cyberporn.com

Eros The leggy, blonde Ankas of Norway have been the archetypal fodder for male masturbation fantasies for decades. Now, thanks to Eros, one doesn't have to fly KLM to make those dreams a semi-reality. This collection of Norwegian erotic magazines is raunchy, and users can access the majority for the price of an international phone call (to obtain a password). Although English translations are only offered for a few of the magazines, the pictures speak for themselves. From lesbians in leather to the playful girls in catsuits, there's a blonde beauty for every walk of life.
WEB http://www.eros.no/english.html

Hustler "'I hate coming home for summer break,' declares botany major Holly, lounging in a favorite secluded nook in her parents' estate." And before you know it, Holly is "thrust[ing] out her bottom, inviting cool water to splash against her little red berry." That's the way things go at *Hustler* online, the electronic version of wheelchair-bound pornographer Larry Flynt's smut mag. You'll have to join *Hustler* online, although membership will cost you ($30 for a three-month membership, $50 for a six-month membership, and $90 for a one-year membership). Drool away.
WEB http://hustler.onprod.com

Mrs. Silk's Magazine for Cross-dressers With its emphasis on humor and role-playing, this magazine is ruled by the fun-loving personality of its indomitable namesake, Mrs. Silk. The mistress entertains readers with stories of her recalcitrant maids and their punishments, as well the tales from her childhood with such titles as "Mummy, I Want to Be a Soldier." Fed-up mistresses can sign up for Mrs. Silk's comprehensive maid-training class.
WEB http://www.cityscape.co.uk/users/av73

Paramour Published in Cambridge, Mass., this magazine features erotic fiction and poetry ("a little cave to explore you come out happier for hav- ing been there"), as well as sponsoring live events, such as erotic-writing workshops.
WEB http://www.paramour.com

Penthouse Bob Guccione isn't just the father of Bob Guccione, Jr. He's also the publisher of *Penthouse*, the *Time* of monthly men's magazines. With an extensive online edition that includes pictorials and the Penthouse Forum— renowned for its hold over the masturbatory fantasies of teen-age boys across the world— this site brings new meaning to the phrase "objectifying women for financial gain."
WEB http://www.penthousemag.com

Playboy Pictures, the *Playboy* cartoon, and even download-able *Playboy* software—includ- ing an archive of *Playboy* interviews, a *Playboy* address book, and the Women of Playboy multimedia screensaver (a.k.a. the Instant Sexual Harassment Suit Kit). For an especially emotional experience, read the philosophy of the Playboy Foundation: "Playboy Enterprises, Inc. is committed to protecting and enhancing the American principles of personal freedom and social justice."
WEB http://www.playboy.com

Erotica

alt.binaries.multimedia.erotica Straight guys and lesbians get erotic video ya-yas here. MPEG B-movie shower scenes and files called "Gigantic Breasts" are the order of the day here. You can even down-

POLYAMORY INDEX
WEB http://www.PlayCouples.com/
picture: WEB http://www.hal.com/~landman/Poly
If you're driven by the belief that sexual love is a powerful force that can't (and shouldn't) be contained within a monogamous relationship, then you're probably feeling your polyamorous oats. Use this site to research how you can sow those oats—and while you're at it, consult the polyamory

FAQ, as well as a list of polyamory-themed organizations, books, magazine articles, movies, and even songs (Prince's "When You Were Mine," John Mayall's "So Hard to Share," and more).

load "Anything You Want." Download all forty parts of "The Nurse" or the single file "Ex-Wife With Bottle in Butt." If your porn tastes match the above, you'll have a field day here.
USENET alt.binaries.multimedia.erotica

alt.binaries.pictures.erotica* Get your pictures here! In the world of Usenet, there are few groups as well-traveled as the alt.binaries.pictures* hierarchy? Why? Well, it's cool to click on a button and watch your computer retrieve an image of a rocketship, or Homer Simpson, or Leonard Nimoy. But let's not be naive about this—there's no picture like an erotic picture. Whether your tastes run to bestiality, blondes, or nude supermodels, there are plenty of softcore and hardcore pictures online, waiting to be downloaded, unencoded, and viewed to your heart's content. Groups with a "d" at the end signify a forum for discussing pictures.
USENET alt.binaries.pictures.erotica*

alt.sex.stories These mostly anonymous postings aren't very different from the Penthouse Forum—there are plenty of camp-counselor stories and sensuous usherettes. Every once in a while, however, an erotic fiction will distinguish itself with such stunningly bad taste that it instantly acquires the feeling of a classic.
USENET alt.sex.stories

alt.sex.stories.bondage The parenthetical notations will let you

know whether this is the place for you: (m/f, f/f, bondage, d/s, paddling, femdom), (mff, light bondage, blindfold, femdom), and (femdom, mff, anal, spanking). Bad boys and girls swap stories here.
USENET alt.sex.stories.bondage

Erotic Literature If you don't want to pay for access to the stories here available "for as little as 25 cents a day" (the same amount you send off to Sally Struthers' starving children), the "wettest spot on the Web" also links to like-minded sites such as Erotic Stories, The Sandmutopian Garden, and Yellow Silk. Guest features here include a bulletin board classifieds page and a collection of free adult files.
WEB http://www.websplash.com /pages/LINK/eroticlit.html

Jimka's Archive of M/M Spanking Stories "Tommy, you've been a very naughty boy. Go to your room and wait for your father...." And that's just from the introduction.
WEB http://agora.rdrop.com/~jimka /spank.html

Interactivity

Hardcore Sex Den If you thought America had a monopoly on the entrepreneurial spirit, think again. Once upon a time, a group of lovely "girls" were working as phone-sex performers in Europe, but the money wasn't good enough. An idea, some backers, and voila! They now have their own site on the

Internet, and spend their days chatting with nice "studs" from around the world. Click on the girl (or, in the case of Jasmine and Lena, girls) of your choice to access their personal phone number. The cost is the price of an international phone call.
WEB http://www.escape.com/~jaf /sexden

HotCat Live Video Conferencing If seeing these strippers in real time, real audio, and real color is enough to convince you they really like you, then HotCat Live is for you. Download the software and talk to your own live private dancer for a mere six dollars a minute and a one-time set-up fee of $9.95.
WEB http://www.hotcat.com/hotcat /guest/hotcat_video.html

LaToya Jackson Dreams If Michael Jackson is the King of Pop, his psychically connected sister is the undisputed Queen of Infomercials. In a family of UFO abductees, LaToya may very well have spent the most time under the alien scalpel. With her wide-eyed Stepford stare and plastic skin, LaToya is a vital part of the Jacksons' quest for world domination. Her position as psychic firmly established, she has now set her sights on the world of Internet smut. LaToya Jackson Dreams, as featured on *The Howard Stern Show*, exemplifies one of many creative ways the Internet has found to further the disembodiment of the female body by the male gaze. Contact the models via

modem, pay a ridiculous sum of money, and watch them on your monitor as they perform live. "We'll do anything you tell us," the girls promise. Even moonwalk naked?
WEB http://www.foreplay.com/Latoyal

SmutLand It ain't Disneyworld. At this virtual adult theme park, "ride" takes on a whole new meaning. Describing itself as the "pig-butt nastiest place on Earth," SmutLand offers live shows, discount shopping, movies and more. And the price of admission is $14.95 a month, a bargain compared to traditional amusement park options.
WEB http://www.smutland.com

Vegas Live Ariel, Jazmine, Chantal, and the other show-girls all have personal pages here for you to preview before you decide to become a member. See the dancers live through the cameras installed at Showgirl Video on the strip or get down and dirty with them via the PC-only one-on-one software offered here. It's $4.99 per minute for an explicit nude dancer and $6.99 per minute for a fea-tured porn star or a two girl show.
WEB http://vegaslive.com/live.html

Images

Alley Katz Online! Owned and operated by porn superstars Janine, Ashlyn Gere, Victoria Paris, and Christy Canyon, Alley Katz Online is a paid

membership page, but offers "censored" hardcore film JPEG clips on a cursory browsing basis. Nothing new here, but very high-quality design, and, of course, naked and very involved females.
WEB http://www.alleykatz.com/home.html

Danish Erotica Get four free samples of hardcore porn here. For the great Danes in all their glory, you'll need a "key" and that'll cost you $10 a month.
WEB http://www.danisherotica.com

Perverted Palace Residing at the Perverted Palace are images of all ilk, including those of les-bians, oral and anal sex, Asian beauties, masturbation, straight sex, fisting, and watersports. Adult links lead to such lascivi-ousness as Pure Perversion, the Little Black Book, and The Bung Hole.

WEB http://www.ingenue.com/pinkpalace/pervert.htm

Slick Chick "I love it when guys and girls tell me what turns them on!" announces this notably un-shy redhead. As if you'll miss the evidence: The top page alone has about six remarkably revealing images of this enthusiastic amateur, along with membership in her per-sonal fan club, links to pal's pages, and, well, more. Like watching your girlfriend's odd, older sister.
WEB http://web.demon.co.uk/slikchic/slick.html

Movies

The Adult Film Database Search this database of more than 9,000 porno flicks by director, stars, or title. Note: Don't be frightened off if the listing states that the performers are

No honey—I said get the vibrator—not the Epilady—oh hell, this will do
http://www.CityScape.co.uk/users/av73

bald—that simply means they are sans pubic hair.
WEB http://homepage.eznet.net /~rwilhelm/asm/dbsearch.html

Adult Movie Reviews A master index of the three major adult movie review sites: The Bio Keeper Archives, Heretic's Adult Movie Site, and The Director's Site. Most use the Imperial Scale—anything below 2 "sucks," anything higher than 3.5 is a keeper, and a 4 is impossible for anything later than 1984.
WEB http://w3.gti.net/director/reviews /all/index.html

alt.sex.movies A recent tour of this site revealed that alt.sex .movies is primarily concerned with Net censorship, finding the Lord Jesus Christ, and where to get the best snuff movies. For those interested in sex at the movies, the site offers quick, helpful answers to questions such as "Has Heather Locklear ever done any nude scenes?" and "Where can I find videos of lactating women?" (*Battle of the Ultra Milkmaids* was one suggestion.) Then there are the Lolita posts that have launched a thousand *Oprahs*. Like "The Young-Girl Watcher's Movies & Ratings," which gives four stars to the young Drew Barrymore's *Firestarter*—"Grips the heart of the girl-watcher through exceptionally arousing and memorable scenes."
USENET alt.sex.movies
FAQ: WEB http://w3.gti.net/director /faqindex.html

This star is porn
http://www.wco.com/~grubenst/ron

The Bare Facts Homepage Looking for nude scenes from your favorite actor or actress? The *Bare Facts Video Guide* helps you locate celebrity nude scenes on video. You'll have to pay for the actual guide, but at this site you can find out which Academy Award nominees have appeared in the buff (Susan Sarandon—yea, Anthony Hopkins—nay), and read the tip of the week and upcoming video releases and scenes to watch for.
WEB http://www.barefacts.com /~chosoda

My Favorite Links to Porn Stars These are a few of his favorite links. When the dogs bite, when the bees sting, when he's feeling sad. He simply clicks on Lori Michaels, Marilyn Star, or Brandy Alexanders, and then he doesn't feel so bad.
WEB http://www.atnet.at/club/jkuhs /links/links.htm

Ron is God, and God is Ron Anecdotes, quotes, and a filmography for Ron "Hedgehog" Jeremy, the magnetic star of more than 1,000 adult-rated films—including *The Flintbones*. He's even been in a few legitimate Hollywood movies, such as *52 Pick-Up* and *Killing Zoe*.
WEB http://www.wco.com/~grubenst /ron

❝ Swingers and the wife-swapping derbies may belong to an earlier era, but why limit your retro fashion to bell bottoms? ❞

Hobbies

WHEN YOU'RE NOT ONLINE, WHAT ELSE IS THERE TO DO? GET ONLINE AND FIND OUT

EVERYONE KNOWS THAT KIDS are supposed to play—it keeps them physically and mentally healthy, stimulates their growth, and all that. But what about adults? With the increasing Dilbertization of corporate America, we've got hardly any recess time. All the same, hobbies—from traditional (collecting, sewing, modeling) to not-so traditional (armor, contortionism, homebrewing)—seem to be as popular, and diverse, as ever. In fact, the hobbies scene is one of the most prolific subsections of Net activity. Fine craftsmanship, a desire to push oneself to the limit, that quest for the perfect piece to augment a collection—all these things rate quite high in bandwidth among folks who share a common passion. So if you have a hobby to which you already devote your free time, or if you're merely looking for a new place to play, your every desire will be satisfied online.

Location: http://www.webpress.net/skybox/cardprod/flusab/usab.html

Fleer USA Basketball

Release Date: June 19
- 52-card regular set.
- Cards will come three cards to a pack–two Flair-quality cards and one lenticular card (like the Hot Numbers insert card for $4.99).

HOBBY CENTRAL
AMERICA ONLINE *keyword* hobby
picture: WEB http://www.webpress.net/skybox
Just about every pastime, craft, hobby, interest, and passion is represented here, somewhere. From antiques to writing, and plenty in between, the busy mini-forums (and some not so mini) gather everything related under AOL's sun and offer plenty of opportunities to reach out and touch a fellow hobbyist. This is exactly the kind of connection that AOL does well: productive discussions among people with something in common.

CLICK PICKS

Starting points

The Exchange It's linked from Hobby Central, but the Exchange is such a unique feature of the AOL hobbyist's experience that it merits special mention. Skip the more general areas like Home & Career or Communities, and go straight to your very own Collector's Corner and Crafts Niche, or try Interests and Hobbies, and Outdoor Fun. Under Collector's Corner, for example, is a discussion area for every collectible under the sun, including dolls, antiques, stamps, coins, and baseball cards. The libraries (one for each topic) feature news articles, software, and lists of people's collections. Sales offers are noticeably absent, and in fact prohibited. **AMERICA ONLINE** *keyword* exchange

Hobbies A popular section of the overarching Home & Leisure section of CompuServe, Hobbies is home to dozens of message boards on topics from astronomy to photography. Some of the areas listed are forums in their own right, while others exist merely as subsets of Hobbies. **COMPUSERVE** *go* hobbies

HobbyWorld Proving once again that the world unconsciously strives toward self-organization, this list of indexes represents a pretty good attempt to link up every hobby on the Web. Each hobby links to a hubsite with links to everywhere. Many of the hubsites chosen aren't necessarily the best, but the idea is excellent. **WEB** http://www.hobbyworld.com

Amateur radio

CB Radio Resources on the Net "Convoy" may be a fading moldy oldie, but the CB craze continues in fine fettle, based on the evidence in this seemingly dashed-together, but exhaustive resource page. Being a sort of punk rock of the communications field—respondents have names like "Red Devil" and "Dynamite Kid"—and with no federal regulations (unlike, say, the Internet), there's a refreshingly rebellious attitude running through these pages. **WEB** http://www.ultranet.com/~bellvill /cb

N2FXZ's Links Page A virtual valentine to the ham radio life, based in Rockland county, New York (and complete with a map of the area). Though still laced with humor, this links page has a serious side; its creator lists affiliation with ham radio organizations RACES, SkyWarn Crystal Radio Club, W2DMC, The Rockland Repeater Association, the NorthEast Digital Association (NEDA), and the American Radio Relay League (ARRL). Of interest to the cyber-browser are a set of links where ham meets Net on pages such as the W2DMC Packet BBS, and The Digital Modes. **WEB** http://www.j5l.com/~richard /hamlinks.html

WWWVirtual Library: Amateur Radio Software downloads, training, interactive technical help, news on FCC regulations, worldwide disaster information: If you're an amateur radio enthusiast, this library page probably has what you need. Created and supported by the American Radio Relay League, the "principal representative of the Amateur Radio Services [in the U.S.], serving members by protecting and enhancing spectrum access and providing a national resource to the public." Combine the aforementioned attributes with near-endless links and you have all the data a (near) literal wire-head could desire. **WEB** http://www.meaning.com /pointers/wwwvl-ham.html

Armor

The Arador Armour Library Some like to make armor, some like to collect it, and others just find the topic interesting. All types, though, will appreciate this comprehensive site, with its facts about armor, pictures of armor, glossary of armor terms, and a daily-updated message board, mostly about construction. **WEB** http://darkstar.swsc.kl2.ar.us /~davidc

Rapier Armor Construction When the Vikings have you pinned and the Celts are at your back, you'll need to protect yourself with a good suit of armor. After all, you wouldn't want to rip a strip in your

chain mail when you bend over to run a fallen foe through, would you? That would be, well, unseemly. Full instructions for constructing a Gaul-proof garment for those simulated battles are here.
WEB http://macl.byte.uh.edu/john/sca /A&S/Rapier.armor.html

Therion's Medieval Arms and Armors Page Care to see what a German Gothic harness circa 1480 was all about? You can and you will, and you'll also view pictures and read descriptions of every kind of armor or weapon imaginable that was made anywhere in the world.
WEB http://www.io.com/~therionl /armor.html

Astronomy

....

AstroWeb When you wish upon a star, it makes no difference where you are. But when you're wishing upon astronomy Net sites, it makes all the difference in (or out of) the world. Weave your way through AstroWeb, which links to Internet astronomy resources of all types—Web sites, gophers, telnet sites, FTP sites, and Usenet newsgroups.
WEB http://marvel.stsci.edu /net-resources.html

The Astronomy Club The sky's the limit for amateur astronomers. The Sky at a Glance and Planet Roundup tell you what to look for in the skies

each week, an FAQ covers everything from "What's the Best Telescope?" to "How do I buy a star?" The discussion board contains active debates on everything from the Big Bang Theory to black holes to supernovas.
AMERICA ONLINE *keyword* astronomy

Cybersky Planetarium Through the magic of shareware, transform your computer screen into a planetarium. This desktop version of the real thing goes it one better though, allowing you to compress days, weeks, and months into minutes, enabling the studious stargazer to learn things about astronomy that would normally require days or weeks of

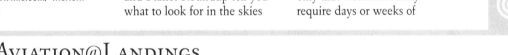

AVIATION@LANDINGS
WEB http://www.landings.com/aviation.html
picture: WEB http://acro.harvard.edu/IAC/images.html
Other aviation sites point to this one as the biggest and best—Aviation@Landings points to every other aviation site. The site's maintainers claim that they "will connect you to virtually every lift-

Location: http://acro.harvard.edu/IAC/images/super_st_600x476.gif

generating Web site on the Net." And while that may seem overwhelming, it's a hobbyist's dream, and the good organization keeps the confusion to a minimum. Use the search engine to find facts and data in the several databases maintained here, or simply visit the directory for the zillions of links under every topic from aerobatics to weather.

SEAM STRESS

The scariest problem that I have encountered as a rapier marshal has been related to improper armor construction. Unfortunately, most fighters do not know how their armor is put together. In one instance, a fighter was showing off his new armor, and when I looked at it, I saw daylight through one of the side seams. On another instance, I was transfering a set of loaner armor from the washing machine to the drier when the side seam opened up like a zipper. I decided that there had to be a better way to build rapier armor. The method I use has several advantages over other methods of construction I have seen. The first is that the seam has 4 layers of coverage at all points. Second, any stress that the seam encounters is distributed across two or more separate lines of stiches. Finally, the seam lays flat due to a minimal amount of bulk at the seam.

—from Rapier Armor Construction

stargazing or repeat trips to a planetarium to observe.
WEB http://www.astro.ucla.edu/staff /stephen/cybersky.html

Pulsar's Cool Links Solar systems and planets, astronomical societies, planetariums, observatories, comet and meteor watches: This link page runs the extraterrestrial gamut with hundreds of quick-loading links.
WEB http://www.users.dircon.co.uk /~jmwebb/links.htm

sci.astro.amateur What's the best beginner's book on astronomy? Where can I find good shareware? What kind of telescope should I buy? This is a user-friendly source of starting points for beginning amateur astronomers, as well as a thriving community for more seasoned star gazers.
USENET sci.astro.amateur

Aviation

The Aviation Home Page As comprehensive as an aviation index can be and then some, the Aviation Home Page will satisfy the desires of any aviation hobbyist. Categories from academies to weather include hundreds of links, and the entire database is searchable. Check out the classifieds, or even link to an aviation poem or two.
WEB http://www.avhome.com

Aviation Web This Web index for aviation enthusiasts is less intimidating than some of the others. It's also very elegant, with an attractive map background, and a nice use of frames to assist with the visual hierarchy. The content is just as pleasing—with links to airlines, flight schools, products and supplies, a photo gallery, and other categories, the Aviation Web certainly ranks as one of the most comprehensive aviation indexes on the Internet.
WEB http://members.aol.com /framehtml/incoming/avweb.html

Homebuilt Homepage Some hobbies are relatively low-stakes—after all, it's difficult to cause major damage as a doll collector. But to make an aircraft in the garage and then fly in it, well, you've really got to trust your own handiwork. This site is for people who enjoy the pastime of homebuilt aircraft and provides lots of leads for builders looking for plans, kits, vendors, clubs, and links to other relevant sites. It's a good starting point for, or worth looking into even if the homebuilt aircraft are stacking up in the tool shed already.
WEB http://www.azstarnet.com /~cmddata/homebuilt

Hot Air Balloon World Grab your sandbags, picnic basket, and your binoculars when you visit this Hot Air Balloon page. Venture to the International Balloon Fiesta in Albuquerque, N.M. and break out the champagne with other hot air balloon enthusiasts. Feel like piloting your own balloon? Inquire at the Foolish Gypsy Balloon section (of course, expect to have about $30,000 lying around). Is the basket on your balloon wearing out? Or maybe you need a more powerful burner. Buy them or exchange info with other airheads. It'll take less than 80 days to peruse the hot air balloon worldwide events section. Also, you might celebrate your anniversary or birthday with a champagne balloon ride for two.

WEB http://www.apci.net/~wag

Birding

Bird Song "Gulp-a-pump!" That's what the American Bittern has to say for itself. And the Brown Thrasher, who obviously works for the government, says, "Drop-it, drop-it, cover-it-up, cover-it-up!: This according to birdsong lover Tom Lorenzin, who is responsible for this method of nomenclature, and says that identifying bird calls is at least as interesting as spotting the little buggers themselves.

Dozens of birds (and their anglicized songs) are listed here, all for free—and that's as "cheep" as things get!

WEB http://www.1000plus.com /BirdSong/birdsong.htm

GeoGraphical Birding Guide Whether you'd like to know about the birds in your backyard or are planning a birding trip elsewhere in the United States or Canada, this site may prove helpful. Click on the map and transport yourself to a local or state birding home page for that area. While not all states and territories are covered, it's much quicker than scrolling through an index.

WEB http://www-astronomy.mps.ohio -state.edu/~ignaz/birds/ABA/ABA.html

GORP—Birding Great Outdoor Recreation Pages (GORP) hosts this guide to birding spots, books, trips, clubs, and more in an attractive format. Featured birding spots link to regional Web sites from Kenya to Massachusetts. Safaris, tours, and birding trips of all kinds (have you ever bird-watched while whitewater rafting?) are indexed here, along with other people's birding sites 'round the Web.

WEB http://www.gorp.com/gorp /activity/birding.htm

The Virtual Birder An online magazine that doesn't fail to remind that "Real birds beat virtual birds anyday." The Virtual Birder is, nonetheless, full

BIRDING ON THE WEB

WEB http://compstat.wharton.upenn.edu:8001/~siler/birding.html

The wise old owl greeting visitors to this site accurately advertises the incredible wealth of intelligence available here. Not an expert yet? No need to hide your head in the sand. This site can help; it is by far the best birding site on the Web, with its **FAQs**, archives of birding mailing list chats, and a complete online version of the Sibley-Monroe bird classification system. If that's not enough, Birding on the Web compulsively links to what simply has to be every possible bird-related site including clubs, exhibits/reviews, geographic regions, and bird families.

Location: http://compstat.wharton.upenn.edu:8001/~siler/birdpix/rdegret.jpg

of good information. Several "On Location" features make birdwatching a Web sport, as they link to featured locales and incorporate pictures and sound clips to emphasize the avian characteristics of the region. "Rants and Raves" reviews other birding Web sites.
WEB http://www.virtualbirder.com /vbirder

Blacksmithing

ABANA: Artist-Blacksmiths' Association of North America Artistic metalwork is the focus of this organization and its home page, focusing on education and the preservation of the craft of its members. Includes an online gallery of works, info on ABANA's international Conference in 1998, and links to local chapters.
WEB http://sunsite.unc.edu/abana /mainindex.html

AFC Blacksmithing Tips A veritable "Hints from Heloise" for blacksmiths. Maybe you need that nifty torch holder or need a way to make your L6 blade cut straight again. Turn those used golf balls into file holders or learn better ways of marking steel than soapstone. Formulas for square and round collaring and ways of determining metal hardness are explained. Create your own rust and copper sulfate patinas and find out what these patinas are anyway. Readers can submit their own tips and have them posted.
WEB http://www.the-matrix.com/afc /tips.html

Collectibles

A-Z Antiques and Collectibles Directory This is, without doubt, the best index available for antique and collectible sites on the Web. Dozens of categories are listed in a style that blatantly, but skillfully, copies Yahoo's organization system and is similarly searchable. The site claims to have more than 1,500 links, and although the small type may hurt the eyes, the sound of that big number is music to the ears.
WEB http://www.eskimo.com/~pither /Web_Directory

Antique Link Can a site that lists more than 33,000 antique dealers possibly be good? Well, of course it can! Especially since you can search by state and then city, making it unnecessary to travel far to find a squirrel-shaped cookie jar or a silver brooch from the Regency period. An online catalog of available pieces is searchable by type of object.
WEB http://www.antiquelink.com

Antiques, Art & Preservation This source of articles and advertisements about the finer things in the world of antiques will be helpful for those who are serious (read: rich) collectors of valuables. For those who only like to window-shop at auctions, and can only dream of Fabergé and early Americana, here's more fuel for the fire of longing. The editors' credentials are impeccable—dropping names like Sotheby's and the National Trust for Historic Preservation—and the free articles, while not exactly plentiful, are very well-written.
WEB http://www.monka.com/antiques

Collecting Where can you go on AOL to actually purchase collectibles from salt shakers to pirate's gold? Where can you talk to people sharing your passion? Start at the Collecting forum, and take a trip to Collectibles Online, a nifty little online catalog of items for sale, or to other related forums (Comics, Stamps, etc.) on AOL. Plus, link to Collector's Corner at the Exchange or AOL-sanctioned Web sites.
AMERICA ONLINE *keyword* hobby → Collecting

rec.collecting* The mother group in the rec.collecting family is, of course, rec.collecting, and it's generically described as a "discussion among collectors of many things." Those bland words can't begin to describe the colorful marketplace atmosphere of all these groups, where everything is collected and everything is for sale. In fact, these groups often resemble nothing more than the classifieds section of a collectibles magazine. However, there is time for questions, answers, and above all, enthusiasm. Besides rec.collecting, the family includes rec.collecting.cards .discuss, rec.collecting.coins, rec .collecting.dolls, rec.collecting .stamps, and several in the rec.collecting.sport category.
USENET rec.collecting*

Contortionism

The Contortionists Home Page So, you want to be a contortionist. This page will either spur you on to acrobatic greatness or completely deter you from pursuing your dream. Why people enjoy watching other people bend their bodies unnaturally remains a mystery, but contortionism, done right, is not really as dangerous or painful as it appears. This site contains several articles on the art of bending and some additional literature on training techniques—contortionism, not surprisingly, doesn't come naturally. There are also resources and contacts, links to other contortionism sites, and photos of contortionists in multitudi-

nous bizarre poses.
WEB http://www.escape.com/~silverbk/contortion

Elainilee's Image Index This non-fancy site bends over backwards to give you images (most from video captures, so not of the highest quality) of female contortionists. They come from such far-off places as *Star Search*, vaudeville, and the Miss America Pageant. When you've seen them all, take a trip to some truly twisted sites elsewhere.
WEB http://members.aol.com/eyetreats/index.html

Cooking

Electronic Gourmet Guide Twelve recipes under "Tomatoes"

alone—the Electronic Gourmet Guide, or eGG as it's usually known, is chock-full of helpful advice. Regular columns like The Culinary Cyber-Sleuth add some spice, and quickies like a food trivia game and a section called Toasts & Quotes make it just like a "real" magazine. The eGGbasket is nice to visit, too—it's an online gourmet store.
WEB http://www.2way.com/food/egg/index.html

Everything Edible! There are plenty of ways to go from this yummy AOL forum. But the real meat, no pun intended, is the AOL Cookbook. More a group of message boards for chef-to-chef chat than an actual cookbook, the Cookbook is

Learn About Antiques & Collectibles
WEB http://www.ic.mankato.mn.us/antiques/Antiques.html

If you've just stumbled upon your first piece of McCoy or Roseville, or you found an old poster in the attic and want to know if it's a collectible—in short, if you are seeking to learn more about the often complex world of the antique and collectibles market, this makes an excellent place to start.

Location: http://www.ic.mankato.mn.us/antiques/furniture/victorian.html

Victorian Furniture

A simple index of categories like Decoratives or Toys and Games links to descriptions and pictures of the types of these items to be found at an auction or dealer store, and often lists highly popular brand names. When you've decided to commit, you'll find plenty of good advice on how to deal with the dealers.

divided into eight sections from Appetizers, Soups, and Snacks to Low Fat/No Fat. Within each section are tens of thousands of messages on every topic imaginable ("SERIOUS FONDANT TROUBLES," shrieks one post) or unimaginable, plus what seem like millions of recipes. Let's hope you're looking for something specific; the cookbook isn't searchable.
AMERICA ONLINE *keyword* food

Gemini and Leo's Meal-Master Software and Recipes If you like more recipes than a little plastic box could ever hold, you'll like the Meal Master shareware (download now, pay later) and the 50,000-plus free recipes that come with it This little program is searchable by ingredient (hungry for artichokes? andouille?), creates shopping lists, and automatically converts ingredient measures. Owners can input their own recipes, and entire mailing lists are devoted to the exchange of Meal Master recipes. One drawback, though: There's no Mac version (none is planned) and the DOS format is, of course, not as popular these days. However, they claim that SoftWindows can run it on a Mac, and that it runs just fine in a DOS window in Windows.
WEB http://www.synapse.net/~gemini /mealmast.htm

Mama's Cucina This award-winning Ragu Web site mixes the best of the old country and the

The Contortion Home Page

This page is dedicated to the wonderful art of Contortion.

Ula - *"How does she do that?"*
Click here or on photo to download an
800x600x24-bit JPEG of the above photo, 106k

Nothing to get bent out of shape about
http://www.escape.com/~silverbk/contortion

new country with a virtual tour of Manhattan's Little Italy, city guides for Italy's hot spots, lessons on Italian art and architecture, family stories gathered from visiting netsurfers, handy phrases translated into Italian, a kitschy Italian-American soap opera called *As the Lasagna Bakes*, and, of course what you're really looking for—a huge cookbook with all of Mama's favorite recipes. There's even a contest where pasta fans can win an all-expense-paid family reunion in the U.S. city of their choice.
WEB http://www.ragu.com

Vicki's Vast List: Food & Drink What's on Vicki's Vast List besides a penchant for alliteration? Why, huge numbers of links to recipes, FAQs, ethnic and vegetarian food sites, and even a dozen or so links to chile peppers and their fans.

Plus, Vicki invites you to visit her recipe collection, and download her converted *USENET Cookbook* to use as your very own.
WEB http://www.gulf.net/~vbraun/food .html

Electronics

Brett Bymaster Circuit and Software An earnest page for the electronics do-it-yourselfer. With easy-to-follow features on building thermostats, alarm clocks, a sound bus and the like, with matching schematics.
WEB http://expert.cc.purdue.edu /~bymas

Information Unlimited Rather loftily proclaiming itself to be "a corporation dedicated to the experimenter and technology enthusiast," this is more of a point-of-purchase page for all manner of unusual, weird, and

sometimes plain disreputable products ranging from tesla coils, tasers, "electronic hypnotizers," "brain controllers," and other "unique" devices. Still, with its animated graphics and febrile text, it's a sort of paranoid paradise, and lots of fun to browse.
WEB http://www.amazingl.com

Firewalking

Firewalking In a cleared wilderness area, a huge roaring fire is dying down, leaving coals glowing with heat in the 1200-degree Fahrenheit range. Suddenly, a group of people start walking on the burning embers, faces transfixed with, of all things, joy. "Just seeing someone walk the coals is a powerful transformative experience," claims the creator of this unique page, a confirmed and longtime firewalker. Whether you're a diehard walker or a newbie, this unique, eye-catching (lots of photos) page supplies plenty of FAQs, the history of F.I.R.E. (Firewalking Institute for Research and Education), tips on how to organize your own fire walk (groups range from 10-50 on the average), and animated chat between firewalking folk who walk the walk because it "builds confidence, lessens fear and creates a sense of transformation." But not all is spiritual sparks here, as one walker warns, "Use your head—firewalking is dangerous."
WEB http://heartfire.com/firewalk /homefire.html

Mastering the Fire Looking at the spiritual practice of walking barefoot over hot coals (meant as a form of transcendence), this is light on graphics, but filled with fascinating details. Culling seemingly divergent sources such as the bushmen of the Kalahari and the firewalkers of ancient Greece, this site explains firewalking in a scholarly but accessible tone, and includes some beautifully poetic bits that make this strange practice make more sense to the average person.
WEB http://www.hway.net/webwzrd /fire.html

Gardening

Cultural Practices in the Vegetable Garden Listing many, many public service links in a whole collection of gardening pamphlets, this page has a pile of practical information, from tips on Minimum Chemical Gardening—use compost, manure, and mulches for soil health; time plantings to avoid maximum insect hatch periods—to advice on managing weeds.
WEB http://www.ext.vt.edu/hort /consumer/pubs/300

The Garden Gate Retrofitted for those who don't know the difference between verbena and vervaine, the Garden Gate is a dummies' guide for first-time gardeners. The witty "Stop me before I kill again" is for those who swear that even a spider plant in the sun room isn't safe from their withering touch. There's a guide to botanical

correctness, detailing how to pronounce Latin plant names, as well as such oddities as a turnip FAQ. Things to do on a really rainy day when you've read every book in the house: Take a tour of Mike's Back Yard. A new, low-cost cure for insomnia.
WEB http://www.prairienet.org/ag /garden

Garden Scape A trove of resources for professionals to keep up on the latest happenings in the nursery, gardening, and landscape businesses. Scroll through Garden Scape informative pages to add to your list of arboreta and herbariums, bone up on how to grow cheeky strawberries, and find out the address of the succulent plant mall. During your off hours, relax and smell the flowers in a virtual tour of St. Thomas's flora, or volunteer your time to help rebuild Bosnia-Herzegovina with the botanically inclined.
WEB http://www.gardenescape.com

The Gardening Launching Pad A bed of more than 700 links, landscaped into well-ordered plots from organic gardening to cacti to butterflies, palms, and just regular tree-huggery. Dig in and join a rousing discussion on tree houses, read a recent issue of the *Arid Lands* newsletter, learn about the Hardy Palm International Organization, or discover how to grow beardless irises—is that a case of arresting development, maybe?
WEB http://www.tpoint.net/neighbor

GardenNet Tired of waiting in the baking sun at the local nursery and straining your back carting those dozens of marigolds to the car? Then order from this nursery in the sky, where you can also swap gardening pointers on new ways to repel rabbits (would you believe a bar of Irish Spring?) and share recipes on low-fat ways to eat a daylily (toss with mescaline and vinaigrette). But before you stuff your shopping cart with plumeria and ginger, remember this motto: "Treat the Goddess like a modest fair, Not overdress, nor leave her wholly bare."
WEB http://trine.com/GardenNet

International Bonsai Guide Bonsai is not just the art of growing very small trees: It's a way of life. Scanning the month-by-month breakdown of the tasks associated with bonsai in the site's calendar, it becomes obvious: There's no rest for either the wicked or the bonsai enthusiast. The links to other bonsai sites and FAQs should help to alleviate some of the pain.
WEB http://www.idiscover.co.uk /bonsai

Internet Bonsai Club What are bonsai? The USDA's answer is simple: Bonsai are miniature trees grown in pots. But there's clearly something more to the pruning and shaping of these tiny trees than meets the eye. Both the practical and aesthetic aspects of this Japanese horticultural art form are considered

at this online club. Learn how to deal with *kannuki-eda* (an ugly branch that must be cut off) and achieve *ko-eda* (very graceful limbs); maybe someday you too can display your beautiful bonsai for at this page, for all the world to see.
WEB http://www.pass.wayne.edu/~dan /bonsai.html

rec.gardens A newsgroup heading with quite a few sub-heads, this is well-tilled territory with active participants who lift the civility level above that sometimes found at other less-cultivated locations. The news, advice, and general information ranging from beginner to expert levels, and people seem to be genuinely interested in answering help posts.
USENET rec.gardens

Yesterday's Rose The site contains illustrations and descriptions of numerous old and old-fashioned rose varieties, including details of scent, flower, growth, and culture. Click onto a thumbnail-sized picture of the Tea Rose, for example, and get a detailed history and a blown-up photo. To get even further detail, choose the list of specific varieties for another photo and a detailed history. Using the Rosefinder, you can locate a list of rose varieties, given such particular criteria as roses that will grow and bloom in as little as five hours of direct sunlight, or apricot- and buff-colored roses. Every rose name on the list brings you to a photo of

that flower, along with its history and growing characteristics. The page links to other rose-related sites.
WEB http://www.halcyon.com/cirsium /rosegal/welcome.htm

Handwriting analysis

Doodles The next time your best friend is yammering endlessly on the phone to you about nothing, look down at your hands. What is that random, desperate doodle saying about you? If it's a cat, you like to defend others. If it's a bus, you desperately need a vacation. All the way from Israel comes this fascinating look at the real reason you're wasting those trees.
WEB http://annakoren.co.il/doodles.html

Graphology/Handwriting Analysis FAQ This is the best, most even-handed document about handwriting analysis on the Web. While it is written by folks who strongly believe in the "science" of graphology, it is not trying to sell you something, and therein lies the difference. It is sensible—for example, under the question "Can Graphology tell [the] Future?" the response is "In a strict sense... No, but in reality... Not really. No." Other interesting points include the tidbit that 80 percent of French businesses use graphology to evaluate job applicants. Aside from the FAQ, you can find out how to sign up for related mailing lists here, also.
WEB http://www.ntu.ac.sg/~tjlow /grapho.html

Handwriting Analysis on the WWW
What does your writing say about you? Well, if you have a little bit of patience, the volunteer analyst members of HWA.ORG (really! that's the name) will be happy to tell you, and for free. Be advised that this has proved to be a popular offer and they are usually running behind, but as the writer notes in Singaporean English, "One exception, though: When we receive a sample containing also a donation, we try to motivate a little better with the incentive!" Plenty of happy customer's survey responses are here—who can complain about free stuff?—as well as links to other related sites.
WEB http://www.hwa.org/~hwa

Homebrewing

Association of Brewers Welcome home brewers! Perhaps you've recently moved to a new state and need to find out if it's legal to crank out more than 800 gallons of beer annually. Refer to the index of state home brewing laws. Break out the beernuts (and possibly aspirin) when you try out the list of lambics, German wheat ales, bocks, porters, stouts, and other neat beer recipes. Beginning brewmakers can try the brew basics section and learn some essentials on the way to becoming a brewmaster. The American Homebrewers Association (AHA not to be confused with AA) also brings its Calendar of Events, home brewing instruction, clubs, and more.
WEB http://www.aob.org/aob/aob.html

The Brewery Other beer sites not hardcore enough for you? This one even has a library for fine-tuning your favorite beer recipes. Evaluate your beer in the Tap Room using the American Homebrewers Association (AHA) guidelines or link to other sites such as the Bud online taste center. Home brew clubs, calendars, suppliers, organizations, even an acronym dictionary for frequently used beer terms. Buy yourself a bottle dryer, bottle capper or a larger primary fermenter from the list of suppliers. Still not

The Armchair Gardener
WEB http://mailer.fsu.edu/~dansley

Want to learn about the green stuff in the back yard? How about the camellias and the roses, the butterflies and the woodlands? With dazzling graphics and insightful commentary, the Armchair Gardener offers terrific information and advice on nearly every aspect of modern gardening and

Location: http://mailer.fsu.edu/~dansley/pre.image1.html

nature watching. Whatever you don't find onsite—whether it be pesticides or the gardens of the rich and famous—can be linked to in a twinkle. Even if you don't get down and dirty in your own yard, the pretty pictures will make your computer screen a window to a greener, quieter, and more peaceful world.

enough detail? Then try the index of technical articles and learn the inside scoop on how much sparging is really necessary after secondary fermentation.
WEB http://alpha.rollanet.org

The Homebrew Experience You have to visit the site that calls itself the "place where recipes and tips flow like fine brew from a party keg." Argue about when to add the bittering hops in Brewtalk or look for a replacement fermenter in Brewmart. The Lexicon has definitions of common beer terms and Brewnet is the place to find recipes and even video clips. Last-minute home brew supplies? Well, Jet Order is the place for you. Maybe you're ready for liquid yeast (maybe you want to culture your own). How about learning how to use your hydrometer correctly? Sure, you can't drink and drive, but you sure can drink and surf.
WEB http://www.brewguys.com /youbrew.htm

How to Brew Your First Beer A simple text page detailing the brewing (emphasis on detail) of a simple ale beer. Matters of cleanliness, brewing terms and techniques, and what brand ingredients to use.
WEB http://www-personal.umich.edu /~spencer/beer/howtobrew1st.html

rec.crafts.brewing Home brewers often sound like a bunch of former chemistry majors— "Suppose isopropanol's effec-

As if you don't have enough to worry about...
http://www.hy.com

tiveness increases linearly with percentage up to 70 percent, whereupon there is some law-of-diminishing-returns involved and 80 percent or 90 percent is negligibly better than 70 percent." But keeping a fermenting process sterile and avoiding having to wash 20 gallons of lumpy ale down the sink is the subject of a good portion of the posts to rec.crafts.homebrewing. Those who like to make home brew like to drink it as well, so plenty of the posts recommend brew pubs and microbrews, too.
USENET rec.crafts.brewing
FAQ: **WEB** http://mashtun.jpl.nasa .gov/beer/general/hbd.html

Juggling

Juggling Information Service Serious jugglers only need apply! Includes instructions on one-handed juggling, torch-

juggling and blind-folded juggling. Shop for that new set of American clubs in the Juggler's Mall. Planning to attend Jonglissimmo in France or the Yale Anti-Gravity Society Juggling Festival? Details are in the Festivals section. Break out your clubs, knives, and bowling balls as you peruse the *Juggler's World* magazine archive. The Juggler's Movie Theater has historical clips, modern techniques, conventions and instructions. Find out what Ren and Stimpy have to say (about juggling of course) in Juggling in the Media and also learn about juggling in films and interviews.
WEB http://www.juggling.org

Learn to Juggle Sure, millions of people want to juggle but don't know how to get started. Well let Mr. Snooter show you how (to juggle that is) with his set of blue balls! Hopefully you won't

start to look like Mr. Snooter if you should actually become a good juggler (bald, weird head and crossed-eyes). This step by step guide includes illustrations and finally a full animation sequence of cascade juggling. Provides clear descriptions and visualization techniques to "Learn to Juggle" the right way. Email the Snootster directly with specific questions.
WEB http://www.c2.org/~carlmm /juggle.html

Kites

Kite Flier's Site With topics such as competition, business, festivals, and galleries, this is the only links page the kite fan should ever need. Loosely affiliated with the rec.kites newsgroup.
WEB http://www.kfs.org/kites

rec.kites Kiting's a serious business, even for folks who pursue it as a part-time hobby. This newsgroup is quite focused on kiting, with little digression and lots of participation. The most recent competition results, debate about the latest model (and how to copy it), and the Q&A about repairing rip-stop nylon (and other oxymorons) can be found here, as well.
USENET rec.kites

Knotting

Knots on the Web Weaving knots, boating knots, climbing knots, even tying that necktie in a dozen different ways—you can find it all just one step away from this, the most complete index of knotting-related sites out there. Besides the typical utilitarian knot-tying sites are Knot Theory sites and Knot Art, making this far more than just a hobby for a Boy Scout.
WEB http://www.earlham.edu/suber /knotlink.htm

Roper's Knots Page With clear, elegant black-on-white diagrams, and links to the sites that describe the many knots in such categories as Stoppers, Bends, Hitches, and Nooses, Roper's Knots Page is one of the best knotty sites around. The creator is even kind enough to remind visitors not to play hangman with the gallows nooses: "It can really kill." These knots are "knot" toys!
WEB http://huizen.dds.nl/~erpprs/kne /kroot.htm

Magic

alt.magic The mother of all magic-related newsgroups, alt.magic comprises a number of subcultures—magic fans who want to talk about David Copperfield and Siegfried and Roy, magic skeptics who want to debunk card and coin tricks, and magic practitioners who want to share tips on forced cards, silks, and mirror boxes.
USENET alt.magic
FAQ: **WEB** http://www.daimi.aau.dk /~zytnia/faq.html

alt.magic.secrets Magicians are notoriously reluctant to share the secrets to their trademark illusions. But as they point out, if your company's survival depended on a top-secret computer code or a secret chemical, would you give away the information just because somebody asked? Anyway, this newsgroup does ostensibly exist for the sharing of these secrets, but much of the actual talk deals with much smaller elements of the trade, like where to find ingredients for a particular trick or whether a certain finale will work in a routine. As for determining the truth behind David Copperfield's greatest illusions, it's not exactly there for an amateur's taking—but maybe if you beg and plead.
USENET alt.magic.secrets

Magic Show The great nineteenth-century magician Robert-Houdin (from whom Harry Houdini took his name) once said that "nothing produces a more marked impression of a conjurer's dexterity than to see so light and airy an object as a card shot from the hand with the speed of an arrow, and impelled into the most distant corners of a spacious hall." Learn to throw cards—as well as collect information about other illusions and the history of the art—with this online magic magazine.
WEB http://www.uelectric.com /magicshow

Magic: The Independent Magazine for Magicians This online version of a popular print magazine for professional and amateur magician doesn't offer the entire contents of the magazine, but the small number of samples posted on the Web site are excellent indeed. They range from feature stories to examples of regular departments like Inside Magic News. **WEB** http://www.magic-mag.com

Miniatures

Historical Miniature Wargames Home Page When tiny soldiers are shooting tiny cannons at tiny little ships, you've got miniature wargames. More than just another excuse for big boys to play with toys, these games are highly elaborate, with rules, structures, and materials far beyond any Bucket O' Soldiers these hobbyists may fondly recall. At this site, war miniaturists can find links to and information about Historical Miniature Gaming Society chapters, newsgroups, rules, manufacturers, book stores, and more. **WEB** http://www.erinet.com/bp/hist.html

The Miniatures Page: A WWW Magazine Fans of gaming miniatures will enjoy this online magazine devoted to their hobby. Frequent new articles on such topics as discontinued miniatures and gaming rules are here, as well as links to plenty of other historical miniature war games sites. **WEB** http://www.eden.com/~tmp

rec.crafts.dollhouses Not particularly busy, but full of dedicated craftspeople, this news-

Watch as this Web site saws itself in half
http://www.uelectric.com/magicshow

group exists mostly in the form of questions and answers. For example, Darla, who was looking for a tiny mirror in perfect 1:12 scale, is somewhere right now making one out of a mylar balloon. Hildegard, on the other hand, is still looking for ways to soften old FIMO, while Pat is in search of the best dollhouse book and plan for a first-timer. **USENET** rec.crafts.dollhouses

Models

Gremlins in the Garage Aliens, dinosaurs vampires, vampirettes, skulls of many species and tons of other creepy-crawlers are the subject at hand (and claw) in "the first Web 'zine dedicated to figure kit modeling including coverage of science fiction, horror, fantasy, and anime from movies, books, comics, and cartoons." Materials, news on conventions, links

to private creature collections, even a Gremlins in the Garage tee-shirt make this one fun for the seasoned model-maker/fan or the merely morbidly curious. **WEB** http://www.gremlins.com

International List of Scale Model Related Web Sites From Canada to the People's Republic of China, from models of *Star Trek* spacecraft to models of ancient Versailles, this is a really fun, almost addictive "sharesite." With more than 100 sites linked, it is truly a don't miss for the modeling maven working at any level. **WEB** http://140.118.103.11/modelhome.htm

The Modeler's Home Page The big feature on this lovingly-laid out page is the incredible gallery of available JPEGs and .GIFs of "aircraft,tanks, cars, spacecraft, figures... whatever!" You'll also find tips, tools, model reviews,

conventions, and links.
WEB http://www.fn.net/~downen

modelrailroad.com Download CAD railroad design programs, chat with a global assemblage of model railroad fans, order miniature scenery, animals, engines and more in this enjoyably cluttered, utterly comprehensive site. This one's an essential bookmark.
WEB http://www.modelrailroad.com /index.html

The R/C Web Directory Airplanes, boats, cars, trucks, helicopters; if it's a miniature and radio-controlled, you'll find articles, answers to FAQs, resources and general "how-to" here. A simple but effective keyword-

based search engine guides you through this enjoyably labyrinthine site.
WEB http://www.towerhobbies.com /rcweb.html

rec.models Just the starting point for a dizzying array of modeling newsgroups, ranging from trains and planes to scale and radio-control models and beyond. An impressive posting rate here.
USENET rec.models

Origami

Alex Bateman's Origami Page
Don't crumple that piece of paper! Get thee to Alex Bateman's Origami Page and fold it into some tessellations. The

diagrams are very clear and large, and range from extremely complicated abstract geometrics to a humble billfold (not guaranteed to make it through the wash). An unexpected surprise at the bottom of the page is a search engine for the entire Origami-L archive as well as one for the text of a large selection of origami books.
WEB http://www.mrc-cpe.cam.ac.uk /jong/agb/origami.html

How to Make an Origami Crane
The sad truth is that if you can't make a crane, you probably won't be too great at a stegosaurus or a giant starburst. So beginners should take this, the ultimate dummy test. In six

DOLLHOUSE CENTRAL
WEB http://www.primenet.com/~meggie/dollcent.htm

Miniaturists everywhere are suddenly appreciating bigness—the bigness of this site, that is. This comprehensive collection of advice, articles, photos, and suggestions for hooking up with other miniaturists is excellent. A Dollhouse Central **FAQ** answers typical beginners' questions like, "Will

Location: http://www.primenet.com/~meggie/nf1.jpg

miniatures purchased in a toy department work in one-inch scale settings?" An events calendar details upcoming mini-occasions. Dollhouse Central also offers a collection of oddball tips like how to make miniature fireworks out of tissue paper and broom straws. The site is sponsored by TEAM, or The Enthusiastic Association of Miniaturists.

easy pages, with each step fully illustrated, the creator of this page takes you through the motions. If you've never done this sort of thing before, you'll want to practice—our first crane looked more like some kind of medieval helmet than a waterfowl.

WEB http://www-personal.umich.edu /~adysart/origami/crane1.html

" Our first crane looked more like some kind of medieval helmet than a waterfowl. "

Jasper's Origami Menagerie Why go to the zoo when you can visit Jasper's Origami Menagerie? He has exhibits of all kinds, be they mammalian, reptilian, or A.A. Milne-ian, accompanied by odd commentary like, "The oliphaunt is charging. Hobbits, Dunedain, and Southrons beware!" The origami, not all of which was folded by Jasper, is spectacular. You wouldn't want to miss Jasper's Guide to Paperfolding Instructions on the Web, and the List O'Links, which branches off into a list of references, organizations, and instruction.

WEB http://www.cytex.com/go/jasper /origami

Location : http://www.goldcanyon.com/photo/outdoor.html

Too bad all the Druids were hiding
http://www.goldcanyon.com/photo/index.html

Photography

A History of Photography Sir John Herschel, a well-known British astronomer, is credited with inventing the word "photography" when the process was first developed in 1839. From its cumbersome beginnings, when capturing an image would take several minutes of absolute stillness on the part of those unlucky subjects—which explains why no one smiled in those old family photos—to the modern days of one-hour processing and digital photography (never mind movies), photography has had a fascinating history. Read about all facets of its sordid past, then visit the photography museums indexed at the top of the home page.

WEB http://www.kbnet.co.uk/rleggat /photo

Focus on Photography Here's an essential how-to guide to photography, which will help even those who are challenged by the words "point-and-shoot." This site asks questions like, "What kinds of photography are there?" reviews Camera Basics, and provides additional references on the Web in an easy-to-understand style.

WEB http://www.goldcanyon.com /photo/index.html

The Photojournalist Coffee House Photographers can't have poetry slams, they don't want to sip espresso and talk about Joyce or Thackeray, maybe some of them can't even string a paragraph together, but that doesn't mean they have nothing to say, as the Photojournalist Coffee House shows eloquently. For the particularly energetic visitor, the coffee

house has also helpfully provided an excellent set of links to related sites.
WEB http://www.intac.com/~jdeck/index2.html

Sight Magazine *Sight* bills itself as "the online magazine for some of the world's finest photography." As such, it's not crowded with ads for a print version of the magazine. Its focus on the Web is a visual treat. The Departments section contains reviews, pictorials, and a chance to talk back. Editorial contains the meat, from photojournalism to documentary photography. A class act.
WEB http://www.sightphoto.com/photo.html

Pottery & sculpture

Clayart An active ceramic arts discussion list. Many of the members are academics, but any topic from kiln-firing to grant-getting is fair game.
EMAIL listserv@lsv.uky.edu ✍ *Type in message body:* subscribe ⟨your full name⟩

The Potter's Page All the way from South Africa comes this index for online ceramics fanatics. It covers everything from wood-fired Japanese stoneware to software that calculates glaze parameters.
WEB http://www.aztec.co.za/users/theo

rec.crafts.pottery No one's more serious about pottery than a recreational potter, and no one has more questions. Amy laments, "I am a novice in pottery/ceramics, and recently made what I think is a fairly common mistake in the craft: The top for a hand-built container was glazed to the container (accidentally)." Several experienced potters leap to her rescue, with techniques ranging from using a diamond-tipped saw to rhythmic tapping. Most questions are about wheels or kilns. Newbies are welcomed warmly.
USENET rec.crafts.pottery

Pyrotechnics

alt.pyrotechnics Whether you're sitting around wondering about

Joseph Wu's Origami Page
WEB http://www.datt.co.jp/origami

Wu deserves recognition, if for nothing else than for his amazing fantasy paper creations. Centaurs, dragons, and other mythical beasts are gathered here for viewing. But there's so much more to this page than examples of good origami, including an extensive history of the art dating

Location: http://www.datt.co.jp/origami/Gallery/JWu/flypig.jpg

back to the first century A.D. and detailed instructions for specialty techniques like wet folding and backcoating. And whether it's shops and suppliers, instructions for every creation imaginable, of links to every origami site under the sun, visitors will find it here on this page, which others refer to as the "mother lode."

where to get a hold of a decent igniter, an ATF-approved Type 3 magazine, or wondering how something will explode over water in humid weather, this is a largely hard-data focused newsgroup.

USENET alt.pyrotechnics

FIREWORKS A link page involving both the Pyrotechnics Guild International (with history and information on joining) and the National Fireworks Association. Lots of animated explosions, downloadable JPEGs of recent and remarkable fireworks exhibitions and some terse complaints about the "mad bomber" contingency creeping into related newsgroups. The Unabomber was unavailable for comment.

WEB http://ezinfo.ucs.indiana.edu /~wwarf/firework.html

Pyrotechnics Home Page Labeling itself as "a not-for-profit fellowship founded in 1969 for the advancement of safety, skill, and artistry in fireworks through communication and for their preservation in America and throughout the world," this is the Pyrotechnics Guild International top page. Along with links to related professional organizations and suppliers, this is worth a gander for some striking .MPEG and .AVI clips and loads of JPEGs of cutting edge pyrotechnic performances worldwide.

WEB http://nickel.ucs.indiana.edu /~flinn/pyro/pyro.html

rec.pyrotechnics FAQ "If you are just getting started, try to get hold of as much information on the subject as you can," this primer on the explosive newsgroup advises. And for good reason, when topics of heated discussion include the effects of certain devices on bystanders, the creation and uses of Nitrogen Tri-Iodide, Thermite "Terminator Bombs," Match Rockets, and more. This group can use all the legal caveats they can come up with. For practitioners, a thorough, info-dense page.

WEB http://www.cis.ohio-state.edu /hypertext/faq/bngusenet/rec /pyrotechnics/top.html

Redzone Firecracker Labels With images of art nouveau bats, rice-paper lobsters, dancing bellboys and a lot more, this gorgeous gallery of a page claims to be "the World's Largest Firecracker Label Collection," and far be it from us to disagree. Prepare for some intense .GIF downloading, as every image here is a crisp evocation of independence days past.

WEB http://www.sky.net/~redzone /labels

Rockets

Dangerous Dave's Handmade Composite Home Page Graphics-heavy (think early Russian propaganda posters) and with a pranksterish tone to the text, this is a unique rocketing resource page that goes beyond. How beyond? Well,

how many sites include as a free bonus .GIFs of "authentic" aliens, not to mention links to other alien-related sites? Weird, fun, and informative.

WEB http://www.ddave.com

Helen's Model Rocket Collection Big Bertha, Mongoose, Maniac: these are the names of a few of this "born again" rocketeer's favorites things. An endearingly slapped-together page packed with "Astrocam" .GIFs of various launches, detailed flight guides (with entries numbering in the hundreds), and related links.

WEB http://hccadb.hcc.hawaii.edu /~cs_rapozo/modroc.html

How to Design, Build, and Test Small Liquid-Fuel Rocket Engines From China Lake California's Rocketlab comes this page of serious tech centering on the creation of the titular engines. With schematics, test routines, safety and legal aspects: not for the amateur in any way.

WEB http://www.im.lcs.mit.edu/rocket

National Association of Rocketry Nifty page aimed at NARs 65,000-plus membership. Keywords link you to pages for joining NAR (which, among other things, allows one to use rocket motors more powerful than those sold to the general public), lists of organized launches, access to liability insurance, related conventions, and lots of helpful rocketry FAQs.

WEB http://www.nar.org/index.htm?s

rec.models.rockets:FAQ A surprisingly sober-toned guide to the newsgroup which dedicates itself to "discussions and topics related to non-professional rocketry of all types." With common queries about topics like the debate over liquid-fueled rockets, legal matters, and what to do when one's rocket engine explodes, it's worth its weight in gun powder.
WEB http://www.dtm-corp.com/~sven /rockets/rmrfaq.toc.html

Sewing & needlework

Crafts@ Woman's Day Pursue this incredible collection of instructions for sewing crafts of all kinds, from quilting (a small quilt showcasing outgrown baby clothes) to sewing (something called a "Victorian Kitty"). Pictures of each craft are available in the libraries, so you don't need to feel "sew" blind. This is the ultimate source for free patterns and ideas—no other site surpasses it, even if many of the crafts are a little bit cutesy.
AMERICA ONLINE *keyword* woman's→ Crafts

Nancy's Notions "The love of sewing is our common thread," says Nancy Zieman, proprietor of Nancy's Notions, a catalog and retail business with a full-blown and excellent Web site. But don't hold it against her. The online catalog offers specials, supplies by the yard, quilting paraphernalia, patterns, and more. In the Sewing Room are a chat room, articles by Nancy, and newsgroups and mailing lists, while in the Sewing with Nancy area are guides to episodes of that long-running PBS show hosted by Nancy herself. Videos of most episodes are available here, too.
WEB http://www.nancysnotions.com

rec.crafts.textiles* Whether your favorite discussion would be on the topic of needlework, quilting, sewing, or yarn, there's a rec.crafts.textiles* newsgroup tailor-made for your needle-and-thread favorite. And of course, rec.crafts.textiles.misc covers none of the above, and everything else.
USENET rec.crafts.textiles

Cmos's Fireworks Pages

WEB http://www.shol.com/users/cmos/index.htm
picture: WEB http://nickel.ucs.indiana.edu/˜flinn/pyro/Pyro.html

An animated grenade greets you, along with the warning "This page and its links are intended for people with a working knowledge of pyrotechnics. Please do not attempt to make any of the things found on this page." And for good reason: here are detailed, easy-to-understand, do-it-yourself tips on making smoke bombs, sugar rockets, M80s, and many other thing that go BLAM! in the night. A tasty recipe for making one's own keg of black powder is also included.

Location: http://www.primenet.com/~dougb/fwk5b.gif

Staceyjoy's Knitting Stitches To overcome an unfortunate name like Staceyjoy must be difficult. This particular, very spirited SJ is attempting to do so by creating the best darn knitting stitches page on the Web. With dozens of printable graphs for handknit cables, machine-knit lace—even a sweater for your Chihuahua (or possibly your cat?), Staceyjoy's collection is admirably complete.
WEB http://www.tiac.net/users/stacey

Wonderful Stitches Quilting, needlework, and decorative stitchery are covered very well at this site, which offers many sample patterns. Particularly of interest are the "CyberSamplers," which show grids for dozens of different pattern-fill stitches.
WEB http://www.needlework.com

The World Wide Quilting Page Whether your quilts are expertly stitched from original hand-embroidered tapestry panels or simply made for warmth out of worn-out flannel pajamas, you'll find plenty to interest you here. Patterns, other quilters' pages, hints and tips, places to buy supplies, and much more are here for folks who love quilting. Even beginners can profit from this page, with its guide to basic quilting techniques. Those who feel that their quilting careers are doomed to failure have a special treat in store—a chance to enter (and view former winners of) the

"Worst Quilt in the World" contest.
WEB http://ttsw.com/MainQuiltingPage .html

Smoking

How to Roll Tobakky As the title implies, a no-frills, downhome, step-by-step (with hand-drawn illustrations) approach to the fine art of rolling leafy greens into tight cylinders for smoking pleasure.
WEB http://www-personal.engin.umich .edu/~vinn/nichowto.html

Pipes Digest Mainly a page of links to personal sites, commercial suppliers, and organizations dedicated to the pipe-smoking lifestyle, with the addition of things like Meerschaum JPEG downloads and and a perversely fascinating subpage examining one hundred and twenty of Sherlock Holmes' favored tobaccos.
WEB http://www.pipes.org

Smoke Magazine Online "A fun, contemporary magazine geared to the rising executive who is interested in cigars and the lifestyle surrounding them," pipes this page's banner, and if this fills your bowl, you probably won't find much better on the web. Mega-hip graphics, features on the cigar habits of The Red Hot Chili Peppers, Berettas (as in guns), and better ways to get caffeinated along with links to other pages makes this an upscale Gen Xer must.
WEB http://www.smokemag.com

The Tobacconist—Your Cigar Web Site Like any hobby, there will be some adherents who will get obsessive about things, but few as charmingly as the creators of this page, which conjures visions of people in suede arm-patch jackets chatting in civilized tones whilst puffing a fine Double Corona. Besides the online ambiance, there's detailed bits about humidors, where to smoke in cigar-negative cities, the uses of molds and worms, and endless other cigar arcana.
WEB http://www.law.vill.edu /~kmortens/humidor

Treasure hunting

The Golden Olde The place where a Radio Shack metal detector is your best friend, and aluminum cans are your enemy (they actually call them "demons"). A monster site with a strong sense of humor (it's subtitled "The Search for the Great Golden Pulltab," a treasure familiar to everyone who has metal detected) The Golden Olde is a bookmark for treasure-hunters to covet. Dozens of articles related to metal detecting are listed here under such titles as "Coin-shooting," "Old Gold," and "Tips for the Detector." And of course, there are lots of links to other treasure hunting sites, making this site one to see.
WEB http://www.iwl.net/customers /norman/index.htm

International Treasure Hunters' Exchange There's gold in them

thar hills (and mountains) and I'm agonna git it! Cybertravel to countries all over the world in the hunt for long lost treasure. Unearth the latest news about the expedition to recover Nuestra Senora de la Concepcion, and don't miss your daily fix of Shroud of Turin news, or an installment of National Geographic treasure hunt online. Serious professionals can relax into an issue of *Treasure Quest* magazine. Post your messages on information resources such as metal detecting, treasure hunting, and shipwrecks. Need more? Give 'em your email address and get the breaking news mailed straight to you.
WEB http://www.treasure.com

The On-line TreasureHunter
"Whether you're an experienced treasure hunter or just getting started, The On-Line Treasure Hunter will help you become productive in your searches." We'd tend to agree, as this concise page offers a well laid-out How To and Equipment-Related and Miscellaneous Treasure tips.
WEB http://onlinether.com

Shipwrecked on the Internet Got a hundred thousand dollars laying around and a couple of years to kill? Dive right in and get the scoop on such sunken treasures as *Aikoko Maru* or *Betty Bomber*. Maybe you've already tried to recover booty from the *Panther* in Lake Superior or *Kamloops* in the Isle Royale? Plenty of nifty pictures and maps, especially in the section devoted to Shipwrecks in the Great Lakes. Links to shipwreck museums, research engines, film festivals, and especially sites about shipwrecks in North America. And yes, that includes the *Titanic* and the *Poseidon*.
WEB http://www.rust.net/~sps/shipwrecked

Treasure Hunter's Paradise If "classics" of the treasure hunting world are what appeals to you—that is, if you're dying to travel to Arizona and hunt up the Lost Dutchman and his mine, or visit Davy Jones to retrieve some pirate's gold—

 ## ALTERNATIVE PLEASURES
WEB http://www.altpleas.com

A neo-macho, post-modern cigar booster page. Peruse texts meditating on the subtext of the cigar as power accessory, the alleged hypocrisy of federal public smoking regulations, and other issues of concern to the connoisseur. This is the first issue of an online magazine, so it's a bit content-lite

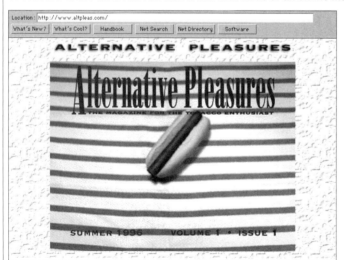

and Zippo-ad-heavy, but the visuals are slick. The publisher comments: "I seriously doubt tourists in New York place the fear of second-hand smoke in between being murdered and getting mugged." Put that in your pipe and smoke it.

you'll enjoy this site, with its updated guides to the lore of these lost treasures. Plus, exclusive articles by treasure hunters, treasure stories from the news, classified ads, and the ever-popular tips on locating your hoard make this a fun and fascinating site for the playground metal detector and the wreck diver alike.
WEB http://macatawa.org/~jmiller /treasure

Woodworking

The Electronic Neanderthal For the uninitiated, "Neanderthal" is woodworking slang for a person who prefers using hand tools in his/her work. The same sense of humor that informs the title of this cool multi-frame page is everywhere, with snappy writing on "Neanderthal" lore, wood suppliers, tools, and interactive group activities.
WEB http://www.cs.cmu.edu/~alf/en /en.html

❝ Do you know what a Stanley No. 386 Jointer Gauge is? If you do, you either need to get out more or you are seriously into woodworking. ❞

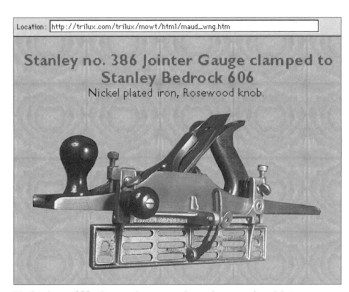

Location: http://trilux.com/trilux/mowt/html/maud_wng.htm

Stanley no. 386 Jointer Gauge clamped to Stanley Bedrock 606
Nickel plated iron, Rosewood knob.

The Stanley no. 386—for use when you need a good, square, clean joint
http://trilux.com/tools.html

The Museum of Woodworking Tools Do you know what a Stanley No. 386 Jointer Gauge is? Well if you do, you either need to get out more or you are seriously into woodworking, in which case this is the perfect place for you. See the fine works of art in the English Shoulder Planes wing, with full explanations and color illustrations. There are even descriptions of how the woodmaking tools themselves were handcrafted. Carpenters, cabinetmakers, joiners, and other wood enthusiasts can view tons of photos and read a wealth of knowledge for the modern wood craftsman.
WEB http://trilux.com/tools.html

rec.woodworking Norm Abrams is a god. Or, he's a sell-out and uses way too many tools just to show that he has them. Belt sanders are a good buy—but

they're nearly useless for the art of woodworking. Pallet wood is a cheap source of good wood—but it's also a cheap way to ruin your tools. Whatever the issue on rec.woodworking, pros and amateurs together are ready to debate it. This newsgroup belongs to serious craftsmen and those who merely suffer from Normenvy alike.
USENET rec.woodworking

Wood Online *Wood* magazine, a *Better Homes and Gardens* spinoff, offers up this well-constructed site, which includes a quick way to zip through old issues, search their lumber and tools database, get ideas for future projects, and take advantage of this fine store of information without having to hit the magazine stand.
WEB http://woodmagazine.com

PART 5
Home & Health

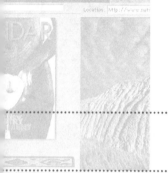

Home & Health

CLICK PICKS
The very best on the Net

Genealogy

LET YOUR PAST LEND MEANING TO YOUR PRESENT
AND DRIVE YOUR FUTURE

SOME PEOPLE SPEND THEIR entire lives trying to get away from their families. Others can't find them to begin with. The former tend to end up on talk shows. The latter take up genealogy as a hobby. Oddly enough, genealogy is one study of the past that has thoroughly embraced the capabilities of the future, fully exploiting the resources that the Information Age brings into the home. The Internet's greatest genius is its ability to connect people around the world, an attribute of great service to genealogists. No more traveling to a distant courthouse to slog through birth records—many are online. No more researching for countless hours to discover that someone in another county is duplicating the effort. And no need to spend thousands of dollars traveling to the homeland just to do research. Tracing a family tree has never been easy, but now those branches aren't so far out of reach.

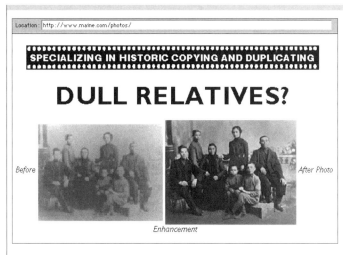

RAND GENEALOGY CLUB

WEB http://www.rand.org/personal/Genea
picture: WEB http://www.maine.com/photos
One of the most comprehensive indexes to genealogy Web sites, the Rand Genealogy Club is also blessed with a searchable database. Want to know if someone is researching the Buttz family of Pennsylvania? Just type in the keywords. The database lists several thousand last names. If yours is one of them, you can try to find your branch and then contact the person who did the research. If your name is simply too unusual, visit the other sections to find out if you're descended from nobility around the world, find government information, visit a genealogical society in any state and most countries, or even find out how to do a tombstone rubbing. The possibilities are as endless as your heritage.

Starting points

CompuServe Genealogy Forum
Susan knows that her grandfather changed his name from Sornberger to Soran, and she wants to know if there's any chance she might be related to a woman named Sorrenburger whom she met at her health club. Antonio, who was adopted by a family named (believe it or not) Cervantes, wants a list of the oldest Spanish surnames. Ophir has some information about how Hebrew names are transliterated into English. And Lucille is curious about whether any other countries have experienced the Ellis Island phenomenon, in which a wave of immigration wreaks onomastic havoc, altering the spellings of thousands of family names. Contribute to the discussion on these active message boards, or consult the library for software and documents pertaining to genealogical research.
COMPUSERVE *go* roots

CompuServe Genealogy Support Forum CompuServe has another forum for people who are conducting their own genealogical research, but this forum targets those who are too overwhelmed (or too lazy) to do it themselves. Organizations at this forum include The New England Historic Genealogical Society, Everton Publishers, and the National Genealogical Society, as well as producers of major genealogical software

products like Wholly Genes, Inc.
COMPUSERVE *go* GENSUP

Cyndi's List of Genealogical Sites on the Internet More than 5,000 links are gathered by genealogist Cyndi, under dozens of geographical categories. It's frequently updated and even contains links to genealogical humor (Anyone for a rousing chorus of "I'm My Own Grandpa?"), ships and passenger lists (including, of course, the *Mayflower*), and cemeteries and obituaries.
WEB http://www.oz.net/~cyndihow /sites.htm

❝ Have any other countries experienced the Ellis Island phenomenon, in which a wave of immigration wreaks onomastic havoc? ❞

Everton's Guide to Genealogy on the World Wide Web The magazine known as *Everton's Genealogical Helper* has been around since 1947. Its publisher's Web site offers a number of introductory documents

for family-tree surgeons, including one titled "20 Ways to Avoid Grief in Your Genealogical Research" (that's research grief, not personal grief). *Everton's* online editions (the most popular publication of its kind in the world) provide a timely look at genealogical research from an Internet perspective. This site will also point you to genealogical archives and libraries on the Net, as well as Everton's extensive catalog of genealogical offerings (books, forms, software, CD-ROMs, and more). As if that wasn't enough, Everton's site will also direct your online research, with annotated sections of links on U.S., international, special (adoptive, ethnic, etc.), and software resources on the Internet.
WEB http://www.everton.com

The Genealogy Home Page An immense annotated list of genealogical resources on the Internet. Offers links to the soc.genealogy* newsgroups as well as to other sites. Particularly useful are the pointers to genealogical research guides and the listings of regional and specific ethnic/religious genealogy sites.
WEB http://ftp.cac.psu.edu/~saw /genealogy.html

GenWeb Database For those researching their family history or wishing to interface with others of the same surname, GenWeb is an index of all known, searchable genealogical databases. Organized

alphabetically, each entry links to a different family name, geographic location, or ethnic group. Not all of these databases have their own Internet home pages, but many of the more common names do, and GenWeb invites you to submit your own page to their listings. Genealogy buffs might also want to look into GenWeb's sponsor: the Frontier Press Bookstore, which specializes in family-history resources.
WEB http://sillyg.doit.com/genweb

Journal of Online Genealogy A brand-new Web and email journal dedicated to the growing science of online genealogy, JOG is aimed toward fledgling and advanced geneal-

ogists. Look for regular sections like Software Trends, Newsgroups & Lists, and Beginner Avenues, written by some of the Internet's best-known genealogists.
WEB http://www.tbox.com/jog/jog.html

National Genealogical Society An introduction to the National Genealogical Society and the services it provides. Read about the library holdings of this Virginia-based organization, its research service (where research assistance is available on a per-hour basis), the charts and aids available from the society, and the home-study class offered by the NGS for learning more about genealogical research.

Also at this site is a selection of documents discussing genealogical research on the Internet.
WEB http://www.genealogy.org/~ngs

The Roots-L Library Do you have a second cousin twice removed? With information for those dabbling in genealogy research, links to Family History Centers nationwide, and special sources for ethnic and religious groups, this is the place for those looking to map their family tree. Best of all, check out the historic and familiar names server and see if anyone famous shared your family name.
WEB http://www.smartlink.net /~leverich/filelist.html

 AOL GENEALOGY FORUM
AMERICA ONLINE *keyword* roots

Genealogical research can often seem like a lonely task. But just on the off chance that someone else knows of your long-lost ancestor or the historical progression of birth records in a particular town, you'd better stop by AOL's Genealogy Forum. Read and post messages to other genealogists on one of several message boards that are organized alphabetically by surname being researched or in terms of geography, time period, and ethnicity. Five chat areas—including Ancestral Digs and Golden Gates—also focus on genealogy, and you can reach them through the forum. There's also

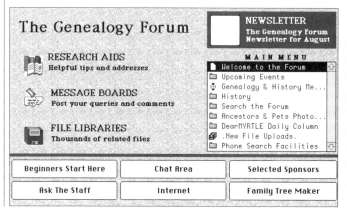

information about weekly moderated and unmoderated topic-specific chat sessions in the two areas, and sometimes there are even "lectures" about genealogical topics. The Genealogy Forum also offers downloadable computer software and software support, as well as a strong section introducing genealogy to beginners.

Regional & ethnic

Cajun Clickers Genealogy SIG
This Louisiana-based organization focuses on computer-aided genealogical research. This site features some of the data being collected from members of the organization, in the form of a surname index and tafel listings (a method of recording research done on surnames of one's own ancestry), as well as links to other genealogical sites on the Web. There aren't any Rodriguezes or Goldfarbs, but if you're a Quackenbush, LeBlanc, Dabney, Colepepper, or DeBleieux, this may be the place for you.
WEB http://www.intersurf.com/~cars

The Gathering of the Clans All things Scottish are here in this colorful tartan-designed resource which includes last-name societies, interactive maps, a history of the Scots, and a large area devoted to Scotch (the drink, not the tape). Questions? Tack 'em up in the Pub. A *Braveheart* fan? Well, the sponsor has a whole shelf of books on William Wallace to send you, all the way from bonnie old Scotland. For those truly brave of heart, there's a recipe for cooking haggis.
WEB http://www.tartans.com

Jewish Genealogical Resources A page devoted to other sites devoted to the study of Jewish genealogy. Don't expect much else. There are four links—three to other Web pages and

one to an FTP site. This is as decent a starting point as any to explore your Jewish roots.
WEB http://sunsite.oit.unc.edu/yiddish/roots.html

" For those truly brave of heart, there's a recipe for cooking haggis. "

Newberry Guide of Topics in Genealogy As an independent research library concentrating in the humanities, the Newberry Library is one of Chicago's intellectual landmarks. Any genealogical researcher will want to take advantage of this online catalogue to review the library's collection and determine the call numbers and availability of useful sources. The Newberry offers extensive information about genealogies in Ohio, Bohemia, Ontario, and Virginia, in addition to considerable Jewish source material.
WEB http://192.231.205.235/ISC75

UK + Ireland Genealogy A guide to genealogical information about the United Kingdom and Ireland, with a good deal of the information—church records and census accounts, for example—available online. Information is divided by region, where appropriate, for

easier research. Users are also pointed to helpful non-Web sources (i.e., books). This site also contains brief guides to general genealogical research and to researching genealogy in the United Kingdom and Ireland from abroad.
WEB http://midas.ac.uk/genuki

Washington State Family History Genealogy Café Did you know that Sweden omitted leap years from the year 1700 until 1740 to complete a gradual transition to the Gregorian Calendar? While that may be nothing more than trivia to some, such a fact can be crucial to those tracing their Swedish heritage. The Genealogy Café has scores and scores of such useful facts that you might not normally think of, as well as advice on beginning your genealogical searches and common stumbling blocks. Taking full advantage of the Internet's huge capacity for storage and referencing, the Genealogy Café is a must for anyone interested in tracing their roots.
WEB http://www.whidbey.net/~jpterry/washngtn.html

Chat

alt.genealogy "Marrying your niece/uncle is or was legal in Italy and possibly some other countries, but it is not permitted in any of the 50 states.... In about half of the states it is permissible to marry a first cousin. In the rest a second cousin is the closest relative you are allowed to marry. Incest is usu-

ally defined as having sexual relations with someone who is in the category of relatives you are not permitted to marry. So if a couple is legally married, the relationship is not incestuous." So much for that skeleton in the closet.... When the subscribers to alt.genealogy aren't worrying about incest law, they're usually asking for software help or trying to track down long-lost relatives—anyone know of Hohners in the Tri-State area or Dvoraks in the Carolinas?
USENET alt.genealogy

soc.genealogy* The network of Usenet newsgroups has been described as one big family. Here, that propaganda becomes a reality. The soc.genealogy newsgroup hierarchy is sorted by region, for the most part (soc.genealogy.methods, which takes a more theoretical approach, and soc.genealogy. surnames, which functions as a sort of entry-level discussion, are the two notable exceptions). If you're Scandinavian, visit soc.genealogy.nordic. If you're Jewish, drop by soc.genealogy .jewish. If you're interested in medieval names, peruse soc.genealogy.medieval. Though there are groups for most major European ancestries—British, German, French, Scandinavian, and the Benelux countries—non-Europeans will have to look elsewhere, probably in the soc.culture* hierar-

chy. One caveat: After you choose the relevant newsgroup, you'll have to wade through hundreds of messages in no particular order to find what you want.
USENET soc.genealogy*

Vicki's Home Page An extensive annotated list of genealogy mailing lists, with subscription information. This index also includes some genealogical newsgroups and home pages.
WEB http://www.eskimo.com/~chance

Dictionary

Genealogy Dictionary Plenty of Latin words like *filium* (son) and *etiam* (also) litter this large glossary of common terms

 ## HELM'S GENEALOGY TOOLBOX

WEB http://genealogy.tbox.com/genealogy.html

You can't build a family treehouse without the proper tools; this site should be the first stop for hardware, software, and iron-clad links to the best genealogy sites around. On your first visit, read the descriptions of the ten major categories, which include surname data, associations, and guides/indexes. Within each category, each link contains a wonderful, detailed annotation, and the entire site is searchable by concept or keyword.

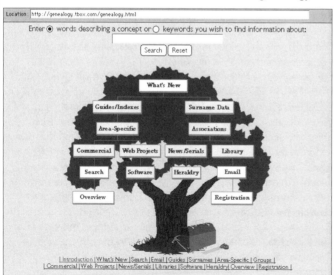

GENEALOGY 101: DAY ONE

Hello there friend...(and likely, genealogist) Don't feel bad if you don't understand "X-Cousin" and "Removed." I didn't either when I started my hobby of genealogy. As you will see, it's all really quite simple.

You know what your cousin (or **FIRST COUSIN**) is, and how they are related to you. (For those of you who use English as a second language: Your cousin is the child of your aunt and uncle; your aunt or uncle is a sibling to one of your parents).

Now, if your cousin has a child, that child is a **FIRST COUSIN ONCE REMOVED** to you, i.e. one generation removed from being a first cousin. If you have a child, your child is a **SECOND COUSIN** to your first cousin's child. If your first cousin has a grandchild, that grandchild is a **FIRST COUSIN TWICE REMOVED** to you, and a **THIRD COUSIN** to your grandchild.

It keeps working the same way. Undoubtedly, you have a 12th Cousin somewhere, and their grandchild is your **TWELFTH COUSIN TWICE REMOVED**.

—from Genealogy Terms & Phrases

genealogists run into. Just remember—sex didn't mean what it does today!

WEB http://www.electriciti.com/~dotts/diction.html

Genealogy Terms and Phrases Did your ancestor die from Milk Sickness? Genealogists come across some rather strange terms when digging through all those old papers; here's the place to find out what they all mean. You'll also find links to related glossaries and even a guide to the symbolism of gravestone markings. Plus, don't miss the ultimate clarification: an explanation of the difference between "cousins" and "removed."

WEB http://www.oz.net/~cyndihow/terms.htm

Software

Genealogy SF Serious tools for the serious researcher, including software information and demos; general genealogical research information (including an indispensable glossary of genealogical terms); collections of genealogical data for the U.S., the U.K., Australia, New Zealand, Africa, Canada, France, and Russia, as well as international Jewish data; and a Tiny-Tafel Matching System, which allows genealogists to check for other people researching the same names.

WEB http://www.sfo.com/~genealogysf

Global Heritage Center Why fight your way through 200 rolls of microfilm or 100,000 pages of

text when you can access the same information on one CD-ROM? That's the question that the people at the Global Heritage Center would like you to ask yourself. This online catalog describes their CD-ROM, which contains millions of birth, death, marriage, and Social Security records; U.S. Census indexes and tax lists; and land records. The Reunion program for Macintosh and Windows is also available.

WEB http://www.ledet.com/genealogy

PAF Review Originally published by the Church of Jesus Christ of Latter-Day Saints, the Personal Ancestry File Review quickly became the essential computer tool for genealogists working with the Internet. Anyone using PAF will find this online newsletter comprehensive and coherent, and the links to shareware programs should be helpful. Researchers looking to connect families via the Internet couldn't ask for a better resource.

WEB http://www.genealogy.org/~paf

soc.genealogy.computing Computers are the greatest thing to happen to genealogy since human procreation. Read about sophisticated database programs, translators that pull names from different languages, and massive databases of public records that have everything from the deaths of medieval Frenchmen to last week's spur-of-the-moment marriage in Vegas.

USENET soc.genealogy.computing

Parenting

BIRDS DO IT. BEES DO IT. THIS IS WHAT YOU GET FOR IMITATING THE BIRDS AND THE BEES

YOU DON'T USUALLY have to interview for the position, it's an easy one to get into, and it's the one you can never quit. Yet raising happy, healthy children in a loving family is no easy task, and only the strong survive with any sanity remaining. How can you entertain the rugrats? What can allay your fears over their every sniffle? What if you're a single parent?

Who can help your children understand what it means to be adopted? How can you protect your kids from growing up too fast? What do you do about non-specific earaches? Why are little girls obsessed with Band-Aids? How do you explain to them how they got here? Why do they keep asking questions? Visit these sites for some answers and a little sympathy.

Location: http://www.parentsoup.com/cgi-bin/genobject/cmp000

Parent Soup Chill Out

Relax
Try these techniques.
A Dad's Life
A new column every Monday!
A Mom's Life
A new column every Monday!
Horoscopes
What's in the stars?
Cartoon Gallery
With New Yorker cartoonist Mort Gerberg
Beyond the Necktie Sweepstakes
Check out our Father's Day Sweepstakes Winners!

PARENT SOUP

WEB http://www.parentsoup.com

If you're a parent with a late-night question, an early-morning gripe, or a need for friendly advice, Parent Soup should help. The 24-hour Soup community discusses everything from the benefits of breastfeeding to the basics of the primal scream (found in the Chill Out section of the Parent Soup Bulletin Board). If you're a single parent interested in a pen pal or date, the Personals section is well-stocked with kindred seekers. Those in the market for budgetary child-rearing advice can grill expert Neale Godfrey, who will steer you toward helpful resources and literature.

Starting points

AOL Families Its name might suggest that it focuses only on parenting issues, but this AOL megaforum, which links to more than 20 smaller ones, treats all issues of family health and welfare—family medicine, child abuse, adoption, education, child safety, Scouting, and more. There's a special entertainment feature that helps parents select movies, records, and books appropriate for their little ones. And parents (as well as anyone interested in online civil rights) should note that this is the place where parents can set up Parental Controls, which allow them to lock out AOL's more salacious features.
AMERICA ONLINE *keyword* families

Facts for Families The collection of essays available at this site sheds light on the topic of psychiatric disorders affecting children and adolescents. Worried that your child might have panic disorder? Watch for a racing pulse and an overwhelming sense of fear. Concerned that your teenage daughter isn't eating the way she should? You should be—an alarmingly high percentage of girls do battle with an eating disorder. Each of the 50 essays describes an illness, its symptoms, and known cures for it. This University of Michigan Department of Psychiatry site offers answers to families facing difficult questions.
WEB http://www.psych.med.umich.edu /web/aacap/factsFam

Sound plans for those in the family way
http://family.com

Family.com Your starting point at Family.com is a friendly, pastel-colored version of our Web-rich country, segmented geographically and surrounded by such headings as Health, Travel, Food, Computing, Entertainment, Activities, Education, and Finance. Dance across this vast land, pick a topic and region, and explore the resources available.
WEB http://family.com

Family Internet A large collection of links that promises to "bring your family and the Net closer together." Click on At Home Dads to link to articles on paternal discipline and the difficult task of entertaining kids on rainy days (draw a picture! invent a game! surf the Web!). In the Kids Korner, children will find a link to the Walt Disney Web, where they can read reviews of the latest megabudget cartoon. And parents who want to expose their

children to less sedentary activities should check out Travel With Blondee, which furnishes reviews of family-oriented hotels and restaurants nationwide.
WEB http://www.familyinternet.com

Family Service Forum Parents sometimes think that kids are possessions. Kids sometimes think that parents are from outer space. Can't we all just get along? CompuServe's Family Service Forum suggests that we can, with the help of extensive electronic resources. The message boards treat sex education, religion, infant diets, and crisis management (Susan's son came home in tears because a bigger boy hit him in the shoulder and said, "You're small!"). And the two dozen libraries range from a repository of family photos to more specific topics: Dad can read about the importance of letting his little girl have her independence, and Mom can explore the male need to monopolize the remote control. **COMPUSERVE** *go* myfamily

Family Surfboard Hang ten on this collection of well-annotated family links. From the Children's Internet Activity Center ("to hone your kids' sleuthing and observational skills") to Kidding around the Keyboard ("for tapping your kids' creativity with drawing programs"), Family Surfboard is a best-of-the-Web introductory page. You'll find reviews, experiences of other parents who've been there, full-length articles, and live links of all kinds—from online museums and science projects to wildlife conservation

programs and an incredible place for kids to publish their own stories online. **WEB** http://www.familysurf.com

The Kids on the Web Parents are well advised to introduce their kids to this exciting funhouse. Kids on the Web features plenty of educational and entertaining books and games for children, and parents are certainly not left out of the loop. It's worth the link-trip to the Cute Kids Page for a helping of amusing stories and quotes. If you're feeling particularly safety conscious, there are numerous useful tips to be found. You can also gain immediate access to the database of the National Center for Missing and

Exploited Children. The advice-oriented and educational links seem limitless, so join in for some family fun. **WEB** http://www.zen.org/~brendan /kids.html

KidSource Online KidSource Online is the place to go to tap into a vast resource base for education, including special education, health care, recreation, forums, organizations, a guide to the best kids' software, and product information for newborns, toddlers, preschoolers, and K-12. Subscribe to the KidSource Online News service for weekly email updates on what's new at KidSource. **WEB** http://www.kidsource.com/index .html

FAMILY PLANET
WEB http://family.starwave.com/index.html

Wanna know about the gum that stops cavities? Maybe you want to sound off because your mom, dad, or kids are driving you crazy. If you'd like to chat live with children's author Erica Silverman, she's here, too. This all-inclusive family page lets you send a birthday ecard, try your hand at

mother-daughter matching games, get family TV reviews, or join Elroy's Netscapade, the "world's first Internet learning adventure." But Family Planet acknowledges that family life isn't all fun and games. Jan Faull, the Parent Advisor, has her own column at the site, where she addresses such problems as what to do when your eight-year-old won't wear shoes.

The National Parenting Center A bright, cheery mishmash of parenting questions and issues. Access the daily newsletter or dial up the various chat sessions and bulletin boards. There's also a shopping directory which highlights books, toys, multimedia items, and accessories that are generally free of the superhero/breakfast cereal/action figure advertising that plagues much of the kiddie merchandise world.
WEB http://www.parentsplace.com /shopping/tnpc

Parent News This sprawling resource contains a huge amount of parenting information, plus online forums for questions, answers, and discussions. While the whole thing could be better organized, it manages to hit many major child-raising issues. The vast articles archive alone is worth a visit—it contains links to information on everything from battling siblings to creative approaches to discipline that get your point across without destroying your child's trust.
WEB http://parent.net

Parenting Magazine Not just an online version of the print version, AOL's version of *Parenting Magazine* offers an active message board and an "Ages and Stages" section that lets you read all about your child as he or she grows. Plus, you still get all that lovable *Parenting* photography: babies galore!
AMERICA ONLINE *keyword* parenting magazine

Parents and Children Together Online Brought to you by the Family Literacy Center at the ERIC Clearinghouse for Reading, English, and Communication, this page encourages parents and children to develop their literacy skills together in an engaging way. There are features, original stories, and articles for children, and, in the once-oral tradition of storytelling, kids can gather 'round the Global Campfire to listen to and exchange wondrous tales.
WEB http://www.indiana.edu/~eric_rec /fl/pcto/menu.html

Parents Place Parents are the best resource for other parents, so if you are one, trying to become one, wish you weren't one, or just want to talk about it, reach out to others like you. You can find things to buy, read, discuss, or just surf though. From the incredibly "interactive"—you punch in dates and it adjusts to your pregnancy period—pregnancy calendar to medical updates on trendy worries like Lyme disease, you'll never stop learning and growing. The Special Events section is home to live chats with your favorite on-site authors—doctors, family therapists, or other parents—discussing such topics as losing weight after pregnancy, childproofing your home, or bringing the Internet to life by introducing sites into activities.
WEB http://www.parentsplace.com

Positive Parenting Home Page When your child's teacher calls home to report that she's raising a ruckus, can you say, "Not my problem?" When your little tyke demands the latest army-sized water pistol, are you capable of turning him down? If you're having a little trouble deciding for yourself, perhaps you should take a look at this site, which wants to make parenting a positive experience, for both parenters and parentees. Information is also available about workshops, books, and videos that can help you out when you're not online.
WEB http://www.fishnet.net/~pparents /index.html

Things to Do With Kids A sweet and practical guide for parents who find themselves running out of entertainment ideas for their children, Things to Do With Kids offers parent-child bonding activities that include rainy-day (and sunny-afternoon) fun. The arts and crafts ideas are simple yet creative, and the necessary supplies cost very little. There's also a decent collection of assorted parenting-related links.
WEB http://www.massey.ac.nz/~KBirks /kids/kids.htm

Adoption

Adoption Forum Beginning the adoption process, adoption for singles and gay couples, and international adoption are topics covered in the libraries at this site. Position papers on open adoption and suggested reading lists are also available.

The message board offers an Adoption Reform Forum, which is full of spirited discussions about ongoing changes in the adoption process. There are also several posts regarding adoption fraud. An entire section of the message board is devoted to adoptees looking for their birth parents.

AMERICA ONLINE *keyword* adoption

Adoption Help According to this site, there are 60 to 100 couples waiting to adopt for every adoptable child. Created by the Independent Adoption Center, this site addresses those wanting to adopt and those with children to put up for adoption. Click through a number of frequently asked questions such as, "Why is it so hard to adopt these days?" (IAC explains that increases in infertility and in the acceptability of single parenthood are the major contributing factors.) Mothers wishing to put a child up for adoption can also find contact information for agencies nationwide.

WEB http://www.webcom.com /~nfediac

Adoption Resources What is the Jewish position on adoption? How can I explain adoption to my child? Any question potential or post-adoptive parents have can be answered at Adoption Resources—even if it's about post-adoption depression. The FAQ format wastes no time, and related links are inserted throughout as appropriate. The site is sponsored by an adoption agency which thankfully keeps the self-aggrandizement to a minimum.

WEB http://www.adopting.org

AdoptioNetwork Volunteers operate this admirable effort. Six FAQs, including "Legal Questions," barely begin to scratch the surface of what's available here. The database contains agencies, publications, local government agencies, legal resources, and plenty of support for the long and arduous adoption process. It should be one of the very first stops for parents who are considering adoption but don't know where to begin.

WEB http://www.infi.net/adopt

INTERNET ADOPTION PHOTOLISTING

WEB http://www.adoption.com

Run by an organization named Precious in HIS Sight, this Christian adoption agency tries to link children from Ethiopia, Russia, and other nations with prospective parents (Christian and non-

Location: http://www.adoption.com/helena.gif

Christian) around the world. Photos of the children are displayed, and a search protocol that can sort children by country, age, agency, and other criteria is available. To find out what life is like for the children, read the touching feature, "My Visit to an Ethiopian Orphanage." Just to make sure you get the message, there's an .AU file of "Jesus Loves the Little Children."

alt.adoption One couple at this newsgroup was recently informed that the child they adopted from the former Soviet Georgia was only two months old, ten months younger than they had been led to expect. Their request for advice on how to prepare for the child was answered in typical Net fashion—consult misc.kids! A healthy number of the entries here are by adoptees looking for their biological parents over the Net.
USENET alt.adoption

Divorce & custody

alt.child-support In some states, a new wife's wages can be garnished if her husband falls behind on child support. This subject is widely discussed at this newsgroup, along with other child-support issues. Digressions are commonplace —the newsgroup veers frequently into conversations about child molestation, divorce, and even rape.
USENET alt.child-support

alt.support.divorce Laura seeks advice on coping with her anger at being divorced and raising two children by herself. Tom wonders what his custody rights will be if he leaves the U.S. Paul is looking for anyone else who divorced his wife for a gay lover. This is the place to go for advice and support when dealing with divorce or the seemingly endless series of repercussions of one.
USENET alt.support.divorce

❝ Divorce Online: Everything you need to rid yourself of the old ball and chain. ❞

Divorce Online Everything you need to rid yourself of the old ball and chain—with links to attorneys, financial planners, and therapists. Divorce Online issues a disclaimer which states that since every divorce is different, surfers should get real advice about the details of their specific situation from a local professional. There's also a section on domestic violence.
WEB http://www.divorce-online.com /index.html

The Divorce Page A voluminous list of links, this quick-serve page offers lots of the divorce basics, but there's a personality at work, too. You've got your American Bar Association listing, and your Debt Counselors of America link—and then there's the Dumping Your Lover Electronically connection.
WEB http://www.primenet.com/~dean /resources.html

Family Law Advisor A divorce lawyer has assembled articles on divorce, alimony, and child custody. Practical information is offered—like tips on composing a watertight prenuptial agreement, dealing with the

"other" lawyer, and courtroom etiquette (spitting is not recommended). This site addresses every possible phase in the life (and death) of a marriage.
WEB http://www.divorcenet.com/law /fla.html

Parents' Little Helper This should be called the Single Parents' Little Helper, because it's a pastel-psychedelic link list for divorcing parents. Created by Patti, an enterprising mother of four kids who wished for a collection of information such as this when she was going through a divorce. She generously decided to share the wealth once she'd done the work, so if you need divorce, custody, or visitation and access information, you know where to go. Patti has not only done a thorough job, she's put it together so nicely that you almost forget the subject.
WEB http://www.carroll.com/p/cazz /index.htm

Single & step-parents

alt.support.single-parents Like so many discussion groups, this one has its share of flamers and monomaniacs, but there are also some genuinely wise and interesting contributions from parents raising kids on their own. Despite the debris of interrupted conversations and shattered rules of civility, some real possibilities exist for posters seeking out like-minded single parents.
USENET alt.support.single-parents

alt.support.step-parents Stepparents don't have an easy time. They have to deal with biological parents returning to claim the love that they feel is rightfully theirs, mates who feel torn between the present and the past, and kids who resist, resent, and rarely restrain themselves from expressing these emotions. This newsgroup offers stepparents a place to vent frustrations, share concerns, and explain (often in exhaustive detail) the legal specifics of domestic situations.
USENET alt.support.single-parents

SinPar Cafe Affecting the atmosphere of a club, SinPar Cafe offers single parents a batch of photos and bios of members, horoscope updates, and links to support groups and newsgroups. There are some amusing graphics, and the clubby atmosphere is first-rate for people who like to join in.
WEB http://www.crl.com/~seajay /sinpar.html

The Stepfamilies Association of Illinois About 40 percent of U.S. children have stepparents or shuttle between divorced parents. This organization is dedicated to strengthening remarried families by providing support, referrals, consultations, and educational materials. Its Web site lists dozens of common expectations held by newly-formed stepfamilies—

"Stepparents and bioparents should always be fair" and "I won't have to put either my new partner or my children 'first' in our new family. I can love and support them all equally!"—then dashes them against the rocks of truth. What can stepfamilies realistically expect? "Legally and socially, remarriage does create a new family. However, it often takes five to eight years for most step-households to feel the closeness, bonding, and loyalty similar to a typical biological family." While five years may seem like a long time to wait, stepfamilies can take their first steps by visiting this site.
WEB http://www.parentsplace.com /readroom/stepfamily/index.html

SAFE-T-CHILD ONLINE
WEB http://yellodyno.safe-t-child.com

How do parents develop the knowledge and tools they need to prevent their children from getting lost, abducted, molested, or abused? At Safe-T, parents can assess their child's street smarts by reading a series of scenarios and deciding how the little one would react to them. Safe-T-Child also

markets products that can enhance your child's security, such as an ID card for kids, and also features excerpts from books such as *Not My Child*, which offers advice that goes beyond "Don't talk to strangers."

Child safety

Adolescence Online Directory

Although the concept of an extended adolescence is relatively new, things in today's world keep getting more complicated—and at a progressively earlier age. Dedicated to helping parents, teens, teachers and the people in their lives get through it all in one piece, this directory presents cleanly organized information, ranging from technical to friendly, academic to self-help style. Topics include mental health, health risks, conflict and violence, and counselor resources.
WEB http://education.indiana.edu/cas /adol/adol.html

Dr. Greene's House Calls A pediatrician hosts a daily Q&A session at this site. His friendly face sets the tone, and his answers are full of both detailed medical information about kids and their treatment, and development advice. One mother worries if her baby is receiving medicine that is malforming her kidneys, and another want to know which toys are appropriate for a 2-year-old—blocks, costumes, cardboard boxes, and puppets are just some of Dr. Greene's suggestions. While the advice may not apply to your particular concerns, a section of links offers nearly infinite spin-off possibilities.
WEB http://www.drgreene.com

KidsHealth From practical advice about dealing with

YOU'RE A LONG WAY OFF, BABY

Advice needed on smoking teenage daughters! Just found out this morning that my 13 yo SD has been smoking for 'quite awhile'... actual time not known. We don't have custody and she is hardly ever here, but I asked her pointblank last night if she smoked, and she said no. But I found cigarettes in her room this morning, and she told her dad they were hers. But she hasn't told her bio mom that she smokes because she doesn't want to get in trouble!

Then when I asked my bio daughter (12) if *she* was smoking too, she admitted she had tried it 'once' but never again. I asked her when, and she said 'a longgggg time ago.' Fast forward to later on, same day: I was talking to bioD to find out details of her first smoking experience and she kept looking at the floor and mumbling, so I knew something was up. Turns out she did first 'try' it about four years ago (when she was 8???!!!)... but she neglected to tell me this morning that she and SD had sneaked off YESTERDAY for a cig break!!!

Right now I feel like going to the store and buying bioD a whole carton and forcing her to smoke them all. Menthols are the crappiest, right? I don't know, because I've never had any desire to smoke and have never even tried it. Need advice please! And flamers be nice! This is NOT about smokers vs non-smokers. This is about two girls are barely 12 and 13 wanting to be 'cool' by going against what we have taught them.

What could be considered appropriate punishment for this? Does anybody have any really gross pictures of... oh, I don't know... maybe someone's LUNGS that have been subjected to tar and nicotine for about 50 years? I could have it made into a T-shirt and force them to wear it to school. Maybe I should stick to the smoke-it-or-eat-it treatment. How about cigars? Do they taste really nasty?"

—from alt.parents-teens

colic—run the vacuum cleaner; it works, even though no one knows why—to discussions about life-threatening issues, KidsHealth has something for everyone. Nicely organized in a simple but clear format and authoritatively written, it's both pleasant to navigate and useful to have.
WEB http://KidsHealth.org

The WonderWise Parent Sweet, gentle, and innovative, WonderWise Parent offers moms and dads the tools they need to

help themselves and their children become everything they want to be. Nicely organized with pretty icons and minimalist text intros to topics, the site includes a Reflecting Pool, which is a space for contemplating the moments of both frustration and joy that come to most parents, and for developing your own reflective powers.
WEB http://www.ksu.edu/wwparent/wondhome.htm

Chat

alt.parents-teens The discussions here sometimes cover ground that is teen-related. One concerned mother worries about her teenager driving all the way from Connecticut to

Florida on Spring Break. A response: "Well, I'd have some reservations about high-school seniors going to Florida for Spring Break, but the driving part would not be my main concern." For parents interested in the Exxon bill and its repercussions on everything from informal sex education to kids' respect for the Constitution, there is an interesting thread about viewing porn on the Net. But largely, this group is a victim of inane cross-postings and obnoxious teens.
USENET alt.parents-teens

misc.kids When do little girls start shaving their legs? When do they start menstruating? Should baby snoring be a con-

cern? Is circumcision a barbaric holdover or a valid modern medical practice? Why does boy's underwear have that little flap in the front, and is it really known as the "pod bay door"? This busy newsgroup doesn't have many posts from kids, but the hundreds of adults posting seem to have little else on their minds—kids' illnesses, kids' behaviors, kids' education, and kids' development are the order of every day.
USENET misc.kids

misc.kids.health Face it: Your infant is an alien. That's the only explanation for those flailing limbs, funny colors, funnier smells, and mood swings you

CHILDREN NOW
WEB http://www.dnai.com/~children

An action group in the old American tradition, Children Now uses the online medium to rally people to get involved in the political process on behalf of children. The site is very much to the point—click here if you want to email the **FCC** about the Children's Television Act, or if you want to contact your legislators about child-related bills. There are also some general policy-and-issue sections, and a free telephone number for people interested in communicating the old-fashioned way.

can't even begin to fathom. But then you post your extraterrestrial concerns to misc.kids .health, and discover that this is what having a kid is all about. Talk to someone who's been there before. Baby vomit? No problem. Toilet-training prodigies? They're represented as well. Discussions are informative, spirited, and generally humorous: "Bilious vomiting in an infant is abnormal. Save some of the vomitus next time, and show it to your doctor, and ask whether it is truly bile."
USENET misc.kids.health

❝ Do your eyes glaze over when you hear the phrases 'breast pump' and 'inguinal hernia'? ❞

misc.kids.info Do your eyes glaze over when you hear the phrases "breast pump," "ear tubes," and "inguinal hernia"? Never fear; not only are there parents out there who've been through it all before, but they're also willing to share their experiences and add to your parenting education. The assortment of topics covered in the FAQ is a bit random, but it's probably worth checking

out the misc.kids.info newsgroup, which, although it doesn't appear to be a place for exchanging messages, does have the full assortment.
USENET misc.kids.info
FAQ: **WEB** http://www.internet-is .com/misckids/index.html

Organizations
....

Administration for Children and Families This federal agency sponsors programs that "promote the economic and social well-being of families, children, individuals, and communities." Hypertext links lead to detailed mission statements and contact information for each of the 20-plus programs offered by the ACF. Some are well-known (Child Welfare Services and Aid to Families with Dependent Children), others less so (Child Support Enforcement, which helps states locate absent parents, establish paternity, and enforce legal orders of support; and Head Start, which offers medical, dental, and mental health services to preschool children from low-income families). Get descriptions and contact information.
WEB http://www.acf.dhhs.gov

D.O.E. Publications for Parents It's your tax dollars at work, so you might as well take a look at the Department of Education's "Helping Your Child" series of pamphlets, which includes such topics as "Helping Your Child Learn Math" and "Helping Your Child Learn

Responsible Behavior." Some of the information may be pretty basic, but it's still worth a look. The pamphlet on writing includes thought exercises and the suggestion that parents encourage children to keep journals so they can simultaneously develop writing and emotional skills. Guides to college financial aid are also offered.
WEB http://www.ed.gov/pubs/parents .html

National Parent Information Network Equal parts parenting supply catalog and discussion archive, this fair-sized site gathers topics appealing to a wide range of parents of young children and teenagers. The book list is eclectic and interesting, including titles of interest to parents concerned about at-risk children and children with self-esteem issues, online interests, and dyslexia. There's also a helpful list of online links.
WEB http://ericps.ed.uiuc.edu/npin /npinhome.html

Office of Child Support Homepage Sponsored by the Federal Office of Child Support, this no-nonsense home page offers an overview of its programs, the latest news and announcements, policy documents, and related information. Although it's not quite like having an online 911 service to assure that deadbeat parents pay what they owe, it's a start.
WEB http://www.acf.dhhs.gov /ACFPrograms/CSE/ocsehome.html

Kids

Pay attention, kids. The Internet isn't just for adults who want to play around

KIDS! DO YOU WANT to chat with or send email to other kids all over the world, take a virtual trip to a foreign country (or even into outer space), or look at pictures of all your favorite animals? Do you like to read? Find places where other kids have posted book reports. Do you like to write? There are loads of places that publish kids' work. If you're interested in sports or science, Barbie or bubbles, you are sure to find something interesting online. And someday you'll be telling your grandchildren about the old days of T1 connections: "When I was your age, I had to wait as long as 30 seconds for a Web page to load...."

Location: http://escrime.en-garde.com/kidpub/

KidPub WWW
WEB http://www.en-garde.com/kidpub
KidPub is filled with hundreds of stories written by kids. New stories are added every few days. Read the editor's picks of best stories, or search by age or place. Want to know what 8-year-old girls in Montana are writing about this year? You can do it at KidPub. Whether you're looking for a place to publish one of your stories or poems, or a place to read other kids' creative work, you'll like this site. More than 4,000 works of prose by young people are archived by date. Read such neo-classics as "The Rotten Pony" and "The Terrible, Horrible, No Good, Very Bad Week."

Starting points

Blackberry Creek Blackberry Creek is a lively place for America Online kids. Look at scrapbooks or make one of your own, featuring your own stories or poems (one recent sample: "Roses are red / Pine trees are green / My mom is as loud / As a washing machine!"), and look at other kids' art or post some of your own. You'll also find some movie and book reviews written by kids.
AMERICA ONLINE *keyword* **blackberry**

The Canadian Kids Home Page Proudly flying the Canadian flag, this huge page is essentially a list of well annotated links, many of which stem from the Great White North. The listings are alphabetical, so you're pretty much on your own in searching out subject areas, but there is a separate pen-pals wanted area, and most of the listings are interesting enough to warrant a visit.
WEB http://www.onramp.ca/~lowens /l07kids.htm

Cyberkids/Cyberteens Launchpad Blast into cyberspace with this easy-to-use introduction to Web crawling. CyberKids has organized a vast amount of information by subject. It's easy for aspiring artists to reach the virtual Louvre—or for aspiring capitalists to connect with Junior Achievement online! There are links to children's literature, games, museums, schools—homework help

too. It's a great place for children learning about the Web to begin.
WEB http://www.woodwind.com/mtlake /CyberKids/Launchpad.html

Kidspace This is a very plain page, but don't let that fool you: there are many links that will lead you to some great sites for kids.
WEB http://main.aisp.net/text/kid.htm

Splash Kids Online This production of Splash Studios is an online magazine that will probably get bookmarked by many kids. You'll find features including a daily joke, environmental updates, news reports by kids, and reviews of kid-friendly software. Try it, you might just like it.
WEB http://www.splash.com

Uncle Bob's Kids' Pages Uncle Bob wants you to stay busy. He's collected hundreds of sites on all kinds of subjects kids like. The one drawback to this page is that the sites are not arranged in an order that makes it easy to find something specific. If you do want to find something specific, go somewhere else. On the other hand, if you're just poking about and don't know what you're looking for, you just might find it here.
WEB http://gagme.wwa.com/~boba /kidsi.html

Yahooligans! This is a section of the Yahoo! search engine that's just for kids. You can type in a subject, and Yahoo! will find

sites that fit their interests. It isn't nearly as good as it should be, and it's cluttered with too many pages that will try to sell something, but it's still the best place on the Web for you to find a site about a particular subject. This would be a good site to bookmark.
WEB http://www.yahooligans.com

Youth Central You'll find discussion boards on music and entertainment, photo essays, artwork, and stories posted by kids and teens, and surprisingly little advertising for Apple, considering that it's an Apple-sponsored site.
WEB http://www.youthcentral.apple .com

Animal world

African Primates at Home Page This page starts well, but it doesn't delve very far into the world of our evolutionary cousins, monkeys and apes. It does, however, have nice pictures and brief factual descriptions of several species, which makes it worth a visit for cursory info on the primate world.
WEB http://www.indiana.edu/~primate /primates.html

Australian A-Z Animal Archive Everything you'd ever want to know about Australian animals, from the antechinuses, (small mouse-like animals), to zyzmomys (rock rats). K is the best letter of the animal archive: It stands for kangaroos, koala bears, and the kul-

tarr, a rare, kangaroo-like mouse.
WEB http://www.aaa.com.au/A_Z/K.html

B-EYE: The World Through the Eye of a Bee A scientist studying the eyesight of the bee has put together this bee-yoo-tiful page that will show you what it's like to see the world through the eyes of a bee. Maybe next time one stings you, you'll understand why.
WEB http://cvs.anu.edu.au/andy/beye/beyehome.html

CELLS Alive! If you're fascinated by microscopic views of the world, check out this page. There are pictures, animated .GIFs, and QuickTime movies of our bodies' cells and the microscopic creatures that

bother them. Some of the views are amazing. You'll never forget to wash your hands again!
WEB http://www.comet.chv.va.us/quill/Indexl.htm

Enoshima Aquarium Not a lot of marine information is available from the home page of this Japanese aquarium, but there are plenty of nice pictures of jellyfish, otters, dolphins, and other oceanic animals. Worth a quick stop.
WEB http://www.iseshima.com/enoshima/index.html

The Froggy Page Frog stories, frog pictures, frog clip art, frog sounds, frog facts, even frog songs are available here. A great link to add to your expanding home pad.

WEB http://www.cs.yale.edu/HTML/YALE/CS/HyPlans/loosemore-sandra/froggy.html

Fun Facts About Tigers Did you know that tigers can see in the dark six times better than humans can? Or that they use their tails to keep their balance during quick turns? If the answer is no, it's time to visit this page and brush up on your tiger trivia. In addition to a page of quick tiger facts, you'll find some longer descriptions about each species of tiger that will be a great help if you should ever need to write up a report for school.
WEB http://www.5tigers.org/coolfac.htm

Gorilla Foundation Home Page The Gorilla Foundation was

BERIT'S BEST SITES FOR CHILDREN
 WEB http://www.cochran.com/theosite/ksites.html
picture: WEB http://www.adventure.com/science_lab/3d_dino/createasaurus
If you're tired of visiting the same old sites, it's time to visit Berit's Best. All the sites on this hub

are rated and have short descriptions that will keep you from wasting a lot of time calling up junk. Berit's Best really are among the best around. Many of the listed sites are also unusual, things you won't find on other lists. The site descriptions are written for parents, but don't let that put you off.

Location : http://207.2.56.10:80/science_lab/3d_dino/crea

Location: http://www.gorilla.org/PhotoVideo/Koko_holding_Smoky.jpg

KoKo goes ape for her pet kitten
http://www.gorilla.org/index.html

established to teach gorillas sign language. Its star pupil, Koko, uses about 500 signs but knows more than 1,000. At this Web site, you'll learn all about the Foundation's fascinating project, as well as facts about gorillas in general. The best part, though, is the page of personal facts concerning three foundation gorillas. Koko's favorite foods are nuts, apples, and corn on the cob. She likes to watch "Wild Kingdom," and she's wild about "Free Willy." Her favorite activities are playing with dolls, playing chase, and drawing.
WEB http://www.gorilla.org/index.html

Hummingbirds If you have a hummingbird feeder but can't seem to attract any of the mighty mites, this page may be able to help. You'll find information on flowers that attract hummingbirds, hummingbird migration patterns, and hum-

mingbirds' favorite colors (fluorescent red and orange).
WEB http://www.inlink.com/~creative /hummers/welcome.html

Interesting Stuff About Opossums This page opens with a picture of a possum with her babies riding on her back and gets better. If you've always thought of possums just as pests, this page will show you that they have their virtues, too. There are lots of facts about possums here (did you know that they are marsupials?), including the one explaining where the phrase "playing possum" comes from.
WEB http://bmewww.eng.uab.edu/BME /MORE/personalities/students /schroeder/opossum.htm

The Lion Gallery You'll enjoy this collection of terrific lion pictures. If you want to see something very cute, take a look at "Cheap Back Rub." Besides the photographs, there's also a

sound file of a lion's roar, a factoid of the month, and links to other lion sites.
WEB http://www.frontiertech.com/gall .htm

Mt. St. Helens and Other Volcanoes: Bats at Ape Cave Bats are the subject of this short but interesting page. The Bats at Ape Cave page will teach you a lot about the mysterious flying mammals, even if you only have a few minutes to spend there.
WEB http://volcano.und.nodak.edu /vwdocs/msh/ov/ovb/ovbacalb.html

Ocean Planet: In Search of the Giant Squid If you were to read about the giant squid in a book, you'd think the author was making it up. For one thing, the giant squid is supposed to be 60 feet long! For another, scientists don't know very much about where in the ocean these animals live. Occasionally, fishermen find them. Often, dead specimens wash up on a beach somewhere. Fantastic illustrations, incredible facts—wrap your tentacles around your mouse and check it out.
WEB http://seawifs.gsfc.nasa.gov/squid .html

Orca Killer Whales You'll learn all kinds of things about the killer whale at this site, including the fact that, although it's well equipped to take a chunk out of a person, there's never been a case of a killer whale swallowing a human being. In addition, there are pictures,

sound files, and book excerpts, all about the dolphin's black-and-white cousin.
WEB http://www.slip.net/~oyafuso /orcinusorca.html

The Penguin Page Unlike many animal pages, the Penguin Page looks great and has a lot of information, too. Anything you want to know about penguins, from where they live to what they eat to how they fight, you can find here.
WEB http://www.vni.net/~kwelch /penguins

The San Diego Zoo There are plenty of descriptions here about America's most famous zoo, and a few pictures of the usual assortment of lions, tigers, and panda bears (not to mention giraffes).
WEB http://www.sandiegozoo.org/Zoo /zoo.html

Sea Otter You won't learn much about the sea otter here, but you will find some very cute pictures.
WEB http://www.ghs.com/ghs/people /jimmy/otter5.html

Sea World/Busch Gardens One of the best features here is Animal Bytes, an encyclopedia of information about a number of different animals. You'll learn all kinds of interesting facts about your favorite animals at this site (Did you know that parrots never mimic sounds in the wild, but only in captivity?).
WEB http://www.bev.net/education /SeaWorld/homepage.html

Sharks This comprehensive and well designed site is a beautifully illustrated FAQ about the "terror of the deep." The webmaster has read about sharks for more than 15 years and here shares all he knows and has been able to find out from marine biologists and other shark specialists. If you're looking for pictures and facts about the shark, you can't do much better than the Shark Web site.
WEB http://www.io.org/~gwshark /sharks.html

Take a Walk in the Rainforest This virtual tour is a good introduction to one of the most amazing habitats in the world, the rain forest. Beautiful photographs of many kinds of rain forest animals and plants are described in short, clear, factual sentences. Definitely worth a stop, but you may leave wanting more.
WEB http://www.pbs.org/tal/costa_rica /rainwalk.html

Virtual Whales At this site, you can watch a variety of movie clips about whales, both animated and real. You'll especially enjoy the animated clips of whales swimming and feeding. There are also sound clips of a variety of whale songs. The songs sound a little like the warm-up chords of a heavy-metal guitarist, but we don't think they'll make the top of the human charts any time soon.
WEB http://www.sfu.ca/~michaec /whales.htm

Whale Information Network This Australian whale information guide is pretty much comprehensive. If you want to know about a specific kind of whale, you can find something about it here, under Whale Facts. If you want to know about a specific whale behavior, you can find that here, too.
WEB http://www.macmedia.com.au /whales

Arts & crafts

Crayola Crayola has just made their 100-billionth crayon, and, to celebrate, they've created a "brand-new, once-in-a-lifetime" color called Blue Ribbon. At the Crayola home page, you can download a QuickTime video of Mr. Rogers helping to make this historic crayon in the Crayola factory. Other fun features include Crayolatrivia, a virtual tour of a kids' museum, and interactive card coloring. There are also tons of contests to enter, like the Storybook Maker Contest, which gives you a chance to publish your own illustrated storybook, both in print and on the Web.
WEB http://www.crayola.com/crayola

Eric's Origami Page You won't learn how to do origami here, but you will find amazing pictures of all kinds of origami creatures. You won't believe what some origami artists are able to do with folded paper. Check out the samurai helmet beetle. If these pictures inspire

WISE WORDS FROM DR. SEUSS

My uncle ordered popovers
from the restaurant's bill of fare.
And when they were served,
he regarded them
with a penetrating stare...
The he spoke great Words of Wisdom
as he sat there on that chair:
"To eat these things,"
said my uncle,
"you must exercise great care.
You may swallow down what's solid...
BUT...
you must spit out the air!"
And...
as you partake of the world's bill of fare,
That's darned good advice to follow.
Do a lot of spitting out the hot air
And be careful what you swallow.

—from CyberSeuss

you, go to the long list of links, where you're sure to find some pages that will tell you how to get started. If you'd rather just look at more online origami galleries, you can find those too.
WEB http://www.netspace.org/~ema /origami.html

Lite Board This online version of the picture-making toy is fun and easy to use. Unlike many drawing programs, it doesn't seem to require any special tools. If you have a mouse, you're in business.
WEB http://asylum.cid.com/lb/lb.html

The Refrigerator: Kids' Art Online For a look at some nice kids' art, stop by The Refrigerator, a gallery of kids' online art.
WEB http://www.aimnet.com/~jennings /refrigerator/index.html

Web-a-Sketch We couldn't get this Web version of Etch-a-Sketch to work, but we're out of practice. Judging from the gallery, a lot of other people are having fun with it.
WEB http://www.digitalstuff.com/web -a-sketch

Books

Book Nook Having trouble deciding what you want to read next? This site is the place to go. You can find short book reports written by kids, post your own book reports, and even visit a conference area

where you can post questions about a particular book you're looking for or want to talk about.
WEB http://www.schoolnet.ca/arts/lit /booknook/index.html

CyberSeuss There's less Seuss on the loose here than you'd expect, but it's still worth a visit to read a little about Dr. Seuss and look at a few good *Cat-in-the-Hat* pictures.
WEB http://www.afn.org/~afnl5301 /drseuss.html

Goosebumps Goosebumps books and calendars such as *The Werewolf of Fever Swamp*, *Monster Blood II*, and *Go Eat Worms!* All the books and merchandise you could ever dream of, are spotlighted here, with the help of some creepy-crawly graphics at the home page of the top-selling book series.
WEB http://scholastic.com/Goose-bumps/index.html

Magic School Bus Fun Place This site almost lives up to its name, with coloring books, puzzles, and games taken from the popular book and television series. You won't find as much fun as the title promises, but you certainly will find some.
WEB http://scholastic.com/Magic SchoolBus/index.html

Nikolai's Web Site This is a great page, with interactive stories and activities about a boy named Nikolai and his cat, Neow-Neow. Along with stories that let you decide what happens next, there are pages

to color, puzzles, and games.
WEB http://www.h-plus-a.com/nikolai/nnn.htm

Redwall Abbey If you're a fan of Brian Jacques's Redwall books, Redwall Abbey will be your cyberhome away from home. Redwall Abbey is the home of the 300-member Redwall Club. David Lindsay, 11, has assembled a great page of links and information on all things related to Redwall.
WEB http://www.islandnet.com/~qnd/redwall/homepage.html

Computer games

Happy Puppy Happy Puppy will have you wagging your tail in no time. It features links to hundreds of gaming sites where you can download games, and links to games you can play right on the Web without any downloading. It's a big site, but don't let that put you off. Go to the bottom of the front page to find the category you want.
WEB http://happypuppy.com

Kid's Shareware and More This is a good place to go the next time you're looking for a new game but don't want to spend a lot of money. Freeware programs for both Mac and PC are yours to take if you want them; you can also download shareware programs, but have to pay a small fee to keep them. There is also a list of links to sites that review software, but these are mostly for parents.
WEB http://www.gamesdomain.com/tigger

Cooking

The Peppered Leopard Let Chef Le Pep at the Peppered Leopard show you how to cook. New lessons are added continuously.
AMERICA ONLINE *keyword* kids→Hobbies & Clubs→Egg for Young Chefs

Tasty Insect Recipes If you're always hungry, this might help. It's a collection of recipes from Iowa State University in which worms and beetles are the ingredients!

THE YUCKIEST SITE ON THE NET

 WEB http://www.nj.com/yucky/index.html

Some people eat cockroaches fried in oil and garlic as a cure for indigestion. South American Earth Worms can grow up to nine feet long. These and other disgusting facts are at your fingertips. Worm World gives you exclusive interviews with celebs like Tommi Tapeworm. Add to the collection of classic worm humor (Q: What's worse than biting into an apple and finding a worm? A: Finding half a worm!), or view QuickTime vids of a real worm birth. Cockroach World shows you a day in the life of Rodney Roach and how to collect and keep roaches as pets (won't Mom love that?). So much infotainment is stuffed into this spot, it would take a year to explore. So get going!

WEB http://www.ent.iastate.edu/Misc/InsectsAsFood.html

Dinosaurs

Charlotte, the Vermont Whale In 1849, railroad workers in Vermont accidentally found the skeleton of a mysterious creature that scientists later identified as a whale. That's right: a whale. How did a whale get to Vermont, more than 150 miles from the ocean? Find out here.
WEB http://www.uvm.edu/whale/whalehome.html

The Field Museum The dinosaur models aren't quite ready for Jurassic Park, but you'll like them anyway. This site isn't just an introduction to the famous Chicago museum; it's an online museum in itself. You can learn everything you ever wanted to know about those big lizards and other creatures of the past by logging onto this site.
WEB http://rs6000.bvis.uic.edu/museum

Royal Tyrrell Museum Tired of animations of dinosaurs? Take a look at the real thing. Well, part of the real thing: This Calgary, Canada, museum has plenty of great skeletons.
WEB http://tyrrell.magtech.ab.ca/tour/dinohall.html

The earth

Energy Quest This California-based site is designed to give kids a sense of the whole world of energy sources and alternatives. The individual sections aren't especially detailed, but if you just want an overview of the various forms of energy, this is a good site to visit. In addition to the descriptions of different energy sources, you'll find an Ask Us section, where you can ask an energy expert any question you may have on the subject.
WEB http://www.energy.ca.gov/energy/education/eduhome.html

Volcano World This is an amazing site. Even if you aren't overwhelmingly interested in volcanoes, you should visit Volcano World, just to see some of the great pictures and movie clips of volcanoes around the world collected by webmasters. Other features include descriptions of the forces that cause volcanoes, and a section in which you can post your questions about volcanoes to a volcanologist.
WEB http://volcano.und.nodak.edu

Girls only

Amber's Place—Girls Only! Amber's home page has links to a number of girls' clubs, magazines, and keypal groups. If you're a girl, and, want to make friends with other girls online, this is the place to go.
WEB http://www.davelash.com/amber/girlpage.html

American Girl You'll find features from this terrific magazine, along with ideas of things to do, and an interactive advice column ("Help from Me") in which online girls post their solutions to another *AG* reader's problem.
WEB http://www.pleasantco.com

Club Girl Tech At one time, the Internet just had stuff for boys. No longer! Now there are plenty of sites for girls, too. When this site is finished, it will probably be one of the best, but even now it's pretty good. It features special Java games and puzzles, a pen pal server, and an advice column.
WEB http://www.girltech.com

History

A Walking Tour of Plimoth Plantation What was life really like for the Pilgrims? Find out by taking a tour of Plimoth Plantation, an outdoor museum that tries to recreate the Pilgrims' village in every detail—right down to the funny spelling of Plymouth. Look at pictures of the reconstructed village and the reconstructed Native American village next door.
WEB http://spirit.lib.uconn.edu/ArchNet/Topical/Historic/Plimoth/Plimoth.html

Reeder's Egypt Page This site will fascinate you. Greg Reeder has put together a page that shows you pictures and tells you interesting facts about ancient Egypt, all of which are displayed in an interesting way. If you've been looking for information about ancient Egypt, but keep running into dreary encyclopedia articles, this is a good place to turn.

WEB http://www.sirius.com/~reeder/egypt.html

SPQR A plot threatens the future of the Roman Empire. You can save it. You'll love the graphics on this game—they're as good as anything you may have seen on CD-ROM, and more mysterious than those offered by *Myst*.
WEB http://pathfinder.com /twep/rome

The Viking Home Page If you're writing a report on Vikings, this is a great place to start your research raid. There's not much at this page itself, but you will find a long list of links to other Viking pages.
WEB http://www.control.chalmers.se/vikings/viking.html

Holidays

Cake Time What famous person shares your birthday? Jim Carrey? Albert Einstein? George Washington? Search this database to find the star born under your star.
WEB http://oeonline.com/~edog/bday.html

Cybercalifragilistic Birthday Greeting Announcement Page Post a birthday greeting to a pal here, or post one to yourself.
WEB http://www.webcom.com/~getagift/Birthday_Page.html

Halloween-O-Webbery Decorating ideas, costume ideas, spooky music recommenda-

tions, and more, from a woman in Minnesota who's crazy about the scariest holiday of all.
WEB http://www.primenet.com/~trix/hallo.htm

North Pole Web Send an email to Santa, read some reindeer recipes (recipes for your reindeer friends, that is), and listen to "'Twas the Night Before Christmas."
WEB http://north.pole.org/santa

Kids' writing

CyberKids Space Look at other kids' artwork, read kids' stories, or listen to kids' compositions. You can also submit your own work. The older kids may

⊚ ZooNet
WEB http://www.mindspring.com/~zoonet

If you want to find information about animals or zoos, this is the first place you should go. You'll find links to hundreds of different zoo and animal pages here, from the Birmingham Zoo in Alabama to the Milwaukee County Zoological Gardens in Wisconsin. Pictures of all your favorites are here, as well as some you may not have heard of yet (ever see a gaur or a kudu?) or some you didn't know were real (the kookaburra *does* sit in old gum trees).

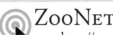

Location: http://www.nol.net/~wqent/zoonet/jackson/pictures/elephan2.jpg

want to read the fantasy novel *The Chosen Ones*, which is appearing in serial form on the site, one chapter at a time. The graphics are nothing special, but, on the other hand, they don't take long to download.
WEB http://www.cyberkids.com

Kidworld Another site where you can find kids' stories, a serialized novel, and puzzles.
WEB http://www.bconnex.net/~kidworld

Positively Poetry In a world where most poetry journals have only a few hundred readers, 13-year-old Kellie Vaughn's *Positively Poetry* site stands out: *Positively Poetry* has had more than 4,500 readers in the past six months alone! *Positively Poetry* publishes kids' poems, usually around 30 every month.
WEB http://iquest.com/~e-media/kv/poetry.html

Maps

Xerox Parc Map Viewer This looks pretty complicated, but be patient. It's actually a great zoom map of the world. Point an arrow anywhere on the map and keep on clicking until you've zoomed into that particular dot on the globe.
WEB http://mapweb.parc.xerox.com/map

Yahoo! Maps Type in any street address in the U.S. and a map of that area will pop up. Technology—it just keeps getting better.
WEB http://www.proximus.com/yahoo

IN THE KITCHEN WITH RUDOLPH

Rudolph loves to cook and is considered the epicure of the pointed hooves set! Try a few of his better known creations:

MOSS SNAPS
A tasty concoction of the best from the frozen tundra. Rudolph says the green slimy moss works the best. He mixes in the exotic taste of ginger and penguin feathers to create a true taste treat.

ALGAE NEWTONS
Um, Um, Um! Just like Mom used to make! A cookie is just a cookie, but Algae Newtons are lichen and cake!

ELF LOGS
Rudolph isn't a big fan of those elves so he made what he proudly calls an "Elf Log." No storebought cookies these, tundra logs are (quoting out of context Joseph Mitchell, the famous writer for the *New Yorker* magazine): "coated inside and out with a lush furry growth made up of algae, sea moss, tube worms, barnacles, horse mussels, sea anemones, sea squirts, sea mice, sea snails, and scores of other organisms."

—from North Pole Web

Meeting places

International Kids' Space If you're tired of running into the same old kids at different sites, come to the International Kids' Space and meet kids from around the world through their stories, artwork, compositions, and home pages. Kids' home page listings are found in a section called the Web Kid's Village, and are categorized by topic, which will make it easy for you to find a key pal somewhere in the world who might share some of your particular interests.
WEB http://plaza.interport.net/kids_space

KIDLINK If you like getting email, check out Kidlink. More than 60,000 kids in 87 countries have participated in Kidlink since it first began. Once you're signed up, you'll get messages from lots of kids who are interested in talking about various topics, and you can write back to one of them or to all of them at once.
WEB http://www.kidlink.org/home-std.html

Movies & video

Children's Television Workshop Family Corner This is mostly for Mom and Dad right now, but there are some free computer

games here for kids and a downloadable alphabet coloring book.
WEB http://www.am.wpafb.af.mil /museum/zone/dz.html

Disney.com Home Page The Disney page—like the company—is big, but dull. Except for some great movie pages and a story section that features stories taken from the movies, most of the site is devoted to selling one Disney product or another, from videos to vacations. Unless you're a hardcore Disney fan, this won't be somewhere you'll want to stay very long. One good feature of the page is that the movie clips can be downloaded fairly quickly.
WEB http://www.disney.com

Disney!!! Simply, Absolutely, Mostly Simply, Absolutely, Mostly is nicely, nicely done. Much less cluttered than many sites (including Disney's official home page), this is a great place to start your search for Disney pictures and information. Disney's webmasters know that you are just looking for pictures and information about the world of Disney, not Disney the media company. Features range from "official" Disney empire links—studios, parks, and hundreds of archived pics—to info on every movie Disney has made in its 60-year history. Be sure to check out Meeko's Bag o' Biscuits for the site of the week.
WEB http://www.columbia.edu/~zm4 /index3.html

Science & inventors

Bill Nye the Science Guy's NYE LABS ONLINE Episode guides, complete with film clips and a Demo of the Day from that wacky wizard, Bill Nye the Science Guy. If you accidentally learn something, we promise it won't be painful. Try downloading the theme song, or the clip of "Dr. Nyeski" explaining nuclear fission in the style of the classic movie *Dr. Strangelove*.
WEB http://nyelabs.kcts.org

Discovery Channel Online This isn't specifically for kids, but, if you're interested in history, nature, science, people, technology, or animals, you'll definitely find something interest-

 ## ARCTIC DAWN: THE JOURNEY OF SAMUEL HEARNE
WEB http://web.idirect.com/~hland/sh/title.html

In 1768, an ex-sailor named Samuel Hearne set out on a voyage through the far north of Canada, where no Europeans had ever been. At this site, you can read about his adventures over the following four years, in his own words. There are also modern photographs of the places he saw and

hypertext links in which Hearne explains at greater length certain customs of the Native American tribes he met, and describes the animals he encountered. If you're interested in history, culture, animals, or all three, you'll like this page.

THERE ARE NO STUPID QUESTIONS

Question: A steel nail sinks. But a steel ship floats. How can that be?

Answer: Floating is a lot like a shoving match. The boat is pushing down on the water and the water is pushing up, holding the boat up. If the water pushes up harder than the boat pushes down, the boat floats. If the boat presses down harder than the water pushes up, it wins the shoving match and sinks. (It's not much of a victory.) Which ever pushes harder, wins. Water pushing up. Boat or nail pushing down. A steel boat hull is not as heavy as the amount water that the boat hull pushes away, or displaces. Imagine the boat as making a hole in the water. If the boat weighs less than the water it would take to fill that hole, it floats.

Question: Where do farts come from? Why do they smell bad?

Answer: This is one of those rude-word questions that I might get in trouble for talking about. Still, it's an excellent question—in fact, one of the questions we get the most. This question was the No. I question the *Beakman's World* TV show received. That's why I think you deserve an answer. The TV show people thought it was too controversial a subject and didn't do it. (Controversy means when people think different things about the same thing and talk about it. A lot.) The syndicate that distributes You Can decided that this question would make newspaper editors angry and decided to withold it from newspapers unless they specifcally asked for it. As few as four newspapers published this. The formal word for farts it is flatulence (FLA-chu-lentz). People don't use that word much, however. Flatulence is mostly air mixed with the gas methane. Other gases mixed in are the stuff that make it smell. Methane doesn't have a smell.

—from You Can with Beakman and Jax

You Can with Beakman and Jax You'll find a Shockwaved interactive experiment, a preview of upcoming episodes of the popular science cartoon, and some pictures of the solar system from the Hubble Telescope, but the heart of this page is a list of 50 science questions (well, 38 right now—the page is still under construction). The questions are surprisingly interesting. Question 1, for example, is "how does soap work?" Answers are given along with experiments that demonstrate the solutions to the questions.
WEB http://www.nbn.com/youcan

Scouting

Boy Scouts of America There have been 90 million since 1910. Here's everything else you ever wanted to know about Boy Scouts.
WEB http://www.bsa.scouting.org

Girl Scouts of the U.S. Whether you're a Girl Scout, would like to be one, or are the parent of one, this friendly, stripped-down and easy-to-use resource will have answers to all your GS questions. The info covers the national organization, local sites, and, of course, cookie sales. There's also an email link for personalized responses to your queries.
WEB http://www.gsusa.org

Ships, planes & trains

Marine Sounds Add a foghorn, sailors' shouts, or some other

ing. A new story is introduced every day on this nicely designed site, with a different category for every day of the week.
WEB http://www.discovery.com

Invention Dimension Ever wonder if you have what it takes to be an inventor? Find out here.

This site from MIT, which features an inventor of the week, a short biographical essay on some famous and not-so-famous inventors thoughout history, from that guy who invented the lightbulb to the woman who invented Liquid Paper.
WEB http://web.mit.edu/invent

sea-related sound to your collection of weird sound clips.
WEB http://www.marineart.com/www.shtml#s

The Original Titanic Page Once it's out of dry dock, this is going to be a great page again. Even now, as it's being rebuilt, this is a terrific place to look at pictures and read about the unsinkable ship that sank. You can find out many interesting facts, from the crucial, like the rudder that was too small for the ship, to the not so crucial (provisions included 40,000 eggs and 16,000 lemons).
WEB http://gil.ipswichcity.qld.gov.au/~dalgarry

Steam Locomotives You've seen steam locomotives in Westerns, but what about all those trains that rolled the rails between the time the West was won and the time the diesel years began? Here are some pictures of those black beauties.
WEB http://www.inmind.com/people/teague/steamtrains.html

USAF Museum Discovery Zone Ever wonder how an airplane really works? Let the U.S. Air Force explain it all for you.
WEB http://www.am.wpafb.af.mil/museum/zone/dz.html

Web Battleship It's not *Doom*, but it's still fun. Test your wits against the computer in this

computer version of the old peg game.
WEB http://info.gte.com/gtel/fun/battle/battle.html

Fun stuff

The Official LEGO World Wide Web If you love Lego, this is the toy for you. You'll find out all kinds of interesting facts about Lego. For example, did you know that children spend an estimated five billion hours a year playing with Lego?
WEB http://www.lego.com

Professor Bubbles' Bubblesphere This incredible site tells you everything you ever wanted to know about blowing bubbles,

National Geographic Online
WEB www.nationalgeographic.com

Explore South Africa's parks. Excavate ice treasures of the Inca. Features like these from the National Geographic Society's magazines and television show are lushly translated to the Web in highly interactive fashion. In case your hard drive isn't fully outfitted, head first to Gear, where you can download all the Shockwave, RealAudio, and QuickTime you'll need to experience National Geographic Online. Then, just click on the passport, and begin your digital journey. Diversions has

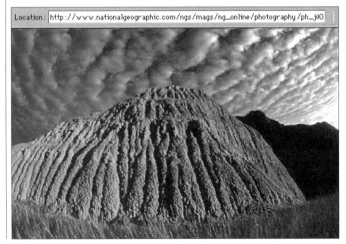

Location: http://www.nationalgeographic.com/ngs/mags/ng_online/photography/ph_jü0

handy maps, trivia questions, and that fun little brain teaser from *World* magazine, where you try to guess what an object is from a very close-up picture. You can even send a postcard with a message to anyone on the Web! This section of the site also houses a Gold Mine of Information, where questions and answers from "Glad You Asked" are archived.

including how you can make bubble solution and bubble wands yourself. There is also a bubble FAQ ("Why are bubbles always round?"), and some amazing pictures—check out the one of Professor Bubble inside a huge bubble.
WEB http://bubbles.org

Space

NASA—Apollo 11 NASA stands for National Aeronautics and Space Administration. It might also stand for National Amazing Site Agency. Here at the Apollo 11 home page, you'll find sound clips, movies, and some great stories by the astronauts from the mission that first took men to the moon.
WEB http://www.gsfc.nasa.gov/hqpao /apollo_11.html

NASA Homepage If you're looking for a liftoff from your ordinary online routine of chat and cartoon pages, check this one out. The NASA home page will lead you to all of NASA's official pages. The best parts are the pictures and the videos.
WEB http://www.nasa.gov/NASA _homepage.html

Space Coloring Book If you like rockets and space stations, you may appreciate this online coloring book. Just print these pictures out from your computer, staple them together, and you'll have plenty of extraterrestrial artwork to keep you coloring.

WEB http://tommy.jsc.nasa.gov /~woodfill/SPACEED/SEHHTML /color.html

Views of the Solar System Mars, Venus, Jupiter, Saturn—maybe you've seen a picture or two, but at this site, you can look at more than 950 pictures and animations of various bodies in the solar system, along with short descriptions of each one. Be sure to take advantage of the chance to look directly into the sun without hurting yourself.
WEB http://bang.lanl.gov/solarsys /homepage.htm

Sports

Sports Illustrated for Kids This online edition of the great kids' magazine is one of the only sports sites on the Net written with kids in mind. You'll find it's a great source of information about sports and pro players, and also a good place to play some fun games.
WEB http://pathfinder.com/SIFK

Virtual tours

Around the World in 80 Clicks Click on any of the red dots on the map of the world at this site and send yourself on a visit to a different part of our planet.
WEB http://www.coolsite.com/arworld .html

Japanese Schools with English Web Pages Be an exchange student for five minutes. Visit the English-language Web pages of a few of these schools and

get an idea of what life is like for Japanese kids.
WEB http://wacky.ccit.arizona.edu /~susd/jschools.html

Kid's Window (on Japan) Kids interested in Japan will have a great time, with cultural and language lessons accompanied by bright graphics. There's an online storybook in English and Japanese, a picture dictionary, and an arts and crafts section with a Let's Learn Origami lesson. Kid's Window makes learning about this big world and the people in it a fun thing—now, that's cool.
WEB http://jw.stanford.edu/KIDS/kids _home.html

TerraQuest If you're in the mood for an adventure, TerraQuest should be one of your stops. TerraQuest produces virtual adventures for the Web. The latest: The story of a blind man who climbs a mountain.
WEB http://www.terraquest.com

Virtual Tours Travel Center Who cares if you're grounded? Take a trip around the world and while away the time until you're allowed to leave the block again. From the Virtual Tours Travel Center, you can set off on hundreds of virtual tours around the world.
WEB http://www.virtuocity.com/travel /tours.html

Virtual World Tours Choose a city, a country, or a museum to visit from the long list of sites.
WEB http://www.dreamscape.com /frankvad/world.html

Gen ral Medicin

From diet advice to the latest alternative cure-all, get better online

THESE DAYS, politicians talk about "family values" as if they're going out of style—and perhaps they are—but in focusing solely on moral issues, it's easy to take for granted basic material necessities like sound, affordable family health care. The rapidly-expanding network of digital medical resources makes it possible for families to access invaluable advice on health and medicine, occasionally even saving themselves a costly and time-consuming consultation with a professional. Doctors are flocking to the Net in droves, and, while it's not quite the same as a home visit, many can offer consultations, advice or second opinions via email. While online advice should only ever be considered supplementary to your relationship with your health provider, there is a lot you can learn here. Heal thyself.

Location: http://www.medaccess.com/better_info/better_info.htm

Better Information for Your Health and Wellness

Healthy Children   Just for Seniors

MedAccess

WEB http://www.medaccess.com/home.htm
Another site that is bogged down with accolades (top 5 percent, *NetGuide* 4 Stars, etc.), but for good reason. MedAccess promotes family health by providing downloadable health workbooks to keep track of children's immunizations and illnesses (user-friendly for the organizationally challenged) and a health and safety alert section direct from the Federal Food and Drug Administration for the latest toxins reports on common household goods. A section called You Are What You Eat investigates just what's in that chicken and rice casserole.

Starting points

Achoo Online Healthcare Services
Gesundheit! This is actually a springboard to all sorts of health and medicine sites all over the world. With more than 6,600 links, it provides a good starting point for answering such burning questions as, "why does it hurt when I go to the bathroom." The latest beef on "mad cow" disease? The Healthcare Headline News should be able to help. If there isn't enough time to examine all the related sites then peruse through the critiques of Web sites, Web Site Kudos, or the Site of the Week. Cybermedical professionals can also get help with their Web site construction with Achoo's Web Site Design and Development Packages.
WEB http://www.achoo.com

America's Housecall Network An online nursing station for everything from nosebleeds to acne. Covers colds, flu, and stomach ailments in detail. People in perfect health can try some of the preventative medicine material in the Wellness and Nutrition section. Learn about the contents of your medicine cabinet (not including that moldy retainer from high school) in Drugs and Medications. Getting old? Reference Older Adults and learn about care and feeding of the elderly. If you can't find it on the shelves, you can always ask the online Librarian. Includes links to dentistry,

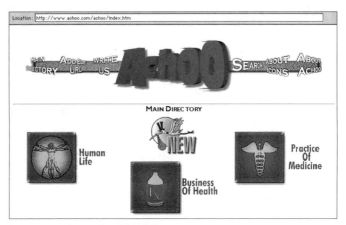

Location: http://www.achoo.com/achoo/index.htm

Blesses you with more than 6,600 links
http://www.achoo.com

pharmacology, and dermatology sites as well as links to medical associations.
WEB http://www.housecall.com

Health Resources Focusing on "reliable and practical" health and fitness information, this site offers an excellent set of Net-wide links on everything from deafness and depression to sex and smoking. The collection of links to health-care publications is particularly extensive, as is the listing of state and national health-care organizations. In addition, the site offers documents and links of interest to health care providers.
WEB http://www.ihr.com

Health Support Forums A central spot on CompuServe for discussion areas devoted to cancer, diabetes, disabilities, multiple sclerosis, muscular dystrophy, attention deficit disorder, and recovery. The issues and problems addressed in the

Recovery section include nicotine addiction, alcohol abuse, and eating disorders. "I'm angry at this disease that prevents me from stuffing my face to stop my feelings," wrote Tom. "I'm angry that I have to take responsibility and can't let myself be out of control." Tom apologized for whining, but Beth, responding to him, wrote: "Just sounds like good honest recovery work to me— the kind that helps you." Much support offered in these active areas. Lively discussions in the Message sections, while the Libraries include studies, reports, and other information.
COMPUSERVE *go* hlt-13

HealthNet An excellent health and medical reference, with a library divided into such section heads as disorders and diseases, tests and procedures, symptoms, and drugs. Poison ivy a problem? Cold compresses are great and don't worry about the little ones

scratching—once all the resin has been washed off, the rash is contained. New summer pumps giving you ingrown toenails? Cut the nail straight across and wedge cotton between skin and nail to relieve pain before going to a doctor. Wondering about that dizziness you've been feeling? Check the "dizziness" selection, and read an entry discussing major causes, evaluation, and treatment. There's even a sports medicine department.
COMPUSERVE *go* hnt

Information USA/Free Health Information and Care Why spend money at the bookstore when you can get free books, pamphlets and even videos that are more complete and more up-to-date? Information USA aims to help you find "the latest information, for free, on any health-related topic." The database includes sections devoted to finding free treatment information and legal help. The section on free information is particularly comprehensive, listing more than 1,500 diseases and health issues from acupuncture to yellow fever. It also provides information on over 4,500 sources of referral networks, organizations, publications, and videos. The site includes state health stats and information on how to get prescriptions filled for free.
COMPUSERVE *go* ius-5996

National Health Information Center Helps put people with general health questions in touch with organizations that can provide the answers. Its Health Information Resource Database lists 1,100 organizations and government offices; it allows you to search for the resource you need, and provides a wide selection of toll-free numbers and contact information for organizations from the American Lung Association to the Vestibular Disorders Association. The site's New Media Resource Locator provides a selection of health-related computer applications. Other topics at the site include a set of links for publications and information on worksite

MEDICINENET
WEB http://www.medicinenet.com
Don't be put off if the Health Fact of the Week ("Elderly—Think Fluids!") doesn't apply to you. With a better bedside manner than many human doctors, this free medical resource will advise you on what does ail you. Find out about diseases and treatments for everything from acne to steroid

withdrawal. Educate yourself about medications and side effects in the Pharmacy. Take part in the chat and message groups of the Viewer Interactive Center. But if it's professional advice you need, Ask the Experts by email. Others have asked about everything from poison ivy to blood in the semen to vulvadynia (if you don't know what that means, look it up in the site's medical dictionary).

health promotion.

WEB http://nhic-nt.health.org

Patient Information Handouts A great informational resource from the University of Iowa, the site provides essays on more than a dozen common family illnesses from asthma to urinary tract infections. Questions are generally very basic—"What is the flu"—but include helpful suggestions for at-home treatment.

WEB http://www.uiowa.edu/~famprac /med.html

U.S. Department of Health and Human Services A clearinghouse for the various divisions of the department, this site provides links to the Administration on Aging and the various sections of the Public Health Service, including areas focused on mental health, substance abuse, and disease prevention.

WEB http://www.os.dhhs.gov

Patient info

CenterWatch Patient Notification Service A fascinating and useful site for those who wish to track the actions of the FDA, a government agency oft-maligned for being slow and out of touch in its approval of drugs. But look at this site and see how many "good" drugs America has besides all the "bad" drugs those men on TV always talk about. Register to be informed of clinical trials on everything from acne treatment to glomerulonephritis, or be the first to take part in clinical trials

for the new drug that fights Internet addiction. There's also a list of drugs newly approved by the FDA, not all of which catch the attention of the mainstream media.

WEB http://www.centerwatch.com /PATEMAIL.HTM

HealthTouch Online A one-stop wellness center, HealthTouch provides a searchable database with specs on all your favorite prescription drugs, as well as summary and contact information on reputable non-profit health organizations and government agencies including the National Council on the Aging and the National Institute of Health. The National Digestive Diseases Information Clearinghouse is here too, but it, like the rest of HealthTouch, is not highly interactive.

WEB http://www.healthtouch.com /level1/menu.htm

HospitalWeb Looking for a hospital with a certain specialty? The email address of a particular doctor? A good starting point would be HospitalWeb, a compilation of links to U.S. and foreign hospitals on the Web. HospitalWeb also features an "interesting medical site of the week."

WEB http://neuro-www.mgh.harvard .edu/hospitalweb.nclk

The body

Muscle Charts of the Human Body Whether or not you can locate your gluteus maximus, this site is a handy index of detailed

information about the muscles of the human body. Visitors can select muscles in three ways: via an image map, textual hierarchy, or alphabetical list. The standard anatomy test info is here: origin, insertion, action, blood supply, and nerve information for each muscle, though there are no pictures besides the initial image map. The site does offers a couple of bonuses: Anyone with an Adobe Acrobat PDF reader (which is free) can download the information laid out in table format; users of Microsoft Word 6.0 for Windows or Windows 95 can download a medical terms dictionary for their spell-checker.

WEB http://www.pathway.net/hws /muscles.htmll

Aging

Age Net Soon to be renamed the "SWT AGE PAGE," (SWT standing for Southwest Texas University), this is a good starting point for older adults and their children to research everything from selecting a long-term care facility to the latest on laws that affect the elderly. The possibilities seem endless, from ordering a special bed at the virtual healthcare industrial park in the commercial link to finding a pet at Father's Cattery, an organization run by an order of Notre Dame monks that gives abandoned cats to the elderly. The Library has titles dealing with health among the elderly and WidowNet offers advice and support for those who have survived their spouses.

WEB http://elo.mediasrv.swt.edu /Departments/Honors_Program/Age _Net/agenetf/AGENET

Alzheimer Web Home Page Maintained by an Australian Molecular Neurobiologist, this is a great site for those interested in the science of Alzheimer's. Dr. David Small has links to the most up-to-date and pertinent articles, grant opportunitites, conferences, patents, and books, and his dedication makes for an uplifting visit.

WEB http://werple.mira.net.au/~dhs/ad .html

Alzheimer's Association Alzheimer's is the leading cause of dementia, and the fourth leading cause of death in adults. Affecting men and women equally, its impact on both sufferers and those around them can be ravaging. The AA "is the only national voluntary health organization dedicated to research for the causes, treatments, cures and preventions of Alzheimer's disease" and provides "education and support services to people with AD, their families and caregivers." The claim is backed by a stack of important basic information and coverage of current events relevant to the topic. Conferences, research, and grant opportunities are also well covered.

WEB http://www.alz.org

American Association of Retired Persons Online One look at the AARP forums on America Online and CompuServe tells you that getting older isn't what it used to be. Forums cover dozens of contemporary issues, including grandparents raising grandchildren, choosing sides on health care issues, and divorce after fifty. While there are no forums devoted exclusively to health and geriatrics, these issues come up througout the site. Check out the Home, Family & Daily Living section for folders on caregiving, long term care and healthy living. Social Security and Medicare discusses legislation, and the message boards are even more fruitful with folders on

Visible Human Project

WEB http://www.nlm.nih.gov/research/visible/visible_human.html

The Visible Human Project creates complete 3-D digital models of a human male and female from radiographic and photographic images. The models can then be rotated a full 360° and viewed on any plane, thus making them powerful tools for exploring the human body for scientific, education-

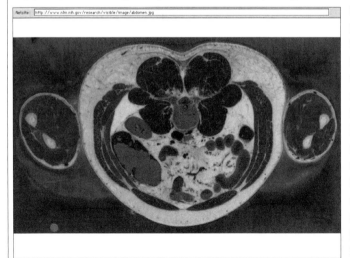

al, or simply recreational purposes. The applications of this technique promise to revolutionize medicine, both in the way it's taught and in the development of noninvasive treatments. The National Library of Medicine's Web site offers a fact sheet, FAQs, and sample images of this fascinating project. The Web site also offers a list of links to other endeavors based on the Visible Human Project, such as the Interactive Knee Program.

Alzheimer's, Aging Issues, Caregiving, and Fitness. A main focus of the site's health discussion is that mental health is the importance of both physical and mental health.

AMERICA ONLINE *keyword* aarp
COMPUSERVE *go* aarp

National Osteoporosis Foundation
One in two American women will develop osteoporosis—the condition in which bones become thin and brittle and break—here's a quick course in the disease, treatment and prevention. Definitions of the disease are displayed in dictionary-like entries, in large type with black-and-white medical illustrations. Clear, easy-to-follow entries on how to prevent and treat the disease are also included.

WEB http://www.nof.org

SeniorNet Online "I have been one of those insomniacs who would fall asleep easily at any time of nite or day, now I take 3 mg of Melatonin at 10 and by 10:30 have drifted into a deep, peaceful sleep." "Maggie, your loss is a terrible loss even if your husband is physically alive, he is no longer the husband you knew." "Last October I began acupuncture treatments along with taking herbal meds for asthma. Trouble is, my med. insurance does not cover the treatment." SeniorNet is a close-knit community dedicated to giving support and advice on every aspect of health, both mental and physical.

AMERICA ONLINE *keyword* seniornet

Location: http://www.ada.org/

ADA ONLINE™

The American Dental Association

Today's News: April 24, 1996

Welcome to **ADA ONLINE**, the American Dental Association's Home Page. If you would like a complete table of contents, or if you have a non-graphical browser or have graphics turned off, use the text-only overview of this site.

News

Products & Services

Practice & Profession

Consumer Information

Open up this page and say ahh
http://www.ada.org

Dentistry

American Association of Pediatric Dentistry A glossy Web site that sells itself on the promise of an America populated by children with megawatt grins, this is a user-friendly waltz through the latest news in pediatric dentistry. For dental surgeons eager to adopt the AAPD's online hard sell, there's a list of Web dos and don'ts, and for parents wanting only the most luxurious graphical representation of their children's oral maladies, there's a well-appointed page of hints, tips, and software.

WEB http://aapd.org

American Dental Association
Updated daily, this is a full-service multimedia extravaganza covering all areas of American dentistry under four main headings: News; Practice and Professionals; Products and Service; and Consumer

Information. But while the "Financial Impact Analysis of Plan Contracts" spreadsheet under "Product of the Month, April '96," no doubt floats some boats, the lure for junior visitors must be the AVI animations in the Consumer section. There you can watch 30-second movies of Dudley the dinosaur explaining how to eat properly (keep off the raw stegasauri) or Cal Ripken Jr. alerting junior spitters to the dangers of chewing tobacco.

WEB http://www.ada.org

Dentistry On-Line A scrubbed, sanitary, and professional home page the color scheme of a dream dentist's reception area, Dentistry On-Line is a near-encyclopedia of tooth truth. Patients' pages explain exactly what happens during, say, a root canal—while the pro forum addresses issues the rest of us are truly better off not

knowing—although "Halitosis and its Management in the Dental Office" may yet have applications at a workplace near you. With a catalog of links to other dentistry sites, this is a good place to start when your thinking of having some oral work done.
WEB http://www.cityscape.co.uk/users/ad88/dent.htm

Men's health

Ask NOAH About: Vasectomy If not the vasectomy bible, then surely one of the testaments. All the tough questions are answered at this New York Online Access to Health site: "What is it? Is it expensive? Does it hurt? Am I right for it? Can it be reversed?" Links to related sites for even more information.
WEB http://www.noah.cuny.edu/wellconn/vasectomy.html

Doctor's Hospital Health Source "The baldness pattern seen in many men is hereditary and inevitable." "Almost every man, at some point in his life, has one or more bouts of impotence." "Testicular cancer is the most common form of cancer in men between the ages of 15 to 35." "As men age, it is common for the prostate to enlarge." This rather cheery outlook is provided by the Web site of an Ohio-based physician network, alongside more reassuring discussion of men's health issues.
WEB http://www.doctors-10tv.com/alt/men/men.htm

The Hairloss Information Center Aims to become "a digital *Consumer Reports*" on hair loss. Find out about new baldness drugs, whether spray-on hair really works, where to get a hair transplant, and how to have hair replaced nonsurgically. Get questions answered by email and gain access to free stuff online.
WEB http://hairloss.com/index.htm

Impotence: It's Reversible First the bad news: More than 30 million men in America suffer from impotence. Given that the majority of men prefer "making love" to any other home activity, this is a problem that needs to be addressed. And the good news? Impotence is reversible. Find out what to do about erection problems, retrograde ejaculation, and a host of other male sexual dysfunctions.
WEB http://www.cei.net/~impotenc

Men's Issues For concerned men MSN offers up this site which, among quality-of-life features, scatters forums on domestic violence and prostate cancer, and *M.E.N. Magazine*, which emphasizes personal growth topics and "inner work." Beat your drum for this site.
MSN *keyword* men

The Prostate Cancer InfoLink What does "maximal androgen deprivation" mean? What is "estramustine phosphate"? What is the medical term for "enlargement of the male breasts"? Refer to Infolink's

Prostate Dictionary to bone up on words used by health professionals in managing prostate cancer and related conditions. This comprehensive site provides the latest news on the world of prostate cancer, current clinical reviews, and where to find help. If in doubt, "Ask Arthur" who provides a jolly forum for health questions.
WEB http://www.comed.com/Prostate

Prostate Pointers The Ayatollah Khomeini had prostate cancer. So did Frank Zappa. Prostate Pointers not only maintains a list of famous people who suffered from the disease, but also supplies a wealth of clinical abstracts, books, and journals for health professionals and consumers alike. This extremely user-friendly site provides access to mailing lists, support groups, and stuff written by regular Joes, and includes all the hypertext links you'll ever need.
WEB http://rattler.cameron.edu/prostate/prostate.html

Orthopedics

Medical Multimedia Group Read the latest on the symptoms, diagnosis, and treatment of common orthopedic disorders such as Carpal Tunnel Syndrome, lower back pain, knee pain, and cumulative trauma disorder.
WEB http://www.cyberport.net/mmg/homepage.html

Musculoskeletal Diseases An index of Web sites that cover

bone diseases (ostopenia), joint diseases (arthritis, bursitis), and the occasional cartilage disease (chondomalacia). Anybody looking for the Charcot-Marie-Tooth disease—the rare hereditary disease that strikes palsy into the feet, legs, and hands of its victims? There are links here.
WEB http://www.mic.ki.se/Diseases/c5.html

UW Bone and Joint Sources What joints are bothering you today? Shoulder? Knees? Hands? Back? Search this page by location of the actual physical problem to find short Quick-Time movies of therapeutic exercises for stiff joints and brittle bones.
WEB http://www.orthop.washington.edu/bonejoint/zzzzzzzl_l.html

Pediatrics

Adolescent Directory On Line (ADOL) Are you enduring adolescence either personally or proximally? If so, use this site to help you navigate through pertinent sites on the Web. With sections on Mental Health, Health-riskFactors, Conflict and Violence, Counselor Resources, and Teens Only, this directory is meant for kids, parents, and all professionals who deal with adolescents, from doctors and researchers to teachers and counselors. All sections have hot links with commentary and the mental health section is especially useful for linking to information on specific condi-

tions, such as attention deficit-hyperactivity disorder and autism. The Teens Only section focuses more on recreational sites, such as teen 'zines.
WEB http://education.indiana.edu/cas/adol/adol.html

The American Academy of Child & Adolescent Psychiatry Homepage Besides providing extensive information about the workings of its group, the home page of The American Academy of Child & Adolescent Psychiatry also offers parents a number of resources. The 46 information sheets that comprise "Facts for Families" discuss an extremely wide range of topics, including bedwetting, children's exposure to violence on TV, how to discuss adoption, and what to do when your child refuses to go to school. Also at this site are a publications brochure, offering information on print and video available through the Academy, and legislative alerts to promote political activism.
WEB http://galen.library.ucsf.edu/kr/subs/psychiatry/aacap.html

Family Practice/Pediatrics/OB-GYN The fact that family practice and obstetrics-gynecology are covered in the same message and library sections as pediatrics might make it more difficult to find the information you're looking for, but this little corner of CompuServe's Med-SIG Forum does manage to cover a variety of pediatric issues. At the message board, expect to find parents and doc-

tors trading information and anecdotes. Topics in the family practice/pediatrics/OB-GYN section of the library run the gamut, from "Pediatric Surgery Update" to "How to avoid picking up pinworms."
COMPUSERVE go medsig→Libraries or Messages→FP/Ped/OB-GYN

Our Kids Online support groups, descriptions of adaptive technology and toys, and medical information are just some of the resources available via links at this Web page designed as a Net hub for parents of children with special needs. Effectively just a list of links, the site offers a range of pages from those dealing with specific conditions (such as Fragile X and Ataxia-Telangiectasia) to those dealing with the more general issues surrounding raising a special-needs child. This site also provides information about subscribing to the Our Kids mailing list.
WEB http://wonder.mit.edu/ok

Pedinfo To call this site just a collection of links would be misleading, because its usefulness to medical professionals, medical students, parents, and researchers makes it one of the most comprehensive pediatric sites on the Web. Links are divided into Institutions; Subspecialties and Areas of Study; Conditions and Diseases; Education; Publications; Software; and Parenting. Also available is information about subscribing to the Pedinfo mailing list,

which covers "pediatric medical informatics," which translates to "computers in pediatrics."
WEB http://W3.LHL.UAB.EDU/pedinfo

Child safety

Sexual Assault Information Page
The Sexual Assault Information Page provides a large number of links to information regarding sexual assault and violence. The section on child sexual abuse is one of the most extensive, and links to information ranging from statistics to coping strategies for adult survivors.
WEB http://www.cs.utk.edu/~bartley /saInfoPage.html

Public health

American Public Health Association "The oldest and largest organization of public health professionals in the world," APHA is one of the best sources of health information on the Internet. The group is committed to bringing people together in a multidisciplinary environment, so its home page contains a huge array of information for everyone from the scientist to the activist. For those interested in getting more specific, links abound.
WEB http://www.apha.org

Global Health Network "The Global Health Network is now a complete 'virtual entity'... we have a consciousness... we exist and are having impact in the area of global health." So

WHO's online and healthy
http://www.who.ch

reads a recent newsletter from the Global Health Network, which gathers a massive set of health-related resources from around the world. The section of resources for global health issues is particularly valuable, with links on topics ranging from tuberculosis to the Ebola virus.
WEB http://www.pitt.edu/HOME /GHNet/GHNet.html

Public Health Forum CompuServe's Public Health Forum contains a varied message board section, with topics ranging from drug policies to disasters. There is also a "health workers' lounge" to promote discussion between professionals. The library section is equally diverse, and includes articles for both the medical professional and those seeking more general information on issues ranging from rabies to Lyme disease.
COMPUSERVE *go* public health

United States Public Health Service Consolidates information from the variety of agencies of the Public Health Service, including the Food and Drug Administration, the Agency for Health Care Policy and Research, and the National Institutes of Health. A section on news and public affairs includes press releases with titles such as "FDA Licenses Chickenpox Vaccine" and "Health Education Loan Defaulters Listed." The selection of general health information runs the gamut from substance abuse and preventive medicine to organ sharing and toxic hazard identification.
WEB http://phs.os.dhhs.gov/phs/phs .html

World Health Organization
Whether you're looking for information on the Ebola virus, World Health Day, or advice about health concerns when traveling around the world,

you'll find answers at the WHO site. The archived press releases focus on topics such as tuberculosis and injectable contraception, while recent issues of WHO newsletters deal with influenza, AIDS, and other topics. The site also offers links to an extensive selection of health-related Web servers.
WEB http://www.who.ch

Emergency medicine

American Association of Poison Control Centers "Danger! Danger!" the skeletons and spiders adorning this groovy-looking site scream. In reality, however, AAPCC's home page is nothing if not user-friendly. Featuring the addresses of poison control centers in every state, a poison prevention resource guide, and an impressive array of related links, the AAPCC's site proves that poison control is about more than hard-to-open pill bottles.
WEB http://www.nlu.edu/aapcc

American Red Cross You just can't beat the ARC for consistence, quality and staying power. Visit the group's home page to learn about their latest activities. Ironically, the number for a hotline offering emotional support for Oklahoma City bombing survivors juxtaposes an archive of articles on the tragedy which may reopen old wounds.
WEB http://www.redcross.org

Global Health Disaster Network Disaster watchers in Ehime,

First on the scene with the Band-Aids
http://www.redcross.org

Japan have put together this sister home page of the Global Health Network. Why? Because "a major difficulty in a disaster is knowing where to find accurate information to help coordinate efforts in a quick and organized way." While it's not terribly likely that the Red Cross will be turning to the GHDN when disaster strikes, it is a fine source for the rest of us. The site includes a call for papers from experts in the field of disaster management, and contributors will be invited to participate in an online conference later this year, entitled "Electronic Communication and Disaster Management."
WEB http://hypnos.m.ehime-u.ac.jp /GHDNet/index.html

HazardNet With a repertoire of hazards organized by category (geophysical, meteorological, insect infestation, etc.), HazardNet invites users to check

out the potential for disaster in the area of their choice. Wondering if your Hawaiian vacation will end in fiery doom? Simply find Hawaii on the world volcano map, click on its icon, and check out the status of Mt. Kilauea. Planning a flight over far eastern Russia? Be warned: Your plane may have to increase its altitude to avoid ash layers from Kliuchevskoi. With its images of lava-spouting volcanoes and satellite weather patterns, the site is an aesthete's gold mine.
WEB http://hoshi.cic.sfu.ca/hazard

International Committee of the Red Cross Visitors to this site can learn out about the IRC's campaign against landmines, read the text of the International Humanitarian Law and review its applications, and view photos of the IRC's work around the world. The IRC's gopher provides contact information for branches of the group in

more than 50 countries.
URL gopher://gopher.ifrc.org/l
WEB http://www.icrc.ch

Safety Related Internet Resources
Including access to mailing
lists, newsgroups, Web and
gopher sites, and more, this
site is a must for anyone looking to access safety-related
resources on the Internet.
WEB http://www.sas.ab.ca/biz/christie
/safelist.html

Sexual health

SHAPE Not the magazine, but
the Sexual Health Advocate
Peer Education program of the
University of Missouri
(Columbia) student-health
center. The site covers a variety
of sexuality topics directed at
the campus community, ranging from what to do if you get
a sexually transmitted infection
to how to decide whether or
not to have sex in the first

place. There's also a Question
of the Week feature, which
solicits answers to quandries
like: "What's the most romantic way to ask your partner to
put on a condom?"
WEB http://www.missouri.edu/~shape

Birth control

Coalition for Positive Sexuality
Advocating a positive attitude
toward sexuality, this pro-sex
Web site was developed from
"Just Say Yes: A Pro-Sex, Safer
Sex Guide for Teens," a pamphlet written by the Coalition
for Positive Sexuality in
Chicago. Topics include myths
and realities ("masturbation
will not make you blind"); how
to talk about sex, safe sex, and
birth control; a brief glossary;
and links to more safe-sex
resources. There's plenty of
practical information, such as
the chart on the symptoms and
treatments of common STDs.

"Just Say Yes: A Pro-Sex, Safer-Sex Guide for Teens"
http://www.positive.org/cps

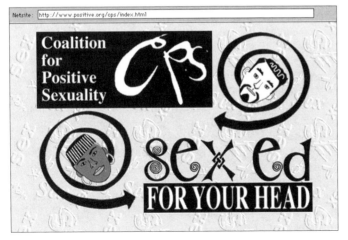

WEB http://www.positive.org/cps •
http://www.actwin.com/aids/jsyIndex
.html • http://www.webcom.com/~cps
/jsy/jsy.html

Planned Parenthood Online Reminiscent of a trip to one of the
clinics decked out with cheesy
cartoonish decor, this Web site
gives the standard Planned
Parenthood rap on abortion,
birth control, and sexually
transmitted infections, plus a
public affairs section on repro-
ductive-health issues and links
to other Web sites. The site's
online women's health newsletter has tips on managing PMS,
shopping for condoms, and
doing a breast self-exam.
WEB http://www.ppca.org

The Safer Sex Page Info on safe
sex, condoms, health issues,
and counseling. The Quickie
Roundup of Birth Control
Options describes what works
and what doesn't (condoms do,
douching doesn't). The site's
multimedia gallery also features
video clips on how to put on a
condom, how condoms are
made, and safer sex techniques
for lesbians.
WEB http://www.safersex.org

Women's health

alt.support.menopause A spot for
women to discuss the effects of
menopause and share experiences with various treatment
options. One woman's post
about the lack of talk in the
newsgroup spurred a few others to speak up.
USENET alt.support.menopause

Ask A Woman Doctor All health questions are answered, not just those related to breast health or gynecology. Some receive a succinct reply: "I am 17 and haven't gotten my period yet. Am I abnormal?" is answered, "I am sure you are not abnormal. Rather it is unusual to not have started menses by your age. I would suggest that you make an appointment with a gynecologist or adolescent medicine specialist." Other questions receive more elaborate treatment: "The new drug for osteoporosis—Fosamax (alendronate sodium)—does it really work?" is answered with both a primer on osteoporosis and an article about the drug detailing how it increases bone density, helps reduce vertebral fractures, and its potential side effects.
WEB http://www.healthwire.com /women/ask.htm

Avons's Breast Cancer Crusade "Breast lumps are very common. More than 80 percent of breast lumps are not cancerous, but biopsy is the only way to know for sure." FAQs and fact sheets are quick fixes, but go to the message center for serious discussion from doctors, survivors, family, and friends. Lots of information for support groups and charitable organizations.
AMERICA ONLINE *keyword* cancer→ Avon's Breast Cancer Awareness Crusade

Breastfeeding Articles and Resources Are you an expectant

> ## " Are you an expectant mom anxious about breast-feeding? "

mom anxious about breast-feeding? A new mother having difficulties? Don't be embarrassed, the most natural thing in the world sometimes requires instruction and practice. This site is full of Q&As on milk production, pumping, and fitting feedings around your work schedule, as well as a detailed guide to positions and "Latch-On" technique. The site also provides articles on the socio-politics of breast-feeding, and the legality of public breast-feeding.
WEB http://www.parentsplace.com /readroom/bf.html

misc.health.infertility From family planning software to infertility and blame to Madonna-resentment, you'll get all kinds of news and views from people trying to conceive. A lot of crossposts from alt.fertility.
USENET misc.health.infertility

National Alliance of Breast Cancer Organizations In 1996, 184,300 new cases of female breast cancer will be diagnosed, and 44,300 women will die from the disease. Breast cancer is the second leading cause of cancer death for African-American

women, and the leading cause of cancer death for all women between the ages of 35 and 54. These and other disturbing facts are provided in one of NABCO's enlightening fact sheets. Drug trial news is also a big draw for this page, as is a finder that offers contact information for breast cancer support groups nationwide.
WEB http://www.nabco.org

PEN Women's Health A number of sex, diet, and nutrition folders here, but the Women's Health Issues & Concerns folder has a healthy serving of articles on such topics as artificial insemination, reconstructive breast surgery, eating disorders, menopause, and ovarian cancer. Links to more women's health Web sites.
AMERICA ONLINE *keyword* pen→ Women's Health

Drugs

A Simple Fact Sheet—Protease Inhibitors A thorough, PWLA-friendly article on protease inhibitors. An overview links to other reports on resistance, clinical trials, AZT and other nucleoside analogs. The page also offers separate simple fact sheets for the Big Three: although there are more than 20 protease inhibitors, Invirase, Crixivan, and Norvir are the most well-known. These individual fact sheets offer trial summaries, describe side effects, warn of drug interactions, and link to patient assistance programs.

WEB http://www.aidsnyc.org/network/simple/protease.html

Drug InfoNet Ever wonder what exactly is in those jagged little pills you pop without thinking every morning? Well this helpful site will tell all, and even provide the chemical formula ($C_{17}H_{17}NC_{12}$–CH sound familiar?). Lovely benzene ring diagrams, pharmacodyamics, pharmacokinetics and all kinds of other technical information about dosage, side effects and precautions is also available here. Search by brand name, manufacturer, or generic name and have the manufacturers fill you in on their product.
WEB http://www.druginfonet.com/phrminfo.htm

PharminfoNet This site is really a friendly neighborhood online pharmacist. Search for information on a specific drug by generic or trade name, and read reviews from the *Medical Sciences Bulletin* which compare prices between different brands of pill. You'll also get down to earth advice from archived threads taken from sci.med.pharmacy. Plus there's an easy to use Drug FAQ from those who know how to keep your drug-taking a beneficial act.
WEB http://pharminfo.com/drg_mnu.html

Exercise and fitness

Balance Fitness On The Net An online fitness magazine that appeals to the casual exerciser, the serious athlete, and the health professional, this site offers rotating articles on the myth of "low-fat" foods, serial features such as "Yoga In Your Home," and extensive, hypertext studies on applied kinesiology. Forums let readers discuss everything from winter training to the benefits of antioxidants. Women be warned: The forum doesn't make much of an effort to address your special concerns, but merely herds all the questions submitted by women under a section called "Fe-Mail." A single post about the beauty paradigm shifting from Kate Moss to Gabrielle Reece is surrounded by general ques-

ATLANTA REPRODUCTIVE HEALTH CENTRE

WEB http://www.ivf.com//index.html

"Thank you for this wonderful site. My husband and I have been trying to get pregnant for 10 years now, and although we have achieved 6 pregnancies, all have ended in miscarriage or stillbirth. I am so scared, mad, angry, etc. and was very pleased to find this site at a time when I truly needed it.

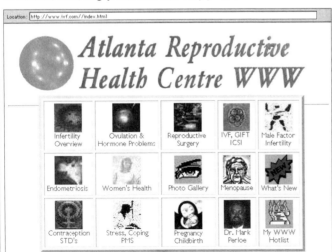

Thank you." This enormous hubsite deals with every aspect of reproductive health: infertility, IVF, endometriosis, contraception, sexually transmitted disease, menopause, even stress management and PMS. Resources vary from original material such as articles on normal/abnormal ovulation to links to hundreds of sites from Condom Country to Menopause Weekly.

tions about foot cramps and infrequent exercise.
WEB http://hyperlink.com/balance

Escaping to Nature An invaluable guide to what to bring, what to wear, and how to leave the wilderness as wild as you found it. Whether you're hiking in the Himalayas or traipsing through a Texas state park, don't count on your survival instincts to kick in. First check out this page to gear up for the trek. Every month brings a spotlight on a different park or hiking spot, so check back often to find your dream trip.
WEB http://www.netxpress.com/users/jwmoor

Health Resources Focusing on "reliable and practical" health and fitness information, this site offers an excellent set of Netwide links on everything from deafness and depression to sex and smoking. The collection of links to health-care publications is especially extensive, as is the listing of state and national health-care organizations. In addition, the site offers documents and links of interest to health-care providers.
WEB http://www.ihr.com

Health Zone Subscribers of all fitness levels and interests are welcome at this forum, which covers a wide range of health topics in seven target sections—zNutrition, zFitness, zSpa, zShopping, zClinic, zBuddies, and of course, zScope (a curious blend of

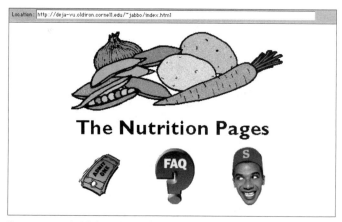

Location: http://deja-vu.oldiron.cornell.edu/~jabbo/index.html

Your recommended daily intake of nutrition info
http://deja-vu.oldiron.cornell.edu/~jabbo/index.html

Susan Powter and Uri Geller). One main difference between this fee-based service and other AOL forums is its surplus of "professional" advice and articles intended to offset user posts, but not replace the advice of a physician. There are also lots of chat rooms: The fitness personals at the zBuddies section matches partners-in-training (the platonic posts outnumber the romantic at about 1,000 to 1). Click onto "Those Last @#$%* Ten Pounds" or "Fit & Fat" to find online encouragement from someone in a similar situation.
AMERICA ONLINE *keyword* health zone

Nutrition

alt.support.big-folks Despite what the title suggests, this newsgroup is more like a comfortable Sunday brunch than a group therapy session. A very interesting cross-section of people and ideas reside here, discussing fashion, medical

issues (an otherwise healthy woman getting intrusive pressure from her OB/GYN to lose weight is urged to find a new doctor), exercise tips (for health, not weight loss), sizism politics, even entertainment media—when Alicia Silverstone, at a whopping 120 pounds, was called "fat" on a tabloid show, the resulting thread took up half the page.
USENET alt.support.big-folks

alt.support.diet (FAQ) List "What do the terms 'overweight' and 'obese' mean?" "Is Promise Ultra Fat Free Margarine really fat-free?" "I've started a diet and exercise program, but I'm finding it really hard to stay on track. Any suggestions?" This is a great resource for dieters, offering sound, moderated advice on healthy eating while smashing a lot of diet myths to bits. The FAQ also encourages lifestyle changes as opposed to short-term diets. In answer to the question "Can I lose weight without dieting?" the FAQ answers "If by 'dieting' you mean a temporary regimen of eating measured portions of raw veggies and expensive, funny-tasting 'dietetic' foods, then the answer is yes. Your goal should be to adopt healthy eating and exercise plans that you can live with for the rest of your life; these two factors can be enough to cause gradual weight loss in most overweight people, without the need for regimented diets." Hallelujah.

WEB http://www.ionet.net/~kchurch/asd-faq.shtml

Fatloss-Support Another extremely positive support group that encourages moving toward permanent healthy eating habits. This group actively discourages regimented diets, and offers a great amount of nutritional info to support their promotion of a low-fat diet and increased exercise. From the group's founder: "The diet industry could care less about making the fat *stay* off of the body, since they love repeat customers. The only thing the diet industry can offer is motivation, but again, this is something they can distort. If they base your fat loss directly upon your emotional response, they have conditioned you to make it a psychological crutch (just as the scale does). But if you can find your own inner moti-vation, then you are the one with direct control over YOU!" In addition to receiving public posts and/or digests, sub-scribers can also receive personal support and direction from a "fatloss guru." To get a list of the gurus, email major-domo@list.stanford.edu and type "info fatloss-support" in the message body.

EMAIL majordomo@lists.stanford.edu

✍ *Type in message body:* subscribe fatloss-support

International Food and Information Council (IFIC) The homepage for the IFIC holds a tremendous amount of information for parents, educators, health professionals, and consumers.

⊚ Acupuncture.com

WEB http://www.acupuncture.com

Acupuncture is that prickly species of Chinese medical therapy in which needles are stuck into the skin to cure pain and disease. Paradoxical? Yes, but apparently it works, although it's still not clear why. The classical Chinese explanation is that pricking needles into certain points on the body is like opening and closing doors of the body's "meridian" channels through which Qi (energy) flows.

Location: http://www.acupuncture.com/

The Tao begot one.
One begot two.
Two begot three.
And three begot the ten thousand things.

-Tao Te Ching
Here are some of those things.

Welcome to Acupuncture.com

Western scientific theories say that the needle-pricks either cause a reflex nerve-reaction signalling the brain to suppress the pain center or stimulate the production of actual pain-killing hormones. At this Web site, information is broken down into levels of interest. For curious consumers, there is an Acupuncture FAQ, a comparison of Western and Eastern Medicine, and other basic information.

Linked in a circular manner, the same nutritional information for children can be accessed via the parents page, the educators' page, the Food Safety and Nutrition Information page, and the consumer page. The section on information for consumers is particularly useful, with documents such as "Ten Tips to Healthy Eating" and "What You Should Know about Caffeine." Other topics deal with food allergies, food biotechnology, and what you should know about MSG.
WEB http://ificinfo.health.org

Why should I exercise when it's such a pain in the ass?

Nutrition Pages This great page gets kudos for both design and well-produced content. There are a series of articles on such topics as Aspartame and Neurotoxicity, The Great Saturated Fat Scam, Militant Vegetarianism, and Amputees and Powerlifting (OK, so it's a little off-topic, but what a great water cooler conversation!). Visitors can comment on articles and send in their own. There are also three excellent FAQs on Basic Stuff (What do the terms RDA, RDI, and USRDA stand for?), Lifestyle (Why should-

n't I just take vitamin pills to balance my diet?) and Sports Nutrition (Why should I exercise when it's such a pain in the ass?).
WEB http://deja-vu.oldiron.cornell.edu /~jabbo/index.html

Vegetarian Pages Buddha was a vegetarian! OK, so you knew that one, but what about Elvis Costello? Brad Pitt? Leonardo Da Vinci? William Shatner? Martin Luther King Jr.? The Captain & Tenille—both of them? But this great veggie/vegan hubsite doesn't stop with a celeb list, it links to FAQs, news from the front, recipes, vegetarian and veg-friendly orgs (Veggies Unite, PETA, The Body Shop), even a vegetarian white pages for the Web. The Mega Index is a huge alphabetical link list with dozens of super-specific sites from articles on Vegetarian Christmas dinners, to Vegetarian Pets, to the Vegan Bikers Home Page.
WEB http://www.veg.org/veg

Alternative medicine

Algy's Herb Page Visitors to this page are greeted with a choice of viewing in "color" or black-and-white for the "slow of link." But both options reward the viewer with delightfully artful renditions of herbs and flowers, and a cornucopia of links to advice boards, herb and recipe exchanges.
WEB http://www.pair.com/algy • http:// frank.mtsu.edu/~sward/herb/herbpic .html

The Alternative Medicine Home-page Dissatisfied with the local M.D.? Wondering if something a bit less traditional might help? This award-winning site gathers spots across the Net devoted to unconventional, unorthodox, alternative, innovative, and complementary therapies. The topics covered include massage, homeopathy, acupuncture, and herbal medicine, with info on everything from "self development" to Kombucha ("a popular health-promoting beverage made by fermenting tea").
WEB http://www.pitt.edu/~cbw/altm .html

HealthSource Catalogs hundreds of Internet sites related to natural health, including directories of services, schools, and organizations; bibliographies of books and magazines; lists of recipes and restaurants; and a calendar of events. An Alternative Humor section links users to the most natural medicine of all—laughter.
WEB http://www.healthsource.com

misc.health.alternative In the largely unregulated world of alternative health products, the most cautious and sound advice often comes from consumers themselves. This popular newsgroup contains plenty of tried-and-true advice from real people. Hot debates frequently center around the efficacy of various herbal cures including Cat's Claw, chaparral, and belladonna.
USENET misc.health.alternative

PART 6
The Digital World

The Digital World

CLICK PICKS
The very best on the Net

Computers

COMPUTERS: CAN'T LIVE WITH THEM, CAN'T LIVE WITHOUT THEM

RESEARCHING COMPUTERS on the Net is—to use a favorite Bill Gates-ism—like drinking from a firehose. This is where the techies, the hackers, the solder-addicts, the code-hogs go to talk about what they spend all day thinking about with their oversized, overheated brains. Fear not: You don't need neural implants to make sense of it all. But what exactly is out there? The enormity of the resources about computers online makes it more appropriate to ask, what isn't out there? The Web is the largest showcase of computerware in existence, bar none, and it can breathe life into your hardware with freebies, FAQs, expert advice, shopping sites, and shareware, not to mention accessories, peripherals, or any products you might want to shower your CPU with, be it an Apple or a ZX80.

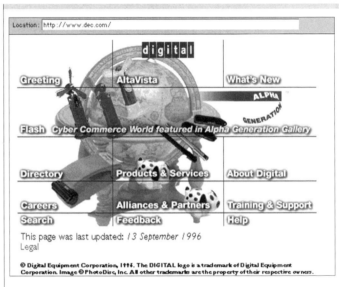

Location: http://www.dec.com/

digital

Greeting · AltaVista · What's New
ALPHA GENERATION
Flash Cyber Commerce World featured in Alpha Generation Gallery
Directory · Products & Services · About Digital
Careers · Alliances & Partners · Training & Support
Search · Feedback · Help

This page was last updated: 13 September 1996
Legal

© Digital Equipment Corporation, 1996. The DIGITAL logo is a trademark of Digital Equipment Corporation. Image © PhotoDisc, Inc. All other trademarks are the property of their respective owners.

VIRTUAL COMPUTER LIBRARY

WEB http://www.utexas.edu/computer/vcl
picture: WEB http://www.dec.com
When it comes to computers, it's a galaxy out there. These boxes of steel, plastic, wire, and silicon just love to talk about themselves. It's a good thing computers are by nature pretty organized; it'd be a real mess if they weren't. Nevertheless, it always helps to have a road map. If the Net were a great big library, this would be the computing section's card catalog. It's an easy-to-use site that has links to thousands of computing resources: animation archives, a glossary of computer term, dozens of computer FAQs, and too much more to list.

Starting points

Computer Hardware and Software Phone Numbers If you're desperately searching for technical support from almost any company, from Acer to Zeos, the folks behind this compilation have your number. The list contains phone numbers for a ton of computer hardware and software companies.
WEB http://www.mtp.semi.harris.com /comp_phl.html

> **❝ Ahh, the comforts of your own commercial service. With a go word and computing curiosity, you can find most everything on CompuServe. ❞**

Computer Library Online Part of the Ziff/Davis Publishing Group's extensive Compu-Serve database, this useful site is an information retrieval service designed to provide a complete reference and assistance resource for computer users. It consists of three searchable databases: Computer Database Plus, for magazine and newspaper articles related to computers; Computer's Buyer's Guide, for those in the market to buy computer hardware, software, or peripherals; and Support on Site, a searchable database for technical support. All of these databases specialize in Macintosh and IBM-compatible products and the search engines are, frankly, amazing.
COMPUSERVE *go* complib

Computers/Technology Ahh, the comforts of your own commercial service. With a go word and computing curiosity, you can find most everything here. No commercial service comes close to CompuServe's mega-computer offerings: computing reference guides, hundreds of hardware and software forums (Hewlett-Packard forums to the Quark Online User Forum), a software catalog, platform-related forums, gaming forums, computer news magazines, and an extensive range of ZiffNet services.
COMPUSERVE *go* computers

Computing A good place to start exploring AOL's computer resources—its software libraries, computer news magazines, vendor support area, family computing center, and many platform-oriented forums. If you're accessing AOL from a Windows machine, the computing menu will focus on PC computing sites (if, for instance, you were to enter the keyword "software" you would move to the PC Software Center). Macin-

tosh users will see a menu oriented toward Mac computing sites. In either case, you have full access to all sites (Windows users could enter the keyword "mac software" to get to the Mac Software Center). The AOL help desk, available from this menu, offers nightly live conferences to help new users.
AMERICA ONLINE *keyword* computing

The Free On-Line Dictionary of Computing With more than 300 contributors and thousands of entries, this is the most comprehensive computer dictionary available online. Just remember—comprehensive doesn't always mean convenient, and you may find yourself baffled at the fact that the dictionary includes separate entries for the singular and plural versions of terms, as well as the occasional misspelling. Still, there's no better place to look when you need to find out the proper usage of "nagware" (shareware that reminds you incessantly to register), "My Favorite Toy Language" (the hobbyhorse of an overzealous programmer), or "zigamorph" (Hex FF when used as a delimiter or fence character).
WEB http://wombat.doc.ic.ac.uk

Gargantuan Guide to Cyber History The Gargantuan Guide offers "just about everything you could want to know (and maybe some you didn't) about the computer's past" through a voluminous list of links. Some samples: the Homepage for the

History of Computing at Los Alamos; services for Historians (in the Netherlands); the Eniac Virtual Museum at the University of Pennsylvania; Computer History and Folklore by Michael Stillwell (Australia). Believe us, there's more—lots more.

WEB http://www.quiknet.com/~merlin

History of Computing You wouldn't ordinarily think of computing as a science with a history—things happen so fast that a new technology is likely to appear in the time it takes you to down your morning bowl of Cheerios. But this site proves that your thinking machine has a deep past, beginning with counting and shamanistic tradition; working through primitive calendars, abacuses, Pascal, Babbage, Hollerith, and Turing; and then moving on to ENIAC, EDVAC, and John von Neumann's famous Stored Program Concept. Microsoft bigshot Bill Gates even gets a chapter for his role in the birth of BASIC programming.

WEB http://calypso.cs.uregina.ca /Lecture

The Microsoft Knowledge Base Don't risk being put on hold as your Word document disintegrates. Why wait until the next morning to find out how to fix an Excel report that appears to be corrupted? Microsoft has put several thousand technical articles online with answers and troubleshooting advice for questions about all their products (On CompuServe, the articles also sometimes refer to software updates and programming aids that can be downloaded from the Microsoft Software Library). The articles, which CompuServe members can easily search by topic and date and AOL members can search by topic, are the same documents used by Microsoft technical support staff to answer calls—and chances are good that if you've owned a PC for more than a few weeks, you've made one of those calls.

URL ftp://ftp.microsoft.com
AMERICA ONLINE *keyword* knowledgebase

COMPUTING VIRTUAL LIBRARY
WEB http://src.doc.ic.ac.uk/bySubject/Computing/Overview.html
picture: WEB http://www.dell.com/prodinfo/desktops/optgen.html
Whether you're looking for an **FAQ** for the Linux system or a Web site that offers a basic overview of artificial intelligence, the Virtual Library of Computing should keep you digging for hours. The main index is separated into the following broad categories: Miscellaneous, Specialized Fields, University Computer Science Departments, Institutes, Centres and Laboratories, Other Organizations, Particular Systems, Vendors, and Magazines and Books.

Location: http://www.dell.com/prodinfo/desktops/optgen.html

| Dell Home | Buy a Dell | Order Status | Tech Support | Search | **DELL** |

The Dell® OptiPlex™ Desktop Systems
Dell Cuts Prices Again On Corporate PCs

MIT Athena Consulting Stock Answers Though it's still evolving, this site plans to be a repository of answers to frequently asked questions about all aspects of computers—everything from email to mainframes to microcomputers.
WEB http://consult-www.mit.edu /stock-index/index.html

" Need repairs? Take a look at the list of local repair shops. Feeling lonely? A long list of Mac user groups is at your fingertips. Bored? Catch up on the latest issue of your favorite Macintosh magazine. "

Webster's Dictionary of Computer Terms Need to learn more about abbreviated addressing? Confused about the history of Arpanet? Just jump right into *Webster's Dictionary of Computer Terms*, available in an easy-to-search format on AOL.

From arrival rate to ascending order, from daisy-wheel printer to data diddling, Webster's offers clear and concise definitions of thousands of computer words, phrases, and acronyms. And those AOLers on the leading edge of technolinguistics can supplement the dictionary with the special Add-a-Definition function. The area includes a message board for sharing definitions of new and familiar computer terms with America Online members and newbies.
AMERICA ONLINE *keyword* computerterms

Yahoo! Computing Reviews The search engine we all know and love has dug a little deeper into the Web. This page narrows its expertise to computing resources, brandishing bite-sized reviews to tantalize your computer thirst for knowledge. Delve into the archive of "over 800 sites," complete with gold-star sites and bubble-gum ads on hardware, shareware, shopping, networking, and all else computer-oriented.
WEB http://www.zdnet.com/yahoo computing/filters/reviews.htm

Support

Computer User Groups on the Web User groups sponsor classes, lectures, get-togethers where users can swap software (if they're so inclined), and job boards where experienced users can advertise their skills. This site brings together contact information about user

groups for several computer platforms and products. If a user group has a site online, odds are high that this site has a link to it.
WEB http://www.melbpc.org.au/others

Industry Connection Need support for Claris FileMaker Pro? Curious about Hewlett-Packard peripherals? Hundreds of forums sponsored by hardware and software companies, The Industry Connection is dominated by Macintosh vendors, but still includes a healthy representation of IBM-compatible manufacturers and designers. Vendor forums usually provide a description of the company, press releases, product information, a customer support message board, user discussion boards, and libraries of software. The Industry Connection lists companies both alphabetically and by category (product, specialty, etc.). You can also search for vendors using related keywords, such as "sound and multimedia."
AMERICA ONLINE *keyword* industry-connection

Macintosh Vendor Directory The star of the site is the alphabetical list of authorized Macintosh vendors and consultants; but that's just the beginning. Need repairs? Take a look at the list of local repair shops. Feeling lonely? A long list of Mac user groups is at your fingertips. Bored? Catch up on the latest issue of your favorite Macintosh magazine.

WEB http://www.macfaq.com/faq/vendor.html

Support Directory Can't figure out how to use that new, expensive program? Not sure which modem to buy? Did you know that more than 800 vendors and organizations offer technical support for their products on CompuServe? You can search this database of online vendors via company name, company type, product name, product category, operating system, or language. When you've found the company, link to its forum for product information, updates, and demos, or technical support via the message boards.
COMPUSERVE *go* support

News

BYTE Magazine The venerable *Byte* magazine has chronicled the computer industry since it was in swaddling clothes, and its online version pretty much mirrors the newsstand edition: You'll find the same solid, no-nonsense reporting style and attention to the many details of the latest microprocessor wars. A search engine allows readers to dredge up the *Byte* archives. For company information, visit the Virtual Press Room, where you can search press releases and product announcements and find links to advertisers and key computer-related sites.
WEB http://www.byte.com

Computing Print & Broadcast This is the central location for commercial computer magazines, radio shows, and television shows on AOL. The majority of the publications have their own software libraries, computing tips, and message boards. You can search back issues, renew your subscription, or send a letter to the editor online. The news library is nicely designed and allows you to search for articles by keywords, read late-breaking stories, or download photographs. There's a "Computing Print & Broadcast Tour" which walks you through the collection of publications, but you're better off browsing on your own.
AMERICA ONLINE *keyword* cp&b

 ## CMP's TechWeb
WEB http://techweb.cmp.com

Obsessed with computing news, this is a pretty super technology site, with the latest computing stories on tap. The main function is to steer you toward more in-depth updates at CMP's digital magazines with "click picks," a Tech Calendar, Guide, and Search. Peruse electronic versions of

many of the most popular computer-related magazines on the newsstands. Read selections from the current issues of *NetGuide*, *Interactive Age*, *Windows* magazine, *Computer Retail Week*, *Home PC*, *InformationWeek*, and others.

Interface Magazine With a New Age look, this online mag from Victoria, British Columbia, offers a quirky blend of art, hard news, reviews, and musings. The stated premise is to bridge the gap between user and computer. The site may never meet its lofty goal, but it has some strong points, including coverage of communications issues by Brock Meeks, "the best cyber-reporter on the planet."
WEB http://vvv.com/interface

Interface—your stop for Net news in cyberspace
http://vvv.com/interface

MagNet An index with links to computer-related magazines around the world. Drop by if you're looking for online versions of popular computing magazines such as *Amiga Power*, *Computer Shopper*, *HotWired*, *Information Week*, *Internet Daily News*, *MacWeek*, and *NetGuide*.
WEB http://annarbor.apcug.org

Product reviews

Computer Buyer's Guide Online computer product information for more than 70,000 hardware and software products, including detailed information about each product's manufacturer. Looking for info about Tele-Port Mercury modem from Global Village Communications, Inc.? Search by product or manufacturer, but be prepared to pay $1 for each report you download or view. You'll receive product and company specifications, including current retail price, the address and phone numbers of the

company, and a listing of the product's features.
COMPUSERVE *go* compbg

Computer Buyer's Guide In the market for a new system? Can't decide between a Mac or a PC? Search this database for product reviews from more than 200 magazines, newspapers, and journals. Contains a meticulous and easy-to-use search engine that will help you narrow your search down to that perfect machine. The only thing this great resource doesn't do is go out to the computer store and buy the new system for you.
COMPUSERVE *go* znt:buyers

Family News Product Reviews Do a little research before you buy. Reviews of computer books, commercial software, and shareware are online here. If you don't find a review for the product you're interested in, post a request on the message board.

AMERICA ONLINE *keyword* familynews →Reviewer's Corner

ZiffNet Reviews Index You saw an article a few months ago about personal digital assistants in an issue of *PC Magazine* that you'd really like to read again. Too bad you threw your copy away. Search a database of more than 40,000 Ziff/Davis articles from such magazines as *PC Week*, *PC Magazine*, and *PC Computing* by magazine name, product name, or company name.
COMPUSERVE *go* znt:index

Family

Computer Life The most general (and in some ways, the most generous) of Ziff's computer magazines, *Computer Life* is oriented toward home and personal computer use. Consult a list of the best products for Macs and PCs. Follow the step-by-step projects to learn more about a variety of com-

puter issues—Ziff will riff on everything from how to upgrade memory to how to do your taxes. Browse back issues to see what computer developments you might have missed ("John, this is Pentium; Pentium, John. I hope you two can be great friends").
WEB http://www.zdnet.com/~complife
COMPUSERVE *go* life

The Family Computing Forum
Splashy graphics and a homey theme are intended to make novice computer users and children comfortable. The effort isn't entirely unsuccessful, though more experienced users may wonder if the operative term here isn't family, but "fluff." Click the Tip-of-the-Day icon for explanations on how to do simple computer tasks such as lock files, name Mac folders, or send email. The Life's Workshop icon links to a dictionary of computer terms, hints on uploading, a dictionary of online terms, and the Novice Playground where AOLers can practice posting messages and downloading from software libraries without being charged for online time. The Rec Room has libraries of gaming software and often sponsors contests; the forum also features holiday-theme activities for kids (make a Mother's Day card, for instance). And what would a home be without a family room? In this forum's version of that place where parents and children bond, AOLers are invited to get to know each

other—chat live, post messages on the Front Porch board, and upload their pictures to what's known here as the Family Photo Album. For both the best and worst of the forum, visit the Computers & Everyday Life area; an archive of utilities for PC and Mac users and a folder of articles about using America Online for important tasks (choosing a college, keeping a diary, making friends, etc.) will be of interest to many forum visitors.
AMERICA ONLINE *keyword* fc

Public Brand Software Home Forum A vacuum cleaner? Of course. A refrigerator? A must. A PC? What family doesn't need one? More and more households are relying on software to help them organize their finances, make decisions about dinner or college, and entertain the children. And cost-conscious families are

buying shareware. The libraries in this forum are packed with wedding planners, patterns for children's crafts, programs to memorize Bible verses, Girl Scout troop databases, nutrition programs, meal planners, to-do lists, and personal finance programs. Download them. Try them. And if you like, register them.
COMPUSERVE *go* pbshome

CD–ROM

CD Archive Those three-and-a-quarter-inch floppies are headed for the museum, right between the abacus and the vacuum tube. One of the new technologies ready to take their place is the recordable CD-ROM. CD Archive has the hardware and the software for recording CD-ROMs, and they support PC, Mac, and UNIX. The Archive of the title refers to the ability to archive

One big happy family PC
http://www.zdnet.com/~complife

your own data. The only CD-ROM software they currently carry are programs for CD-ROM writers.
WEB http://www.cdarchive.com

CD-ROM FAQ Looking for a good CD-ROM drive and rec-ommendations for where to buy it? Want to know how to transfer your 10,000-page doc-ument onto a CD-ROM? How do you mount an ISO-9660 disc on Sun? Okay, so maybe you just came to find out what CD-ROM stands for ("Compact Disks Read Only Memory"). Whatever the question, from Photo CDs to CD-ROM jukeboxes, you'll probably find the answers here.
WEB http://www.cis.ohio-state.edu /hypertext/faq/usenet/cdrom-faq /faq.html

Modems & printers

Cable Modem Resources on the Web To a dedicated netsurfer, this page resembles an oasis after a hot, dusty trek. Oh, to have a cable modem! But if you can't buy one right now, David Gingold's site will at least bring you up to speed on their development, through a remarkably comprehensive col-lection of articles, papers, and links to pages about manufac-turers and system trials. Don't despair—some day you'll prac-tically fly through the Web.
WEB http://rpcp.mit.edu/~gingold /cable

comp.dcom.modems Modems can be pesky and uncoopera-

tive, so it's nice to have a place where you can vent your frus-trations over the little hissing box that helps you to get online. Modem users post queries and recommendations on a variety of modem-related topics. For instance, did you know that the high voltage of phone lines in Singapore allegedly causes U.S. modems to burn out when they are used over there?
USENET comp.dcom.modems

comp.periphs.printers Tom is flustered because the ink car-tridge for his HP FaxJet 100 keeps clogging up. So he posts a query to this newsgroup spe-cializing in printers and fax machines and gets two responses: "Is it one of the 'longer life' cartridges? When we switched to those we found

that at least every second one had clogging problems. We just took it back to the store and asked for a replacement." and "Did you remember to remove the white and green piece of tape that is along the side and bottom? Failure to do so will shorten the life of the cartridge." People who keep abreast of the printer scene hang out here, so it's a good place to read product updates and swap industry news.
USENET comp.periphs.printers

SCSI FAQ Excuse me, but do you know what a SCSI port is for? Known in some circles as a Small Computer Systems Interface and in others as a plain old "scuzzi," it's a stan-dard port for connecting peripherals to your computer. In other words, it's that funny-looking thing on the back of your computer with a lot of little holes that your monitor plugs into. If you have any other questions about the exciting world of SCSI, refer to this enlightening two-part FAQ.

WEB http://www.cis.ohio-state .edu/hypertext/faq/usenet/scsi-faq /top.html

Security

Cryptography, PGP, and Your Privacy An excerpt from the World Wide Web Virtual Library, this entry concerns itself with keeping information private, and it offers (among other things) resources for private-citizen cryptography. Skip the pompous, overblown open-ing quote from Ayn Rand and proceed directly to the links, which range from fiercely serious to downright hilarious.

WEB http://world.std.com/~franl /crypto.html

Hackers Yes, hackmeisters, this is the promo page that real-life hackers tapped into and de-faced, with disparaging comments about the film and Hollywood's attempt to market it to an uninterested audience. MGM preserved the hacked page and made it accessible from their Web site. Other-wise, this is your standard fan club, shrine, and general info spot, opening with a toll-free number for ordering the soundtrack, a couple of reviews, correspondence about hacking, and links to info about the cast, crew, and pro-duction. Light, tight, and bright, the overall feel is friendly and the hype is mini-mal.

WEB http://www.mgmua.com /hackers/index.html

Security FAQ Internet Security Systems, Inc., in Norcross, Ga. maintains this index of FAQs, aimed primarily at system administrators. There's infor-mation about and links to many of the big software and hardware vendors, patches for various systems, check lists to follow when security is com-promised, an FAQ on sniffing (intercepting messages intended for other machines), and information on how to set

SHAREWARE.COM
WEB http://www.shareware.com

Let's face it, a computer user's favorite word, like any consumer, is "free." With all the cash one shells out for hardware, connections, etc., it's always great to find a giveaway; there are more than

190,000 of them here at *c|net*'s Shareware.com, a searchable index of shareware sites around the world. When you find the program you're looking for, up pops a compre-hensive list of transfer sites. It's your choice: get a local copy or make the server get it all the way from Timbuktu.

Location: http://www.macplay.com/

Just one of the resources linked via The Ultimate Macintosh
http://www.velodrome.com/umac.html

up a secure anonymous FTP site.
WEB http://iss.net/~iss/faq.html

talk.politics.crypto A forum for debating the political implications of cryptography. Take a side on the Clipper debate or the distribution of RC4 on this newsgroup.
USENET talk.politics.crypto

Virus FAQ This large document is divided into seven sections: sources of information and anti-viral software; definitions (e.g., "What is a Trojan Horse?"); tips on detecting and eliminating viruses; tips on infections; Facts and Fibs, ("Can a virus infect data files?"); answers to miscellaneous questions ("What is the plural of virus, anyway?"); and information about specific viruses and anti-viral programs. Although the preface indicates that this document is supposed

to be constantly changing, it hasn't been updated since Nov. 18, 1992.
WEB http://www.cis.ohio-state.edu /hypertext/faq • http://www.cis.ohio -state.edu/hypertext/faq/usenet /computer-virus-faq/faq.html
URL ftp://rtfm.mit.edu/pub/usenet-by -hierarchy comp/virus

Software
....

The Software Site Remember how you claimed you were getting the computer as an educational and productivity tool? What you really meant was you wanted to play games day and night, right? The Software Site specializes in games. They have, in total, only a few hundred titles, but they're guaranteed to be the best and most useful. If you want them all, the company is willing to send you a CD-ROM for a paltry shipping cost.
WEB http://www.softsite.com

Wuarchive Software Archive Pick a system, any system. This mammoth archive has directories for dozens of operating systems like the Amiga, the PC, the Mac, and OS/2. While the site houses several thousand of its own programs, it also mirrors many of the biggest software archives on the Net. In the Mac directory, for instance, you have the option of accessing the vast resources of the Info-Mac and U. Mich archives as well as an original Macintosh archive with applications ranging from PostScript programs to virus detectors to education programs.
URL ftp://wuarchive.wustl.edu /systems

Macintosh
....

The Apple II Info Web Home Page It's not pretty (too many icons), but it brings together many resources for Apple II users—from shareware archives to information on dozens of system and hardware topics (post-patching and GSBug, Apple Superdrive repair, Using a Syquest SCSI on IIe, etc.) to links to other Apple II sites on the Internet.
WEB http://www.visi.com/~nathan /a2/faq/index.html

Apple Information Need that system software update? How about the specs on the new QuickTake 150 camera? You'll find it here, along with everything else Apple, whether you're interested in product

descriptions, software updates, or developing the next "killer app." The Smorgasbord area includes links to the Apple Virtual Campus, a list of employment opportunities, and an archive of QuickTime movies.
WEB http://www.info.apple.com
URLftp://ftp.info.apple.com

Apple Support Forum Want to read about what the Multimedia Tuner's got to offer? Or maybe you're trying to locate a new version of an old favorite—Hypercard, for example? If you're looking for software updates, Apple press releases, or info on how to contact Apple, this is the place. The area includes a compre-

hensive library for information and software, whether it's for the Newton, the Mac, or an Apple II.
COMPUSERVE *go* aplsup

Everything Macintosh OK, maybe not everything. But they do have links to so many places, they may have everything once removed. The best way to approach this is with a general goal, like picking up a new game, because their index uses general categories only, and browsing is too randomly organized to be much fun. You can put yourself on a mailing list (as if you don't get enough junk mail), download some stuff for your Mac (games, shareware, fonts), and check

the address book for newsgroups and FTP sites. Basically, there's not much at the site, and they don't make it easy to find what little there is.
WEB http://www.cs.brandeis.edu/~xray/mac.html

Mac Internet Helpers Suspect you may not be getting all you can out of the vast splendor that is the Net? You won't find chills and thrills here, but you will find anything and everything you're looking for to use your Mac on the Internet, along with a few things it never before occurred to you to want, and which you now realize you can't possibly live without. Search and sample browsers and plug-ins, emailers, FTP

 CULT OF MACINTOSH
WEB http://cult-of-mac.utu.fi

Mac user paradise is lost no more. Although it's all in frames, there are so many Mac items available (the super huge shareware and freeware archive includes games, fonts, and utilities) that the site, however clumsy, is well worth negotiating. If you don't find what you're looking for in their

archive, the Indices section not only links to a variety of other Mac pages, it also has a keyword search engine to help you get to the right one for your needs. Also, if you're the obsessive-type, you may appreciate the Mac O/S propaganda and the top 20 list of Mac-oriented sites.

rograms, and HTML editors and converters. Choose from a large assortment of newsreaders, IRC clients, PPP/TCP utilities, and much more. As the name implies, these guys are tremendously helpful.
WEB http://www.wp.com/mwaters /machelp.html

MacWorld Online Some articles or excerpts mix with freeware or shareware to make this online sampler of the print magazine a great example of the less-is-more philosophy. MacWorld Daily will clue you in to new insights in the computer cult. Free registration permits you to post and receive items on their (logically enough) Mac-oriented message board, or get great new stuff from their huge and well-indexed shareware and freeware library.
WEB http://www.macworld.com

The Ultimate Macintosh Self-touted as "the best Macintosh page on the Web," this spot offers some pretty neat stuff, but calling it "best" might be pushing it a bit. But not by much. Check out What's Hot to pick up the newest applications, games, and other fun features, or just read up on the latest-breaking news about Apple and its products through the many Mac-oriented publications, newsgroups, and vendors linked to from the site. Best of all is the large shareware and freeware library.
WEB http://www.velodrome.com/umac .html

PC

Build Your Own PC Yes, literally. Throw off the yoke of the hardware giants and put together your own personal computer. It's easier and more cost-efficient than you might expect, and this page contains all the information you could possibly need to do it. Select your components based on piece-by-piece comparisons and descriptions. Pick the place you think offers the best deal from the list provided. Decide on an operating system, and you're off and running. A cool and inexpensive do-it-yourself project, if you think you have the knack.
WEB http://www.verinet.com/pc

PC/Computing Online Even the limited, online version of the magazine that brings you the best the PC environment has to offer is comprehensive. Reviews and a map of the Web help you to recognize and find the "1,000 best sites," as per *PC/Computing Online*, while downloads are available for Internet tools and games. Articles review hardware and software and cover Internet issues and PC usage.
WEB http://www.zdnet.com/pccomp

PCNet Online CompuServe has recently started linking many of its forums together. In this case, they've linked Novell's forums, Microsoft's forums, the graphics forums, and even most of the PC-related forums (PCNet). From the PCNet

menu, you can go to the PC Communications Forum, the PC Hardware Forum, the PC Applications Forum, the PC Fun Forum, the PC Programming Forum, the PC Utilties/ Systems Forum, the PC Bulletin Board Forum, the ASP Shareware Forum, several PC vendor forums, and LAN vendor forums. A file finder searches several thousand PC files and programs in libraries all over CompuServe. In addition to its role as a jumping-off point, PCNet Online offers its own selection of indispensable software such as ARC-E (for extracting files from ARC archive files) and VuePrint 3.3 (a fast Windows JPEG/.GIF viewer). Veteran users can also test their knowledge in the trivia contest for the prize of the week—an HP 200LX 1Mb palmtop perhaps?
COMPUSERVE *go* pcnet

System Optimization You won't notice the bland design once you discover the content. If you're committed to getting the most out of your PC for the least possible money, System Optimization has a tremendous amount of on-the-money information. Comparative performance evaluations are simple to do, using the site's benchmark-comparison list; they've stocked plenty of tips to help you with performance problems or to take the next step in an upgrade. System-component information and FAQs let you browse to find the customized system you use (or are thinking of using) and troubleshoot in advance. Links to software companies make it easy to shop around to find what suits you best.

WEB http://www.dfw.net/~sdw /index.html

ZiffNet ZiffNet on CompuServe is one cyberspot that PC users should not miss. Several of the large Ziff-Davis magazines have forums here, including *PC Magazine, PC/Computing, PC Week, Computer Shopper, Interactive Week, Computer Life, Computer Gaming World, MacUser,* and *MacWeek.* Members can discuss articles or related topics on their message boards and hit the libraries for software and selected

articles. In addition, *PC Week, MacWeek,* and *Newsbytes* offer full-text daily computer news.

COMPUSERVE *go* ziffnet

PC-DOS

Garbo PC Archive Computer acting funny? Pick up an antivirus program. Can't find important files? Download a file finder. Heard that the Net is filled with fabulous images and sounds? Get a sound player, a graphics viewer or two, and start exploring. The archive carries hundreds of astronomy .GIFs. Broken down into dozens of directories, from hypertext programs to communications programs

to system utilities, Garbo is the other huge DOS archive online—besides SimTel.

URL ftp://archie.au/micros/pc/garbo
• ftp://wuarchive.wustl.edu /systems/msdos/garbo.uwasa.fi

Microsoft MS-DOS Forum Running DOS 6.2 and out of disk space? Have an autoexec.bat file that won't load? Installing, networking, optimizing memory, running software, and other MS-DOS issues are covered in this forum. Documentation and instructions, addons, and a fairly large selection of MS-DOS shareware—soccer games to phone dialers to recipe databases—are available in the library.

COMPUSERVE *go* msdos

 INTEL

WEB http://www.intel.com

Intel invites you to "Open the Door to the World Within Your PC" at its Web page. Try it—you won't be disappointed. To sample Java, VRML (Virtual Reality), or Shockwave, click on demos of 3-D spaceships, virtual conference calls, or voice-activated help desks. Or read "The Mobile Story"

and learn how a sales account executive uses mobile technology to the max. Although these demos are designed for business users, home users shouldn't be shy. Where else can a techno-junkie download free Java and Shockwave software, or see what's "On the Edge of Web Development"?

PC-OS/2

OS/2 e-Zine No, *e-Zine* is not a character from a cheesy anime, it's an online magazine exclusively for OS-2 users. Available freeware includes mouse and keyboard lockout software and a host of OS-2 utilities. Download such hard-to-find card games as Milles Bornes or Dungeon Chess. Link to places to download financial, office, and graphic software. Subscribers also can be notified when new installments are launched, and new users can scroll through old issues (as of this printing, however, there are only seven—submissions welcome).
WEB http://www.haligonian.com/os2

The OS/2 Homepage If it's not linked to this page, it's probably not about OS/2. Besides offering links to major software archives, other OS/2 Web pages, and the OS/2 newsgroups, the site has a large list of OS/2 user group home pages.
WEB http://web.mit.edu/afs/athena /activity/o/os2/www/os2world.html

Windows

comp.os.ms-windows.misc A very active newsgroup with a broad range of questions and discussions about Microsoft Windows.
USENET comp.os.ms-windows.misc

The Windows FAQ The number of questions and answers in this FAQ is directly propor-

tional to the number of Windows users out there, and that's a lot of answers. There are descriptions of several versions of Microsoft Windows, information on Windows 95 (previously known as Chicago), links to Windows resources on the Net, information on setting up and configuring Windows systems, hundreds of tips and tricks, and troubleshooting advice for many Windows applications (uh, oh, "Page-Maker 4.0 font selection box won't scroll").
WEB http://scwww.ucs.indiana.edu /FAQ/Windows

Windows Forum Features numerous message boards, with separate symposiums for Windows NT, Windows 95, and Visual Basic Windows, as well as workgroups, databases, and multimedia, to name but a few. The software libraries offer thousands of Windows files for users to download. The libraries are separated into categories, so you can easily locate the utility, game, or font you desire. There is also a Top Picks listing of the most popular downloads, a downloading Hall of Fame listing, access to feature articles from *Windows* magazine, and regularly scheduled live chat sessions.
AMERICA ONLINE *keyword* winforum

Windows Information Network If you haven't heard enough about Microsoft from the papers, radios, and TV shows, visit W.I.N.'s site. They're a nonprofit organization and PC

user group "dedicated solely to the promotion and demonstration of MS Windows, Windows products, and applications."
WEB http://www.mbnet.mb.ca/win /winhome.html

Unix

comp.unix.questions Whether you're sitting down at your first Unix machine and don't know how to list a directory, or you're having trouble compiling that pesky new software package, go ahead and ask the experts. Most questions get a polite and knowledgeable reply.
USENET comp.unix.questions
FAQ: **WEB** http://www.cis.ohio-state .edu/hypertext/faq/bngusenet/comp /unix/questions/top.html

Sun Microsystems Infocentral for Sun's ever-increasing product line, seminars, and usergroups with a special focus on their most widely popular software to date, Java. Try *Sunworld Online* (the company's zine), stop in for new product bulletins and press releases (even brief demo-permissions and ordering are available), or updates and FAQs on your old standbys. But don't expect to come here for fun or get much out of it if you're a Mac user.
WEB http://www.sun.com

Unix FAQs A collection of dozens of FAQ documents about Unix.
WEB http://www.cis.ohio-state.edu /hypertext/faq/bngusenet/comp /unix/top.html

Portables

comp.sys.laptops Although ostensibly for discussing laptops, there is a tremendous amount of buying and selling activity—"My Desktop for Your Laptop"—on this newsgroup. Nonetheless, it's also the place to get answers to questions about upgrades, accessories, and add-ons for your Powerbook, Thinkpad, or one of the less popular laptop models. The majority of the messages are queries from prospective laptop buyers seeking advice about which machine to choose.
USENET comp.sys.laptops

comp.sys.mac.portables Got problems with your 520C freezing up? Wondering about PowerPC upgrades for that Duo? And what do you do if your Duo gets stuck in its mini-dock. If you want to talk about portable Macs, here's the spot. You'll also find computers and memory for sale, info on jacking up your machine for maximum speed, and answers to questions about battery woes, AC adapters, and other PowerBook-related dilemmas.
USENET comp.sys.mac.portables

Multimedia

Audio Virtual Library Links from here to sound repositories, newsgroups, software, and documented support for audiophiles and sound junkies. The software links will take you to sites on the Web where you can download sound utilities. Then, visit the sound repository, which features links to places with sound clips for your new player.
WEB http://www.comlab.ox.ac.uk /archive/audio.html

Macintosh Music and Sound Forum Want to make music on the Mac? Go to the Macintosh Software Center's Greatest Hits area in the software libraries to download reliable, easy-to-use sound players like SoundMaster and Now Hear This. Attend a weekly conference or engage in real-time chat with a fellow forum member about both the technological and aesthetic issues of digital sound. The software

CALTECH'S OS/2 SITE
WEB http://www.ccsf.caltech.edu/~kasturi/os2.html

If you're looking for information about OS/2, everything you could ever possibly need is available through this single resource center. This is an exceptionally well-organized Web site, with links to

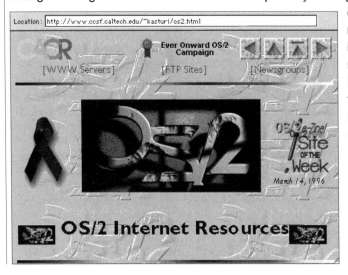

every imaginable Internet resource relating to OS/2, including several different mirror sites for the "OS/2 Pharmacy." You'll find descriptions of, as well as links to, international Web servers, FTP sites, and newsgroups.

libraries are filled with sound files. Use the America Online sounds to customize your AOL software or explore the world of pop culture with TV, music, movie, cartoon, and science fiction. Beginners should head to the message boards for some sound advice: "I can't play MIDI files!" screams one post: "Buy a sequencer program that can play standard midifiles (SMFs)! All the good ones will play SMFs!" shouts back another.
AMERICA ONLINE *keyword* mms

Macromedia.com This brilliant software manufacturer has, unsurprisingly, a great offering online as well. A well-organized overview helps you navigate the maze of interesting features, including an extensive freeware section and the "shocked" site of the day; it highlights the best use of the Macromedia program Shock-

wave, a Netscape plug-in which permits your computer to view Director movies, and is available here for downloading free. Today's News and Headlines, and a variety of industry articles keep you up to date on what's new with Macromedia and multimedia in general, and an Interactive Gallery offers great uses of all these multimedia-creation programs.
WEB http://www-1.macromedia.com

The MIDI Home Page Dedicated to both the budding MIDI enthusiast and the veteran digital composer, the MIDI Home Page has enough information to please even the most jaded Web traveler. Heini Withagen, the author of this remarkable page, has included more data and links than are physically possible to digest in one sitting. After perusing text files on the history, application, and specifications of the communi-

cation protocol, you can advance your MIDI knowledge by following links to other MIDI pages, FTP sites, and related newsgroups.
WEB http://www.eeb.ele.tue.nl/midi/index.html

Databases

comp.apps.spreadsheets
Whichever spreadsheet you use to crunch your numbers, chances are it's a topic of discussion in this high-traffic newsgroup devoted to software troubleshooting and gossip. The emphasis is on Microsoft Excel, but there are plenty of posts about Quattro Pro and Lotus 1-2-3. If you're looking to convert files from one spreadsheet program into another, this group will serve you well. File conversion appears to be everyone else's quandary, too.
USENET comp.apps.spreadsheets

comp.databases Do you want to keep track of the programs and movies you've videotaped? Ask members of the newsgroup which database products are best for the job. Speaking of jobs, database consultants and those in need of consulting turn to this newsgroup to find each other. You can also ask questions about specific databases ("Can I define my database structure, relations, reports, forms, and queries in MS-Access and implement my code in its Visual Basic language?").
USENET comp.databases

The 'wave of the future
http://www-1.macromedia.com

Desktop publishing

DTP Internet Jumplist A hypertext list of resources on the Internet containing links to FAQs, fonts, clip art, and other DTP-related sites. This electronic trampoline lets you search by topic or allows you to jump directly to font and clip art archives or related discussion groups. A good place to start exploring desktop publishing resources on the Internet.
WEB http://www.cs.purdue.edu/homes/gwp/dtp/dtp.html

PC DTP Resource Center Typefaces, images, and formatting tips for desktop publishers who work in an IBM-compatible environment. And that's just the beginning. Worried about copyright issues for the *X-Files* newsletter you're working on? Turn to the libraries for texts on copyright law or post a question on the message boards. Need to learn the professional lingo? Pick up a glossary of desktop publishing terms. And if you don't know how to convert a JPEG to a .GIF, read the graphics file tips. You can also directly access popular vendors through the Industry Connection or post questions and observations pertaining to practically every desktop publishing program in the world.
AMERICA ONLINE *keyword* dwp

Publish RGB A sizzling ezine to pump up your publishing powers. This site is colorfully and simply divided into Tools, Talk, Treasury, and Techniques, with a cutting-edge, exciting approach. Find out the best types of paper to use, read consumer reports on printers, and get font recommendations. It's all here to make you look the best on paper.
WEB http://www.publish.com

Programming

comp.lang.misc Discussion about and help with any computer language, from C++ to JAVA, from the cyber-polyglots of the Net (who will, no doubt, be attending the USENIX 1997 Annual Technical Conference).
USENET comp.lang.misc

POWERBOOK ARMY!
WEB http://www.net-army.com/pba

Journalist and Japanese telecommuter Atsushi Iijima spends five hours a day on the train going to and from work. With PowerBook in hand, they're five hours well spent. At this site, which has three

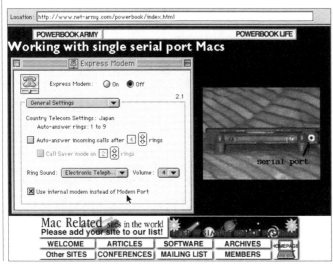

separate servers in Tokyo, Hawaii, and New York (each with localized information), Iijima passes on tips and tricks for making the most of Mac portables. He has also made the PowerBook utilities and extensions that he's collected available.

Developer's Resources A Web site for software developers working with MS-DOS, MS-Windows, and OS/2 platforms. The site includes links to source code libraries, FAQs, and other programming-related resources on the Internet.
WEB http://www.mind.net/jfs/devres.html

The Language List A searchable list of more than 2,300 published computer languages. Successful searches return brief explanations of the languages, reference works written about the languages, and online resources related to them.
WEB http://cuiwww.unige.ch/langlist

The Netlib Scientific Computing Repository Software and documentation to compute functions, simulations, and algorithms in a variety of programming languages.
WEB http://netlib.bell-labs.com

PC MagNet Programming Forum Oriented toward PC users, this Ziff-Davis forum is a rich resource for programmers and programming students. In the library, there are hypertext tutorials for C++, FAQs for BASIC, Pascal source code, tools for Visual Basic, and a wide range of other programming files. The message boards include topics about the philosophy of programming, utilities coding, corporate software development, and C++.
COMPUSERVE *go* program

Location: http://www.publish.com/0996/productwatch/

Product Watch

Tools

Fast, EZ Storage

The **EZFlyer 230**, the latest removable hard drive from SyQuest, provides 230-MB capacity per 3.5-inch cartridge and claims an average access time of 13.5 ms, as well as a burst data transfer rate of up to 4 MB per second. For **$299** you get the drive, cables, software, and one cartridge. Additional cartridges are $29.95 each. SyQuest Technology Inc., 510-226-4000 or 800-245-2278.

A Gem of a Scanner

The redesigned and upgraded **Topaz ($49,000)** flatbed transparency scanner for the Power Mac scans up to 200 percent faster with a maximum optical resolution of 5,080 dpi. The **Topaz Robot ($64,000)** can batch-scan up to 225 35mm transparencies; both models come with LinoColor 4.1 software and a $19,000 option for Copix, for digitizing and descreening film separations and line art. Linotype-Hell Co., 516-434-2000 or 800-842-9721.

Topics / Techniques / Talk / Tools / Treasury / Search

Publish RGB is a must for serious DTP
http://www.publish.com

Programmer University Self-paced introductory, intermediate, and advanced online courses for those interested in learning C or Pascal programming. The courses consist of a weekly online conference with an expert and regular programming assignments.
AMERICA ONLINE *keyword* programmeru

Software Development Forum Run by *Software Development* magazine, the forum's message boards carry discussions about object-oriented programming, public domain shareware, language tools, software development conferences, game development, and other programming topics. The libraries are full of programming instructions and source code, including language FAQs, the source code published in *Software Development* magazine, and public domain software.
COMPUSERVE *go* sdforum

Virtual Library's Computer Programming Languages An A-Z hypertext index to programming resources online. The site includes links to an introduction to the ABC programming language, FAQs about Perl, LISP, and other languages, source code for C++ programs, and other programming indexes.
WEB http://src.doc.ic.ac.uk/bySubject/Computing/Languages.html

Utilities

PBS Utilities Forum Run by Ziff-Davis staff members, the Forum is a goldmine for PC users with questions about utilities ("how do you use the 'regular expression searches' featured in ProFind?") and utility needs. The library features system, hardware, printer, and file utilities for DOS, Windows, and OS/2 platforms.
COMPUSERVE *go* pbsutilities

Utilities and Tools To tackle a world of file extensions (.ARJ, .LHA, .ZOO, .ZIP, .HQX, etc.), savvy computer users come equipped with files to unencode, uncompress, unzip, unstuff, and convert. This site carries most of the important programs for Mac, Amiga, PC, and Unix users.
URL ftp://ftp.tex.ac.uk/pub/archive/tools

Word Processing
....
comp.os.ms-windows.apps.word-proc Microsoft Word for Windows, better known in this newsgroup as "WinWord," is the main topic of discussion. How do you create a bibliogra-phy in WinWord? Export to HTML? Manage large documents? Advice is doled out by MS Word gurus on these and other topics (macro writing, printer drivers, etc.). Computer users looking for hints and advice about WordPerfect, AmiPro, and other Windows word processing programs are also welcome.
USENET comp.os.ms-windows.apps.word-proc

Mac Word Processing In the world of the Macintosh, word processing usually means Microsoft Word, and while there is plenty of discussion about Word (including a very active Word 6.0 Nightmare folder), MacWrite, Write Now, Nisus, and even WordPerfect for the Mac have their own message folders in this forum. But writers can turn to this forum for more than program support; general advice about word processing and recom-mendations for dictionaries, file conversion utilities, and index programs are also covered on the message boards—in the libraries, there is an archive of shareware utilities for your Macintosh, including typing tutors, a screenplay formatter, and an HTML convertor that translates Word 6.0 files into text files with hypertext mark-up language tags.
AMERICA ONLINE *keyword* mdp →

AMBROSIA CAFÉ
WEB http://www.AmbrosiaSW.com/Cafe.html
All right, it's a commercial boost for a software company, but they do make great games, many of which are downloadable and discussable right here. From straightforward classic arcade "homages" to elaborate strategy "homages" to *Star Wars*, Ambrosia always packs a punch and always with a good sound-track. You've already got one? Check the game-specific FAQs, peruse *Mac Media Monthly* or the *Real MacOy* ezines to find out who's talking about what, then join the discussion in the Share the Mac users group. Sections focus on Internet fea-tures (TCP/PPP, FTP, etc.) and provide PowerMac ideas and downloads.

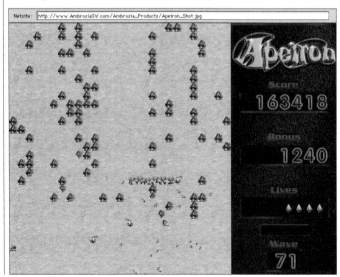

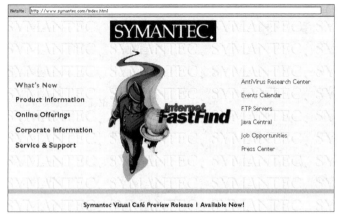

Netsite: http://www.symantec.com/index.html

SYMANTEC.

What's New
Product Information
Online Offerings
Corporate Information
Service & Support

AntiVirus Research Center
Events Calendar
FTP Servers
Java Central
Job Opportunities
Press Center

Internet FastFind

Symantec Visual Café Preview Release | Available Now!

Check out Symantec's site to get the dish on most known viruses
http://www.symantec.com/avcenter/index.htm

Message Boards→DWP Message Boards→List Categories→Word Processing • *keyword* mdp→Software Libraries→Utilities→Word Processors

PC Word Processing The PC Applications Forum has a shareware archive full of software add-ons for word processors, including AmiPro, WordPerfect, and Word for Windows. Need a poetry generating program? Drop into the Utilities area and download PoeTrio, an application that coaches you through the process of writing free verse, cantonas, and haiku. How about a bibliography management program (BibLogic 3.02) or the useful Cliché Finder, which scans your document in search of overused words? The forum also has a message board where word processing and word processing programs are discussed.
AMERICA ONLINE *keyword* APPS→ Word Processing→pcapplications→ Message Boards→Word Processors

Word Processing/DTP For most people—designers excepted—the line between word processing and desktop publishing is blurry if not meaningless. The goal, after all, is the same: to produce a business plan, write a resume, or, perhaps, send a memo. To do the job, you'll use a word processor, fonts, and maybe clip art or scanned images. Located in the Working from Home Forum, this discussion area and library section offers members support, advice, templates, and sample projects to help them flesh out project ideas and troubleshoot problems with word processing and DTP tools.
COMPUSERVE *go* work→Libraries *or* Messages→Word Processing/DTP

Viruses

Anti-Virus Resource Center On this resourceful page, the software company Symantec offers warnings about widespread viruses, and, of course, Syman-

tec anti-virus products. A section under construction promises hints for implementing anti-virus protection on networks.
WEB http://www.symantec.com /avcenter/index.html

comp.virus Keeping computers virus-free (and healing those already infected) is the mission of this newsgroup—sort of the Center for Disease Control of the computer world. The relative merits of anti-viral programs, information on specific viruses, warnings about new viruses, and questions about the best ways to prevent viral infection are common topics ("How many anti-viral programs does it take?" asks one writer plaintively; the not-terribly-reassuring answer: three should cover you "reasonably well"). Although Mac users aren't specifically excluded, almost all messages are posted by PC users.
USENET comp.virus

❝Keeping computers virus-free is the mission of this newsgroup— sort of the CDC of the computer world. ❞

The Net

YOU DON'T HAVE TO BE BILL GATES TO BE THE MASTER OF YOUR DOMAIN

DOES IT EVER FEEL like the Internet is just one big country club, and you've been blackballed? So much of the Web seems to be ruled by its own technology, and if you don't understand it, the technology begins to rule you. That's OK, really, because the portion of the Web devoted to helping people catch up on the lingo and the techie stuff is significant indeed.

Whether it's the great browser wars, the difference between Java and Shockwave, or even that between the Internet and the World Wide Web, there's an FAQ, a Web site, a newsgroup, or a rule book somewhere to teach you about it. And of course, once you've mastered the technology, the culture of the Net is even more fascinating. What's netiquette all about? Where's the Internet headed? Is cybersociety a real entity or just the creation of story-needy journalists?

Location: http://netday.iworld.com/simba/

media daily
A Service of Cowles New Media

Media Central
http://www.mediacentral.com

1996
- January
- February
- March
- April
- May
- June
- July

1995
- May
- June
- July
- August
- September
- October
- November
- December

CIA Web Site Hacked

The Central Intelligence Agency seems to be lacking a little World Wide Web intelligence. The nation's covert operations agency was forced to pull the plug on its Web site after a hacker broke in and replaced it with a parody.

COWLES/SIMBA

WEB http://netday.iworld.com/simba
AMERICA ONLINE *keyword* cowles

When the *Village Voice* and the *L.A. Weekly* announced the launch of their online guide to nightlife in the two cities, Cowles/SIMBA had a story on it the next day. When AT&T announced a series of consumer products and billing options merging telephone and computer technologies, Cowles/SIMBA covered it. And when Prodigy announced that its members could create home pages, guess who covered it? Each weekday, new stories about online media are added to both the Internet and AOL sites.

Starting points

alt.newbie/alt.newbies/news.newusers.questions/comp.unix.questions Newsgroups created especially for Internet novices to post questions. The FAQ directory includes guides about email, FTP, Internet access providers, creating a signature file, and reading newsgroups.
USENET alt.newbie/alt.newbies/news .newusers.questions/comp.unix .questions
WEB http://www.cis.ohio-state.edu /hypertext/faq/bngusenet/news /newusers/questions/top.html

EFF's Extended Guide to the Internet EFF's (extended) guide to the Internet is a very basic primer for the Internet. The guide covers Internet providers, email programs and email addresses, Usenet culture and newsreaders, mailing lists, telnet instructions and sites, FTP instructions and sites, gophers and sites, IRC and MUDs, netiquette, the EFF, and much more.
WEB http://www.eff.org/papers/eegtti /eegttitop.html • http://www.eff.org /pub/Net_info/EFF_Net_Guide /netguide.ef
URL ftp://ftp.lib.ncsu.edu/pub/stacks /guides/big-dummy/bdg_toc.html
COMPUSERVE →go inetforum→libraries →*Search by file name:*ntgd3l.zip

How to Select an Internet Service Provider Rick Adams, CEO of UUNet Technologies, tells you what questions to ask and how best to evaluate Internet services, whether you're looking for a bare-bones plan for the kids or a high-speed backbone for your small business. The site could use a glossary for all the turgid techno-prose, but at least you'll sound like you know what you're talking about when you ask potential ISPs about network topology and whether the firm is a member of the Commercial Internet Exchange Association.
WEB http://www.cnam.fr/Network /Internet-access/how_to_select.html

Information Sources: the Internet and Computer-Mediated Communication A huge, well-organized guide to Internet resources about the very broad topic of computer-mediated communication. The guide links to hundreds of sites with information or discussion about the Internet, including mailing lists about the Web, Internet tutorials, Internet search engines, and information about Internet protocols.
WEB http://www.december.com/cmc /info/index.html

Internet Café A useful, no-non-sense collection of Internet instructional guides and software. Download files like TurboGopher, "Setting up a WWW Home Page," and even the "Internet Downloading Guide."
AMERICA ONLINE *keyword* mcm→ Software Libraries→Internet Cafe

Internet Services From within CompuServe, members can telnet, FTP, and read newsgroups. The main Internet menu also links to a trio of active Internet forums where netters discuss all facets of the Internet. In the New Users Forum (go inetforum) novices are introduced to Internet Web browsers, email, telnet programs, IRC channels, FTP, and CompuServe via PPP connections. They can ask questions on the boards or turn to the libraries to download Internet guides, tutorials, and software. More experienced surfers should head straight to the Internet Resources Forum (go inetresource) for more technical discussions of Internet software and navigational tools. The strength of the Resources Forum lies with its libraries which are packed with FAQs on Net topics such as TCP/IP, firewalls, and cryptography as well as lists of mailing lists, Web browsers and HTML editors, telnet and gopher clients, and much more. The third forum, the Internet Publishing Forum (go inetpub), is exclusively for CompuServe members interested in Web design and creating home pages.
COMPUSERVE *go* Internet Services→ internet

InterNIC If you're looking to be the master of your own domain, you had better stop here. InterNIC is the place to come to claim a new domain. InterNIC provides information on costs and protocol, and tells you if that URL you so craved is already taken.
WEB http://www.internic.net

The List Trying to guess the number of Internet Service Providers (ISP) is a lot like speculating about the number of jelly beans in the jar. The List has counted more than 2,600 ISPs, but that number waxes and wanes depending on the day you visit. Despite the fact that not all listings are complete and necessarily accurate, you can assemble a good rundown of ISPs in your area code or state, or look up Galactic Gewgaws, a good place to comparison shop and discover some of Galactic's offerings.
WEB http://thelist.iworld.com

World Wide Web FAQ A valuable resource about the Web. The FAQ describes and links to Web browsers, guides to writing HTML, HTML editors, and documents about designing a home page.
WEB http://www.boutell.com/faq
• http://www.cis.ohio-state.edu/hypertext/faq/usenet/www/faq/faq.html

Zen and the Art of the Internet
This guide is often considered the granddaddy of all Internet manuals. Generations of Internet users started with this compact reference tool that covers topics ranging from Archie file searching to the Internet domain name system.
AMERICA ONLINE *keyword* internet→ Zen & the Art of the Internet
URL ftp://ftp.internic.net/pub/internet-doc/zen.txt

WEB http://www.cs.indiana.edu/docproject/zen/zen-I.0_toc.html

News & commentary

alt.wired A newsgroup where some people debate about whether Kurt Cobain was a genius or an overrated jerk, while others consider Einstein's theory that a fully functional brain could do fifty times the work that he did, and still others trade back issues of *Wired* magazine. Occasionally, *Wired* itself posts announcements to this unofficial and unmoderated newsgroup.
USENET alt.wired

c|net Online What's new in computerdom? This elabo-

WEBMONKEY
WEB http://www.webmonkey.com

A *This Old House* for the wired bunch from the *Wired* folks. Webmonkey offers the Net set the tools and methods to deal with modern problems such as whether to incorporate server-push, and whither to surf with a fully loaded browser. If frames have you frazzled or your browser's got you

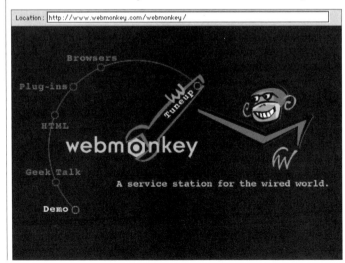

bummed, Webmonkey can help you out, acting as either a quick reference guide or an in-depth tutorial center. The site performs with *HotWired's* usual high level of user interaction. Just a baby when we visited, however, Webmonkey has a long way to go in terms of depth and content if it wants to live up to its own hype.

rately produced home page—where Silicon Valley meets Hollywood—is the place to find out. From sales estimates on Intel's Pentium Pro microprocessor selling to 55 Netscape tips to a Web-celeb profile of Laurie Plaksin (who emoted on *The Spot*, an online soap-opera), it's all here. The c|netters, who also have a TV program on USA Network and the Sci-Fi Channel, incorporate audible computer news (with a RealAudio download) and television footage.
WEB http://www.cnet.com

Global Internet News Agency
GINA—the Global Internet News Agency—has a rather spiffy site, with all the intro mumbo-jumbo fitting on a single, efficient page. If you want to access the Internet wire, the technology news tips, the ExpertNet, or the rest of the links, you can choose from simple text links or a lovely solar-system effect, with each of the heavenly bodies serving as an icon, in a design in which the medium is truly the message.
WEB http://www.gina.com

HotWired An innovative electronic "magazine" produced by the *Wired* organization. It's hip, well-designed, and packed with original editorial content. The site features a continuously changing mix of features like the recent profile of independent record labels using the Web (with sound clips of their musicians), a Net Surf column

highlighting new sites, a gossip column called Flux about the online medium and media, Club Wired for live symposiums with special guests, and much more. And did we mention that it's completely free and that the "cover" changes each time you access it?
WEB http://www.hotwired.com

Interactive Age A hybrid of a digital 'zine presented with a print publication's front page and summary-style table of contents, this page offers online access to Web-industry news and gossip in a slightly breathless but info-packed and easy-to-use format. You can subscribe or continue to glom onto the free Web version; it's your choice.
WEB http://techweb.cmp.com /techweb/ia/current

The Mesh Very slick, very high concept, and accompanied by a full explanation of what it thinks it's doing, The Mesh is a good place to go if you're seeking a greater understanding of hot Web issues, online or in print, whether you're a clueless newbie or an oldtimer. Mac users get special attention. Oh, yeah—there's a chat component, too.
WEB http://www.albany.globalone.net /theMESH

NetGuide On-line What sites are worth visiting? Who's making news on the Net? And what tips would make your Net life a lot easier? The monthly print magazine is pitched to answer

exactly these questions. Its online counterpart includes listings of all the Web sites reviewed in the Cyberguide (reviews and live links are available online) as well as the full text of a selection of articles from the current issue.
WEB http://www.wais.com

Packet At *HotWired's* ever-evolving site, Signal (one of their oldest areas) has finally been replaced by Packet, which now aspires to provide "a good idea, every day" to the Web community with rotating daily columns. Ned Brainard's poison pen remains poised, delivering the inside scoop on the business of the Net in Flux on Monday. On Tuesdays, Michael Schrage explores online business models and markets. Wednesdays, Simson Garfinkel, covers the technical inner workings of the Net. Andrew Leonard takes over on Thursdays with reports on emerging Web cultures and trends. And on Fridays, Packet offers *HotSeat*, a 30-minute RealAudio program interviewing the key players in the digital revolution.
WEB http://www.packet.com

Suck The vitriolic editors of this 'zine declare it "an experiment in provocation, mordant decontructionism, and buzz-saw journalism... a dirty syringe hidden" in the shallow waters of the Net. At the sign of the fish, the barrel, and the smoking gun, you'll find a smattering of articles and

essays laced with biting sarcasm, wit, and satire amidst the general mayhem of text and graphics. Continually updated, *Suck* features two new pieces every 24 hours. For particularly scathing commentary on the new media industry, Web trends, and hypersophisticated cybercriticism, check our the work of Ersatz and CGI Joe.
WEB http://www.suck.com

Upside Online This ezine features "provocative, insightful analyses of the individuals and companies leading the digital revolution." Also includes an archive of back issues. *Upside* is hardly as jargon-heavy as one would expect. In fact, this magazine features some of the most entertaining business and technology-related writing around.
WEB http://www.upside.com

Web Week Industry news that you can use, presented in a

headline-and-summary format that takes up a couple of screens but is rich with information. It's a useful read for anyone hoping to stake a claim to a piece of the info frontier. The section subheads helpfully break up the entries, for which eyes everywhere are grateful.
WEB http://pubs.iworld.com /ww-online

Web picks

Cool Site of the Day Been staring at too many hideous, boring sites? Don't waste your time looking; let someone else's fingers do the walking. A recent winner was the Simon Wiesenthal Center's site.
WEB http://cool.infi.net

The High Five Award Page Dave Siegel's place in the annals of Web design is well assured. Here he brings his tenets and his lofty tone to yet another "Best of the Web" site. But this

one does distinguish itself from other sites in that Siegal actually works with designers toward a better site before he awards them his hallowed High Five. Submit your own URL to see if you too can be among the few, the proud, the Dave Siegel disciples.
WEB http://www.highfive.com

Project Cool If you're looking for the best of the Web, Project Cool might be able to take you there. With sections on Business, Computers, Entertainment, News, Science, Travel and more, Project Cool offers its own subjective rating of the best there is to surf. Also offered up, in Developer Zone are helpful tips for Web designers whether you're a novice or a seasoned veteran.
WEB http://www.projectcool.com

Spider's Pick of the Day An incredibly popular site for netsurfers, the site features a new Web site everyday. Past Spider picks have included a tour of the Sixteenth Chapel, *People* magazine online, a Frisbee page, a page dedicated to Timothy Leary, and a gallery of space shots.
WEB http://gagme.wwa.com/~boba /pick.html

Mailing lists

The List of Lists This is by far the most comprehensive tool to search for mailing lists on the Internet. Offering more than 6,000 entries and revised on a weekly basis, it's the quickest

Turkey Chariot, from *HotWired*'s gallery
http://www.hotwired.com

Location: http://www.hotwired.com/gallery/96/29/c.html

way to find a good mailing list.
WEB http://alpha.acast.nova.edu
/cgi-bin/lists

Tile.Net ListServ Lists It's late in
the evening and you have a
need to discuss underwater
basket-weaving. Why not join
a mailing list? Tile.Net has cataloged thousands of ListServ
mailing lists that are run by a
ListServ program. The site lets
you search by subject or list
name and sort alphabetically or
by number of subscribers.
WEB http://www.tile.net/tile/listserv
/index.html

Anonymous remailers

**Anonymous Remailer Non-techni-
cal FAQ** Have a hot tip about
your company but don't want
people to know who you are?
Want to post to an alt.sex*
group without anyone else
knowing? Use an anonymous
remailer, a program that lets
you send email without tipping
off anyone as to who you are.
This cogent FAQ by Andre
Bacard, author of *The Computer Privacy Handbook*, offers
clear explanations and breaks
down the options. Happily, the
very first question is, "What is
a remailer?" and Bacard proceeds accordingly, taking no
previous knowledge for
granted.
WEB http://www.well.com/user
/abacard/remail.html

List of Anonymous Remailers
Raph Levien offers up this
comprehensive list of remailers.
Levien has also included an

options and features section to
help users choose the optimum
remailer for their purposes.
WEB http://www.cs.berkeley.edu/~raph
/remailer-list.html

BBS

BBS Sites on the Internet More
than 154 bulletin boards from
the Anarchists to the Floating
Pancreas to Grinning Evil
Death—all those BBSs you
wanted to join but were unable
to find elsewhere in the under-
belly of the Net. Also, the ones
nobody you know would know
about—LaToya Jackson's
Dreams, anybody?
WEB http://aug3.augsburg.edu
/~schwartz/ebbs.html

Tech

**Entering the Worldwide Web: A
Guide to Cyberspace** Cyberspace
and the Web are not synony-
mous, despite what this site
says. That mistake aside, this
online guide offers an overview
of Web technology, describes
the Web's place in Internet
history, and features a timeline
of the hypertext history.
WEB http://www.hcc.hawaii.edu/guide
/www.guide.html

Macintosh Internet Software
Both AOL and CompuServe
have large libraries of Internet
software, FAQs, and other
information for Macintosh
users with a SLIP or PPP connection. The standard programs such as MacWeb, TurboGopher, and CU-SeeMe are
available.

AMERICA ONLINE *keyword* mcm→
Software Libraries→Internet Cafe
COMPUSERVE *go* inetresource→
Libraries→*Search by file name:* Mac
Internet S/W

NETLiNks More links than
Jimmy Dean sausages are
available to help new Internet
users, covering such topics as
shareware, downloading, and
kid-safety lockouts for Mom's
Playgirl gallery. For squeamish
beginners there are a few
quirky sites to check out, such
as the alternative 'zines in
Canada, which list the hottest
happenings in the frozen
North, you betcha.
NETLiNks is like a paint-by-
numbers scheme for newbies.
WEB http://www.interlog.com/~csteele
/netlinks.html

Newbie Information Runs the
gamut of introductory information for newcomers, from cryptography and FAQs on Internet Relay Chat to Usenet
writing style. The netiquette
test is a white-glove inspection
for Net freshmen: memorize
the ten commandments of the
Computer Ethics Institute,
insert an "_" before and after
book titles, and never, never,
email anything you would
mind seeing on the evening
news, warns Arlene Rinaldi,
the anti-Miss Manners of the
Internet.
WEB http://www.infi.net/~dolores
/newbie.html

Starting to Use the WWW If you
need to get up to speed on the
Web quickly, this site defines

essential Web terms and concepts, and also offers a basic guide to coding Web documents. There are also links to other Web authoring resources.
WEB http://www.sils.umich.edu/~fprefect/inet/using/html.html

The World Wide Web Inititative A central repository for software and information about the Web. The site links to documents about HTML programming, Web browsers for several platforms, resources on Web security, Web development tools, and links to other Web resources.
WEB http://www.w3.org/pub/WWW

World Wide Web Tools Information about Web browsers and a good collection of links to information about Web authoring—an HTML style guide, coding standards, HTML writing tools, and more.
WEB http://www.ziff.com:8002/~pcweek/navigator/webtools.html

Protocols

Anonymous FTP FAQ How do I use the FTP program? What is Archie? How do I automate FTP sessions? The guide features fairly detailed instructions for FTPing.
WEB http://www.cis.ohio-state.edu/text/faq/usenet/ftp-list/faq/faq.html

Anonymous FTP Site List A listing of more than 2,300 FTP sites. Each listing includes an FTP address, information about the institution where the site is located, and a brief descripiton of the FTP site's contents. Use one of the first two addresses if you want to search the list.
URL ftp://rtfm.mit.edu/pub/usenet-by-hierarchy/news/answers/ftp-list/sitelist
WEB http://www.cis.ohio-state.edu/text/faq/usenet/ftp-list/sitelist/top.html • http://www.info.net/Public/ftp-list.html

Charm Net Personal IP Page From the MacTCP FAQ to the Winsock Beginners Guide, from the PPP FAQ to PPP software, the site is a good place to find information and software for cruising the Net

 # DYNAMITE SITE OF THE NITE

WEB http://www.netzone.com/~tti/dsotn.html

picture: WEB http://www.roadsideamerica.com

Next to "I'll still love you in the morning," there's not an emptier promise on the Net than "check out my list of cool sites," but the Dynamite Site is one that delivers on its name. Why bother saving

endangered species? Why can't we predict tornadoes better? If you have any such questions rattling around your head, there's plenty of fun fodder for you, Curious George. Try BlenderWeb, *Cocktail* magazine, or the Abilitoys Museum, where you can learn about the genealogy of the Green Giant, and other advertising-icon collectibles. Their motto: "We will serve no Web site before its time."

with a SLIP, PPP, or over a T1.
WEB http://www.charm.net/ppp.html

comp.protocols.ppp Golden Richard is "having a weird problem getting PPP going between a Linux box with a direct Internet connection and a 28.8K modem and [his] home machine." Al recommends checking the BPS rate and using the flow control and asyncmap options. Netters post requests about PPP software, ask for advice configuring their PPP, and troubleshoot conflicts with client software. Oh, and you won't find any FAQs here. Instead, you'll find "Frequently Wanted Information." Those darned PPP people have different terms for everything.
USENET comp.protocols.ppp
FAQ: **WEB** http://www.cis.ohio-state.edu/text/faq/usenet/ppp-faq/top.html
URL ftp://rtfm.mit.edu/pub/usenet/comp.protocols.ppp

The PC-Mac TCP/IP & NFS FAQ List An incredibly comprehensive FAQ covering TCP/IP and related the two major platforms—the Mac and PC. The hypertext document links to information about setting up TCP/IP, defines many of the most common TCP/IP terms, and describes and links to shareware and public domain versions of email packages, Web browsers, newsreaders, FTP clients, and finger servers.
WEB http://www.rtd.com/pcnfsfaq/faq.html

PPP FAQ It isn't pretty, but there's a lot of technical infor-

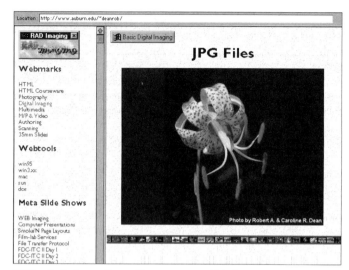

RAD Imaging helps sew the seed for your very own Web site
http://www.auburn.edu/~deanrob

mation about PPP in this FAQ. The document includes an introduction to PPP, a description of PPP's features, a glossary of terms, configuration questions and answers, and Net addresses for PPP.
URL ftp://ftp.merit.edu/internet.tools/ppp/documents/pppfaq-3.9

Veronica The Web has many good search engines. The gopher world has one—Veronica. This powerful tool searches most public gopher-server menu titles and file names.
URL gopher://futique.scs.unr.edu/ll/veronica • gopher://info.psi.net:2347/7 • gopher://veronica.utdallas.edu:2348/7
WEB http://www.einet.net/gopher/gopher.html

WAIS-Discussion A moderated discussion about electronic publishing and WAIS.
EMAIL listproc@wais.com ✍ *Type in*

message body: subscribe wais-discussion (your full name)

Web design

alt.hypertext Is HTML truly a hypertext language or something slightly different? What hypermedia seminars are coming soon to a convention center near you? Find out the answers to these questions in this well-trafficked newsgroup, then ask anything you want about drag-and-drop HTML for Windows.
USENET alt.hypertext alt.hypertext

The Art of HTML If you're looking for information on HTML, it's a good bet you'll find it here. A plethora of links—from beginners' essentials to HTML validation, tutorials, graphic resources, and Web designers—can be found at this address. In the tutorial section

alone, there are more than 20 different links.
WEB http://www.thecoo.edu/~menon /html.html

Beginners Guide to HTML This primer assumes that you have some knowledge of Web sites, servers, and browsers. For the most part, this is a step-by-step guide to producing files in HTML on the Web. It breaks down everything you'll need to know to create a file. And while it's just a general overview, it still has some detailed information. There are also links to other sites that will give you more information on HTML and related topics.
WEB http://www.ncsa.uiuc.edu /General/Internet/WWW /HTMLPrimer.html

Carlos's Forms Tutorial What began as a college project on computer-aided instruction is now a comprehensive tutorial available to all on the use of HTML "fill-in forms." Most of the lessons discuss the tags associated with forms while exploring passwords, menus, options, scrolled lists, button types, and how a server uses the information gathered from your forms. If you need to back up a few steps, Carlos even provides a review of the basics for HTML newbies.
WEB http://robot0.ge.uiuc.edu/ ~carlosp/cs317/ft.l.html

RAD Imaging RAD is dedicated to photography, digital imaging, and multimedia development. Robert A. Dean's (or

RAD's) online tutorial on Basic Digital Imaging covers image file types, sources for images, common formats, bitmap editors, and detailed instructions for creating .GIFs and JPEGs, transparent-background .GIFs, thumbnails, and reducing file sizes. Besides dozens of links to imaging resources and meta slide shows, there are several clickable image indexes (mostly animal or horticultural). Get the picture?
WEB http://www.auburn.edu/~deanrob

State of the Art Review on Hypermedia Issues and Applications All about hypertext and issues in hypertext programming, including implementation, interfaces, and information retrieval issues. Perhaps not

 # Newbie NET
WEB http://www.newbie.net

If you find that your first experience on the Internet is like "trying to eat noodle soup with chopsticks," if you got your ego singed by hotshot flamers, take a load off at this refuge that promises

to turn "newbies into knowbies," with info on **HTML** programming and more general technical tips. By the time you're done taking the cybercourse, you'll know a shell prompt from a price tag, and you'll be loop-de-looping from link to link with the best of them.

Location: http://www.auburn.edu/~deancar/show1/1.htm

A wildflower slideshow demonstrates the power of images at **RAD Imaging**
http://www.auburn.edu/~deanrob

surprisingly, the review itself is in hypertext.
WEB http://www.isg.sfu.ca/~duchier /misc/hypertext_review/index.html

Shockwave

Cool ShockeR Site Find out all that's new in Shockwave applications. This weekly updated page boasts a wide range of features, including a list of new ShockeR sites, instructions for downloading the Shockwave application, a ShockeR emailing list, and lists of sites that use the Shockwave application (you can add your site to the list, if applicable). There's also an immediate listing of Previous Cool ShockeR Web sites.
WEB http://www.shocker.com/shocker /cool.html

Java

Java World Check out the latest issue of *Java World*, IDG's periodical contribution to the Java community. To give you a taste, *Java World* lets you download full-text articles from the *Java World*'s Nuts & Bolts and News & Reviews sections (from both current and back issues). The resources section includes applet reviews, events calendars, DOS and Macintosh utilities, and related articles from *Java World*'s sister publication, *SunWorld* online. If you like what you see, subscriptions are a click away.
WEB http://www.javaworld.com

JavaSoft If you're into creating applets and applications with Java, you'll find a lot brewing at this Sun Microsystems page, such as FAQs, online documentation, upcoming training and educational events, and product information. There are also links to Java newsgroups and tech-support via email. Serious Java addicts will want to download the Developers' Kit or visit the Developer's

Corner for workshops, news, and updates.
WEB http://java.sun.com

Sound

alt.binaries.sounds.utilities Can't figure out how your sound player or MIDI sequencer works? Post a query in this newsgroup and wait for a cybersound authority to reply with an answer. This is a good place to find out about sound-related software upgrades, too.
USENET alt.binaries.sounds.utilities

Audio Virtual Library Links from here to sound repositories, newsgroups, software, and documented support for audiophiles and sound junkies. The software links will take you to sites on the Web where you can download sound utilities. Then visit the sound repository, which features links to places with sound clips for your new player.
WEB http://www.comlab.ox.ac.uk /archive/audio.html

The Music & Audio Connection A large collection of links to many of the audio sites on the Net. The Connection includes a mall with audio-related merchandise, links to dozens of audio newsgroups, and a group of MIDI files and software.
URL gopher://nor.com:7l
WEB http://nor.com/music

Real Audio Sometimes sounds can be so aggravating. They take hours to download, then you have to move them

through a sound player. Or at least you had to. Now, though, the waiting is over. With Real Audio, sounds play as they download—your computer merely creates a buffer file that it deletes after the entire sound is played. Download a Real Audio test version and link to pages with Real Audio Sounds, from NPR's *Morning Edition* to college radio.
WEB http://www.realaudio.com

Sound And Music/MultiMedia File Formats on the Internet A good resource for newbies who want to learn about the sound capabilities of their PC. Includes a list of recommended sound players and converters, with links to where they can be

downloaded on the Web. Recommended players and converters include Music Sculptor, MOD4Win, GoldWave, Scoptrax. WHAM and SOX10.
WEB http://ac.dal.ca/~dong/music.htm

Chat

IRC-Related Resources on the Internet Though it doesn't have the sexiest name, this Web site may feature the most comprehensive listing of IRC resources online. All the basics are here (FAQs, manuals, primers, history, etc.), and that's just the beginning. Essays on IRC sociology, articles on IRC events, links to home pages of many IRC channels, links to telnet IRC

clients, logs of big IRC happenings (the 1992 Russian revolution, the 1994 California earthquake, various online weddings, etc.), and links to other IRC Web pages and FTP sites are just some of the resources available at this site.
WEB http://urth.acsu.buffalo.edu/irc /WWW/ircdocs.html

The Undernet Directory IRC is known to be addictive, but if you're willing to risk being drawn into a world of chat channels that run 24 hours a day, then you need to get equipped. After you've secured an Internet connection that gives you IRC access, take a trip to this directory. Beginners can pick up the well-regarded

AFTERSHOCK
WEB http://www.ashock.com

If you want to see just what Shockwave can do for you, a visit to AfterShock is a must. The idea here is self-promotion; and why not? That's the whole point for AfterShock, a creative-design firm

focused on multimedia and the Internet that utilizes Shockwave to its true potential. The company designed this promo page, which contains links to several publications reviewing and praising AfterShock's admittedly stunning site. If you're not looking to get professional help to spice up your Web site, you may want to pass. But if you do, you'll be missing the fun arcade corner, which contains such games as Web Frog and Web Invaders.

IRC primer, an IRC history, and the IRC and Undernet FAQs. Netters with an Internet connection that lets them run client software (SLIP, PPP, ISDN, etc.), should download clients and manuals. Client programs (e.g., mIRC for Windows and Homer for the Mac) are available for several operating systems, including the Amiga, Mac, Windows, OS/2, and DOS. Running a client makes following and participating in IRC discussions much easier and usually more fun. This directory also stores images of IRC chatters, codes for IRC servers, documents on IRC netiquette, and more.
URL ftp://ftp.undernet.org/irc
WEB http://www2.undernet.org:8080/~cs93jtl/Undernet.html

WebChat A real-time chatting environment on the Web that allows users (providing that they have a Web browser that supports forms) to include .GIFs of themselves in their messages. Everyone in the Main Hallway chooses a room (e.g., the watercooler, the twilight zone, tech talk), and joins in the discussions. There's an option to see who's here, a picture and icon library to illustrate messages, and even mailing lists to keep up-to-date on the site's development.
WEB http://www.irsociety.com/webchat/webchat.html

List of USENET FAQs Links to versions of hundreds of Usenet FAQs, from the Olympics FAQ to the ZyXEL U 1496

Cool ShockeR parades the latest in Shockwave sites
http://www.shocker.com/shocker/cool.html

series modem resellers FAQ.
WEB http://www.cis.ohio-state.edu/hypertext/faq/usenet

news.announce.newusers There are two kinds of computer users: those who read the manuals and those who don't. The former should drop by this newsgroup where the updated versions of Usenet's "manuals" are kept. Postings include Hints on Writing Style for Usenet, the Anonymous FTP FAQ, and even FAQs about FAQs.
USENET news.announce.newusers
FAQ: **WEB** http://www.cis.ohio-state.edu/hypertext/faq/bngusenet/news/announce/newusers/top.html

news.answers The Chocolate FAQ, the alt.polyamory FAQ, the Fat Free Vegetarian Resource List, and the MPEG FAQ are just a few of the hundreds of posts in this newsgroup which serves as a

repository for FAQs.
USENET news.answers

news.groups.questions A newsgroup to help netters find the right newsgroup. "Is there a newsgroup for WordPerfect?" (bit.listserv.wpcorp-l) "Is there a newsgroup for new parents?" (alt.parenting*) "Who built Egyptian pyramids?" (soc.culture.egyptian, sci.archaeology, or alt.mythology).
USENET news.groups.questions
FAQ: **WEB** http://www.cis.ohio-state.edu/hypertext/faq/bngusenet/news/groups/questions/top.html

Information
All-in-One Search Page A Web page with more than 100 search tools. You can certainly search with the Lycos and Yahoo search engines from here, but you can also search a database of mailing lists, the largest software archives on the

Net, a weather database, CMP's technical articles, the full-text of Shakespeare's works, a movie database, White House documents, the Bible, and a thesaurus.

WEB http://www.albany.net/~wcross /alllsrch.html

Clearinghouse for Subject-Oriented Internet Resource Guides
Netters are incredibly generous with information—and their time. This collection of subject guides cataloging Internet resources testifies to that generosity. David Brown has created a guide to children's literature on the Web, Michele Pfaff and David Bachman have authored a guide to resources about individual rights, and Tricia Segal and Julie Lea have authored a guide to women's health issues. More than 100 of these guides with information on newsgroups, Websites, mailing lists, and FTP sites, are available here in hypertext or ASCII format.

WEB http://www.lib.umich.edu /chhome.html

The WWW Virtual Library It's the first Web directory, and still one of the largest, with comprehensive coverage of online resources about subjects ranging from chemistry to wireless computing. Unfortunately, the breakdown by subject areas is not hierarchical and there are a clutter of topics on the first page.

WEB http://www.w3.org/hypertext /DataSources/bySubject/Overview .html

Cybersociety

WELCOME TO THE MOST DEMOCRATIC, EGALITARIAN CLUB YET

Location: http://www.eff.org/pub/EFF/Graphics/crypt02.gif

 EFF
WEB http://www.eff.org

The "digital revolution" is transforming our lives, traditions, and institutions. We may need an entirely new way of thinking regarding law, medicine, advertising, even personal identity. That's precisely the ambitious mission of the Electronic Frontier Foundation—not only to catalog those new concepts but to exert some critical control over them. This forum functions as an **EFF** storefront.

Society

alt.politics.datahighway Sign an online petition to stop the Communications Decency Act, read the latest issue of *EFFector Online* (a newsletter published by the Electronic Freedom Foundation), or read someone's rant about the new Web site maintained by the Christian Coalition. Tap into the group for insight on how how the online masses feel about electronic legislation and its implications.
USENET alt.politics.datahighway

Blue Ribbon Campaign If you've been wondering where those Free Speech blue ribbons festooning the Web come from, this is the place. Sponsored by a cross-cultural coalition of old and new civil-libertarian groups, the campaign is clearly explained here as a protest movement against encroachments on cyberspeech. The idea is simple: "We insist that anything that's legal in bookstores, newspapers, or public libraries must be legal online." You can get your own blue ribbon here.
WEB http://www.eff.org/blueribbon.html

comp.org.eff.talk Whether censorship, child pornography, data security, or digital cash is the civil liberties debate of the moment in cyberspace, this electronic soapbox known as a newsgroup carries some of the best iconoclastic and passionately argued opinions. Writes

one anti-gun control advocate: "I'm a radical libertarian. I'm willing to accept the risks that go with widespread firearms possession just as I'm willing to accept the frightening risk of terrorists and pedophiles on the Net, as a small practical price to pay for adherence to a principle." Other hot topics of late include the transmission of child pornography over the infobahn. Should people be prosecuted? If so, should it be the system administrators? Should it be the Internet carrier? Cases are sometimes discussed in painful detail. Hosted by the Electronic Frontier Foundation.
USENET comp.org.eff.talk
URL listserv@eff.org ✍ *Type in message body:* subscribe comp-org-eff-talk (your full name)

comp.society.development Are computers contributing to or detracting from our social development? James T. votes for the former, and he can't wait for cable TV-access to the Internet because "Knowledge should be accessible to all." A different James posts a *New York Times* story about connecting Vietnam to the Internet—the government worries about opening up channels to dissident voices and pornography but also seeks the connection to the modern world. Announcements for conferences about computer technology and development are also posted to this low-traffic newsgroup.
USENET comp.society.development

comp.society.futures Futuristic predictions are the order of the day in this philosophical newsgroup that addresses technological advances and their implications on society. "I'm conducting research pertaining to society's battle with its modern 'conveniences'" announces Nick M. "Read *Islands In The Net* by Bruce Sterling or *Neuromancer* by William Gibson," replies a somewhat disgruntled Craig N. "Read them, look around you, and come up with some of your own answers." John S. was kind enough to post an article he found in *Cybernautics Digest* called "Kiss Your Branch Bank Goodbye," in which interactive banking takes the place of bank tellers. No more free lollipops!
USENET comp.society.futures

Computer Professionals for Social Responsibility Eschewing the belief that technology alone will improve our world, CPSR, an organization of computer scientists founded in 1981, goes after government organizations hellbent on tapping your telephone or raiding your computer's database. Take the case of the Clipper chip, an encryption device for the next generation of telephones, a device that makes it impossible for amateur techno-voyeurs to tap your phone, but opens a backdoor to secret service and military agencies to listen in. The CPSR Web site has an automated letter of protest against the Clipper chip that users can send to the White House. The heart of the site, however, is its archive of academically-oriented texts on computing responsibility in such areas as computer crime, the Freedom of Information Act, privacy and encryption, MUDs and MOOs, and more; it's a good clearinghouse for information on the sociology of the online world. CPSR also maintains a list of 20 plus mailing lists covering specific issues from security in the workplace to Bay Area CPSR member concerns. **EMAIL** listserv@cpsr.org ✍ *Type in message body:* subscribe cpsr-announce (your full name)

Cyberlaw/Cyberlex Each month important legal issues related to

computer technology—Microsoft's anti-trust case to the Scientology suit—are reported at these sites. In the form of either short news briefs (Cyberlex) or long features (Cyberlaw), the reports describe both the rulings and their implicatons. **AMERICA ONLINE** *keyword* cyberlaw **WEB** http://www.cyberlaw.com • http://www.portal.com/~cyberlaw/cylw_home.html

Electronic Privacy Information Center Operating kind of close to the frontier, where computer crime becomes art and art becomes crime, this self-described public-interest research center makes available information ranging from for-

merly classified government documents to updates on computer cryptography, wire tapping, and caller ID. The information is nicely organized and comes in a headline-and-summary form that makes it easy to assess how deep into all this you want to venture. **WEB** http://epic.org

Ethics and Law on the Electronic Frontier The online version of an MIT course, this is an excellent source for reading material, discussion archives and other materials related to the topic of cyberspeech and the law. The material includes references to *Neuromancer*, the cybernovel close to so many hackers' hearts, mass-media

 # THE PROGRESS & FREEDOM FOUNDATION
WEB http://www.pff.org
picture: WEB http://aspen.pff.org/cyber/guests/gilder.html
Clubby visionaries convene at this veritable think tank, founded in 1993 by Jeffrey A. Eisenach and George A. Keyworth. The foundation, loosely allied with Newt Gingrich and with a distinctly conservative slant, has quickly become one of the more innovative and creative idea fonts in the country on the future and impact on society of the Information Revolution. Armed with "the

Location: http://aspen.pff.org/cyber/guests/gilder.html

American idea that... progress is the belief that Mankind has advanced in the past, is presently advancing, and will continue to advance through the foreseeable future," the foundation brings together futurists, politicians, scientists and other players to guage the present so as to better forecast the future.

articles, and some more esoteric stuff. Think of the site as an opportunity to participate in distance-learning without paying the tuition.
WEB http://www-swiss.ai.mit.edu /6095/index.html

The Magna Carta for the Knowledge Age This tome, released by the Gingrich-related Progress & Freedom Foundation in August of 1994, was the work of four of the day's giant cyberpundits: Esther Dyson, George Gilder, George Keyworth, and Alvin Toffler. With Toffler's ideas on the three waves of civilization setting the tone, the four make the case for the Information Revolution already upon us, what it portends, and how societies and governments should respond. As national boundaries fall, dynamic relationships develop, and conflicts become rare, we are primed for an age when, "The powers of mind are everywhere ascendant over the brute force of things."
WEB http://www.pff.org/pff/position .html

The Netizens and the Wonderful World of the Net: An Anthology An online book about the history of Usenet and how it helped to create wholly new academic and scientific fields and disciplines, not to mention a clearinghouse for free information for netizens around the world. Anyone interested in the sociological implications of the Internet should check out

Chapter 7 ("The Impact the Net Has on People's Lives") and Chapter 10 ("The Computer as Democratizer").
WEB http://www.cs.columbia.edu /~hauben/netbook

Rights, Camera, Action Consider yourself warned: This is a long-winded essay. It's worth it if you can find the time. This piece should be of particular interest to anyone interested in the implications of wired interconnectivity on social structures, in particular the underlying legal issues with regard to the Web. It's an excellent rumination by U. Mass. Amherst Professor Ethan Katsh, which was first published in the *Yale Law Journal* in May, 1995.
WEB http://www-unix.oit.umass.edu /~eleclaw/ylj.html#FN8REF

World Future Society—Boston Chapter It makes sense that Boston has an aura of intellectual ferment given the number of excellent universities and related think tanks in the city. Then again with the Web, where you are doesn't matter so

> **"Are you unable to place the face or attach any kind of identity to the name William Gibson?"**

much. Keeping both in mind, come here to find an excellent list of links to institutions, individuals, and publications trying to anticipate what will be. (Note: The domain name is a little worrying).
WEB http://www.lucifer.com/~sasha /refs/wfsgbc.html

Cybergurus

Panelists at the Aspen Summit '95 A great resource. This one's a list of experts that the Progress & Freedom Foundation was able to gather for the 1995 Aspen conference. Among them you'll find bios of many of cyberspace's great visionaries, including John Perry Barlow, Esther Dyson, Kevin Kelly, and Jeffrey Eisenach.
WEB http://aspen.pff.org/cyber/guests /guests.html

William Gibson Homepage Are you unable to place the face or attach any kind of identity to the name William Gibson? Are people dropping his name into conversation wherever you go? Are you beginning to feel like a social outcast, or that you've really missed out on something? Help is at hand in the form of the William Gibson Homepage, a primer on the putative godfather, if not father, of cyberpunk. Thumbnail sketches of the man and his work will help you to bluff your way through your next encounter with a *Sprawl Trilogy* fanatic, and might even entice you into

reading the books for yourself.
WEB http://www2.cibola.net/~michaela/gibson

George Gilder George Gilder is yet another guru whose status was confirmed when *Wired* placed him on the cover of their March 1996 issue. While his politics run to the right, his predictions for the future are anything but conservative. He's advised and addressed many a media mogul, futurist, and president—of both countries and companies. This *HotWired* site is a good place to start if you want to get giddy about Gilder, with links to other features on the man.
WEB http://www.hotwired.com/wired/4.03/gilder/index.html

Marshall McLuhan In the beginning there was the word. Then there was Gutenberg. And then there was Marshall McLuhan. McLuhan's writings on the power and future of language, such as *The Medium is the Massage* and *Understanding Media* have served as the springboard for much of today's thinking about media and the information age. If Nicholas Negroponte is the apostle of *Wired* magazine, then Marshall McLuhan is its patron saint. McLuhan's long career and prodigious writing sprung from the University of Toronto and it's here where his legacy lives on in the form of The McLuhan Program in Culture and Technology, an entire program devoted to examining both old and new media in the context of McLuhan's work.
WEB http://www.mcluhan.toronto.edu

Nicholas Negroponte Home Page This is a concise introduction to Negroponte, relating his early years as an MIT graduate student and professor to his later experiences founding the Media Laboratory, serving as the senior columnist of *Wired*, and his writing of *Being Digital*. It has two links of interest: the first to every column he's ever written for *Wired*; the second features a series of pictures of the maestro with his own best friend and so-called collaborator, his droopy-eyed dog.

THE MCLUHAN PROBES

WEB http://www.mcluhan.ca/mcluhan
picture: WEB http://www.voyagerco.com/catalog/mcluhan/indepth/live.html
McLuhan's influence on modern media is well-documented. Institutions such as the center at the

University of Toronto and The Herbert Marshall Foundation are doing their best to ensure his continued relevance. The Foundation, thanks to his wife Corinne McLuhan, holds the electronic rights of all her husband's work and hopes to raise enough money to make it electronically accessible to all. The Probes themselves are a series of beautifully designed scrims upon which McLuhan's writings have been posted.

Great minds look alike. You'll also find his email address inside.
WEB http://nicholas.www.media.mit.edu/people/nicholas

Wired Interview-Being Nicholas A man of considerable ego, talent, and arduous but seminal prose, Negroponte is one of cyberspace's most prominent thinkers and doers—he spearheaded the MIT Media Lab and was an early contributor to *Wired* magazine's pockets. In this authoritative and wide ranging piece from the magazine, Thomas A. Bass finds out what makes Negroponte tick.
WEB http://vip.hotwired.com/wired/3.II/features/nicholas.html

❝ Negroponte is a man of considerable ego, talent, and arduous but seminal prose. ❞

Paul Saffo Lucky is the man who gets to spend all his time examining the future. Saffo has been at it for more than 25 years at The Institute for the Future, a consulting firm he founded. On the subject of the Web, his favorite tagline is "Context over Content." We'll leave it to you to figure it all out—it's outlined in this

Location: http://www.microtimes.com/toffler.html

"We are living through the birth pangs of a new civilization whose institutions are not yet in place. A fundamental skill needed by policy makers, politicians, and politically active citizens today--if they really want to know what they are doing--is the ability to distinguish between proposals designed to keep the tottering Second Wave system on life-support from those that spread and smooth our transition to the Third Wave civilization."

--Alvin and Heidi Toffler, *Creating a New Civilization*

Surfing the Third Wave
http://www.microtimes.com/toffler.html

HotWired feature, as is Saffo's forecast for the Web and what it augurs. Take the "context" link to get a clearer definition of Saffo's emphasis on context over all else.
WEB http://www.hotwired.com/club/special/transcripts/10-16-04.saffo.html

Alvin Toffler in Microtimes Not the first, nor the last, but certainly the big daddy of all futurists, Alvin Toffler became a household name in the early nineties when Newt Gingrich deemed his *The Third Wave*, co-written with his wife Heidi, an important and prophetic book. The Tofflers have an uncanny ability to get it right and have presaged many of today's social trends in such books as *Future Shock*, *Power Shift*, and *War and Anti-War*. *The Third Wave*, written in 1980, has particular relevance: It addressed the advent of a third wave of social change—

the move to a post-industrial, high-tech, information-based economy. It's hardly visionary today, but 15 years ago the suggestion of a non-industrial America was considered mildly blasphemous. Toffler also explains his association with Newt Gingrich and the Progress & Freedom Foundation. This interview is an excellent introduction to the ideas of the two Tofflers, of whom the male counterpart gets more of the credit on the Web.
WEB http://www.microtimes.com/toffler.html

Alvin Toffler: Still Shocking After All These Years This interview, published in *The New Scientist* in March 1994, is yet another good introduction to Alvin Toffler from the man himself. He weighs in on the relevant implications of chaos theory, and the future of international conflict.
WEB http://httpl.brunel.ac.uk:8080/~ph92szh/toffler.html

PART 7
Education & Culture

Education & Culture

CLICK PICKS
The very best on the Net

Physical Sciences

FRUSTRATED BY YOUR INERTIA? GET TO KNOW THE LAWS THAT GOVERN YOUR EXISTENCE

So you're convinced that science has nothing to do with magic? Tell that to Albert Hoffman, the great Swiss chemist who synthesized LSD. Like many a scientific revelation, it happened by accident, but the microscopic molecule went on to challenge traditional notions of human consciousness, thereby contributing to a social and cultural revolution that gave the world acid house music and Pucci ties. The physical sciences have long been the bastion of experiment, enlightenment, and progress, while at the same time unleashing some of the most destructive forces on earth. These links are your keys to exploring the netherworlds and abstract realms, where beings made of massless light-cone particles dwell beyond the space-time continuum—just watch your step, keep your synapses intact, and don't stumble into any black holes along the way.

DISCOVERY CHANNEL ONLINE
WEB http://www.discovery.com

If you're curious about your world, there's no better place to start than the Discovery Channel Online. Special features, daily articles, bulletin boards, fact sheets and more make this the site around which all others revolve. Discovery devotes a day to each of seven sections: Nature-Tuesday, Science-Wednesday, etc. A late summer special feature provided daily updates from a new expedition to the wreckage of the Titanic. Another allowed visitors to query scientists involved with Galileo's mission to Jupiter. Also available—information on Discovery CD-ROMS, videos, and collectibles, a place to register for Discovery Channel School, and a Discovery search engine.

Starting points

Franklin Institute Virtual Science Museum The science museum that never closes and doesn't charge admission. View such virtual exhibits as "The Heart: An Online Exploration", "An Inquirer's Guide to the Universe", and "Benjamin Franklin: Glimpses of the Man". The institute also spotlights stories each month like "Web Gardens" (some beautification projects on the information superhighway), "Science Fairs: Love Them or Hate Them" (start-to-finish help with your experimental endeavors), and "The North Pole" (what it's really like to be on top of the world).
WEB http://sln.fi.edu

General Science Plants and magnetism, metric measurements, how water is made, and misused science terms. Just a few of the popular topics of discussion at this basic science forum. Put your two cents in at the Messages section or browse the Libraries to find a primer on virtual reality or downloadable files to test your brain power.
COMPUSERVE go science→general science→messages and libraries

InQuiry Almanack What's new at the Franklin Institute? InQuiring minds want to know. The Almanack not only offers the scoop on the Institute's latest offerings but also includes a monthly Spotlight story; Fistful of Favorites, FI's five featured

links; Caught in the Web, the online school of the month; and Science News.
WEB http://sln.fi.edu/qanda/qandall .html

MendelWeb Mendel meets hypermedia. This site, modeled around Gregor Mendel's 1865 paper, "Experiments in Plant Hybridization," integrates elementary biology, discrete mathematics, and the history of science. An English translation of Mendel's paper, which is considered to mark the birth of classical and evolutionary genetics, is presented in hypertext, with links to traditional reference material (glossaries, biographies, and the original German text) as well as images, tutorials, active commentaries, notes, homework sets, related Web sites, and animation. Cyberstudents will learn about more than genetics and nineteenth-century botany though— Mendel's paper presents a context for learning more about techniques of data analysis, the rhetorical strategies of scientific literature, and a variety of topics in the history and philosophy of science.
WEB http://www-hpcc.astro .washington.edu/mirrors/MendelWeb

National Academy of Sciences Offers a range of information on scientific topics from agriculture to space. The biology section, for example, has articles such as "Biologic Markers Show Pollution Effects on the Immune System." The earth

sciences folder informs the visitor on subjects like "Radioactive Waste Issues." The site also houses the NAS archives, a bookstore, a lecture hall, and a chat forum. A search engine simplifies research.
AMERICA ONLINE keyword nas

ScienceWeb Find out what our neighbors to the north are accomplishing in science. Science Web presents the spectrum of science and technology activities going on in Canada, in an attempt to expose its thriving science culture to the rest of the world. There's plenty in it for you— links to the coolest Canadian science sites, cybertours, the latest news, and scholastic resources.
WEB http://scienceweb.dao.nrc.ca /can/can.html

Biology

The ABCs of DNA The University of California at San Francisco knows how difficult science can be, which is why they've developed a series of Web sites under the rubric of "Science Made Easy." This reader-friendly page on DNA is simple enough even for those who plan to major in English in college.
WEB http://www.ucsf.edu/research /science_made/abc_dna.html

The Amazing Body Pavilion This virtual tour of Houston's Museum of Health & Medical Science walks visitors through the human body. The page

only features photographic simulation of real museum visitors enjoying such attractions as the 27-foot intestine, the 10-foot brain, and the skeleton riding a bicycle, but those with active imaginations may glean some form of vicarious pleasure.
WEB http://www.mhms.org/amazing.html

Anatomy Pick a body part, any body part, and connect to close-up images of the part in anatomical splendor. You have a choice of six highlighted areas to select on the human figure, which is not anatomically correct. Each highlighted area leads to more choices. Click on the brain, for exam-

ple, and find juicy pictorials of the left, right, anterior, superior, and inferior regions. Then you'll understand the term "grey matter."
WEB http://rpisunl.mda.uth.tmc.edu/se/anatomy

CTC Math/SciGateway: Biology
Cornell Theory Center has collected a trim set of links to basic bio resources. Click onto Cells Alive! and watch phagocytosis in action by a human macrophage cell or take a photographic Greenhouse Tour of the University of Georgia's Botany Department and discover the relationships among some major land plant groups. For the frog lover, there's the Interactive Frog Dissection

which includes an actual lab manual and step-by-step photos of the frog. If insects are your thing, there's a collection of images and movies on beetles, mosquitos and ticks. For an excellent explanation of how the brain deduces what we should see, click on Blind Spots: The Eye and the Brain.
WEB http://www.tc.cornell.edu/Edu/MathSciGateway/biology.html

Evolution: Theory and History
Everything you would ever want to know about evolution and then some. Learn about the theory behind systematics (study of the evolutionary interrelationships between living things) and taxonomy (scientific naming system). Click

DR. BOB'S INTERESTING SCIENCE STUFF
WEB http://ny.frontiercomm.net/~bjenkin/science.htm
Weird Science. Did you know that in the distant future the sun that lights our solar system will die a violent death? Were you aware that the ears of a cricket are located on its front legs, just below the knee? Or that the most powerful laser in the world, the Nova laser, generates a pulse of energy equal to 100,000,000,000,000 watts of power for .000000001 second to a target the size of a

grain of sand? You would if you made regular appointments to see Dr. Bob. The only thing that ties together the tidbits of scientific trivia found here is the fact that Dr. Bob, a chemist by trade, finds them fascinating. But random as they are, they're guaranteed to get the scientific side of your brain whirring.

onto the history of vertebrate flight and learn how evolution has perfected the act of flying. The Web Lift will transport you to any Taxon, Period, Topic, or just the glossary.

Links to notable naturalists and scientists are also provided.
WEB http://ucmpl.berkeley.edu /exhibittext/evolution.html

HUMEVO You might not feel it personally, but humans are constantly evolving. This mailing list on human evolutionary research examines the details, including adaptation, variation, and evolutionary medicine.
EMAIL listserv@gwuvm.gwu.edu ✍
Type in message body: subscribe HUMEVO (your full name)

Insects & Human Society An engaging virtual lecture on how insects have changed major battles, altered governments, and generally proved influenial in shaping human history.
WEB http://www.ento.vt.edu/IHS

Microscopy UK Netsurfers who've got a pair of blue-and-red 3-D glasses handy can check out pictures of fossils, insects, and even the tip of a syringe as they appear to jump off the screen at this site, which calls itself the "home of amateur microscopy on the Web." This truly comprehensive and innovative site has microscopic resources for everyone from the mildly curious student to the professional microscopist. Students can go "scoping" and examine the teeth of a snail, or take advantage of more onsite features, like the SEM (scanning electron microscopy) pictures of mildew, leaves, and other perennial favorites. Swimming

in a pond will never be the same after seeing what lives there.
WEB http://www.microscopy-uk.org.uk

The Origin of Species by Charles Darwin It's Pat Buchanan's favorite site. The classic of evolutionary theory in its entirety online.
WEB http://www.wonderland.org /Works/Charles-Darwin/origin

Chemistry

Center for Polymer Studies What does lightning have in common with shattering plastic? Lichtenberg patterns. Watch movies of this and other fingering-and-branching patterns in the Dance of Chance Exhibit Hall at this Web site put together by Boston University and the Boston Museum of Science. Is composed music based on the rhythm of the heartbeat? Download MIDI files by Zack Goldberger and find out. More advanced budding scientists can see simulations of molecular networking, including Wasser and Lehnhard-Jones models.
WEB http://cps-www.bu.edu

Internet Chemistry Resources Does wondering what a molecule of aspirin looks like give you a headache? Does your idea of a fun experiment involve an exploding can of methane (kaboom!) or a nuclear reactor (bigger kaboom!)? Curious lay chemists will find links to online chemistry courses (including all the AP chemistry

exams from 1970 to 1995) and a section on images that links to many 3-D models, such as one illustrating the origami of folding proteins. If your lungs hurt just thinking about the effect of the chemical industry on the ozone layer, vent your frustrations by linking up to the corporate Web pages like those of Shell, Ciba, Dow, and Mobil.
WEB http://rampages.onramp.net /~jaldr/item03.html

sci.chem A newsgroup for those who "truly love science" in general, and chemistry in particular. Hot topics have included the chemical composition of diesel, compressed polystyrene, and whether a hotter or colder ping-pong ball will bounce higher.
USENET sci.chem

Understanding our Planet Through Chemistry How old is the earth? Is a Jurassic Park really possible? What caused dinosaurs to become extinct? This Web site offers a collection of documents organized into a "book," which explains how chemical analysis can tell us many things about our world. Interested folks can take a look at the current research on amber (tree sap) and fossils, learn how to predict volcanic eruptions, and read about the destuctive effects of acid rain. The information ranges from the contemporary (see how robots perform many of the repetitive tasks of the analytical chemist) to the historical (did you know that in the early 1900s, horse-drawn carriages were used to determine ele-

ments in the field?). Perhaps this was the original meaning of the term "mobile laboratory."
WEB http://helios.cr.usgs.gov/gips /aii-home.htm

The World of Materials What exactly are semiconductors? Are the ceramic tiles on a space shuttle the same as the ones in your bathroom? What about ceramic superconductors? In simple jargon, this site defines four classes of materials—metals, ceramics, semiconductors, and polymers. Three-dimensional molecular diagrams illustrate how the variable stiffness of polyester makes it suitable for everything from fabric to two-liter Coke bottles. Examine the chemical structure of pantyhose (nylon) and see how it compares to the

The Visible Human Project
WEB http://www.nlm.nih.gov/research/visible/visible_human.html

Get to know your body, if you haven't already. The Visible Human Project creates 3-D digital models of a human male and female from radiographic and photographic images. The models can then be rotated a full 360 degrees and viewed on any plane, making them powerful tools for scientific,

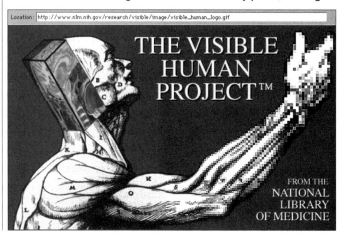

educational, or simply recreational purposes. The project is intended for medical professionals, but is so fascinating that anyone with the bandwidth and the necessary multimedia packages can't help but find the work both engaging and beautiful.

Kevlar (aromatic nylon) found in tires and bullet-proof glass. After learning about Teflon, frying an egg will never be the same.
WEB http://tantalum.mit.edu/struc_mater/material_structures.html

Earth science

Earth Pages Who's better qualified to help you out with navigation than NASA? NASA's Earth Pages contain a search tool that allows users to delve into their database of Earth Science WWW sites using keywords, returning a list of matching URLs with a short description of each site.
WEB http://epserver.gsfc.nasa.gov/earth/earth.html

Earth Sciences The WWW Virtual Library houses hundreds of links to earth science organizations around the globe, currents events, resources, software, and reference materials.
WEB http://www.geo.ucalgary.ca/VL-EarthSciences.html

Ecology Channel Only here would a fabled frog make the front page. One of the lead stories on the Ecology Channel's Greenwire Eco Update was news that the California red-legged frog was listed as threatened under the Endangered Species Act. The Ecology Channel not only keeps on top of the latest environmental news, but also offers such features as Eco Travel and Eco Business.
WEB http://www.ecology.com

EnviroLink Every aspect of EnviroLink hints at man's innate connection to the earth, right down to the icons—they're actually ancient artwork from indigenous cultures worldwide. Get in touch with your own dependence on the planet by visiting the EnviroLink Library, reading EnviroNews, shopping at the Internet Green Marketplace, taking in some EnviroArts, or talking with other tree huggers in the online forum. Envirolink also rates other ecosites and online events in What Soars, What Snores (And What Bites).
WEB http://www.envirolink.org

Energy

Department of Energy This branch of the U.S. government informs the public about coal, nuclear, solar, electric, petroleum, natural gas, and other types of fuel. Those afraid of the day when gas runs out can refer to the section on fuel efficiency, which explains the short- and long-term effects of depleting the earth's resources. For people who want the bottom line on what effect energy depletion will have on the economy, a page has been devoted to the topic. Informed citizens can help the community by participating in one of the outreach programs outlined.
WEB http://www.eia.doe.gov/energy

Hydro Power Find out more about the nature of Hoover Dam by visiting this site, which provides basic explana-

tions of alternative ways of obtaining power from nature. Small and large hydroelectric systems are explained as well as geothermal, wind, and solar. Plenty of pictures illustrate the no-nonsense overview of each alternative form of energy, including its applications, theory, case studies, and even economics.
WEB http://solstice.crest.org/renewables/re-kiosk/hydro/index.shtml

Mr. Solar Home Page Mr. Solar and his wife have been working for 18 years on letting the sun shine in. Ways to obtain environmentally friendly equipment for the solar age are avilable at their trilingual (English, Spanish and French) Web site. Browse the library of articles about progressive forms of energy, culled from the "Ask Mr. Solar" columns. Connect to other "enlightened sites" all over the globe and learn the specifics of configuring a home solar system.
WEB http://www.netins.net/showcase/solarcatalog

Nuclear Energy If you've discovered uranium in the backyard and are wondering what to do with it, visit the Nuclear Energy Web site. Learn facts about nuclear fusion. Study the advantages of nuclear energy (no air pollution, it's abundant in all countries). Find out about the magnetic fields in a tokamak (the plasma confiner) and other recent research in the field. The China Syndrome was once just a possibility, but can be a reality.

WEB http://www.pppl.gov/oview/pages /fusion_energy.html

Geology

A Decade of Notable California Earthquakes "I'm going back to Cali" raps LL Cool J, but he may change his mind after reading about the foreshocks, mainshocks, and aftershocks that have occurred in the Golden State in the last ten years. This page also includes a map of probable future earthquakes in Southern California through the year 2004.

WEB http://www.westworld.com /~shorose/califneq.html

Ask A Geology Question Get a geology answer. What killed the dinosaurs? Why do beaches change from year to year? What can scratch a diamond? Scientists, engineers, and support staff who study the geology of eastern Canada are standing by to satisfy your earth science curiosity.

WEB http://agcwww.bio.ns.ca/schools /classrm.html

National Earthquake Information Center What important establishment is located in Golden, Colo.? Not the Coors Brewing Company, the National Earthquake Information Center— the national data center and archive for all seismic information. Cyberseismologists can access current worldwide seismic maps, earthquake facts and statistics, explanations of plate

tectonics and the Richter Magnitude Scale, and a glossary of quake terminology.

WEB http://gldss7.cr.usgs.gov

Rockhounds Information Page Members of the rockhounds mailing list have set up shop on the Web with links to images and pictures, rock shops and galleries, books and magazines, software and mailing list archives, general earth science info, paleontology pages, collecting sites and trips, and geology clubs and societies. Something for everyone, from the amateur rock collector to the professional geologist.

WEB http://www.rahul.net/infodyn /rockhounds/rockhounds.html

Smithsonian Gem & Mineral Collection For the hard-core geologist, a trip to see the precious stones here is better than breakfast at Tiffany's. Some of the more remarkable rocks include a 98.6 carat Bismark Sapphire, one of the world's largest; an uncut corundum crystal, second only to diamond in hardness; and a spectacular and rare "Canary" diamond.

WEB http://galaxy.einet.net/images /gems/gems-icons.html

Volcano World So you want to be a volcanologist. Be warned, it involves more than living in Hawaii. Volcano World describes the details of this consequential career choice. The site is expansive and explosive, containing data on

volcanoes in the form of news, facts, volcanic parks and monuments, contests, links, and the ask-a-volcanologist pages.

WEB http://volcano.und.nodak.edu

Meteorology

Explores! Basic Skills and Activities Although Aristotle didn't coin the word "meteorology" until 340 B.C., the first meteorologists were probably prehistoric farmers and hunters, who were dependent upon atmospheric conditions for their existence. Although they couldn't adequately explain many atmospheric phenomena (a problem even the best weather forecasters have today), a collection of weather "signs" were accumulated and handed down from generation to generation. This Florida State site explores the history of weather science and provides activities that assist in understanding atmospheric composition, the hydrologic cycle, thermometers, and that dynamic duo—latitude and longitude.

WEB http://thunder.met.fsu.edu /explores/skillmenu.html

Oceanography

Aquatic Network A virtual clearinghouse of underwater wisdom, covering all the subjects of the sea—aquaculture, conservation, fisheries, marine science, oceanography, maritime heritage, ocean engineering, and seafood. The Aquatic Network covers news and events, contains information on related publications, and houses the AquaStore.

WEB http://www.aquanet.com/aquanet

Marine Biology Database Did you know that flatworms are the most primitive animals to have bilateral symmetry? Useful facts such as this are at your fingertips at this excellent cybersource of information on the major marine animal classes. Find out about the flatworm's other invertebrate friends, as well as arthropods, birds, echinoderms, fishes, mammals, mollusks, plants, and reptiles.

WEB http://www.calpoly.edu:8010 /cgi-bin/db/db/marine-biology/: /templates/index

Ocean Planet More than 99 percent of living space on earth is ocean, all habitable by plants and animals. This traveling Smithsonian exhibition plumbs the workings of our watery planet. The culmination of a four-year effort to study and understand environmental issues affecting the health of the world's oceans, the exhibit will be touring from 1996-1999, but is available for private viewing in cyberspace.

WEB http://seawifs.gsfc.nasa.gov /ocean_planet.html

Paleontology

Amber, A View of The Past How can you ensure that you'll be around for the next 40 million years? Get stuck in tree sap. That's what happened to the insects featured at A View of

the Past. Interesting articles are also posted on other amber-encased fossils, like mammalian bones and a 94 million-year-old mushroom.

WEB http://kadets.d20.co.edu /~lundberg/amber.html

❝ How can you ensure that you'll be around for the next 40 million years? Get stuck in tree sap. ❞

Paleontology Without Walls Most people think paleontology is strictly the study of fossils. In fact, it incorporates many kinds of data from diverse fields. This University of California Museum enlightens about paleontology's facets beyond fossils with three online exhibits: a family tree connecting all organisms that ever lived, explanations of evolutionary topics and scientists from Darwin to da Vinci in their historical context, and "Geology and Geologic Time." A multi-volume, multimedia virtual glossary is available to help you with any new words.

WEB http://www.ucmp.berkeley.edu /exhibit/exhibits.html

Stewart Wright's Paleo Page Stewart Wright's cool site features dinosaur art, pictures

from the Royal Tyrrell Museum's Field Experience Program, and links to a different paleontology page each month.

WEB http://www.GEB.com/net/sw.html

World's First Dinosaur Skeleton A complete history of *Hadrosaurus foulkii*, the world's first nearly complete dinosaur skeleton found in 1858 in Haddonfield, N.J., by Victorian gentleman and fossil hobbyist William Parker Foulke. Learn how he found the site while attending a dinner party at the house of his friend, John E. Hopkins. A map of Haddonfield let's you see where the actual site was located.

WEB http://www.levins.com /hadrosaurus.html

Physics

Contemporary Physics Education Project Those looking for a solution to an infinite source of energy such as fusion should visit this site. Download deluxe full-color charts and software. Ever wonder what makes the universe stay together or how atoms were discovered? This site has the answer. Learn how to win the Nobel Prize at the small particle section which details the discovery of the neutrino and the lepton. Build a nuclear warhead in the basement (or at least get a better idea of how to do this) by checking out the section on fundamental paricles.

WEB http://www-pdg.lbl.gov/cpep.html

sci.physics In the world of sci.physics, the question "Does light have mass?" exists side by side with "Does tapping Coke can keep fizz from exploding?" But as was the case in high school, when you first studied physics, this newsgroup's participants self-segregate into cliques. The "brains" confine themselves to such topics as hypersurfaces, infinite subdivisibility, and wave-particle duality, while the more recreational-minded are more interested in how to use practical physics to subvert police radar or cool their bedrooms.
USENET sci.physics

The Speed of Light: A Limit on Principle Find out if the speed of light can be exceeded and if so, what would happen if you turned on the headlights? Are *12 Monkeys* and *The Terminator* scenarios actually possible or is there too much conflict with simultaneity? Use clocks and mirrors to shed some light on the problem. Physicist Laro Schatzer provides diagrams and arguments covering all these questions and more in one "easy treatise." It will make the old Minkowskian versus Galilean space-time controversy seem as challenging as the "tastes great, less filling" debate.
WEB http://monet.physik.unibas.ch /~schatzer/space-time.html

Theory of Relativity In four short weeks, any student with a grasp of ordinary algebra can learn Einstein's Theory of Relativity, which revolutionized physics about a century ago. Topics covered include inertial reference frames, four-dimensional space-time, length contraction, time dilation, accelerating frames, general relativity, and gravitation through the Equivalence Principle. Sound incomprehensible? According to the course description, the relativity theory is quite straightforward; then again it's all relative.
AMERICA ONLINE *keyword* courses→ Science & Nature→Theory of Relativity

Zoology

African Primates at Home Seven different African primates are featured in their natural habitats at this Web page. Sound files let you listen to the scream

EcoNet Endangered Species Resources
WEB http://www.econet.apc.org/endangered
picture WEB http://blues.helsinki.fi:80/whale/rock.html
Saving wild salmon is just one of the Econet causes at this Web site. Find out why dams and wild salmon don't mix and then get involved by contacting endangered species organizations and emailing to key politicos. The Datalink contains documents such as the U.S. Endangered Species Act or the Kempthorne ESA Bill of 1995. Links to more conservation resources make this a great starting point for conscientious citizens.

Location: http://www.physics.helsinki.fi/whale/images/whabab.gif

Location: http://164.116.102.2/mms/homepage/amphibiar

Gee I really like this game
http://164.116.102.2/mms/homepage/amphibians.html

of the *Pan troglodytes schwein-furthii*, otherwise known as the common chimpanzee, and learn about its habitat, its eating patterns, and how it moves. Links to more East African information and other zoological sites are provided.
WEB http://www.indiana.edu/~primatez/primates.html

❝ Listen to the scream of the *Pan Troglodytes Schweinfurthii.* ❞

Endangered Species Want to know what's endangered in your part of the country? The regional map at this Web site shows which species are threatened and endangered in each state and lists fact sheets for some of those species. The page also links to international conservation sites and WWF's Ten Most Endangered Species of 1994.
WEB http://www.nceet.snre.umich.edu/EndSpp/Endangered.html

Cyber Zoomobile Learn about distribution, individual characteristics, life cycles, reproduction and sex, endangered species status, and many other interesting aspects of the animal kingdom. The section on Unusual Alliances explains how leopards and tigers can dwell within the same habitat though it's not big enough for both of 'em. The worldwide links include search engines, zoos and wildlife parks, animal related educational materials, and federal and state agencies.
WEB http://www.primenet.com/~brendel/index.html

Rainforest Amphibians The frog is the star of the show. Link to The Froggy Page for even more information on the most common amphibian in the world. Frog photos are accompanied by specific information on the marine toad, the leaf toad, and the poison arrow frog.
WEB http://164.116.102.2/mms/homepage/amphibians.html

Twenty of the Most Endangered Animals The numbat, the golden bamboo lemur, the woolly spider monkey. Not the "Top Twenty" most threatened animals in the world, but the ones "which are of popular interest," as chosen by the World Conservation Monitoring Centre. Judging criteria probably had a lot to do with their cute-sounding names. Those who don't think animal conservation is a popularity contest can link to the 1994 IUCN Red List of Threatened Animals which lists all 6,000 threatened species, of which 1,184 are endangered.
WEB http://www.wcmc.org.uk/infoserv/species/sp_top20.html

Zooary Get to know your animals! An online zoo aimed at educating people in the area of zoology. Choose from five animal categories: Amphibians, Arthropods, Birds & Mammals, Reptiles, and Miscellaneous. Click on Birds & Mammals, for example, and find a color image of a guinea pig. Read about its habitat, breeding habits, and gestation period. In the Career Corner, find out what an apiculturalist or a herpetologist does all day.
WEB http://www.poly.edu/~duane/zoo/mission.html

Social Sciences

ONLINE MAPS OF BOTH THE PHYSICAL WORLD AND THE MENTAL ONE

PEOPLE WHO ARE INTERESTED in social sciences are actually an anti-social bunch, right? They spend all day and night hunched over dusty books, shuffling papers, right? Nope. On the Net, at least, they're a vocal, even contentious lot. Their discussions, debates, and diatribes are carried out in newsgroups and mailing lists, each more specific than the last to a genre, historic period, or finer point of economic theory. And as befits bookworms, they're thorough: Salaried social scientists and weighty institutions, closet historians and weekend dabblers, museums and schools all contribute thousands of informative posts a day, enough to coax any amateur philosopher or historian into the quagmire of academic pursuit. If Lord Carnarvon, Margaret Mead, and Immanuel Kant could venture out into the world and do it for real, certainly you can use the Net to do your own social spelunking.

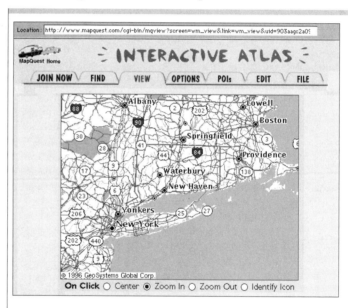

MAPQUEST

WEB http://www.mapquest.com

Whether you're planning a road trip, hunting for the perfect map to illustrate your project report, or merely trying to figure out on what street that girl or guy you met last night lives, you will never want to leave this entertaining site. It features an interactive atlas: Just type in your street address and watch your neighborhood pop up in full color. Then, back up to see the region, the state, or the world, with your house marked for posterity. Also try TripQuest, which will provide driving instructions from place to place. Are we there yet?

Anthropology

ANTHAP—The Applied Anthropology Computer Network According to this site, anthropologists are actually everywhere, applying what they know about human social interaction to advertising, corporate management, forensic science, and more. Could it be that one of the social sciences has—gasp!—a practical application? Find out all about it here.
WEB http://www.acs.oakland.edu/~dow/anthap.html

Anthropology and Culture Rice University's merged gopher collection of anthropology and archeology sites on just about any subtopic.
URL gopher://riceinfo.rice.edu/11/Subject/Anth

Archeological Fieldwork Server Anyone with an overwhelming urge to spend a summer digging in the dirt with a toothbrush should check out this directory to fieldwork opportunities around the world. Who knows? A dig may be taking place right in your own backyard.
WEB http://durendal.cit.cornell.edu

Classics of Out(land)ish Anthropology This unusual site applies anthropological principles to modern advertising and journalism by nit-picking at inaccurate borrowings from the field of anthropology and pointing visitors to where they can find resources on the real thing. Nothing is safe, from

Indiana Jones to the Nissan Pathfinder ads.
WEB http://www.lawrence.edu/dept/anthropology/classics.html

Perseus Project Want to see the Sanctuary of Apollo at Delphi or learn all the Greek words that end in -sis (Now there's a project for a really rainy day.)? You're in luck. This thorough multimedia library of information about archaic and classical Greece will help you get Hellenic in a hurry.
WEB http://www.perseus.tufts.edu

Society for American Archeology The best part about this pretty site is the very clear introductory information about the science of archeology, which is a whole lot more than just digging. Also check out the section on Participating in Archeology for tips on how to get

your hands dirty.
WEB http://www.saa.org

Stone Pages Millions of otherwise normal people are fascinated by stone circles, standing stones, and other ancient manifestations of the human need to organize (Tetris is a modern one). This site, which is not just for wide-eyed moon worshippers, contains links to archeological sites in England, Ireland, and Scotland.
WEB http://joshua.micronet.it/utenti/dmeozzi/homeng.html

Summer Institute of Linguistics "To study language is to study humanity," say the people at the Summer Institute of Linguistics in Texas. The study of living and dead cultures implies living and dead languages, too, and that's what the SIL site is all about. Download the Eth-

Stonehenge-by-the-Sea
http://joshua.micronet.it/utenti/dmeozzi/homeng.html

Location: http://joshua.micronet.it/utenti/dmeozzi/Scotland/Inglese/StonesofStennessHl.html

nologue of Languages of the World, or check out the multitude of links to sites on linguistics, anthropology, and literacy. **WEB** http://gopher.sil.org

U. PENN Museum of Archaelogy and Anthropology Ever consider the significance of grass socks? They are just one of the many cultural adaptations made by Eskimos to deal with the Artic environment. The museum is not just home to beautiful collections, but also serves as the base for Penn's anthropologists and archaeologists. Wait until you see what Professor Alan Mann has discovered about human evolution in his work with Neanderthal teeth. **WEB** http://www.upenn.edu/museum

Economics
....

Adam Smith's Wealth of Nations
Smith is the old-fashioned capitalist's guru. He coined the terms "division of labor" and "natural progress" in his 1776 master work, available at this site. The text is as dry as dust, but if you haven't been forced to read it at some point in your life, you ought to know what the rest of us had to suffer through. So dig in, as the economy grows with no end in sight.
WEB http://www.duke.edu/~atm2 /SMITH

Bri's Economics Page A high school social studies teacher in Pennsylvania put up this index

page to help his economics students. Lucky them, and lucky for students who don't go to Westmont Hilltop High and others who want to learn about economics. The index is a concise and well-organized list of places economics buffs will want to visit, from PC Quote to the FDIC.
WEB http://westy.jtwn.kl2.pa.us/~brm /briecon.html

Capitalism FAQ The no-frills text housed at this site provides an accurate portrayal of capitalist concerns, beginning with "What is capitalism?" and ending with "How do I get my piece of the pie?" In between are academic questions explained in a digestible fash-

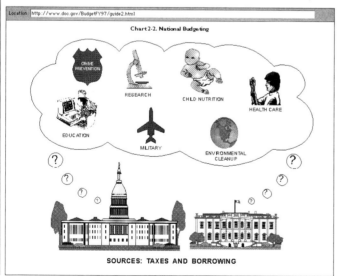

A Citizen's Guide to the Federal Budget
web http://www.doc.gov/BudgetFY97/guidetoc.html

In the first three years of its existence, the U.S. Government spent only $4 million. We spend just a little—well, maybe a lot—more than that now, as this simple guide, written for the average person, indicates. The information applies not only to our ever-expanding budget, but to economics in general. For a government pamphlet, this is a pretty good read that takes anyone with the faintest interest on a non-patronizing tour of our national profits and losses.

ion by a professor at the University of California at Berkeley. A suggested reading list is also available.
WEB http://www.ocf.berkeley.edu /~shadab

Collected Works of Marx and Engels The communist forefathers' key economic writings are available for your perusal. A lovely rainbow-colored picture of Marx is on view, should the budding enthusiast for communist thought require visual inspiration.
WEB http://english-www.hss.cmu.edu /marx

Dead Economists Society The society is very much in favor of free market capitalism, hence its choice of Adam Smith's face on a penny as its emblem. Promoting "classical liberal economists" is the ultimate goal of this page featuring pretty portraits and biographies for every economist from Smith to H.L. Mencken, along with text excerpts and links to relevant Web sites.
WEB http://cac.psu.edu/~jdml14

Economic Democracy Information Network An invaluable source of "alternative" economics and business information for the concerned consumer, EDIN is devoted to delivering information that has an impact on economics and business, but doesn't often show up in the business pages. The Web site offers documents on human rights, education and training, political organization, labor organization, health care, race, and the environment.
WEB http://garnet.berkeley.edu:3333

FinWEB In need of a refresher course in Econ 101? This collection of links is heavily weighted toward the academic side of economics, but there's a healthy selection of links to more general-interest sites, including stock quote services, economic databases, and investment houses on the Web.
WEB http://www.finweb.com

Post-Keynesian Thought Is unemployment a public policy problem? Paul doesn't think so, but Randy does. So leave the peacemaking to Steve, who steps in to opine that "Both Paul and Randy seem to agree that inflation is mismeasured to some degree." This mailing list, devoted to post-Keynesian economic theories and thoughts, is populated mostly by academic economists.
EMAIL listproc@csf.colorado.edu ✍
Type in message body: **subscribe pkt ⟨your full name⟩**

Resources for Economists on the Internet An extensive collection of links to economic resources gathered by a Mississippi college professor. The emphasis is on academic research, but there's something for everyone, from online journals to newsgroups to economic societies.
WEB http://econwpa.wustl.edu /EconFAQ/EconFAQ.html

sci.econ Home to debates and discussions about the economy, particularly the political economy. Gets ugly, but stays intelligent.
USENET sci.econ

Geography

Condé Nast Photo Gallery Another gorgeous place to see the world from the comfort of your desk chair. This gallery is part of *Condé Nast Traveler* online, and for budding geographers, it is the best part. Click on an area of the world like the Arctic or the South Pacific, and be rewarded with *CN Traveler*'s brand of eye candy. If you like the picture (which tends to be a close-up shot of blue sky and happy native folks), click on the text beneath it for a map and detailed information about the region. Then, book your flight. (Ah, don't you wish?)
WEB http://www.cntraveler.com /photo_gallery/photo_gallery.html

Connected Traveler A view of the bold and the beautiful in world photography is waiting at this magazine. Russell Johnson, who does with travel what J. Peterman does with clothes and Martha Stewart does with housework, narrates his journeys with lush and enviable photos. Other notables such as Arthur C. Clarke of sci-fi fame contribute (he now lives in Sri Lanka pondering this and other worlds). One of the best things about the *Connected Traveler* is that while it does paint the world in pastel hues, it is packed with information

about the respective countries. Of particular note is the online guide to the Mekong countries. A restful place to contemplate geography.
WEB http://www.well.com/user/wldtrvlr

Country Maps from W3 Servers in Europe This is very simple: Pick a country from the list, click on the country's icon, and go to a map of the country. There may even be other goodies, such as the photos and info on the Bosnia Home Page.
WEB http://www.tue.nl/europe

Finding Your Way With Map and Compass For those of you who didn't join the Boy or Girl Scouts because the uniforms were too geeky, the U.S. Geological Survey gives you another shot at honing your navigational skills. This online pamphlet is actually quite readable, and the kind of thing that your mother would say "may come in handy some day," especially if you need to find your way out of your messy kitchen or bedroom.
WEB http://info.er.usgs.gov/fact-sheets/finding-your-way/finding-your-way.html

Geography Ready Reference The Internet Public Library's enormous—but searchable—collection of geography links, provides a nice introduction to some of the geographic possibilities on the Web. The glos-saries and FAQs are invaluable, and a section on atlases leads to some of the places mankind has gone before.
WEB http://www.ipl.org/ref/RR/GEN/geography-rr.html

GeoNet Game If you ignore the goofy premise of this geographical trivia game—something about the Grunddargh, a group of aliens that wants to take over Earth—a gimmick that wouldn't reel in a 5-year-old—then you may find a genuine challenge. As with the game of Tetris, you choose the difficulty level, so once you know all the answers you can move on to higher ground. The game encompasses several categories from physical to politi-

CITY NET
WEB http://www.city.net

Combining tourism and cultural information on cities worldwide, City.Net is a mandatory stop for armchair travelers. You can explore the world by region or by site name (listed alphabetically); for example, a jaunt to Paris rewards you with street and subway maps, an insider's guide to the city,

subway navigators, and hotel and restaurant recommendations. For a less urban trek, visit the Grampian Highlands of Scotland via online pictures and narrative, including a visit to a twelfth-century cathedral and a trip down the Malt Whiskey Trail.

cal geography.
WEB http://www.hmco.com/hmco
/school/geo/indexhi.html

The Great Globe Gallery They're
not kidding. There are hundreds of views of the whole
world here. Click on Projection
(just one choice out of dozens)
and receive a menu of available
globes from Albers Equal Area
Conic to Transverse Mercator.
Too complicated? Then select
The Most Popular View to
receive the famous photo shot
from the moon. This site is
guaranteed to fulfill all your
global needs.
WEB http://hum.amu.edu.pl/~zbzw
/glob/globl.htm

The Hall of Geography Not Arse-
nio Hall, not Hall's Menthola-
tum, but the Hall of Geography. The links at this Web site
range from Cape Cod to Portugal, from Rwanda to Wilming-
ton, and provide great midnight inspirations for that next
vacation, research topic, or virtual visit.
WEB http://www.tenet.edu/academia
/geog.html

**TIGER Mapping Service & the US
Gazetteer** This incredible public resource will take the name
of any town, county, city or
river in the U.S., determine its
longitude/latitude, and generate a high-quality, detailed
map of the location and its surrounding terrain. The maps are
downloadable, but be prepared
to wait—the graphics files are
very large.
WEB http://tiger.census.gov

Pick a state, any state
http://www.hmco.com/hmco/school/geo/indexhi.html

The World Factbook 1995 Country profiles, compiled by the
CIA, for every nation on the
planet. The site includes geographical, political, economic,
and social information about
countries ranging from
Afghanistan (its infant mortal-
ity rate for the year 1995 was
152.8 deaths per 1,000 live
births) to Zimbabwe (its government is a parliamentary
democracy). A map is linked to
each profile, and the site also
maintains information on
weights and measures conversion, international organizations, the United Nations, and
environmental agreements.
WEB http://www.odci.gov/cia
/publications/95fact/index.html

Philosophy

No Dogs or Philosophers Allowed
How can anyone resist the title
of this British TV show, which
was borrowed from a famous

London pub, whose frustrated
owner erected it to deter poor
philosophers who would sit for
hours talking, but not ordering.
The sign's namesake has put
up an excellent Web page with
lots of facts about the show, its
host, and most importantly,
contextual background for each
of the show's topics, which
range from "Time" to "God."
If you're lucky, the show may
be airing in your area, so check
the listings here.
WEB http://www.access.digex.net
/~kknisely/philosophy.tv.html

Philosophy Archive For those
who need to hear it from the
horse's mouth, this is a great
place to find the actual texts of
philosophical works. They're
well-sorted, so a click on
Enlightenment brings up Fou-
cault and Kant, while a click
on Descartes yields the thinking man himself. A few links to
critiques are included.

WEB http://english-www.hss.cmu.edu/philosophy.html

Philosophy In Cyberspace All the way from Monash University in Australia comes this exhaustive index of all things philosophical. Beginning with a very basic introduction to Net navigation, the site then lists links, including mailing lists, newsgroups, online texts, journals, and organizations.
WEB http://www.monash.edu.au/cc/staff/phi/dey/WWW/phil.html

The Realm of Existentialism Do you ever feel like you're not really here? Do you constantly contemplate the quality of simply being? If so, you may be an existentialist (just like Sartre and Kierkegaard). Go to this

page and read more about the most angst-ridden of philosophies. Its basic guide to the philosophy and its proponents might make you feel more substantial.
WEB http://www.cris.com/~Huntress/philo.shtml

The Sovereign Grace Theology Resource Page Go directly to Hell. Do not pass GO. Do not collect $200. Okay, so the guys who put up this Web site have a definite agenda and they aren't shy about it. But this page can't be beat for an exposition on the Calvinist and Reformation philosophy that played such an influential role in the early history of the United States.
WEB http://www.conline.com/sovgrace

ThinkNet Philosopher's Guide Probably the best source for philosophy in a nutshell on the Web, this easy-to-use guide has photos, a biography, major works, and a list of links for each of the great philosophers, from Aquinas to Wittgenstein.
WEB http://server.snni.com/~palmer/philosophy_guide/philos.htm

Psychology

American Psychological Association Of all the special interest groups standing on soapboxes in Washington these days, this is one of the most vocal, which seems appropriate, and not just because of the current debates over the proper treatment of the mentally ill. The APA's Web site is a treasure trove of

 # The Realm of Existentialism
WEB http://www.cris.com/~Huntress/philo.shtml

Do you ever feel like you're not really here? Do you constantly contemplate the quality of simply being? Do you stare at a bus seat and find yourself imagining it the upturned corpse of a dead

Location: http://www.cris.com/~Huntress/soren.html

Soren Aabye Kierkegaard

donkey floating downstream into a terrible lifeless void? If so, you may be an existentialist (just like Sartre). Go to this page and read more about the most angst-ridden and deeply satisfying of philosophies. This basic guide might make you feel more substantial.

reader-friendly articles about the profession, with info on psychological disorders and their treatment. The site strikes a balance between catering to professionals, educating students, and supporting those desperate for mental comforting. Visitors can come away with plenty of insight.
WEB http://www.apa.org

FreudNet His theories have been widely rejected lately (no doubt due to his detractors' sexual repression in early childhood), but someone had to get the psychoanalysis ball rolling and no one could have done the job better than the charismatic Sigmund Freud. Unfortunately this Web site fails to include a picture of the famous velvet-draped sofa (on display at Siggy's London home-turned-museum), but there is plenty to send a Freudian investigator spinning away in all kinds of (id-iotic)

patterns. Now, how does that make you feel?
WEB http://plaza.interport.net/nypsan

General Psychology—an Introductory Course Here's a chance for anyone to telecommute to Indiana University East, which offers its introductory psych course online. A high school diploma and a few tuition dollars are the only requirements. Those with a fear of commitment can peruse assignments and a class outline before making a decision.
WEB http://www.indiana.edu/~iuepsyc/PI03Psyc.html

JungWeb He's got personality, dreams, he's in touch with his feelings. He's not Prince Charming, but fans of Jung, the so-called father of modern psychotherapy, think he's the greatest thing since the invention of the superego. At this cybertribute to Jung, visitors can take the Meyers-Brigg per-

sonality typing test (which does not involve a gauge of words per minute), participate in discussion of dream analysis, subscribe to a newsletter, and much more.
WEB http://www.onlinepsych.com/jungweb

Sociology

A Sociological Tour Through Cyberspace The tour begins at Texas' Trinity University, where a professor has set up this fantastic page of links and commentary to every imaginable social topic in cyberspace. If all tours were this complete, they'd be worth the price of admission and the cramped buses.
WEB http://www.trinity.edu/~mkearl/index.html

American Sociological Association While this site is largely about the ASA, rather than sociology itself, it contains some valuable articles on such topics as the social causes of violence. A little note at the bottom hints that more information for the general public is forthcoming, so this is a site to watch.
WEB http://www.asanet.org

The Gallup Organization It's the undisputed watchdog of social trends, with polls on topics ranging from elections to religion. Gallup wants to know what makes you tick, so fill out a Gallup Poll here, then search for all kinds of vital stats and articles from the Gallup newsletter.
WEB http://www.gallup.com/index.html

The father of psychoanalysis at play
http://plaza.interport.net/nypsan

Location: http://plaza.interport.net/nypsan/freudarc.html

Sigmund Freud and the Freud Archives

History

LET THE MEDIUM OF THE FUTURE BRING YOU THE EVENTS OF THE PAST

WHETHER YOU AGREE with Tolstoy that history is not made by great individuals, but is the sum of an infinitesimal series of causes and effects, or, if you prefer Teddy Roosevelt's maxim that history is bunk, you can't help but be blown away by the abundance of resources relating to Herodotus's favorite pastime on the Net. No more frustrating peregrinations through the labyrinthine maze of library stacks. Akhenaton, Bonaparte, and Caesar have joined the digital revolution, so delving into the past is as easy as ABC. If you have about as much faith in historians as you do in politicians, cut straight to the primary sources and weave your own narrative tapestry from the eyewitness accounts of those who were on the scene. To understand the world of tomorrow, check out these links to yesteryear, for, as Orwell aptly put it, "Whoever controls the past controls the present, and whoever controls the present, controls the future."

Location: http://rubens.anu.edu.au/imageserve/images/egypt/299011.JPG

HISTORY AT U. KANSAS
WEB http://ukanaix.cc.ukans.edu/history
picture: WEB http://rubens.anu.edu.au
This is it—the repository of all things past, a massive site which takes the mandate "history is everything" literally. Luckily, it also features a search engine to help historians navigate the wealth of Web pages on art, culture, war, and politics. Netsurfers can explore what it was like to be Buzz Aldrin at the U.S. National Space Agency Historical Archives, visit a Roman fort in Scotland, or discuss the Warsaw Ghetto uprising. There are literally hundreds of links to other fascinating sites.

Starting points

A Selection of History Pages A Net-savvy history buff has put together a list of pages of interest to historians. The author's interests are decidely catholic: you'll find links to the National Library of Medicine, the Armenian Research Center, a Sardinian museum, and the Magna Carta.
WEB http://www.cm.cf.ac.uk/User /Gwyn.Price/history.html

Archives and Archivists Need to find the records of the Third Municipality Guard in New Orleans from 1836-1846? They're online at the New Orleans Archives, and you can link there from here. Want to trace the South African Constitutional Court's recent decision? They're easily reached, too. How did Gerald R. Ford spend his day as president? Head to the Ford exhibit to find out.
WEB http://miavxl.acs.muohio.edu /~ArchivesList/index.html

Groningen Historical Electronic Text Archive (GHETA) An ever-growing collection of articles and documents from numerous points on the historical map. Documents include late eighteenth-century shipping records from Amsterdam. The bulk of historical data, however, appears to originate in America, dating from the Revolution to the Civil War. Telnet links take you to the History Network at the University of Kansas and the Institute for

Historical Research in London.
WEB http://grid.let.rug.nl/ahc/gheta .html

H-Ideas Intellectual history has been called the cocktail-party field—and reading the list will certainly give you some juicy, erudite-sounding tidbits to drop over the canapés. You won't, however, get simple answers. Ask about modern life in Athens and follow a trail of ideas in the ensuing discussion that includes Byron, Hitler, Catherine the Great, and architecture. Don't be frightened away: List members decry pretentiousness.
EMAIL listserv@vuicvm.uic.edu ✍
Type in message body: subscribe h-ideas (your full name)

H-Net Archive An archive of historical debate, and insight from popular history mailing lists. Some lists provide complete collections of dialog, others select popular threads. The H-

Women discussion of Lizzie Borden's guilt is a must-read.
URL gopher://gopher.uic.edu/ll /research/history/hnetxx

H-State One of the busiest history lists around. Participants are eager to discuss anything that touches on the history of "the state"—social welfare policy, crime and punishment, and public education. The list has a strong international base, which makes for good cross-cultural comparisons of social programs and social needs. H-State is friendly to newcomers.
EMAIL listserv@uicvm.uic.edu ✍
Type in message body: subscribe h-state (your full name)

Hargarett Library Rare Map Collection A collection of maps spanning almost 500 years, from the sixteenth to the early twentieth century. Most of the maps are of the American South during the Civil War era.
WEB http://scarlett.libs.uga.edu/lh /www/darchive/hargrett/maps.html

Mapping the world in a less prosaic time
http://scarlett.libs.uga.edu/lh/www/darchive/hargrett/maps.html

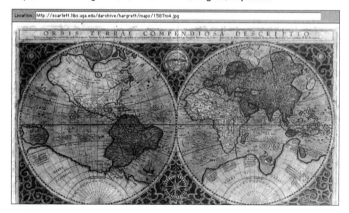

The Historical Text Archive From the Arctic Circle to Zimbabwe, the Historical Text Archive covers history and culture in modern process. Understand imperialism, women's history, and ethnic issues in ways you never thought you could. From tracing the roots of African genealogies to a cross-cultural women's history page, this site offers sophisticated information. More conventional resources like George Washington's speeches are also included as a bonus.
WEB http://www.msstate.edu/Archives/History/index.html

History Sate your appetite for information on history topics from Attila the Hun to the Bay of Pigs. A collection of academic articles has been placed online, and are complemented by primary documents and personal musings. Even Disney makes a showing, with Walt's testimony before the House Un-American Activities Committee. Mickey Mouse indeed.
WEB http://english-server.hss.cmu.edu/Histry.html

> **" Want to know the best place to study the sexual practices of Woodrow Wilson? "**

"And when attatched to the front of a plane the propeller you see here rotates."
"Patronizing creep."
http://lcweb.loc.gov/spcoll/spclhome.html

History Departments Around the World Want to know the best place to study the grooming habits of the Emperor Vespasian, the sexual practices of Woodrow Wilson, the subtext of The Federalist Papers, or the tactics of Napoleon in Russia? Use this hubsite to link to universities from Dusseldorf to Hong Kong to learn more about history.
WEB http://gopher.gmu.edu/other/history/research/depts.html

History Forum If you want to pick a fight on the merits or lack thereof of history, the messages section of CompuServe's History Forum may be the good place to start. The libraries section is a bit less even, however. For example, the Napoleon in Love folder supplies some juicy historical tidbits, but other folders, such as History and Science Fiction or Latin American History, remain empty.
COMPUSERVE go past→Libraries or Messages

History Resources This historical catch-all organizes links into source material, collections, searchable indexes, individual projects, and discussion lists. There is a lot to choose from—the AHC Home Page which serves historical statisticians, the Labyrinth for Medievalists, *American Memory*'s archival collections, and the Renaissance Dante Project are just a few of the resources available. Good annotations make this an easy-to-use gateway to history.
WEB http://www.arts.gla.ac.uk/www/ctich/histlinks.html

Institute of Historical Research
This venerable institution, famous for its research into British social history, has been one of the forerunners in using the Net for historical research. A good collection of links leads scholars to online resources worldwide, and a primer on Net navigation instructs newbies on how to get to them. An ongoing electronic seminar touches on the hot spots of historical debate, and information is available about the Institute's own projects.
WEB http://ihr.sas.ac.uk:8080/ihr/ihrOlOl.html

Library of Congress American Special Collections Brief descriptions of the resources available in the Library of Congress archives. The collections, which range from twentieth-century comic books to photos of cowboys to the maps of explorer William Clark, are organized by subject, format, and chronology.
WEB http://lcweb.loc.gov/spcoll/spclhome.html

> ## 66 Resources in the Library of Congress Archive range from comic books to the maps of explorer William Clark. 99

Around the World Culture in 80 frames
http://www.wsu.edu:8080/~dee

World Cultures from Antiquity to 1500 A professor at Washington State University wants his students to use the World Wide Web to discover the whole wide world, and invites all to come along. You can do the class reading, participate in online discussions on everything from Mesopotamia to The Analects of Confucius, and even take the quizzes—you just won't get a grade. There are resources available for those interested in the history of Greece, Rome, ancient China, the Near East, and Native American culture as well as information on the Middle Ages and the Renaissance. Some of the resources are fabulous, including a hypertext essay on Da Vinci that leads to the master's own words and work, and links to other Renaissance Web sites.
WEB http://www.wsu.edu:8080/~dee

World History Find out everything you need to know on the Middle Ages, the history of France, or any other world history topic at this section of the AOL Academic Assistance Center. Post questions on the bulletin board or sign up for basic tutoring. If you need to know something and you need to know it right now, email a question to the Teacher Pager.
AMERICA ONLINE *keyword* aac→World History

Living history

alt.history.living If you're the sort of pervert who has always wanted to wear thigh-high black leather SS boots or imagine yourself as Rhett Butler—but in that white-and-green hooped number Scarlett wore to the picnic—there are other places on the Net for you. If you are serious about recreating the past, uncomfortable shoes and all, alt. history.living is a good place to meet like-minded people. Most participants are men who like to play soldier, but who are also concerned about authenticity—which leads to earnest debates. The place of women in battle, the value of "amateur" history, and the "correct" way to act out the past, are discussed with fervor and intelligence.

USENET alt.history.living

Living History Forum If you've ever thought that you may have been born in the wrong century, you might want to start hanging out in Compuserve's Living History Forum which is dedicated to

"the re-enactment of selected periods of history." Topics of discussion include: how laundry was done in 1198 A.D.; the medical practices of seventeenth century England; and the hidden agendas behind witch trials and burnings. These people are serious about living as history—even to the point of doing without the spin cycle. The Society for Creative Anachronism gathers here to play lords, ladies, and lance victims.

COMPUSERVE go living

Ancient history

ABZU: Guide to Resources for the Study of the Ancient Near East ABZU makes writing a paper

on ancient Mesopotamia easy. In addition to links to ancient history and archaeological sites, this collection holds an impressive collection of text documents indexed by author and subject. The University of Chicago's Oriental Institute, ABZU's sponsor, has uploaded incredible artifacts and illustrations to enrich the Near Eastern experience.

WEB http://www-oi.uchicago.edu/OI /DEPT/RA/ABZU/ABZU.HTML

ABZU Regional Index—Egypt Visit the land of the pharaohs. Archeological treasures include the Nubian wall paintings of Abdallah-Irqi, works by the most famous names in Egyptology, including the Oriental

ANCIENT WORLD WIDE WEB

WEB http://atlantic.evsc.virginia.edu/julia/AncientWorld.html

picture: WEB http://pharos.bu.edu/Egypt/Alexandria/

Providing links to hundreds of terrific ancient history sites, as well as descriptions of related newsgroups and mailing lists, this Web page author stays on top of what's new in the ancient

Location: http://silicon.montaigne.u-bordeaux.fr:8001/IMAGES/EGYPT/CPA

world, offering netsurfers the very latest from antiquity. If anthropology is more to your taste, the Aboriginal Database and North American Native Culture sites are just a link away. Learn about the Coptic Church, read some of Virgil's works, or stroll through a virtual rendition of the Emperor Diocletian's ornate palace at Spalato with equal ease.

GET REAL

People should feel free to engage in historically inspired fantasy activities but if they claim a historical validity for these activities then they are working against the efforts of re-enactment groups. A case in point is the Society for Creative Anachronism, whose King Arthur/Hollywood antics have created an environment where it is difficult, if not impossible for medieval and early modern re-enactment societies in America to be taken seriously. People who see these sort of groups either believe what they are seeing what actually happened or realise that what they are seeing is fantasy and regard re-enactment with derision.

Nobody is expecting re-enactment groups to be perfect, but I would like to see groups consider what they claim outside their own closed events. Don't claim to represent a group of people from history unless you actually look like they did or unless your aim is to attack history and re-enactment. Do some more work. Gain an acceptable standard of authenticity. If you are not prepared to do this then perhaps you would be better off playing Dungeons and Dragons or Paintball.

—from alt.history.living

Institute of Chicago and the Aegyptischen Museum in Berlin. In addition to the assortment of scholarly articles, visitors can imagine they are Queen Hatshetsup and wander through a computer model of the Giza Plateau.
WEB http://www.oi.uchicago.edu/OI /DEPT/RA/ABZU/ABZU_REGINDX _EGYPT.HTML

Ancient History Resources Not just old stuff, but really old stuff—articles about ancient history in Africa, the Americas, Asia, Australia, and Europe.
WEB http://history.cc.ukans.edu/history /subtree/ancient.html

Annual Egyptological Bibliography Home Page If Cleopatra and mummies pique your interest, this site is a good place to begin. The page offers reviews of the new Egyptological studies, and links to other resources.
WEB http://www.leidenuniv.nl/nino /aeb.html

Archaeological Reports Online Dig through this collection of illustrated archeological reports from the Near East. Choose from the Tall-E Bakun dig in Iran, the Titris Hoyuk in Turkey, or the Valley of the Kings in Egypt, among others.
WEB http://www.oi.uchicago.edu/OI /DEPT/RA/ABZU/ABZU_SUBINDX _ARCH_SITES.HTML

Archeology of Northeastern North America Get a sense of what life was like for Priscilla Mullins or

Squanto by taking a Walking Tour of Plimoth Plantation and Hobbamock's Homesite. Connect to one of the other sites dedicated to pre-expressway New England, such as the dig at Grove Street Cemetery in New Haven, Conn.
WEB http://spirit.lib.uconn.edu/ArchNet /Regions/Northeast.html

Classics and Mediterranean Archaeology Home Page A large searchable collection of links, journals, articles, archeological reports, image catalogs, and databases, the Classics and Mediterranean Archaeology Home Page will thrill visitors with the research short cuts provided.
WEB http://rome.classics.lsa.umich .edu/welcome.html

The Institute of Egyptian Art and Archeology Take a look at a 4,000-year-old loaf of bread placed in a tomb to nourish a king in the afterlife. This attractive sight offers a full-color tour of Egypt and many insights into the ancient culture. The details are the highlights—an image of a small statue of Nedjemu (c. 2544-2407 B.C.), or stone fragments from the grinding of flour that left ancient Egyptians toothless at a young age. The Book of the Dead is available for those wishing to mummify their nearest and dearest.
WEB http://www.memst.edu/egypt /main.html

Papyrology Home Page Want to bone up on papyrology, the

American History

FROM HONEST ABE TO TRICKY DICK TO SLICK WILLIE

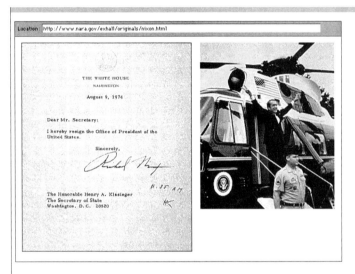

study of manuscripts written on paper made from the Egyptian papyrus plant? This site offers a chance to scrutinize writing and images from thousands of years ago. Many of the world's largest papyri collections can be accessed from this site, which also houses scholarly literature.
WEB http://www-personal.umich.edu /~jmucci/papyrology

Scrolls From the Dead Sea After remaining hidden in jars in a desert for thousands of years, and enduring 50 years of seclusion in the hands of scholars, the Dead Sea Scrolls have surfaced to be scanned by the entire Net world. Read the fascinating story of the discovery of the Scrolls, and the speculation on the society that created them. View images of selected scroll fragments dating from the third century B.C. to 68 A.D.—1,000 years before the earliest known Biblical manuscripts.
WEB http://sunsite.unc.edu/expo /deadsea.scrolls.exhibit/intro.html

Worlds of Late Antiquity You don't have to be a member of Professor O'Donnell's class to learn from his superb Web course. Lavishly illustrated hypertext essays explore the worlds of St. Augustine, Boethius, and Cassiodorus. The critical works of literary and artistic lights are at your fingertips—take a peek at Priscus's account of a visit to Attila the Hun.
WEB http://ccat.sas.upenn.edu/jod /wola.html

AMERICAN ORIGINALS

WEB http://www.nara.gov/exhall/originals/original.html
"We find the defendant, Alphonso Capone, guilty..." The original verdict paper (with signatures) with which Capone was found guilty for tax evasion is available at this site, alongside many more original American documents. See the determination in Washington's handwriting of his first inaugural address, which talks about how he will make democracy a success. History buffs' wallets will fly out of their pockets when they get to see the Lousiana Purchase deed. Bring back Dick with Nixon's resignation letter or read the police blotter for Lincoln's assassination. Then, sink into the report made by a U.S. Navy officer upon discovering the *Titanic*'s collision.

Starting points

American History Get the 411 on everything from the Civil War to presidential addresses at this section of AOL's Academic Assistance Center. Post questions on the bulletin board or sign up for tutoring. The truly desperate can access a history teacher by email using the forum's Teacher Pager.
AMERICA ONLINE *keyword* aac→ American History

American Memory Pulled from the vast and valuable collections of the Library of Congress, American Memory carries a series of excellent searchable online exhibits. Experience the Civil War through photos of historical battles. Relive WWII with posters of Rosie the Riveter on a fuselage. Meet ex-slave Mandy Long Roberson in one of the thousands of Depression-era interviews transcribed online. All collections are fully cross-indexed for an easy search.
WEB http://rs6.loc.gov/amhome.html

From Revolution to Reconstruction A great resource of articles by historians, with hypertext links to primary sources, this Web site covers American history from the settlement of the colonies through the Reagan presidency. Choose the link labeled "The search for religious and political freedom" for an illustrated outline of early colonization, the Mayflower Compact, the

Location: http://rs6.loc.gov/pnp/perm1/4a/4a10000/4a16000/4a16700/4a16765r.jpg

Give me your wired, your 14.4, your AOL masses yearning to break free
http://rs6.loc.gov/amhome.html

Charter of Massachusetts Bay, colonial maps, and a law code from the Virginia Colony.
WEB http://grid.let.rug.nl/~welling/usa/revolution.html

Presidential Addresses Did you know that when Andrew Jackson was 13, he was captured by the British during the Revolutionary War? Or that Woodrow Wilson called the government a "debauched instrument of evil" in his first inaugural address? This site is a great resource for presidential info. Look for biographies of all the presidents, inaugural addresses, and selected State of the Union addresses.
WEB http://grid.let.rug.nl/~welling/usa/presidents/addresses.html

U.S. Historical Documents The biggies are all here—the Dec-

laration of Independence, the Mayflower Compact, the Monroe Doctrine, and the Declaration of War on Japan.
URL gopher://wiretap.spies.com/11/Gov/US-History

Early America

Abolition Exhibit Details slavery and how it ended with the help of key figures and parties. Learn about Jonathan Edwards Jr.'s involvement in the early anti-slavery movement and how the issue of black mothers being separated from their children was used to gain sympathy from women abolitionists. Documents, petitions and anti-abolitionist sentiment—it's all presented in black and white.
WEB http://www.loc.gov/exhibits/african/abol.html

Abraham Lincoln Was it the beard? The hat? Or maybe it was the suit that made Lincoln's brief speech at the Gettysburg Address so memorable. This site has pictures, history, and a quiz section for those who need to test their trivial knowledge, plus an oh-so-zany Madlib Gettysburg Address. Find out about Lincoln's family tree, famous quotes, and other things that made Lincoln a great leader. Celebrate Lincoln for the next four score and seven years by checking out the section on Birthday Events. **WEB** http://deil.lang.uiuc.edu/web .pages/holidays/Lincoln.html

The American Antiquarian Society Three nights prior to the Battle of Lexington and Concord, Isaiah Thomas, friend of the common man and active Whig, smuggled his printing press out of Boston and set it up in Worcester, Mass., and the AAS was born. Since its auspicious beginings, the AAS has become one of the greatest research libraries and societies in the United States. Specializing in the American history to 1877, the AAS is also thought to have the finest collection of American newspapers anywhere. This site houses online searchable catalogs, email addresses of its accommodating staff, seminar information, and the latest Massachusetts weather. **URL** gopher://mark.mwa.org:70/I

An Ongoing Voyage It may not be so important to know that Columbus lost his shoe in 1492—but Americans should know that he brought tobacco, potatoes, and the hammock back from the New World, in exchange for horses, disease, and destruction. This Web site features a section on pre-Columbian society, and illustrated histories that tell the story of conquest and exploration. **WEB** http://sunsite.unc.edu/expo/1492 .exhibit/Intro.html

Archiving Early America Why is the word "vessel" printed as "veffel"? "Same" as "fame"? The short answer is that printers used "f"s when a long "s" was used. What is a long "s"?

A TIMELINE OF THE COUNTER-CULTURE

URL gopher://gopher.well.sf.ca.us/11/Community/60sTimeline
picture: WEB http://icarus.shu.edu/HyperNews/get/vp/protest.html
A timeline of significant events for baby boomers, bohemians, beatniks, and hippies, focusing especially on the sixties. Too much '60s indulgence may have temporarily affected the memory loss of

Location: http://icarus.shu.edu/gallery/V_Portfolio/protest/img0091b.html

this aging hippie, but the author has nonetheless put together a useful timeline including the age of Aquarius, Woodstock, the Weathermen, and Spiro Agnew. Celebrate the advent of the sexual revolution—the Pill came on the market in December, 1960. Relive the drug culture—Timothy Leary took his first tab of acid on Aug. 9, 1960. And in 1966, John Lennon met Yoko Ono.

That requires the long answer, and it's available at this site which archives original eighteenth-century documents.
WEB http://earlyamerica.com

Ask Thomas Jefferson Even though he's been dead for more than 150 years, Thomas Jefferson is happy to answer queries about rebellion, the price of freedom, divine right, slavery, and scores of other topics. The quotes are all authentic. The selection shows the political leaning of the page's author: libertarian.
WEB http://www.mit.edu:8001/activities /libertarians/ask-thomas-jefferson /jefferson.html

Cherokee National Historical Society Follow the Cherokees to the time before thousands were killed by European colonists. Take a cybertour of the ancient village of Tsa-La-Gi or visit present day Oklahoma to see the Adams Corner Rural Village. Find out why the Cherokees called their trek across the country the "Trail of Tears." Then sign up for membership to the Cherokee National Historical Society and help preserve the history of this nation.
WEB http://www.Powersource.com /powersource/heritage

Columbus and the Age of Discovery It's 1492 and time to set sail for India. This site lets users find out about the intrepid explorer who stumbled upon the American continent and the myths surounding him. Check out research papers written by stu-

I could've sworn I parked the spaceship right here
http://www.osf.hq.nasa.gov/apollo/apoll.html

dents and take a course on Colonial Latin America.
WEB http://www.millersv.edu /~columbus

Frederick Douglass Museum and Cultural Center Take a cybertrip to Rochester (a mecca for information about black and women's history) and learn about Frederick Douglass, leader and statesman. The site contains a timeline of his life and a calendar of important events in black history. Links to other Douglass sites include one to soundclip of an actor reading the speech, "An Appeal to the British People."
WEB http://www.vivanet.com/freenet /f/fdm/index.html

The World of Benjamin Franklin Come here to appreciate the genius of Ben Franklin, scien-

tist, inventor, statesman, printer, philosopher, musician, and economist. You can download a movie about this master of kite-flying, or explore his life and works through a series of hypertext essays.
WEB http://sln.fi.edu/franklin/rotten .html

Twentieth century

Apollo 11: One Giant Leap Houston didn't have a problem when it launched the *Apollo 11* mission. Reach for the moon by visiting this site which includes images from the actual mission (takeoff, picking up samples, coming off ladder onto moon, and that sort of thing). Take off to the Air and Space Museum to learn about what Armstrong, Aldrin, and Collins discovered on the

moon's surface and what they brought back with them.
WEB http://www.osf.hq.nasa.gov /apollo/apoll.html

The Cuban Missile Crisis: Walden's Paths Go to the brink of war with this progression of the events leading to the Cuban Missile Crisis. Learn about Kennedy, Khrushchev, and Castro and their involvement in this potential prelude to full-scale atomic war. Read the actual letters between Kennedy ("Let us not negotiate out of fear") and Khrushchev. Includes facts about the geography that made it possible as well as a brief tour of Cuba.
WEB http://csdl.cs.tamu.edu/cgi-bin /walden/path_server?cmc-path+

Ellis Island Immigration Exhibit The University of California at Riverside obtained tons of great black and white photos of pre-Statue of Liberty Ellis Island for this online exhibit. You'll feel like an immigrant entering the country at the turn of the century when you see the detailed pictures of baggage inspection and even Christmas celebrations at the port of entry. Observe U.S. inspectors examining the eyes of immigrants to enforce the Chinese Exclusionary Act. Boat, port, and aerial views of Ellis Island from 1900 to 1920 are plentiful, along with some shots of Brooklyn and the immigrants who were allowed into the country.
WEB http://cmpl.ucr.edu/exhibitions /immigration_id.html

World History

THE INFORMATION AGE MEETS THE MIDDLE AGES

Location: http://mistral.culture.fr/lumiere/documents/files/oeuvres/Girodet.gif

THE AGE OF ENLIGHTENMENT
WEB http://mistral.culture.fr/lumiere/documents/files /cadre_historique.html

The French seem able to make almost anything beautiful and chic (who else could make frogs' legs a delicacy?), and it is therefore no suprise to find that the French Cultural Ministry has put together a stunning online guide to the Age of Enlightenment that has been beautifully illustrated and enlivened by a careful selection paintings. With the emergence of secular philosophy, and the rise of the bourgeoisie, French culture shifted from decadence to classical virtue. Explore this evolution at this site fantastique (it's in English).

African

H-Africa Scholars, students, librarians, and teachers participate in this moderated discussion group for the study of African history and humanities. Sponsored by the University of Illinois at Chicago and Michigan State, the H-Africa Home Page contains instructions and tips for subscribing to the list, as well as its discussion logs. Reports, dissertations, and other academics resources are linked there, too.
EMAIL listserv@msu.edu ✍ *Type in message body:* subscribe H-Africa (your full name)
WEB http://h-net.msu.edu/~africa

Asian

A Brief History of China Can there be such a thing as a "brief history" for one of the oldest cultures in the world? The site's author admits that his intention is less a full-fledged history and more like the Cliffs Notes version. Nevertheless, the site covers the origins of Chinese civilization

 Can there be such a thing as a "brief history" for one of the oldest cultures in the world?

Location: http://moni.net/~mitch/mong/images/genghis2.gif

By G. Radnaabazar

Genghis Khan, warmongol from the north
http://www.bluemarble.net/~mitch/mong/cult.html

from 221 B.C., the early empires, the later empires, through the birth of modern China.
WEB http://www.hk.super.net/~paulf/china.html

Chinese History A collection of Chinese historical documents, articles about Chinese history, and sound clips (Mao speaks). The best resources are those related to the democracy movement. Remember Tiananmen Square?
WEB http://darkwing.uoregon.edu/~felsing/cstuff/history.html

The Great Game: Afghanistan and the Asian Sub-Continent The story is of one of those conflicts that just won't end. The site documents the relationship between Afghanistan and its invaders, from the Crimean

War of the 1850s to the Afghan "conflict" of the 1970s. Official studies of her majesty's troops, VD and Kipling's imperialist stories sit alongside modern news coverage and CIA reports.
WEB http://www.deltanet.com/users/llambert/great_game.html

Japanese History A series of articles on Japanese history covering ancient times, the feudal age, isolationism, restoration, and the modern period.
URL gopher://gan.ncc.go.jp/II/JAPAN/History

Mohandas Gandhi Perhaps one of this century's greatest advocates of non-violence and religious toleration, Gandhi managed to lead India out of colonial rule and addressed

conflicts between Hindu and Moslem. This very basic page introduces the great man who has been an inspiration to politicians, peaceniks, and vegetarians alike.
WEB http://www.maui.com/~lesslie/gandhi.html

Mongolia "It would be no exaggeration to say that Mongolia is the only one of the ancient nomad states to retain the tenets of its original nomadic civilization, including the classic migration of livestock and closeness to nature." Though much of the country still lives a traditional nomadic lifestyle, the twentieth century has brought several Communist invasions and the insurgence of democracy. Made famous by the Huns, Mongolia's history is well described at this site.
WEB http://www.bluemarble.net/~mitch/mong/cult.html

Nanjing Massacre Some things are neither easy to forget, nor to deny. This site memorializes the 300,000 victims of the 1937-38 massacre of the Chinese of Nanjing by Japanese soldiers. Graphic photos of the carnage are included, along with eyewitness accounts, monographs, and examples of Japanese "historical revisionism."
WEB http://www.arts.cuhk.hk/NanjingMassacre/NM.html

Thai History: Ayutthaya Period Sure, you know of a quaint little Thai food place around the corner, but did you know that after King Narai's reign in the 1600s, European relations with the country virtually ceased? The Ayutthaya Period is the main focus of this report on Thailand's history, from the fourteenth to eighteenth centuries. Read about Cambodia's influence during the reign of Ramathibodi I, the royal founder of the Thai Kingdom, and the destruction of the capital of Ayutthaya by invaders from Burma in 1767.
WEB http://sunsite.au.ac.th/thailand/history_of_thai5.html

The Turks in History This essay, with sparse hypertext, chronicles the Turkish civilization through its initial rise and on to the fall of the Ottoman empire. Starting in 1300 B.C., it flies through the ages reaching the present day or, more accu-

 UNIVERSITY OF PENNSYLVANIA AFRICAN STUDIES
WEB http://www.sas.upenn.edu/African_Studies/AS.html

A terrific resource from one of the best African Studies departments in America. With links to academic and nonacademic sites, a gallery of photographs, direct links out of Africa, and the Web pages of each African country, this site is indispensable for those getting into the study of Africa. One section includes a country-by-country breakdown, from Algeria to Zimbabwe, with links to relevant resources.

Location: http://www.sas.upenn.edu/African_Studies/Horn_GIFS/Ark_13218.gif

rately, 1920. Storytellers will enjoy the Turkish epic *Dede Korkut* with its positive female view and documentation of the Islamic religion. The devoutly religious might be intrigued by the Church of Aya Sofya and why it was significant to the Turks at the peak of their reign in the 1400s. Even a top military strategist would have to reread some of the passages related to warfare because of the different factions involved.
WEB http://www.cs.utk.edu/~basoglu /history/tihist.html

European

Aldus The early modern period in England, otherwise known as the English Renaissance, is brought to life with paintings and writings. The well-balanced menu of texts, which include poems written by Elizabeth I, is complemented by a beautiful selection of images.
WEB http://www.jhu.edu/~english /aldus

The Berlin Wall Falls The crumbling of the Berlin Wall has become the symbol for the end of the Cold War. This site gives you German, American, and European perspectives on the event. Download QuickTime movies and pictures of the wall, as well as newsreels and personal accounts, including some from those who were kidnapped by East German Police. Present-day Berlin is also covered.
WEB http://sti.mit.edu/brc/bigdig /Berlin_contents.html

Bosnia Homepage Get involved in the Bosnian crisis. Download newsgroup threads or listen to some of the NEXUS radio broadcasts or CNN reports. You can virtually feel the pain in some of the Bosnian survivors' accounts. Take a look at artwork inspired by the Bosnia/Sarajevo war and learn about U.S. involvement. This site also provides a form to send messages to people surviving the conflict.
WEB http://www.cco.caltech.edu /~bosnia/bosnia.html

The Dreyfus Affair This isn't about Richard Dreyfuss (although there is some resemblance,) it's about Alfred Dreyfus, the falsely imprisoned French officer who eventually became recognized as a martyr of anti-semitism. Check out his scholastic activities at the Ecole Polytechnique. Find out how he attempted suicide in prison by bashing his head into a wall. This site also accounts for other participants in the Dreyfus Affair, including Zola, Colonel Piquart, and Colonel Henry.
WEB http://www.well.com/user/vision /proust/DREYFUS.HTML

Eighteenth-Century Resources The perfect source for studying the era of Voltaire, Mozart, and Hogarth, this site gathers sites dedicated to literature, history,

Michelangelo's masterpiece online—no need to crick your neck
http://viper.idbsu.edu/courses/hy309

Location : http://www.idbsu.edu:80/courses/hy309/pics/sistine1.jpg

philosophy, art, music, architecture, and even landscape gardening. You can ask Thomas Jefferson for his opinions on slavery or read *Paradise Lost*. A collection of home pages of scholars working on eighteenth-century issues provides a unique resource for historians.
WEB http://www.english.upenn.edu/~jlynch/18th.html

Electric Renaissance Designed for a college course, this site recreates the Renaissance with an electronic flair. Essays introduce Renaissance social relations, economics, politics, and religion, to inform readings of *The Canterbury Tales*, *The Decameron*, or Montaigne's *Essays*. Connect to related sites on the luminaries of the Renaissance—Botticelli, Michelangelo, and Machiavelli. Maps, pictures, and sounds make this a comprehensive multimedia experience.
WEB http://viper.idbsu.edu/courses/hy309

The Gregorian Chant Home Page A Web site for serious research in medieval music and Christianity, with hypertext essays on ethnomusicology, medieval religious practices, art, and archeology. Sound files will be available soon.
WEB http://www.music.princeton.edu/chant_html

Irish Republican Socialist Movement This site documents the 20-year struggle of the Irish Republican Socialist Move-

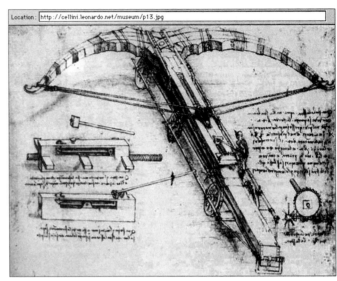

Location: http://cellini.leonardo.net/museum/p13.jpg

DaVinci's early version of the Cruise missile
http://cellini.leonardo.net/museum/main.html

ment. While reading about some of the obstacles the party faced, such as repression from the Official Irish Republican Army and the British Army, you'll learn the meanings of acronyms such as INLA, IRSP, and SDLP. Find out exactly what Sinn Fein, Nicky Kelly, and Devlin McAlisky had to do with anything, and then push forward to the future of Ireland as the Provisionals find allies in the SDLP, call a ceasefire, and try to figure out the voice of the working class.
WEB http://www.serve.com/IRSCNA/irsm20yr.htm

Leonardo da Vinci Museum Exchange punches with the undefeated champion of the Renaissance, Leonardo DaVinci. Sure everyone knows about his "Mona Lisa" or "The Last Supper" but what about

his designs for the multi-barrel gun or the giant crossbow? Soloflex has nothing on this da Vinci site, illustrated with plenty of anatomical sketches. Trace the history which includes his meetings with Michaelangelo and Raphael. Forge to the past to find this futurist's helicopter designs and engineering feats that included channeling the course of the Adda River.
WEB http://cellini.leonardo.net/museum/main.html

Louis XIV, King of France The Sun King, Louis XIV was the longest reigning monarch in European history, and ruled in regal style from his famous palace, Versailles. Besides his commitment to the arts, Louis XIV was an active politician: He took power from the nobility and parliament, rendering himself his own government. Read the details of his life at this site, including the notorious 1685 Edict of Nantes, which forbid Protestants from worshipping freely.

WEB http://129.109.57.188/louisvix.html

The Napoleon Series Napoleon fanatics will find their Waterloo at this site. Find out the details of that historic day in 1815. Download paintings of Napoleon or visit the Napoleon Museum. Links lead to more sites about this charismatic military figure. Diehard war buffs can check out the battle sequences of Waterloo and the attack on Russia, then prepare to go to war at The Historical Miniature Wargame Home Page.

WEB http://www.ping.be/~ping5895

NetSERF This site manages to merge the '90s with the medieval era with a compendium of sites. The section on medieval social history is particularly good.

WEB http://www.cua.edu/www/hist/netserf

Nineteenth Century British Timeline Actually, this site has several timelines of events in British history. The Humanitas Romantic Chronology covers all the major British literary figures, from Wordsworth to Huxley, and the publications that made them famous. The Victorian Web Timeline covers 1700 to 1983, including such notable events as the abolition

Location: http://www-philosophy.ucdavis.edu/ph

Karl Marx: big beard, big ideas
http://www-philosophy.ucdavis.edu/phil5l/phil5l.htm

of slavery and the Battle of Waterloo. Links to relevant Web sites and a syllabus about British Empire lead to even more historical info.

WEB http://athena.english.vt.edu/Brinlee/TIMELINE.HTML

Nineteenth Century Philosophy Get out the *2001: A Space Odyssey* soundtrack when you read the online text of *Thus Spake Zarathustra*. This site includes black and white illustrations of the notable nineteenth-century philosophers as well as some of their writings. From Kierkegaard to Marx, there are plenty of ways to sit at the computer screen and think about thinking. Cross the boundaries between mind and brain by checking out the philosophy lectures.

WEB http://www-philosophy.ucdavis.edu/phil5l/phil5l.htm

The Peninsular War and the Constitution of 1812 In 1808, Napoleon forced the abdication of the Bourbon monarchy in order to install his own relatives in its place. The Spanish people mobilized, and the Spanish War of Independence began. Lasting for six years, the brutal war was memorialized in the paintings of Goya. The essay at this site provides an excellent introduction and overview of this period of Spanish history.

WEB http://www.DocuWeb.ca/SiSpain/history/peninsul.html

The Prague Spring, 1968 This details the events which led to the disappearance of Czecho-

slovakia and then its re-emergence after WWII, and highlights the creation of the KSC, the Czechoslovak National Socialist Party and the Czechoslovak Social Democratic Party. Visitors can virtually feel the usurping of power from the Communist dissidents and independent activists. Stalinization and other political currents are traced through the Third Republic. Read about Brezhnev, Dubcek, The Warsaw Pact and, of course, The Prague Spring.
WEB http://lcweb2.loc.gov:8080 /country-studies/cz_0I_06.html #cz_0I_06A55

Richard III Society Richard III was the 12th of 13 children,

and the youngest of 7 siblings to survive childhood. When his family, the Yorks, came into power, it didn't seem likely that young Richard would end up on the throne. Yet he did, and his reign and death became the subject of Shakepeare's famous play. This page is an excellent resource for those interested in Richard III or fifteenth-century England.
WEB http://www.webcom.com /~blanchrd/gateway.html

Tito's Home Page Who the heck is Tito? This experiment in creating a cult following via the Web traces this historical figure through his illustrious career. Check out "A Song for Tito," "Flag of the Party" and

other songs that can be downloaded. How well-connected was he? See the pictures of him with Nixon, Sadat, Gandhi, Kissinger and others. Plenty of speech files let you hear about how Tito felt about the Cold War, fraternity, equality and unity.
WEB http://www.fri.uni-lj.si/~tito /tito-eng.html

Vatican Exhibit Chances are good that most of us won't ever get a library card for the Vatican's collection, so visit it through this Library of Congress electronic exhibit. More than just a catalog of this famous repository that held 3,500 books by 1481 B.C., the exhibit is a walk through the

The World of the Vikings

web http://www.demon.co.uk/history/index.html
picture: web http://home.sn.no/~perkaa/what/vestvaag/lofotr/vikera.html
They may have been the world's first "wind surfers," as one contributor to this site calls them, but Vikings weren't catching waves. This site compiles a number of fascinating Viking-related sites. The Electronic Beowulf Project of the British Library uses modern technology to retell the tale of

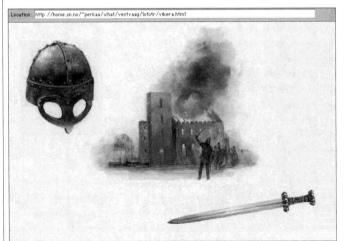

Location: http://home.sn.no/~perkaa/what/vestvaag/lofotr/vikera.html

Grendel and the she-monster with a new vigor. At other sites, netsurfers can learn medieval ship-building and Runic writing. There's a Bryggen Runic font available for downloading and a Runecaster to tell the future; and if the sea is in your blood, you might try to join the Viking Network.

history of the city itself, from the ravages of the fourteenth century through archeology, music, and medicine of the last five centuries. The text is accompanied by illustrations from the collection, including the love letters of the many-wived Henry VIII and botanical illustrations by Renaissance masters.
WEB http://sunsite.unc.edu/expo /vatican.exhibit/Vatican.exhibit.html

> ❝ **Raids hardly made the Vikings the most popular in the world, but hey, it's lonely at the top.** ❞

The Victorian Web Furniture is one commonly recognized Victorian contribution, but that plush velvet chaise longue is only part of the story, as this site explains. Such philosophies as feminism, Marxism, and socialism are attributed to this nineteenth-century movement. Agnostics can read about Tennyson's doubt in God. Carpenters might want to look at the section on architecture. Regress with the moderns who write in Victorian literary style (e.g. Thackeray) or compare today's attitudes with what used to be considered sexual crimes.
WEB http://www.stg.brown.edu

/projects/hypertext/landow/victorian /victov.html

The Vikings An excellent essay on the history of the legendary invaders from the North. Raids in England, Ireland, France, Russia, Iceland, Greenland, and North America hardly made the Vikings the most popular in the world, but, hey, it's lonely at the top. This essay explains why the Scandinavian warriors were so powerful and successful.
WEB http://odin.dep.no/ud/nornytt /uda-302.html

Latin American

Cuba A variety of info on Cuba is available at this site. The featured article is "The Cuban Nation, 1898-1959," but there are also links leading to the Cuban History Archives and

info on Cuban current events and Fidel Castro.
WEB http://www.msstate.edu/Archives /History/Latin_America/cuba.html

The Early History of Haiti Learn about the first republic in the world to have been led by a person of African descent. Illustrations of early Haiti depicted include a visit by Christopher Columbus (this guy turns up everywhere in this hemisphere), the transfer of 500,000 slaves from West Africa, and Jean-Jacques Dessalines' revolution over French rule. Parallel the interesting similarities of Haiti to America and also learn about some of the key figures in Haitian history such as Toussaint, Napoleon, Bookman (a voodoo priest), and Sonthonax.
WEB http://pasture.ecn.purdue.edu /~agenhtml/agenmc/haiti/history.html

The Tainos, Haiti's first settlers
http://pasture.ecn.purdue.edu/~agenhtml/agenmc/haiti/history.html

Location: http://pasture.ecn.purdue.edu/~agenhtml/agenmc/haiti/images/native.1.gif

Latin America Mississippi State University has compiled this excellent set of sources on Latin American history. Read about the region's discovery and conquest and national histories on individual countries in the region from Argentina to Venezuela. There are also links to numerous articles on contemporary subjects like Manuel Noriega and drug trafficking.
WEB http://www.msstate.edu/Archives /History/Latin_America/latam.html

Middle Eastern

A Basic Help for Middle Eastern Historical Research For those being introduced to the history of the Middle East, this page links to starter bibliographies. The basic research paper method is provided, including descriptions of primary, secondary and tertiary sources and of course, the five Ws (who, what, when, where, and why). Also find out additional information by checking the Library of Congress, people's names, and periodicals on the subject. Includes links to all sorts of Middle East sites (none of which are in the Middle East) such as the Middle East Studies Association Bulletin and the University of Texas.
WEB http://alexia.lis.uiuc.edu/~lsmith /history.html

A Brief History of Mecca "Fulfill the inner spiritual void by learning about the place where God's will was revealed to Muhammad (peace be upon him)." Find out why Muslims pray to the East when in America and West when in India. Get down with your holy, bad self by calling out the list of 11 alternative (but still holy) names for Mecca. This site has a history of Mecca and a brief description of the surrounding mountains and entrances to the site of the holy mosque and the Kaaba. In case you're planning a visit, conversion to Islam is suggested. Also links to Saudi Arabia and Islam pages.

Jewish Culture & History through the Ages
WEB http://www.igc.apc.org/ddickerson/judaica.html

Shalom! Hear this greeting by downloading the sound file. Then break out the Yiddish dictionaries: It's time to learn about the Jewish culture. Travel to Tour of Israel or the Jerusalem One WWW

Location: http://www.igc.apc.org/ddickerson/judaica.html

Jewish Culture and History

Łańcut, Poland: *Bimah* of Synagogue

Network to see pictures of the Western Wall and link to sites with loads of historical and cultural information. Construct an online family tree using the Jewish Genealogy Home Page. Visit the Nozyc and Rema synagogues in Poland (pictures included). *Mazel Tov!*

MELTDOWN IN CHERNOBYL

Ranking as one of the greatest industrial accidents of all time, the Chernobyl disaster and its impact on the course of Soviet events can scarcely be exaggerated. No one can predict what will finally be the exact number of human victims. Thirty-one lives were lost immediately. Hundreds of thousands of Ukrainians, Russians, and Belorussians had to abandon entire cities and settlements within the thirty-kilometer zone of extreme contamination. Estimates vary, but it is likely that some 3 million people, more than 2 million in Belarus alone, are still living in contaminated areas. The city of Chernobyl is still inhabited by almost 10,000 people. Billions of rubles have been spent, and billions more will be needed to relocate communities and decontaminate the rich farmland.

Chernobyl has become a metaphor not only for the horror of uncontrolled nuclear power but also for the collapsing Soviet system and its reflexive secrecy and deception, disregard for the safety and welfare of workers and their families, and inability to deliver basic services such as health care and transportation, especially in crisis situations. The Chernobyl catastrophe derailed what had been an ambitious nuclear power program and formed a fledgling environmental movement into a potent political force in Russia as well as a rallying point for achieving Ukrainian and Belorussian independence in 1991. Although still in operation, the Chernobyl plant is scheduled for total shutdown before the year 2000. The power station will be replaced by a thermal energy giant.

—from Soviet Archives Exhibit

Middle East Studies Association of North America MESA, a non-profit organization with international membership, allows all sorts to flip through its newsletter online. Interested parties can read optimistic papers such as "Is there a future for Middle East Studies?" and the ever-popular, "The End of Civilization is Not So Bad." But there are good sources of information, both practical and historical: Britannica has got nothing on the Encyclopedia Iranica. The devoted Muslim can reach the highest level of ecstasy possible by looking through the index of Koran recitations. The latest Arabic word processor (Arabic system 6.1) is featured and information on the Project for the Translation of Arabic is available by contacting the University of Pennsylvania. MESA membership information is also available.
WEB http://www.cua.edu/www /mesabul/selarts.htm

Russian

H-Russia A good place to make contact with scholars, writers, and retired spies in the former Soviet-bloc countries, H-Russia also provides a translated-news service from Moscow, with daily updates from the republics. Join members in their efforts to analyze the updates and explain the process of history in the making.
EMAIL listserv@uicvm.uic.edu ✍
Type in message body: subscribe h-russia (your full name)

WEB http://darkwing.uoregon.edu /~kbatarfi/makkah.html

Algeria Allah has stated: "Do not incline toward those who do evil, for hellfire will seize you." These words opened a communiqué by Abdelrezak Rejjam in 1993 to the Muslim people of Algeria, the ruling Junta and the rest of the globe. Venture to the past to examine another historic milestone such as the Proposal for the Establishment of a Native Army in

Algeria, written in 1830. Then zoom to 1954 to browse the first passionate proposal for the Algerian Front. Mississippi University has archived these three documents and translated them into English. Try to determine why Islamic Salvation Front is abbreviated FIS and why Algerian National Liberation Front is abbreviated FLN. Includes links to the Africa page.
WEB http://www.msstate.edu/Archives /History/Africa/algeria/algeria.html

Russian History If the word "Russia" conjures images for you of men drinking vodka and eating at McDonald's in Red Square, this site will open your eyes to Russia's very rich history. From an early history of ethnic diversity to periods of royal tyranny, to the Communist revolution of this century, Russian history gives new meaning to "war and peace." This wonderful site has compiled essays on some of the most fascinating moments of the Russian timeline. Extremely helpful for almost all time periods.
WEB http://www.bucknell.edu /departments/russian/history.html

Soviet Archives Exhibit The Cold War's on display in cyberspace. For the first time in more than 70 years, the inner workings of the Soviet system are open to view via official documents of the former U.S.S.R., ranging from the October Revolution of 1917 to the failed coup of '91. Take a guided tour through the Communist state with exhibits focused on the KGB, the Gulag, propaganda, Chernobyl, and collectivization. Each is illustrated with documents, letters, and photos. The section on U.S. and Russia relations features the rebuking letter sent by Khrushchev to Kennedy during the Cuban Missile Crisis. Each document in this extensive exhibit is accompanied by an English translation.
WEB http://sunsite.unc.edu/expo /soviet.exhibit/soviet.archive.html

War

EVEN THE SWISS CAN'T REMAIN NEUTRAL ON THIS ONE

Location: http://rs6.loc.gov/pnp/perm3/04a/04a30000/04a39000/04a39900/04a39955.jpg

AMERICAN CIVIL WAR PAGE
WEB http://funnelweb.utcc.utk.edu/~hoemann /cwarhp.html
A site dedicated to making sure no one forgets the War Between the States, this is an immense collection of Civil War-related links and includes a minute-by-minute chronology of the five-year conflict, a multimedia exhibit, maps, photos, letters, and diaries. This is an exemplary piece of Web work that breathes life into the Great Conflagration. Battle buffs can search for great-great-grandpa's unit at the several sites devoted to troop rosters, or arm themselves with info before re-enacting the Battle of Antietam with an online soldier's slang dictionary, artillery and small arms glossaries, as well as sartorial advice for Rebs and Yanks alike.

Starting points

alt.war "Is the Yugoslav Civil War petering out?" "Is 'Debt of Honor' evidence?" "Does Proof Exist Of the Rosenberg's GUILT!?!" This newsgroup switches from one war to another more quickly than you can say "ceasefire," but if you're looking for an argument, or a kindred spirit, you'll find both.
USENET alt.war

MIL-HIST Provides a searchable, chronologically organized infoserver for academic research in military history, from ancient and medieval times to the twentieth century. An invaluable resource for the battle buff or academic war historian wannabe.
WEB http://www.olcommerce.com /cadre/milhist/index.html

MILHST-L Diverse souls meet here—an ex-colonel and a teenager discuss WWII battle plans; a military librarian posts a tidbit about a Civil War general's ground-breaking use of the insanity defense. The list entertains discussion about things nobody could possibly remember, like the dietary requirements of medieval crossbowmen. There are many ex-servicemen on this list, which makes for a friendly rivalry and fosters nostalgia. Newcomers and noncombatants are welcome.
EMAIL listserv@ukanvm.cc.ukans.edu
✍ *Type in message body:* **subscribe milhst-l** ⟨your full name⟩

soc.history.war.misc Battle strategy, favorite generals, and lethal weapons are the subjects at hand. There are many ex-military men here, and in their eyes your credibility rises with trench experience. This is especially evident when the arcane discussion of castle sieges is replaced by modern issues—women in the military is a particular favorite.
USENET soc.history.war.misc

Civil War

alt.war.civil.usa For some, Gettysburg is more familiar than the Gulf War. All the old controversies are here, but much of the debate slides over into the present—to the issues of contemporary guilt "imposed" on the South. The effects of 130 years of brooding are quite clear. "States' rights" are referred to in the present tense and the Confederate flag remains a rallying point.
USENET alt.war.civil.usa

Civil War Battles Get your uniform pressed for the reenactment or the annual Shiloh party. This site lists the battlefields, from the famous (Antietam) to the not-so-famous (Boonsborough). Each conflict is described, its casualties listed, and results noted.
WEB http://www.cr.nps.gov/abpp /battles/Contents.html

Civil War Diaries The whole bloody story of the Civil War is told here through excerpts of the diary of George Molin-

eaux, a 26-year-old volunteer. The site features a hypertext timeline linked to maps, troop orders, and casualty figures for his unit (the 8th Illinois Volunteer Infantry Regiment).
WEB http://www.augustana.edu /library/civil.html

AOL Civil War Forum Meet at specific times in the Mason-Dixon room to chat about Robert E. Lee. Download photos of old battlefields. Link up to terrific Web sites. America Online's Civil War forum is a great place to learn about this favorite subject of American history buffs.
AMERICA ONLINE *keyword* civil war forum

Compuserve Civil War Forum Encompasses a wide range of Civil War topics. From Antietam to Gettysburg, the relevant documents are available, but what makes this site useful are the chat rooms and message boards. Questions are asked, debates rage, and information is exchanged. Civil war buffs share their passions, and can be found giving directions to a particularly well-preserved gravestone, or recommending an authority on battle fields.
COMPUSERVE *go* civil war forum

The United States Civil War Center Saddle up the horse, put out the flag (yes, even the Confederate one) and break out the bayonet, it's time for the Civil War. Inquiring minds might take a sneak peek inside some of the soldier's diaries from

both sides of the battle. Evocative images of battles, weapons and even Stonewall Jackson's bible bring the war to life. Not sure when the Battle of Shiloh took place? Try the Calendar of Events section which chronicles even some of the most minor conflicts. Collectors can find that miniature soldier attacking with a rifle at the games and entertainment department. Includes all sorts of links to books, films, museums, maps, organizations, etc.
WEB http://www.cwc.lsu.edu/civlink.htm

World War I

Fourteen Points Speech Text and commentary on Woodrow Wilson's "Fourteen Points" speech of 1918, which outlined the basic premise of a just and lasting peace.
WEB http://www.edshow.com/civnet/Teaching/Basic/part8/5l.html

Gallipoli Seeing the movie would be easier but a more accurate portrayal of the events can be obtained by visiting this site. The beginnings of a world at war are explained, including the Ottoman Empire's shift from the possibility of joining the Triple Entente (Britain, France, and Russia) to joining the Triple Alliance (Germany, Austria-Hungary, and Italy). Read about the naval, land, Ariburnu, Anafartalar, and Seddulbahir battles and thank the heavens that war is not on the horizon after reviewing the details of the death toll.

WEB http://www.focusmm.com.au/%7Efocus/anzac_0l.htm

Lost Poets of the Great War "The rest is silence." What happens to the people who are wholly against something and yet are compelled to participate? World War I bred these lost poets (who died in action) and this site explains their inner conflict. Discuss the Christian imagery in John McCrae's "Flander's Fields." Search for the hidden meaning in Edward Thomas' "The Cherry Trees," "The Owl" or "Rain" and find out about his bizarre death, two years after joining the war. A relatively thorough chronology is provided.
WEB http://www.emory.edu/ENGLISH/LostPoets

WWI-L An international discussion list devoted to the history of the First World War in its broadest aspects. The period under discussion is generally restricted to the years 1900-1920, particularly the military conflicts of the period.
EMAIL listserv@ukanaix.cc.ukans.edu
✍ *Type in message body:* subscribe wwi-l ⟨your full name⟩

World War II

alt.revisionism Revisionists are historians of a sort—unregenerate polemicists who suggest that Nazi war atrocities were exaggerated by self-serving Jews looking to reap the benefits of a planet's pity. While the newsgroup wanders into related topics—general anti-semitism, "identity" Christianity (the theory that God's favor is reserved for the direct descendants of Adam)—it spends a great deal of time

Egalité, *fraternité*, and *liberté*
http://meteora.ucsd.edu/~norman/paris/Expos/Liberation

Location: http://www.paris.org.:80/Expos/Liberation/

Paris Libéré !

haggling over factual questions of the Holocaust. For example: Was it really six million who perished? Weren't some of the Jews common criminals?

USENET alt.revisionism

FAQ: **WEB** http://www.cis.ohio-state .edu/hypertext/faq/usenet/holocaust /auschwitz/part01/faq.html

Cybrary of the Holocaust This educational site is dedicated to making sure that no one forgets the six million who perished. Historical essays on anti-semitism, Nazism, and the Holocaust are rendered terrifyingly real by the personal recollections of survivors and the mute testimony of photographs.

WEB http://www.pinsight.com/~write /cybrary/index.html

Holocaust Archives The files here allow documents and perpetrators to speak for themselves. Netsurfers can read through the cold-blooded testimony of captured S.S. officers, the Wansee Protocols, prison diaries, and trial testimony from Nuremberg to the Demjanjuk Trial. Or they can view holocaust .GIFs, death camp rolls, and blueprints for ovens. Perhaps most poignant are the photos and stories of European Jewish communities annihilated by the war. Historians and Holocaust apologists both have their say in essays and published articles.

URL gopher://israel-info.nysernet .org:70/11/hol

Holocaust Memorial Museum While this brief virtual tour of

the new Holocaust Memorial Museum's exhibits and research facilities doesn't do it justice, it is a decent introduction and a good source for information on obtaining tickets and reservations.

WEB http://www.ushmm.org

Paris-Expos-Liberation Rejoice with the crowds at the Arc d'Triomphe through this bilingual photo essay on the liberation of Paris in 1944. A map of the assault, profiles of the major players, and documents of surrender are all linked to a chronology and glossary.

WEB http://meteora.ucsd.edu/~norman /paris/Expos/Liberation

> **ff Nazism and the Holocaust are rendered terrifyingly real by the personal recollections of the survivors. JJ**

soc.history.war.world-war-ii Researching the Battle of Stalingrad and need some help? How about the Battle of Britain? Post a question here, and prepare to be flooded with helpful responses. A heavily-trafficked list with readers from all over the world.

USENET soc.history.war.world-war-ii

The White Rose The heroic story of the White Rose, an anti-Nazi resistance group led by students Hans and Sophie Scholl, is told through their pamphlets, letters, photos, and eyewitness testimony.

WEB http://neuromancer.ucr.edu| /beauty/rose.html

World War II FTP Archive A collection of World War II resources that include numerous primary documents—the "Green Book" from the Battle of the Bulge, a list of active aircraft carriers, peace treaties, and even an article on the fates of Japanese battleships.

URL ftp://byrd.mu.wvnet.edu/pub /history/military/wwii/Battle.of.Bulge

World War II—Keeping the Memory Alive Want to know what Hitler was doing on this day 50 years ago? (Hint: he was dead.) This site features a daily column detailing what was happening on specific days during WWII, both on the battlefronts and on the American homefront. Links to photograph collections, and personal reminiscences of battles from soldiers and civilians, enliven the war chronology.

WEB http://members.gnn.com/jbdavis /ww2.html

World War II: The World Remembers A collection of essays, memoirs, and primary sources from both sides of the fatal D-Day invasion. Government documents, photos, *Stars and Stripes* articles, speeches and newsreels make the fateful days

of 50 years ago come alive.
WEB http://192.253.114.31/D-Day
/Table_of_Contents.html

Vietnam

alt.war.vietnam "Napalm bomb" could accurately describe the flame wars that ignite in alt.war.vietnam. It is not just the class of '68 butting heads with the ROTCs—several generations of ill-will meet up here. These people definitely do not see the war in Indochina (or the Cold War) as over. (When is the last time you called someone "commie pinko scum"?) Simple questions like "What if the U.S. hadn't entered Vietnam?" invite discussions that quickly devolve into name-calling and

dogma-slinging. There is also a sharp divide between the "been there" and the "others." Many participants have complained that discussions often deteriorate into to attacks on a single individual—and are attempting to correct this. For now, let it just be said that President Clinton probably should choose to discuss the 1960s and the Vietnam War in another forum.
USENET alt.war.vietnam

Images of My War An infantry officer's retrospective on his strange odyssey from a jungle training camp in Panama to the real thing in Vietnam. His struggles to maintain morale among his men during this much-hated conflict are espe-

cially interesting.
WEB http://www.ionet.net/~uheller
/vnbktoc.shtml

soc.history.war.vietnam This Web site chronicles cultural debates surrounding the American "experience" in Vietnam, and the resulting emotional fallout. Essentially the same as alt.war.vietnam except that soc.history.war.vietnam is frequented by more civilians, academics, and other people who would be called "commies" on alt.war.vietnam.
USENET soc.history.war.vietnam

Vietnam Archives Includes the *Nam Vet* newsletter, info about how to obtain casualty files and service records, and lyrics to many songs of the Vietnam

 # THE WARSAW UPRISING
WEB http://www.princeton.edu/~mkporwit/uprising/top.html

To call the Warsaw Uprising a failure is an understatement. This site shows why war truly is hell. The Polish were so underequipped and undertrained that even Boy Scouts were among those

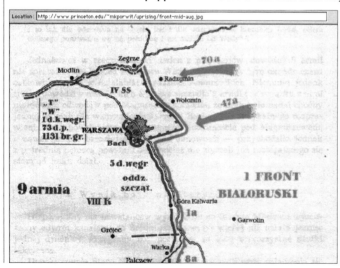

fighting against the tanks and tremendous artillery of Hitler's finest. The site covers "W hour" at 17:00 on Aug. 1, 1944, when the slaughter began, to its gruesome end on Sept. 2, 1944. To better understand the conflict, maps and brief descriptions of the main participants are provided.

Location: http://users.aol.com/andyhosk/reup.html

The front line for George Bush's Gulf War
http://users.aol.com/andyhosk/gulf-war.html

war era.
URL ftp://ftp.msstate.edu/docs
/history/USA/Vietnam

Vietnam Related Government Documents The words that started it all, and kept it going for ten long years—they're all here. Start with the ever-popular Gulf of Tonkin "all necessary measures" Resolution, then move to the State Department White Paper from 1965, entitled "Aggression from the North." The most recent Senate POW/MIA report is available in its entirety.
URL gopher://wiretap.spies.com/11
/Gov/US-History/Vietnam

VWAR-L A mailing list formed to facilitate communication among scholars, teachers, veterans, and anyone else interested in the Vietnam War.

WEB listserv@ubvm.cc.buffalo.edu ✍
Type in message body: subscribe
VWAR-L (your full name)

The Incredible PBS Gulf War Home Page The online version of the television broadcast that aired in January, 1996. Listen to or read about the war according to key players, pilots and soldiers in the battlefield. The site links to tapes, transcripts, maps, weapons lists, and the BBC Radio series, "Voices in the Storm."
WEB http://www2.pbs.org/wgbh/pages
/frontline/gulf/index.html

Gulf War

The Operation Desert Storm Debriefing Book Where did we leave that SCUD missile? It has to be lying around here somewhere. Powell and

Schwarzkopf fans, get ready to be debriefed, and military buffs be on guard—this site has plenty of artillery and machinery statistics, including a list of the helicopters and major missiles used. Chuck Norris has nothing on some of the actual accounts of POWs in the conflict. Find out about all the major players (and some of the minor ones like the media and the anti-war movement) and the countries they came from, as well as a week-to-week breakdown of the important events before and during the war.
WEB http://www.nd.edu/~aleyden
/contents.html

Ronald A. Hoskinson's Gulf War Photo Gallery A collection of snapshots of the Desert Shield and Desert Storm missions (third and thirteenth battalions) and the online text of Ronald A. Hoskinson's *Gulf War Diary.* Enjoy the relaxing bath at the Desert Hilton (actually, it's just a tent). Visit some of the scenic sites such as the "antenna farm" and the many destroyed Iraqi tanks. After shaking sand out of hair, shoes, and clothing, relax with a game of cards or better yet, mail call. This photo album is more personal than most online galleries, with candid shots of soldiers and the situations they faced. Includes a neat little map of the "March Through Hell" and other campaigns.
WEB http://users.aol.com/andyhosk
/gulf-war.html

Literature

THE NET HASN'T SPELLED THE END OF PRINT. IF ANYTHING, IT'S HELPED THE CANON TO EXPAND

As Thomas Carlyle once said, "In books lies the soul of the whole Past Time: the articulate audible voice of the Past, when the body and material substance of it has altogether vanished like a dream." But the voice of the past, however wedded to plot, languages, and character it may be, is not the only thing that draws us to good literature: It's the voice of the writer, which leads us to laugh, cry, or punt the book out the window. Since the computers that make up the Net are limited in their capacity to hold large works of literature, the emphasis of literary Web sites tends to fall on the authors and on resources related to their biographies. So while reading is in itself an inherently antisocial activity, don't forget that there's a world of other readers waiting to lock critical horns with you over the Lives of the Great Ones.

Location: http://www.ee.mcgill.ca/~nverever/hem/writer.html

THE PAPA PAGE

WEB http://www.ee.mcgill.ca/~nverever/hem/pindex.html
The Papa in question is, of course, Ernest Hemingway, hard-drinking Midwesterner turned expatriate. Created by a Hemingway scholar/fan, the site was the first to post pictures of the author, inspiring others to follow. The site contains an extensive biography of the man, as well as images culled from books on Hemingway, including those by A.E. Hotchner and Anthony Burgess. There are numerous links as well, allowing users to join mailing lists, access a timeline of Hemingway's life, or find out more about that ancient yet oh-so-modern virulent rite of passage, the running of the bulls.

GET ME REWRITE!

Does anyone have any opinions about the rewriting of some of the classics—doing them up in modern language and form to make them more accessible to the modern reader? If it's acceptable to make a film in modern language of a Jane Austen novel, why not a total prose rewrite? Austen might be delighted.

I personally "love" rewrites. My favorite is from the Bible (I actually once read it in several versions).There's a passage in the King James Version which says "obey the higher powers." Okay, room for interpretation. The "higher powers" could refer to holy people or bishops or such, not necessarily to the government. When Billy (one-world government) Graham's group rewrote it to make it "modern and accessible", they changed this passage to "obey the government," because all governments were put on earth by God. I think there's a lesson in here somewhere.

—from rec.arts.books

Starting points

alt.books.reviews Is Stephen King a serious writer? What is a serious writer anyway? Inquiring bookworms want to know. Wandering consistently from the topic at hand, posters

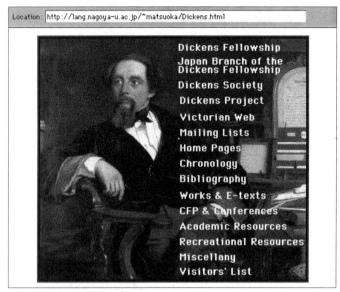

Location: http://lang.nagoya-u.ac.jp/~matsuoka/Dickens.html

Dickens Fellowship
Japan Branch of the Dickens Fellowship
Dickens Society
Dickens Project
Victorian Web
Mailing Lists
Home Pages
Chronology
Bibliography
Works & E-texts
CFP & Conferences
Academic Resources
Recreational Resources
Miscellany
Visitors' List

What the Dickens is this about?
http://lang.nagoya-u.ac.jp/~matsuoka/Dickens.html

to this newsgroup concentrate less on reviewing than on discussing books. Befuddled students and hapless homework help-seekers, are savagely censured by the snooty intellectual types. A thread titled, "Why Do My Own Homework When People on the Net Can Do it for Me?" explores the issue, as students write in to defend their interests ("Why so anal? How long ago was it that you were in high school?"). **USENET alt.books.reviews**

AmLit-L This mailing list attracts mostly academic users, a situation that has both benefits and drawbacks. On the plus side, academics generate a uniformly high level of discourse, with detailed and often fascinating meditations on American literature. How is

Beat poetry related to the projective verse of Charles Olson and the Black Mountain School? What were the factors involved in the rise and fall of African-American poet Melvin Tolson? But the same intellectual rigor that produces diligent investigations of these issues also gives rise to a stultifying self-importance. If you can overlook the the pretension, you'll find that the heavier material is offset by a number of lighter entries—graduate students confessing their weaknesses for (gasp!) popular authors, professors relating humorous classroom anecdotes, and ordinary citizens celebrating the simple pleasure of reading literature. **EMAIL** listserv@mizzou1.missouri.edu ✍ *Type in message body:* **subscribe amlit-l (your full name)**

Literary If you're kept awake at night by apocalyptic visions of Shakespeare's bald pate overrun with circuitry, take heart in this mailing list, which proves not only that readers of fine literature are alive and well, but also that technology can aid their pursuits. Thanks to the synthetic community of mailing lists, bibliophiles can debate first editions of Saul Bellow's novels, recommend favorite plays, and even address more arcane matters. If you're interested in an extended conversation about the linguistic basis for sexual identity in Proust's *Recherché*, this mailing list—textured and thoughtful—is the place to go.
EMAIL listserv@bitnic.cren.net ✍

Type in message body: subscribe literary ⟨your full name⟩

rec.arts.books This baggy newsgroup debates matters such as whether Yeats was an obscurantist, who belongs on a list of the top ten poets of this century, and the delicately inflected ambiguities of *Go, Dog, Go!* Amateurs post reviews on everything from sci-fi to Michael Ondaatje, although sometimes one suspects the handiwork of a publishing house's paid flunky. Several camps—sci-fi and fantasy, hermetic postmodern novels, poetry, and long, fat British books—coexist peacefully but fairly separately. On the evidence here, American readers are not as stick-in-the-muddish as the *New York Times Book Review*. If you rant about academic cabals, for instance, you will politely but firmly be advised to read Jonathan Culler and Terry Eagleton, and then try again.
USENET rec.arts.books

Nineteenth century

Jane Austen Information Page
Everybody's favorite posthumous Hollywood screenwriter, Jane Austen was—believe it or not—also a fairly well-known nineteenth-century writer. While some may opt to wear out their Blockbuster card when confronted with an Austen assignment, those who

◎ AUTHOR'S PEN
WEB http://www.books.com/scripts/authors.exe
picture: WEB http://charon.sfsu.edu/TENNYSON/tennyson.html
This virtual salon is the home base for literary lights past and present. The large collection of links will take you to sites dedicated to the life and works of authors from Lewis Carroll to Douglas Adams. Another great feature: literary and chatty surfers can contribute to ongoing forums on such subjects as poetry, mystery, and science fiction. You can even vote for your favorite young American novelist—Chabon? Powers? Minot?

Location: http://charon.sfsu.edu/TENNYSON/tennyson.html

Jane Austen: Not quite Gwyneth Paltrow
http://uts.cc.utexas.edu/~churchh/janeinfo.html

crack a book may be pleasantly surprised. Replete with irony, subtle humor, and even hints of feminism, her novels have inspired volumes of criticism, a great deal of which can be found at this site. The scope of the material is somewhat daunting. Along with the comprehensive set of links to etexts (annotated and otherwise) of Austen's novels, minor work, and letters, there are notes on her period in history, images,

and quotes, organized by category. Failed pick-up lines, for example, includes such excerpts as Darcy's heavy-handed marriage proposal in *Pride and Prejudice*. From this site, one may also sign up for the Austen mailing list.
WEB http://uts.cc.utexas.edu /~churchh/janeinfo.html

Brönte-L Although they're hardly Harlequin material, these books give one a window

onto the Romantic origins of the modern romance novel. The Brönte sisters clustered on the Yorkshire moors, indulging their fevered imaginations in creating dark, mysterious heroes and passionate, head-strong heroines. On this list, seasoned world travelers meet Ph.D. candidates. Professors seek advice on college syl-labuses. Subscribers share travel tips and book reviews. Modern Brönte readers argue over the ideal cast for a film of *Jane Eyre*. No flames generally, but woe unto the subscriber who confuses Catherine, Heathcliff's inamorata, with Cathy, her daughter, in *Wuthering Heights*. This is exactly the sort of mistake that suggests that the poster is a fan of the vilified Olivier-Oberon film which rendered the dis-tinction moot.
EMAIL majordomo@world.std.com ✍
Type in message body: **subscribe bronte (your full name)**

The Dickens Page The prom queen is your life-long neme-sis, the Beastie Boys show is for the 21 and older crowd, and, of course, your parents just don't understand. Before you start bemoaning your plight, check out childhood à la Dickens. Overworked, underfed, and generally mis-treated, the Oliver Twists, David Copperfields, and Pips of Dickensian London will put your problems in perspective before you can say, "child labor laws." Providing unparal-leled insight into the author's

bleak world, this site is the major Dickens resource on the Net, with links, etexts, and criticism.
WEB http://lang.nagoya-u.ac.jp/~matsuoka/Dickens.html

Thomas Hardy Resource Library
Hardy souls will find etexts, criticism and reviews of the author's work at the Hardy Resource Library. If you're parched after all the intellectual stimulation, follow the brewing instructions for Thomas Hardy's ale.
WEB http://pages.ripco.com:8080/~mws/hardy.html

Nathaniel Hawthorne A fan of the author garnered this fantastic collection of Hawthorne's writ-ing, writings on Hawthorne, and other "Hawthorneana." If you prefer visual aids, check out the site's collection of art, including portraits of the artist and illustrations from editions of his books. The lazy student may opt to order the audio book version of *The Scarlet Letter*. The ultra-lazy may even go for the comic book. Hey, it may not be *Batman*, but at least it's more accurate than the Demi Moore vehicle.
WEB http://www.tiac.net/users/eldred/nh/hawthorne.html

Herman Melville From his early days as a seafaring adventurer to his maturity as a writer—which produced some of the most vivid works on spiritual crisis in the history of American literature—Herman Melville was a compelling figure, and while the early twentieth century forgot him almost entirely, F.O. Matthiessen and other critics soon returned him to prominence. Join the search for the white whale at this excellent Web site, and learn more about the creator of *Typee, Omoo, Pierre, The Confidence-Man, Billy Budd*, "Benito Cereno," and "Bartleby the Scrivener" (not to mention a piece of fluff called *Moby Dick*). There's a biography and a generous and diverse collection of links on everything from sailing to whales to French Polynesia.
WEB http://www.melville.org

 # F. SCOTT FITZGERALD
WEB http://www.sc.edu/fitzgerald/index.html

The original preppy, F. Scott Fitzgerald, once said that, "an author ought to write for the youth of his generation, the critics of the next, and the schoolmasters ever afterward." True to his aspiration, Fitzgerald's masterpiece, *The Great Gatsby*, is a canonical high school must-read, while *Tender is*

Location: http://www.sc.edu/fitzgerald/gifs/fitz_portrait.gif

the Night often acts more as an introduction to the wacky world of Freudian literary analysis. This site celebrates Fitzgerald's centenary and contains an extensive biography, several complete short stories online, a bibliography, quotes, and more, all sponsored by the University of South Carolina, keepers of a large Fitzgerald collection. Sadly, the only things missing from this beautifully designed site are pictures of Scott and Zelda.

Location: http://www.tiac.net/users/eldred/ptx/ozg256.jpg

Nathaniel Hawthorne—meet the twentieth century
http://www.tiac.net/users/eldred/nh/hawthorne.html

Mark Twain Resources on the World Wide Web Huckers and Trekkers alike will appreciate the breadth of this Mark Twain clearinghouse, which includes an analysis of his character's appearance on *Star Trek: The Next Generation* along with other popular culture references. Of course, for those in search of more traditional fare, there's a raft of etext links, biography, and criticism resources. Also included is a list of maxims from Twain's writing, from the terse ("Tell the truth or trump—but get the trick.") to the convoluted and rambling.
WEB http://web.syr.edu/~fjzwick /twainwww.html

Twain-L "Clothes make the man. Naked people have little or no influence..." Mark Twain is America. Almost everyone knows Huck and Tom or can quote a pithy statement or two. On this active mailing list, academics and amateurs meet to interpret Twain's work and worship at his shrine. These people love Twain and want him on their side. Thus, a recent thread about Twain's meeting another nineteenth-century wit, Oscar Wilde, sparked a long discussion about Twain and his probable attitude toward homosexuality. Those who saw Twain as liberal cited his acceptance of Walt Whitman (Twain was "a sexual libertarian"); the other side pointed toward his "moral" family life ("Twain was an honorable man"). Sometimes the list is academically high-toned—how Huck's raft becomes a site of homoerotic friendship—sometimes it's just an exchange of favorite stories.
EMAIL listserv@vml.yorku.ca ✍ *Type in message body:* subscribe twain-l ⟨your full name⟩

Twentieth century

Literary Kicks Leave the material world behind and enter a realm where Beat Poetry is still revered as the acme of artistic expression. The site was created by fiction writer Levi Asher and in spite of his instructions to visitors—"turn your mind off, relax, and float downstream"—the site is a clearinghouse of pragmatic information. There are extensive bios on everyone from the well-knowns to the lesser known Beats, such as Gregory Corso.
WEB http://www.charm.net/~brooklyn /LitKicks.html

ModBrits These scholars of modern British writers (Joyce,

Wilde, Woolf, Conrad, etc.) are a tad hip and not overly cerebral. In addition to discussions of the subtext of *To the Lighthouse,* you will find information on how to run a *Ulysses* scavenger hunt ("a pin for her drawers"). A recent, long thread sought opinions on texts that crack you up and times that you have trouble keeping a straight face while in class.
EMAIL listserv@kentvm.kent.edu ✍
Type in message body: subscribe modbrits (your full name)

Ralph Ellison's Invisible Man This page, created by the University of Pennsylvania English Department, contains a chapter summary of the novel as well as excerpts from various reviews and critical essays, including that of Saul Bellow, Ellison's former flatmate.
WEB http://www.english.upenn.edu /~afilreis/50s/ellison-main.html

William Faulkner A guide to Yoknapatawpha County, with a bibliography of Faulkner's oeuvre (novels, short stories, and essays), maps of his fictional Mississippi landscape, and an essay on Faulkner's time in Hollywood.
WEB http://www.mcsr.olemiss.edu /~egjbp/faulkner/faulkner.html

FWake-L "And so they went on, the fourbottle men, the analists, unguam and nunguam and lunguam again, their anschluss about her whosebefore and his whereafters and how she was lost away." What is there to say about a group of people who spend time trying to figure out what was probably a big practical joke? Actually, FWake-L, which occasionally talks about Joyce's other works, is a very friendly list—congratulations flowed in from around the world for a daughter born on Bloomsday. In the spirit of Joyce, FWake-L welcomes all manner of enthusiasts and helps them "catch up." When they finally get down to business, members generally analyze the novel one paragraph at a time, focusing on the "vertical" axis of the text—its many "levels" of playful discursive,

PROUST SAID THAT

 WEB http://www.well.com/user/vision/proust

Settle back with a plate of madeleines and start clicking through this online 'zine, which brings a dash of humor to the great Gallic obsessive. Did you know that the French choreographer Roland Petit once met with the members of Pink Floyd to discuss a ballet based on *Remembrance of Things Past*? Did you know that Proust lined his apartment walls with cork? And why do all the women in the novel have feminized versions of men's names, anyway? You might well ask. You can even download a recipe for Nesselrode Pudding, a chestnut-flavored dessert favored by the narrator's dinner guests.

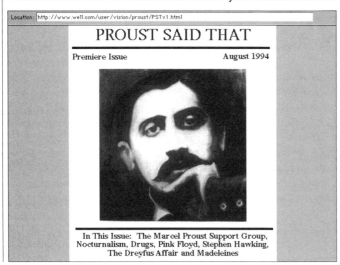

Location: http://www.well.com/user/vision/proust/PSTv1.html

PROUST SAID THAT

Premiere Issue   August 1994

In This Issue: The Marcel Proust Support Group, Nocturnalism, Drugs, Pink Floyd, Stephen Hawking, The Dreyfus Affair and Madeleines

BIBLIOKLEPTOMANIA

Recently I happened upon a very humorous and enlightening book titled Bibliologia Comica, by Lawrence S. Thompson. A chapter on Bibliokleptomania tells the stories of famous book thieves. "The prototype of the collector-biblioklept is perhaps Sir Edward Fitzgerald," according to Thompson. "Born of an illustrious English family, wealthy, and with powerful political ties within his family, he started out on a promising diplomatic career which, however, never came to fruition. He began his infamous hobby by stealing books of his friends. On one occasion his wife caught him stealing from the library of a castle in Northumberland and denounced him, but he escaped the net of justice and escaped to France. Here his unfortunate passion pursued him, and towards the middle of the nineteenth century he was well known among Parisian bouquinistes as l'Anglais. They tolerated his minor depredations on their stock, but one day he overstepped the bounds of their patience when he appropriated a polyglot Bible. He was apprehended and sentenced to two years in the penitentiary."

Speaking of which, "in the United States, librarians have had a considerable amount of trouble with ministers of the Gospel and with theological students. W.F. Poole remarked that he had been annoyed especially by clergymen who unlawfully coveted the books in libraries of which he was custodian. A.R. Spofford reported that antiquarian dealers in Boston had caught ministers stealing pamphlet sermons and that, as of 1900, the Union Theological Seminary had lost 1,000 volumes." Bibliokleptomania respects no class or profession, apparently.

—from Authors Pen

punning experimentation—rather than the "horizontal," or narrative, axis. ReJoyce.
EMAIL listserv@irlearn.ucd.ie ✍ *Type in message body:* subscribe fwake-l ⟨your full name⟩

James Joyce in Cyberspace
Stately, plump Buck Mulligan would certainly have been a netsurfer, and might have stopped taunting Stephen long enough to come to this page,

which serves as a clearinghouse for Joyce resources, including links to Joyce discussion groups, and mailing lists and information about the hypertext journal of Joyce criticism, Hypermedia Joyce Studies.
WEB http://www.2street.com/joyce

HyperArts (Thomas Pynchon)
Thomas Pynchon probably loves the Net. Why wouldn't

he? It encourages polyphony, produces paranoia, and allows for the transmission of information quicker than you can say "Trystero." It also has a page devoted to Pynchon's works. Web Guides to *V.* and *Gravity's Rainbow* are the stars here, along with related "Pynchonalia" (including a link to a Pynchon mailing list) and an FTP site.
WEB http://www.hyperarts.com

Alice Walker A comprehensive site detailing the Pulitzer Prize-winning author's varied life, with annotated works, excerpts from an interview, and critical essays.
WEB http://www.alchemyweb.com/~alchemy/alicew

Mythology

Greek Mythology The Ancient Greeks liked their gods petty, vengeful, and angst-ridden; in other words, human. To learn about Zeus' thunderbolts, Athena's sagacity, and Aphrodite's libidinousness, explore this many-faceted reference work on the residents of Mount Olympus. Having trouble keeping up with Hera's fecundity? A family tree is provided to allay the confusion. A limited selection of myths is included, along with biographical rundowns of the gods, the heroes, and the creatures. Could Ares beat up Mars? A fact sheet explores the differences between Greek and Roman mythology. If studying mythology seems like a trip to

Hades, let this site shed some light on the matter.
WEB http://www.intergate.net/uhtml /.jhunt/greek_myth/greek_myth.html

Women writers

19th Century American Women Writers Web Why were Louisa May Alcott's women so little? Was it the corsets? Malnutrition? Find the answers at this informative site, where etexts, critical journals, and a message board are devoted to the likes of Alcott, Emily Dickinson, and Harriet Beecher Stowe.
WEB http://www.clever.net/19cwww

A Celebration of Women Writers An online exhibit honoring women's prose and poetry. New texts are being added, but there is already an impressive collection of works, including biographies of significant women. Don't miss the hypertext version of Austen's *Pride and Prejudice* or anarchist Emma Goldman's essay on patriotism. A Celebration of Women Writers even offers illustrated mysteries by Mary Roberts Rinehart.
WEB http://www.cs.cmu.edu/Web /People/mmbt/women/writers.html

Women's Reading Room When's the last time you read *Daddy Long Legs*, *A Few Figs From Thistles*, or *Mansfield Park*? Try this growing online library of fiction, history, nonfiction, and academic writing by women.
WEB http://www.inform.umd.edu /EdRes/Topic/WomensStudies /ReadingRoom

Poetry

FEAR NOT—THE NET'S NO WASTELAND

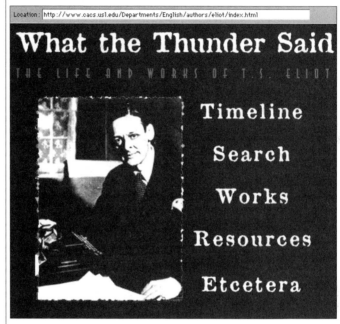

Location: http://www.cacs.usl.edu/Departments/English/authors/eliot/index.html

What the Thunder Said
THE LIFE AND WORKS OF T.S. ELIOT

Timeline
Search
Works
Resources
Etcetera

WHAT THE THUNDER SAID
WEB http://www.cacs.usl.edu/Departments /English/authors/eliot/index.html

One of the best literary sites around. "Like a patient etherised upon a table," the reader of T.S. Eliot is often rendered catatonic with confusion. Sure, the guy is responsible for the decidedly anti-intellectual musical, "Cats", but he also wrote "The Wasteland," "A Song for Simeon," "Gerontion," and many other cryptic stanzas. Fortunately, this site is no wasteland. It is an excellent resource has tools for the student and casual reader alike, making it the ultimate Eliot site, "Now and Forever!"

Starting points

A Procession of Poets This collection of works, reprinted without permission from the *Norton Anthology of Poetry*, is the lazy student's dream. Why lug your books home when you can read, print, and study poems online? Who knows if Donne and Pound would have approved of such step-saving industry, but it'll do wonders for your social life.
WEB http://www.internet-ireland.ie/maryanne

American Verse Project A collaboration of the Michigan Humanities Text Initiative and the University of Michigan Press, the American Verse Project is in the process of assembling an archive of American poetry prior to 1920. Already quite comprehensive, the archive allows users to search by a single word, words, or artist. From standbys like Emerson to lesser-known patriots, the poets are a prolific bunch, reflecting the diversity of the American landscape.
WEB http://www.hti.umich.edu/english/amverse

British Poetry 1780-1910 "A hypertext archive of scholarly editions," this site includes illustrated, annotated texts by poets including Lewis Carroll, Coleridge, Dickinson, Keats.
WEB http://etext.lib.virginia.edu/britpo.html

Poets' Corner What do 1,068 poems from 283 poets mean to

Location: http://www.ilt.columbia.edu/projects/dante/index.html

ILTweb Digital Dante Project

What floor of hell is your apartment on?
http://www.ilt.columbia.edu/projects/dante/index.html

you? If you're a poetry lover, it means that you'll want to visit Poets' Corner (named, naturally, for a morbid but awe-inspiring portion of Westminster Abbey). Both traditional Norton-style poems, like Blake's "The Tiger" or Matthew Arnold's "Dover Beach," and more obscure poems like Eilean Chuilleanain's "Swineherd" are gathered here by a slightly obsessed poetry fanatic. The index is searchable by keyword, so those who have forgotten if Byron's "she" walks in beauty like the "night" or the "armadillo" needn't agonize.
WEB http://www.lexmark.com/data/poem/poem.html

ILTweb Digital Dante Project The project in question is an online, multimedia translation of

Dante's *Divine Comedy*, developed by the Institute for Learning Technology at Columbia University. Each canto includes an illustration and notes; the translation is by the nineteenth-century poet Longfellow. So, whether you choose to enter the Inferno, Purgatory, or Paradise, your trip to hell is bound to be a little easier.
WEB http://www.ilt.columbia.edu/projects/dante/index.html

The Milton-L Home Page If Beelzebub and company had this kind of resource at their disposal, maybe their little rebellion would have met with more success. As it is, the perplexed fan of *Paradise Lost* should check out the mailing list's home page before entering the inferno that is Milton's epic of good and evil. Of

course, the zealous Milton fan can sign on for epistolary hell (i.e. the mailing list proper).
WEB http://www.urich.edu/~creamer /milton.html

Romantics

Romantic Circles An ambitious assembly of top scholars in the field of Romantic poetry has undertaken this project, and it promises to be exciting. They want it to be "open-ended, collaborative, and porous," to remain in keeping with the medium of the Web itself. Shelley (both of them), Keats, Byron, Wollstonecraft, and their contemporaries will all be represented when the site officially launches in November of 1996. Online texts, scholarly essays and articles, mailing lists, and very complete bibliographies of Romanticism-related resources will be searchable, either as a whole or by author. Rather rare for literary academic Web pages, Villa Diodati, a five-room MOO named for Byron's famous summer home and the place where Frankenstein was composed, will be host to both "serious professional exchange" and "casual conversation among friends." Romantic Circles is a site to watch.
WEB http://www.inform.umd.edu:8080 /RC/rc.html

The Blake Multimedia Project As the site is quick to point out, William Blake would have been a bona fide Internet junkie. One of the most innovative multimedia artists, even without the benefit of hypertext, the early Romantic adorned his verse with trippy, codified illuminations. Sadly, his psychedelic visual artistry loses something in the translation to screen, but the Cal Poly students who authored this site use the technology admirably, inviting both detailed and general exploration of Blake's words and images.
WEB http://luigi.calpoly.edu/Marx /Blake/blakeproject.html

Selected Poetry by George Gordon, Lord Byron Who was the first to be "mad, bad, and dangerous

THE ATLANTIC MONTHLY'S POETRY PAGES

WEB http://www.theatlantic.com/atlantic/atlweb/poetry/poetpage.htm

Take an informal, nostalgia-driven journey into the *Atlantic Monthly*'s past, where the emphasis is less on critique and analysis than on the magazine's personal connection with artists in question. The magazine prides itself on "a history of bringing new literary talents to light." Indeed, a young Emily Dickinson was so inspired by an *Atlantic* article, that she began writing to its author. In 1891, after Dickinson's death, these letters were published, and are included in their entirety. In a 1902 article, a journalist recalls his friendship with Walt Whitman. There are also articles on Frost, as well as a collection of poems by Emerson, Longfellow, and Lowell, which appeared in the magazine's first issue.

Location: http://www.theAtlantic.com/atlantic/atlweb/poetry/frost/frostint.htm

ATLANTIC UNBOUND
THE MAGAZINE
THE EXCHANGE
ELECTION CONNECTION

Robert Frost in
The Atlantic Monthly
The First Three Poems
and One That Got Away

- A Group of Poems by Robert Frost (*Atlantic*, August, 1915), with readings by Peter Davison.
- "A New American Poet," by Edward Garnett (*Atlantic*, August, 1915)
- "Reluctance," by Robert Frost (1913), with a reading by Peter Davison.
- A Note on the Recordings and the Text
- A Note on the Audio

to know?" The epithet was originally attached to the itinerant poet, Lord Byron, in all of his rabble-rousing glory. The artist responsible for the immense oceans of appealling but uneven verse that are "Childe Harolde" and "Don Juan," Byron raised hell as a playboy/adventurer, had an affair with his half-sister, and generally embodied the cult of the artist-as-glamorous-outcast. **WEB** http://library.utoronto.ca/www /utel/rp/authors/byron.html

Coleridge Where is Xanadu? And what kind of sick mariner goes around killing seabirds? Reading Coleridge evokes many such questions: A visit to this site yields a few answers. **WEB** http://www.lib.virginia.edu/etext /stc/Coleridge/stc.html

The Poetical Works of John Keats It is the rare high school student who escapes the English classroom un-urned; that is, without decrypting, deciphering, and generally anatomizing Keats's "Ode on a Grecian Urn." The poem often acts as an introduction to the big league of literary criticism, a symbol that the playful puns of Nash and Silverstein are not entirely welcome in the adult world of metaphor and alliteration. But at least the Keatsian wake-up call is a gentle, lyrically beautiful one. The odes, the epics, and the dedications are here for perusal and appreciation. **WEB** http://www.cc.columbia.edu/acis /bartleby/keats/index.html

Complete Works of Percy Bysshe Shelley The complete works of the moody, doomed Romantic are featured, along with a lengthy biographical sketch and an unflattering, bloated-looking portrait. **WEB** http://www.cc.columbia.edu/acis /bartleby/shelley/index.html

Completed Poetical Works by William Wordsworth Wordsworth's obsession with childhood memory and imagination—particularly his own—makes for some interesting reading. His twelfth book, *The Prelude*, is a metaphorical trove for the English scholar and the Freudian alike, spanning western Europe from Cambridge to the Alps. For those interested in exploring the Romantic fascination with the self, Wordsworth is the reigning king of introspection. **WEB** http://www.cc.columbia.edu/acis /bartleby/wordsworth/index.html

Nineteenth century

Elizabeth Barrett Browning Web "How do I love thee?" In case you forgot how to count the ways, visit this Web site, which furnishes the complete texts of "Sonnets from the Portuguese" and "Poems of 1844." **WEB** http://www.inform.umd.edu:8080 /EdRes/Topic/WomensStudies /ReadingRoom/Poetry/Barrett Browning

Emily Dickinson With links to more than 350 of her poems online, this Dickinson site, created by students at Brigham

---

1,900 LEAVES OF GRASS

BEGINNING my studies, the first step pleas'd me so much, The mere fact, consciousness—these forms—the power of motion, The least insect or animal— the senses—eyesight—love; The first step, I say, aw'd me and pleas'd me so much, I have hardly gone, and hardly wish'd to go, any farther, But stop and loiter all the time, to sing it in exstatic songs.

—from Walt Whitman

Young University also includes an FAQ, a biography of the cloistered poet, and access to the Dickinson mailing list. **WEB** http://lal.cs.byu.edu/people /black/dickinson.html

Rudyard Kipling: "The White Man's Burden" and Its Critics Crossing that hazy line between a healthy foreign policy and outright imperialist racism, Kipling is one of the world's most insidious colonists, hiding aggressively Eurocentric tendencies behind a facade of cute talking animals. This site explores one of Kipling's most patently imperialist efforts, "The White Man's Burden," and includes responses to the work upon its timely publication in 1899. The satirical "Brown Man's Burden," "The Poor Man's Burden," and

"The Black Man's Burden" were all written within weeks of the Kipling poem. The site also includes cartoon responses and more recent criticism of the poem.
WEB http://web.syr.edu/~fjzwick /kipling/whiteman.html

The Tennyson Page One needn't be a card-carrying member of the Society for Creative Anachronism to appreciate a good Arthurian legend. Everyone loves a vicarious search for the Holy Grail, as Alfred Lord Tennyson knew well. The "Idylls of the King" is his most ambitious work, but most of Tennyson's poems deal with some palatably heroic subject, from the journeys of Ulysses to

the Arabian nights. The site also includes a timeline of the poet's life and a bearded, scowling portrait of the man.
WEB http://charon.sfsu.edu /TENNYSON/tennyson.html

Walt Whitman A guide to the premier American bard of the nineteenth century, including an autobiographical note, the full text of *Leaves of Grass*, and an index of first lines.
WEB http://www.cc.columbia.edu/acis /bartleby/whitman/index.html

Twentieth century

Early Modernist Poets What is modernism? A word invented to perplex hapless students? A blanket term for any number of

> ## ❝ What is modernism? A word invented to perplex hapless students? ❞

ghastly paintings? Visit this site for the dictionary definition of the word, a cogent explanatory essay, and a collection of works by a group of poets— Eliot, Pound, Moore, Stevens and Williams—who exemplify some of the characteristics of early modernist verse.
WEB http://ccwf.cc.utexas.edu/~trog /english.html

QRISSE'S POE PAGES

WEB http://www.cs.umu.se/~dpcnn/eapoe/ea_poe.html

"Nevermore," quoth the Raven—but in fact the poem, and many of Poe's works, are doomed by their greatness to be eternally exhumed and re-read. You've got to admire the guy's commitment to everything grisly. More than a century before Jason started slashing coeds, Poe was scaring up proper society with his talking birds, disfiguring plagues, and morgue murders. One young goth has erected an impressive site in honor of his literary hero. Etexts, a message board inhabited by the likes of "Darth" and "VampuBro," and biographical pages are included at a site that is both comprehensive and suitably dark.

Location: http://www.cs.umu.se/~dpcnn/eapoe/images/front.gif

EDGAR A. POE
Mournful and Never-ending Remembrance

Dr. Maya Angelou Angelou may be the poet du jour, having read a rousing piece for the 50th anniversary of the U.N. and a triumphant verse for Clinton at his 1993 inauguration ceremony, but she also has staying power. *I Know Why the Cage Bird Sings* was published more than 25 years ago, and Angelou's not finished yet. Robert Daeley's Angelou site contains a short biography, as well as links to related sites and online texts.
WEB http://web.msu.edu/lecture/angelou.html

Location: http://www.ozemail.com.au/~kyeemagh/dyl&cait.htm

No wallflower, this Dylan
http://pcug.org.au/~wwhatman/dylan_thomas.html

e.e. cummings page if you've an interest in the undisputed master of lowercase lettering and rampant punctuational eccentricity (cummings revolutionized the look and feel of poetry) here you'll find a collection of the poet's works (as well as one example of his painting prowess) the author promises to include a short bio of the poet (in the) future
WEB http://www.unc.edu/~jyandle/cummings

The Robert Frost Web Page Why is Frost North America's most famous poet? Who among us has not stood at the proverbial crossroads, contemplating "the road less traveled" with a wistful, yearning eye? Frost's most famous poem captures the spirit of rebellious longing that is central to America's popularly touted national identity. This Web page, "dedicated to one of America's Greatest poets," is a family affair, cre-

ated by Jay and Sue M. and their Uncle Danny Clayton. Including a biography of the poet, a selection of poems, recordings of Frost reciting his own work, and papers and critiques, the site is an excellent place to begin exploring the life and times of a poetic hero.
WEB http://pronews.pro-net.co.uk/home/catalyst/RF/rfcover.html

Pablo Neruda Want to woo the girl/guy of your dreams? Sadly, there's no magic formula, but a working knowledge of one or two Neruda poems can't hurt. The Chilean poet turned socialist penned some of the most romantic verse this side of Barrett Browning, even as he devoted himself to the Republican cause during the Spanish Civil War. Already the subject of the award-winning, if sappy, *Il Postino*, Neruda is clearly

slated for commercial rediscovery. The sage student would do well to check out this selection of poems.
WEB http://www.cris.com/~Huntress/neruda.shtml

Sylvia Plath Making depression fashionable and artsy, Sylvia Plath was nevertheless genuine in her poetic laments, ripe as they are for psychoanalytic vivisection ("Daddy, I have had to kill you..."). Many of Plath's poems are included in this site, giving the reader insight into one of the most creative depressed minds of the century.
WEB http://www.informatik.uni-leipzig.de/privat2/beckmann/public_html/plath.html

Carl Sandburg The complete, text of the Chicago Poems ("Hog Butcher for the World,

Tool Maker, Stacker of Wheat...") is here.
URL gopher://wiretap.spies.com/00 /Library/Classic/chicago.txt

The Anne Sexton Archive Anne Sexton wrote nearly a dozen books of poetry in her too-brief career before dying by her own hand in 1974. The introduction to this selection of her poems is shamelessly maudlin ("Anne Sexton's life and work is an open wound of confession..."), but there's no tainting the brilliance of her work.
WEB http://www.crl.com/~miko/sexton .html

The Dylan Thomas Place The hackneyed motif of uplifting films the world over—especially those having to do with inspirational teachers—"Do Not Go Gentle Into That Good Night," is just one of Dylan Thomas's diverse poems. Many others can be found at this site, along with photographs, recordings of the poet, and related links.
WEB http://pcug.org.au/~wwhatman /dylan_thomas.html

Yeats Home Page For information on Yeats, why not go right to the source—Sligo (Sligo, Ireland, that is)? The Yeats Society Sligo's aim is "to promote, celebrate and foster the works of W.B. Yeats and his family." Towards that end, it provides images and essays detailing the poet's numerous artistic achievements.
WEB http://www.rtc-sligo.ie/rtc_ug /yeats.html

Drama

To surf or not to surf? That is the question

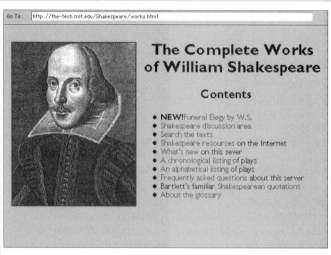

Go To: http://the-tech.mit.edu/Shakespeare/works.html

The Complete Works of William Shakespeare

Contents

- **NEW!**Funeral Elegy by W.S.
- Shakespeare discussion area
- Search the texts
- Shakespeare resources on the Internet
- What's new on this sever
- A chronological listing of plays
- An alphabetical listing of plays
- Frequently asked questions about this server
- Bartlett's familiar Shakespearean quotations
- About the glossary

THE WORKS OF SHAKESPEARE
WEB http://the-tech.mit.edu/Shakespeare/works.html
Everyone knows that *Macbeth* begins with chanting witches and funky lighting, and most Shakespeare buffs know that the mock trial scene in *King Lear* did not appear in the First Folio. But how many know that part of *Coriolanus* takes place in a Volsican camp, or that stage directions (including the infamous "Enter **PERICLES**, wet") have been vexing textual issues since the seventeenth century? Read or act along with this collection of the Bard's works, encoded in hypertext so readers can grasp the subtleties of sixteenth-century English. Readers solely interested in the clichés can check out Bartlett's list of famous Shakespeare quotations.

Starting points

Drama Gopher There's a center-stage-seeking diva living inside of all of us. Come on, admit it! You know you've been dying to play all seven roles from Sophocles' *Electra* in the shower, to crank up the music and sing along with *The Beggar's Opera*. This gopher accesses a limited but varied selection of full scripts, aiding and abetting the inner thespian that, in many cases, might be better left alone.
URL gopher://eng.hss.cmu.edu:70/II ftp%3AEnglish.Server%3ADrama%3A

rec.arts.theatre FAQ Sadly, the rec.arts.theatre newsgroup has gone the way of the dodo, but nostalgic *Les Mis* junkies can relive the glory days at their FAQ. While some questions are only relevant to current and aspiring Broadway ticket holders (e.g. "What should I wear to ‹insert name of pricey musical›?"), others pertain to online resources, the location of drama-related bookstores, and how to access scripts.
WEB http://www.lib.ox.ac.uk/internet /news/faq/archive/theatre.part1.html

rec.arts.theatre.plays Oh, those theater people and their endless jabber about plays, playwrights, and play production—they're what make this newsgroup fun. It's a good place to partake in debate on the literary and philosophical merits of plays from *Hamlet* to *Waiting for Godot*.
USENET rec.arts.theatre.plays

Theatre and Drama From the recesses of the World Wide Web Virtual Library to your computer console, let this well-stocked theater and drama clearinghouse open your eyes to a world of costumes, divas and puppetry. With links to mailing lists, newsgroups, and electronic text archives, the site is an excellent first stop in your journey—behind the cybercurtain. An encore? Head to Journals, where you'll find many of the best theatrical ezines on the Internet.
WEB http://www.brookes.ac.uk/VL /theatre/index.htm

Thomas Middleton Middleton's *Women Beware Women* (1621) and *The Changeling* (1622) are among the bloodiest and most delicious Jacobean tragedies, lacking the richness of Shakespeare's late work, but with a firm grasp of the conventions of the genre—sexual betrayal, double identity, and physical brutality. This page is part of an initiative to put all of Middleton's works online.
WEB http://dayhoff.med.virginia.edu /~ecc4g/middhome.html

The Plays of Sophocles Project Gutenberg's e-text of Freud's great inspiration, *The Oedipus Trilogy*.
WEB http://www.stud.his.no/~odd-arne /oedip10.txt

Shakespeare

humanities.lit.authors.shakespeare Amazing, isn't it, how contentious literary types can be in

> ## There's a center-stage-seeking diva living inside of all of us.

the comfort of their own esoteric newsgroup. "Hamlet's a wimp!" one poster exclaims, and others are quick to jump to their favorite procrastinator's defense. With all of the talk of term papers and study carrels, it's clear that the group is populated by college types, but anyone can get a question answered. Appeal to the superior knowledge of these bookworms, and they'll be sure to respond with helpful hints.
USENET humanities.lit.authors .shakespeare

Shakespeare In the Shakespeare section of CompuServe's Living History message forum, literary experts and neophytes rub elbows, exchange opinions, and clamor to answer trivia questions. Is *The Merchant of Venice* anti-Semitic—and if so, should it be included in the canon? Who has this week's trivia answer? Can anyone help Jeff with a particularly cryptic crossword question involving a Shakespearean jester? These are the questions that keep the Bard's most zealous fans awake at night.
COMPUSERVE *go* living history

Shakespeare Illustrated If you like your classes heavy on slides and light on lectures, this may very well be your gateway to Shakespeare nirvana. Exploring the relationship between the Bard and his visually artistic peers, the site wastes little time on verbose theorizing, and, instead, cuts right to the chase, displaying a selection of artwork influenced by various plays and sonnets. According to the introduction, "pictures from Shakespeare accounted for about one-fifth—some 2,300—of the total number of literary paintings recorded between 1760 and 1900." How did the painters, actors, directors, and critics of the Bard's era influence one another? Although

the site focuses primarily on one author, it answers a number of more general questions about the relationships at work in the artistic world.
WEB http://www.cc.emory.edu /ENGLISH/classes/Shakespeare _Illustrated/Shakespeare.html

William Shakespeare's Sonnets
Homoerotic love poetry or overblown self-laudatory verse? Whatever your opinion of the Bard's sonnets, there's no denying their resonance within the literary and popular culture of the English-speaking world. What desperate Romeo has not attempted to woo the prom queen with a little, "Shall I compare thee to a summer's day?" or something along those lines. Along with the hack-

neyed standards included in this site, some lesser known sonnets work the magic of poesy. The etymologically curious may be interested in the site's discussion of the word, "sonnet."
WEB http://www.eecs.uic.edu /~mocampo/sonnets.html

Nineteenth century

Faust Never make a deal with the Devil, 'cause the Devil always gets his due. And never, ever challenge God to arm-wrestling. Why is it that mortals—from the builders of the Tower of Babel to Dr. Frankenstein—are pathologically incapable of learning the Faustian lesson? The vainglorious quest for omnipotence can only end

STRINDBERG
WEB http://www.jmk.su.se//jmk/stud/H93-120/d-hedjon/index.html
A long address—but worth it. The eminently quotable, long-suffering, multi-talented bad boy from Sweden, August Strindberg wrote plays and novels, painted and drew, and raised hell around

Location: http://www.jmk.su.se//jmk/stud/H93-120/d-hedjon/bio2.html

"this long and boring walk trough the shadow land of memory"

Europe with the likes of Munch and Gauguin. Late in his life, Strindberg developed an interest in the occult, and some of the most interesting pages of this site include excerpts from his Occult Diary, in which he describes nocturnal visitations from the spirit of his remarried ex-wife ("Is she literally two persons? And do I possess one? The better one?").

in tragedy. Just ask the protagonist of Goethe's *Faust*. Of course, one might have trouble finding him—he's in Hell.
URL gopher://gopher.vt.edu:10010/02/102/1

Peer Gynt The script of Ibsen's play, spanning six years in the fantastical life of a Norwegian peasant boy, is presented in its drawn-out entirety.
URL gopher://gopher.vt.edu:10010/02/102/1

Wild Wilde Web Oscar Wilde's plays revolutionized the art of conversation, paving the way for such repartee-driven popular standbys as *Seinfeld* and *Cheers*. Plagued by public scandal and prejudice, Wilde was nevertheless a sought-after dinner guest at a time when being a sought-after dinner guest was the be-all and end-all of social eminence. Once he was challenged to make a clever remark on a subject chosen at random. Somebody suggested "the Queen"; "The Queen," Wilde ad-libbed, "is not a subject." This site both educates and entertains, even as it encourages reverence for the multi-talented author in question.
WEB http://www.clients.anomtec.com/oscarwilde

Twentieth century

English Contemporary Theatre 1950-1990s Learn about the lives, times and works of British playwrights such as Orton, Pinter, and Churchill at this well-organized, somewhat limited site.
WEB http://weber.u.washington.edu/~redmama/barry/titlejm.html

Samuel Beckett Home Page When the grotesque slave Lucky does a weird, flailing dance in *Waiting for Godot*, Estragon asks Pozzo what it's called. "The net," replies Pozzo. "He thinks he's caught in a net." Well, if he wasn't caught in it before, he is now—by one Katerie Prior, a U of Mich. undergrad, whose attractive memorial page includes a biography, a chronology of Beckett's work, a photo or two of the famously handsome Irish author, and some brief critical notes on his work (paraphrased from the Encyclopedia Americana).
WEB http://www-personal.umich.edu/~kadaca/beckett.html

Arthur Miller Although to some, sitting through a production of *The Crucible* may seem like an inquisition and a witch-hunt all rolled into one, there is no refuting Miller's influence in the literary and popular culture of the United States. Just as *The Crucible* is inextricably linked in the popular imagination with Salem, *Death of a Salesman* has become the uber-narrative of American failure and disillusionment. Of course, if that doesn't earn the guy respect, there's always the little matter of his marriage to Marilyn Monroe...
WEB http://www.danbury.org/org/sherman/ArthurMiller.html

Travesties Thomas Stoppard has been pushing the boundaries of the dramatic arts for years. Just as Rosencrantz misuses free speech "to prove that he exists" in *Rosencrantz and Guildenstern Are Dead*, Stoppard invokes the conventions of traditional theater merely to flout and criticize them. For more information on the playwright who dared to parody *Hamlet* and get away with it (he also co-wrote Terry Gilliam's movie *Brazil*), check out the Stoppard home page.
WEB http://www.sff.net/people/mberry/stoppard.htp

Thornton Wilder Be glad it's not your town, because nothing much ever seems to happen in *Our Town*. A funeral here, a lengthy monologue there, and one has the basic elements of the most frequently produced play in the history of student theater. This is a suitably bare-bones page, with a bibliography of his works and little else.
WEB http://www.sky.net/~emily/thornton.html

Tennessee Williams Get off the roof, Maggie, and Stella, let Stanley in the house before he has your sister committed. Alcoholism, dysfunctional families, and hints of incest abound in Williams' plays, and all before breakfast. Focusing on *The Glass Menagerie*, the site includes a fairly long biography of Williams as well.
WEB http://www.susqu.edu/ac_depts/arts_sci/english/lharris/class/WILLIAMS/bio.htm

The Arts

At long last, the various strands of the art world have found a happy medium

WHEN MARCEL DUCHAMP, under the alias of Richard Mutt, entered his first "ready-made" work of art, a urinal that he'd found among garbage on the street, in an exhibit sponsored by the New York Society of Independent Artists in 1917, it was rejected on "moral" grounds. Mr. Mutt responded to such charges by commenting, "It is a fixture that you see every day in plumbers' show windows... The only works of art America has given us are her plumbing and her bridges." Whether or not you agree with him, Duchamp changed the international art scene forever with this shot heard around the world, sounding the call to arms for Dada revolutionaries with his "redefinition" of the art object. Today the creative community is not so divided; on the Net, actors, artists, architects, dancers, historians, photographers, and designers have all found common ground.

ÄDA'WEB
WEB http://adaweb.com

The creators of this cybercollage of self-expression seem to have no method to their madness, and they obviously like it that way. The design is impeccable, bursting with images and as sleek as any corporate site, if only it didn't take forever to load the intricate graphics. But patience pays off; these are serious artists, and they've assembled a brilliant collection of continuously changing aphorisms relating to art and life, as well as some exciting creative projects. As you would with master abstractionists, the best way to approach it is to go with the flow—don't even try to impose sense or rational order, you'll only be frustrated.

Starting points

1200 Years of Italian Sculpture
View images by period or by sculptor—dozens of options and hundreds of images are offered. Whether you need to find a good fig leaf to model or prefer your sculpture like Michelangelo's David (*au naturel*) you're guaranteed to find something inspiring.
WEB http://www.thais.it/Scultura

alt.artcom Art aficionados exchange information about Internet art resources, art college versus university education, and employment opportunities; discuss creative blocks and the pending dismantlement of the NEA; and digress, digress, digress.
USENET alt.artcom

Art History: A Preliminary Handbook Dr. R.J. Belton, a professor at Okanagan University College in British Columbia, has written this helpful little guide to studying art history. While there is no information about periods or artists, reading this handbook is ideal for getting into the artistic mindset and learning how to write about art. "Why Study Visual Culture?" and "What is Art?" along with "Some Basic Reference Materials" are just a few of the topics.
WEB http://oksw01.okanagan.bc.ca /fiar/hndbkhom.html

The Art Line With one of the best online illustrated guides to periods and styles from Neo-

Location: http://www.hotlava.com/media/covers/09.jpg

ART
MUSIC
PHOTO
STYLE

Hot Lava: a font of artistic output
http://www.interverse.com/interverse/lava/index.html

classical to Dada, this hubsite has enough art history resources to fill a textbook. But don't forget to scroll down on that black, purple, and green home page to the encyclopedic index of museums, university departments, and artists—both the masters and contemporary. If you knew nothing about art when you dialed this page, you'd be ready for that Advanced Placement Test by the time you're done reading.
WEB http://grimmy.santarosa.edu /~sfaught/art.html

Artcrit An art criticism discussion forum. Strike a pose with cumbersome prose.
EMAIL listserv@yorku.ca ✍ *Type in message body:* subscribe artcrit ⟨your full name⟩

Artdeal If you've ever felt self-conscious about your ignorance regarding all things arty, click on "Stupid About Art" and you're sure to be inspired with renewed confidence and a

fresh outlook. For in truth, claim the authors of this beautiful digital shrine to creativity, there are no authorities in the art world. But if you do hope to hold your own in contemporary art discourse, they offer a glossary of terms like Minimalism, Surrealism, and Postmodernism, accompanied by brief histories of various movements that made waves in the art world. Features include essays on method and technique, art expositions, and interviews with contemporary masters suchas Leon Polk Smith, Porfirio DiDonna, and Rosemarie Trockel. The emphasis of the site is on painting and drawing, though it is by no means limited to them.
WEB http://home.earthlink.net/~wntl /artdeal

Fine Art Forum This is an active place, host to images, tools and techniques, and discussion on the creative process. As a forum, it is a mixing bowl for art criticism, chat rooms, interactive galleries, and much more. Check out the libraries for a large number of .GIFs and .JPEGs in all styles from Florida Wildlife to Portraiture. **COMPUSERVE** *go* fineart

fineArt forum online This electronic news service reports on art and technology. It is available in three formats: a monthly email digest, an online gopher database, and a fully interactive color version on the Web. In addition to current and back issues, the site has an online gallery and links to individual artists, museums, mailing lists, newsgroups, and international associations and events.

WEB http://www.msstate.edu/Fineart_Online/home.html

Hot Lava Magazine This graphically intense (many thumbnails and JPEGs) monthly displays the works of independent artists and photographers, poets, and musicians. There are links to artists' home pages and information on designing one of your very own.
WEB http://www.interverse.com/interverse/lava/index.html

The Incredible Art Department Some of this site is geared for elementary and middle school-aged students, but it's a must-see for anyone who fancies art. This is the spot for anything creative, from Art Games and

Lessons to Public Domain Pictures. Plus, there are plenty of annotated links to Museums/Galleries, Artists, Art Magazines/Journals, Architecture, Art Styles/Periods... do we need to continue or are you already typing in the URL?
WEB http://www.geocities.com/TheTropics/1009/index.html

NEA Grant Awards—State by State Listing This site, organized by state and city, is a detailed list of grant recipients, including award amounts and nature of programs funded. A rare opportunity to see exactly where and how our tax dollars are spent.
URL gopher://gopher.tmn.com:70/Artswire/Govarts/NEA/NEAINO

WebMuseum

 WEB http://sunsite.unc.edu/wm

One of the most comprehensive art resources available on the Net. New exhibits, curated by Nicolas Pioch, are presented several times a week. In one recent week, significant paintings by Giorgio De Chirico, Edward Hopper, Wassily Kandinsky, Paul Klee, Amedeo Modigliani, Pablo Picasso, and Jean Renoir were shown. The site also offers a Famous Paintings collection, which

heavily emphasizes Impressionism. There is an index of more than 100 artists (from Josef Albers to Joseph Wright of Derby) with biographies and several images of the artists' prominent paintings. Works are also cataloged by style (Early Gothic, Fauvist, Cubist, and Abstract Art); pieces that best exemplify the various styles illustrate the catalog.

POP ART REDUX

The paintings of Lichtenstein, as well as those of Wesselman, Rosenquist, and Warhol, share not only an attachment to the everyday, commonplace, or vulgar image of the modern industrial America, but also the treatment of this image in an impersonal, neutral manner. They do not comment on the scene or attack it like social realist, nor do they exalt it like the ad men. They seem to be saying simply that this is the world we live in, this is the urban landscape, these are the symbols, the interiors, the still lifes that make up our own lives. As opposed to the junk sculptors, the assemblage artists who have created their works from rubbish, the garbage, the refuge of modern industrial society, the pop artists deal principally with the new, the "store-bought," the idealized vulgarity of advertising, of the supermarket, and of television commercials.

—from The Art Line

Oversight Magazine Los Angeles's alternative arts community is the primary focus of this online magazine, featuring profiles of individual artists and information on local shows. Visit the Studios section (featuring such artists as Bertha Big Butt), or links to *Over-sight's* critical 'zines, which include *Coagula, Frame-Work,* and *Caffeine*. If time permits, visit the multi-roomed Galleries, especially the ever-popular Empty Gallery.
WEB http://home.earthlink.net /~oversight

The PartheNet It's got Impressionism. It's got Ancient Egypt. It's got Man Ray, the Vatican, and the Taj Mahal. In short, it's got a helpful index to all of art history on the Net. All you have to do is take a look.
WEB http://home.mtholyoke.edu /~klconner/parthenet.html

The World of Art The World of Art is home to a Masterpiece of the Week, with a review. Also featured are Q&As about current arts events and a nice set of links to museums. The Masters contains an exhibition of Michelangelo, Rodin, David, Raphael, and Bernini. All told, it's a site that's as pretty as its subject.
WEB http://ezinfo.ucs.indiana.edu /~mworkman

The WWW Virtual Library-Art History The University of London's Birkbeck College comes through again, with a dazzling array of constantly updated art history links. It's not very well-organized, but is definitely worth wading through since some of the links—The Unicorn Horn for Liverpool Museum, for example—probably won't be found elsewhere.
WEB http://www.hart.bbk.ac.uk /VirtualLibrary.html

The Zeitgeist Hundreds of messages on art events, recent shows, art movements, the imperiled NEA, and issues such as death (suicide, AIDS) within the artistic community. The site will soon have an online museum: Enter your art in its competition and win five free hours online.
AMERICA ON LINE *keyword* afterwards→ The Zeitgeist→CafeMenu

Art school

The Alphabet of Art Learn a new alphabet here, one that will help you describe and work with art to your fullest. "Alphabet" is a misnomer, since the site is more of a course in art criticism and creation, but read it anyway, starting with Line and working all the way through The Picture Plane. You'll never look at, create, or talk about art in the same way.
WEB http://www.atl.mindspring.com /~massa/alphabet.html

Art 101: Art Appreciation Southern Utah University offers this course on an ongoing basis. It's entirely online and even includes virtual field trips. The course is self-paced and fully interactive, including discussion via email.
WEB http://www.suu.edu/WebPages /MuseumGaller/artapp.html

Photography & design

A History of Photography Sir John Herschel, a well-known British astronomer, is credited with inventing the word "photogra-

phy," when the process was first developed in 1839. From its cumbersome beginnings, when capturing an image would take several minutes of absolute stillness—which explains why no one smiled in those old family photos—to the modern days of one-hour processing and digital photography (never mind movies), photography has had a fascinating history. Read about it, then visit the photography museums indexed at the top of the home page.
WEB http://www.kbnet.co.uk/rleggat /photo

Sight Magazine *Sight* bills itself as "the online magazine for some of the world's finest photography." As such, it's not crowded by ads for a print version of the magazine. It's focus on the Web is a visual treat. The Departments section contains reviews, pictorials, and a chance to talk back. Editorial contains the meat: from photojournalism to documentary photography. This is a class act; not to be missed.
WEB http://www.sightphoto.com /photo.html

@tlas magazine This online magazine for photography, multimedia, design and illustration features a new and radically different design for each seasonal issue. The most recent was all lower-case Courier and featured plenty of ASCII art, taking you back to the bad old days of the Net. But a click on the Photo section reveals a whole new side of @tlas, and a great exhibit of photography by contemporary artists. The same exists for design, multimedia, and illustration.
WEB http://atlas.organic.com

Galleries

Art on the Net This site, created by and for artists, is a studio for 100 artists throughout the world. It displays the work of visual artists, sculptors, and animators, as well as poets, musicians, and bands. Stroll

WORLD WIDE ARTS RESOURCES

WEB http://wwar.com

picture: WEB http://www.mcs.net/~sculptor/jpeg/silverdl.jpg

Don't miss this incredible source for everything on the Net. "You will notice that WWAR offers the most comprehensive information available," assures the home page. They're not just tooting their own horn—it's the truth. If you know exactly what you want, you can save time with the handy search engine. Otherwise, scroll through galleries or art schools, artist home pages, museums, festivals, and more. In the Asian Arts section alone, you'll find more than sixty annotated links.

Location: http://www.mcs.net/~sculptor/jpeg/silverdl.jpg

1994 Walter S. Arnold   sculptor@mcs.com

through the virtual gallery to
view works-in-progress, or listen to sound clips and new
music from alternative bands.
Art is blossoming in the sculpture garden (a recent addition
to the site), and the presence of
video art will be expanding in
the near future. There are links
to other artists online, as well
as a list of events planned
worldwide. It's also possible to
submit your work for review,
and to open an online studio of
your own.
WEB http://www.art.net

ArtCity Recent exhibits at
ArtCity have included "Pierced
Hearts" and "True Love: A
Century of Drawings for Tattoos" as well as others both
mainstream and offbeat. The
galleries and artists listed are
paying for the privilege, but
the work is quality and the presentation sumptuous. There
are articles from *Art & Auction*
magazine, a Newsstand, and a
small but intriguing index.
Visit, though, for the pictures.
WEB http://www.artcity.com

Artnet Worldwide Have money
to burn? Maybe not, but still a
devoted art buyer that frequents auctions? Well, going
once... going twice... sold to
the lady in Nome, Alaska with
the 28.8 kbps modem! It's Artnet Auctions Online—a place
to cast your bid and find that
Cubist oil on canvas you so
crave. Artnet is also a showcase
for aspiring Arps to present
their works on the Web in
Artists Online. Looking to

Your art on the Web—a leap of faith?
http://www.sightphoto.com/photo.html

appraise a painting that was
stashed in your great grandfather's attic for decades? Visit
Art Market Analysis Online.
Art professionals can visit Galleries online and download
computer renderings (zoom in
and out).
WEB http://www.artnet.com/magazine
.html

Artplace Browse ArtPlace with
student and professional artists,
dealers and the like. Drop in
on Clark Kelley Price's studio
at 24 Artplace to have a look at
some of his western oil paintings, cruise the student art
area, where middle and high
school students exhibit their
best work, or post a classified
net-ad. Visit the Virtual
Gallery where you can show
up to five of your paintings or
drawings for free. If you're
ready for the big time, you can
"rent" a Web studio,
(designed, built and maintained by Artplace, Inc.),
where prospective buyers can

see your work, read your bio
and descriptions—and
maybe—make a purchase.
WEB http://www.artplace.com

Museums

The Akron Art Museum Works
from the permanent collection
(Frank Stella's "Diepholz" and
Chuck Close's "Linda") are
displayed. The color and detail
quality of the images is outstanding. Upcoming museum
events are also available.
WEB http://www.winc.com/~aam

Allen Memorial Art Museum Want
to see some lesser-name, quality works? Try Allen, home to
14,000 pieces. The images,
which include some big names
like Monet and Klimt, too, are
large and detailed.
WEB http://www.oberlin.edu/wwwmap
/allen_art.html

The Brooklyn Museum From the
second-largest art museum in
New York comes a rewarding

set of images from their permanent collection, organized by period and artist. Explore painting, sculpture, prints, drawings, and photography, or perhaps the Arts of Africa. Want more than a virtual visit? Location and hours are provided.
WEB http://wwar.com/brooklyn_museum

The Butler Institute of American Art It's "America's Museum," situated in Youngstown, Ohio. A good portion of Butler's collection is online, and some of America's best artists are represented. See Edward Hopper, Winslow Homer, Mary Cassatt, and many others of varying degrees of fame. Of course,

there's plenty of background on the museum and its programs, too.
WEB http://www.butlerart.com

The Chrysler Museum This museum isn't dedicated to the auto. It holds a collection of 30,000 objects, spanning almost 4,000 years, including a world-renowned glass collection, art nouveau furniture, and works from African, Egyptian, pre-Columbian, Islamic and Asian cultures. There is also an extensive collection of European and American painting, sculpture, and decorative art.
WEB http://www.whro.org/cl/cmhh

Cleveland Museum of Arts This classy site hosts a selective

exhibit from the museum's 30,000 works, and provides a detailed "Curator's Choice" article (changed periodically) describing a particular artwork. Collection highlights include Picasso, Caravaggio, Rubens, several works of antiquity, and works by Impressionists like Degas and Renoir. It's a beautiful, comprehensive grouping.
WEB http://www.clemusart.com

Dallas Museum of Art Online Reproductions of works from a number of periods and cultures; major pre-Columbian and contemporary works are featured. More than 200 digital images are currently available, and the site's still expanding. Every gallery, the sculpture

 ZONEZERO
WEB http://www.zonezero.com
One of the premier sites for photography and photojournalism on the Net, this well-organized digital portfolio is alternately a feast for the eyes, a startling revelation, and an insightful critique of human civilization and current glaring disparities of wealth, both nationally and internationally. A

dazzling exhibition gallery features photo essays on subjects ranging from the cocoa harvest in Bolivia to the postmodern Wild West gangland of East Los Angeles. Photographs are accompanied by text written by the artist. Articles deal with everything from the mechanics of photgraphy to artistic manifestos by individual photographers. An excellent collection of links, including one to the Latin American Colloquium of Photography.

garden, and even the Dallas skyline and local tourist attractions are displayed. The .GIFs are all quite large (visiting online could take more time than walking through in person). There is also information about the museum's comprehensive programs and resources.
WEB http://www.unt.edu/dfw/dma/www/dma.htm

Detroit Institute of Arts There's more to the Motor City than cars and Motown, as the DIA artfully demonstrates. Almost every period of Western art is featured. Click on images to reveal the artist, period, and medium of any painting in the exhibit. Information on museum-sponsored events is also available.
WEB http://www.dia.org

The Guggenheim Museum Home to one of the world's finest collection of modern and contemporary art, the museum (the one that looks like a big, white spiral) is almost as famous for its architect (Frank Lloyd Wright) as for its exhibits. It's also the world's first international museum, comprised of the Solomon R. Guggenheim Museum, the Guggenheim Museum SoHo, and the Peggy Guggenheim Collection in Venice.
WEB http://math240.lehman.cuny.edu/gugg

Heard Museum Contemporary and historical Native American and Southwestern art is fea-

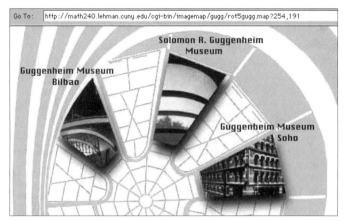

The Guggenheim site is less likely to induce vertigo than the museum
http://math240.lehman.cuny.edu/gugg

tured at the Heard Museum.
WEB http://hanksville.phast.umass.edu/defs/independent/Heard/Heard.html

High Museum of Art Nestled on one of Atlanta's 23 Peachtree Streets is the High Museum, famous for its diverse collection of traditional and contemporary European and American art. The Information page teases with an image of the museum's acclaimed facade; unfortunately, the graceful interior is currently not displayed. The online gallery samples the permanent collection—from the work of the Italian Renaissance masters (Bellini's "Madonna and Child") to modern artists (a Warhol silkscreen of Marilyn Monroe). Pieces from the furniture galleries are also represented. Special exhibitions have featured Jacob Lawrence's "Migration" series and "The Treasures of Venice."
WEB http://isotropic.com/highmuse/highhome.html

Indianapolis Museum of Art Thumbnail images from the museum's special exhibitions are featured, including "Art By Four African-Americans" (contemporary artists John Wesley Hardrick, William Majors, William Edouard Scott, and Hale Aspacio Woodruff), "Juxtapositions," and "Dutch and Flemish Painting from the Royal Library, Windsor Castle." You can't download images, but color and sharpness are excellent.
WEB http://ws2.starnews.com/ima

Internet Arts Museum For Free (IAMFREE) A multimedia (paintings, music, photography, video art, and literature) art site. Read *A TriAngle of Stories*, a collection of short stories by Kevin McCaughey. Listen to albums created for the site by composers like Mike Frengel. Past "exhibited" albums have included "The Dance of Antoine," reportedly the first album created specifically for the Internet. .GIFs and short video clips are also available.

WEB http://www.artnet.org/iamfree/index.html

Los Angeles County Museum of Art This site is filled with artistic masterpieces from L.A.'s premier art museum, including selections from decorative and Eastern art, costumes and textiles.

WEB http://www.lacma.org

Luxembourg National Museum of History and Art Visiting Le Musée National d'Histoire et d'Art will expand your knowledge of the tiny Grand Duchy, a nation roughly the size of Jacksonville, Fla. The site's

elegant entry hall leads to exhibits on the art and lifestyles of Luxemburgers. Special exhibitions include the collection of the Prince of Liechtenstein (Liechtenstein is an even tinier European nation than Luxembourg). There are also links to several other online museums worldwide. Some information at this site is available only in French.

WEB http://www.men.lu/Musee/LUXMUSE.HTML

Montreal Museum of Fine Arts "Masterpieces in Motion: A Century of Automobile Design" and "The Symbolists" (works by Rodin, Munch, Maurice Denis, and Alfons Mucha) is a collection of works

that has been exhibited at this site. The permanent online collection, which emphasizes modern Canadian and European art, is growing; images are being cross-referenced with an index of artists.

WEB http://www.interax.net/tcenter/tour/mba.html

The Palmer Museum of Art ONLINE A wonderful collection of American landscapes, sculpture, and portraits. The online catalog represents only a portion of this Centre Hall, Pa. museum's holdings, displaying art by Milton Avery, Edward Hopper, John Sloan, and others. The Online Catalog Preview contains more than 40 thumbnail images (some with

MOMA: The Museum of Modern Art
WEB http://www.moma.org

Click on that stark red logo, and head to the menu of the online guide to the mother of all modern art museums. MOMA began with eight prints and one drawing, and has mushroomed into a museum housing approximately 100,000 pieces, not to mention the thousands of films and books in the library. Visit Mondrian, Matisse, and van Gogh, just to name a few, and find out all about exhibits such as the huge Picasso and Portraiture.

Location: http://www.moma.org/filmvideo/pages/lang.metropolis.html

links to larger versions).
WEB http://cac.psu.edu/~mtdl20/palmer

Philadelphia Museum of Art A few of the museum's more prominent works are shown, such as Vincent Van Gogh's "Sunflowers" and Marcel Duchamp's "The Large Glass (The Bride Stripped Bare by Her Bachelors, Even)." Image sizes (39K, for example) are small, making it difficult to appreciate the detail of pieces such as "The Large Glass."
WEB http://pma.libertynet.org

Smithsonian Institution Navigating the Web pages and floor plans at this site requires patience and skill. But if you are persistent, you can view

paintings and sculpture as if you were actually inside the immense complex. The site is expanding as the museum adds new collections (e.g., the Royal Benin Gallery in the National Museum of African Art). There are links to all the galleries in the Smithsonian complex (the National Portrait Gallery and the Museum of American Art are particularly rich), as well as to off-site museums (such as the Cooper-Hewitt in New York City). The resources at this site are extensive. America Online's Smithsonian site also offers links to Smithsonian publications and an excellent photo archive.
WEB http://www.si.edu
AMERICA ONLINE *keyword* smithsonian

The Philadelphia Museum of Art's collection includes the best of American, European, and Asian Art
http://pma.libertynet.org

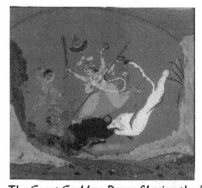

Location: http://pma.libertynet.org/html/durga.html

Indian Art

The Great Goddess Durga Slaying the Buffalo Demon
Kotah School, Rajasthan, c. 1750
Opaque watercolor with gold and silver or tin on paper
Philadelphia Museum of Art: Stella Kramrisch Collection
1994-148-

Architecture

The Aesthetic Movement A charmingly-rustic looking links page guides visitors through favored architects and artists from the 1870s to the 1930s. Posted by an architecture firm with offices in New York, Denver, and Los Angeles, that specializes in historical styles and period additions, the site puts a heavy emphasis on handtooling and craftsmanship, evoking a feeling of nostalgia for a time when people actually made things. Links include a guide to American gothic architecture, the Prairie School and, inevitably, Frank Lloyd Wright.
WEB http://www.fswarchitects.com/links.html

The AIA/AAF Website This dual home page for both the American Institute of Architects and its some 58,000 members and the American Architectural Foundation endeavors to make design professionals, and their craft, more accessible to the general public. With furthering the "cause of American architecture" as its imprimatur, the page offers descriptions of careers in architecture, resources for curious teenagers, and proffers advice for those contracting architects. Includes a well maintained and quickly expanding collection of links.
WEB http://www.aia.org

ARCH-Online An online connection service for architects, artists and consultants based in

the northeast. With direct links to employers, product and fabrication manufacturers, related organizations, this page also offers advice on cost-effective web-design.
WEB http://www.arch-online.com

Architecture and Urbanism A lecture even Bernard Tschumi could love: Huw Thomas, an architect with Norman Foster and Partners, delivered this contemplative talk on emerging technologies, and cultural and design trends. Juxtaposing masterplans and buildings in London, Germany, Spain, France, Greece and Japan, he alleges a global change in the way architects conceive community, the home, and the work space. A highlight here is a very active world discussion subpage, and though a bit stripped-down visually, this is full of some refreshing insights on our architectural and urban future.
WEB http://www.Austria.EU.net/gv95/HuwThomasText.html

Architecture & Architectural Sculpture of the Mediterranean Basin Plumb the pages of this site for some 2,000 exquisite images of classical and Hellenistic architecture in Italy, Greece, and Turkey, and Medieval and Renaissance architecture in Italy and France. Each image is fully annotated. Pergamum, Pliny, Palladio—the list of classically inspired architects, buildings, and locales never ends.
WEB http://www.ncsa.uiuc.edu/SDG/Experimental/anu-art-history/architecture.html

Architecture ONLINE As one might expect from MIT—it's a somewhat stodgy but info-rich source featuring, in pictures and text, the university museum's most popular exhibits. Of particular interest is the photo-packed online exhibit detailing the history of that most American of architectural innovations: the skyscraper. With all these wonderful old renderings, lengthy histories, and detailed biographies—it's a dissertation writer's dream page.

THE FRANK LLOYD WRIGHT PAGE
WEB http://www.mcs.com/~tgiesler/flw_home.htm
picture: WEB http://www.envirolink.org/orgs/fallwater/index.html
The admirable work of **FLW** obsessives across the land, this page attempts to cover every conceivable cranny of the life and works of America's most famed and persnickety architect. The Frank

Lloyd Wright Tourist has loads of personal photos taken by the devoted of most every building designed by Wright. Also included are a single page dedicated to The Master's three-legged chair, downloadable QuickTime clips, JPEGs, .GIFs, and even a page on Wright's personal typeface, Eaglefeather. Exhaustive, to say the least.

WEB http://web.mit.edu/museum/www /architecture_online.html

Art and Architecture Network

Based in Japan, this communications collective is designed to connect digital artists and programmers with engineers, urban planners, and architects via the Net. A nifty, literal map of collaborative users, their locations and equipment and software illustrates one of many ways "the CAD environment may be regarded as not only the means that provides a new possibility for designers, but also a 'porthole' through which we see how multimedia network society can be developed in the future."
WEB http://www.bekkoame.or.jp /~arthiweb/index.j.html

artNtec A sense of play informs the layout of this page dedicated to the needs of both professional and amateur computer-aided architectural designers. Mosey past the home page and you'll find an amusing "houseplan" that links you to various marketplace, gallery, and educational resources.
WEB http://www.students.uiuc.edu /~p-chen2

The Barcelona Pavilion Enig-

matic, starkly beautiful, prescient—all these words could describe this masterpiece of modern architecture designed by Mies van der Rohe for the 1929 World Exposition in Barcelona. Then add to that list of adjectives "mysterious,"

because six months after the exhibit, the dismantled structure disappeared in transit back to Germany. Now, using QuickTime movies of a computer-generated model, one can tour this fabulous bit of architectural history. A haunting, not-to-be-missed online experience, as you become "a bodiless subject/observer reveling in uninterrupted reflections..."
WEB http://archproplan.auckland.ac .nz/People/Mat/barcelona

Department of Architecture, University of Hong Kong "Society

looks to the architect to design the physical settings that enable people... and society as a whole to realize their potential to create better and more fulfilling lives." So goes the opening manifesto of this intriguing look at Asian architectural thought and theory. Exotic projects on view in photos and plans in the Student Gallery give this page visual luster, while the online "virtual tutor" makes this useful for anyone interested in HTML, Java, and other computer-assisted design modalities.
WEB http://www.arch.cuhk.hk.

IAWA Home Page Or, spelled out, the home site for the International Archive of Women in Architecture. Established in 1985 by the College of Architecture and Urban Studies, the University Libraries at Virginia Polytechnic Institute, and Virginia Tech, the IAWA examines women's involvement in the traditionally glass-ceilinged

fields of architecture, landscape design, and design criticism and history. With a comprehensive biographical database of women in the field, inventories of works worldwide, and related links.
WEB http://scholar2.lib.vt.edu/spec /iawa/iawa.htm

Interior Design Council Founded in 1970, IDC represents some 200 architects and interior designers. It's an invaluable resource for those listed professionals, providing an interactive Issues Forum (with topics ranging from population density and accompanying design problems to queries on CAD gear). With info on membership in IDC, job openings, and links to related firmsand resources.
WEB http://www.voicenet.com/~idcnl

Islamic and Arabic Arts & Architecture Gilt domes of Shi'i sanctuaries, towering buildings of packed earth, walled cities with mighty gates made of unbaked brick and stone: the thousand-year iconography and traditions of Islamic architecture are powerfully evoked on this page. "Architecture," says one of the authors of this page, "is the solemn identity of peoples and civilizations... the shape and the tone of a society." That might sound a bit dour to Western ears, but Islamic design is inextricably tied to religious belief, which is just one of many subjects explored with academic authority in this eye-opening page.

WEB http://venture.cob.ohio-state.edu:IIII/khalid

Manifesto of Futurist Architecture "The supreme imbecility of modern architecture, perpetuated by the venal complicity of the academies, the internment camps of the intelligentsia, has become in their hands a vacuous stylistic exercise, a jumble of ill-mixed formulae to disguise... the supreme imbecility of modern architecture." And you thought modern architects were opinionated. At least nobody can accuse Antonio Sant'Elia, who wrote the preceding rant in 1914, and his Futurist friends of understatement. This page zeroes in on this radical movement via incredible quasi-fascistic/neo-expressionist imagery, and links to similar Futurist pages and an astonishing Futurist Hate List. Not to be missed.
WEB http://www-personal.washtenaw.cc.mi.us/~ssusnick/futurism/architecture.html

National Building Museum Sometimes it seems America suffers from a cultural inferiority complex regarding its built environment: this page is an effort to redress the problem. Billing itself as "the only institution in the United States dedicated to American achievements in architecture, construction, engineering and design," the NBM offers a comprehensive overview of American achievements in design, while offering keywords that lead you to photo-filled pages focusing on uniquely American structures packed with historical background. Of particular use to the more casual browser are succinctly written pages on everything from gardening to an ongoing discussion about inner city architecture and the NEA to a lecture transcription series. There's also a fun series of do-it-yourself workshops led by professionals teaching skills ranging from faux-finishing to blueprint-reading.
WEB http://206.I.7I.59/program.htm

Perseus Art and Archeology Yale, Harvard, the Rhode Island School of Design, and other

MUSIC'SPACE

WEB http://musicspace.com/musicspace/welcome.html
An utterly unique page dealing with the idea of music, "space," architecture, and the ephemeral overlapping of all three. One could say they're talking about "ambiance," but it gets headier than that. The multi-frame environment supplies many a fascinating and perplexing idea on composing music based on room designs and making art based on music and design. Okay—so it may all seem like a bunch of arty goo-gah, but let yourself float into the abstracted, dark images—the hypnotic nature of this page, inspired by research done at the UCLA Department of Architecture and Urban Design, may just challenge more staid notions of architecture.

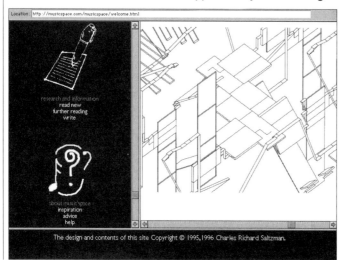

academic havens pooled their talents to create this veritable online encyclopedia covering everything from ancient vases, coins, and other anthropological artifacts, to classical and modern architectural modes. With 13,000 images of coins, vases, sculptures, sites, buildings, and descriptions to match, one can confidently say this covers the associated fields well.
WEB http://www.perseus.tufts.edu/art&arch.html

siteX Out of the McGill School of Architecture Web site comes this absorbing, appropriately spare looking sampling of CAD designs, or as the page phrases it, "places in cyberspace." Neat feature: click on a part of a featured floorplan detail, and find yourself inside that designated room. Very spacey, very hip stuff. Might have made Howard Roark happy; then again, probably not.
WEB http://architecture.mcgill.ca/siteX/homepage.html

The Slammer For Penn Jilette, the taller, talking half of magic and comedy bad-boys, Penn and Teller, even a page on the construction of his house is an exercise in deadpan surrealism. Built on a patch of land somewhere outside Las Vegas, The Slammer looks like just the sort of place to house such a loony loner—it's a small adobe and stone pen in the middle of nowhere. In the detailed floor plans, to go along with the

Netsite: http://sgwww.epfl.ch/BERGER/Jardin/bois-sacre2_english.html

Abandon all hope, ye who enter here
http://sgwww.epfl.ch/BERGER/Jardin/index_english.html

jacuzzi and band rehearsal room, there's also a mention of a dungeon and "secret room" (So that's why Teller is so quiet and obedient on stage). As the page's designer readily admits, "This project is what happens when an eccentric New Yorker builds in the desert."
WEB http://www.sincity.com/house

UNIT 19 Art, architecture and theory meet in this glossy, unique page. Originally a "cyberspatial mirror" gallery installation that closed after a scant two weeks, its designers (from The Bartlett School of Architecture) have installed it on the Web "permanently." Very avant-garde, Unit 19 examines the semiotics of living spaces with questions like "Is the self identity of the creative individual strangled within a physical spatiality informed by rational theory?"

Sounds like Koolhaas territory. But still, a visually arresting, intellectually bracing change of architectural pace.
WEB http://doric.bart.ucl.ac.uk/web/unit19/unit19.html

Landscape architecture

alt.landscape.architecture
Attracting both landscaping amateurs and professionals alike, this is a very chatty group, posting everything from requests for internships to bids for land sales. And who would have thought that landscape design could stir such emotions?—"Aspen... is only really good for making bent wood furniture, smoking fish, and toilet paper," opines one respondent with an apparent chip on the shoulder about *Populus tremuloides*.
USENET alt.landscape.architecture

eLAN Breezy, tropical-hued graphics make this a visual treat. Created by eLAN, a Britain-based education and communication electronic co-op, this site is mainly for the use of emerging landscape artists in Europe (complete with multiple language options, joblinks, and lots of impressive CADs), but also of interest to anyone starting down this path. A good selection of links adds to the page's usefulness.
WEB http://www.netiink.co.uk/users/elan

Enchanted Gardens of the Renaissance This site offers a portal into three Renaissance gardens of Italy: the Sacred Garden of Bomarzo, the Villa Lante Gardens at Bagnaia, and the Villa d'Este gardens in Tivoli. Included with images of the gardens is a philosophical discussion of the gardens' meaning with art works of the period also incorporated into the intellectual matrix. And the explanations are clear, even for those who never took an art history class.
WEB http://sgwww.epfl.ch/BERGER/Jardin/index_english.html

GardenNet: Gardens Online Absolutely everything for the serious landscape designer: an interactive Q&A with "The Ardent Gardener," a guide to notable gardens by type and state (including estimated walk-through time!), and an impressive collection of purchase points for those seeking quality gardening products.
WEB http://www.trine.com/GardenNet/home.htm

Japanese Gardens Database From the delicately beautiful karesangui gardens of Ryoanji, to the sprawling imperial villas of the Shugakuin, Japanese horticultural design has undergone a renaissance in the post-World War II years. Though perhaps overly-ambitious, with many listed topics still undefined, this site still aspires to be the interactive database of the majestic gardens of Japan, supplying an impressive array of Japanese garden history, a sci-

Shoestring Radio Theatre
WEB http://www.shoestring.org

A nonprofit, tax-exempt corporation that produces two weekly, nationally syndicated radio shows, the San Francisco-based Shoestring Radio Theatre's site links fans, supporters, and friends to Shoestring in several ways—through email, through the home pages of the two weekly shows

(*Shoestring Radio Theatre* and *Movie Magazine International*), and through 24-hour, six-days-a-week RealAudio simulcasts. Information about downloading Real Audio players is provided.

entific overview of indigenous plants, and photos of exotic species. You'll even find tips on growing your own traditional garden.
WEB http://dolphin.upenn.edu /~cheetham/jgarden/intro.html

LandNET Though a bit dense and dry in text—but with more graphics and more frequent updates promised soon—this is the official page for the American Society of Landscape Architects and its 12,000 members. Still, if you're here, it's not for flash; it's to check out the latest environmental issues and legislation, cruise through ASLA's joblinks, its bookstore, discussion groups, and other information aids.
WEB http://www.asla.org/asla

Landscape Architecture The link page for the Planning and Architecture Internet Resource Center (PAIRC). 52 topic-related sites listed A-Z, from university research efforts to state ecological resource associations.
WEB http://www.arch.buffalo.edu /pairc/landscape_architecture.html

Landscape—Virtual Library The Centre for Landscape Design Research of the University of Toronto has created this resource in the hope of "collating all existing electronic resources for the landscape architecture professional." Dive into this seemingly bottomless well of professional services and information on degree programs, history, earth sciences,

legislation, and more.
WEB http://www.clr.toronto.edu:1080 /VIRTUALLIB/larch.html

PlantAmerica A charmingly enthusiastic, multi-media resource for horticulture and design information. What it lacks in slickness it makes up for in gorgeous plant photography, product info, and scads of horticultural data. The guy who designed this page owns more than 92,000 plant photos, so he obviously knows his stuff.
WEB http://www.plantamerica.com

Virtual Library: Landscape Architecture Quite often, professional association sites are, shall we say, a bit dull. This page, fortunately, rises above the rest of the crop. In addition to the perfunctory coverage like Jobs, Shop Talk, and Professional Resources, there's a bevy of interesting research institutes to tap, like the Cliff Ecology Research Group, a history section with Archaeological CD-ROMs, an account of the building of Central Park, and a look at such hot plots as the landscape design of Vatican City.
WEB http://www.clr.toronto.edu:1080 /VIRTUALLIB/larch.html

Theatre

The Dramatic Exchange Written a play that you'd like someone to produce? Need a script for a play you want to direct? While the site makes no guarantees about the quality of the works,

it does bring playwrights and producers together for mutual advantage. Plays are organized into categories such as comedies, tragedies, dramas, mysteries, one acts, full-length, musicals, and experimental. Note: files with .SIF attached are summary information files which briefly describe the play and offer information for contacting the playwright.
WEB http://www.dramex.org
URL ftp://ftp.cco.caltech.edu/pub/plays

Gilbert and Sullivan Archive During Gilbert and Sullivan's 25-year collaboration, they produced 14 light operas, many of which, such as *Pirates of Penzance*, are still being performed today. The site offers song scores, librettos, images, reviews of the operas, parodies, and a searchable database of worldwide performances of Gilbert and Sullivan productions.
WEB http://diamond.idbsu.edu/GaS /GaS.html

Headquarters Entertainment Index Designed as a clearinghouse for performing arts information frequently sought by professionals and audiences, this high-concept index is part theater directory, part hiring hall, part backlot, and part tech resource guide. Whether you want to see the resumes of actors and technical workers, find out what's on in New York and London, or get the name of the union for theater and film designers (United Scenic Artists Local 829), you can link to it. The site uses minimal graphics and packs maximum information into its lists of links.

WEB http://www.hqe.com/netlink /net-link.htm#index

Playbill The famous bible of Broadway, *Playbill* has made it online, and with more than a hint of attitude. An emporium of what's what and who's who in the world of Broadway theater, *Playbill* also features an online ticket ordering service, travel and dining packages for after the show, and trivia galore for Broadway fans.

WEB http://www.playbill.com

The Really Useful Theater Company Presents Andrew Lloyd Webber

There are two kinds of people in the world—those who worship Andrew Lloyd Webber and those who don't. This is clearly a page for the former. Webber, the guiding force behind such shows as "Cats", "Phantom of the Opera", and "Sunset Boulevard", is also the wizard behind the Really Useful Theater Company, his corporate manifestation for business and production purposes. That makes the site a public relations outlet, a recruiting ground for non-Webber works the company would like to produce, and a promotional vehicle for similar money-making endeavors.

WEB http://www.reallyuseful.com /index.html

Saturday Review Download an annotated musical theater bibliography from the library, contribute to an ongoing discussion about Michael Crawford's performance in "Phantom of the Opera" on the message board, browse the large collection of theater reviews, or let This Month On Stage satisfy your curiosity about the theater world with its Box Office statistics, reviews, and feature articles.

AMERICA ONLINE *keyword* saturday review

Theatre Central Whether you're dialing up Theatre Central for its postings about auditions and job openings or just want to read the *Journal*, an online

New York City Ballet

WEB http://www.nycballet.com

One of the country's most prominent dance organizations has one of the Web's most gorgeous home pages, but the beautiful graphics take lots of time to load. It's worth it, however, for photos of the company's lead dancers in action. The information is well organized, from the alphabetical

topic index to the program notes on individual ballets. The company's history veers a little far in the direction of hagiography, but this is, after all, the house that Mr. Balanchine built. The site makes available box-office and performance information, previews the upcoming season, and invites the public to subscribe to the New York City Ballet.

monthly magazine that contains discussions of everything from design and directing to acting, Theatre Central is the ticket. The graphics are unobtrusive, the links are nicely grouped, and the general ambiance is all-embracing enough for listing-seeking patrons and job-hunting actors to feel comfortable.
WEB http://www.theatre-central.com

Tower Lyrics Archive Lyrics from the world's most famous musicals, including Andrew Lloyd Webber's "Cats" and "Phantom" Boublil and Schoenberg's "Les Miserables" and "Miss Saigon", Gilbert and Sullivan's "Pirates of Penzance".
WEB http://www.ccs.neu.edu/home/tower/lyrics.html

Dance

alt.arts.ballet Aspiring dancers and avid ballet fans gather in this newsgroup to talk dance. Discussions can be informational (Meagan is looking for a dance school in Dallas), emotional ("I'm so sad that The Joffrey will no longer continue to exist"), and even defensive (in response to the question "What's so interesting about a bunch of men in tights?" Bill wrote, "Friend, the reason for my tights is so that my teacher can see my legs and know whether I'm really projecting like a laser beam and sufficiently crucifying my flesh of this body *qui a soixante six ans*. Try it sometime. If you have a tad of a masochistic streak,

Location: http://www.abt.org/images/jpegs/imperial.jpeg

Christine Dunham in performance of Ballet Imperial with the American Ballet Theater
http://www.abt.org

you're sure to like it").
USENET alt.arts.ballet
WEB http://www.math.ucla.edu/~eijkhout/aab/faq.html
Archives: **URL** ftp://ftp.std.com/customers/nonprofits/dance/ballet-modern
FAQ: **WEB** http://www.math.ucla.edu/~eijkhout/ballet_faq.html

American Ballet Theater Along with dramatic images of classically trained bodies in motion, ABT's site offers tour and schedule information, a company history, intros to the dancers, and thumbnail histories of pieces in the company's repertoire. Whether you're planning to catch a performance at the company's New York City home, or hoping to see a road performance, ABT offers plenty of information in a clearly organized, easy-to-use format.
WEB http://www.abt.org

Calendar of Upcoming Dance Events Around the world or

around the block, there are plenty of choices for dance spectators; this calendar keeps track of most of them, up to four months in advance with information on workshops, performances, musicals, ethnic dances, dance festivals, and the like. Many of these offerings are free to the public. Pick your dance pleasure: acrobatic rock and roll? Ballet Creole? Dogs in Space? It's here, as is an email feature for ordering tickets.
WEB http://www.weblink.com/nyibc/Events/events.html

Contemporary/Modern Dance Companies A link-fest that brings you to sites for dance projects from the Alaska Dance Theater to the Zephyr Dance Ensemble, billed as "Chicago's best all-female modern-dance company." The voluminous listings bring up home pages that combine snippets of reviews with bits of self-description, plus information

about tour dates and performances. Think of it as a national Arts and Leisure section specializing in modern and contemporary dance.
WEB http://users.aol.com/aablisting/modern.htm

Cunningham Dance Foundation
Merce Cunningham is a driving force in modern dance, and the list of people with whom he's worked is a virtual who's who of high culture. You can rummage through his electronic basement of dance information—he has decades of it. Much of the information at this arty, philosophical site is geared toward top-level pros, especially those who can actually make it to his New York City classes. For those not as overwhelmingly enthusiastic about dance, this eclectic fountain tells you about the early computer experiments that took place in the building his dance school occupies.
WEB http://www.merce.org

Dance Ink Glossy and slick, the Dance Ink site combines articles from the archives of Dance Ink with links to many things dance-related. One of the coolest features is a handy search engine of Dance Ink's Web pages. Primo links include such nifty places as an introductory tour of the New York Public Library for the Performing Arts. There's also an appreciation of the late Lincoln Kirstein, and many dance links sorted by category.
WEB http://www.webcom.com/~ink

Dance Links An incredible collection of links to Web sites for dance companies, organizations, university departments, and schools as well as to sites with dance news, discussions, and funding information. Whether it's a site dedicated to the Royal Ballet, an electronic magazine dedicated to dance in New York City, or a homage to belly dancing, there's a link here. Perhaps most helpful are the many links to calendars listing local dance performances (e.g., Dance Theater and Performance in Berlin, Dance in Vancouver, Dance in Halifax, etc.)
WEB http://bohr.physics.purdue.edu/~jswhite/dance_links.html

Dancing on a Line An electronic magazine dedicated to new dance. The 'zine features essays on dance, interviews with performers, reviews of performances, and calendar listings of upcoming events in New York City.
WEB http://www.danceonline.com

English National Ballet While the patron of the English National Ballet is none other than Diana, Princess of Wales, royal watchers won't find any links to Di pages. What ballet lovers will find here is one of the most lush, best laid-out sites for any dance company. Download 80 full-size color photos of the dancers, in mid-jete or pirouette, or follow the company's schedule of performances around the globe. Everything's presented on a lush, royal-blue velvety stage with handsome black-and-white photos as links.
WEB http://www. en-ballet.co.uk

George Balanchine A virtual coffee-table tome sure to delight devotees of the late ballet choreographer. Everything's

Dance on a Line photo gallery
http://www.danceonline.com

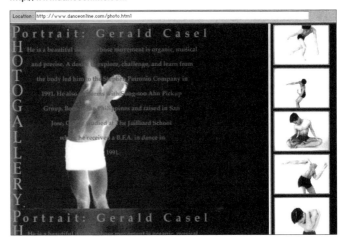

included: a basic bio for all his ballets, accompanying illustrations for each entry, premiere dates, music-score entries, a brief essay on Balanchine, and links to the world's greatest choreographers and the Balanchine Library. It's a remarkable gift for those who can never get enough of the founder of the New York City Ballet.
WEB http://www.ens-lyon.fr/~esouche /danse/Balan.html

Mark Morris Dance Group Ever have the feeling that you're a rat in a maze, and some cruel researcher keeps moving the cheese around simply to frustrate you? The Mark Morris Dance Group has built such a place for culturally elite Web surfers. It has that creepy abandoned feeling, welcoming you with a list of long-gone performances. Clicking on anything takes you back to the starting point.
WEB http://www.emerald.net/cf /output.htm/Mark_Morris_Dance _Group.htm

Martha Graham This site— dedicated to one of the great inventors of modern dance— includes summaries of Martha Graham's biography and resume, and lists (and provide links to sites on) some of her most important works, online dance resources, and reference works.
WEB http://www.ens-lyon.fr/~esouche /danse/Graham.html

Paris Opera Ballet The Paris Opera Ballet is one of the old-

Location: http://www.en-ballet.co.uk/pictures/full/cind1.jpg

"Cinderella": It's tough to ballet in glass slippers
http://www.en-ballet.co.uk

est ballet companies in the world, established in 1661, and, as such, has seen the company of the world's most famous male dancers. Louis XIV, The Sun King, often danced with the company, performing as a nymph, a star, and—you guessed it, the sun. Nureyev was director of the company in 1983. For Francophiles, the home page of the Paris Opera Ballet gives a rundown of this year's dances, profiles of its most famous dancers, and links to a schedule of ballet events in the City of Light.
WEB http://www.ens-lyon.fr/~esouche /danse/POB.html

rec.arts.dance The music's on, and men and women are moving to the beat. In fact, on this newsgroup, they're moving to quite a few beats. Ballroom dancers, line dancers, swing dancers, and slow dancers all

share the group. Fairly active, the group gets questions about where to dance, dancing steps, and dancing competitions, but by far the majority of posts can be filed in the how-do-I-dance-at-the-wedding category.
USENET rec.arts.dance

The Royal Ballet For a basic primer on dance, you could do a lot worse for a starting point. The Royal Ballet site is not too fancy, but it makes up for its sparse graphics by having the real goods on European dance companies—show dates, dancer bios, and general background on virtually every ballet in existence. If you plan on going to the ballet but are a little shaky on the basics, spending a few minutes here first might make your night out a lot more worthwhile.
WEB http://www.ens-lyon.fr/~esouche /danse/Royal.html

College

RESEARCHING AND APPLYING TO COLLEGES ONLINE
LENDS NEW MEANING TO "DESKTOP APPLICATION"

GETTING INTO COLLEGE is never going to be a stroll in the park, but preparation for those four years on a lovely, ivy-draped campus has taken on an aspect of one-stop shopping that didn't even exist a mere three or four years ago. These days, there are online SAT tutorials, guides to the best col-leges, and links to every college on the Net. So whether you use the fee-based services or the free ones, you'll find your modem worth its weight in gold. Now, about those tuition costs... Go to http://www.ypn.com /college to get the latest statistics, test dates, admissions and financial information, and reviews of the Web sites of more than 300 of the country's best colleges and universities.

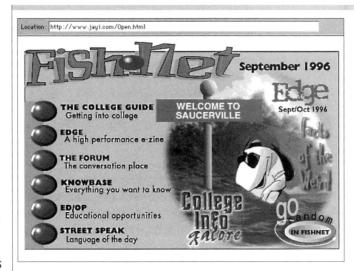

FISHNET
WEB http://www.jayi.com/jayi

In the sea of online college search resources, FishNet is a real catch. Without paying a penny, you can request information from selected schools, build your own profile, seek electronic guidance from an admissions guru, or access an array of articles on the admissions process. FishNet also has its own ezine, *Edge*, with informative, if not quite edgy, content for college-bound high-school students on dorm life, academics, and social concerns.

College search

College and University Home Pages MIT provides access to alphabetical and geographical listings of college and university sites worldwide, with several mirror sites from Austria to Australia available for faster access. An FAQ details how schools come to be included on the list and where to go for information not contained here.
WEB http://www.mit.edu:8001/people/cdemello/univ.html

College Assist Utilize the college database, search functions, college web sites, and helpful tips about the admissions and financial aid processes as a guest or become a member (for $39) and College Assist will personalize the planning process with college matching, a personal organizer, and connections to college admissions offices.
WEB http://www.edworks.com/index.htm

CollegeEdge Even if you have no intention of purchasing the CollegeEdge Software, a trip to this site can be worthwhile. You can tour college home pages, link to financial aid resources, or access tips and information on majors and careers. If the whole college search procedure has got you a little stressed out, take a break at their art gallery, play some games, and laugh at a joke or two.
WEB http://www.collegeedge.com

CollegeNET Your father wants you to go to Sacred Heart; your mother prefers Wellesley; and you want to head south to Mardi Gras and Tulane. Who's going to win? This online database may help you find a school that's right for the whole family. Simply choose the state, a maximum enrollment and maximum tuition, and you'll be rewarded with in-depth profiles on a number of schools. Financial aid info and other academic resources are currently being added.
WEB http://www.collegenet.com

Colleges and Universities Search this database of more than 3,000 entries for links to institutes of higher learning by entering your keywords of choice.
WEB http://www.universities.com

CollegeXpress Register for free at CollegeXpress and you can search for info on private colleges by profile, geographic location, or alphabetically. Run by the Howard Greene Group, this site gets you in the mood for higher education by operating on the backpack system— you cram all the schools you're interested in into your cyber-school bag, and you'll get more information directly from the institutions. Also accessible are articles on the college search ("How About a Women's College?", "Private Colleges: The Significant Advantages"), admissions ("Writing the Essay," "The Application as a Reflection of You"), and finan-

cial aid ("Scholarships You Can Win," "FAFSA Express").
WEB http://www.collegexpress.com

ExPAN College Search The sovereigns of standardized testing are out to help you find the school that best suits you. Using the College Board's ExPAN database of schools, you can search for two- or four-year institutions with specific geographic locations, enrollment sizes, majors offered, admissions or aid policies, student activities, etc. ExPAN will return a list of matching schools with expanded information on enrollment, financial aid, admissions policies, student life, and academic offerings at each institution.
WEB http://www.collegeboard.org/csearch/bin/chOl.cgi

Higher Ed Home Page A hodge-podge of higher education links. If you're willing to wade through the rather long link list, you'll find over 200 sites related somehow to college, from EDUCOM and CollegeNet to Higher Education Gophers and the Syllabus Top 20 Education Sites.
WEB http://128.250.89.9/highered.html

Internet College Exchange Ideally, you'd like to attend a small liberal arts college in the Southwest, and you can spend up to $20,000 per year. Or maybe you'd rather go to a large, public school in the

Midwest for under $10,000? What are your options? Just plug in the pertinent criteria and search a database of college info compiled by the U.S. Department of Education. There's also practical information for parents, students, and guidance counselors—all designed to make the process of choosing a college a little less daunting.
WEB http://www.usmall.com/college

National Liberal Arts Colleges A list of schools fitting the Carnegie Foundation for the Advancement of Teaching's definition of "national liberal arts college." Here, you're a click away from the home pages of hundreds of sources of

a liberal arts education.
WEB http://www.aavc.vassar.edu /libarts.colleges.html

U.S. News College Fair The much-hyped and oft-contested college rankings from *U.S. News and World Report* are now available online. Also included are features from the best-selling perennial, like "Grad School Best Buys," and a series on new cyberjobs. Unique to the College Fair is Ask the Advisor—submit your college queries to the managing editor of the *U.S. News* guides, and he and his team of experts will answer you electronically.
WEB http://www.usnews.com/usnews /fair/home.htm

Worldwide Classroom You don't have to join the Navy to see the world. Worldwide Classroom has amassed an impressive compilation of intercultural and educational programs. These courses, stemming from educational facilities around the globe, include university study, foreign language immersion, adult enrichment programs, internships, volunteer programs, and teen camps. Also on site is a planning guide to make the passage from one country to another a bit easier, with information on everything from dealing with culture shock to money matters to global weather.
WEB http://www.worldwide.edu

THE PRINCETON REVIEW: THE BEST COLLEGES
WEB http://www.review.com/undergr/best_colleges.html
picture: WEB http://www.cc.swarthmore.edu/

The PR's guide to the best 309 colleges in the U.S. What do they mean by the best? Well, yes editors took all the usual statistics, but they also gathered responses from at least 100 students at every college for a behind-the-brochures look at campus life. Here you'll find out: whose professors bring material to life and whose suck all the life out of the material; where things run smoothly and where there is red tape; where students are bookworms, and where students are party hounds. For each school, you'll find quotes from students, quality of life ratings, demographics info, and a list of what's hot and what's not.

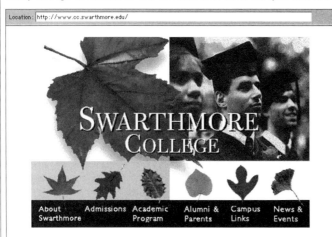

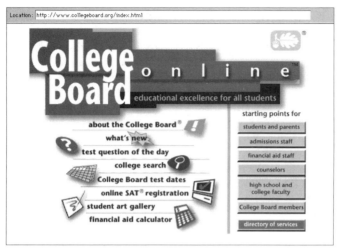

Great, yet another reminder that the SAT awaits you
http://www.collegeboard.org

Testing

The College Board Online (America Online) Like its Internet counterpart, America Online's College Board service allows students to register for the SAT. The Ask the College Board section invites specific testing and college-related questions.
AMERICA ONLINE *keyword* student center - 〈college and beyond 〉- college board online

The College Board Online Home Page No, this isn't a clever trap, nor does entrance to the site require knowledge of 1950s television trivia; the enemy really has rolled out the red carpet for its impending torture victims. The College Board Home Page welcomes high and middle schoolers with open arms in a vain attempt to curry favor with those for whom their very name is anathema. The sentiment is

appreciated, but there are no secrets to be learned here; no cheat sheets or recipes for a Ritalin cocktail. However, along with the public relations gloss, visitors to the College Board Home Page can do the following: register for the SAT online, access test dates, and even try their hand at the Test Question of the Day. There is also specific information on Advanced Placement Exams and the PSAT.
WEB http://www.collegeboard.org

Kaplan The Kaplan Web site is almost daunting in scope, offering a wide range of services, including the opportunity to take a sample SAT or GRE online, free of charge. Kaplan's services don't end with test preparation, however. The College Simulator invites postmatriculators to tour a virtual campus and face day-to-day scenarios, while the Hot

Seat simulates a nerve-racking job interview. A new package, SAT RoadTrip Multimedia, promises to prepare students for the test via an in-depth software package. The cost: $30.
WEB http://www.kaplan.com

One-on-One with the S.A.T. In yet another desperate move to negate the influence of those costly SAT classes, the College Board has designed its own brand of online SAT preparation software. And, of course, they do have one very real claim to fame: One-on-One "is the only program with hundreds of real SAT questions." This may seem akin to accepting aspirin from a flu bug, but there is something to be said for test vérité. The program features an advisor from the hallowed halls of the College Board, who promises to guide students through the painful process. The program requires an IBM-compatible personal computer and costs $49.
WEB http://www.collegeboard.org/library/html/oneonone.html

The Princeton Review Its name a nod to ETS territory, the Princeton Review debunks the SAT mystique through utter mockery of its writers, Jim and Pam, and all they represent. Process of elimination techniques focus on wiping out the worst answers rather than finding the best ones. A character named "Joe Bloggs" teaches students how to avoid falling into pitfalls designed

for average-scoring students. The company's Web site includes information on courses, books and software for the anxious college hopefuls.
WEB http://www.review.com

The Princeton Review Online (America Online) Learn about the course, browse the message boards, or shop till you drop at the Princeton Review store. The company's America Online presence does not differ substantially from that of its Internet Web site.
AMERICA ONLINE *keyword* Princeton

Applying

Academic Counseling Services, Inc. The staff of ACS claims to be able to "fit students' strengths, weaknesses, needs, interests, and financial resources to appropriate college opportunities... in a careful, organized manner while understanding the importance of this decision in relation to personal satisfaction and career development." Nowhere in the site does ACS publicize the price of its professional help, but if you're truly interested in finding out more, you can fill out their email information request form.
WEB http://www2.interaccess.com /nichenet/acs

Be Real, Get In Applying to college makes most students feel like nothing more than a nameless, faceless, bunch of numbers and statistics. SATs, GPA, AP Tests, class rank... This

---

THE POT CALLS THE KETTLE BLACK

If there was an award for the "worst inter-sororital campus" it would be mine. My sorority is relatively new on campus and we have received no help from other greeks. We are a very old and well-established name in the greek world, but we have received nothing but insults for being "new." Is a sorority bad for expanding? Does that mean that when they get a chapter at Harvard, Stanford, Cornell, or Northwestern that my sorority is supposed to bad mouth them and not welcome them to the campus? Also, during rush, this one sorority is infamous for promising bids and threatening to cancel them if the girl looks at any other houses. They also tell the rushees that the other houses and I quote "suck." Why is this house still operating on our campus without punishment? That is a good question. I think they should have been suspended for at least one rush. I also think that sororities should have more mixers and philanthropy functions together. After all, we don't exist for the fraternities. Does it really matter who is doing what with which fraternity? One fraternity has forbidden us to step foot in their house because we are "new," even though we were practically in Canada by the time they were founded. If I sound bitter, yes, I am. The bottom line is that you should respect another person's choice. What should have been a good experience for me because I made a good choice, was ruined by ignorant greeks who don't know how the system should work.

—from alt.college.sororities

---

article has much to say about just being yourself and gives advice about presenting the true you to colleges, who often do make admissions decisions entirely subjectively. It's written by a true authority—an admissions official who estimates he has read 150,000 applications by *real* people just like you. Believe it or not, in ten years no one will care what your verbal scores were.
WEB http://www.jayi.com/ACG/articles /Be_Real.html

Cambridge Essay Service Did cranking out that first draft make you long for a cool breeze? Welcome to Cambridge Essay Service. They're editors. They will help you find your voice so that the person you present to that admissions staff is the best possible you. Check out the seven tips for writing an essay and the free evaluation offer for your first draft.
WEB http://world.std.com/~edit

CollegeLink Avoid college application induced writer's cramp or carpal tunnel syndrome and download the free CollegeLink software. You can apply to as

many colleges as you wish while entering your vital stats only once, and each application is customized to fit the institution's requirements. Although the software and first application are on the house, it's $5 for each additional school. But the convenience may be worth the cost. Check and see if your colleges of choice are on the list of hundreds of schools that accept applications using CollegeLink. The current list of participants includes colleges from Adelphi to Xavier, with several lowering or waiving their fees for CollegeLink applicants.
WEB http://www.collegelink.com

Dear Admissions Guru "There is a rumor going around my school that if you get accepted to Yale you won't get accepted to Harvard and vice versa. Is it true that these two schools share admissions information?" One desperate student asks the Admissions Guru (actually several senior admissions officers.) Admissions Guru responds: "No way." Anyone with a specific question or problem regarding the admissions process should read here, and if the question's not already answered, ask away.
WEB http://www.jayi.com/jayi/ACG /ques.html

Electronic Common Application Do any of the schools you're applying to accept the Common Application? Many probably do. Wesleyan University

provides an electronic, downloadable version of the application here for Macintosh, DOS, or Windows.
WEB http://www.admiss.wesleyan.edu /ecommon.html

soc.college.admissions Learn what's more important—good grades, good standardized test scores, a good essay, or a long list of extracurriculars. And find out how many AP exams you should take. The helpful advice just keeps coming and, amazingly enough, there are plenty of people around who stop by just to offer helpful tidbits of wisdom. Just remember—no matter how much you learn, there's still plenty of work to do offline; in the words of one message writer, "The colleges certainly aren't going to read a stupid newsgroup to find good students!"
USENET soc.college.admissions

Undergraduate Admissions E-Apps* Plenty of schools have online applications, IF you can find them in the maze of the college's Web site. E-Apps* makes it easy. At this site, find the college in the alphabetical

❝ Do you really get a 4.0 if your roomate dies during the term? ❞

list, and click on the appropriate icon to go straight to that school's email application. Plus, visit the college's home page, downloadable application, printable application, and tuition information. Very helpful stuff, huh? Yes, except that the number of colleges is pretty small, although that's bound to change.
WEB http://www.eapp.com/UNIV /UGLIST.HTM

US News CollegeFair Forum Why do they call it a Personal Statement, anyway? (By the time you're done with it, it sounds pretty stilted and impersonal!) Should you write one of those "human interest," cute essays, or a more serious essay which conveys your intent to save the world? The folks in this forum have a lot to ask about the most dreaded part of the college application. Fortunately, there are experts here to answer the questions.
AMERICA ONLINE *keyword* college→ College Search→US News CollegeFair Forum→Browse Messages→College Essay

Student life

alt.college.food Some college students post recipes here, others are looking to meet people, and others still are hocking vitamins, or trying to get students to work on their pyramid scheme. But, quickie recipes abound, so if you need to whip together a tuna casserole, and perhaps meet a fellow coed from around the globe, you

may want to check in.
USENET alt.college.food

alt.college.fraternities In addition to old-boy greetings and meetings, this newsgroup hosts debates on the instutition itself. Hazing, the single-sex policy, and date rape are consistently hot topics up for discussion and division.
USENET alt.college.fraternities

alt.college.sororities Less controversial than the fraternities newsgroup, the distaff half of the Greek newsgroups usually consists of friendly contact between "sisters"—both present students and alums.
USENET alt.college.sororities

alt.flame.roommate Practical and serious discussions are not the rule. While this newsgroup does occasionally address such real problems as the Roommate Who Will Not Pay Her Share, the Roommate Who Will Not Clean the Bathroom, and the Roommate Who Will Not Spend One Second Without Her Annoying Boyfriend Rick, many of the postings are consumed by hollow rage, filled with the sort of baseless griping that any student knows all too well. Still, roommate bashing is an unavoidable part of college life, and all members of the college set should know about this electronic opportunity to mock your bunkmate mercilessly.
USENET alt.flame.roommate

alt.folklore.college Do you really get a 4.0 if your roommate dies during the term? For answers to this and other myths of college life, just dive into this newsgroup. In addition to charting past folklore, the group invites participants to contribute new experiences to the annals of college folklore. Some of them are so extreme (sex in a carillon tower that drowned out the bells) that they sound like lies, but that's the beauty of the Net: epistemologically bankrupt, it makes every story an equal.
USENET alt.folklore.college

Campus Newspapers on the Net
The University of Tennessee's *Daily Beacon* shines its searchlight on more than 100 college papers that are online, from *The Hustler* at Vanderbilt University to *OSI-Zeitung* at the Free University of Berlin. Cyberpapers are sorted by frequency of circulation.

NCAA
WEB http://www.ncaa.org

The National Collegiate Athletics Association page is the place to start for anything and everything to do with college sports. Its coverage spans the sports spectrum with a seemingly endless battery of statistics, current records, and championship information. Of particular interest to the high

school student is the College Bound section, which details eligibililty requirements for Division I and II schools, and features an FAQ on recruiting, advice on how to approach schools, and a suggested list of questions to ask coaches. Sports covered include football, soccer, baseball, softball, hockey, and more.

WEB http://beacon-www.asa.utk.edu
/resources/papers.html

Campus Voice The Serious section at Campus Voice is particularly good for collegiates. One wouldn't think that it was possible to write an article on choosing a major without sounding patronizing, but it has been done here. Plus, the feature on cool professors is really interesting. The Culture Vulture section has links to entertainment mags, Lollapalooza, the ultra kitschy *Hollywood and Vine*, and other au courant sites.
WEB http://www.campusvoice.com

The Link Digital Campus Are colleges still hotbeds of radicalism and sexual experimentation? This site gives you a window on life in the ivy-covered world. Hit the news briefs link for updates on fraternity hazings and affirmative-action sit-ins on campus. Or head to the news map and link to hundreds of college newspapers nationwide—for example, the *Missouri Miner*, the *Yale Daily News*, and the *Daily Texan*. Talk to college students from all over the country about date rape or financial aid at the site's bulletin board—or just hang back and discuss music in the Pub.
WEB http://www.linkmag.com

The Main Quad The Main Quad is not some "corporate fajita." It is not an ezine either. The Main Quad is an "environment," and in its charter it

Jazz up your social life with a little help from your Campus Voice friends
http://www.campusvoice.com

stresses that it hopes to bring students together to start companies, meet, and be political. They have a Dean's List page of links that address hip issues without insulting one's intelligence, an excellent collegiate media newswire. There is an on-site emphasis on using the Net for job searches.
WEB http://www.mainquad.com

soc.college There are always hundreds of messages on this newsgroup devoted to "the fine art of procrastination" and other weighty college issues. Despite the slacker veneer, this newsgroup is also useful for guerrilla research: just ask questions about a particular school of your choice and then lurk in the shadows, listening to the opinions of students who know the answers. Between their alternately jaded and naive insights and the glossy, misleading college brochure you've received in the mail, you may actually start to

get a clearer picture of the place. The group's FAQ is a how-to guide to finding student's email addresses.
USENET soc.college
FAQ: URL ftp://rtfm.mit.edu/pub
/usenet-by-group/soc.college

t@p College Sports How's the women's lacrosse team doing at your university? Here are links to countless pages of baseball, gymnastics, hockey, swimming, soccer, track and field, wrestling, Ultimate Frisbee—you get the idea—college sports clubs and organizations nationwide. There's plenty of stuff to keep you fit: lists of college sports events, team standings, championship predictions, and a viewpoint column. If that's not enough, lose yourself in the wonders of the Division I Collegiate Volleyball Update, or the remarkable section devoted to Australian Rules football.
WEB http://www.taponline.com/tap
/csports.html

PART 8
Identity & Society

Identity & Society

CLICK PICKS
The very best on the Net

Religion

SAINTS, IMMORTALS, GURUS, LAMAS, MASTERS, AND DISCIPLES ALIKE CAN FIND THEIR WAY ONLINE

So THINGS HAVEN'T BEEN GOING too well of late. You're beginning to doubt if your luck will ever change. Even Job didn't have it this bad. Or did he? Why not do a comparison to see how far one can push the limits of faith? Go to the Bible Gateway, plug "Job" into the appropriate search form, and you'll get every single passage in the Holy Bible describing the trials and tribulations of the unlucky man. Make a pilgrimage to the CyberMuslim Information Collective for the latest news from the world of Islam. Where to find the world's best matzoh—inquire within! What other all-inclusive library of links can give you the name, address, and phone number of every Zen Center in the world, allow you to browse through elaborate archives of koans and sutras, study the electronic Bhagavad-Gita, and "Do-nothing" with Taoist sages Lao-tzu and Chuang-tzu on the eternal I-Way?

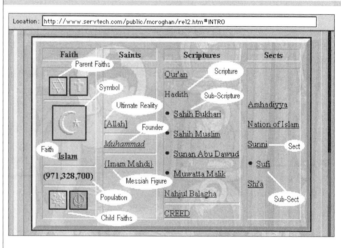

MIKE'S RELIGION PAGE

WEB http://www.servtech.com/public/mcroghan /religion.htm

As open-minded as a Unitarian meeting house, Mike's Religion Page attempts to list, discuss, and categorize the world's religions, with all due respect to local beliefs and practices. Mike— yes, there is a Mike behind the page—invites fellow seekers to send him their spiritual musings for online publication, and he lists lots of links to everything from the Egyptian Book of the Dead to a pagan 'zine. Mike organizes everything into a fabulous table of religions from Adidam to Zorarastrianism with their respective Saints, Scriptures, and Sects. The only drawback to this religious smorgasbord is that is takes a devil of a time to load.

Starting points

APS Research Guide What the APS Research Guide lacks in prettiness it makes up for in serious, high-grade theological resources, ranging from the texts of Archbishop Desmond Tutu to bibliographical listings of papyrus manuscripts and academic e-journals. Just reading the list of links is an educational experience.
WEB http://www.utoronto.ca/stmikes /theobook.htm

Comparative Religion Big-time intellectuals and fairly serious religious scholars will find links, links, and more links here—to libraries, academies, sites discussing women and religion, sites chronicling the history of art and religion, and much, much more. If your idea of a heavy religious question is asking if God can make a rock so big that even He can't lift it, the stuff here is probably a little bit over your head.
WEB http://weber.u.washington.edu /~madin

Facets of Religion Opening with pretty iconic links to eight of the world's most populous religions (listed in order of the faith's longevity), Facets of Religion is that rare site: elegant and efficient, well designed, and quick to load. Think of the content as an online survey course in faiths of the world, and you're on the right track.
WEB http://sunfly.ub.uni-freiburg.de /religion

The Monk Page From info about St. Benedict's beer to Monty Python links, this collection of monk esoterica and various other stuff reflects the interests of its compiler, who writes in his official disclaimer that he claims no authority, just a pronounced interest in various subjects and the need to post the fruits of his research in cyberspace. And we are all the better for it—especially since Russell's taken to posting where monk wannabes can find a retreat from modern life.
WEB http://www.efn.org/~russelln

Ontario Centre for Religious Tolerance An excellent place to begin your spiritual journey on the Net. The site focuses not only on religious tolerance and freedom, but also on religious abuse, intolerance, and issues relating to religious tolerance (e.g., school prayer). Documents written by the center provide extensive analyses of religions and their views on various controversial issues and a religious news section tracks political pronouncements and Papal bulls. Don't miss the indispensable glossary of religious terms.
WEB http://www.kosone.com/people /ocrt/ocrt_hp.htm

Religion Forget the prayer over wine for Passover? Need a new ritual for Beltane (the Wiccan Spring Rite)? Want to brush up on your liturgy skills? No matter your faith, from Islamic to Baptist to Hindu and back, it's all here in lively BBS

forums, ZIP downloads, and even chosen chapters from an online Bible.
MSN *keyword* religion

Wiretap Library It's like a library, only the texts are electronic. The big religious texts like the Book of Mormon, the Qur'an, and the Bible are organized by faith.
URL gopher://wiretap.spies.com/ll /Library/Religion

Religion & politics

American Family Association, Inc. The American Family Association, Inc. claims to have been founded "for people who are tired of cursing the darkness and who are ready to light a candle." That darkness is societal elements, particularly the media, which the AFA feels assault their Christian values. Go to their Web representative to keep track of the AFA's various candles—like their Boycott Box of companies that promote pornography and homosexuality, or their Dirty Dozen list of "the top 12 sponsors of prime-time filth." Whether you support the AFA's campaigns or not, this is essential reading for anyone interested in how religion can clash with a democratic culture.
WEB http://www.gocin.com/afa/home .htm

Christian Coalition As one of the most well-organized and influential political entities in the nation, the Christian Coalition fully understands the impor-

tance of getting the word out to their supporters. While their Internet site may not be much to look at, interested visitors will find information about membership, training seminars, speeches, press releases, and excerpts from the Coalition's monthly magazine, *The Christian American*. Their most intriguing feature is the Congressional Scorecard, a meticulous tracking of how each state's Senators and Congressmen have voted on issues concerning the Coalition's "pro-family agenda."
WEB http://cc.org

The Talk.Origins Archive It's creationism vs. non-creationism, Buchananites vs. Darwinists. This newsgroup discusses issues related to biological and physical origins, i.e., evolution, creation, biogenesis, catastrophism, cosmology, and theology. Not sure what the argument is all about? Read the FAQ section and when you're ready there's a handy set of guidelines to help facilitate intelligent, thoughtful interaction. Search previously posted questions (scientific evidence that what was thought to be Noah's Ark really isn't). If you find your interest peaked, many sources are listed.
WEB http://earth.ics.uci.edu:8080

Bible studies

The Bible: God's Word, Wholly Inspired and Infallible A phenomenal and fully developed experience of biblical proportions. This resource for bible study and appreciation includes a dictionary of terms and references specifically geared to the King James Version (along with ample analysis), and individual research and discussion sections on the Kingdom and Jesus Christ. A beautiful Bible library for the gospel-literati.
WEB http://users.aol.com/bible2007/index.html

World Wide Study Bible An excellent resource for Bible study online with access to books of the Bible, different translations, and commentary. For some sections there are also bibliographies and pictures.
WEB http://ccel.wheaton.edu/wwsb

The WWW Bible Gateway Not only can you search the Bible

FINDING GOD IN CYBERSPACE
WEB http://users.ox.ac.uk/~mikef/durham/gresham.html
picture: WEB http://users.ox.ac.uk/~mikef/durham/gresham.html
Sometimes the title is the best part of a site. In the case of this British page, though, the content lives up to the name. Need Web pages? Journals? Gophers? Electronic conferences hosted by notable theologians and scholars? They're all just a click away; before you know it, you'll be off to the Islamic Resources Gopher, the library catalog of the Jewish Theological Seminary of America, or the Guide to Early Church Documents, and on your way to being a true believer.

Location: http://www.isomedia.com/homes/geekboy/

for specific words in specific passages and display the corresponding verses, but you can do it in English, German, Swedish, Latin, French, Spanish, and Tagalog. Now you can also perform topic searches on the Bible—what exactly does the good book say about sex— the answer's just a click away. **WEB** http://www.gospelcom.net/bible

Atheism

Atheist Contacts Around the World Open up this world atheism atlas and surf your way around the metaphysical globe. Of course, you could also just use the list to find other atheists from Argentina to the USA at the speed of scroll bar. Don't expect too much in the way of substantive philosophizing here, however—it's just a fancy email address book for individual atheists (no organizations). Still, the live links to addresses all across the world make it easy to find someone to talk to if atheism's your bag, and you can post yours so you might get some meaningful mail once in a while. **WEB** http://www.sdsmt.edu/caa-bin /contact

Joel's Atheism Page It's easy to say that you don't believe in atheism, but the proof that it exists is on Joel's Atheism Page, where the links explore the rejection of traditional religion through an FAQ, discussion groups and clubs, and personal testimonials. If there is in fact a God, He has not yet

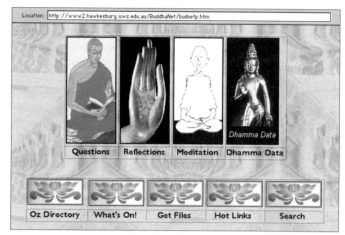

Location: http://www2.hawkesbury.uws.edu.au/BuddhaNet/budnetp.htm

Questions   Reflections   Meditation   Dhamma Data

Oz Directory   What's On!   Get Files   Hot Links   Search

Open your chakras to BuddaNet options
http://www2.hawkesbury.uws.edu.au/BuddhaNet/budnetp.htm

chosen to prove it by upgrading the graphics on the page. **WEB** http://www.public.iastate.edu /~elcid/atheism.html

Man is Man Made One U.K. contribution to the primarily American presence of atheists on the Web—with the desire to form some cohesive community contact a la theist religious groups. Visit, share, and discuss beliefs and issues of existence. Check into the live talk area—the participants are seriously deep, and take on such topics as the scientific analysis of New Testament literature, science as the basis for belief systems, and what, if anything, our religions might share with those of "people" from other solar systems. There is a lighter side in the page of celebrity atheists, which features quotes from non-believers like Woody Allen and Stanley Kubrick. **WEB** http://www.csv.warwick.ac.uk /~mauie/manmade

The Secular Web Itching to rally with other non-believers? Eager to meet other Net-savvy atheists, agnostics, and apathetics? Can't wait to read criticism, debates, and feature articles, including the ever-popular "Sixteen Reasons Why God Never Received Tenure at a University"? The Secular Web is nothing less than the Holy Grail of free thought with links to sites netwide. Plus who wouldn't want to hang out with a group that calls themselves The Internet Infidels? **WEB** http://freethought.tamu.edu

Baha'ism

The Baha'i Faith WWW Page In addition to general information about the Baha'i faith and some assorted links, this site offers the *Baha'is Magazine*, an online magazine that approaches the Baha'i faith. Explore a number of critical articles such as "Women:

Unambiguous Equality," "Heaven and Hell: A Baha'i View of Life After Death," "How Many Baha'is Are There?" and "The Persecution of Baha'is in Iran."
WEB http://oneworld.wa.com/bahai /index.html

Rob Hain's Baha'i Page In 1863 the Baha'u'llah declared himself the Messenger of God. More than a century later, believers around the world are still spreading his message of universal peace and the oneness of God. A devout follower himself, Rob Hain has created a series of visually striking and thankfully non-proselytizing pages to spread the teachings of Baha'i while offering links to other acolytes. Learn about the creation of this faith, read some of its prayers, and consider its spiritual and philosophic fundamentals. "Everyone should discover Baha'u'llah for themselves," the lessons assert, and here is a relaxing way to explore the faith.
WEB http://www.calligrafix.co.uk /RobHain

Buddhism

alt.religion.buddhism.nichiren A newbie wants to know the difference between the various schools of Buddhism; someone with a scanner is in search of software that will recognize Tibetan. Elsewhere, there's a discussion going on about the politics of the Soka Gakkai. Both this newsgroup and alt.religion.buddhism.tibetan will put you in touch with others who want to discuss the many aspects of Buddhism.
USENET alt.religion.buddhism.nichiren

alt.religion.buddhism.tibetan Newcomers to Buddhism will be lost among the questioners, teachers, and multiple interpretations in this very serious newsgroup. But if you're willing to be enlightened cyber-Bodhisattvas abound, with informed postings and intelligent discussion that should get you up to speed in no time.

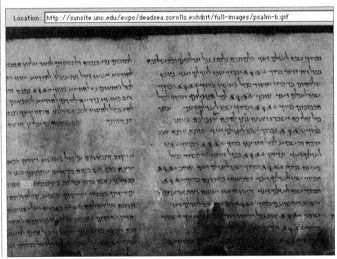

AFTFL Project: Bibles
WEB http://humanities.uchicago.edu/homes/BIBLES.html
picture: WEB http://sunsite.unc.edu/expo/deadsea.scrolls.exhibit/intro.html
Scholars, stop here. Saints, keep browsing. **AFTFL** is a University of Chicago linguistics project. The purpose of this collection of Bibles in different languages is to present the Good Book as one of the most translated and interpreted books in human history, rather than as a religious reference.

Location: http://sunsite.unc.edu/expo/deadsea.scrolls.exhibit/full-images/psalm-b.gif

The builders of these bibles (so far, **KJV** English, French, German, and Latin are available) neither espouse nor catalog online theology of any kind, but, using the canonical referencing system built into the book, have built a tremendous search engine which should make researching "the Bible as literature" a snap.

Get advice on how to choose a personal guru, discuss rebirth, read up on the recent activities of the Dalai Lama, and find dharma centers in Paris.
USENET alt.religion.buddhism.tibetan

BuddhaNet Put Buddhism on the Net, and voilá, it's BuddhaNet. Check out the answers to commonly asked questions about Buddhism and Buddhist teachings, learn about Buddhist meditation, or link to other Buddhist sites. Since BuddhaNet is "Australia's Buddhist Communications Link," Buddhist organizations and meditation practice groups across Australia are just a kangaroo hop away. And BuddhaNet also contains information about BuddhaNet BBS, a network of bulletin board systems.
WEB http://www2.hawkesbury.uws .edu.au/BuddhaNet/budnetp.htm

Daily Zen Sutras You'll find everything but the *Tao of Pooh* here. This site provides the text and translations for approximately two dozen Zen sutras, from the Vandana ("I venerate the Sacred One, the Great Sage, the Truly Enlightened One") to the last lines of the Shodoka ("The carriage of the elephant moves like a mountain/How can the mantis block the road?").
WEB http://coombs.anu.edu.au /WWWVLPages/BuddhPages /Daily-Zen-Sutras.html

Gyuto Tantric Choir It's a feast for the senses: Let your eyes

take in the color photo of this choir of Buddhist monks from Tibet while samples of their music bathe your ears. The music, as well as some recordings of various speakers' discussions of the choir, are encoded in aiff format. General information about the choir, including its performance schedule is also available.
WEB http://www.well.com/user/gyuto

NCF Buddhism Home Page Be kind to yourself: Find out how by reading about kindness meditation practice at this Ottawa-based Web site. Kindness meditation is just one of the exercises described here; the page even includes a set of graphics showing proper meditating positions. Also accessible at this site are an introduction to the Theravada tradition of Buddhism (especially useful are hypertext definitions), a set of photographs of Buddhist leaders, and a directory of Buddhist groups in Canada.
WEB http://www.ncf.carleton.ca /freenet/rootdir/menus/sigs/religion /buddhism/introduction/home.html

Shin Buddhist Resource Center Translations of Shin Buddhist texts and essays relating to Shin Buddhism, as well as the newsletter of the Shin Buddhist Resource Center, and links to other Buddhist resources online are available at this site.
WEB http://www.well.com/user /shinshu/SBRC

Zen Buddhism FAQ "Why do Zen writings seem like nonsense?"

The answer has something to do with the slavery of normal thought, ego pain, and rigid linear discursivity (the clinical term for "square"). Other questions answered in this document include "What is Zen?" and "What is meditation?"
URL ftp://coombs.anu.edu.au /coombspapers/otherarchives /electronic-buddhist-archives /buddhism-zen/information/zen-faq.txt

Catholicism

AlaPadre's Catholic Corner This page offers advice and information for Catholics seeking links to other Catholics, as well as for recent converts to Catholicism who want to make an online connection. This site features its own built-in search function. There's also a kiddie section and some helpful hints for clueless Internet newbies.
WEB http://www.wsnet.com/~alapadre

Catholic Apparitions of Jesus and Mary Paris, France and Phoenix, Ariz. are just two of the places where apparitions of Jesus and/or Mary have been recorded, according to this Web site. The site lists apparitions from 1347 to the present; a handful are linked to documents describing the full circumstances of the apparitions.
WEB http://web.frontier.net /Apparitions/apparitions.html

Catholic.Net Opening with a graphics-heavy image of the crucified Christ and links to Catholic media, Catholic teachings, and a Pro-Life

Directory, Catholic.Net is a suitable entry point for people wishing to immerse themselves in all things Catholic. There's a lot of stuff out there, and this page indexes much of it.
WEB http://www.catholic.net

Catholic Online Forum Returning Catholics, the Youth Ministry, apologetics, the Knights of Columbus, and women are just a few of the Catholic groups with their own discussion topics and libraries in this hyper-active forum. While these groups provoke a steady stream of discussion, the pro-life, prayer, doctrine, liturgy, and general discussion topics dominate the forum's activity.

Debates on the message board can erupt over controversial Creeds, the Pope's political agenda, and a priest's advice to a Protestant woman marrying into the Church. Catholics also turn to the forum for support with home schooling, Bible trivia, and religious affirmation. In the libraries, members can download the full text of Pope John Paul's open letter to the women of the world, articles on celibacy, hints on how to deal with anger, hymns and homilies, Noah's Ark clip art, the Catholic Digest, and more. Everything Catholics need to get from Sunday to Sunday.
COMPUSERVE *go* catholic

The Holy See: Vatican Web Site
This official online site for the Catholic Church offers news and views on religious questions of the day. The site features the Pope looking, well, Pope-ish. Due to the Church's multinational status, News from the Holy See is available in several languages, including Spanish, German, French, Italian, Dutch, and Portuguese.
WEB http://www.vatican.va

The Mary Page The Blessed Virgin Mary is not only the most important female in the Christian faith but also one of the most popular figures in Western art. With grace and style, the Marianists at the Univer-

Buddhist Studies WWW Library

WEB http://coombs.anu.edu.au/WWWVL-Buddhism.html
picture: WEB http://www.cs.uidaho.edu/~marc9442/buddha.html

Brew a nice, hot pot of tea and find enlightenment at this meditative site. What is the sound of one hand clapping? Maybe this is where to find the answer and also learn about other koans. Bust out your Boddhisattvas and try the online research guide or track down thatancient translation. The

library covers everything from early Buddhism to Zen Buddhism including Chinese, Korean, Western, Tendai, and Theravada. Tired of those other Buddhist sites that have you meditating until you saw off both arms and legs? Well, maybe it is time to enter one of the chat rooms or network with other resources and databases.

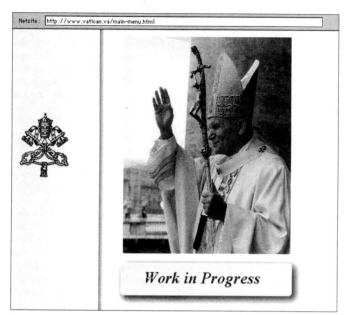

Netsite: http://www.vatican.va/main-menu.html

Work in Progress

His work is never done
http://www.vatican.va

Shroud of Turin Home Page "For believers no amount of proof is necessary. For non-believers, no amount of proof is sufficient." If you're still on the fence, though, how about reading the information about the Shroud of Turin provided at this site? The alleged history of the Shroud is given, along with information about research being done to determine the Shroud's authenticity.
WEB http://www.cais.net/npacheco /shroud/turin.html

Christian Science

Christian Science on the Web You'll find a rather helpful search-engine system on all things Church of Christ, Scientist. Unlike the keyword searches you're probably accustomed to, this one is set up by topic in alphabetical sequence. It's actually a bit slower if you know exactly what you're looking for, but it's still interesting for browsers who want to learn more about the religion, its history, and its practitioners.
WEB http://www.ultrasite.com/csindex

The Church of Christ, Scientist The Church of Christ, Scientist makes use of QuickTime VR technology on its well-designed, eye-pleasing home page. You'll be able to visit the First Church of Christ, Scientist in Boston, access an FAQ board on the religion, link to several newspapers, including The Christian Science Monitor, and learn more about the church's founder, Mary Baker

sity of Dayton have assembled an impressive Web site to celebrate and study Mary. Visitors can browse through prayers, view the history of Mary in art, and peruse the Marianists' course catalog of Mary studies. There's even an FAQ section, covering a broad range of topics, from discussions of her impact on the Catholic faith to the reasons for her frequent depiction in light-blue garb.
WEB http://www.udayton.edu/mary

Partenia So, you're a French bishop who has irked the Vatican with your public pronunciations on the state of the country's homeless. And despite repeated admonitions from *Il Papa* himself, you continue mouthing off. Be careful, or you may be conveniently assigned

to another post—in this case, Partenia. (Partenia doesn't exist on any map of France, or even Europe. It's known as a titular see and hasn't existed since about the sixth century.) So, what do you do? If you're Bishop Jacques Gaillot you transform that rather uninspiring Partenia posting into the world's first virtual diocese. Although virtual sacraments are still not available, the bishop's monthly letters serve as online homilies. Gaillot also answers questions from his parishioners, in all their infinite numbers. This Web site also has links to good works organizations around the world, as well as to other religious, non-Catholic sites. Notre Dame was never like this.
WEB http://www.partenia.fr

Eddy. Did you know she's the only American woman to ever found a worldwide religion?
WEB http://www.tfccs.com

Cyberreligions

First Church of Cyberspace
Although the First Church of Cyberspace has an affiliation with the Central Presbyterian Church of Montclair, New Jersey, this site does not function as the home page for a church; rather, this site is the church. The sanctuary contains text versions of sermons written expressly for this cyberaudience; the gallery links churchgoers to religious artwork across the Web (including the Sistine Chapel). The library also links you to

other Christian sites on the Web. Web surfers are encouraged to join the congregation and email their responses and thoughts.
WEB http://execpc.com/~chender

Evangelical

Christian Broadcasting Network (700 Club) Every day approximately one million Americans watch programming produced by Pat Robertson's TV ministry, the Christian Broadcast Network. Now CBN watchers can continue their spiritual viewing on the computer screen, with links to a monthly program guide, online scripture, and transcriptions of CBN's news and information program *Newswatch*. You can

also email questions that Pat might answer on the air, and anyone interested in Bible studies will want to peruse the "700 Scripture References" that cite key passages for everything from Afflictions to Wisdom.
WEB http://the700club.org

Gospel Communications Network
Something of a clearinghouse for Christian ministries of various denominations, this easy-to-use, quick-loading resource encompasses interests ranging from the Children's Bible Hour programs and Gospel Films, Inc., to the InterVarsity Christian Fellowship, Youth for Christ, and various evangelistic resources.
WEB http://www.gospelcom.net

 THE GREAT GOD CONTEST
WEB http://www.islandnet.com/~luree/contest.html

Jihads getting you down? Tired of those same old my-God's-better-than-your-God arguments? Enter your God (or a proxy deity) in this (holy) mother of all contests, and settle religious acrimo-

ny for all time. Entrants must impregnate virgins, raise corpses, and choose between feeding a multitude or healing the sick; meanwhile, you (the sponsor) won't get bored waiting for God to step up to the plate if you visit the ample section on things to do while waiting for God. Truly tasteless. Certainly blasphemous. And totally hilarious.

I'LL TAKE OPTION 8, PLEASE

The Religious Tolerance Test

Suppose that a person of another faith has moved in next to your house or apartment. Some of your options are to approach your neighbor and...

Option 1: Ask them to describe their religion to you; offer to describe yours to them, if they are interested. Ask them whether you could attend one of their services. Invite them to yours, if they are interested. We believe that this is would exhibit religious tolerance; in fact, it goes beyond passively accepting a person's religion and actively promotes religious harmony in your community.

Option 2: Ask them to describe their religion to you, and offer to reciprocate. We believe that this also actively promotes tolerance.

Option 3: Treat them no differently than any other neighbor; ignore your religious differences. This passively promotes tolerance.

Option 4: Suggest that they should convert to your religion; express no interest in learning about their religion. This expresses religious intolerance.

Option 5: Forcefully suggest that they should convert to your religion; repeat this often; express no interest in learning about their religion. This would be an annoying level of religious intolerance to your neighbor.

Option 6: Tell your neighbor that this is a God-fearing neighborhood, and that she/he should move on. This would be a serious level of religious intolerance and harassment.

Option 7: Organize your fellow neighbors to make life miserable for this person with the goal of getting them to move away. This would be a very serious level of religious intolerance and harassment.

Option 8: Take more direct action: vandalize their home or apartment; leave a dead rat at their front door; commit arson, shoot at their windows. This would be an extreme level of religious intolerance and criminal harassment.

—from The Ontario Centre for Religious Tolerance

Hare Krishna

The Bhagavad Gita PostScript files of the chapters of the book *Bhagavad Gita As It Is*, a Krishna work in which the speaker is Lord Sri Krishna. This site is also linked to an English translation and an introduction which explains the work.
WEB http://www.cc.gatech.edu/gvu /people/Phd/Rakesh.Mullick/gita/gita .html

Hare Krishna An impressively professional graphic representation of Krishna greets you at Hare Krishna, where the authors are seeking to become the HK community's "Village Green" on the Net, giving you access to HK resources, research, organization lists, and manifesto. You can even look for individual devotees—all as that famous chant scrolls along the bottom of the page, ceaseless as an electronic tide.
WEB http://www.algonet.se/~krishna

Hinduism

Hindu Tantrik Home Page Even to the uninitiated, this stunning home page packs a spiritual wallop. The artwork is arresting, and if the language unique to these religious practices seems opaque, there's a handy glossary. There are texts on yogi, images of gods and goddesses, meditation techniques, bibliographies, and glossaries and links to other sites. One page guides you to The Triple Goddess, Lalita, who "dwells

on a paradise island in a sea of nectar."
WEB http://www.hubcom.com/tantric

Hinduism Today Full text of current and back issues of *Hinduism Today*, an international news journal are archived here. Also available is information on various Hindu organizations.
WEB http://www.HinduismToday.kauai .hi.us/ashram/htoday.html

Overview of Hinduism For spiritual seekers, or simply those who need material for a comparative-religions class, this presentation is enlightening. The author's lucid explanation of Hinduism is aided by an approach that assumes no prior knowledge and lets outsiders get an overview of the deities and practices. The site also is

seeded with links, answering such questions as whether Hinduism is monotheistic and providing heavy helpings of data on yoga practices. Quotes and poems fill out the page.
WEB http://www.geocities.com /RodeoDrive/1415/indexd.html

Islam

Caltech Muslim Students Association Much broader than its name sounds, this is not a pretty site. It *is* an extensive and intelligent discussion of Islam that starts at the very beginning, with a basic introduction to the beliefs and sects of Islam, and then provides Muslim surfers or researchers with every possible type of Islamic information, from religious discussion and database

to Halal meat shops and restaurants. There are also religious links, prayer times, links to pages of like-minded seekers, and lists of faith-related books and videos. Too dull a presentation for proselytizing, this is just serious news and conversation for those who are already serious about the religion.
WEB http://www.cco.caltech.edu /~calmsa/calmsa.html

Defenders of Aal-Ulbait and the Companions, Islamic Homepage A comprehensive index (with links) to Islam-related material on the Web, including various Qur'an translations, Arabic software, information on Muslim countries, pictures, and even 800 numbers for Islamic information! The majority of

 ## GLOBAL HINDU ELECTRONIC NETWORK
WEB http://www.hindunet.org

Sponsored by the Hindu Students Council, this site features information about Hindu festivals, Hindu organizations, India, as well as information about a variety of other Hindu-related topics—

Location: http://users.aol.com/hindunet/pics/gods/shiva03.jpg

from yoga to vegetarianism. HinduNet offers up-to-the-minute news, and has an email link for those who want to keep abreast of new developments. Whether you're a devotee or a newbie, you'll find everything you need at this enlightening Hindu hub.

Netsite: http://www.webcom.com/~ara/col/art/swing.html

Krishna and Radha—one swingin' couple
http://www.webcom.com/~ara

items listed here are articles about Islam, such as descriptions of Heaven and Hell, and a discussion of the differences between Islam and the Nation of Islam. There's even a category of articles at this site called "Mankind's Corruption of the Bible."
WEB http://web.syr.edu/~maalkadh

The Holy Qur'an The special feature of this English translation of the Qur'an is that it includes an index of specific references in the text. An essential tool for the believer or the scholar.
WEB http://chestnut.enmu.edu /~stjeanp/quran.index.html

International Association of Sufism Sufism is the school of Islam which focuses on the goal of spiritual truth; in addition to explaining the history and philosophy of Sufism, the

IAS's home page provides a wealth of information about Sufism-related events and publications.
WEB http://www.ias.org

Islam's Homepage It's tempting to say that if you can't find info on Islam here, it doesn't exist. In addition to an extensive collection of original articles about elements of Islam, this site also includes information about and selected text from Islam-related books and magazines, programming info for Muslim Television Ahmadiyya, an English translation of the Qur'an, selected prayers, and pictures.
WEB http://www.utexas.edu/students /amso/indext.htm • http://www.utexas .edu/students/amso/indexg.html

soc.religion.islam Well-trafficked newsgroup discussing a broad range of Islamic issues, from

the role of women to intermarriage to the fate of non-Muslims on the Day of Judgement. The FAQ, with its 15 parts, is equally far-reaching; besides an extensive discussion of Islamic beliefs, there are sections on Islamic Internet resources, human rights, and Farrakhism.
USENET soc.religion.islam
FAQ: **WEB** http://www.cis.ohio-state .edu/hypertext/faq/usenet-faqs /bygroup/soc/religion/islam/top.html

Judaism

Jewish Post of New York This cyberspace version of the *Jewish Post of New York* offers an array of stories on religion, culture, and news of Jewish interest. The paper makes an ambitious effort to utilize the online medium, and so, unlike most other online papers which lean heavily on text, The *Post* uses QuickTime movies, sound files, animations, and graphics. The site offers a preview of the multimedia future.
WEB http://www.jewishpost.com /jewishpost

The Judaica Web World A potpourri of Jewish culture. Find out how to take a kosher vacation to Costa Rica or Yosemite; study the Torah (the first five books of the Bible) read the only kosher comic book; or find a Jewish Internet site for your kids. The only thing missing is a decent cyberpastrami sandwich.
WEB http://www.nauticom.net/users /rafie/judaica-world.html

Shamash Home Page Its goal is to "help bring the Jewish community into the center lanes of the 'Information Superhighway'" and they've done an excellent job thus far. Links are provided to Reform, Conservative, and Orthodox sites covering everything from Israeli politics to Jewish book lists. Information is also available about the Shamash project itself.
WEB http://shamash.nysernet.org

soc.culture.jewish "While Jews have argued forever about whether Judaism is more of a 'culture' or a 'religion' or a something else, the choice of name for this newsgroup is not proof of anything," declares the FAQ to this newsgroup. "So if you start arguing 'but this group is soc.culture.jewish, so...,' please, as a well known character in a 1970s U.S. television comedy series says, 'Just stifle.'" In other words, this is the place to discuss just about everything Jewish.
USENET soc.culture.jewish
FAQ: WEB http://www.cis.ohio-state .edu/hypertext/faq/usenet-faqs /bygroup/soc/culture/jewish/top.html

Mormonism

LDS Info on the Internet Quick to note its unofficial status, this text- and info-heavy page offers Latter-Day Saints material ranging from introductory discussions to more advanced books and articles, links for young men and women, mission alumni pages, and a list of LDS-related colleges, universities, and ongoing projects.
WEB http://205.162.176.69/links/main .html

Protestantism

Anglicans Online! This site has evolved into an excellent virtual newspaper for the Anglican community—from the death of a Kenyan bishop to the embezzlement trail of a fallen U.S. Anglican. Anglicans online also provides a vast number of links to other parts of the Web and is probably the best place to go if you're looking to have all of the cyber-Anglican world at your finger-

CyberMuslim Information Collective

WEB http://www.uoknor.edu/cybermuslim
picture: WEB http://jeru.huji.ac.il/moslems_sites.htm
Welcome CyberMuslims, devotees of Islam on the Internet! Your guide is Selim the CyberMuslim (a graphical character). And what can you do here? Join the Digital Jihad to rally against anti-Muslim prejudices in the wake of the Oklahoma City bombing; read a newspaper clipping about

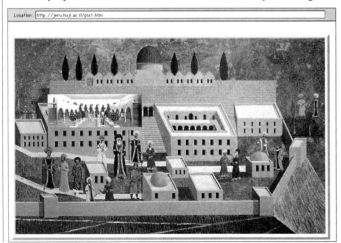

Bosnia; experience a photo-narrative essay on Muslims in nineteenth-century Russia; and listen to recitations of Al-Fatiha, the beginning of the Qur'an. Some of the sounds on the site are more random than others (especially the one about a cappuccino bar!), but all in all, this site is a feast for the senses.

THE FRACTAL GOD

I've often thought of the trinitarian/unitarian duality as analogous to the wave/particle duality in physics. Is the universe made of waves of energy or particles of matter? If we set up an experiment to look at it in terms of particles, we see particles. If we look at it in terms of waves, we see waves. Which is correct? Both, depending how we look at it. Is God one or three? Maybe both, depending on how we perceive Him (/Her/It?). For that matter, maybe God is simultaneously One and Many: the Many referring to that of God in each of us, the One being the being that created the universe —just as a particle occupies a single point in space but its wave function acts simultaneously over a large area. (I don't mean to equate God with a particle, but perhaps some characteristics of the top level are reflected in lower levels, kinda like fractals.)

—from soc.religion.quaker

tips. There's even an interactive forum for discussion of all things Anglican.
WEB http://infomatch.com/~haibeck /anglican.html

Episcopal Church Home Page
Unofficial home page of the Episcopal Church, with infor-

mation about the Episcopal tradition. Geared to the non-Episcopalian, this site describes the origins of the Episcopal Church, its relationship to the Anglican Church, the various elements of worship, and the belief system. Religious texts, information about some of the religious orders of the Episcopal Church, writings by various Episcopal leaders, and other Episcopal-related material are accessible on-site or by links to other sites.
WEB http://www.ai.mit.edu/people/mib /anglican/anglican.html

Presbyterian Church USA Like most officially sponsored, endorsed and created Web spots, the Presbyterian Church's entry is filled with useful links to all manner of things. Quietly slick in its no-frills presentation, it offers news and information about all things Presbyterian and features an email contact for people seeking the church closest to home.
WEB http://www.pcusa.org

Project Wittenberg Responding to a perceived lack of Lutheran material on the Net, the people responsible for Project Wittenberg have created a site which provides a retrospective on Lutheran texts.
WEB http://www.iclnet.org/pub /resources/text/wittenberg /wittenberg-home.html

United Methodist Information
Refreshingly simple, unclut-

tered, and to the point, this guide to United Methodist resources touches on everything from news and upcoming events to information about church money at work, official UM contact points, statements about the organization's beliefs and structure, and video and media links.
WEB http://www.umc.org

Quaker

The Religious Society of Friends Online Resources You won't waste any time waiting for graphics to download—the Religious Society gets to the point quickly and cleanly. Although the Quakers' history in the United States dates back to colonial days, it remains one of the least-known faiths, and this page hopes to change that with numerous links and FAQs addressing a wide range of practices and beliefs.
WEB http://www.misc.org/geeks /bnorum/quaker

soc.religion.quaker Twentysomething coffee drinkers aren't the only Friends who can sit around and chat. There are plenty of people at this newsgroup willing and ready to discuss issues relating to the Society of Friends, such as what the moral obligations of Friends are and how to take a marriage "vow" without taking an oath.
USENET soc.religion.quaker
FAQ: **WEB** http://www.cis.ohio-state .edu/hypertext/faq/usenet-faqs /bygroup/soc/religion/quaker/top.html

Satanism

Hell—The Online Guide to Satanism It's slick, it's snazzy, and it makes Satan proud: Hell is the only Satanic Web site you'll ever need. An excellent resource for information, publications, and merchandise pertaining to Satanism, including the Satanic bible and the alt.satanism newsgroup. Don't miss the text of a 1978 U.S. Army religious manual describing Satanism. ("Worship in the Church of Satan is based upon the belief that man needs ritual, dogma, fantasy, and enchantment. Worship consists of magical rituals and there are three basic kinds: sexual rituals, to fulfill a desire; compassionate rituals, to help another; and destructive rituals, used for anger, annoyance, or hate.")
WEB http://webpages.marshall.edu/~allenl2/index.html

> **❝ It's slick, it's snazzy, and it makes Satan proud: Hell is the only Satanic Web site you'll ever need. ❞**

Scientology

alt.religion.scientology Scientology is, of course, the fever dream of the late ex-Navy man L. Ron Hubbard. And while opponents deride it as a spiritual farce that borders on being either a cult or an out-and-out cash cow, Scientology adherents like John Travolta and Lisa-Marie Presley insist that it's a legitimate religion. Participants in alt.religion.scientology agree—sometimes. While there's a small amount of conversation about the spirtual tenets of the religion, most of the newsgroup is devoted to either condemning or commending Hubbard for

ARTICLES FROM THE JEWISH STAR

WEB http://www.ucalgary.ca/~elsegal/Shokel/Art_Index.html
picture: WEB http://www.virtual.co.il/city_services/snapshot/views/
A collection of erudite newspaper columns by Eliezer Segal, a professor at the University of Calgary and writer for Canada's *Calgary Free Press.* The columns cover the Sabbath, weddings, holidays, and community issues but with a historical and etymological perspective rare in both

Netsite: http://www.virtual.co.il/city_services/snapshot/views/babyflag.htm

journalism and scholarship. In addition to the thought-provoking columns are links to Segal's home page, which in turn links to the course outlines and notes for university classes on comparative religions as well as specialized Jewish courses. Care to take a midterm? It's at the site. Just make sure you study first.

his avaricious vision. Did he really say, "The best way to make a million dollars is to start a religion"?

USENET alt.religion.scientology

FAQ: WEB http://www.cis.ohio-state.edu/hypertext/faq/usenet-faqs/bygroup/alt/religion/scientology/top.html

" The best way to make a million dollars is to start a religion. "

Scientology Home Page No modern religion has grown as significantly as has the Church of Scientology in its mere 50 years of its existence. With increasing membership rolls (and ever-expanding bank accounts), the Church has sponsored this graphically appealing, if bluntly beatific, Internet site. Behind all the pretty pictures are acres of spiritual philosophy by L. Ron Hubbard, plus plenty of information concerning the Church and its various branches around the world. Skeptical visitors will quickly note the links to the Scientology bookstore and to Hubbard's best-selling *Dianetics*.

WEB http://www.scientology.org

Unitarianism

Eyebeams Magazine for Unitarian Universalist Opinion "What does it mean to be a Unitarian Universalist today?" This online magazine attempts to answer the question by exploring issues relating to religion, ethics, society, politics and law, the arts, education, family and youth, science and technology, and the parish. The editor's note and FAQ page discuss the nuts and bolts of the magazine, including its mission and future direction.

WEB http://www.wolfe.net/~uujim/eyebeams/magazine.htm

Unitarian Universalist Association The home page of the UUA provides clear and concise information on its belief system and serves congregations throughout North America. An outline of Unitarian beliefs and a brief history of Unitarian-Universalism provide a grounding for the uninitiated. The site also offers links to individual congregations and pages addressing specific concerns, such as the AIDS crisis and racial diversity.

WEB http://www.uua.org

Zoroastrianism

World of Traditional Zoroastrianism This imposing page declares the tenets of Zoroastrianism. The believers write, "All our Scriptures are sacred... We pray all of them in our Fire temples, before the Sacred Fire, and they have immense spiritual power, their very utterance in the sacred Avestan language serving to further righteousness and fight evil." Also described is the prescribed method of corpse destruction, and why practitioners of the faith are commanded to marry within their religion.

WEB http://www.zip.com.au/~porushh/tenets33.html

The Dark Lord speaks fluent HTML
http://webpages.marshall.edu/~allen12/index.html

Race & Ethnicity

CONFUSED ABOUT WHERE YOU COME FROM? LOOK TO OTHERS TO GET A CLEARER SENCE OF SELF

IN CASE YOU HAVE BEEN locked in an Age of Aquarius time capsule and have spent the last two decades singing "The World is a Melting Pot" over and over, you should know that homogeneity is out—now roots, multiculturalism, and diversity are in. But even then, the questions aren't so simple. Assimilate or acculturate? Tow the line or fight for your distinct identity? Then there are the more complex problems. Is everyone ethnic in America? Even white people? How important is ethnicity anyway? Reflecting this particular form of bio-diversity, the Web is a melting pot all it's own, so dive into the cultural stew and see how your own roots are cooking.

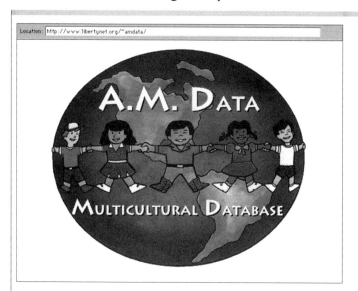

DIVERSITY
WEB http://latino.sscnet.ucla.edu/diversity1.html
picture: http://www.libertynet.org/~amdata
Your well-researched and comprehensive source list for links and info on the many different cultures and alternate lifestyles that make the Web truly worldwide. Listservs, gophers, sites, and newsgroups pertaining to the variety of racial/gender/sexual orientation issues that seem to proliferate in the U.S. are all listed and linked. North America's indigenous peoples are also represented in an intelligent and informative manner. Try something socially conscious while techno-cruising: Stick around, and you might learn something.

Starting points

Interracial Voice In a strange way, cyberspace seems the perfect place for an interracial community magazine. Published every two months, *Interracial Voice* features well-considered and politically correct articles, editorials, and poetry discussing the personal elements of race relations. Get involved, learn something, or send in your own interracial story. If you've had cross-racial experience and have something to say about it, they'd love to hear it. One of the more worthwhile and thought-provoking places on the WWW.
WEB http://www.webcom.com /~intvoice

ITI's Multi-Cultural Network Art, books, business, and education links for African-American, Irish-American, Jewish-American, Puerto Rican-American, and Native American communities. More hyphenated ethnicities to come.
WEB http://www.fcg.com/iti/iti_cultnet .html

Minority Affairs Forum Do you have immigration, affirmative action, bilingual and multicultural education, or race relations on your mind? See what's been said on all sides of these issues in this forum devoted to comparing and contrasting views. Each topic is discussed in depth, affording the visitor a comprehensive assortment of facts and opinions that the mainstream media does not

explore. The diversity of ideas is so profound, you cannot help but come away with many new thoughts and perspectives; it's an eye-opening experience for even the most socially-aware Americans.
URL ftp://heather.cs.ucdavis.edu/pub /README.html

MOLIS: Minority Online Information Service If you're in the market for information on Historically Black Colleges and Universities and Hispanic Serving Institutions, (HBCU and HSI, respectively), MOLIS will satisfy your queries. Learn about the federal government's funding obligations to minority-dominated institutions or, for a more socio-political perspective, compare the U.S. Department of Education's monetary commitments with those of the agency for International Development. Other related departments can give you crucial scholarship and fellowship information and update you on current seminars, meetings, campus lectures, and job opportunities. If environmental issues spark your interest, you'll want to head to the Environmental Technical Capabilities Statement, where the latest efforts in the areas of environmental technology and waste management solutions are discussed. There's a sea of informational resources available, ranging from government institutions to private foundations.
WEB http://web.fie.com/web/mol

African

Africa-L "You should all remember that when they first came to our lands and said 'Let's pray' they spelt the word pray with an 'e,' i.e., prey." Africa-L is an intensely political and left-leaning mailing list and an interesting place to get cross-cultural perspectives of Africa in the twentieth century.
EMAIL listserv@vtvml.cc.vt.edu ✍
Type in message body: subscribe africa-l ⟨your full name⟩

African National Congress Home Page It seems strange that a few years ago, the words of Nelson Mandela and the ANC were considered illicit. Now the official page of South Africa holds the findings of the African Communist Party, the Congress of South African Trade Unions, and the Human Rights Committee—all illegal not long ago. Mandela's voice is here too—from the 1955 Freedom Charter to his speeches as president. Finally, the page provides local election information and email links to government offices.
WEB http://www.anc.org.za

Country-Specific Pages for Africa U. Penn's Africa pages are the most comprehensive in cyberspace. They're all here—home pages for countries from Algeria to Zimbabwe. Each page offers a map and U.S. State Department and *CIA World Factbook* assessments. On the Zambia page, there are links to a national news service, a lan-

guage database, and an article on the fertilizer industry. Wander to Marrakesh and explore Moroccan culture at Tamazight: The Berber Culture and Language page. Book a tour on a gorilla safari, or take a look at the flora and fauna of Madagascar. Frequent updates make these pages among the most valuable African resources around.
WEB http://www.sas.upenn.edu /African_Studies/Home_Page /Country.html

U. Penn African Studies WWW Links The annotations make this collection of African and African-American links among the most useful on the Web. Organized by topic, there are

links here to sites focusing on everything from trade to wildlife. There are places to chat (meet with other Rastafarians at Virtual Niahbingi), places to learn (visit The University of South Africa), and places to look (see the African Mask Collection).
WEB http://www.sas.upenn.edu /African_Studies/Home_Page/WWW _Links.html

Asian

Asian Arts There are several spectacular online exhibits housed here. Explore the world of Mongolian art in "The Legacy of Chinggis Khan," learn about the relationship between religion and sculpture

in "India in Images of Faith," or meander through 1,000 years of Chinese textiles. Scholarly articles are also online here, along with links to galleries from London to Santa Fe specializing in Asian art.
WEB http://www.webart.com/asianart /index.html

China Home Page Welcome to the real thing—courtesy of the Institute of High Energy Physics in Beijing. There are the expected scientific links to universities, research institutes, and businesses, but culture and community are not neglected. Various sites bring together Chinese students, scholars, and just plain folks for cyberchatter. A sound archive holds samples

 ## The Heritage Project
WEB http://heritage.excite.sfu.ca/hpost.html

What makes you think of Canada—a moose, a maple leaf, or a mountain? This online magazine is devoted to the preservation and promotion of Canadian national identity. In both English and French, readers will find a discussion of things that symbolize Canada, listings of heritage fairs,

and features on Canadian culture, such as "Flight," a history of Canadian aviation, or "Water Pump," an article about Canada's contribution to global development. Take the Canadian history quiz and win Heritage Project prizes.

BALIKBAYAN MANIFESTO

The reason I INSIST on being referred to as a Filipino-American is because it explains volumes about my indivi - dual - ity. Having been born and RAISED in the Philippines and being an American citizen it wouldn't be fair to insist that I choose one. Of course one can be more to my advantage than the other on a given occasion for example when I go out and vote. I do so because I get to (I don't always get my way though!) When in the process of deciding HOW to vote I admit that I do so in ways in which I believe will best suit the general welfare of minorities and the Filipino community/communities all over the U.S., so I guess you can say I vote as a Filipino American.

But when you see me eyeballing the halo-halo or ginataan (mm sarap!) or the turon or the dinuguan or the SISIG at the table next to me in a pinoy restaurant, or when after a long 10 hour drive from Southern Cal to Northern Cal I get out of the driver's seat to stretch and say "Ay! Kawawa naman ang puwet ko!", you won't need to ask whether I'm American or not because you'll know na sa loob-loob nitong tisay, pinay talaga.

—from soc.culture.filipino

group, you can brag that your *sensei* is wiser, stricter, or older than anybody else's. Experts offer advice on Japanese bookstores abroad, visas and the INS, and job hunting in Japan (tip: add a photo and your marital status to your resume). **COMPUSERVE** *go* japan

Japan Window The window is a cooperative sight with information on technology, business, government, and living in Japan. Kids visiting the site are invited to learn *hiragana* and origami. Adults can read about the Japanese diet, review tax law, find out what's playing at the theater, or meet in an online live chat room to talk about the Kobe earthquake or last night's baseball game. **WEB** http://jw.nttam.com/HOME/index .html

soc.culture.china/soc.culture.hong kong/soc.culture.taiwan No, they aren't the same. In fact, that's one of the most frequent topics in these three newsgroups— the distinctions and political hostilities among the "three Chinas." Soc.culture.china is dominated by Chinese students doing study-abroad programs in the States. Most are taking the time to freely post anti-government messages, since they are safely out of reach of rolling tanks; Tiananmen and its aftereffects remain high-volume topics. Much conversation is conducted with embedded Pinyin phrases. Soc.culture.hongkong, on the other hand, is more evenly bal-

of music and voices, including one folder labeled "post-Gang of Four." There's a lot more to explore here, especially if you cybertour China's cities and provinces. **WEB** http://solar.rtd.utk.edu/~china /china.html

Hong Kong Terminal The Terminal holds information for those living in the bustling island city and those who would like to. Business types will find end-of-the-day stock reports so they can play the volatile "1997 is coming" market with confidence. A restaurant database reveals where to find Italian food in Hong Kong, while a culinary guide discusses the proper preparation of dim sum.

Events calendars list what's on in the clubs—a top-40 list says what's hip on the radio. But the highlight is a real-time chat room where visitors can converse in English or Mandarin about Hong Kong and just about anything else. **WEB** http://zero.com.hk/z.html

Japan Forum *Gaijin* and Japanese trade stories about Japanese waiters sent to Paris's finest culinary schools to learn to be surly, and debate whether the H2 rocket is an expensive flop or a prescient investment in the space market. Twentysomething tourists come here to be shocked that their favorite Tokyo nightclub, Juliana's, has closed. In the martial arts

anced between Chinese-Americans with Hong Kong roots and Hong Kong citizens studying in America; it also draws a certain number of non-Hong Kongers who are fans of Hong Kong film or music. Don't expect to talk about Hong Kong movies after a single viewing of *Hard Boiled*, either—the fans here know what they're talking about, and will use the original Cantonese versions of movie and star names just to drive you mad. Soc.culture.taiwan is one of the Asian newsgroup family's most contentious members. TIs (those demanding Taiwanese Independence) square off against WSRs (those Wishing to Stay a Republic), lobbing bazooka blasts across the Net

with the regularity of shots fired in a free-fire zone along the Maginot Line during World War II. If you don't care about Taiwanese politics, there's discussion of Little League baseball scores and pop singers, as well as the movies of Ang Lee.
USENET soc.culture.china/soc.culture .hongkong/soc.culture.taiwan

Soc.Culture.Filipino—The Phillipine Cyberbayan There are more than 200 links at this excellent site for Filipinos at home and abroad. Make your voice heard with a visit to the Philippine Senate Online, or head to the rec.music.filipino home page for a hot discussion of the latest release by Gil Lopez Kabayao. Movers and shakers meet at

Phillipine Business On-line, and those with satellite dishes look for the Pinoy TV listings.
WEB http://www.mozcom.com/SCF /SCF.html

soc.culture.japan Of all of the major soc.culture Asian newsgroups, soc.culture.japan is the only one that seems largely dominated by non-Asians. Quirky discussions of cultural difference (why are there fewer bald men in Japan than in the U.S.?) prompted by questions from returned tourists or exchange students are common. The handful of regulars posting from Japan are vested with a sort of guru status; they're asked to deliver Solomonic decisions on who's right and who's wrong about

Caribbean Art Center

WEB http://www.nando.net/prof/caribe/Caribbean_Art_Center.html

Get a taste of the Caribbean artistic flavor in the works of artists such as Jose Morales, Guillo Perez, and Diogenes Ballester. The Antilles gallery provides photos of their work, as well as photos of the artists themselves. Interviews with the artists (in Spanish, for now) offer glimpses into their creative processes, and links to other Caribbean Cultural sites on the Internet are provided to give you a deeper understanding of their art. A brief biography of Jose Morales, written by a fellow artist, explains his difficult road to success.

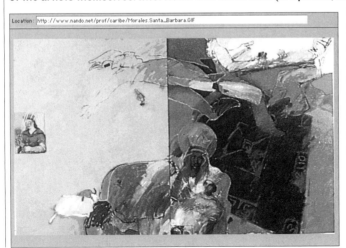

Location: http://celtic.stanford.edu/images/Narada/cl400.jpg

The Ceolas Web site gets its name from the Irish/Scots Gaelic words for music (*ceol*) and knowledge (*eolas*). Here, an album cover featured at the site http://celtic.stanford.edu/ceolas.html

various aspects of Japanese culture. A fair amount of spillover from the newsgroup rec.arts .anime also visit the site.
USENET soc.culture.japan

Australian

soc.culture.australian Imagine that you've captured an Australian and you can ask him anything you want. "As a black American, how would I be treated in Australia as opposed to a white American?" "How do Aussies feel about the Queen?" You're probably thinking of visiting Australia, aren't you? So drill the natives: Where do I stay? What do I see? When do I go? And, of course, what about Oz beer? Discussion sometimes becomes very serious—"I have another question before I actually move

in late October: Is the *Star Trek* series readily available in Australia, and if so, what season are they on?"
USENET soc.culture.australian

Canadian

Ethnologue Database: Canada Every single member of the Atikamekw tribe of northern Quebec (3,225 people in all) speaks the tribal tongue. Get a brief description of the language and culture of all Canadian tribes here.
WEB hhttp://www-ala.doc.ic.ac.uk /~rap/Ethnologue/eth.cgi/Canada/

soc.culture.canada While U.S. citizens can't resist posting their border-crossing experiences, Canadians dominate the group with discussions about domestic politics, the environ-

ment, the country's bilingualism, trade relationships, and the debate over Quebec's sovereignty. Boorish Americans often jump in with anti-Canadian comments. But for every Maple enemy, there are many more enthusiastic posts about our Great Northern Neighbor.
USENET soc.culture.canada

Caribbean

MIT Caribbean Home Page An immense collection of links to various Caribbean-related resources. Stop at De Shop Corner to get in touch with other Islanders. From there it's just a jump to Caribbean-related newsgroups. Turn the corner to a list of home pages of West Indians. The Papa Bois database allows for even greater interaction—post your profile, look up old school chums, or find a local Caribbean grocery in your neighborhood by just plugging in a search term.
WEB http://caribbean-www.lcs.mit.edu /caribbean-www

soc.culture.caribbean Mary reminds everyone when the Boston Carnival will happen this year. Dan posts two more sites for watching the Chance's Peak volcano in Montserrat. The debate rages in Spanish over Cuba, and Foster seeks other Vincies (from St. Vincent) for a discussion of the homeland. Lots of islands, lots of people, and a wide range of topics here.
USENET soc.culture.caribbean

European

Albanian WWW Homepage A separate entity within the obscure territiory of what is commonly referred to as The Balkan Region, Albania has a distinct ethnic personality as well as its own history. What is the story behind the doubleheaded black eagle on a scarlet field that stands proudly as the emblem of this country's flag? Where are Tirana and Kosova? Read about the news, places, history, and people in what some have called "The Switzerland of the Balkans." Take a virtual tour through the mountainous terrain of Albania, while stopping at links that will lead to mailing lists, Albanian newspapers, home pages of Albanians around the world, and some interesting facts such as: Mother Teresa is a famous Albanian. Did you know that?
WEB http://www.albanian.com

Balt-L The Baltic mailing list not only includes up-to-the-minute news postings, but also tireless dissections of moves on the international chessboard. Conversations can become impassioned, and sentiments often collide with calls for reform.
EMAIL listserv@ubvm.cc.buffalo.edu
✍ *Type in message body:* subscribe balt-l ⟨your full name⟩

Ceolas-Celtic Music on the Internet Ceolas rightfully boasts that it is the most complete collection of Celtic music information on the Net. There are links to online 'zines, listings of radio stations carrying *Thistle & Shamrock*, album reviews, sound bytes, artist profiles, concert listings, and hundreds of tunes in .GIFs, MIDI and PostScript. There are a number of music-writing software packages—even one for bagpipes.
WEB http://celtic.stanford.edu/ceolas.html

European Forum Doom-mongering Europeans worry that Americans "kill for fun, sport, and revenge." You can agree that the worst is true or instead ask, "Are we dysfunctional, or do we just need good hair-

EUROPEAN COMMUNITY HOME PAGE

WEB http://s700.uminho.pt/ec.ng.html

The page is here, whether the Tories and the Danes like it or not. Simply click on the proper flag, and you'll be rewarded with a comprehensive list of Internet servers and a clickable map full of local information. A cultural European home page is linked to this site, a visit to Slovenia provides ski tips, a trip to France yields a virtual tour of the Pompidou Center, and a jaunt to Germany offers a comprehensive beer guide. Widely regarded as one of the most efficient, clear, and effective central resources of information on the member states, this has a depth most Euro MPs can only imagine.

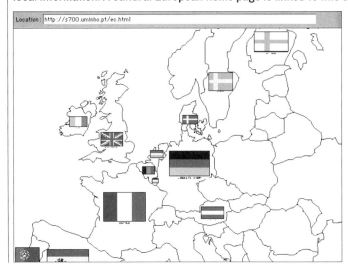

IT AIN'T NO PLAIN BANJO

The Braguinha is a small guitar that was made by the Portuguese residents on the island of Madeira. In the Canarie Islands a related instrument, the timple, was, and is, made and played.

In 1879 the Braguinha came to Hawaii with immigrants from Madeira, among whom were Manuel Nunes, Augustos Dias and Jose do Espirtu. These men were the first ukulele makers in Hawaii.

The metal strings of the Braguinha were replaced with gut (and later, nylon) strings and the tuning was changed to make the instrument easier to play. Thus was born the ukulele. Another Portuguese immigrant, Joao Fernandes helped to popularize the ukulele by playing it wherever he went. The ukulele became very popular among the people of Hawaii. "Ukulele" in Hawaiian can be translated as "jumping flea".

As Hawaiian music and culture became more widely known in the early 1920s, the ukulele became popular all over the world, with such well-known instrument makers as Martin and Gibson producing excellent instruments.

The modern ukulele comes in 4 sizes:
Soprano or Standard: This is the smallest one.
Concert: A bit larger than the soprano uke.
Tenor: The most popular size in Hawaii.
Baritone: The biggest size; like a small guitar.

The basic ukulele has 4 strings. In Hawaii 6 and 8 string ukuleles are popular. Some or all of the strings are doubled (either in unison or octaves) on these ukes. Ukuleles have been made with 5, 6, 7, 8, 10 and even 12 strings. The ten string ukes are called "tiples" and are not popular today in Hawaii.

Builders in Hawaii today are experimenting with new shapes and sizes and amplified electric models, as well as the traditional forms. Ukuleles are becoming more and more popular here in Hawaii as well as the Mainland and the world.

—from A Brief History of the Ukulele

someone's wife and kids, walk each other through the French scuba-permit bureaucracy, and ask which are the best seats in Prague's Strahov stadium for the upcoming Pink Floyd concert. Be prepared for threads to bounce in and out of English. **COMPUSERVE** *go* eurfor

Hellas List Home Page More than just a travel site, this page of links is the Web counterpart to the popular Hellas mailing list, whose logs and newsfeed are easily accessed here. Head to the soc.culture.newsgroup for immediate discussion of important topics like "Why Greeks hate Turks" and "Is Hellinism racist?" Additional links allow you to make your own Greek calendar, contact a Greek embassy, and keep up with the Greek Epikairo cartoon. **WEB** http://velox.stanford.edu/hellas

Interactive Slovakia Slovakia is working hard to counter its image as the lesser half of the former communist state. Virtual visitors will be impressed by the interactive map, virtual tour of Bratislava, and rent-a-cottage-in-the-Urals features at this site. Slovaks worldwide are encouraged to add material or home page connections. **WEB** http://www.savba.sk/logos/interactive/list.html

Les Carnet de Route de FranceWeb Francophiles will find much to please them here, with links to news services and government agencies. There are links here for children, shoppers, travel-

cuts?" In this wide-ranging, neighborly forum, members also volunteer to translate "baking soda" and "condensed milk" into German, find an apartment in Stockholm for

ers, scientists, and even a job bank. The cultural listings are diverse—everything from new bands to employment opportunities to shopping bargains to science fiction—and are not to be missed.

WEB http://www.francenet.fr/france web/FWCarnetRoute.html

Mideur-L A mixture of contemporary political debate, historical discussion, and ethnic bonding. List members include scholars from around the world and middle Europeans in and outside the borders of their countries. Emotions run high during talk of ethnic strife. Scholars step in every once in a while to moderate discussions of how hate builds over time.

There is also an element of support here—a young American seeks prayers in Croatian to ease his dying grandfather's mind.

EMAIL listserv@ubvm.cc.buffalo.edu ✍ *Type in message body:* subscribe mideur-l ⟨your full name⟩

The Nordic Pages Home to all things Scandinavian—fish, ice, blondes, and fjords—this site offers extensive links to the Great European North. Step through Mofile Place to reach the *Finnish Web* magazine. The daily news from Reykjavik is available, as are the proceedings of the Norwegian Parliament. Read the classics of Sweden (in Swedish) or meet some barbar-

ians online at the Viking Network Web.

WEB http://www.algonet.se/~nikos /nordic.html

Poland Home Page Need to know when the next flight to Krakow leaves? That information is at hand with this excellent collection of Polish-related links. A nationwide Polish railway schedule, a virtual tour of the Tatra mountains, and the latest numbers from the Polish stock exchange are also here. Poles at home and abroad can meet to discuss the country's economy or the Pope through a link to the newsgroup soc.culture.poland, or they can catch up with old friends by searching the online

ELECTRIC MERCADO

WEB http://www.mercado.com

What is a "*Dole-oroso*"? How about a "*Mexikitsch*"? The answer is a link away when you visit this showcase of Latino resources. This hot and spicy site serves up a dish of Latino culture like no other. Introduce yourself to the beat of the New Poetry Movement and literature of writers such as

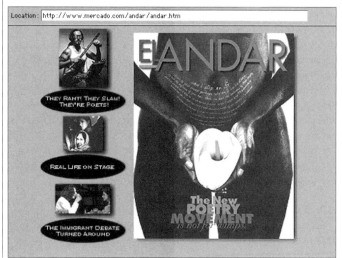

Odilia Galvan Rodriguez, Sergio Troncoso, and many others. Visit Los Puestos for a peek at Latino art. Get cooking at the Comida Corrida where you can learn how to make *Arroz con Pollo a la Chorrera* (that's chicken with yellow rice and beer for all of you non-Spanish speaking epicureans), as well as other delicacies of the Latino kitchen. Magazines, music, and debates make this site a stand-out.

email database. There's much more of interest—daily newspapers, a cinema database, art galleries, and even a Polish TV guide.
WEB http://info.fuw.edu.pl/pl/Poland-Home.html

St. Petersburg Web St. Petersburg sounds so much friendlier that Leningrad, right? The Russian Internet provider, Reclom, has created a virtual city café featuring copies of the English-language paper, a hip Russian magazine entitled *Beat?*, and a weekly culture, restaurant, and bar guide that can't be beat. Russians living aboard will appreciate the taste of home provided by the cartoons of Victor Borgorad and short stories about life in the city of the Tsars.
WEB http://www.spb.su

UK Forum An American reading the Politics section here might think she stepped into a parallel universe, where the Clinton health plan has passed and is running as smoothly as the post office: Social Security is—for some reason—called National Insurance, and elected officials actually participate in political discussions on the Internet. Don't worry: It's not the future; it's just Britain. In Rover's Return Pub, Brits pretend to be drunk and fondle each other boozily. Recently, forum members met offline in Manchester, London, and Los Angeles. Tourists share tips on places to visit such as the Dylan Thomas house in Wales

and the hedge mazes at Hever Castle or arrange to rent a converted barn in Cornwall. Oddly, John Cleese's name pops up in nearly every thread.
COMPUSERVE *go* ukforum

Welcome to Tweednet Warning: This is a tartan-free zone. There are thousands of sites listed here—including organizations dedicated to restocking the salmon in the Tweed, a guide to national poet Robbie Burns, and a business directory. Further links take visitors rock climbing and stargazing at the Royal Observatory. Head to the Internet 13 Café for updates on the Edinburgh Fringe Festival.
WEB http://www.scotborders.co.uk

Windows On Italy This site is a large collection of bilingual links for Italians in the homeland and on Mott Street. The daily newspapers—right, center, and communist—are just a jump away, as are virtual tours of every Italian city from Milan to Naples. A trip to the general subject tree yields lots of links in Italian. From here you can read about the latest in Italian chemical engineering, find a long lost relative in Sicily, and contact the Catholic Church in Rome.
WEB http://www.mi.cnr.it/WOI

Hawaiian & Polynesian

A Brief History of the Ukulele This quintessential Hawaiian instrument was actually introduced by Portuguese immi-

grants in the 1800s. Read all about the history, construction, and tuning of this tiny guitar.
WEB http://hookomo.aloha.net/~jimad/uke.html

Hawai'i—Independent & Sovereign Nation-State In 1993, President Clinton apologized for the illegal overthrow of the native Hawaiian government. Now everyone can read expert testimony that contends the apology makes reclamation action against the U.S. government not only legal, but possible. This home page is a clearinghouse for the Hawaiian independence movement, with a collection of newspaper articles and email links to government officials.
WEB http://www.aloha.net/nation/hawaii-nation.html

Kualono Most of the resources on this page—and they include a news service, bulletin board, and community information—is written in Olelo Hawaiian. Try the online lessons in the language of paradise to decipher the rest of the site.
WEB http://www.olelo.hawaii.edu

Hispanic

CiberCentro Ciber Centro hosts a customized newspaper/index. If you want newsgroups for Argentinians or a map of Peru, you can get exactly that. You can also find people who are online (and might be able to answer your questions) at the Ciber Citizens page for each country. Although the main

menu of the site is in English, knowledge of elementary Spanish is needed.
WEB http://www.cibercentro.com

IPRNet Home Page This is basically an information service on Puerto Rican issues where you'll find a *Journal of Puerto Rican Policy and Politics*, a socio-economic profile for Puerto Ricans in the U.S., (including a new feature that allows you to find out statistics on the city's 21 Latino neighborhoods, including population projections to the year 2000). There is a directory of 500 Puerto Rican community organizations in the U.S. and Puerto Rico, a calendar of events, festivals, and historical

dates, essays, poems, and stories on the Puerto Rican experience. If that's not enough to satisfy your interest, you can get on a mailing list for more.
WEB http://www.iprnet.org/IPR

Hispanic & Latino

The Azteca Web Page Among the many questions you can have thoroughly answered are, "What is a Chicano?" "Where is Aztlan?" and "How many people speak indigenous languages in Mexico?" Would you like to view Mexican images, download a PC game or an Aztec game (*Patolli*), learn more about immigration policy, or just hear some interesting stories? It's all possible

at The Azteca Web Page.
WEB http://www.directnet.com/~mario/aztec

Hispanic Heritage Connect to countries of origin here—virtual Spain, Argentina, Peru, and Mexico. Or read brief biographies of famous Hispanics like Gabriela Mistral, Salvador Dali, and Carlos Fuentes. A primer on bullfighting explains the sport and gives current bullfighter rankings (scored in numbers of ears held).
WEB http://www.clark.net/pub/jgbustam/heritage/heritage.html

Hispanic/Latino History A series of hypertext essays on Hispanic history open this site.

PAKISTAN STUDENTS ASSOCIATION
WEB http://www.rpi.edu/dept/union/paksa

Homesick Pakistanis stuck at school in upstate New York have created this excellent interactive map full of illustrations and information. Simply click on Lahore and say "there's no place like home." This site is not only for natives, though. It is also a great resource for those ignorant about the government, culture, tourism, and sports that are most commonly played in the mystical land of Pakistan. Don't miss the Pakistan National Anthem sound file, accompanied by lyrics displayed in Urdu.

SUNG BEFORE CRICKET GAMES

National anthem:

Pak sarzamin shad bad
Kishware haseen shad bad
Tunishane azmealishan arze Pakistan
Markazeyaqin shadbad.
Pak sarzamin ka nizam quwate akhuwati awam
Qaum, mulk, Sultanat
Painda ta binda bad shad, bad man zele murad.
Parchame sitarao hilat
Rahbare tarraqio ka mal
Tarjumane mazishane hal jane istaqbal
Sayyai, khudae zul jalal.

Translation:

Blessed be the sacred land,
Happy be the bounteous realm,
Symbol of high resolve, Land of Pakistan.
Blessed be thou citadel of faith.
The Order of this Sacred Land
Is the might of the brotherhood of the people.
May the nation, the country, and the State
Shine in glory everlasting.
Blessed be the goal of our ambition.
This flag of the Crescent and the Star
Leads the way to progress and perfection,
Interpreter of our past, glory of our present,
Inspiration of our future,
Symbol of Almighty's protection.

—from The Pakistan Page

What were the Flour Wars? Find out about the "near apocalyptic," pre-Columbian feud in the Aztec Empire. There is a link to the Library of Congress exhibit "1492: An Ongoing Voyage," which presents the long history of Spain in the new world. Other links lead to mission churches in California, the Alamo, and a Mayan museum.
WEB http://latino.sscnet.ucla.edu /research/history.html

LatinoWeb Looking for a loan to build a bridge in Buenos Aires? Go straight to the business section here and find the home page of Banco Inter-

americano de Desarrollo. Some of the other diverse links take cultural explorers to the Andean Music page or the Ballet Folklorico. No fewer than six sites hold recipes for *chimichangas* and *psole*—but if taste dictates otherwise, the *Wall Street Journal* and *Las Journada* are just a jump away.
WEB http://www.catalog.com/favision /latnoweb.htm

Mundo Latino This page is one substantial link list. CubaWeb tells you all you want to know about doing business in Cuba, or you can link yourself to such diverse sites as those for Costa Rican coffee, a detail of the Honduran participation in the global marketplace, the *Mex-Assist Financial Newsletter*, a Brazilian Business Directory, Latin American/Spanish language Resources, or the Lambda Theta Phi Latin Fraternity's national home page.
WEB http://www.mundolatino.org /latingle.htm

Indian subcontinent

The Beauty of India—Unity in Diversity This site presents its large collection of links in a unique manner—through a hypertext essay on the past and present of the largest democracy in the world. Click on a "population" and find a gopher with the latest Indian census data. Many Indian religions and languages have several associated pages for perusal. Find out more about the East India Company and the tea

trade, or view some ancient sculpture. Link to an archive of sound files from Indian movies or the page dedicated to the cuisine of Tamilnadu. The Hindu newspaper and a number of community-action groups round out the collection.
WEB http://www.cs.clemson.edu /~nandu/india.html

The Nepal Homepage Practical information is at your fingertips here—a Nepalese phone directory, email links to other Nepalese, embassy locations, and a list of Nepalese organizations in the West. There is culture from the heights of Kathmandu here, too—recipes for *momo*, extensive travel and trekking information, and a literature collection written in a Nepalese font. Nepalese natives far from home will find news links, like *Nepal Digest*, or the soc.culture.nepal discussion group, where the most recent thread was about caste and Hinduism.
WEB http://www.cen.uiuc.edu/~rshresth /Nepal.html

Pakistan Page Miscellaneous links here lead to PACA-WOMEN, dedicated to improving the position of Pakistani women, and a page dedicated to the political father of Pakistan, Jinnah. Sound files of Pakistani music are available, as are elementary lessons in Urdu. Keep up with local news courtesy of the dial location for Radio Pakistan given here.
WEB http://www.exit109.com/~fazia /Pakistan.html

Mosaic nation

THE WEB IS PURE DEMOCRACY— A PLACE WHERE ALL CAN SPEAK

AFRO AMERICAN NEWSPAPERS
WEB http://www.afroam.org

The **AANC** boasts the most extensive collection of twentieth-century African-American history. So when its Web site, which is a massive storehouse of information, suggests registering for the biweekly updates, it may be worth your while. The What's New section gives you the statistics detailing Farrakhan's popularity (as well as that of O.J. Simpson and Jesse Jackson), and encourages you to vote for the most influential living musician in black culture. If you're young and on the scene, or at least trying to find one, Freaknik will tell you where the phattest parties are happening nationwide.

African-American

A Deeper Shade of Black This page is a growing repository of black history—from minutiae to movements. Check the chronology of events to celebrate achievements in black history, or re-read Dr. King's "Letter from a Birmingham Jail" for inspiration. Heroes, both celebrated and unsung, are here too, including Nelson Mandela and G.F. Grant, the inventor of the golf tee.
WEB http://www.ai.mit.edu/~isbell/HFh /black/bhcal-toc.html

AFAM-L This scholarly list for those studying African-American culture has evolved into an active place to discuss the here and now of African-American life. A news release about the firing of the head of the NAACP sparked immediate debate about the specific incident, the history of the organization, and its current direction. When the Fox network canceled five black-oriented shows, a week-long discussion of media images and media power ensued. AFAM-L is an essential gathering place for scholars, activists, and anyone else interested in the African-American experience.
EMAIL listserv@mizzou1.missouri.edu
✍ *Type in message body:* **subscribe afam-l (your full name)**

Africa This collection of links encourages African Americans to delve deep into African issues and culture. Pick a country and explore. Leap

---

A PIECE OF MIND

The Black Man is America's newest gross national product. We are the court jesters of television and radio, the meat on the field of sports competition (Denise Rodman, David Robinson and even Michael Jordan) and the convicts from which the new city economies will be built. We disrespect our black queens, we kill our young and neglect our old. Look at some of our entertainers that are looked up to by our young people, such as LL Cool J or R. Kelly and ask yourself why they must make such songs as "Bump and Grind" and "Doing It" and prostrate themselves and our young black queens before the public as they do? Songs like those mentioned only encourage more actions and create an atmosphere that will lead to more teenage pregnancies. I seem to remember one song and accompanying video, old school, as our young refer to it, entitled "Face Down Ass Up: That's the way I like it" one of the most horrible songs that made it to the market place. These types of songs and images contribute to the fact that 2 out of 3 black kids today are born without a father in the home.

We must deal in today's reality, as I pointed out in one of my earlier articles, "If the White Man is attempting to kill us off with Drugs, we can thwart the attempt by just not taking the drugs. If he doesn't want to give us jobs, we should create our own jobs and hire one another. If he is trying to make us the next economic commodity—the convict—don't commit any crimes that will put you at risk of being jailed, etc., etc., etc." The white man doesn't need to kill us off. All he need do today is, in most cases, stand back and watch us commit self-genocide.

—from **AFRONET**

---

from here to the Algeria page, or wander through the Abyssinian Cyberspace Gateway. Lean back and listen to the music: choose from West African, Algerian Rai, Cuban, calypso, reggae, jazz, blues, or hip-hop sounds. Check out the link to African art. A number of Caribbean-related sites can also be reached from here.
WEB http://www.seas.upenn.edu /~cardell/africa.html

African American History Archive at Mississippi State University Read Frederick Douglass's autobiographical *My Escape from Slavery*, or Henry Louis Gates's recent article on the backlash against affirmative action. You don't have to stop reading because of the site's limited resources: a plethora of links to newsgroups, mailing lists, art sites, and other interesting sites like Black History

on the Web and the African-American Shopping Mall are provided as well.
WEB http://www.msstate.edu/Archives/History/USA/Afro-Amer/afro.html

Afro-American Culture & Arts Forum The Salon, a general chitchat board, is the most active section in the forum. It's where parents discuss how to deal with a teen "indefinitely homebound" (a euphemism for grounded) and where everyone picks apart the media image of the single black mother. Recent immigrants go to Caribbean Meeting to talk about the old country. The forum also includes serious political talk about Rush and O.J., occasional accusations of "blacker than thou" posturing, and a group that periodically shares its favorite items from *Weekly World News*—like the one about the 50-foot Jesus terrorizing a small town. The big draws here are the culture topics: art, history, film, theater, and music.
COMPUSERVE *go* afro

AFRONET This online newspaper serves a wide variety of interests, without the fluff. It also promotes active participation in the proceedings, inviting feedback. If you want to talk racism in Hollywood (with or without Spike Lee), current African-American flicks you like or loathe, politics, or local news, this is the place. The "junior posse" gives you all of the relevant fashion news, R&B grooves, hip hop singles,

and fraternity, sorority, and college scholarship info. Also available is an African-American product catalogue.
WEB http://www.afronet.com

ASA-L Provides an opportunity for African-American students worldwide to share ideas, wisdom, and humor. Predictably much more active during the school year, the list members are young, smart, and impassioned. Keeping abreast of international developments, the ASA-L often creates networks for relief work and political action. Students can form friendships with their counterparts in other countries and check out opportunities for travel (e.g., Mark from the U.S. discusses the Egyptian club scene with a new friend in Cairo). The chat is often fun—how about a long re-evaluation of fairy tales from a modern perspective?

EMAIL listserv@tamvml.tamu.edu ✍
Type in message body: subscribe asa-l (your full name)

Black African Related Resources A lengthy and thorough list of online information storage sites (ftp, gopher, telnet, WWW, BBS, and database) concerning black or African people, culture, and issues worldwide. There are additional resources relating to Ethnic and Intercultural Relations, International and Sustainable Development, and Social and Progressive Activism. From this starting point you can vault into the WELL, an experiment in cyberspace magazine creation; head off to Norway via Electronic Frontier Norway; or peruse the Tropical Database for regional information on microbial strains.
WEB http://www.sas.upenn.edu/African_Studies/Home_Page/mcgee.html

At the Black Info Network, you can have the whole world in the palm of your hand
http://www.bin.com/homepage.htm

Black Information Network This sprawling mass of listings and articles has everything from names of ministries on the Gospel World Wide Network, to members of the Association of Black Accountants, to stats on black-owned broadcasting companies to a section on adoption, missing children, employment opportunities, real estate, and friends (with the romantic potential emphasized). You'll also come across compelling articles covering issues such as transgenderism and politics. If it's talk you want, there's no lack of opinion-swapping.
WEB http://www.bin.com/homepage.htm

Black Voices The *Orlando Sentinel*'s "Black Voices" is a good place to go for the latest news affecting the African-American community and topical discussion of the issues. When we visited, there were special folders for the black church fires, the '96 election, and the O.J. Simpson civil trial. For a look at the lighter side of black life, there are special areas such as For Lovers Only, Sports Rap, and Brothers and Sisters.
AMERICA ONLINE *keyword* black voices

The Book Stunning graphics are only a hint of the wealth of African-American culture and history you'll find at this dynamic page. Through text, images, and sounds, you're taken through a vast library of popular music, photos, video clips, famous speeches, and twentieth-century icons. The educational and entertainment opportunities are updated regularly and are easily navigated. Perhaps the most impressive aspect of the site is its thoroughly researched and highly useful compilation of "the best." Web locations, from comics and cartoons to arts and sciences to "wild stuff." For those new to the Web or fed up with fruitless searches, this tool could prove beneficial.
WEB http://www.blackhistory.com

Café Los Negros Not your average café, this moody, black and Latino Web joint offers a potent cup of art, performance, poetry, fashion, and music. Be advised—unlike most cafés, this one has a cover charge. But like most, there are some juicy conversations worth hearing. Take a peek at the Negro-file, a gossip-style, daily diary on the life of a "cybernegro." With the help of a black-and-white photo guide, you can see the hottest threads, play the latest grooves (depending on what's currently available), and get the historical lowdown on LL Cool J, Dove Shack, Method Man, and Public Enemy. If you missed a local multimedia performance or poetry reading, you just might be able to download it from this funky place.
WEB http://www.losnegroes.com

ClubNubia Online Magazine This self-described "unifying, uplifting," and musically-based Net paper is geared toward people of color worldwide. As with its hard-copy competition, you'll find related features, reviews and commentaries, letters from the editor, and reader responses. A typical feature may discuss your rights as an artist, while other less traditional sections of the paper offer poetry and a stream of consciousness-like page entitled "Bruhhman's Perspective." Special events, bulletin boards, round out the standard fare.
WEB http://www.directhit.com/clubnubia

The Faces of Science: African-Americans in the Sciences This page is dedicated to African-American scientists. Read about Dr. Herman Branson, who mapped the Alpha and Gamma helical structure of proteins. Join in Afritech, '95, an email online conference on African-Americans and technology, and connect with peers and colleagues. Or read the extensive bibliographies and funding guides available here.
WEB http://www.lib.lsu.edu/lib/chem/display/faces.html

MELANET: Your Commerce & Information Center Subtitled "the UnCut Black Experience," Melanet offers a nexus for black business as well as general resources of interest to the black community. The business directory is of most use for those in the greater Washington, DC, area, where you can find an African-American contractor or personal fitness instructor. Visit the virtual marketplace, with links to vendors ranging from a skin-care consultant to a funeral home. A good collection of service links lead to scholarship databases and demographic and economic data.

WEB http://www.melanet.com/melanet

The Million Man March Here's where you'll get: details about the unprecedented and historical event led by Reverend Farrakhan. Extolling the virtues of their controversial leader, Nation of Islam followers excerpt key segments of the reverend's speech and deliver commentary on its intent and effect. If you'd rather draw your own conclusions, the speech is available in its

entirety, to be downloaded from the Nation of Islam home page. For those less familiar with the NOI rhetoric, or for those with preconceived notions of its greater implications, you might be well served by delving into the discussion section for a better look at the fundamental dichotomy of this massive movement.

WEB http://www.socool.com/~rkennedy /march.html

NAACP Before you go anywhere else on the site, you'll want to get a first-hand account of the NAACP's origins from its first and foremost member, Mary White Ovington. The history, as recounted in 1914 by this fascinating woman, is essential

for anyone wanting to understand in greater depth what the NAACP is all about. From there, you might want to familiarize yourself with their current commitments, crusades, and community activism, including the legislative work and contact with federal agencies, the power of the black vote, civil rights laws, and their continued attack on restrictive zoning ordinances. Other topics include prison reform, modern "lynching" practices, desegregation, military justice, and the group's recent efforts to introduce low- and moderate-income housing into the suburbs.

WEB http://www.bin.com/assocorg /naacp/naacp.htm

FILIPINAS ONLINE

WEB http://www.filipinasmag.com

The most compelling thing about the Internet edition of *Filipinas* magazine is the Your Community section, which has created a venue for Filipino community interaction here and abroad through "facts, figures, and hyperlinks." There's a community calendar of local events, links to newsgroups

Location: http://www.filipinasmag.com/heat.html

Scapegoats: Filipino farm laborers became magnets for racial hostility as the economy got worse

and mailing lists, community news and issues, a study of Filipino-American consumer behavior, and a guide to where to send your literary and art submissions around the world. Buy a FoneCard, win a *Filipinas* subscription with your trivia acumen, comment, suggest, or chat—whatever your pleasure, your options are many.

Location: http://www.amagazine.com/at.live/amagazine/magazine96.02/15mins/15.mins.html

A. Magazine @Mall Discussion Areas Subscribe! Main Menu

Feb/Mar 1996 ▶ Contents ▶ 15 Minutes ◀

2 of a Kind

Martin Wong talks with Ming-Na Wen and

Eric Michael Zee—the hardest-working couple

in show business.

The gal from *The Single Guy* has a guy of her own
http://www.amagazine.com

One ON-Line A letter from Osaka chronicles a black teacher's mission to challenge stereotypes in Japan; a black Brit living in America questions the relationship between black Americans and black foreigners—these are but a few of the letters found in the One Nation section of this page. Other headings include One Music, Film, Marketplace, and Links. Letters aside, it's not a particularly distinct version of Web page basics.
WEB http://www.clark.net/pub /conquest/one/contents.html

soc.culture.african.american The African Americans here can be more insightful critics of black politics than any talk-show right-winger. But politics takes a back seat to the topic of all topics—the relationship between men and women. In a recent discussion about love and marriage, "What is it about marriage that women want so desperately?", more than 100 people weighed in. Stay around the group long enough, and you'll grow accustomed to the monthly "What is racism?" or its sibling discussion "Is that really racism?" After one participant (not an African American) asked, "Could it be that the funny looks you get in the elevator are more about being male?" an exasperated regular wrote back: "I really think you need a vacation from this group." Perhaps as many as half the regulars on this newsgroup are not African-American.
USENET soc.culture.african.american

Asian American

A. Magazine *A. Magazine* takes you inside the Asian-American community through highlighted features and special supplements. Although you won't be able to get the meat of the magazine, you will get a taste of what's inside. If it's Japanese animation you want, or hard-to-find classics in Asian-American literature, the @mall is the place to go, offering one-stop Net shopping for must-have, pop-culture Asian items. There's also the @Mall video box, where you can get a glimpse of the latest Asian asimation, complete with thematic descriptions; and @Mall music has the most popular tunes? Take a virtual tour of Asian-American resources, or weigh in on the ruling topics of the discussion area, if you're so inspired.
WEB http://www.amagazine.com

ACON: Asian Community Online Network What can the Asian Community Online Network offer you? Essential political, social, civil-rights, education, employment, arts, and health service references. They have created a network that allows members of the APA community to exchange ideas on current events, publicize campaigns, coordinate political strategies, announce events, and provide other relevant info. The site is slanted toward the progressive-minded—whether you're actively involved in any of the member organizations, or just interested in learning about PeaceNet or the Anti-Asian Violence Network.
WEB http://www.igc.apc.org/acon

Asian-American Mall Everything you might expect from a mall and more. Check out the Cosmetics, Popular People, Jewelry, Magazines, and even a Personals section (named Singles Solutions), where you'll find products and resources for the single Asian-American, among other resources for male and female Asian-Americans that make this site truly jammin'. Stop by the sunglasses shop and pick up a pair (you can order right from here), or order a movie from Hong Kong Video. It's cool, it's hip, and with a section called "Sexy, Sassy Stuff (18+ only)," it's more than a little racy. **WEB** http://www.stw.com/amm/amm .htm

Asian-American Resources It's not surprising that one of the links here is titled Diversity on the Web—these resources are from all over the Asian continent. Leap over to the Hmong Homepage to learn more about this Laotian mountain tribe, or find other Hmong online. Preview a new film by a Chinese director, or take a peek at Queer Asian/Pacific Resources. **WEB** http://www.mit.edu:800I/afs /athena.mit.edu/user/i/r/irie/www/aar .html

Asian-American Studies Center Founded in 1969, the UCLA Asian-American Studies Center has active programs in research, teaching, publications, archival collections, and public educational programs focusing on Asian Pacific Americans in Southern California and the nation. The Center has the largest faculty in the U.S., and the site links to online AA studies resources. **WEB** http://www.sscnet.ucla.edu/aasc

Chinese Community Information Center This is a center for, among other things, information on Chinese Community Publications and their affiliate organizations. Up to 20 papers, in Chinese and English, are available for downloading. They also serve up substantial reference lists of Chinese associations, societies, and alumni listings, and ample resources for literature, music, language, religion, and Internet directories. And kudos to CCIC for creating a link where you can seek out a former classmate, acquaintance, or even an old, undisclosed crush, from here all the way to China... literally. **WEB** http://www.ifcss.org

Chinese CyberWorld The land of Mao and Deng meets the homeland of hypertext. The library houses Chinese magazines and newspapers with a cyberpresence. The arts and entertainment page links to sites like the Chinese Zodiac, the Asian Electronic Magazines & CD Center, and the Chinese Television Network. Life in the USA connects to employment and financial assistance resources. Other pages include Community Organizations, The Youth Center, Religion, Homeland, and Opinion. For enhanced viewing, you'll want to download the Chinese software. **WEB** http://www.aan.net/chinese.htm

Phillipine News Online So you were seeking the largest Filipino newspaper in North America? You found it. Since 1961, *Philippine News* has been providing the Filipino community with headline news, worldwide reporting, community and business news, and entertainment info. Now, thanks to the Web, it offers commlink, where you can learn, on a more personal level, about who's doing what—and where. You can write letters to the webmaster, get a calendar of events, or read hometown datelines which give updated news flashes from Antipolo to Zamboanga. **WEB** http://www.philnews.com

soc.culture.asian.american Believed to be the granddaddy of identity newsgroups, soc .culture.asian.american has survived years of flesh-searing flame wars to become one of the most exciting newsgroups on the Net. Topics include English-only legislation, immigration questions, the media portrayal of Asian Americans (any recent movie, TV series, or, for that matter, comic book with Asian-American characters is likely to get a thorough going-over), issues of violence and cooperation among races and interracial dating. Sometimes these discussions function as mere triggers for flame wars between the two armed camps that dominate the group. The primary factional breakdown is simple: non-Asians who consider the group

DECONSTRUCTION GLOSSARY

Mexikitsch:
Decor heavy on the velorios (candles with saint images), Frida Kahlo coffee mugs, Zapatista posters. Art used to make a quick buck off of one's culture.

Generación Dos Equis:
n. drunk Latino twentysomethings.

Dole-oroso:
painful right-wing political leanings, or a stiff pain in your right butt cheek.

—from Frontera

to be a place for all who admire or concern themselves with Asian-American issues versus Asian Americans who consider the group to be a haven for intra-Asian discussion and bonding. Most people are truly concerned with the issues here, and they post what they feel and think with passion. They're also pretty regular about it: a few hundred new posts a night is not uncommon. Regional RL get-togethers by soc.culture.asia.american members in the Bay Area, Boston, and New York are common.
USENET soc.culture.asian.american

WWW Hmong Homepage The Hmong hail from Laos, are descendants of the southwestern Chinese, and have, like the rest of the world, their very own Web page. The lives, ideas, and experiences of this exotic culture are presented in detail, covering both their Asian homelands (Laos, Cambodia, and Thailand all have substantial Hmong populations) and their experience as immigrants in American communities. Upcoming Hmong events, newsgroups, and publications are posted, and the culture and photo sections show Hmong art (poetry, drawing, textile, and quilt-making) and landscape. For a closer look at the Hmong culture, you could, if so inclined, use their ample travel info to plan your own trip to Asia.
WEB http://www.stolaf.edu/people/cdr/hmong

Caucasian American

Center for the Study of White American Culture This is not a group for people who like to wear bedsheets and dunce caps. Instead, it is a multiracial organization operating on the premise that knowledge of one's racial heritage (even if it is the so-called mainstream) is essential to establishing understanding among races. The CSWAC also believes that people of all races are required in a group to foster a balanced knowledge of a particular race. Follow links to other resources on white culture, and be surprised at how politically correct a group like this can be.
WEB http://www.euroamerican.org/index.htm

Latino & Hispanic American

CLNET (Chicano-Latino Net) Head to this site for information, networking, cultural edification, and a good time. Start at the community center, which provides general assistance on housing, education, labor, and social services information. Stop off at the museum section for a breathtaking view of the murals of Los Angeles and the works of Frida Kahlo, or listen to some mariachi, dance the tango, and get a Spanish-language film review. Then, finish at the library for a quiet read.
WEB http://latino.sscnet.ucla.edu

LatinoLink Open the pages of this weekly ezine to find timely hypertext news articles and political commentary in English and Spanish. But all is not politics here—links to lifestyle, travel, and entertainment pages provide excellent diversions with stories about the struggle over Eva Peron's remains, the Tejano music boom, and the documentary *Carmen Miranda: Bananas is My Business*. In addition, a business section provides online commerce and a growing job bank.
WEB http://www.latinolink.com

LatinoWeb: Education & History Material on university organizations, fraternities, educational projects, cultural resources, and related articles are woven into this Web site. Some assorted Latino links include *Dia de los Muertos* (Day of the Dead), Electric Mercado: Literature (highlighted works of Latino authors), and Hispanics in the American Revolution.

WEB http://www.catalog.com/favision /history.html

Los Angeles Murals Homepage

SPARC (The Social and Public Art Resource Center) will take you on a tour of the spectacular murals and street art of of the greater Los Angeles area. View with wonder the art that started as political protest and ended up bringing beauty to the community.

WEB http://latino.sscnet.ucla.edu /murals/indexl.html

Things Latino-CyberRaza from EgoWeb Felipe, the creator of this vast collection of Latino links, has assembled a "discovery point" for cyberexplorers. Country-page links take visitors and expatriates to virtual Guatemala, Peru, and other nations. And then there are the places to meet—The Latino Connection, El Mundo Latino, and Hispanic.Com offer Spanish-language discussions. Political links, history links, and music and art links round out an impressive collection or resources. End the day with a samba and a cocktail at Alberto's Nightclub.

WEB http://edb518ea.edb.utexas.edu /html/latinos.html

Native American

A Guide to the Great Sioux Nation

It's not enough to have seen *Dances with Wolves* to begin to understand Sioux culture; you need to hear the Sioux speak for themselves as they relate the history of the buffalo hunt, the battle with Custer at Little Big Horn, Ghost Dance movement, and the massacre at Wounded Knee. Lavish illustrations of artifacts and landmarks bring the plains alive. Members of the nation will appreciate links to government and other Native American Net sites.

WEB http://www.state.sd.us/state /executive/tourism/sioux/sioux.htm

 FRONTERA

WEB http://www.mercado.com/frontera/frontera.htm

What does *tripiar* mean? To bug out. How about *slackeria*? It's a *taqueria* that caters to a mostly white (mostly unemployed) clientele. And what would it mean if you called a guy a *chongista*? Probably that he was an avant-garde Latino with a pony tail, dressed all in black (most likely sporting a goatee and reciting poetry). It's all covered in *Frontera*'s glossary of the latest lingo. This

monthly Latino ezine also includes features like an interview with Frost, the godfather of Latino hip-hop, a look at the lack of Latinos on network TV, and an assortment of reviews and short articles on the Refried Nation page.

Native American Resources The Native American experience, past and present, is presented in this far-reaching collection of links. Ponder the mysterious demise of an ancient civilization at the Anasazi site, or connect and converse with other Shoshone through the Inter-Tribal Network. Links are also provided to the powers that be—the Bureau of Indian Affairs and the U.S. Senate Committee on Native American Issues.
WEB http://www.uark.edu/depts /comminfo/www/native.html

American Historical Images on File: The Native American Experience This large collection of images tells the story of American Indians through engravings of the Battle of Bad Axe, a photo of Sioux prisoners, and a pictogram by Sitting Bull. Each of the several hundred images is annotated.
WEB http://www.csulb.edu/gc/libarts /am-indian/na

Chatanooga InterTribal Association History is ongoing for this intertribal congress. Re-read the last resolution of the original Cherokee Nation written in the face of Indian Removal in the last century, or a current article detailing a battle with a Coca-Cola heir over his proposed development atop Native American graves. Links lead to other sights dedicated to preserving Native American rights.
WEB http://www.chattanooga.net /CityBeat/politics_f/cita_f/index.html

Constanoan-Ohlone Indian Canyon Resource Learn the story of the Native Americans who "provided the human raw material for Mission Santa Cruz." A group of their California descendants has created a spectacular site dedicated to gaining tribal recognition, and to the rescue of their sacred waters from the vineyards of Northern California. You'll learn their history through hypertext links to documents and essays, and watch the falls dwindle in pictures and movies. Email links take your protests to the White House, and the Virtual Lodge links Native Americans on an active bulletin board.
WEB http://www.ucsc.edu/costano

Fond du Lac Tribal Gopher Look here for information on the current Senate Indian Affairs Committee and the reservation education program. If the need arises, this is also the place to translate English into Ojibwe and vice versa: money is zhooniyaa, and god is manidoo. (But money does not equal god.)
URL gopher://asab.fdl.cc.mn.us

Index of Native American Resources on the Internet Deceptively simple, this site holds hundreds of pointers to social, cultural, artistic, economic, educational, and political resources. Well worth a visit is the collection of electronic Native American texts which holds everything from turn-of-the-century *Atlantic Monthly*

stories to the current issue of the ezine *Red Ink Online*. Other pointers lead to language lessons, archeological dig sites, and museums. The selection of U.S. and tribal government sites collected is among the best on the Web.
WEB http://hanksville.phast.umass .edu/misc/NAresources.html

Lakota Home Page This collection of documents and bibliography represents efforts to right some wrongs—removing Crazy Horse's image from beer cans, and creating a park honoring the martyrs at Wounded Knee. Debates over teaching religion outside a spiritual setting and a "Declaration of War Against Exploiters of Lakota Spirituality" attempt to protect Native religion and culture in the face of a New Age onslaught.
WEB http://maple.lemoyne.edu/~bucko /lakota.html

The Native American Culture Home Page This is an outsider's guide to the world of the Pueblos of Northern New Mexico. A historical essay takes the reader through the 800 years of history held in the adobe compounds. The calendar of events highlights feast days like the Corn Dances of Santa Clara and the feast of San Geronimo at Taos where Catholic and native religions combine. Read the online etiquette guide before attending.
WEB http://LAHS.LosAlamos.K12.nm .us/sunrise/work/piaseckj/homepage .html

LGBT

ALL YOU WANT IS A LITTLE RESPECT. QUEERS ON THE WEB ARE CERTAINLY DOING THEIR PART

OVER THE PAST FEW YEARS the gay, lesbian, and bisexual communities have gone online in full force and in characteristic style, so if it tickles your fancy, tune in to the links that follow for the latest social, cultural, and political LGBT happenings worldwide. Students can get in touch with countless resources and activist groups on hundreds of college campuses. Prospective travelers can get tips and pointers from those who have gone before, from accommodations listings to gay tour operators. On the political front, the same-sex marriage debate is heating up across the nation and there's no time like the present to organize. Humor, gossip, coming-out stories, true confessions, and more are out there as well. Dykes, queens, trannies, and those of you who don't yet have your own buzzword, log on! You may just find the most accepting community yet.

Location: http://www.sappho.com/lart/tamara4.htm

WWW CYBERQUEER LOUNGE

WEB http://cyberzine.org/html/GLAIDS/glaidshome page.html • *picture:* WEB http://www.sappho.com/lart /1911_on.htm

Pride, politics, and purchasing power are the main focuses of the CyberQueer Lounge. It's one of the best places on the Net to find interactive activism issues and it contains an encyclopedia that will take you to everything even remotely related to LGBT life online. A paid membership at the lounge gives you access to locked areas, private chat rooms, and more. One of the most unique resources is the Pride Mall, which links you to queer-centric and queerfriendly merchants and merchandise.

Starting points

....

Alternative Sexuality/Sexual Politics Resource List A collection of links to gay, lesbian, transgender, polyamory, body design, and S/M sites online. Well-organized with cheap, cheerful graphics. Stars denote recommended pages, and the site author has pretty eclectic tastes—favorites include Bisexual Hell, The Sandmutopian Garden, and Transsexuals in the Work Place—A Guide for Employers, among others.
WEB http://www.infoqueer.org/queer /qis/vl-queer.html

The Gay and Lesbian Community Forum One of the largest and most complete resources for the gay community available on the Net, the Gay and Lesbian Community Forum covers every imaginable subject, from community activism to cooking to classifieds. You can discuss boycotts or find a roommate on the Community Issues board; and in the Dialogue between Gays & Straights folder you'll find gays and straights engaging in a surprisingly intelligent discussion, with nary a flame from bashers or religious zealots. If it affects you, it's in here.
AMERICA ONLINE *keyword* **glcf**

The Gay Cafe For about $5 a month you can receive this premium social service, with live Java chat rooms, exclusive erotic image galleries, a library of queer fiction, and dozens of forums. The entire LGBT

community doesn't really benefit from all these fantastic services and fun features, however, since the site is definitely male-centric. The names of the membership packages, including "Valueman" and "Sugardaddy," are especially telling. Obviously, the service does not exclude women and women-lovers, it's just the way the site happens to be coming together.
WEB http://www.gaycafe.com

infoQueer Not just another pretty index. While infoQueer does contain hundreds of links to mags and ezines, health info, international and regional gay resources, transsexual resources, cultural and political pages, and other queer sites, it also hosts a unique feature—Home Pages of People OUT on the Net. This is a link list of over 100 men and women who've come out to the online world. Meet Sue Lacey's cat, currently slinking around Adelaide, Australia. Get some online insight into Bård Kjos of Trondheim, Norway. And explore the virtual playground of Las Vegas' Lenadams Dorris. Then submit your own home page to the list—you'll be getting hits, and maybe hit on, in no time.
WEB http://server.berkeley.edu/mblga

NetWatch Top Ten—Gay Interest Not just a collection of the biggest directories on the Web; they put a little thought into their selections. From multimedia soap operas to the Human

Rights Campaign, lesbian hotlists to Gay TV listings—this is an eclectic little guide to the best queer sites online.
WEB http://www.pulver.com/netwatch /topten/tt8.htm

Planet Out Available in Spanish, French, Dutch, Russian and German (and English), this is a truly world-wide gay, lesbian, bi and transgendered digital community. Major gay rights organizations like GLAAD (Gay and Lesbian Alliance Against Defamation) have a strong presence here, while innumerable topic-specific forums and support groups make this an invaluable addition to the MSN fold.
MSN out

Queers 101 Want to know what other netizens think of queers and queerness? You'll find every voice on the airwave spectrum at Queers 101. The Facts & Opinions section links you to sites offering a variety of views on queerness and its relation to religion, science, government, and history. The Advice Column offers links to support for the queer-curious and queer-confused, coming out stories, and resources for intra-lifestyle concerns like lesbian battering and workplace issues. Warm Fuzzies links to dozens of gay-positive sites, and people, around the Net. The forums are up now, and they're still pretty empty, but when they start filling up, Queers 101 will be one of the best places online for open discussion of all aspects of sexuality.

WEB http://www.webcom.com/kris/queer.html

Newsstand

The Advocate Unlike another big offline queerzine, *The Advocate* doesn't offer much in the way of orginal material. But just to tease you, the contents section has one-sentence descriptions of articles available in the offline publication. There are also a handful of events listings here, for stuff like the Paula Poundstone tour and the $200 per-person AIDS fundraiser, Take Off 96. An interactive quiz asks your opinion about gay content in mainstream movies. If you so desire, you can buy a subscription to the print version of the *Advocate* online. The only saving grace here is a relatively active forum which discusses everything from a new study on the effects of aminoacridine on AIDS to dykes in the Olympics. The cover scans are pretty nice, too.

WEB http://www.advocate.com

The Brain That Wouldn't Die "Welcome to the new format for The Brain That Wouldn't Die, the Web site that achieves enlightenment by contemplating the question, 'If you write a bunch of essays, pepper them with HTML, stick them on the Web, and no one browses them, do they make a sound?'" This 'zine is a spout hooked up to one man's mouth, spilling over with eclectic rants, raves, reviews and responses to the times in which we live. Only three editions of the Brain are available, "Kill the Fascists?!?" "No Fats, No Fems," and "Ecclecticism with Elcat," but they're pretty darn entertaining, and sometimes even enlightening. Features range from a

 Q WORLD

WEB http://www.qworld.org

This is the heart of queer cyberspace. The site leads off with two fantastic lesbian ezines (see the lesbian subheader for reviews), and an **LGBT** inclusive mag called *Qzine* that offers exhaustive features (Pride Month), quotable quotes ("... God forbid a straight person should acknowledge that there are pleasures associated with their anus...."), and articles on politics, sports, and news. QWorld hosts three **IRC** chat sections devoted to the community, gay men, and lesbians, with special events like gay teachers chat, transtalk, house of style, and lesbian family chat. There are also

a dozen forums with more than a hundred folders ranging from GLBVA (Gay Veterans) to Dear Madame Lesbo, queer-friendly churches to computer help, personals to pets. Finally, the Qlinks page provides link lists for every community and activity (there's even a section for "straight, but cool" sites), if for some strange reason you haven't found what you were looking for at QWorld.

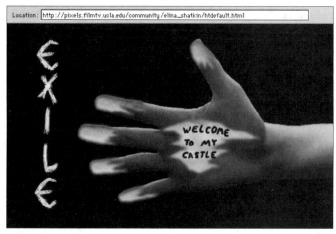

Location: http://pixels.filmtv.ucla.edu/community/elina_shatkin/htdefault.html

Exile could use a hand
http://pixels.filmtv.ucla.edu/community/elina_shatkin

review of *The Last Supper* to an Interactive Song Writers Corner, from Homo-Language Hints to Chubby Chasers Tell All, from the Battle of the Sexual Orientations to Newt's World. The site also includes literary links and a java game where you can blow the head off Pete Wilson, Ronnie Reagan, and other upholders of the Great Straight Way.
WEB http://www.he.net/~jbeek/index.html

Exile A high-concept punk 'zine with lesbian leanings. *Exile* contains a few really cool features and a lot of dumb prattle. The high-tech version of the site, for some reason, only carries the actual ezine: This is where the dumb prattle—collected from netizen submissions—is located. We love free-thought forums, and would never want to discourage anyone from mouthing off, but please people, make it

interesting! Occasionally you'll stumble onto well-formed rants, but more often you're left with deadly dull lists about why someone hates their boss.
WEB http://pixels.filmtv.ucla.edu/community/elina_shatkin

Gay Source One of the best magazines online, queer or otherwise, but perhaps too slick and mainstream for young guerilla warriors—Zima and Stoli advertise here, 'nuff said? The Happenings section includes news reports culled from around the Web, including everything from "CA Transsexual Expelled from Public Park" to "House of Representatives passes Anti-Marraige Bill." Aesthetica houses interviews with gay authors, collections of essays by PWLAs, and album reviews.
WEB http://www.gaysource.com

Holy Titclamps Rush, Pat, and Newtie's worst nightmare is

Larry-Bob, queerzine connoisseur. He keeps track of all the on- and offline home brews at *Queerzine Explosion*, and his own dish is *Holy Titclamps*, a hardcore little 'zine with a big mouth. Articles on prison rape, road trips, AIDS, and nightclub utopia rub elbows with editorial rants on anti-assimilation and quitting smoking, more radical fairie stuff than you can handle, book and music reviews, a link list with some personality, and best of all, tons of brilliant underground comics strips and original artwork.
WEB http://www.io.com/~larrybob

Queer Zine Explosion *Bimbox, Chicken Coop, Diseased Pariah News, Eidos, Fucktooth, Gay Saivite Hindu Brotherhood Zine, Harvard Gay & Lesbian Review, I'm Not A Feminist But..., Jurryrig, Lickety-spit:, My Car Pinto, Naked Teenagers That Fight Crime, Oh...: Tomboy, The Polished Knob, Queer Action Figures, Skyjack: For Gay People Who Fly, Thorn, Venus Infers: A Leatherdyke Quarterly, Waffle Stomper, X-it Press, Yes, Ms. Davis.* No, they're not college bands, they're queerzines! Dozens of reviews offered by the inimitable Larry-Bob. Also offers ordering info.
WEB http://www.qrd.org/qrd/www/media/print/queerzine.explosion

The U Report Many communities come together in this splashy mess of a magazine (we mean mess in the nicest

possible way) full of pop culture and the people who create it. It does lean toward the queen, but it still speaks to everyone. Editions range from a buncha fierce photos of San Fran queens and a fantastic interview with Justin Bond/Kiki Durain, to reports on the Kombucha Mushroom Culture, lit reviews, dead celebrity gossip, Web art, U Report Sports with Gym and Kneel, and oh so much more. One warning: *U* can take a camp attitude toward anything, even (gasp!) politics. The irony-impaired should abstain. It's daily mantra;"The only thing I can really trust is my own self-indulgence."
WEB http://www.hooked.net/ureport

Lesbians

Caryl's Lesbian Links A pride purple index gives you a healthy helping of lesbian links. The sites are all reviewed and rated, from First Base (includes some lesbian content, but it's buried) to Home Run ("just as dykey as you can get").
WEB http://www.columbia.edu/~vk20 /links.html

Fat!So? Fellow fatty Rush Limbaugh would not approve of this site. The front door is covered with pics of big bare bottoms, and the content inside is just as confrontational. While this is supposed to be the open arms version of the ezine *Fat-Girl*, embracing not just fat

dykes, but everyone, regardless of sex or sexuality, it's still very dyke-centric. *FatGirl*'s caustic sense of humor and "pride-purple" design makes weight politics truly entertaining, with features such as "Mighty Morphin' Oprah," a trés-friendly chat cafe, and articles on everything from talk show titles— "Fat women and families who hate them for it"—to the dark side of Weight Watchers.
WEB http://www.fatgirl.com

Girlfriends—The Magazine Of Lesbian Enjoyment Created by a group of mutineers from *On Our Backs*, *Girlfriends* is a more inclusive lesbian lifestyle magazine offering news, editorials, parenting support, enter-

A DYKE'S WORLD

WEB http://www.qworld.org/DykesWorld/index.html

This is the mothership, baby! You must go here for all your lesbian resources online, not simply because it's comprehensive, but because it has lots of funky animation, a friendly conversational tone, a number of femme-force features, and happens to be one of the best-designed pages online, period. Links are annotated and split into several pages. Features include CartoonCorner, a gallery

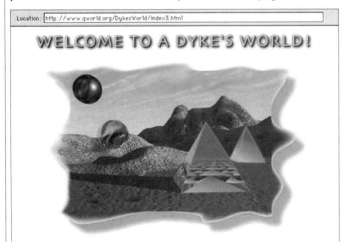

of the site authors, graphic creations, a forum called Let's Talk, Sista!, Eva Dahlgren Page, African Goddesses, and the very exciting Eurosappho Picturebook, showcasing the thoughts and images of Eurosappho subscribers. A definite bookmark for the discerning dyke.

tainment coverage, fiction and more. Right now, they only have a few of the offline articles and artwork online, but if the fare is this consistently impressive, *Girlfriends* is sure to be the word in the next wave.
WEB http://www.gfriends.com

Kinky Women Expanding Boundaries Want to get the lowdown on B&D safety? Just coming out of the kinky closet and need support? Or do you just want to read some dirty stories about femme-to-femme S&M? A sexy and supportive spot for D/S. S&M, and B&D. Lots of erotica, real and fictional, discussion of safety and health issues, merchandise and personals, and articles on being lesbian and kinky and on being a kinky mom.
WEB http://www.kweb.org

Lesbian Avengers—The London Chapter The London chapter of the lesbian activist group really knows how to tell the tale of its campaign: performances of "Juliet and Juliet" in Hackney, a suburb; placement of surplus mannequins in department store windows holding signs saying, "chic lesbian" and "S&M dyke"; and a chain-in to the *Sunday Times*' file cabinets. The site serves as an advertisement for the group's activities.
WEB http://www.cs.ucl.ac.uk/students/zcacsst/LA.html

The Lesbian History Project Southern Californian lesbians and lesbians of color are the

focus here, but the scope of medium, era, and experience is broad enough to include all lesbians, everywhere, at any point in time, and of any persuasion. Hundreds of articles and theses, oral histories, journals, interview, biographies, chronologies, and histories. Check out the small but growing photograph section, a dramatic connection to your past, and a reassurance of your future.
WEB http://www-lib.usc.edu/~retter/main.html

Lesbian Safer Sex As if lesbian issues could get any more invisible, lesbian safe sex and AIDS are rarely addressed even in non-mainstream press. Get the guidelines, and some really nice photos, here. Safe sex is hot sex, indeed.
WEB http://www.cmpharm.ucsf.edu/~troyer/safesex/lesbianss.html

Lesbians A fascinating interactive multimedia project. Click on any letter in "lesbians" and you are faced with a request for any kind of material on a certain topic—sex, dreams, politics, biographies, relationships, spirituality and more. There are only a handful of entries for each letter at the moment, but the entries range from a single paragraph of personal erotica about the Palladium's Night of 5,000 Women, to a Quick-Time movie on breast cancer. But don't just browse the archives, leave your mark!
WEB http://www.echonyc.com/~lesbians

Yoohoo Lesbians! Another stellar annotated link list covering a dozen topics, including Protecting Our Rights, Daily Living, and Celebrating Diversity, to name but a few. Hundreds of resources.
WEB http://www.sappho.com/yoohoo

Gays

Esteem Are you a gay or bisexual man with feelings of low self-esteem? This list explores the consequences of and factors involved with low self-esteem.
EMAIL listserv@queernet.org ✍ *Type in message body:* subscribe esteem (your full name)

The House of Clarice House Mother Miranda Clarice's children have gone online and all out at this fabulous site. Or rather, they will very shortly— right now they only have a link list, some fascinating images, and an online form for House of Clarice Membership. Be willing to part with some very private information, sisters. The site promises to be a mecca for the whole queer spectrum, but the opening graphic seems to have a rather targeted appeal.
WEB http://www.geocities.com/WestHollywood/3407

Out And Proud A meeting place and forum exclusively for gay and bi men, *Out and Proud* forms a spirited, supportive community. Pen Pals and Pen Pal PowWows are your access to communication, with hundreds of interesting, available guys. Real Life Writing ranges from coming out stories to erotica, with some really touching pieces from teenagers. The Help Center offers online advice from a queer-friendly psychologist, a more social "Dear Abby" type advice column, and an article on things to consider when coming out of the closet. Links, employment classifieds, and calls for submission round out the site. **WEB** http://catalog.com/outproud

The Site of the Gay Male Body Is Its History Howard Smith's fascinating abstact media piece. Believe us: you have to experience it for yourself. **WEB** http://www.usc.edu/dept/finearts /hs/SITE.html

Why Is Earring Magic Ken So Controversial? Because many people were convinced that the first pierced Ken doll wore a chrome cock ring around his neck, Earring Magic Ken's value has "risen steadily" among Barbie collectors. Here you'll find a brief history of gay clone activist rave fashion, circa 1988, and denials by various Mattel spokespersons: "It's a necklace. It holds charms he can share with Barbie. C'mon, this is a doll designed for little girls; something like that would be totally inappropriate." **WEB** http://deepthought.armory.com /~zenugirl/cockringken.html

Bisexuals

Anything that Moves The infamous offline magazine makes a wonderful online debut here, starting out with some clarification about their name: "We deliberately chose the radical approach. We are creating dialogue through controversy. We are challenging people to face their own external and internal biphobia. We are demanding attention, and are re-defining anything that moves on our own terms. This is one of the

OUT.com
WEB http://www.out.com

America's No. I gay and lesbian magazine is now a top-flight gay and lesbian site online. If you like your Web sites oh-so-slick, exhaustively comprehensive, and just a wee bit commercialized, there's no better way to keep up with queer culture, stay informed on queer issues, or meet a new friend, longtime lover, or online fling. There's an entire network of forums in the Community section, organized by region, country, and social group—L, G, B, & T, teens, people of color, marriage and parenting, and clean and sober queers each get their own forum. The Culture section offers archived articles and current features on everything from Iggy Pop to Anna Sui's fall line, to hot new non-fiction like *The Girls Next Door: Into the Heart of Lesbian America*. The News section may be the best in cyberspace for gay issues: It's updated daily and offers articles on topical issues ranging from school prayer to employment and housing discrimination to religious concerns, from media visibility to AIDS news. Given that the offline mag only comes out once a month, it's an impressive accomplishment.

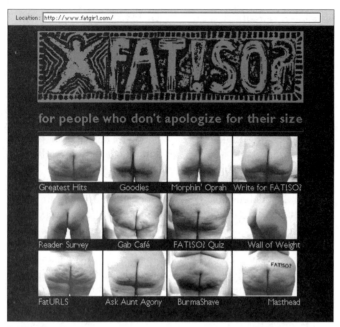

Location: http://www.fatgirl.com/

for people who don't apologize for their size

Greatest Hits   Goodies   Morphin' Oprah   Write for FAT!SO?

Reader Survey   Gab Café   FAT!SO? Quiz   Wall of Weight

FatURLS   Ask Aunt Agony   BurmaShave   Masthead

Baby's got back. A dozen times over
http://www.fatgirl.com

more polished (read: well-produced, not commercial) queerzines out there, with articles, editorials, fiction, art, comics, and poetry that range from the personal anecdote "I Was A Teenage Homophobe" to a huge illustrated history of bisexuality behind the iron curtain titled "Shades of Red and Pink."
WEB http://www.hooked.net/users/jonesey/atm.html

BiAct-L Elaine, the "list dominatrix," leads her troops in the fight against bi-ignorance. Add your two cents to *Coming Out Bi*, a pamphlet under development; sign up for Fox TV's open auditions for a real-life bisexual couple; or find out how to enroll your local queer

activist group in your state's Adopt-a-Highway program. Recent campaigns have included educating the parents' group PFLAG and telephoning support to Visa, under attack from the religious right for contributing to Gay Games IV.
EMAIL listserv@brownvm.brown.edu ✍
Type in subject line: subscribe biact-l (your full name)

BiDay BiNight "We'd like to meet OTHER bi/open-minded, non-sexist, happy, groovy, together, PUNK, artsy, silly, friendly, non-MaCHo, nice people to be friends and explore 100 percent safe things, like Net/phone sex, massage, mastrubation, and maybe other stuff. We are ONLY interested in people

who are PUNK at heart (looks don't matter, although piercings and tattoos are interesting to look at, and I happen to shave)." Check out hundreds of personal ads from all over the U.S., link to other bisites and bimail lists, and add a personal anecdote from the heart (or lower) to bistories.
WEB http://www.kirstens.com/bipages/bipage.html

Bisexual Hell A poorly organized hotlist of bi and poly sites from Annie Sprinkle's Homepage, to A Brief History of the Bisexual Movement, to Bearpaw's polyamory page.
WEB http://www.tiac.net/users/danam/bisexual.HTML

Bisexual Options One of the most interesting features in this enormous page is the biographies listing, where hundreds of men and women have offered their vital statistics and email addresses. It's like an in-depth personal ad. City Bi City gives links to regional bi sites. In BiWorld International News, people from all over the world offer personal insight into the bi scene in their native country, with recent queer newsflashes and on/offline resources.
WEB http://205.216.138.19/~websites/fritzk

Bisexual Resource List This is the biggest bi-list out there, kids, with offline contact info and online links to newsletters, radio shows, literature, HIV/AIDS education, Usenet,

general info, mags, home pages, Fight the Right sites, and much more.
WEB http://www.qrd.org/qrd/www /orgs/brc/brl-toc.html

Bisexuality & Related Topics
From the Bisexual Purity Test to Slippery When Wet, this is a long hotlist of graphics, resources, essays and articles, 'zines and organizations for the bi, the bicurious, and the bifriendly.
WEB http://coos.dartmouth.edu /~jcollins/kataBisex.html

soc.bi Archives Along with this very informative bisexuality FAQ, the soc.bi archives Web site offers dozens of soc.bios with details (intimate and otherwise) on soc.bi posters, an eclectic poetry collection, newsgroup stats, an archive of digests, some queer humor, and lots of recipes involving chocolate.
WEB http://serf.org/~jon/soc.bi

Transgendered

Above and Beyond Gender
Another source for resources— merchandise, personals, articles, regional pages, newsgroups, and general transgenedered sites.
WEB http://www.abmall.com/cb/tg /res.html

alt.transgendered/soc.support.tra nsgendered "The Social Security administration has told me they must still process any paperwork I send them with me listed as 'male.' How many

states still force a TS to either go around with a 'Scarlet Letter' showing their born gender, or seek an illegal birth certificate as the only possible options?" Two serious but friendly newsgroups that constantly cross-post. The support newsgourp also tends to get a few more posts about both loneliness/depression and beauty secrets .
USENET alt.transgendered • soc .support.transgendered

Gender 3 A fascinating media project based on Pr. Martine Rothblatt's book entitled "The Apartheid of Gender." The text explores and deconstructs the political, scientific, psychological, and sociological meanings of gender, promoting a future of liquid sexual identity and sexuality, in some ways spurred on by the virtual revolution. Photographs, magazine covers, and advertisements reflecting our changing cultural impressions of gender illustrate this daring and convincing piece.
WEB http://199.171.16.53/gender3.html

Tstar A great index of transgendered resources, ranging from general resources, to newsgroups, from support groups to activism, and from hormones to personal trannie home pages.
WEB http://travesti.geophys.mcgill.ca /~tstar

Youth

Elight! "The point I'm hoping to make is, more people are beginning to support gay

rights. Sure, some people will refuse to accept that we are equals, but they are being shot down by the large number of gays and straights that support gay rights. Support can be found in many unexpected places." A collection of sometimes painful, sometimes positive coming-out stories is only part of this great magazine for gay teens. There are personals from all over the world, poetry and fiction, articles on news and personal experiences with gay issues, rants and raves, and more. But don't just read, contribute!
WEB http://www.youth.org/elight

International Gay & Lesbian Youth Organization If you're under 26, you can join the IGLYO, which aims to provide support networks for gay and lesbian youth and to aid in their emancipation. Though the group's activities find their strongest support in Europe, plans are in the works for expansion into North America. Besides information on becoming a member and details on the annual IGLYO conference, the site carries a press release outlining the organization's anti-NAMBLA stance.
URL gopher://uclink.berkeley.edu:1901 /11/other/intern/iglyo

Resources for Parents of Gay, Lesbian, Bisexual, and Transgendered Youth Coming out of the closet is a difficult experience for parents of queer kids as well as for the kids themselves. Many parents, even supportive ones, have questions and issues. This is a great place to start your education and look for support. In addition to the FAQ, you'll also get resources and advice on how to help your kid with problems at school or in the community, as well as activism links to parents like who've joined the fight for their kids' rights, your kids' rights, and the rights of all LGBTs.

WEB http://www.pe.net/~bidstrup /parents.htm

soc.support.youth.gay-lesbian-bi
"I'm 19 and my only connection to other gay or bisexual people is my computer. I need to know if other bisexual people go through phases. Sometimes I'm only interested in guys and sometimes I only like girls. Does that mean sometimes I'm gay and other times I'm straight?" "As far as being gay or straight vs. being bi, labels don't mean that much, and I wouldn't use any of them, except queer if you like (but that's only helpful around other queers; it doesn't tell str8 people anything positive). Accepting yourself comes first; explaining yourself to others can come later, and that's all labels are good for." Coming-out stories, confusion and angst met with supportive advice, and a few tidbits of politics and news flashes. With suicide rates as high as they are among queer teens, this is an invaluable resource.

USENET soc.support.youth.gay -lesbian-bi

Square Pegs—Queer Youth Zine
What started out as a little Santa Cruz queerzine is now one of the coolest ezines online for young people. The biggest, and best part of the mag is the homo(genius) section offering some of the most accomplished, effective artworks and articles on the Net—interviews, poetry, images, cartoons, and fiction from the front. What's Up gives mostly local info on LGBT happenings about town. Kool Queer offers reviews for reels, reads, and records. Political links include all of your "representatives" (yeah, right) in the House and Senate.

WEB http://arts.ucsc.edu/squarepegs /home.index.html

Ethnic

Arena "According to reports received by the International Gay and Lesbian Human Rights Commission, gay men and transvestites in the Mexican city of Chihuahua began to suffer an intense campaign of harassment and repression beginning sometime in October 1994. That repression continues today. Urgent and strongly worded letters are needed insisting that all government attacks against sexual minorities in the state of Chihuahua cease immediately." Urgent actions, legal info, and advice for travel in Latin America and Spain, a list of influential LGB Hispanics, and the history of the diversity flag, are all available here in

both Spanish and English. Some articles are available only in Spanish.

WEB http://www.indiana.edu/~arenal /Homepage.html

Black Homies Page A calendar of community events, classifieds with everything from employment to personals, community links, and both lesbian and gay erotica—they want your pics for the site! Articles on the Dallas scene and queer rants of the week give a moment of levity between news stories like these: "Tyrone 'Tyra' Hunter died of injuries incurred in an automobile accident last August. Witnesses stated emergency workers laughed upon discovering that Hunter was actually a black male, and that the emergency workers began calling him names. Although, the Fire Chief personally interviewed 16 firefighters who witnessed the incident, no one would identify which rescue worker stopped treating Hunter."

WEB http://www.blk.com/blk

The Blacklist A stirring, well-presented list of lesbian, gay, bisexual, and transgendered people of African descent, with brief biographies and meditations on what it means to be black and gay.

WEB http://www.udel.edu/nero/lists /blacklist.html

Jewish GLBT Archives Link lists for regional queer-friendly synagogues here and abroad, inter-

national organizations, Web sites and chat, shopping, health issues and more. The Virtual Newspaper will take you to topical sites on every thing from AIDS to culinary arts. Entire indexes of reviews and links are available for films, novels, and plays. There's a growing link and bio list of Members of the Tribe, and lots more. Check out the background on the offline archives, one man's vision of collecting the experiences, history and images of Jewish LGBTs.
WEB http://www.magic.ca/~faygelah /Index.html

Isis Want to know which women are shining a spotlight on the black-out in Hollywood? You'll find links to film projects and filmmakers, including the likes of the African Film Festival and Vertamae Grosvenor. Want to know where you came from, so you can see where you're going? The OurStory page links to general resources, covering historical and cultural icons from Kagendo Murungi to Rosa Parks to FloJo. Links to fan pages of sisters on stage and screen from Josephine to Urban Bush Women. Audre Lorde is online, too, and so is *Callaloo*, a diaspora lit journal. Written-word sites are linked in the lit section. Spirituality comes in all forms, from the Egyptian book of the dead to a painting of the "Black Madonna."
WEB http://www.netdiva.com/isisplus .html

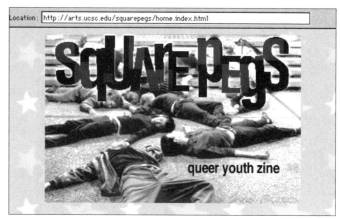

This is *not* about Lauren and Patty at Weemawee High School
http://arts.ucsc.edu/squarepegs/home.index.html

ULOAH—United Lesbians of African Heritage An organizational profile and mission statment, mailing list info, and a little herstory: "In March 1989, a group of Black women convened to plan a Black lesbian conference which would be infused with women's energy and spirit. Through our work together, a new vision evolved: a vision of an organization for Black lesbians based on principles of sisterhood and empowerment."
WEB http://members.aol.com/uloah

Utopia A slick, professional mag with a personal touch. Gasian & Lezian of the month features a photo and bio of the winner plucked from hundreds of Web submissions—regular people with something to say (or something to show!) You can meet your next friend or lover at the message center. There's AIDS & HIV info and contacts for eight Asian countries, and safe sex rules in six

Southeast Asian languages. The travel section covers Thailand, Cambodia, Singapore, Hong Kong, Taiwan, Indonesia, Korea, Malaysia, and Vietnam, with links to info and personal queer-friendly city guides. The Women's Space offers info on organizations, publications, and travel tips for various regions, provides a lesbian message center, and a link list. And last but not least, there is a fantastic online gallery of queer Asian art.
WEB http://www2.best.com/~utopia

Partners and marriage

Domestic Partners For gays, lesbians, or bisexuals interested in or concerned about issues like employment benefits for domestic partners.
EMAIL domestic-request@cs.cmu.edu
✍ *Write a request*

Domestic Partnerships and Same-Sex Marriages Domestic and international news, articles,

Netsite: http://www.webworqs.com/g3/warning.html

WARNING
ONLY 2 SEXES
ALLOWED!

It's the law that creates an apartheid of sex.

Queers took to the Net to protest DOMA
http://199.171.16.53/gender3.html

and case reports about issues such as the definition of a family, domestic partner policies, same sex marriages, and adoption. Some of the policies most often discussed are those set up, proposed, or denied by academic institutions.
WEB http://www.cs.cmu.edu/afs/cs.cmu.edu/user/scotts/domestic-partners/mainpage.html

The Equal Marriage Rights Home Page The best place to get information and resources about same-sex marriages. The site leads off with a map and chart of the progress of same-sex marriage rights in the U.S., indicating the states which have passed laws or are trying to pass laws against same-sex marriages. It then provides information on each state's legal position on gay marriage and its pending legislation. Links lead to lobbying groups, mailing lists, sociological

reports, and bibliographies. Articles are available on gay marriage from such diverse sources as the Log Cabin Republicans, the Texas Human Rights Foundation, and Camille Paglia. There is also information about donating to HERMP, the Hawaii Equal Rights Marriage Project. For $17.50, you even get a T-shirt!
WEB http://www.nether.net/~rod/html/sub/marriage.html

Marriage A mailing list set up by activists concerned about ensuring the right of a man to marry a man and a woman to marry a woman.
EMAIL majordomo@abacus.oxy.edu ✍
Type in message body: subscribe marriage (your email address)

Partner's Task Force for Gay & Lesbian Couples A very well-produced collection of resources and information about same-

sex marriages, including the full texts of reports and essays, explanations of legal issues, advertisements for videos and books about gay and lesbian couples, a gallery of couple photos, quotes about same-sex couples, contact info for religious ceremonies and wedding planners, and more.
WEB http://www.eskimo.com/~demian/partners.html

Parenting

Children Of Lesbians and Gays Everywhere "There is absolutely no evidence that children are psychologically or physically harmed by having gay, lesbian or bisexual parents.—Rofes, E.E., 1983, Herdt, 1989." Membership and services information, as well as information on the COLAGE mailing list and their annual conference is available.
WEB http://www.colage.org

Gay Dads A few of the men here chose to become fathers after living for years as out gay men. They want to know at what age they should come out to their children, trade titles of gay children's books, and share the joys of staying up until 2 a.m. to the tune of "Rock-a-Bye, Baby" instead of "I Will Survive." Most, however, are men who married before they were comfortable with their gay identity, hoping marriage would straighten them out. These men are more concerned about their relationships with their wives than with their chil-

dren, despite the group's name. Bisexuals are welcome.
EMAIL majordomo@vector.casti.com
✍ *Type in message body:* subscribe gaydads

The Lesbian Mom's Homepage Want to know the pros and cons of anonymous sperm donors? Worried about potential legal problems surrounding adoption? This page offers comprehensive resources and personal experience, a contact info list, as well as information on doctors and sperm banks. All aspects of insemination including terminology, diet and health issues, and adoption.
WEB http://www.lesbian.org/moms

The LesBiGay Parenting Home Page The most comprehensive annotated index to LGB parenting issues on the Net. It also has general LGBT resources,

kids pages, and domestic violence links. A must-have bookmark for any queer family.
WEB http://www.albany.net/~gelco /welcome.htm

Parents and Friends of Lesbians and Gays Information on PFLAG's activities and how to get involved with the national association for parents and friends of lesbians and gays.
URL gopher://uclink.berkeley.edu:1901 /00/other/national-orgs/pflag/pflag

International

France Queer Resources Directory A guide to having a gay ol' time in Paris, from descriptions of Gai Pied's Bastille Day Ball to the Salon de l'Homosocialité. Decide whether you'd rather hang out with Father Jacques Perotti at the Centre Lesbienne et Gai's weekly *homosexualité*

et spiritualité event or camp it up on the dance floor at Le Queen. In addition to listing queer symposiums, rallies, support groups, and parties, this site includes profiles of queer events in Paris and news coverage of queer issues both locally and abroad.
WEB http://fglb.qrd.org:8080/fqrd /fqrd-e.html

Gay Quebec A guide to lesbian and gay resources in the province. Hotels, B&Bs, restaurants, bars and clubs, organizations, publications, and even personals can be found here. Links connect to other sites, including Montreal's Lesbian and Gay Center (located in the Gay Village there). The site is bilingual and primarily covers Montreal, Quebec City, and Hull.
WEB http://www.gaibec.com

MICHELLE'S MID-DAY BREAK
WEB http://www.imagin.net/~crashit/midday

"The fantasy shape is indistinct; gauzy: shivering with fabric of an alien, exciting chrysalid sex. These my boundaries defined: each plane sharp, unambiguous; purpose, obvious at a glance or inquiring touch, at least. And alone in, the madding—who looks beyond the public play?—DAVID"

Though at first it may seem like one trannies tribute to blatant self-promotion, a closer look shows that it is, in fact, one of the more comprehensive sites on the Net. Whether you're looking for support, expressive artwork, or girl talk, you can find what you want here, and be who you want, as well.

The Gay Traveler Seeking a homo-friendly vacation? America Online's complete gay and lesbian traveler resource features listings of queer tour operators, events calendars, and IGTA (International Gay Travel Association) member listings. The member listings give you the names of hotels, airlines, and cruise lines, as well as links to gay travel World Wide Web pages. For recommendations, helpful hints, and warnings about destinations from other travelers, head to the message board here. You'll get insider information from the best sources, and the opportunity to make new friends online.
AMERICA ONLINE *keyword* glcftravel

Outrageous Tokyo Tokyo isn't exactly a mecca for gay-rights activists—only 1,200 people showed up at the annual Gay Pride Parade in one of the world's most populous cities. But underneath the woodwork, and with a little help from *Outrageous Tokyo*, an English-language gay quarterly, you'll find a few outlets for the non-political majority. Shinjuku 2-chome, gay-lesbian central in Tokyo, boasts approximately 20 gay bars (but only three for lesbians). If you have Adobe Acrobat, you can download a map of the district and take a virtual walk through the streets yourself, as well a really cool print version of the new offline mag.
WEB http://shrine.cyber.ad.jp/~darrell /outr/home/outr-home.html

Queer in Israel A small but growing collection of information about gay life in Israel, informally presented, including a mini-essay about the gay scene in Israel, information about community centers, and recent legal decisions affecting gay issues.
WEB http://qrd.tau.ac.il

SchWeb—Schwul im Web *Schwul* means "faggot" in German, but the word seems to have been reclaimed from the gay-bashers. Most of this page is for events in Germany, but you'll find information on pride celebrations throughout Europe. And even if you haven't planned on a trip abroad to alleviate boy trouble, the "Dear Boy" advice column might still make this site worth a visit.
WEB http://www.casti.com/GQRD/svsk /svsk.html

Trikone (Lesbian and Gay South Asians) Pink *trikones* (*trikone* is Sanskrit for triangle) flourish in the South Asian gay and lesbian worldwide community, thanks to this organization for bent folk from Afghanistan, Bangladesh, Bhutan, Burma, India, the Maldives, Nepal, Pakistan, Sri Lanka, and Tibet. The Web page carries highlights from *Trikone* magazine, information on speakers of interest to the South Asian gay and lesbian community, and the details on the annual *Trikone*-sponsored Pride Utsav convention. If you're looking to hook up with local organizations from Bombay to Boston,

check out *Trikone*'s South Asian Queer Resources list.
WEB http://www.rahul.net/trikone

Culture

GALA Choruses Got a hankering to sing Sondheim's greatest hits with your queer brothers and sisters? There's probably a GALA chorus in your area. This site offers a FAQ on the organization, articles and reviews, chorus and community links, and extensive, searchable databases of performances, recordings, choruses, and online GALA members.
WEB http://www.csun.edu/dlt /CHORUS

Homo Radio List For those interested in producing or writing radio shows aimed at gays, lesbians, bisexual, or transgendered people.
EMAIL majordomo@abacus.oxy.edu ✍
Type in message body: subscribe homoradio (your full name)

In a Different Light "The resonance of gay and lesbian experience in twentieth-century American art has been profound in ways we are just beginning to realize. At the same time... the younger generation of artists is telling us that our definitions of sexual identity are changing in unforeseen ways. Now may be the right time to reflect on our collective history while we still have one foot planted in "gay," "lesbian," and "straight" experience and the other stepping into a new world whose defini-

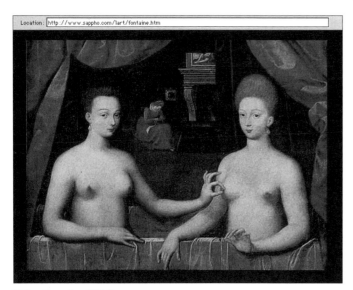

Location: http://www.sappho.com/lart/fontaine.htm

Sixteenth-century titillation
http://www.sappho.com

tions—and pleasures—are, as yet, unknown." This online, annotated version of an exhibit put on at UC Berkeley premiered in 1995 and would surely be striking and vibrant if the images of the originals weren't so small and poorly scanned. Nevertheless, an exciting collection.
WEB http://www.uampfa.berkeley.edu /exhibits/idl/dlhome.html

Isle of Lesbos Profiles, selected works, and bibliographies for lesbian poets, from that proto-dyke Sappho to Elsa Gidlow. High quality images of lesbian and lesbian-suggestive artwork from Toulouse-Lautrec and Picasso to Georges Callot and Tamara de Lempicka. Also, enjoy quotes by everyone from Rita Mae Brown, to Colette, to Eleanor Roosevelt.
WEB http://www.sappho.com

Lesbian and Gay Bands of America If you want to do more than just march in the next pride parade, blow your horn in one of America's 22 gay and lesbian marching bands. From Rochester, New York's Basically Treblemakers to the Mile-High Freedom Band in Denver, queer marching bands are putting the message in the music. If there isn't an LGBA member band in your area, this site explains how to start one.
WEB http://agora.rdrop.com/users/joe /lgba.html

New York Lesbian & Gay Film Festival Another year, another slew of queer films come and gone. This page dares to ask the tough questions: The Question of Borders, The Question of Gender, The Question of Race, and The Question of History. You can get info on

the films and their creators—from *Stonewall* to *Shinjuku Boys*, *Queer Colored Girls* to *Boy! What a Girl!* Then check the calendar to see when you missed it—and when next year rolls around, get there in time.
WEB http://www.newfestival.com

Tinsletown's Queer Web Site "Yes, Tinseltown IS Burning, because in Hollywood, perhaps eight out of ten people know that homophobia is wrong, yet so few—SO FEW—seek to FULLY express this truth to the people whom they influence. The entertainment industry, which so easily commands the global spotlight, is potentially the greatest fire-fighting force on the planet. Yet, by virtue of our silence—the withholding of our true Selves for the sake of market share, Q-ratings and big box office, or simply because of fear—we are, in fact, the greatest proponents of this firestorm." Info on the public access sensation, the movement, and the man—Nicholas Snow.
WEB http://www.gaywired.com /ttownqueer

YouthArts Write it, draw it, play it, say it, scream it: you finally have a place to put it. Read excerpts from *Girl Power*, Hillary Carlip's collection of real stories, writings, and rants by brilliant young dykes. Get the last word on the music scene with QueerCore Beat. Find out about the "Reflections of Our Community Project" and see the winning shots. Peruse the collection of poetry written by young, gay African-Americans. And finish it off with a youth-issue diatribe by Patricia Neil Warren. **WEB** http://www.qcc.org/yap

Activism

ACT-UP New York The AIDS Coalition to Unleash Power has Web pages across the country, but the New York site is the mother of them all. You want local action? Check out the plans for a massive demonstration against New York Governor Pataki's AIDS, health-care, and welfare policies, on the governor's own estate, no less. You want national headlines? "Stadtlander's Pharmacy = AIDS Profiteer, click here to read about corporate greed." You want information? There's an array of publications including the Civil Disobedience Manual, YELL (Youth Education Life Line), DIVA TV (Damned Interfering Video Activists), AIDS Cure Project papers, and more. You want to help? You'll find urgent actions, contact info for donations, Silence = Death merchandise, and interactions on how to start an ACT-UP chapter in your home town. **WEB** http://www.actupny.org

Digital Queers What Act Up and Queer Nation were to the '80s, Digital Queers is to the '90s. If the talk of the times is technology, then DQ wants to get the

queer community wired. Besides throwing the best parties at the MacWorld Expo (Robin Williams showed up at one), DQ's aim is to provide anything, from a state-of-the-art modem or printer to a "complete computer beauty makeover," to gay, lesbian, bisexual, and transgender organizations across America. If you're frustrated with the fax machine or an obsolete, constantly crashing computer at your local queer organization, this is where to get information on getting an upgrade. The DQ site also carries announcements about upcoming queer events, press clippings covering DQ activities, a list of chapters, and instructions on starting a local chapter in your area. **WEB** http://www.dq.org/dq

Gay Men's Health Crisis On the Web Once sexually active, you have now decided that the only way to be safe from AIDS is to stop having sex completely. Out of fear of contracting AIDS, you stop seeing friends and don't participate in activities of your community. You find yourself constantly worrying about your health and refuse to believe your physician's assurances that any medical conditions you might have are not AIDS-related, or you refuse to believe the negative results of an HIV antibody test. You begin to think that there is something wrong with being gay or bisexual. If you display a number of these

ISN'T IT IRONIC, DON'T YOU THINK

You would think that those who are always talking about family values would want to create an environment of permanent relationships for people of the same sex. But they're not advocating family values. They're advocating their values.... I still get this shit full-time.... They just are haters, period.

—San Francisco Mayor Willie Brown to The Advocate, from Q World

"symptoms," you're suffering from a state of paranoia GMHC calls "AIDS fear." Find out how to combat the fear and the condition. Positive but never passive, the GMHC tells you how to volunteer, advocate, and contribute; where to get tested, get support, or get treatment; what to know and what not to believe. **WEB** http://www.gmhc.org

GLAAD: Gay and Lesbian Alliance Against Defamation The media watchdogs for the gay community are online at this Web site with the full-text versions of the current and back issues of the *GLAAD Newsletter*, which monitors the representation of gays and lesbians in the media. In addition, the site features an extensive list of media contacts,

and announcements about gay-related media coverage archived in categories such as online (AOL adds a Transgender Community Forum), advertising, radio, print, TV (the lesbian couple on the show *Friends* has made "a notable contribution"), etc.
WEB http://www.glaad.org/glaad/glaad .html

Lambda Legal Defense and Education Fund Next time you need professional advice on gay, lesbian, or AIDS-related litigation, consult the oldest national gay political organization in the

U.S., founded in 1972. Lambda's impressive casework includes the recent Amendment 2 anti-gay initiative in Colorado and the ongoing gays-in-the-military debate. The site carries contact numbers and press releases describing recent high-profile cases.
URL gopher://uclink.berkeley.edu:1901 /00/other/national-orgs/lldef/lldef

NGLTF A site worthy of the country's oldest national gay and lesbian civil rights organization. The National Gay and Lesbian Task Force is a civil rights organization with far-

reaching issues and influence. Not only do they sponsor a youth leadership training workshop, which helps young activists hone their skills, to best serve projects in their communities, they also actively fight the Republicans' platform for welfare reform. The NGLTF will ask you to flex your political muscle by emailing your representatives, not just on queer-targeted issues like the DOMA, but on the Church Arson Prevention Act. The site also offers info on their many publications, a schedule of important community events,

 PopcornQ
WEB http://www.planetout.com/kiosk/popcornq

Even if you saw most of these movies at film festivals, on video, in porn houses, for film class, or in your friend's basement, none of these could equal the glam treatment **LGBT** film culture gets here. First and foremost is the incredible database of queer film info, searchable or browsable by nationality, date, or subject matter (Body Issues, Class, Role Play, Asian Images etc...). There's a film fest directory, queer top tens from critics and filmmakers, and lots of links. There is also a memorial feature on Mark Finch, the highlight of which is the Ainagram, a pop-culture tree diagram. This week it's "Why Olivia Newton-John is Still Popular." The Olivia core branches out into things like

"Xanadu," "paved way for exploitation of male bodies in pop video," and "spookily reminds me of...," which then branches out into "E.L.O.," "Weather Girls," "a less exuberant Goldie Hawn" etc., etc... And every little connection has a link to a sympathetic page. Great for stumbling onto retro-value sites you would never have found otherwise.

THE DR. SEUSS PURITY TEST

Have you done it on a boat?
Have you done it with a goat?

Have you done it in a bed?
Have you done it with the dead?

Have you done it in the ass?
Have you done it, high on grass?

Have you done it in the car?
Have you simply gone too far?

Have you done it on the beach?
Have you done it with the teach?

Have you done it on your back?
Have you done it strapped to a rack?

Have you done it in a box?
Have you done it with a fox?

Have you done it in a tree?
Have you done it with more than three?

Have you done it in the rain
Have you done it for the pain?

—from soc.bi Archives

employment opportunities, and an online membership form. Every voice is needed in this election year, so join today.
WEB http://www.ngltf.org

Queer Immigration List Only six countries (Australia, New Zealand, Sweden, The Netherlands, Denmark, and Norway) guarantee same-sex partners the right to immigrate. Discuss strategies for changing gay immigration policies in the rest of the world.
EMAIL majordomo@abacus.oxy.edu ✍
Type in message body: subscribe qi

Homophobia

alt.politics.homosexuality Before you enter the fray, check the .SIG files of the debaters: Generally speaking, those who quote Nine Inch Nails are not on the same team as those who quote Saint Paul. In the rare, quieter moments, gay politics are discussed, with an overwhelming number of posts devoted to bible interpretation/refutation, and of course, the hot topic of gay marriage. Essentially this newsgroup is a battlefield, hand-to-hand combat between gays and the religious right. You'll hear all sorts of interesting facts: Simon LeVay, the gay neurologist, is actually Anton LeVay, former leader of the Satanic Church. Same-gender sex is impossible, because of the American Heritage Dictionary's definition of the word. One of this group's regular homophobes actually managed to get himself banned from alt.flame., but don't worry, there are plenty more to go around. One hint—know from whereof you speak. The idiots and intellectuals from both sides of the fence are here

in droves, but if you happen to hit a resourceful fundamentalist, be ready to spit bible passages right back at him/her. One misquote or misinterpretation and you're sure to receive a thousand triumphant gloating posts.
WEB alt.politics.homosexuality

alt.sex.homosexual As alt.sex newsgroups go, this one is pretty straight (pun intended). Despite a smattering of postings about homosexual erotica, this group is mostly informative, with detailed discussion and debate about gay-rights developments worldwide—it's the only place in the alt.sex world you're likely to read about jailed Italian activists. Many posters are newbies, unsure whether they're ready to come out or not and unclear about the details of safe sex, so the group is a little reminiscent of a gay dive bar—where the painfully naive meet the jaded. If you're new to cyberqueer culture, try one of the "MOTTS" groups instead, preferably a local one.
WEB alt.sex.homosexual

Family Q Home Page One of the best sources for gay parenting information online or offline. Starting Out helps you explore a range of options, from adoption, to AI , to fostering, to surrogate mothering. Legal info offers contact information on dozens of sympathetic lawyers across the U.S. Organizations provides annotated link lists and contact informa-

tion lesbigay family support orginizations, both national and regional. Partnership offers links to queer marriage and domestic partnership sites. Books and Articles offers an annotated bibliography along with contact info for ordering. And Kidstuff is a big collection of links that will distract your progeny for days at a time.
WEB http://www.athens.net/~familyq

Homosexuality-Ethics and Religion Folder One of the longest-running, most active, and most flame-prone of all the topics, where members argue the religious objections to homosexuality with Bible citations, insults, and threats of damnation. The threads rarely go anywhere or reveal anything new, which makes you wonder why anyone bothers, but some thoughtful posts by reverent gays and non-gays alike keep it worthwhile. If you feel like offering an intelligent, point-by-point refutation of hate-speech thinly veiled as the Gospel of Love, or if you just feel like throwing a well-aimed punch to let off steam, this is the place to do so.
AMERICA ONLINE *keyword* ethics → Debate →List Topics→Homosexuality

Kitsch and camp

Blair A campy Web 'zine named after the *Facts of Life* blond bombshell (Too bad Tootie couldn't make it). Put together by Richard ("*Blair*'s macho frontman") and Bryan!

("shy 'Captain'-like counterpart to Richard's sassy Tenille"), *Blair* includes an audio archive of Parker Posey quotes, Pippy Longstocking worship, a Gay or Eurotrash? quiz, a *Sassy* parody aptly named *Sissy*, and the "Cute Skater of the Month" award. You'll also find audio and video samples from classics like *V: The Miniseries*, and *Faster Pussycat! Kill! Kill!* Pop culture vultures will plotz over this splashy kitsch-fest, a fantastic frivolous pick me up when you're done flaming on alt.fan.newt-gingrich. A distinct '80s retro feel may turn off not only granola lesbians, but even camp-queens with a few more miles on their Ferragamos. For Genqueeration X only.
WEB http://www.blairmag.com/library .html

DataLounge Mon cher, you've found the best little haunt on the Net, this page serves the driest martinis in town, and the waiters are gorgeous! Trudy, the owner and your charming hostess, will take your name and get you acquainted with the lounge. Why not have a cocktail at the bar and watch a fierce little soap called *Barbaras* on the telly while you wait to be seated. When you're called, Trudy will show you your seats. And no, she won't put the napkin on your lap, naughty boy. The menu for today starts off with an aperitif of Pride Parade pictures, replete with catty captions such as "I wasn't aware that Greenpeace sold muumuus," and "An usherette! But where have you hidden your flashlight?" We recommend the house whine— er, wine, out of Sir Lancelot's

It's a family affair
http://www.athens.net/~familyq

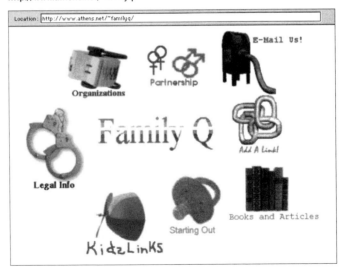

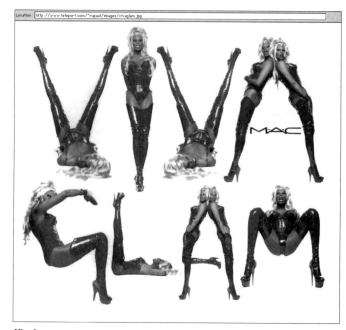

Viva ham
http://www.teleport.com/~rupaul

Pretty Boy's Home Page This fabulous page has everything and whipped cream with a maraschino cherry on top. Pretty Boy has created a terribly thrilling design for the page: A dozen pulp novel covers and B-movie posters link to various aspects of his terribly thrilling life. Features are offered on his friends the Evil Blond Temptress, and Diva du Web, catty site-review maven. Enemies like Pretty Boy's last ex are trashed and thrashed for your amusement. Links to other saucy sites, as well as your comments on Pretty Boy's accomplishment (the sweet ones only, naturally), round out this campy site.
WEB http://fox.nstn.ca/~mmacleod

Crate. Today's special is Miss World Wide Web contest, where you can vote for your favorite site in the categories of Poise, Talent, Evening Gown, and Swimsuit. Would you care for a Darling Diary sorbet to clean the palate in between courses? You can relax and eavesdrop on the table next to you, where Trudy is being interviewed by *OUT* reporter Elise. Now for dessert (forget the diet, sweetheart, your days under the football bleachers aren't going to come back if you skip the flan) there is the Dragnatrix, so orgasmic you won't even remember your name afterwards. And 'Lectric Letters make a refreshing after-dinner mint. Till tomorrow darling. And don't forget to leave

your Calling Card, I won't go through Giorgio again to find you, the little beast. Ta Ta!
WEB http://www.datalounge.com

The GabPage It's nothing but hot air from the windy city. This Chicago rag is one of the best nastEzines on the Net, with the downright frightening adventures of Mary Jane Rotten Crotch, fascinating fetish fantasy-cum-abstract art in the Bar-Basement Collection, another half-dozen words you can't say in front of your mom in Sister Edilie's Diction, Rico—Reckless Ruff Trade (need we say more), and gossip with Grey Pucenda, just for starters.
WEB http://users.aol.com/gabpage /index.html

RuPaul's House of Love It's official, darlings, but what do you expect? She's got the best body in the business and her PR company ain't too bad either. RuPaul is still in the spotlight, but her rhetoric may be a little dated. The House of Love is filled with slightly misappropriated hipster vocab, like using "dish" to mean publicity calendar and "accessorize" to mean cheesy T-shirts (we were hoping for Pink Pussycat!) The word "*fierce*" is sadly overused, and the tired old question of How She Tucks It In gets dragged out for another voyeuristic go-round. Well, everything gets corrupted eventually, peaches, most of us only wish we could be exploited like this!
WEB http://www.teleport.com/~rupaul

Women & Feminism

ONLINE AS WELL AS OFF, SISTERS ARE DOING IT FOR THEMSELVES

THE STATISTICS HAVE BEEN saying the same thing for years: The Net is the playground of pale males and women scarcely ever get a look in. Well, time's up boys, because women with modems are becoming a force to be reckoned with. Taking to the online world with a passion, women aren't simply trying out the boytoys and falling for the allure of the latest multimedia browser plug-in. Instead they are educating, studying, enlightening, and helping one another through all areas of life: culture; politics; health; sexuality; the workforce; and the family. From humorous remarks to serious disscusions, whether your an arch-feminist or traditional homemaker, someone online has something for you.

Location: http://www.inform.umd.edu:8080/EdRes/Topic/WomensStudies

Women's Studies Resources

The women's studies database, created in September 1992, serves those people interested in the women's studies profession and in general women's issues. The database contains collections of conference announcements, calls for papers, and employment opportunities, as well as a picture gallery, and a significant number of government documents, and much more. If you have questions or comments, please contact the database coordinator at megan@info.umd.edu

 ### INFORM'S WOMEN'S STUDIES
WEB http://www.inform.umd.edu/EdRes/Topic/WomensStudies

If for some obscure reason you can only visit one woman-related Web site, make it this one. It links to almost all the female interest sites in cyberspace and is a terrific compendium of women's studies resources in its own right. You can find a job here, a conference on Gender and Law, the text of "A Vindication of the Rights of Women," a feminist film review of *Die Hard*, and the email address of your congressperson.

Starting points

A Web of One's Own Its name a take-off on Virginia Woolf's essay on writing and women, this Dutch and English Web entry serves as a publishing forum for feminist thought, inviting visitors to contribute any past articles of their own, formerly gathering dust in relative obscurity. Articles on the latest in French feminist thought, trendy as it is, are also available.
WEB http://www.reference.be /womweb/index.html

Cicely's Place for Women Cicely, in a previous incarnation a short-story character created by Andrea Foster, is currently the virtual hostess of a down-home chat room. Cicely's motto: "I do not wish women to have power over men, but power over themselves."
WEB http://www2.vivid.net/~cicely

The CyberMom.com CyberMom Dot Com, as it is referred to onsite, has a surreal atmosphere with graphics that are mostly '50s kitsch and a tone somewhat along the lines of the Stepford Wives. Organized as a (nuclear) home, with attic, basement, kitchen, family room, bedroom, and other coffee-table pages, one gets the sense that most of the visitors are happy housewives of the "old school." The books reviewed are mass market; the decorating tips not so sophisticated; the film survey was about favorite Moms in film.

RAPE RAGE

"So it's my responsibility as a woman to dress so that I don't "turn you on." I recently read of a nun who was raped... I wonder what provocative article of *her* wardrobe gave her rapist an annoying erection and *made* him rape her—that teasing veil, perhaps, or the Madonna-like crucifix, or the flirty wimple? I suppose that little girls who are raped are asking for it by dressing in Lolita-like children's frocks. Housewives who are raped at home are "asking for it" by wearing those come-hither, devil-may-care jeans and sweatshirts. And, of course, the working woman who's raped on her way home from the office is at fault for wearing a tailored business suit—power being the ultimate aphrodisiac and all, right?"—Sally

"Rape is not about sex. It's about power. It's about men who get off on overpowering and humiliating women—women of every age, occupation and, yes, sartorial style. Your posting is obscene and an insult to any woman who's ever been sexually assaulted. Men, being free agents blessed (one hopes) with free will, have the ultimate responsibility for their behavior. Deal with it. And stop giving aid and comfort to rapists by posting enabling hogwash like your previous post."—Becky

—from AOL's Women's Board

Savvy sex talk won't be found here, but real-life advice and anecdotal amusement will: "When our son was about four years old he walked in on us once. He said, 'Mommy, what's daddy doing on top of you?' As casually as possible, I said, 'I don't know. He has the whole bed, and this is where he sleeps.'"
WEB http://www.thecybermom.com

Nrrd Grrl! Nrrd Grrl! is designed for women "who think, talk, and act for themselves. Nrrd Grrl!'s only politics are your own. No rules, no dogmas, no ideological rights or wrongs. Just individuals try-

ing to reclaim the word normal." Nrrd Grrl! maven Amelia just wants to be loved and heard. Overwhelmed by the "confusing, impossible, societal yardstick," she has started this group for women who just want to "be." If you're fed up and need a space to do and say and think whatever you want, Nrrd Grrl! is your answer. Amelia may be fed up, but she's assembled a great rack of 'zines and chosen some truly funky graphics.
WEB http://www.winternet.com /~ameliaw/nrrdl.html

soc.women If you ignore the cross-postings from those

groups with the dreaded word feminism in their title, then soc.women is a very different—casual and warm—place to be. The group only has a few lurking male malcontents. This down-home chat about the "business" of being a woman has a good deal of joking about shaving legs, the ordeal of housework (Jeanne doesn't find it demeaning, just "utterly unnecessary"), and the other "species" with good humor toward all.
USENET soc.women

Women in Cinema: A Reference Guide Women and film are linked in complicated ways. Women, as historical objects of desire and the male "gaze,"

should have a vested interest in the way in which they have been, and still are represented on the big screen. Spectatorship and visual desire are important themes to feminists. Women in Cinema: A Reference Guide is essentially an annotated bibliography, and a good place to start exploring these issues.
WEB http://poe.acc.virginia.edu /~pm9k/libsci/womFilm.html

Women's Board Some women visit the center to discuss their favorite novels. Others discuss dating in the age of AIDS. A feminist activists network gives women a space to discuss change without the Limbaugh-loving interlopers found in

most online feminist forums. Political debate is confined to the Women's Issues folder— which proceeds in spite of intrusions by the likes of LuvGangsta, who thinks sexual harassment regulations take all the fun out of the office.
AMERICA ONLINE *keyword* exchange→ communities→women's board

Women's Net Women's Net Internet Resources for Women is a multitude of resources designed to help women make it in a man's world. Head to the Abortion & Reproductive Rights page to keep track of the ongoing battle in Washington and around the country. The Domestic Violence gopher is a valuable resource for

 # FILM AND DESTROY
WEB http://www.olywa.net/otterpop/filmdes1.htm

Film and Destroy sets out to end the sexist ways in which women can be represented visually in film and other media by presenting and encouraging independent work by, for, and about women. Highlights include art from abuse shelters, information on filmmaking, and the fascinating and dis-

turbing essay "One Out of Eight," which claims that one in eight Hollywood movies depicts a rape scene. Not only that, but "8 million girls and 5 million boys are sexually abused before they are 8 years old and 8% of women have been sexually abused by an adult relative, acquaintance, or stranger before age 18." Chastening stuff, smartly presented.

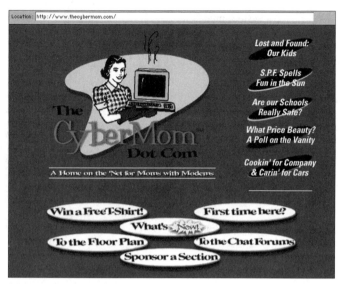

Cybermom, baked fresh daily
http://www.thecybermom.com

women seeking pertinent information and advice. And the Women's Health Resources gopher reports on breast cancer and other health issues.
WEB http://www.igc.apc.org /womensnet

Women's Network A hub for AOLers of the female variety. Areas covered include career, family, leisure, personal life, and well-being. While most articles toe the mainstream line, some more interesting features recently included "Women and Their Cars" and "Transgender Warriors."
AMERICA ONLINE *keyword* women

The Women's Page at Social Cafe Where else could you find the Mother Tongue, a feminist bookstore, but at the Social Cafe? Rush Limbaugh would probably have a "feminazi"

field day, but for those who are looking to find a group of women anglers in their hamlet, want to invest in the Global Fund for Women, or are looking to join the Society of Women Engineers, this place is an eclectic locale for getting up to speed on feminology online, from the Electra Pages to the Assault Prevention Information Network. You'll also find an interactive discussion area for women's issues.
WEB http://social.com/social/women .html

Women's Wire A crash course of sorts in '90s women's issues, with forums and BBSs addressing reproductive health, alternative birth control techniques, and financial issues. There's even a "Pregnancy Q & A" for the nervous or excited, a fairly conservative

fashion section, and a truly helpful forum discussing STDs.
MSN *keyword* women

Women's Wire CompuServe's women's hub is a forum for females to discuss personal and professional topics, hosting discussions on everything from workplace issues to weddings. There are live conferences every month with experts, celebrities, authors, and other special guests and a extensive library of articles, lists, book excerpts, and expert columns. Recent articles covered how to find a trainer, an alternative to hysterectomy, and breaking the debt cycle.
COMPUSERVE *go* women

Women's Wire Great features for women abound at Women's Wire: career profiles, stories about women to watch, and Web-related articles. Lighter topics are also covered, touching upon fashion, sex, and gossip. The wide range of topics covered by Women's Wire give it a really progressive feel, but some of the advertising— such as the one for "slimming" bathing suits—puts a slight damper on the enlightened-woman vibe.
WEB http://www.women.com

Feminism

alt.feminism Much of this group is devoted to the abortion debate, with pro-choicers and pro-lifers duking it out online. But you'll also find discussion

of other issues like women and religion, politics, and the Internet scattered throughout. Posters seem to be equally feminist and anti-feminist.
USENET alt.feminism

Bluestocking When this 'zine first loads, "Unabashedly Feminist" comes up followed by an image of blue jeans and black boots that evokes skinheads. Combine the two and you get Feminazi, a fervent brand of feminism subscribed to by *Bluestocking*'s editors. Mostly a collection of essays and links on topics like abortion, menstruation, and people like Susie Bright and Annie Sprinkle, the print version of this Portland-based 'zine recently went into nationwide distribution.
WEB http://www.teleport.com /~bluesock

Feminism and the Net Touting itself as "a guide for fun feminists" this is actually a great starting point for serious feminists new to the Net. Several mailing lists, newsgroups, gopher addresses, and Web sites, from the Feminist Economists mailing list to the ftp directory of the Washington State NOW, are linked as well. Those interested in firing off cyberprotests will find addresses of the House of Representatives, the White House, and Newt Gingrich.
WEB http://www.eskimo.com /~feminist/nownetin.html

Feminist The domain of the American Librarians Associa-

tion Feminist Task Force, this list is actually geared to a general discussion of women's issues—abortion, equal pay, sexual harassment. But it is not just theory here; Sharon from Ohio offers her story of harassment at work and is inundated with strategies and sympathy. Because many participants are librarians, the list often feels like a reading group. Discussions are long and intelligent, and often about books of interest to feminists. Reading *The Morning After* sparked a long and heated debate among women and men on the issue of date rape.
EMAIL listserv@mitvma.mit.edu ✍ *Type in message body:* subscribe feminist (your full name)

FemSuprem Women and men are encouraged to join a discussion based on the premise that "perhaps women are superior to men, whether in a few ways, or in everything." Formerly called gynosupremacy, female supremacy should not be confused with female domination. Each week the list takes on a new topic. You'll automatically receive a FAQ and help file upon subscribing.
EMAIL femsuprem-request@renaissoft .com ✍ *Type in message body:* subscribe femsuprem (your full name)

Leslie's World O' Chicks It may sound like yet another of the thousand of sex services online. Instead, WOC is "an eddy of estrogen in that vast sea of testosterone known as the Internet." Rather than

highlighting the traditional feminist sites, Leslie's links tend to be pro-sex, pro-queer, pro-camp, pro-fashion, and anti-censorship and include sites that see physical exertion (sports) and physical force (including guns) as viable options for "real feminists."
WEB http://www.fearless.net/woc

soc.feminism Postings to this moderated newsgroup include the usual topics up for discussion and debate, as well as topical issues such as the 1996 election and general information related to feminism.
USENET soc.feminism

Women Created to provide a forum for women worldwide to discuss their concerns. No topic is forbidden, from dance to child care to menopause to sexuality.
WEB majordomo@world.std.com ✍ *Type in message body:* subscribe women

Law & government

EMILY's List An acronym for "Early Money Is Like Yeast" (it makes the dough rise), EMILY's list identifies pro-choice democratic women candidates for key offices. For a $100 contribution you can join the list, or you can sign up for the free email network.
WEB http://www.emilyslist.org

Feminist Theory and Feminist Jurisprudence on the WWW Jurisprudence is an especially important area for women, as

Location: http://www.sm.rim.or.jp/~shioko/Edappi.html

Japanese working women are a force to be reckoned with
http://www.sm.rim.or.jp/~shioko/Edappi.html

they tend to be vastly under-represented in the legal profession. Feminist Theory and Feminist Jurisprudence on the WWW features a few feminist law courses and lists relevant bibliographies and indexes. Biographies of Hillary Rodham Clinton, Ruth Bader Ginsberg, Sandra Day O'Connor, and Janet Reno are featured. **WEB** http://lark.cc.ukans.edu /~akdclass/femlit/femjur.html

Women's Legal and Public Policy Info Head to this fabulous site to research rights and redress wrongs. Annotated connections to gophers dedicated to many women's issues (health care, violence, work) and special interests (lesbians, women of color, disabled women, and mothers) are featured. The site also links to women's organizations and chat groups. **WEB** http://asa.ugl.lib.umich.edu /chdocs/womenpolicy/womenlaw policy.html

Sexual Harassment Resources A list of pamphlets, books, and videos from the Equal Employment Opportunity Commission that seeks to inform, educate, and affect change. A good manager's must-read list. **URL** gopher://eng.hss.cmu.edu:70 /00ftp%3AEnglish.Server%3A Feminism%3ASexual%20Harassment %3ASexual%20Harrassment%20 Resources

Washington Feminist Faxnet The *Washington Feminist Faxnet* is a newsletter, distributed via fax, to those concerned with women's issues. Founded by prestigious Washingtonian Dr. Martha Burk, president of the Center for Advancement of Public Policy, *Faxnet* makes political activism easy—concise explanations of issues, followed by the pertinent phone numbers or addresses, make it simple to lend a voice or a pen. But activism comes at a price—$35, to be exact. You

can read excerpts here. **WEB** http://www.feminist.com/ffn.htm

International

Dappi A collection of essays of interest to Japanese working women. Dappi addresses the issues of marriage, domestic violence, and reproductive choice. **WEB** http://www.sm.rim.or.jp/~shioko /Edappi.html

The Fourth World Conference On Women If you weren't able to attend the United Nations' Fourth World Conference on Women in Beijing in the fall of 1995, you can still catch up with the international women's movement. The page features important news that's hard to find at other sites, focusing on the current status of women in development efforts, human rights, and emigration issues. Other sites seem myopic in scope once you surf though this spot, sponsored by the UN's Division for the Advancement of Women. **WEB** http://www.undp.org/fwcw/dawl .htm

International Women's Groups A list of email addresses for women's interest groups worldwide. Discover how to contact the Synergie Femmes et Developpement in Senegal, the Feminist International Radio Endeavor in Nicaragua, or the Women's World Banking Organization. **URL** gopher://gopher.igc.apc.org:70 /II/women/directory

South Asian Women's Net

SAWNET has put together a site that's full of links and resources for women, particularly for those with an interest in or allegiance to South Asia. The book and film reviews are Asian-focussed, and cover territyory less familiar to North American feminists. Similarly, links tend to be more exotic—hence the hookup with the Women's Caravan and Cyberharem.

WEB http://www.umiacs.umd.edu /users/sawweb/sawnet

Women in India Though the world's first female prime minister was Indian, discrimination and the general treatment of a great number of women in India is still an issue of grave concern to women around the world. Wife burning, rape, female infanticide—all of these take place in the world's largest democracy. Women in India focuses on the positive steps being taken to eradicate these abuses.

WEB http://www.webcom.com /~prakash/WOMEN/WOMEN.HTML

Women of Africa Resources

Leave it to an anthropologist to choose a variety of interesting links, covering art, politics, literature, and Web culture. WAF is a terrific choice for those researching African women. An outstanding selection of bibliographies, articles, and pages has been compiled by this Lawrence University academic. Notable links point to information on female genital mutilation.

WEB http://www.lawrence.edu /~bradleyc/war.html

ZAN ZAN features such articles as PMS and Iranian Women—subjects that aren't likely to suffer from overexposure. On the other hand, this seems to be the only hubsite specifically for such topics. Featuring art, poetry, and literature by Iranian women, and networks of professional Iranian women, ZAN (which means "woman" in Farsi), is an important site for those in search of a cyber-community for Persian women.

WEB http://www.zan.org

BITCH

WEB http://www.bitchmag.com

The cybersister to the San Francisco-based 'zine is not nearly as hostile as the name would lead you to expect; in fact, it's one of the most woman-friendly hubs on the Web. "*Bitch* is a constantly evolving Web 'zine and community space where feminists, Internet gluttons, media addicts and thoughtful folks in general can talk about women, pop culture, advertising, and just about anything

else." You'll find weekly rants about Tori Amos, lipstick, and women who wear glasses alongside attacks on mainstream media articles like "How Cosmo Girls Eat and Stay Skinny" and praise for the Avon ad featuring Jackie Joyner-Kersee. Weigh in at the chat group on such topics as the representation of female Olympians at Atlanta's Summer Games.

News & 'zines

Catt's Claws, a Frequently-Appearing Feminist Newsletter Whose claws? Why, the descendants of suffragist Carrie Chapman Catt, of course. When it was revealed that taking increased doses of the Pill after sex was an effective birth control method, the newsletter was outraged. *Catt's Claws* charged that it was a "betrayal of American women by doctors, medical practitioners of all kinds, the Food and Drug Administration, and our own feminist movement's leaders." Another article exposed a recent police raid in Beijing of an ice cream factory where 18,000 plastic ice cream sticks were found shaped like naked women. Another criticized the lack of breast cancer research in the U.S. Access the most recent issues of the newsletter or receive them via email. Comments are welcome.
WEB http://worcester.lm.com/women/is/cattsclaws.html
EMAIL listserv@netcom.com ✍
Type in message body: (subscribe catts-claws)

gURL Sort of cyber-*Sassy* (the original one) for the wired young woman, this is one girls' 'zine guaranteed not to wreak havoc on her body image. With departments like Looks Aren't Everthing, Deal With It, and Where Do I Go From Here, *gURL* has attitude and spunk, even as it informs and entertains.
WEB http://www.itp.tsoa.nyu.edu/~gURL

Ladies' Home Journal Online Read the latest issue, browse back issues, or sound off on recent articles you loved or loathed at the cyber version of the mainstream women's powerhouse publication.
WEB http://www.lhj.com

Redbook All the usual issues you've come to expect from *Redbook* can now be found online: love and marriage, your career, you and your child, beauty and style, stars and entertainment, food and nutrition, health, and the only horoscope exclusively for married women.
WEB http://homearts.com/rb/toc/00rbhpcl.htm

VOW World: Voices of Women This two-year-old online magazine examines the latest in alternative medicines, the state of the feminist movement, and even the gender of God. Check the calendar for workshops to help you realize your "sacred inner space" or learn how protect your outer space with self-defense demos.
WEB http://www.voiceofwomen.com

Woman's Day Donna Reed would have felt right at home in the virtual edition of *Woman's Day*. There's a Recipe of the Day, a Tip of the Day (what to do if you've overdone the perfume), the current table of contents, and an archive of previous articles on shopping, parenting, health, and crafts.
AMERICA ONLINE *keyword* Woman's Day

SUCK IT UP STEVE

Hearing John Tesh refer to the US women gymnasts as "little girls" over and over was enough to make me want to plant my foot up his ass (can you imagine the uproar if the men's gymnastics team had been introduced as "little boys"??), but the most appalling moment came when Steve Nunno approached Shannon Miller moments after she messed up her floor routine in the individual all-around competition. Shannon was doubled over crying (with good reason, I think-- I'd have had a similar reaction had it been me), and Nunno says "Stop crying! There's people watching everywhere! Suck it up!" I was pissed at his callousness, but mostly I was overwhelmed with sadness that this is the only kind of emotional life that these young women have known so far. I truly hope they soon find some depth in their lives.

—from Bitch

The Women's Desk How did the media represent Paula Jones (of Bill Clinton fame)? Part of *FAIR*, a magazine that focuses on media representation of women, The Women's Desk columns are archived here and cover everything from the connection between far-right militias and anti-abortion violence to the media's assault on poor women in their coverage of the welfare debate.

WEB http://www.fair.org/fair/womens-desk.html

Women's Feature Service The Women's Feature Service reminds us that the women's movement exists on an international scale. This New Delhi-based service compiles articles about women in developing countries. Third World women tend to be underrepresented in the media, so the Women's Feature Service is extremely valuable for the committed or interested. You can browse the articles here or receive the entire WFS feed of six features a week by email subscription for $6 a month.

WEB http://www.igc.apc.org/wfs

Organizations

The ElectraPages A database of more than 7,000 women's organizations and businesses that is searchable by subject, name, or region.

WEB http://www.electrapages.com

Heartless Bitches International Natalie is not a nice girl; she'd consider it a compliment if you told her so. Her club and Web site, Heartless Bitches International is not for the passive. Not sure if you're belligerent enough to become a card-carrying member of HBI? "You ever get tired of those whiners in the newsgroups? Or the guys who hit on you and you politely decline, and they keep pestering you and pestering

you, and pestering you like some obnoxious, festering, pus-filled sore, until you finally have to WHAP them over the head with a VERY LARGE CLUE (tm)... ?" If your answer is a resounding yes, then Heartless Bitches is for you. With articles like "No More Fucking Flowers" and "The Myth of the Sensitive New Age Nice Guy," HBI takes man-hating to a whole new level.

WEB http://www.heartless-bitches.com

The League of Women Voters Founded in 1920, The League of Women Voters encourages participation in government and public policy through advocacy and education. Non-

ELECTRIC ANIMA HOME PAGE
WEB http://www.io.com/~ixora

This new ezine proclaims itself "the 'zine for smart women and the men who love them" and is marked by in-your-face colors and editorial. On a recent visit, *Electric Anima* included an article on women's boxing, with links to a list of gyms and an exercise plan. "Lingerie Meander" mused on the

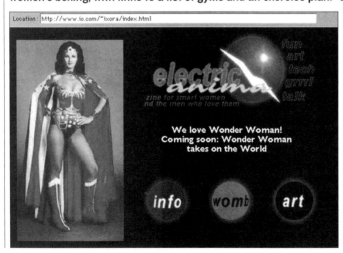

meaning of teddies in today's world and linked to an online catalog for ordering studded leather bustiers. A healthy, happy collection of essays, anecdotes, poems, and rants for the cybersavvy woman led, in spirit, by Linda Carter's Wonder Woman.

partisan but definitely political, the league generally aligns itself with the liberal lobby. For those itching to join in, the local branches—with their sites linked here—may have more specific activities and events in which to participate.
WEB http://www.lwv.org/~lwvus /index.html

National Organization for Women If there was ever a time for women's political action it is NOW! Peruse the hypertext women's issues forums for the latest on court decisions and NOW projects from abortion rights to economic equality. An electronic version of the *NOW Times* newsletter is also available. Find out how to join NOW online or whom to contact in your area.
WEB http://now.org

Women Leaders Online From the organization dedicated to mobilizing women over the Internet in their efforts to empower women politically and stop the anti-women agenda of the extreme right, the WLO site includes news, information on anti-women bias in the media, and the history of the organization.
WEB http://worcester.lm.com/women /women.html

Religion

Feminist Theology Women, scholars, and spiritualists meet in this unmoderated forum to discuss alternatives to traditional relationships between

women and God. Announcements are posted to keep up to date on publications and research on Christian and Jewish feminist theology.
EMAIL mailbase@mailbase.ac.uk ✍
Type in message body: **subscribe feminist-theology (your full name)**

Kol-Isha Moderated discussion focuses on women's roles in traditional Judaism. Two guidelines must be observed: Respect for the belief of Orthodox women in Halaka and a commitment to exploring new Halakic topics.
EMAIL listproc@shamash.org ✍
Type in message body: **subscribe kol-isha (your full name)**

Under Shekhina's Wings Most monotheist religions worship male gods, but nonetheless, strong female elements persist. Where was Jesus without Mary? The God of Judaism may be the paragon of patriarchy, but Jewish rituals and customs often celebrate and depend on the female. Some belief systems (like Wicca) center around the sacred knowledge of women, and this Web page tries to present any such religious themes that celebrate women. Links to general women's spirituality sites exist here, too.
WEB http://www.geocities.com /Athens/1501

WMSPRT-L If you have an 18-inch python skin and would like to learn how to preserve it for your pagan altar, you've come to the right place.

Women's Spirituality and Feminist Oriented Religions is a relatively active list (check for new posts daily or weekly, perhaps depending on planetary alignment) of "Pagans, neo-Pagans, Goddess worshipers, and feminist Christians of both genders." The active discussion ranges from the morality of buying African animal handicrafts to how to deal with "those pesky electric experiences that move you to a higher plane." Advice is freely given on planning pagan ceremonies, channeling and raising ecoconscious inner (and real) children, and how to deal with your mother (Earth and earthly). Feminists should be warned that this is a "Wild Woman" inner-voice list. Issues like abortion are discussed in "spiritual" terms. Although the readership is divided, the discussion is not dogmatic.
EMAIL listserv@ubvm.cc.buffalo.edu ✍ *Type in message body:* **subscribe wmsprt-l (your full name)**

Women in Islam For women, strict Islamic law requires veils, celibacy, and absolute obedience to one's husband. Divorce is rare, and women aren't allowed to pray in mosques. Does Islam subordinate women? Women in Islam approaches this question; articles on abortion, rape, and comparative religion are available and don't take conventional feminist stances.
WEB http://www.d.umn.edu/~sahmed /woman.html

Scholarship

American Association of University Women The official page for an association dedicated to equality of girls and women in education includes a list of current research projects, scholarships, and legal advocacy for sex discrimination lawsuits. There's also information on how to get involved if you're concerned about the academic gap in the classroom—starting at age 12—that exists between boys and girls.
WEB http://www.aauw.org

Feminism and Women's Studies The English Server offers up a hodgepodge of gender-related material, including wry articles such as "Dead Doll Humility" or "The Girls' Guide to Condoms." Philosophical and political tracts such as "Equal Pay" and "Feminists and Cyberspace" are also available.
WEB http://english-www.hss.cmu.edu /feminism

Gender and Sexuality A collection of documents covering a broad range of topics—e.g., musings on nymphomania, the marketing of angry women in popular culture, sex and the cybergirl, sexual harassment, and body image.
WEB http://english-www.hss.cmu.edu /gender.html

Voice of the Shuttle: Women's Studies Terrific links to sites of interest to women, from pop culture to the most erudite areas of women's studies. Sites also cover gay, lesbian, and queer studies; men's movements; and cybergender and techgender.
WEB http://humanitas.ucsb.edu /shuttle/gender.html

Women in Higher Education Read snippets from this extremely thorough journal devoted to women in all areas of academia, from those in athletics to those on the tenured track. The site was founded on the premise that gender and academia are deeply enmeshed and, as such, affect ideas of authority and knowledge from reading to books to interaction in

GUERRILLA GIRLS
WEB http://www.voyagerco.com/gg/gg.html

The higher the social class, the less sleep a working woman gets and the more a working man gets. About 96 percent of top executives are white males. The average salary of a black female college graduate is less than that of a white male high-school dropout. The Guerrilla Girls are women

artists who make posters citing such statistics, dubbing themselves the female counterparts to Robin Hood, Batman, and the Lone Ranger. Why the gorilla masks? To focus on the issues rather than on their personalities, not to mention it makes one hell of an impression. Check out and buy some of their posters, read a diary from their travels, and correspond with the masked mystery women via email.

RECLAIMING THE GIRL

At 24 years old, I'm not afraid to call myself a girl. But if someone had called me a girl even a few months ago, you bet I would have given them hell. See, I spent a year at Mills, a women's college, and that was a place where one became extremely well-versed in correcting anyone who dared refer to females over the age of 16 as "girls." But something has changed.

Being called a girl just doesn't seem so bad anymore. In fact, the idea of reclaiming my girlhood in all its freshness and limitless potential is incredibly appealing. I'm not talking here about docile, timid, self-effacing girlhood. I'm talking about re-claiming the girl who swung with abandon from the monkey bars, who spent hours telling wild and creative stories into a tape recorder, who gloried in strange costumes, who danced in a skill-less frenzy, who wasn't afraid to cry when upset, nor yell insults when angry.

I see that girl captured repeatedly in the black and white images my mother caught with her Leica as she snapped hundreds of photos throughout my childhood. But frozen on film as well is the sulky adolescent who came after. The one who thought girls shouldn't speak their minds for fear of ridicule or play tennis with the speed of the boys. I study that sullen 13-year-old face, masked in makeup and a pout, and wonder where did the knowledge that "girls could do anything" go? Where did the enthusiasm go? Where did the girl go? I'm still wondering how to get her back...

—from VOW World

information on the glass ceiling, women's studies syllabi, or feminist film reviews.
URL gopher://peg.cwis.uci.edu:7000 /11/gopher.welcome/peg/women

Women & cyberspace

The Cybergrrl Webstation This page is billed as "your first stop on the Web" with tools and tips for going online. You can see what the second sex has been up to in site design with Webgrrls Unite!, a collection of links to Net-savvy women's home pages. Choose an intriguing title (Venus Envy?) or wander over to the Grouchy Cafe for Bijou's Tofu Scramble recipe. Or jump to Angela Gunn's Seven Deadly Sins of the Web and indulge all your vices. And WomenSpace is the first site devoted to the health concerns of young women. At the Cybergrrl Webstation, you can also join the Cybergrrl Network, a diverse group of women exploring the Web or working in new media, and participate in cybergrrl chat or join the mailing list.
WEB http://www.cybergrrl.com

F-Email A British list dedicated to probing the relationship between gender and cyberspace. Promotes the point of view that although the Net is predominantly male, it may actually be a form of communication more suited to women.
EMAIL mailbase@mailbase.ac.uk ✍
Type in message body: subscribe f-email (your full name)

the classroom. Intelligently written, the page should be of interest to all feminists.
WEB http://www.itis.com/wihe

Women's Studies Roadmap
Admit it. You're lost in cyberspace. If you're looking for women's resources, this meta-index is huge and easy to use. Each entry is carefully annotated and gives a brief sampling of the resource. Mailing lists, Usenet newsgroups, Web pages, and gophers are all part

of this reference guide.
WEB http://reks.uia.ac.be/women /roadmap/women/w0000000.html

Women Studies Gopher This catch-all gopher lets intrepid parties visit the electronic resources of women's studies departments worldwide—from Gettysburg College in Pennsylvania to the Koordinationasstelle fur Frauenforschung in Linz, Austria to the Chicana-Latina Studies department at UCLA. Gather

Geekgirl What is cyberfeminism? "An intimate and possibly subversive element between women and machines—especially the new intelligent machines—which are no longer simply working for man as women are no longer simply working for man." So says Dr. Sadie Plant of the University of Birmingham. This hip online journal combines cyberculture with women's issues. Learn about the chromo-phallic patriarchal code or electronic salons for women only. Try Lemon Links for lesbian networking. The campy illustrations make this site a lot more fun.
WEB http://www.next.com.au/spyfood /geekgirl

Virtual Sisterhood A global women's electronic support network, this site explains the goals of cybersisterhood—networking and creating greater access for women on the information superhighway, sharing online communications skills, controlling and shaping cyberspace, and breaking through language barriers. Instructions for joining the group's mailing list are included.
WEB http://www.igc.apc.org/vsister /vsister.html

Voxxen Worx Who are the voxxen? "We are a collective of smart, funny, and foxy babes with modems. All of us are former or current members of MindVox, a New York City

BBS about which many of us are ambivalent." Browse the avant-garde home pages of the cybergals, each packed with links to personal obsessions (hound dogs, ballet, Star Trek) and favored sites. Or, if you fit the requirements outlined above, become a voxxen yourself.
WEB http://www.phantom.com /~barton/voxxen.html

Workforce

Advancing Women Home Page An arena for getting ahead by forging ties and sharing information with other women determined to break through the glass ceiling. In addition to numerous chat rooms and an

 # THE FEMINIST MAJORITY ONLINE
WEB http://www.feminist.org

Get that domain name and check out the latest-breaking feminist news, hot off the press. Campaigns in need of political activists look for the latest-breaking feminist new at **FMO**. And while it's an important site for women, it doesn't fall into the overly academic or political trap. Hip and contemporary, this site includes links to **Rock 4 Choice** and on-campus organization programs. The tone can sometimes be intense, as in a 911 feature that links to domestic abuse and harassment hot lines, but the detailed articles on such issues as breast cancer are a must-visit for fledgling and old-school feminists alike.

Self-dubbed babes with modems
http://www.phantom.com/~barton/voxxen.html

international bulletin board, there are sections on disproving myths about women in business. One such section argues that men are twice as likely to suffer from alcoholism as women, which is costly to business. Case in point: How many maternity leaves could Exxon have funded with the billions of dollars it spent because the captain of the Valdez was drunk?
WEB http://www.advancingwomen.com

Association of Women Industrial Designers At first, the sight of a sleek, industrial-style kitchen may seem to reinforce the stereotype that a woman's place is right there. However, the Association of Women Industrial Designers is a think-tank for woman-powered design ideas, and the site is a chronicle of women in design through the decades. Case

studies of new works are inspiring, like the design of an all-natural general store, complete with ostrich egg-shell lights and counters made of soy-protein resin. Learn that as early as 1943, a group called Damsels in Design was designing cars for General Motors, with women's needs in mind. Or take a peek at a recent exhibit, Goddess in the Details, where you'll learn that a woman designed the infamous Shaq Attack sneakers.
WEB http://www.core77.com/AWID

Equal Opportunity Publications A major publisher of informative magazines for women and minority communities since 1968 (Women Engineer, Minority Engineer, Careers & the disABLED, Workforce Diversity) provides information for companies dedicated to diversity hiring, a list of career

fairs, and job hints and articles from each magazine.
WEB http://www.eop.com

Oasis The creator of this Web site has written a book, *Kidding Ourselves: Breadwinning, Babies, and Bargaining Power*, about the inability of women to achieve economic equality with men while undertaking the lion's share of childcare. Read excerpts from the book and other related works here, such as an article from *Nature* about how women's brains are "different" or a recent study on the relationship between breast-feeding and IQ. Or help the author out with her new project about women in computing.
WEB http://www-leland.stanford.edu /~rmahony/index.html

Wired-Woman Network A searchable directory enabling women to collaborate, find a mentor, or advance their careers by Networking with women in their profession.
WEB http://www.sdsu.edu/wit

Women and Computer Science A compilation of issues and answers concerning women and computing, including a catalog of academic treatises on whether computer classrooms are female-friendly and how girls respond to electronic games. There's a little levity amidst the academic gravity, including nerd songs, theme songs for the digerati, gender benders, and real-life harassment horror stories in the busi-

ness and academic trenches.
WEB http://www.ai.mit.edu/people
/ellens/gender.html

The Women's Center for Employment Dr. Katherine Jordan presides over this online employment site for women. Women have a unique set of job concerns, and this site posts research on women and work (What's the relationship between marital status and career advancement?); reviews job search guides from a woman's perspective; and features information useful to professional women on industry trends, corporate outlooks, and the top companies for working moms. Currently, women can upload their resume to PLUS

20, The Internet Resume Registry System. Best of all, an interactive form provides women with online career counseling. Simply send in a question and Dr. Jordan will respond within 24 hours. Peruse previous queries for job tips and advice.
WEB http://amsquare.com/america
/wcenter/center.html

The World's Women Online An online directory and art gallery of women artists from Pakistan to Peru, in conjunction with the United Nations' Fourth World Conference on Women, which took place in Beijing in 1995—in case you missed the news reports that week.
WEB http://wwol.inre.asu.edu

Indexes

fem•mass "No commercial sites. No men. No fluff." fem•mass brings you a well-chosen collection of women's pages on the Web. From Alice the artist to Denise, mild-mannered software engineer by day and kick-butt aerobics instructor by night, Leigh Ann the motorcycle mama to Amber whose favorite pastime is skincare, Web-savvy women of all walks of life are highlighted. If you like what you see, check out the accompanying list of links to other creative and Web-active women around the Net.
WEB http://users.aimnet.com/~mijo
/Femmass.html

 ## BRILLO
WEB http://www.virago-net.com/brillo
The first page is a spoof of a box of tampons; the second, of Brillo pads—Brillo, the Web site, is caustic and bold. The tampon graphics continue, adorning articles that deal with how the Net marginalizes women and minorities, and how these problems are being addressed and corrected.

Topics include issues such as women and minority access to technology or how cyberspace perpetuates sexist and misogynistic paradigms. A brief scan of some of the Web's more popular pages might lead you to the same conclusion, but this site cogently qualifies your unease, as a good virago ought.

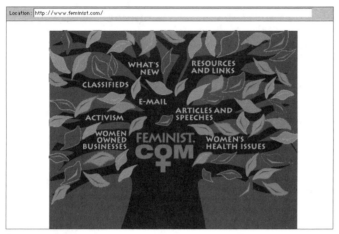

Strong roots make strong women
http://www.feminist.com

Femina A wonderful, user-friendly database of links relating to women's issues. The topics may be basic (education, business, finance), but the chosen links show a wide vision—for example, the art index houses the Guerrilla Girls (famous New York feminist activists) along with the home page of a Web grrl from the Bronx.
WEB http://www.femina.com

Feminist.com With sections on health, activism, classifieds and professional networking, this page should prove to be a good lure to get more women online. The Articles and Speeches page is a particularly excellent collection of commentary from the likes of Hillary Rodham Clinton and Betty Friedan.
WEB http://feminist.com

Feminology—Women's Resources on the Net A rather massive mix of links to those of the female persuasion. Some of the many categories covered are art and culture, conferences and education, health and history, and literature and sports.
WEB http://www.einet.net/editors /Stephanie-Walker/women.pages .html

General Sources of Women's and Feminist Information As one of a number of women's Web indexes, this one distinguishes itself with good site descriptions and email addresses for the authors of many sites. In addition, there are links to sites not specifically about women. Try *Mother Jones*'s list of not-for-profits, the Activists' Toolkit, or the National Child Rights Alliance.
WEB http://asa.ugl.lib.umich.edu /chdocs/womenpolicy/feminist.html

Gender-Related Electronic Forums An annotated collection of mailing lists pertaining to gender-related discussion top-ics including Jane Austen, women and ecology, meno-pause, and materialist feminism.
WEB http://www-unix.umbc.edu /~korenman/wmst/forums.html

Women's Literature and Art Links A terrific set of links covering topics from art to multimedia to theater. Lots of literature sites are listed for those in search of pages relating to women writers.
WEB http://www.zoom.com/personal /staci/litart.htm

Women's Resources on the Internet This site is a great place to start exploring women's resources online. Links to NOW, *Ms.*, women's health sites, bisexual and lesbian resources, bibliographies, biographies, legal resources, support groups, and women's colleges. But stay onsite for an online collection of paintings by women artists, sound clips of readings by famous women writers like Maya Angelou, and a calendar of links to women's events ranging from a martial arts training camp for women to WisCon 19: The World's Foremost Feminist Science Fiction Convention.
WEB http://sunsite.unc.edu/cheryb /women/wresources.html

WWWomen A directory devoted to sites for and about women, from pages about child rearing and pregnancy to sites about civil liberties and careers. Browse descriptions by subject area or search by keyword.
WEB http://www.wwwomen.com

PART 9
Virtual
Newsstand

Virtual Newsstand

CLICK PICKS
The very best on the Net

News

GONE ARE THE DAYS OF THE NEWSWIRE. TODAY,
ANYONE CAN ACCESS UP-TO-DATE NEWS AND REPORTS

EXTRA! EXTRA! Finding up-to-the-minute news on the Internet isn't hard anymore. Neither is finding interesting stories and probing commentary. There are over 1,400 newspapers online, not to mention dozens of news agencies, and several news radio networks whose broadcasts can be listened to in real time, right on your computer. There are even personalized news services available to help you choose the news sources you want most. And coverage isn't limited to just the U.S. Foreign papers are posting to the Web at a greater rate than those in the states, many with English-language sections. With access to so much information, what may be harder for the news junkie is logging off.

CRAYON
WEB http://crayon.net

If information overload is a problem, Crayon (Create Your Own Paper) can help you manage it. While it's scarcely an advanced search tool for people who need specific information, it does allow you to choose the sections you want from dozens of online news sources. For example, if you like the sports section of the *Philadelphia Inquirer* but want the front page of the *New York Times*, or like the *Times* but don't want to give up comics, this is the place for you. It's also possible to add your own URLs to the lists for particular sections. And all for one low price: nothing but your time. The software was initially developed by an undergraduate at Bucknell University—between classes.

Starting points

AJR NewsLink For links to a variety of news sources, and commentary on those sources, the *American Journalism Review*'s NewsLink is a good place to turn. More than 3,500 different news- and magazine-related sites are listed here, including URLs for many college newspapers. Other sites may be more comprehensive for specific categories, but NewsLink is a good hub for the less than maniacal. The front page is a little confusing because some important features are listed in tiny print in the left column, but once you're past that and down to the lists, the organization gets much better. One feature, a readers' top-ten list of news sites, may be of special interest to Net news newbies just looking for some good basic news sites. There are also a few features from NewsLink's mother magazine.
WEB http://www.newslink.org/mag .html

Online Newspapers *Editor & Publisher*, the newspaper trade magazine, estimates that there are now more than 1,400 newspapers online. For a comprehensive directory of them all, you won't find a more complete source than *E&P*'s own database.
WEB http://www.mediainfo.com /ephome/npaper/nphtm/online.htm

WebOvision's News and Magazine Links Less comprehensive than

Home to the best of Beantown news
http://www.boston.com/globe/glohome.htm

the *E&P* list, but also less daunting to use, WebOvision's links include some broadcast and radio sites not found on the *Editor & Publisher* list or at NewsLink.
WEB http://www.webovision.com /media/sd/pubnmail.html

National newspapers

The Boston Globe The best source of New England news online, and a good place to catch AP's news feed. Some stories include a column of hypertexted links outside the *Globe* on related subjects. A recent story on a shark attack included links to the Florida Museum of Natural History, International Shark Attack File, Shark Facts, and a Shark FAQ. Readers may also search by keyword for today's paper, or any word for the past seven days' paper, or participate in threaded discussions on a

variety of topics.
WEB http://www.boston.com/globe /glohome.htm

Financial Times The online version of the *Financial Times*'s U.S. edition, the *Wall Street Journal*'s English competitor, is still free at the moment, but subscriber information indicates that this can change with three hours' notice. The *Financial Times* is best on business news, of course, but there are other features as well. The international news, for example, is very good.
WEB http://www.usa.ft.com

Los Angeles Times The home page of the *Los Angeles Times* is decidedly low-tech, but you will find many current stories from one of the largest U.S. dailies. There are many better news sites online, but if you're looking for an antidote to the East Coast point of view of

most major news sources, this may be a remedy.
WEB http://www.latimes.com

New York Times Fax Sponsored by AT&T, Lexis/Nexis, Advil, Mobil, and Radisson, Times-Fax is a short (eight-page) version of the day's *New York Times,* which can be downloaded from the World Wide Web for free in Adobe Acrobat .PDF format.
WEB http://nytimesfax.com

The New York Times on the Web
The *New York Times* on the Web features the solid *Times* analysis and writing, which make it worth a stop, but the site lives up to its print parent's reputation for lousy layouts.

One front page screen, for example, shows the day's top headlines, sans stories, laid out as attractively as a ransom note. It's possible to click on the headline and get each story, which is good, but if you're already a regular reader, this may not be your first online choice. On the other hand, occasional special features may compensate, including deeper looks at a particular issue. The recent Web special on Bosnia, for example, included a photo essay, audio files from NPR, QuickTime movies, and forums keynoted by various experts in the respective field. It also included a lively discussion by people who seemed to know whereof they spoke. The

Times on the Web is free for now but judging from the elaborate password system, the gates may soon come crashing down.
WEB http://www.nytimes.com

The Philadelphia Inquirer In addition to the reporting that makes this one of the country's stronger newspapers, there are fun features you can't find everywhere online, such as a horoscope and a personalized comics page. This could be a great homepage if you're the kind of newspaper reader who starts reading from the lighter inside sections, then works up the courage to face the front page.
WEB http://www2.phillynews.com

 # Christian Science Monitor
WEB http://www.csmonitor.com

The *Monitor* has long been considered one of the best papers in the U.S., particularly for international news and perspective; the entire issue is now available online every day, along with RealAudio links to Monitor Radio and an Associated Press news feed. The Email from Our Bureau section, which look suspiciously like stories that didn't make the main paper for space reasons, is

another strong feature. In addition, there are issue forums and an interactive crossword puzzle. Researchers will find the *Monitor* an invaluable resource, because of its searchable archive of every issue going back to 1980.

San Jose (CA) Mercury News The *San Jose Mercury News* used to be just another large-circulation newspaper covering a suburban sprawl, but that was before Silicon Valley became the capital of the computing industry. Although it is still not a prominent paper in print, the virtual *Mercury* is one of the stronger online newspapers, particularly for Internet and computer industry news. Parts of the paper are slated to become accessible by subscription only in September, at $2.95 a month. Subscribers may also download archived stories since June 1984, for 25 cents a story. *Mercury* claims to have a million stories in its searchable database.
WEB http://www.sjmercury.com

Trib.com—The Internet Newspaper
Another little paper, this one out of Wyoming, tries to make the big time in cyberspace. *Trib.com* makes good use of links to other news organizations, but like the *Nando Times* it is being outclassed by larger organizations that couldn't be bothered about the Internet before.
WEB http://www.trib.com

USA Today The paper that changed the face of American news is now just one of the pack on the Web, with a site that looks much like other online papers, and in a medium that just may suit it better. There are no film or sound bites, but special Web features include a column on

McPaper—beautiful graphs, and all—fast food for the eyes
http://www.usatoday.com

Internet news and happenings, a special department for ongoing stories. In addition to longer stories, readers will also find the news McNuggets that made this paper popular on the street and infamous in the better journalism schools.
WEB http://www.usatoday.com

The Wall Street Journal Interactive Edition One of the most successful of the daily online news sites, the *Wall Street Journal* will undoubtedly find loyal online readers. One reason is because of the excellent *Journal* writing. The other is that the editors have built some special interactive features into their online edition that could prove extremely useful, particularly for people who follow the market. Perhaps the most useful is the Personal Journal, a computerized clipping service that will not only save articles about topics of key interest to a reader—by newspaper section, word, and company—but even

let you set up a clipping file for later retrieval. But a subscription here will cost you: $49 for one year for non-print *WSJ* subscribers.
WEB http://www.wsj.com

Washington Post The glory days may be behind the *Post* now that Ben Bradlee has retired, but it's still a good source for Washington news. The online *Post* looks like many online newspapers, with somewhat snappier graphics. It features both political stories and stories from its well-regarded Style section.
WEB http://www.washingtonpost.com

Southern

North Carolina News and Observer/ The Nando Times The *Nando Times* used to be considered one of the premier news sites on the Net, but now that the big boys have joined the game, it's not looking so special.
WEB http://www.nando.net

Southwestern

The Dallas Morning News
Promises to offer the most complete north Texas news online, but for now there is only one screen.
WEB http://www.pic.net/tdmn/tdmn.html

The Houston Chronicle
The home page features three buttons, to Houston, Chronicle, and Interactive. Houston leads to local sites, Chronicle to the online edition of the *Chronicle*, and Interactive to special online interactive features of the *Chronicle*. Interactive is just a hitlist of great sites. The online *Chronicle* is not pretty, but is still a good source for Houston news.
WEB http://www.chron.com

Midwestern

Chicago Tribune "There's no subscription fee yet..." Java-enhanced bells and whistles. Message boards. Includes neighborhood news, sports.
WEB http://www.chicago.tribune.com

Detroit News The usual features of a large daily, plus the famous auto section. If you want to read up on what's going on in the auto industry, this is the place to look. Another unusual feature: the Rearview Mirror. From Father Coughlin to Ice Cream Fountains, Motor City residents can respond to stories about their city's history, posting memories of their city in response to a specific article, culled from the archives of the *Detroit News*. Responses are posted on the Rearview Mirror bulletin board.
WEB http://www.detnews.com

Minneapolis Star-Tribune What's new in the Twin Cities? In addition to the ordinary features of a large online daily, the *Minneapolis Star-Tribune* keeps an archive of special features handy. This year's included a comprehensive fishing guide and an interesting article on how European countries handle welfare.
WEB http://www.startribune.com

THE TIMES
WEB http://www.the-times.co.uk

The *Times* beats The *Telegraph* in the category of best foreign newspaper by a nose, largely because of a few interactive features. The best feature is the Personal Times, which tailors each issue to a reader's interests by keyword. There is also an interactive version of The *Times*'s famous crossword puzzle. The look of the site may enchant or irritate, depending on how the reader feels

about sleek, black British design that looks lifted from a single malt scotch ad (complete with a Jeeves-like droid in the Personal Times section). But for all the posturing of exclusivity, the online *Times* is democratic where it really counts: unlike some of its American cousins, it plans to stay free.

DAD. HUNGRY. SEND FROGS. SPASIBO.

Students of the Ussurisk Academy of Agriculture have started to eat frogs and snakes, when late scholarship payments leave them short of cash. Third-year veterinary student, Alexei Chetvergov, started eating them after getting particularly hungry while experimenting on a frog. He kept the legs, fried them, ate them and liked the taste. Before long the 20-year-old cooked up a snake that he'd finished experimenting on. He says the animals taste so good that more and more students are now eating them.

—from Vladivostok News

Northwestern

Tacoma (WA) News-Tribune
News and features from Tacoma and beyond. One special feature: trade with Russia is growing very important in the Seattle-Tacoma area, and the *News-Tribune* has responded online with a special section devoted to Russian news, especially news from Vladivostok, the key Siberian port.
WEB http://www.tribnet.com

International

Asahi Shimbun English language and Japanese versions available; look for the tiny English Here. Good source for news and commentary from this Tokyo daily.
WEB http://www.asahi.com

Central European Online Navigator
This daily news site in English follows Central European news much more thoroughly than even the largest American dailies, culling from a number of English-language news sources in Central Europe, including that alliterative trio, *The Prague Post, The Slovak Spectator*, and *The Warsaw Voice*.
WEB http://www.ceo.cz

El Nacional Mexico City's daily newspaper.
WEB http://www.el_nacional.com.mx

Granma (Cuba) Biweekly news from our commmunist neighbors, available in English, Spanish, French, Portuguese, and German—but not Russian.
WEB http://www.cubaweb.cu/granma /index.html

Hong Kong Standard Until the *South China Morning Post* site wraps up construction (http://www.scmp.com), this is your best choice for Hong Kong news.
WEB http://www.hkstandard.com

The Independent What's the face of the new South Africa? The not entirely reassuring mugs of Wallace & Gromit are plastered all over the welcome page of this site. Why? "Because I like them," says webmaster Andrew Morris. Aside from that idiosyncratic note, most of the site is a straightforward online news site for one of South Africa's largest newspaper syndicates.
WEB http://www.inc.co.za

India Web Post An excellent source for news from India, geared specifically to the overseas Indian community.
WEB http://www.indiawebpost.com

The Indian Express (Bombay)
Nicely designed pages featuring English language news of India, including a leisure section and classifieds. Think our personals are complicated with DWF and GJM and GBMs? Check out the Bride Wanted section of the classifieds, where personals are classified by caste, ethnic origin, and profession.
WEB http://express.indiaworld.com

The International Herald Tribune (Paris) The hometown paper of American expatriates is now on the Web; the *Herald-Tribune* is a joint effort of the *New York Times* and the *Washington Post*, and includes the features of both along with other reports written by its own staff.
WEB http://www.iht.com

The Irish Times (Dublin) In addition to current Irish news and weather, homesick Irish will find a picture of Dublin City,

updated every 30 seconds.
WEB http://www.irish-times.com

The Jerusalem Post Jersualem's only English daily.
WEB http://www.jpost.co.il

La Nacion (Buenos Aires, Argentina) News on Argentina from this Buenos Aires journal.
WEB http://www.lanacion.com.ar/index.htm

Le Monde (Paris) Lafayette, we are here! France's famous paper, as brought to the Web by the *Boston Globe*.
WEB http://www.lemonde.fr

The Monitor (Uganda) A recent issue included a story on the naming of this year's Miss Uganda(she won a Hyundai, a round trip ticket to London, and a round trip ticket to Sun City, South Africa, among other prizes), a rebel attack on government troops, and the banning of Rwenzori mineral water to Rwanda because a Uganda Revenue Authority chemist found something in it—and that something was growing. "This growth is a sign that these solids are living things," the chemist said. A nicely laid-out site, which will shortly be accessible by paid subscription only.
WEB http://www.africanews.com

Moscow News Weekly English language news weekly. Check up on the latest Kremlin capers.
WEB http://www.vol.it/RU/EN/MOSCOW

Southam@Canada For news on Canada turn to media conglomerate Southam and their 11 dailies across Canada, from the *Vancouver Sun* to the *Montreal Gazette*.
WEB http://www.southam.com/nmc

The Sydney Morning Herald In addition to newspaper features, the online edition has RealAudio interviews with Australian Internet leaders, as well as video conferences.
WEB http://www.smh.com.au

The Telegraph Lacks the cozy twee look of the *Times*, but may have more inches of news. If you're looking for a good source of news without an American bias, this is definitely a good resource. Web features

 # CNN Interactive
WEB http://www.cnn.com

What's the difference between an online newspaper and an online cable news network? More sound bites and movies, mostly, and no comics. It may also be a little faster. As a headline service, CNN Interactive keeps up with Reuters and AP, but serves the same dish, but more stylishly. The

stories are shorter, but many readers may find the audio-visual goodies more than make up for the lost inches of copy. Many stories include links to relevant Web sites.

include NetLife, an attractive column of top Web site picks, and a searchable index going back to 1994.
WEB http://www.telegraph.co.uk

Vladivostok News A joint venture of the *Vladivostok*, the *Vladivostok News*, and Tacoma, Washington's *News-Tribune*, in English, from the capital of Russia's wild, wild east. Some of the local news will give you a glimpse of a side of Russian life almost never seen in western journalism. A recent issue, for example, contained a report on how hungry veterinary students at a local agricultural school had begun to eat the frogs and snakes they had experimented on because their scholarship checks had not arrived for two months and they were hungry.
WEB http://vlad.tribnet.com

Yomiuri Shimbun With more than ten million copies sold every day, it's the most widely read newspaper in Japan. Available online in English and Japanese.
WEB http://www.yomiuri.co.jp

Newswires

ABC RadioNet It's still in Beta, but if the test goes well, listeners will still be able to get ABC Radio updates on the hour, and ABC News *World News Tonight* (in its entirety), as well as *This Week with David Brinkley*, through the magic of RealAudio.
WEB http://www.abcradionet.com

Must-C TV
http://www.c-span.org

Associated Press A news feed to the Associated Press updated every 30 minutes, from the *Boston Globe*.
WEB http://www.globe.com/globe /cgi-bin/globe.cgi?ap/apnat.htm

C-Span If you're tired of summaries of what's going on in Congress, come listen for yourself. RealAudio feeds of the House and Senate are available courtesy C-Span, in live time, whenever the House or Senate is in session. Still photos in synch are also promised.
WEB http://www.c-span.org

MSNBC Although it took some raps in the trade press when it first went up, MSNBC may prove to be one of the more innovative news sources in the coming year. The downside is that reader-viewers may spend half their time online downloading files. A 3-D virtual photo essay on the Olympics that requires 1 MB of space to

download and five steps of work to set up may be amazing, but not many people outside of Microsoft and NBC will ever know. Gates might take the example of marketing whiz Thomas Edison: if you build it, they will come.
WEB http://msnbc.com

National Public Radio *All Things Considered* and the other excellent radio news programs from National Public Radio are now available online. Listen to the entire broadcast, or to separate stories, on the free RealAudio plug-in. Just catch the last part of an *All Things Considered* story last winter? Now you can go back and hear the whole thing, from the archives—as long as it wasn't broadcast before January 1, 1996. NPR can be heard through the NPR home page at http://www.npr .org, but this is the better access. Here, you'll be able to listen to the day's broadcast in

its entirety, or story by story, browsing the same way you would an online newspaper. You'll need a password from RealAudio, but it's free.
WEB http://www.realaudio.com /contentp/npr.html

New Century Network This service filters the best stories every day from 225 newspapers across the country, held by nine of the U.S.'s largest media companies, including Knight-Ridder and the *New York Times*.
WEB http://www.ncn.com

Yahoo—Reuters News Summary Breaking stories in a variety of categories are available on Yahoo! through a feed from Reuters, the world's largest news organization. Archived stories are available for several days after the fact, but that's not really what will make this site such a great resource for

the typical newshound. What will make it useful are reliable, up-to-the-minute news summaries, along with links to complete news stories. For fast, authoritative wire reporting, Reuters is a good choice with a reputation for being slightly ahead of the competition, particularly when it comes to business news.
WEB http://www.yahoo.com/headlines

Video

CBS Up to the Minute in VDO A new VDOLive feed every day, plus a weekly VDOLive feed from *Wired* magazine.
WEB http://uttm.com/vdo/cbs0.vdo

France 3 News This site features a six-minute France 3 news broadcast that you can watch without downloading, using the free VDOLive player, available here. The talking *têtes* move with a disjointed, *Max*

Headroom quality, but you will be able to tell what's going on. Dedicated Francophiles will also find a special edition for Rennes and Brest.
WEB http://www.sv.vtcom.fr/ftv/fr3 /video/newvid.html

❝ The talking *têtes* move with a disjointed, *Max Headroom* quality. ❞

News magazines

The Economist Although print subscriptions are expensive, this British institution has had loyal fans in America for years because of its incisive writing and thoughtful analysis. If you get tired of reading newsweeklies that seem only marginally less sensational than daytime talk shows, the *Economist* may be a good choice for you. Unfortunately, at the moment, only a few sections from the print version are featured in its online incarnation.
WEB http://www.economist.com

The Onion If online news begins to sound all the same to you, this satirical weekly/biweekly from Wisconsin may bring you out of your news fugue.
WEB http://www.theonion.com

Time Features from the newsmag, plus daily updates at

The Onion: where you'll laugh so hard, you'll cry
http://www.theonion.com

Time daily. Unfortunately, *Time* online lacks the memorable photographs that made the magazine famous. Without many soundbites or movies, *Time* isn't as high tech as its competitor, *U.S. News*. Good if you like *Time Magazine* writing, but if you're not particularly attached you may want to go to a more visual page.
WEB http://www.time.com

U.S. News In addition to features and columns from the print magazine, readers will find some soundbytes and outside links. A lot like CNN, actually, but not quite as high tech. Much prettier than *Time*'s site, and with an AP feed updated hourly, probably more useful as well.
WEB http://www.usnews.com

Personalized

ClariNet An electronic news service that claims a 1.5 million circulation, ClariNet lets its subscribers choose between thousands of different newsletters. Features are drawn from UPI, Reuters, ClariNet's own reporters, and other news sources, delivered to the subscriber's computer in the Usenet news format. A single user subscription costs $15 per month—for "two thousand stories a day, classified for efficient personalized review and reading."
WEB http://www.clari.net

I/spy Internet News Search Not a personalized news paper per se, this site is another useful way to retrieve news. Search for current and past stories

from many of the most important sources of online news using any word and call them up one after another without leaving the site. News is drawn from dozens of Internet sources. If you need information on a particular topic or company, this is a great place to start your search. One aspect that slows it down but may make it more useful (compared to going directly to a search engine), is that different sources have to be searched separately.
WEB http://www.oneworld.net/ispy /main.htm#techweb

PointCast Not a Web site, PointCast is an advertiser-supported service that provides PC users with frequently updated news and weather feeds, which are shown as part of a screensaver. Users select the news sources they would like from a number of sources, including Reuters.
WEB http://www.pointcast.com

Timecast The free Net radio news service offered by Timecast allows you to personalize your own radio newscast from a variety of sources. Sponsored by the Progressive Network, the company that brought RealAudio to the Web, this service began just a few months ago. There aren't all that many sources to choose from yet, but there will most likely be more in the future, given the stampede to supply sound through RealAudio.
WEB http://www.timecast.com

Time Magazine **goes daily on the Web**
http://www.time.com

Magazines

Online magazines have only one downside— you can't read them in the bath

As hundreds of periodicals flock to the Net, the print medium, according to some, is beginning to look like an anachronism. The problem, however, is that too many of them don't take advantage of the numerous tools that the new medium has to offer, resorting instead to what industry professionals refer to as "shovelware": text and pictures indiscriminately dumped online in unmodified form. In the digital realm, editors and publishers have the opportunity to expand the linear, two-dimensional, printed entity into a dynamic bazaar of hypertext, multimedia, and interactive forums. But ironically, some of the most prestigious print mags have the worst Web sites, for the simple reason that they've refused to adapt creatively. Don't take our word for it: check their techniques for yourselves. The good news is that if you don't like what you see, you can talk back.

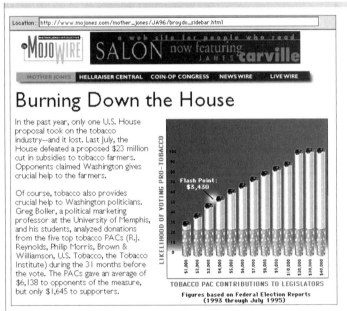

Location: http://www.mojones.com/mother_jones/JA96/broydo_sidebar.html

MOJOWIRE — SALON now featuring JAMES carville — a web site for people who read

MOTHER JONES | HELLRAISER CENTRAL | COIN-OP CONGRESS | NEWS WIRE | LIVE WIRE

Burning Down the House

In the past year, only one U.S. House proposal took on the tobacco industry--and it lost. Last July, the House defeated a proposed $23 million cut in subsidies to tobacco farmers. Opponents claimed Washington gives crucial help to the farmers.

Of course, tobacco also provides crucial help to Washington politicians. Greg Boller, a political marketing professor at the University of Memphis, and his students, analyzed donations from the five top tobacco PACs (R.J. Reynolds, Philip Morris, Brown & Williamson, U.S. Tobacco, the Tobacco Institute) during the 31 months before the vote. The PACs gave an average of $6,138 to opponents of the measure, but only $1,645 to supporters.

Flash Point: $3,430

LIKELIHOOD OF VOTING PRO-TOBACCO

$1,000 $2,000 $3,000 $4,000 $5,000 $6,000 $7,000 $8,000 $9,000 $10,000 $20,000 $30,000 $40,000

TOBACCO PAC CONTRIBUTIONS TO LEGISLATORS

Figures based on Federal Election Reports (1993 through July 1995)

MojoWire

WEB http://www.mojones.com

The admirable home of *Mother Jones* Interactive offers the content-starved surfer exclusive online material as well as extensive excerpts from the print magazine. Photo essays, effective use of hypertext, and aggressive investigative reporting are combined to generate an in-depth picture of American politics that puts many publications to shame. MoJo 400 offers readers a database of the nation's biggest political donors while Live Wire is a chat forum open to public debate on new and emerging issues.

CLICK PICKS

Starting points

Big Magazines A simple but useful page of links to major magazines organized by category. From the *Economist* to *Entertainment Weekly* to *Esquire*.
WEB http://www.bigpages.com/links/magazines.html

HomeArts The Hearst publishing empire moves online, tapping the collective wisdom of *Redbook, Good Housekeeping, Country Living,* and *Popular Mechanics* to proffer the best possible advice on topics such as Health, Relationships, Food, Pastimes, Home, and Garden. The cyberdelic smorgasbord of Planet Lunch is the place to go for recipe ideas and quick-fix snack tips. Special features include Great Home Gardens, Film Nation, and HomeCare Advisor. InnFinder is a handy resource, offered in conjunction with American Historic Inns, Inc., which allows you to click on a national map to locate and make reservations at the B&B or country inn of your choice.
WEB http://homearts.com

News & politics

The American Prospect The liberal journal of politics and culture is online in the staid, sober, and self-important manner one would expect of such hard-core policy wonks. Political pundits cover such topics as the media, money, healthcare reform, socio-economic policy, family values, and the

Netsite: http://www.thenation.com/

The Nation. DIGITAL EDITION

Sept 5 - 11, 1996   *Beta Release*

The Phony Drug War
Drug policy has made it to the campaign trail but the Democratic and Republican fixes are the same.

by JOSHUA WOLF SHENK

When the Clinton Administration released statistics showing an increase in drug use by the nation's youth -- 105 percent since the President took office -- Secretary of Health and Human Services Donna Shalala implored that "this is a bipartisan issue" and "these are all of our children." "The one thing we can't do," cautioned White House spokesman Michael McCurry, "is to turn drug use among young people into a political football."

- This Week
- Subscribe!
- About The Nation
- Nation Alert
- Forums
- Nation Audio
- Archives
- Search
- Hot List
- Marketspace
- User Survey

CONTENTS

Picking apart politics, byte by byte
http://www.thenation.com

future of the democratic party. Politically correct with a vengeance, TAP serves up a generous dose of Gingrich-bashing. The links to the Electronic Policy Network and Idea Central, liberal-democratic brainstorming forums, allow readers to actively participate in the discussions.
WEB http://epn.org/prospect.html

The Atlantic Monthly The one big improvement you'll find in the online version of the *Atlantic*—devoted to "Politics, Society, the Arts, and Culture"—is the seahorse. Every article marked with the seahorse icon is supplemented by links to related pieces that have appeared in previous issues, conveniently archived at the site. And after you've read five or six articles on a particular subject of interest, you'll be armed with ideas and ready to enter Post & Riposte, the interactive forum

for polite (and not-so-polite) discussion of contemporary issues. For arts, culture, and literature, tune in at Atlantic Unbound, or, if you'd rather just shop, pull out the plastic and go to the Exchange.
WEB http://www.agtnet.com/Atlantic

The Economist The name is enough to put some people to sleep, but this magazine's truly global outlook on politics and business with a dash of dry British humor makes it the intellectual's alternative to the standard news weeklies. The Web site is still experimental, and consists primarily of a handful of articles from the latest issue and a monthly review of books and multimedia. Interactivity? Sorry, old chap. See the "Business This Week" column for a wrap-up of the week's events around the world.
WEB http://www.economist.com

George It certainly isn't politics as usual at this rag with an unrepentant predilection for parody. Editor-in-Chief John Kennedy Jr. manages to patch together an eclectic assortment of featured articles on the issues of the day, the likes of which include "If I Were President" by the infamous F. Lee Bailey and "Why Kids Are Ruining America" by Bret Easton Ellis. Find Your Rep is a convenient way to quickly locate your state's representatives and senators in congress—simply click on the color-coded, interactive map. Virtual Politics is an entertaining and easy-to-use guide to political organizations on the Web such as the United Nations, NATO, federal and state governments, as well as major parties. A bastion of democratic spirit, this 'zine conducts frequent polls and surveys, and actively encourages reader participation.
WEB http://www.georgemag.com/hfm/index.html

Maclean's Canada's premier news magazine is also available on CompuServe. Readers will find features from the magazine and an interactive online forum.
COMPUSERVE *go* Macleans

The Nation The left-leaning, political biweekly is now available in a well-organized digital incarnation featuring periodically updated Special Sections comprised of extensively researched articles, forums, and photo essays. The table of contents includes This Week, a review of top news stories; Nation Alert, a political activist's bulletin; a link to RadioNation, the syndicated weekly radio show; and a searchable archive of past issues.
WEB http://www.thenation.com

National Review The time-honored, right-wing political journal's site opens with an intriguing headline: "Think the War on Drugs is Succeeding? Think Again!" The curious who follow the link will find that this bastion of conservatism is now advocating decriminalization, a policy that would save $75 billion worth of taxpayer's money, relieve inordinate strains on the legal system, and channel resources into rehabilitation and damage control rather than incarceration as a solution to addiction.

 # TIME WARNER'S PATHFINDER
WEB http://pathfinder.com

Pathfinder packs the entire Time Warner empire's publishing output onto one page, and sometimes it's difficult to know just where to click. Aim your mouse just about anywhere and you'll be ushered off to one among the legions of 'zines, news wires, weather centers, stock reports, and shopping malls squeezed into this site. It's the home of *Time, Money, People, Sports Illustrated, Entertainment Weekly, Fortune*, and the *Netly News*, just for starters. Restaurant reviews are courtesy of Zagat. Subject-oriented buttons connect to arts, entertainment, games, hobbies, kidstuff, music, shopping, and the Site Seeker Internet Guide.

In addition to proffering highlights of the print edition, *NR* contains a special Online Exclusive, with news and gossip from Capitol Hill, an Outrage du Jour, and William F. Buckley's Word of the Day.
WEB http://www.townhall.com/nationalreview

New Republic This respected journal of politics and opinion, available at AOL's electronic newsstand, is unfortunately confined to that commercial service's spartan, one might even say philistine, digital interface. Reading those stark text files, set in that lackluster Helvetica font, with no accompanying graphics or photos, is a little like eating corn flakes without the milk. Not that the writing doesn't live up to the standards of the 82-year-old publication. It delivers excellent insider coverage of events in the nation's capital, informative investigative reporting, and a forum for debate on issues and current events provides quality content. If only the presentation weren't so dull.
AMERICA ONLINE *keyword* newrepublic

Time The confusing and somewhat arbitrary organization of *Time* World Wide, the new media hub for Time, Inc., leaves a lot to be desired. The full text of the print magazine is now online, but the articles are strictly text and lack photos or hyperlinks. Apart from the magazine replica, the *Time* Daily section features photographs accompanied by cur-

Netsite: http://www.utne.com/

The Utne Lens: A Web publication --- **Café Utne**: A Web community

WELCOME

Sept./Oct. Cover Section	Café Utne Navigation
JUST QUIT! The Fine Art of Breaking Free	**INFORMATION & REGISTRATION** Joining is easy and free

Alternative journalism and meaningful chat
http://www.utne.com

sory text-bytes, which are subsequently archived in the Special Features area. How about a litte old-fashioned innovation?
WEB http://time.com

U.S. News Choose from a few headline stories or go straight to the subject-oriented sidebar, which links you to a number of special departments. Newswatch is a quick source for breaking news and current events, Washington Connection serves up a full platter from the corruption capital of the world, News You Can Use covers special interest stories and consumer reports, Colleges & Careers has those controversial school rankings and reviews, and the electronic Town Hall is where you get to talk back to the editors and other readers. Conventional news, mainstream opinions,

and good organization make this a palatable if unoriginal site.
WEB http://www.usnews.com

The Utne Reader "The best of the alternative press." An amalgamation of the *Utne Reader*, the Utne Lens (with exclusive online content), and Café Utne (an interactive community), this site should serve as an example to those publications which, for lack of vision, merely import text from their printed editions and attempt to spice it up with a few graphics. A digital center for alternative journalism, *Utne* articles cover topics as varied as art, travel and culture, mind and spirit, community and society, and media and technology. The cybercafe is the place to discuss issues, with a wide range of cultural forums, special panels, guest participants, and an

archive featuring the "best of Café Utne conversations."
WEB http://www.utne.com

Art & culture

Art and Antiques What does the electronic version of this magazine have over its sister edition in print? Well, there's the Forum, a global bulletin board where netsurfers can communicate with art dealers and collectors from around the world. And the archives, which give you access to articles from back issues. Unfortunately, there are few photos and

graphics to liven up the lackluster design, and the emphasis is on brief text-bytes over substantial content. *A&A* online is a somewhat abridged version of the original, and it doesn't go out of its way to explore the multimedia potential of the Web.
WEB http://www.artantqmag.com

The Paris Review The highbrow journal of art and literature has teamed up with Voyager, the multimedia powerhouse, to put together an appropriately sophisticated, though graphically dull, digital edition brim-

ming with the work of a familiar group of international illuminati. Interviews include such celebrated writers as Chinua Achebe, Woody Allen, Garrison Keillor, and Czeslaw Milosz. Excerpts from the magazine are also available, but the prestigious quarterly will apparently need some time to figure out that there's more to the new media than simple text.
WEB http://www.voyagerco.com/PR

Smithsonian Magazine The Smithsonian Institute has been studying, diagramming, ana-

NATIONAL GEOGRAPHIC SOCIETY

WEB http://www.nationalgeographic.com

The virtual home of the **NGS** features an abundance of exclusive online content in addition to a generous sampling of material from print publications like *National Geographic* and *Traveler*. An exceptional graphical interface, intelligent use of hypertext, and investigative reporting are combined to create an entertaining and educational multimedia tool. A featured article on the wreck of the Spanish galleon *Concepción*, for example, offers such links as an interactive map charting the route of the ship's final voyage, a profile of the captain and crew, cutaway diagrams of the vessel, and details regarding the treasure contained within. The more geographically inclined can click on the Map Machine to explore an archive of maps.

Cowboy: Montana 1993

lyzing, measuring, scratching, and sniffing across the planet for more than 150 years. Art, history, and the natural sciences are its usual beats, and now they're blasting off into cyberspace with an exclusive story from President Clinton himself, who imagines what it would be like to travel back through the mists of time to join explorers Lewis and Clark on their pioneering journey across North America. Articles are accompanied by a convenient "informative links" sidebar, which allows users to move swiftly to related stories and other sites. An eclectic collage of art and photography is located in the Image Gallery, while Smithsonian Museum exhibitions, study tours, seminars, and special events are enumerated in the Events section.

WEB http://www.smithsonianmag.si.edu

The Tricycle Hub The interactive (and they really mean it) forum of the independent quarterly *Tricycle: The Buddhist Review* is the ultimate hub for the beginning student, layperson, monk, or anyone else interested in Buddhist teachings and ways of life. The Monk's Bag offers a variety of means by which readers can actively participate in the ongoing dialogue, including features like Turning Words, an expanding, annotated glossary of Buddhist terms with contributions from esteemed teachers and individual readers (often lay practitioners who write from their

Location: http://www.smithsonianmag.si.edu/smithsonian/issues96/sep96/o

Big wheels keep on turnin'
http://www.smithsonianmag.si.edu

own experiences). Buddhism 101 is an excellent primer for the newbie, complete with a historical portrait of the Buddha, a glossary, Zen poetry, and various ABCs of Buddhahood. The Poll provides a forum for readers to post responses to specific questions about reconciling the practice of Buddhism with everyday life, while the Dharma Center Directory guides you to the flesh-and-bones Sangha nearest you. Dharma Connections presents a calendar of upcoming events, and has links to the virtual community of Buddhists worldwide. A fine starting point for exploring "the Way that is not a Way" on the Web.

WEB http://www.tricycle.com /index.html

Entertainment

Entertainment Weekly Drugs, sex, rock 'n' roll, movies, and all the gossip that's fit to print about the latest antics of the Hollywood glitterati. Choose from an extensive hypertable of contents, including featured articles, movie and multimedia reviews, and entertainment news. A bulletin board service provides a forum for topic-oriented discussions in four general categories: movies, television, books, and multimedia. EW Metro is a new monthly editorial section that focuses on "what's hot, hip, and happening" in major cities nationwide. The Latest covers all the breaking news from Tinseltown.

WEB http://pathfinder.com/ew

High Times Can you feel the high? *High Times*'s digital smoking lounge for unabashed marijuana aficionados from all walks of life. If you're a hemp activist, a cannabis connoisseur, or a marijuana horticulturist with the prohibition blues, at last, you can take the trip of your dreams. Take a cybertour along the canals of Amsterdam, sampling some of the world's finest strains from the notorious Northern Lights to heady Hawaiian Indica. Visit the virtual gardens of Holland's expert growers for cultivation tips, or learn some new recipes for cooking with ganja from Chef Ra. And show of your homegrown at the Pot Shot. The site has an assortment of links to reefer madness ranging from how to roll a joint to the history of hemp. A detailed FAQ provides everything you need to know about the renowned weed.
WEB http://www.hightimes.com

People As you would expect, you'll find the usual celebrity profiles, along with a sprinkling of plain-folks hometown heros, and supplemented with glossy galleries and gossip forums. Cyber Celebs presents links to other star-studded sites.
WEB http://pathfinder.com/people

Premiere Your digital guide to life on and off the Silver Screen. Go straight to the Marquee for reviews of movies coming soon, now playing, and new on video. Check out On the Set for sneak previews and the ongoing filmmakers series with such high-profile directors and producers as Joel and Ethan Coen, Oliver Stone, and Martin Scorsese. Armchair critics and movie aficionados can be found in Schmoozing, taking their art to the next level.
WEB http://www.premieremag.com

Saturday Evening Post Ben Franklin's bust greets you on the front page of this familiar bimonthly, though its online form is hyperabridged. A preview of the upcoming print

VIBE ONLINE
WEB http://pathfinder.com/vibe

When you zero in on the home of *Vibe* online, don't expect to find a conventional table of contents with articles listed according to the traditional linear model. Instead you'll be greeted with an eclectic collage of photographs, each one linking to articles, essays, fashion pages, and song

lyrics, as well as hip-hop and R&B music reviews. The site features a sampling of pieces from the current print edition, a celebrity chat forum, a guide to the latest styles on the street, the Vibewire interactive feedback zone, sound and video clips from recent music industry galas, and a hotlist of independent ezines selected by the editors. A well-designed, flavorful multimedia experience.

issue is followed by condensed versions of traditional segments, including the Medical Mailbox, with health tips for the layperson: Humor, featuring jokes, spoofs, and cartoons; and the Art Gallery, with the spotlight on Norman Rockwell, among others.
WEB http://www.satevepost.org

Women's magazines

Elle Get down with the trendsetters of the virtual fashion world for '96 and beyond at this glamorous Web site. A model gallery is complemented by reels of revealing images of such celebrated nymphs as Claudia, Naomi, Cindy, Christy, and Elle. Behind-the-scenes profiles uncover the "beauty secrets" that took them to the top, and they testify to the trials and tribulations of life as a jet-set supermodel. We should all have their problems! The Online Exclusive features interactive videos of the latest styles from the trendiest boutiques. Test your sophistication with the Fashion Quiz, and don't forget to visit the numerology section to determine the perfect day and time for that crucial rendevous.
WEB http://www.ellemag.com

Harper's Bazaar The magazine must not have much of a budget set aside for electronic publishing, because online *Bazaar* is more like a flea market, peddling a few articles recycled from old print editions. The site welcomes you with a

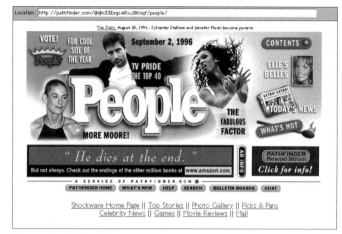

Who are they kidding? Celebs aren't people
http://pathfinder.com/people

promising graphic flashing the past year's covers before your eyes, only to follow it up with an insolent "purchase a subscription" link preceding a paltry selection of interview and article summaries. The online editors, in the words of DJ Premier, had better "check the technique."
WEB http://mmnewsstand.com/Bazaar

Ladies Home Journal Health and psychology, marriage and family, beauty and fashion—it soon becomes quite clear that *LHJ* likes a catchy pairing, but the online product just doesn't deliver as far as content is concerned. Poorly scanned, blurry images of the glossy edition in miniature serve as headers for the five-minute synopses of the articles that you'd pay for on the newsstand. It's clear the site was put up primarily for advertising purposes, which is fine as far as the industry goes, but don't expect much more

than shovelware.
WEB http://www.lhj.com

Redbook You have to hunt around inside the HomeArts site to find *Redbook*, a magazine that's mostly for married couples. It presents a retrographical interface harkening back to the fifties, with headings like Love & Marriage, You & Your Child, Health, Beauty & Style, Star & Entertainment, and Food & Nutrition. The articles are so utterly succinct that they seem to be intended for people with little time or a short attention span. You can get through the whole site in a matter of minutes, but don't miss the horoscopes created exclusively for married women.
WEB http://homearts.com/rb/toc /00rbhpcl.htm

Food

Bon Appétit Recipes, restaurants, wines, and spirits—it's

❝ Could common chemicals be causing the recent epidemic of shrunken genitalia among alligators? ❞

the epicurean's delight, free and open to the public. Take a peek inside this month's magazine or peruse the special seasonal supplement, which contains brunch, luncheon, and dinner suggestions. Best Cellars features a wine of the month and Going Out to Eat highlights the cuisine of a particular region or city. The most useful section may be the Epicurious Dictionary of Food, which you can search by subject or alphabetically, and has everything you've wanted to know about food but were afraid to ask.
WEB http://www.epicurious.com/b_ba /b00_home/ba.html

Science & nature

Discover Could another great meteorite like the one thought to have wiped out the dinosaurs strike the earth in the soon? Could common chemicals be causing the recent epidemic of shrunken genitalia among alligators—and is this cause for concern among

humans? These are some of the questions examined in the online version of this popular science magazine. It's full of well-researched articles written in clear, straightforward prose for the benefit of the non-specialist. An archive library contains an index of back issues, and the editor's Web tour will take you to the science sites deemed to be the best and brightest by the *Discover* staff.
WEB http://www.enews.com /magazines/discover

Nature Everything from molecular biology to quantum physics is fair game for discussion at *Nature*'s digital theory center. The editors claim that it is the "most cited science journal" in the world, with research papers covering topics such as immunology, earth sciences,

chemistry, astrophysics, and space sciences. Its database is full of science-policy news, and extensive listings of international science-related jobs, lectures, events, and announcements. One of the most interesting sections is the weekly Science Update, which recently featured an article on researchers in Germany who discovered a way to grow diamonds inside of onions. Unbelievable? See for yourself.
WEB http://www.nature.com

Omni Magazine Welcome to the new media lab of science, technology, and the future, split into six submodules: humor, fiction, columns, live science, gallery, and talk. Technophiles, science fiction enthusiasts, futurists, scientologists, and others of that ilk gather here to

Eat this
http://www.epicurious.com/b_ba/b00_home/ba.html

QUANTUM CAT TRICKS

ERWIN SCHROEDINGER, the brilliant Austrian physicist who was among the founders of quantum mechanics, once dreamed up a paradoxical thought experiment to highlight one of the stranger aspects of quantum theory. Put a cat in a box, he proposed, along with a vial of poison and a lump of some radioactive element. After a certain period of time, depending on the element used, there's a fifty-fifty chance that an atom will decay and emit a particle, triggering a device that smashes the vial, releases the poison, and kills the cat. There is, of course, an equal chance that the atom will not decay, thus sparing the cat. But during the entire time, according to quantum mechanics, the atom is simultaneously in the decayed and undecayed states. Not until someone makes a measurement of the atom is it forced into one mode or the other.

And the cat? Schroedinger said that one would have to "express this situation by having the living and the dead cat mixed, or smeared out (pardon the expression) into equal parts," living and dead.

—from Discover

Netsite: http://www.omnimag.com/emedia/dr_moreau/

Genetics and ethics at *Omni*
http://www.omnimag.com

discuss things like the recent adaptation of the old H.G. Wells' classic, *The Island of Dr. Moreau*. In The Omni Mandate the editors express the vision of the 'zine, which is currently being reorganized and expanded to provide "a completely interactive habitat that taps the full potential of cyberspace" and will "shed the tether of print for the medium of the future." Well, they've already succeeded at the latter, but we're still waiting on the former.
WEB http://www.omnimag.com

Scientific American "The Advocate of Industry and Enterprise, and Journal of Mechanical and Other Improvements." Talk about progressive visionaries—if this sounds like something out of another century,

well, it is. *SA* gives you a bit of history with an electronic version of its first issue, which appeared on Aug. 28, 1845. Recent issues investigate such questions as "What If a Comet Hit the Earth?" and "How Big a Threat Is Mad Cow Disease?" Ask the Experts gives you the opportunity to post your queries on science and technology to the professionals, while Explorations takes you on a hypertextual investigative journey into new discoveries and topical research projects. For example, when that small bit of embriotic rock was found, suggesting life on Mars, *SA* covered both sides of the story. Are terrestrial amino acids really little green men or are they just another bacteria run amuck?
WEB http://www.sciam.com

Weather

THERE'S NOT MUCH YOU CAN DO, EXCEPT TALK
ABOUT IT, OR WAIT FOR YOUR BROWSER TO LOAD

F YOU'RE A CHRONIC NETHEAD, you may have already figured out that you can do without the natural world. Why should you care about the weather? The only radiation that might concern you is the kind emanating from your computer monitor. Wind, rain, and snow shouldn't faze you at all, unless they knock out the phone lines. But should you decide to venture out of doors, having weather information at your fingertips is a necessity. And there's certainly no lack of meteorological data online, from current weather to long-range forecasts, international outlooks to local atmospheric conditions, and the latest weather-related news to updates on ongoing meteorological disasters. And even if you decide not to venture into the great outdoors, your time spent at the weather sites won't be a complete waste; you'll have something to talk about with the strangers you meet in the chat rooms.

Netsite: http://www.weather.com/weather/us-maps/maps/images/delta/natrad.gif

NATIONAL RADAR
LIGHT ▬▬▬▬▬ HEAVY
THE WEATHER CHANNEL

NATRAD 5 Sep 1996, 11:24 EDT

THE WEATHER CHANNEL
WEB http://www.weather.com

A perfect site for the weather neophyte, The Weather Channel allows you to check out current conditions and the forecast for your favorite U.S. city; you can also view nifty national weather maps of the same. Submit your weather-related question to the site's Met on the Net, follow weather links across the Web in search of answers by yourself, or best of all, fulfill your secret dream of becoming a meteorologist and explore TWC's Meteorologist's toolbox. You'll also find a short history of TWC, bios of your favorite forecasters, a monthly programming guide, and a list of TWC contacts.

Starting points

The Daily Planet Not to be confused with a certain fictional newspaper of the same name, this *Daily Planet* is a product of the University of Illinois Department of Atmospheric Sciences. The Online Guide to Meteorology is a virtual textbook on weather. For those who master that and see forecasting in their future, there's the Weather Visualizer which allows you to customize your own daily weather maps and images and the Weather Machine which offers satellite products.
WEB http://wx3.atmos.uiuc.edu

Interactive Weather Browser The Interactive Weather Browser lets you choose graphically, by way of a point-and-click map, what U.S. weather information you wish to view. Get the report on the weather in your city, without any static.
WEB http://rs560.cl.msu.edu/weather /interactive.html

Live Weather Images Current weather images from across the

> ❝ **The Weather Visualizer allows you to customize your own daily weather maps and images.** ❞

Who needs Willard?
http://www.usatoday.com/weather/wfront.htm

country gathered via Doppler radar, that instrument of weather-forecasting wizardry that's taken the country's meteorologists by storm. Also available are forecast maps, seismic activity updates, and hurricane warnings and watches.
WEB http://www.geocities.com/Sunset Strip/7033/weather.html

Weather News Daily weather maps, a dazzling exhibition of interesting statistics, satellite maps, thunderstorm outlooks, precipitation potential for the continental U.S., and an index of U.S. forecasts. The information is displayed with slick, easily understood online graphics. Additional resources include a weather-related current events section, a foreign cities' forecast section, and a ski condition report area. Weather News also boasts an

impressive Weather Discussion Area, where weather watchers meet to discuss long-range forecasting methods, instrumentation, and software.
AMERICA ONLINE *keyword* weather

Weather Reports Weather reports for most major cities in the United States, including national maps and radar reports.
COMPUSERVE *go* weather

Weather Underground In case you've been living underground (or at your computer desk) you can find out the current temperatures, humidity, pressure, and conditions for cities from Hilo, Hawaii, to Bangor, Maine.
WEB http://www.wunderground.com

Weathernews Yahoo!'s weather page, brought to you by

Weathernews, lets you search for weather info by city or airport code (e.g., LAX=Los Angeles) and will provide temperatures in Celsius or Fahrenheit. Or you can search both hemispheres by area for current and forecasted conditions.
WEB http://www.wni.com/yahoo

Weather in the news

CNN Weather No need to wait in front of your TV for the next weather segment to air on CNN—Ted Turner brings it to the Web. It's all here all the time, from U.S. and international forecasts to the CNN storm center to in-depth meteorological stories.
WEB http://www.cnn.com/WEATHER

INTELLiCast Home Page Offering detailed international weather information, this MSNBC weather Web site includes U.S. weather reports, national (and international) weather forecasts, selected city forecasts from Amsterdam to Warsaw, links to local weather resources, and detailed ski condition reports. The SunCast service predicts daily levels of ultraviolet rays, the form of radiation most responsible for "adverse health effects," as well as allergy alerts and yesterday's extremes.
WEB http://www.intellicast.com

USA Today Weather *USA Today* has put the colorful weather maps (that made their back

page famous) on the Web. Graphics-intensive maps and charts complement the site which offers the latest weather news, U.S. and world forecasts, and the "Ask Jack" column which provides answers to email queries from those wondering about weather.
WEB http://www.usatoday.com /weather/wfront.htm

Weather Events and Natural Disasters In line with the old saw, "No news is good news," Yahoo! provides a rundown of the latest shake-ups in the weather realm each day. When we visited, 12 people had been killed and 3 others were injured by rock and mud slides triggered by heavy rains over

NATIONAL WEATHER SERVICE HOMEPAGE
WEB http://www.nws.noaa.gov

Although you may have to try a few times to get through to this popular U.S. weather site, it's definitely worth the effort for the detail that's available. The site offers local and regional temperature, humidity, and "comfort index" info for locations across America. You'll find the two-, five-, ten-day, and monthly forecasts helpful to varying degrees, especially when making travel plans. Specialized NWS data on topics such as weather bulletins, tropical cyclone warnings, fire weather, and Alaska products also reside here.

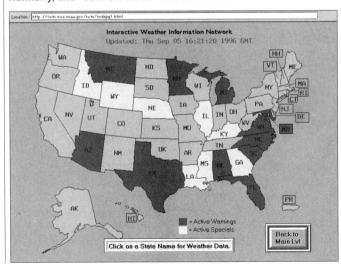

A TALE OF TWO TWISTERS

Has anyone watched the film *Twister*? It is a meteorological phenomena rare in Hong Kong. I have some questions about tornadoes:

Is the tornado more violent if two combine into one ?

"Two tornadoes combining into one" is known as a multiple vortex tornado. These are usually the most violent types of tornadoes. Most of the very violent tornadoes that have occurred have been multiple vortex tornadoes.

Do tornadoes disappear suddenly and appear again suddenly ?

For a tornado to survive, it requires an inflow of air. There is something called the "rear flank downdraft" (RFD) that descends with the tornado. The RFD will gradually wrap around the tornado and cut off its inflow. After the inflow has been cut off, the tornado dissipates. A storm that does this is called a "cyclic supercell."

—from sci.geo.meteorology

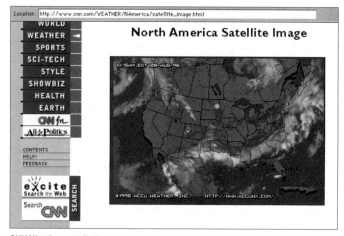

CNN Weather—to die for
http://www.cnn.com/WEATHER

Weather talk

sci.geo.meteorology The most technical of the weather news groups (a frightening concept), sci.geo.meteorology is visited primarily by 'ologists (geologists, meteorologists, etc). A recent thread concerning dew points drew upwards of 50 posts.
USENET sci.geo.meteorology

Indexes

Current USA Weather Map A National Weather Service forecast, updates on extreme weather conditions across the country, and more.
WEB http://www.arc.com/wx.html

Organized Weather Links: North America Whether you're looking for marine forecasts, satellite images, surface maps, or upper air charts (and who isn't?), this index of meteorology-related links will point

you in the right direction.
WEB http://www.comet.net/weather

Weather Information Superhighway A collection of links to weather report sites around the world. Find out if it's sunny in the Sudan, raining in Remagen, or snowing in Sydney.
WEB http://thunder.met.fsu.edu/~nws/wxhwy.html

WeatherNet Sponsored by the slightly sinister-sounding Weather Underground at the University of Michigan, this is the Internet's premier source of weather links. With more than 250 sites listed and new links added every day, WeatherNet is the most comprehensive and up-to-date on-ramp to the world of Web weather data. From here you can access weather reports and forecasts for just about any location which can be reached by plane, train, or automobile.
WEB http://cirrus.Sprl.Umich.Edu/wxnet

the weekend in El Salvador, and Hurricane Dolly forced the closure of 29 Mexican ports.
WEB http://newspage.yahoo.com/newspage/yahoo3/005idx.html

Ezines

In the '60s, there was the mimeograph. In the '90s, the Web is the ultimate 'zine machine

AN ONLINE 'ZINE is nothing like a magazine. First, it needs no paper, print, or postage. Second, it's void of glossy advertisements you have to thumb through to find the story that piques your interest. Best yet, it's free. At least, most of the time. A 'zine is not so much a thing, as an event, a happening. And yet, most 'zines have tables of contents, articles, essays, departments, features, photos, and letters to the editor—just like regular magazines. But 'zines have something their print counterparts lack, chat. With the Net, readers and writers can now achieve an immediate level of intimacy previously unheard of. And for those plagued by deficits not of the pocketbook, but of the attention span, hypertext provides instantaneous links to perpetual info-tainment.

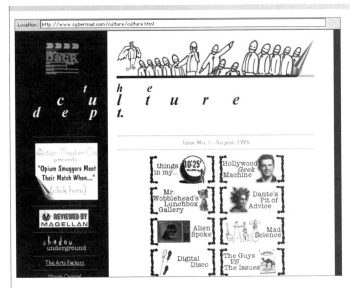

CYBERMAD
WEB http://www.cybermad.com

It seems that every online 'zine has a one-liner packed with choice adjectives to characterize its style and content. So, if "100% groovy" and "pop-culture" whet your appetite, then this Madison-based electronic collage of kitsch might be your dream come true. A virtual storehouse of trivia, froth, frivolity, and just plain nonsense, *Cybermad* may leave you wondering, "What's the point?" But that's precisely it, says ubiquitous editor Alan Smithee: "It could be our mantra."

Starting points

John Labovitz's E-zine List An annotated directory of over a thousand electronic 'zines updated monthly and organized alphabetically and by keywords. An invaluable resource for keeping track of what's being published online.
WEB http://www.meer.net/~johnl /e-zine-list

Art & literature

The Acid-free Paper Judging from the hallucinatory, psychedelic images found in this Ontario-based 'zine, not all the artists featured in the Acid-free Gallery are acid-free, though the "paper" certainly is. Each issue has a short story, a poem, and a work of art. School is a special section highlighting artwork from schools in the North Bay area.
WEB http://tnt.vianet.on.ca/pages /smithk

Addicted to Words The focus here, as the title implies, is on text, so as long as you prefer your images in the form of simile and metaphor, you'll love it. To multimedia technophiles, however, the spartan quality of the site might seem downright reactionary. Definitely oriented toward the literary purist, *ATW* offers stories, poems, author profiles, 'zines of the month, and a quirky collection of word miscellany called Oddities.
WEB http://www.morestuff.com/words /a2wortop.htm

Agnieszka's Dowry Don't be deceived by the dull, lusterless home page of this online magazine of arts and letters. Each of the colored buttons leads to a poem or story, and all of them are prefaced by exotic graphics. As for the poems, there may be a few gems tucked away among the dreamy ramblings of these amateur romantic surrealists.
WEB http://www.mcs.net/~marek/asgp /agnieszka.html

The Art Bin Straight out of Stockholm, a 'zine of art, literature, music, and cultural politics, organized in a "structured heap of articles, documents, pictures and so on." An introduction to Guillaume Apollinaire's 1917 manifesto, "The New Spirit and the Poets," six photographics from Ted Warnell, and seven collages by Edward Derkert are among the featured virtual exhibits.
WEB http://www.nisus.se/artbin /aaehome.html

Art Crimes The writing's on the wall—graffiti artists and street bombers from around the globe have found an electronic forum to display their work, share ideas and discuss the future of spray-can method, one of the most ephemeral of all art forms. Articles and interviews featuring artists "specialized to vandalize." From the walls of the concrete jungle to subway cars and trains, everything is game for the guerrillas of the Aerosol Armageddon. Manifestos and meditations on the state of dig-

ital graffiti, plus contacts and links to related sites.
WEB http://www.gatech.edu/desoto /graf/Index.Art_Crimes.html

The Blue Penny Quarterly "Ramble up to the barrista, order a cup of your favorite poison, and be prepared to defend your views... amongst writers, readers, and editors alike." This is the welcome you'll receive at the door to Café Blue, the *Blue Penny*'s special forum for the digital literary community, where you can discuss everything from Dostoevsky to dime-store romances. Narrative ficition, poetry, essays, book and CD-ROM reviews, and interviews with prominent poets and writers.
WEB http://ebbs.english.vt.edu/olp /bpq/front-page.html

Glossolalia Be forewarned: this is an experimental publication. The word alchemists of this online journal don't play—they strip flesh from bone, distilling the elements of language into a potent and sometimes volatile essence. Editor J. Lehman is also the founder of Cyanobacteria International, the anti-organization for communication irrationalism. The ultimate abstract aesthetician, his far-out perspective flavors the selection of prose, poetry and graphic arts.
WEB http://www.thing.net /~gristhomecyan.htm

Gutter Voice The home of "dangerous Web fiction," this sampling of prose and poetry is

compiled by the editors of Gutter Press. It is intended as an exposition of the "most talented and compelling" short works on the Net, featuring only one or two pieces in each issue.
WEB http://www.io.org/~gutter/voicenew.html

Kudzu Taking its name from the tenacious vine known for mercilessly ravishing forests and choking off all herbaceous competitors while at the same time serving as one of nature's great healing medicines, this 'zine is about as down-to-earth as they come. Several of the editors are graduate students at the University of Arkansas; featuring fiction, poetry, and essays. The emphasis is on the texts: the work of card-carrying MFAs encased in so plain a

package that its bound to be somnific.
WEB http://www.etext.org/Zines/Kudzu

The Mississippi Review A literary monthly published by the Center for Writers at the University of Southern Mississippi that features professional writers. Whether you're interested in slow-paced, old-fashioned narrative or the instant gratification of hypertext, this site features short stories and poetry by some of the most talented digital authors of the electropolis.
WEB http://sushi.st.usm.edu/mrw

ZipZap A snazzy presentation and delectable offering of poetry and fiction make this an interesting and worthwhile read. It features lesser-known writers that may have been

ignored in mainstream literary publications but whose work deserves attention nonetheless.
WEB http://www.dnai.com/~zipzap

Zuzu's Petals A beautifully organized online quarterly (named after Jimmy Stewart's daughter in *It's a Wonderful Life*) that aims to "unearth and present the best resources for creative people on the Internet." Specializing in fiction, poetry, and the literary arts, it sponsors poetry contests and offers a healthy healping of literary news and information on writer workshops. *Zuzu's* also provides an extensive collection of more than 1,500 links for artists, poets, researchers, and the otherwise arty-minded.
WEB http://www.hway.net/zuzu/zu-link.htm

HotWired

 web http://www.hotwired.com

Forget the magazine metaphor because it really doesn't apply to this de-centered, decidedly non-linear rag. *HotWired* consists of a collection of catchy headlines, supplemented by teaser links to a number of associated sites that each have a unique identity and subject matter: *Netizen* for poli-

tics, *Pop* for movies, music, videos and other miscellany from the culture industry, *Wired* for the latest technoculture news, *Cocktail* for those seeking a new twist on an old poison, *RoughGuide* for travel and tourism, and *Ask Dr. Weil* for health and medical advice. You'll find interviews of the gurus of cyberspace. The authoritative source for commentary on the Information Age.

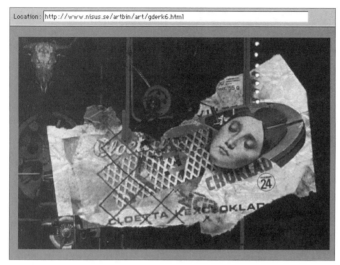

Location: http://www.nisus.se/artbin/art/gderk6.html

New trash from Stockholm
http://www.nisus.se/artbin/aaehome.html

Alternative culture

Adze Mixxe's Astrology Zine How will you fare in the Age of Aquarius? This is the premier astrology site on the World Wide Web, with seemingly endless links, in-depth sun sign profiles, analysis of the four elements, takes on triplicities, angles on aspects, tours of the planets, essays, quotes, and advice. What's in store for you now that the planet Pluto is traveling through the astrological sign of Sagittarius? Well, you may want to find out, since it will affect the course of your life through 2008. If you want your chart done, or a more personalized analysis, fill out the simple email form.
WEB http://www.adze.com/zine /adzezine.html

altX From the armed bunker of Avant-Pop, a creative move-ment that springs like maggots from the freshly interred body of Postmodernism, *altX* director and "cyber-prophet" Mark Amerika contemplates the "teleportation of narrative consciousness into the electrosphere." In addition to essays on cyberculture, Amerika's rant includes "The Electronic Beat," with input from the likes of Amiri Baraka, Allen Ginsberg, and Ken Kesey. Delve into the massive archive of interviews with writers, critics, and new media celebs like R.U. Sirius & St. Jude, Dame Darcy, Paul Krassner, Leslie Marmon Silko, Douglas Coupland, and Martin Amis. Another highlight is HyperX, an experiment in hypertextual narrative.
WEB http://www.altx.com

American Cheese This cut-and-paste, hypertext rag has taken its cue from Primus and set out to sail the seas of cheese. Indeed, they've got it all: ignorance, stupidity, irrelevance, obsolescence, triteness, contradiction, arrogance, authoritarianism... and a bizarre selection of links to the Net's most precious oddities.
WEB http://www.amcheese.com

Firehorse Attributed in the credits to "An Unknown Species Production," this radical 'zine opens with a quote from the Buddha: "Believe nothing, no matter where you read it, or who said it, no matter if I have said it, unless it agrees with your own reason and your own common sense." It is home to the Unofficial William Burroughs Home Page, with some fantastic pics of the old master of subversion. The metaphysically minded can turn to the Electrik Philosophy section with its magical interweaving of hypertext and graphics. News from around the Net, regularly updated columns, and "running" commentary from the Teknomad Road-Crew.
WEB http://www.peg.apc.org /~firehorse

geekgirl The womyn (sic) who write for this Australia-based, feminist 'zine include high flying cyberpunks, pagan earth goddesses, jaded witch types, cynical glam-pop princesses, and a horde of other "ambitious bitches." Get ready for high-octane entertainment as well as more serious, insightful

articles and interviews with writers, intellectuals, and everyday people from the land of Oz. Excellent graphics and a fair amount of technical tips for prospective Web authors.
WEB http://www.next.com.au/spyfood/geekgirl

Hempworld The latest news from the banned hemp industry, including stories on organizing, activism, farming, fashion, and cuisine. The 'zine's archive is packed with interesting stories, like one about the fate of a cannabis advocate who sent a parcel of marijuana to President Clinton, followed by a carton of home-made hemp ice cream to Hillary. Insightful essays on the potential of hemp as a major agricultural product that can be used (instead of wood pulp) in the making of paper, clothing, oil, and fuel.
WEB http://www.crl.com/~hemplady/hwarch.html

nrv8 Hook up a blender to your brain, flick the switch to high speed, and scramble the contents. What do you get? An alphabet soup of ideas and opinions that comes packaged Fresh Daily, Bottled Monthly, or Frozen Forever. Opinions, of course, do not always make for satisfying reading—especially if you disagree. That's where Feedback Now! comes into play, inviting you to spill your own guts on the issues of the day.
WEB http://www.nrv8.com

Stim Somehow these monosyllabic "S" words came into vogue as titles for ezines, all claiming to be radically jaded in their narcissistic, hipper-than-thou prose. This latest clone has about as much variety and flavor as airline food, with the usual articles on the agony and ecstasy of virtuality by cyber-rebels. Specifically, this means in-depth analytical nostalgia on childhood favorite TV shows, and tongue-in-cheek pieces on fashion, culture, and the coming apocalypse. Several opinion columns, listed under obscure, "cutting-edge" headings like Phenom, Trender, Eyebot, and Automedia, apparently serve only to create the illusion of depth. *Stim*'s notion of style

SUCK

WEB http://www.suck.com

The vitriolic editors of this 'zine declare it "an experiment in provocation, mordant deconstructionism, and buzz-saw journalism... a dirty syringe hidden" in the shallow waters of the Net. And this doesn't embarrass them one bit. At the sign of the fish, the barrel and the smoking gun, you'll find

articles and essays littered with sarcasm and satire contained within an ordered mayhem of graphics. Continually updated, *Suck* features two new pieces every 24 hours. For particularly scathing commentary on the new media industry, Web trends, and hypersophisticated cybercriticism, check out the work of Ersatz and CGI Joe.

and innovation is to replace every "f" with "ph." So if you want to actually find out who writes it, click on Meat the Staph.
WEB http://www.stim.com

Thought Crime "Sacred cows make the best hamburger." This piece of acerbic wit from Mark Twain serves as the proud motto of this entertaining and iconoclastic 'zine, which takes its name from the phrase coined by George Orwell in *1984*. Gnosticism, Zoroastrianism, conspiracy theory, Fundamentalism, Mysticism and Magick—all injected with a powerful dose of outright literary rebellion—are among the subjects of essay, commentary, and criticism authored, for the most part, by Brits. The criminal-minded architects of this eclectic melange of texts give precedence to the realm of ideas, and consequently little space is wasted on graphics or other technological bells and whistles.
WEB http://deoxy.org/tcrime.htm

Total New York Some people think that New York is full of beautiful people. Everyone, it seems, is a closet rock star, wannabe model, struggling actor, an aspiring somebody. *Total New York* perpetuates this myth: each interface is more beautiful and original than the last. But, the real surprise of *Total* is that it's rich in content too. Hosting some of Manhattan's fashionistas, such as photographer Dan Lecca

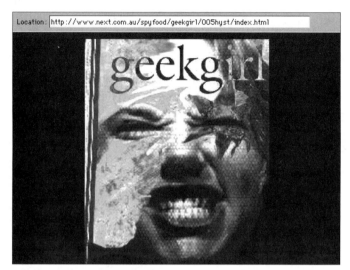

Location: http://www.next.com.au/spyfood/geekgirl/005hyst/index.html

Geekgirl: not just another pretty face
http://www.next.com.au/spyfood/geekgirl

and his account of the spring fashion shows, *Total* declares itself the chicest New York-centric site around. *Total New York* is really worth a visit, just by virtue of its interface. You'll never confuse it with supermodel.com.
WEB http://www.totalny.com

Traffic A 'zine largely written and produced by g. beato, whose writings have also appeared at *Suck*, *Traffic* is chock-full of cultural commentary by its critics-at-large. In the Museum of Corporate Folly you'll find a witty piece on Starbuck's imperialistic tendencies. The Wayward Web offers critiques of Net culture and a "Complete Guide to Automythology," while the Serial Theater presents the brave new world of cyberdrama.
WEB http://www.microweb.com/traffic/contents.html

Underground eXperts United An independent, irregularly published 'zine based in Sweden (though all articles are in English). It's a smorgasbord of writings that includes fiction, poetry, non-fiction, politics, satire, lyrics, and art. Authored by *uXu* members and outside contributors, the texts are largely subjective and narcissistic, inducing pleasure, pain, and indifference. The lack of organization and randomness of form and content makes anything other than casual browsing next to impossible.
WEB http://www.lysator.liu.se/~chief/uxu/index.htm

Urban Desires The highlight of this New York-based "interactive magazine of metropolitan passions" is Andrew Watts' "The Talking Feds" cartoon, somewhat by default because so many of the articles pack too

many words and not enough punch. The 'zine itself is split into a whopping ten subdivisions: Word, Art, Tech/Toys, Sex and Health, Music, Performance, Food, Style, Travel, and the ubiquitous Feedback. You're bound to find something worthwhile with so many choices, but the editors seem to spread themselves a bit thin, sacrificing quality for quantity and breadth. Book reviews, fiction, rants, raves, travel essays, opinion, cultural critique, art, pulp—it's all stuffed into a glitzy package for your viewing pleasure.
WEB http://www.desires.com

Zaius Words of wisdom from the Zaius Foundation publish-

ers: "Upside down in a net a man isn't worth much." (It appears as if the post-literate have forgotten women.) This "Post-Human Culture Zine" consists of three parts: Beatkit, Annexia, and This. Tune in here for "4th dimensional branding strategies, nowhere plans, Toxist works and lifestyle assemblies." If you enjoy nonsense with a Dadaist slant, check out this bizarre accumulation of words and images.
WEB http://www.qinet.com/zaius

Zero News The all-in-one megasite for politics, cyberculture, virtual voodoo, Subterranean Warfare, Hollow Earth Theories, paranormal experience, brainwashing, techno music,

smart-drugs, neurohacking, art, philosophy, fiction, aliens, and the cattle mutilation phenomenon. The creators must be out of their minds! A seemingly inexhaustible collection of links.
WEB http://www.t0.or.at/zero.htm

Politics & society

The Anarchives The hippy gang that graces the front page of this anarchist site is not one of the lost tribes of the Woodstock Nation and any resemblance to the Manson family reunited is strictly unintentional. The long-hairs are members of the TAO Media Collective, your friendly neighborhood anarchist commune.

 ## Feed
WEB http://www.feedmag.com

Feed has all the techno-frills that herald the electronic age: interactivity, reader participation, hyperlinks, and multimedia. The Filter section attempts to decode mediaspeak in the age of the sound bite. Feedline is devoted to "bite-sized analysis and opinion." Feature serves up longer, analytical articles on culture and society. Document is a page set aside for critics and pundits to annotate selected texts. Dialog is like an electronic roundtable, a forum in which "experts" discuss issues of the day. Recent debates include "One Nation Underpaid," which focused on wage stagnation and downsizing, and "Wiring the Fourth Estate," a forum on the future of Web journalism.

The radical thinkers at TAO have put together this electronic journal of militant idealism with the lofty goal of "transcending the exploitation and domination of our civilization." Study the origins and evolution of these semiological guerrilla warriors, visit The Shack for an archive of articles on the evils of capitalism, the threat of the concentration of corporate power, the similarity between Orwell's world and ours, along with a colorful collage of revolutionary rhetoric. Consult The Hermit for a fine selection of related links. Bakunin would have been pleased.
WEB http://www.lglobal.com/TAO /anarchives.html

The Big Gun Project Responding to an embittered email accusing the writers of this 'zine of being right-wing militia sympathizers, The Big Gun Project's editor writes: "25 years ago you'd be accused of being a Pro-Vietnam Marxist, 50 years ago as a Russian Communist, 80 years ago as a Socialist Labor Agitator, and 300 years ago as a witch." Big Gun intends to be the boogeyman of the nineties (are you scared yet?), and it's doing a great job, with cutting social commentary and intense scrutiny of the mass media. Its contributors, representing the emerging anarchist front on the Net, are a curious amalgamation of revolutionaries based on a reclaimed oil rig off the Pacific Coast.
WEB http://www.biggun.com

Gray Areas "We explore subject matter which is illegal, immoral, and/or controversial." This underground 'zine cuts right to the issues with articles, columns, and cartoons on topics passed over by the mainstream media. Recent features include such titles as "The Entrapment Debate," "Dominance and Submission: How The Police Use Psychological Manipulation to Interrogate Citizens," "Conversations In Prison," and "I'm a Vegetarian... In Love with a Butcher." Serious, insightful Web journalism.
WEB http://w3.gti.net/grayarea /gray2.htm

Postmodern Culture One must approach with caution any publication that has an entire section devoted to dense paragraph-long abstracts oozing with -ologies and -isms that attempt to summarize the content of featured articles. But those blessed with long attention spans will be pleasantly surprised. Though written and edited by academics, this 'zine contains provocative articles, novel uses of hypertext, and some of the most insightful social and cultural criticism on the Net. Keep in mind, however, that all discussions of "good" and "bad," "up" and "down," and "inside" and "outside" are heavily indebted to Derrida—and don't you forget it. Postmodern Culture is a joint effort sponsored by North Carolina State University, Oxford University Press, and the University of Virginia's Institute for Advanced Technology in the Humanities.

Pull up a leather couch in a corner of *Salon*
http://www.salon1999.com/11/bookfront/salon.html

WEB http://jefferson.village.virginia
.edu/pmc/contents.all.html

Salon The *New York Times*
called it "an electronic magazine that seeks civilized
exchanges on the Internet." If
that doesn't scare you away,
this eclectic panoply of essays,
opinion, interviews, and music,
book, and movie reviews generates ample food for thought.
The discourse takes in a wide
swath of social, political, and
cultural issues, with a decidedly literary slant that emphasizes style as much as content.
On a more personal note, Anne
Lamott's online diary, Word by
Word, affords inspirational
advice for victims of the
dreaded mid-life crisis.
WEB http://www.salon1999.com

Slate What's in a name?
Apparently nothing, according
to editor Michael Kinsley, who
also claims that "good magazines are exercises in serendipity." Well, serendipity and a
little PR. *Slate* was the beneficiary of arguably the most bal-
lyhooed debut on the Web
when it first appeared in June
1996. In any case, unlike much
of the gratuitous fare on the
Net, these ideas and essays
from a medley of professional
journalists, columnists, and
pundits will come at a cost—
$19.95 a year, to be exact. As
for content, the weekly is organized by departments that are
devoted to news about the
news (Briefings and In Other
Magazines), analysis and
deconstruction of the tradi-

STILL SUCKING AFTER ALL THIS YEAR

It was the best of hype, it was the worst of hype. This year the web
hit the big time, an amphetamine sneeze of annoyance punishing
innocent TV viewers, newspaper readers, and widemouth-beer guz-
zlers across the globe. Right around the time Tampax started printing their URL on their product wrappers, we realized the predictions
of an industry-size bubble-bursting were frightfully optimistic—the
web, or whatever it becomes in these times of IE 4.0 desktop annex-
ation and Pointcast-inspired transaction theory, is here to stay. We'd
try to cough up a cowed "God help us all" if we weren't certain He's
busy enjoying His joint programming with NBC.

But if the current crop of banana-headed programming geniuses
can't claim to have shared in the wealth, their attempts to cast
blame on the industry, the economic models, the users, or their
staffs only illuminate insofar as they value-add our daily laffs. It's
almost too bad net terrorists waste their time spamming mainstream
media pundits—it would've been amusing to see blame for this
year's content disasters squarely on their own shoulders. Web
Review, MCI/Delphi, Virtual City, Blow, even Spiv - all dead. No wonder the hottest new content meme is the "gravesite of the day."

—from Suck

tional media (Varnish
Remover), economics (The
Dismal Scientist), and a Features section with long articles
focusing on political, social,
and cultural themes. The more
entertaining, less discursive
sections include Doodlennium,
a weekly cartoon, and Diary, a
daily entry authored by a different writer, artist, or "interesting mind" every 24 hours.
Another treat is The Back of
the Book where you might find
artwork by Jenny Holzer or a
poem by Seamus Heaney,
downloadable with RealAudio.
Although *Slate* claims to have
no ideological mission or
agenda, its editors plan to take

a "fairly skeptical stance
toward the romance and
rapidly escalating vanity of
cyberspace" in favor of serious
journalism, which, to be honest, is quite refreshing.
WEB http://www.slate.com

Word How to sum it up in three
words? "Issues. Cultures. X."
Of course, "X" may not be a
word, per se, but it is a variable, and the crux of *Word* is
that it is constantly in flux. Not
to worry, you can always find
the obsolete texts in Dead
Words. A more abstract presentation than most 'zines, editor
Marisa Bowe prefers first-person, documentary-style writing

by non-professionals as opposed to traditional journalism. Broken down into general categories like Habit, Gigo (Garbage In, Garbage Out), Pay, Machine, Place, and Desire, there's not much chance that the writing will be mistaken for journalism. The solipsistic docudramas range from an account of sex in an airplane to the trials of a bicycle messenger in New York City. Simple, straightforward, and occasionally entertaining pieces by twentysomething amateurs.
WEB http://www.word.com

Student 'zines

Citizen Poke Under the glare of the transcendental eyeball, a group of creative Amherst students with a virtual arsenal of verbal and graphical skills have put together a hip little 'zine

that is updated with new stories and articles each day. The young, pop-intelligentsia crank out cultural commentary on familiar and more obsure topics, featuring titles like "Willy Wonka as Pimp Daddy: The Subversion and Perversion of a Classic Pop Icon." A heavy dose of digital wizardry, metaphysical chitchat, and just plain fun.
WEB http://www.amherst.edu/~poke

The Other Voice Trinity College's "other" student 'zine isn't merely one voice, but a gallimaufry of well-articulated opinions on everything from Buchaninism and gun control to "New Age Yuppie Trash" and the "truth" about Castro's Cuba. Formal academic essays and pop-criticism in addition to fiction and poetry. The textual smorgasbord is supple-

mented by a fascinating gallery of art, graphics, and electronic collage.
WEB http://www.trincoll.edu/othervoi

The Spoke Live from the Fish Bowl at Emory U., the Spokers spew out their infectious blend of wit, humor, and parody with such style it makes *National Lampoon* look like an academic journal. Comical spoofs on cults, militias, chain fast food outlets, politicians, and other cultural flotsam from post-ism America, with a focus on the greater Atlanta metropolitan area.
WEB http://www.emory.edu/SPOKE

think An electronic journal of the literary and visual arts published by the Getting The Word Out Group, a student organization at the University of California at Davis. Fiction, poetry, and .JPEG images of sculpture, painting, and art installations. Not much use of hypertext or other new media features, but an interesting selection of young and unpublished writers.
WEB http://think.ucdavis.edu

Trincoll Journal The "Amazing" 'zine from the Trin kids featuring text, art, graphics, audio, video, hypertext, multimedia, and other luxuries of technotopia. First published on the Web in 1992 as an alternative to the stodgy campus print press, the staff enthusiastically documents campus life as well as examines cultural trends.
WEB http://www.trincoll.eu/tj

Those in glass houses...
http://www.amherst.edu/~poke

Location: http://www.amherst.edu/~poke/

CITIZEN POKE

FREAKS OF THE WEEK

EMMETT ARCHIVES

Freaks of the Week
Click on the picture

Beef Today

Beef Today

There's a web 'zine for beef farmers, and we found it. Check out the latest in custom cattle feeding, or maybe just head down to the "chat corral" to chew thefat.

PART 10
Politics & Government

Politics & Government

CLICK PICKS
The very best on the Net

Issues & Debate

ANGRY? GET YOUR VIEWS ON ABORTION, WELFARE, AND MUCH MORE OFF YOUR CHEST

YOU'VE SEEN THE COMMERICIALS, heard the stump speeches, read the editorials, and listened to the pundits on TV. Now, at long last, you have the spotlight. So get ready to rant, rave, and spew out all your cherished opinions to the world at large. Whether it's animal rights, civil rights, women's rights, gun-owner's rights, inmates's rights, immigrant's rights, reproductive rights, or just plain human rights, the Net has a forum for you. So many forums, in fact, that the most difficult choice you face may be picking the one that's right for you. Are you more inclined to discuss the spotted owl, or the pros and cons of armor-piercing bullets? Do you like a debate filtered through a polite moderator, or do you prefer to fight tooth and nail, going straight for the jugular? Take your time, peruse our reviews, then dust off your ideals and give free reign to your need to bleed.

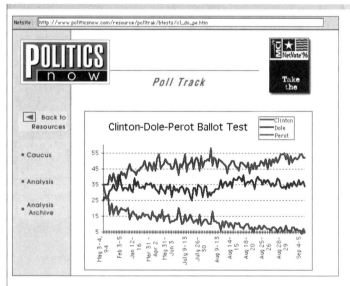

POLITICSNOW
WEB http://www.politicsnow.com

Make a visit to this site for your daily dose of that bitter medicine we call American political life. Along with news from the bayous of Louisiana to the coal fields of Pennsylvania (EPA support), there are plenty of issue and party links. But the real meat here is the interactive caucus—just register, and you can discuss all things political with voters from across the country. Prominent guests often drop by—recent visitors have included GOP strategist Ed Rollins. Virtual polls are posted weekly. The Virtual Voter Booth poses new questions every day, so you can express yourself directly on late-term abortions, or the popularity of the Newt.

TRICKLE UP ECONOMICS

Just how big is this "Lifetime Welfare" crowd? I've never met one, and I doubt you have, either.

Sure you have. Every time you've spoken to a middle manager in a defense industry that makes overpriced military equipment. Every time you've talked to a rancher feeding his cattle on public land. Every time you've met a miner who got a sweetheart deal from the Dept. of Int. Every time you've talked to a logger who clearcuts public land. Every time you've met a clergyman who doesn't pay taxes but demands public services. Every time you've met a manufacturer who dumps his waste and expects someone else to clean up for him. Every time you've met a pentagon official who is busy promoting worthless defense projects in a desperate attempt to keep his monthly dole coming in. Every time you meet a farmer who gets a subsidy for not planting. Every time you've met an S&L executive out of jail. Most of these folks are devout conservatives.

Conservative/GOP types aren't against welfare. They're just against giving it to folks who need it.

—from talk.politics.misc

Starting points

Capital Connection With links to *Congressional Quarterly*, the ACLU, and the NRA, this large non-partisan site contains a wealth of information for the politically aware. Track the 1996 presidential campaign. Read about the Heritage Foundation. Email the president. Drop by the message boards to weigh in on everything from health care to crime. Or visit the libraries and download a transcript of Congress's balanced-budget debate. **AMERICA ONLINE** *keyword* capital

Interactive Democracy Home Page A forms-based Web site that sends emails to your favorite political figures—Newt, Bill, Jesse, Rush—as well as political commentators and others who bear upon the political process. **WEB** http://www.cgx.com/id.html

talk.politics.misc For better or for worse, talk.politics.misc lives up to its subtitle: "Political discussions and ravings of all kinds." Why don't more women own guns? Does capitalism truly benefit the American worker? What should be done about Whitewater? While the hot topics are the same as elsewhere on the Net—more than 600 subscribers posted responses to an essay titled "Is Health Care a Right?"—there's an entertaining diversity, including brief but impassioned discussions of Scientology, Prozac, pornography, and Nixon's anti-Semitism. **USENET** talk.politics.misc

White House Forum Is Bill Clinton linked to gangland slayings? Should the White House be renamed the Sleaze House? Is it true that Bob Dole and Hillary had lunch last week, and that Hillary even ordered an "eclair" for dessert? All these questions and more are handled with great passion and a bare minimum of tact on AOL's White House Forum. Encompassing both domestic policy and international affairs, the White House Forum also has two special message boards devoted to Current Legislation and Media Watch. But the real meat of the forum is in its libraries, which collect a mass of press releases and transcripts on everything from education to health care to housing. **AMERICA ONLINE** *keyword* whitehouse

Yahoo Daily Politics Summary Don't waste time watching TV or soiling your hands with unsightly newsprint—Yahoo! has gone to the trouble of collecting all the daily political news from Reuters and serving it up hot. Find out just which congressperson is embarrassing which party this week, or which popular industry is under the cosh. Check in every morning—the leftovers archive lasts only three days.

WEB http://www.yahoo.com/headlines/current/politics

Animal rights

Animal Rights Resources

Reprinted from the *Vegan*, this site details the injustices and cruelties perpetrated against animals, including their confinement as pets, their killing for food, killing for fashion, and killing for amusement. Are humans superior to animals? Can animals reason? Maybe, but most of them can't point and click, and none of them can vote; you'll have to read up on these ethical issues for them.

WEB http://www.waste.org/~lanshark

PETA The popular animal-rights organization diverges from its enormously effective offline strategies—shock-tactic images and celebrity endorsements by the likes of Ricki Lake, Christy Turlington, and several other supermodels—with its Web site, which is short on pictures of animals and fur-clad celebs but long on news and analysis. The one exception to this toned-down strategy is the interactive tour of Animal Research Laboratories, which bludgeons visitors with images of dead animals and stomach-churning text: "At Wright State University in Dayton, Ohio, one dog was cut open and an autopsy was performed

while another live dog watched, waiting his turn on the bottom shelf of a stainless steel cabinet."

WEB http://www.envirolink.org/arrs/peta

Capital punishment

alt.activism.death-penalty What kinds of homicide are justifiable? How do other nations treat their criminals? When does the statute of limitations expire on an unpremeditated killing? What does the Ehrlich study say about deterrence? And who is being executed in the near future? Dominated by virulent foes of capital punishment, this newsgroup sometimes veers into tangential top-

⊚ All Things Political

WEB http://www.federal.com/Political.html

picture: WEB http://library.whitehouse.gov

Sponsored by *Washington Weekly*, this site has articles with titles like "The Anti-Newt Agenda of the Liberal Media" and offers free subscriptions to talk-show hosts. Hmmmmm. If you're not troubled by this, you can use this gateway to reach political newsgroups, candidates' home pages, and

other political sites. You can also take a detour into the *Weekly*'s scandal section which, in addition to the traditional Whitewater fare, includes information on something called The Mena Scandal, which attempts to link Governor Clinton to the Iran-Contra Affair and drug-running. Next stop: *The X-Files*.

A page from a Black Panther coloring book of the 1960s
http://www.cybergate.com/~bpcb/index.html

ics like freedom of speech and Jeremy Bentham's panopticon.
USENET alt.activism.death-penalty

Death Penalty Information Part of the Critical Criminology Homepage, this Web site provides death penalty statistics and information. Get death row stats for each state, find out which ones use the death penalty and what methods are employed, and read the arguments for and against. Is the death penalty cheaper, and is it a good deterrent to crime? The answers may surprise you. Phone numbers for those wanting to get politically involved on either side are provided.
WEB http://sun.soci.niu.edu/~critcrim /dp/dp.html

Executions in the USA in 1996 An up-to-date list, including the name and race of the execu-

tionee, the state doing the executing, and the method. More general stats on the death penalty in 1996 are also provided, including the number of women on death row and their names. You can also take advantage of the helpful links to other death penalty pages.
WEB http://members.magnet.at/k .sand/amnesty/usa/dp96/index.html

Links Toward Abolition Links to sites against the death penalty including Amnesty International, the ACLU, and the NAACP.
WEB http://www.wco.com/~aerick/dp .htm

Civil liberties

alt.society.civil-liberties Much of this newsgroup revolves around issues relating to civil liberties in cyberspace, particu-

larly the Exon bill, which was aimed at regulating online obscenity. Occasionally, though, Usenet's civil libertarians look beyond the scope of their monitor and mouse to address three-dimensional issues, such as the scheduled execution of cause célebre Mumia Abu-Jamal.
USENET alt.society.civil-liberties

Civil Liberties and Human Rights Links to national and international resources for the protection and preservation of our precious civil liberties.
WEB http://www.ping.be/~ping0044 /civlib.html

Individual Rights in America: A Citizen's Guide to Internet Resources Information wants to be free, and so does your average American. Enhance your autonomy with these links to information resources available on the Web that explain and describe the rights of Americans under federal law, or under nationally applicable legal principles. These include some links to the text of the Constitution and the Bill of Rights, rights under select federal statutes, rights of Americans by status and group, and particular rights arising under various federal programs. A sampling of general legal resources rounds out the site.
WEB http://asa.ugl.lib.umich.edu /chdocs/rights/Citizen.html

alt.discrimination Along with the usual commonsensical exposure of injustice ("Mistreatment is wrong"), this newsgroup is the venue for a tremendous amount of new-fangled, more dubious claims —complaints by male victims of affirmative action, a revisionist complaint that *"Schindler's List* falsifies history," and even a posting that tries to give new teeth to the old saw that girls can't do math.

USENET alt.discrimination

American Civil Rights Review It's always a challenge for a single forum to present any issue in a truly non-partisan fashion, and when the forum is dealing with a subject as charged with tension as civil rights, it gets damn near impossible, but the *American Civil Rights Review* does its level best to put forward "positive civil rights vs. negative civil rights issues." The *Review* publishes articles and position papers on both sides of questions like "Diversity & Multiculturalism in International Areas." It also links the reader to documents related to the Geneva Conventions, Hague Conventions, League of Nations, Mideast, including the Israeli-PLO Peace Agreement, and the Law of the Sea.

WEB http://www.anet-stl.com/~civil

Black Panther Coloring Book The author of this page found this Black Panther coloring book in a supply closet in Fresno City College in 1993 and estimates that it dates from the late '60s. The book, which is displayed in actual size online, reproduces Black Panther Party tenets along with large black-and-white (or is that black-and-non-black?) illustrations. Print them out for your kids, so that the little ones will know that "The Junior Panther defends his Mother," "The Pig is afraid of the Black Man. He strikes out against little children," and "Power comes

ACLU
WEBhttp://www.aclu.org

The American Civil Liberties Union doesn't exactly have customers to cater to or a product to promote, but they've created an informative online outpost that puts the customer service and public relations departments of most major businesses to shame. With a crisp and clean design, the ACLU outlines its main program—links to Congressional action, Supreme Court decisions, and a

state-by-state rights review, all of which help civil libertarians cry freedom—but doesn't skimp on community orientation (features about online issues position the organization as an expert in the new-born field of cyberliberties). There's also plenty of interactivity; visitors can email a character named Sibyl Liberty to get answers to topics ranging from drug testing to the laws requiring parental notification of daughters seeking abortions.

through the barrel of a gun."
WEB http://www.cybergate.com/~bpcb /index.html

Creationism vs. evolution

Institute for Creation Research
This self-described "Christ Focused Creation Ministry" is both up-front and upbeat about its positions. Its many candy-colored buttons take you to bibliographies, tracts, pamphets, an FAQ, and a number of areas still under construction and evidently aimed at children.
WEB http://www.icr.org

Politics and Religion Much of the message board is devoted to the irreconcilable differences between the doctrines of evolution and creation, and the equally problematic gap between faith and verifiable "fact." The debate is surprisingly learned and respectful, and there's an exceptionally handsome archive of past discussions, replete with links, lectures, and pictures of fossils.
COMPUSERVE *go* issues→Messages→ Politics & Religion

talk.origins The great debate between evolutionists and creationists. In one corner, the Grubaugh Polar Configuration model, the "indisputable truth of fossilized remains," and the fact that "research has fixed the point at which man emerged from other forms of life." In the other corner, the word of God. And that, in short, is the prob-

lem with this newsgroup, which is less a discussion than a collision of faiths: one in scientific research, the other in spiritual documents. Futile polemics notwithstanding, there's still some fascinating material, such as an attempt to reconcile the biblical account of The Flood with available geological evidence.
USENET talk.origins

Cyberliberties

Freedom Forum What do Daniel Ellsberg, Rush Limbaugh, and Murphy Brown have in common? They all owe their ability to reach the public to the media Doberman watchdogs at the *Freedom Forum*. Find out about all their programs to keep speech, the press, and the spirit free. Don't miss the *Forum* magazine article "Should your T-shirt have freedom of speech?" There's quite a bit of informative reports and articles about freedom of the press, media studies, and the information revolution.
WEB http://www.freedomforum.org

Jake Baker Information Page
University of Michigan undergraduate Jake Baker made national headlines in the winter of 1995 when sexually explicit, violent stories about the rape and dismemberment of a classmate were posted in the alt.sex.stories newsgroup under his name. Though criminal charges stemming from the stories were eventually dropped, Baker became a poster child

for civil liberties in cyberspace, despite the fact that many of his defenders expressed personal disgust toward the very material they sought to protect. This carefully measured page includes documents pertaining to the case, pictures of Baker and university officials, reprints of relevant newsgroup threads, and even the stories themselves.
WEB http://krusty.eecs.umich.edu /people/pjswan/Baker/Jake_Baker .html

National Campaign for Freedom of Expression Some may wonder why Rush Limbaugh is allowed to equate feminists with Nazis with impunity on the airwaves, while birth-control information is still censored as immoral. This page is using the online medium to its greatest potential while it still can. Email your senator to demand the right to look at naughty binaries in peace.
WEB http://www.tmn.com/Artswire /www/ncfe/ncfe.html

Education

alt.education Parents and teachers come to blows over whether reading should be taught before, during, or after kindergarten (or at all). Much considered discussion comes across the Net at alt.education, and it's often dedicated to the many available options for reforming the American educational system, whether by school choice, multiculturalism, or plain old phonics. The

presence of actual education professionals adds a certain extra spice.
USENET alt.education

Education Policy Analysis Archives The education scholar's take on the practice of education. Read the latest in policy, reform, and analysis in this electronic journal from the College of Education at Arizona State University.
WEB http://seamonkey.ed.asu.edu /epaa

Environment

Environmental Forum The forum divides environmental issues into national and global topics. The former helps explain what

ordinary citizens like Donna ("I try to recycle but sometimes my neighborhood doesn't help me with regular pickups") and Saul ("Are there any environmental drawbacks to email?") can do to improve their environment. As for the latter, the Global Action and Information Network uses this forum as a base, publishing regular news releases and updates on environmental breakthroughs, and encouraging all kinds of "green" activism. Live conferencing happens in the Environmental Chat room.
AMERICA ONLINE *keyword* eforum

League of Conservation Voters Be an American Lorax and speak for the trees by voting "green"

this time around. This handy site provides environmental ratings for every Congressperson. For example, Connecticut Representative Delauro is a friend to all things leafy (with a rating of 100 percent), but colleague Franks gets 0 percent. The site also contains press releases and ready-to-email missives.
WEB http://www.lcv.org

talk.environment "I want to be green / recycle my mail / I'm hoping to be / a friend to the whale." It's just a song, of course, but it accurately summarizes the dominant sentiment on this newsgroup, which speculates on both the small (recycling your newspapers) and the

ELECTRONIC FRONTIER FOUNDATION

 WEB http://www.eff.org

"Click this button to change the world!" proclaims the Electronic Frontier Foundation's home page. In addition to an extensive archive of material on first amendment rights in the electronic age, the page links to EFF's Action Alert page, which serves as a sort of hotline to the ACLU of cyberspace.

Location: http://www.eff.org/pub/Graphics/aero-eff_shirt.jpg

What is electronic crime? How can it be punished? Who enforces? Who suffers? Find resources (if not answers) and up-to-the-week (if not up-to-the-minute) news about free speech, encryption, privacy, and intellectual property issues. The resident authority on cyberlegalese.

Location: http://www.indirect.com/www/warren/flag/burn2.html

She's blazing, and Newt's not gonna like it.

Keep it burning...

Stars and stripes and flames
http://www.indirect.com/user/warren/flag.html

large (nuclear power) things that we can do to clarify our responsibility to the earth. The participants are the usual suspects: older activists who want to provide for the future, and younger activists who worry that the world won't bear their weight. And remember, online conferences are ecologically airtight (except for the electricity used and the radiation from your monitor).
USENET talk.environment

Flag burning

Virtual Flag-Burning Page One of the best examples of symbolic imagery available in cyberspace, this page chronicles the history of flag-burning and traces the fate of current anti-flag-burning legislation. But the political wallop of this site

resides in the virtual flag-burning link, which loads an image of Old Glory and then torches it with the help of Web animation. Mindful of its pro-liberty stance, the page contains a number of different animations, from a more provocative version in which accompanying text taunts the amendment supporters ("She's blazing and Newt's not going to like it") to an image-only burning. And because democracy is paramount, the site invites readers' comments, which range from admiring appraisals of the page to considerations of some of the more absurd extensions of the proposed law ("How about those flag postage stamps? Would postmarking one be considered desecration?").
WEB http://www.indirect.com/user/warren/flag.html

Gun control

Guide to Internet Firearms Information Resources A huge collection of gun-related Net sites ranging from regional mailing lists to Web sites to BBSs. Want to join a concealed weapons mailing list? How about one devoted to the history of black-powder cartridge guns? Their addresses are here.
WEB http://www.portal.com/~chan/firearms.faq.html

Gun Politics/SRA "Hurry, hurry, all amendments must go! Order now, while you can still get some!" That sentiment, expressed by one participant, seems to be the dominant attitude on CompuServe's Gun Politics message board. Along with the usual disparagement of the Brady Bill and the frequent use of firearm jargon— "They offer the P94 in 9mm and .40 for civilian sale without the laser light"—these bullet-heads seem to be mainly interested in defeating gun-control arguments by means of reductio ad absurdum. To wit: "One of the anti-gunners' arguments is that our Founding Fathers did not foresee the advancement of technologies of the next 200 years. They would have us believe that the Second Amendment limits us to black-powder muskets and the like. Of course, that might also limit and ban radio, TV, electronic communication, and modern printing presses." And maybe even personal computers.

GunFree Site Anyone who's against guns can find something here. This site makes it easy to keep up with what Congress is or isn't doing to prevent gun violence. There's a state-by-state list of activities and pending firearm laws, and the calendar of these activities is updated once a month. For the most recent information on legislation, call your state capital information number and ask for the Bill Status Office.
WEB http://www.gunfree.inter.net

National Rifle Association Rather than loading up and firing at anti-gun forces, the NRA has chosen to use its site to build a sense of community for supporters and sympathizers. Low on graphics and high on text—including hundreds of articles, legislative reports, federal delegation info, state firearms alerts, a firearm glossary, and a bibliography—the site also includes ads for NRA multimedia (a gun safety program for children, with fun-filled activity books and a Jason Priestley-hosted video), an NRA store, and a large library including some books on banned firearms.
WEB http://www.nra.org

talk.politics.guns In addition to hosting a large volume of passionate debate, this newsgroup does its part to counteract common stereotypes by passing the microphone to segments of America one doesn't often hear from. There are urban hunters and rural pacifists, Republican gun-control supporters and Democratic riflemen. On talk.politics.guns, the various pro-gun and anti-gun postings square off and fire barely controlled rhetorical bursts at one another: "If we accept the Brady Bill, we allow the feds to dictate law enforcement," "I would much rather see people like you beaten, raped, and murdered than give up my Second Amendment rights," and "All you gun supporters don't mind the prospect of accidental shootings because you already have holes in your heads."
USENET talk.politics.guns

 ## GREENPEACE
WEB http://www.greenpeace.org

There's no better place in cyberspace for the latest in environmental news and environmental science worldwide. The Greenpeace site is peppered with small, friendly icons—a radioactivity sign for nuclear power, a skull-and-crossbones for toxic waste—that lead you through the details of the organization's commitment to environmental protection. To build a sense of community, the site also provides online membership enrollment and a chat room where environmentalists across the globe can discuss the latest laws, disasters, and victories.

Location: http://www.greenpeace.org/~comms/pics/0213.gif

IT'S THE LAW

A militia, when properly formed, are in fact the people themselves... and include all men capable of bearing arms... To preserve liberty it is essential that the whole body of the people always possess arms and be taught alike... how to use them.
—Richard Henry Lee

A well-regulated Militia, being necessary to the security of a free State, the right of the People to keep and bear Arms, shall not be infringed.
—Amendment II, Constitution of the United States

—from the National Rifle Association

Health care

Global and Domestic Health
Essays range from a treatise by the Carter Center on Tobacco to a report on fair treatment for the mentally ill to one detailing the horrible guinea-worm outbreak.
WEB http://www.emory.edu/CARTER _CENTER/health.htm

Idea Central Health Policy Page
One of the best health-care sites online, this Electronic Policy Network page is basically an online journal devoted to issues of medical privacy legislation, preventive medicine, children's health, and sex education including the article

"Does Liberalism Cause Sex?"
WEB http://epn.org/idea/health.html

Intergovernmental Health Policy Project All this talk about national health care has had a number of beneficial effects, but one of the deleterious ones has been the deflection of attention from state and local health-care plans. The IHPP, located at George Washington University, attempts to remedy this oversight by tracking economic and legislative developments affecting health care at the state level—not just insurance regulations, but also laws directing the creation and monitoring of managed-care businesses.
WEB http://www.gwu.edu/~ihpp

Policy Information Exchange
Though it's relatively costly by research-services standards, and exorbitant by the standards of the Web (a year-long subscription runs $335 for a non-profit organization and $435 for a for-profit organization), PIE may be worthwhile if you want access to the largest database of health-care information available online. In addition to collecting thousands of articles each week from health-care organizations nationwide, PIE has created a public bulletin board where its subscribers (and even visitors) can share their opinions on health-care issues. And whether or not you subscribe, you'll have access to PIE's comprehensive list of health links.
WEB http://www.pie.org

Right-To-Die Organizations in the U.S.A. Kevorkian Central. Looking for that final exit, but can't find the door? There's a growing movement pushing for living wills, right-to-die laws, and assisted-suicide provisions, and you'll find it here, organized at regional and national levels.
WEB http://www.efn.org/~ergo/USA.dir .html

Rock the Vote—HIV/AIDS Breaking it down for the masses, MTV personalizes AIDS with a scary story of a white, twenty-something woman who became an AIDS activist. "Sandy apparently had contracted HIV 5 years earlier, at 21, from boyfriend No. 4. An estimated 60,000 other Americans were also stricken that year. One in four of them was under 22. The day Sandy was infected—as every day since—40 more young people contracted the virus. If she had been a prevention activist then, she might not be a drafted-treatment activist today." Information on medical care options follows.
WEB http://www.iuma.com/RTV /HIV-AIDS.html

Homelessness

Homeless Home Page The pointed irony of the title notwithstanding, this is an excellent collection of resources about homelessness, with statistics, fund-raising ideas, and articles and reports such as "The Criminalization of Poverty" and "Non-Recreational Campers: Homeless

People Who Use Public Lands." If you're interested in discussions of homelessness, check out the information and archives of the "homeless" mailing list. The site also includes a varied set of links to information about homelessness elsewhere on the Net.
WEB http://csf.colorado.edu/homeless/index.html

National Coalition for the Homeless While there's a spare, almost skeletal look to the National Coalition for the Homeless Home Page (no irony intended, presumably), the organization's Web site includes two excellent multimedia features that help communicate the terrors of homelessness. "One Family's Path to Homelessness" presents the actual story of a clean-cut, white suburban family's road to homelessness, using

scanned letters, email, images, and more. The feature is updated every day to intensify the sense of urgency. The other feature, "Homeless Voices," collects images and sound clips of real homeless people, of all races, ages, and educational and economic backgrounds.
WEB http://nch.ari.net

Overview of 54 Ways You Can Help the Homeless Written by Rabbi Charles A. Kroloff, this list aims to answer the question, What can I do to help the homeless? It provides practical tips on volunteering, giving to the homeless, and getting others involved in the cause. Specific suggestions include volunteering at a soup kitchen, playing with the children in a shelter, and joining Habitat for Humanity.
WEB http://ecosys.drdr.virginia.edu/ways/54.html

Rock the Vote's HIV/AIDS page
http://www.iuma.com/RTV/HIV-AIDS.html

Netsite: http://www.iuma.com/RTV/HIV-AIDS.html

Human rights

Amnesty International Online Renowned offline for its human rights letter-writing campaigns, Amnesty hasn't changed its tune in its move to the online world: thanks to the speed of the Web and the convenience of email, Amnesty can now reach more supporters and get quicker responses than ever before. In addition to the Worldwide Appeals section, Amnesty includes a special section targeted at women's rights, reports on the status of human rights worldwide, links to other resources, and provides information on Amnesty's interactive CD-ROM.
WEB http://www.amnesty.org

Directory of Human Rights Resources Interested in prison issues? How about reports on human rights from the State Department? This site gathers an eclectic set of links, including connections to Amnesty International, PeaceNet's Human Rights gopher, and the Minnesota Human Rights Library.
WEB http://www.igc.apc.org/hr

Human Rights Organizations Physicians for Human Rights, the Committee to Protect Journalists, and Human Rights in China are just a few of the non-governmental agencies represented at this site, which serves as a clearinghouse for information on organizations that work on a range of human rights issues. The materials

from these groups include action alerts, newsletters, press releases, and other documents.
URL gopher://gopher.humanrights .org:5000

Human Rights Web The site opens with a quote from Auden ("Acts of injustice done / between the setting and the rising sun / In history lie like bones / each one"), setting the serious tone for the topics dealt with here. The materials include biographies of prisoners of conscience, a history of the human rights movement, and a variety of documents related to legal and political issues, debates, and discussions. There's also a Human Rights Resource Page with a great set of links and info.
WEB http://www.traveller.com/~hrweb /hrweb.html

soc.rights.human Human-rights abuses are up for discussion, whether the abuses are taking place in Tibet or Brazil.
USENET soc.rights.human

Immigration

Affirmative Action for Immigrants Affirmative action wasn't created to help immigrants, but this article from *National Review* magazine points out that non-U.S. citizens are increasingly becoming its beneficiaries. Congress "accidentally" wrote in the Immigration Reform and Control Act of 1986 language which made it illegal to bar immigrants from affirmative-action programs.

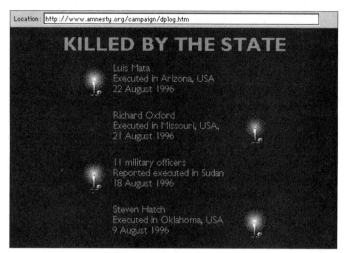

Location: http://www.amnesty.org/campaign/dplog.htm

KILLED BY THE STATE

Luis Mata
Executed in Arizona, USA
22 August 1996

Richard Oxford
Executed in Missouri, USA,
21 August 1996

11 military officers
Reported executed in Sudan
18 August 1996

Steven Hatch
Executed in Oklahoma, USA
9 August 1996

Amnesty lists America's dead men walking
http://www.amnesty.org

Read the Executive Summary of "Affirmative Action for Immigrants—The Entitlement Nobody Wanted," and find out how to order a copy of the book.
WEB http://www.netcom.com/~jimrobb /affirmative.html

The Immigration and Population Page from Charlotte's Web The Reform Party's take on immigration reform (they're for it), along with good coverage of relevant legislative action and media coverage of immigration, capped off by loads of online articles.
WEB http://emf.net/~cr/immigration .html

Militia

Militia Info Page Information and Web links on militia groups across the country.
WEB http://www.well.com/user /srhodes/militia.html

misc.activism.militia Should arms be kept in the home? Should they be used against a government threat? Who should be given the right to decide when a weapon is owned for recreational purposes and not out of some scarcely contained urge to commit murder? And who decides when the government is threatening the individual and when it's merely observing its duties as an administrative body? Debate the constitutional, cultural, and political role of various military and paramilitary organizations across the country.
USENET misc.activism.militia

Public policy

Committee for a Responsible Federal Budget Yet another "bipartisan, nonprofit, grassroots" organization wanting to balance the federal budget. The one major difference here is that these folks publish *Exercise in Hard Choices* every year to prove that they're serious. Get your basic contact information through the site.

WEB http://sunsite.unc.edu/concord /info/cc_crfb.html

Statistical Assessment Service Interested in the use of statistics by the media? Check out the site for the Statistical Assessment Service, an organization devoted to "the accurate use of statistical and quantitative information in public policy debate." As part of its mission, the service aims to help journalists by analyzing statistical disputes.

WEB http://www.proxima.com:8080 /stats

Taxpayer Assets Project Yet another program founded by the busy bee (or some would say gadfly) of American consumer activism, Ralph Nader. Discover what's up with the management and sale of your minute portion of government property (they're charging *what* for grazing cows in Yellowstone?).

WEB http://essential.org/tap/tap.html

Term Limits Throw the bums out—every six or so years. That's the cry at this collection of links, which includes pro and con articles from major newspapers, Supreme Court rulings, and even proposed Constitutional amendments.

WEB http://www.vote-smart.org/issues /Term_Limits

Reproductive rights

Abortion and Reproduction Rights Internet Resources Links to resources on both sides of the abortion debate, including the *ChoiceNet Report*, Catholics for A Free Choice, Operation Rescue National, and the *Pro-Life News*. You can also re-read the pronouncements of the Supreme Court in *Roe v. Wade*, and of the Pope in *Humanae Vitae*.

WEB http://www.caral.org/abortion .html

alt.abortion.inequity The inequity appears to consist in the fact that the abortion decision rests mainly with women. This newsgroup essentially consists of a few men (the same names are always present) sitting around debating the sentience of the zygote and the viability of the fetus outside the womb. When threads are titled "The Overpopulation Myth Is Bull Pucky," it shouldn't be surprising that although there's vociferous debate going on, there's little movement on either side.

USENET alt.abortion.inequity

CARAL Web Page The California Abortion and Reproduction Rights Action League-North hosts this multi-faceted page. Read the full text of the Clinic Access Law, keep up-to-date with court challenges, and connect to other abortion-related sites. Or, hey, download a pro-choice movie.

WEB http://www.caral.org/caral.html

Lifelinks The right-to-life movement is online, making its case against abortion. The site links to the *Feminists for Life* publication ("Abortion does not Liberate Women") and statements from public personalities, such as *Village Voice* writer Nat Hentoff on third-trimester abortions and Mother Teresa on abortion and peace.

WEB http://www.nebula.net/~maeve /lifelink.html

Roe v. Wade, 410 U.S. 113 (1973) "A pregnant single woman (Roe) brought a class action challenging the constitutionality of the Texas criminal abortion laws..." So begins the most controversial Supreme Court ruling of our lifetime. Refresh your memory with the complete hypertext of the ruling opinion and dissensions.

WEB http://www.law.cornell.edu/supct /classics/410us113.ovr.html

talk.abortion "We've been subjected to 21 years of being told that a woman has a right to do with her body as she wishes," writes one exasperated man. "Can you present any compelling reasons why she should not be allowed to control her own body?" queries an equally annoyed man. Count on it. The abortion debate here is not pretty, and some of it is even quite volatile. On the other hand, its obnoxiousness is not entirely unentertaining either. Why shouldn't a woman be allowed control of her body, for instance? Well, you know, "in the U.S. no one controls

his/her own body totally. You can be called to jury duty..."
USENET talk.abortion

Terrorism

alt.security.terrorism Primarily a discussion about ways to combat terrorism and reports on recent terrorist attacks.
USENET alt.security.terrorism

The Counter Terrorism Page The worldwide war against terrorism is being waged as much over phone lines as anywhere else, by means of the rapid distribution of information, and this well-designed Web page is leading the way. Reprints of case studies of terrorists and extremist groups are the main event, but the site uses chat rooms and links (to other anti-terrorist sites and to the U.S. State Department's Travel Advisories) to fight the good fight.
WEB http://www.terrorism.com

Emergency Net's Counter Terrorism Page A chronological listing of acts of terrorism, with special sections devoted to the modern-day fathers of terrorism: Carlos the Jackal, Saddam Hussein, and Qaddafi.
WEB http://www.terrorism.com

State Department Terrorist Profiles A reprint of the U.S. State Department's "The Profiles of Global Terrorism," which is indexed by the homeland of the terrorist.
WEB http://www.tezcat.com/~top /Terrorist

Welfare reform—another brick in the wall?
http://www.sar.usf.edu/~sevenet

Welfare reform

HandsNet Welfare Reform Watch HandsNet is the premier site for keeping up with welfare reform on all levels. You'll find detailed comparisons between House and Senate bills, as well as the studies that each side likes to quote during high-visibility debates. HandsNet has an extensive searchable archive.
WEB http://www.igc.apc.org /handsnet2/welfare.reform/index .html

Poverty & Welfare Homepage The site's liberal agenda is immediately apparent—check out the image of a "No Reagan" sign spray-painted on a brick wall (the author does, however, point the disoriented back to the Rush Limbaugh Home Page at absolutely no charge). But there's more here than

polemics—the site provides poverty and income statistics, and an active message board where visitors can post their own reform plans and ideas.
WEB http://www.sar.usf.edu/~sevenet

Welfare and Families This section of the Electronic Policy Network's online journal is a forum for thoughtful analyses on all issues that come under the welfare reform umbrella, such as the role of charity, welfare time limits, the minimum wage, workfare, and educational assistance. A quick glance at the list of contributors—Frances Fox Piven and the Center for Law and Social Policy among them—suggests a liberal bent, but dissent is duly presented in every case. Good links are provided to studies and other publications.
WEB http://epn.org/idea/welfare.html

International Politics

(EXIT STAGE LEFT) THE COLD WAR.
(ENTER STAGE RIGHT) WHO KNOWS?

GENOCIDE IN EAST TIMOR and Bosnia-Herzegovina. Rebel uprisings in the former Soviet republics. Tribal wars in Africa. Outcries against corporate irresponsibility and environmental destruction in the U.S. Starving nations flirting with nuclear arms in North Korea and the Middle East. Widespread graft and corruption. Welcome to the World Theater of the Absurd, where the curtain has been drawn and the stage set for the perpetual drama that is global politics. The cast features a motley assemblage of international politicos and power-brokers who play hardball the likes of which would tweak the conscience of even the most cynical Machiavellian. For intrepid global citizens who are concerned enough to join the fray, dive in and feed your head with this world of links.

Location: http://www.oneworld.org/gallery/zimbabwe/september.html

ONE WORLD ONLINE
WEB http://www.oneworld.org

Definitely trying to make the world a better place (see the Stop Torture Now section), this site dubs itself "the Web's Alternative News Service." More than just a regular news service, it links to photo galleries, media criticism, other world peace groups, guides to important issues, and even a section on how to get involved (instead of just sitting there and reading about it). The City, for example, details the hazards of urban life and offers possible remedies. One World Online presents stories with a Discovery Channel-type feel, addressing many of the day's most pressing issues and is an excellent place to start your tour of the global community, both its failures and its successes.

Starting points

International Issues Forum Massive and messy, this forum lumps together everything from the Gaza Strip to Cuba, from extradition to female circumcision, and while this can be a liability—threads tend not to develop into sophisticated discussions—the breadth of coverage is exhilarating.
AMERICA ONLINE *keyword* issues

The Internationalist Info on international affairs, divided into well-annotated sections on research organizations, publications, the U.S. government, other national governments, and international organizations; the links direct you to the European Union, the Organization of American States, articles from *Foreign Affairs* magazine, and other spots.
WEB http://www.duke.edu/~gilliatt /internatl/index.html

Political Parties Around the World Links to Web sites for hundreds of political parties worldwide, including Norway's Progress Party (Fremskrittsparti), South Africa's Communist Party, Portugal's Socialist Party, and even the United States' own Democratic Party.
WEB http://www.luna.nl/~benne /politics/parties.html

Political Resources on the Net One world is enough for all of us... and this site has links which just might make that

possible. If amnesia has kicked in and visualizing the flag of Brunei seems difficult, enter its initial and link to its Web page. Unlike other world information sites, this one divides the world into those familiar parts from grade school. Of course, page one only gives you two initial choices: the European Union or International. Also has listings of links to political parties, organizations, and national governments, and more from around the globe.
WEB http://www.agora.stm.it/politic

News

clari.world newsgroup descriptions A listing of the ClariNet news feeds from Africa, the Americas, Asia, Europe, Middle East, and Oceania. Clari-

Net will drop a load of relative news in your lap (top) every day in the feeds you've selected. Some notable sections include clari.world.briefs (newsbriefs from around the world) and clari.world.top which relays the top stories on the international slate. For information on international institutes, coalitions, and other organizations turn to clari .world.organizations. One thing, it will cost you: a single user subscription is $15 per month.
WEB http://www.clarinet.com/descr-2 .html#world

News Resource Entitled "NeWo" for the New World, the general idea here is that eventually, world news won't be such an alien concept and everyone will have access to a

---

Reflect on the African continent at Africa 2000
http://www.africa2000.com

news event, whether it's taking place in a fishing village in rural China or the City of London. A map of the world allows you to choose continent and country of interest. This in turn provides you with the relevant news sources, market indicators, radio links, and much more. An excellent and helpful hub for international newshounds. Includes weather tracking links for those actually venturing into foreign lands.
WEB http://newo.com/news

Online Intelligence Project The Online Intelligence Project proffers its world news site for anyone with a nose for interna-

tional news, commerce, and references. The site has somewhat of a focus on world security with direct links to DefenseNet as well as the CIA home page. Several regional news sources are also provided for each country and region as well as links to embassies abroad, policy statements, and the text of international accords.
WEB http://www.icg.org/intelweb /index.html

Africa

Africa 2000 Africa 2000 contains info about "foreign aid programs, policy objectives,

political intervention, military affairs, covert operations, propaganda, and population activities in the southern hemisphere," plus it uses friendly green and red colored text. The X-Files has documents from the racist right, while the Conscious Rasta Perspective is a guide for how developments in science affect people of color.
WEB http://www.africa2000.com

Bosnia

BosniaLINK If the coverage of the war in the former Yugoslavia left you a bit confused about what was really going on, BosniaLink should help

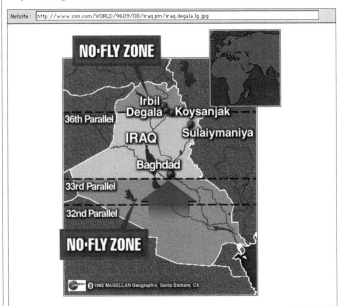

@ CNN—WORLD NEWS
WEB http://www.cnn.com/WORLD/index.html

What could bring you world news faster than the Cable News Network? CNN Online of course. Capitalizing on the vast resources and immediacy of the medium, **CNN** gives concise summaries, stories, and soundbytes for those in a hurry. Not the place to come for discursive analysis, World News is nevertheless still the first place to go for breaking stories and recent news events as they play out around the world. The only things missing are the anchors and James Earl Jones' booming "This is CNN" intonation.

A CASTLE BUILT OF SAND?

CASTLE D'AIANO, Italy (CNN) —GOP presidential nominee Bob Dole has loyal supporters in the United States, but he also has an ardent fan club in a small town in northern Italy.

Castle D'Aiano is holding a "Bob Dole for President" festival that ends Friday with parachutists, majorettes and a big-screen video of the Republican National Convention that nominated Dole this week. To the town's citizens, Dole represents liberation in World War II.

In that area 51 years ago, Dole was injured by German shrapnel that permanently injured his right arm. So Castle D'Aiano has decorated itself with U.S. flags and "Dole for President" banners in support of its adopted son.

Despite not having a single eligible U.S. voter, Castle D'Aiano is hoping an honorary local boy who made good will make better.

"Because he was one of the 10th mountain division soldier and come to give freedom and democracy and we (are) very affectionate to him," said Pietro degli Esposti of the Dole for President Committee.

—from CNN World News

Location: http://www.echonyc.com/~leila/Wei.html

WEI JINGSHENG CHINA'S SPIRIT OF DEMOCRACY

The Wei to go
http://www.echonyc.com/~leila/Wei.html

with maps and charts to show the division of land as well as fact sheets from the U.S. military. The site also hosts *The Talon*, which was the paper for the U.S. soldiers in the Bosnian conflict. For visual illustration, there's a photography section. Don't expect to see any probing photo essays of the conflict; they're mostly a collection of PR photos for the U.S. operations. Speeches and Testimony includes policy statements from Defense Secretary William Perry and others. Also armed with a BosniaLink search engine.
WEB http://www.dtic.dla.mil/bosnia /index.html

Court TV War Crimes Tribunal
Mass graves and ethnic cleansing in former Yugoslavia are a far cry from Court TV's last triumph—the Simpson spectacle—but perhaps in the long-

run much more important. This site holds weekly summaries of testimony, backed by an excellent glossary, a Who's Who of trial participants, a history of the conflict, court documents, and interviews with the major players.
WEB http://www.courttv.com/casefiles /warcrimes

International Criminal Tribunal for the Former Yugoslavia Come here for the latest from the International Criminal Tribunal for the Former Yugoslavia's press office. Resources include informational releases, UN resolutions, rules of procedure, and excerpts from actual case files.
WEB http://www.igc.apc.org/tribunal

Welcome to Bosnia Homepage A diverse and impressive guide to the Bosnian conflict, with links to a war history, maps, pho-

tographs, and even the Bosnian weekly *Ljiljan*. In Bosnia, anti-war songs became as common as war tragedies; there's one here with a verse that translates roughly as "Houses on fire / shots to the head / defiant children / faces of the dead."
WEB http://www.cco.caltech.edu /~bosnia/bosnia.html

China

Human Rights in China An independent, non-governmental organization devoted to monitoring human rights abuses in China. Includes reports in both English and Chinese.
URL gopher://gopher.igc.apc.org:5000 /II/nat/hric

Support Democracy in China Based in Silicon Valley, this volunteer community organiza-

tion attempts to promote democracy in China through a number of avenues, including community outreach, dissident relief, education, and information technology. With a link to a huge site for Harry Wu, jailed in the summer of 1995 for allegedly misrepresenting the government's human rights violations, and a link to a smaller site commemorating the sixth anniversary of the Tiananmen Square uprising, the page strikes a balance between an activist and an archival tone.
WEB http://www.christusrex.org/wwwl /sdc/sdchome.html

Wei Jingsheng: China's Spirit of Democracy This page is devoted to the Chinese human rights activist Wei Jingsheng, who has been jailed (off and on)

since 1978 for his opposition to the autocratic practices of the Chinese government. Learn about Wei, view some soulful pictures, and email a note to the Norwegian Nobel Committee urging them to award Wei the Nobel Peace Prize.
WEB http://www.echonyc.com/~leila /Wei.html

Cuba

Castro Speech Database Assembled by the University of Texas, this rich resource collects English-language translations of every single public speech of Cuba's head of state, from his assumption of power on Jan. 3, 1959 ("Compatriots of all Cuba, we have finally reached Santiago de Cuba. The road was long and difficult, but we finally arrived.") to

@ THE NATO OFFICIAL HOMEPAGE
WEB http://www.nato.int

The North Atlantic Treaty Organization welcomes you to the Web. Who was the NATO Secretary General in 1969 or who are some of the permanent members? Find answers to these questions in Who is Who at NATO. Operation Joint Endeavor shows the connection of NATO to other alliances including NATO AFSOUTH and OFCE. Looking for a conspiracy today or in from the past? The NATO archive should a least be a start with loads of Fact Sheets and Press Releases. Read the buzz on weekly international affairs in The Latest at NATO.

Netsite: http://www.nato.int/docu/review/pictures/9605-1j.jpg

Location: http://crisny.org/users/siegelm/picture.html

Jerusalem's Western Wall
http://crisny.org/users/siegelm/israel.html

an October 1994 comment on the U.S. blockade of the island ("Before, nobody dared to oppose it; today, the most influential media outlets do so"). If there is a problem with this collection, it lies in presentation—the speeches are organized by date, with very little annotation, although the site does offer a keyword search.
URL gopher://lanic.utexas.edu/ll/la/Cuba/Castro

European union

EU and the Internet A simple, well-organized selection of documents on the Net that relate to the European Union, including resolutions from the European Parliament and copies of the Maastricht Treaty. The site is divided into sections providing official information, details on research and development activities, and info on related newsgroups

and mailing lists. In addition, it contains a series of links to maps and flags of Europe.
WEB http://www.helsinki.fi/~aunesluo/eueng.html

The EU FAQ Wondering about the differences between the European Union and the European Community? This FAQ has answers to those questions, and many others, whether you're wondering about something basic ("What countries are members of the EU?") or more involved ("What is the Court of Auditors?").
WEB http://eubasics.allmansland.com/index.html

Europa Can you name all 15 states that belong to the European Union? Find the answer at this Web site, and learn all about the news and history of this less than perfect marriage. The section on European Institutions describes the Monetary

Institution and European Parliament. On the Political Agenda details current initiatives and policies, including external affairs and legislation that should allow free movement between the participating countries. On the Record offers official documents drafted since the union, while Newsroom carries the latest news flashes as well as a the daily midday briefing from the Union's spokesman.
WEB http://europa.eu.int

The Maastricht Treaty A copy of the treaty on European Union signed at Maastricht on Feb. 7, 1992. The treaty is divided into sections on foreign policy, security, justice, home affairs, economic issues, and other salient matters.
URL gopher://wiretap.spies.com/ll/Gov/Maast

Middle East

Islamic Association for Palestine With a Middle Eastern focus, this site offers news and information on politics, diplomacy, and current events in the region. The documents here include political cartoons, "20 Basic Facts about the Palestine Problem," and interviews with Dr. Hanan Ashrawi and other pro-Palestinian advocates. The news section of the page includes links to such organizations and publications as the Muslim Student Association, the *Muslim World Monitor*, and *The Palestine Times*.
WEB http://www.iap.org

Israel and the Peace Process

Assembled by a student who's pursuing a master's degree in Israeli Politics, this has links to just about everything related to Israel. For questions about policy and politics, consult the list of Israeli Agencies and Ministries. Planning a trip to the Holy Land? Be sure to visit the Israeli Ministry of Tourism. If you're a history buff interested in Israel, you are advised to read the Camp David Accords or the Agreement about the Gaza Strip and the Jericho Area.

WEB http://crisny.org/users/siegelm /israel.html

The Mideast Peace Process

Established in 1948 and often at war with its Arab foes, the State of Israel, along with its neighbors, has made great strides in recent years. This guide begins to describe some of the details with a focus on the Madrid Conference (1991), a continuation of the peace initiative of 1989. Studying the Interim Agreement between the Israeli and the Palestinians? See all the Annexes and Maps regarding the possession of land. Read about the assassination of Itzhak Rabin and its consequences on the struggle for peace. From the Camp David Accords in 1978 to the current state of affairs, this Web site gives many highlights.

WEB http://www.israel.org/peace /index.html

International organizations

NATO Handbook The handbook begins by answering the simple question, "What is NATO?" From there, things get a lot more complex, as the publication describes various aspects of the organization's operations in great detail. This guide to the North American Treaty

 THE WORLD BANK
WEB http://www.worldbank.org

If the pundits have it right we're in for an age of fewer wars and greater economic cooperation. And while the imprimatur of Cold War outfits like **NATO** has grown hazier, that of organizations like the World Bank and the International Monetary Fund (**IMF**) have taken on new relevance and importance. For more than 50 years, the World Bank has been lending monies from First World countries to developing nations. Its site is an encyclopedic resource for catching up on issues facing the developing world, with information on povery-reduction programs, education initiatives, and sustainable development as well as region-specific reports, monthly commodities reports, and more. Go to the Public Information Center for more than you could ever possibly want on development projects around the globe.

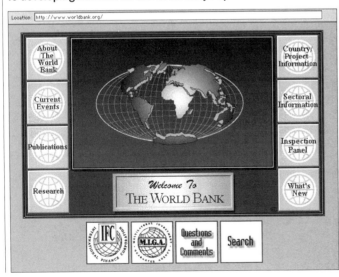

FOR THE COST OF A CHEAP BEER

The budget for the UN's core functions—the Secretariat operations in New York, Geneva, Nairobi, Vienna, and five Regional Commissions - is $1.3 billion a year. This is about 4 per cent of New York City's annual budget—and nearly a billion dollars less than the yearly cost of Tokyo's Fire Department. It is $3.7 billion less than the annual budget of New York's State University system.

The USA's share of the UN's regular budget is $321 million a year—the equivalent of $1.24 per American.

The New York Headquarters of the UN requires the services of 4,831 people. The Swedish capital of Stockholm, by contrast, has 60,000 municipal employees.

—from United Nations

Netsite: http://www.un.org/UN50/Photos/un50-016.gif

Stalin, Roosevelt, Churchill, and others at the 1945 Yalta Conference
http://www.un.org

Organization covers everything from fundamental operating principles and strategies of economic cooperation to the workings of the Military Committee Meteorological Group and the Advisory Group for Aerospace Research and Development.
URL gopher://wiretap.spies.com/II /Gov/NATO-HB

UN Fiftieth Anniversary Founded at the close of World War II, the United Nations isn't even as old as Mick Jagger. This site serves as a basic guide to links having to do with the United Nations and its 50th anniversary. The information gathered here includes an overview of anniversary activities, a statement by the U.N. secretary general, anniversary-specific newsletters, and a variety of links to background info on institutions such as the World Bank and the Academic Council on the United Nations System.
WEB http://www.amdahl.com/internet /events/un50.html

United Nations Visit this virtual United Nations, and soon you'll be reading the U.N.'s charter, perusing the Universal Declaration of Human Rights, and learning about the history of the organization. The site includes information on all aspects of world affairs, from political conflict to economic development. The documents available here provide details on U.N. member states (at last count, there were 185), peace-keeping operations, agencies related to the U.N., and various conferences. Also open for perusal are the latest resolutions from the General Assembly and the Security Council.
WEB http://www.un.org

United Nations (UNESCO) Peace-keeper to the world or harbinger of the dark New World Order? You can decide with a simple visit to the United Nation's site, where you'll find out about all their benign activities, from the Fund for Agriculture Development to the Educational, Scientific, and Cultural Organization (UNESCO).
WEB http://www.unicc.org

Ideologies & Parties

DID SOMEBODY SAY PARTY? WHAT'S TO CELEBRATE IN U.S. POLITICS TODAY?

DONKEYS AND ELEPHANTS and Trotskyites, oh my! The Net has become the equal-time medium par excellence: anybody with a server and a political ideology can set him or herself up as a pundit, a pedagogue, or a Pope, and wait for the world to rally round. The result? A pluralistic carnival of zeal the likes of which history has never seen. Democrats and

Republicans are of course the twin towers, but why stop there? The Reform Party lays out its plans to run the government like a business; while the Libertarian Party rails against Big Government from its cyber-soapbox. But it's not all partisan platitudes: serious political discussion thrives on the newsgroups, so choose sides, grab your balloons and confetti, or just plain nominate yourself: The Net is off to the races!

Location: http://www.vote-smart.org/

"It's Time to Hire the Help"

PROJECT VOTE SMART

WEB http://www.vote-smart.org

Project Vote Smart goes a long way toward keeping the public apprised of what the "hired help" is up to in that party town on the Potomac. The resources here are truly admirable in their scope. Simply plug in any Congressperson's name or state and a complete profile pops up, with bios, special interest funding sources, contact information, voting records, and performance evaluations by special interest groups. Vote Smart also follows state governments and the Court, providing analysis of decisions by everyone from Sandra Day O'Connor to the Court of Appeals judge for Skagit County. There's even a primer on how the government works, from bills up on Capitol Hill to budget appropriations. Should all this not be enough to answer your question on your local rep's opinion on the spotted owl or how the local circuit court ruled on the new barking dog ordinance, there's an 800 number that will connect you with Vote Smart's research staff.

Starting points

Voter Information Services, Inc.
Where do the nominees stand on the issues that are important to you—the right to bear arms, the right to join a union, the right to choose an abortion? VIS can ease the cumbersome voting process. Plug in your state, ZIP code, or rep's name, and you'll be rewarded with his or her ratings by special interest groups (based on voting record) since 1989. You'll have ample ammunition, knowing how Representative X voted on Desert Storm or NAFTA.

> ❝ **Where do the nominees stand on the issues that are important to you—the right to bear arms, the right to join a union, the right to choose an abortion?** ❞

Complete records of specific votes can be ordered for $1 each (and it's cheaper if you buy bulk—records are half price for more than 50!). The list of groups rating the candi

Rep. Dick Armey

Progress for Religious Freedom Amendment

The drive for a Religious Freedom Amendment to the U.S. Constitution cleared a major hurdle on July 16. That's when House Majority Leader Dick Armey introduced to the House of Representatives legislation authorizing the amendment. Armey, along with the amendment's chief architect, Illinois Rep. Henry Hyde, hopes H.R. 184 will end decades of religious discrimination. The amendment reads in part:

Proposing an amendment to the Constitution to further protect religious freedom, including the right of students in public schools to pray without government sponsorship or compulsion £ In order to secure the right of the people to acknowledge and serve God according to the dictates of conscience, neither the United States nor any State shall deny any person equal access to a benefit, or otherwise discriminate against any person, on account of religious belief, expression, or exercise.

"Fundamentally this is a free speech issue," said Brian Lopina,

Yet another of Ralph Reed's friends in the Senate
http://www.cc.org

---

dates is hypertextual, and you can link to dozens of organizations ranging from the Christian Coalition to the AFL-CIO.
WEB http://world.std.com/~voteinfo

The Yankee Citizen Joe DiMaggio was the Yankee Clipper. Mark Twain wrote *A Connecticut Yankee in King Arthur's Court*. And The Yankee Citizen is a no-nonsense Web guide to American politics, with links for information on both major parties and a variety of guides to American government. Other categories include the 1996 elections, U.S. government agencies, and the executive, legislative, and judicial branches.
WEB http://www.tiac.net/users/macgyver/pols.html

Republicans

alt.politics.usa.republican Republicans convene in this news

group to debate the pros and cons of candidates, to comment on party policy initiatives, and to sound off on topics ranging from morality to isolationism. A typical day in the newsgroup includes discussions with subject headers like "Bubba's speech on affirmative action," "Libertarians should join the Republican Party," and "Abortion IS murder." You'll find some off-topic posts here, along with quite a few intended to get the extremists riled ("Republicans Stick It to the Constitution"), but generally the discussion is vigorous and varied, with opinions spanning the political spectrum.
USENET alt.politics.usa.republican

Christian Coalition Interactive This is the home of the ever-so-righteous Right. Choose from stories about how chastity and phonics will save America

("Godly Principles Will Restore Our Independence"), weekly columns by those next to God (and Pat) like Ralph Reed, and other features. No stranger to aggressive lobbying, the Christian Coalition uses its Web presence to keep the faithful up to date on the Presidential campaign, religious rights, and Congressional voting on sanctified issues like abortion and school prayer.
WEB http://www.cc.org

Conservative Corner A collection of files described as "non-mainstream conservative" and gleaned from the Birch Bark BBS. Many of the files come from conservative organizations, such as Accuracy in Media, the Future of Freedom Foundation, and the Lincoln Heritage Institute. Topics include the Vincent Foster case, government regulation, and the failure of socialism.
WEB http://www.execpc.com/~jfish

The Conservative Network Deceptively low-tech in appearance, this homepage spends more time analyzing and using the Net for political ends than loading its page with fancy gizmos or dancing elephant animations. Here you'll find thoughtful examinations of how the Internet influences politics with changing feature stories—from the French Usenet strike to Government cryptography options. The Network also attempts to put that power to use through its mailing list and other activist venues. The Conservative Candidate Support Group (not a 12-step program for also-rans like Alan Keyes or Bob Dornan) puts out a call for local Republicans nationwide. A Calendar of Upcoming Events makes sure that those "Clinton Did Inhale" and "Abortion = Murder" placards never miss an oppotunity to shine.
WEB http://www.cais.com/dc/tcn

 ## THE JEFFERSON PROJECT
WEB http://www.voxpop.org/jefferson

This site is a veritable cornucopia of political delights. Savvy voters can link to candidate pages from all over the nation. Party links lead to the Libertarian Party of Alachua County and the Democratic National Committee. The virtual newsstand offers both *The Brooklyn Metro Times* and *The New Republic*. Link to political watchdogs to find those who make it their life's work to hound Bob Dole or the media. Government links abound—to the FBI, CIA, Greens, even virtual Zapatistas. If all this isn't enough, old Tom has a list of political mailing lists to touch every heart—from chronic fatigue syndrome activists to the Conservative Coffeehouse. Bewildered? Try the Gumball Machine, which pops out a new political page at every visit.

Cyber-Republicans Subscribe to this newsletter for heavy doses of Net-savvy conservatism that details the progress of the Republican conquest of the Internet. Although Bob Dole doesn't laugh, there's a daily conservative cartoon treat here, and also a handy definition of a Republican, just in case you were confused. The Web site archives the newsletter.
EMAIL listserv@netcom.com ✍ *Type in message body:* subscribe cyberep-newslette (your full name)
WEB http://www.rpi.edu/~scotta/republican.html

Eagle Forum Remember Phyllis Schlafly, the woman who called the atomic bomb God's gift to a righteous America? Well, she doesn't like those Democrats much, especially that horrible Hillary. But she does like conservatism, and she wants the Right to take back the White House in 1996. Read her monthly newsletter for the word on timely topics—"The United Nations: An Enemy in Our Midst," "The NEA Proves Itself Extremist Again." Sign up the kids at Eagle Forum Collegians and "become a traditional voice for a new generation."
WEB http://www.basenet.net/~eagle/eagle.html

The Future of Freedom Foundation From the publishers of *Freedom Daily* comes a collection of essays on jury trials (for), patriotism (for), Social Security (against), the NEA (against), and NATO (against).

WEB http://www.execpc.com/~jfish/fff/index.html

GOP In-fighting Update A series of stories on GOP in-fighting with the aim of exposing "the fact that the right wing that has taken over the GOP does not allow intra-party discussion" and does not reflect the views of all Republicans. Topics include "GOP Fireworks Predicted," "Republican Delusions Squashed," and "The Religious Reich Has Declared War on Congress!" Where have you gone, Dwight D. Eisenhower?
WEB http://www.webcom.com/~albany/infight.html

The Heritage Foundation Home page for the powerful and influential think tank that considers political issues ranging from federal budgets to family values. The Heritage Foundation publishes the journal *Policy Review* six times a year, and selections are released weekly to the Web. Read articles about school reform, citizenship, land trusts, health care, and politics in America from the most conservative voices in America, including Dinesh D'Souza, author of *The End of Racism*. Besides policy papers and journal articles, the site also includes "Top Ten Facts for the Week," a feature that includes public opinion polls, crime rates, and other statistics that relate to the concerns of conservatives. ("Marital Status of Nation's 3.8 million mothers receiving

AFDC—48% never married.") Internship information is also available.
WEB http://www.heritage.org

Republican Forum The Grand Old Party has its very own CompuServe forum, and while it's slightly less bustling than its Democratic counterpart, the Republican Forum has considerable coverage of issues ranging from the defense budget to health care to the crime bill. Since the gains in the 1994 elections, action has picked up somewhat, and the GOP is looking hungrily toward the possibility of unseating Clinton. As a result, Big Bill is under fire constantly in this forum—for Whitewater, for Hillary, for his adjustable girth, and more. The libraries contain information on most of the major Republican candidates, as well as mementos of the Bush, Reagan, and Nixon Administrations.
COMPUSERVE *go* republican

Republicans Web Central "Hope Isn't in Arkansas—It's In 1996" proudly proclaims this site's home page. Here you can view all the pretty candidates sitting in a row—Bob, Pat, Phil—and link to their Web pages. The impressive list of conservative Web resources will provide hours of fun; others are labeled "non-partisan" to help those who don't like their politics slanted. The organization here also offers assistance to cyberconservatives hoping to reach the faithful via

mailing lists or Web sites.
WEB http://republicans.vt.com

The Right Side of the Web You know you've arrived at "the right side" when the far right isn't right enough, when the Thought for the Day can criticize Republican Orrin Hatch, insinuating he's "in bed with Louis Freeh." The site includes an astonishing amount of info, links, and interactive features, including a conservative comic strip ("DeMOCKracy"), the Speaker's Corner (fans of Newt Gingrich start drooling), and the unofficial Alan Keyes for President page. Other highlights include a Question of the Week, solicitations for ideas on casting *Whitewater: The Mini-Series*, and the Right Side

Message Wall, where you'll see items like the following "scrawled" on the screen of your Web browser: "Those liberals are at it again. Now they want African-American English to be taught in our schools. I guess we need to teach color coding for gang recognition."
WEB http://www.clark.net/pub/jeffd /index.html

Town Hall Gathered here are the best and brightest of American conservatives—from Newt's own Progress and Freedom Foundation to Empower America. There are news links and conservative columnists like Pete du Pont and the timeless William F. Buckley. You can also calculate your flat tax or order a Town Hall T-Shirt

and wear conservative sleeves. Other links lead to sanctioned organizations and a search engine capable of finding any mention of "Hillary," "multiculturalism," and other dirty words in the publications of sixteen conservative entities.
WEB http://www.townhall.com

We, the People: An Unofficial Republican Homepage The American Eagle pictured here is mighty feisty—signifying this site's objective of combating Democratic Web presence and rectifying the lack of "liberal-bashing" on the official GOP site. Here you'll find loads of right-wing fun. Pick out Bosnia on a map or join in the "anniversary celebration of Clinton's letter to the draft

 BOB DOLE FOR PRESIDENT
WEB http://www.dole96.com

Campaign '96 Part One: He may or may not be America's choice for the highest office in the land, but he should certainly be America's choice for Hard-Bitten Washington Insider Whose Dedicated Staffers Know How to Make the Most of the Internet. The official Bob Dole home page is the best

candidate Web site online, hands down. Why? Because it has a lavish biography of ol' Bob. Because it lets you track the Dole campaign's progress with an interactive map of the U.S. Because it includes a trivia quiz about the candidate. And because it's even beautiful, in a faux-Rockwellian way.

board by joining in the Smoke-Along or Saigon-Along, (traditional activities described in full). Other links leads to conservative gathering places throughout the Net.
WEB http://www.netrunner.net/~covers/republic

Democrats

A Democrat's Source Page Need some ammunition to counter those Republican claims that all Democrats are do-nothing, tax-and-spend liberals leading the nation down the road to fiscal and moral ruin? Look no further. Not only is there a list of Clinton's accomplishments here, but also those of Gore, and more, more, more! Link to other "politically enlightened" Web sites like the Democratic National Committee, legislative alerts, and the Progressive Policy Institute. Grassroots organizations, email links to Congress, and several online polls invite democratic participation. And there's always fun to be had at Newt Watch and the GOP In-Fighting Updates Series. Put your money on the guy in the red, white, and blue trunks.
WEB http://www.wp.com/lookn2it/home.html

A Trip Down Democrat Lane Whistle as you walk the lane, from the White House to the Bruin Democrats at UCLA. The large collection of links to Democratic sites also lead the enthusiastic to the Senate, a list of President Clinton's accom-

plishments (more than can fit on the head of a pin), and party organizations. Associated groups promoting the New World Order (read United Nations), cultural decadence (the Corporation for Public Broadcasting), and the liberal media elite (National Press Club) are also just a click away.
WEB http://www-leland.stanford.edu/group/sudems/links.html

alt.politics.democrats.d The right-wing Net is well in evidence in this allegedly Democratic forum, which is filled with postings about "creeping socialism," the federal government discouraging the rich, "the real truth from Rush." The tax-the-rich folks can hardly be heard over the squalling of Newt defenders.
USENET alt.politics.democrats.d

An American Legacy: The Kennedys This mini-memorial offers brief biographies of America's royals, links to related sites (Ted's Senate Office), somewhat-related sites (John F. Kennedy Space Center), and beefcake pictures of Jack the Zipper and his brothers.
WEB http://www.webcom.com/locke/kennedy

Democratic Forum What is a Democrat? Well, someone who believes in welfare, for one ("In the richest nation in the world, it is our obligation to support those whose misfortunes enable the rest of us to be suc-

cessful"). Someone who despises Pat Buchanan ("His red-meat rhetoric brings out the worst in people, inspires fear and loathing"). Someone who resists being a slavish ideologue by gently needling rad-lib oracles like Noam Chomsky ("Is he still mad at himself for being Jewish, or has he calmed down in his anti-Israel diatribes?"). And, above all, someone who posts on CompuServe's Democratic Forum. Issues range from domestic economy to crime to international affairs, and the opinions come from all over the country—from the D.C. insider who suggests that Bill Clinton is "quietly assembling one of the more impressive Administrations of the last thirty years" to the Oregon man who disparages his state for deeming it "'unnecessary' to offer women breast reconstruction after breast cancer." There are dissenting voices, of course, but they're usually drowned out within a day or two. The libraries contain a wealth of resources for Democrats, including the party platform, a list of important election dates, and a number of documents relating to the Clintons.
COMPUSERVE *go* democrat

Democratic Leadership Council This is the place to prime for those "liberal/conservative dialogues" that many families have over the dinner table. All the hot-button issues are here—Democratic policy papers on health care, trade,

and affirmative action. Weekly updates include news summaries and the official word on touchy issues like Bosnia. If you're really serious, you can join the leadership council and get into the secret clubhouse on the Net where they probably discuss the Bulls and Baywatch. And best of all, membership is tax deductible!
WEB http://www.dlcppi.org

Democratic Party Activists With sections for Democratic Party clubs, state and county party organizations, and government officials of all types, this site makes it easy to find info about the Democratic party, its leaders, and politics in general. Lots of links here, whether you're looking for college Democratic clubs or members of Congress.
WEB http://www.webcom.com/~digitals

Justin's Political Infopage Justin is one of those young liberals who is still shocked and appalled by the things politicians get up to. His site is, however, a useful collection of links and updates on the doings of the Republican Revolution. Of an activist bent, Justin favors environmental groups like Greenpeace and Net Freedom Fighters EFF. He also provides bedtime reading. Try "Breach of Faith: How the Contract's Fine Print Undermines America's Environmental Success."
WEB http://www.cs.cmu.edu/~jab /politics.html

Greens

alt.politics.greens Some come here to pose rather fatuous questions like "why do the greens dislike nuclear power?" Kind of like asking why the Republicans dislike capital gains taxes, isn't it? Others come to practice the fine art of

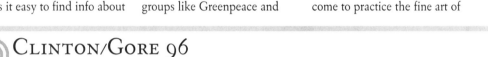

Clinton/Gore 96

web http://www.cg96.org

Campaign '96 Part Two: Bill really knows how to win supporters—opening his site with graphs of how much better life is than it was four years ago. Then it's on to a fancy slide show of Bill looking Presidential. The wealth of information here is also presented to remind visitors that these are the

incumbents with a proven track record (there's a briefing room and a section entitled "meeting America's problems"). There are the requisite biographies of the fab four (Whitewater and Gennifer aren't to be found). Everything is backed with facts and figures—and full color photos that make the site somewhat cumbersome. A downloadable treats section includes campaign buttons, video clips, and a grassroots action kit.

in-fighting—who's greener than whom, etc. And then there's the unfortunately all too common, all too necessary, doom-saying about Arctic oil drilling and rain forest desecration. As Kermit the frog so eloquently said, "It ain't easy being Green."
USENET alt.politics.greens

Green Parties of North America

It's not easy being environmentally conscious during a supposed Republican era. But these tree huggers are giving it a really good try. Read the world's take on Ralph Nader's Green candidacy (the only man who is less exciting than Michael Dukakis: just take a look at the online transcript of his David Frost interview). Other pointers lead to an explanation of Green politics, the Green's Clearinghouse of local activists and the online Econet conference, where people meet to discuss spotted owls, French atom bombs, and strip mining in Yellowstone.
WEB http://www.rahul.net:80/greens

Lefties

alt.politics.radical-left Where else in the world can you get into a debate on the politics of Slim Fast? Yes, there's a bunch of guff about weapons, welfare, interracial crimes, prayer in the schools, and misogyny in political rhetoric. But who wouldn't be drawn to the discussion of whether Rush Limbaugh is fat because he is morally and physically weak or because he

is the embodiment of capitalist greed? Slim Fast evidently backed the Bush campaign, but the verdict is still out on Jenny Craig.
USENET alt.politics.radical-left

alt.politics.socialism.mao Got some green PJs, a little red book, and a collection of Gang of Four albums? Then this is the place for you—and for discussion of the peasant revolution and its impending reform.
USENET alt.politics.socialism.mao

alt.politics.socialism.trotsky With posts from a "Capitalist Worker" equating socialism with parasitism and internecine debates on socialism and imperialism (Lenin and Gramsci notwithstanding), this group reminds one of the old joke in which Trotsky writes to Lenin, "You were right? I was wrong? This is socialism?"
USENET alt.politics.socialism.trotsky

Democratic Socialists of America

The site offers details on the DSA—the largest socialist group in the U.S.—and provides materials on the DSA's local groups, committees, and publications. A section labeled "Left Resources" offers a set of links, divided into sections on cyberpolitics, the Democratic Party, activism, and leftist talk, thought, and history. And you can even join the organization with the online forum. The Radical Parenting Page is bound to put Pat Buchanan and friends into a tizzy.
WEB http://www.dsausa.org/index.html

Liberalism Described as a "quasi-FAQ," this site attempts to present readers with the basic tenets of liberalism. Admittedly oversimplified in its answers, the document responds to such questions as "How do liberals differ from 'socialists' and 'Communists'?" and "What is the liberal position on gun control?" Highly readable and well organized.
WEB http://www.cs.ncl.ac.uk/people /chris.holt/home.informal/lounge /politics/liberalism.html

Socialist Party CybercenterUSA

Wondering "how to be a socialist"? Find out at this site, with answers to the questions "Will I be attacked by my friends for being a socialist?" and "What does my being a Socialist Party member do for me?" The site includes general information on the party ("The Socialist Party: Who We Are"), a statement of principles, membership information, and contact info. The documents available at the site cover the history of the Socialist Party, socialist economics, and related topics.
WEB http://sunsite.unc.edu/spc/index .html

Spamily's Politics Page With sections labeled "Privacy and Free Expression" and "Rights for Women, Queers, and Everyone Else," this site offers a unique and idiosyncratic collection of links to sites focused on reproductive rights, resources for bisexuals, online activism, and more. Other highlights of the site include sections offering general political resources and "sites to help you appreciate the outdoors." **WEB** http://www.io.org/~spamily /SocPolEnv.html

Libertarian

alt.politics.libertarian Give me libertarianism or give me death. Or something like that. Why do we need birth certificates? Are we people or "subjects?" Why don't we have very, very short-term limits? All in all, governments in general take a beating, and virtually every administrative action is seen as an attack on personal liberties. Newsgroup members do sometimes attempt to recon-

cile the libertarian hard line with real-world concerns. For instance, after one post insisted that taxation equals extortion—"Taxation is unjust, and only despotic governments tax, and, since all governments tax, all governments are despotic." —dozens of other participants wonder aloud how a libertarian government would raise money. **USENET** alt.politics.libertarian

Libertarian FAQ "Do libertarians support gun ownership as a personal liberty?" "Are people better off with free trade than with tariffs?" Find the answers to those questions—"yes" to both, if you can't wait—in the Libertarian FAQ. The FAQ

also includes information on the Libertarian Party, libertarian mailing lists, and related organizations. **WEB** http://www.cis.ohio-state.edu /hypertext/faq/usenet/libertarian/top .html

Libertarian Party Talk about libertarian issues—the cowed press, the overprotected flag, the highway robbery that is income tax. Where it stops, nobody knows. **AMERICA ONLINE** *keyword* election→ Message Boards→Libertarian Party

Libertarian Web A well-ordered selection of libertarian resources includes the Libertarian Party program, an article titled "Understanding the Lib-

 ## DEMOCRATIC NATIONAL COMMITTEE
WEB http://www.democrats.org

The committee's site serves as an excellent spot if you're looking for information about the Democratic Party, whether on the national, state, or county level. The "What's Hot" section

includes press releases and talking points from the DNC, while the area called "Connecting with America" offers audio clips from the President and the DNC's chairman. Sensibly arranged, with lots of info for left-leaning cybercitizens. Everybody do the Donkey Stomp!

PRIVATE INTEREST, PUBLIC GOOD?

It's not clear what your point is. Can government magically determine the cause of pollution better than the private sector? If not, then how does this in any way argue against libertarian approaches? If "it's not clear WHO polluted" something, it seems either it isn't possible for anyone to determine this, or if it *is* possible but difficult, then it seems private entities that have been either harmed by this or who stand to profit by helping collect damages from the polluter have a greater incentive to determine the source of the pollution than a government bureacrat who isn't personally affected.

—from talk.politics .libertarian

ertarian Philosophy," and a variety of leaflets and press releases. The site provides links to Web pages for a diverse selection of political groups, nonpartisan organizations, student clubs, and publications.
WEB http://w3.ag.uiuc.edu/liberty /libweb.html

talk.politics.libertarian If you're interested in talk of free markets, government regulation, and taxes, here's your discussion. Lurk for a while, getting a feel for the tenor of the

group's lengthy, argumentative discussions on topics such as "The Liberal Lapdog Press" and "The First Amendment, the Flag, and Matches." Wildy active and flame-friendly.
USENET talk.politics.libertarian

World Wide Libertarian Pages The site gathers libertarian resources of all types, including links to libertarian-owned businesses, periodicals, clubs, political parties, and organizations. One interesting feature, called "Libertarian People," allows you to link your home page to the site. If you're a newbie, check out "A Very Brief (400 Words) Introduction to the Libertarian Movement."
WEB http://www.libertarian.com/wwlp

Reform

alt.politics.perot Chock full of cross-postings about the Vince Foster suicide and the questionable conjugal loyalties of Speaker of the House Gingrich, this group has precious few posts specifically about H. Ross here. Why? Perhaps his mole-like features and shrill proclamations about the fate of the nation have ceased to warm the hearts of Americans everywhere.
USENET alt.politics.perot

Charlotte's Web Home Page Don't come here expecting an intellectually gifted spider and a friendly pig. This site is a clearinghouse for information on the Reform Party's drive to change

the face of American politics. You'll also find the party's stand on the debt, lobby reform, immigration, and welfare.
WEB http://www.emf.net/~cr/home page.htm

Independence Party News The news briefs posted here are hardly anything to get excited about, consisting of what Ross Perot has to say about everything from the fracas on Air Force One returning from Jerusalem to his call for a "George Washington" political fitness test.
WEB http://www.fosters.com/FOSTERS /cgi-bin/walk.cgi/FOSTERS/info/dl /d7/d8

Reform/Independence Party Web Site "Little parties have big ears," as the old saying goes. Find out what Ross and crew are up to here—follow their campaign for ballot access and their search for a replacement candidate. Read the party's principles of reform—high ethical standards for the White House and Congress, balanced budget, a consensus on Medicare and Social Security, term limits, and a paperless tax system. If convinced, you'll find an organization desperate for financial support.
WEB http://www.reformparty.org

Ross Perot '96 Why did Perot name his organization the Reform Party? Because there wasn't another name that tickled the fancy of all volunteers. And, see, under the inefficient political system, you have to come up with all this crazy paperwork. It's like being a jackal on an escalator—by the time you turn around your lunch is far away from you. Jackal? Escalator? Huh? Follow H. Ross Perot's tortuous populist metaphors here. **AMERICA ONLINE** *keyword* election→ Message Boards→Ross Perot '96

The other sides

Constitution Action Party "This is probably not the Web site you were looking for if you believe the Democrats or the Republicans, or both, are doing a good job" states the frank introduction to this third-party home page. They don't like the way FDR "messed up the constitu-

tional masterpiece of Madison and Monroe." They don't like the global marketplace. And they especially hate the judiciary. But the CAP's answer of who might be better qualified to sit in the Oval Office may surprise you. Their first operating principle? "God is the source of all authority. Those who seek to displace or ignore God in the public forum are working de facto against the interests of the nation. We will strive to make this fact clear at every turn to our fellow citizens." Enough said, right? If you want to keep up with their position on sex outside of marriage, you'd better start burning your Henry Miller now. **WEB** http://www2.ari.net/home/CAP

The Natural Law Party Not since your sociology class in college have you heard so many references to the collective consciousness. According to the guiding ideas of the Natural Law Party, if we can just fix that troublesome old collective consciousness, all will be right with America. "The Natural Law Party promotes education that develops intelligence, creativity, moral reasoning, and higher states of consciousness for all students... By eliminating stress in the collective consciousness of society, by promoting education that develops the creativity and intelligence of every person, and by providing effective rehabilitation of prison inmates, the Natural

THE LIBERTARIAN PARTY

WEB http://www.lp.org/lp

Lady Liberty graces every page here—pages of philosophy and positions, official documents, history, and more. A list of libertarian candidates is available, as well as information on the national

Location: http://www.lp.org/lp/

The Libertarian Party

- Overview
- Philosophy and Positions
- Membership Information
- Current Activities
- Directories and Lists
- Official Documents
- Info by State
- History

1996 LIBERTARIAN PRESIDENTIAL NOMINATING CONVENTION

HARRY BROWNE
for President

JO JORGENSEN
for Vice President

convention in Washington, D.C. Libertarian alternatives to GOP and Democratic strategies for fighting crime are in evidence too. (They want to "end drug prohibition" and allow everyone to carry concealed weapons.) They even have a health care proposal—free-market, of course.

❝ We'll just meditate away those assault weapons and all that nasty poverty. ❞

Law Party is unique in its ability to eliminate the root causes of crime." We'll just meditate away those assault weapons and all that nasty poverty. Heighten your consciousness and follow the fate of John Hagelin and the other NLP candidates from here.
WEB http://www.fairfield.com/nlp

The New Party Yet another self-proclaimed majority—there was the silent, the moral, Perot's, and now the New Majority. This site is loaded with the New Party's statement of principles, essays on how liberals and democrats have failed, and press clips. And (surprise!) the party wants to "return power to the people" and fix all the social ills too.
WEB http://www.newparty.org

Patriot Party Internet Home Page Welcome to a good old boy named David Schultz's labor of love. Here he posts, not only his home phone number, but the newly adopted principles of the Patriot Party. (Constantly humming "America the Beautiful" and never wearing red

without white and blue are, oddly enough, not high on the list.) The Patriots are for campaign reform, getting rid of the electoral college, no Congressional mailing at public expense, balanced budget (except during war), tax reform, and market rates for grazing your cows on public lands.
WEB http://www.epix.net/~dschultz/patriotl.html

Third Parties '96 Want to help build a new political mainstream? This bunch of regular guys and gals stands for the exciting principles of proportional representation, open access to the ballot, and voting on non-work days. They're also against racism, for full employment, and staunchly pro-choice. Find out more about their principles and their upcoming convention here.
WEB http://www.envirolink.org/greens/3rd-p96

United We Stand America This organization is not the current vintage of Ross Perot's populist juggernaut—that's the Reform Party. But this site does contain assorted op-ed columns and legislative updates.
WEB http://www.uwsa.org

We the People Home Page—Jerry Brown Tired of being viewed as the space-case outsider of the Democratic Party, Jerry Brown decided to launch one of his own parties into electoral orbit in 1992. In 1996 the platform is still "in progress"—after all, Brown is a laid-back Californian. How far he'll get with a slogan like "Restore Humility to Government!" is questionable, but who wouldn't vote for the only candidate who favors doubling the budget for the National Endowment on the Arts? See you on Planet Koozebane, Jerry.
WEB http://www.hia.com/hia/wtp

"Ya hear what I'm sayin', don't ya?"
http://www.reformparty.org

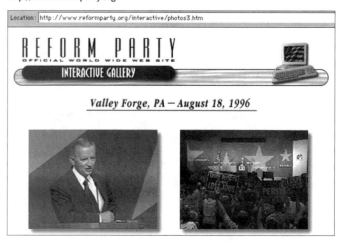

Location: http://www.reformparty.org/interactive/photos3.htm

REFORM PARTY
OFFICIAL WORLD WIDE WEB SITE
INTERACTIVE GALLERY

Valley Forge, PA — August 18, 1996

U.S. Government

HE WANTS *YOU* TO TAKE HIS AVUNCULAR ADVICE.
GET TO KNOW HIM FIRST

IN THE LATE TWENTIETH-CENTURY Uncle Sam isn't quite the hallowed icon he once was. These days he's more the black sheep of the national family. He can be greedy, belligerent, intrusive, overbearing, and occasionally just plain stupid. Sometimes it's hard to tell if he'll make it into the next millennium intact, assailed as he is on all sides by anarchists, libertarians, fundamentalists, terrorists, cyberpunks, and just plain everyday Americans who detest taxes. Nevertheless, he's got Web pages like everybody else, and those without serious ideological objections can find some pretty useful information there. These links provide the citizen, activist, and would-be reformer with a window on what it is your tax dollars are actually doing.

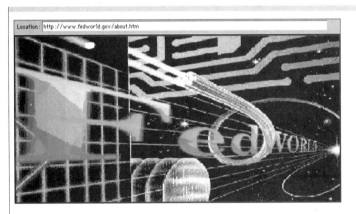

Location: http://www.fedworld.gov/about.htm

FEDWORLD
WEB http://www.fedworld.gov
Perhaps in these days of near universal calls for "smaller government," civil service Web designers ought to reconsider this site's logo—a giant globe with FedWorld branded on it. But FedWorld does have a wealth of information, from tax forms to the FDA's report on fat-free potato chips, and it makes a solid attempt to resell the government to its owners with a user-friendly site. They have provided lots of guides—resources are listed both by agency and subject (Department of Agriculture and soybeans)— and there are FTP and telnet options to ensure availability to the greatest number. Big government seems less like Big Brother and more like a cyberpal here.

CLICK PICKS

Starting points

Federal Government Agencies
Divided into executive, legislative, judicial, independent, and quasi-official, this list of federal agencies provides links to more than 200 government sites.
WEB http://www.lib.lsu.edu/gov /fedgov.html

Federal Web Locator Billed as "one-stop shopping for the Federal Government," this site collects links to virtually every branch and agency, from the CIA (Central Intelligence Agency) to the FAA (Federal Aviation Administration) to the SEC (Securities and Exchange Commission). A built-in search application aids in locating everything from farm subsidies to federal court judges.
WEB http://www.law.vill.edu /Fed-Agency/fedwebloc.html

Government Agency Web Servers
An alphabetical list of government agencies online, whether it's NASA's Jet Propulsion Laboratory, the city of Palo Alto, or the U.S. Patent and Trademark Office.
WEB http://www.eit.com/web/www .servers/government.html

Executive

A Day in the Life of the President
So you thought being a president was all gala receptions, troop deployments, and pocket vetos? Well, think again. Here you can find out about the daily grind of being Commander in Chief from the diary of

Location: http://sunsite.unc.edu/lia/president/

Linking America's citizens to leaders past and present
http://sunsite.unc.edu/lia/president

that most exciting of Chief Executives, Gerald R. Ford. Here's a taste of the treats to come: "10:19: The President went to the President-General's Room. He was escorted by Mr. Smith, Mr. Booth, Mr. Morrison, Mr. Nielson..." Gripping, isn't it?
WEB http://www2.sils.umich.edu /FordLibrary/DayInTheLife.html

66 Who wouldn't want to hear Tricky Dick's many resignation speeches? 55

Historical Speech Collection How could they have wanted to take that cute little puppy away from Tricia and Julie? Relive some of the most glorious moments of American political

history at this wonderful sound and film archive. The Nixon collection is especially good— who wouldn't want to hear Tricky Dick's many resignation speeches and fumbled defenses? Other highlights include an incoherent debate between Bill Clinton and Newt Gingrich, H. Ross Perot's paranoid ramblings, and Pat Buchanan's fire-breathing castigation of sinners. Don't miss George Bush's ode to broccoli or Spiro Agnew's explanation of the Kent State tragedy.
WEB http://www.webcorp.com/sounds /index.htm

Inaugural Addresses of the Presidents of the United States An amazing resource for students of American history, this archive collects the inaugural addresses of all the presidents of the United States. George Washington comes out full of high rhetoric—"Such being the impressions under which I have, in obedience to the public summons, repaired to the present station, it would be peculiarly improper to omit in this first official act my fervent supplications to that Almighty Being who rules over the universe, who presides in the councils of nations, and whose providential aids can supply every human defect, that His benediction may consecrate to the liberties and happiness of the people of the United States a Government instituted by themselves for these essential purposes, and may enable every instrument employed in its administration to execute with success the functions allotted to his charge." George Bush is all earthy plainspokenness—"I come before you and

assume the Presidency at a moment rich with promise. We live in a peaceful, prosperous time, but we can make it better." There's also some general information about inaugurations, and a list of presidents who were never inaugurated.

WEB http://www.cc.columbia.edu/acis /bartleby/inaugural/index.html

Information From the White House
Want the word right from the horse's mouth? Press releases, State of the Union addresses, U.S. Budgets, and more are available here.

WEB http://sunsite.unc.edu /white-house/white-house.html

President A lemon-yellow site dedicated to the celebration of

all things presidential. Pick a smiling president from the online portrait gallery to link to a presidential library. Limited to presidents of this century, this archive includes snapshots (of Tricia and Daddy, Fala and Eleanor), sounds (fireside chats and Star Wars speeches), and documents (the Camp David Accord and the Civil Rights Act of 1964). Get up close and personal with Presidents of the Past with a visit to other memorial sites, from George Washington's not-so-humble birthplace to Thomas Jefferson's Monticello home to the James K. Polk Elementary School in Alexandria, Va.

WEB http://sunsite.unc.edu/lia /president

THE WHITE HOUSE
WEB http://www.whitehouse.gov/WH/Welcome-nt.html

Our president's online home has been completely updated for 1996 and now, like Clinton, seems a bit more grown up. No longer does poor Socks Clinton have his own home page (although a cartoon version of the First Kitty does host the tour of the new White House for Kids). Chelsea, too, despite her recent public appearances, is almost nowhere to be found. But there are recorded greetings from the president, vice president (that's Bill and Al to you), Hillary, and Tipper, plus

candy-coated biographies of all four. There's also a tour of the grounds, a history of the building, and even an Interactive Citizen's Guide to the Federal Government. A lot less crowded than a stroll down Pennsylvania Avenue.

TO WHOM IT MAY CONCERN

Do you have any hints for writing to legislators?

- In the first paragraph, state your purpose for writing. Make it short and to the point. If you are writing about a certain bill, specify its number.
- Then, build your case—explain why you feel as you do. Use facts, not emotional arguments to support your position. Explain the ramifications of the matter in question.
- If you are writing in opposition to something, say so. Explain why it is wrong, and suggest alternatives.
- If you admire your legislator for a particular reason, mention it in your letter.
- Ask your legislator his or her view on the subject.
- Be sure to include your name and complete address.

What about hints for writing to the media?

- Be brief. Focus on one issue. Be succinct. The more concise the letter, the less chance it will be edited beyond recognition.
- Be accurate. Do your homework. Check your facts as well as spelling, grammar, and punctuation.
- Be pertinent. There should be a clear reason for the letter (e.g., in answer to a letter or editorial).
- Be prompt. Daily papers want immediate answers. Weeklies are not as strict.
- Be courteous. Avoid insults. Criticize facts, not opinions.
- Be interesting. Have something original to say, even on an old subject.
- Be humorous. An entertaining letter is more memorable (and more apt to be printed) than an angry one.
- Be patient. If at first... keep trying.
- Be professional. Remember to sign it and include typed name, address, and daytime and evening phone numbers.

—from The Electronic Activist

Texas A&M's White House Archives A true example of electronic democracy, this site collects a wealth of information on the White House and the presidency, ranging from transcripts of informal remarks made by the Chief Executive during photo ops to detailed accounts of progress in health care lobbying to lists of awards and ceremonies held on the White House lawn. The archives can be searched, though the information contained only covers the Clinton Administration.
WEB http://www.tamu.edu/whitehouse

Judicial

Federal Court Locator A home page for all federal courts, including the Supreme Court, the Third, Fifth, and Eleventh Circuit appellate courts, and links to related executive agencies, such as the Department of Justice.
WEB http://www.law.vill.edu/Fed-Ct /fedcourt.html

Federal Courts A tutorial on the operation of the federal court system, selected articles from *The Third Branch* (the newsletter of the Federal Courts), and a link to the Directory of Electronic Public Access, which permits citizens to retrieve federal court information.
WEB http://www.uscourts.gov

The National Center for State Courts Founded in 1971 at the urging of Chief Justice Warren Burger, this organization seeks to strengthen communication among state courts in the hope of improving the efficiency and accuracy of justice nationwide. This page includes a mission statement, a history of the NCSC, and links to descriptions of most of the center's programs.
WEB http://www.ncsc.dni.us/ncsc.htm

Supreme Court Decisions Few historic decisions of the court are in the principal archives of the Legal Information Institute. Justice has been on patrol since the eighteenth century, and the Cornell database didn't

begin until 1990. But the organization has also collected prominent pre-1990 decisions, including *Roe v. Wade* (reproductive rights) and *Engel v. Vitale* (school prayer).
WEB http://www.law.cornell.edu/supct

Legislative

Electronic Activist Guidelines for writing letters to congresspeople, along with email addresses.
WEB http://www.berkshire.net/~ifas/activist

House of Representatives A mother lode of information on the lower house, including information on the legislative process, schedules for legislators, a member director, committee profiles, legislative data, and even tourist information for those visiting Capitol Hill.
WEB http://www.house.gov

Library of Congress The Library of Congress isn't just a gigantic collection of books; it's also a legislative agency, entrusted with maintaining the documents that bear the nation's laws. Find out all about the library—its holdings, exhibits, and electronic card catalog.
WEB http://www.loc.gov

List of Congressional E-mail Addresses Various lists of email addresses for members of the 104th Congress.
URL gopher://una.hh.lib.umich.edu/0/socsci/poliscilaw/uslegi/conemail
WEB http://www.webcom.com/~leavitt/cong.html

United States Senate Government gripe? Write your Congressperson! Don't know who that is? Well, this Web site can help. Planning a trip to visit the United States Senate? Pick up some tips on what to look for (besides learning that Washington D.C. has a lot more exciting things to see). The Glossary will help you to better understand what all that gobbledegook on the Senate floor is all about. For taxpayers who want to know where the heck all that money is going, consult the Senate Calendar (also check out C-SPAN once in a while). Select, special, and joint Senate commitees are fully explained in detail, for your viewing pleasure.
WEB http://www.senate.gov

THOMAS & THE CONGRESSIONAL RECORD ONLINE

WEB http://thomas.loc.gov

Are your elected representatives spending all their time in the House barbershop, or eating cheese danishes in the Senate cafeteria? If so, they're missing these bills currently before Congress.

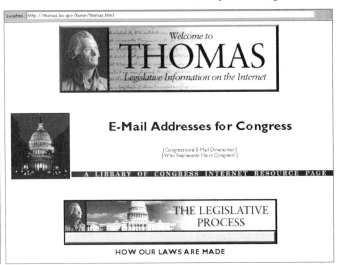

Trendy citizens will want to head to the Hot Legislation section, which tracks bills on issues from abortion to terrorism to welfare. If all these committees, negotiations, riders, and roll calls leave you confused, **THOMAS** also provides a nice little legislative manual, *How Our Laws Are Made.* You'll even find such seminal documents as the Federalist Papers and the Declaration of Independence.

Federal agencies

Centers for Disease Control
WEB http://www.cdc.gov

Consumer Products Safety Commission
URL gopher://cpsc.gov

Department of Agriculture
WEB http://www.usda.gov

Department of Commerce
WEB http://www.doc.gov

Department of Education
WEB http://www.ed.gov

Department of Energy
WEB http://www.doe.gov

Department of Health and Human Services
WEB http://www.os.dhhs.gov

Department of Housing and Urban Development
WEB http://www.hud.gov

Department of the Interior
WEB http://info.er.usgs.gov/doi/doi.html

Department of Justice
WEB http://www.usdoj.gov

Department of Transportation
WEB http://www.dot.gov

Department of the Treasury
WEB http://www.ustreas.gov

Department of Veteran's Affairs
WEB http://www.va.gov

Environmental Protection Agency
WEB http://www.epa.gov

Federal Aviation Administration
WEB http://www.faa.gov

Federal Communications Commission
WEB http://www.fcc.gov

Federal Deposit Insurance Corporation
WEB http://www.fdic.gov

Federal Emergency Management Agency
WEB http://www.fema.gov

Federal Trade Commission
WEB http://www.ftc.gov

Food and Drug Administration
WEB http://www.fda.gov

General Services Administration
WEB http://www.gsa.gov

Indian Health Services
WEB http://www.tucson.ihs.gov

Internal Revenue Service
WEB http://www.irs.ustreas.gov/prod

National Aeronautics and Space Administration
WEB http://www.nasa.gov

National Institutes of Health
WEB http://www.nih.gov

National Oceanic and Atmospheric Administration
WEB http://www.noaa.gov

National Park Service
WEB http://www.nps.gov

National Science Foundation
WEB http://www.nsf.gov

National Transportation Safety Board
WEB http://www.ntsb.gov

Nuclear Regulatory Commission
WEB http://www.nrc.gov

Peace Corps
WEB http://www.peacecorps.gov

Securities and Exchange Commission
WEB http://www.arc.com/sec/sec.html

Small Business Administration
WEB http://www.sbaonline.sba.gov

Smithsonian Institute
WEB http://www.si.edu

Social Security Administration
WEB http://www.ssa.gov

U.S. Fish and Wildlife Services
WEB http://www.fws.gov

U.S. Geological Survey
WEB http://www.usgs.gov

U.S. Information Agency
WEB http://www.usia.gov

U.S. Patent and Trademark Office
WEB http://www.uspto.gov

U.S. Postal Service
WEB http://www.usps.gov

Law

IS YOUR LEGAL KNOWLEDGE OUT OF ORDER? GET YOURSELF A BRIEFING ONLINE

WE LIVE IN AN AGE OF LITIGATION; lawyers swarm across the planet like locusts bringing a plague of suits and counter-suits, often clogging our legal system for years. These days you have to protect yourself, and there's no better way to do that than to study the laws and statutes that have mushroomed over the past century. Our legal system is currently one of the world's most elaborate and complex, making the U.S. the world's leading incarcerator with more than a million of its citizens behind bars. Netizens, with their libertarian bent, seem to have taken particular interest in law —they think there's too much of it. If you do hope to someday take the law into your own hands, the info on these sites will dazzle any jury and perhaps the odd regulator, too.

LEGAL RESOURCE GUIDE

WEB http://www.ilrg.com

The Internet Legal Resource Guide welcomes readers by claiming to be equally useful for lay persons and legal scholars alike, and that it is under heavy quality control, presenting only the best online resources. Happily, the site's founder, Presscott Caballeron, has made sure that his site lives up to its promise. Enter the What's News in the Legal Community section, and you'll find concise summaries of legal developments written with a clarity for which lawyers aren't usually known. If this isn't the most comprehensive legal site on the Net, it comes close.

NOT LIKE THERE WERE FLIES IN HER SOUP

I've come across foreign objects in food before—but have just tried to ignore and forget about it... However, it seems more and more, I'm finding odd things in store purchased foods than before. Today, while eating a "very raisin oatmeal" cookie, I ended up scratching the top of my mouth with... what appears to be [a soft matchstick-sized dark piece of] wood... something... I can't really recognize... [p]ossibly a dead stem of a stalk [of some kind and] I would like some advice as to what I should do and say in contacting the company to inform them of this experience.—Janet

The important question here is not the "legal" one as such but, instead, why the poster would want to "contac[t] the company to inform [it] of this experience"—since the experience as described is so utterly innocuous and, indeed, to be expected.

When one purchases a "natural" product, especially a dried berry-fruit product like raisins, one ought to expect that, occasionally, one will encounter a small piece of barely and harmless detritus, like a tiny piece of stalk... and, So what?

Even the most ardent proponent of aggressive regulatory action would be hard-pressed to find in the story recited even the slightest evidence of manufacturer misconduct or even carelessness nor, indeed, any oversight whatever, and no sensible person, not even a first-year-law-student, would consider this report legally or in any other way significant.

—from misc.legal.moderated

Starting points

Bill's Law Library Bill is obviously a man who's done his homework. Along with a healthy dose of international links, there are generous offerings for those looking into Canadian legal questions. Things, however, get eclectic in Bill's world, where you can survey legal decisions of the UN court and, while you're at it, check out some astronomy links or newsgroups devoted to discussions of aboriginal life.
WEB http://www.io.org/~jgcom /librlaw.htm

Christo's Law Links Page Christo, a Greek-American computer consultant, knows from whence all things legal come— the U.S. Constitution, which is the first link here, just before the Seamless Web disclaimer. And it's well worth following the links to the Virtual Magis-

trate and the MacCrate Report on Mandatory Continuing Education if you haven't already seen them. The other links are extensive but run-of-the-mill, including the Justice Department, and congressional and American Bar Association sites.
WEB http://www.nauticom.net/www /balouris/law.html

The Law Source This publisher of guides to online legal sources claims to have "the most complete and most current cumulative listing of primary source legal resources available free on the Internet," which includes federal, state, and international resources, as well as legal resources categorized by subject. Download Adobe Acrobat Reader to check out sample issues of the Source's newsletter. Subscription costs range from $79 to $99 per publication, but they offer a volume discount if you subscribe to more than one. Costs increase if you want the guides in print format. Free, but just as valuable, are links to law firm and attorney directories, law school directories, associations, consultants, publishers, references sites, and other law-related sites.
WEB http://www.thelawsource.com

The 'Lectric Law Library You're out of order! At least you will be if you come to visit this online library, with its irreverent and breezy take on legal research. First, your law librarian takes you on a tour and leaves you in the rotunda. From there you can wander into the Law for Business Lounge, the News Room, the Legal Professional's Lounge, or the Reference Room, home of the 'Lectric Lawcopedia (for humor, try the Rubber Room). In these rooms you'll find information fit for the legal professional or novice alike. For example, in the Business Lounge you will find a solid study of the pros and cons of forming a C corporation, an S corporation, or a Limited Liability Corporation. The Laypeople's Law Lounge is a must-visit for every regular Joe or Jane; there's plenty of information on the implications of law in our day-to-day lives—"When can my landlord enter

my residence?" and "The Law on Grocery Store Rain Checks"—with a little humor thrown in for good measure.
WEB http://www.lectlaw.com

Villanova Center for Information Law and Policy This center, affiliated with the Villanova University School of Law, studies the role of the Internet and works with other law schools to propagate legal information and education via the Internet. In addition to information from the law school, the site provides links for locating federal and state government agencies and the federal and state judiciary as well as areas on more esoteric topics, such as a joint effort with the University of Sarajevo law faculty to create a

legal information infrastructure for Bosnia-Herzegovina.
WEB http://ming.law.vill.edu

World Wide Web Virtual Law Library: Law Produced by W3C, an industry consortium which develops standards for the Web through its specifications and reference software, this law page provides subject and type search functions and links to all the major online legal search tools. It looks and behaves very much like a standard-bearer's product.
WEB http://www.law.indiana.edu/law/v-lib/lawindex.html

Areas of practice

Advertising Law Is it legal to advertise that your company

U.S. HOUSE OF REPRESENTATIVES LAW LIBRARY
WEB http://law.house.gov

Sure, Congress makes the laws; here they're willing to tell you a bit about them. Isn't the government great? The House Law Library contains a full-text, searchable version of the U.S. Code, and its "sister publication," the Code of Federal Regulations. While these are far from summer reading,

they are comprehensive. And, if the government's lawbooks aren't what you need, the library's webmasters have cobbled together more than 6,600 sources of legal information—some on the House server, some as links to other sites. Now that's complete.

GOD ON LAWYERS

„"Woe unto you, lawyers! For ye have taken away the Key of knowledge: ye entered not in yourselves, and them that were entering in ye hindered."—St. Luke II:52

[Note: In reaction to our publishing the above we were contacted by the Planetary Bar Assn. who, after intensive negotiations with our highly respected legal counsel, Rinkle & Rinkle, PC., Esqs., Inc., LP., Ltd., offered us $1,000,000,000 to remove the material... to which we hesitantly agreed. However, the agreement's strict confidentiality clause—that we also get a retraction from the author—has presented some problems; She refuses to reply to our email. Any help our beloved visitors can provide in resolving this will be greatly appreciated.—Staff]

—from The 'Lectric Law Library

sells "the best damn widgets on the planet?" Find out with this collection of material from the government, the courts, and other sources on the legal guidelines and boundaries for advertising claims. And in case you were wondering, the widgets slogan might be legally categorized as "puffery," which means you might be able to get away with it—depending on the context of the ad.
WEB http://www.webcom.com /~lewrose/home.html

Center for Corporate Law
Located at the University of Cincinnati, the recently established Center for Corporate Law includes the full text of some of the most important corporate acts of the post-depression era: the Securities Acts of 1933 and 1934, the Public Utilities Holding Company Act of 1935, the Trust Indenture Act of 1939, and the Securities Investor Protection Act of 1970.
WEB http://www.law.uc.edu/CCL

Criminal Law Links Set up by a public defender with Kentucky's Department of Public Advocacy, along with links to federal law sites and legal-news resources, this page's unique contribution is a cluster of Kentucky law links. Feature articles contain links to recent studies on criminal law in the U.S. and archives contain similar material dating back to the summer of '95.
WEB http://dpa.state.ky.us/~rwheeler /archives/archive.htm

Family Law Library The first thing one finds here is a bit of good advice: "You should only discuss your legal problems confidentially with a licensed attorney, and never rely solely on information or advice you find or receive over the Internet." Makes perfect sense. Links include the California and Colorado Bar Associations'

sites (which dispense advice on choosing a family lawyer and getting what you pay for), divorce support pages, newsgroups, and a host of other popular professional and state links. If you want to loosen the ties that bind, this is a fine place to begin your research.
WEB http://www.value.net/~markwelch /famlaw.htm

GayLawNet Although this page's information—about personal safety, health and HIV, immigration, business and home ownership—is of broad interest to all gay and lesbian netizens, the details of most of the legal issues discussed at the site are relevant only in Australia. Still, the countries represented in the list of gay lawyers is growing, and will eventually become a useful resource for gay Internet users worldwide.
WEB http://www.labyrinth.net.au/~dba

The International Law Page
Beyond the international law library, where legal experts can read international law journals online, the name of this page is a bit of a misnomer, for the resources are heavy on European law, and lacking with regards to the rest of the world. Read up on treaties from Maastricht to the mother of all, Westphalia; take a shortcut to any embassy page on the Web; or crib up on a country you'll be visiting soon by visiting the CIA Fact Book.
WEB http://www.noord.bart.nl /~bethlehem/law.html

Psychiatry and the Law University of Alabama pages give psychiatrists and lawyers the kind of reciprocal information each might need when dealing with the fascinating area where mental health and the law intersect. They also give laypeople the kind of information they can use for knowledgeable cocktail party chit-chat about high-profile cases which use the insanity defense or John Grisham's latest legal thriller.
WEB http://ualvm.ua.edu/~jhooper /tableofc.html

Sex Laws This extensive, albeit somewhat less-than-comprehensive, survey of sex law in Canada, the United States, Australia, and some Islamic countries, is designed for those with an itch for some for the absurd arcana of sex and society. If you were wondering about the legal duties of Islamic women when it comes to menstruation, this is where you'll find the answer. If you're sympathetic to the claim that American society is sheepish when it comes to sex, learn about historical persecutions of bestialists.
WEB http://www.cc.gatech.edu/grads /g/Mark.Gray/Sex_Laws.html

WEB Multimedia Law With the help of slick graphics, this page offers legal resources for the information age. In addition to legal search engine links, its content focuses on emerging laws on all aspects of multimedia. Topics such as Internet telephony and its legal implications are covered, as are Malaysia's planned multimedia super-corridor.
WEB http://www.batnet.com/oikoumene

Law school

FindLaw FindLaw is much like a general Web search engine, except that its universe is limited to legal sites, resources, and law reviews. Interested in the Iroquois Constitution, the Lanham Act (trademarks), or the use of peyote in Oregon? Chances are you'll find a citation on these pages. The process is transparent and the

LAW JOURNAL EXTRA
WEB http://www.ljextra.com

LJE's news articles are cleanly written reports of intriguing legal issues, such as one piece that examined how easy it is for convicted lawyers to be readmitted to the bar. Speaking of the stuff that cynicism is made of: Take one of LJE's recent Decision of the Day articles, a transcript of a recent decision by the Eighth Circuit's Court of Appeals—a dispute raged between insurance companies and the Catholic Diocese of Winona, Minn. The issue: Whether compensatory and punitive damages awarded against the diocese in a sexual-abuse suit were covered by the diocese's insurance policies.

content is deep enough for professionals, but not too intimidating for novices.
WEB http://www.findlaw.com/index.html

Law School Dot Com Sponsored by West Professional Training, this virtual law-school campus offers a wealth of resources, including a financial-aid office, a bookstore, and free study outlines. There's also a searchable database of law firms, and both students and attorneys can create personal profiles. If you're a little shark who's just starting out, you may want to refer to the list of legal employment links. For law news updates, read the Daily Lawyer.
WEB http://www.lawschool.com

The Seamless Website This commercial page claims to have 3,000 HTML files and more than 4,000 links to other Web sites. While a significant section is dedicated to Internet law, there are many links to law firms' home pages. The site also offers a "grab bag" of destinations, chosen by the webmasters for intrepid virtual voyagers.
WEB http://seamless.com

Law talk

misc.legal If you want to greet your colleagues once they've shaken off their wing tips and checked their bone-dry legalese at the door, you'll find that lawyers moonlight as champion Internet flamers. But be advised, no one can be held in

Welcome to West Publishing!

Shine a light across the shadowy world of the law
http://www.westpub.com

contempt here. No matter if the topic is a discussion of whether child pornography should be republished by Internet service providers or a debate on how Clinton's world trade policy is jeopardizing sales of South American gasoline exports, the banter is legally incorrect. Recent barbs: "If you ever wanted to really learn something, the NRA might have to take away your Golden Eagle membership." or "By your uninformed opinion, I'd say you're either: 1) a politician; 2) management; or 3) unemployed."
USENET misc.legal

misc.legal.moderated Imagine if there was a place you could go for free legal advice, without having to tug on some lawyer's sleeve at a cocktail party. Well, this is the place, and it's also a good pit-stop for law students, researchers, and type-A lawyers. The latter in particular

should appreciate the handy "road map for the impatient" FAQ, where no question is too dumb to ask, and where there won't be a colleague hanging around to make you feel even dumber—it's filled with perfect short cuts for looking up a Supreme Court case or finding a bilingual guide to Greek citation lingo.
USENET misc.legal.moderated

Legal publishers

West Publishing This St. Paul-based legal publisher is best known for slicing and dicing case law and statutes to make the information accessible to the legal profession via books and computer-assisted research services. Its commercial-oriented site does a yeomanly job of outlining the company's history, highlighting its products, and providing contacts for further information.
WEB http://www.westpub.com

Military

THERE'S A VIRTUAL ARMY OF ARMED FORCES SITES ONLINE. SO BE ALL THAT YOU CAN VIRTUALLY BE

HAD TOLSTOY HAD HAD ACCESS to the wealth of military minutiae on the Internet when he was writing *War and Peace*, the novel would probably be several thousand pages longer than it already is, much to the horror of college students everywhere. Virtually anything and everything you could possibly want to know about humanity's most tragic and horrific pastime is a mere click away—from the exact technical specifications of a patriot missile to the most heart-wrenching confessions of a Vietnam War veteran. Purple Hearts and Bronze Stars, M-16's and Sherman tanks, V2s and ICBMs and Scuds, Patton and Powell, POWs and MIAs, blood, guts, and gas chambers—take your pick. The Net is a virtual quartermaster's storehouse of military intelligence.

Location: http://www.dtic.mil/defenselink/photos/24896_960

DefenseLINK
WEB http://www.dtic.dla.mil/defenselink

The Department of Defense has several ready-made audiences (veterans, contractors, war buffs), and its crowded home page offers something for everyone. Style is key here: The DOD enables everyday citizens to play online general with its current hit, BosniaLINK, which follows the campaign tank by tank. The site has also retained GulfLINK, to attract those interested in reminiscing about past glories. Contractors and taxpayers alike can take advantage of the site's easy to use search function to find out about upcoming rocket contracts and Star Wars research, which thankfully isn't written in "Pentagonese."

Starting points

alt.military.cadet The future leaders of our armed forces talk about current events, hazing, and student life as cadets at the various military academies worldwide.
USENET alt.military.cadet

Journal of Electronic Defense (JED) Not for the neophyte, this electronic magazine focuses on electronic warfare in all its daunting complexity. Includes articles about technologies and systems for self-protection, electronic counter-measures, electronic counter-countermeasures, intelligence collection and dissemination, and other aspects of command and control warfare. Just register here, and you can be the first kid on your block to harden your bedroom against EMP weapons.
WEB http://www.jedefense.com/jed .html

Air Force

The Air Combat Command (ACC) The largest Major Command (MAJCOM) in the U.S. Air Force, comprised of 156,000 active-duty/civilian and 110,600 Guard and Reserve personnel, four numbered air forces, two direct reporting units, 28 installations, and 11 major units on non-ACC installations. The ACC has 3,487 aircraft and almost 1,000 intercontinental ballistic missiles (ICBMs). Does the catchphrase "peace through superior firepower"

Touch down at AFLink for info on U.S. forces in the air
http://www.dtic.dla.mil/airforcelink

come to mind? This page has lots of fairly unsurprising info about ACC, including biographies of some of the staff, but not everything here is accessible to the non-military surfer.
WEB http://www.acc.af.mil

Air Education and Training Command (AETC) AETC's fundamental mission is to recruit, train, and educate USAF personnel. It is thus ironic that they are the clear winners of the Netscape Enhanced Hall of Shame Award, in the Military home page category. On the plus side, the site features a nifty, searchable map of all USAF bases in the world.
WEB http://www.aetc.af.mil

Air Force Home Page This site is brought to you by the Air Force News Service (AFNS). Discover what happened when a B-2 bomber was struck by lightning. Read about the starting of the Alternate Master

Clock in Falcon, Fla. which is as accurate as the master clock in Washington D.C. Love learning about military aviation? Try the story on the retiring of the F-111 (the *Aardvark*) which flew for more than 30 years on missions throughout the Vietnam war, the Cold War and the Gulf Crisis. This site is updated with fresh Air Force News every day.
WEB http://www.dtic.dla.mil /airforcelink

Headquarters Air Force Reserve. (HQ AFRES) Provides a wide range of information as a service to the general public, including (logically enough) information on how you can join the Air Force Reserve. The sales pitch? "A great way to serve."
WEB http://www.afres.af.mil

Headquarters U.S. Pacific Command (PACAF) Learn about the flyboys responsible for patrol-

ling more than half the earth's surface (from the West Coast of North America to the East Coast of Africa, and from the Arctic to the Antarctic).
WEB http://www.hqpacaf.af.mil

rec.aviation.military Was the P-38 a worthless fighter plane? The guys on rec.aviation.military want to talk about it—that and anything to do with any military or civilian aircraft of the past, present, and future, from the *Enola Gay* to the stealth bomber. A lot of ex-fly-boys can be found here congenially talking shop.
USENET rec.aviation.military

Space Information Network (SPin) A low-tech page for a high-tech military outfit. Links to all SPin unit nodes, including the

USAF's 45th Space Wing. May the force be with you.
WEB http://www.pafb.af.mil/index.htm

USAF Academy (USAFA) The USAF's version of West Point, and home to its Officer Cadet Corp, the Academy sits along the eastern ridge of the Colorado Rocky Mountains, perfect terrain for jet exercises and even a little recreational skiing. This site provides information about Academy athletics and admissions resources, as well as links (via FTP or Telnet) to the USAF's library catalog system.
WEB http://www.usafa.af.mil

Army

U.S. Army Home Page For crop-tops who think all other mili-

tary branches are full of wimps, here it is: the place to find "the most modern weapons and equipment the country can provide." See full-color pictures of the men in charge, including General Dennis Reimer (don't you just love a man in uniform?). Those who just can't get enough of those gripping war stories can read the AUSA Luncheon speech. Also, pick up fascinating documents on the desk of the Chief of Staff, including the scintillating "Dental Changes for Family Members." Hackers are kindly asked not to infiltrate DOD computers.
WEB http://www.army.mil

United States Military Academy (USMA) Better known as West Point, the USMA has been in

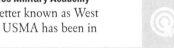

DEFENSE NEWS
WEB http://www.defensenews.com

Decorate those bare white walls with fabulous prints of military aircraft and vehicles, available in the Marketplace, or maybe order a CD-ROM about Vietnam. Trying to find other members of the

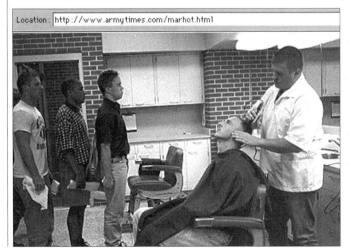

32nd Tactical Fighter Squadron? Converse with them at their reunion in the Military City. A painless registration process is the only price you pay. Links to the *Federal Times*, *Space Times*, *Army Times*, and Military City Online. Feedback (not about the military division in general but just this Web site) is available to registered users.

From the cyberhalls of Montezuma
http://www.usmc.mil

the business of training the Army's officer corps for more than 175 years, and its alumni include figures as diverse as Edgar Allan Poe and Robert E. Lee, as well as several presidents. You'll find admissions information, a brief history, alumni links, an email directory, and plenty of bronze eagles.
WEB http://www.usma.edu

Navy

Flagship The official publication of the world's largest navy base (in Norfolk, Va.), *Flagship* is of interest primarily to base residents and employees, although it does contain tidbits of general information about the Navy.
WEB http://www.infi.net/flagship

NavyOnLine While not as comprehensive as ArmyLINK or AirForceLINK, the official Web site of the United States

Department of the Navy still provides useful links to the Navy's other online resources, including the Official Navy FAQ, the Navy News Service, the Navy Public Affairs Library, and the Navy Terminal Access Program (Nav-TAP), as well as a slightly disorganized index of all Navy-related Web pages. Need to find a needle in this haystack? Use the Search NavyOnLine function, which allows you to search all this information by keyword.
WEB http://www.navy.mil

United States Naval Academy Established in 1845, the United States Naval Academy at Annapolis is the undergraduate naval college that prepares young men (and recently women, as well) to become professional officers in the U.S. Navy and Marine Corps. The site provides resources of interest to both the USNA's acade-

mic body and the general public. Come to Alumni Day and see if you can spot former president Jimmy Carter or H. Ross Perot in the crowd.
WEB http://www.nadn.navy.mil

Marines

MarineLINK "From the halls of Montezuma to the shores of Tripoli," brags the official United States Marine Corps Web site. You'll find news, gossip, history, and individual links to the Army, Navy, and Air Force. Supplemental features such as BosniaLink and GulfLink provide the latest information from the former battle zones, events calendars, and more specific info on veterans' issues like the mysterious Persian Gulf War illnesses. Even more engaging for the prospective marine, seasoned veteran, or curious civilian is Marine Doom, where you can shoot up the enemy in 3-D, with RealTime and RealAudio technologies.
WEB http://www.usmc.mil

National Guard

Guardlink OK, so it isn't the Army, Navy, Air Force, or Marines but let's face it, the National Guard can kick some butt. Let Lt. Gen. Edward D. Baca explain to you what it means to be a National Guard member. Want to sign up? Find out if you qualify (and if you have to do 500 sit-ups). Trying to infiltrate a drug operation? Maybe you should leave

it up to the Counter Drug (CD) division. You can actually obtain their email addresses and telephone numbers. Perhaps you're already an Administrative Technician Sergeant, and you're looking to relocate? The job listings are updated regularly.
WEB http://www.dtic.dla.mil /defenselink/guardlink

Coast Guard

U.S. Coast Guard Once, they protected our nation's shores from pirates and foreign invaders. Now, they protect us from illegal drugs and illegal aliens. Who said things never change in the military? The

Coast Guard's site includes general information about the USCG and its current mission, pointers to other sites of interest, and current navigation and travel information of use to all mariners.
WEB http://www.dot.gov/dotinfo/uscg

LGBs in the military

Homo Base Come out of the closet at this page for gays in the military. Newt Gingrich would flip if he saw Match.com or Manfinders— search tools to help gays find a partner—in the Observation Lounge. Looking for "alternative lifestyle" publications? Find 'em in the Rack at the

Electric Library. Vacationers can check out the Flight Deck and read about GayDay at Disney, or even learn about Gay Las Vegas. Let your fingers do the walking in the Pink Pages of Amsterdam or catch up with *Gay Daze*, a daily soap opera on the Web. Of course, the latest gay/military issues are covered in the Briefing Room, and the Infirmary has the latest scoop on AIDS-related subjects.
WEB http://members.aol.com /surfsdown/index.html

Veterans for Human Rights Forget "Don't ask, don't tell" for this site from the Veterans for Human Rights (VFHR). This

MILITARY COMMAND ONLINE (MCO)

AMERICA ONLINE *keyword* mco
picture: AMERICA ONLINE *keyword* mco→Communications Center→Bosnia Deployment Resource Center→Photographs→Aircraft

A virtual city unto itself, the **Military Command Online's** massive resources are aimed primarily at current military personnel and their families. Visit the Communications Center, with message boards devoted to the Q & A's of the military community. Drop by The Times Newsroom, which con-

tains the current week's issues of *Army Times*, *Navy Times*, *Navy Times—Marine Corps Edition*, and *Air Force Times*. Buff up your credit card for the Shopping Center, which is divided into the Military Only Mall and the Open Market. Finally, consult the list of military benefits for the perks that await those in uniform (hotel discounts, government-paid moving expenses, etc.).

WHO WEARS THE STRIPES IN THIS RELATIONSHIP?

It could have been worse. When I was growing up at Hahn AB in the late 1980s it was almost impossible to get a date because most of the high school girls preferred to date Gi's. I do remember being turned down for a date by a girl because her dad was a LTC and a pilot and mine was just a lowly Major and the commander of the Services Squadron.

I wasn't allowed to date soldiers—I wasn't allowed to call them GIs, either, because that means 'government issue,' which soldiers aren't, my dad insisted firmly. But I was allowed to date any boy I wanted to and mention was never made of his dad's rank. It's amazing to me to hear all these stories. I knew tons of officers' daughters and never knew one who turned a guy down because of his dad's rank. Heck, most of us were thrilled when *anybody* asked us out! You have to remember that the sword cuts both ways; lots of guys were hesitant to ask us out because of our dads' rank.

—from alt.culture.military-brats

site has updates on nationwide activities, with an emphasis on gay, lesbian, and women's rights. Whether you're trying to find a forum to discuss military discrimination, or you want to learn about veteran volunteering opportunities in Washington and Oregon, this is the place. Proudly wave your American flag while reading the Defenders of Liberty Statement. Give your own review of the site and see how it compares to others (including friends of the Board of Directors). Connects to women's fun links (unrelated to the military) and also homosexual links, including Out and Proud and the Queer Resources Directory.
WEB http://www.solnlogic.com/VFHR2

Military families
....
alt.culture.military-brats Children of military families trade war stories and try to locate old friends. Beverly Bryant of Nurenberg and Ft. Sill, Okla. circa 1955? Your old boyfriend is calling.
USENET alt.culture.military-brats

POW & MIA
....
The POW/MIA Forum Sure, you've been driving along and seen one of those MIA-POW stickers on the back of some car, and wondered if prisoners are still out there. But are they? The people who maintain this site believe they are. Examine their evidence, such as the transcript of Quang 1205, or

maybe some government memos sent in March of 1996. Find out why William "Billy" Hendon handcuffed himself to the Hanoi Compound last March. Learn what Operation Smoking Gun is doing about MIAs. The organization is comprised of the POW Network, the National Alliance of Families for the Return of America's Missing Servicemen, The Heart of Illinois, and a network of independent researchers.
WEB http://pages.prodigy.com /powforum/pwmiaf.htm

Vietnam POW/MIA Database Operated by the Library of Congress, this database contains more than 120,000 records pertaining to the fates of missing or imprisoned Vietnam-era American soldiers.
WEB http://lcweb2.loc.gov/pow /powhome.html

Veterans
....
Australian Vietnam Veterans Organizations United States Commander General Westmoreland said of the Australian troops, "I have never seen a finer group of men. I have never fought with a finer group of soldiers." Of course, he's specifically referring to the 423 Australians who died during the conflict, not to mention nearly 2,500 others who were wounded. Read about the 10 years of intensive training and fighting that the Australians went through. Australian Vets

can find addresses and telephone numbers where they can get help dealing with the effects of the Vietnam conflict, and others can develop a deeper appreciation of the 10,000-day war. Also links to the Vietnam home page.
WEB http://grunt.space.swri.edu /ozorgs.htm

Department of Veterans' Affairs
Opening with a quote from Abe Lincoln—"To care for him who shall have borne the battle and for his widow and orphan"—the Department of Veterans' Affairs home page reviews the history of the country's support for veterans, reviews veterans' benefits, and lists VA facilities by state.

Links to archives of veteran-related legislation and hearings are also available.
WEB http://www.va.gov

Gulf War Veteran Resource Pages
The most immediately appealing feature of this site is a forum called Gulf Chat, where surfers can discuss the House Committee's findings on the Gulf War Syndrome and the counter-arguments in the Department of Defense's CCE10K report. Need to find the answer to a Gulf War-related dispute? Try the Gulf War Web Search. What's better than seeing a man in uniform? How about a woman like Dr. Sandra L. Bonchin (a couple of men also provided their photo

albums, but, thankfully, they didn't provide their karaoke audio files). Budding Gulf War writers (who were there and didn't just watch it on TV) can publish online by submitting their experiences to Traces in the Sand.
WEB http://gulfwar.org

Gulflink—Persian Gulf War Illnesses Home Page Get that Saddam Hussein dartboard out to prepare for this site. Pore over declassified Iraqi documents as well as U.S. documents to better understand the Gulf Crisis. Read about the nerve agent prophylaxis and immunization, and think about why some of the military came back ill for unknown reasons, and how

VETERAN NEWS AND INFORMATION SERVICE

WEB http://www.vnis.com

Probably the best Web site for vets who are just trying to try to find their way on the Web, this includes polls, surveys, chat groups, newsgroups, and the like. It also addresses legislation pending in the current Congress, gives toll-free telephone numbers for veterans' services, and it has some nifty .GIFs and RealAudio files for netheads to download. Read the latest from the Veterans' News and Information Service—you might learn something about the insurance scams that are enticing some unsuspecting veterans. You can also link to all sorts of Veterans of Foreign Wars (VFW) sites nationwide.

YOU'RE IN THE CIVILIAN RANKS NOW

I felt a great sense of pride in myself and the American Military as the War ended. But it seemed the closer I got to home, the worse I felt about returning to a regular civilian life. Upon returning as a civilian, I grew very angry and withdrawn. I felt like everyone around me was watching me. I didn't feel safe. Everyday tasks frustrated and angered me more.

—from Gulf War Veteran Resource Pages

that led to the establishment of an 800 number for dealing with their mysterious syndromes. Plenty of fact sheets, press releases, bibliographies, and speeches, all declassified for your viewing pleasure. Links to Air Force features and news as well as other links pertaining to the Department of Defense.
WEB http://www.dtic.dla.mil/gulflink

Korean War Project The only major resource for information about America's "forgotten war," this site features a Korean War casualty file, a listing of Korean War veterans' groups, an index of Korean War history resources (both online and offline), and several personal testimonies by veterans.
WEB http://www.onramp.net/~hbarker

Military and Vets Club Not just a club for veterans, this forum admits anyone with an interest in Military or Veterans' Affairs; the club's message boards contain posts exploring a range of topics. From its libraries, military buffs can download programs, military graphics files, and transcripts of weekly meetings. These meetings (which occur every Thursday night from 10 p.m. to 11 p.m. EST) address topics as diverse as Vietnam vets, Gulf War support, and spouses' support. On the lighter side, the Club also sponsors Military Trivia Games and a "Humor, In and Out of Uniform" joke contest.
AMERICA ONLINE *keyword* military

New Zealand/Australian Vietnam Vets With the serene Maya Lin memorial and the scars on our national memory, we tend to forget that plenty of other countries sent men to die in Vietnam, including New Zealand and Australia. These two pages pay tribute to the Allied Forces from Down Under.
WEB http://grunt.space.swri.edu /nzorgs.htm

soc.veterans Amid the flood of newsletters from anti-imperialists and exposers of military atrocities (remember, this is Usenet), military men reminisce, search for old buddies, and debate the pros and cons of national service. The quality of today's soldiers and military policy are popular topics, and political talk is pretty much all conservative. Not a fast-mov-

ing newsgroup by any means, the group blossoms when someone mentions the name of a military vessel, base, or other touchstone to which members can relate.
USENET soc.veterans

Women

U.S. Servicewomen A basic, low-budget, text-heavy hub honoring U.S. servicewomen. The lack of pictures or graphics is compensated for by the diversity of surprisingly good links. Take a peek at the ground-breaking ceremony at the brand new Women in Military Service Memorial in Washington, D.C. at Arlington National Cemetery. If you're trying to locate a friend in the service, here's where to get the addresses you need. You can also take a look at health information for veterans with a focus on breast cancer, a lesbian veteran mailing list, and a collection of Just for Fun links, the majority of which are to lesbian resources.
WEB http://solnlogic.com/VFHR2 /vfhr-women.html

Women in the Military Is it "this man's army" anymore? Get a quick overview of the role women are playing in today's Army with this modest collection of documents. As an interesting sidelight, you can also review the Tailhook scandal findings here.
WEB http://www.inform.umd.edu:8080 /EdRes/Topic/WomensStudies /GovernmentPolitics/Military

PART II
Dollars & Sense

Dollars & Sense

Business

HOPING TO BE THE NEXT TED TURNER? THE NET CAN GIVE YOU A HEAD START

EVERYONE'S STARTING A BUSINESS THESE DAYS, and for some reason, these entrepreneurs are falling over themselves to help you do the same thing. whether you're a young Silicon Valley adventurer on the lookout for venture capital or a wizened business buccaneer searching for tips to keep your company in the black, you'll find plenty of information and get expert answers to your questions, current economic forecasts, software for planning and book-keeping, and much more. So, if you're looking to patent your new invention, incorporate your baby of a company, or check out the demographics of your local neighborhood, the Web, unlike those pesky tax laws, can help.

 ## INC. ONLINE
WEB http://www.inc.com

The Net offspring of *Inc.* magazine is one of the best friends of small business in cyberspace. Unlike many sites that offer a little help and a lot of hype, *Inc.* Online is a site of real substance. Topic-threaded bulletin boards, interactive worksheets written by experts, and a database of 4,000 articles from *Inc.*, among other features, make this one of the most useful and attractive sites on the Web for the small-business owner.

Starting points

alt.business.misc Mostly a place for advertisements (some hard-sell, some thinly veiled), this newsgroup also includes discussion of products and strategies: Want to know what makes for the most effective calling cards? How to go about importing exotic fruit juices? Many questions and almost as many answers.
USENET alt.business.misc

The Information Economy A professor from Berkeley's School of Information Management has placed his entire course online. Here, eager Net business types will find lots of interesting links, in-depth research on Net commerce, and fun electronic developments. An entire page focuses on the laws of electronic commerce, another of the newest technology in site-traffic measurement. For the serious marketing analyst, there is no better source.
WEB http://www.sims.berkeley.edu/resources/infoecon

Public Relations and Marketing Forum Talk here revolves around how to put the best spin on a product, the pros and cons of electronic seminars, the costs and benefits of traditional advertising, and the growing popularity of online marketing techniques. There's also basic software and a library of articles for downloading. There are longer posts on a variety of subjects, from

---

COFFEE TALK WITH A YAHOO!

Rhonda: How'd you and David get the idea for Yahoo!?

Jerry: We started on the Web in late 1993, but didn't really get into it until early 1994. We got frustrated (trying to find their way around). We had more time on our hands than anybody else. David put a database system together to keep track of sites. We figured other people would have an interest, too. It was pretty humble at the beginning.

Rhonda: When did you realize there was a business here?

Jerry: We never intended it to be a business. We just wanted it to be a product people could use. We were happy running it as a service for people and seeing it grow. But by late November last year (1994), it was severely hampering our human resources. It was hard to keep up with the hardware and software. We approached Stanford University to see if they wanted to take it over or whether we could take it and find our own resources. They were gracious about letting us take it.

Rhonda: Stanford is pretty aggressive about keeping technology invented there. Do you think Stanford regrets not taking Yahoo! over?

Jerry: No. It's not a patentable technology. If they wanted to keep it, it would have been hard. At the time, it was hard to see that Yahoo! would be a real business, and it was too expensive as a service. We still have a lot of ties to Stanford and get a lot of support from them. We owe everything to Stanford.

—from The Idea Café

---

the poster's own resume to the history of humor in speech writing (it apparently started with the Greeks).
COMPUSERVE *go* prsig

Stanford Business School Magazine Reprints from the hard-copy of the Ivy-credentialed quarterly. Recent articles by leading economists and business gurus cover human resources practices in emerging companies, the perils of naive

netsurfing, and the effect of pay on productivity.
WEB http://gsb-www.stanford.edu/sbsm/sbsm.html

Entrepreneurship

The Entrepreneur's Forum Entrepreneurs of all shapes and sizes populate this forum, browsing a menu that offers advice on start-up strategies, contacts, market research, franchising, and more. Take a break at a

message board that attempts to duplicate the atmosphere of the office water cooler.
COMPUSERVE *go* usen

Entrepreneurial Edge Online The publishers of *Entrepreneurial Edge* magazine offer a place for self-starters to look for advice, news, and even venture capital. The Interactive Edge forum lets users send questions to experts in finance and business or post their own responses to the Question of the Week. There's also a large chat area for aspiring Richard Bransons.
WEB http://www.edgeonline.com

Entrepreneurs on the Web The site features a good selection of Internet resources, with a brief

description of each one.
WEB http://www.eotw.com

Idea Café: The Small Business Channel Chat rooms, bulletin boards, news, and features by and for entrepreneurs, angled toward the sensitive, Ben & Jerry's side of the business spectrum.
WEB http://www.IdeaCafe.com

Financing

Entrepreneurial and Business Funding How do you get federal grants? Why is venture capital simpler than it seems? What are sources of state money? The Information USA database, based on the book of the same title, gives you the names

and addresses of the sources of information. Even if you don't have a business, you may enjoy following some of author Matthew Lesko's other tips on where to get videos from Uncle Sam, entrepreneurial advice, and free help for the disabled.
COMPUSERVE *go* ius-8679

FinanceHub For a fee, you can search a database of venture-capital firms eager to invest in startup companies. Free services include articles on venture-capital funding and a wide assortment of business and finance links, including links to the Web pages of a number of venture capital firms.
WEB http://www.FinanceHub.com/welcomef.html

SMALL BUSINESS ADMINISTRATION HOME PAGE
WEB http://www.sbaonline.sba.gov

In recent years, the federal government has been getting out of the business of helping people. One throwback is the Small Business Administration, a support organization for people who are

trying to get a small business off the ground. You'll find listings here of the services this agency offers (including loans for qualifying businesses), FAQs and other information about starting or running a small business, as well as .ZIP files of business shareware and freeware. Some of the advice offered is fairly basic (keep good records and choose your location carefully, for example), but major businesses founder every year by not following it.

Venture Capital Finance Master Resources Page A no-frills hub-site for entrepreneurs hunting for venture capital. Dozens of venture capital firms are listed from A.C.I. to Yozma.
WEB http://www.autonomy.com/venture.htm

Small business

Microsoft Small Business Center Whether you already own a small business or are thinking about starting one, you'll find ample assistance here: a message board analyzes small businesses, home businesses, and consulting opportunities, and a real-time conference room enables you to converse with others about legal issues, marketing and advertising, sales, and women in business. Members of the Service Corps of Retired Executives visit the conference room every Wednesday from 7-11 p.m. (EST) to give wise counsel.
AMERICA ONLINE *keyword* small business

NetMarquee Here is another Net venue for small businesses, with a special emphasis on family-owned operations. It provides a place for small-business executives to share advice on issues such as how to be an effective public speaker and how to keep a family business going through the generations. NetMarquee also hosts a family-business mailing list. As Prince Charles says, "small is beautiful."
WEB http://nmq.com

smallbiznet This service of the Edward Lowe Foundation provides a number of online resources for entrepreneurs. There is a lot of information here, but much of it is available only by $2 download via fax.
WEB http://www.lowe.org

SOHO Central Not a trendy neighborhood, but "Small Office/Home Office," this site has great resources for people who telecommute or run a business from their homes. Covered topics include technology, taxes, raising capital, and home-business ideas. Sponsored by the Home Office Association of America, it will set you up with lots of perks and a home page for a fee.
WEB http://www.hoaa.com

Your Business AOL's area for small business resources, with special forums and databases for a range of industries. A special section covers businesses on the World Wide Web. The area also hosts interactive chats with business and financial experts. At the Web Diner, you can get advice for putting up a free 2 MB home page.
AMERICA ONLINE *keyword* Your Business

Your Company A virtual magazine created by the people at Time Inc. for small-business owners. Recent topics have included how to reel in giant firms as business partners, how to pick the best laser printer for your small office,

and how to find a trustworthy overseas distributor for your products.
WEB http://pathfinder.com/money/yourco

Accounting

AuditNet A monster list of Web sites, mailing lists, and gophers devoted to the people who count the money.
WEB http://www.unf.edu/students/jmayer/arl.html

Rutgers Accounting Web A major Internet hub for accountants, auditors, and financial managers. Resources include professional associations, courses, mailing lists.
WEB http://www.rutgers.edu/Accounting/raw.htm

Bankruptcy

The Bankruptcy Lawfinder Should you file Chapter 7 or Chapter 11? This site has lots of links, including recent legal decisions involving bankruptcy, the full text of laws, and pending legislation, all courtesy of a law firm. If you can decipher the abundance of legal info, you should consider starting your own practice.
WEB http://www.tiac.net/users/agin/blawfind.html

InterNet Bankruptcy Library Much of this information seems designed for lawyers and others who stand to benefit from the woes of what are euphemistically referred to as "troubled companies." One

useful resource is a directory of bankruptcy experts in such fields as public relations, law, and accounting. Other options at this library are news stories and background information on public and private companies that have gone under.
WEB http://bankrupt.com

Incorporation

The Company Corporation Have an idea that just can't wait? Incorporate your business online in 48 hours, for just $45 plus filing fees. In addition to the Company Corp.'s services, this page offers general information on the whys and wherefores of incorporation, including 16 reasons to incorporate in Delaware.
WEB http://www.incorporate.com/tcc

Corporate Agents, Inc Besides answering common incorpora-

tion questions, Corporate Agents, Inc. can incorporate your business in all 50 states or anywhere in the world—for a fee. Acting from your online instructions, Corporate Agents, Inc. will incorporate you in Delaware for $85 in 24 to 48 hours, including filing fees.
WEB http://www.corporate.com

List of Registered Agents You may have to get offline and use a phone or fax, but you can get incorporated in Delaware—or anywhere—quickly and cheaply through one of the hundreds of incorporation agents listed on this Delaware-based page.
WEB http://www.inet.net/deldoc /agents.html

Legal issues

Advertising Law Is it legal to advertise that your company

sells "the best damn widgets on the planet?" The short answer is "it depends." The widgets slogan might be legally categorized as "puffery," which means you might be able to get away with it, depending on the context of the ad. Find out the answers to other such questions with this collection of material from the government, the courts, and other sources on the legal guidelines and boundaries for advertising claims.
WEB http://www.webcom.com /~lewrose/home.html

Center for Corporate Law Located at the University of Cincinnati, the recently established Center for Corporate Law includes the full text of the most important corporate laws enacted since the Crash of '29: the Securities Acts of 1933 and 1934, the Public Utilities Holding Company Act of 1935, the Trust

U.S. Business Adviser

WEB http://www.business.gov

Advertising itself as the "one-stop electronic link to government for business," the U.S. Business Advisor lives up to its name. This site links to information about taxes, exports, postage, the Federal Communications Commission, and other business-related arms of the federal government. How-tos range from how to get a passport to how to make your building compliant with asbestos safety rules.

Indenture Act of 1939, and the Securities Investor Protection Act of 1970.
WEB http://www.law.uc.edu/CCL

Legal Research Center These days you can't swing an accountant without breaking a tax law. Quick and easy access to databases of more than 750 law journals, as well as publications and studies from the worlds of criminal justice, criminology, and law enforcement. So what does all this have to do with taxes? Well, many of the publications—including *Tax Notes Today*—address recent legislative, regulatory, judicial, and policy developments in the area of federal taxation.
COMPUSERVE *go* las $

SEC's Small Business Information The Securities and Exchange Commission isn't just for the big guns. Although most of its regulations protect investors of larger public companies, there are also some regulations to protect investors of small, privately-owned businesses. This site also includes information on pending changes in regulations pertinent to small businesses.
WEB http://www.sec.gov/smbusl.htm

Uniform Commercial Code Whether you're selling furs or leasing Fords, you must obey the provisions of the Uniform Commercial Code. Articles 1-9 of this imposing document are on display in a hypertext document at Cornell University

Got a great idea? Get the ball rolling
http://www.spo.eds.com/patent.html

Law School. Learn about bills of lading, bulk transfers, and chattel paper.
WEB http://www.law.cornell.edu/ucc/ucc.table.html

Virtual Library: Law The Indiana University School of Law presents this large alphabetical hotlist of legal sites, with a short description of each.
WEB http://www.law.indiana.edu/law/lawindex.html

Patents & trademarks

Patent FAQ One of the best basic guides to the patent process available online, with chapters on career opportunities for the inventor, the history of the patent process, the necessity of a patent, the cost of a patent, and tips for the inventor.
WEB http://www.sccsi.com/DaVinci/patentfaq.html

Shadow Patent Office A searchable database of all U.S. patents issued since 1972,

updated weekly with new entries. Full access costs a fee, but a limited free search can locate patents dated 1993 and later. Input a number, and the database will find other patents similar to that item. The search engine also accepts descriptions in plain English, such as "gadget to keep the potato chips from getting stale."
WEB http://www.spo.eds.com/patent.html

Trademarkscan Combining federal and state databases, Trademarkscan indexes well over a million registered trademarks. Enter a keyword, and for $10 the service will return five trademark names containing the word. The retrieval is a bit slow, but it provides full reports on topics such as international and U.S. product classifications, serial numbers, filing dates, orginal applicants, and filing correspondents. Be warned: Even if a trademark is not listed in this database, it

may still be a common-law trademark currently controlled by a business or individual.
COMPUSERVE *go* trd $

U.S. Patent and Trademark Office

The official scoop from the government on how to patent your new mousetrap. It runs from the basics of the patent and trademark routine to the specifics of putting together a patent application, including downloadable forms in Acrobat format. There are links to the full text of the Patent Act and other statutes. A patent database, which includes all patents from 1976 on, is also featured.
WEB http://www.uspto.gov

Demographics

American Demographics Browse the current issue of *American*

Demographics magazine, search an archive of previous issues by keyword (the archive holds articles from the past year), download a data table of America's Hottest Markets, or pick up details on how to subscribe to the offline version of this demographics magazine. There's a lot of information here, but it's a surprisingly clumsy and low-tech site for a high-tech industry.
WEB http://www.marketingtools.com

Business Demographics If you're thinking of opening a supermarket in northern Wyoming, or selling office equipment in Maine, you'll probably want to know all about the business conditions—not only how many competing businesses there are, but how many people they employ, and how they

compare to other industries and services. This service offers reports by ZIP code, county, state, metropolitan statistical area, Arbitron TV Market, or Nielsen TV Market, and furnishes basic statistical information on utilities, retail, wholesale, and financial businesses.
COMPUSERVE *go* busdem $

FIND/SVP This fee-based service offers demographic/industry reports online. Browse hundreds of reports on groups ranging from African Americans to the college market to the affluent. The service also collects information on hundreds of industries, including manufacturing, chemicals, and the Internet. Read descriptions of the reports and, if interested, purchase them online. Prices

BIG YELLOW

WEB http://www.bigyellow.com

Find all the pizza parlors in Brooklyn, all the jazz clubs in New Orleans, or every taxidermist in Montana (all 110 of them). This nifty site, courtesy of **NYNEX**, gives you free access to a nationwide yellow pages directory containing 16 million entries. Searches are easy and fast. Narrow your search by specifying area codes or streets. The Web Business Guide even offers a professionally executed guide to getting your new business on the Internet.

DILBERT FIRED! STARTS NEW BIZ

Email interview of Scott Adams by *Inc.*

Inc.: What has it been like to go from being an employee to an *Inc.*-type guy who owns his own business?

Adams: It was unsettling at first. I had to build a little cardboard fort at home to wean myself away from the security of the cubicle I had left behind. But since I've gotten used to the change in physical surroundings, it's been great. I hardly ever have to deal with idiots. I never do status reports or have United Way meetings or form task forces. I never reengineer my core processes or brainstorm quality initiatives. Almost everything I do is useful. The only downside is that I end up working ridiculously long hours.

Inc.: Nobody spends all day doing useful things. Surely you must have already begun dreaming up policies, rules, dress codes, and the like.

Adams: My dress code is mandatory pajamas until 10 a.m. My cats hate it. You should see them struggle when I try to get them up to code. Here are some of my other rules: (1) I have a "no-talk zone" from 6 a.m. to 8 a.m., when I do the majority of my creative work. (2) I will not pose for photographers while wearing a Dilbert-like necktie. They have to think of something more creative. (3) I will not conduct interviews over email.

—from Inc. Online

for these studies vary widely (anywhere from $10 to $2,000).
WEB http://www.findsvp.com

Neighborhood Demographics What do you want to know about a neighborhood before you open a business there? Population breakdowns by age, race, family status, occupation, and income? The age of the buildings? Reports, which can be broken down by ZIP code, are $10 each.
COMPUSERVE *go* neighbor $

State-County Demographics Basic census information by state, county, or neighborhood (ZIP code), as well as special neighborhood reports on civic and leisure activities. The reports sell for a flat fee of $10 each.
COMPUSERVE *go* state $

Supersite Demographics You can select any combination of ZIP codes, counties, and states for up to 50 geographic areas, and retrieve detailed demographic data consolidated into a single report. Ideal for the businessperson who wants to explore the profitability of a number of different neighborhoods. Reports cost about $45 per category; more extensive reports, with data on socioeconomic status, racial background, and age breakdown, are more expensive.
COMPUSERVE *go* supersite $

Software

Classifieds Software Library If you've just placed an ad on a classified board and expect a flood of responses, you may want to pick up some software to manage the influx. Packed with shipping and tracking software, the library has an assortment of postal calculators, ZIP code databases, invoice generators, and address managers for Mac and PC owners.
AMERICA ONLINE *keyword* classifieds Software Library

Humor

The Dilbert Zone Who's the symbol of business in the 1990s? Forget Ted Turner and Bill Gates. If you work in an office, you know that Dilbert is the man. For seven years, Scott Adams's cartoon has entertained hapless paper pushers with his view of the life within corporate America. At this official page, you'll find information about Adams, the latest comic, downloadable Dilbert Zone icons.
WEB http://www.unitedmedia.com /comics/dilbert

Investment

INDUSTRIAL REVOLUTION: TIME = MONEY
ONLINE REVOLUTION: INFORMATION = MONEY

HOPING TO BE THE NEXT Warren Buffet? Now, you too can get instantaneous and constant quotes, as well as the latest news and research, whether it's coming from New York, London, Hong Kong, or Tokyo. The rapid and universal dissemination of data is the very stuff of which financial markets are made, and it's only natural that they should gradually merge with the substance of the Net. So whether you're in it for your living, your nest egg, or your weekly adrenaline rush, the Net is the fastest and cheapest way to feel the pulse of markets the world over. And checking stock quotes is just the beginning. The world of investments has gone online, and it neither can nor ever will go back.

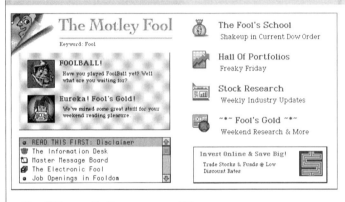

THE MOTLEY FOOL

AMERICA ONLINE *keyword* fool

Friendly, down-to-earth investment advice delivered with a bad case of Dadaist hiccups. For instance, in this forum "foolish" is the greatest honorific for an insight or money-making stock trade. The hard-working staff has created what some consider to be the finest online corrective to the macho mumbo-jumbo that characterizes most stock tip services. Highlights include the Novice Investor area, site of a small library of background reading for new investors; a Monthly Novice Quiz; and a special message board area where no question goes unanswered—no matter how foolish. Then, there's the Fool Portfolio, a fully-managed, real-money, online portfolio. Unlike most show portfolios, "intentions to buy, sell, or sell short a stock are announced the night before doing so." This makes it possible to follow right along with your own investments, rather than learn at the end of the day that you missed getting in on a rally or out of a crash.

Investment DOLLARS & SENSE

Investment basics

AAII Online Sponsored by the nonprofit American Association of Individual Investors and featuring hundreds of articles on investing basics. Articles are organized in folders on the forum's opening screen (International Investments, Insurance, Managing Your Portfolio, etc.); the collection can be searched via an icon at the bottom of the forum. See the Reference Library for suggested financial reading, names of brokers, investment terms, and the like. The Reference Shelf contains cut-to-the-bone surveys of software, services, and discount brokers for computerized investing. The Software Library stores a growing archive of mostly public domain programs for managing investments, and is divided into such categories as Technical Analysis, Portfolio Management, and Fundamental Analysis. Stock Selection and Computerized Investing dominate the AAII Message Area, but there are also busy threads on such subjects as dealing with brokers.
AMERICA ONLINE *keyword* aaii

E*Trade Stock Market Game Ever wonder what it would be like to have $100,000 to play the market? With E*Trade's market game, you can dabble in stocks and options just like the big boys. The E*Trade program uses actual market data and prices to determine your success or failure over the

Where Wall St. and Main St. intersect
http://www.better-investing.org

course of four weeks, and keeps track of commission costs for extra-realistic profit and loss calculation. Join this month's game to compete against other CompuServe subscribers, and try to win the monthly $50 cash prize.
COMPUSERVE *go* etgame

eINVEST A popular mailing list for non-experts, devoted to discussions of investment strategies and research methods. The list is chaired by Joseph Friedman, professor of economics and finance at Temple University.
EMAIL listserv@vm.temple.edu ✍
Type in message body: **SUB E_INVEST** ⟨your full name⟩

Fidelity Investments With more than ten million customers served, Fidelity Investments is the McDonald's of mutual funds. Its Web site is appropriately elaborate and informative, even for investors who aren't

Fidelity customers. It covers the basics of investment, with a retirement-planning FAQ, mutual-funds info, and articles addressing the investment options for people in specific situations, such as newlyweds or single mothers. An interactive checklist lets you find out what kind of saver you are, and their snappy, animated magazine, *@82DEV*, keeps you up to date on developing investment issues. Of course, there's plenty of information on Fidelity's range of mutual funds, including downloadable prospecti and daily price updates. Don't forget to enter the Guess the Dow contest.
AMERICA ONLINE *keyword* Fidelity
WEB http://wwwl.fid-inv.com

FinWEB This collection of links is heavily weighted on the academic side of economics—journals and such—but there's a healthy selection of connections to more general-interest

sites, such as stock-quote services, economic databases, and online investment houses.
WEB http://www.finweb.com

The Investment FAQ The mammoth Investment FAQ offers a concise introduction to investment in the electronic age: everything you always wanted to know about stocks, bonds, options, mutuals, brokers, and markets, but didn't know what to click on.
URL ftp://rtfm.mit.edu/pub/usenet-by-group/misc.answers/investment-faq
WEB http://www.cis.ohio-state.edu/hypertext/faq/usenet/investment-faq/general/top.html

Investment/Financial Services Learn where to find valuable information (primarily addresses and phone numbers

of contact organizations) on an extensive number of financial topics, including stocks, bonds, and commodities.
COMPUSERVE *go* ius-506I

InvestorWEB Beginning Investors Page Maintained by a consulting company in Illinois, InvestorWEB, is basically a file of articles by experts and financial journalists on such topics as "Individual Stock Investing for the Small Investor." There's nothing elaborate or innovative about this resource, but it does give you the straight dope with no hassles.
WEB http://www.investorweb.com/begin.htm

National Association of Investors Corporation "Where Wall Street

and Main Street meet" is the slogan of this organization, which encourages individual investors to keep educating themselves about the markets and join investment clubs. There's not much here for non-members, but you don't have to be a member to join the investment-club electronic-mailing list, which hosts discussions on stock-selection strategies.
WEB http://www.better-investing.org

nVESTOR You can actually make money out of this simulation run by the League of American Investors—if you choose to pay a monthly fee. If not, all the money involved is strictly virtual. When you sign up to participate, you're given a simulated portfolio with

BARRON'S

WEB http://www.barrons.com

A product of Dow Jones & Co., publishers of the *Wall Street Journal*, this weekly financial newspaper has taken an ambitious approach to online journalism. Their Web site combines the primary content of the print mag—investment analysis and data, delivered in *Barron's* characteristically

blunt, straightforward style and aimed at individual investors—with daily performance updates and a searchable archive of back issues. You'll also find links to various corporate sites, and dossiers on all the companies, equities and mutual funds mentioned in the articles sections, as well as about I5,000 others.

HIGH ANXIETIES

There are many types of investment styles. We will attempt to outline a few of the choices and decisions here. To determine your investment style, you need to ask yourself one question. CAN YOU SLEEP AT NIGHT? Is the type of investing you are doing causing you to think about it when you wake up in the middle of the night?

Do you worry about what will happen if you make a bad decision? Which style or combination best suits your inner nature, your true self? A bit of philosophical self-reflection here is a valuable exercise for an investor. Find a guru.

—from InvestorWEB Beginning Investors Page

"shares" in companies that are sponsoring the contest. You can sell these right away if you want; stay with them and the companies will send you annual reports and other propaganda so that you can learn more about them.
WEB http://www2.investorsleague.com/investorsleague

Securities Screening If you know what kind of investments you want to make but don't know where to find them, this will help you narrow the field. Specify your needs in any of

ten different categories (price, earnings, dividends, risk, capitalization, highs and lows, exchange, and industry), and the service will find the appropriate securities.
COMPUSERVE *go* screen

U.S. Securities & Exchange Commission: What Every Investor Should Know The graphics may be unattractive, but at least you know you can trust the source. The U.S. Securities and Exchange Commission is responsible for enforcing laws governing financial markets, so their tips on avoiding investment fraud carry a lot of weight. The firm, avuncular advice from Uncle Sam is basic but sound, and includes an introduction to mutual funds, advice on how to choose an investment firm, and what to do if you have a dispute with your broker.
WEB http://www.sec.gov/invkhome.htm

Investment news

Bloomberg Personal Market pros pay more than $1,000 a month to get a Bloomberg news and data terminal on their desks. Bloomberg's site brings a generous sampling of their services to your desk for free. Summaries of the top business stories are updated every hour, and there are entire special categories on World Markets and Financial Analysis (for a downer, check out the Expected Future Education Cost Calculator). But check under Bloomberg News for

coverage of mutual funds and an archive of daily and weekly columns on various industries and world regions. Market reports from news bureaus around the world are also included.
WEB http://www.bloomberg.com

Briefing.com—Live Market Insight This is the kind of service that really narrows the information-flow gap between the investment professionals and the little guys. Briefing provides minute-to-minute coverage of financial markets, letting you know what people on the trading floors are talking about. For example, the service will let you know what Microsoft's newest earnings report says, what investors are saying about it, how the stock's reacting, and where it could go from there, with updates throughout the day. The format is nothing fancy, but with valuable "live" data and information like this, it doesn't matter.
WEB http://www.briefing.com

CNNfn There's nothing terribly deep about this site, but it's great for a quick fix of business news. Besides text versions of broadcast stories, about a page long, there are news and market reports from Reuters and Knight-Ridder. Top stories on the front page are updated regularly, along with a graph showing today's fluctuations in the Dow. The Speak Up and Interact sections let you submit your thoughts on a topic of the day, and read what others have

to say. Check out Grapevine for a selection of quirky and fun business stories. Despite its breezy, stylish feel, this site has an enormous amount of information in it, all in bite-sized pieces.
WEB http://cnnfn.com

Dow Jones Clipping, Tracking & Alert Services Dow Jones, the infinitely respectable business information provider, offers two different customizable news delivery services. DowVision, the more popular option, puts current investment news data on your desktop and on the desktop of everybody in your company, drawn from the major sources of financial news (you know—the *Wall Street Journal*, the *Financial Times*). The data are tailored to your individual information needs, according to a profile that you fill out that covers the companies, issues, markets, industries, and people that you need to keep track of. You can also subscribe to DowJones CustomClips, which culls articles from more than 1,600 trade and industry publications, chooses the ones dealing with topics that are relevant to your own needs, and distributes them to different computers on whatever network you happen to be running.
WEB http://bis.dowjones.com/clipping/index.html

Dow Jones Investor Network Dow Jones offers sample interviews with corporate executives and investment analysts, taken from

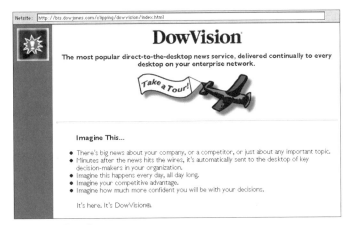

How now cash cow?
http://bis.dowjones.com/clipping/index.html

its pricey desktop video service for professional investors. Is Donald Trump thoroughly washed-up? Hear the answer from the man himself, in an audio-on-demand interview in RealAudio format. There's an archive of past interviews, many with text transcripts and QuickTime video clips, as well as reporting on breaking stories and corporate presentations.
WEB http://www.djin.com

Executive News Service With access to clips from the *Washington Post* and major wire services (AP, UPI, Reuters), this service provides general business news as well as news sorted by company ticker symbol. In addition, it offers a few perks—for instance, sorting stories into folders for later perusal.
COMPUSERVE *go* ens $

Fortune Although it's basically an advertisement for the magazine, the order of the day on

Fortune's garish Web site is light financial news, with a few human-interest details thrown in: You can also access an archive of special issues of Fortune, with themes like "Pacific Rim," and "The Global 500." The magazine takes a stab at multimedia with a daily financial and business-news update via RealAudio. Download the famous Fortune 500 list in an Excel spreadsheet.
WEB http://pathfinder.com/fortune

Investor's Business Daily *IBD*'s brand of business journalism is targeted a bit more at individual investors than its competitor, the *Wall Street Journal*. The newspaper's Web site is clearly organized, but you won't find anything here that isn't in the daily paper: no market updates during the day. *IBD*'s offerings on AOL are a bit more substantial and are supplemented by lively message boards. Check out the discussions and rumor-swap-

ping on individual stocks.
WEB http://ibd.ensemble.com
AMERICA ONLINE *keyword* IBD

UK Newspaper Library If you
find yourself obsessed with
U.K. news, fretting over the
price of petrol or the FTSE
100, you might want to put
your mind at ease by reading
through the British press.
Contains searchable full-text
versions of the *Daily
Telegraph*, the *Financial Times*,
the *Guardian*, the *Observer*,
the *Independent*, and the
European.
COMPUSERVE *go* ukpapers $

**Wall Street Journal Interactive
Edition** The bible of Wall Street
sets new standards for newspapers on the Web with an
entirely natural extension of the
print version, right down to the
handsome design and clear layout. Unlike the dead-tree version of the *Journal*, this one
never stops changing. What's
News, the column on the left
side of the screen, gives quick
summaries of the day's business activity, with links to full
stories. The right side offers
links to special features and
lengthier articles from the
morning's paper. A customizable search function lets you
create your own daily paper.
Alas, all this splendor is no
longer free, unless of course
you've signed on with
Microsoft Explorer's assault
on Netscape in the ongoing
browser war: However, free
trial subscriptions are available.
WEB http://update.wsj.com

Investment advice

Decision Point Daily analysis on
150 stocks, weekly charts on a
variety of stocks, popular proprietary market indicators, and
ample regular market commentary. To those uninitiated into
the finer points of financial
analysis, the reports of moderator Carl Swenlin might seem a
bit labyrinthine. Hang in there,
though, and soon you'll be
talking about apparent and
actual bottoms forming on the
"Short-Term Volume Oscilla-
tor." Decision Point comes to
life with a busy message-based
forum (fundamentalists and
techies trading "I-told-you-
so"s), a real-time chat conference area, and a mid-sized
library of charts and other data.
Who knows, you might even
enjoy Carl's conservative
political postscripts.
AMERICA ONLINE *keyword* dp

**Frank Armstrong's Investment
Strategies for the 21st Century**
Armstrong, a portfolio manager
and investment counselor, presents a number of investment
ideas in a clear, clever style,
complete with diagrams and
charts. Topics include assessing risks, allocating assets, and
selecting mutual funds.
WEB http://gnn.com/gnn/meta/finance
/feat/21st

Investor's Network Combines
chatroom/newsgroup-style bull
sessions with hard financial
data resources and features-
style analytical articles. It's a
truly enormous resource, with

forums, statistics, and advice
on a dizzying array of topics,
and they're adding more. If you
can find your way around,
you'll find what you need. For
general-interest investing
advice, drop in on the Investing Today Message Board,
hosted by Mike McCarthy.
Check out the New Guru
Review area for advice from
investment advisors still trying
to establish themselves.
AMERICA ONLINE *keyword* investors

Investors' Forum Whether you
dabble in stocks and bonds or
pour tens of thousands annually into commodities and
mutual funds, there's sure to
be a discussion tailored to your
needs. Topics on the message
boards range from Stocks/The
Market to Options Trading to
Newsletters/Theories. The
forum also offers real-time
conferences with various
financial experts, a wide range
of financial software for downloading, and an extensive
library that archives newsletters and introductory documents.
COMPUSERVE *go* invforum

misc.invest Examines general
investment topics ranging from
stocks and bonds to mutual
funds to the vagaries of e-trade.
If you want to discuss retirement planning or complain
about the mistreatment of the
tobacco industry—"Congress
and the anti-smoking lobby are
driving the tobacco industry
out of business in the U.S."—
put your two cents in, and see

what they yield. A few committed newsgroup participants upload market reports—the same info that you're paying for on other services.
USENET misc.invest

National Association of Investors Corporation Forum The National Association of Investors Corporation is a friendly nonprofit organization that promotes better investing through investor education and self development. In other words, it caters to people looking to invest responsibly as a means to long-term stability, not to get rich quick. As a result, the forum features down-to-earth talk about down-to-earth matters—for example, investing for col-

lege funds. Forum members recommend stocks, and discuss their picks in software and opinions on other financial matters.
COMPUSERVE *go* naic

Nest Egg The investment advice magazine *Nest Egg* perpetuates its "lifestyles of the rich and famous" attitude online with articles about real estate, living abroad, and glamorous golf getaways. But there's serious content here as well: a wealth of interesting articles from their publication, including a column on Web finance, and highly useful links to well-respected names "on the street," such as a Smith Barney Wall Street Watch, news from

the editors of *Investment Dealers Digest*, and Dow Jones performance information. *Nest Egg* appeals to those who both have (or want) money and are serious about managing it.
WEB http://nestegg.iddis.com

Worth Online A companion forum to the financial magazine —"the place to find financial intelligence"—*Worth* Online includes both articles from the magazine and exclusive online features and news items, as well as daily articles (Mutual Fund Friday! and so on) by financial celebrities like Peter Lynch, market snapshots, and fairly casual postings from readers, often with an offbeat spin—for instance, how to

INVESTORAMA
WEB http://www.investorama.com

Investorama is a surprisingly stylish site put together by Douglas Gerlach, a private investor and financial journalist. He gives short descriptions of many of the 2,163 links he lists, which is an improvement over most collections of investment links. Investorama covers most of the major top-

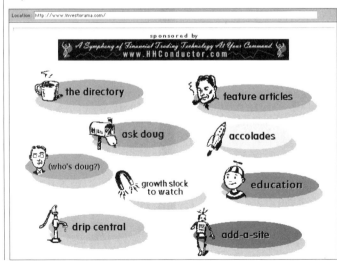

ics—taxes, technical analysis, real estate—and it also includes a stock pick of the week, an advice column, and Gerlach's feature articles, which describe stock-selection techniques and offer plenty of examples. Check out the section on investment mailing lists—they can often be hard to track down on your own. This is a great resource for individual investors exploring the Internet.

choose a choice lobster.
AMERICA ONLINE *keyword* Worth

Research

Business Wire: Company News on the Net Business Wire allows you to search for the latest press releases issued by its customers, organized by company name. Links to corporate Web sites are also included, where appropriate. Companies obviously try to put the best possible spin on things in press releases, so for a more complete (if jargon-laden) account of what's going on, check corporate filings in the Securities & Exchange Commission's EDGAR database.
WEB http://www.businesswire.com/cnn

" Find exchange rates for more obscure currencies, from Afghanistan to Zimbabwe. "

European Company Library This service supplies address, personnel, and financial information on more than two million European companies, as well as updates on business-related European Community legislation, all culled from several worldwide business databases.
COMPUSERVE *go* eurolib $

Industry.Net Check out Industry.Net Report for news and corporate press releases organized by field: business, manufacturing, and computing. It's also searchable by company name, product, and location. In the Newsroom, daily features track breaking stories and developing trends. A RealAudio clip of the day's news is also available.
WEB http://www.industry.net

PR Newswire: Company News On Call A wire service that specializes in rapidly distributing press releases from public and private companies to the news media. Companies often make major announcements and release their earnings reports through PR Newswire and/or Business Wire, a competing service. PR Newswire's Web site lets you look up press releases filed by company name.
WEB http://www.prnewswire.com/cnoc.html

S&P Online Distills the recent business histories of more than 5,000 companies to bring you essential information, including recent market activity, dividend information, product line summaries, and earnings estimates. Info is believed to be accurate, but not guaranteed.
COMPUSERVE *go* s&p $

The economy

Bloomberg: Key Cross Currency Rates A nifty table of 11 major currencies, cross-referenced

and updated regularly. Elsewhere on the site, find rates for more obscure currencies, from Afghanistan to Zimbabwe.
WEB http://www.bloomberg.com/cgi-bin/tdisp.sh?markets/fxc.html

Bureau of Economic Analysis Data & Methodology These are the friendly folks charged with keeping an objective eye on the state of the national economy—the Nation's Accountants, they call themselves. The Bureau provides all kinds of tables and charts on the regional, national, and international scale, including quarterly gross-domestic product figures, savings and consumption, and corporate profits.
WEB http://www.bea.doc.gov/bea/beadata.html

Dr. Ed Yardeni's Econimics Network Dr. Ed, the chief economist of Deutsche Morgan Grenfell, a major investment bank, whips up loads of charts to help you track every wiggle in the economic indicators, including interest rates, inflation, and exchange rates, all out of the goodness of his heart. And for the good PR. Most of the big, handsome charts are in Adobe Acrobat format—the applications are free and downloadable. Check out the Best Charts of the Month wrap-up for some interesting analyses, as well as the weekly Economic Analysis, Economic Briefing, and Economic Indicators.
WEB http://www.webcom.com/~yardeni/economic.html

Economic Democracy Information Network Devoted to delivering information that has an impact on economics and business but doesn't often show up in the business pages, EDIN offers dozens of documents on human rights, education and training, political organization, labor organization, health care, race, and the environment. EDIN is invaluable as a source of "alternative" economics and business information—news about Internet sites in Cuba, for instance.
URL gopher://garnet.berkeley.edu

STAT-USA The Commerce Department comes to the Web with a site that promises quick access to the latest government economic data—Foreign Government Tenders, Agricultural Trade Leads, Treasury Yield Curve Rates. Unfortunately, you'll have to pay for it; an individual subscription is $50 per quarter or $150 for a full year.
WEB http://www.stat-usa.gov

Summaries of Current Economic Conditions Straight from the Economics Bulletin Board, which is a general clearinghouse for economic stats about the U.S., overseen by the Department of Commerce's Office of Business Analysis. This gopher, just one among many, gives you a composite index of 11 leading economic indicators, as well as summaries of other financial and economic factors—including housing starts, personal income, producer prices, and durable goods orders.
URL gopher://una.hh.lib.umich.edu:70 /II/ebb/summaries

World Bank Public Information Center (PIC) Yes, it's the U.N. piggy bank. Includes national economic reports, environmental assessments and projections, and explanations of new World Bank Projects.
WEB http://www.worldbank.org
URL gopher://gopher.worldbank.org

Stocks

American Stock Exchange This competitor to the New York Stock Exchange provides a

Hoover's Business Profiles

AMERICA ONLINE *keyword* hoover • COMPUSERVE *go* hoover
• WEB http://www.hoovers.com

Search the full text of *Hoover's Handbook* for detailed profiles of nearly 2,000 of the largest and fastest-growing public and private companies in the U.S. and the world. Profiles are exhaustive, with info that includes assets, sales figures, number of employees, CEO and CFO salaries, and company products. The profiles also feature long and gossipy descriptions of a company's history and culture; you can use them to get the location of a company, its goals and ongoing programs, its recent stock prices, plus phone, address, and fax information. It's the ideal way to get to know the market, one company at a time. Note: To search the database on the Web, you have to subscribe at a cost of $9.95 per month.

summary of market activity every trading day at about 6 p.m., including a rundown of the most active issues and the greatest advancers and decliners. Check out a graph of the Inter@ctive Week Internet Index, tracking a cross-section of companies involved in building cyberspace. Unfortunately, real-time stock quotes aren't provided, since the Exchange makes money selling quote feeds to other information distributors. Every Monday the Amex Trendline appears: a summary of domestic and international markets—currency rates, important commodity rates—in one neat table. The Amex Newsmaker Exchange is a transcript of a moderated conference call between a group of financial journalists and a financial luminary—Robert Reich was a recent guest.
WEB http://www.amex.com

Charles Schwab Schwab's portfolio management service keeps track of your holdings, automatically downloading price information and updating portfolio positions every time you connect. Issues can be organized by type, market value, yield, or gain and loss. In addition to graphing and formatting portfolio reports, the program can export its data to Excel, Lotus, and Quicken, and reports can be saved in several formats. If you want to speculate a bit, the program can also track hypothetical holdings.
WEB http://www.schwab.com

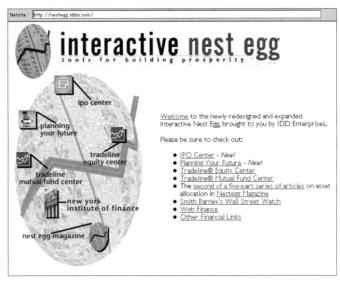

Hoping to lay a golden egg?
http://nestegg.iddis.com

Closing Bell This service presents itself not as the trader's tool with the fastest real-time quotes, but rather as the email alternative to the newspaper where John Q. Investor can track his five shares of IBM. What you get is a daily email containing closing prices and news on a personalized portfolio of market indexes, mutual funds and securities from the three major U.S. exchanges. You'll also get a daily sample report with news briefs on selected companies. The free two-week trial will undoubtedly appeal to the small investors that make up Closing Bell's market.
WEB http://www.merc.com/cbell2.html

Current Quotes Get prices for NYSE, AMEX, and NASDAQ issues, but be warned: Delays of "at least 15 minutes"

can stretch up to 90 minutes or even half a day. Quotes are listed by symbol only, and contain 52-week highs and lows, yield, and P/E ratio. AOL's portfolio tracking tools can watch up to 100 investments, listing issues alongside their purchase price and current price and calculating the net gain or loss.
AMERICA ONLINE *keyword* quotes

Dow Jones News/Retrieval Let the grand old man of business info providers turn your computer into a stock ticker. Dow Jones News/Retrieval—Private Investor Edition offers market trading prices for stocks from the New York, American, Pacific, and Chicago exchanges, and the NASDAQ National Market and small-cap issues. You can also get access to one of the largest historical

pricing databases available, with historical quotes and volume information on actively traded NYSE, AMEX, NASDAQ, and OTC securities. A screening feature lets subscribers select stocks, and the data-retrieval options allow users to either plot onscreen charts or download the quotes to most types of offline charting software.
WEB http://bis.dowjones.com

Holt Stock Report A daily compilation of market activity, including 29 indexes and averages, and the most actively traded stocks and changes in foreign currency. Of special interest to short-term traders is the list of growth stocks with sudden increases in trading volume. You can have the Holt Report sent to you via email; it also has its own gopher site, and it appears daily on the misc.invest newsgroup, as well as in the eINVEST mailing list.
WEB http://207.67.198.21/holt
URL gopher://wuecon.wustl.edu:671/11/holt

Latest Market Action A component of CompuServe's Personal Finance Center, this column provides continuous updates of stock prices, along with nifty graphs of the Dow Jones Industrials, the American and Nasdaq exchanges, and the S&P 500.
COMPUSERVE *go* finance

NetInvestor Leading with their "Best on the Net" award, this online brokerage follows up its kudos with an emphasis on cheapness and control. The word "free" is scattered all over the site, always in bold type (a potent attraction even when not technically true—these "free" services come with a fee-based package). NetInvestor also focuses on the personal access of Net investing—portraying its cash management (checking, Visa, money markets), financial news, and brokerage services as the very best way to keep a 24-hour watch on matters that once resided exclusively in the hands of unknown Wall Street professionals. Real-time quotes are available only to active accounts.
WEB http://pawws.com/tni

Quote.com This commercial service will provide, at no charge, up to five quotes a day on U.S. stocks and mutual funds. A basic subscription ($9.95 a month) gets you up to 200 quotes a day, unlimited closing quotes, and emailed updates and price alerts. Keep adding services, including real-time news feeds and historical data, and your home PC will soon have as much market info as the trading terminals of the Wall Street pros. Just hope your trading profits offset your subscription fees.
WEB http://www.quote.com

The Stock Room Clear, fast, historical graphs of all major U.S. stock indexes, plus selected foreign indexes, bonds, commodities, and interest rates, updated daily. Special pages compare the performance of Fidelity's sector-specific funds to the S&P 500 index. A free personalized stock quote email service is provided. This self-described "neat little free service" was created by a "molecular biologist who likes to mess around with stocks."
WEB http://loft-gw.zone.org/jason/stock_room.html

Online brokers

AGS Financial Services AGS has set itself the difficult task of playing both the small investor's advocate and insider's information source. A section titled "What discount brokers don't want you to know" tells amateurs how to avoid large fees (by using AGS, of course). But the group that just placed itself squarely on the side of the consumer follows up with a "for stockbrokers only" description of how to get the "best payout package in the industry." Aside from this mixed message, AGS does serve up some perks—a weekly $10 contest, and free trade for first-timers with accounts over $25,000. All in all AGS's most potent lure is probably its "one price" brokerage fee, though it gets lost somewhere in the translation.
WEB http://ags-financial-services.com

e.Schwab Online Investing An impressively comprehensive investment services package including the ability to trade stocks, mutual funds, bonds,

Are you in the industry?
http://www.industry.net

and options through Schwab's own linkup. You can issue just about any instruction you would leave with a live broker—orders to buy or sell, short, switch, limit or stop, day or good-till-canceled, and change or cancel (open orders can be revised until executed)—for a low commission rate: $29.95 on stock trades up to 1,000 shares. The service also offers extensive portfolio management features and research facilities, including real-time quotes during market hours, and dividend histories.
WEB http://www.eschwab.com

E*Trade One of the many discount brokers, the beginner-friendly E*Trade site features a trading demo that lets you try out their system, access stock quotes, and, for those not quite ready to take the plunge and invest real money, a stock market game.
WEB http://www.etrade.com

Investment Brokerages Guide
Should you go with a discount broker, or one that offers more services? How do you find one with reasonable commission fees? This page provides contact information for brokers in the U.S. and abroad, with some information about commissions and links to home pages. IBG also offers a nice, impartial explanation of the different types of brokerages out there, how to pick one, and what to do if you end up with a dud.
WEB http://www.cs.cmu.edu/~jdg/invest_brokers

NETWorth This investment service for mutual funds, equities, and college and retirement planning has a ready-made audience courtesy of its place in the popular money management software Quicken's online universe. NETWorth plugs into Quicken's self-help formula and enables visitors to tailor management options

through a combination of features including Atlas, a mutual fund; free 15-minute delayed stock quotes; company research; and Net links. Once lured into online dollar watching, visitors are pointed toward its fee services. These include crack investment advisors, a life insurance company, and a group of "tax-conscious" managers who promise to minimize IRS "success penalties." There's also a link to Quicken's online store where you can purchase all the software any cybertycoon could ever want.
WEB http://networth.galt.com/www/home

Wall Street Internet Address Book
Investment Dealers' Digest provides this useful collection of links, listing cut-rate discount brokers as well as big-name financial institutions that are now available on the Net. Articles addressing concerns over online trading are accessible under "Wall Street Wires into the Web."
WEB http://iddmz3.iddis.com/iddmag/web/sites.html

Mutual funds

Decision Point Daily analysis of 160 mutual funds, weekly charts of a variety of mutual funds, and regular market commentary.
AMERICA ONLINE *keyword* dp

Experimental Stock Market Data
Need to keep track of your IRA? One of the best free

sources of market information, with charts of price movement for major mutual funds.
WEB http://www.stockmaster.com

Fundwatch Online by Money Magazine Sift through more than 4,500 brands of mutual funds and find those that match your "investment philosophy." The funds are classified according to criteria such as investment objective, return over time, dividend yield, risk ratings, and so on. The service has detailed reports on most of the funds listed, with performance information and sector and portfolio holdings updated monthly.
COMPUSERVE *go* fundwatch

misc.invest.funds This newsgroup discusses any and all kinds of funds—college funds and mutual funds, gold funds and 401(k) funds. Are load funds better in the long run? Can currency funds serve as an inflation hedge? And what about those infomercials for fidelity funds? Sometimes the postings get very specific—one man wants to know if his wife's company, a small nonprofit whose 403(b) plan is invested in a family of loaded mutuals, is paying too much to its administrator. But if you like to talk about annuities and no-load mutuals, the fun will never end.
USENET misc.invest.funds

FAQ: **URL** ftp://rtfm.mit.edu/pub /usenet-by-hierarchy/misc/invest /funds/misc.invest.funds

Mutual Fund FAQ Concise answers to 26 basic questions about mutual-funds investing. Is there any disadvantage to investing in a mutual fund? What is a socially responsible fund?
WEB http://www.moneypages.com /syndicate/faq/index.htm

Mutual Fund Interactive This independent home page comes pretty close to living up to its claim as "The Mutual Funds Home Page." It includes articles designed to appeal to the fund novice as

NASDAQ STOCK MARKET
WEB http://www.nasdaq.com

By far the slickest and most useful Web site of the three major U.S. stock exchanges, as befits the only one of the three that's fully electronic. The site is about data, data, and more data, with live

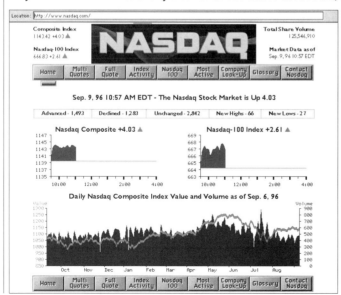

graphs of major-market indexes and delayed price quotes for stocks. The list of most active issues includes corporate logos and links to more quote data. Even first-time users can find what they're looking for in seconds. The only background information on the exchange itself is buried in the investment glossary.

And now... a Schwab for your eyes
http://www.eschwab.com

maturity, prevailing interest, and the relationship between bonds and interest rates. Other files of bond wisdom are available, including tracts on more specific topics and downloadable bond-related shareware.
COMPUSERVE *go* invforum→Libraries→ Bonds/Fixed Income→BONDS.THD

" Stop and set a spell with the Bond Professor. He's here to help. "

well as the more experienced investor. There's a moderated newsgroup that people actually use to discuss fund issues, such as the best way to calculate total return if you're investing a small amount in a fund each month. The site also publishes unique interviews with mutual fund managers.
WEB http://www.brill.com/funds.html

NETworth: The Internet Resource for Individual Investors With tie-ins to financial analysis firms like Chicago-based Morningstar, this service allows users to download no-load mutual fund marketing information, prospectuses, and financial newsletters. With free quotes on over 5,000 mutual funds, as well as educational forums and industry news, the service provides a solid entry into the world of mutual funds.

Snoop around in the Mutual Fund Market Manager area, a set of documents that addresses the concerns of mutual-funds investors; in particular, such issues as fund selection and maximum-security strategies.
WEB http://networth.galt.com

Bonds

Bond Prices and Ratings Enter the ticker symbol or CUSIP number of one or more issuing companies, and this service will list all bonds (with ticket symbols and CUSIP numbers), their issue type and date, identifier number, price, and yield, as well as the Standard & Poor's and Moody's ratings.
COMPUSERVE *go* bonds $

Bonds Made Easy This catechism explains such basic but vital issues as market values,

Bonds Online From the folks at 21st Century Municipals, Inc., Bonds Online is an absurdly complete directory of bond-related Net resources, with links to a galaxy of brokers and information providers with statistics on municipals, corporates, treasuries—whatever you're into. Stop and sit a spell with the Bond Professor, Dick Wilson. You can pose a question for him, or just read his FAQ and consult his library. He's here to help.
WEB http://www.bondsonline.com

Briefing Bond Quotes Free price quotes on bonds issued by corporations and government agencies like Fannie Mae, updated every 10 to 15 minutes. No frills, no waiting.
WEB http://www.briefing.com /bondquotes

Personal Finance

Lifestyle of the rich and famous? Not quite yet, but...

MANAGING MONEY IS NO FUN, but there are times when we all have to go it alone. Fortunately, if you can log on, you're never entirely alone, and you might be surprised to find out that it's not such a jungle out there. Online financial magazines sites are a useful if familiar way to go, but, there are greater rewards to be reaped for those prepared to be a little more adventurous. Many a site, whether the creation of a benign individual or of a profit-seeking company, can lend a helping hand when it comes to actually being able to afford that arduous trek called life. There's advice here for every occasion, from paying for college, buying a new car, mortgaging a new home, and saving for retirement, to writing that seminal prose your relatives will slaver over. No, not your first novel—your will.

Location: http://gnn.com/gnn/meta/finance/feat/brain/index.html

brain trust

Featuring Eric Forster

WELCOME TO THE *BRAIN TRUST*, where guest experts respond to your questions and opinions on various topics related to personal finance. The focus of our third *Brain Trust* forum, hosted by Eric Forster, was homebuying. Throughout the forum, which ended on May 10, questions and answers were posted here.

GNN Personal Finance
WEB http://gnn.com/gnn/meta/finance/index.html

The **GNN** people have put together a collection of articles that reads like the best of the personal-finance magazines. Regular features include The Internet Investor, which looks beyond the megahype surrounding Internet-related stocks and attempts to find out which ones are actually worth investing in, and the Brain Trust forum, in which financial experts answer emailed questions from readers. Most features are updated every two weeks, and there's a regularly updated list of the ten most-linked-to sites, so you can see where other users are heading for the latest finance info. If you're really into this page, you can join the mailing list to get weekly updates on what's here.

Starting points

Financenter Financenter has accumulated loads of information on the best way to buy, finance, or refinance major assets such as cars and houses, all presented in a clean, handsome format. Credit cards are another major focus: Comparisons are displayed that clarify the many options out there and suggest ways to manage cumbersome debts. The site includes financial decision calculators that help you decide whether it's better to buy or rent, or how much money you should put down on a house. You can even apply online for loans from various finance companies, some of which offer discounts and special deals to Financenter users.
WEB http://www.financenter.com

Financial Calculators These calculators, part of the home page of financial services company Centura Banks, offer a quick and simple way to get an idea of what kind of personal, home or auto loans you should apply for, what your monthly payments will be, and how much return you can expect from your savings over a given period.
WEB http://www.centura.com /formulas/whatif.html

Green *Green* is slacker-bait: a personal finance magazine directed at recent college grads who are just too alternative to deal with the money scene, man. This plucky startup's

Web page is really just an advertisement for the print magazine ($10 for four issues per year), but there are current articles here (you only get to read about half of the full piece) as well as an archive of past issues. The articles seem to be divided into two categories: the serious, plain-talking, worth-reading kind ("How to Buy Life Insurance") and the jokey, content-free, please-read-this-magazine kind ("How to Look Busy At Work").
WEB http://members.aol.com/green zine/INDEX.I.HTM

iGuide's Your Work, Your Money
The jewel in the crown of this regular-guy-oriented page is the Figure It Out area, a priceless collection of online worksheets that help you figure out key aspects of your financial situation. The worksheets deal with such brass-tacks issues as debt analysis, asset allocation, calculating your net worth, and the value of your home, just to name a few. For thrills and chills, play the Longevity Game, a worksheet that uses actuarial tables to estimate your life expectancy. Other areas of this truly useful page give you stock quotes, financial news, first-job anecdotes, and beginning investor tips.
WEB http://www.iguide.com/work_mny /index.sml

Money The people at *Money* magazine have obviously made an effort to prevent their site from becoming just another print magazine slapped onto

> **❝ For thrills and chills, play the Longevity Game, a worksheet that uses actuarial tables to estimate your life expectancy. ❞**

the Web. Articles incorporate such interactive treats as calculators and a worksheet to determine your chances of getting audited by the IRS. There's a daily audio report from money editors giving a rundown of the day's top business stories; you can also sign up for a free subscription to *Money Daily*, which will be rushed to you via email every evening complete with a quick recap of the day's market activity.
WEB http://pathfinder.com/money

Money Matters The Exchange is a network of bulletin boards that covers everything under the sun, but come to the Money Matters area for home budgeting and consumer chats. The forum advocates down-to-earth economic responsibility. Members praise frugality and exchange cost-cutting hints, worry over the safety of safe-deposit boxes, struggle to patent their inventions, and question the practices of church accounting.

AMERICA ONLINE *keyword* exchange→ Home/Health Careers→Money Matters

Personal Finance Network Feature articles on subjects like retirement planning, pensions, 401(k) plans, personal savings, and changes to Social Security are the order of the day here. The content is very much slanted toward older readers, and, interestingly, it's presented in a half-text, half-audio format. The site is divided into eight or nine separate sections, with titles like Financial Tips and Women and Pensions. There's a section devoted to tracking developments in Washington that could affect the way you invest and save, and, in addition, the site hosts

virtual town meetings with public officials and finance experts.

WEB http://www.wwbroadcast.com/pfn

The Personal Net Worth Program This service calculates your worth by asking extensive questions about assets and liabilities, and then subtracting the latter from the former. In addition, it projects your future net worth, assuming a certain rate of growth. The service is free, unless you want a printed report mailed to you for $3.50.

COMPUSERVE *go* hom-16

Real Life Parts of Real Life feel a bit like an extremely practical Oprah Winfrey show online. Average folks send in a description of their financial

situation, or problem, along with pictures of themselves. Then the audience (meaning you) is invited to respond with feedback and advice via the message boards. Topics range from employment to relationships to investing. There's more here, though, than vicarious thrills: Everyman-oriented financial news, features on topics like family finances, links, advice for the individual investor—everything you need to make a messy life neat.

AMERICA ONLINE *keyword* real life

Buying a car

All Things Automotive Directory When one imagines a comprehensive online car directory, the image of a loping, over-

PERSONAL FINANCE CENTER

COMPUSERVE *go* finance

A wealth of information, conveyed in a reassuring tone of voice. Features include the Budget Doctor, a.k.a Lesley Alderman, a staff writer for *Money* magazine, who doles out "prescriptions" in response to emailed questions from CompuServe subscribers about personal finance and budget-

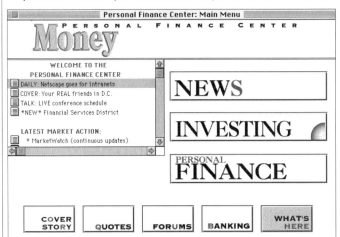

ing issues. Topics covered in Your Goals include ways to cut down on the food bill and to find out a used car's worth. One recent saving-for-college feature included a list of 75 mutual funds in which to invest while the kids grow up. You're going to need it. Also included are daily updates on market news.

STRAIGHT FROM THE ASS' MOUTH

I used to work as a car salesman. I got out of the business because I became tired of playing the game (the lying game). There was a point in my career when I told people the truth about buying a car (financing, leasing, warranties, dealer cost) and guess what happened? I almost starved to death. I went back to my old ways and started making a killing again. Not only was I making a lot of money for my self but I was making money for the dealer, the manufacturer, and the leasing company. And just guess where that money came from? It came from you and people just like you.

You might be thinking that I'm stretching the truth just a little. But if you knew all the facts about the banking business surrounding leasing and financing you would never buy a car again (that is, if you did not have to). And yes, I said the banking business, not the car business. The laws that pertain to financing and leasing are not in favor of the consumer, they're in favor of the lender and its representatives. Did you know that the usury laws of your state do not pertain to your federal bank, savings and loan, credit union, and many specialized lenders? The rules were rewritten in the '80s. The laws pertaining to leasing are absolutely in the favor of the leasing company and the car dealer. These laws are supposed to be in the interest of the public in general, that is what most Americans believe, and that is why most Americans get ripped off: because they assume that they're protected by the banking laws.

—from alt.autos

flowing dump truck comes to mind. But not with the All Things Automotive Directory—a sleek, mega-horsepower semi, barreling down the information superhighway. Every category from Auto Clubs to Sales and Service is listed, in clear alphabetical order, so all searching is performed in high gear. Car-lovers love car magazines, and online fans are no different—check out the international array of ezines. Finally, if you're sick of your gas guzzler, drive by the Miscellaneous heading for solar and electric car information.
WEB http://www.webcom.com/~autodir

alt.autos Discuss a variety of models and makes here—from hot rods to RVs, from the building to the buying to the maintaining to the selling to the scrap heap.
USENET alt.autos

Auto Site If you can spare a few bucks from your new-car fund, registering with Auto Site is money well spent. A high-octane server offering more than 30,000 pages of automotive statistics, guidelines, and directories, Auto Site will tell you everything about the car of your choice, from its options to its crash-test ratings. The information offered is truly all-encompassing, and the free services (maintenance references, basic buying tips) are handy as well. It's all delivered with cheery graphics and intelligible organization, so pull over for all the automotive data you could ever need.
WEB http://www.autosite.com

Auto Web Interactive Ever driven by a suburban auto mile, where a seemingly endless array of new and used-car dealers' signs pollute the horizon? This is the Internet equivalent. With comparable information, but none of the "charm" of a real car salesman, this site will help you find the new or used car you're looking for through a dealer in your state. There's even a worksheet at the bottom of the page for generating new-car price quotes or figuring trade-in values. Once you've done your window-shopping, we're sure the folks on your local auto mile will be glad to see you.
WEB http://www.autoweb.com

Automobile Forum One of the best online sources of general information about cars—with libraries and message boards on performance, safety, shopping, financing, maintenance, and insurance. What's the best used Nissan? Is the Taurus a good deal? Why does the Neon say "Hi" all the time? And why hasn't anyone invented a device to turn off a turn signal after 20 minutes of infernal blinking? **COMPUSERVE** *go* cars

Calling all Cars Cars for sale by owners nationwide. Organized by manufacturer and model, a wide variety of cars are available here, including classic Ford Woodies, Mustangs, Hondas, Saabs, and Subarus. Between 40 and 70 new ads are added to this site each week. Also available here is a sample of *Calling All Cars* magazine, along with subscrip-tion information.
WEB http://www.cacars.com

Car and Driver The premier automotive review magazine, *Car and Driver* has put the complete text of their definitive buyer's guide online, reaffirm-ing a 40-year tradition of dependability. The next best thing to a test drive, this online guide is pleasantly easy to use. Many of the magazine's latest car reviews are offered as well, in addition to a roadmap of links to car shows, races, and other automotive hot spots.
WEB http://www.caranddriver.com /hfm/index.html

The Car Place This page is assembled by Robert Bowden, who has test-driven over 500 cars in his life and whose words of wisdom are updated weekly. Bowden's reviews are not written in the language of dry technical manuals; he rates the cars on a scale of one to four "James Deans," four being as good as it gets. The Car Place covers a wide range of makes and models. Bowden also photographs cars in rather unique locales—check out his photo album.
WEB http://www.cftnet.com/members /rcbowden

Car Talk The popular National Public Radio car mechanics, Tom and Ray, take their irrev-erent sense of humor into cyberspace with this cartoonish

 THE AUTO CHANNEL
WEB http://www.the-autochannel.com

Rev up your engines and fasten your seat belts—The Auto Channel is *the* Internet site for automo-tive enthusiasts. Cruise through hundreds of new car reviews (with real-time videos), race into the latest automotive news, and burn rubber in The Auto Channel's comprehensive motor-sports cov-erage. These guys offer indexes and reviews of other pages for everything from off-road vehicles

to remote-controlled car rac-ing. Best of all, you can clank wrenches with other gear-heads in the chat rooms and take advantage of some free automotive repair advice. But remember, you get what you pay for.

car site. If you missed the most recent radio episode, you can find bits in RealAudio format. Poke around under the hood, and you'll find a surprising amount of such useful information as test-drive results and four years of searchable mechanics' tips hidden among the jokes.
WEB http://www.cartalk.com

Car-link Used-car shoppers will find an illustrated list of hundreds of autos, listed by individuals and dealers. Because the photographs are such an essential part of this site, the people at Car-link have posted hardware requirements—jalopy computers don't have the horsepower.
WEB http://www.car-link.com

Consumer Reports Reports on road tests, new car profiles and ratings, reliability, and recall information, in addition to articles with titles such as "How to Drive Home a Bargain" and "Should You Lease?" Good, solid, basic information for the prospective buyer.
AMERICA ONLINE *keyword* consumer reports→automobiles
COMPUSERVE *go* csr-l

Cyberspace Automotive Performance This collection of automotive links claims to be the most comprehensive server of its kind on the Net. Use the site's calculator to determine monthly car payments. Learn which cars are on manufacturer's recall and why. Or read about the turbo oiler and how

to install it, in the Technical Guru's Corner. Links to online magazines (like *Chrysler Power* magazine and *Racer* magazine) make this site complete.
WEB http://cyberauto.com

DealerNet "A world of personal transportation on your desktop," DealerNet links to dealers and showrooms for all types of autos. Search for parts, accessories, and affordable service.
WEB http://www.dealernet.com

Edmund's Automobile Buyer's Guides You want to sound as if you know something about cars when you first step onto the showroom floor. Edmund has been helping car buyers for 30 years and has the online goods. Pick a model and spend the next hour reading the relevant details, then peruse the solid price-haggling and negotiating tips that will arm you with the knowledge of dealer's cost and other essentials. With millions of hits a month, the word is out about the usefulness of Edmund's guides.
WEB http://www.edmunds.com

rec.autos Tom is looking for third-party replacement roll pads to give his 4x4 truck the "fat look." Joel wants to know if a hole in the muffler of his Mustang will hurt the car's engine (besides being loud). Two Accord owners compare their cars (one was built in Japan, one in Ohio). Automotive enthusiasts meet here for car talk of all kinds. The newsgroup's FAQ is a tremendous

resource as well, answering questions from "What is this threshold breaking business?" to "How often should I change my brake fluid?"
USENET rec.autos
FAQ: **WEB** http://www.cis.ohio-state .edu/text/faq usenet/rec-autos /top.html

Webfoot's Used Car Lot Collecting vintage Bentleys? Need a new headlight for your 1984 Honda? Webfoot links to dozens of sites for used-car sales, used car parts, and general automotive information.
WEB http://www.webfoot.com/lots /international.car.lot.html

College costs

ASKERIC The federally funded Educational Resources Information Center (ERIC) is an immense clearinghouse of educational information. ASK-ERIC, the center's online presence, is a helpful virtual library that points fund-seekers in the direction of relevant information, publications on education, and discussions of college testing and admissions.
WEB http://ericir.syr.edu

Don't Miss Out The handbook, entitled *The Ambitious Student's Guide to Financial Aid*, from Signet Bank, takes would-be students step by step through the quest for college funding, from defining their monetary need through successful financing. Included are tricks of the trade for tilting the financial aid process in your favor, like reducing the family contribution or increasing the cost of education in order to up your award.

WEB http://jerome.signet.com /collegemoney/tocl.html

Education Planning A simple but informative introduction (including an FAQ, articles, and message board) to legal gifts to children, trust funds, and tax shelters. Learn the nitty-gritty of college savings as parents try to grapple with the most pertinent question of all: how much is enough? The feature also carries links to Ask the College Board, where anxious students and parents get advice directly from the College Board, along with a link to the 2,500 institutions profiled

in the searchable version of the College Handbook.
AMERICA ONLINE *keyword* your money →Education

fastWEB! (Financial Aid Search Through the Web) Fast it's not. This financial aid search requires you to give up screen after screen of personal details before providing you with information about scholarships and loans. However, it finally pays off with a personally tailored search that you can check for updates (according to the site, approximately 1,200 awards are added to the database each day and additions matching your profile are added to your "mailbox." Best of all, it's free.
WEB http://www.fastweb.com

The Financial Aid Information Page Links to the financial aid and admissions offices of several American colleges and universities. You can also access information on scholarships, fellowships, and grants, or retrieve a bibliography of resources for offline reading on college funding.
WEB http://www.finaid.org

Financing College A primer from the renowned Princeton Review, starting with a comprehensive explanation of the financial aid process. Also included: information on grants and scholarships, explanations of state and federal loan and grant programs, and a Q&A covering such queries as "Will applying for aid jeopar-

SALLIE MAE
WEB http://www.salliemae.com

Having trouble distinguishing your SAR from your EFC? A presentation of one of the leading providers of higher-education loans, Sallie Mae will help you straighten out your financial aid confusion. (And just so you're not left hanging, SAR refers to your student-aid report, while EFC is

your expected family contribution.) Sallie Mae's glossary contains such commonly tossed-about financial aid acronyms as FAFSA and PLUS. The interactive calculators will help you plan for college or estimate loan repayments. There's even a page designed specifically for financial aid administrators who may get a little discombobulated every now and then.

dize my chance of admission?" and "Should I hire a professional to help me fill out the forms?" This site also allows you to search The Princeton Reviews' college database for even more information on the general college thing.
AMERICA ONLINE *keyword* princeton→College→Financing College
WEB http://www.review.com/faid/college_faid.html

The Loan Counselor From Purdue University, a site with all the benefits of a trip to the financial aid office without the impertinent student receptionists, long lines, and curt counselors. Purdue provides prospective students with loan counseling, ways to manage educational loan debt before your payments begin, a list of lenders, and alternative financing options. And you don't have to go to Purdue for the information.
URL gopher://oasis.cc.purdue.edu:2525/11/student/cnslr

Minority Scholarships and Fellowships No matter what kind of program you're in, there's probably financial aid for which you're eligible. Search financial aid opportunities by school, state, degree program, or sponsoring institution.
WEB http://web.fie.com/htbin/cashe.pl

Parent Soup: College Planning One of the best guides to financial planning of a college education, whether you have six years or six months to go. It answers questions like "What

if You Come Up Short?" and provides both detailed and general advice about investment strategies, including such areas as Scholarships and Grants, Setting Up an Investment Plan Now!, and How Can My Children Help Pay for College?
WEB http://www.parentsoup.com/cgi-bin/genobject/gtsx000

Petersen's Education Center: Financing Education All right, face it: You're stressed. Being a high school junior or senior isn't easy—you figure it's time to enjoy the privileges of being an upperclassman, for example, unqualified respect and a better locker, but everyone's bugging you about this college thing and asking how you're going to afford it. Luckily, Petersen's has the financial aid scene down to a science. Besides a general description of types of aid and a glossary of useful terms, there's a month-by-month college admissions calendar for both high school juniors and seniors, so they can make sure they're not so consumed with worry about the prom and the yearbook that they can't remember to file their FAFSA. At this site you can also read up on other financial aid sources—including, of course, Petersen's own *Paying Less for College*.
WEB www.petersens.com/resources/finance.html

Scholarships and Grants A gateway to educational funding sources, including the *Grant*

Getter's Guide, the *Catalogue of Federal Assistance*, and FEDIX. For science scholars and researchers, the site links to the National Institutes of Health, the National Science Foundation, and the Science and Technology Service. The online version of the *Scientist* is also available here.
URL gopher://riceinfo.rice.edu:70/11/Research

Schools & Money Aimed at college trendsters, Schools & Money has articles about handling money while in school, wake-up calls about avoiding credit card debt and filing taxes, and an online book exchange to help students dodge the ruinous costs of textbooks. You can also hook up to the Student Services database of grants, scholarships and loans.
WEB http://www.taponline.com/tap/higher.html

The Student Guide from ED Got questions about how you're going to finance your education? Ask your Uncle Sam. This is the official guide from the U.S. Department of Education's Office of Postsecondary Education, updated each academic year. General information on student eligibility for federal aid, the application process, and borrower's rights and responsibilities are available. You'll also find specifics on Pell Grants, Stafford Loans, PLUS Loans, and other federal assistance programs. A glossary helps future freshmen interpret the financial aid lingo.

WEB http://www.ed.gov/prog_info/SFA/StudentGuide

U.S. News College Fair Forum The equivocal financial status of middle-class kids may be the most prevalent theme of discussion in this forum, but it's not the only topic in the air. When a divorced parent asks for advice about filling out financial aid applications, others in similar situations respond. And when someone asks for ideas for funding a Russian exchange student, the forum is flooded with responses. *U.S. News* has staff online to help answer financial aid questions and provide information on grants and scholarships. They'll also point you in the direction of more

detailed sources. All options are explored here, from gaining "independent status" to staying in state for payment breaks.

COMPUSERVE *go* usncollege→ Messages and Libraries Financial Aid

Consumer power

Better Business Bureau The BBB brings its helpful consumer publications to the Web, offering consumer alerts, an opportunity to file complaints online, and advice on avoiding scams. If you're thinking of using a company's services, the BBB in your area may be able to tell you if the company has a good reputation. The bureau makes available publications for businesses, too, including material on the ethics of advertising.

WEB http://www.bbb.org

clari.living.consumer Anyone who has ever watched in horror as his or her new car was recalled by its manufacturer, or felt the sting of an unfair return policy, will feel comfortable here on this pay-to-read newsgroup.

USENET clari.living.consumer

CONSSCI A mailing list for family and consumer economists, consumer educators, and consumer-affairs specialists.

EMAIL listserv@ukcc.uky.edu ✍ *Type in message body:* subscribe CONSCCI (your email address)

Consumer Information Center Originally created to provide the media with access to consumer-oriented press releases, this Web site is now a massive clearinghouse of consumer information, providing not only

THE CONSUMER LAW PAGE

WEB http://consumerlawpage.com

An excellent selection of resources, stylishly displayed for easy consumption. The Consumer Law Page falls into four major sections: a large collection of articles (not in legalese) about consumer news and legal issues; a set of over 100 brochures full of advice for consumers on topics such as

Location: http://consumerlawpage.com/securities/index.html

Stocks & Securities

D e f r a u d e d   I n v e s t o r s

DEFRAUDED

Recent Allegations of Corporate Misconduct

Contained on this page are news summaries that document recent allegations of corporate fraud and misconduct in relation to securities investors. Please bookmark this page. It will be updated often.

filing a complaint and repairing lousy credit; links to other pages—none as good as this one—with similar resources; and, last but not least, a big, angry red button you can push for advice on filing complaints, whether it's a fair trial in small claims court or a class action suit.

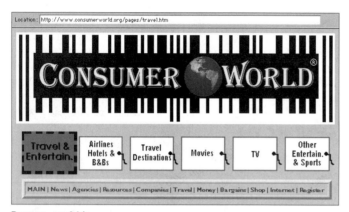

Buy now—pay fairly
http://www.consumerworld.org

consumer-news updates, but also access to hundreds of free federal publications, such as "How to Buy Canned and Frozen Vegetables," "Child Health Guide," and "U.S. Marshal's Property List."
WEB http://www.pueblo.gsa.gov

Consumer World Consumer advocate Edgar Dworsky put together this amazing collection of links to consumer information sites. Large and well-researched, this site is superbly organized and even fun to use; it includes online shopping venues as well as consumer advice. Dworsky breaks up the long lists of links with tags indicating new items, "Hot Sites," and "Best Bets," speeding up the search for useful, current info. Categories include consumer agencies, resources, money and credit, and company connections.
WEB http://www.consumerworld.org

FTC Consumer Brochures Don't get scammed. Here's the full

text of more than 100 consumer brochures issued by the Federal Trade Commission's Office of Consumer and Business Education, as well as a large file of articles on advertising law. Find out what to do if you just had plastic surgery and you still look terrible, among other things.
WEB http://www.webcom.com /~lewrose/brochures.html

General Consumer Information A library of basic consumer documents, including the Consumer Information Catalog, a consumer quiz, updated consumer information, and mutiple documents outlining consumer resources.
COMPUSERVE *go* consumer→ Libraries→General Consumer Information

HomeArts Consumer News Tidbits of consumer information from Hearst magazines; this includes sections on credit cards, pharmaceuticals, and buying a new car.

WEB http://homearts.com/depts/fresh /00consfl.htm

misc.consumers This newsgroup reads like one huge whine cellar, with hundreds of consumers from all walks of life complaining about airfares, lamenting the scourge of telemarketers, and discussing credit policies. While attitudes and tones vary wildly, everyone shares the desire to illuminate the often shadowy world of consumer spending—in short, to put their mouths where their money is.
USENET misc.consumers

National Fraud Information Center The snake-oil salesmen have found a new home on the Internet, but don't worry: the no-nonsense NFIC is looking out for us. Read the daily update on new scams, report suspicious-seeming businesses, or find out what to do if you believe you have been scammed online. NFIC also offers contact information for seniors who feel vulnerable to fraud.
WEB http://www.fraud.org/report.htm

Nolo Press Self-Help Law Center This publisher of books and software on consumer law topics presents excerpts from its products in jargon-free prose. Legal tip: Some states have "lemon" laws that apply to pets, protecting you if the lovely dachshund you just bought turns out to be terminally ill. You can also learn how to defend yourself in court, and what your rights are

as a tenant.
WEB http://www.nolo.com/catalogue
/index.html

U.S. Consumer Products Safety Commission The USCPSC is the government agency that issues alerts when toys or other products turn out to be potentially dangerous. Check out their latest press releases or ask to be put on the agency's electronic mailing list for new announcements. The USCPSC Publications folder has safety tips for items ranging from power tools to backyard pools.
URL gopher://cpsc.gov

Credit & debt

Cheapskate Monthly What is essentially an ad for a non-free print publication is itself of some use. Mary Hunt, former debtor, passes on tips and financial wisdom for the debt-ridden. You can drool over the horror stories, rejoice over Mary's success story, and, most importantly, view an online sample copy of the magazine itself, a subscription to which costs $16 a year and which features dollar-stretching tips and tea-and-sympathy encouragement. The page also tries to sell you books from a line of self-help titles, but take a page from Mary's own book and decline.
WEB http://www.cheapsk8.com

The Consumer Law Page Informational Brochures An independent law firm put together this

---

DEBT OF HONOR

I am considering some type of debt consolidation for my credit cards and medical bills. I need information on consumer credit counseling services. I have heard from some that this is a great way to manage debt and from others that it is not. If anyone has had any experience with this type of debt consolidation service I would appreciate a reply.

The way CCC works is this: they get all your info, such as who you owe & how much you owe them, & your income info. Then they set up a payment plan based on a percentage of your total amount owed to each creditor. Your creditors are not required to accept this payment arrangement, since CCC holds out 10% of the payment amount for their fee. The creditor then has to eat that amount. Also, the payments they make usually aren't the same as your contract amount, so your account falls further & further behind each month unless the creditor is willing to alter your accounts each month to show current. Therefore, your credit report shows delinquent status until all debts are paid.

—from Credit Libraries

---

collection of useful brochures on a whole range of credit-related issues; the brochures themselves are mostly authored by the Federal Trade Commission. "How to Dispute Credit Report Errors" is notable among them; it tells you what to do when you're refused a loan because someone with your name racked up a giant credit card bill and fled to the Maldives.
WEB http://seamless.com/alexanderlaw
/txt/brochure/index.html#credit

Credit FAQ This comprehensive FAQ is garnered from the newsgroup misc.consumers, and covers topics ranging from the differences between various credit cards to understanding

credit reports. The FAQ also contains concise instructions for obtaining and revamping your credit report, battling billing errors, and making sure your cards are working for you and not solely for the credit company. For straight, well organized, old-fashioned, heart warming honesty in a field dominated by oily scam artists, you can't beat the FAQ.
URL ftp://rtfm.mit.edu/pub/usenet-by
-group/misc.answers/consumer
-credit-faq

Credit Libraries Here, you'll find Federal Trade Commission publications addressing such issues as how to get a credit history, repair bad credit, combat false credit reports, and avoid credit scams. The files Credit Card Blocking and Credit Repair Scams help you make sense of all those offers that arrive in the mail each day for "preapproved credit." If you've been wrongly denied credit, the file "How to Dispute Credit Report Errors" describes what you need to do to fix it and whom to contact for help. Citizens' rights under the Fair Credit Reporting Act, Equality in Lending and Truth in Lending Acts are clearly explained. "Women and Credit Histories" offers useful tips to fiancees, wives, divorcees, and widows for getting and keeping credit record of their own. A highlight is "Ten Steps to Improving Your Credit"—strictly for those not averse to using credit laws to their own advantage. This is trench warfare strategy for those with bad credit histories. Example: "Since credit rating companies have only 30 days to verify a bad risk incident, keep ques-

❝ The first thing you'll notice when looking into credit agencies online is how stridently everybody promises to cure what ails you. ❞

tioning them until they miss the deadline."
COMPUSERVE *go* conforum→ Libraries→Banking & Credit

Credit Repair Scams This page is a vital tool if you're looking for help with your credit on the Web. The first thing you'll notice when looking into credit agencies online is how stridently everybody promises to cure what ails you. There's a subsection of something called the Advertising Law Page, where you'll benefit from the research of the Federal Trade Commission into the question of just what is and isn't legal (and possible) for credit repair services to promise you.
WEB http://www.webcom.com /~lewrose/brochures/creditrepair.html

Credit Reporting Agencies It says what it does, does what it says. Links to home pages of credit agencies in the U.S. and overseas.
WEB http://www.teleport.com/~richh /agency.html

Debt Counselors of America The nonprofit organization Debt Counselors of America offers to retrieve your credit records from major rating agencies and review them with you for $50. Nowhere on the site, however, do they inform you that credit agencies are legally required to let you review your credit history once a year at little or no cost—a DCA spokesman insisted that they inform callers of this fact. This makes DCA's collection of tips on recovering

from debt seem like a little less than the straight dope. Despite this, the site is crawling with happy cartoons and testimonials from people who say they've been helped by DCA's services.
WEB http://www.dca.org

Electronic Credit Repair Kit Many caveats and legal disclaimers accompany what is actually a refreshingly excellent product in a field where scams abound. It was created by one Michael Kielsky, "not a lawyer," who collects $30 a pop if you decide to write to him for a hard copy—though you can view it on the Web for free. The repair kit itself is just a no-nonsense batch of good sense, made up of simply presented information about credit and credit agencies, designed to arm the average debtor against his or her natural foe. You'll also find useful items like effective sample letters to credit agencies, and links to legal and credit wisdom.
WEB http://www.primenet.com /~kielsky/credit.htm

Insurance

clari.biz.industry.insurance Provides reports on various facets of the insurance industry, including the earnings of specific companies and the regulations guiding the risk-management business as a whole.
USENET clari.biz.industry.insurance

Insurance Companies & Resources on the Net Links to more insurance-related sites than you can

possibly imagine, in a simple alphabetical list, compiled by a Loyola student.
WEB http://lattanze.loyola.edu/users /cwebb/insure.html

Insurance Information Institute
Triple-I offers a series of brochures on property and casualty-insurance topics, including "Insuring your home business" and "Tornado safety." Soporific, but that's the nature of the beast. If only Dorothy had been on the Net.
WEB http://www.iii.org

Insurance News Network INN's reams of data, including sample rates organized by state, could prove useful to careful consumers seeking a new auto,

home, or life-insurance policy. Yet, while the majority of the databases found through INN (which was developed by a financial journalist) can be accessed for free, a few fee-based services are included, and are clearly marked as such.
WEB http://www.insure.com

InsWeb Search for insurance agents in your area that sell the kind of policy you're looking for, and get tips from the National Insurance Crime Bureau on how to prevent and avoid insurance scams. Also featured is a glossary of several hundred insurance terms. Online rate-quote services and applications for personal, business, and professional insur-

ance are in the works.
WEB http://www.insweb.com/main /OI-ci/default.htm

ITT Hartford With a home page that emphasizes the company's long tradition of insurance and financial services—clients have included Abraham Lincoln and Robert E. Lee—ITT Hartford's site is most noteworthy for its interactive financial-service features, for example, the Retirement Time Machine, which helps netsurfers plan for a secure future.
WEB http://www.itthartford.com

Legi-Slate Law Center Insurance is one of the most heavily regulated industries; this site contains a wealth of information

QUICK QUOTE
WEB http://www.quickquote.com

The online shopping revolution meets the insurance industry at Quick Quote, where you can freely access a database of insurance products and shop around for the best rates on term life insurance or fixed annuities. Fill in some basic demographic information on a form and you'll be pre-

sented with the best bargains from a database of more than 1,500 plans. One feature will even provide a quick and easy estimate of your insurance needs. And if you're interested, you can sign up for *Quick Quote Notes*, a free quarterly insurance industry newsletter.

STEP 1: FLUSH THE TOILET

"Does anyone have a check-list of things to look for when doing a new house walk-through?"—Helen

"As soon as you get there, start the dishwasher and let it run a full cycle. Have a lamp or something you can plug in to every outlet to check. Check all light switches. Open and close all doors and windows. Check window screens for tears or holes. Run all faucets and check that the drains drain. Flush the toilets. Generally check anything mechanical."—Richard

"All excellent suggestions, but instead of a lamp, go to your local hardware store and buy a gadget known as a **TLT** (three light tester). It is a little whiz-bang about the size of a three-pronged plug with three lights (I wonder why the call it a TLT ;-). This thing is easy to carry and will warn you of mis-wired outlets. Also flush all toilets, and run water from as many widgets as possible simultaneously, but your home inspector should have already done this. BTW, I had my son check the house we were selling three years ago, and, yep he found a mind-fart of mine. Hot and neutral reversed."—Bob

—from misc.consumers.house

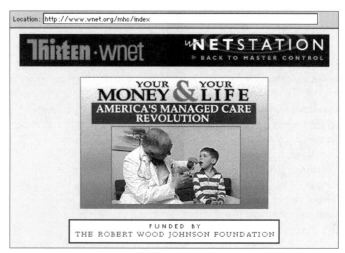

PBS's *Your Money and Your Life* tells Junior how HMOs actually work
http://www.wnet.org/mhc/index.html

on every piece of insurance legislation currently pending in Congress. Though some of the information is available through subscription only, much of it is free, and the breadth of resources is stunning. Along with the full text of every bill, the service provides sponsorship information, remarks by supporting and dissenting Congressmen, a history of related legislation, and links to pertinent press clippings. Insurance topics include auto insurance, health insurance, life insurance, and liability, as well as less common risk industries, including bank insurance, crop insurance, flood insurance, and survivors' old-age insurance.
EMAIL legislate@gopher.legislate.com
✍ *Write a request*
URL gopher://gopher.legislate.com:70/1

Long-Term Care Insurance This Web site answers the most

common questions about long-term care, the difficult health-insurance decision more commonly (and less euphemistically) known as "putting Mom and Dad in a nursing home." In addition, it lists a set of support organizations and pamphlets that treat the issue in greater detail.
WEB http://www.service.com/answers/health_insurance.html

The New England This Northeastern insurance company offers more than just the traditional policy information and mission statement, providing an extensive glossary of insurance terms, from AD&D to zero-coupon securities.
WEB http://www.tne.com

Your Money & Your Life A companion site to the 1995 PBS television series of the same name, Your Money provides a primer on managed care and all the other buzzwords rocking the world of medicine. The spot also includes "How do HMOs work?" and a series of real-life stories from people who have been affected by changes in health care.

WEB http://www.wnet.org/mhc/index.html

Real estate

alt.home.repair If your dream home is starting to seem like the disastrous house in the movie *The Money Pit*, you might want to post your laments at this newsgroup, where home-improvement experts will solve your particular dilemma or, at the very least, comfort you with horror stories of their own. Posts run from the somewhat technical (Re: Dewalt 18.0 V Cordless Drill) to the plaintive (Shower Grout Repair?). Wide-ranging and informative, this newsgroup should be mandatory for anyone who is thinking of tiling over that old floor or rewiring the guest room.

USENET alt.home.repair

The Electronic Mall Insurance, Finance, Real Estate Compuserve gives you access to a fair-sized selection of online services, including Homefinder by AMS, which can size up a prospective community for you in terms of schools, employment possibilities, real estate agents, and more, for only a few dollars a pop. There's also a home equity service, from Chase Manhattan.

COMPUSERVE *go* Shopping→Insurance/Finance/Real Estate

Internet Real Estate Directory An excellent collection of real estate sites online. In addition to rating the sites (from "outstanding" to "don't bother"), the page also divides them by state and country, and maintains a top-ten list. Tidbits and features on real estate news make IRED more than a barebones directory. A good first stop.

WEB http://www.ired.com

Living Home A beautifully made online magazine where the

HOME FAIR
WEB http://www.homefair.com/homegrap.html

There's probably a question about buying, renting, selling, mortgaging, and moving your place of residence that HomeFair's extremely beige page doesn't deal with, but it's hard to think of one. HomeFair is a thoroughgoing online introduction to the whole infernal process. You want easy, helpful tools? Try the Salary Calculator, the Moving Calculator, or the Mortgage Qualification cal-

culator (the Java-heavy Intelligent Mortgage Agent looks promising, but it's still a little buggy). The Relocation Wizard will make up a personalized timeline for you. There's also a feature especially for first-time buyers that's a godsend, and a menu of free services provided by the page's various sponsors.

A WRINKLE IN TIME

I will be 62 in December. If I file for SS retirement, how much am I allowed to make per year at my present job? Is the benefit amount considered as part of the restricted limit?

The limit on "earned income." i.e., W-2 income NOT investment or SS income, at age 62 is approximately $8,300 annually. For every $2.00 over that figure, your SS payment is reduced by $1.00. In the year that you reach 62 and start your SS, the earned income figure limitation is waived if you certify that you didn't work over so many hours to receive it and most everyone so certifies. There is, however, one wrinkle that was once "explained" to me by my SS advisor that is something to the effect that if at age 65 you haven't received because of the earned income requirement any money, you are given credit at that time and your payments at 65 are adjusted upward. One other "wrinkle": If you elect to take SS at age 62 (and most everyone is advised to do so) and you subsequently change your mind because of high earned income, you can elect to renege on your election and wait until you're older. You must, however, return all SS funds received up to that time.

—from Retirement Living Forum

emphasis is on building and decorating a home, although it does touch on the problems of buying homes as well. If Web pages could have beveled edges, this one would. Simple online calculators help you map out the financial obligations involved with wallpapering a room, putting in a new kitchen floor, breaking ground on a new site, and everything in between. Helpful links and engaging personal narratives flesh out this elegant page as a pleasing, practical resource.
WEB http://www.livinghome.com

misc.consumers.house While the bulk of threads in this high-volume newsgroup relate to

home repair, you have to buy a home before you can fix it up, and many messages deal with that traumatic experience. The couple that lost their ideal home when the seller went bankrupt gets a sympathetic response from others stuck in the closing process. A woman refinancing her home is evicted by the first owner when he decides she is "in default during changeover." With tips on buying, avoiding penalties, and assessing value, this is a useful resource.
USENET misc.consumers.house

misc.invest.real-estate Discussion of real estate as an investment, including financing,

restoration, and property leads. Government real estate auctions are also announced here.
USENET misc.invest.real-estate

MLS—Sell, Buy, Rent, Exchange A broad spectrum of properties is offered for sale here, from homes in Blue Hill, Maine (5 BR/ocean view), to Hilo, Hawaii (1 BR/dishwasher and carport). All entries contain information about property taxes, amenities, and utility rates. To list your home, fill out the online form and email it to MLS. There's no charge. Rentals are also admissible, but not for periods less than a month. Brokers and salespeople may use the service if they identify themselves and follow special guidelines.
AMERICA ONLINE *keyword* mls

Mortgage Rates A brief introduction defines the types of mortgages—30-year fixed; 15-year fixed; jumbo (more than $203,150); negative amortization (deferred interest); and adjustable-rate (ARMs). Specialized loan programs like those from the Veterans' Administration and the FHA are also listed. With this information in hand, prospective home buyers can begin to explore the individual bank listings, which are updated on a daily basis. Each bank involved furnishes the current rate on most or all types of mortgages, contact information, and details on its lending program.
AMERICA ONLINE *keyword* mortgages

Real Estate Dictionary Definitions for about 100 real estate terms—from "appurtenance" ("anything attached to the land or used with it passing to the new owner") to "pipestem lot" ("a lot connected to a public street by a narrow strip of land"). Helpful links within the dictionary let you click around between related terms.
WEB http://199.182.58.42/dictionary.html

The Real Estate Library Like many of America Online's libraries, this one gives you access to almost more information and resources than you know what to do with. One first stop is the Reading Room, wherein you'll find fea-

ture articles on a variety of current real estate topics (CA Condo Defect Law Enacted!), and a link to AOL's real estate classified section. The text library has all kinds of friendly and helpful documents, with tips on every imaginable real estate topic. Another real find is the shareware and freeware library, which is divided into different sections for PC and Mac. Hot apps include the Home Inspector (HOME-INSP.ZIP DOS), which is basically a set of electronic home, buying checklists and information to help you evaluate a prospective home, and Rent Wizard, which assists you in keeping accurate records of your property trans-

actions. For more current, topical tips, the Home section of the Real Life forum is also definitely worth a look.
AMERICA ONLINE *keyword* real estate→ Library

Retirement

American Association of Retired Persons Pensions, taxes, and home equity are all hot topics in the Finance area of this well organized online resource, which has meetings, a software library, and a wealth of other nonfinance-related activities as well. Browse the consumer resources section, for information about credit and debt and scams that prey on seniors.
AMERICA ONLINE *keyword* aarp

 RETIREMENT LIVING FORUM
COMPUSERVE *go* senior
picture: WEB http://www.maturityusa.com
This forum run by SPRY (Setting Priorities for Retirement Years) provides retirement advice in two formats. First, there are the libraries, which contain a wealth of information for downloading. There's the Pension Rights Center, with its files on pension plans, Medicare, and the Employee

Retirement Income Security Act (ERISA); H&R Block's tax information for seniors; primers on Mutual Funds and IRAs; and Social Security libraries filled with useful programs on benefit calculation, disability and survivor benefits, and benefit adjustments. In the forum itself, participants pose specific questions about retirement issues and are answered by online experts and other retirees.

Guide to Retirement Living Online If you're sorting out a suitable retirement lifestyle, this guide can help. It's got descriptions of the kinds of facilities available, details on how to find an affordable home, and listings of facilities in Maryland, Virginia, D.C., Pennsylvania, New Jersey, and Delaware. There's also a section for those who choose to continue living at home in their later years.
WEB http://www.retirement-living.com

Life Span Web: In Memoriam A resource for information about the things for which we'd rather not have to plan: living wills, funerals, death benefits, and the like. LSW is developing an electronic safe-deposit-box system, where users will be able to store digitized versions of important documents (i.e., wills, marriage certificates, etc.) in password-protected accounts. The electronic reproductions are acceptable in most courts, should you lose the originals to flood or fire.
WEB http://www.twoscan.com/2scan /lifespanweb/memoriam/memoriam .html

Maturity USA A monthly online magazine, *Maturity USA* features articles on the financial concerns of the aging.
WEB http://www.maturityusa.com

Retirement Planner Software Download a shareware program that will help you develop a savings strategy for your 401(k) plan. You can use a simplified version of the pro-gram right on the Web; it tells you if you're saving enough to meet your retirement goals. If not, it provides suggestions on how to get back on track.
WEB http://www.awa.com/softlock /tturner/401kplan.html

Retirement Planning Come here with your retirement questions. The message board is a great place to ask for help with your 401(k) or to discuss your child's retirement planning, but be sure to check the FAQ first—forum members have already asked and answered questions about the number of times an IRA account may be changed each year, the rules about taxing Social Security, and the invesments you can't make with an IRA account.
AMERICA ONLINE *keyword* yourmoney

The Retirement Zone A few helpful excerpts of articles from *Kiplinger's Personal Finance* magazine, covering the basics of retirement planning, are featured. A worksheet designed to help you calculate your retirement needs is available, but you have to do the math yourself.
WEB http://www.researchmag.com /investor/zone.htm

RetireWeb Tips on the financial implications of retirement. While the site is geared toward Canadian seniors, there are enough links and information to make a virtual visit north of the border well worth it. Calculators are included to help you figure out how big a nest egg you're going to need before you can start spending your weekdays on the golf course.
WEB http://www.retireweb.com

SeniorNet Forum Seniors exchange advice and strategize together about money matters in the investment and finance section of this forum. Although they may be living on fixed incomes, most of the regulars here seem to be practiced, savvy investors, market veterans who monitor their stocks, bonds, and mutual funds every day of the trading week. Two widows discuss the wisdom of moving from high-yield money market investments to more conservative funds; two elderly men compare stock tips. Not all decisions depend on a bottom line; one man bought IBM because his kids work there.
AMERICA ONLINE *keyword* seniornet

Seniors Internet Mall Page You can't get a Cinnabon, but this mall lists products and services especially for seniors, as well as special rates and discounts. The companies represented are about equally divided between the U.S. and Canada.
WEB http://www.seniorsnet.com /mall.htm

Social Security Online Curious about just exactly how much money you've put into Social Security over the years? The official Web site of the Social Security Administration tells you how to find out, and answers many other questions in a long and detailed FAQ.
WEB http://www.ssa.gov

Taxes

THERE'S NOTHING CERTAIN EXCEPT DEATH, TAXES, AND UNIMPLEMENTED TRAPS

TAXES ARE NO ONE'S IDEA OF fun—except perhaps the occasional Elliot Ness. But there are ways to ease the pain of shelling out your hard-earned dollars to The Man. The Web holds warehouses of paperwork, software, and other resources that can help you simplify and expedite the tax-paying process. Listen to discussions about W-2 forms and deductibles, download invaluable shareware, and consult the tax wizards, prophets, and professionals who dot the i's and cross the t's on every black and white government tax form. Suck it up, get online, and pay your debt to society; the dreaded deadline will pass much more quickly and painlessly.

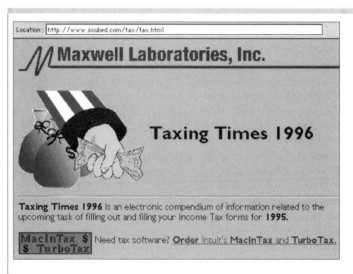

Location: http://www.scubed.com/tax/tax.html

Maxwell Laboratories, Inc.

Taxing Times 1996

Taxing Times 1996 is an electronic compendium of information related to the upcoming task of filling out and filing your Income Tax forms for **1995**.

MacInTax $ $ TurboTax   Need tax software? **Order** Intuit's **MacInTax** and **TurboTax.**

TAXING TIMES
WEB http://www.scubed.com/tax/tax.html
Taxing Times is the premier tax information resource online. Created by Maxwell Labs, a leading developer of defense technology, the site carries more than 750 official federal and state tax forms in different formats. Any graphics program will handle the TIFF format, and any PostScript laser printer will handle Post-Script formats, but you must download the Adobe Acrobat Reader to view and read .PDF files. Even without the ability to download files, you can order forms and instructions by email. You can even order the tax preparation software MacInTax/TurboTax; download the U.S. Tax Code; and link to the misc.taxes newsgroup, tax software FTP sites, and the archives of the *Tax Digest* newsletter.

Starting points

CompuServe Tax Connection A menu linking to all of CompuServe's tax resources, including H&R Block tips, support forums for tax software, and an electronic filing service.
COMPUSERVE *go* taxes

The Department of the Treasury: Internal Revenue Service Web site If only the IRS made the tax process as easy to navigate as this Web site. Stop by the Information Highway outpost of the country's most hated government agency if you want tax forms, instructions, information about where to file, IRS telephone numbers, Adobe Acrobat Readers, and more. The site links to the IRS-UTL Library on Fed-World, which is packed with fact sheets and articles about taxation and IRS services.
WEB http://www.irs.ustreas.gov

Individual Income Are you withholding the right amount? Is your college scholarship taxable income? If you sell your old home, then use part of the money to put a roof on your new home, is that money still considered capital gain? Not for tax theorists, this message board is an active source of discussion about practical tax questions.
AMERICA ONLINE *keyword* naea

State Tax Information Serves as a gateway to government information for the 41 tax-happy

Location: http://www.irs.ustreas.gov/prod/cover.html

PRINTED DAILY AND IT'S FREE!

DEPARTMENT OF THE TREASURY
Presenting The Fastest, Easiest

INTERNAL REVENUE SERVICE
Tax Publication On The Planet

AND YOU DON'T HAVE TO RECYCLE!

THE DIGITAL DAILY

FASTER THAN A SPEEDING 1040-EZ... JUN 12, 1996 (307 DAYS UNTIL APRIL 15TH).

IN TODAY'S ISSUE
Tax Info For You.
(Select Exactly What You Need.)
Comments & Help.
Forms And Publications.
(It Pays To Stay In Good Shape With Your Taxes.)

Woman From Lake Calm Gets Off The Hook By Filing Her Taxes On-Line.

Jeepers! This Is A Life Saver!

A kinder, friendlier IRS?
http://www.irs.ustreas.gov

states in the Union; income tax information is easily retrievable from state-by-state menus.
WEB http://www.loc.gov/global/state/stategov.html

Tax Forum America Online's tax forum unites some of the biggest players in the tax world—government agencies like the Internal Revenue Service, software companies like Intuit, financial analysts like Kiplinger, accounting firms like Ernst & Young, and professional organizations like the National Association of Enrolled Agents—and delivers enough tax information and advice to stun an ox. With a newsfeed dedicated to tax-

related articles, an archive of tax shareware, and a full complement of tax forms, this is the main center for tax information on AOL. The Tax Forum even offers taxpayers a wealth of more general personal finance software, from budget planners and mortgage calculators to utilities like Adobe Acrobat Readers, which enable the viewing and printing of tax forms in .PDF format. During tax season, the forum includes a link to a service that lets taxpayers file their taxes electronically.
AMERICA ONLINE *keyword* tax

Tax World A professor at Northeastern University maintains

this Web site for NU students and for the Internet community. Designed to introduce students to the various aspects of taxation, the site links to a history of taxation, an international glossary of tax terms (in Germany, you are a *steuerzahler*, in Hungary, an *adofizeto*, and in America, a plain old beleaguered taxpayer), and a hypertext outline of rudimentary tax topics (audits, flat tax, property taxes).
WEB http://omer.cba.neu.edu/home

Tax advice

Ask the CPAs Open year-round, this forum collects the wisdom of thousands of accountants, and dispenses it on a broad range of accounting topics, from forensic accounting to S corporation issues. But Ask the CPAs comes to life in the winter, when America goes into its annual tax frenzy. So if you're not sure which software to use to generate W-2s and 1099s, or which forms to file if you gave private piano lessons in your home last year, calm down and come on over.
COMPUSERVE *go* accounting→ Messages and Libraries→Ask the CPAs

Net Tax The DeLellis & Company accounting firm prepares federal and state tax forms for netizens. If you want this firm to prepare your taxes, you must fill out the appropriate worksheets online and respond later (probably by telephone) to any questions the firm may have. The site features worksheets for the 1040, self-employed individuals, and individuals with rental properties. Your prepared taxes are then mailed to you. The site also includes a fee schedule.
WEB http://www.vcnet.com/DeLellis/HowTo.html

Tax news

Nest Egg Tax Information An index of tax articles ("This April... Help Ease the Paying,"

MISC.TAXES
USENET misc.taxes

picture: WEB http://www.irs.ustreas.gov/prod/forms_pubs/forms.html

Who knew there was so much to say about taxes? From heated debates about the verity of tax facts (true or false: 95 percent of all Americans don't really have to pay taxes) to huge, ongoing discussions about the right to protest taxes (more than 300 posts in a week) to questions about tax software (is TaxWare as good for tax professionals as TurboTax?), this newsgroup is incredibly active year-round. The accountants, lawyers, and tax preparers online here offer informed answers to most questions.

TAKE THAT HOME TO THE MILITIA

Spambo wrote: "3. Taxation is theft, enforced through extortion."

So, you can drive on our roads, feel (marginally) protected by the local police, ambulances, and fire depts., be educated in public libraries or schools, breathe the air we all breathe (or pollute it), or otherwise benefit from your relationship to the world... but you don't want to contribute to the community's prospects for growth through taxation.

Do you live in a vacuum? Or on an island? Now, I hate that a person's income is gouged by the current tax-codes and implementation, and I'd rather see the community needs met more by sales taxes rather than by taxing the individual incomes of the citizenry. But I think that taxes are a fair price to pay to live and do business with other human beings in a practical local economy/community.

To assert that it is theft is an egregious fallacy, as each individual "takes" plenty from the community in various intangible ways. Drive 400 miles to the West, along the Pecos river in West Texas, miles from any town and think to yourself "I could survive all by myself out here without ANYONE around to help." That ought to put things into perspective for you.

—from misc.taxes

"Tax Planning for Mutual Fund Profits," etc.) that have been printed in the monthly financial magazine *Nest Egg*. The index links to the full text of articles dating back to 1993.
WEB http://nestegg.iddis.com/nestegg/nestind/taxes.html

Tax News An impressive collection of archives of press releases and news briefs about tax issues. The material is culled from several tax organizations, including the IRS, Tax Management Inc., and the National Association of Enrolled Agents.
AMERICA ONLINE *keyword* tax

Tax Notes Newswire Updated three times a day, the Web site features brief reports on tax news worldwide. The Tax Analysts organization, which sponsors the TaxNotes news wire, also publishes a series of databases and publications that are widely used among tax professionals.
WEB http://205.177.50.2/news.htm

Forms

Federal Tax Forms Maxwell Labs has created a hypertext list of links to tax forms with brief descriptions of each form next

to the file name. Forms are all in .PDF format and compressed.
WEB http://www.scubed.com/tax/fed/1996/fed.html

Nest Egg IRS Tax Information Center *Nest Egg* magazine carries (in .PDF format) the same tax forms, instructions, and publications as the IRS Web site. While it's not as frequently updated as the IRS site, it is much better designed and includes descriptions of each file.
WEB http://nestegg.iddis.com/irs/irsdown.html

Getting audited

Criminal and Civil Tax Violations Discussion Group Taxpayers, no matter how nice they are, often try to defraud the IRS. And the IRS, no matter how bureaucratic, still catches them. This moderated list carries summaries, reports, and court case synopses relating to how the IRS combats fraud.
EMAIL criminal.group@tax.com ✍
Type in message body: subscribe (your full name)
Archives: **WEB** http://205.177.50.2/crimel.htm

What You Need to Know If You Fear an IRS Audit Assuage your fear by requesting in-house audit manuals from the IRS (the ones they use to teach their people how to do it!). This article lists all available titles, their prices, and where to get them. Read the manuals and you'll know as much about your audit as the auditor. Knowledge is, after all, the best defense.

COMPUSERVE *go* infousa→Libraries→ *Search by file name:* audit.txt

Tax fun

A History of Taxation A very sketchy history of taxation from the time of the Roman Empire to Colonial America to post-revolutionary America. Quick: What year was the Stamp Act imposed? The shocking answer? It was in 1765, roughly 203 years before the Beatles recorded *Sgt. Pepper's Lonely Hearts' Club Band.*
WEB http://omer.actg.uic.edu/Tax History/TaxHistory.html

Tax Trivia Take your mind off the pain of tax time with a doc-

ument of tax trivia. Did you know that when Abraham Lincoln calculated his federal income tax for the first time, he overpaid by $1,279.15?
COMPUSERVE *go* hrb

Test Your Tax I.Q. Last year *Money* magazine asked 500 people a set of 15 tax questions by telephone. No one answered all 15 correctly, and most answered at least six incorrectly. If you're curious to see if you could have done better, the questions are online in hypertext format. Click the answer you think is correct—if it is, there will be a brief explanation of the implications of this tax fact. If not, you'll hear about it.
WEB http://pathfinder.com/Money /features/taxquiz_0295/taxquiz.html

Software

BBS software If your primary interest is building your collection of finance—or business-related applications—you may want to subscribe to a BBS specializing in shareware. The larger BBSs have collections as extensive as those on the commercial services, at competitive prices. On most boards, the main menu has an option to go to the file collection. The collection is usually divided into several file directories: The BBS PC-Ohio, for instance, has 230 directories, including Finance-Accounting, Finance-Business. Finance-Personal, Finance-Taxes, Law/Legal, and Windows-Business. A selection of some of the country's

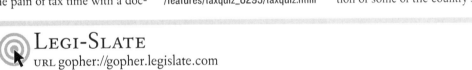

LEGI-SLATE

URL gopher://gopher.legislate.com

picture: WEB http://www.legislate.com

This database of legislation chronicles the passage of every tax bill proposed in Congress. The site is updated daily and carries archives that date back to the 103rd Congress. Taxpayers can follow legislation; read drafts of proposed bills; view roll-call votes; access Federal Register documents, as well as specific bills and resolutions; and research *Washington Post*, *National Journal*, and *Congressional Quarterly Weekly Report* articles. The service offers two levels of access—one to the public and the other to paid subscribers. See "About the LEGI-SLATE Gopher Service" for a description of what the public and the subscription services offer.

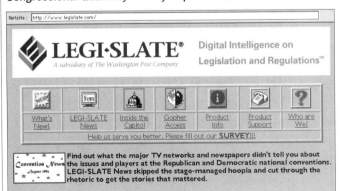

biggest and best finance BBSs follows.

BBS 414-789-4210

comp.os.ms-windows.apps .financial This lightly populated newsgroup is dedicated to questions about financial and tax software running under Microsoft Windows. The bulk of the discussion concerns Quicken, with scattered references to Peachtree and Excel.

USENET comp.os.ms-windows.apps .financial

Intuit An extensive range of resources for all Intuit products, including Quicken, TurboTax, and MacInTax. For company and new product information, head to the folders on the main menu. If you're having a problem using Turbo-Tax, installing MacInTax, or downloading tax data from Quicken, the Intuit Messaging

Center is a good place to get support (Curious about how to enter a large number of Schedule D transactions or how to print blank forms from the software, for instance? Post a message on the board and either Intuit's technical support staff or other users will offer step-by-step advice). Intuit features software libraries with FAQs, instructions, forms, and update information. The forum also links to an area for electronic filing that includes instructions, a library with forms, Adobe's Acrobat Viewer, and during tax season, an option to transmit your electronic return to an IRS-authorized electronic filing center.

AMERICA ONLINE *keyword* intuit

NetTaxes 1996 Software Reviews Throughout the tax season, the editors of *NetTaxes* keep track of how the major computer and

financial publications rate tax software. A list of the software ratings has been compiled, with links to the full text of all reviews that are published online.

WEB http://www.ypn.com/taxes /reviews.html

PC Applications The software libraries are jam-packed with business and financial applications for PCs. In the Productivity library there are sections for address and phone applications and desktop and time programs (there's even a Mayan calendar). The Databases library has sections filled with templates and add-ons for major PC database languages including Clipper, dBASE, and Paradox, as well as an entire section devoted to Windows PIMS and Databases. The Financial library seems endless, with sections devoted to home financial programs, investment programs, and Windows financial software. The forum's active message boards make this site even richer, providing a constant flow of questions, answers, and feedback on the applications.

AMERICA ONLINE *keyword* pc applications→Software Libraries

Personal Finance Software Forum Offers a generous selection of financial software, with hundreds of programs relating to accounting, career and job hunting, financial planning, home management, investment, loan calculation and amortization, organization,

Financial advice, quick as you please
http://wwwl.qfn.com/quicken

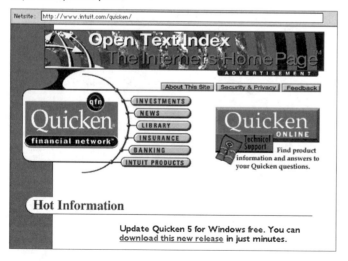

portfolio management, real estate, and taxes. America Online provides download assistance and reviews of especially popular programs. A software support section covers more than 50 companies whose wares range from market analyzers to personal organizers. Each company provides a corporate history and product list; many provide message boards for customers and technical FAQs.

AMERICA ONLINE *keyword* pf software

66 How can you get in on the IRS's sale of confiscated jewelry? Matthew Lesko answers this and other questions. 99

Quicken Home Page Taxes may be inevitable, but preparing for them can be manageable. In the continuum of personal-finance management software, Quicken is the be-all and the end-all, the alpha and omega. Quite simply, Quicken is the most popular personal finance management program in the world, fully equipped with banking, budgeting, and organizing features. The site offers

Location: http://www.vcnet.com/DeLellis/HowTo.html

A world of tax advice from DeLellis & Company
http://www.vcnet.com/DeLellis/HowTo.html

answers to questions about Quicken—"What is a locked transaction?" "Can I use Online Banking to enter data in Quicken?"—plus product updates, links to business news, and online product ordering.

WEB http://wwwl.qfn.com/quicken

Simply Money This software package contains several useful budgeting, investment management, and organizational features. The forum contains updates, demos, and documentation for the various versions of Simply Money. Program users can also post software suggestions or complaints.

AMERICA ONLINE *keyword* simply

Tax libraries
....

Business Tax Information Many taxpayers want to know what

they can deduct if they use their homes for business, whether as a sole proprietor they need an employer identification number, and whether they have to pay estimated taxes. In fact, so many taxpayers want answers to these questions, that the IRS has created a brief FAQ addressing them.

URL ftp://ftp.fedworld.gov/pub/irs-utl /btifaq.txt

TELNET telnet://fedworld.gov→go irisbti

Information USA: Taxes Where's your refund? What do you do if you get an overdue tax bill from the IRS? What are the advantages of filing electronically? How can you get in on the IRS's sale of confiscated jewelry? Matthew Lesko, the author of this database of government information and contacts, answers these and dozens of other questions in a series of

THE LIFESTYLE AUDIT

The IRS has recently instituted training for its auditors that will expand the information that auditors will request during taxpayer audits. Instead of just comparing taxpayer records with information on file, the auditor will also ask taxpayers' questions about such topics as weddings of children, cultural background, vacations, address and neighborhood, and home furnishings. These new procedures are an attempt, on the part of the IRS, to raise voluntary taxpayer compliance to 90 percent (from 83 percent) by the year 2001. With the new procedures the auditor is looking for inconsistencies between reported income and taxpayer characteristics that suggest unreported income. For example, when a taxpayer reports $40,000 of income but drives a $60,000 automobile, the auditors will question the taxpayer about how the automobile was acquired.

Because of the estimated 127 billion dollars of uncollected taxes, taxpayers that voluntarily comply with the tax law bear more than their fair share of the nation's tax bill. If the IRS is successful in reducing the amount of uncollected taxes, all taxpayers should benefit. On the other hand, is the IRS going too far? The trade-off appears to be, government intrusion versus potentially lower tax costs. What do you think?

—from Tax World

informative and entertaining articles. Organized around subjects like "Learning Loopholes," "Avoiding Audits," "Making Money from the IRS," and "Getting Free Tax Preparation Help," the site offers detailed instructions for taxpayers on how to handle the IRS and the tax process.
COMPUSERVE *go* ius-5494

IRS Guidelines for Independent Contractor and Employee Status Is the woman who works for you three days a week in your home required to follow instructions about when, where, and how she works? Does she have to wear a uniform? If so, the IRS may classify her as an employee. Or does this woman accomplish certain ends, but follows her own instructions? Then she might be an independent contractor. This is a list of IRS guidelines for determining whether an individual should be classified as an employee or an independent contractor.
WEB http://www.primenet.com/~laig/proserve/bulletin/bu0001.htm

misc.taxes FAQ This FAQ doesn't stop at answering common tax questions—"I've received an old chair and $3,000 as an inheritance. Are they taxable?" It also lays out the protocol for participating in the misc.taxes newsgroup, explains how to contact and receive information from the IRS, and provides a list of other Web sites containing tax-related information.
WEB http://www.cis.ohio-state.edu/hypertext/faq/usenet/taxes-faq

U.S. Tax Code Online Title 3 of the United States Code is the body of law covering the operations of Congress. Title 39 is the body of law covering the operations of the Postal Service. And Title 26 covers the procedures of the Internal Revenue Code. The full text of Title 26 is available here in hypertext format.
WEB http://www.fourmilab.ch/ustax/ustax.html • http://www.tns.lcs.mit.edu/uscode • http://www.fourmilab.ch/ustax/www/t26-A-I-D-I-A.html

Indexes

The Insider: Taxes For the internationally taxed, here's a directory of tax sites on the Web broken down into federal, state, Canadian, and British.
WEB http://networth.galt.com/www/home/insider/tax.htm

Tax Sites A long list of links to tax-related sites. The list is frequently updated and is divided into sections such as directories, federal tax, state tax, international tax, and commercial tax sites.
WEB http://www.uni.edu/schmidt/tax.html

Jobs

GETTING A JOB NEEDN'T BE A JOB IN ITSELF. WITH THE NET, IT CAN EVEN BE A PLEASURE

IT'S A DOG-EAT-DOG WORLD out there—and that's never more clear than on the job front. But there is an upside. Whether you're braving the market for the first time or are headed once more into the breach, the resources of the Net can give you an incredible advantage over the competition. More than 100,000 job openings are listed on the Web every week and the background information available—on hundreds of industries and thousands of companies—allows you to be both better prepared for interviews and better positioned than your competitors. Selling yourself is never easy: To make the most of your chances, you'll also find lots of help on prepping for the interview, writing your resume, and even choosing the job that's right for you.

NATIONJOB
WEB http://www.nationjob.com

NationJob has everything a good job site should have: an extensive, searchable database of jobs, a searchable database of company profiles, and links to other job resources. But it also has one feature that sets it apart from other sites: P. J. Scout. Even when you get discouraged, P.J. Scout will stay on your case. Every few days, the free Personal Job Scout service sends you email updating job possibilities within your field. Just fill out a form with your name, email address, and job criteria, and P.J. Scout will send you descriptions of job opportunities which might interest you.

Starting points

Career Development Manual If you are looking for someone to take you by the hand in the job hunting process, from building a resumé to pounding the pavement, the Career Development Manual developed by the University of Waterloo in Canada may be the right site for you. It's not flashy, not Web-integrated, and not especially fun, but if you climb its pyramid of job-hunting steps one by one, it's sure to help.
WEB http://www.adm.uwaterloo.ca /infocecs/CRC/manual-home.html

Career Magazine The resources here are truly impressive. That's probably why close to 200,000 people visit the site every month. They search the site's listings of thousands of jobs (mostly for engineers and programmers) which are updated daily; shop for new employees; drop off resumés in the resumé bank; research one of the close to 200 companies listed in the site's Company Profiles section; and read employment-related articles on subjects ranging from job fairs to head hunters to interviews.
WEB http://www.careermag.com

Career Mosaic Clean graphics make this site easy to use. A Career Resource Center offers tips on creating the ultimate resumé and acing an interview. A calendar of Online Job Fairs invites you to "come to the hire happenings." The CollegeConnection collects

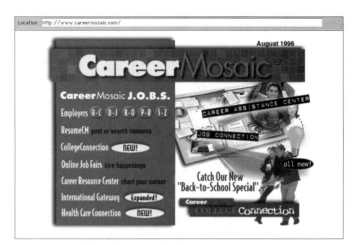

Looking for a job? CM will help you put all the pieces together
http://www.careermosaic.com

job listings and internship opportunities for students and recent graduates. In ResuméCM you can post your resumé, or, if you're an employer, search for the candidate to fill your job opening. An A-to-Z list of companies lets visitors familiarize themselves with important companies. Finally, a searchable database of jobs lets you look for hot jobs in over 60 different fields. The newest section is the International Gateway for jobs overseas. Jobs in Hong Kong and other places in Asia can be found here, but other country-based career Mosaics are not yet in place.
WEB http://www.careermosaic.com

careerWEB Although it has only been around since May 1995, careerWEB has already assembled an impressive collection of employment resources. Besides a growing number of job listings in a wide range of fields

(transportation, sales, marketing, engineering, and computers, among others), the site also offers a list of about 50 company profiles, and a job-search newsletter called *Connections* (which is packed with online job-search tips). Best of all, careerWEB recognizes that job searching can be a bit depressing at times, so they offer a Career Readiness Inventory, which is actually a thinly veiled job-search pep talk.
WEB http://www.cweb.com/welcome .html

Heart "Connecting employers and candidates throughout the world... or around the corner," Heart makes the comforting suggestion that your job search will be a short one. The site has a database of job openings in about 75 fields which you can search by company, location, or discipline. Heart also sponsors regular online job fairs with leading companies like Unisys Corporation and Fidelity Investments; visit the site for a calendar of upcoming fairs. Hint to users: Heart is heavily geared toward college students.

WEB http://www.career.com

IntelliMatch For job seekers and employers in the fields of engineering, accounting, telecommunications, computers, and software, IntelliMatch offers a worldwide database of positions wanted and offered. Employees sleuthing out the ideal job can visit the Watson section to post or build their own Web resumés, while companies seeking the perfect candidate can post recent openings in the Holmes area.

Another handy security feature allows workers to block certain companies from seeing their resumés; all contact information can be withheld upon request.

WEB http://www.intellimatch.com /index.html

Job Hunt This mega-list of jobs is a great place to begin your search. You'll find everything here, from lists of great job sites to lists of recruiters' sites. One particularly useful feature is a page of search engines to the top 11 job databases on the Web.

WEB http://rescomp.stanford.edu/jobs

Job World If you've ever felt frustrated by the condensation

of your entire work into one meager page, the entry field at Job World's CV site may be welcome indeed. Feel free to include that special merit badge you earned in the Webelos while in Cub Scouts, or any other vitae, for that matter. The problem is, it's awfully tough to get a sense of what industries are well-represented at Job World, so enter as many key words as you want to see if your dream job magically appears. There's also an email service which drops recent postings of new jobs right into your mailbox.

WEB http://www.job-search.com

JobWeb Yet another general job resource with separate sections

AOL CAREER CENTER
AMERICA ONLINE *keyword* career

Every college and university, most libraries, and many community centers and churches offer career guidance and resources to assist job seekers. America Online's Career Center can compete with the best of them. To help the newbie, the center publishes monthly articles about trends in the job market and online job searching. For those not sure what they want do with their lives (or what they are qualified to do), an online database based on the *Occupation Outlook Handbook*, a feder-

al publication, lists descriptions, average earnings, and entrance qualifications for more than 250 of America's most popular occupations. When you've narrowed your interests, but need to find employers, the Center's Employer Contact Database provides info on thousands of American companies.

for college students, recent graduates, experienced job seekers, and human resources professionals. Click into the appropriate category for career counseling, job databases, career fairs, online research sites, and bibliographies. This is a good point to begin a search, but not a place to post a resumé or use a search engine to call up a specific job.
WEB http://www.jobweb.org

Career assessment

Career Planning Assessments
The Career Services department at Bowling Green State University has set up a series of Web exercises to help job-seekers assess their values, needs, motivational levels, and personality traits; consider their academic and career options; reflect on their relevant practical work experience; prepare for graduate school; and consider a career change. For instance, the first exercise, the "Self-Assessment Exercise," asks the job seeker to rate how important certain lifestyle issues are to him or her— including the importance of political activity and access to movies. It then lists some concrete suggestions for improving self-confidence and other important competency areas related to self-assessment.
WEB http://www.bgsu.edu/offices /careers/process/process.html

Keirsey Temperament Sorter: Jungian Personality Test Jungian personality tests are all the rage

On the right track to the twenty-first century?
http://www.jobtrak.com

in management, and appear to have some degree of validity. Some corporations are now using the tests to determine how to make working groups more efficient. Find out if you're an INFP (introverted, "N-tuitive", feeling, and perceiving), an ESTJ (extroverted, sensitive, thinking, and judging), or one of the many other personality types.
WEB http://sunsite.unc.edu/jembin /mb.pl

Learning Style Take this short test to find out the way you learn best. This is short and doesn't seem at all definitive, but its questions may give you some idea of how you learn best: If you have an idea of how you learn, you may be able to get a better idea of what kind of work may suit you best. For instance, if you're an auditory learner, you may not be cut out for actuarial work.
WEB http://www.gse.rmit.edu.au /~rsedc/learn.html

The hunt itself

America's Job Bank With its links to the Employment Services of all 50 states, this board offers a job database of close to 250,000 listings. There is no cost either to the job seekers or employers who utilize this service (the site is funded through the Unemployment Insurance taxes paid by employers). Those looking for work can choose to browse the listings under the Military Specialty, Job Code, or Federal Opportunities sections; or they can execute a self-directed search by choosing from a detailed menu of job criteria (industry, title, location). America's Job Bank also maintains links to the job boards of about 100 companies from ADEPT, Inc. to Zeitech, Inc. Job hunters will also find the Occupational Outlook Handbook at this site, which forecasts the future of particular jobs by industry and category.
WEB http://www.ajb.dni.us

Best Jobs in the USA Today Can't get motivated for that job interview? Consult these two books to learn about at the *USA Today* site: *Hire Power* and *101 Answers to the Toughest Interview Questions*. Expand your career horizons by picking up the latest issue of *Employment Review* magazine. Or, if you're having a bad work day, skim the jobs database to see if there's something better out there for you in your field.
WEB http://www.bestjobsusa.com

Careerpath.com Careerpath.com features help-wanted classifieds from the newspapers of 19 major cities—from the *New York Times* to the *Sacramento Bee*—searchable by category and location. More than 90,000 jobs are featured every week.
WEB http://www.careerpath.com

Hoover's Online A database of 10,000 companies, with separate databases listing 2,577 corporate Web sites and 685 corporate job opportunity sites. The job opportunity list should have a search engine shortly, which will make it much more useful to the job seeker than it is now.
WEB http://www.hoovers.com

Job Hunting on the Internet Links to recruitment pages for 491 major companies online.
WEB http://copper.ucs.indiana.edu/~dvasilef/jobsearch.html

JobTrak This job service is targeted specifically at job-seeking college graduates and older alums. The webmasters claim that 2,100 new jobs are posted on Jobtrak each day. Most of those jobs are sorted by college, and can only be viewed if you have a password from the placement office of your college. Get them connected if they're not already.
WEB http://www.jobtrak.com

Interview preparation

E-Span's Tips Instead of listing rudimentary tips ("Don't smoke during the interview"), E-Span assists with the second layer of interview preparation. The Questions Behind the

VIRTUAL JOB FAIR
WEB http://www.careerexpo.com

Fancy graphics, good organization, and high-quality information make the Virtual Job Fair a must-see site for job seekers. Currently, 400 U.S. companies list approximately 9,000 job opportunities at the page; more than half of them are in the computer industry. This searchable database of job listings is updated every month. There's also a Resumé Center that helps candidates create a password-protected resumé; if a company is interested, the candidate is contacted through the

site, ensuring complete confidentiality. The site is also closely associated with the magazine *High Technology Careers*, and it offers a link to the full text of the publication. Rounding out the Virtual Job Fair is a collection of links to other employment-related job sites.

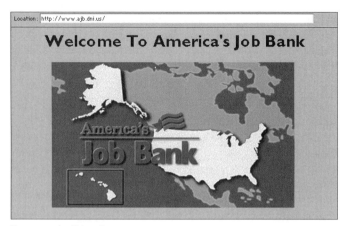

Location: http://www.ajb.dni.us/

Welcome To America's Job Bank

America's Job Bank

Have resumé, will travel
http://www.ajb.dni.us

Questions section will make you think like an interviewer and help you anticipate the questions you might be asked. E-Span even offers Interviewing Practice, a series of 16 frequently asked questions along with four or five possible responses. Choose an answer, and a link will take you to a brief essay on why your response was good or bad. There is also a useful checklist of information you should know about your prospective employer before you walk in for an interview.
WEB http://www.espan.com/docs

Job Hunting Secrets of a Corporate Headhunter A corporate headhunter gives tips on interviewing that go beyond the standard advice. If you're the type who becomes self-conscious if you get too much advice, don't look at this. But if you've been through a few interviews and are looking for a way to make your interviews

more effective, this is a good place to turn.
WEB http://www.cja-careers.com /getjob.htm

Job Interview If you don't mind the human resource-speak ("You must transition yourself across that boundary...") this is another list of helpful interviewing tips.
WEB http://www.wm.edu/catapult /enelow-i.html

Job Interviews Because Job Interviews assumes that "the only purpose of a first interview is to get a second interview" the bulk of its helpful hints are found under the Second Interview topic. Learn how to emphasize strengths in your responses, convey a good attitude during an interview, and answer questions briefly.
WEB http://www.next.com.au/libjobs /succeed_at_int.html

LEG's Interview Tips for Job Seekers Pretty standard tips, but

worth a review before you interview. It's helpful, though some of the advice is probably a little more aggressive than may be considered prudent for a non-sales position: "A very effective interviewing technique is simply to ask for the job. One way to do this is to ask the employer, 'Do you think I can do the job?' If the answer is yes, say, 'Great! When can I start?'"
WEB http://www.netaccess.on.ca /%7Eleg/appintvw.htm

Thank You Letter Template Even if you think the interview was a bomb, the advice of most professionals is to send a thank-you note. This form letter will help you compose your thank-you letter with style.
WEB http://www.hood.edu/cfscenter /cfsjobs/covthank.htm

Resumés

Career Dimensions Page Two General tips and advice on resumés and cover letters from articles published in the *Wall Street Journal*'s *National Business Employment Weekly*.
WEB http://www.cweb.com/dimensions /Career_Dimensions2.html#Letters

Cover Letters Concise and direct, the document offers basic advice on writing cover letters and supplies two finished samples.
WEB http://www.rpi.edu/dept/llc /writecenter/web/text/coverltr.html

Creating a Functional and Reverse Chronological Resumé Still can't

make up your mind whether to write a functional or a chronological resumé? This article explains how to combine the approaches.
WEB http://www.espan.com/docs /combform.html

How to Write An Electronic Resumé Excerpts from the book *How to Write an Electronic Resumé* by Joyce Lain Kennedy.
WEB http://www.occ.com/occ/JLK /HowToEResumé.html

Quick Guide to Resumé Writing A sample resumé with hypertext links to detailed preparation and writing advice. Very helpful, but don't be intimidated by the sample—chances are you won't be competing with this

M.Ed. in higher education with a 3.95 GPA. who speaks Mandarin and Bulgarian, and designs Web pages.
WEB http://www.jobweb.org/catapult /guenov/sampleres.html

Resumé Builder Want a quick, simple way to build your resumé? This site features a program that creates standard resumés for use in electronic resumé banks and databases. Just fill out the form with the pertinent information, and the site will format it for you. It doesn't give resumé-writing advice, however, so be sure to gather some Net-friendly resumé words beforehand.
WEB http://www.resumix.com/resumé /resumé-form.html

Resumé Formats The big debate is on once again, and it has nothing to do with presidential hopefuls or beer—it's about functional versus chronological resumés. Which is best for you? Consider the issues.
WEB http://www.espan.com/docs /resform.html

Resumé Writing *Career* magazine has collected a number of articles on resumé and cover letter preparation such as "How to Make Your Resumé Irresistible," and "The Truth about Cover Letters." How's this for a bitter pill: "Cover letters are extremely limited in value, even when used properly."
WEB http://www.careermag.com /careermag/newsarts/resumé.html

 # MONSTER BOARD
WEB http://www.monster.com

Monsters are scary. But never fear, this monster is here to help you find a job. In fact, this accommodating beast has assembled a collection of job-hunting resources that will take the bite out of looking for a job. The main attraction of the page is its database, and with more than 48,000 listings accessible through its "Career Surfari" search engine, it's a job force to be reckoned with. To add listings to the database, potential employers should first read the directions on the page. The Monster Board also maintains a resumé bank called Resumé On-Line. Instructions at the Web site

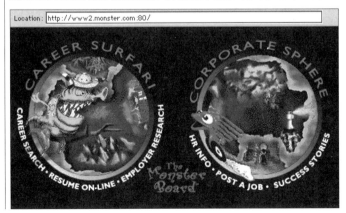

will tell job seekers how to develop and submit their resumés for perusal by employers. But it's not all work and no play at the Monster Board—a section of the board dedicated to the "next generation" offers links to music and film sites.

Top Secrets of Resumé Writing
Wonder why those resumés you're mass-mailing aren't eliciting the response you'd hoped for? Look here for some solid tips about resumé writing.
WEB http://amsquare.com/america/advance2.html

HTML guides

A Beginner's Guide to HTML For those of you who don't even know that HTML stands for Hypertext Mark-Up Language, this is a good way to put a resumé online. Head to this page for step-by-step lessons on understanding, using, and creating HTML code.
WEB http://www.ncsa.uiuc.edu/General/Internet/WWW/HTML Primer.html

HTML Manuals Resumés are becoming standard fare on many home pages. Learn how to make an electronic resumé that's interactive and informative. This site includes basic instruction, tips, and advice, and plenty of templates and samples.
WEB http://www.webcom.com/~webcom/html/tutor/welcome.html

The Hot Seat From Stanley Kaplan, the college board study course guru, comes The Hot Seat. This interview game is only half serious, but parts of it are funny and it's good practice. The game is part of a larger career planning site, Kaplan's Career Center.
WEB http://www.kaplan.com/career/hotseat

CAN I BRING A GUN TO WORK?

The "most unusual" questions that have been asked by job candidates:

What is it that you people do at this company?

What is the company motto?

Why aren't you in a more interesting business?

What are the zodiac signs of all the board members?

Why do you want references?

Do I have to dress for the next interview?

I know this is off the subject, but will you marry me?

Will the company move my rock collection from California to Maryland?

Will the company pay to relocate my horse?

Does your health insurance cover pets?

Would it be a problem if I'm angry most of the time?

Does your company have a policy regarding concealed weapons?

Do you think the company would be willing to lower my pay?

Why am I here?

—from **Job Interview Shenanigans**

Humor

Job Interview Shenanigans The vice presidents and personnel directors of the 100 largest corporations in the U.S. reveal their strangest interviewing experiences. Arms are a recurring theme: One candidate fell and broke his arm during an interview; another challenged the interviewer to an arm-wrestling contest; yet another offered to prove his loyalty by tattooing the company logo on his forearm. Hilarious.
WEB http://www.oberlin.edu/~consult/jeremy/text/job.html

Appendix

INDEX

Index

Index

Index

C

Index

Index

E

Index

Index

Index

Index

Index

Index

Index

Index

Index

Index

Index

Index

Index

X, Y, Z

Index

Notes

WOLFF NEW MEDIA

Wolff New Media is one of the leading providers of information about the Net and the emerging Net culture. The company's NetBooks series includes such titles as *NetGuide*, *NetGames*, *NetChat*, *NetMoney*, *NetTrek*, *NetSports*, *NetTech*, *NetMusic*, *Fodor's NetTravel*, *NetTaxes*, *NetJobs*, *NetVote*, *NetMarketing*, *NetDoctor*, *NetStudy*, *NetCollege*, *NetSpy*, and *NetSci-Fi*. In the coming year the series will add new titles such as *NetShopping*, *NetKids*, *NetLove*, *NetBaseball*, *NetOut*, *NetWine*, *NetFix-It*, *NetInvesting*, and *NetRoots*. The entire NetBooks Series is available on the companion Web site YPN—Your Personal Net (http://www.ypn.com). And *Net Guide*—"the *TV Guide*® to Cyberspace," according to *Wired* magazine editor Louis Rossetto—is now a monthly magazine published by CMP Publications.

The company was founded in 1988 by journalist Michael Wolff to bring together writers, editors, and graphic designers to create editorially and visually compelling information products in books, magazines, and new media. Today, the staff consists of some of the most talented and cybersavvy individuals in the industry. Among the company's other projects are *Where We Stand—Can America Make It in the Global Race for Wealth, Health, and Happiness?* (Bantam Books), one of the most graphically complex information books ever to be wholly created and produced by means of desktop-publishing technology, and *Made in America?*, a four-part PBS series on global competitiveness, hosted by Labor Secretary Robert B. Reich.

The company frequently acts as a consultant to other information companies, including WGBH, Boston's educational television station; CMP Publications; and Time Warner, which it has advised on the development of Time's online business and the launch of its Web site, Pathfinder.

Who are the most influential Asian Americans in the U.S.?

Who are the Asians making waves in Corporate America, in Cyberspace, in Hollywood?

What are the issues, challenges, and opportunities that face America's fastest-growing ethnic group?

Turn to A. Magazine for the answers! From politics to pop culture, from trends to technology, from our disparate past to our promising future, we'll take you inside Asian America in every issue. The hottest writers. The timeliest topics. Stunning design and photography. Get them all, six times a year, direct to your door.

GET A FREE PREVIEW COPY OF A. MAGAZINE, AND START YOUR NO-OBLIGATION TRIAL SUBSCRIPTION! USE THE COUPON BELOW OR CALL 1-800-346-0085 X 477 AND MENTION CODE MNB961.

If after getting your free copy, you don't like what you read, simply call us toll-free, or write "cancel" on your invoice and you'll owe absolutely nothing – the free issue is yours to keep. Otherwise, you'll receive six more issues of A. Magazine – a full year – for the low rate of $11 – 25% less than the regular subscription rate, and 38% lower than the newsstand price

"A. Magazine captures the life and times of Asian America, and gives them what they want — widely acclaimed editorial covering trends, leaders, culture, and style."
— *Inside Media* magazine.